Take The Collegiate Investment Challenge!

Win Cash Prizes!

Manage a $500,000 simulated portfolio in real-time

EXPERIENCE WALL STREET . . . FIRST HAND

20% – 33% Discount when you register with your Access Code.

Imagine being given half a million dollars to experience the world of investing while assuming absolutely no risk. Now consider the valuable experience you'll gain from buying and selling equities to performing more sophisticated transactions like trading options, short selling and purchasing on margin — all at current market prices. Experience the excitement of Wall Street in the Collegiate Investment Challenge, the nation's most realistic stock market simulation. Form a team, or do it individually, for as little as $29.95!*

Playing the Collegiate Investment Challenge is easy. We'll give you all the resources you'll need to make your experience a hit. By the end of the Challenge you'll be able to walk, talk and act like you work on Wall Street. Who knows? You may even win your share of thousands of dollars in prizes and get recognized in a national newspaper. This semester don't just read about it - experience it.

FREE trial offer for Professors:

The Collegiate Investment Challenge provides all the resources professors need to easily and effectively implement the program into their classrooms:
- Free Professor Portfolio
- Classroom Reports (including ROI, # of trades, types of trades, etc.)
- Ability to view students' accounts
- Toll–Free Professor Support Line
- Professor Chat Room

For More Information:

Challenges are offered each semester. For information, please call The Investment Challenge at 1–800–487–3862 or visit the website at <www.ichallenge.net/prenticehall>.

* prices subject to change

How Does It Work?

The Collegiate Investment Challenge mimics the daily operation of a real brokerage firm. With a $500,000 fictional brokerage account, you get to experience the markets just like the professionals. Implement your own investment strategies by buying and selling equities and options listed on all the major exchanges (NYSE, NASDAQ, AMEX, CBOE, PSE, and PHLX). In addition, you can try your hand at purchasing on margin and short selling. The Challenge is so realistic—it even incorporates commission schedules, dividends, and stock splits. Trades can be placed on–line, via the Investment Challenge Website at **<www.ichallenge.net/prenticehall>**, or by fax, answering machine, or through live brokers using the toll–free number **1–800–487–3862**. For maximum authenticity, every trade is placed using real–time prices (i.e., no delay).

If Investing Intimidates You . . . Don't Worry.

The Investment Challenge's staff of brokers are there to answer all your questions by phone or e-mail. They can guide you through the basics—from buying a stock to even the most sophisticated option trades. Whatever your needs or questions, the Investment Challenge staff is there to help.

The Right Account For You.

WebTrader Account
- Exclusive Internet trading
- On–line Investment Manual
- On–line Newsletters
- On–line stock research information
- Full e-mail support

TradersEdge Account
- All WebTrader features plus:
  - Access to live brokers
  - Biweekly mailed newsletters
  - Biweekly mailed account statements

National Competition

Compete against college students from across the country for a chance to win thousands of dollars in prizes:
- Prizes for top performers
- Weekly prizes
- Recognition in a national newspaper
- Special prizes and rankings for Investment Clubs

Your Resume's Secret Weapon

The Collegiate Investment Challenge provides the kind of hands–on experience that looks great on a resume, and makes an excellent topic of conversation in interviews. Whether you are thinking about a career in the financial services industry, or just want to learn more about the stock market, participating in The Collegiate Investment Challenge will be a valuable asset.

Register Today. Call 1-800-487-3862
or register on–line at www.ichallenge.net/prenticehall
and enter your Prentice Hall Student "access code"
Save 33% off WebTrader Accounts
Save 20% off TradersEdge Accounts

©1999, 0–13–021226–1

ISBN 0-13-021226-1

FUNDAMENTALS
OF INVESTMENTS

PRENTICE HALL FINANCE SERIES

Personal Finance
Keown, *Personal Finance: Turning Money into Wealth*
Winger/Frasca, *Personal Finance: An Integrated Planning Approach*
Trivoli, *Personal Portfolio Management: Fundamentals and Strategies*

Investments
Alexander/Sharpe/Bailey, *Fundamentals of Investments*
Fabozzi, *Investment Management*
Fischer/Jordan, *Security Analysis and Portfolio Management*
Haugen, *Modern Investment Theory*
Taggart, *Quantitative Analysis for Investment Management*
Winger/Frasca, *Investments*
Haugen, *The New Finance*
Haugen, *The Beast on Wall Street*
Haugen, *The Inefficient Stock Market*
Sharpe/Alexander/Bailey, *Investments*

Portfolio Analysis
Alexander/Sharpe/Bailey, *Fundamentals of Investments*
Fischer/Jordan, *Security Analysis and Portfolio Management*
Haugen, *Modern Investment Theory*
Sharpe/Alexander/Bailey, *Investments*

Options/Futures/Derivatives
Hull, *Introduction to Futures and Options Markets*
Hull, *Options, Futures, and Other Derivatives*

Risk Management/Financial Engineering
Hull, *Financial Engineering and Risk Management*
Mason/Merton/Perold/Tufano, *Cases in Financial Engineering*

Fixed Income Securities
Van Horne, *Financial Market Rates and Flows*
Handa, *FinCoach: Fixed Income* (software)

Bond Markets
Fabozzi, *Bond Markets, Analysis and Strategies*
Van Horne, *Financial Market Rates and Flows*

Capital Markets
Fabozzi/Modigliani, *Capital Markets: Institutions and Instruments*
Van Horne, *Financial Market Rates and Flows*

Corporate Finance, Survey of Finance, & Financial Economics
Bodie/Merton, *Finance*
Gallagher/Andrew, *Financial Management: Principles and Practices*
Haugen, *The New Finance: The Case Against Efficient Markets*
Shapiro/Balbirer, *Modern Corporate Finance: A Multidisciplinary Approach to Value Creation*
Keown/Martin/Petty/Scott, *Basic Financial Management*
Keown/Martin/Petty/Scott, *Foundations of Finance: The Logic and Practice of Financial Management*
Emery/Finnerty/Stowe, *Principles of Financial Management*

Emery/Finnerty, *Corporate Financial Management*
Van Horne, *Financial Management and Policy*
Van Horne/Wachowicz, *Fundamentals of Financial Management*

International Finance
Baker, *International Finance: Managements, Markets, and Institutions*
Grabbe, *International Financial Markets*
Rivera-Batiz/Rivera-Batiz, *International Finance and Open Economy Macroecomomics*

Capital Budgeting
Aggarwal, *Capital Budgeting Under Uncertainty*
Bierman/Smidt, *The Capital Budgeting Decision*

Mergers/Acquisitions/Takeovers
Hill/Sartoris, *Short Term Financial Management*
Weston/Chung/Siu, *Takeovers, Restructuring and Corporate Governance*

Short-Term Finance
Hill/Sartoris, *Short Term Financial Management*

Taxes and Corporate Financial Decision Making
Scholes/Wolfson, *Taxes and Business Strategy: A Global Planning Approach*

Insurance
Black/Skipper, *Life and Health Insurance*
Dorfman, *Introduction to Risk Management and Insurance*
Rejda, *Social Insurance and Economic Security*

Financial Markets and Institutions
Arshadi/Karels, *Modern Financial Intermediaries and Markets*
Dietrich, *Financial Services and Financial Institutions*
Fabozzi/Modigliani/Ferri/Jones, *Foundations of Financial Markets and Institutions*
Kaufman, *The U.S. Financial Systems*
Van Horne, *Financial Market Rates and Flows*

Commercial Banking
Dietrich, *Financial Services and Financial Institutions*
Sinkey, *Commercial Bank Financial Management*
Arshadi/Karels, *Modern Financial Intermediaries and Markets*

Entrepreneurial Finance
Adelman/Marks, *Entrepreneurial Finance*
Vaughn, *Financial Planning for the Entrepreneur*

Cases in Finance
May/May/Andrew, *Effective Writing: A Handbook for Finance People*

Financial Statement Analysis
Fraser/Ormiston, *Understanding Financial Statements*

Finance Center
For downloadable supplements and much more . . . visit us at www.prenhall.com/financecenter

THIRD EDITION

FUNDAMENTALS OF INVESTMENTS

GORDON J. ALEXANDER

University of Minnesota

WILLIAM F. SHARPE

Stanford University and Financial Engines Inc.

JEFFERY V. BAILEY

Target Corporation

Prentice
Hall

Upper Saddle River, New Jersey

Alexander, Gordon J.
    Fundamentals of investments / Gordon J. Alexander, William F. Sharpe, Jeffery V.
Bailey.—3rd ed.
       p.   cm.
    Includes bibliographical references and index.
    ISBN 0-13-292617-2
    1. Investments. I. Sharpe, William F. II. Bailey, Jeffery V. III. Title.
HG4521 .A419 2000
332.6—dc21   99-048069

VP/Editorial Director: James C. Boyd
Editor-in-Chief: P. J. Boardman
Senior Editor: Maureen Riopelle
Managing Editor: Gladys Soto
Assistant Editor: Holly Jo Brown
Editorial Assistant: Cheryl Clayton
Senior Marketing Manager: Lori Braumberger
Director of Production: Michael Weinstein
Production Manager: Gail Steier de Acevedo
Production Coordinator: Kelly Warsak
Manufacturing Buyer: Natacha St. Hill Moore
Senior Manufacturing and Prepress Manager: Vincent Scelta
Cover Design: Bruce Kenselaar
Cover Art: Photo Disc
Full Service Composition: Omegatype Typography, Inc.

10 9 8 7 6 5 4 3 2
ISBN 0-13-292617-2

In memory of my mother and father
GJA

To Kathy
WFS

To Ann, Stephen, and Megan
JVB

Brief Contents

Contents

PART III   MODERN INVESTMENT THEORY   119

CHAPTER 7   The Portfolio Selection Problem   119

CHAPTER 8   Portfolio Analysis   147

Preface

Writing a textbook is never easy. For a subject as diverse as investments, the task is particularly difficult. The undisciplined writer could fill volumes and never finish. How does an author best go about organizing the many topics that constitute the field of investments? We chose to start by establishing a basic set of principles to guide our development of *Fundamentals of Investments*.

We sincerely believe that the serious student of investments should acquire a balanced knowledge of both investment theory and practice. Granted, someone desiring only an introductory exposure to investment practice could get by with a minimal discussion of theory and focus almost exclusively on institutional details and personal finance applications. That approach, however, would leave the student unable to appreciate the many subtle and important issues faced daily by the investment professional.

We have structured *Fundamentals* to present students taking their first course in investments with the basic building blocks of modern investment thought. Although the text is meant to present a thorough discussion of investments, we have constantly tried to remain faithful to three principles:

1. Keep the material practical and relevant.
2. Make the text easy to comprehend.
3. Design the text for modular use by instructors.

First, we have written *Fundamentals* to give students a working knowledge of the financial instruments available to investors and the ways in which markets for these instruments operate. We have avoided tangential discussions of issues not germane to the primary subject at hand. Second, we want the text to be accessible to students unfamiliar with investments. Therefore, we have tried to write in a clear, concise style, keeping mathematical notation to a minimum, and including numerous examples to explain the concepts presented. Finally, we want instructors to be able to use the text in a modular fashion. Although we have organized the text in what we believe to be a logical order, some instructors may wish to change that order or skip certain sections or chapters entirely. The organization of the text accommodates such preferences.

This is the third edition of *Fundamentals*. As any textbook author will attest, a previous work can always be improved. Each time after the first and second editions were published, we received many helpful suggestions from instructors, readers, and reviewers regarding ways in which we could make *Fundamentals* better. In response, we have made a number of changes that we believe substantially enhance *Fundamentals* in terms of our goals of practicality, ease of comprehension, and flexibility. Specifically, the third edition contains the following differences from the second:

- *Updated material.* Where appropriate, we have updated the text to keep students abreast of the latest developments in investments. We have revised tables, graphs, and illustrations to incorporate current information. Furthermore, we have added discussions of recent important academic research.
- *Revised Money Matters.* In each chapter we have updated and in some cases replaced the Money Matters features, which are topical discussions designed to show students how some of the concepts described in the text are applied in the "real world."
- *Improved the book's focus.* We have concentrated on the most important concepts by eliminating those that have become less important over time.
- *Added statistical concepts review section.* In order to understand investments it is important for students to have a solid grounding in basic statistics. We have introduced this review section at the end of Chapter 7 to help refresh the reader's memory.
- *Expanded and improved coverage of efficient markets.* This concept plays a central role in modern thinking about investing regardless of ones beliefs. We have approached the subject differently than other texts. Instead of treating the subject in one lengthy section of the book, Chapter 4 provides a concise summary of efficient markets concepts. A review of the literature is then placed in chapters where that discussion is most relevant.
- *Added international content.* The globalization of investments is occurring at a rapid pace. It is imperative that students become familiar with an increasingly broad array of international investing concepts. Chapter 26 deals directly with international investing. Moreover, throughout the text we have considerably expanded the discussions of research and data on international securities and securities markets. There are also new discussions of currency management and interest-rate parity.

Many people ask us how *Fundamentals* differs from our other book, *Investments.* After all, *Investments,* now in its sixth edition, has been one of the most successful finance textbooks published. Why another version of such a popular text?

Both *Fundamentals* and *Investments* are comprehensive, covering all of the major aspects and theories of investing, while avoiding excess detail. Furthermore, both books contain similar features, such as a glossary of terms introduced in the text, and both books offer an instructor's manual and investment software.

Investments, however, is written primarily for students who have stronger backgrounds in economics, statistics, and accounting. We felt that most students in their first investments course could benefit from a textbook designed to provide a less theoretical and technical approach to investments. Therefore, although we have not ignored the quantitative nature of modern investment theory and practice, we have considerably reduced the mathematical content from that contained in *Investments.* Moreover, we have organized *Fundamentals* in a different manner. Specifically, *Fundamentals* is organized in a modular fashion, as mentioned earlier, whereas *Investments* has a presentation style that is more integrated.

Fundamentals contains several teaching aids that we believe instructors will find valuable. The terms highlighted within the text and noted marginally in each chapter emphasize important concepts. The glossary allows students to quickly reference terms discussed earlier in the text, thereby creating a continuity of concepts across chapters.

The point-by-point chapter summaries permit students to easily identify essential thoughts developed in each chapter.

We are particularly proud of the Money Matters articles presented in each chapter. Specifically written for *Fundamentals,* these articles are designed to give students a sense of how various investment issues are approached by practitioners as well as a glimpse of the techniques that are used. For example, the Money Matters box in Chapter 2 compares the various types of brokers, ranging from full-service to discount to on-line brokers; Chapter 18 discusses assessing manager skill; and Chapter 26 considers the controversial issue of whether to hedge a foreign investment portfolio. Furthermore, Ann Sherman, a recent faculty member of the Hong Kong University of Science and Technology for six years, wrote the Money Matters feature in Chapter 13 about raising capital in the world's largest emerging economy—The People's Republic of China. In addition, the Chartered Financial Analyst program is described in the Chapter 14 Money Matters. We believe the Money Matters articles provide both interesting reading for students and a stimulating source of classroom discussion material.

An extended supplements package accompanies the third edition of *Fundamentals.* Included in this package are

- *Instructor's Manual.* Prepared by the authors, the Instructor's Manual contains detailed solutions to all end-of-chapter questions and problems in the text. A set of course outlines designed to accommodate a variety of teaching approaches is also presented.
- *Test Bank.* Completely revised and rewritten by Joseph F. Greco of California State University, Fullerton, the test bank contains approximately 1,400 multiple-choice and true/false questions. The third edition Test Bank contains more even coverage of topics and provides three levels of difficulty: knowledge, comprehension, and application/analysis.
- *Prentice Hall Test Manager.* The Test Bank is designed for use with the Prentce Hall Test Manager, a computerized package that allows instructors to custom design, save, and generate classroom tests. The test program permits instructors to edit, and, or delete questions from the test bank; organize exams; analyze test results; and create a database of student results.
- *PowerPoint Lecture Presentation.* Created by Joseph J. Greco, the PowerPoints provide detailed lecture outlines and summaries that can be tailored for individual use. The PowerPoints can be downloaded from the *Fundamentals* web site at www.prenhall.com/financecenter.
- *Financial Engines Investment Advisor^{sm} Service.* With every new purchase of *Fundamentals of Investments,* third edition, students can enjoy a 25 percent discount on a subscription to the Financial Engines Investment Advisor Service. With this service students will receive the following: the ability to forecast their investments and see what their results may yield, professional investment advice, and the ability to monitor their investments to stay on track as the markets change. To subscribe or to receive additional information, please go to www.prenhall.com/alexander or www.prenhall.com/financecenter.

Many people have assisted us in preparing the third edition of this book, and we would like to acknowledge them as well as those who helped us with earlier editions. Specifically, we would like to thank Seth Anderson, Ted Aronson, Ann Bailey, Ed Baker, Michael Barclay, Kenneth S. Bartunek, Jeffrey Born, E. Taylor Claggett, John Cone, James Conley, Thomas Eyssell, Mark Edwards, Joe Finnerty, Charlie Freund, Ping Hsiao, Robert Jennings, Lee Jones, Steven L. Jones, Dougles R. Kahi, Ed Keon,

Jaroslaw Komarynsky, Linda Kramer, K. C. Ma, S. Maheswaran, Linda J. Martin, Carl McGowan, Ronald Melicher, John Nagorniak, Tom Nohel, Thomas O'Brien, Martha Ortiz, James A. Overdahl, Lynne Pi, Maggie Queen, Sailesh Ramamurtie, Peter Robbins, Scott Rosen, Frank Roszkiewicz, Anthony Sanders, Frederick P. Schadler, Jandhyala L. Sharma, Arlene Spiegel, Len Washko, Tony Wilkins, Robert Wolf, Steve Wunsch, Fernando Zapatero, Emilio Zarruk, and Ken Zumwalt.

We would like to give a special thank you to Henry Hecht for his many constructive comments and sharp-eyed "catches"; to Ann Sherman for writing one of the Money Matters features; and the following reviewers: Victor Abraham, FIDM; Grace Allen, Western Carolina University; Carol Billingham, Central Michigan University; Howard Bohnen, St. Cloud State University; Stephen Brown, New York University; Don Cox, Appalachian State University; Marcus Ingram, Clark Atlanta University; Reinhold Lamb, University of North Carolina at Charlotte; David Louton, Bryant College; Linda Martin, Arizona State University; Byron Menides, Worcester Polytechnic Institute; and David Upton, Virginia Commonwealth University. We are also especially grateful to the people at Prentice Hall, particularly Maureen Riopelle, senior editor; Gladys Soto, managing editor; Cheryl Clayton, editorial assistant; Lori Braumberger, senior marketing manager; Kelly Warsak, production coordinator; and Katherine Evancie, copy editor; and to Robert Howerton of Omegatype Typography, Inc., for their work in preparing the text for publication.

We have learned much by writing this book and hope that you will learn much by reading it. Although we have done our best to eliminate errors from the book, experience tells us that perfection is unattainable. Thus, we encourage those students and instructors with constructive comments to send them to us at either galexander@csom.umn.edu, wfsharpe@leland.stanford.edu, or jeff.bailey@target.com.

GJA
WFS
JVB

About the Authors

GORDON J. ALEXANDER

Gordon J. Alexander is professor of finance at the University of Minnesota, having recently completed a two-year consultancy to the Office of Economic Analysis at the Securities and Exchange Commission that followed a two-year stint as an in-house senior research scholar. Alexander has published articles in *Financial Management, Journal of Banking and Finance, Journal of Business, Journal of Finance, Journal of Financial Economics, Journal of Financial and Quantitative Analysis,* and the *Journal of Portfolio Management.* He received his Ph.D. in finance, M.A. in mathematics, and M.B.A. from the University of Michigan, and his B.S. in business administration from the State University of New York at Buffalo.

WILLIAM F. SHARPE

William F. Sharpe is the STANCO 25 professor emeritus of finance at Stanford University, and chair of the board of Financial Engines, Incorporated, a firm that provides investment advice to individuals via the Internet. He has published articles in a number of professional journals, including *Management Science, Journal of Business, Journal of Finance, Journal of Financial Economics, Journal of Financial and Quantitative Analysis, Journal of Portfolio Management,* and the *Financial Analysts Journal.* Sharpe is past president of the American Finance Association, and in 1990 he received the Nobel Prize in economic sciences. He received his Ph.D., M.A., and B.A. in economics from the University of California, Los Angeles.

JEFFERY V. BAILEY

Jeffery V. Bailey is director of benefits finance at Target Corporation. Previously he was a principal at the pension fund consulting firm of Richards & Tierney, Inc. Before that he was the assistant executive director of the Minnesota State Board of Investment. Bailey has published articles in the *Financial Analysts Journal* and the *Journal of Portfolio Management.* He has contributed articles to several practitioner handbooks and has co-authored a monograph published by the Research Foundation of the Institute of Chartered Financial Analysts. Bailey received his B.A. from Oakland University and his M.A. in economics and his M.B.A. in finance from the University of Minnesota. He is a Chartered Financial Analyst.

FUNDAMENTALS OF INVESTMENTS

CHAPTER

Introduction

T his book is about investing in marketable securities. Accordingly, it focuses on the investment environment and process. The **investment environment** includes the kinds of marketable securities that exist and where and how they are bought and sold. The **investment process** is concerned with how an investor should make decisions about what marketable securities to invest in, how extensive the investments should be, and when the investments should be made. Before discussing the investment environment and process in detail, the term **investment** is described.

Investment, in its broadest sense, means the sacrifice of current dollars for future dollars. Two different attributes are generally involved: *time* and *risk*. The sacrifice takes place in the present and is certain. The reward comes later, if at all, and the amount of the reward is generally uncertain. In some cases the element of time predominates (for example, with government bonds). In other cases risk is the dominant factor (for example, with call options on common stocks). In yet others both time and risk are important (for example, with shares of common stock).

A distinction is often made between real and financial investments. **Real investments** generally involve a tangible (physical) asset, such as land, machinery, or factories. **Financial investments** involve contracts written on paper, such as common stocks and bonds. The financing of an apartment building provides a good example. Apartments are sufficiently tangible ("bricks and mortar") to be considered real investments. But where do the resources come from to pay for the land and the construction of the apartments? Some may come from direct investment. For example, a wealthy doctor who wants to construct an apartment building may use some of his or her own money to finance the project. The rest of the resources may be provided by a mortgage loan. In essence, someone loans money to the doctor, with repayment promised in fixed amounts on a specified schedule over some period of time. In the typical case the "someone" is not a person, but an institution acting as a financial intermediary. Thus the doctor makes a real investment in the apartment building, and the institution makes a financial investment in the doctor.

As a second example, consider what happens when General Motors (GM) needs money to pay for plant construction. This real investment may be financed by the sale of new common stock in the **primary market** (the market in which securities are sold at the time of their initial issuance). The common stock itself represents a financial investment to the purchasers, who may later trade these shares in the **secondary market** (the market in which previously issued securities are traded). Although transactions in the secondary market do not generate money for GM, the fact that such a market exists makes the common stock more attractive and thus facilitates real investment. Investors would pay less for new shares of common stock if there were no way to sell them quickly and inexpensively at a later date.

investment environment
investment process

investment

real investments

financial investments

primary market

secondary market

These examples introduce the three main elements of the investment environment—securities (also known as financial investments or financial assets), security markets (also known as financial markets), and financial intermediaries (also known as financial institutions). They will be discussed in more detail next.

1.1 The Investment Environment

1.1.1 SECURITIES

When someone borrows money from a pawnbroker, the borrower must leave some item of value as security. If the borrower fails to repay the loan (plus interest), the pawnbroker can sell the pawned item to recover the amount of the loan (plus interest) and perhaps make a profit. The terms of the agreement are recorded on pawn tickets. When a college student borrows money to buy a car, the lender usually holds formal title to the car until the loan is repaid. In the event of default, the lender can repossess the car and sell it to recover his or her costs. In this case the official certificate of title, issued by the state, serves as the security for the loan. A person who borrows money for a vacation may simply sign a piece of paper promising to repay the loan with interest. The loan is unsecured because there is no collateral, meaning that no specific asset has been promised to the lender in the event of default. In such a situation the lender would have to take the borrower to court to try to recover the amount of the loan. Only a piece of paper called a promissory note stands as evidence of such a loan.

When a firm borrows money, it may or may not offer collateral. For example, some loans may be secured (backed) with specific pieces of property (buildings or equipment). Such loans are recorded by means of mortgage bonds, which indicate the terms of repayment and the particular assets pledged to the lender in the event of default. However, it is much more common for a firm to pledge all of its assets, perhaps with some provision as to how the division will take place in the event of default. Such a promise is known as a debenture bond.

Finally, a firm may promise a right to share in its profits in return for an investor's funds. Nothing is pledged, and no irrevocable promises are made. The firm simply pays whatever its directors deem reasonable from time to time. However, the investor is given the right to participate in the determination of who will be directors. This right protects the investor against serious misconduct by the firm. A share of common stock represents the investor's property right. The stock can be sold to someone else, who can then exercise that right. The holder of common stock is considered an *owner* of the corporation and can, in theory, exercise control over its operation through the board of directors.

security

Usually, only a piece of paper represents the investor's rights to certain prospects or property and the conditions under which he or she may exercise those rights. This piece of paper, serving as evidence of property rights, is called a security. It may be transferred to another investor, and if it is, all its rights and conditions are transferred as well. Thus, everything from a pawn ticket to a share of GM common stock is a security. Hereafter the term **security** will be used to refer to a *claim to receive prospective future benefits under certain conditions.* The primary task of security analysis is to evaluate securities by determining their prospective future benefits, the conditions under which those benefits will be received, and the likelihood of the occurrence of such conditions. Simply put, security analysts attempt to understand the risk and return characteristics of securities.

The focus here is on securities that may be easily and efficiently transferred from one owner to another. As a result, common stocks and bonds are studied rather than pawn tickets, although much of the material in this book applies to all three types of instruments.

Figure 1.1 and Table 1.1 show the year-by-year results of investing in four types of securities during the 100-year period from 1899 through 1998. The middle four columns show the percentage change in a hypothetical investor's wealth from the beginning to the end of each year. This amount, known as the **holding period return** (or, simply, the *return*), is calculated as follows:

holding period return

$$\text{Return} = \frac{\text{End-of-period wealth} - \text{Beginning-of-period wealth}}{\text{Beginning-of-period wealth}} \tag{1.1}$$

where in this case the holding period is one year. In calculating the return on a security, assume that a hypothetical investor purchased one unit of the security (for example, one bond or one share of common stock) at the beginning of the period. The cost of such an investment is the value entered in the denominator of Equation (1.1). Then the value in the numerator is the answer to a simple question, How much better (or worse) off is the investor at the end of the period? For example, assume that Widget Corporation's common stock was selling for $40 per share at the beginning of the year and for $45 at the end of the year and that it paid dividends of $3 per share during the year. The annual return on Widget for the year would then be calculated as [($45 + $3) − $40]/$40 = .20, or 20%.[1] Note that the numerator includes both a capital gain component ($5 = $45 − $40) and a dividend component ($3).

Treasury Bills

The first type of security in Figure 1.1 and Table 1.1 involves lending money on a short-term basis to the U.S. Treasury. Such a loan carries little (if any) risk that payment will not be made as promised. Moreover, although the rate of return varies from period to period, it is known with certainty at the beginning of any single period. These investments, called Treasury bills, produced returns ranging from a high of 14.71% per year in 1981 to a low of almost zero (−.04%) in 1939 and 1940, with an average value of 4.15% during the entire period.

Long-Term Bonds

The second and third types of securities in Figure 1.1 and Table 1.1 are bonds and also involve lending money. Each type of bond represents a fairly long-term commitment on the part of the issuer (that is, the borrower) to the investor (that is, the lender). This commitment is to make cash payments each year (the coupon amount) up to some point in time (the maturity date) when a single final cash payment (the principal plus a coupon) will be made. The amount for which such bonds can be bought and sold varies from time to time. Thus, whereas coupon payments are easily predicted, the end-of-period selling price of the security is quite uncertain at the beginning of any period (except the period in which the bond matures), making it difficult to predict the return in advance.

The second type of security (long-term government bonds) are approximately 15-year loans to the U.S. Treasury and are called Treasury bonds. The third type of security (long-term corporate bonds) are 15-year loans to high-quality U.S. corporations and are simply referred to as corporate bonds. To date both types of bonds had their highest annual returns in 1982, reaching 47.35% for government bonds and 39.31% for corporate bonds. The lowest annual returns were reached in different years. For government bonds the lowest return occurred in 1994 (−6.94%), and the lowest return for corporate bonds was in 1969 (−10.01%). On average, government bonds have had a higher return (4.97%) than Treasury bills (4.15%), and corporate bonds have had a higher return (5.48%) than government bonds (4.97%). Although the second and third types of securities have considerable variability, they usually provide larger returns than Treasury bills.

TABLE 1.1	Annual Returns: Stocks, Bonds, Treasury Bills and Changes in the Consumer Price Index				
	Treasury Bills	*Government Bonds*	*Corporate Bonds*	*Common Stocks*	*Change in CPI*
1899	4.55	7.63	2.01	11.07	4.17
1900	4.35	3.94	−7.94	18.97	1.33
1901	4.24	3.31	4.18	20.00	2.63
1902	4.93	2.00	1.88	4.50	2.56
1903	5.51	2.75	1.76	−15.52	0.00
1904	4.13	2.16	6.75	30.10	1.25
1905	4.27	2.99	3.78	19.02	2.47
1906	5.64	3.15	1.49	6.43	4.82
1907	6.46	−0.18	−3.37	−29.72	3.45
1908	4.22	4.35	12.05	45.37	0.00
1909	3.90	1.58	3.52	19.55	5.56
1910	4.73	3.38	2.94	−7.86	0.00
1911	3.91	2.95	4.06	6.19	2.11
1912	4.75	3.59	2.50	8.68	3.09
1913	5.52	2.92	0.06	−7.15	2.04
1914	4.70	3.03	1.49	−1.93	0.98
1915	3.29	3.94	7.80	34.16	1.98
1916	3.34	3.65	5.55	7.22	12.63
1917	4.75	1.41	−8.76	−26.57	18.10
1918	5.92	4.77	10.28	22.18	20.45
1919	5.13	−6.84	−6.61	18.15	14.53
1920	6.25	0.27	−1.92	−21.55	2.65
1921	5.79	15.57	19.34	10.39	−10.82
1922	4.40	6.02	12.74	24.88	−2.31
1923	4.72	4.13	5.07	3.57	2.36
1924	4.02	8.41	7.63	25.36	0.00
1925	3.84	5.67	6.83	27.57	3.46
1926	3.30	6.40	7.98	9.30	−1.12
1927	3.11	7.73	8.82	33.01	−2.26
1928	3.56	0.37	1.87	37.84	−1.15
1929	4.71	4.64	3.73	−12.08	0.57
1930	2.41	4.89	8.42	−27.20	−6.38
1931	1.43	−4.06	−9.78	−43.44	−9.32
1932	0.88	10.27	20.72	−10.63	−10.28
1933	0.50	1.41	6.07	56.84	0.75
1934	0.27	9.25	17.44	2.69	1.51
1935	0.17	4.72	11.48	49.01	3.01
1936	0.17	6.05	10.67	31.54	1.45
1937	0.27	0.96	1.42	−34.46	2.85
1938	0.06	4.83	6.05	26.05	−2.77
1939	0.04	4.40	6.11	2.75	0.00
1940	0.04	7.05	7.11	−6.18	0.70
1941	0.15	−4.53	0.21	−10.70	9.92
1942	0.34	2.60	3.52	16.89	9.05
1943	0.38	2.49	4.31	24.59	2.94
1944	0.38	2.74	3.64	18.74	2.32
1945	0.38	4.09	4.90	40.35	2.24
1946	0.38	3.33	2.56	−6.06	18.12
1947	0.62	0.18	−2.92	2.99	8.84
1948	1.08	2.25	5.06	2.23	3.00
1949	1.12	5.15	6.99	18.70	−2.08
1950	1.22	0.03	0.67	29.47	5.93
1951	1.54	−1.20	−4.87	19.60	6.00
1952	1.75	2.17	4.09	15.97	0.75
1953	1.88	3.53	0.29	0.61	0.75
1954	0.90	4.14	7.32	49.55	−0.74
1955	1.79	−0.60	−1.92	31.53	0.38
1956	2.69	−2.40	−8.76	6.90	2.98
1957	3.27	5.53	5.17	−10.45	2.90
1958	1.71	−2.64	−3.01	43.43	1.77
1959	3.46	−0.88	−4.95	11.99	1.72
1960	2.83	9.61	9.48	0.48	1.37

	Treasury Bills	Government Bonds	Corporate Bonds	Common Stocks	Change in CPI
1961	2.39	1.30	2.76	26.78	0.67
1962	2.81	6.43	8.47	−8.72	1.33
1963	3.22	0.78	1.71	22.65	1.64
1964	3.61	4.46	3.37	16.39	0.98
1965	4.04	1.11	−0.83	12.36	1.92
1966	4.93	3.69	−5.97	−10.02	3.46
1967	4.42	−3.23	−7.26	23.92	3.04
1968	5.48	0.62	1.96	11.01	4.72
1969	6.91	−4.35	−10.01	−8.39	6.20
1970	6.45	14.85	13.43	4.00	5.57
1971	4.37	11.87	11.39	14.29	3.27
1972	4.17	4.74	9.05	18.93	3.40
1973	7.20	−1.20	−0.67	−14.74	8.71
1974	8.00	4.18	−5.24	−26.36	12.34
1975	5.89	4.04	12.20	37.14	6.94
1976	5.06	6.72	18.66	23.67	4.86
1977	5.43	0.23	3.57	−7.25	6.70
1978	7.46	0.32	−2.37	6.58	9.02
1979	10.56	−1.33	−6.44	18.55	13.29
1980	12.18	−2.43	−9.07	32.41	12.51
1981	14.71	−1.11	8.19	−4.85	8.92
1982	10.84	47.35	39.31	21.53	3.83
1983	8.98	−0.21	5.95	22.44	3.79
1984	9.89	16.72	18.03	6.23	3.95
1985	7.65	33.13	36.36	31.66	3.80
1986	6.10	27.74	28.48	18.61	1.10
1987	5.89	−4.94	−7.67	5.27	4.44
1988	6.95	8.90	15.58	16.55	4.42
1989	8.43	19.19	18.56	31.62	4.65
1990	7.72	5.79	7.93	−3.07	6.11
1991	5.46	16.57	19.96	30.37	3.06
1992	3.50	9.28	12.64	7.61	2.90
1993	3.04	18.67	20.84	10.04	2.75
1994	4.37	−6.98	−9.87	1.29	2.67
1995	5.60	27.37	34.40	37.65	2.54
1996	5.13	0.59	0.67	22.67	3.32
1997	5.22	10.97	12.84	33.43	1.71
1998	5.06	13.77	11.76	28.59	1.61
Average Return	4.15	4.97	5.48	11.86	3.31
Standard Deviation	2.83	7.98	9.55	19.60	5.01

Source: Copyright 1999 by Global Financial Data. This data can be accessed on the Internet at www.globalfindata.com.

Common Stocks

The fourth and final type of security is common stock, which represents a commitment by a corporation to pay periodically whatever its board of directors deems appropriate as a cash dividend. Although the amount of cash dividends to be paid during a year is subject to some uncertainty, it is generally relatively easy to predict the amount that will be paid. However, the amount for which a stock can be bought or sold varies considerably, making the annual return difficult to predict. Figure 1.1 shows the return from a portfolio of large, well-established common stocks selected to represent average performance. Returns ranged from an exhilarating 56.84% in 1933 to a depressing –43.44% in 1931 and averaged 11.86% per year during the entire period. Such investments can provide more substantial returns than the returns provided by corporate and government bonds. However, they are much more volatile than either type of long-term bond.

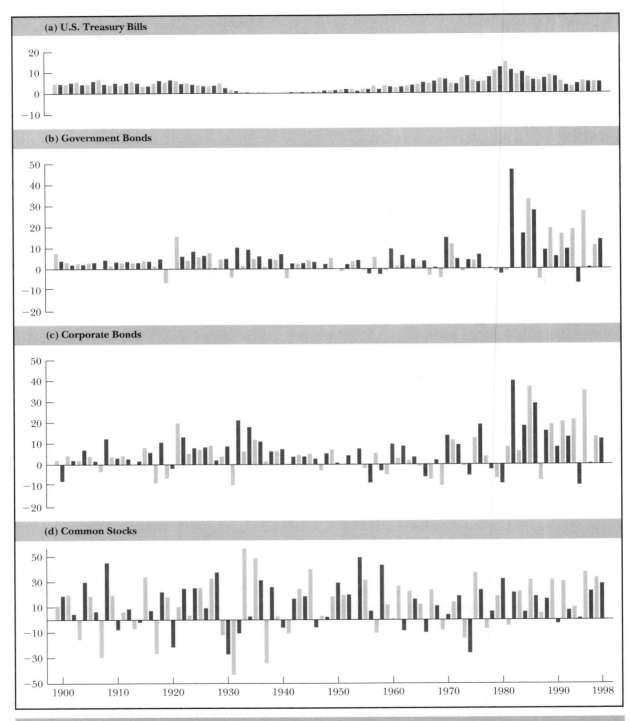

FIGURE 1.1 Annual Returns, 1899–1998

Source: Copyright 1999 by Global Financial Data. This data can be accessed on the Internet at www.globalfindata.com.

Cost of Living

In addition to annual returns on the four types of securities, Table 1.1 also includes the annual percentage change in the Consumer Price Index (CPI), which indicates changes in the cost of living. These changes ranged from –10.82% in 1921 to 20.45% in 1918 and averaged 3.31% per year.

1.1.2 RISK, RETURN, AND DIVERSIFICATION

Average annual returns are shown at the bottom of the table. Below these values are the standard deviations of annual returns, which measure the variability of the returns on the respective securities.[2] Table 1.2 provides average annual returns and standard deviations for securities from the United States, Japan, Germany, and the United Kingdom from 1970 to 1998. The historical record revealed in Figure 1.1, Table 1.1, and Table 1.2 illustrates a general principle: When sensible investment strategies are compared with one another, risk and return tend to go together. That is, securities that have higher average returns tend to have greater amounts of risk.

It is important to note that historical variability is not necessarily an indication of prospective risk. The former deals with the record over some past period; the latter has to do with uncertainty about the future. The pattern of returns on Treasury bills provides one example. Although the values have varied from period to period, in any given period the amount to be received at the end of the period is known in advance and so it carries little or no risk. However, the annual return on a common stock is very difficult to predict accurately. For such an investment, variability in the past may provide a fairly good measure of the uncertainty surrounding the future return.[3]

To see how difficult it is to predict common stock returns, cover the portion of Table 1.1 from 1941 on, and then try to guess the return in 1941. Having done this, uncover the value for 1941, and try to guess the return for 1942. Proceed in this manner a year at a time, keeping track of your overall predictive accuracy. Unless you are very clever or very lucky, you will conclude that past patterns of stock returns are of little help in predicting future returns. It will later be seen that this apparent randomness in security returns is a characteristic of an efficient market—that is, a market in which security prices fully reflect current information (discussed in Chapter 4).

Is one of these four types of securities better than the others? No. The right security or combination of securities depends on the investor's situation and preferences for return relative to his or her risk tolerance. There may be "right" or "wrong" securities for a particular person or purpose. However, it would be surprising to find a security

TABLE 1.2 Summary Statistics for U.S., Japanese, German, and U.K. Securities, 1970–1998

	Average Return[a]				*Standard Deviation*			
	U.S.	*Japan*	*Germany*	*U.K.*	*U.S.*	*Japan*	*Germany*	*U.K.*
Short-term interest rates	6.94%	5.56%	6.15%	10.44%	2.70%	3.42%	2.42%	3.14%
Government bonds	9.82	7.08	8.08	12.32	12.52	5.13	5.09	12.45
Common stocks	14.65	11.60	12.12	18.69	16.18	28.93	25.57	31.86
Inflation	5.25	4.26	3.48	8.07	3.31	5.02	2.08	5.69

[a]Foreign returns are calculated in local currencies. Foreign stock returns include dividend income adjusted for the tax rate applicable to U.S. investors. Government bonds include maturities greater than one year.

Source: U.S. financial market data provided by Global Financial Data. Foreign financial market data provided by Brinson Partners.

that is clearly wrong for everyone and every purpose. Such situations simply do not exist in an efficient market. Figure 1.2 illustrates the tradeoffs between risk and return. Note that the securities with higher historical returns also have higher levels of risk, suggesting that no security dominates any other by having both higher return and lower risk. "Blend" at the right in Figure 1.2 is the risk-return performance of a portfolio that, at the beginning of each year, had one-half of its funds invested in corporate bonds and the other half in common stocks. The portfolio's average return of 8.62% equals one-half of the average return of corporate bonds and one-half the average return of common stocks. However, the risk of the portfolio is 12.19%, which is less than half the risk of corporate bonds plus half the risk of common stocks, which equals

diversification

14.57%. This illustrates the fundamental principle of **diversification.** When securities are combined into a portfolio, the new portfolio will have a lower level of risk than the simple average of the risks of the securities because when some securities are doing poorly, others are doing well. This pattern tends to reduce the extremes in the portfolio's returns, so there is less fluctuation in the portfolio's value.

1.1.3 SECURITY MARKETS

Security markets bring together buyers and sellers of securities; they are mechanisms created to facilitate the exchange of financial assets. There are many ways security markets can be differentiated. One way has already been mentioned—primary versus secondary markets. The key difference between primary and secondary markets is whether the securities are being sold by the issuer. The primary market can be subdivided into *seasoned* and *unseasoned* new issues. A seasoned new issue refers to the offering of an additional amount of an already existing security to the public, whereas an

FIGURE 1.2 Risk and Return, 1899–1998

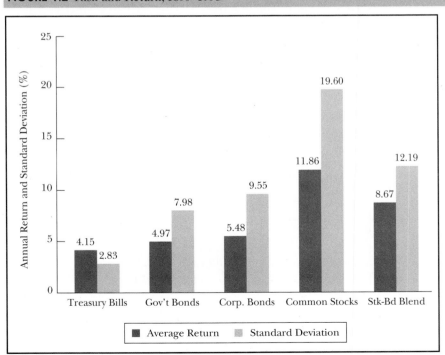

Source: Copyright 1999 by Global Financial Data. This data can be accessed on the Internet at www.globalfindata.com.

unseasoned new issue involves the initial offering of a security to the public. Unseasoned new equity issues are often referred to as *initial public offerings,* or *IPOs.*

 Another way of differentiating security markets is the life span of the financial assets. **Money markets** usually involve securities that expire in one year or less, whereas **capital markets** usually have securities with life spans greater than one year. For example, Treasury bills are traded in a money market, and Treasury bonds are traded in a capital market.

money markets
capital markets

1.1.4 FINANCIAL INTERMEDIARIES

financial
intermediary
financial
institution

Financial intermediaries, also known as **financial institutions,** are organizations that issue financial claims against themselves (they sell financial assets representing claims on themselves in return for cash), and they use the proceeds from these issuances to purchase primarily the financial assets of others. Financial intermediaries position themselves between providers and users of funds. Because financial claims simply represent the right-hand side of the balance sheet (liabilities and stockholders' equity) for any organization, the key distinction between financial intermediaries and other types of organizations involves what is on the left-hand side of the balance sheet (assets).

 For example, a typical commercial bank issues financial claims against itself in the form of debt (such as checking and savings accounts) and equity, but so does a typical manufacturing firm. However, commercial banks invest most of their money in loans to individuals and corporations as well as in U.S. government securities such as Treasury bills, whereas typical manufacturing firms invest their money mostly in land, buildings, machinery, and inventory. Thus the banks invest primarily in financial assets, whereas manufacturing firms invest primarily in real assets. Accordingly, banks are classified as financial intermediaries, and manufacturing firms are not. Other types of financial intermediaries include savings and loan associations, savings banks, credit unions, life insurance companies, mutual funds, and pension funds.

 Financial intermediaries provide an indirect method for corporations to acquire funds. As illustrated in Figure 1.3(a), corporations can obtain funds directly from the general public using the primary market, as mentioned earlier. Alternatively, they can obtain funds indirectly from the general public using financial intermediaries, as shown

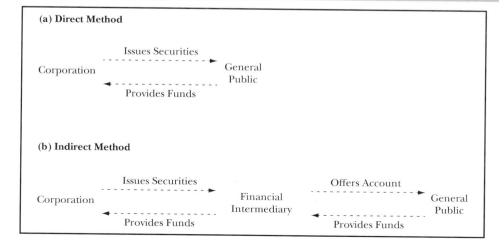

FIGURE 1.3 Corporate Funds Acquisition

(a) Direct Method

Corporation — Issues Securities → General Public
← Provides Funds

(b) Indirect Method

Corporation — Issues Securities → Financial Intermediary — Offers Account → General Public
← Provides Funds   ← Provides Funds

MONEY MATTERS

In Search of Past Performance

"Those who do not remember the past are condemned to repeat it," asserts a famous maxim. From the investor's perspective, those words of wisdom might be rephrased as "those who do not remember the past are condemned to invest unwisely."

Developing a basic knowledge of historical security markets' performance is not simply an exercise in cocktail party conversation trivia. Rather, that information is a critical element in many phases of the investment process. Most importantly, it permits the investor to recognize and profit from the relationship between risk taking and economic reward inherent in the structure of security markets.

From a theoretical standpoint, the existence of this risk–return trade-off is central to models of asset pricing (see Chapters 10 and 12). From a practical stance, an investor should understand the nature of the relationship between investment risk and return if he or she is to allocate his or her funds among various asset classes optimally over the long term, consistent with his or her level of risk tolerance (see Chapter 17). Moreover, to effectively evaluate the success of an investment program, an investor must be able to place absolute results in the context of the risk–return characteristics of that investment program (see Chapter 18).

Despite the importance of security market performance data, the availability of comprehensive historical performance information on various types of assets is relatively new. Even today, continuing efforts notwithstanding, the historical investment results of many asset types in which investors are placing ever larger amounts of money—such as venture capital—are relatively unknown.

Extensive historical return data on U.S. security markets became widely available to investors with the work of Roger Ibbotson and Rex Singquefield (I&S) in the late 1970s. Prior to the I&S research, only a few narrowly focused studies concerning interest rates and stock prices had been conducted in the United States and Europe.

The I&S research brought together the returns on U.S. stocks, bonds, Treasury bills, and inflation. Their study directly compared the performance of the U.S. security markets and quantified the risk premiums historically earned by investors in those markets.

The I&S research has had a number of important consequences for the investment profession:

1. It was widely disseminated, reaching a broad audience of investment practitioners.

2. It permitted investors to attach hard numbers to previously held beliefs about the risk premiums earned in various asset classes and the correlation of returns between those asset classes.

3. It provided a rationale for investors, particularly large institutional investors, such as pension and endowment funds, to increase their investments in equity assets.

4. It stimulated research into the past performance of nontraditional investments, including gold, real estate, and commodities.

5. It created a thriving business for brokerage and consulting firms to collect historical performance data on various asset types and distribute that data to their interested clients. (Global Financial Data, whose data are used in Table 1.1, is an example.)

In the past 20 years, the growing popularity of foreign investing by individuals and institutions has spurred the demand for information about the past performance of foreign security markets. Both academics and practitioners have responded with increased research efforts. That research, however, has been hampered in many countries by fragmented and nonautomated recordkeeping procedures. Even in countries with well-established security markets, reliable data cannot be gathered from earlier than the 1960s. Countries with "emerging" security markets may have little more than a decade of security market data available under the best of conditions. Nevertheless, in the near future, investors can expect to find increasing access to foreign security markets' performance data, a development that will reinforce the trend toward the globalization of investments.

A growing body of performance data is being collected for other types of assets as well. Various investment organizations, anxious to stimulate investor interest in particular asset types, have been willing to bear the expense necessary to collect, process, and disseminate past price data and then maintain those databases on a continuing basis. Price indices for certain forms of commercial real estate are now available stretching back over 20 years. Performance information has also been compiled for speculative-grade bonds (so-called junk bonds) and investments in venture capital, leveraged buyouts, and oil and gas properties, to mention only a few. Although the performance history for these asset types is not as comprehensive as it is for U.S. stocks and bonds, the increasingly broad nature of performance databases for nontraditional assets will allow investors to make more intelligent investment decisions.

in Figure 1.3(b). Here the corporation gives a security to the intermediary in return for funds. The intermediary, in turn, acquires funds by allowing the general public to maintain such investments as checking and savings accounts with it.

1.2 The Investment Process

As mentioned previously, the investment process involves how an investor should make decisions about what marketable securities to invest in, how extensive the investments should be, and when the investments should be made. A five-step procedure for making these decisions is the basis of the investment process:

1. Set investment policy.
2. Perform security analysis.
3. Construct a portfolio.
4. Revise the portfolio.
5. Evaluate the performance of the portfolio.

1.2.1 INVESTMENT POLICY

investment policy

The first step, setting **investment policy,** involves determining the investor's objectives and the amount of his or her investable wealth. Because there is a positive relationship between risk and return for sensible investment strategies, it is not appropriate for an investor to say that his or her objective is to "make a lot of money." What is appropriate is for an investor to state that his or her objective is to attempt to make a lot of money while recognizing that there is some chance that large losses may be incurred. Investment objectives should be stated in terms of both risk and return.

This step in the investment process concludes with the identification of potential categories of financial assets to be included in the portfolio. This identification will be based on, among other things, the investment objectives, amount of investable wealth, and tax status of the investor. For example, as is discussed later, usually it does not make sense for individual investors to buy preferred stock or for tax-exempt investors (such as pension funds) to invest in tax-exempt securities (such as municipal bonds).

Investment policy is the cornerstone of the investment process. Without it, investors have no appropriate context in which to make decisions. Unfortunately, however, investment policy often receives the least attention from investors.

1.2.2 SECURITY ANALYSIS

security analysis

The second step in the investment process is performing **security analysis.** It involves examining several individual securities (or groups of securities) within the broad categories of financial assets previously identified. One reason to examine securities is to identify those that seem mispriced. There are many approaches to security analysis. However, most of these approaches fall into one of two classifications. The first classification is **technical analysis;** analysts who use this approach to security analysis are called technicians, or technical analysts. The second classification is **fundamental analysis;** those who use it are known as fundamentalists, or fundamental analysts. In discussing these two approaches to security analysis, the focus will be first on common stocks and then on other types of financial assets.

technical analysis
fundamental
analysis

In its simplest form, technical analysis involves the study of stock market prices in an attempt to predict future price movements. Past prices are examined to identify recurring trends or patterns in price movements. Then more recent stock prices are analyzed to identify emerging trends or patterns that are similar to past ones. This analysis is done in the belief that these trends or patterns repeat themselves. By identifying an emerging trend or pattern, the analyst hopes to predict accurately future price movements for a particular stock.

In its simplest form, fundamental analysis begins with the assertion that the "true" (or "intrinsic") value of any financial asset equals the present value of all cash flows the owner of the asset expects to receive. Accordingly, the fundamental stock analyst attempts to forecast the timing and size of these cash flows and then converts the cash flows to their equivalent present value using an appropriate discount rate. More specifically, the analyst attempts to estimate the discount rate and to forecast the dividends a particular stock will provide in the future; this process is equivalent to forecasting the firm's earnings per share and payout ratios. Once the true value of the common stock of a particular firm has been estimated, it is compared with the current market price of the common stock to determine whether the stock is fairly priced. Stocks whose estimated true value is less than their current market price are known as overvalued, or overpriced, stocks, whereas those whose estimated true value is greater than their current market price are known as undervalued, or underpriced, stocks. The magnitude of the difference between the true value and the current market price is important because the strength of the analyst's conviction that a given stock is mispriced will depend, in part, on it. Fundamental analysts believe that any notable cases of mispricing will be corrected by the market in the near future, meaning that prices of undervalued stocks will show unusual appreciation and prices of overvalued stocks will show unusual depreciation.

1.2.3 PORTFOLIO CONSTRUCTION

portfolio
construction

selectivity
timing

The third step in the investment process, **portfolio construction,** involves identifying specific assets in which to invest and determining how much to invest in each one. The issues of selectivity, timing, and diversification need to be addressed by the investor. **Selectivity,** also known as microforecasting, refers to security analysis and focuses on forecasting price movements of individual securities. **Timing,** also known as macroforecasting, involves forecasting price movements of common stocks in general relative to fixed-income securities, such as corporate bonds and Treasury bills. Diversification, as mentioned earlier, involves constructing the investor's portfolio in such a manner that risk is minimized, subject to certain restrictions.

1.2.4 PORTFOLIO REVISION

portfolio revision

The fourth step in the investment process, **portfolio revision,** concerns the periodic repetition of the previous three steps. Over time the investor may change his or her investment objectives, which, in turn, would make the currently held portfolio less than optimal. The investor may create a new portfolio by selling certain securities and by purchasing others. Another motivation for revising a portfolio would be if the prices of securities changed—some securities that initially were not attractive may become attractive and others that were attractive at one time may no longer be so. The investor may want to add the former to his or her portfolio and eliminate the latter. Such decisions depend on, among other things, transaction costs incurred in making changes and the magnitude of the perceived improvement in the investment outlook for the revised portfolio.

1.2.5 PORTFOLIO PERFORMANCE EVALUATION

portfolio performance evaluation

The fifth step in the investment process, **portfolio performance evaluation,** involves determining periodically how the portfolio is performing in terms of the return earned and also the risk experienced by the investor. Thus, appropriate measures of return and risk as well as relevant standards (or benchmarks) are needed.

1.3 Globalization

The "globalization" of the investment business has become a recurring theme in recent years. The U.S. economy is much more integrated with the rest of the world than it was several decades ago. Similarly, U.S. financial markets are more sensitive to events abroad than they were previously. The growth in foreign security markets has significantly increased international opportunities for U.S. investors.

When looking at stock markets around the world, most striking is the tremendous growth in the last three decades. Since 1970, the total value of the world's major equity markets has grown from less than $1 trillion to more than $20 trillion. Although the U.S. stock market has participated in this growth, Figure 1.4 shows that non-U.S. stock markets have expanded even faster. As a result, the total proportion of the world's common stocks represented by the United States has declined during the past 25 years from roughly 66% to roughly 49% today. With the formation of vibrant stock markets in Eastern Europe, Latin America, and the Far East, non-U.S. capital markets may continue to grow in relative importance.

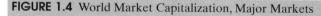

FIGURE 1.4 World Market Capitalization, Major Markets

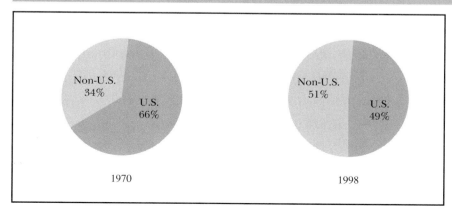

Summary

1. Because this book is about investing, it focuses on the investment environment and the investment process.
2. An investment involves the sacrifice of current dollars for future dollars.
3. Investments may be made in real assets or in financial assets (securities) through either primary markets or secondary markets.
4. The primary task of security analysis is to identify mispriced securities by determining the future benefits of owning those securities, the conditions under which those benefits will be received, and the likelihood that such conditions will occur.
5. The rate of return on an investment measures the percentage change in an investor's wealth due to owning the investment.
6. Studies of the historical rates of return on various types of securities demonstrate that common stocks produce relatively high but variable returns; bonds generate lower returns with less variability; and Treasury bills provide the lowest returns with the least variability.
7. In an efficient market, security prices reflect information immediately. Security analysis will not enable investors to earn abnormally high returns.
8. Security markets exist in order to bring together buyers and sellers of securities.
9. Financial intermediaries (financial institutions) are organizations that issue financial claims against themselves and use the proceeds primarily to purchase the financial assets of others.
10. The investment process describes how an investor makes decisions about what securities to invest in, how extensive these investments should be, and when they should be made.
11. The investment process involves five steps: setting investment policy, performing security analysis, constructing a portfolio, revising the portfolio, and evaluating portfolio performance.
12. There has been a tremendous growth in equity markets around the world since 1970, particularly in those located outside the United States.

Questions and Problems

1. Why do secondary security markets not generate capital for the issuers of securities traded in those markets?
2. Colfax Glassworks stock currently sells for $36 per share. One year ago the stock sold for $33. The company recently paid a $3 per share dividend. What was the rate of return for an investor in Colfax stock during the past year?
3. At the beginning of the year, Ray Fisher decided to take $50,000 in savings out of the bank and invest it in a portfolio of stocks and bonds; $20,000 was placed into common stocks and $30,000 into corporate bonds. A year later, Ray's stock and bond holdings were worth $25,000 and $23,000, respectively. During the year $1,000 in cash dividends was received on the stocks, and $3,000 in coupon payments was received on the bonds. (The stock and bond income was not reinvested in Ray's portfolio.)
   a. What was the return on Ray's stock portfolio during the year?
   b. What was the return on Ray's bond portfolio during the year?
   c. What was the return on Ray's total portfolio during the year?
4. Why are Treasury bills considered a riskfree investment? How do investors bear risk when they own Treasury bills?
5. The following table shows the annual returns on a portfolio of small stocks during the 20-year period from 1976 to 1995. What is the average return and standard deviation of this portfolio? How do they compare with the 1976 to 1995 average

return and standard deviation of the common stock portfolio whose annual returns are shown in Table 1.1?

1976:	57.38%	1981:	13.88%	1986:	6.85%	1991	44.63%
1977:	25.48	1982:	28.01	1987:	−9.30	1992	23.35
1978:	23.46	1983:	39.67	1988:	22.87	1993	20.98
1979:	43.46	1984:	−6.67	1989:	10.18	1994	3.11
1980:	39.88	1985:	24.66	1990:	−21.56	1995	34.46

6. Does it seem reasonable that higher-return securities historically have exhibited higher risk? Why?
7. Give an example, outside of the financial markets, in which you commonly face a trade-off between risk and return.
8. Examining Table 1.1, you can find many years in which Treasury bills produced greater returns than common stocks. How can you reconcile this fact with the statements made in the text, citing a positive relationship between risk and return?
9. Again referring to Table 1.1, in terms of total returns, what was the worst single calendar year for common stock investors? What was the worst year in the 1970s? Compare these two years in terms of return in "constant dollars" (that is, purchasing power). Does this comparison show that the stock market slump of the 1970s was not as disastrous as the crash associated with the Great Depression? Explain.
10. Why might it be reasonable to believe that including securities issued in foreign countries will improve the risk–reward performance of your portfolio?
11. Describe how life insurance companies, mutual funds, and pension plans each act as financial intermediaries.
12. What are the five steps in the investment process? What is the importance of each step to the entire process?
13. Why does it not make sense to establish an investment objective of "making a lot of money"?
14. Financial advisers often contend that elderly people should invest their portfolios more conservatively than younger people. Should a conservative investment policy for an elderly person call for owning no common stocks? Discuss the reasons for your answer.
15. What factors might an individual investor take into account in determining his or her investment policy?

Endnotes

1. In general any cash received during the period is treated as if it were received at the end of the period. However, this treatment typically causes the actual return to be understated. For example, if the dividends on Widget were received at midyear, the investor could have put them in a bank savings account and earned, say, 5% interest on them for the rest of the year. This interest then would have amounted to $.15 (= .05 × $3.00), resulting in the annual return being equal to 20.375% {= [($45 + $3 + $.15) − $40]/$40 = $8.15/$40}. One method of handling dividends is to subtract half of them from the beginning-of-period price and add half of them to the end-of-period price; in this example, the return would be 20.78% {= [($45 + $3/2) − ($40 − $3/2)]/($40 − $3.2)}. See Maria Crawford Scott, *Portfolio Building* (Chicago: American Association of Individual Investors, 1998).

2. The standard deviation was calculated as equal to the square root of

$$\sum_{t=1}^{100} (r_t - \bar{r})^2 / 99$$

where r_t is the return for a year t (so $t = 1$ corresponds to 1899, $t = 2$ to 1900, and so on) and $\bar{r}$ is the average return over the 100-year period. A larger standard deviation means a greater amount of dispersion in the 100 returns and, hence, indicates more risk. Standard deviation will be discussed in greater detail in Chapter 7.

3. Studies have found that (1) stocks have not become more volatile recently and (2) stocks tend to be more volatile during recessions (particularly during the Great Depression of 1929 to 1939).

CHAPTER 2

Buying and Selling Securities

broker

When a security is sold, many people are likely to be involved. Although it is possible for two investors to trade with each other directly, it is more common for brokers, dealers, and markets to perform the transactions. A **broker** acts as an agent for an investor and is compensated with a commission. Many individual investors deal with brokers in large retail or "wire" houses—firms with many offices that are connected by private wires with their own headquarters and, through the headquarters, with the major markets. The people in these brokerage firms with prime responsibility for individual investors are called **account executives,** or **registered representatives.** Institutional investors, such as mutual funds and pension funds, also deal with these large retail brokerage firms, but they typically do so through separate divisions designed to handle their specific trading needs. Institutional investors also conduct business with smaller firms that maintain only one or two offices and specialize in institutional business.

account executives
registered
representatives

regional brokerage
firms
discount brokers

Two other types of brokerage firms are **regional brokerage firms** and **discount brokers.** The former concentrate on transactions within a specific geographic area; the securities traded in a regional brokerage firm have a special following in that area of the country because the issuers of those securities are located in that area. Discount brokers offer "bare-bones" services at low cost; they provide fewer services than full-service brokerage firms, such as Merrill Lynch and Salomon Smith Barney. Investors who simply want to have their orders executed and do not seek investment advice can substantially reduce the commissions they pay by using a discount broker. Lately a special type of discount broker has emerged who accepts, executes, and confirms orders electronically over the Internet for lower commissions than those of the generic discount broker. (See the Money Matters box later in this chapter for an additional discussion of discount brokers.)

commissions

An account executive's compensation is usually determined by **commissions** his or her customers pay; these commissions are directly related to the amount of turnover (trading) in his or her customers' accounts. This arrangement may tempt some account executives to recommend frequent changes in customers' holdings, and because commissions on various investments differ, account executives may also be tempted to recommend changes in investments with the highest rates. Account executives who encourage excessive turnover (or "churning") often lose customers and may even encounter lawsuits.[1] Nonetheless, such behavior may be profitable in the short run.

It is easy to open an account with a brokerage firm: Simply appear at (or call) the local office. Someone (perhaps an account executive) at the office will help you fill out some forms.[2] After these forms have been signed, everything else can be done by mail

17

or telephone or via the Internet. Transactions are posted to your account just as they are to a bank account. For example, you can deposit money, purchase securities using money from the account, and add the proceeds from security sales to the account. Brokers exist (and charge fees) to make security transactions as simple as possible. All that the investor has to do is to provide the broker with **order specifications.**

order specifications

In discussing order specifications, assume that the investor's order involves common stock. In this situation the investor must specify

1. The name of the stock
2. Whether the order is to buy or sell shares
3. The size of the order
4. How long the order will be outstanding
5. What type of order will be used

The last three specifications are discussed next in more detail.

2.1   Order Size

round lot
odd lot

When buying or selling common stock, the investor places an order involving a round lot, an odd lot, or both. Generally, a **round lot** is for an order of 100 shares, or a multiple of 100 shares.[3] **Odd lot** orders generally are for 1 to 99 shares. Orders for more than 100 shares, but that are not multiples of 100, are a mixture of round and odd lots. Thus an order for 259 shares should be considered an order for 2 round lots and an odd lot of 59 shares.

2.2   Time Limit

day orders

The investor must specify a time limit on his or her order—that is, the time within which the broker should attempt to fill the order. For **day orders** the broker will attempt to fill the order only during the day in which it is entered. If the order is not filled by the end of the day, it is canceled. If a time limit is not specified by the investor, the broker will treat the order as a day order. Week and month orders expire at the end of the respective calendar week or month during which they are entered provided they have not been filled by then.

open orders
good-till-canceled (GTC) orders
fill-or-kill (FOK) orders
discretionary orders

Open orders, also known as **good-till-canceled (GTC) orders,** remain in effect until they are either filled or canceled by the investor. However, during the time before the order has been filled, the broker may periodically ask the investor to confirm the order. In contrast to GTC orders, **fill-or-kill (FOK) orders** are canceled if the broker is unable to fully execute them immediately.

Discretionary orders allow the broker to set the specifications for the order. The broker may have complete discretion on all the order specifications, including which stocks to buy and sell, or limited discretion, in which case he or she decides only on the price and timing of the order.

2.3   Types of Orders

There are several types of orders that investors can place with their brokers. The most common types are market and limit orders, although stop and stop limit orders can also be used. There are other special types of orders that are rarely used; readers interested in them should contact their broker.[4]

2.3.1 MARKET ORDERS

market order

The most common type of order is the **market order,** wherein the broker is instructed to buy or sell a stated number of shares immediately. The broker is obligated to act on a "best-efforts" basis to get the best possible price (as low as possible for a purchase order, as high as possible for a sell order) when the order is placed. An investor placing a market order can be fairly certain that the order will be executed but will be uncertain of the price. However, there is usually reliable information available beforehand about the likely price at which such an order will be executed. Not surprisingly, market orders are day orders.

2.3.2 LIMIT ORDERS

limit order
limit price

The second type of order is the **limit order,** wherein a **limit price** is specified by the investor when the order is placed with the broker. If the order is to purchase shares, the broker is to execute the order at a price less than or equal to the limit price. If the order is to sell shares, the broker is to execute the order at a price greater than or equal to the limit price. Thus, the investor specifies a ceiling on the price to purchase shares and a floor on the price to sell shares. In contrast to a market order, an investor using a limit order cannot be certain that the order will be executed. Hence there is a trade-off between these two types of orders—immediacy of execution with uncertain price versus uncertain execution with bounded price.

For example, assume that the common stock of ABC Corporation is currently selling for $25 a share. An investor placing a limit order to sell 100 shares of ABC with a limit price of $30 per share and a time limit of one day is not likely to have the order executed because this limit price is well above the current price of $25. Only if the current price becomes more favorable (if the stock price rises by at least $5 per share) will the limit order be executed.

2.3.3 STOP ORDERS

stop order
stop price

There are two other kinds of orders: stop orders (also known as stop-loss orders) and stop limit orders. For a **stop order** the investor must specify a **stop price.** If it is a sell order, the stop price must be below the market price when the order is placed. Conversely, if it is a buy order, the stop price must be above the market price when the order is placed. If someone later trades the stock at a price that reaches or passes the stop price, the stop order becomes, in effect, a market order. Hence a stop order can be considered as a conditional market order.

Continuing with the $25 ABC Corporation example, a stop sell order at $20 would not be executed until a trade involving others had taken place at a price of $20 or lower. Conversely, a stop buy order at $30 would not be executed until a trade involving others had taken place at a price of $30 or more. If the price does not fall to $20, then the stop sell order would not be executed. Similarly, if the price does not rise to $30, the stop buy order would not be executed. In contrast, a limit order to sell at $20 or a limit order to buy at $30 would be executed immediately, because the current market price is $25.

Stop orders can be used to "lock in" paper profits. For example, assume that an investor had purchased ABC stock at $10 per share two years ago and now has paper profits of $15 (= $25 − $10) per share. Entering a stop sell order at $20 per share means that the investor will be sure of realizing a profit of roughly $10 (= $20 − $10) per share if the stock falls in price to $20. If instead of falling the stock price rises, then the investor's stop order will be ignored and the investor's paper profits will increase in size. Thus, the stop order will provide the investor with a degree of profit protection.[5]

One risk with stop orders is that the actual price at which the order is executed may be much higher or lower than the stop price. This discrepancy occurs if the stock price moves rapidly in one direction. For example, ABC may have an industrial accident that results in a spate of lawsuits and causes the stock price to fall rapidly to $12 per share. In this situation a stop sell order at $20 may be executed at $16 instead of near the stop price of $20.

2.3.4   STOP LIMIT ORDERS

stop limit order

The **stop limit order** helps investors know with more certainty the execution price associated with a stop order. With a stop limit order the investor specifies not one but two prices—a stop price and a limit price. Once someone trades the stock at a price that reaches or passes the stop price, then a limit order is created at the limit price. Hence stop limit order can be viewed as a conditional limit order.

Continuing with the example, the investor could place a stop limit order to sell ABC stock with a stop price of $20 and a limit price of $19. In effect, a limit order to sell ABC stock at a price of $19 or higher would be activated for the investor only if others trade ABC at a price of $20 or less. Conversely, the investor could enter a stop limit order to buy ABC stock with a stop price of $30 and a limit price of $31. In this case a limit order to buy ABC stock at a price of $31 or lower would be activated for the investor only if others trade ABC at a price of $30 or more.

If the stop price is reached, execution is assured for a stop order but not for a stop limit order. In the ABC example, the industrial accident may cause the stock price to fall to $12 so rapidly that the stop limit order to sell (with the stop price at $20 and the limit price at $19) might not have been executed, whereas the stop order (with the stop price at $20) would have been executed at $16. There is a trade-off between these two types of orders that is similar to the trade-off between market and limit orders. Once activated, the stop order provides certain execution at an uncertain price, whereas a stop limit order provides uncertain execution at a bounded price.

2.4   Margin Accounts

cash account

margin account

hypothecation agreement

street name

A **cash account** with a brokerage firm is like a regular checking account: Deposits (cash and the proceeds from selling securities) must cover withdrawals (cash and the costs of purchasing securities). A **margin account** is like a checking account with overdraft privileges: If more money is needed than is in the account, a loan (with limits on the amount) is automatically made by the broker.[6] When opening a margin account with a brokerage firm, an investor must sign a **hypothecation agreement**, also known as a customer's agreement. This agreement allows the brokerage firm to pledge the investor's securities as collateral for bank loans, provided the securities were purchased using a margin account. Most brokerage firms also expect investors to allow them to lend their securities to others who wish to "sell them short." Short selling is described later in this chapter.

In order to facilitate either pledging or lending securities, brokerage firms request that securities purchased through a margin account be held in **street name**.[7] This means that the registered owner of the security, as far as the original issuer is concerned, is the brokerage firm. In the case of common stock the issuer sends all dividends, financial reports, and voting rights to the brokerage firm, not to the investor. The brokerage firm then simply forwards the items to the investor.[8] Accordingly, an investor holding a security in street name will be treated basically the same as if the investor were holding the security in his or her own name.[9]

Securities Brokers: Full-Service to Self-Service

 The Internet has affected the way many businesses deliver goods and services to their clients, but in few places has its impact been more dramatic than in the brokerage industry. In a very short period of time the Internet has forced brokerage firms to significantly restructure the types of services they offer and the prices they charge for those services.

It was not long ago (as recently as the early 1990s) that the brokerage industry was segmented neatly into full-service and discount brokers. Full-service brokers, such as Merrill Lynch and Paine Webber, offer clients a wide range of financial services including investment research and advice, financial planning, home equity loans, life insurance, and cash management accounts. Perhaps more importantly, their clients receive the personal touch, with individual account representatives assigned to their accounts. Conversely, discount brokers, such as Charles Schwab or Quick & Reilly, offer a narrower range of investment services. "Deep" discount brokers focus on only one type of service, such as executing stock trades cheaply and efficiently. Other discount brokers may provide a wider variety of services, such as trading a full range of bonds (government, municipal, and corporate); trading options; and selling insurance, limited partnerships, and mutual funds. Customer interaction with discount brokers is less personal than with full-service brokers because salespersons are not assigned to client accounts. In making a choice between full-service and discount brokers, investors have to weigh service against costs. Those firms with the lowest commissions tend to offer the fewest opportunities to do anything but trade common stocks, whereas higher commission firms offer a wider range of services.

These formerly neat distinctions have blurred with the increasing use of the Internet. The number of primarily online brokerage firms has exploded. Firms like E*Trade and Ameritrade have become household names. With their low overhead, these firms work under different profit formulas than their counterparts on the full-service and traditional discount side. Online brokers have been able to slash trading commissions. Consider the following: The American Association of Individual Investors' 1999 Survey of Discount Broker Commissions and Services reported that for a 100-share trade, the average online broker charged $15. By comparison, the average traditional discount broker charged $42 for the same trade. A full-service broker would charge roughly $100. Stated as a percent of the total dollar amount traded ($5,000), the differences in costs are eye-catching: The online brokerage cost is .30%, the traditional discount brokerage cost is .84%, and the full-service cost is 2.00%.

The convenience and lower costs of online trading have caused many investors to migrate to the Internet, which, in turn, has forced a competitive response from full-service and traditional discount brokers. Many now offer their own online trading services along with their standard trading procedures. Merrill Lynch, for example, had initially scorned the idea of online trading but began offering such services in 1999. Charles Schwab, one of the original traditional discount brokers, reported that in 1999 well over half of its trading was done online.

How should you as an investor choose between the various types of brokerage services offered in the marketplace? For starters, all brokers feature a number of common services. All are registered with the SEC and all provide SIPC insurance. Most offer margin loans (discussed in this chapter). Trade execution varies little in quality from one broker to another for small trades. Many of these trades are handled automatically through the computer systems of the NYSE and Nasdaq (discussed in the next chapter).

Most financial advisers suggest that investors consider a number of factors in selecting a broker. Commissions, of course, are at, or near, the top of everyone's list. However, you should also consider other fees that a broker might charge, such as fees for issuing stock certificates or wiring funds. Margin loan rates should be monitored if

(continued)

you trade on margin. Some firms offer more an-cillary services than others, such as sweeps of cash balances to money market funds, checkwriting privileges, and debit cards. In addition, the ability to buy no-load mutual funds varies among bro-kers. Research and investment recommendations are another important way brokers distinguish themselves. The full-service brokers and some traditional discount brokers offer research pro-duced by their own teams of analysts. Other bro-kers may offer research by third parties, such as Value Line or Standard & Poor's.

In the end, the choice of a broker will be highly personal. If you are the type of investor who knows precisely what securities to buy or sell, does his or her own research, requires no "hand-holding," and buys "plain vanilla" securities, then it does not make sense to pay the heavy commis-sions charged by full-service brokers or even those charged by traditional discount brokers. A bare-bones online broker may serve all of your needs. But if you trade in uncommon securities—unlisted stocks or foreign stocks, for example—or if you are an investing novice and want counseling and recommendations from your broker (with all the caveats attached to relying on a broker for invest-ment advice), then it may pay to use a full-service broker.

A margin account allows investors to make certain types of transactions that are not allowed with a cash account. These transactions are known as margin purchases and short sales.

2.4.1   MARGIN PURCHASES

With a cash account an investor who purchases a security pays the entire cost of the purchase with cash. However, with a margin account the investor pays only a percent-age of the cost and can borrow the rest from the broker.[10] The amount borrowed from the broker as a result of such a **margin purchase** is referred to as the investor's **debit balance.** The interest charged on loans advanced by a broker for a margin purchase is usually calculated by adding a service charge (for example, 1%) to the broker's **call money rate.** The call money rate is the rate paid by the broker to the bank that loaned the broker the cash that ultimately went to the investor to pay for part of the purchase.

margin purchase
debit balance
call money rate

For example, the bank may loan money to the broker at a rate of 10%, and the bro-ker may loan this money to the investor at a rate of 11%. The call money rate changes over time as market interest rates change. The interest rate investors are charged for loans used to finance margin purchases changes correspondingly. The securities pur-chased by the investor serve as collateral on the loan made by the broker. In turn, the broker uses these securities as collateral on the loan made by the bank. Thus the bro-ker is acting as a financial intermediary in the lending process by facilitating a loan from the bank to the investor. Sometimes, however, the broker will use the brokerage firm's own funds to make the loan. Regardless, the investor will be treated as if a bank made the loan

Initial Margin Requirement

initial margin requirement

The minimum percentage of the purchase price that must come from the investor's own funds is known as the **initial margin requirement.** Regulations T, U, G, and X, prescribed in accordance with the Securities Exchange Act of 1934, give the Federal Reserve Board the responsibility for setting this percentage when either common stocks or convertible bonds are purchased.[11] However, the exchanges that fill the pur-chase orders are allowed to set a higher percentage than the one set by the Federal Re-serve Board, and brokers are allowed to set it even higher. Hypothetically, the Federal

Reserve Board could set the initial margin requirement at 50%, the New York Stock Exchange could make it 55%, and the broker could make it 60%. Table 2.1 shows that the initial margin requirement since 1934 as set by the Federal Reserve Board has ranged from 25% to 100%. In 1999 it was 50%.[12]

Consider, as an example, an investor who purchases on margin 100 shares of Widget Corporation for $50 per share. With an initial margin requirement of 60%, the investor must pay the broker $3,000 (= .6 × 100 shares × $50 per share). The remainder of the purchase price, $2,000 [= (1 − .6) × 100 shares × $50 per share], is funded by a loan from the broker to the investor.[13] Table 2.2 presents the investor's balance sheet immediately after the margin purchase. The investor has assets of $5,000 corresponding to the value of Widget stock. Those assets are partially offset by liabilities of $2,000 representing the margin loan, leaving $3,000 in equity. Keep in mind that the 100 shares of Widget are kept as collateral on the $2,000 loan to the investor. If the price of Widget drops, the value of the collateral will decline, causing the broker to become nervous. For example, if the price dropped to $15 per share, the broker would have collateral

TABLE 2.1   Initial Margin Requirements of the Federal Reserve Board

Period		*Initial Margin Requirement (%)*		
Beginning Date	*Ending Date*	*Margin Stocks*	*Short Sales*	*Convertible Bonds*
Oct. 15, 1934	Jan. 31, 1936	25–45	(a)	(b)
Feb. 1, 1936	Mar. 31, 1936	25–55	(a)	(b)
Apr. 1, 1936	Oct. 31, 1937	55	(a)	(b)
Nov. 1, 1937	Feb. 4, 1945	40	50	(b)
Feb. 5, 1945	Jul. 4, 1945	50	50	(b)
Jul. 5, 1945	Jan. 20, 1946	75	75	(b)
Jan. 21, 1946	Jan. 31, 1947	100	100	(b)
Feb. 1, 1947	Mar. 29, 1949	75	75	(b)
Mar. 30, 1949	Jan. 16, 1951	50	50	(b)
Jan. 17, 1951	Feb. 19, 1953	75	75	(b)
Feb. 20, 1953	Jan. 3, 1955	50	50	(b)
Jan. 4, 1955	Apr. 22, 1955	60	60	(b)
Apr. 23, 1955	Jan. 15, 1958	70	70	(b)
Jan. 16, 1958	Aug. 4, 1958	50	50	(b)
Aug. 5, 1958	Oct. 15, 1958	70	70	(b)
Oct. 16, 1958	Jul. 27, 1960	90	90	(b)
Jul. 28, 1960	Jul. 9, 1962	70	70	(b)
Jul. 10, 1962	Nov. 5, 1963	50	50	(b)
Nov. 6, 1963	Mar. 10, 1968	70	70	(b)
Mar. 11, 1968	Jun. 7, 1968	70	70	50
Jun. 8, 1968	May 5, 1970	80	80	60
May 6, 1970	Dec. 5, 1971	65	65	50
Dec. 6, 1971	Nov. 23, 1972	55	55	50
Nov. 24, 1972	Jan. 2, 1974	65	65	50
Jan. 3, 1974	Present	50	50	50

[a]Requirement was the margin "customarily required" by the broker.

[b]Initial margin requirements for convertible bonds were not adopted by the Federal Reserve Board until March 11, 1968.

Source: Federal Reserve Bulletin, various issues.

TABLE 2.2	Investor's Balance Sheet after Margin Purchase		
Assets		*Liabilities and Net Worth*	
Widget stock	$5,000	Margin loan	$2,000
		Equity	$3,000
Total assets	$5,000	Total liabilities and net worth	$5,000

worth $1,500 [= $15 × 100 shares], but the amount of the loan is still $2,000. If the investor skipped town, the broker would still have to make good on the bank loan of $2,000, but would have only $1,500 of the investor's assets to pay off the loan. The broker would have to bear the $500 difference and hope to track down the investor and recoup this amount at a later date.

Marking to Market and Maintenance Margin Requirements

maintenance margin requirement

Brokers require investors to keep collateral in their accounts that is worth more than the amount of the loan. This amount is based on a **maintenance margin requirement.** It is set by the exchanges, not by the Federal Reserve Board, and brokers can set it as high as they want. As of 1999, the New York Stock Exchange set this requirement for common stock and convertible bond purchases at 25%. The formula for determining the minimal amount of collateral that the investor must keep in his or her account is calculated as follows:

$$\text{Minimum collateral required} = \frac{\text{Loan}}{1 - \text{Maintenance margin requirement}} \qquad (2.1)$$

marking to market

Calculating the current market value of the assets and liabilities in the investor's account is known as **marking to market;** in this case it is the assets that will be marked to market to see if they are worth more than the minimum collateral that is required. If an account's collateral falls below the minimum collateral, then the account is said

undermargined margin call

to be **undermargined,** and the broker will then issue a **margin call** requesting the investor to either (1) deposit cash or securities into the account, (2) pay off part of the loan, or (3) sell some securities in the account to pay off part of the loan. These actions will either increase the collateral in the account or reduce the loan, thereby lowering the minimum collateral required shown in Equation (2.1).[14] If the investor does not respond, then, in accordance with the terms of the account, the broker will sell some (or all) of the securities in the account to make the collateral equal to at least the minimum amount required.

If, instead of falling, the stock price rises, the investor can take part of the increase out of the account in cash because the collateral in the account will have risen above the initial margin requirement [that is, the collateral will exceed an amount equal to Loan/(1 − Initial margin requirement)].[15] In this situation the account is considered

unrestricted overmargined

to be **unrestricted** or **overmargined.**

The foregoing discussion considered cases in which the stock price of the shares purchased on margin either (1) fell to such a degree that the collateral was below the maintenance margin requirement (the account was undermargined) or (2) increased, leaving the collateral above the initial margin requirement (the account was overmargined). One more situation should be considered: What if the stock price falls but not by enough to make the collateral drop below the maintenance margin requirement? In this case no action by the investor is necessary since the collateral in the account is below the initial margin requirement but above the maintenance margin

restricted account

requirement. Now, the account will be **restricted;** any transaction that would decrease the collateral further (such as withdrawing cash) will not be allowed.[16]

Table 2.3 shows possible margin account conditions in which the investor in Widget stock might find himself or herself. In the example, 100 shares of Widget stock have been purchased on margin for $50 per share, with an initial margin requirement of 60%. Assume further that the maintenance margin requirement is 30%. Three possible current prices for the stock are presented along with the resulting outcomes for the margin account and potential actions that the investor might take.

Holding Period Return

financial leverage
The use of margin purchases allows the investor to engage in **financial leverage.** That is, by using debt to fund part of the purchase price, the investor can increase the expected rate of return on the investment. However, there is a complicating factor in the use of margin: the effect on the risk of the investment.

Consider Widget again. If the investor believes that the stock will rise $15 per share during the next year, then the expected holding period return on a cash purchase of 100 shares of Widget at $50 per share will be 30% $[= (\$15 \times 100 \text{ shares})/(\$50 \times 100 \text{ shares}) = \$1,500/\$5,000]$, assuming that no cash dividends are paid. A margin purchase would have an expected return of 42.7% $\{= [(\$15 \times 100 \text{ shares}) - (.11 \times \$2,000)]/(.6 \times \$50 \times 100 \text{ shares}) = \$1,280/\$3,000\}$, where the interest rate on margin loans is 11% and the initial margin requirement is 60%. Thus, the investor has increased the expected return from 30% to 42.7% by the use of margin.

But what will happen to the return if the stock falls $10 per share? In this case the investor who made a cash purchase would have a rate of return equal to -20% $[= (-\$10 \times 100 \text{ shares})/\$5,000 = -\$1,000/\$5,000]$. The margin purchaser would have a rate of return equal to $-40.7\%\{= [(-\$10 \times 100) - (.11 \times \$2,000)]/\$3,000 = -\$1,220/\$3,000\}$. Thus the margin purchaser will experience a much larger loss than the cash purchaser for a given dollar decline in the price of the stock.

TABLE 2.3   Potential Margin Account Conditions and Actions for Margin Purchaser

Purchase price = $50
Initial margin requirement = 60%
Maintenance margin requirement = 30%

	Current Stock Price		
	$25	*$45*	*$60*
Actual collateral:			
Market value of 100 shares	$2,500	$4,500	$6,000
Check to see if acount is undermargined:			
Minimum collateral required = $2,000 loan/(1 − .30)	$2,857	$2,857	$2,857
Difference with actual collateral	($357)	$1,643	$3,143
Check to see if account is restricted:			
Minimum collateral required = $2,000 loan/(1 − .60)	$5,000	$5,000	$5,000
Difference with actual collateral	($2,500)	($500)	$1,000
Condition:	Undermargined	Restricted	Overmargined
Potential actions:	1. Add cash or securities	1. Do nothing	1. Do nothing
	2. Pay off part of loan		2. Withdraw excess cash
	3. Sell some shares and use proceeds to pay off part of loan		

Margin purchases are usually made in the expectation that the stock price will rise in the near future, meaning that the investor thinks that the stock's current price is too low. An investor who thinks that a given stock is not too low but too high may engage in a short sale.

2.4.2 SHORT SALES

short sale

"Buy low, sell high" is an old adage from Wall Street. Most investors hope to do just that by buying securities first and selling them later.[17] However, with a **short sale** this process is reversed: The investor sells a security first and buys it back later. In this case the Wall Street adage might be reworded as "sell high, buy low."

Short sales are accomplished by borrowing stock certificates for use in the initial trade, then repaying the loan with certificates obtained in a later trade. Note that the loan here involves certificates, not dollars and cents (although the certificates do have a certain monetary value). The borrower must repay the lender by returning certificates, not dollars and cents (although an equivalent monetary value, determined on the date the loan is repaid, can be remitted instead as it will be used to buy the requisite number of shares), and there are no interest payments to be made by the borrower.

Rules Governing Short Sales

Any order for a short sale must be identified as such. The Securities and Exchange Commission (SEC) has ruled that short sales may not be made when the market price for a security is falling because the short seller could worsen the situation, cause a panic, and profit therefrom. This assumption is inappropriate for an efficient market with astute, alert traders. The precise rule, known as the **up-tick rule** (Rule 10a-1), states that a short sale must be made on a **plus-tick** (or "uptick," meaning the sale must be for a price higher than that of the previous trade) or on a **zero-plus tick** (meaning the sale must be for a price equal to that of the previous trade but higher than that of the last trade at a different price).[18]

up-tick rule
plus-tick
zero-plus tick

Within three business days after a short sale has been made, the short seller's broker must borrow and deliver the appropriate securities to the purchaser. The borrowed securities may come from

- The inventory of securities owned by the brokerage firm itself
- The inventory of another brokerage firm
- The holdings of an institutional investor (such as a pension fund) that is willing to lend its securities
- The inventory of securities held in street name by the brokerage firm for investors who have margin accounts with the firm

The life of the loan is indefinite; there is no specific time limit on it.[19] If the lender wants to sell the securities and thus needs them back, then the short seller will not have to repay the loan if the brokerage firm can borrow shares elsewhere because the loan will be transferred from one lender to another. However, if the brokerage firm cannot borrow the shares, the short seller will have to repay the loan immediately. Interestingly, the identities of the borrower and the lender are known only to the brokerage firm. The lender does not know who the borrower is, and the borrower does not know who the lender is.

An Example

An example of a short sale is indicated in Figure 2.1. At the start of the day, Mr. Lane owns 100 shares of XYZ Company, which are being held for him in street name by Brock, Inc., his broker. During this particular day, Ms. Smith places an order with her broker at Brock to short-sell 100 shares of XYZ. (Mr. Lane believes that the price

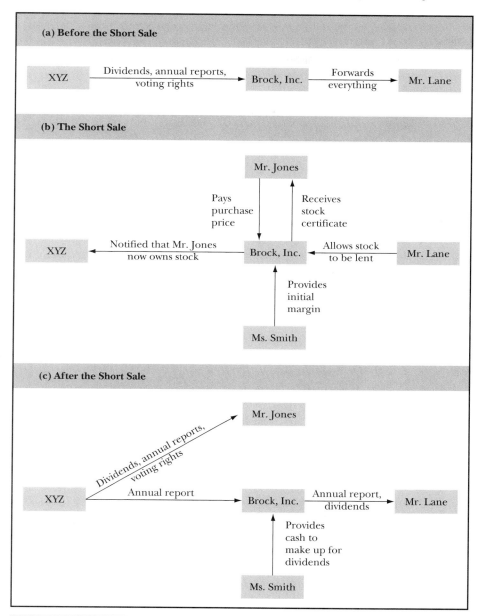

FIGURE 2.1 Short Selling of Common Stock

of XYZ stock is going to rise in the near future, whereas Ms. Smith believes that it is going to fall.) In response, Brock takes the 100 shares of XYZ that it is holding in street name for Mr. Lane and sells them for Ms. Smith to some other investor, in this case Mr. Jones. At this point XYZ will receive notice that the ownership of 100 shares of its stock has changed hands, going from Brock (remember that Mr. Lane held his stock in street name) to Mr. Jones. At some later date Ms. Smith will tell her broker at Brock to purchase 100 shares of XYZ (perhaps from Ms. Poole) and to use these shares to pay off her debt to Mr. Lane. At this point XYZ will receive another notice that the ownership of 100 shares has changed hands, going from Ms. Poole to Brock, restoring Brock to its original position.

Cash Dividends

What happens when XYZ declares and subsequently pays a cash dividend to its stockholders? *Before the short sale* Brock would receive a check for cash dividends on 100 shares of stock. After depositing this check in its own account at a bank, Brock would write a check for an identical amount and give it to Mr. Lane (or, Brock could deposit the dividend in Mr. Lane's brokerage account). Neither Brock nor Mr. Lane is worse off having the shares held in street name. *After the short sale,* XYZ will see that the owner of those 100 shares is no longer Brock but is now Mr. Jones. So XYZ mails the dividend check to Mr. Jones, not Brock. However, Mr. Lane will still be expecting his dividend check from Brock. Indeed, if there was a risk that he would not receive it, he would not have agreed to have his securities held in street name. Brock is required to mail him a check for the same amount of dividends that Mr. Jones received from XYZ—that is, for the amount of dividends Mr. Lane would have received from XYZ had he held his stock in his own name. When Brock mails Mr. Lane such a check, it will be losing an amount of cash equal to the amount of dividends paid. What does Brock do to avoid incurring this loss? It makes Ms. Smith, the short seller, give it a check for an equivalent amount.

Consider all the parties involved in the short sale now. Mr. Lane is content because he has received his dividend check from his broker. Brock is content because its net cash outflow is still zero, just as it was before the short sale. Mr. Jones is content because he received his dividend check directly from XYZ. What about Ms. Smith? She should not be upset with having to reimburse Brock for the dividend check given by Brock to Mr. Lane because the price of XYZ's common stock can be expected to fall by an amount roughly equal to the cash dividend, thereby reducing the dollar value of her loan from Brock by an equivalent amount.

Financial Reports and Voting Rights

What about financial reports and voting rights? Before the short sale these were sent to Brock, who forwarded them to Mr. Lane. After the short sale Brock no longer receives them, so what happens? Financial reports are easily obtained by brokerage firms free of charge, so Brock will probably get copies of them from XYZ and mail a copy to Mr. Lane. However, voting rights are different. These are limited to the registered stockholders (in this case, Mr. Jones) and cannot be replicated like cash dividends by Ms. Smith, the short seller. When voting rights are issued, the brokerage firm (Brock) will try to find voting rights to give to Mr. Lane if he asks for them. (Perhaps Brock owns shares, or manages a portfolio that owns shares of XYZ, and will give the voting rights from these shares to Mr. Lane.) Unless he is insistent, however, Mr. Lane may not get his voting rights once his shares have been borrowed and used in a short sale. In all other matters he will be treated as if he were holding the shares of XYZ in his own name.

Initial Margin Requirement

As mentioned previously, a short sale involves a loan, implying there is a risk that the borrower (in the example, Ms. Smith) will not repay the loan. What would happen in this situation? The brokerage firm would be left without the 100 shares that the short seller, Ms. Smith, owes the firm. Either the brokerage firm, Brock, is going to lose money or the lender, Mr. Lane, is going to lose money. This loss is prevented by not giving the cash proceeds from the short sale, paid by Mr. Jones, to the short seller, Ms.

Smith. Instead, they are held in her account with Brock until she repays her loan. Will holding the proceeds assure the brokerage firm that the loan will be repaid? No, unfortunately it will not.

In the example assume that the 100 shares of XYZ were sold at a price of $100 per share. The proceeds of $10,000 from the short sale are held in Ms. Smith's account, but she is not allowed to withdraw them until the loan is repaid. Now imagine that at some date after the short sale, XYZ stock rises $20 per share. Now Ms. Smith owes Brock 100 shares of XYZ with a current market value of $12,000 (= 100 shares × $120 per share), but has only $10,000 in her account. If she skips town, Brock will have collateral of $10,000 (in cash) but a loan of $12,000, resulting in a loss of $2,000. How will Brock protect itself from experiencing losses from short sellers who do not repay their loans? By the use of margin requirements. Ms. Smith must not only leave the short sale proceeds with her broker, but she must also give her broker the initial margin applied to the amount of the short sale.[20] If the initial margin requirement is 60%, she must give her broker $6,000 (= .6 × $10,000) in cash.[21]

Table 2.4 shows the investor's balance sheet immediately after the short sale. The investor's assets total $16,000 made up of the cash proceeds from the short sale and the initial margin. The investor has liabilities of $10,000 representing the market value of the short sold stock, leaving $6,000 in equity.

Marking to Market and Maintenance Margin Requirements

In the example XYZ stock would have to rise in value to a price above $160 per share in order for Brock to be in jeopardy of not being repaid. The initial margin provides the brokerage firm with a certain degree of protection. However, this protection is not complete because it is not unheard of for stocks to rise in value by more than 60% [= ($160 − $100)/$100]. The maintenance margin requirement and the process of marking to market protect the brokerage firm from losing money in such situations. In order to examine the use of the maintenance margin requirement and marking to market in short sales, the minimal amount of collateral required in a short sale is defined as

$$\text{Minimum collateral required} = \text{Loan} \times (1 + \text{Maintenance margin requirement}) \quad \textbf{(2.2)}$$

Note that the loan is multiplied by 1 plus the maintenance margin requirement, whereas for margin purchases it was divided by 1 minus the maintenance margin requirement. In the case of a short sale, the loan is marked to market because it is based on the current market price of the borrowed shares.

If XYZ stock rises to $130 per share, the minimal collateral required in Ms. Smith's account will be $16,900 [= ($130 × 100 shares) × (1 + .3)]. Because the actual collateral is $16,000, the account is undermargined, which causes Ms. Smith to receive a margin call. Just as with margin calls on margin purchases, she will be asked to deposit more collateral by adding cash or securities to her account. If the stock price falls instead of rising, the short seller can take a bit more than the drop in the price out of the account in cash. This is because the loan has fallen so that the collateral now exceeds the initial margin requirement, resulting in the account being overmargined (unrestricted).[22]

TABLE 2.4	Investor's Balance Sheet after Short Sale		
Assets		*Liabilities and Net Worth*	
Cash proceeds from short sale	$10,000	Market value of short sold stock	$10,000
Initial margin	$ 6,000	Equity	$ 6,000
Total assets	$16,000	Total liabilities and net worth	$16,000

The foregoing discussion considered the cases for short sales in which the stock price either (1) fell and the account was thereby overmargined or (2) rose so much that the maintenance margin requirement was violated and the account was thereby undermargined. There is one case left to be considered: What happens if the stock price goes up but not to such a degree that the maintenance margin requirement is violated? In this case the initial margin requirement has been violated and therefore the account is restricted. Here restricted has a meaning similar to its meaning for margin purchases: Any transaction that has the effect of further decreasing the collateral in the account will be prohibited.

Table 2.5 shows possible margin account conditions in which the investor in XYZ stock might find himself or herself. In the example, 100 shares of XYZ stock have been sold short for $100 per share with initial margin and maintenance margin requirements of 60% and 30%, respectively. Three possible current prices for the stock are presented along with the resulting outcomes for the margin account and potential actions that the investor might take.

What happens to the cash in the short seller's account? When the loan is repaid, the short seller will have access to the cash. (Actually, the cash is typically used to buy the shares that are needed to repay the loan.) Before the loan is repaid, however, the short seller may be able to earn interest on the portion of the cash balance that represents margin. (Brokerage firms will typically accept certain securities, such as Treasury bills, in lieu of cash for meeting margin requirements.)

Regarding the cash proceeds from the short sale, sometimes the securities may be borrowed only on the payment of a premium by the short seller; in other words, the short seller not only does not earn interest on the cash proceeds but must *pay* a fee for borrowing the shares. When large institutional investors short sell stock, they typically negotiate a split with the brokerage firm of the interest earnings on the cash proceeds, thereby *receiving* a fee. However, securities are generally loaned "flat" to small investors.

TABLE 2.5   Potential Margin Account Conditions and Actions for a Short Seller

Short sale price = $100
Initial margin requirement = 60%
Maintenance margin requirement = 30%

	Current Stock Price		
	$90	*$105*	*$130*
Actual collateral:			
Short sale proceeds plus initial margin	$16,000	$16,000	$16,000
Check to see if acount is undermargined:			
Minimum collateral required =			
Loan value × (1 + .30)	$11,700	$13,650	$16,900
Difference with actual collateral	$4,300	$2,350	($900)
Check to see if account is restricted:			
Minimum collateral required =			
Loan value × (1 + .60)	$14,400	$16,800	$20,800
Difference with actual collateral	$1,600	($800)	($4,800)
Condition:	Overmargined	Restricted	Undermargined
Potential actions:	1. Do nothing	1. Do nothing	1. Add cash or securities
	2. Withdraw excess cash		2. Buy shares to pay off part of loan

The brokerage firm keeps the cash proceeds from the short sale and enjoys the use of this money, and neither the short seller nor the lender receives any direct compensation. When this happens, the brokerage firm makes money not only from the commission paid by the short seller but also on the cash proceeds from the sale. (The brokerage firm may, for example, earn interest by purchasing Treasury bills with these proceeds.)

Holding Period Return

Short selling results in holding period returns to the investor that are opposite to what would be earned if the shares were purchased on margin [ignoring interest on the margin loan and assuming that (1) the initial margin requirement for the short sale is met by depositing cash and (2) the short loan is flat]. Hence short sales also involve the use of financial leverage.

Consider XYZ once again, where Ms. Smith short sold its stock at a price of $100 per share. If she later repays the short loan when the stock is selling for $75 per share and just after XYZ has paid a $1 per share cash dividend, then her return will equal 40% $[= (\$100 - \$75 - \$1)/(.6 \times \$100) = \$24/\$60]$. In contrast, note that the return for someone who had purchased the stock of XYZ on margin would be -40% $[= (\$75 + \$1 - \$100)/(.6 \times \$100) = -\$24/\$60]$, whereas the return for someone who had purchased the stock without using margin would be -24% $[= (\$75 + \$1 - \$100)/\$100 = -\$24/\$100]$.

However, if Ms. Smith incorrectly predicted the future price movement of XYZ and it went up to $120 per share just after paying a $1 per share cash dividend, then her return will equal -35% $[= (\$100 - \$120 - \$1)/(.6 \times \$100) = -\$21/\$60]$. Conversely, if the stock had been purchased on margin, her return would have been 35% $[= (\$120 + \$1 - 100)/(.6 \times \$100) = \$21/\$60]$. Without margin, the return on the stock purchase would be 21% $[= (\$120 + \$1 - \$100)/\$100 = \$21/\$100]$.

What happens to these return calculations if interest is earned on both the initial margin and the short proceeds? The rate of return to the short seller increases. Consider the example where XYZ fell to $75, and assume that the short seller earned 5% on the initial margin deposit and 4% on the short proceeds. In this case the return to the short seller would be 51.7% $\{= [\$100 - \$75 - \$1 + (.05 \times .6 \times \$100) + (.04 \times \$100)]/(.6 \times \$100) = \$31/\$60\}$, which is notably higher than the 40% previously calculated. Hence financial leverage is even more apparent when either form of interest is paid to the short seller.[23]

Summary

1. Investors typically buy or sell securities through brokers who are compensated for their services with commissions.
2. For a security transaction, an investor must specify the following: the security's name, buy or sell, order size, time limit, and type of order.
3. The four standard types of orders are market, limit, stop, and stop limit. Market orders, followed by limit orders, are the most common types of orders.
4. Investors may purchase securities with cash or may borrow from brokerage firms to buy securities on margin.
5. Investors must make down payments on their margin purchases, maintain minimum collateral levels in their margin accounts, and pay interest on margin loans.
6. If an investor's collateral falls below the maintenance margin requirement, the investor's account is undermargined. The investor will receive a margin call and must increase the collateral or decrease the loan in the account.
7. Buying on margin results in financial leverage, thereby magnifying (positively or negatively) the impact of a security's return on the investor's wealth.

8. Short selling involves the sale of securities that are not owned, but rather are borrowed by the seller. The borrowed securities must ultimately be purchased in the market and returned to the lender.

9. A short seller must deposit the proceeds of the short sale and initial margin with his or her broker. The short seller must also maintain a minimum level of collateral in his or her margin account or face a margin call.

Questions and Problems

1. Discuss the advantages and disadvantages to the investor of the following:
   a. Market order
   b. Limit order
   c. Stop order

2. Lollypop Killefer purchases on margin 200 shares of Landfall Corporation stock at $75 per share. The initial margin requirement is 55%. Prepare Lollypop's balance sheet for this investment at the time of purchase.

3. Buck Ewing opened a margin account at a local brokerage firm. Buck's initial investment was to purchase 200 shares of Woodbury Corporation on margin at $40 per share. Buck borrowed $3,000 from a broker to complete the purchase.
   a. At the time of the purchase, what was the collateral in Buck's account?
   b. If Woodbury stock subsequently rises in price to $60 per share, what is the collateral in Buck's account?
   c. If Woodbury stock subsequently falls in price to $35 per share, what is the collateral in Buck's account?

4. Snooker Arnovich buys on margin 1,000 shares of Rockford Systems stock at $60 per share. The initial margin requirement is 50% and the maintenance margin requirement is 30%. If the Rockford stock falls to $50, will Snooker receive a margin call?

5. Lizzie Arlington has deposited $15,000 in a margin account with a brokerage firm. If the initial margin requirement is 50%, what is the maximum dollar amount of stock that Lizzie can purchase on margin?

6. Explain the purpose of the maintenance margin requirement.

7. Penny Bailey bought on margin 500 shares of South Beloit Inc. at $35 per share. The initial margin requirement is 45% and the annual interest on margin loans is 12%. Over the next year the stock rises to $40. What is Penny's return on investment?

8. Ed Delahanty purchased 500 shares of Niagara Corporation stock on margin at the beginning of the year for $30 per share. The initial margin requirement was 55%. Ed paid 13% interest on the margin loan and never faced a margin call. Niagara paid dividends of $1 per share during the year.
   a. At the end of the year, if Ed sold the Niagara stock for $40 per share, what would Ed's rate of return be for the year?
   b. At the end of the year, if Ed sold the Niagara stock for $20 per share, what would Ed's rate of return be for the year?
   c. Recalculate your answers to parts (a) and (b) assuming that Ed made the Niagara stock purchase for cash instead of on margin.

9. Beauty Bancroft short sells 500 shares of Rockdale Manufacturing at $25 per share. The initial margin requirement is 50%. Prepare Beauty's balance sheet as of the time of the transaction.

10. Through a margin account, Candy Cummings short-sells 200 shares of Madison Inc. stock for $50 per share. The initial margin requirement is 45%.
    a. If Madison stock subsequently rises to $58 per share, what is the equity in Candy's account?
    b. If Madison stock subsequently falls to $42 per share, what is the equity in Candy's account?

11. Dinty Barbare short sells 500 shares of Naperville Products at $45 per share. The initial margin and maintenance margin requirements are 55% and 35%, respectively. If Naperville stock rises to $50, will Dinty receive a margin call?

12. Eddie Gaedel is an inveterate short seller. Is it true that Eddie's potential losses are infinite? Why? Conversely, is it true that the maximum return that Eddie can earn on his investment is 100%? Why?

13. The stock of DeForest Inc. sold at the beginning of the year for $70 per share. At that time Deerfoot Barclay short sold 1,000 shares of the stock. The initial margin requirement was 50%. DeForest stock has risen to $75 at year-end, and Deerfoot faced no margin calls in the interim. Further, the stock paid a $2 dividend at year-end. What was Deerfoot's return on this investment?

14. Calculate Candy Cummings's rate of return in parts (a) and (b) of Problem 10, assuming that the short loan was flat but the initial margin deposit earned interest at a rate of 8%, and that the prices of $58 and $42 were observed after one year during which the firm did not pay any dividends.

15. Distinguish between an investor receiving a margin call and having his or her margin account restricted.

Endnotes

1. For more on churning, see Seth C. Anderson, Sue L. Visscher, and Donald A. Winslow, "Guidelines for Detecting Churning in an Account," *AAII Journal,* 11, no. 9 (October 1989): 12–14. Rewards in the brokerage business are heavily skewed toward brokers who generate the largest trading volume from their customers. In general, brokers earn the greatest compensation by selling products affiliated with their employers.

2. For more on opening an account, see Bruce Sanking, "The Brokerage Account Form: Handle with Care," *AAII Journal,* 13, no. 6 (July 1991): 15–16.

3. Occasionally, a round lot is for less than 100 shares. When this happens, it is usually for stocks that are either high priced or traded infrequently.

4. An example of a special order is a "market on close" order, which is executed at the close of trading at the best price available at the time.

5. Stop buy orders can be used to lock in paper profits generated from short sales, which will be discussed later in this chapter.

6. There are other types of accounts. Furthermore, an investor may have more than one type of account with a brokerage firm. An interesting type is the "wrap" account (started in 1980 by E. F. Hutton & Co.) where the broker, for an annual fee, helps the investor select money managers. See Albert J. Golly, Jr., "The Pros and Cons of Brokerage Wrap Accounts," *AAII Journal,* 15, no. 2 (February 1993): 8–11.

7. Investors with cash accounts may voluntarily elect to have their securities held in street name. Reasons offered for doing so include reduced risk of theft of securities that the investor might otherwise hold in his or her physical possession and improved record keeping. Typically the brokerage firm will send monthly statements detailing the investor's holdings. See J. Michael Bishop and Henry Sanchez, Jr., "Reading and Understanding Brokerage Account Statements," *AAII Journal,* 14, no. 10 (November 1992): 7–10.

8. The investor may not receive the voting rights, particularly if the stock has been loaned to a short seller. This situation is discussed later in this chapter.

9. The investor whose securities are held in street name may be concerned about what would happen if the brokerage firm were to go bankrupt. If this were to happen, the Securities Investor Protection Corporation (SIPC), a government-chartered firm that insures investors' accounts against brokerage firm failure, would cover each individual investor's losses up to $500,000. Some brokerage firms have also purchased private insurance in addition to the insurance offered by SIPC. See Henry Sanchez, Jr., "SIPC: What Happens If Your Brokerage Firm Fails," *AAII Journal,* 12, no. 10 (November 1990): 13–16.

10. With either a cash or a margin account, the investor usually has up to three business days after an order is executed to provide the broker with the necessary cash. The third business day after execution is known as the **settlement date.** For margin purchases, the loan value of certain other securities can be used instead of cash as a down payment, in which case these securities must be provided by the settlement date. Sellers of securities must also provide their brokers with their securities by the settlement date. If requested, an investor may be able to get an extension of the settlement date.

11. Regulation T covers credit extended by brokers and dealers; Regulation U covers credit extended by banks; Regulation G covers credit extended by anyone other

than brokers, dealers, or banks; and Regulation X covers borrowers. All common stocks and convertible bonds that are listed on a national securities exchange (for example, the New York Stock Exchange, the American Stock Exchange, or the National Market System of Nasdaq) can be purchased on margin. Furthermore, four times a year the Federal Reserve Board publishes a roster of other securities that can be purchased on margin. The firms that are put on this roster depend on such factors as number of shareholders and firm size.

12. Initial margin requirements on nonconvertible bonds are set in a similar fashion, except that the Federal Reserve Board is not involved. Typically the investor wishing to purchase nonconvertible bonds on margin faces a lower initial margin requirement (for example, 10% for purchases of U.S. Treasury securities).

13. In general at the end of each month the interest on the loan is calculated and added to the amount of the loan. For simplicity, this fact is ignored in the examples given here.

14. The broker may ask the investor to immediately (in some cases within three business days, in other cases even sooner) bring the actual margin up to a level corresponding to the maintenance margin requirement, or to a level that is even higher, ranging up to the initial margin requirement.

15. Alternatively, the cash could be used as part of the initial margin requirement on an additional margin purchase by the investor. In fact, if it was large enough, it could be used to meet the entire requirement.

16. There is an exception to this rule if the account was overmargined before it became restricted. In such a situation, the broker will create a *special memorandum account* for the investor; the balance in this account can be withdrawn in cash or used to purchase more securities.

17. After purchasing a security, an investor is said to have established a *long position* in the security.

18. The Nasdaq Short Sale Rule, recently extended on a temporary basis (subject to SEC approval), covers the larger stocks in the over-the-counter market. Under this rule, short selling is prohibited at or below the current bid when that bid is lower than the previous different bid. Here the bids that are referred to are the "best bids," meaning the highest ones being quoted. The Nasdaq market is discussed in Chapter 3.

19. The New York Stock Exchange, the American Stock Exchange, and Nasdaq publish monthly lists of the **short interest** in their stocks. (Short interest refers to the number of shares of a given company that have been sold short where, as of a given date, the loan remains outstanding.) To be on the NYSE or AMEX list, either the total short interest must be equal to or greater than 100,000 shares or the change in the short interest from the previous month must be equal to or greater than 50,000 shares. The respective figures for Nasdaq are 50,000 and 25,000.

20. Table 2.1 also presents the initial margin requirement for short sales. Note that it has been set at the same level as for margin purchases of common stocks in the postwar period.

21. There are other forms of collateral that can be substituted for cash.

22. Alternatively, the short seller could short sell a second security and not have to put up all (or perhaps any) of the initial margin.

23. An investor with a margin account may purchase several different securities on margin or may short sell several different securities. He or she may also purchase some on margin and short sell others. The determination of whether an account is undermargined, restricted, or overmargined depends on the total activity in the account. For a discussion of aggregation of an investor's margin account, see William F. Sharpe, Gordon J. Alexander, and Jeffery V. Bailey, *Investments,* 6th ed. (Upper Saddle River, NJ: Prentice Hall, 1999), pp. 38–40.

CHAPTER 3

Security Markets

security market
financial market

A **security market,** or **financial market,** can be defined as a mechanism for bringing together buyers and sellers of financial assets in order to facilitate trading. One of its main functions is "price discovery"—that is, to ensure that security prices reflect currently available information. The faster and more accurately price discovery is achieved, the more efficiently financial markets will direct capital to its most productive opportunities, thereby leading to greater improvement in public welfare. **Secondary markets** involve trading financial assets previously issued. This chapter is devoted to such markets; Chapter 13 discusses securities issued in the **primary market.**

secondary markets

primary market

3.1 Call and Continuous Markets

3.1.1 CALL MARKETS

call markets

In **call markets,** trading is allowed only at specified times. When a security is "called," individuals interested in either buying or selling it are physically brought together.[1] There may be an explicit auction in which prices are announced until the quantity demanded is as close as possible to the quantity supplied. Alternatively, orders may be left with a clerk, and periodically an official of the exchange will set a price that allows the maximum number of shares from the previously accumulated orders to be traded.

3.1.2 CONTINUOUS MARKETS

continuous markets

In **continuous markets,** trades may occur at any time. Although only investors are needed for such a market to operate, it would not be effective without intermediaries. In a continuous market without intermediaries, an investor who wanted to buy or sell a security quickly might have to either spend a great deal of money searching for a good offer or run the risk of accepting a poor one. Because orders from investors arrive randomly, prices in such a market vary considerably, depending on the flow of buy orders relative to the flow of sell orders. However, anyone willing to take temporary positions in securities could make a profit by resolving these transitory variations in supply and demand. This is the role of intermediaries known as dealers (also known as market-makers) and specialists. In the pursuit of personal gain, these intermediaries reduce fluctuations in security prices that are unrelated to changes in value and in doing so provide **liquidity** (or marketability) for investors. Liquidity allows investors to convert securities into cash at a price similar to the price of the previous trade, assuming no new information has arrived since the previous trade.

liquidity

Secondary security markets for common stocks (as well as for certain other securities) in the United States typically involve dealers or specialists. The next section presents a detailed description of how these markets function and the role played by

organized exchanges

dealers and specialists. Although the focus is on markets for common stocks, many of their features are applicable to the markets for other types of financial assets (such as bonds). **Organized exchanges,** which are central physical locations where trading is done under a set of rules and regulations, are discussed first. Exchanges for common stocks include the New York Stock Exchange (NYSE), the American Stock Exchange (AMEX), and various regional exchanges.

3.2 Major Markets in the United States

3.2.1 NEW YORK STOCK EXCHANGE

The New York Stock Exchange is a corporation with 1,366 full members. It has a charter and a set of rules and regulations that govern its operation and the activities of its members. A board of 26 directors that is elected by the membership supervises the exchange. Of the directors, 12 are members and 12 are not; the latter are known as "public directors." The remaining two directors are full-time employees: a chairperson who also functions as the chief executive officer and a vice chairperson who also functions as president.

seat

In order to become a member, a person must purchase a **seat** (comparable to a membership card) from a current member.[2] Members are allowed to execute trades using the facilities provided by the exchange. Because most trades of common stocks, in both dollar size and number of shares, take place on the NYSE, this privilege is valuable.[3] Not surprisingly, many brokerage firms are members, meaning that an officer (if the brokerage firm is a corporation), a general partner (if the brokerage firm is a partnership), or an employee of the firm could be a member. Indeed, many brokerage firms have more than one member. A brokerage firm with one or more NYSE memberships is often referred to as a **member firm.**

member firm
listed security

A stock that is available for trading on the NYSE is known as a **listed security.** A company must apply to the NYSE for it's stock to be listed. The initial application is usually informal and confidential. If approved, a formal application is announced publicly and approval of the formal application is almost certain. The general criteria used by the NYSE in approving an application include the following:

- The degree of national interest in the company
- The company's relative position and stability in the industry
- Whether the company is engaged in an expanding industry, with prospects of at least maintaining the company's relative position[4]

delist

Companies that are approved for listing must agree to pay a nominal annual fee and provide certain information to the public. After listing, if trading interest in a company's stock declines substantially, the NYSE may decide to **delist** the company so its stock will no longer be available for trading on the exchange. Delisting also occurs when a listed company is acquired by another company or is merged into another company because the originally listed company no longer exists. A company may also ask to have its stock delisted even though it is still eligible for listing. In order to request delisting, the company must first acquire approval from its audit committee and a majority of its directors, according to NYSE Rule 500. After the approval is granted, the company must notify its shareholders and allow 20 to 60 business days for them to react (for example, shareholders may ask the board to reconsider its decision).

Table 3.1 shows the specific criteria that are used by the NYSE to determine whether to list or delist a U.S. stock (tighter standards are applied to non-U.S. stocks). Because companies may apply for listing on more than one exchange, the NYSE has

TABLE 3.1   NYSE Criteria for Listing and Delisting a Security

(a) Initial Listing Requirements of the NYSE for a Domestic Company[a]

1. Either (a) the pretax income for the most recent year must be at least $2,500,000 and the pretax income over each of the preceding 2 years must be at least $2,000,000 or (b) the pretax income over the most recent 3 years must be at least $6,500,000 in total with a minimum of $4,500,000 in the most recent year, and all 3 years must have been profitable.
2. Net tangible assets must be worth at least $40,000,000.
3. There must be a least 1,100,000 shares outstanding that are publicly held, and these shares must have an aggregate market value of at least $40,000,000 (this amount is subject to periodic adjustment based on market conditions).
4. There must be either (a) at least 2,000 stockholders who each own a minimum of 100 shares or (b) at least 2,200 stockholders with the monthly trading volume averaging at least 100,000 shares over the most recent 6 months or (c) at least 500 stockholders with monthly trading volume averaging at least 1,000,000 shares over the most recent 12 months.

(b) NYSE Conditions for Delisting a Security[b]

1. There are fewer than 400 stockholders.
2. The number of stockholders falls below 1,200 and average monthly trading volume is less than 100,000 shares over the most recent 12 months.
3. The number of shares that are publicly held falls below 600,000.
4. The aggregate market value of publicly held shares falls below $8,000,000 (this amount is subject to periodic adjustment based on market conditions).
5. The aggregate market value of shares outstanding falls below $12,000,000 and earnings after taxes over the past three years are less than $600,000.
6. Net tangible assets falls below $12,000,000 and earnings after taxes over the past three years are less than $600,000.

[a]In general, all these requirements must be met for initial listing.

[b]Normally a security will be considered for delisting if any of these conditions occur. However, under certain circumstances a security may be delisted even though none of the conditions occur.

Source: Adapted from *Fact Book: 1998 Data* (New York Stock Exchange, 1999).

some companies listed on it that are also listed on other U.S. exchanges or on foreign exchanges. Companies listed on U.S. exchanges are usually U.S. companies, and those listed on foreign exchanges are usually foreign companies (a notable exception is the London Stock Exchange, as will be seen later in this chapter). Under certain conditions an exchange may set up "unlisted trading privileges" for transactions in a stock already listed on another exchange.

Trading Halts and Circuitbreakers

trading halt

Whereas delisting refers to the permanent suspension of exchange trading for a particular firm's shares, occasionally the need arises for a temporary suspension of trading in a firm's shares, which is known as a **trading halt.** Trading halts typically are issued by the NYSE when trading in a stock becomes disturbed because of rumors or news releases (such as rumors of a takeover attempt or the announcement of unexpected poor quarterly earnings) or if a large imbalance of orders has accumulated. The opening of trading can be delayed for similar reasons.

circuitbreakers

The NYSE can also temporarily halt trading simultaneously in all its listed stocks (or a large number of them). This is done automatically using **circuitbreakers** when circumstances indicate that there is a need to reduce market volatility and to promote investor confidence. Under Rule 80B, as revised in April 1998, if the Dow Jones Industrial

Average (DJIA) declines 10% in a day before 2 P.M. Eastern time, the NYSE shuts down for one hour (if the decline occurs after 2:30 P.M., the market does not shut down; if it occurs between 2 P.M. and 2:30 P.M., the market closes for 30 minutes). If the DJIA continues to decline after it reopens making the total decline for the day at least 20% by 1 P.M., the market closes for two hours. (If the continued decline occurs after 2 P.M., the market closes for the rest of the day; if it occurs between 1 P.M. and 2 P.M., the market closes for one hour.) If the DJIA again continues to decline after it reopens, making the total decline that day 30%, the market shuts down for the rest of the day.[5]

In summary, the current trigger points and NYSE reactions for the Rule 80B circuitbreaker are as follows:

DJIA Trigger	*When Reached*	*Reaction*
10% decline	Before 2 P.M.	One-hour halt
20% decline	Before 1 P.M.	Two-hour halt
30% decline	Any time	Closed for rest of day

These trigger points are converted into DJIA points at the beginning of each quarter based on the average closing price of the index during the last month of the previous quarter and rounded to the nearest 50 points. Thus, if in June 1999 the average closing price of the DJIA was 10,700, then the trigger points for the July–August–September quarter would be 1,050 (10% of 10,700 is 1,070), 2,150 (20% of 10,700 is 2,140), and 3,200 (30% of 10,700 is 3,210).

Whether Rule 80B actually reduces market volatility, as its originators intended, is debatable. The large intraday price decline implied by Rule 80B has occurred only once since the rule's inception. On October 27, 1997, the DJIA plunged 554.25 points (7.2%). Under Rule 80B's provisions at that time, a half-hour shutdown was triggered, followed quickly thereafter by a one-hour shutdown. Because the last trading halt took place at 3:30 P.M., the NYSE closed for the rest of the day. The next day the DJIA rose 337 points. Critics claimed that the existence of the circuitbreakers actually destabilized the market. They argued that after the first trading halt, investors rushed to submit sell orders to beat the anticipated next shutdown, which accelerated the market's decline. Despite recent changes in Rule 80B, many market participants continue to call for elimination or substantial restructuring of the circuitbreakers.

New York Stock Exchange Members

Members in the NYSE fall into one of four categories, depending on the type of trading activity in which they engage. The categories are commission brokers, floor brokers, floor traders, and specialists. Of the 1,366 members of the NYSE, roughly 700 are commission brokers, 400 are specialists, 225 are floor brokers, and 41 are floor traders. The trading activities of members in these categories are as follows:

commission brokers

1. **Commission brokers.** These members take orders that customers have placed with their respective brokerage firms and ensure the orders are executed on the exchange. The brokerage firms they work for are paid commissions by the customers for their services.

floor brokers

2. **Floor brokers** (also known as two-dollar brokers). These members assist commission brokers when there are too many orders flowing into the market for the commission brokers to handle alone. For their assistance, they receive part of the commission paid by the customer. (Sometimes both floor brokers, as defined here, and commission brokers are lumped together and called floor brokers.)

floor traders

3. **Floor traders.** These members trade only for themselves and are prohibited by exchange rules from handling public orders. They hope to make money by taking advantage of perceived trading imbalances that result in temporary mispricings,

which allows them to "buy low and sell high." They are also known as registered competitive market-makers, competitive traders, or registered traders.

specialists

4. *Specialists.* These members perform two roles. First, any limit order that the commission broker cannot execute immediately because the current market price is not at or better than the specified limit price will be given to the specialist for possible execution in the future. If this order is subsequently executed, the specialist is paid part of the customer's commission. The specialist keeps these orders in what is known as the **limit order book** (or specialist's book). Stop and stop limit orders are also left with the specialist to enter in the same book. In this situation the specialist is acting as a broker (that is, agent) for the customer's broker and can be thought of as a "broker's broker."

limit order book

Second, the specialist acts as a **dealer** (or **market-maker**) in certain stocks (in particular, for the same stocks in which he or she acts as a broker). In this role the specialist buys and sells certain stocks for his or her own account and is allowed to seek a profit in doing so. However, as a dealer, the specialist is required by the NYSE to maintain a "fair and orderly market" in those stocks in which he or she is registered as a specialist. Thus, the NYSE expects the specialist to buy or sell shares from his or her own account when there is a temporary imbalance between the number of buy and sell orders. (Specialists are allowed to short sell their assigned stocks, but they still must follow the up-tick rule.) Even though the NYSE monitors the trading activities of the specialists, this requirement is so ill-defined that it is difficult, if not impossible, to enforce.

dealer
market-maker

As might be inferred from the preceding discussion, specialists are at the center of the trading activity on the NYSE. Each stock that is listed on the NYSE has one specialist assigned to it.[6] (In the past, two or more specialists might have been assigned to the same stock.) There are about 3,000 common stocks listed on the NYSE and only about 400 specialists. As those numbers suggest, each specialist is assigned more than one stock.

trading post

All orders involving a given stock must be taken physically or electronically to a **trading post,** a spot on the floor of the NYSE where the specialist for that stock always stands while the NYSE is open.[7] It is here that an order is either executed or left with the specialist.

Placing a Market Order

The operation of the NYSE is best described using an example. Mr. B asks his broker for the current price of General Motors (GM) shares. The broker punches a few keys on a PC-like quotation machine and finds that the current **bid** and **asked prices** on the NYSE are as favorable as the prices available on any other market at $61 and $61\frac{1}{4}$, respectively. In addition, the quotation machine indicates that these bid and asked prices are good for orders of at least 1,500 and 3,000 shares, respectively. These quotations mean the NYSE specialist is willing to buy at least 1,500 shares of GM at $61 a share (the bid price) and is willing to sell at least 3,000 shares of GM at $61\frac{1}{4}$ (the asked price).[8] After getting this information, Mr. B instructs his broker to "buy 300 at market," meaning that he wants to place a market order with his broker for 300 shares of GM. The broker transmits the order to his or her firm's New York headquarters, where the order is relayed to the brokerage firm's "booth" on the side of the exchange floor. When the order is received, the firm's commission broker goes to the trading post for GM.

bid price
asked price

A standing order to buy at $61 means that no lower price need be accepted, and a standing order to sell at $61\frac{1}{4}$ means that no higher price need be paid. The only negotiation left is the spread between the two prices. If Mr. B is lucky, another broker (for example, one with a market order to sell 300 shares for Ms. S) will "take" the order at a price "between the quotes," say at $61\frac{1}{8}$, resulting in "price improvement." (This happens often, as about one-third of the volume in NYSE-listed stocks is traded between the bid and asked quotes.) Information will be exchanged between the two brokers and the sale made. Figure 3.1 illustrates the procedure used to fill Mr. B's order.

double auction

If the gap between the quoted bid and asked prices is wide enough, an auction may take place among commission brokers, with sales made at one or more prices between the specialist's quoted values. This auction is known as a **double** (or two-way) **auction,** because both buyers and sellers participate in the bidding process.

What if no response came from the floor when Mr. B's order arrived? The specialist would then "take the other side" and sell 300 shares to Mr. B's broker at $61\frac{1}{4}$ per share. The actual seller might be the specialist or another investor whose limit order is being executed by the specialist. Sometimes the specialist will "stop" the order, meaning that the order will not be filled immediately but the specialist will guarantee that a price that is no worse than his or her quote will be obtained for the investor before the

FIGURE 3.1 Order Flow for a NYSE-Listed Security

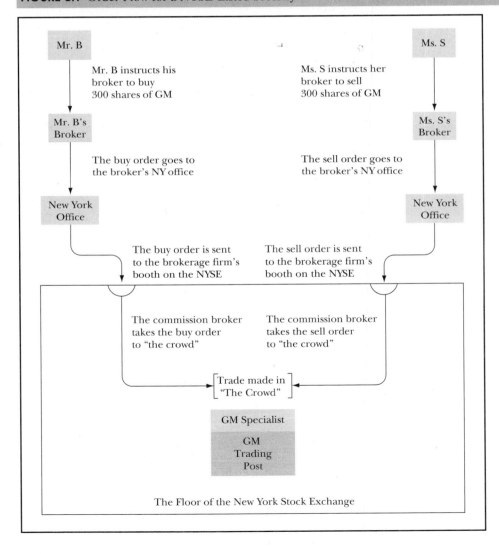

day is over. Such orders are sometimes filled at better prices than the quotes initially posted. The specialist might also take the other side at 61\frac{1}{16}$, 61\frac{1}{8}$, or 61\frac{3}{16}$ for strategic reasons even though the quote is 61\frac{1}{4}$. (Sometimes a specialist wants an order to be recorded at a specific price and time; for example, a trade at 61\frac{1}{8}$ would make it subsequently easier to execute a short-sell order under the up-tick rule than if the trade were executed at 61\frac{1}{4}$.)

tick

If the bid–ask spread on a stock is no wider than the standard unit in which prices are quoted, known as a **tick** (in 1999, typically $\frac{1}{16}$ of a point or 6.25 cents), market orders are generally executed directly by the specialist at the prevailing quote because there is little room for price improvement.[9] In the example, if the specialist had quoted bid and asked prices of $61 and 61\frac{1}{16}$, there would have been little incentive for Mr. B's commission broker to try to get a better price for the purchase order than 61\frac{1}{16}$ because any seller could have obtained a price of $61 from the specialist. To entice someone other than the specialist to sell GM to Mr. B, his commission broker would have to offer a better price than $61—the price the seller could obtain from the specialist. Given that the next highest price is 61\frac{1}{16}$, and that the specialist is willing to sell at that price, Mr. B's commission broker will typically deal with the specialist at the specialist's bid quote rather than deal with "the crowd." (In some instances, the specialist will provide price improvement in $\frac{1}{16}$-point markets—perhaps for strategic reasons—by executing the trade at the opposite side quote, which is $61 in the example.[10])

Placing a Limit Order

So far the discussion has been concerned with what would happen to a market order placed by Mr. B. What if Mr. B placed a limit order instead of a market order? Consider a buy limit order in which the specialist is quoting GM at $61 bid and 61\frac{1}{4}$ asked with order quantities of 1,500 and 3,000 shares, respectively (the concepts to be illustrated also apply, but in reverse, for a sell order). Three possible situations exist. The limit price associated with a limit buy can be either

- At or above the asked price of 61\frac{1}{4}$
- Below the asked price of 61\frac{1}{4}$, but at or above the bid price of $61
- Below the bid price of $61

The first case involves a "marketable limit order," meaning that the limit price is not a constraint given the existing bid and asked price quotations. It will be handled like a market order because the specialist is willing to fill the order at a price that is at least as favorable as the limit price. For example, a limit buy of 300 shares at $62 would be filled immediately by the specialist at 61\frac{1}{4}$ (or perhaps at an even better price by someone in "the crowd").

In the second case, in which the specialist is quoting prices of $61 and 61\frac{1}{4}$, assume that Mr. B has placed a limit order with his broker to buy 300 shares of GM at a limit price of 61\frac{1}{8}$ (or $61). When this order is carried to the trading post, it could be executed by the commission broker for the limit price of 61\frac{1}{8}$ if someone in the crowd (or even the specialist) were willing to take the other side of the transaction. After all, anyone with a sell order can transact with the specialist at the specialist's price of $61. To these people, the limit price of 61\frac{1}{8}$ looks more attractive because it represents a higher selling price to them. They would prefer doing business with Mr. B's commission broker rather than with the specialist. However, if nobody is willing to trade with Mr. B's commission broker, his order is recorded in the limit order book by the specialist within 30 seconds of receipt and the bid quote is increased from $61 to 61\frac{1}{8}$. (If the limit buy order had a limit price matching the specialist's bid of $61, the quote would then be good for not 1,500 but 1,800 shares.)

In the third case, assume that Mr. B has placed a limit order to buy 300 shares of GM with a limit price of $60. When this order is carried to the trading post, the commission broker will not even attempt to fill it because the limit price is below the specialist's current bid price. Anyone with a sell order can deal with the specialist at a price of $61, so there is no chance that anyone will want to sell to Mr. B for the lower limit price of $60. Thus, the order will be given to the specialist to be entered in the limit order book for possible execution in the future. (As in the second case, any limit orders that cannot be immediately executed must be entered by the specialist in the book within 30 seconds of receipt.) Limit orders in the book are executed in order of price. For example, all purchase orders with limit prices of $60\frac{1}{2}$ will be executed before Mr. B's order is executed. If there are several limit orders in the book at the same price, they are executed in order of arrival time (first in, first out). Furthermore, public limit orders take priority over the specialist's orders if they are at the same price.

It may not be possible to fill an entire order at a single price. For example, a broker with a market order to buy 2,000 shares might buy 500 shares at $61\frac{1}{8}$ and have to pay $61\frac{1}{4}$ for the remaining 1,500. Similarly, a limit order to buy 2,000 shares at $61\frac{1}{8}$ or better might result in the purchase of 500 shares at $61\frac{1}{8}$ and the entry of a limit order in the specialist's book for the other 1,500 shares.

Large and Small Orders

The NYSE has developed special procedures to handle both routine small orders and exceptionally large orders. In 1976 the NYSE developed an electronic system known as Designated Order Turnaround (or DOT) to handle small orders, defined at that time as market orders of 199 or fewer shares and limit orders of 100 or fewer shares. DOT was later replaced by the **Super Designated Order Turnaround** system (or **SuperDOT**), which accepts market orders of 30,999 or fewer shares and limit orders of 99,999 or fewer shares. Member firms must be participating subscribers to use Super-DOT. With this system, the New York office of the customer's brokerage firm can send the customer's order directly to the specialist, whereupon it will be exposed to the crowd and executed immediately (if possible), with a confirmation of the execution sent to the brokerage firm. Although SuperDOT usually sends relatively small market orders directly to the specialist for execution, it has been programmed to send certain other orders directly to the firm's floor brokers for execution.[11] In deciding where to send the order, SuperDOT examines such things as order size and type of order. For example, market orders and limit orders whose limit price is far from the current quotes of the specialist would be sent directly to the specialist. Each member firm sets the parameters that it wants SuperDOT to use in making such decisions.

SuperDOT has greatly facilitated the execution of "basket" trades in which a member firm submits orders in a number of securities all at once. Before SuperDOT, brokers from member firms would carry trade tickets with preprinted amounts that were to be used if the firm suddenly launched a basket trade. These tickets had to be brought by hand to the appropriate trading posts for execution. With SuperDOT, all trades in a basket can be sent simultaneously to the various trading posts on the floor for immediate execution.

Exceptionally large orders, known as **blocks,** generally involve at least 10,000 shares or $200,000, whichever is less. Typically, these orders are placed by institutional customers and may be handled in a variety of ways. They may be taken directly to the specialist and a price negotiated for them. However, if the block is large enough, the specialist will likely lower the bid price (for sell orders) or raise the asked price (for buy orders) by a substantial amount because specialists are prohibited by the exchange from soliciting offsetting orders from the public and, thus, do not know how easily they can obtain an offsetting order. Even with these disadvantages, this procedure is used on occasion, gen-

Super Designated Order Turnaround (SuperDOT)

blocks

erally for relatively small blocks, and is referred to as a **specialist block purchase** or **specialist block sale,** depending on whether the institution is selling or buying shares.[12]

Larger blocks can be handled using an **exchange distribution** (for sell orders) or **exchange acquisition** (for buy orders). Here a brokerage firm attempts to execute the order by finding enough offsetting orders from its customers. The block seller or buyer pays all brokerage costs, and the trade price is within the current bid and asked prices as quoted by the specialist. A similar procedure, known as a **special offering** (for sell orders) or **special bid** (for buy orders), involves letting all brokerage firms solicit offsetting orders from their customers.

Another way of selling a block is through a **secondary distribution,** in which the shares are sold off the exchange after the close of trading in a manner similar to the sale of new issues of common stock. The exchange must give approval for such distributions and usually does so if the block could not be absorbed easily in normal trading on the exchange. Accordingly, secondary distributions generally involve the sale of exceptionally large blocks.

Although all these methods of handling block orders are used at one time or another, most block orders are handled in the **upstairs dealer market.** Using **block houses,** which are set up for large orders, institutions can get better prices for their orders. A block house, when informed that an institution wants to place a block order, will line up trading partners (including itself) to take the other side of the order. Once the trading partners have been identified, the block house will attempt to reach a mutually acceptable price with the original institution. If the price is reached, then the order will be "crossed" on the floor of the exchange, meaning the specialist can fill any limit orders in the specialist's book at the block's selling price.[13] (If such a price is not reached, the institution can take the order to a different block house.) However, there is a limit of 1,000 shares or 5% of the block, whichever is greater, that can be used by the specialist to fill these limit orders.

For example, suppose that the PF Pension Fund informs a block house that it wishes to sell 20,000 shares of GM common stock. The block house proceeds to find three institutional investors that want to buy, say, 5,000 shares apiece; the block house decides that it too will buy 5,000 shares of GM from PF. Noting that the buyers have said that they would be willing to pay $70 per share, the block house subsequently informs PF that it will buy the 20,000 shares for $69.75 each, less a commission of $8,000. If PF accepts the deal, then the block house becomes the owner of the shares but must first "cross" them on the NYSE because the block house is a member of the exchange. In this example assume that when the block is crossed at $69.75, the specialist buys 500 shares at this price for a limit order in his or her book. After the cross, the block house gives 5,000 shares to each of the institutional buyers in exchange for $350,000 (= 5,000 shares × $70 per share) and hopes that the remaining 4,500 shares it now owns can be sold in the near future at a favorable price. Needless to say, the possibility of not being able to sell them at a favorable price is one of the risks involved in operating a block house.

3.2.2 OTHER EXCHANGES

Table 3.2 shows the total trading volume of the securities listed on each of the active stock exchanges in the United States in 1998. Not surprisingly, the NYSE dominates the list. Second in importance is the AMEX, which lists shares of somewhat smaller companies of national interest (a few of which are also listed on the NYSE). The others are called **regional exchanges** because historically each served as the sole location for trading securities primarily of interest to investors in its region. However, the major regional exchanges now depend to a large extent on transactions in securities that are also listed on a national exchange. Interestingly, the regional exchanges are now

TABLE 3.2 Trading Volume of the Stock Exchanges

(A) TRADING VOLUME (in shares)

	NYSE	*AMEX*	*Regionals*[a]	*Nasdaq*	*Third Market*[b]
Annual (trillions)	170	7	18	202	16
Daily (millions)	674	29	71	802	64

(B) FIVE-YEAR COMPARISON

	NYSE			*Nasdaq*		
Year	*Companies*	*Issues*	*Daily Share Volume*[c]	*Companies*	*Issues*	*Daily Share Volume*[a]
1998	3,114	3,773	674	5,068	5,583	802
1996	2,907	3,285	412	5,556	6,384	544
1994	2,570	3,060	291	4,902	5,761	295
1992	2,088	2,658	202	4,113	4,764	191

[a]Regionals consist of the Boston, Chicago, Cincinnati, Pacific, and Philadelphia Stock Exchanges.

[b]The third market figures represent the volume figures reported on the Consolidated Tape as over-the-counter market in NYSE-listed securities.

[c]In millions.

Source: Adapted from *Fact Book: 1998 Data* (New York Stock Exchange, 1999); *1999 Nasdaq-Amex Fact Book & Company Directory* (National Association of Security Dealers, 1999); <www.nyse.com>; and <www.nasdaq.com>.

larger than the AMEX. (The AMEX merged with Nasdaq in 1998 and is part of the Nasdaq–Amex Market Group but operates as a separate market.) There are five major regional exchanges currently in existence: the Boston, Chicago, Cincinnati, Pacific, and Philadelphia exchanges. All the regional exchanges use procedures similar to those of the NYSE. The role of specialists and the extent of automation may differ slightly, but the approach is basically the same.

Options exchanges and futures exchanges use some procedures that differ significantly from those used by stock exchanges. Futures exchanges often have daily price limits instead of specialists with directions to maintain "fair and orderly markets." The Chicago Board Options Exchange separates the two functions of the specialist: An order book official maintains the book of limit orders, and one or more registered market-makers act as dealers. These exchanges are discussed in more detail in Chapters 24 and 25.

3.2.3 OVER-THE-COUNTER MARKET

In the early days of the United States, banks acted as the primary dealers for stocks and bonds, and investors literally bought and sold securities "over the counter" at the banks. Transactions are more impersonal now, but the term is still in use for transactions that are not executed on an organized exchange but, instead, involve a dealer. Most bonds are sold over the counter, as are the securities of small (and some not so small) companies.

National Association of Securities Dealers (NASD) National Association of Securities Dealers Automated Quotations (Nasdaq)

Nasdaq

The over-the-counter (OTC) market for stocks is highly automated. In 1971 the **National Association of Securities Dealers (NASD),** which serves as a self-regulating agency for its members, put into operation the **National Association of Securities Dealers Automated Quotations** system **(Nasdaq).** This nationwide communications network allows brokers to know instantly the terms currently offered by all major dealers in securities covered by the system.

Dealers who subscribe to Level III of Nasdaq use electronic terminals to enter bid and asked prices for any stock in which they "make a market." Such dealers must be prepared to execute trades for at least one "normal unit of trading" (depending on the security, this can be as large as 1,000 shares) at the prices quoted. As soon as a dealer enters a bid or an asked price for a security, it is placed in a central computer file and may be seen by other subscribers (including other dealers) on their own terminals. When new quotations are entered, they replace the dealer's former prices.

When there is competition among dealers, those who are not well informed either price themselves out of the market by having too wide a spread between bid and asked prices or go out of business after incurring heavy losses.[14] In the first situation, nobody does business with such a dealer because there are better prices available with other dealers. The second situation occurs when the dealer accumulates a large inventory at too high a price or disposes of inventory at too low a price. Thus, the dealer will be doing the opposite of the familiar advice of "buy low, sell high."

It is argued that the interests of investors are best served by a market in which multiple dealers with unlimited access to all sources of information compete with one another. This would lead to narrow bid–ask spreads around the "intrinsic" value of a security and provide investors with the "best" prices. However, organized exchanges argue that their system provides the "best" prices because all orders are sent to a central location for execution where they can be matched and bid on. Although trades on Nasdaq take place at the "best" quoted prices, the exchanges note that they have only one source of quoted prices (the specialist), and that trades can (and often do) take place "inside" these prices. Thus, the exchanges argue that, unlike Nasdaq, they provide investors with the chance for "price improvement."

Most brokerage firms subscribe to Level II of Nasdaq for their trading rooms, obtaining terminals that display the current quotations on any security in the system. All bid and asked quotations are displayed, with the dealer offering each quotation being identified, so that orders can be routed to the dealer with the best price. Imagine how difficult it would be to get the best price for a customer without such a terminal (as was the case before Nasdaq existed). Brokers would have to contact dealers one by one to find the best price. After determining what appeared to be the best price, the broker would have to contact that dealer again. But by the time the dealer was contacted again, the price might have changed and the previously quoted price might no longer be the best one.

inside quotes

Level I of Nasdaq is used by individual account executives to get a sense of market conditions. It shows the **inside quotes,** meaning the highest bid and the lowest asked price for each security, along with last-sale reports and market summary data. Sometimes the inside quotes are known as the **NBBO** (national best bid or offer; **offer price** is often used instead of *asked price* in reference to the price at which dealers are willing to sell, or "offer," a specific security).

NBBO
offer price

National Market System

Nasdaq classifies stocks with large trading volumes (which also meet certain other requirements) as belonging to the **National Market System** (Nasdaq/NMS). Every transaction made by a dealer for such a stock is reported directly, providing up-to-date detailed trading information to Nasdaq users. Furthermore, any stock included in Nasdaq/NMS is automatically eligible for margin purchases and short selling. Less active issues belong to the **Small Cap Issues** (Nasdaq Small Cap) section of Nasdaq; these issues generally are automatically "phased into" NMS when they meet the higher listing standards of NMS. For these issues, dealers report only the total transactions at the close of each day, and only certain ones are eligible for margin purchases and short sales. (The Federal Reserve Board determines which ones are eligible four times a year.)

Small Cap Issues

markup

markdown

As its name indicates, Nasdaq is primarily a quotation system. The price paid by a customer buying shares is likely to be higher than the amount paid by the broker to procure the shares. In the case where the broker's firm acts as a *principal,* or dealer, selling shares from inventory, the difference is called the **markup.** Conversely, when selling shares, the customer receives a price less than that received by the broker, with the difference being known as a **markdown.** However, if the broker's firm is acting as an *agent* where the broker is executing the order with a dealer who works for a different firm, then the customer will be charged a commission. Markups, markdowns, and commissions are examined periodically by the Securities and Exchange Commission (the SEC is a federal agency that regulates U.S. security markets) to ensure they are "reasonable."

A security must have at least two registered market-makers (dealers) and a minimum number of publicly held shares to be included in Nasdaq. The issuing firm must also meet stated financial requirements. As shown in Table 3.2, at the end of 1998, 5,583 issues were included in the system.[15] Although this total is substantially more than the total for the NYSE, trading volume is less than that of the NYSE, especially when measured in dollars.

SOES

Small Order Execution System (SOES)

During the market crash of October 1987, many investors' orders involving Nasdaq stocks could not be executed because their brokers were unable to reach the appropriate dealers by telephone. As a result, NASD established the **Small Order Execution System (SOES),** an electronic order-routing system in which all Nasdaq dealers must participate. With SOES, brokers can electronically route a customer's order to the appropriate dealer for quick execution and confirmation. Large orders are typically not handled through SOES because dealers only accept orders up to 1,000 shares. (Currently, the limit is 100 shares for 50 large Nasdaq/NMS stocks but 1,000, 500, and 200 shares for the remainder of the Nasdaq stocks, depending on trading volume, number of dealers, and best bid price.) Instead, most large orders involving Nasdaq stocks are handled by negotiation over the telephone with one of the dealers.

OTC Bulletin Board and Pink Sheets Stocks

Pink Sheets

The Nasdaq system covers only part of the outstanding OTC stocks. Brokers with orders to buy or sell other OTC securities rely on quotations that are published daily either on Nasdaq's OTC Bulletin Board or in **Pink Sheets** to get "best execution" for their clients. (There are also less formal communication networks.) The OTC Bulletin Board is an electronic quotation forum run by Nasdaq, where brokers and dealers can find current price quotes, trading data, and a list of market-makers in several thousand securities. Although companies listed on the Bulletin Board typically cannot meet Nasdaq's standards (they meet less demanding standards), they must file quarterly financial statements with the SEC, banking, or insurance regulators (such filings were made mandatory in 1997). Pink Sheets are published electronically by the National Quotation Bureau, an organization unaffiliated with Nasdaq. They contain dealer quotations for thousands of unlisted stocks, but, unlike the OTC Bulletin Board, they do not provide trading data. Trading in both OTC Bulletin Board and Pink Sheet stocks takes place over phone lines rather than electronically.

3.2.4 THIRD AND FOURTH MARKETS

Until the 1970s the NYSE required its member firms to trade all NYSE-listed stocks at the exchange and to charge fixed commissions. For large institutions, meeting this requirement was expensive. In particular, the required minimum commission rate created a serious problem because it exceeded the marginal cost of arranging large trades.

third market

Brokerage firms that were not members of the exchange faced no restrictions on the commissions they could charge and thus could compete effectively for large trades in NYSE-listed stocks. Such transactions were said to take place in the **third market.** The term *third market* refers to the trading of any exchange-listed security in the OTC market. Trading hours are not fixed in the third market (unlike exchanges), and it can trade securities even when trading is halted on an exchange. As Table 3.2 shows, on average, 64 million shares were traded in the third market during each day of 1998.

Instinet and SelectNet

fourth market

Instinet

Many institutions have dispensed with brokers and exchanges altogether for transactions in exchange-listed stocks and other securities. Trades in which the buyer and seller deal directly with each other are sometimes said to take place in the **fourth market.** In the United States some of these transactions are facilitated by an automated communications system called **Instinet,** which provides quotations and automatic execution.[16] A subscriber can enter a limit order in the computerized "book," where it can be seen by other subscribers who can, in turn, signal their desire to take it. Whenever two orders are matched, the system automatically records the transaction and sets up the paperwork for its completion. Subscribers can also use the system to find likely partners for a trade, and then conduct negotiations by telephone. Instinet became popular because it allowed institutions to trade securities inside the bid–ask quotes established by dealers. Many dealers trade through either Instinet or a dealer-only computer network called SelectNet to manage their inventories inexpensively while maintaining standard bid–ask quotes for their customers. Since 1997 orders posted on Instinet and SelectNet have been available to the public to enhance the competitiveness of dealers' quoted prices.

Crossing Systems

In recent years automated electronic facilities have been developed to permit institutional investors to trade *portfolios* of stocks, rather than individual securities, directly with each other. The two largest systems are POSIT and the Crossing Network. Some large investment managers also maintain their own internal crossing systems. These managers invest billions of dollars for many institutional clients. On any given day, some clients will be withdrawing funds from such a manager and other clients will be contributing funds. The manager simply exchanges the contributing client's cash for shares from the withdrawing client. The shares are usually valued at closing market prices on the day of the "cross." A nominal commission is charged to handle the transactions.

Electronic Communications Networks

electronic communications networks (ECNs)

Electronic communications networks (ECNs) are fourth-market organizations designed to automatically execute investors' buy-and-sell orders by computer without the intervention of specialists or dealers. Instinet was actually the first ECN and remains the largest. In recent years, however, ECNs have proliferated, with several attaining rapid growth in trading volume, including Island, Archipelago, and Tradebook. Investors submit individual trade requests to ECNs, often through online brokerage firms. Most stocks traded on ECNs are Nasdaq securities. For a commission, the ECNs attempt to match buy-and-sell orders submitted to them and execute market order trades at prices within the NBBO during the hours that the Nasdaq market is open. Trades are also handled after Nasdaq closes, although prices may range far from the respective closing Nasdaq prices. Unmatched market orders are typically submitted to dealers through SelectNet for execution. (ECNs are discussed further in the chapter's *Money Matters* box.)

3.2.5 INTERNALIZATION

Until 1976 NYSE member firms were prohibited by Rule 394 from either acting as dealers in the third market or executing orders involving NYSE-listed securities for their customers in the third market. In 1976 Rule 394 was replaced by Rule 390, which permits the execution of orders for NYSE-listed stocks in the third market but still prohibits member firms from acting as dealers in the third market. In 1979 the SEC issued Rule 19c-3, permitting member firms to act as dealers in securities that were listed on the NYSE after April 26, 1979. This rule led to **internalization** in which NYSE-member broker-dealers take their customers' orders in 19c-3 stocks and fill them internally instead of sending them to an exchange floor for execution. Internalization can also involve broker-dealers who are not NYSE members and who can execute their customers' orders in any NYSE-listed stock internally. Furthermore, Nasdaq stocks can be internalized when customers' orders are filled by a brokerage firm in its dual role as a dealer instead of sending the trades to other dealers. Thus, internalization can be thought of as *routing orders to oneself* because the orders never leave the customer's brokerage firm for execution.[17]

internalization (margin)

Controversy over Rules 390 and 19c-3 led to their repeal in 1999, which will likely spur further competition between the NYSE and Nasdaq. Now NYSE member firms can act as dealers in any NYSE-listed security. Hence, they are no longer required to take any order to the NYSE for execution.

3.2.6 FOREIGN MARKETS

The two largest stock markets in the world outside New York are in London and Tokyo. During the past fifteen years both of these markets have undergone major changes in their rules and operating procedures. Both have active markets in foreign securities. At the end of 1998 the London Stock Exchange listed 522 foreign companies (in addition to 2,399 U.K. companies) and the Tokyo Stock Exchange listed 52 foreign companies (in addition to 1,838 Japanese companies). Also of interest is the Toronto Stock Exchange, which, by market value of securities listed, is the third largest stock market in North America (after the NYSE and Nasdaq, according to the *Toronto Stock Exchange 1997 Annual Report,* p. 1). Its electronic trading system has been adopted by many foreign markets either directly (by Paris) or indirectly (by Tokyo). At the end of 1998 the Toronto Stock Exchange listed 1,384 companies, 53 of which were foreign companies.

London

In October 1986 the "Big Bang" introduced several major reforms to the London Stock Exchange. Fixed brokerage commissions were eliminated, membership was opened to corporations, and foreign firms were allowed to purchase existing member firms. An automated dealer quotation system similar to Nasdaq was also introduced. This system, known as **SEAQ** (Stock Exchange Automated Quotations), involves competing market-makers whose quotes are displayed over a computer network. Small orders can be executed using **SAEF** (SEAQ Automated Execution Facility), which functions like Nasdaq's SOES; large orders are handled over the telephone. Limit orders are not handled centrally but rather by individual brokers or dealers who note when prices have moved enough for them to be executed.

The London Stock Exchange's reforms have been highly successful. The exchange has attracted trading in many non-U.K. stocks, thereby enhancing its status as the dominant European stock market. Even U.S. stock markets have felt the competition. In an attempt to recapture some of the lost trading in U.S. securities lost to the London Stock

The Evolution of the Fourth Market

Scientists define the evolution of a species as its gradual adoption of features that facilitate its long-term survival. In this context it is fitting to refer to the evolution of the fourth market. From its rudimentary beginnings the fourth market has evolved into a sophisticated set of electronic trading mechanisms in which hundreds of millions of shares change hands daily. Furthermore, the fourth market is posing a threat to existing species: the organized security exchanges. How this competition plays out will influence the nature of trading well into the twenty-first century.

The fourth market, where investors deal directly with one another, began in response to high commission rates charged by brokerage firms. In 1969, Institutional Networks Corporation, later renamed Instinet, developed a novel product: a computer trading system that permitted institutional investors to trade listed and Nasdaq stocks among themselves without the intervention of a market-maker. Instinet allowed these investors to remain anonymous, thus guarding their trading strategies from other market participants. Just as importantly, Instinet's commissions were only a small fraction of those charged by brokers.

Despite (or perhaps because of) its revolutionary design, Instinet was far from an overnight success. Liquidity was initially quite limited. Because investors submit buy or sell limit orders (see Chapter 2) on individual securities at irregular times, if an interested investor on the "other side" of the trade happens to access the system at the right time, the trade may be completed. There is no guarantee, however, that the transaction will take place. In recent years, volume and, hence, Instinet's success at matching orders have grown as more traders, including Nasdaq dealers, have accessed Instinet.

Nevertheless, the odds that an institutional investor can complete large trades in numerous securities are small. These investors insisted that they needed a system that allows them to trade entire portfolios instead of individual stocks. In 1987, the fourth market evolved to accommodate

this need through a mechanism generically known as a *crossing system*. Several electronic crossing systems now conduct regular market sessions in which investors may submit large packages of securities for trade. These crossing systems involve regularly scheduled, widely announced trading sessions (effectively, call markets). Before each session, investors anonymously submit lists of stocks they wish to buy or sell and the associated quantities. At the scheduled times (some while the organized exchanges are open and some after they are closed), the lists of desired trades are compared automatically by computer and offsetting buys and sells are matched. Trade prices are based on current market prices as set on the organized security exchanges or Nasdaq. When buy orders do not equal sell orders for a security, matches are allocated on the basis of total dollar value of trades entered by each investor, which encourages the submission of large trading volume requests. Investors are notified of the completed trades, and the system handles the transfer of stocks. Unmatched trades are returned to the investors for resubmission or execution elsewhere.

Although crossing systems offer low cost and anonymous trading of portfolios, they present some serious drawbacks as well. They do not provide liquidity in many stocks. Investors may not be able to complete trades in certain securities even after days of submitting those securities to the crossing networks. This problem is particularly acute for smaller capitalization Nasdaq stocks. In addition, the crossing systems require a certain amount of technological sophistication. Investors must submit trades computer to computer. Trading packages must be readied for entry at the appropriate times, and arrangements must be made for handling trades that cannot be completed through the crossing systems.

Crossing systems were designed to meet the needs of institutional investors. It was inevitable, however, that the fourth market would evolve to meet the needs of retail investors as well. Since they first appeared in 1997, Electronic Communi-

(continued)

cations Networks (ECNs) have begun to fill those needs. Like their progenitor, Instinet, all ECNs allow anonymous buy and sell orders for individual securities to be matched electronically. When a match cannot be found, an ECN posts the bid or ask, depending on the order, on Nasdaq's trading screens. If it is the best bid or ask available for that security, it will likely be executed with a Nasdaq market participant. Although only brokerage firm members of an ECN can trade through its facilities, retail investors' trades reach ECNs through their brokers. Because many online discount brokers (see Chapter 2) are members of ECNs, the surge in online trading has corresponded with the rapid growth in trading volume on ECNs. The synergy between Internet trading and ECNs cannot be overemphasized. Online traders, particularly the infamous day traders who move quickly in and out of stocks, seek to avoid the high commissions charged by traditional brokerage firms. The existence of ECNs allows online brokers to offer low-cost trade execution and hence attracts more Internet trading. Further, the technological flexibility of trading on ECNs has allowed them to offer trading hours not served by the organized exchanges and Nasdaq. This flexibility, in turn, has put pressure on those organizations to extend their hours of trading.

Most ECN trading activity to date has taken place in Nasdaq stocks. In large listed names, where bid–ask spreads are low and specialists charge commissions primarily for the service of bringing buyers and sellers together, there is little advantage to executing small trades through an ECN. On the other hand, in the decentralized Nasdaq market, with dealers making a living on the bid–ask spread, it can pay to trade through an ECN. The drawback, of course, is that a match is not always available, particularly for large trades.

Organized exchanges and Nasdaq have been warily eyeing ECNs as they have begun to eat into the exchanges' trading volume. In 1999, the SEC estimated that alternative trading systems (including Instinet, other ECNs, and crossing systems) accounted for roughly 20% and 4% of Nasdaq and NYSE trading volumes, respectively, and those numbers are growing rapidly. Just as some traditional brokerage firms have entered the online trading business, they have also begun to make minority investments in fledgling ECNs, perhaps hoping to stay in front of, or at least not fall too far behind, the rapid developments taking place in the fourth market. The crossing systems have made connections to ECNs to improve the proportion of their orders that are matched. In early 1999, the NYSE itself was rumored to be interested in creating its own ECN to capture trading in Nasdaq stocks. The situation has become so fluid that joint ventures or even mergers between the NYSE and either Nasdaq or Instinet, which were once unthinkable, are now being seriously discussed. Some observers contend that ECNs are pushing major U.S. stock exchanges to adopt a central limit order book system, long a holy grail sought by the SEC. The only outcome that is certain is that trading in U.S. common stocks will be radically different in the near future.

The trading mechanisms available to investors continue to grow as per-unit trading costs continue to fall. Crossing systems and ECNs have played an important role in these declining costs. Interestingly, both are beginning to conduct global operations. Given that transaction costs on foreign markets are usually many times higher than they are in the United States, the room for fourth-market growth in those markets appears enormous. Inexorably, the evolution of the fourth market continues.

Nasdaq International

Exchange, NASD received approval from the SEC for a computer system like Nasdaq that involves trading many of the stocks listed on the NYSE, AMEX, or Nasdaq/NMS. This system, known as **Nasdaq International,** opens for trading six hours before the NYSE, which corresponds to the opening time of the London Stock Exchange, and closes a half-hour before the NYSE opens.

Tokyo

CORES

The Tokyo Stock Exchange has also experienced major reforms. **CORES** (Computer-assisted Order Routing and Execution System), a computer system for trading all but

FORES

the 150 most active securities, was introduced in 1982. In 1986 the exchange began to admit foreign firms as members, and in 1990 **FORES** (Floor Order Routing and Execution System) was introduced as a computer system to facilitate trading in the most active stocks.

The system of trading both the most active and the relatively less active securities is different than any system found in the United States or the United Kingdom. Members, known as *saitori,* act as auctioneers in that they are intermediaries who accept orders from member firms and are not allowed to trade in any stocks for their own account. Thus, they are neither dealers nor specialists.

The exchange is open from 9 A.M. to 11 A.M. and from 12:30 P.M. to 3 P.M. As a result, there are two openings each day. At each opening the *saitori* set a single price so that the amount of trading is maximized (subject to certain constraints). This method is called *itayose,* and it operates like a call market. Setting the price effectively involves constructing supply and demand schedules for the market and limit orders that have been received; it notes where the two schedules intersect. (This process is described and illustrated in Chapter 4.) After the opening of the exchange, orders are processed continually as they are received; this process is known as *zaraba.* Market orders are set against previously unfilled limit orders. New limit orders are filled, if possible, against previously unfilled limit orders. New limit orders that cannot be filled are entered in the limit order book for possible future execution. Unlike the NYSE, the Tokyo Stock Exchange prohibits trading at prices outside a given range based on the previous day's closing price. Hence it is possible that trading in a stock may cease until the next day (when the price range is readjusted) unless two parties decide to trade within the current range.

Toronto

CATS

In 1977 the Toronto Stock Exchange began to use **CATS** (Computer-Assisted Trading System) on a trial basis with 30 stocks. Two years later CATS was expanded to include about 700 stocks and became permanent. All other listed stocks were traded in a specialist-driven system like the one in New York. The success of CATS led to the inclusion of more and more stocks until all listed stocks were traded on it. CATS now uses decimal pricing where stocks priced above $5 trade in $.05 increments and those priced below $5 trade in $.01 increments.

With CATS, orders are entered electronically in brokers' offices and then routed to a computer file. The computer file displays limit orders against which other investors may trade. Market orders are matched against the limit order with the best price in the file (that is, a market order to buy is matched against the lowest priced limit order to sell, and a market order to sell is matched against the highest priced limit order to buy). If insufficient volume is available in the file at the best price, the remainder of the market order is put in the file as a limit order at that price. However, brokers, responding to the wishes of the investor, can change this price at any time.

At the daily opening CATS, like *itayose* in Tokyo, sets an opening price to maximize the number of shares that are traded. Although both market and limit orders are accepted, there are constraints on the size of each market order, and these orders must be from the public (hence member firms are not allowed to submit opening market orders).

3.3 Stock Quotations

Figures 3.2 through 3.4 provide examples of quotations summarizing a day's transactions in stocks traded on Nasdaq and on various stock exchanges.

3.3.1 NASDAQ

Activity in stocks traded on Nasdaq is summarized in Figure 3.2. Transactions in securities designated "National Market Issues" are detailed in Figure 3.2(a). High and low prices for trades during the preceding 52 weeks are given, along with the annual per share amount of dividends, in dollars, based on the latest declared amount. (Letters refer to footnotes providing details concerning extra or special dividends and yields. The footnotes also explain the sporadic entries in the extreme left column and why certain rows are either emboldened or underlined.) This dollar amount is divided by the **closing price** (the price at which the last trade of the day was made) to obtain the figure shown for **dividend yield.** The price–earnings ratio (the closing price divided by the past 12 months' earnings per share) is given next. The remaining entries summarize the day's transactions in the major markets in which the stock is traded: sales volume, in hundreds of shares; the highest and lowest prices at which trades were completed during the day; the closing price; and the difference between the day's closing price and that of the preceding day.

closing price
dividend yield

Nasdaq stocks with less activity, which are referred to as "Small Cap Issues," are summarized in Figure 3.2(b). Annual per share dividends are reported first, followed by trading volume (in hundreds of shares) and the price at which the last trade of the day took place. The net change in the last price from the previous day is shown in the right column. Investors in these securities, like investors in National Market Issues, transact with dealers paying the asked price when purchasing shares and receive the bid price when selling shares (unless the order is relatively large). Hence the last price and net change figures may reflect bid or asked prices. Investors may also have to bear markdowns or markups and commissions, which may be added on by retail brokers.[18]

3.3.2 U.S. STOCK EXCHANGES

Activity in stocks traded on U.S. stock exchanges is shown in Figure 3.3. Stocks listed on the NYSE are shown in Figure 3.3(a). Stocks listed on the AMEX are shown in panel (b). The information provided for both of these exchanges is identical in format to the information provided for Nasdaq National Market Issues shown in Figure 3.2(a).

Figure 3.3(c) shows various regional stock exchanges in the United States. Any trading that involves securities that are also listed on either the NYSE or AMEX ("dually listed securities") is excluded because those trades are reflected in either panel (a) or panel (b). Less information is provided for trading on the regional exchanges than on organized exchanges; only daily sales volume and the high, low, and closing prices, along with the change in the close from the previous day are reported.

3.3.3 FOREIGN STOCK EXCHANGES

Figure 3.4 displays the trading activities in various foreign stock markets including the two major Canadian markets (Toronto and Montreal), the major Mexican market (Mexico City), and several other foreign markets based on the area of the world in which they are located. The prices are given in the local currency of the country in which the exchange is located.

3.4 Information-Motivated and Liquidity-Motivated Traders

Perhaps the single major concern of a dealer is the adverse consequences he or she experiences as a result of buying from or selling to an informed trader. When a trader approaches a dealer, the dealer cannot tell whether the trader knows something about

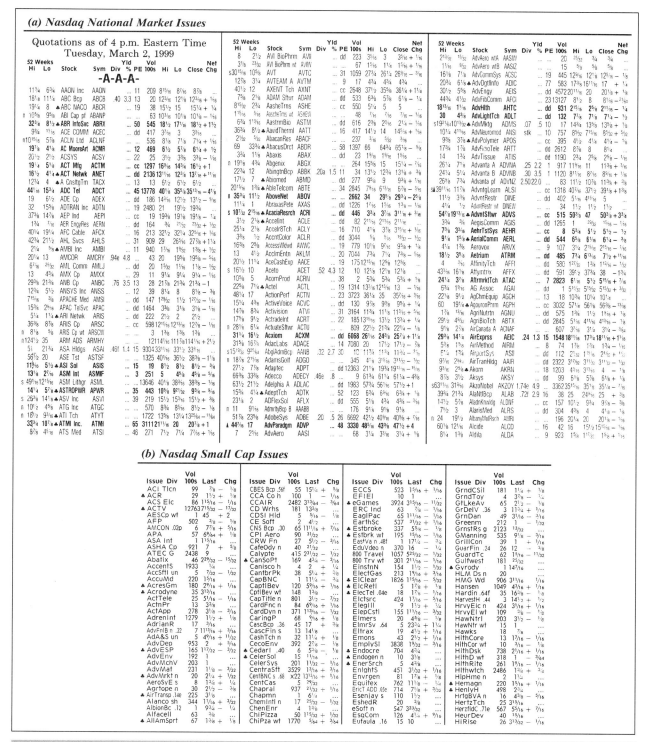

FIGURE 3.2 Summary of Stocks Traded with the Aid of the Nasdaq System (excerpts)

(a) Stocks Listed on the NYSE

Quotations as of 5 p.m. Eastern Time
Tuesday, March 2, 1999

-A-A-A-

52 Weeks Hi	52 Weeks Lo	Stock	Sym	Div	Yld %	PE	Vol 100s	Hi	Lo	Close	Net Chg
30 3/8	14 5/8	AAR	AIR	.34	2.1	11	3377	16 7/16	15 5/8	16	+ 3/8
37	25	ABM Indus	ABM	.56f	1.9	22	207	29 5/16	29	29	− 1/8
27 9/16	14 1/4	ABN Am ADR	AAN	.62e	3.1	...	726	20 1/16	19 11/16	19 3/4	− 1/4
n▼ 26 5/8	24 5/8	ABN Am pfA		1.88	7.3	...	394	25 13/16	24 5/8	25 3/4	+ 1/16
s 43	**24 3/8**	**ACE Ltd**	**ACL**	**.36**	**1.3**	**8**	**3012**	**28 13/16**	**27 3/8**	**28 11/16**	**+ 1 1/2**
11 1/2	7 5/8	ACM Gvt Fd	ACG	.90	10.1	...	514	8 15/16	8 13/16	8 7/8	...
8 3/4	7 3/8	ACM OppFd	AOF	.63a	8.4	...	58	7 1/2	7 7/16	7 1/2	+ 1/16
10 13/16	7 1/2	ACM SecFd	GSF	.90	10.8	...	1220	8 5/16	8 3/16	8 5/16	+ 1/16
6 7/8	5 15/16	ACM SpctmFd	SI	.54	9.0	...	517	6 1/8	6	6	...
14 1/2	7 3/4	ACM MgdDlr	ADF	1.35a	13.7	...	552	9 15/16	9 11/16	9 7/8	...
10 7/16	7 7/8	ACM MgdInco	AMF	1.02f	11.3	...	525	9 1/4	8 13/16	9 1/16	+ 3/16
14 11/16	13 3/8	ACM MuniSec	AMU	.87	6.2	...	52	13 15/16	13 13/16	13 15/16	+ 1/16
25 13/16	9 5/16	♣ACX Tch A	ACX		...	18	597	13 1/4	12 7/8	13	+ 3/16
58	23	♣AES Cp	AES		...	21	9140	36 7/8	35 7/16	35 15/16	− 3/16
s 50 1/2	**25 1/8**	**♣AFLAC**	**AFL**	**.26**	**.5**	**21**	**7369**	**49 5/16**	**45 13/16**	**49 3/16**	**+ 3 1/16**
30 7/16	5 1/4	AGCO Cp	AG	.04	.6	7	3740	6 5/8	6 1/4	6 1/2	− 1/16
23 3/8	17 11/16	AGL Res	ATG	1.08	5.8	15	1337	20	18 5/8	18 11/16	− 9/16
18 1/2	11 5/8	AgSvcAm	ASV		...	12	63	14	13 15/16	13 15/16	+ 1/16
26 1/4	24	AICI CapTr pf		2.25	9.1	...	27	24 13/16	24 3/4	24 13/16	− 1/16
13	4 1/8	AIM EstEurFd	GTF		...	...	53	5 7/8	5 7/8	5 7/8	− 1/8
39 1/2	17 5/8	AIPC	PLB		...	...	530	24 3/4	24 1/8	24 7/16	− 3/16
24 3/8	13 5/8	♣AK Steel	AKS	.50	2.3	11	2690	22 9/16	21 7/16	21 3/4	+ 3/16
26	20 3/4	AMB Prop	AMB	1.37	6.5	17	770	21 1/4	21 1/16	21 1/8	− 1/16
n 25 7/16	22 1/4	AMB Prop pfA		2.13	8.9	...	33	24 1/8	23 7/8	24	..
16 3/8	8	AMCOL	ACO	.24	2.4	13	366	10 3/16	9 1/2	10 1/8	+ 7/16
31	3 7/8	AMF Bowlng	PIN		...	dd	94	4 7/8	4 5/8	4 5/8	− 1/8
23 15/16	18 7/16	♣AMLI Resdntl	AML	1.80f	9.0	14	396	20 1/16	19 7/8	20	+ 1/16
53 15/16	28 1/8	AMP	AMP	1.08	2.0	cc	9560	53 1/2	52 9/16	53 1/2	+ 11/16
s 89 15/16	45 5/8	AMR	AMR		...	8	25479	59 1/4	57 3/4	57 7/8	+ 1 3/4
n 26	24 1/2	ANZ pf		2.02	7.9	...	156	25 5/8	25 1/2	25 5/8	+ 1/16
n 26 5/16	25 7/16	ANZ II pf		2.02	7.8	...	203	25 13/16	25 11/16	25 13/16	+ 1/8
14	2	APT Satelt	ATS		...	...	322	2 5/8	2 9/16	2 5/8	...
25 5/8	12 7/16	ARM FnlGp A	ARM	.16	1.0	11	1896	16 7/16	16	16 1/8	...
26 5/8	13 5/8	ASA	ASA	.60f	3.7	...	736	16 3/8	15 15/16	16 3/16	+ 3/8
34 3/4	27 3/8	♣AmWtrWks	AWK	.86	2.8	19	918	30 5/8	30 5/16	30 9/16	+ 3/16
24 3/4	20	♣AmWtrWks pfA		1.25	5.9	...	z1930	22 3/4	21 1/4	21 1/4	− 1 1/4
s 18 5/8	6 5/8	♣AmeriCredit	ACF		...	11	2393	11 7/8	11 1/4	11 3/8	− 1/4
26 7/16	21	Amerigas	APU	2.20	10.0	73	269	22 3/8	21 1/2	21 15/16	+ 7/16
82 3/4	44 7/16	♣AmeriSrc A	AAS		...	34	1096	75 3/8	74 5/8	74 5/8	− 1/8
69 3/8	41 1/4	Ameritech	AIT	1.27f	2.0	19	13199	63 3/4	61 1/8	63	− 1/2
62 3/4	33 3/8	AmeronInt	AMN	1.28	3.3	8	15	39 1/2	39 3/8	39 3/8	− 1/16
34 13/16	14 3/8	AmerUsLf A	AMH	.40	1.9	11	786	21 1/8	20 13/16	21	+ 1/8
n 31 15/16	17	AmerUsLf un			...	...	857	22 5/8	22	22 3/8	+ 3/8
31 3/8	15 3/4	Ametek	AME	.24	1.4	11	292	17 3/8	17 1/16	17 3/16	+ 1/8
▼ 19 1/4	9 1/4	AmpcoPgh	AP	.40f	4.4	6	255	9 3/8	9 3/16	9 3/16	− 1/8
64	27	Amphenol	APH		...	17	52	36 5/16	35 5/8	35 5/8	− 1/2
10 1/2	5 1/2	AMREP	AXR		...	6	106	7 1/8	7	7 1/8	+ 1/8
s 49 15/16	30 11/16	AmSoBcp	ASO	1.00	2.1	22	5083	48 3/4	47 13/16	48 7/16	+ 5/8
s 62 1/4	21 1/2	Amvescap	AVZ	.97e	2.0	...	138	50	49	49	+ 1
21 1/16	7	AmwayAsia	AAP	j	...	dd	151	7 1/2	7 1/4	7 1/4	− 3/16
10 5/8	3 1/2	AmwayJpn	AJL	.39e	9.2	...	3015	4 5/16	4 1/16	4 1/4	+ 1/8
s 44 7/8	24 3/4	♣AnadrkPete	APC	.20	.7	dd	2670	28 1/4	27 5/16	27 1/2	...
39 5/8	12	AnalogDevcs	ADI		...	38	22088	26 9/16	25 5/16	25 9/16	− 3/16
23 1/2	10 1/4	EAndinA ADR	AKOA	.31e	2.4	...	122	13	12 3/4	12 15/16	− 3/16
21	8 3/8	EAndinB ADR	AKOB	.34e	2.9	...	50	11 5/8	11 1/2	11 5/8	...
24 1/2	14 1/8	♣Angelica	AGL	.96	6.2	16	165	15 15/16	15 1/2	15 1/2	− 1/2
n 31	16	Anglogold ADS	AU	1.27e	6.7	12	750	19 1/4	18 7/8	19	+ 9/16
▲ 77 3/4	45 1/16	AnheuserB	BUD	1.12	1.4	31	14467	78	76 1/4	77 13/16	+ 1 3/16
22 3/4	10 5/8	AnixterIntl	AXE		...	9	4792	12 7/8	12 5/8	12 11/16	...
11 5/8	6 1/8	AnnalyMtg	NLY	1.22e	12.9	8	507	9 9/16	9 1/4	9 7/16	+ 1/8
42 1/8	13 1/2	AnnTaylor	ANN		...	35	3110	39 3/4	38 9/16	39	+ 1/4
n 15 1/2	3 5/8	AnthracitCap	AHR	.92e	12.8	...	262	7 1/4	7 1/16	7 3/16	− 3/16
75 9/16	48 1/4	AonCp	AOC	1.12	1.9	19	4057	60 1/2	58 1/2	59 11/16	+ 11/16
38 3/4	17 5/8	ApacheCp	APA	.28	1.4	dd	2948	20 1/16	19 13/16	19 7/8	− 1/8
41 5/8	30	♣ApartmtInv	AIV	2.50f	6.5	43	819	38 3/4	38 1/2	38 3/4	+ 1/16
25 5/8	20 1/2	ApartmtInv pfC		2.25	9.9	...	52	22 3/4	22 1/4	22 5/8	...
25 11/16	19 7/8	ApartmtInv pfD		2.19	10.1	...	73	21 7/8	21 5/8	21 5/8	− 1/4
n 24 7/8	21 1/2	ApartmInv pfG		2.34	10.0	...	114	23 1/2	23 5/16	23 7/16	...
n 24 5/8	21 3/16	ApartmtInv pfH		2.38	10.2	...	29	23 1/2	23 5/16	23 5/16	− 3/8
n 25 1/8	24 3/8	ApartmtInv pfK	AIVK		...	...	127	24 11/16	24 7/16	24 1/2	− 1/8
13 3/4	7 1/8	♣ApexMtg	AXM	1.20f	9.8	13	112	12 1/4	11 3/4	12 1/4	+ 3/8
10 7/8	9 7/8	ApexMunFd	APX	.63e	6.1	...	268	10 7/16	10 1/4	10 3/8	...

(b) Stocks Listed on the AMEX

Quotations as of 5 p.m. Eastern Time
Tuesday, March 2, 1999

-A-B-C-

52 Weeks Hi	52 Weeks Lo	Stock	Sym	Div	Yld %	PE	Vol 100s	Hi	Lo	Close	Net Chg
27 3/4	10 1/4	AMC Entn	AEN		...	dd	138	17 5/8	17 1/4	17 3/8	...
2 1/2	3/4	AMTEC	ATC		...	dd	615	1 7/16	1 3/8	1 7/16	...
6	1	ARC Int	ATV		...	dd	961	1 9/16	1 3/8	1 1/2	...
14 5/8	2 3/4	ARV AsstLvg	SRS		...	dd	26	4 5/8	4 3/8	4 3/8	− 1/8
14 7/8	4 3/4	AT Cross A	ATX	.24j	...	dd	618	6 1/2	6	6 1/8	− 3/16
▼ 9	5	AT Plastics g	ATJ	.18	...	...	5	4 15/16	4 15/16	4 15/16	− 1/16
25 3/4	14 3/4	Acadiana	ANA	.44	2.4	15	25	18 1/8	18 1/8	18 1/8	+ 1/8
6 1/2	**1 3/8**	**AcmeUtd**	**ACU**		**...**	**dd**	**9**	**2**	**1 7/8**	**2**	**− 1/8**
14 3/4	5 1/4	AdamsRes	AE	.10	1.7	11	10	6	6	6	...
13 1/2	4 1/4	♣AdvMagnet	AVM		...	dd	39	4 15/16	4 3/4	4 7/8	+ 3/16
1 9/16	1/2	♣AdvPhotonix	API		...	16	10	5/8	5/8	5/8	...
12 1/4	8 3/8	AegisRlty	AER	.96a	10.2	...	116	9 1/2	9 3/8	9 7/16	− 1/16
10 1/4	4	Aerocent	ACY		...	12	1	9 1/4	9 1/4	9 1/4	...
20 1/8	6 1/2	Aerosonic	AIM		...	97	43	14 7/8	14 1/2	14 5/8	− 1/16
s 28 7/8	3 1/16	AlbaWaldn	AWS	.15	.7	11	10	22 1/4	22 1/4	22 1/4	− 3/8
s 16 5/8	9	♣AllncBcpNE	ANE	.20	1.9	10	18	10 1/2	10 3/8	10 1/2	...
13 1/2	6	AlldRsch	ALR		...	4	10	7	7	7	− 1/8
16	3 3/8	♣AllouHlth	ALU		...	17	354	8 7/8	8 5/8	8 3/4	+ 1/16
35 1/4	16	AltLvgSvc	ALI		...	22	1238	20 1/2	19 3/4	20	− 1/4
s 33	17 7/8	AmBkCT	BKC	.84f	3.9	10	72	21 3/4	21 1/8	21 5/8	+ 9/16
31 3/4	20 1/2	AmBiltrite	ABL	.50	2.0	11	6	25 1/2	25 3/8	25 3/8	− 3/8
9 5/8	7 5/8	AmMtg86	AIJ	1.66e	20.9	12	27	8	7 7/8	7 15/16	− 1/16
14 1/4	10 1/2	AmMtg88	AIK	.96a	9.0	11	132	10 15/16	10 5/8	10 5/8	− 1/8
20	11 7/8	AmRlEstInv	REA	1.06	8.2	7	60	13 9/16	13	13	− 9/16
16 1/2	9 3/8	♣AmSciEngrg	ASE		...	13	8	11	10 7/8	10 7/8	− 1/8
16 7/8	5 7/8	AmTchCeram	AMK		...	13	13	6 5/8	6 5/8	6 5/8	− 1/8
203 1/4	125 1/4	AT&T Fund	ATF	2.93	1.6	...	71	185 1/2	182 3/8	182 3/8	− 1 7/8
9 7/8	4 1/2	AmVngrd	AVD	.07e	1.1	9	22	6 1/4	6 1/4	6 1/4	− 1/8
5 3/4	**3 1/4**	**♣AmpalAm A**	**AIS**		**...**	**cc**	**73**	**4 3/16**	**4**	**4**	**− 5/16**
5 5/8	**11/16**	**AmpexCp A**	**AXC**		**...**	**15**	**1887**	**3 3/16**	**2 15/16**	**3**	**− 3/16**
26 1/8	4	AndreaElec	AND		...	dd	393	7 1/2	7 1/4	7 1/4	− 1/8
13	6 3/4	ApexSilvr	SIL		...	dd	344	9 1/2	9	9 3/8	− 1/8
16 1/2	**2 1/4**	**AppleOrth**	**AOI**		**...**	**18**	**141**	**2 7/8**	**2 1/2**	**2 11/16**	**− 3/16**
3 3/8	1 1/8	AquaAllnc	AAI		...	dd	227	1 3/8	1 5/16	1 3/8	...
n 10 1/2	9 5/8	ArgoCapTr pf		.20p	...	...	15	9 7/8	9 7/8	9 7/8	+ 1/4
7 3/16	5 3/8	ArizLand	AZL	.40	6.7	21	13	6	6	6	− 1/8
14 15/16	**8 7/8**	**ArmorHldg**	**ABE**		**...**	**27**	**593**	**14 7/16**	**13 3/8**	**13 1/2**	**− 15/16**
2 1/8	7/8	♣ArrhythRsch	HRT		..	dd	14	1 1/4	1 3/16	1 1/4	...
21 5/8	4 1/8	AssistLivng	ALF		...	45	583	4 15/16	4 3/4	4 15/16	− 1/16
16 1/4	6 3/4	AtlTeleNtwk	ANK	.60	5.9	...	51	10 5/8	10 1/4	10 1/4	− 1/2
9 1/4	5 3/4	AtlsPlas A	AGH		...	10	16	9	8 7/8	9	+ 3/16
20 7/8	3 3/8	AudioBook	KLB		...	dd	2182	11 5/8	10 3/8	11 3/16	− 3/16
7 7/16	3 5/8	Audiovox	VOX		...	6	108	6 13/16	6 3/4	6 3/4	− 1/16
▼ 9 3/8	7/8	AutoBond	ABD		...	dd	329	1	13/16	13/16	− 1/8
11	**2**	**Autobond pfA**		**1.50**	**57.1**	**...**	**12**	**2 11/16**	**2 5/8**	**2 5/8**	**+ 1/8**
3 1/16	1 1/8	♣Autotote A	TTE		...	dd	345	1 15/16	1 3/4	1 7/8	+ 1/8
n 9 1/2	5 11/16	AvlnHldg A wi			...	...	7	6 1/8	6 1/8	6 1/8	...

(c) Stocks Listed on Regional Stock Exchanges

U.S. REGIONAL MARKETS

Dually Listed Issues Excluded. Sales in Hundreds.
Tuesday, March 2, 1999

CHICAGO

Sales	Stock	High	Low	Close	Chg
25	NAIC Gt	10 5/8	10 1/2	10 5/8	+ 1/8
4	PionRail	1 1/2	1 1/2	1 1/2	− 1/8
10	UtdFinMtg	3	3	3	− 3/8

CBOE

Sales	Stock	High	Low	Close	Chg
369	SalSB SP06	10 1/16	10	10	...
23	SalSB S&P05	10 3/16	10 3/16	10 3/16	...

Sales	Stock	High	Low	Close	Chg
116	SSB DJ05 n	15 5/8	15 5/8	15 5/8	...
3	SB S&P02	23 1/16	23 1/16	23 1/16	− 5/16
4	TgtCSCO n	43 3/4	43 3/4	43 3/4	− 1/8

PACIFIC

Sales	Stock	High	Low	Close	Chg
2	GoldCyc	7 1/4	7 1/4	7 1/4	+ 1/8
29	LTC Hlth n	2 9/16	2 1/2	2 1/2	− 1/16
10	LincHerit	4 1/4	4 1/4	4 1/4	+ 1/8
19	MesaOffsh	1/32	1/32	1/32	...
12	OrigSix	7/8	3/4	7/8	+ 1/8
2	SecCapCp	3 7/8	3 7/8	3 7/8	+ 1/8

BOSTON

Sales	Stock	High	Low	Close	Chg
40	CstlCarib	1 5/16	1 1/4	1 1/4	...

TOTAL SALES

BOSTON	14,199,000
CBOE	51,500
CHICAGO	35,954,000
PHILADELPHIA	5,672,000
PACIFIC	15,860,000

FIGURE 3.3 Summary of Activities in Stocks Traded on U.S. Exchanges (excerpts)

Source: Reprinted by permission of *The Wall Street Journal,* Dow Jones & Company, Inc., March 3, 1999, pp. C3, C13. All rights reserved worldwide.

Americas

MONTREAL in Canadian dollars

	CLOSE	NET CHG.
Bio Pha	34.50	– 0.10
BombrdrB	21.75	– 0.30
Cambior	6.20	+ 0.25
Cascades	7.50	– 0.05
Donohue A	30.50	– 0.50
NatBk Cda	20.50	– 0.25
Power Corp	29.40	– 0.15
Quebecr B	33.00	– 0.25
Quebecr P	33.25	– 0.95
SNC-Lavalin	12.10	– 0.10
Teleglobe	46.45	– 0.20
Videotron	24.50	– 0.75

TORONTO in Canadian dollars

	CLOSE	NET CHG.
Abitibi C	11.75	– .30
AirCanada	6.15	+ .05
Alcan	35.80	– 1.20
AltEnergy	31.25	– .90
Anderson	11.95	– .20
Atco I f	40.00	+ .50
Aur Res	1.92	+ .02
BC Gas	29.25	...
BCE Inc	61.00	– 1.40
BCE Mobl	42.50	– .50
BCT Tels	41.80	– .45
BGR A	9.65	+ .15
Bank Mtl	62.85	– .30
Bank N S	30.35	– .55
Barick gld	26.80	+ .05
C Util B	48.50	+ .20
CAE	8.35	– .15
CCL B f	16.10	– .10
CIBkCom	34.65	– .05
CP Ltd	26.10	– 1.05
CTire A f	37.80	+ .25
Cambior	6.20	+ .25
Cambridg	9.00	...
Cameco	31.65	– .35
Canfor	4.50	– .15
Cdn Airlne	1.93	+ .04
Cdn Tire	54.00	+ 2.00
CdnNatRes	20.00	– .20
Co Steel	11.50	...
Cominco L	20.25	– .25
Crestar	10.45	+ .40
Dia a o f	15.00	...
Dofasco	17.95	– .65
Domtar	9.00	+ .10
DundeeAf	14.75	– .25
Dupont A	46.25	+ .25
Dylex Ltd	4.20	+ .15
Enbridge	69.50	– 1.00
Euro Nev	21.75	– .25
F Season	54.60	+ .10
Fairfax f	504.00	– 24.00
Falcnbrg	15.85	– 1.05
Finning	9.00	– .10
FletCCanA	12.90	– .75
Franco	23.35	+ .10
GeacComp	21.45	– .15
Gendis A	3.45	– .30
GoldcorpAf	9.15	– .10
Gulf Can	3.71	– .13
H Bay Co	14.35	– .05
I Comfort	10.65	+ .45
IForestAf	2.95	+ .04
Imasco L	32.25	– .45
ImperialOil	23.95	+ .20
Inco	17.70	– 1.05
Ipsco	25.50	– .25
Ivaco A f	2.35	+ .05
Jannock	15.25	– .25
Loblaw Co	39.40	+ .75
MDS B	32.90	– .10
Mackenzie	17.10	– .65
Macmilan	14.90	– .20
Maritime f	38.50	– .30
MolsonAf	21.55	+ .10
Moore	15.70	– .10
NatBkCan	20.45	– .35
Noma A f	9.00	– .05
Noranda I	16.00	+ .05
Onex C f	45.75	– .25
PanCan P	16.30	– .35
PetroCCV	15.60	– .15
PlacerDm	16.75	...
Poco Pete	8.90	...
Ptash Cor	84.55	– 1.90
Ranger	4.05	– .20
Renisanc	12.65	– .30
RogersBf	23.55	– .50
Royal Bnk	72.90	+ .50
Sears Can	21.30	...
Shell Can	22.20	– .25
Spar Aero	9.50	...
Stelco A	8.30	+ .10
TIPS	34.60	– .60
Talisman	22.50	– .15
Teck B f	10.40	– .30
ThomCor	36.45	– 1.05
TorDmBk	61.20	– 1.20
TorstarBf	15.75	– .10
TrAlt corp	23.30	– 1.30
TrCan PL	20.10	– .45
Trilon A	11.15	+ .15
Trimac	7.00	...
TrizecHaf	29.15	– .25
Wcoast E	29.50	...
Weston	60.00	– .75

MEXICO CITY in pesos

	CLOSE	NET CHG.
Alfa A	23.80	– 0.50
Apasco A	42.80	– 0.45
Banacci B	15.10	+ 0.40
Bimbo A	19.22	– 0.28
Cemex B	29.55	– 0.15
Cifra C	12.48	+ 0.18
Cifra V	12.60	+ 0.12
ComerciUBC	8.18	– 0.24
Femsa B	26.40	....
Gcarso A1	33.80	+ 0.30
GModeloC	22.50	+ 0.10
Kimber A	30.85	– 0.30
Maseca B	8.38	– 0.02
Tamsa	61.80	– 0.20
Telecom A1	41.90	– 0.40
Televisa	136.20	– 1.30
Telmex L	27.55	– 0.55
Vitro	14.60	– 0.10

BRAZIL in real

	CLOSE	NET CHG.
BcoBrdscoPfd	8.55	+ 0.05
BrahmaPfd	790.00	+ 20.00
CemigPfd	27.80	+ 0.10
ItaubancoPfd	765.00	....
LightServ	109.40	– 3.60
PetrobrasPfd	169.50	– 1.50
Sabesp	80.00	– 2.00
TelebrasPfd	132.80	– 3.20
TelespPfd	193.00	– 3.90
ValRioDocPfd	26.35	– 0.18

CHILE in pesos

	CLOSE	NET CHG.
Cervezas	1920.00	– 30.00
Chilectra	2400.00	– 25.00
Copec	1050.00	– 10.00
CTC-A	2730.00	+ 10.00
D&S	365.00	....
Endesa	209.50	– 2.50
Enersis	244.00	– 2.00
Falabella	240.00	– 10.00
Gener	105.00	– 3.40
Santander	31.60	– 0.40

VENEZUELA in bolivars

	CLOSE	NET CHG.
BcoPrvincial	605.00	+ 5.00
CANTV	1268.00	+ 11.00
ElecCaracas	180.50	– 1.50
Sivensa	18.00	– 0.70
Vancemos	228.00	– 7.00

Europe

AMSTERDAM in euros

	CLOSE	NET CHG.
ABN Amro	18.05	....
Aegon	94.50	+ 0.75
Ahold	34.15	– 0.55
Akzo Nobel	32.50	– 0.90
AMEV	33.55	– 0.25
DSM	77.75	....
Elsevier	14.70	+ 0.15
Hagemeyer	27.65	– 0.15
Heineken	47.40	+ 1.15
Hoogovens	26.80	– 0.10
Hunter Douglas	28.10	– 1.40
ING Groep N.V.	49.50	– 0.15
KLM	26.55	+ 0.95
KNP BT	17.20	+ 0.40
Nedlloyd	10.20	– 0.30
Oce-van Grntn	24.25	– 0.65
Pakhoed Hldg	21.50	+ 0.20
Philips Elec	62.60	– 0.20
Randstad	46.50	+ 0.30
Robeco	109.65	....
Rodamco	22.45	+ 0.25
Rolinco	94.05	+ 0.05
Rorento	60.80	+ 0.05
Royal Dutch	39.30	– 0.10
Royal PTT	45.70	– 0.80
Unilever	65.85	+ 0.10
Van Ommeren	26.95	– 0.20
VNUVerBez	37.80	+ 0.05
Wessanen	12.00	– 0.35
Wolters Kluwer	167.20	– 3.50

BRUSSELS in euros

	CLOSE	NET CHG.
Arbed	64.60	– 0.90
BarcoNV	156.60	+ 7.00
Bekaert	372.50	+ 4.50
CBR	84.50	+ 4.20
Delhaize	85.50	+ 0.35
Electrabel	363.00	– 7.00
Fortis	32.40	– 0.10
Gevaert	68.50	– 1.50
GIB	38.26	+ 0.46
KBC Bk	68.15	– 0.45
Petrofina	426.00	+ 6.20
Solvay	62.30	– 0.05
Tractebel	152.80	+ 1.80

FRANKFURT in euros

	CLOSE	NET CHG.
Adidas Salmn	86.00	– 1.50
Allianz	269.50	– 3.50
BASF	31.54	+ 0.75
Bayer	32.85	+ 1.55
Beiersdorf	66.90	+ 0.10
BMW	624.00	– 16.00
Byr Vereinsbk	50.50	+ 2.00
Commerzbank	24.62	– 0.33
Continental	21.30	....
Daimler Chrysler	83.65	+ 0.45
Degussa	30.70	+ 0.35
Deutsche Bank	46.40	+ 0.80
Deutsche Tel	43.54	+ 1.54
Dresdner Bank	31.50	+ 1.00
Gehe	51.30	....
Heidlbg Zemnt	58.30	– 3.00
Henkel	75.00	+ 2.99
Hochtief	29.90	– 0.10
Hoechst	39.20	– 2.03
Karstadt	326.00	– 10.00
Linde	496.00	....
Lufthansa	20.47	+ 0.47
MAN	23.70	+ 0.20
Mannesmnn	118.30	– 1.70
Metallges	16.40	– 0.40
Metro AG	61.30	– 0.69
Munchen Rk	176.25	+ 1.75
Porsche	1860.00	....
Preussag	439.50	+ 10.10
RWE	39.15	– 0.55
SAP	311.50	+ 1.00
SAP Pfd	339.00	+ 0.75
Schering	111.00	– 0.95
SchwarzPhar	50.50	....
Siemens	55.50	– 0.11
Thyssen	162.50	– 3.85
Veba	46.49	– 0.01
Viag	473.00	+ 2.00
Volkswagen	56.00	+ 0.64

LONDON in pound/pence

	CLOSE	NET CHG.
3-I Group Plc	6.050	+ 0.025
Abbey National	11.980	+ 0.110
Allied-Domecq	4.770	+ 0.040
AlliedZurich	8.955	– 0.065
Arjo Wiggins	1.280	+ 0.035
Assoc Brit Fds	4.550	– 0.115
BAA Plc	7.040	+ 0.090
Barclays	16.790	+ 0.150
Bass	8.630	+ 0.110
BG	3.558	– 0.028
Blue Circle	3.070	+ 0.010
BOC Group	8.335	+ 0.105
Body Shop	0.965	– 0.035
Boots	9.980	+ 0.030
BPB Indus	2.235	– 0.035
Brit Sky Brd	5.625	– 0.088
BritAmTob	5.690	– 0.110
British Aero	3.910	– 0.045
British Airwys	4.380	– 0.083
British Land	5.295	+ 0.210
British Pete	8.505	– 0.120
British Steel	1.275	+ 0.025
British Telcom	10.740	+ 0.110
Burmah Castrol	9.090	+ 0.500
Cable&Wireless	8.440	– 0.100
Cadbury Schwp	9.320	– 0.020
Caradon	1.470	– 0.018
CGU	9.280	+ 0.430
Charter Plc	3.480	– 0.020
Coats Viyella	0.380	+ 0.005
Compass	7.465	– 0.445
Cookson Group	1.535	– 0.125
Diageo	6.955	+ 0.060
EMI	4.470	+ 0.040
Eng Ch Clay	2.415	+ 0.015
Enterprise Oil	2.673	– 0.008
Euro Tunnel	0.855	– 0.010
Gen Electric	5.360	+ 0.200
GKN	8.475	+ 0.085
Glaxo Wellcome	19.280	+ 0.120
Granada	12.600	– 0.075
Great Universl	8.220	+ 0.260
Guardian Royal	3.500	– 0.003
Hanson Plc	5.240	+ 0.083
Hillsdown	0.690	....
Imp Chem Ind	5.160	– 0.135
Imperl Tobac	7.490	+ 0.145
Inchcape Plc	1.440	– 0.029
Jefferson Smurf	1.280	– 0.036
Johnson Mathy	4.435	– 0.023
Kingfisher	7.395	– 0.280
Ladbroke Grp	2.858	+ 0.008
Land Securs	8.375	+ 0.140
LASMO	1.213	– 0.003
Legal & Genl	7.495	– 0.010
Lloyds TSB Grp	9.035	+ 0.200
Lucas Varity	2.838	+ 0.003
Marks & Spencr	3.950	– 0.163
MEPC	4.800	+ 0.100
Nat Power Plc	5.045	+ 0.120
Nat Wstmn Bk	12.710	+ 0.210
Next Plc	7.235	+ 0.035
NFC	1.530	– 0.010
P & O	7.135	– 0.185
Pearson	13.650	– 0.020
Pilkgtn Bros	0.635	– 0.015
PowerGen Plc	7.630	+ 0.015
Prudential	8.220	+ 0.020
Rank Gp	2.398	+ 0.023
Reckit&Colman	8.145	+ 0.110
Reed Intl	5.840	– 0.088
Rentokil	4.008	– 0.480
Reuters	8.625	+ 0.175
Rexam Plc	1.940	– 0.010
Rio Tinto	7.965	– 0.035
RMC	7.150	+ 0.060
Rolls Royce	2.720	+ 0.020
Royal and Sun	5.333	+ 0.218
Royl Bk Scot	11.920	+ 0.420
Safeway	2.638	+ 0.015
Sainsbury J	3.645	+ 0.030
Scottish Pwr	5.925	+ 0.175
Severn Trent	8.960	....
Shell	3.290	– 0.058
Siebe Plc	2.633	+ 0.020
Smith & Nephew	1.810	+ 0.015
SmithKline B	8.540	+ 0.070
Smiths Ind	9.625	– 0.105
Std Chartrd	8.050	– 0.020
SunLife & Prov	4.900	+ 0.035
Tarmac	1.080	+ 0.020
Tate & Lyle	4.278	– 0.223
Tesco	1.685	– 0.003
Thames Wtr	10.150	+ 0.090
TI Group	3.820	+ 0.020
Tomkins	2.188	– 0.068
Unilever	5.960	– 0.010
United Util	7.785	+ 0.010
Utd Biscuits	1.830	+ 0.058
Utd News	6.560	– 0.005
Vodafone	11.205	+ 0.035
Williams	3.768	– 0.075
Wolseley	4.063	+ 0.113
WPP Group	5.028	+ 0.043
Zeneca Grp	25.190	– 0.120

MADRID in euros

	CLOSE	NET CHG.
ACESA	12.75	+ 0.22
Argentaria	21.79	+ 0.19
Bco Bil Viz	13.17	– 0.07
Bco Cntrl Hisp	10.56	– 0.04
Bco de Sntdr	17.60	– 0.23
Bco Inter Esp	32.28	– 0.04
Bco Populr Esp	59.20	– 0.45
Centr Com Pry	20.20	+ 0.20
Crp Mapfre	19.25	– 0.17
ENDESA	23.96	– 0.02
Fomnto Constr	60.80	– 0.40
Gas Natrl SDG	87.95	– 0.65
Iberdrola I	13.50	– 0.48
Petroleos	32.49	– 0.08
Repsol	47.60	+ 0.46
Sevillana Elec	12.70	– 0.04
Tabacalera A	20.15	– 0.06
Telefonica	41.88	+ 0.44
Valen Cem Port	11.00	– 0.27

MILAN in euros

	CLOSE	NET CHG.
Alleanza	9.39	– 0.08
Banca Com	5.49	– 0.11
Benetton	1.43	– 0.04
CIGA	0.63	+ 0.00
CIR	0.98	– 0.02
ENI	5.38	+ 0.04
FIAT Com	2.62	– 0.02
FIAT Pref	1.34	– 0.04
Generali	34.50	+ 0.05
Instituto Naz	2.27	+ 0.01
Mediobanca	10.10	....
Montedison	0.89	+ 0.02
Olivetti Com	2.99	+ 0.14
Olivetti NC	2.79	+ 0.11
Pirelli Co	1.50	– 0.02
Pirelli SpA	2.66	+ 0.04
RAS	9.32	– 0.05
Rinascente	7.70	– 0.32
Rolo Banca	22.10	+ 0.05
Saipem	3.15	+ 0.04
Snia	1.25	+ 0.01
Telecm Ital	6.01	+ 0.05
Telecm Itl Ord	9.61	– 0.19
UniCredito Ital	4.58	– 0.09

PARIS in euros

	CLOSE	NET CHG.
Accor	215.00	+ 5.70
Air Liquide	135.00	+ 2.20
Alcatel Alstm	101.50	+ 5.15
AXA Group	112.20	– 2.60
Bic	47.85	+ 0.59
BNP	74.50	+ 3.60

FIGURE 3.4 Summary of Trading Activities on Selected Foreign Exchanges (excerpts)

Source: Reprinted by permission of *The Wall Street Journal,* Dow Jones & Company, Inc., March 3, 1999, pp. C14.

the stock that he or she does not know. That is, the dealer does not know if the trader has an information advantage. However, the dealer understands that if the trader is informed, it is likely that any information will soon be disseminated, which is good news for the stock if the informed trader bought it and bad news if the informed trader sold it.

For example, assume that the bid and asked quotes for Widget are $20 and $21 and an informed trader (at this point the dealer does not know whether the trader is informed) arrives and sells 1,000 shares to the dealer at $20. Typically, negative information about the company will be released shortly thereafter that will cause the dealer to lower his or her quotes to, say, $18 and $19. The dealer has bought 1,000 shares for $20 but now is offering and likely will sell them for $19, a potential loss of $1,000. (In this example it is also assumed that the dealer cannot quote an asked price of $20 because there are other dealers who would undercut him or her at that price.) Conversely, if an informed trader arrives and buys 1,000 shares at $21, typically there will be positive news announced shortly thereafter that will cause the dealer to raise his or her quotes to, say, $22 and $23, resulting in an opportunity loss of $1,000. In both of these cases, the dealer has been "picked off" by informed traders, losing money in the process.

So how does the dealer earn a profit? By transacting with uninformed traders, because their trades are not consistently followed by news of any particular type. After an uninformed trader buys 1,000 shares when the quotes are $20 and $21, it is equally possible that good or bad information (if any) about the company will be released. The dealer, on average, will not be adversely affected by transacting with an uninformed trader. Consequently, dealers set spreads so their expected losses from dealing with informed traders balance out with expected gains from dealing with uninformed traders. In the language of financial economists, dealers cope with this *adverse selection problem* by setting a spread so that the losses from trading with *information-motivated traders* are offset by the gains from trading with *liquidity-motivated traders* (so called because they either have excess cash to invest in stocks or need cash and sell stocks to raise it).[19]

3.5 Central Market

The Securities Acts Amendments of 1975 mandated that the Securities and Exchange Commission (SEC) implement a truly nationwide competitive central security market:

> The linking of all markets for qualified securities through communication and data processing facilities will foster efficiency, enhance competition, increase the information available to brokers, dealers, and investors, facilitate the offsetting of investors' orders, and contribute to best execution of such orders.[20]

consolidated tape

Implementation of these objectives has proceeded in steps. In 1975 a **consolidated tape** began to report trades in stocks listed on the New York and American stock exchanges that took place on the two exchanges, on major regional exchanges, in the OTC market using the Nasdaq system, and in the fourth market using the Instinet system. Since 1976 this information has been used to produce the **composite stock price tables** published in the daily press.

composite stock price tables

The second step involved commissions charged to investors by brokerage firms that are members of the NYSE. Before 1975 the NYSE required its members to charge all investors the same commission for a given order. However, as a result of an SEC order and the subsequent Securities Acts Amendments of 1975, this system of fixed commissions was abolished and all brokerage firms were free to set their own commissions.

The next step involved quotations. A broker must know the prices currently available on all major markets in order to get the best possible terms for a client. To reach this objective, the SEC instructed stock exchanges to make their quotations available in the **Consolidated Quotations System** (CQS). With the implementation of this system in 1978, bid and asked prices (along with the corresponding volume limits) became accessible to subscribers of quotation services. In most situations, brokers now rely on electronics to find the best available terms for a trade, eliminating extensive "shopping around."

Consolidated Quotations System

In 1978 the **Intermarket Trading System** (ITS) was inaugurated. This electronic communications network links eight exchanges (NYSE, AMEX, the Boston, Chicago, Cincinnati, Pacific, and Philadelphia stock exchanges, and the Chicago Board Options Exchange) and certain OTC security dealers, thereby enabling commission and floor brokers, specialists, and dealers at various locations to interact with one another. The ITS display monitors provide the bid and asked prices quoted by market-makers (these quotes are obtained from the CQS), and the system allows the commission and floor brokers, specialists, and dealers to route orders electronically to the best price at a given moment. However, the market-maker providing the best price may withdraw it on receipt of an order, and the customer's broker is not required to route the order to the market-maker with the best price.

Intermarket Trading System

In 1996 the SEC passed a series of initiatives known as order handling rules. Among other things, these rules require that (1) NASD establish a central limit order book for investors and (2) quotations posted on ECNs be made available to all investors; previously, ECNs such as Instinet and SelectNet had made their quotations available only to certain investors such as institutions or dealers.

3.6 Clearing Procedures

Most stocks that are sold the "regular way" require delivery of certificates within three business days. On rare occasions a sale may be made as a "cash" transaction, requiring delivery the same day, or as a "seller's option," giving the seller the choice of any delivery day within a specified period (typically, no more than 60 days). On other occasions extensions to the three-day limit are granted.

It would be extremely inefficient if every security transaction had to end with a physical transfer of stock certificates from the seller to the buyer. Fortunately, certificates can be almost completely immobilized. The **Depository Trust Company** (DTC) maintains computerized records of the securities "owned" by its member firms (brokers, banks, and so on). Members' stock certificates are credited to their accounts at the DTC, and the certificates are transferred to the DTC on the books of the issuing corporation and remain registered in its name until a member withdraws them. Whenever possible, one member will "deliver" securities to another by initiating a simple bookkeeping entry in which one account is credited and the other is debited for the shares involved. Dividends paid on securities held by the DTC are simply credited to members' accounts based on their holdings and may be subsequently withdrawn from the DTC as cash.

Depository Trust Company

3.7 Insurance

The Securities Investor Protection Act of 1970 established the **Securities Investor Protection Corporation** (SIPC), a quasi-governmental agency that insures the accounts of clients of all brokers and members of exchanges registered with the SEC against loss

Securities Investor Protection Corporation

due to a brokerage firm's failure. Each account is insured up to a stated amount ($500,000 per customer in 1999). The cost of the insurance is supposed to be borne by the covered brokers and members through premiums. If its financial resources prove insufficient, SIPC can borrow up to $1 billion from the U.S. Treasury. A number of brokerage firms have also arranged additional coverage from private insurance companies.

3.8 Commissions

3.8.1 FIXED COMMISSIONS

In the 1770s people interested in buying and selling stocks and bonds met under a buttonwood tree near present-day 68 Wall Street in New York City. In May 1792 a group of brokers pledged "not to buy or sell from this day for any person whatsoever, any kind of public stock at a rate less than one-quarter percent commission on the specie value, and that we will give preference to each other in our negotiations."[21] A visitor to the New York Stock Exchange today can see a copy of this "buttonwood agreement" publicly displayed. This view of the exchange is not surprising because the exchange is a lineal descendant of the group that met under the buttonwood tree. Also, until 1968 the exchange required its member brokers to charge fixed minimum commissions for stocks, with no "rebates, returns, discounts or allowances in 'any shape or manner,' direct or indirect."[22] The terms had changed, but the principle established 174 years earlier remained in effect.

In the United States most cartels that limit competition by fixing prices are illegal. This one, however, was exempted from prosecution under antitrust laws. Before 1934 the exchange was, in essence, considered a private club for its members. This situation changed with passage of the Securities Exchange Act of 1934, which required most exchanges to be registered with the SEC. The Commission, in turn, encouraged exchanges to "self-regulate" their activities, including the setting of minimum commissions.

3.8.2 COMPETITIVE COMMISSIONS

May Day

As mentioned earlier in this chapter, the system of fixed commissions was terminated by the Securities Acts Amendments of 1975 (but only after repeated challenges by the NYSE). Since May 1, 1975 (known in the trade as **May Day**), brokers have been free to set commissions at any desired rate or to negotiate with customers concerning the fees charged for particular trades. The former procedure is more commonly used in "retail" trades executed for small investors, whereas the latter is used more often when handling large trades involving institutional investors.

After May Day commissions for large trades fell substantially, as did those for small trades by firms offering limited brokerage services. However, full-service firms that provide extensive services to small investors for no additional fee continued to charge commissions like those specified in the earlier fixed schedules. More recently, the emergence of discount brokers, particularly online discount brokers, has provided small investors with low-cost alternatives to the full-service brokers.

No legal restriction gave monopoly power to the NYSE. The NYSE's dominance has been attributed to economies of scale in bringing many people together (either physically or via modern communications technology) to trade with one another. The increasing institutionalization of security holdings and the progress in communications and computer technology have reduced the advantages of a centralized physical exchange. Thus, the removal of legal protection for fixed commissions may have accelerated a trend already under way.

Increased competition among brokerage firms has resulted in a wide range of alternatives for investors. After May Day, some firms "unbundled": They priced their services separately from their pricing of order execution. Other firms "went discount": They dropped almost all ancillary services and cut commissions accordingly. Still others "bundled" new services into comprehensive packages. Some of these approaches have not stood the test of time, but just as mail-order firms, discount houses, department stores, and expensive boutiques coexist in the retail clothing trade, many different combinations are possible in the brokerage industry.

3.9   Transaction Costs

3.9.1   BID–ASK SPREAD

bid–ask spread

Commission costs are only a portion of the total cost associated with buying or selling a security. Consider a "round-trip" transaction, in which a stock is purchased and then sold during a period in which no new information is released that would cause investors to collectively reassess the value of the stock (the bid and asked prices quoted by dealers do not change). In this case, the stock will be purchased typically at the dealers' asked price and sold at the bid price, which is lower. The **bid–ask spread** thus constitutes a portion of the round-trip transaction costs.

How large is the spread between bid and asked prices for a typical stock? The spread generally amounts to less than 1% of the price per share for large actively traded stocks—a reasonably small amount to pay for the ability to buy or sell in a hurry. However, not all securities enjoy this type of liquidity. Shares of smaller firms tend to sell at lower prices but at similar bid–ask spreads. As a result, the percentage transaction cost is considerably higher.

Spreads are inversely related to the amount of trading activity in a stock. Stocks with more trading activity (trading volume) tend to have lower spreads.[23] The inverse relationship between the amount of trading activity (market value) and spread size can be explained by the fact that the spread is the dealer's compensation for providing investors with liquidity. The smaller the amount of trading, the less frequently the dealer will capture the spread (by buying at the bid and selling at the asked). Hence the dealer needs a wider spread to generate a level of compensation commensurate with more frequently traded securities.

3.9.2   PRICE IMPACT

price impact

Brokerage commissions and bid–ask spreads represent transaction costs for small orders (typically 100 shares). For larger orders the possibility of **price impacts** must also be considered. According to the law of supply and demand, the larger the size of the order, the more likely the investor's purchase price will be higher (or sale price lower). Furthermore, the more rapidly the order is completed and the more knowledgeable the individual or organization placing the order, the higher the purchase price (or lower the sale price) set by the dealer.

market capitalization

Table 3.3 offers a profile of trading activity conducted by a sample of institutional investors during the 12-month period ending June 30, 1996. The table presents information on 1.3 million trades on both the NYSE and Nasdaq/NMS markets. Stocks traded are divided into three groups based on their **market capitalization,** which equals

TABLE 3.3   Price Impact Analysis of Institutional Trades

(a) NYSE Trades

	Size	Percent of Total	Avg. Price Impact	Avg. Commission	Avg. Market Capitalization (billions)	Avg. No. of Traded Shares	Avg. Price/ Share
Large market capitalization	More than $10 billion	28	$.10 (.17%)	$.045	$34.4	24,000	$75
Midmarket capitalization	$1–$10 billion	51	.09 (.25%)	.046	4.4	24,000	35
Small market capitalization	Less than $1 billion	21	.07 (.36%)	.044	0.6	17,000	19
Small trades	0–10,000 shares	63	.04 (.10%)	.040	15.2	2,000	41
Medium trades	10–50,000 shares	26	.055 (.14%)	.044	13.6	23,000	39
Large trades	More than 50,000 shares	11	.105 (.27%)	.046	18.7	133,000	39

(b) Nasdaq/NMS Trades

	Size	Percent of Total	Avg. Price Impact	Avg. Commission	Avg. Market Capitalization (billions)	Avg. No. of Traded Shares	Avg. Price/ Share
Large market capitalization	More than $10 billion	7	$.17 (.35%)	N.A.	$34.5	38,000	$48
Midmarket capitalization	$1–$10 billion	32	.19 (.52%)	N.A.	3.4	28,000	37
Small market capitalization	Less than $1 billion	61	.16 (.80%)	N.A.	0.5	17,000	20
Small trades	0–10,000 shares	58	.06 (.23%)	N.A.	5.5	3,000	28
Medium trades	10–50,000 shares	32	.125 (.43%)	N.A.	4.6	22,000	29
Large trades	More than 50,000 shares	10	.22 (.68%)	N.A.	11.1	128,000	32

Source: Plexus Group, 1997. All rights reserved.

the market value of the firm's outstanding equity (its share price times the number of shares outstanding). For example, large capitalization stocks are those with market capitalizations more than $10 billion. The table also segments the trades themselves into three groups based on the number of shares involved in the transactions. For example, large trades involve more than 50,000 shares.

The table indicates that similar commissions are charged on NYSE trades regardless of the stocks' market capitalizations. However, because average price per share tends to be directly related to market capitalization, commissions, stated as a percentage of the dollar value of a trade, increase as market capitalization decreases. Further, the smaller the market capitalization of a traded stock, the greater the price impact of the trade. Similarly, the larger the trade in terms of shares traded, the greater the price impact.

Figure 3.5 provides estimates of the average cost of institutional trading. All three sources of costs are included: brokerage commissions, bid–ask spreads, and price impacts. The figure refers to the total cost of a "round trip" for a purchase followed by a sale. It illustrates the round-trip cost for stocks with varying market capitalizations and varying trade sizes, with the trade size expressed relative to the daily volume of trading carried out in that stock on a typical day. Transaction costs increase as both market capitalization declines and the proportion of a day's trading volume consumed by the trade rises.

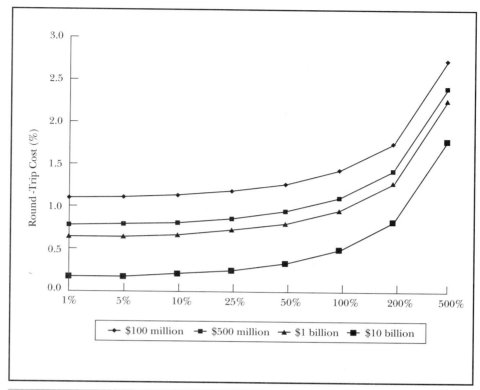

FIGURE 3.5 Transaction Costs versus Percent of Daily Trading Volume (by market capitalization)

Source: Plexus Group, 1997. All rights reserved.

3.10 Regulation of Security Markets

Directly or indirectly, security markets in the United States are regulated under both federal and state laws. Figure 3.6 illustrates the four main laws that regulate U.S. security markets.

1. The Securities Act of 1933 was the first major legislation at the federal level. Sometimes called the "truth in securities" law, it requires the registration of new issues and the disclosure of relevant information by the issuer. The act prohibits misrepresentation and fraud in security sales.

2. The Securities Exchange Act of 1934 extended the principles of the earlier act to cover secondary markets and required national exchanges, brokers, and dealers to be registered. It also made possible the establishment of self-regulatory organizations (SROs) to oversee the securities industry. Since 1934 both acts (and subsequent amendments to them, such as the Securities Acts Amendments of 1975 discussed earlier in the chapter) have been administered by the **Securities and Exchange Commission (SEC),** a quasi-judicial agency of the U.S. government established by the 1934 act.[24]

Securities and Exchange Commission (SEC)

3. The Investment Company Act of 1940 extended disclosure and registration requirements to investment companies. These organizations' total assets at the end of 1998 amounted to more than $5 trillion. (Investment companies use their funds primarily

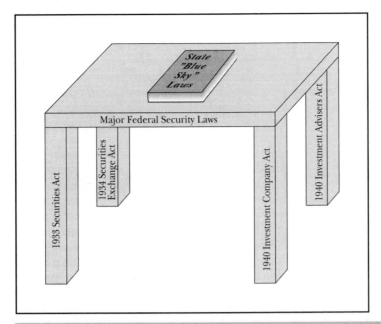

FIGURE 3.6 Pillars of Security Legislation

to purchase securities issued by corporations as well as the U.S. and state governments; they are discussed in Chapter 23.)

4. The Investment Advisers Act of 1940 required the registration of individuals who provide others with advice about security transactions. Advisers are also required to disclose any potential conflicts of interest.

self-regulation

As mentioned earlier, federal securities legislation relies heavily on the principle of **self-regulation.** The SEC has delegated its power to control trading practices for listed securities to the registered exchanges. However, the SEC has retained the power to alter or supplement any of the resulting rules or regulations. The SEC's power to control trading practices in OTC securities has been similarly delegated to NASD, a private association of brokers and dealers in OTC securities.[25] The SEC usually discusses proposed changes with both NASD and the registered exchanges in advance. As a result, the SEC formally alters or rejects few rules.

The Banking Act of 1933, also known as the Glass-Steagall Act, is an important piece of legislation that has made security markets in the United States different from those in many other countries. This act prohibited commercial banks from participating in investment banking activities because it was felt that there was an inherent conflict of interest in allowing banks to engage in both commercial and investment banking. Consequently, banks have not played as prominent a role in security markets in the United States as they do elsewhere. Recently, however, their role has increased, as the federal government has taken action to spur competition among various types of financial institutions. Many banks now offer security brokerage services, retirement funds, and the like via subsidiaries of their holding companies. Furthermore, long-standing limitations on rates paid on deposits and checking accounts were removed. Moreover, in 1999 many features of the Glass-Steagall Act were abolished. As a result the line between commercial banking and investment banking is becoming more blurred every day.

Initially, security regulation in the United States was the province of state governments. Beginning in 1911, state *blue sky laws* were passed to prevent "speculative schemes which have no more basis than so many feet of blue sky."[26] Although such statutes vary substantially from state to state, most of them outlaw fraud in security sales and require the registration of certain securities as well as brokers and dealers (and, in some cases, investment advisers). Some order has been created by the passage in many states of all or part of the Uniform Securities Acts proposed by the National Conference of Commissions on Uniform State Laws in 1956. Furthermore, the North American Securities Administrators Association (NASAA), an organization of state securities regulators based in Washington, D.C., monitors federal regulation and attempts to coordinate state regulation.

Securities that are traded across state lines, as well as the brokers, dealers, and exchanges involved in such trading, typically fall under the domain of federal legislation. However, significant aspects of security trading still fall under the exclusive jurisdiction of the states. In general, federal legislation only supplements state legislation; it does not supplant it. Some critics argue that the investor is overprotected as a result. Others suggest that the regulatory agencies (especially those that rely on "self-regulation" by powerful industry organizations) in fact protect the members of the regulated industry against competition, thereby damaging the interests of their customers instead of protecting them. Both positions undoubtedly contain some elements of truth.

Summary

1. Security markets facilitate the trading of securities by bringing buyers and sellers of financial assets together.
2. Common stocks are traded primarily on organized security exchanges or on the over-the-counter (OTC) market.
3. Organized security exchanges provide central physical locations where trading is done under a set of rules and regulations.
4. The primary organized security exchange is the New York Stock Exchange (NYSE). The American Stock Exchange (AMEX) and various regional exchanges also exist.
5. Trading on organized security exchanges is conducted by members who transact only in listed securities.
6. Exchange members fall into one of four categories, depending on the type of trading activity in which they engage. Those categories are commission broker, floor broker, floor trader, and specialist.
7. Specialists are charged with maintaining an orderly market in their assigned stocks. In this capacity they perform two roles. They act as brokers, maintaining limit order books for unexecuted trades, and they act as dealers, trading in their stocks for their own accounts.
8. In the OTC market, individuals act as dealers in a manner similar to specialists. However, unlike specialists, OTC dealers face competition from other dealers.
9. Most of the trading in the OTC market is done through a computerized system known as Nasdaq.
10. Trading in listed securities may take place outside the various exchanges on the third and fourth markets.
11. Foreign security markets each have their own particular operating procedures, rules, and customs.
12. Daily information regarding transactions in publicly traded stocks can be found in business newspapers and the business sections of most local newspapers.

13. Dealers typically make money trading with liquidity-motivated traders and lose money trading with adept information-motivated traders. A dealer must set a bid–ask spread that attracts sufficient revenue from the former group to offset losses to the latter.

14. Following legislation in 1975, the Securities and Exchange Commission (SEC) mandated procedures designed to create a truly nationwide central security market.

15. For most U.S. security transactions, the transfer of security ownership, known as clearing, is now done electronically.

16. SIPC is a quasi-governmental agency that insures the accounts of clients of all brokers and members of exchanges registered with the SEC against loss because of a brokerage firm's failure.

17. Since May Day (May 1, 1975), commissions have been negotiated between brokerage firms and their larger clients.

18. Transaction costs are a function of the stock's bid–ask spread, the price impact of the trade, and the commission.

19. The most prominent security market regulator is the SEC, a federal agency. Regulation of the U.S. security markets involves both federal and state laws.

20. The SEC has delegated to the various exchanges and NASD the power to control trading practices through a system of self-regulation with federal government oversight.

Questions and Problems

1. Virtually all secondary trading of securities takes place in continuous markets as opposed to call markets. What aspects of continuous markets cause them to dominate call markets?

2. Differentiate between the role of a specialist on the NYSE and the role of a dealer on the OTC market.

3. Describe the functions of commission brokers, floor brokers, and floor traders.

4. Pigeon Falls Fertilizer Company is listed on the NYSE. Gabby Hartnett, the specialist handling Pigeon Falls stock, is currently bidding $35\frac{3}{8}$ and asking $35\frac{5}{8}$. What would be the likely outcomes of the following trading orders?
   a. Through a broker, Eppa Rixey places a market order to buy 100 shares of Pigeon Falls stock. No other broker from the crowd takes the order.
   b. Through a broker, Eppa places a limit order to sell 100 shares of Pigeon Falls stock at 36.
   c. Through a broker, Eppa places a limit order to buy 100 shares of Pigeon Falls stock at $35\frac{1}{2}$. Another broker offers to sell 100 shares at $35\frac{1}{2}$.

5. Bosco Snover is the NYSE specialist in Eola Enterprises' stock. Bosco's limit order book for Eola appears as follows:

Limit—Sell		Limit—Buy	
Price	*Shares*	*Price*	*Shares*
$30.250	200	$29.750	100
30.375	500	29.000	100
30.500	300	28.500	200
30.875	800	27.125	100
31.000	200	26.875	200

The last trade in the stock took place at $30.
   a. If a market order to sell 200 shares arrives, what will happen?
   b. If another market order to sell 100 shares arrives just moments later, what will happen?

    c. Do you think that Bosco would prefer to accumulate shares or reduce inventory, given the current orders in the limit order book?

6. Because specialists such as Chick Gandil are charged with maintaining a "fair and orderly" market, at times they will be required to sell when others are buying and buy when others are selling. How can Chick earn a profit when required to act in such a manner?

7. Why is Nasdaq so important to the success of the OTC market?

8. Prices on the NYSE were once quoted in units of $\frac{1}{8}$ of a dollar (or $.125). Why would a change to smaller price increments be expected to increase opportunities for price improvement?

9. How might a dealer attempt to discern whether a trader is information-motivated?

10. What are some of the major steps that have been taken toward the ultimate emergence of a truly nationwide security market?

11. The NYSE has strongly opposed the creation of alternative market trading structures such as off-exchange crossing systems. The NYSE claims that these alternative structures undermine its ability to offer "best execution" to all investors. Discuss the merits of the NYSE's contention.

12. Why was May Day such an important event for the NYSE?

13. What is the purpose of SIPC insurance? Given the late 1980s experience of banking and savings and loan deposit insurance programs, under what conditions might SIPC insurance be expected to be effective? Under what conditions might it fail to accomplish its objectives?

14. Immediately after May Day, why did commission rates fall so sharply for large investors, but decline so little (or even increase) for small investors? More recently, why have online discount brokers driven down commissions for small investors?

15. Why does the price impact of a trade seem to be directly related to the size of the trade?

Endnotes

1. Enough time is allowed to elapse between calls (for example, an hour or more) so that a substantial number of orders to buy and sell accumulate by the time of the auction.

2. The applicant for membership must also pass a written examination, be sponsored by two current members of the exchange, and be approved by the board. The NYSE also allows members to lease their seats to individuals acceptable to the exchange. In addition to the 1,366 full memberships, there are a few individuals who hold special memberships that, in return for an annual fee, give them access to the trading floor.

3. During 1998 daily trading volume on the NYSE averaged 674 million shares, worth about $29 billion. AMEX, the second largest organized exchange, had daily values of less than one-tenth that amount.

4. <www.nyse.com/listed/listed.html>, 1999.

5. There is one other circuitbreaker known as Rule 80A, which restricts the execution of certain kinds of index arbitrage orders (a form of program trading). Readers are encouraged to check the NYSE's web page (www.nyse.com) for the current status of the various circuitbreakers, as they are subject to change.

6. The assignment is made by the board of directors and also includes any preferred stock or warrants that the company has listed on the exchange. At the end of 1998 there were 3,114 companies listed on the NYSE, with 3,773 stock issues being traded, meaning that there were more than 600 different issues of preferred stock and other classes of common stock being traded on the NYSE. There were also warrants on some of these companies' stock that were traded. Bonds are also listed on the NYSE but are traded in an entirely different manner that does not involve the use of specialists.

7. The NYSE is currently open from 9:30 A.M. until 4 P.M. Competitive pressure from rivals including Nasdaq, regional exchanges, electronic communication networks, and foreign stock markets (such as London) is forcing the NYSE to consider extended trading hours. Changes to its trading hours are likely by 2001. The NYSE does allow certain computerized trading to take place after the close in Crossing Session I (4:15 P.M. to 5 P.M.) and Crossing Session II (4 P.M. to 5:15 P.M.). Trades in Crossing Session I are based on 4 P.M. closing prices, whereas each trade in Crossing Session II must involve a "basket" of at least 15 NYSE-listed stocks and an aggregate price of $15 million (prices are set for the baskets, not for individual stocks).

8. The NYSE has rules that the specialist must follow regarding the minimum size associated with the quoted prices. These quotations may represent either orders for the specialist's own account or public orders, but they may not be the "best" ones because under certain circumstances specialists are not required to display

orders on the screens of quotation machines. However, such "hidden orders" would appear in the limit order book and would be on the exchange floor. According to NYSE policy, only the specialist is allowed to see the contents of the limit order book. However, in 1991 the NYSE began to allow the specialists to disclose some information about buying and selling interest to others on the floor.

9. In late 1999, the Securities Industry Association (a trade group representing the major U.S. stock exchanges) announced plans to move to full decimalization in pricing securities by the end of 2000.

10. Evidence of price improvement in minimum spread markets (as well as in markets with larger spreads) is provided in Lawrence Harris and Joel Hasbrouck, "Market vs. Limit Orders: The SuperDOT Evidence on Order Submission Strategy," *Journal of Financial and Quantitative Analysis,* 31, no. 2 (June 1996): 213–231; and Katharine D. Ross, James E. Shapiro, and Katherine A. Smith, "Price Improvement of SuperDOT Market Orders on the NYSE," NYSE Working Paper #96-02.

11. Odd lot market orders are executed immediately by the specialist at the quoted bid or asked price. Odd lot limit orders are held by the specialist and executed immediately after there has been another trade at the limit price. Typically, odd lot orders use the facilities of SuperDOT. There are special features of SuperDOT that are used to execute opening orders; that is, orders that are received up to the time the NYSE opens in the morning.

12. One alternative for the institution planning to place the block order is to place many small orders sequentially. However, institutions generally do not want to do this because their block order will not be executed with due speed. Furthermore, other traders may anticipate these additional transactions and develop strategies to take advantage of them.

13. The order must be crossed on an exchange where the stock is listed, provided that the block house is a member of that exchange.

14. In 1996 the Department of Justice and the SEC reached settlements with NASD after concluding that dealers had engaged in anticompetitive behavior by colluding in the setting of spreads in large Nasdaq stocks. Interestingly, the investigation was triggered by an academic paper by William G. Christie and Paul H. Schultz, "Why Do Nasdaq Market Makers Avoid Odd-Eighth Quotes?" *Journal of Finance,* 49, no. 5 (December 1994): 1813–1840. For press articles describing the settlement, see Anita Raghavan and Jeffrey Taylor, "Will NASD Accord Transform Nasdaq Market?" *The Wall Street Journal,* August 8, 1996, pp. C1, C6; and Floyd Norris, "Tough Crackdown on Nasdaq Market Announced by US," *New York Times,* August 9, 1996, pp. A1, D16.

15. Of this total, 484 were foreign securities consisting of 157 ADRs (American Depositary Receipts) and 327 non-ADRs. (Many of the non-ADRs were Canadian securities.) ADRs are discussed in Chapter 26.

16. The use of an intermediary, such as a computer system, makes it difficult to categorize such trades. Some people refer to the market where trades involving a "matchmaker" take place as the "3.5 market." The term *fourth market* would then be used only when referring to the market where no matchmaker is involved.

17. There is another way that internalization can take place. Broker-dealers can be specialists in NYSE-listed securities on either the NYSE itself or on a regional exchange. They can take their customers' orders and send them to their own specialists for execution. This practice is particularly common on certain regional exchanges where the specialists can make markets in many stocks (often several specialists will make a market in the same stock).

18. ADRs (see footnote 14) that are traded on Nasdaq are displayed in *The Wall Street Journal* after the Small Cap Issues under the heading *ADRs.* Exchange-listed ADRs are not shown separately. They are integrated into the tables with listed U.S. securities. ADRs are also discussed in Chapter 26.

19. Other classifications of traders often used by financial economists include (1) informed speculative traders who possess both public and private information, (2) uninformed speculative traders who possess just public information, and (3) noise traders whose trades are not based on information. The first two types are information-motivated traders, and the third is a liquidity-motivated trader. See Sanford J. Grossman and Joseph E. Stiglitz, "On the Impossibility of Informationally Efficient Markets," *American Economic Review,* 70, no. 3 (June 1980): 393–408.

20. From *Securities Acts Amendments of 1975,* section 11A.

21. See Wilford J. Eiteman, Charles A. Dice, and David K. Eiteman, *The Stock Market* (New York: McGraw-Hill, 1969), p. 19.

22. ———, *The Stock Market,* p. 138.

23. Roger D. Huang and Hans R. Stoll, *Major World Equity Markets: Current Structure and Prospects for Change,* Monograph Series in Finance and Economics 1991–93 (New York: New York University Salomon Center, 1991), p. 11.

24. The Commodity Futures Trading Commission (CFTC) was established in 1974 by Congress to regulate futures markets, and the Municipal Securities Rulemaking Board (MSRB) was established in 1975 to regulate trading in municipal securities.

25. The Maloney Act of 1938 extended the SEC's jurisdiction to include the OTC market and recognized the NASD as a self-regulatory organization (SRO).

26. See *Hall v. Geiger-Jones Co.,* 242 U.S. 539 (1917).

4

Efficient Markets, Investment Value, and Market Price

Payments provided by securities may differ in amount, timing, and risk level. A security analyst must estimate the amount of these payments as well as when and under what conditions the payments will be received. This estimate typically requires a detailed analysis of the firm involved, the industry (or industries) in which the firm operates, and the economy (either regionally, nationally, or internationally).

Once such estimates have been made, the overall investment value of the security must be determined. This determination generally requires conversion of uncertain future values to certain present values. The current prices of other securities can often be used in this process. If it is possible to determine the value of a similar set of payments, then this value provides a benchmark for the investment value of the security being analyzed. An investor would neither want to pay more than this amount for the security nor want to sell it for less. In some cases, however, equivalent alternatives may not exist. When this happens, the investor will have to estimate the appropriate discount rate to apply to the forecasted cash flows in order to estimate the security's investment value.

Later chapters discuss in detail the manner in which estimated future payments can be used to determine a security's current investment value. Methods for estimating the payments and finding equivalent alternatives are discussed after the characteristics of the securities have been introduced. In this chapter some general principles of investment value and how they relate to market prices in an efficient market are presented, leaving valuation methodology for specific types of securities for later.

4.1 Demand and Supply Schedules

Although there are more than one billion shares of AT&T common stock outstanding, on a typical day only a few million shares will be traded. What determines the prices at which such trades take place? A simple (and correct) answer is demand and supply. A more fundamental (and also correct) answer is investors' estimates of AT&T's future earnings and dividends, as such estimates strongly influence demand and supply. Before dealing with such influences, it is useful to examine the role of demand and supply in the determination of security prices.

As shown in Chapter 3, securities are traded by many people in many different ways. Although the forces that determine prices are similar in all markets, they are slightly more obvious in markets using periodic "calls." One such market corresponds to the *itayose* method of price determination that is used by the *saitori* at the twice-a-day openings of the Tokyo Stock Exchange.

4.1.1 DEMAND-TO-BUY SCHEDULE

demand-to-buy schedule

At a designated time all brokers holding orders to buy or sell a given stock for customers gather at a specified location on the floor of the exchange. Some of the orders are market orders. For example, Mr. A may have instructed his broker to buy 100 shares of Minolta at the lowest possible price, whatever it may be. His personal **demand-to-buy schedule** at that time is shown in Figure 4.1(a): He wishes to buy 100 shares no matter what the price. Although this schedule captures the contractual nature of Mr. A's market order at a specific point in time, Mr. A undoubtedly has a good idea that his ultimate purchase price will be near the price for which orders were executed just before he placed his order. Thus his true demand schedule might be sloping downward from the upper left portion to the lower right portion of the graph. This schedule is shown by the dashed line in Figure 4.1(a). It indicates his desire to buy more shares if the price is lower. However, to simplify his own tasks as well as his broker's tasks, he has esti-

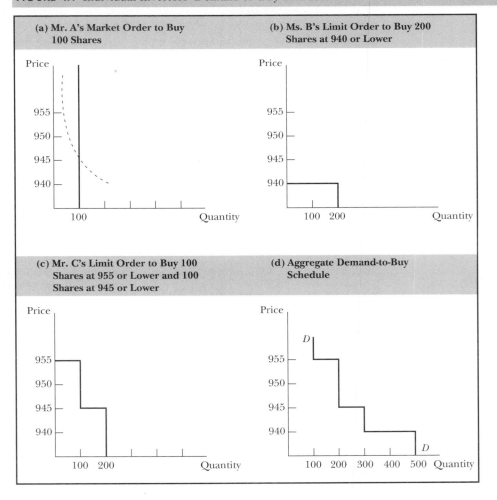

FIGURE 4.1 Individual Investors' Demand-to-Buy Schedules

mated that the price at which his order will be executed is in the range that he would choose to hold 100 shares. In the example shown here, this price is 945 yen per share.

Other customers may place limit orders with their brokers. Thus, Ms. B may have instructed her broker to buy 200 shares of Minolta at the lowest possible price if and only if that price is less than or equal to 940 yen per share. Her demand schedule is shown in Figure 4.1(b).

Some customers may give their broker two or more orders for the same security. Thus Mr. C may wish to buy 100 shares of Minolta at a price of 955 or less, plus an additional 100 shares if the price is at or below 945. To do this, Mr. C places a limit order for 100 shares at 955 and a second limit order for 100 shares at 945. Figure 4.1(c) portrays his demand schedule.

If all the orders to buy Minolta (both market and limit orders) could be examined, it would be possible to determine how many shares would be bought at every possible price. Assuming that only Mr. A, Ms. B, and Mr. C have placed buy orders, the resulting aggregate demand-to-buy schedule will look like line *DD* in Figure 4.1(d). Note that at lower prices more shares would be demanded.

4.1.2 SUPPLY-TO-SELL SCHEDULE

supply-to-sell schedule

Brokers will also hold market orders to sell shares of Minolta. For example, Ms. X may have placed a market order to sell 100 shares of Minolta at the highest possible price. Figure 4.2(a) displays her **supply-to-sell schedule.** As with market orders to buy, customers place such orders on the supposition that the actual price will be in the range in which their true desire would be to sell the stated number of shares. Thus, Ms. X's actual supply schedule might look more like the dashed line in Figure 4.2(a), indicating her willingness to sell more shares at higher prices.

Customers may also place limit orders to sell shares of Minolta. For example, Mr. Y may have placed a limit order to sell 100 shares at a price of 940 or higher, and Ms. Z may have placed a limit order to sell 100 shares at a price of 945 or higher. Panels (b) and (c) of Figure 4.2 illustrate these two supply-to-sell schedules.

As with the buy orders, if all the orders to sell Minolta (both market and limit orders) could be examined, it would be possible to determine how many shares would be sold at every possible price. Assuming that only Ms. X, Mr. Y, and Ms. Z have placed sell orders, the resulting aggregate supply-to-sell schedule will look like line *SS* in Figure 4.2(d). Note that at higher prices more shares would be supplied.

4.1.3 INTERACTION OF SCHEDULES

The aggregate demand and supply schedules are shown on one graph in Figure 4.3. In general no one would have enough information to draw the actual schedules. However, this limitation does not diminish the schedules' usefulness as representations of the underlying forces that are interacting to determine the market-clearing price of Minolta.

What actually happens when all the brokers gather together with their order books in hand? A clerk of the exchange "calls out" a price—for example, 940 yen per share. The brokers then try to complete transactions with one another at that price. Those with orders to buy at that price indicate the number of shares they wish to buy. Those with orders to sell do likewise. Some deals will be tentatively made, but as Figure 4.3 shows, more shares will be demanded at 940 than will be supplied. Specifically, 300 shares will be demanded, but only 200 shares will be supplied. When trading is completed (meaning that all possible tentative deals have been made), there will be a number of brokers calling "buy," but nobody will stand ready to sell to them. The price of 940 is too low.

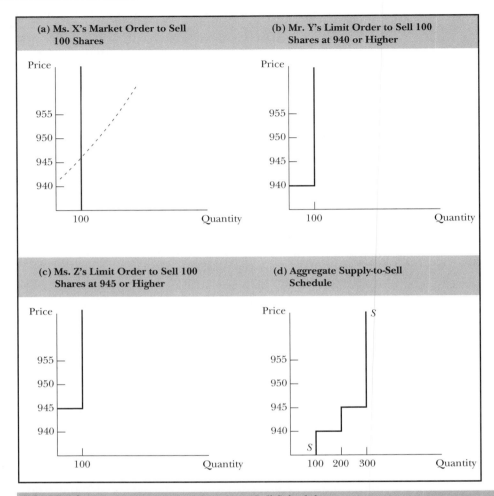

FIGURE 4.2 Individual Investors' Supply-to-Sell Schedules

As the situation develops, the clerk calls out another price, for example, 950. The previous trades are all canceled at this point, and the brokers consult their order books again and indicate how much they are willing to buy or sell at the new price. Figure 4.3 shows, when trading is completed, there will be a number of brokers calling "sell," but nobody will stand ready to buy from them. Specifically, 300 shares will be supplied, but there will be a demand for only 200 shares. The price of 950 was too high.

Undaunted, the clerk tries again. And again, if necessary. When there are only a few unsatisfied brokers, the price (and the associated tentative deals) will be declared final. As Figure 4.3 shows, 945 is the price. At 945, customers collectively want to sell 300 shares and there is a collective demand for 300 shares at this price. Thus, quantity demanded equals quantity supplied. The price is "just right."

4.1.4 ELASTICITY OF THE DEMAND-TO-BUY SCHEDULE

How elastic (flat) will the aggregate demand-to-buy schedule for a security be? The answer depends in part on how "unique" the security is. Securities are unique when they have few close substitutes. Securities are less unique when they have more close sub-

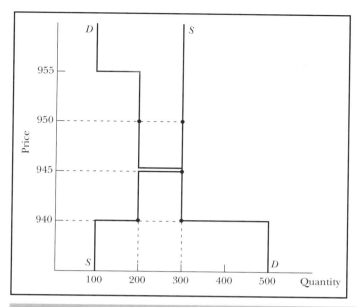

FIGURE 4.3 Determining a Security's Price Based on the Interaction of the Aggregate Demand-to-Buy and Supply-to-Sell Schedules

stitutes. The aggregate demand-to-buy schedule will be more elastic (flatter) for less unique securities. Equivalently, the less unique a security is, the greater the increase in the quantity demanded for a given fall in price because these shares produce a smaller increase in the typical portfolio's risk when substituted for other shares. At the extreme, other securities are viewed as perfect substitutes for the one being analyzed. In this case the security's demand-to-buy schedule will be horizontal, or perfectly elastic. At the other extreme where there are no substitutes, the security has an almost vertical (or almost perfectly inelastic) demand schedule.

4.1.5 SHIFTS IN THE DEMAND-TO-BUY AND SUPPLY-TO-SELL SCHEDULES

If one investor becomes more optimistic about the prospects for a security and another investor becomes more pessimistic about the same security, they may trade with one another with no effect on the aggregate demand-to-buy and supply-to-sell schedules. In this situation there will be no change in the market price for the security. However, if more investors become optimistic than pessimistic, the demand-to-buy schedule will shift to the right (for example, to $D'D'$ in Figure 4.4) and the supply-to-sell schedule will shift to the left (for example, to $S'S'$ in Figure 4.4) causing an increase in price (to P'). Correspondingly, if more investors become pessimistic than optimistic, the demand-to-buy schedule will shift to the left and the supply-to-sell schedule will shift to the right causing a decrease in price.

Some investors regard sudden and substantial price changes in a security as indications of changes in the future prospects of the issuer, which complicates this analysis. In the absence of additional public information, some investors may interpret such a change as an indication of **asymmetric information,** meaning "someone knows something that I don't know." While exploring the situation, these investors may revise their

asymmetric information

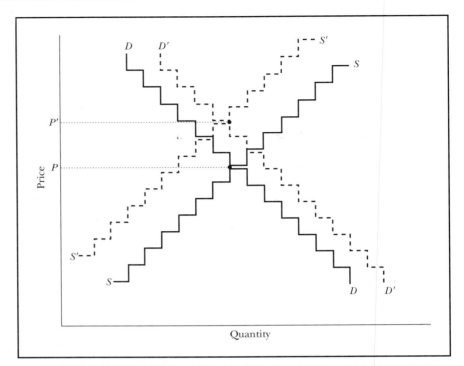

FIGURE 4.4 Shifts in the Aggregate Demand-to-Buy and Supply-to-Sell Schedules

own assessment of the issuer's prospects and may subsequently alter their demand-to-buy or supply-to-sell schedules. For this reason, few investors place limit orders at prices substantially different than the current price for fear that such orders would be executed only if the security's prospects changed significantly. If such a large price change occurred, it would imply the need for a careful reevaluation of the security before buying or selling shares.

4.1.6 SUMMARY

Trading procedures used in security markets vary from auction markets to dealer markets and from call markets to continuous markets. However, the similarities are more important than the differences. In the United States, for example, specialists at the NYSE and dealers on Nasdaq provide some of the functions of the *saitori* at the Tokyo Stock Exchange, and trades can take place at any time. Nevertheless, the basic principles of security price determination still apply. In general, market price equates quantity demanded with quantity supplied.

4.2 Market Efficiency

Market efficiency has been and is likely to continue to be a topic of intense debate in the investment community. In order to understand and participate in this debate, one must understand what market efficiency is. Most financial economists agree that capital should be channeled to the place where it will do the most good. One goal of government policy is to encourage the establishment of **allocationally efficient markets** in which the firms with the most promising investment opportunities have access to the

allocationally efficient market

externally efficient market

internally efficient market

needed funds. However, in order for markets to be allocationally efficient, they need to be both internally and externally efficient. In an **externally efficient market,** information is quickly and widely disseminated, which allows each security's price to adjust rapidly in an unbiased manner to new information so that it reflects investment value (a term that will be discussed shortly). In comparison, an **internally efficient market** is one in which brokers and dealers compete fairly, making the cost of transacting low and the speed of transacting high. External market efficiency has been the subject of much research since the 1960s, but internal market efficiency has only recently become a popular area of research.[1] Indeed, the SEC has adopted polices aimed at improving the internal efficiency of markets, primarily by setting rules and regulations that affect the design and operations of security markets. Henceforth, the term *market efficiency* will be used to denote external market efficiency (also known as informational efficiency) because this is the subject that has generated the most interest among practitioners and academics.

4.2.1 THE EFFICIENT MARKETS MODEL

investment value

Imagine a world in which (1) all investors have costless access to currently available information about the future, (2) all investors are capable analysts, and (3) all investors pay close attention to market prices and adjust their holdings appropriately.[2] In such a market a security's price is a good indicator of its **investment value,** where investment value is the present value of the security's future prospects, as estimated by well-informed and skillful analysts who use the information that is currently at hand. (Investment value is often referred to as the security's "fair" or "intrinsic" value.) That is,

efficient market

an **efficient market,** defined as one in which every security's price equals its investment value at all times, will exist.

In an efficient market a set of information is fully and immediately reflected in market prices. But what set of information? Eugene Fama offers the following distinctions:[3]

Form of Efficiency	Set of Information Reflected in Security Prices
Weak	Previous prices of securities
Semistrong	All publicly available information
Strong	All information, both public and private

The formal definition of an efficient market is as follows:

> A market is efficient with respect to a particular set of information if it is impossible to make abnormal profits (other than by chance) by using this set of information to formulate buying and selling decisions.

weak-form efficient

semistrong-form efficient

strong-form efficient

That is, in an efficient market investors should expect to make normal profits by earning a normal rate of return on their investments. For example, a **weak-form efficient** market would be one in which it is impossible to earn abnormal profits (other than by chance) by using past prices to make buying and selling decisions. Similarly, a **semistrong-form efficient** market would be one in which it is impossible to earn abnormal profits (other than by chance) by using publicly available information to make buying and selling decisions. Lastly, a **strong-form efficient** market would be one in which it is impossible to earn abnormal profits (other than by chance) by using any information whatsoever to make buying and selling decisions. When people refer to efficient markets, they usually mean semistrong-form efficient markets because the United States has strict laws governing the use of insider information (a form of private information) to make buying and selling decisions. Hence, it is interesting to consider whether markets are semistrong-form efficient because that involves restricting the analysis to the publicly available information that analysts use in making recommendations.

Why have the preceding statements included the qualifying phrase "other than by chance" in the definitions of efficient markets? Simply because some people may invest on the basis of patterns in past prices and end up making extraordinarily high returns. However, in an efficient market this outcome would have had nothing to do with the investor's use of past price information. Instead, it would have been merely luck, just as someone who wins a lottery after using a method for picking a number does not necessarily have a successful method for picking winning lottery numbers.

Figure 4.5 illustrates the three forms of efficiency. Note how in moving from weak- to semistrong- to strong-form efficiency, the set of information expands. Thus, if markets are strong-form efficient, they are also semistrong- and weak-form efficient. Similarly, if markets are semistrong-form efficient, then they are also weak-form efficient.

4.2.2 SECURITY PRICE CHANGES ARE RANDOM

What happens when *new* information arrives, such as an announcement that a company's earnings have experienced a significant and unexpected decline? In an efficient market, the actions of investors will result in the new information's being incorporated immediately and fully into security prices. New information is just that: new, meaning a surprise. (Anything that is not a surprise is predictable and should have been anticipated; hence it is old information.) Because good surprises are as likely as bad ones, price changes in an efficient market are as likely to be positive as negative. A security's price should move upward by an amount that provides a reasonable return on capital (when considered in conjunction with dividend payments), but anything above or below such an amount would, in an efficient market, be unpredictable. Consequently, price changes are random in a perfectly efficient market.[4] This randomness does not mean that prices are irrational. Because information arrives randomly, changes in prices that occur as a consequence of that information will seem random, being sometimes positive and sometimes negative. However, price changes are simply the result of investors' reassessing a security's prospects and adjusting their buying and selling appropriately. Hence, price changes are random but rational.

As mentioned earlier, in an efficient market a security's price is a good indicator of its investment value, where investment value is the present value of the security's future prospects as estimated by well-informed and capable analysts. In a developed and

FIGURE 4.5 Information and the Levels of Market Efficiency

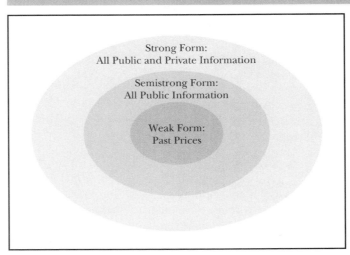

free market, major disparities between price and investment value are noted by alert analysts who seek to take advantage of their discoveries. Securities priced below investment value (known as underpriced or undervalued securities) will be purchased, creating pressure for price increases caused by the increased demand to buy. Securities priced above investment value (known as overpriced or overvalued securities) will be sold, creating pressure for price decreases caused by the increased supply to sell. As investors seek to take advantage of opportunities created by temporary inefficiencies, the inefficiencies are reduced, and the less alert and less informed have less of a chance to obtain large abnormal profits. As a result of the efforts of such highly alert investors, at any time a security's price can be assumed to equal the security's investment value, and security mispricing will not exist.

4.2.3 OBSERVATIONS ABOUT PERFECTLY EFFICIENT MARKETS

Some interesting observations can be made about *perfectly* efficient markets.

1. *Investors should expect to make a fair (or normal) return on their investment but no more.* Looking for mispriced securities using either technical analysis (whereby analysts examine past price behavior of securities) or fundamental analysis (whereby analysts examine earnings and dividend forecasts) will not be fruitful. Investing money on the basis of either type of analysis will not generate abnormal returns (other than for those few investors who turn out to be lucky).

2. *Markets will be efficient only if enough investors believe that they are not efficient.* The reason for this seeming paradox is straightforward: Investors who carefully analyze securities will make prices reflect investment values. However, if everyone believed that markets are perfectly efficient, then everyone would realize that nothing is to be gained by searching for undervalued securities, and hence nobody would bother to analyze securities. Consequently, security prices would not react instantaneously to the release of information but instead would respond more slowly. Thus, in a classic "Catch-22" situation, markets would become inefficient if investors believed they were efficient, yet they are efficient because investors believe them to be inefficient.

3. *Publicly known investment strategies cannot be expected to generate abnormal returns.* If a strategy generated abnormal returns in the past and the strategy was revealed to the public (for example, through a book or article), then the usefulness of the strategy will be destroyed. The strategy, whatever it is based on, must provide some means of identifying mispriced securities. Investors who know the strategy will try to capitalize on it, and in doing so will force prices to equal investment values the moment the strategy indicates a security is mispriced. The action of investors following the strategy will eliminate its effectiveness at identifying mispriced securities.

4. *Some investors will display impressive performance records.* However, their performance is merely due to chance (despite their assertions to the contrary). Think of a simple model in which half the time the stock market has an annual return greater than Treasury bills (an "up" market) and the other half of the time its return is less than T-bills (a "down" market). With many investors attempting to forecast whether the stock market will be up or down each year and acting accordingly, in an efficient market about half of the investors will be right in any given year and half will be wrong. The next year, half of those who were right the first year will be right the second year too. Thus, $\frac{1}{4}$ ($= \frac{1}{2} \times \frac{1}{2}$) of all the investors will have been right both years. About half of the surviving investors will be right in the third year, so that in total $\frac{1}{8}$ ($= \frac{1}{2} \times \frac{1}{2} \times \frac{1}{2}$) of all the investors will have been right all three years. Thus, $(\frac{1}{2})^T$ investors will be correct every year over a span of T years. For example, if $T = 6$, then $\frac{1}{64}$ of the investors will have been correct all five years, but only

because they were lucky, not because they were skillful. Anecdotal evidence about the success of certain investors is misleading, and fees paid for advice from such investors are wasted.

5. *Professional investors should fare no better in picking securities than ordinary investors.* Prices always reflect investment value, so the search for mispriced securities is futile. Professional investors do not have an edge on ordinary investors in identifying mispriced securities and generating abnormally high returns.

6. *Past performance is not an indicator of future performance.* Investors who have done well in the past are no more likely to do better in the future than are investors who have done poorly in the past. Those who did well in the past were merely lucky, and those who did poorly merely had a streak of misfortune. Because past luck and misfortune do not have a tendency to repeat themselves, historical performance records are useless in predicting future performance records. (Of course, if the poor performance was due to incurring high operating expenses, then poor performers are likely to remain poor performers.)

4.2.4 OBSERVATIONS ABOUT PERFECTLY EFFICIENT MARKETS WITH TRANSACTION COSTS

The efficient markets model assumed that investors had free access to all information relevant to setting security prices. In reality, it is expensive to collect and process such information. Furthermore, investors cannot adjust their portfolios in response to new information without incurring transaction costs. How does the existence of these costs affect the efficient markets model? Sanford Grossman and Joseph Stiglitz considered this issue and arrived at two important conclusions.[5]

1. *In a world where it costs money to analyze securities, analysts will be able to identify mispriced securities.* However, their gain from doing so will be exactly offset by the increased costs they incur (perhaps associated with the money needed to procure data and analytical software). Their gross returns will indicate abnormal returns, but their net returns will show a fair return and nothing more. Of course, they can earn less than a fair return if they fail to use the data properly. For example, by rapidly buying and selling securities, they may generate large transaction costs that would more than offset the value of their superior security analysis.

2. *Investors do just as well using a passive investment strategy where they simply buy securities in a particular index and hold onto the investment.* Such a strategy will minimize transaction costs and can be expected to do as well as any professionally managed portfolio that actively seeks out mispriced securities and incurs costs in doing so. Indeed, such a strategy can be expected to outperform any professionally managed portfolio that incurs unnecessary transaction costs (for example, by trading too often). Note that the gross returns of professionally managed portfolios will exceed those of passively managed portfolios having similar investment objectives but that the two kinds of portfolios can be expected to have similar net returns.

4.3 Testing for Market Efficiency

Now that the characteristics of perfectly efficient markets have been described, it is useful to consider how to conduct tests to determine if markets actually are perfectly efficient, reasonably efficient, or not efficient at all. There are a multitude of methodologies available, but three stand out. They involve conducting event studies, looking for patterns in security prices, and examining the investment performance of professional money managers.

MONEY MATTERS

The Active versus Passive Debate

The issue of market efficiency has clear and important ramifications for the investment management industry. At stake are billions of dollars in investment management fees, professional reputations, and, some would argue, even the effective functioning of our capital markets.

Greater market efficiency implies a lower probability that an investor will consistently identify mispriced securities. Consequently, the more efficient a security market is, the lower the expected payoff is to investors who buy and sell securities in search of abnormally high returns. In fact, when research and transaction costs are factored into the analysis, greater market efficiency increases the chances that investors "actively" managing their portfolios will underperform a simple technique of holding a portfolio that resembles the composition of the entire market. Institutional investors have responded to evidence of significant efficiency in the U.S. stock and bond markets by increasingly pursuing an investment approach referred to as *passive management*. Passive management involves a long-term, buy-and-hold approach to investing. The investor selects an appropriate target and buys a portfolio designed to closely track the performance of that target. Once the portfolio is purchased, little additional trading occurs, beyond reinvesting income or minor rebalancings necessary to accurately track the target. Because the selected target is usually (although not necessarily) a broad, diversified market index (for example, the S&P 500 for domestic common stocks), passive management (see Chapter 17) is commonly referred to as "indexation," and the passive portfolios are called "index funds."

Active management, on the other hand, involves a systematic effort to exceed the performance of a selected target. A wide array of active management approaches exists, far too many to summarize in this space. Nevertheless, all of these approaches involve the search for mispriced securities or for mispriced groups of securities. Ac-

curately identifying and adroitly purchasing or selling these mispriced securities provides the active investor with the potential to outperform the passive investor.

Passive management is relatively new to the investment industry. Before the mid-1960s, it was taken for granted that investors should search for mispriced stocks. Some investment strategies had passive overtones, such as buying "solid, blue-chip" companies for the "long term." But even these strategies implied an attempt to outperform some nebulously specified market target. The concepts of broad diversification and passive management were, for practical purposes, nonexistent.

Attitudes changed in the 1960s with the popularization of Markowitz's portfolio selection concepts (see Chapters 7 and 8), the introduction of the efficient market hypothesis (see this chapter), the emphasis on "the market portfolio" derived from the Capital Asset Pricing Model (see Chapter 10), and various academic studies proclaiming the futility of active management. Many investors, especially large institutional investors, began to question the wisdom of actively managing all of their assets. The first domestic common stock index fund was introduced in 1971. By the end of the 1970s, roughly $100 million was invested in index funds. Today, hundreds of billions of dollars are invested in domestic and international stock and bond index funds. Even individual investors have become enamored of index funds. Passively managed portfolios are some of the fastest growing products offered by many large mutual fund organizations.

Proponents of active management argue that capital markets are inefficient enough to justify the search for mispriced securities. They may disagree on the degree of the markets' inefficiencies. Technical analysts (see Chapter 14), for example, tend to view markets as dominated by emotionally driven and predictable investors, thereby creating numerous profit opportunities for creative and disciplined investors. Conversely, managers who use highly quantitative investment tools often view profit opportunities as smaller and less

(continued)

persistent. Nevertheless, all active managers possess a fundamental belief in the existence of consistently exploitable security mispricings. As evidence they frequently point to the stellar track records of certain successful managers and various studies identifying market inefficiencies (see the appendix in Chapter 13, which discusses empirical regularities).

Some active management proponents also introduce into the active–passive debate what amounts to a moralistic appeal. They contend that investors have an obligation to seek out mispriced securities because their actions help remove these mispricings and thereby lead to a more efficient allocation of capital. Moreover, some proponents derisively contend that passive management implies settling for mediocre, or average, performance.

Proponents of passive management do not deny that exploitable profit opportunities exist or that some managers have established impressive performance results. Rather, they contend that the capital markets are efficient enough to prevent all but a few with inside information from consistently being able to earn abnormal profits. They claim that past successes are more likely the result of luck than skill. If 1,000 people each flip a coin 10 times, the odds are that one of them will flip all heads. In the investment industry, this person is crowned a brilliant money manager.

Passive management proponents also argue that the expected returns from active management are actually lower than those for passive management. The fees charged by active managers are typically much higher than those levied by passive managers. (The annual difference is typically between .30% and 2% of the managers' assets under management.) Further, passively managed portfolios usually experience very small transaction costs whereas, depending on the amount of trading involved, active management transaction costs can be quite high. Thus, it is argued that passive managers outperform active managers because of cost differences. From this perspective, passive management involves settling for superior, as opposed to mediocre, results.

The active–passive debate will never be totally resolved. The random "noise" inherent in investment performance tends to drown out any systematic evidence of investment management skill on the part of active managers. Subjective issues therefore dominate the discussion, and as a result neither side can convince the other that its viewpoint is the correct one.

Despite the rapid growth in passively managed assets, most domestic and international stock and bond portfolios remain actively managed. Many large institutional investors, such as pension funds, have taken a middle ground on the matter, hiring both passive and active managers. In a crude way, this strategy may be a reasonable response to the unresolved active–passive debate. Assets cannot all be passively managed—who would be left to maintain security prices at "fair" value levels? However, it may not take many skillful active managers to ensure an adequate level of market efficiency. Further, the evidence is overwhelming that managers with above-average investment skills are in the minority of the group currently offering their services to investors.

4.3.1 EVENT STUDIES

Event studies can be performed to determine how fast security prices actually react to the release of information. Do they react rapidly or slowly? Are the returns after the announcement date abnormally high or low, or are they simply normal? Note that the answer to the second question requires a definition of a "normal return" for a given security. "Normal" is defined using some equilibrium-based **asset pricing model,** two of which are discussed in Chapters 10 and 12. An improperly specified asset pricing model can invalidate a test of market efficiency. Thus, event studies are really joint tests, as they simultaneously involve tests of the asset pricing model's validity and tests of market efficiency. A finding that prices react slowly to information might be due to markets' being inefficient, or it might be due to the use of an improper asset pricing model, or it might be due to both.

asset pricing model

As an example of an event study, consider what happens in a perfectly efficient market when information is released. When the information arrives in the marketplace, prices react instantaneously and, in doing so, immediately move to their new investment values. Figure 4.6(a) shows what happens in such a market when good news arrives; Figure 4.6(b) shows what happens when bad news arrives. Note that in both cases the horizontal axis is a time line and the vertical axis is the security's price, so the figure reflects the security's price over time. At time 0 ($t = 0$), information is released about the firm. Observe that shortly before the news arrived, the security's price was P^B. With the arrival of the information the price immediately moves to its new equilibrium level of P^A, where it stays until additional information arrives. (To be more precise, the vertical axis represents the security's abnormal return, which in an efficient market would be zero until $t = 0$, when it would briefly be either significantly positive in the case of good news, or significantly negative in the case of bad news. Afterward, it would return to zero. For simplicity, prices are used instead of returns because over a short time period surrounding $t = 0$, the results are essentially the same.)

Figure 4.7 shows two situations that cannot occur with regularity in an efficient market when good news arrives. (A similar situation, not illustrated here, cannot occur when bad news arrives.) In Figure 4.7(a) the security reacts slowly to the information, so that it does not reach its equilibrium price P^A until $t = 1$. This situation cannot occur regularly in an efficient market because analysts will realize after $t = 0$ but before $t = 1$ that the security is not priced fairly and will rush to buy it. Consequently, they will force the security to reach its equilibrium price before $t = 1$. Indeed, they will force the security to reach its equilibrium price moments after the information is released at $t = 0$.

In Figure 4.7(b) the security's price overreacts to the information and then slowly settles down to its equilibrium value. Again, this situation cannot occur with regularity in an efficient market. Analysts will realize that the security is selling above its fair value and will proceed to sell it if they own it or to short sell it if they do not own it. As a consequence, they will prevent its price from rising above its equilibrium value, P^A, after the information is released.

Many event studies have been conducted concerning the reaction of security prices, particularly stock prices, to the release of information, such as news (usually referred to as "announcements") pertaining to earnings and dividends, share repurchase programs, stock splits and dividends, stock and bond sales, stock listings, bond rating changes, mergers and acquisitions, and divestitures. Indeed, this area of academic research has become a virtual growth industry.

4.3.2 LOOKING FOR PATTERNS

A second method to test for market efficiency is to investigate whether there are any patterns in security price movements attributable to something other than what one would expect. Securities can be expected to provide a rate of return during a given time period in accord with an asset pricing model. Such a model asserts that a security's expected rate of return is equal to a riskfree rate of return plus a "risk premium" whose magnitude is based on the riskiness of the security. If the riskfree rate and risk premium are both unchanging over time, securities with high average returns in the past can be expected to have high returns in the future. However, the riskfree rate and the risk premium are likely to change over time, making it difficult to see if there are patterns in security prices. Indeed, any tests conducted to identify the existence of price patterns are once again joint tests of both market efficiency and the asset pricing model used to estimate the risk premiums on securities.

In recent years, many of these patterns have been identified and labeled as "empirical regularities" or "market anomalies." For example, one of the most prominent

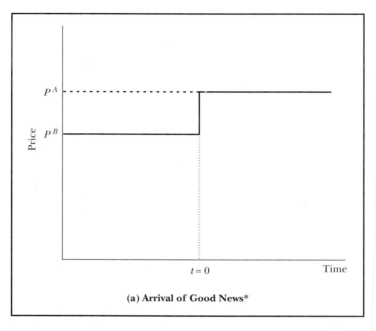

(a) Arrival of Good News*

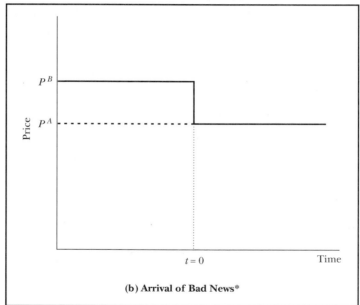

(b) Arrival of Bad News*

FIGURE 4.6 The Effect of Information on a Firm's Stock Price in a Perfectly Efficient Market

*Information is assumed to arrive at time $t = 0$.

market anomalies is the January effect. Security returns appear to be abnormally high in the month of January. Other months do not show similar returns. This pattern has a long and consistent track record, and no convincing explanations have been proposed. (The January effect and other market anomalies are discussed in Chapter 13.)

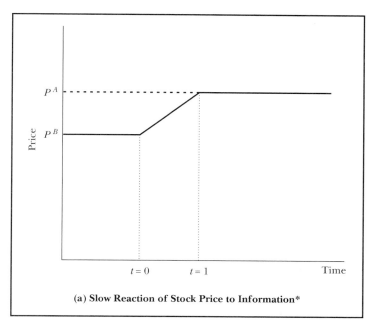

(a) **Slow Reaction of Stock Price to Information***

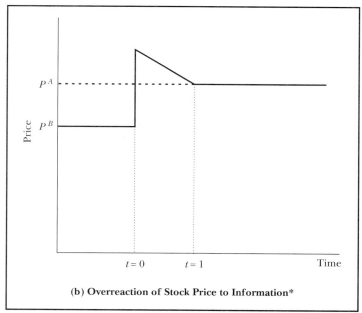

(b) **Overreaction of Stock Price to Information***

FIGURE 4.7 Possible Effects of Information on a Firm's Stock Price in an Inefficient Market

*Information is assumed to arrive at time $t = 0$.

4.3.3 EXAMINING PERFORMANCE

The third approach for testing market efficiency is to examine the investment records of professional investors. Do more of them earn abnormally high rates of return than one would expect in a perfectly efficient market? Do more of them consistently earn abnormally high returns period after period than one would expect in an efficient market? There are difficulties in conducting these tests because they require the determination of what constitutes abnormal returns, which, in turn, requires the determination of just what are "normal returns." Because normal returns can be determined only by assuming that a particular asset pricing model is applicable, all such tests are joint tests of market efficiency and an asset pricing model.

4.4 Market Efficiency Test Results

Many tests have been conducted over the years examining the degree to which security markets are efficient. Rather than laboriously reviewing the results of those tests at this point, the most prominent studies are discussed in later chapters in which the specific investment activities associated with the studies are considered. However, a few comments about the general conclusions drawn from those studies are appropriate here.

4.4.1 WEAK-FORM TESTS

Early tests of weak-form market efficiency failed to find any evidence that abnormal profits could be earned trading on information related to past prices. That is, knowing how security prices moved in the past cannot be translated into accurate predictions of future security prices. These tests generally concluded that technical analysis, which relies on forecasting security prices based on past prices, was ineffective. More recent studies, however, have indicated that investors may underreact to certain types of information in the short term, but overreact in the long term, driving security prices away from their investment values. As a result, it may be possible to earn abnormal profits by buying either securities that have recently risen in price or those that have fallen in price over a longer time period. These two strategies are known as "momentum" and "contrarian" strategies, respectively. It should be pointed out, however, that considerable questions surround both strategies, and they have not been universally accepted.

4.4.2 SEMISTRONG-FORM TESTS

The results of tests of semistrong-form market efficiency have been mixed. Most event studies have failed to demonstrate sufficiently large inefficiencies to overcome transaction costs, and the performance of the portfolios (such as mutual funds) managed by professionals has not been clearly superior to the performance of passively managed portfolios. However, various market "anomalies" have been discovered whereby securities with certain characteristics or during certain time periods appear to produce abnormally high returns. For example, as mentioned, common stocks in January have been shown to offer returns much higher than those earned in the other 11 months of the year.

4.4.3 STRONG-FORM TESTS

One would expect that investors with access to private information would have an advantage over investors who trade only on publicly available information. In general, corporate insiders and stock exchange specialists, who both have information not readily available to the investing public, have been shown to be able to earn abnormally high profits. Less clear is the ability of security analysts to produce such profits. At times, these analysts have direct access to private information, and in a sense, they also "manufacture" their own private information through their research efforts. Some studies have indicated that certain analysts are able to discern mispriced securities, but whether this ability is based on skill or chance is an open issue.

4.4.4 SUMMARY

Tests of market efficiency demonstrate that U.S. security markets are highly efficient, impounding relevant information about investment values into security prices quickly and accurately. Investors cannot easily expect to earn abnormal profits trading on publicly available information, particularly once the costs of research and transactions are considered. Nevertheless, numerous unexplained abnormal returns have been identified, guaranteeing that the debate over the degree of market efficiency will continue.

Summary

1. The forces of supply and demand interact to determine a security's market price.
2. An investor's demand-to-buy schedule indicates the quantity of a security that the investor wishes to purchase at various prices.
3. An investor's supply-to-sell schedule indicates the quantity of a security that the investor wishes to sell at various prices.
4. The demand and supply schedules for individual investors can be aggregated to create aggregate demand and supply schedules for a security.
5. The intersection of the aggregate demand and supply schedules determines the market clearing price of a security. At that price the quantity traded is maximized.
6. The market price of a security can be thought of as representing a consensus opinion about the future prospects for the security.
7. An allocationally efficient market is one in which firms with the most promising investment opportunities have access to needed funds.
8. Markets must be both internally and externally efficient in order to be allocationally efficient. In an externally efficient market, information is quickly and widely disseminated, thereby allowing each security's price to adjust rapidly in an unbiased manner to new information so it reflects investment value. In an internally efficient market, brokers and dealers compete fairly so that the cost of transacting is low and the speed of transacting is high.
9. A security's investment value is the present value of the security's future prospects, as estimated by well-informed and capable analysts, and can be thought of as the security's fair or intrinsic value.
10. In an efficient market a security's market price will fully reflect all available information relevant to the security's value at that time.
11. The concept of market efficiency can be expressed in three forms: weak, semistrong, and strong.
12. The three forms of market efficiency make different assumptions about the set of information reflected in security prices.
13. Tests of market efficiency are really joint tests about whether markets are efficient and whether security prices are set according to a specific asset pricing model.
14. Evidence suggests that U.S. financial markets are highly, but not perfectly, efficient.

Questions and Problems

1. Using aggregate demand-to-buy and supply-to-sell schedules, explain and illustrate the effect of the following events on the equilibrium price and quantity traded of Fairchild Corporation's stock.
   a. Fairchild officials announce that next year's earnings are expected to be significantly higher than analysts had previously forecast.
   b. A wealthy shareholder initiates a large secondary offering of Fairchild stock.
   c. Another company, quite similar to Fairchild in all respects except for being privately held, decides to offer its outstanding shares for sale to the public.

2. Imp Begley is pondering the statement, "The pattern of security price behavior might appear the same whether markets were efficient or security prices bore no relationship whatsoever to investment value." Explain the meaning of this statement to Imp.

3. We all know that investors have widely diverse opinions about the future course of the economy and earnings forecasts for various industries and companies. How then is it possible for all these investors to arrive at an equilibrium price for any particular security?

4. Distinguish between the three forms of market efficiency.

5. Does the fact that a market exhibits weak-form efficiency necessarily imply that it is also strong-form efficient? How about the converse statement? Explain.

6. Consider the following types of information. If this information is immediately and fully reflected in security prices, what form of market efficiency is implied?
   a. A company's recent quarterly earnings announcement.
   b. Historical bond yields.
   c. Deliberations of a company's board of directors concerning a possible merger with another company.
   d. Limit orders in a specialist's book.
   e. A brokerage firm's published research report on a particular company.
   f. Movements in the Dow Jones Industrial Average as plotted in *The Wall Street Journal.*

7. Would you expect that fundamental security analysis makes security markets more efficient? Why?

8. Would you expect that NYSE specialists should be able to earn an abnormal profit in a semistrong efficient market? Why?

9. Is it true that in a perfectly efficient market no investor would consistently be able to earn a profit?

10. Although security markets may not be perfectly efficient, what is the rationale for them being highly efficient?

11. When a corporation announces its earnings for a period, the volume of transactions in its stock may increase, but frequently that increase is not associated with significant moves in the price of its stock. How can this be explained?

12. In 1986 and 1987 several high-profile insider trading scandals were exposed.
   a. Is successful insider trading consistent with the three forms of market efficiency? Explain.
   b. Play the role of devil's advocate and present a case outlining the benefits to financial markets of insider trading.

13. The text states that tests for market efficiency involving an asset pricing model are really joint tests. What is meant by that statement?

14. In perfectly efficient markets with transaction costs, why should analysts be able to find mispriced securities?

15. When investment managers present their historical performance records to potential and existing customers, market regulators require the managers to qualify those records with the comment that "past performance is no guarantee of future performance." In a perfectly efficient market, why would such an admonition be particularly appropriate?

Endnotes

1. A burgeoning field of research in finance is known as *market microstructure,* which involves the study of internal market efficiency.

2. Actually, not all investors need to meet these three conditions for security prices to equal their investment values. Instead, marginal investors need to meet these conditions because their trades correct the mispricing that would occur in their absence.

3. Eugene F. Fama, "Efficient Capital Markets: A Review of Theory and Empirical Work," *Journal of Finance,* 25, no. 5 (May 1970): 383–417.

4. Some people assert that daily stock prices follow a **random walk,** meaning that stock price changes (say, from one day to the next) are independently and identically distributed. The price change from day t to day $t + 1$ is not influenced by the price change from

day $t-1$ to day t, and the amount of the price change from one day to the next can be determined by the spin of a roulette wheel (with the same roulette wheel being used every day). Statistically, in a random walk $P_t = P_{t-1} + e_t$, where e_t is a random error term whose expected outcome is zero but whose actual outcome can be thought of as being determined by the spin of a roulette wheel. Stock prices do not need to follow a random walk in order for them to fully reflect information and for markets to be efficient.

5. Sanford J. Grossman and Joseph E. Stiglitz, "On the Impossibility of Informationally Efficient Markets," *American Economic Review*, 70, no. 3 (June 1980): 399–408.

CHAPTER 5

Taxes

Taxation should not be regarded as an unmitigated evil. It provides benefits to some individuals that may outweigh the associated costs that others have to bear. Regardless of whether the benefits outweigh the costs, however, taxes have a significant impact on investment decisions and results. This chapter provides an overview of some of the more important aspects of taxation from the investor's viewpoint.

Federal and state tax laws play a major role in the way securities are priced in the marketplace because investors are understandably concerned with after-tax returns, not before-tax returns. Accordingly, the investor should determine the applicable tax rate before making any investment decision. This tax rate is not the same for all securities for a given investor: It can be as low as 0% in the case of certain tax-exempt securities issued by states and municipalities or well over 40% for corporate bonds when both federal and state taxes are considered. After determining the applicable tax rate, the investor can estimate a security's expected after-tax return and risk. Only then can the investor make a wise investment decision.

Many of the specific tax rates and provisions in the United States were enacted with the Tax Reform Act of 1986, the Omnibus Budget Reconciliation Acts of 1990 and 1993, and the Orwellian-named Taxpayer Relief Act of 1997. Because changes occur from year to year, current regulations should be examined when preparing tax returns or considering major investment decisions. However, the material given here can be considered broadly representative of current taxation (primarily federal) in the United States.

In general, the most important taxes for investment decision-making are personal and corporate income taxes. In this chapter the essential elements of each are described, and the manner in which they influence the pricing of securities is considered.

5.1 Corporate Income Taxes

There are three forms of business organizations in the United States and in most other countries:

1. Corporations
2. Partnerships
3. Proprietorships

The corporate form of organization is the largest in terms of the dollar value of assets owned, even though there are more firms organized as partnerships or as single proprietorships. Legally, a corporation is regarded as a separate entity, whereas a proprietorship or partnership is considered an extension of its owner or owners. Income earned by proprietorships and partnerships is taxed primarily through personal income taxes levied on owners. Income earned by a corporation may be taxed twice: once when it is earned through the corporate income tax, and again when it is received as dividends by holders of the firm's common and preferred stock through the personal income tax.[1]

The double taxation of corporate income at first may seem inefficient, if not unfair. It also raises questions about the efficiency of the corporate form of organization. Suffice it to say that limited liability and the ability to transfer shares of subdivided ownership seem to be of sufficient value to more than offset the tax law disadvantages. Moreover, without the corporate income tax, personal tax rates would probably have to be increased if the level of government expenditures were to remain constant without increasing the national debt.

5.1.1 CORPORATE TAX RATES

Before 1993 the corporate income tax was relatively simple in one respect; there were only a few basic rates. However, in 1993 even this feature was complicated by the creation of eight basic rates. The 1998 rates and applicable levels of taxable annual income are as follows:

1. A tax rate of 15% is applicable to the first $50,000
2. A tax rate of 25% to the next $25,000
3. A tax rate of 34% to the next $25,000
4. A tax rate of 39% to the next $235,000
5. A tax rate of 34% to the next $9,665,000
6. A tax rate of 35% to the next $5,000,000
7. A tax rate of 38% to the next $3,333,333
8. A tax rate of 35% on all additional income

marginal tax rate
average tax rate

Figure 5.1 illustrates what are known as the **marginal tax rate** and **average tax rate** schedules for corporations. A corporation's marginal tax rate is the tax rate that it

FIGURE 5.1 Marginal and Average Corporate Tax Rates, 1998

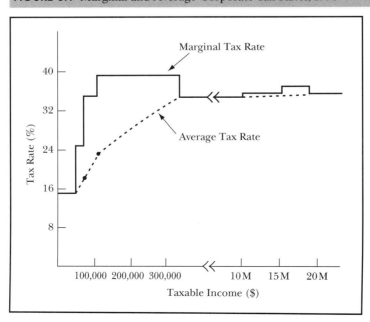

would pay on an additional dollar of income. For example, a corporation earning $85,000 would pay $17,150 in income taxes:

$$
\begin{aligned}
0.15 \times \$50,000 &= \$ \ 7{,}500 \\
0.25 \times \ \ 25{,}000 &= \ \ \ 6{,}250 \\
0.34 \times \ \ 10{,}000 &= \underline{\ \ \ 3{,}400} \\
\text{Total income tax} &= \$17{,}150
\end{aligned}
$$

For this corporation, the marginal tax rate is 34% because an additional dollar of income would be taxed at this rate. In other words, if this firm's income were $85,001 instead of $85,000, its tax bill would be $17,150.34 instead of $17,150. Thus $.34 (= $17,150.34 − $17,150.00) more in taxes would be paid as a result of earning $1 (= $85,001 − $85,000) more in income.

The average tax rate is equal to the total amount of taxes paid divided by the total income subject to tax. The average tax rate for the previous example would be 20.18% (= $17,150/$85,000). That is, 20.18% of this firm's total income would be paid to the government in the form of corporate income taxes. As can be seen in Figure 5.1, the average rate is exactly equal to the marginal rate at three places: (1) The rates are equal to 15% for incomes below $50,000; (2) the rates are equal to 34% for incomes between $335,000 and $10,000,000; and (3) the rates are equal to 35% for incomes above $18,333,333. Indeed, the purpose of the relatively high fourth and seventh marginal rates of 39% and 38%, respectively, is to equate the average and marginal rates.

The average rate measures the overall impact of taxes, but the marginal rate is more relevant for most decisions. For example, if a corporation were considering an investment that would increase its income from $85,000 to $90,000 each year, the increase in income after taxes would be $3,300 [= (1 − .34) × $5,000], not $3,991 [= (1 − .2018) × $5,000].

5.1.2 CORPORATE INCOME FROM DIVIDENDS, INTEREST, AND CAPITAL GAINS

Congress has provided that 80% of the dividends received by a corporation can be excluded from income when calculating the corporation's income tax liability.[2] The effective tax rate on an additional dollar of dividends received by a corporation with income in the 35% range is 7% [= (1 − .80) × .35]. This special treatment of dividends is to avoid triple taxation of income. Consider how dividends would be taxed if the 80% exclusion did not exist. Corporation A is taxed on its income and then pays dividends to one of its stockholders, corporation B. Corporation B then pays taxes on its income, which includes the dividends received from A. Finally, the stockholders of B pay income taxes on the dividends received from B. Thus, a dollar of income earned by A would be taxed three times—a tax on A, then a tax on B, then a tax on the stockholders of B—if the dividend exclusion did not exist. With the dividend exclusion, a dollar of income earned by A is taxed, for all practical purposes, "only" a little more than twice.

5.1.3 BONDS VERSUS PREFERRED STOCKS

No deduction is allowed for interest received on bonds bought by a corporate investor. It is simply added to income and taxed at the regular rates. For corporations in the 35% tax bracket, the effective tax rate on interest received from bonds is substantially greater than the 7% effective tax rate on common and preferred stock dividends. This differential tax treatment affects the relative prices corporate and individual investors are willing to pay for these securities because their concern is with relative after-tax yields.

Table 5.1 provides an example of preferred stock that illustrates the before-tax and after-tax yields for both a corporate investor with a marginal tax rate of 35% and an individual investor with a marginal personal tax rate of 28%. Note that the preferred stock has a lower before-tax yield despite being riskier than the bond. The table shows that the individual investor will be better off purchasing the bond because its after-tax yield of 5.76% exceeds the after-tax yield of 5.04% on the preferred stock. (Careful scrutiny reveals that this is true for *any* marginal tax rate for the individual investor because dividend and interest income of any individual are taxed equally.) However, the corporate investor will be better off purchasing the preferred stock because its after-tax yield of 6.51% exceeds the after-tax yield on bonds of 5.20%.

5.1.4 TAX-EXEMPT ORGANIZATIONS

Many organizations are wholly or partly exempt from federal income taxes. Nonprofit religious, charitable, or educational foundations generally qualify. A small tax (2% in 1999) is levied on the net investment income of such a foundation. In addition, the foundation should pay out either all income received by the end of the year in which it was received, or a minimum percentage of its assets (5% in 1999), whichever is higher. Failure to pay the higher amount can result in a confiscatory tax on the difference between the two.

Investment companies, often called *mutual funds,* may elect to be treated as regulated investment companies for tax purposes. This privilege is granted if certain conditions are met. For example, the assets of the investment company must be invested primarily in securities, without undue concentration in any security. Thus its income takes the form of dividends and interest received on its investments, as well as capital gains from price appreciation realized when investments are sold at a price higher than their purchase price. A regulated investment company pays income tax only on income and realized capital gains not distributed to its shareholders. As a result of this tax treatment, such companies distribute substantially all income and gains and, therefore, do not have to pay income taxes.

TABLE 5.1 Comparison of Yields on Preferred Stocks and Corporate Bonds

	Investment	
	Preferred Stock	*Corporate Bond*
(a) Feature		
Price	$10 per share	$1,000 per bond
Annual dollar yield	$.70 per share	$80 per bond
Aggregate investment	100 shares	1 bond
Cost of aggregate investment	$1,000	$1,000
Aggregate annual dollar yield	$70	$80
Before-tax percentage yield	7% = $70/$1,000	8% = $80/$1,000
(b) Corporate investor[a]		
After-tax dollar yield	$65.10 = $70[1 − (.20 × .35)]	$52 = $80(1 − .35)
After-tax percentage yield	6.51% = $65.10/$1,000	5.20% = $52/$1,000
(c) Individual investor[b]		
After-tax dollar yield	$50.40 = $70(1 − .28)	$57.60 = $80(1 − .28)
After-tax percentage yield	5.04% = $50.40/$1,000	5.76% = $57.60/$1,000

[a]Assuming a marginal corporate income tax rate of 35%.

[b]Assuming a marginal individual income tax rate of 28%.

Employee pension, profit-sharing, and stock-bonus plans may entrust their assets, which are usually securities, to *fiduciaries* (for example, banks; a fiduciary is entrusted with the securities of a person or entity and is to act in that person's or entity's best interests). The fiduciary receives new contributions, makes required payments, and manages the investments owned by the plan. A qualified plan (that is, a plan that meets all the requirements of applicable legislation) pays no taxes on either income or capital gains.

Another example of a tax-exempt entity is the *personal trust.* Here, funds are provided for the benefit of one or more individuals by another individual or individuals, with a fiduciary serving as a trustee. Some trusts are created by wills, others by contracts among living persons. Whatever the origin, trusts generally pay taxes only on income that is not distributed to the designated beneficiaries.

Income and capital gains earned by investment companies, pension funds, and personal trusts do not go untaxed forever. Payments made to investment company shareholders, pension fund beneficiaries, and the beneficiaries of personal trusts are subject to applicable personal income tax rules. The exemptions apply only to taxes that might otherwise be levied at the previous stage.

5.2   Personal Income Taxes

Although the corporate income tax is an important feature of the investment scene, its impact on most individuals is indirect. Individuals, however, directly bear the personal income tax. Few investors avoid dealing with it in detail, at both an economic and an emotional level. Its provisions have major and direct effects on investment behavior.

5.2.1   PERSONAL TAX RATES

Taxes must be paid on an individual's income, defined as "all wealth which flows to the taxpayer other than as a mere return of capital. It includes gains and profits from any source, including gains from the sale or other disposition of capital assets."[3] Certain items are excluded from the definition of income; others are deducted from income before the tax due is computed. Capital gains and losses are subject to special treatment, which is described in a later section. Deductions and exclusions of special importance for investment purposes are described in this section as well as in later sections.

Personal taxes are based on an individual's or family's taxable income. Taxable income is determined by initially computing gross income. From that point, adjusted gross income is obtained by subtracting certain allowed adjustments (for example, business expenses and contributions to certain retirement funds). This amount, less a number of personal expense deductions (such as personal exemptions), equals taxable income. The resulting tax must be paid unless the taxpayer is able to claim tax credits, which may be subtracted directly from the tax liability to obtain a final amount due to the government. In summary, after-tax income is determined as follows:

Gross income

− Adjustments

Adjusted gross income

− Deductions

Taxable income

− Taxes

+ Tax credits

After-tax income

Although the Tax Reform Act of 1986 (as amended in 1990 and 1993) brought sweeping changes aimed at simplification, the Taxpayer Relief Act of 1997 brought many complications. Consequently, most people believe that almost nothing about personal income taxes in the United States is simple. Four different schedules of tax rates are currently in effect. The applicable one depends on whether the particular taxpayer is single, married and filing a joint return with his or her spouse, married but filing a separate return, or the head of a household. Table 5.2 shows the tax rates in effect for income earned in 1998 for the first two types of taxpayers. (The figures shown here—and elsewhere—are indexed to inflation and will change over time.) The rates are plotted in Figure 5.2.[4] For comparison, the 1913 federal tax form applicable to individuals, the first one ever needed by U.S. taxpayers, is shown in Figure 5.3. Its relative simplicity is striking and emphasizes the complexity of modern personal income taxation.

The solid line in each panel of Figure 5.2 shows the marginal tax rate, which was defined earlier. The marginal personal tax rate is the tax rate paid on an additional dollar of taxable income. Although this rate is constant over certain ranges of income, it increases as the taxpayer moves to higher taxable income brackets, to a maximum of 39.6% for income over $278,450 in 1998 for both individuals and married couples filing jointly. Interestingly, Figure 5.3 indicates that the highest marginal tax rate in 1913 was 6% and was applicable to any income over $500,000 that was earned by individuals.

The dashed line in both panels of Figure 5.2 shows the average tax rate, which was also defined earlier. The average personal tax rate is the ratio of total tax paid to total taxable income and is generally smaller than the marginal tax rate. Although the average rate is less than the marginal rate for all levels of income above that specified for the lowest tax bracket of 15%, it approaches the top marginal rate of 39.6% as income becomes very high.

Earlier, it was mentioned that, for corporations, the marginal tax rate is generally more relevant than the average tax rate in making certain decisions. This observation is also true for individuals and married couples. For example, consider a married couple with taxable income of $80,000 who are evaluating an investment opportunity that is expected to increase their taxable income by $3,000. This increase in taxable income

TABLE 5.2   Personal Income Tax Marginal Rates, 1998

At Least	Taxable Income But Not More Than	Amount of Taxes
(a) Single Taxpayers		
$ 0	$ 25,350	$ 0.00 + 15% of income over $ 0
25,350	61,400	3,802.50 + 28 of income over 25,350
61,400	128,100	13,896.50 + 31 of income over 61,400
128,100	278,450	34,573.50 + 36 of income over 128,100
278,450	. . .	88,699.50 + 39.6 of income over 278,450
(b) Married Taxpayers Filing Jointly		
$ 0	$ 42,350	$ 0.00 + 15% of income over $ 0
42,350	102,300	6,352.50 + 28 of income over 42,350
102,300	155,950	23,138.50 + 31 of income over 102,300
155,950	278,450	39,770.00 + 36 of income over 155,950
278,450	. . .	83,870.00 + 39.6 of income over 278,450

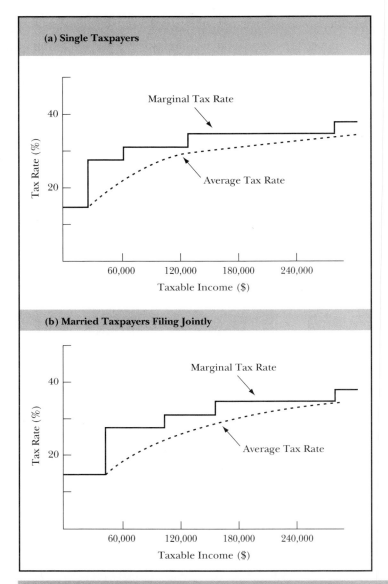

FIGURE 5.2 Marginal and Average Personal Tax Rates, 1998

will result in an increase of $840 (= $3,000 × .28) in taxes, leaving a net increase in spendable income of $2,160 (= $3,000 − $840). The calculations for this particular example are simple because the change in taxable income left the taxpayer in the same bracket. Thus, 28% of the additional income will be taxed away, leaving 72% to be spent. The average tax rate before and after the increase is irrelevant to this couple in deciding whether to make the investment.

When an investment moves income into a higher bracket, the computations are more complex. For example, assume that the opportunity in question would increase the couple's income by $30,000. This increase in taxable income will result in an increase of $8,631 [= (.28 × $22,300) + (.31 × $7,700)] in taxes, leaving a net increase in

TO BE FILED BY COLLECTOR

List No...........................

..................*District of*.......................................

Date received...

FORM 1040

INCOME TAX

THE PENALTY
FOR FAILURE TO HAVE THIS RETURN IN THE HANDS OF THE COLLECTOR OF INTERNAL REVENUE ON OR BEFORE MARCH 1 IS $20 TO $1,000
(SEE INSTRUCTIONS ON PAGE 4.)

TO BE FILLED IN BY MUNICIPAL COUNTY CLERK

File No...

Assessment List..

Page.................... *Line*..........................

UNITED STATES INTERNAL REVENUE.

RETURN OF ANNUAL NET INCOME OF INDIVIDUALS.

(As provided by Act of Congress, approved October 3, 1913.)

RETURN OF NET INCOME RECEIVED OR ACCRUED DURING THE YEAR ENDED DECEMBER 31, 191....
(FOR THE YEAR 1913, FROM MARCH 1, TO DECEMBER 31.)

Filed by (or for) -- *of* --
(Full name of individual) (Street and No.)

in the City, Town, or Post Office of -- *State of* --
(Fill in page 2 and 3 before making entries below.)

1. GROSS INCOME (see page 2, line 12)	$
2. GENERAL DEDUCTIONS (see page 3, line 7)	$
3. NET INCOME	$

Deductions and exemptions allowed in computing income subject to the normal tax of 1 percent.

4. Dividends and net earnings received or accrued, of corporations, etc. subject to like tax. (See page 2, line 11)	$
5. Amount of income on which the normal tax has been deducted and withheld at the source. (See page 2, line 9, column A)	
6. Specific exemptions of $3,000 or $4,000, as the case may be. (See Instructions 3 and 19)	

Total deductions and exemptions. (Items 4,5 and 6)	$
7. TAXABLE INCOME on which the normal tax of 1 per cent is to be calculated (See Instruction 3).	$

8. When the net income shown above on line 3 exceeds $20,000, the additional tax thereon must be calculated as per schedule below:

	INCOME	TAX
1 per cent on amount over $20,000 and not exceeding $50,000	$	$
2 " " $50,000 " " $75,000		
3 " " $75,000 " " $100,000		
4 " " $100,000 " " $250,000		
5 " " $250,000 " " $500,000		
6 " " $500,000		

Total additional or super tax	$
Total normal tax (1 per cent of amount entered on line 7)	
Total tax liability	

FIGURE 5.3 1913 Federal Income Tax Form 1040

spendable income of $21,369 (= $30,000 − $8,631). Thus, 28.8% (= $8,631/$30,000) of the additional income will be taxed away, an amount greater than the 28% figure that was applicable in the previous example. As before, average tax rates are irrelevant to the couple in making their decision.

5.2.2 TAX-EXEMPT BONDS

tax-exempt bonds

A major consideration for investors with large taxable incomes is the possibility of obtaining tax-exempt income. The simplest way to accomplish this goal is to purchase **tax-exempt bonds.** These securities exist because the notion of federalism has been interpreted to imply that the federal government should not tax states and municipalities or the income produced from their bonds.[5] Although the legal basis is complex, the facts are simple. Interest income from most bonds issued by states, municipalities, and their agencies need not be included in taxable income in determining the amount of federal taxes that are owed. The benefit for a high-bracket taxpayer is significant.

Consider again the couple in the previous example. Assume that for the same cost they can obtain an increase in taxable income of $30,000 per year by investing in corporate bonds or a tax-free increase in income of $24,000 per year by purchasing tax-exempt bonds. As shown earlier, their effective tax rate on an increase of $30,000 in taxable income would be 28.8%, leaving 71.2%, or $21,369, to be spent. But all $24,000 in tax-exempt income could be spent—clearly a preferable investment opportunity.

This relationship is no secret. Not surprisingly, tax-exempt bonds offer lower before-tax rates of interest than taxable bonds. Thus, they are not attractive for investors with low marginal tax rates. For example, if the couple had a marginal tax rate of 15% instead of 28%, they would prefer the corporate bonds because their after-tax return would be $25,500 [= $30,000 × (1 − .15)], an amount greater than the $24,000 provided by the tax-exempt bonds.

If couples with a marginal tax rate of 28% find the tax-exempt bonds more attractive, and couples with a marginal tax rate of 15% find the corporate bonds more attractive, then there should be a marginal tax rate in between these two rates that makes couples in that bracket indifferent to the two types of bonds. In this example, if the couple had a marginal tax rate of 20%, they would be indifferent between the corporate bonds and the tax-exempt bonds because both would provide an after-tax return of $24,000. However, a 20% marginal tax rate does not currently exist. Couples with rates equal to or greater than the next highest tax rate (28%) would prefer the tax-exempt bonds; couples with rates equal to or less than the next lowest tax rate (15%) would prefer the corporate bonds (unless the additional income from the bond pushed them into the 28% bracket).

The 20% marginal tax rate figure was determined by solving the following equation for t:

$$\$30{,}000 \times (1 - t) = \$24{,}000$$

Generally, the marginal tax rate that makes an investor indifferent between a taxable and a tax-exempt investment can be determined by solving the following equation for t:

$$\text{Taxable bond yield} \times (1 - t) = \text{Tax-exempt bond yield} \tag{5.1a}$$

or

$$1 - t = \text{Tax-exempt bond yield}/\text{Taxable bond yield} \tag{5.1b}$$

or

$$t = 1 - \text{Ratio of tax-exempt to taxable bond yields} \tag{5.1c}$$

Figure 5.4 shows the ratio, over time, of the yield-to-maturity for a group of tax-exempt bonds issued by municipalities to that of a group of taxable bonds issued by public utilities.[6] On this basis, tax-exempt bonds appear to be competitive with taxable bonds for investors subject to marginal tax rates between 20% (when the ratio of bond yields is 80%) and 40% (when the ratio of bond yields is 60%). For those wealthy enough to be con-

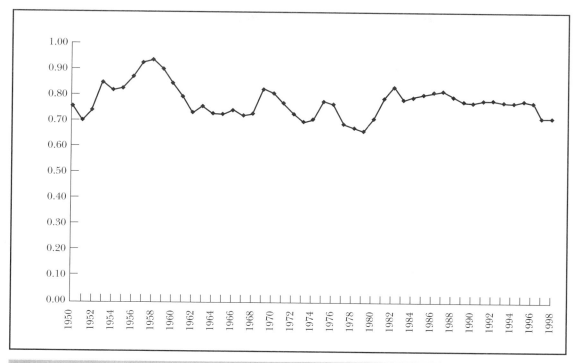

FIGURE 5.4 Ratio of High-Grade Municipal Bond Yields to High-Grade Corporate Bond Yields (1950–1998)

Source: 1999 Economic Report of the President (Washington, DC: GPO, 1999): p. 412.

sidering investments that provide income subject to the higher ranges, tax-exempt bonds are worth investigation. Less wealthy investors are likely to find them unattractive.

5.2.3   CAPITAL GAINS AND LOSSES

The provisions of the personal income tax laws that deal with capital gains and losses have had a great impact on investor behavior. Only the basic elements of these provisions can be described here. A complete understanding of the details would require an effort sufficient to keep many lawyers, tax accountants, and investment advisers busy, especially with the complexities introduced by the Taxpayer Relief Act of 1997.

realized capital gain
unrealized capital gain

  A change in the market value of a capital asset is not relevant for tax purposes until it is **realized** as a **capital gain** (or loss) by sale or exchange. If a security purchased for $50 appreciates to a value of $100 in a year, no tax is due on the **unrealized capital gain.** But if it is sold for $120 two years after purchase, the difference of $70 must be declared as a capital gain realized at the time of sale, and tax must be paid at the rate applicable to it.

  This rule can make the end of the year an interesting time for investors. Depending on their situations, taxpayers may be either eager or reluctant to realize capital gains or losses before a new tax year begins. Consider, for example, a taxpayer who earlier in the year sold 1,000 shares of stock *A* for $50 per share, having purchased it three years ago for $20 per share. This investor has a capital gain of $30,000 [= 1,000 × ($50 − $20)] and will have to pay taxes on this gain if nothing is done. However, it is now December, and the investor currently owns 1,000 shares of stock *B,* which is selling for $65 per share. Having purchased it four years ago for $95 per share, the investor has an unrealized loss of $30,000 [= 1,000 × ($65 − $95)] on the investment in *B*. Nevertheless, the investor believes that stock *B* will rebound in the near future and, hence, wants to continue owning it. It might seem at first glance that the investor should sell *B* on December 31 and then buy it back on January 1, thereby establishing a capital loss of $30,000 on *B* to offset the capital gain on *A*. This action would remove the tax liability associated with the investor's gain on *A*, while essentially maintaining the position in *B*. However, the same stock cannot be bought and sold simultaneously in such tax exchanges because the tax laws preclude a deduction associated with a loss on a **wash sale**, in which a security is sold and a "substantially identical" one is bought within 30 days.

wash sale

Brokerage firms publish lists pairing similar stocks for investors who wish to sell a particular stock for tax purposes. By selling a stock and simultaneously purchasing the matching stock, the investor may be able to continually maintain a portfolio with similar investment characteristics. In the previous example, a brokerage firm may have stocks *B* and *C* matched together. These two stocks have different issuers but may be in the same industry and, in the opinion of the brokerage firm, be poised for a similar rebound next year. Accordingly, the investor might sell *B* and purchase *C*.

End-of-year sales and purchases motivated by tax considerations are fairly common. At this time, securities that experienced substantial price changes during the year tend to have large numbers of trades as investors sell to realize gains or losses. If buyers recognize that the sellers are motivated by knowledge of the tax laws, and not some previously unrecognized bad news affecting the company in question, such "selling pressure" should not seriously depress the company's stock price.

capital gains and losses

Capital gains and losses involve, of course, capital assets, but the regulations define capital assets rather narrowly. Capital assets include all kinds of property except that held in conjunction with the taxpayer's trade or business (for example, inventories). Gains or losses on property that are an integral part of a taxpayer's business are considered regular income. Pro rata appreciation of a fixed-income security issued at a significant discount (for example, a 90-day Treasury bill) may also be considered income, as it is more like interest than capital gains.

The capital gain or loss realized when an asset is sold or exchanged is the difference between the value received and the asset's *basis*. For an asset purchased outright, the (initial) basis is equal to the actual cost of the asset. For an asset received as a gift or inheritance, the recipient's basis will be the donor's basis, or the value at the time of receipt, respectively. Gains and losses are categorized as *short-term* if the asset is held for a year or less and *long-term* if the asset is held for more than a year. The treatment of long-term gains and losses is complex because there are several categories of long-term gains and losses that depend on the length of time the assets were held, when they were bought, and the marginal income tax rate of the investor.

The ability to control the realization of capital gains and losses has some obvious advantages. Most important, tax can be paid at the most opportune time. The clearest case involves the realization of capital gains around the time of retirement. Shortly before retirement is usually a time when the taxpayer's income is relatively high, which in turn means that the taxpayer's marginal tax rate is relatively high. After retirement the taxpayer's income and, in turn, marginal tax rate are usually substantially lower. Accordingly, it is generally advantageous for the taxpayer who is near retirement to wait until after retirement to realize any capital gains.

The tax treatment of capital gains begins by bringing all short-term capital gains and losses together to obtain either a net short-term capital gain or a loss. Similarly, all long-term gains and losses are brought together for each category to obtain either a net long-term capital gain or a loss for that category. For the tax year 1998, here are the categories and the tax rates involved, assuming there is a net gain:

1. Holding period: Less than one year.
   Taxation: The aggregate gain is taxed as ordinary income.

2. Holding period: More than 12 months.
   Taxation: The aggregate gain is taxed at a rate of 20%, unless the taxpayer is in the 15% income tax bracket, in which case the rate is 10%.

3. Holding period: Five years or more; asset must be purchased in 2001 or later.
   Taxation: The aggregate gain is taxed at a rate of 18%. An exception is allowed for any taxpayer who is in the 15% income tax bracket, in which case the 2001 restriction on when the asset was purchased is replaced with a restriction that the asset must have been sold in 2001 or later. For these taxpayers, the rate is 8%.

As an example, assume that Mr. and Mrs. Smith have taxable income of $400,000, which includes $50,000 of capital gains. Their tax bill can be determined by first noting in Table 5.2 that the marginal tax rate for $400,000 of income appears to be 39.6%. Because this rate is greater than the marginal rates for long-term gains given in cases 2 and 3, their tax bill will depend on the nature of the $50,000 capital gain. Note that if the $50,000 is attributable to short-term capital gains, then the full $400,000 will be treated as ordinary income, resulting in a tax bill of $132,004 [= $83,870 + .396 × ($400,000 − $278,450)]. In this case, the net capital gain is taxed at a rate of 39.6% and amounts to $19,800 because the Smiths are unable to take advantage of the lower long-term capital gains tax rates.

In case 2, the $50,000 is associated with the sale of capital assets after owning them for at least 12 months. Referring to Table 5.2, the Smiths' taxable income before the long-term capital gains is equal to $350,000 (= $400,000 − $50,000) and will be taxed at a marginal rate of 39.6% with taxes amounting to $112,204 [= $83,870 + .396 × ($350,000 − $278,450)]. However, the long-term capital gains will now be taxed at a rate of only 20%, producing taxes of $10,000 (= .20 × $50,000). Hence the Smiths' total tax bill comes to $122,204 (= $112,204 + $10,000).

In case 3, the $50,000 is derived from selling capital assets after holding them at least five years and having initially purchased them in 2001 or later. Once again, the Smiths' marginal income tax rate is 39.6%, resulting in income taxes of $112,204. Now, the long-term capital gains tax rate is only 18%, and the capital gains taxes are $9,000 (= .18 × $50,000), resulting in a total tax bill of $121,204 (= $112,204 + $9,000). (It goes without saying that Congress changes the tax laws frequently. As a result, it might be unwise to count on the current rules applying to assets purchased after 2001 and held for five years.)

In summary, note that the total tax bill of the Smiths is different in all three cases because of the difference in the amount of tax paid on the $50,000 capital gain.

	Total Taxes Paid	*Income Taxes Paid*	*Capital Gains Taxes Paid*
Case 1	$132,004	$112,204	$19,800
Case 2	122,204	112,204	10,000
Case 3	121,204	112,204	9,000

The total tax bill amounts to either $132,004 or $122,204 or $121,204, depending upon how long the asset was owned and, in the last case, when it was initially bought. The best situation from the Smiths' viewpoint is if the $50,000 is due entirely to five-year long-term capital gains (the tax bill would thus be minimized at $121,204), whereas the worst situation is if the $50,000 is due to short-term capital gains (the tax bill would thus be maximized at $132,004).

5.2.4 STATE INCOME TAXES

Most states levy personal income taxes similar to that of the federal government. Although the amounts are lower, state taxes are also likely to be progressive. The impact of these taxes is not quite as large as it might first appear because state income taxes may be deducted from income before computing federal income tax. For example, consider an investor whose marginal rates for state and federal income taxes are 10% and 31%, respectively. Assume that federal taxes are not deductible in computing state taxes. An additional $100 of income will result in $10 of state tax. This leaves $90 subject to federal income tax, thereby increasing the investor's federal income taxes by $27.90. Overall, $37.90 will be taxed away, giving an effective combined marginal rate of 37.9%. More generally,

$$\text{Combined marginal tax rate} = s + (1 - s)f \tag{5.2}$$

where s and f denote the marginal state and federal tax rates, respectively.

cross-deductibility

The situation becomes a bit more complicated if the state allows the taxpayer to deduct the amount of federal taxes paid in determining the amount of taxable income. In this situation there is **cross-deductibility,** because state taxes are deductible for federal tax purposes and federal taxes are deductible for state tax purposes. Now, using the previous $100 example, $7.12 {= $100 × [.1 − (.1 × .31)]/[1 − (.1 × .31)]} will be paid in state income taxes, and $28.79 {= $100 × [.31 − (.1 × .31)]/[1 − (.1 × .31)]} will be paid in federal income taxes, for a combined total of $35.91. Thus, the effective combined marginal tax rate is 35.91%. More generally, the amount of state tax paid for each additional dollar earned equals $[s - (s \times f)]/[1 - (s \times f)]$, and the corresponding amount of federal tax paid equals $[f - (s \times f)]/[1 - (s \times f)]$. Therefore

$$\text{Combined marginal tax rate} = \frac{s + f - (2 \times s \times f)}{1 - (s \times f)} \tag{5.3}$$

Another interesting feature of state taxation is that the interest income from bonds issued by municipalities within a state may be exempt from that state's income tax. Some states extend this exemption to include dividends from certain corporations domiciled within the state. Furthermore, cities that levy personal income taxes typically exempt from taxation the interest income on any municipal bonds they have issued. In this situation, the resident of the city who purchases such a bond escapes taxation on three levels: federal, state, and local.

5.3 Before-Tax Investing

There are features of the tax code that virtually all investors should consider. Specifically, investors should consider opportunities to invest money on a before-tax basis where the income earned on the initial investment also grows tax-free. If this strategy is not possible, then they should consider doing only the latter—investing in such a manner that the income earned on the initial investment can grow tax-free.

Keogh plan

Two examples can be used to illustrate the point. First, the tax code allows individuals who are self-employed to set aside as much as 25% of their income each year on a before-tax basis, subject to a maximum of $30,000, in what are known as **Keogh plans.** This money can be invested according to an investor's desires and can be withdrawn after the investor reaches an age of $59\frac{1}{2}$ (such withdrawals must begin by the age of $70\frac{1}{2}$; there are penalties if withdrawals are not taken between the ages of $59\frac{1}{2}$ and $70\frac{1}{2}$). The key feature of Keogh plans is that neither the amount invested nor the income earned on this investment is subject to taxation until funds are withdrawn from the plan, at which point the funds are taxed as ordinary income.[7] Hence the investor

---

MONEY MATTERS

The Capital Gains Tax Rate Controversy

 Should capital gains taxes be reduced? That question has sparked considerable controversy in recent years. Congressional Republicans have made cutting capital gains taxes the centerpiece of their domestic policy agenda. In 1997, they succeeded in enacting legislation that, despite the complexity of the resulting tax structure, effectively lowered the tax rate on a large portion of the capital gains realized by investors. They quickly announced that they intended to push for more cuts. Democrats, including the Clinton administration, have been reluctant to endorse wide-scale capital gains tax reductions, although they went along with the 1997 rate cuts. They have generally used the issue to paint Republicans as the uncaring party of the rich.

Investors have a large stake in the outcome of the capital gains tax debate. Despite all the rhetoric, the true public policy issue is not whether additional capital gains tax cuts will make investors richer as a group (a likely short-run result). Rather, it is whether a capital gains tax cut will make the economy wealthier in the long run.

We will not attempt to provide a definitive answer to this question. Numerous commentators have argued the case long and hard. We will simply summarize the arguments on both sides of the debate. You, as an investor and as a voting citizen, will have to draw your own conclusions.

Economists agree that taxing any commodity or activity reduces the output of that commodity or activity. Taxing gains on capital assets, therefore, undoubtedly reduces the amount of capital assets "produced." However, the government must obtain its tax revenues from some source. Given the required revenues needed to maintain a balanced budget, if capital gains taxes were lowered further, then other taxes would have to be raised (at least in the short run). Here the law of unintended consequences comes into play. If, for example, income taxes were raised to make up for the reduction in capital gains tax proceeds, people would cut back on taxable employment, certainly

a detrimental consequence from the economy's perspective.

The issue boils down to whether one believes that lower capital gains taxes would stimulate sufficient investment (and the benefits derived therefrom) to compensate for the resulting revenue losses. (We note that most proponents of lower capital gains taxes contend that such tax reductions would cause more existing investments to be sold in the short run, increasing tax revenues immediately and negating the need for raising other taxes.)

Advocates of lower capital gains taxes typically decry what they perceive as strong disincentives present in our economy toward savings and investment. Many countries totally exempt capital gains from taxation, whereas others have effective tax rates lower than those in the United States. The arguments of many of these tax cut proponents hark back to the "supply-side" economics of the early Reagan administration. Those proponents assert that lower capital gains taxes will promote investment and encourage savings. As a consequence, the economy will move to a higher long-run growth path. As by-products, stock markets will rise in value and interest rates will decline, generating more capital gains tax revenues than would be the case if rates were not reduced.

Proponents also point to a fairness issue. A significant portion of an investor's return is simply compensation for expected inflation. As a result, capital gains taxes effectively tax an investor's principal as well as earnings on that principal. Cuts in capital gains help in a rather imprecise way to diminish this inequity. (Some countries, such as Australia and the U.K., index capital asset original cost values to the inflation rate when calculating capital gains taxes.)

Opponents of lower capital gains taxes (class warfare demagogues aside) argue that good investments are still amply rewarded in the United States. Under the recently changed tax laws, investors can be taxed as low as 8% (after 2001) on their realized capital gains. Higher income in-

(continued)

vestors who hold their investments for at least 12 months face a 20% tax rate. Further, investors may defer capital gains taxes for years by not selling their assets (thus reducing the present values of their tax liabilities). They may even completely forgo capital gains taxes by passing on their assets to their heirs. Moreover, contend opponents, why should capital gains taxes be lowered on existing investments, the owners of which would be by far the largest beneficiaries of the reduction? Their assets represent investment decisions that cannot be rescinded no matter what the level of capital gains tax rates. Lowering taxes on those assets would do nothing to stimulate future investment and would simply aggravate government revenue shortfalls. Some opponents assert that reducing capital gains taxes encourages a short-run trading mentality on the part of investors, a development they view as detrimental to what they contend are already short-sighted capital markets.

Is there a simple answer to this debate? Clearly, no. The politics of capital gains taxes have become severely entangled with the economics. Given the strong ideological stances of the interested parties, the controversy is likely to rage indefinitely. If nothing else, the debate will provide a continuing revenue stream for a host of tax lobbyists on both sides of the issue.

---

benefits by deferring income tax payments on both the amount invested and the income earned on the investment until a later date.

individual retirement account

The second example is **individual retirement accounts** or IRAs, which can be set up by anyone. According to the tax code, an individual can contribute up to $2,000 per year to an IRA and a married couple can contribute up to $4,000. Although the amount contributed to an IRA is not tax-deductible for anyone whose income exceeds a certain limit (unless his or her employer does not offer a pension plan), the earnings on the investment are allowed to grow without the payment of taxes until withdrawn.[8]

The Taxpayer Relief Act of 1997 created a new type of IRA known as a Roth IRA.[9] With this type of IRA, contributions are not tax-deductible regardless of income level, but withdrawals are tax free provided the taxpayer is at least $59\frac{1}{2}$ when they are made and the account has been open for at least five years. Earlier withdrawals are also tax free provided they are used for either the purchase of a first home or for educational expenses, or are taken from the amount initially contributed. Consider an individual who is thinking about investing $2,000 of gross income in a 20-year bond. This investor is in the 31% marginal tax bracket and anticipates being in it for life. Bonds currently earn 10% and are anticipated to continue earning this amount indefinitely. If the investor deposits the $2,000 in either a Keogh plan or a deductible IRA, which in turn buys the bonds, the investment will grow to be worth $13,455 [= $2,000 \times (1.10)^{20}$] at the end of 20 years. If the money is withdrawn at that time, the investor will receive $9,284 [= $13,455 \times (1 - .31)$] after taxes.

Alternatively, the investor could consider investing in a nondeductible IRA, which, in turn, buys the bonds. However, taxes on the $2,000 amounting to $620 (= $2,000 \times .31$) must be paid first, assuming the investor does not qualify for a tax-deductible IRA. Depositing the remaining $1,380 (= $2,000 - 620) results in the IRA's having a balance of $9,284 [= $1,380 \times (1.10)^{20}$] at the end of 20 years. If the money is withdrawn at that time, the investor will receive $6,834 {= $1,380 + [($9,284 - $1,380) \times (1 - .31)]$} after taxes. However, if a Roth IRA had been used instead, the investor would have received $9,284 [= $1,380 \times (1.10)^{20}$] in after-tax money, assuming the investor was over $59\frac{1}{2}$ and initially was qualified for the Roth IRA.

As a basis for comparison, consider what would happen if the investor avoided using either a Keogh plan or an IRA and invested directly in bonds. In that case, only $1,380 would be available for investment, and each year the investor would get to keep earnings amounting to only 6.9% [$= 10\% \times (1 - .31)$] of the amount invested. Hence after 20 years the investor would have an amount available after taxes equal to $5,241 [$= \$1,380 \times (1.069)^{20}$].

In summary, the after-tax payoffs for the three alternatives discussed are

Keogh plan, deductible IRA, and Roth IRA	$9,284
Nondeductible IRA	6,834
Direct investment	5,241

Note that the Keogh plan, deductible IRA, and Roth IRA provide the investor with 77% more money after taxes than could be earned by investing directly. Another way to view these payoffs is to note that the direct investment would have to earn 14.5% before taxes in order to provide the same after-tax payoff provided by investing in a Keogh plan, deductible IRA, or Roth IRA that earns 10%. Similarly, the direct investment would have to earn 12% before taxes in order to provide the same after-tax payoff provided by the nondeductible IRA. It is no surprise that a popular book on investing advises readers that "one of the best ways to obtain extra investment funds is to avoid taxes legally."[10]

Summary

1. Because investors concern themselves with after-tax returns, federal and state tax laws play a major role in the way securities are priced.
2. Income earned by a corporation may be taxed twice; once when it is earned through the corporate income tax, and again when it is received as dividends by the stockholders through the personal income tax.
3. In the case of both individuals and corporations, the marginal tax rate is more relevant than the average tax rate for making investment decisions.
4. Tax-exempt bonds generally pay lower interest rates than equivalent-risk taxable bonds. Comparable tax-exempt and taxable bonds should be evaluated on an after-tax basis.
5. Long-term capital gains taxes are lower than short-term capital gains taxes; the size of the tax depends on the investor's marginal tax bracket, the length of time the investor owns the asset before selling it, and when it was bought.
6. Because state taxes are deductible on a federal level (and vice versa for some states), the combined marginal tax rate is not the sum of the state and federal marginal tax rates.
7. Some tax shelters, such as Keogh plans and IRAs, permit the deferral of taxes on part of the investor's wage income and all of the investment earnings, subject to certain conditions.

Questions and Problems

1. Why is the marginal tax rate more relevant to investment decision making than the average tax rate?
2. What is meant by the term "double taxation of corporate income"?
3. Given the following income tax schedule, draw a graph illustrating the marginal and average tax rates as a function of income level.

Income	*Tax Rate*
$0–$10,000	10%
$10,001–$20,000	13%
$20,001–$30,000	15%
$30,001–$50,000	20%
$50,001 and above	25%

4. Minneapolis Pipelines pays an annual dividend of $.80 per share on its preferred stock. The stock currently sells for $12 per share. Maplewood Chemicals is considering investing idle cash in either Minneapolis's preferred stock or a bond yielding 9.8%. If Maplewood's marginal tax rate is 34%, which investment is more attractive?

5. U.S. federal personal income tax rates are progressive in that the marginal tax rate increases with income (see Figure 5.2). What is the justification for this tax structure? Make a case for or against progressive tax rates.

6. Footsie Belardi earned $65,000 last year. Using the single filer tax schedule in Table 5.2, calculate Footsie's income tax.

7. Heine Groh expects consumer prices to rise at a 7% rate next year and has negotiated a 9.5% pay increase. Given a 35% marginal income tax bracket, will this pay increase cause Heine's real income (that is, purchasing power) to grow? Explain.

8. A corporate bond is selling for $950. It matures in a year, at which time the holder will receive $1,000. In addition, the bond will pay $50 in interest during the year. What would be the after-tax return on the bond to an investor in the 50% marginal income tax bracket? (Assume that capital gains do not receive preferential tax treatment.) What would be the after-tax return if the bond had been a tax-free municipal bond?

9. Consider a tax-exempt municipal bond yielding 6%. To an investor in the following marginal tax brackets, what is the equivalent before-tax interest rate that a taxable bond would have to offer to be considered equivalent to the municipal bond?
   a. 10%
   b. 28%
   c. 33%

10. Spot Bethea must choose between investing in a tax-free municipal bond yielding 5% and a taxable bond yielding 7.5%. Spot's marginal tax rate is 30%. Which bond should Spot choose?

11. Pinky Higgins and spouse had taxable income of $120,000 last year, which includes a capital gain of $20,000. What is their tax bill if the gain is entirely short-term? What is their tax bill if the gain is derived from assets held for 13 months?

12. What is a wash sale? Why does the IRS prohibit such transactions for tax calculation purposes?

13. Is it true that the combined state and federal personal income tax rate is the sum of the two rates? Why?

14. Jean Dubuc lives in a state where the tax schedule lists an 8% marginal tax rate. The federal tax schedule lists a 25% marginal tax rate. Accounting for cross-deductibility,
   a. What is Jean's effective state marginal tax rate?
   b. What is Jean's effective federal marginal tax rate?
   c. What is Jean's effective combined marginal tax rate?

15. Would you expect tax shelters to be as attractive to lower income persons as to higher income persons? Should lower income persons invest in tax shelters? Why?

Endnotes

1. Certain corporations with 35 or fewer shareholders may elect to be treated as partnerships for tax purposes. Such firms, often called "Subchapter S corporations" (after the enabling provision of the Internal Revenue Code), constitute an exception to the general rule.

2. This provision assumes that the corporate investor owns between 20% and 80% of the stock of the firm issuing the dividends. If less than 20% is owned, then only 70% of the dividends are excluded from income. If 80% or more is owned, then 100% of the dividend is excluded.

3. *1988 Federal Tax Course* (Upper Saddle River, NJ: Prentice Hall, 1987): p. 89.

4. Some subtle yet complicated changes made in 1990 and 1993 cause the tax rate schedules to be slightly different than what is shown here.

5. Chapter 19 describes various bonds that are available for investment and gives a detailed discussion of how they are taxed.

6. These yields are also compared in Chapter 19 (see, in particular, Figure 19.11).

7. Other plans that are treated similarly with respect to taxation are known as 401(k) plans, run by corporations; 403(b) plans, run by certain nonprofit organizations and school districts; and 457 plans, run by state and local governments.

8. Variable annuities, available from many insurance companies, are treated similarly for tax purposes. See the Money Matters box in Chapter 23.

9. The Education IRA was also introduced with the Taxpayers Relief Act of 1997. With this IRA a maximum of $500 per child can be set aside annually. This amount is not tax deductible, but under certain circumstances withdrawals are tax-exempt if used to pay for college expenses.

10. Burton G. Malkiel, *A Random Walk down Wall Street* (New York: W. W. Norton, 1990): p. 279.

6

Inflation

inflation

The previous chapter mentioned that taxation should not be regarded as an unmitigated evil. The same statement can be made about **inflation** because it too provides benefits to some individuals that may outweigh the associated costs that others have to bear. And, like taxes, inflation can have a significant impact on investment decisions and results. This chapter provides an overview of some of the more important aspects of inflation from the viewpoint of the investor.

The story is told of the modern-day Rip Van Winkle who awoke in the year 2050 and immediately called his broker. (Fortunately, pay phones at the time permitted a call of up to three minutes without charge.) He first asked what had happened to the $10,000 he had instructed the broker to put in Treasury bills, continually reinvesting the proceeds. The broker promptly informed him that because of high interest rates and the power of compounding, his initial $10,000 investment had grown to more than $1 million. Stunned, Mr. Van Winkle inquired about his stocks, which were also worth about $10,000 when he dozed off. The broker told him that he was in for an even more pleasant surprise: They were now worth $2.5 million. "In short, Mr. Van Winkle," said the broker, "you are a millionaire 3.5 times over." At this point an operator cut in, "Your three minutes are over, please deposit $100 for an additional three minutes." Although this story clearly overstates the case, there is no doubt that inflation is a major concern for investors. By and large, people have come to fear significant inflation, particularly when it is unpredictable.

This chapter begins by describing how inflation is typically measured. Then the benefits and costs of inflation are discussed, along with who gains and who loses when it is present.

6.1 Measuring Inflation

There is no completely satisfactory way to summarize the price changes that have occurred during a given time period for the large number of goods and services available in the United States. Nevertheless, the federal government has attempted to do so by measuring the cost of a specific mix of major items (a "basket of goods") at various points in time. The "overall" price level computed for this representative combination of items is termed a **cost-of-living index.** The percentage change in this index during a given time period is a measure of the inflation (or deflation) from the beginning of the period to the end of the period.

cost-of-living index

Whether this measure of inflation is relevant for a given individual depends to a large extent on the similarity of this individual's purchases to the mix of items used to construct the index. Even if the individual finds the mix appropriate at the beginning of a period, the rate of increase in the price of the mix during the period is likely to overstate the increase in the cost of living for the individual for two reasons. First, improvements in the quality of the items in the mix are seldom adequately taken into account. Often the end-of-period price for an item is not comparable to the beginning-of-period price because the item is different. For example, a new Toyota may have a 5% higher sticker price than a similar model had the previous year, but the new model may have better tires than the old model. Hence it would be inaccurate to conclude that the price of this particular model rose by 5% during the year.

Second, and perhaps more important, little or no adjustment is made in the mix as relative prices change. Rational customers can reduce the cost of living as prices change by substituting relatively less expensive goods for those that have become relatively more expensive. For example, if the price of beef rises 20% during a given year while the price of chicken rises only 10% during the same year, customers may start to eat more chicken and less beef. Failure to take into account this change in the mix will result in an overstatement in the rate of inflation. Despite these two drawbacks, cost-of-living indices provide at least rough estimates of changes in prices.

6.2   Price Indices

Consumer Price Index

Most governments compute alternative price indices to provide a wider choice for analysis. However, many people focus on only one index as an indicator of the price level. In the United States the **Consumer Price Index** (CPI) often fills this role, despite some attempts by government officials to discourage such widespread use.[1] Because the CPI is so widely used, the composition of the market basket of goods that make up the CPI has been changed from time to time in order to provide a more representative basket. Furthermore, the process by which the relevant data are gathered and verified has periodically been improved.[2] The CPI is calculated monthly by the U.S. Bureau of Labor Statistics in the Department of Labor.

In Chapter 1, Table 1.1 provided some historical perspective on the rate of inflation in the United States. It showed the annual rate of increase in the CPI from 1899 through 1998. As an aid to interpretation, these rates are plotted on the graph in Figure 6.1(a). As can be seen in the figure, the CPI did not grow at a constant rate from 1899 to 1998. After substantial deflation from 1920 to 1933, prices increased almost every year. There were four subsequent subperiods with different rates of inflation: mild (but notably uneven) inflation from 1935 to 1951; negligible inflation from 1952 to 1965; fairly rapid (but somewhat uneven) inflation from 1966 to 1981; and mild inflation from 1982 to 1998. Interestingly, the recent moderation in U.S. inflation has occurred almost simultaneously in most other countries as well, leading some observers to contend (perhaps erroneously) that inflation is no longer a serious macroeconomic problem.

Table 6.1 shows the average annual rate of growth of the CPI for each of the subperiods, measured by the *geometric mean growth rate* of the CPI. This growth rate, when compounded over the subperiod and applied to the beginning index value, results in the ending index value. For example, at the end of 1965 the CPI was 95.5, and at the end of 1981 it was 281.5 (here the CPI was adjusted so that its value in 1967 was 100). Thus the geometric mean growth rate was 7.0% because a CPI of 95.5, when growing at this compounded rate over 16 years, equals 281.5:

$$281.5 = 95.5 \times (1 + .07)^{16}$$

More generally, the geometric mean growth rate (g) can be calculated by solving the following equation for g:

$$C_e = C_b(1 + g)^y \tag{6.1}$$

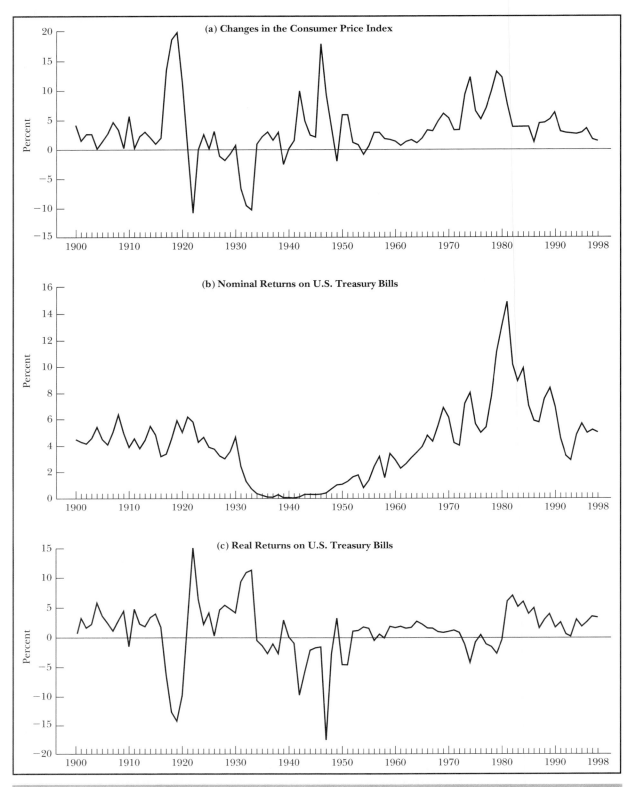

FIGURE 6.1 Nominal and Real Returns on Short-Term Default-Free Investments, 12-Month Periods Ending December, from 1899 to 1998

Source: Copyright 1999 by Global Financial Data. This data can be accessed on the Internet at www.globalfindata.com.

TABLE 6.1	Geometric Mean Growth Rates of the U.S. CPI	
From	*To*	*Rate of Growth (% per year)*
1899	1915	2.2%
1916	1919	16.4
1920	1934	−2.3
1935	1951	4.1
1952	1965	1.3
1966	1981	7.0
1982	1998	3.3
Overall		
1899	1998	3.2

Source: Based on Table 1.1.

which results in:

$$g = (C_e/C_b)^{1/y} - 1 \qquad (6.2)$$

where y denotes the number of years and C_e and C_b denote the ending and beginning CPI values, respectively.

6.3 Nominal and Real Returns

6.3.1 NOMINAL RETURNS

Modern economies gain much of their efficiency through the use of money—a generally agreed-on medium of exchange. Instead of trading corn for a stereo to be delivered in one year, as in a barter economy, the citizen of a modern economy can trade his or her corn for money, then trade this current money for future money by investing it. Later, the future money can be used to buy the stereo. The rate at which a citizen can trade current money for future money depends on the investment and is known as the **nominal return.**

nominal return

6.3.2 FISHER MODEL OF REAL RETURNS

real return

In times of changing prices, the nominal return on an investment may be a poor indicator of the **real return** obtained by the investor.[3] This situation occurs because part of the additional dollars received from the investment may be needed to recoup the investor's lost purchasing power due to inflation that occurred during the investment period. As a result, adjustments to the nominal return are needed to remove the effect of inflation to determine the real return. Frequently, the CPI is used for this purpose.

For example, assume that at the start of a given year the CPI is at 150, and at the end of the year it is at 160. This means that it costs $160 at the end of the year to buy the same amount of the CPI market basket of goods that at the start of the year could have been purchased for $150. Assuming that the nominal return is 9% for this year, the investor who started the year with $150 and invested it would have $150 × 1.09 = $163.50 at year end. At this point, the investor could purchase ($163.50/$160) −1 = .0219 = 2.19% more of the CPI market basket of goods than at the beginning of the year. Thus, the real return for this investment is 2.19%.

These calculations can be summarized in the following formula:

$$\left[C_0 \times \frac{1 + NR}{C_1} \right] - 1 = RR \qquad (6.3)$$

where

$$C_0 = \text{CPI at the beginning of the year}$$
$$C_1 = \text{CPI at the end of the year}$$
$$NR = \text{the nominal return for the year}$$
$$RR = \text{the real return for the year}$$

Alternatively, the investor could note that an increase in the CPI from 150 to 160 can be translated into an inflation rate of $(160/150) - 1 = .0667$, or 6.67%. This inflation rate can be denoted as *CCL* (change in the cost of living), and the real return can be calculated using the following formula, known as the *Fisher model*:[4]

$$\left[\frac{1 + NR}{1 + CCL}\right] - 1 = RR \qquad \qquad \textbf{(6.4)}$$

Note that for the example, $RR = (1.09/1.0667) - 1 = .0219$, or 2.19%.

For a quick calculation using the Fisher model, the real return can be estimated by simply subtracting the inflation rate (*CCL*) from the nominal return:

$$NR - CCL \cong RR \qquad \qquad \textbf{(6.5)}$$

where $\cong$ means "is approximately equal to." In this example, the "quick method" results in an estimate of the real return of $.09 - .0667 = .0233$ or 2.33%. Thus, the error resulting from use of this method is $.0233 - .0219 = .0014$, or .14%.[5]

6.3.3   THE EFFECT OF INVESTOR EXPECTATIONS

Investors are concerned with real returns, not nominal returns. Looking to the future, investors do not know what the rate of inflation will be, nor do they know what the nominal return on an investment will be. However, in both cases they have expectations about these figures, which are denoted as $E(CCL)$ (expected inflation rate) and $E(NR)$ (expected nominal return), respectively. Thus, the Fisher model implies that $E(RR)$ (the expected real return on an investment) can be approximated by

$$E(RR) \cong E(NR) - E(CCL) \qquad \qquad \textbf{(6.6)}$$

If a security is to provide a given expected real return, then the expected nominal return must be larger by the expected rate of inflation for the relevant holding period. This condition can be seen by rearranging Equation (6.6):

$$E(NR) \cong E(RR) + E(CCL) \qquad \qquad \textbf{(6.7)}$$

For example, if the expected rate of inflation is 4% and a given security is to provide investors with an expected real return of 6%, then the security must be priced in the marketplace so that its expected nominal return is approximately 10%. Furthermore, if the expected real rate remains constant, then a 1% increase in the expected rate of inflation from 4% to 5% will result in a 1% increase in the expected nominal rate of return, from 10% to 11%. In summary, if investors are concerned with real returns, then securities will be priced in the marketplace so that expected nominal returns incorporate the expected rate of inflation.[6]

6.4   Interest Rates and Inflation

At the start of a given investment holding period, nominal interest rates for securities having no risk of default should cover both a requisite expected real return and the expected rate of inflation for the period in question. At the end of the period, the real

Inside the Consumer Price Index

 No doubt you have seen reports in the news media such as, "Consumer prices rose last month at an annual rate of 2.1%." If you are like most people, you rarely give such pronouncements much thought. Inflation simply means that what you buy now costs more than it did last year. Have you ever stopped to think about how "what you buy" is determined and how "now costs more" is calculated? For answers to these questions, we have to go inside the Consumer Price Index (CPI).

The CPI is a measure of the average price paid by urban consumers for a specific "market basket" of goods and services. In fact, the Bureau of Labor Statistics (BLS) calculates two versions of the CPI: the CPI for All Urban Consumers (CPI-U) and the CPI for Urban Wage Earners and Clerical Workers (CPI-W). The CPI-U is the most widely quoted version. It covers roughly 90% of the total U.S. population and is based on the expenditures of almost all households of urban and metropolitan areas. The CPI-W covers the subset of households included in the CPI-U whose incomes come from clerical or wage occupations and the households' earners have been employed for most of the previous twelve months.

Because it is an index, the CPI is a relative measure; it compares the price currently paid for a market basket to the price of the market basket in a reference (or base) year. For example, suppose that we have identified a market basket that costs $3 to purchase today. And, suppose that ten years ago, that same market basket cost only $1 to buy. We could express the price of the difference as a ratio: 3 to 1, or 3.0, with ten years ago serving as the base year. For convenience, we could multiply our index by 100 to give it a current value of 300.0.

The BLS computes the CPI in precisely the same fashion. At year-end 1998, the CPI had a value of 163.9. This fact means that the CPI market basket that cost $100 during the base period now costs $163.90. The BLS currently uses the average of prices in the 3-year period from 1982 to 1984 as the base for its CPI calculations. If the CPI rose to 180.9 at the end of 2002, that would represent a 10.4% increase in the market basket's nominal value from the end of 1998, or a 2.5% inflation rate measured on a geometric mean annual basis.

What exactly is this market basket from which the CPI is created? The BLS categorizes goods and services into eight major groups: food and beverages, housing, apparel, medical care, transportation, recreation, education and communication, and other goods and services. Housing represents the largest component of the index with a relative weight (at the time of the 1998 revision) of 39.6%, followed by transportation at 17.6%, and food and beverages at 16.3%. Within each major group is a subset of "items." For example, under the food and beverages product group, breakfast cereal is an item. More than 200 items make up the market basket, ranging from eggs to college tuition. On a monthly basis, BLS field agents across the country gather some 90,000 prices, which are used to compute the index's value.

In order to adjust the CPI for changes in consumers' purchasing patterns, the BLS updates the composition of the basket periodically. The index was first developed during World War I, and since then there have been six major revisions, with the revisions in the past 50 years having been made approximately once a decade. In 1999, the BLS announced that, beginning in 2002, it would undertake market basket revisions every two years in an attempt to make more timely changes in the expenditure weights.

The revision process involves surveying urban consumers to determine their expenditure patterns. In its survey, the BLS interviews what it refers to as "consumer units"—essentially financially independent households—across the country. In its most recent survey, 36,000 consumer units were interviewed regarding both the types and amounts of goods and services they purchased as well as the location in which those pur-

(continued)

chases were made. Based on the results of this survey, the BLS assigns goods and services, and their respective weights, to the CPI. It also develops a sampling process that identifies the specific items to be priced at specific outlets. The CPI's composition (items and their weights) will change from the previous survey because of one or more factors that include population movements, product definition changes, new products, changes in distribution channels, and demand shifts.

Despite (or perhaps because of) the CPI's intricate construction, the BLS must make many estimates and assumptions in collecting price data. For example, the BLS must estimate the imputed rent that homeowners pay to calculate changes in the price of a primary residence. Discerning price changes from the noise generated by continually changing consumer tastes and the introduction of thousands of new goods and services is a daunting task.

The CPI has come under close scrutiny in recent years. A special commission headed by former White House chief economist Barry Boskin issued a controversial report in 1996 that estimated the CPI that overstated inflation by more than 1% per year. The commission stated that roughly half this overstatement came from the index's fixed weight construction, which does not respond to changes in consumer purchasing patterns as prices change. (For example, if the price of chicken rises relative to the price of pork, consumers may substitute pork for chicken in their purchases, yet the fixed weight assigned to chicken and pork in calculating the CPI will not change until the next revision.) The commission claimed that the overstatement also is due to a failure to account for the benefits of improved product quality and newly introduced goods. Partly in response to these criticisms, the BLS made changes in the CPI, including the previously mentioned acceleration in the index revision timetable and a move to an item-weighting system that is less prone to "substitution bias."

Despite its limitations, the CPI represents the government's best estimate of national consumer prices. Other price measures exist, including the Producer Price Index and the Gross Domestic Product Deflator. However, the CPI is by far the most widely recognized price index. It serves as the primary source of inflation data for businesses and government alike. It directly affects the income of approximately 75 million people, including Social Security beneficiaries, food stamp recipients, and Federal Civil Service retirees and survivors, all of whom have changes in their payments tied to the CPI.

return actually received will be the difference between the nominal return and the rate of inflation actually experienced. Only when actual inflation equals expected inflation will the actual real return equal the expected real return on such securities. Figure 6.1(a) indicates the annual rate of inflation, as measured by changes in the Consumer Price Index, during the 100-year period from 1899 to 1998. Figure 6.1(b) shows how short-term nominal interest rates varied during this period; Treasury bill rates, from Table 1.1, are used to measure these rates. Figure 6.1(c), derived by subtracting panel (a) from panel (b), represents real returns.

One cannot help being struck by the fact that those who invested in short-term securities during this period frequently ended up with less purchasing power (particularly if taxes are taken into account) than they started with because the real return was negative in 30 of the 100 years. Perhaps even more surprising is the fact that the average real return during the period was close to zero.

Although expected real returns may vary from year to year, this variation may be relatively small. If it is, investors may have been willing to invest in short-term, highly liquid securities even though they expected to earn very little in real terms. If they are currently willing to do so, such securities will be priced to give a very low expected real return.[7]

If this assumption is made, the "market's" predicted rate of inflation in the near future is calculated by simply subtracting an estimate of the low expected real rate, say

1%, from the nominal interest rate (also known as the yield) on short-term government securities (Treasury bills). The resulting figure represents a consensus prediction of inflation—a prediction that an "average" investor in this market would make, and one that is likely to be more accurate over time than the predictions of any single forecaster.

6.5 The Effect of Inflation on Borrowers and Lenders

Although deviations of actual inflation from expected inflation may have relatively little effect on the real return on investments in general, they may have a significant effect on specific investments. In fact, one would expect a direct impact on the real returns associated with investments whose payments are fixed in terms of dollars to be received.

A simple example illustrates the relationship. Assume that everyone currently expects the rate of inflation to be 5% during the next year and that a lender has agreed to make loans at a nominal rate of 5% (the lender is content with an expected real return of zero). An individual could borrow $100 now and pay back $105 (= $100 × 1.05) one year later for a one-year loan. Note that if actual inflation equals expected inflation, a one-year loan would require a payment equivalent to $100 in constant (or real) dollars (that is, today's purchasing power) a year hence. In this case, the real rate of interest would be zero.

Now, imagine that an individual takes advantage of the lender's offer, borrowing $100 for one year. How will the borrower and lender be affected if the actual rate of inflation differs from the expected rate of inflation? Assume that in the first year prices rise by 9% instead of the expected 5%, meaning that unexpected inflation is 4% (= 9% − 5%). In this situation, the short-term borrower gains at the expense of the lender. Why? The borrower must still repay $105, but, in terms of constant dollars, this is only $96.33 (= $105/1.09), a figure less than the amount of the loan. As a result, the lender receives a real rate of interest of −3.67% [= ($96.33 − $100)/$100], instead of the anticipated rate of 0%.

What if first-year prices had risen by only 3%, meaning that unexpected inflation was −2% (= 3% − 5%)? In this situation, the short-term lender would gain at the expense of the borrower. The borrower would have to repay $105, which, in terms of constant dollars, would amount to $101.94 (= $105/1.03), a figure that is greater than the amount of the loan. As a result, the lender would receive a real rate of interest of 1.94% [= ($101.94 − $100)/$100], instead of the anticipated rate of 0%.

These results can be generalized: When the actual rate of inflation exceeds the expected rate of inflation, those with commitments to make payments fixed in nominal terms (debtors) gain in real terms at the expense of those to whom payments are to be made (creditors). Conversely, when actual inflation is less than expected inflation, creditors gain and debtors lose.[8] This uncertainty in the real return on fixed-income securities that is due to uncertain inflation is frequently referred to as **purchasing-power risk.**

purchasing-power risk

6.6 Indexation

The previous section suggests that even default-free bonds are subject to purchasing-power risk. Contractual nominal interest rates can cover expected inflation, but the subsequent real return from any investment with fixed nominal payments depends on actual inflation. As long as the two inflation rates differ, the real return is uncertain. However, there is a way to design a bond that eliminates this uncertainty. It involves the use of **indexation.**

indexation

6.6.1 GOVERNMENT BONDS

If a specified price index can adequately measure purchasing power, there is no reason a contract, such as a government bond, cannot be written with specified real payments instead of specified nominal payments. Assume the CPI currently stands at C_0, and will be C_1 one year later, C_2 two years later, and so on. Thus, in exchange for a loan of $100 and a 4% real return, the government could promise to pay amounts that are currently unknown but that will be equal to $\$4 \times C_1/C_0$ one year later, $\$4 \times C_2/C_0$ two years later, ..., and $\$104 \times C_{10}/C_0$ ten years later. The values $C_1/C_0, C_2/C_0, \ldots, C_{10}/C_0$ are known as *index ratios,* and represent the quantity (1 + the rate of inflation) from the time the bond is issued (time 0) to the time a given payment is to be made. Conversion of these payments to constant (or real) dollars requires that each be divided by the corresponding quantity (1 + the rate of inflation) since the bond was issued, which is equivalent to C_t/C_0 for a payment made at time t.

Time	Amount in Nominal Dollars	Price Level (CPI)	Amount in Real Dollars
1	$\$4 \times C_1/C_0$	C_1	$4
2	$\$4 \times C_2/C_0$	C_2	$4
.	.	.	.
.	.	.	.
.	.	.	.
10	$\$104 \times C_{10}/C_0$	C_{10}	$104

The real value of each payment is the amount shown in the final column. These payments will have the indicated purchasing power expressed in time 0 prices regardless of what happens to future prices (that is, regardless of the actual values of C_1, C_2, and so on). Thus, the bond is said to be fully indexed because all amounts are tied to a stated price index on a one-for-one basis; when the price index goes up by 10%, for example, all of the subsequent payments go up by 10%. Any investor who buys this bond at issuance for $100 and holds it until maturity will receive an annual *real* return of 4%.

What happens if inflation in the first year is 5% and the investor sells the bond at year-end for $103? This investor's nominal return will be 7.2% $\{= [(\$4 \times 1.05) + \$103]/\$100\}$, for a real return of approximately 2.2% ($= 7.2\% - 5\%$). The new buyer will have an inflation-protected stream of annual cash inflows amounting to $4.20 ($= \$4 \times 1.05$) for the next eight years and $109.20 [$= (\$100 \times 1.05) + (\$4 \times 1.05)$] in nine years. Having paid $103 for this stream, the buyer will receive an annual *real* return of 4.3% if the bond is held to maturity.[9]

inflation-indexed securities

In January of 1997 the U.S. Treasury started a program in which bonds of this nature, dubbed Treasury **inflation-indexed securities,** are sold quarterly (these securities are discussed in more detail in Chapter 19). One of the interesting features of these securities is that a comparison of their yields against the yields of conventional Treasury securities with similar maturities provides a rough measure of the representative investor's expected rate of inflation over the life of the security. In the previous example, when the 10-year, inflation-indexed security was first sold, it provided the investor with an expected real return of 4%. If at the same time a 10-year, conventional Treasury note was sold with an expected nominal return of 7%, then a rough estimate of the expected rate of inflation during the forthcoming 10-year period is 3% ($= 7\% - 4\%$).[10] Table 6.2 indicates the experience of six other countries with similar securities. Note that Israel has made the greatest use of such securities, which is not surprising given its history of relatively high inflation.

TABLE 6.2   Inflation-Indexed Securities in Six Countries

	Israel	*U.K.*	*Sweden*	*Australia*	*Canada*	*New Zealand*
			YEAR FIRST ISSUED			
	1955	*1981*	*1994*	*1985*	*1991*	*1995*
Amount outstanding (in billions of U.S. dollars)	$27.9	$71.1	$5.7	$2.7	$4.3	$.1
Indexed debt as percent of country's total marketable debt	79.0%	17.8%	4.5%	3.8%	1.4%	.7%

Source: Jeffrey M. Wrase, "Inflation-Indexed Bonds: How Do They Work?" *Federal Reserve Bank of Philadelphia Business Review* (July–August 1997): p. 7.

6.6.2   INDEXING OTHER CONTRACTS

Keep in mind that not only government bonds can be tied to inflation. In some countries (two notable examples are Israel and Brazil), many contracts besides bonds are tied to standard price indices. Returns on savings accounts, wage contracts, pension plans, and insurance contracts all have been indexed at various times and places. In the United States, Social Security payments are indexed, as are pension payments of retired federal employees. Some of these payments are fully indexed; others are partially indexed (for example, they might increase by 7% when the price index increases by 10%).

The key advantage of indexation is its role in reducing or eliminating purchasing-power risk. Higher expected inflation usually is accompanied by increased uncertainty about the actual rate of inflation. Increased uncertainty means that potential gains and losses to both nonindexed borrowers and nonindexed lenders are greater. Because both borrowers and lenders dislike the prospect of losses more than they like the prospect of gains, there will be increased pressure for indexation by both borrowers and lenders when a country moves into periods of high inflationary expectations.

When uncertainty about inflation is substantial, one would expect indexation to become widespread. However, laws regulating interest rates may prevent the issuance of fully indexed debt if these laws place a ceiling on the nominal rate but not on the real rate. Such laws lead to predictable inefficiencies when expected inflation increases because credit rationing might be required. Rationing may be necessary because a ceiling on the nominal rate causes the real rate to decline as inflationary expectations increase. The decline in the real rate, in turn, increases the demand for credit and reduces the supply, leading to credit rationing.[11] A notable example occurred in the 1970s in the United States. At that time, ceilings placed on nominal rates paid by savings and loan companies, coupled with increased inflationary expectations, caused a substantial outflow of funds from such companies and a corresponding reduction in the amount of money they made available for home mortgages. On the other side were issuers of securities that were not subject to rate ceilings and that offered an appropriate nominal

disintermediation   rate and, thus, had little difficulty in attracting funds. The term **disintermediation** was invented to describe this pattern of funds flow.

Because inflation is generally hard to predict for long time periods, uncertainty about inflation often leads to a reduction in the average term-to-maturity of newly issued fixed-income securities. For example, the average term-to-maturity of fixed-coupon debt issued in periods of great inflationary uncertainty is usually shorter than in more stable times.

variable rates

Alternatively, debt with long maturities can be written with **variable rates** (also known as *floating rates*) of interest. Such instruments provide long-term debt at short-term rates. Interest payments vary, with each one determined by adding a fixed number of percentage points (say, 2%) to a specified base rate that changes periodically. Two base rates frequently used are the prime rate and the yield on 90-day U.S. Treasury bills. If short-term interest rates anticipate inflation reasonably well, such a variable-rate security is an effective substitute for a fully indexed bond.

6.7 Stock Returns and Inflation

6.7.1 LONG-TERM HISTORICAL RELATIONSHIPS

It is reasonable to assume that investors are more concerned with real returns than with nominal returns because real returns reflect how much better off they are in terms of the purchasing power of their wealth. Accordingly, real returns of securities need to be analyzed. Table 6.3 shows rates of real return for common stocks and Treasury bills for the long-term period of 1802 to 1998 and four relatively long subperiods.

Column (2) of the table shows that, on average, the rate of return on common stocks has substantially exceeded the rate of inflation, providing a real return of more than 8% for the entire period and in excess of 7% in the last 100 years. In comparison, the rate of return on Treasury bills exceeded the rate of inflation by more than 3% for the entire period. However, the subperiods show substantial variation, as the real return on Treasury bills was -1.08% during the 50-year period from 1899 to 1948.

equity premium

Also of interest is the **equity premium** shown in column (4), which is simply the difference between the real rate of return on stocks and bills. In the last 100 years it has been nearly $7\frac{1}{2}\%$, an amount that some researchers believe is inexplicably high. In summary, Table 6.3 shows that common stocks have historically returned substantially more than the rate of inflation and Treasury bills. That is, in the long run, common stocks have had a large positive real return.

6.7.2 SHORT-TERM HISTORICAL RELATIONSHIPS

Another interesting issue concerns the relationship between the short-term rate of return on stocks and the rate of inflation. Conventional wisdom suggests that stock returns should be relatively high when inflation is relatively high and relatively low when

	TABLE 6.3	Rates of Real Return on Common Stocks and Treasury Bills and the Equity Premium		
Period *(1)*	*Length of Period (in years)* *(2)*	*Real Return on Stocks* *(3)*	*Real Return on Bills* *(4)*	*Equity Premium (3) − (4) = (5)*
1802–1998[a,b]	197	8.21%	3.12%	5.09%
1899–1998[b]	100	7.38	−0.01	7.40
1899–1948[b]	50	4.78	−1.08	5.86
1949–1998[b]	50	9.99	1.05	8.93
1974–1998[b]	25	11.45	2.88	8.57

[a]Based on Andrew B. Abel, "The Equity Premium Puzzle," *Federal Reserve Bank of Philadelphia Business Review* (September–October 1991): p. 8.

[b]Based on data in Table 1.1.

inflation is relatively low. Why? Because stocks represent claims on real assets that should increase in value with inflation.

Figure 6.2 displays the relationship between annual stock returns and rates of inflation from 1899 to 1998. The figure shows that there is no discernible relationship between the rate of inflation and stock returns. Indeed, the correlation coefficient between these two variables is –.05, which for all practical purposes is zero.[12] That is, when inflation is relatively high, there is no tendency for stock returns to be either relatively high or low. Similarly, when inflation is relatively low, there is no tendency for stock returns to be either relatively high or low.[13] Accordingly, stocks are not good hedges against inflation in the short term.

A study comparing inflation rates and stock rates of return from 1802 through 1990 confirmed these observations.[14] Using one-year rates, no apparent relationship was found between inflation rates and stock returns. However, when analyzing five-year rates, a significant positive relationship was found. Thus, there appears to be evidence that inflation rates and stock returns are directly related over long periods of time.[15]

Summary

1. Inflation measures the percentage change in a specific cost-of-living index at various points in time.
2. Whether a measure of inflation is relevant for a given individual depends to a large extent on the similarity between that person's purchases and the composition of the price index.

FIGURE 6.2 Annual Stock Returns and Rates of Inflation, 1899–1998

Source: Copyright 1999 by Global Financial Data. This data can be accessed on the Internet at www.globalfindata.com.

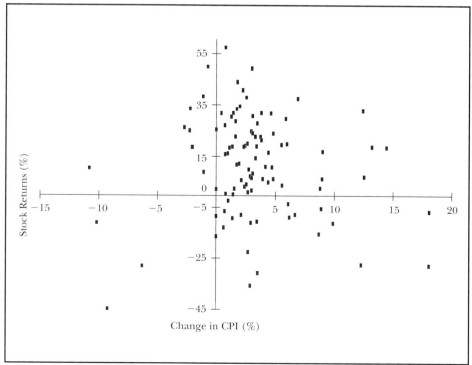

3. An investor's real return is approximately equal to the difference between the investor's nominal return and the inflation rate.
4. Real returns are important to an investor because they represent how much the investor's purchasing power has increased (or decreased) and thus how much better (or worse) off the investor is.
5. If investors are concerned with real returns, then securities will be priced so that expected nominal returns incorporate the expected inflation rate.
6. When the actual inflation rate exceeds the expected inflation rate, debtors gain at the expense of creditors. The opposite is true when actual inflation is less than expected inflation.
7. Investment returns can be indexed by tying security payments to changes in the price level. Indexation reduces or removes an investment's purchasing-power risk.
8. Over long periods of time, common stocks have generated large, positive real returns. Treasury bills have produced much lower, but still positive, real returns.
9. Over short periods of time, stock returns do not seem to be positively related to rates of inflation. However, over long periods of time, stock returns seem to be positively related to rates of inflation.

Questions and Problems

1. If a price index had a value of 340 at the beginning of a particular year and 370 at the end of the year, what was the inflation rate for the year?
2. Given the following beginning and ending values for a particular price index, and the respective number of years between the measurement of the two values, calculate the annual compounded (geometric mean) inflation rates during the three periods.

Price Index Beginning Value	Price Index Ending Value	Years Covered
100	120	1
120	175	3
175	150	2

3. Distinguish between the nominal and real return on an investment.
4. Calculate the arithmetic mean rate of inflation using the data in Table 1.1 for the same time periods given in Table 6.1. What is the relationship between the arithmetic and geometric means?
5. Given the following average compound annual inflation rates, how much would $1 be worth in terms of purchasing power five years from today as expressed in today's dollars?
   a. 5%
   b. 10%
   c. 15%
6. Bingo Binks's portfolio earned an 8% average compound annual return over an 8-year period. The average compound annual inflation rate during this period was 4%. Bingo's portfolio was worth $15,000 at the beginning of the period. At the end of the period, what was the portfolio worth, expressed in beginning-of-period dollars?
7. Kirby Higbe started the year with investments valued at $11,500. At the end of two years those same investments were worth $16,000. During the same time period the price index rose from 210 to 250. What was Kirby's annual real return over the 2-year period?
8. How are economy-wide inflation rates calculated? Are all consumers affected equally by the increase in overall prices measured by the price index? Explain.
9. Assume that your portfolio grows 9% in value per year and annual inflation is 5%. How many years will it take for the nominal value of your portfolio to triple? How many years will it take for the real value of your portfolio to triple?

10. Why is it reasonable to assume that rational investors will build an expected inflation premium into the returns they require from their investments?

11. In the late 1970s and early 1980s, a period of unexpectedly high inflation, Happy Felsch referred to long-term bonds issued by U.S. corporations and the Treasury as "certificates of confiscation." Why would Happy make such a comment?

12. Also in the late 1970s and early 1980s, there was considerable discussion concerning the "quality" of corporate earnings. Straight-line depreciation and the first-in–first-out (FIFO) inventory valuation methods were often cited as the causes of "poor quality" earnings. Further, it was argued that these accounting methods effectively resulted in tax overpayments. Discuss the reasons for both contentions.

13. From the perspective of after-tax returns, typically what is the problem with fully inflation-indexed securities?

14. The returns on bonds have been found to be negatively correlated with unexpected inflation. Explain why this relationship should be expected to occur.

15. Common stocks, in general, do not appear to be effective hedges against either expected or unexpected short-run inflation. Explain why the stocks of some companies might be better hedges against inflation than the stocks of other companies.

Endnotes

1. A number of authorities prefer "deflators" derived from gross domestic product figures, but such indices have not received the publicity accorded the Consumer Price Index.

2. In 1996, a commission headed by former White House chief economist Barry Boskin examined the accuracy of the CPI in measuring inflation. The Boskin commission estimated that the CPI overstates inflation by roughly 1% to 1.5% per year. This conclusion generated considerable controversy. How it will affect public policy remains to be seen. For a summary of the report, see Michael J. Boskin, "Prisoner of Faulty Statistics," *The Wall Street Journal,* December 5, 1996, p. A20. See also the entire issue of the May/June 1997 Federal Reserve Bank of St. Louis Review, which is devoted to the Boskin report and its implications. Also see this chapter's Money Matters box.

3. Here *real return* refers to the increase (or decrease) in purchasing power that the investor has received as a result of making a particular investment.

4. The Fisher model is named after its creator, Irving Fisher, who derived the model in *The Theory of Interest* (New York: Macmillan, 1930).

5. This error will be larger for higher rates of inflation. Thus, in countries with "hyperinflation," the quick method will have a substantial amount of error associated with it. For example, if the nominal return is 110% and the inflation rate is 100%, then the true real return is 5% but the quick method will indicate that it is twice as large, 10%.

6. The model given in Equation (6.7) can be written more precisely as $E(NR) \cong E(RR) + E(CCL) + IRP$ where *IRP* denotes inflation risk premium. Investors will demand to be compensated not only for the expected inflation rate but also for the risk of an uncertain inflation rate. Thus, if the expected rate of inflation is 4% and a given security is to provide investors with an expected real return of 6%, then the security must be priced in the marketplace so that its expected nominal return is more than 10%, such as 10.5% if the inflation risk premium is .5%. Similar adjustments can also be made to Equations (6.3) through (6.5) by replacing *RR* with *RR + IRP*. It should be noted that the Fisher effect reflected in Equations (6.6) and (6.7) tends to underestimate the expected rate of inflation; see Robert G. Schwebach and Thomas S. Zorn, "A Simple Derivation of the Fisher Equation under Uncertainty," *Journal of Financial Education,* 23 (Fall 1997): 84–87, and the references cited therein.

7. There apparently are periods of time when such securities have an expected real return that is relatively large. For example, in the 1981 to 1986 period, Treasury bill returns actually exceeded the rate of change in the CPI by more than 5%. The implication is that investors expected a relatively large positive real return during the latter part of the period.

8. More specifically, long-term borrowers are likely to gain somewhat more than short-term borrowers when actual inflation exceeds expected inflation and to lose somewhat more when actual inflation falls below expectations. Similarly, long-term lenders are likely to lose somewhat more than short-term lenders when actual inflation exceeds expectations and to gain somewhat more when actual inflation falls below expectations.

9. To see that 4.3% is the investor's new real rate of return, begin with a purchase price of $103. Given cash inflows each year for eight years of $4.20 in real dollars and a final payment after nine years of $109.20 in real dollars, the internal rate of return of the investment equals 4.3%.

10. A more accurate determination of the expected rate of inflation would involve comparison of the yields on two stripped bonds. For more on determining expected inflation rates by comparing Treasury inflation-indexed securities with conventional Treasury securities, see Jeffrey M. Wrase, "Inflation-Indexed Bonds: How Do They Work?" *Federal Reserve Bank of Philadelphia Business Review* (July–August 1997): 3–16.

11. An extreme form of rationing might occur if lenders simply refuse to make those kinds of loans that are subject to ceilings when inflationary expectations are high.

12. The correlation coefficient from the 50-year period of 1949 to 1998 is –.30. Similar results occur when monthly data is used. Hence, some people argue that there is an inverse relationship between historical rates of inflation and stock returns.

13. Interestingly, there appears to be a significantly negative relationship between the real return on stocks and the rate of inflation. That is, higher rates of infla-

tion seem to be accompanied by lower real stock returns. A number of explanations (some of them conflicting) have been offered to account for this observation. For a survey, see David P. Ely and Kenneth J. Robinson, "The Stock Market and Inflation: A Synthesis of the Theory and Evidence," *Federal Reserve Bank of Dallas Economic Review* (March 1989): 17–29.

14. Jacob Boudoukh and Matthew Richardson, "Stock Returns and Inflation: A Long-Horizon Perspective," *American Economic Review,* 83, no. 5 (December 1993): 1346–1355.

15. Similar results were obtained when *expected* inflation rates were compared with subsequent stock returns (because expected inflation rates cannot be observed, the authors cleverly estimated such expectations). The results are consistent with those comparing *actual* inflation rates and stock returns. That is, there was a positive relationship over long periods of time but not over short periods.

CHAPTER

The Portfolio Selection Problem

Most securities available for investment have uncertain outcomes and are thus risky. The basic problem facing each investor is to determine which particular risky securities to own. Because a portfolio is a collection of securities, this problem is equivalent to the investor selecting the optimal portfolio from a set of possible portfolios. Hence, this situation is often referred to as the *portfolio selection problem*. One solution to this problem was put forth in 1952 by Harry M. Markowitz in a landmark paper that is generally viewed as the origin of *modern investment theory*.

holding period

Markowitz's approach begins by assuming that an investor has a given sum of money to invest at the present time. This money will be invested for a particular length of time known as the investor's **holding period.** At the end of the holding period, the investor will sell the securities that were purchased at the beginning of the period and then will either spend the proceeds on consumption or reinvest the proceeds in various securities (or do some of both). At this point, Markowitz's approach can be reapplied to those proceeds that are to be reinvested. Thus, this approach is for a single period, where the beginning of the period is denoted $t = 0$ and the end of the period is denoted $t = 1$. At $t = 0$, the investor must decide which particular securities to purchase and hold until $t = 1$.[1] Then, at $t = 1$, the investor must again decide which particular securities to hold until $t = 2$, and so on.

expected holding period return

In making this decision at $t = 0$, the investor should recognize that security returns (and thus portfolio returns) in the forthcoming holding period are unknown. However, the investor could estimate the **expected holding period returns** (or expected returns) on the various securities under consideration and then invest in the one with the highest expected return. (Methods for estimating expected returns are discussed in Chapter 15.) According to Markowitz, this decision would generally be unwise because the typical investor, although wanting "returns to be high," also wants "returns to be as certain as possible." Thus, in seeking to both maximize expected return and minimize uncertainty (that is, **risk**), the investor has two conflicting objectives that must be balanced against each other when making the purchase decision at $t = 0$. The Markowitz approach gives full consideration to both of these objectives.

risk

One interesting consequence of having these two conflicting objectives is that the investor should diversify by purchasing not just one security but several. The ensuing discussion of Markowitz's analytical approach to investing begins by defining initial and terminal wealth.

7.1   Initial and Terminal Wealth

In Equation (1.1) it was noted that the one-period holding period return on a security could be calculated as

$$\text{Return} = \frac{\text{End-of-period wealth} - \text{Beginning-of-period wealth}}{\text{Beginning-of-period wealth}} \tag{1.1}$$

where beginning-of-period wealth is the purchase price of one unit of the security at $t = 0$ (for example, one share of a firm's common stock) and end-of-period wealth is the market value of the unit at $t = 1$, along with the value of any cash paid to the owner of the security between $t = 0$ and $t = 1$. Here any cash inflows, such as dividends, are assumed to be paid at the end of the period.

7.1.1   DETERMINING THE RATE OF RETURN ON A PORTFOLIO

Because a portfolio is a collection of securities, its return, r_P, can be calculated in a similar manner:

$$r_P = \frac{W_1 - W_0}{W_0} \tag{7.1}$$

Here W_0 denotes the aggregate purchase price at $t = 0$ of the securities contained in the portfolio; W_1 denotes the aggregate market value of the securities at $t = 1$, as well as the aggregate cash received between $t = 0$ and $t = 1$ from owning these securities. Again, any cash flows associated with the portfolio are assumed to take place at either $t = 0$ or $t = 1$. Equation (7.1) can be manipulated algebraically, resulting in

$$W_0(1 + r_P) = W_1 \tag{7.2}$$

initial wealth
terminal wealth

Based on Equation (7.2), beginning-of-period or **initial wealth,** W_0, multiplied by (1 plus the rate of return) on the portfolio equals end-of-period or **terminal wealth,** W_1.

Earlier it was noted that the investor must make a decision regarding what portfolio to purchase at $t = 0$. In doing so, the investor does not know what the value of W_1 will be for most of the alternative portfolios under consideration because the investor does not know what the return will be for most of these portfolios.[2] According to Markowitz, the investor should view the return associated with any one of these portfolios as what is called in statistics a **random variable;** such variables can be "described" by their moments, two of which are **expected** (or mean) **value** and **standard deviation.**[3]

random variable
expected value
standard deviation

Markowitz asserts that investors should base their portfolio decisions solely on expected returns and standard deviations. That is, the investor should estimate the expected return and standard deviation of each portfolio and then choose the "best" one on the basis of the relative magnitudes of these two parameters. The intuition behind this assertion is actually quite straightforward. Expected return can be viewed as a measure of the potential reward associated with any portfolio, and standard deviation can be viewed as a measure of the risk associated with any portfolio. Once each portfolio has been examined in terms of its potential rewards and risks, the investor can identify the one portfolio that is most desirable to him or her.

7.1.2   AN EXAMPLE

Consider the two alternative portfolios, *A* and *B,* in Table 7.1. Portfolio *A* has an expected annual return of 8% and portfolio *B* has an expected annual return of 12%. Assuming that the investor has initial wealth of $100,000 and a one-year holding period,

TABLE 7.1 Comparison of Terminal Wealth Levels for Two Hypothetical Portfolios

Level of Terminal Wealth	Percent Chance of Being below This Level of Terminal Wealth	
	Portfolio A[a]	Portfolio B[b]
$70,000	0	2
80,000	0	5
90,000	4	14
100,000	21	27
110,000	57	46
120,000	88	66
130,000	99	82

Note: Initial wealth is assumed to be $100,000, and both portfolios are assumed to have normally distributed returns.

[a]The expected return and standard deviation of A are 8% and 10%, respectively.

[b]The expected return and standard deviation of B are 12% and 20%, respectively.

the expected levels of terminal wealth associated with A and B are $108,000 and $112,000, respectively. It would appear, then, that B is the more desirable portfolio. However, A and B have annual standard deviations of 10% and 20%, respectively. Table 7.1 shows that there is a 2% chance that the investor will end up with terminal wealth of $70,000 or less if he or she purchases B, whereas there is virtually no chance that the investor's terminal wealth will be less than $70,000 if A is purchased. Similarly, B has a 5% chance of being worth less than $80,000, whereas A again has almost no chance. Continuing, B has a 14% chance of being worth less than $90,000, whereas A has only a 4% chance. Going on, B has a 27% chance of being worth less than $100,000, whereas A has only a 21% chance. Because the investor has initial wealth of $100,000, according to this last observation, there is a greater probability of having a negative return if B (27%) is purchased instead of A (21%). Overall, Table 7.1 shows that A is less risky than B, meaning that on this dimension A would be more desirable. The ultimate decision about whether to purchase A or B will depend on the investor's attitude toward risk and return.

7.2 Nonsatiation and Risk Aversion

7.2.1 NONSATIATION

nonsatiation

Two assumptions are implicit in this discussion of the portfolio selection problem. First, it is assumed that investors, when given a choice between two otherwise identical portfolios, will always choose the one with the higher level of expected return. More fundamentally, an assumption of **nonsatiation** is made in the Markowitz approach, in which investors are assumed to always prefer higher levels of terminal wealth to lower levels of terminal wealth. After all, higher levels of terminal wealth allow the investor to spend more on consumption at $t = 1$ (or in the more distant future). Thus, given two portfolios with the same standard deviation, the investor will choose the portfolio with the higher expected return. However, it is not quite so obvious what the investor will do when he or she has to choose between two portfolios with the same level of expected return but different levels of standard deviation. At this point the second assumption enters the discussion.

7.2.2 RISK AVERSION

risk-averse investor

It is assumed that investors are **risk-averse,** which means they will choose the portfolio with the smaller standard deviation.[4] What does it mean to say that an investor is risk-averse? It means that the investor, when given the choice, will not want to take *fair gambles* (or fair bets), where a fair gamble is one that has an expected payoff of zero. For example, consider flipping a coin, with heads meaning you win $5 and tails meaning you lose $5. Because the coin has a 50:50 chance of being heads or tails, the expected payoff is $0 [= (.5 × $5) + (.5 × −$5)]. Accordingly, the risk-averse investor will avoid this gamble. The concept of investor utility helps explain why.

7.3 Utility

utility

Economists use the term **utility** to quantify the relative enjoyment or satisfaction that people derive from economic activity such as work, consumption, or investment. Satisfying activities generate positive utility; dissatisfying activities produce negative utility (or disutility). Because tastes (or preferences) differ among individuals, one person may experience more utility from a particular activity than another person does. People are presumed to be rational and to allocate their resources (such as time and money) in ways that maximize their own utilities. The Markowitz portfolio selection problem can be viewed as an effort to maximize the expected utility associated with the investor's terminal wealth.

7.3.1 MARGINAL UTILITY

The exact relationship between utility and wealth is called the investor's *utility of wealth function.* Under the assumption of nonsatiation, all investors prefer more wealth to less wealth. (Money is indeed assumed to buy happiness.) Every extra dollar of wealth enhances an investor's utility. But by how much?

marginal utility

Each investor has a unique utility of wealth function. As a result, each investor may derive a unique increment of utility from an extra dollar of wealth. That is, the **marginal utility** of wealth may differ among investors. Further, that marginal utility may depend on the level of wealth that the investor possesses before receiving the extra dollar. (A rich investor may value an extra dollar of wealth less than a poor investor does.)

A common assumption is that investors experience diminishing marginal utility of wealth. Each extra dollar of wealth always provides positive additional utility, but the added utility produced by each extra dollar becomes successively smaller. Figure 7.1(a) illustrates the utility of wealth function of an investor. Higher levels of wealth (read off the horizontal axis) produce higher levels of utility (read off the vertical axis). The assumption of nonsatiation requires that the utility of wealth function is always positively sloped no matter what the level of wealth. However, this utility of wealth function is concave (it is bowed downward). As wealth increases, the corresponding increase in utility becomes smaller. That is, marginal utility diminishes. An investor with diminishing marginal utility is necessarily risk-averse. This risk-averse investor is unwilling to accept a fair bet. The utility of wealth function explains that preference.

Smith has been offered the choice of two investments. One is to invest $100,000 and earn a certain return of 5%. The expected terminal wealth of this investment is $105,000. The alternative investment also requires an outlay of $100,000. It has a 50% probability of returning a $10,000 gain (a 10% return) and a 50% probability of returning only the

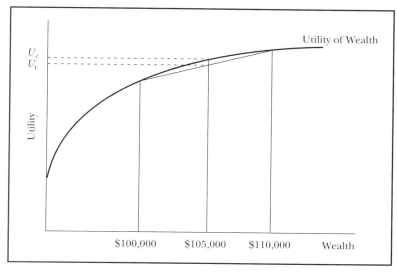

(a) Utility of Wealth

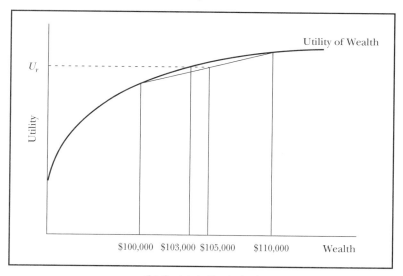

(b) Certainty Equivalent

FIGURE 7.1 Investor's Utility of Wealth Function and Certainty Equivalent Wealth

original investment (a 0% return). The expected terminal wealth of the risky investment is the same as that of the certain investment: $105,000 (= .5 × $100,000 + .5 × $110,000), or a 5% expected return. Which investment will Smith prefer?

The answer is shown in Figure 7.1(a). The utility associated with the certain investment is found by moving up from the terminal wealth axis at $105,000 to the utility of wealth function and then moving across to the utility axis. The utility of the certain investment is identified as U_c. The expected utility of the risky investment is found by connecting the utility of the upper and lower possible outcomes on the investment ($100,000 and $110,000) with a straight line and then moving up from the expected terminal wealth of the investment ($105,000) on the terminal wealth axis to that line and then moving across to the utility axis. The expected utility of the risky investment is labeled U_r. Because U_c is greater than U_r, Smith will choose the certain investment.[5] This conclusion can be generalized for any pair of certain and risky investments with the same expected terminal wealth: A risk-averse investor will derive greater satisfaction from the certain investment than the risky investment.

The reason for this preference is straightforward. A risk-averse investor displays diminishing marginal utility of wealth. Thus, the negative utility (or disutility) associated with a $1 (or $5,000) loss is more than the positive utility of earning $1 (or $5,000). That is, at any point along a concave utility of wealth function, if one moves $1 (or $5,000) to the right, the corresponding increase in utility is smaller than the decline in utility if one were to move $1 (or $5,000) to the left.

7.3.2 CERTAINTY EQUIVALENTS AND RISK PREMIUMS

certainty equivalent

Figure 7.1(b) introduces two additional concepts. Smith is given the chance to enter into the same risky investment described in the previous example. Moving horizontally from the utility axis at the expected utility of the risky investment to the utility of wealth function and then moving down to the terminal wealth axis indicates the **certainty equivalent** wealth associated with this risky investment. In this case that wealth is $103,000. This value is the amount of terminal wealth that, if offered with certainty, would provide the same amount of expected utility as the risky investment. Smith will be indifferent to a $100,000 investment that offers a terminal wealth of $103,000 with certainty (a 3% certain return) and this risky investment, with an expected terminal wealth of $105,000 (a 5% risky return). The additional $2,000 in expected terminal wealth (or additional 2% in expected return) offered by the risky investment over the

risk premium

certain investment is called a **risk premium:** It is the expected increase in terminal wealth (or expected return) over the certain investment required to compensate the investor for the risk incurred. For a risky investment with a given expected terminal wealth, investors who are more risk-averse will have lower certainty equivalents and commensurately higher risk premiums than will investors who are less risk-averse.

Risk-averse investors are willing to forgo some expected terminal wealth (they will accept lower expected returns) in exchange for less risk. Thus, various combinations of expected terminal wealth (or expected returns) and risk will produce the same level of expected utility for an investor. This relationship leads to the concept of indifference curves.

7.4 Indifference Curves

indifference curve

An **indifference curve** represents a set of risk and expected return combinations that provide an investor with the same amount of utility. The investor is indifferent about the risk–expected return combinations on the same indifference curve. Because indifference curves indicate an investor's preferences for risk and expected return, they can be drawn on a two-dimensional figure where the horizontal axis indicates risk as measured by standard deviation (denoted σ_P) and the vertical axis indicates reward as measured by expected return (denoted $\bar{r}_P$).

Figure 7.2 shows several indifference curves a hypothetical risk-averse investor might possess. Each curved line indicates one indifference curve for the investor and represents all combinations of portfolios that provide the investor with a given level of expected utility. For example, the investor with the indifference curves in Figure 7.2 would find portfolios A and B (the same two portfolios shown in Table 7.1) equally desirable, even though they have different expected returns and standard deviations, because they both lie on the same indifference curve, I_2. Portfolio B has a higher standard

Behavioral Finance

 The bedrock on which theories of risky security valuation rest is the presumed existence of rational investors who respond in a predictable manner to the opportunities for gain and the risks of loss. As the text discusses, these investors are assumed to assess potential investments on the basis of expected returns and standard deviations that are derived from estimates of the investments' probability distributions of returns. Furthermore, the investors' estimates are assumed to exhibit no systematic biases relative to the "true" probability distributions. That is, investors do not consistently make mistakes in one direction or another when examining potential investments.

The view of investors as objective decision-makers has traditionally gone unchallenged in the academic world. Although many professional investors have argued that investing is dominated by the emotions of fear and greed, their opinions have been dismissed by many academics as anecdotal and self-serving. More recently, however, a school of thought has developed among certain academics that argues that investors may not deal with risky choices in a totally rational manner. This reasoning is based on a branch of psychology known as *cognitive psychology,* which studies human beings' capacity for perception and judgment.

Applied to the study of economic decision making, and investments in particular, cognitive psychology draws some intriguing conclusions. Most fundamentally, people do not seem to be consistent in how they treat economically equivalent choices if the choices are presented in significantly different contexts. These differences are referred to as *framing effects.* Two prominent cognitive psychology researchers, Daniel Kahneman and Amos Tversky, cite a simple example of framing effects (see "The Psychology of Preferences," *Scientific American,* January 1982).

Suppose you are walking to a Broadway play carrying a ticket that cost $100. On reaching the theater you discover that you have lost your ticket. Would you pay another $100 for a ticket at the door? Now suppose that you were planning to buy the ticket at the door. On arriving you find that you have lost $100 on the way. Would you still buy a ticket?

The economic consequences of these two situations are identical. You have lost $100 and now must decide whether to spend another $100. Interestingly, however, most people would buy a ticket in the second case but not in the first. People appear to "frame" the choices differently. They treat the loss of cash differently from the loss of a ticket.

In terms of investing, framing effects may cause deviations from rational decision making. For example, it seems that people react differently to the prospects of large gains as opposed to large losses. That is, investors are assumed to choose a riskier investment over a less risky one only if the expected return of the riskier investment is greater than that of the less risky one. (This trait is known as risk aversion, as discussed earlier in this chapter.) This assumption seems to hold well for situations involving large gains. For example, consider a situation in which you have invested in a start-up company and have a 90% chance of receiving $1 million and a 10% chance of receiving nothing. The expected payoff is $900,000 [= (.9 × $1 million) + (.1 × $0)]. If somebody offered to buy you out for $850,000, most likely you would accept the offer because it has nearly the same expected payoff but much less risk. That is, you would be exhibiting risk-averse behavior.

Now, however, consider a situation involving large losses. Suppose that you had invested in another start-up company. Things are going poorly, and if nothing changes there is a 90% chance of losing $1 million but a 10% chance that things might work out well enough to not lose (or gain) anything. The expected loss is $900,000 [= (.9 × −$1 million) + (.1 × $0)]. Another investor offers to take over the company if you pay him or her $850,000, resulting in a certain $850,000 loss. Most people would reject the offer and choose to remain with the risky option even though it has a lower expected value (−$900,000 versus −$850,000). In a situation involving large expected losses, people do not seem to exhibit risk-averse behavior—a framing effect.

People also seem to overestimate the probability of unlikely events occurring and to underestimate the probability of moderately likely events occurring. These traits may explain the popularity of lotteries but may also have direct ramifications for the pricing of investments when the chances of success are low—such as with bonds and stocks of bankrupt companies, start-up companies, and options whose strike prices are far above the underlying securities' prices.

Framing effects may also be involved in the observed tendency of investors to overreact to good and bad news (see Chapter 13). That is, some studies suggest that investors bid up the prices of companies reporting unexpectedly good earnings beyond the amount fairly warranted by the improved earnings. The converse seems to occur for companies reporting unexpectedly poor earnings.

Are the observations of cognitive psychologists relevant to the study of financial markets? Do these framing effects produce market anomalies that present exploitable investment opportunities or even undermine commonly accepted theories of security valuation? Or are these framing effects merely interesting stories whose impacts are overwhelmed by the sophistication and profit motive of avaricious investors? Certainly, investors as a whole are far from irrational because large and persistent disparities between "fair" values and market values are difficult to find. Nevertheless, the behavioral observations of cognitive psychologists are likely to provide a better understanding of how investors make decisions and to help explain certain apparent market inefficiencies. Indeed, it has opened up a whole new field known as *behavioral finance.*

deviation (20%) than portfolio *A* (10%) and is therefore less desirable on that dimension. However, exactly offsetting this loss in desirability is the gain in desirability provided by the higher expected return of *B* (12%) relative to *A* (8%).

Because all portfolios that lie on a given indifference curve are equally desirable to the investor, by implication *indifference curves cannot intersect.* Consider two curves that do intersect, such as those shown in Figure 7.3. The point of intersection is represented by *X*. Remember that all the portfolios on I_1 are equally desirable. This means they are all as desirable as *X*, because *X* is on I_1. Similarly, all the portfolios on I_2 are

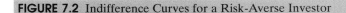

FIGURE 7.2 Indifference Curves for a Risk-Averse Investor

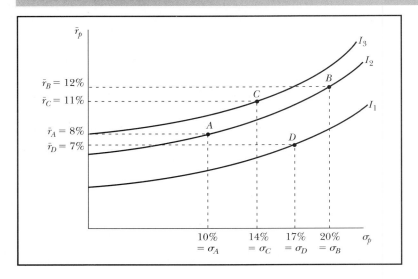

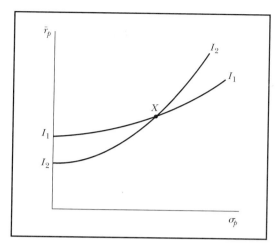

FIGURE 7.3 Intersecting
Indifference Curves

equally desirable, and are as desirable as *X,* because *X* is also on I_2. Given that *X* is on
both indifference curves, all the portfolios on I_1 must be as desirable as those on I_2. But
now there is a contradiction, because I_1 and I_2 are supposed to represent different
levels of utility. Thus, in order for there to be no contradiction, these curves cannot
intersect.

Although the investor represented in Figure 7.2 would find portfolios *A* and *B*
equally desirable, he or she would find portfolio *C,* with an expected return of 11% and
a standard deviation of 14%, preferable to both of them. This preference is because
portfolio *C* happens to be on indifference curve I_3, which is located to the "northwest"
of I_2. *C* has a sufficiently larger expected return relative to *A,* which offsets its higher
standard deviation and makes it more desirable than *A.* Equivalently, *C* has a sufficiently smaller standard deviation than *B,* which offsets its smaller expected return and
makes it more desirable than *B.* This comparison leads to the second important feature
of indifference curves: A risk-averse investor will find any portfolio lying on an indifference curve "farther northwest" more desirable (it will provide greater expected utility) than any portfolio lying on an indifference curve "not as far northwest."

Note that *an investor has an infinite number of indifference curves.* Hence, whenever
two indifference curves have been plotted on a graph, it is possible to plot a third indifference curve that lies between them. As can be seen in Figure 7.4, given indifference
curves I_1 and I_2, it is possible to graph a third curve, *I**, between them. It also implies
that another indifference curve can be plotted above I_2 and yet another below I_1.

How does an investor determine what his or her indifference curves look like?
After all, each investor has a map of indifference curves that, given the previously
noted features, is unique. One method, discussed in Chapter 17, involves presenting the
investor with hypothetical portfolios and their expected returns and standard deviations.[6] The investor would be asked to choose the most desirable portfolio. After the
selection is made, the shape and location of the investor's indifference curves can be
estimated because it is presumed that the investor acted as if he or she had explicit
knowledge of his or her own indifference curves in making the choice, even though
those indifference curves would not have been directly referenced.

In summary, every investor has an indifference map representing his or her preferences for expected returns and standard deviations.[7] Hence, an investor should determine the expected return and standard deviation for each potential portfolio, plot

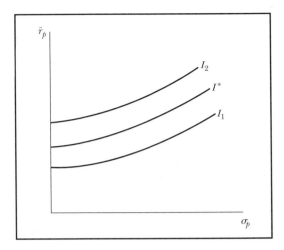

FIGURE 7.4 Plotting a Third Indifference Curve between Two Others

them on a graph such as that shown in Figure 7.2, and then select the portfolio that lies on the indifference curve "farthest northwest." Based on the set of the four potential portfolios in this example—*A, B, C,* and *D*—the investor should select *C.*

The two assumptions of nonsatiation and risk aversion cause indifference curves to be positively sloped and convex.[8] Although it is assumed that all investors are risk-averse, it is not assumed that they have identical degrees of risk aversion. Some investors may be highly risk-averse, whereas others may be only slightly so. Consequently, different investors have different maps of indifference curves. Figure 7.5 displays maps for three investors who are (a) highly risk-averse, (b) moderately risk-averse, and (c) slightly risk-averse. As the figure shows, the more risk-averse an investor is, the more steeply sloped the indifference curves will be.

7.5 Calculating Expected Returns and Standard Deviations for Portfolios

The previous section introduced the portfolio selection problem that every investor faces. It also introduced the investment approach of Markowitz as a method of solving that problem. With this approach, an investor should evaluate alternative portfolios on the basis of their expected returns and standard deviations using indifference curves. In the case of a risk-averse investor, the portfolio on the indifference curve that is farthest northwest would be selected for investment. However, certain questions remain unanswered. In particular, how does the investor calculate the expected return and standard deviation for a portfolio?

7.5.1 EXPECTED RETURNS

With the Markowitz approach to investing, the focus of the investor is on terminal (or end-of-period) wealth, W_1. That is, in deciding which portfolio to purchase with his or her initial (or beginning-of-period) wealth, W_0, the investor should focus on the effect of the various portfolios on W_1. This effect can be measured by the expected return and standard deviation of each portfolio.

As mentioned previously, a portfolio is a collection of securities. The expected return and standard deviation of a portfolio depend on the expected return and standard

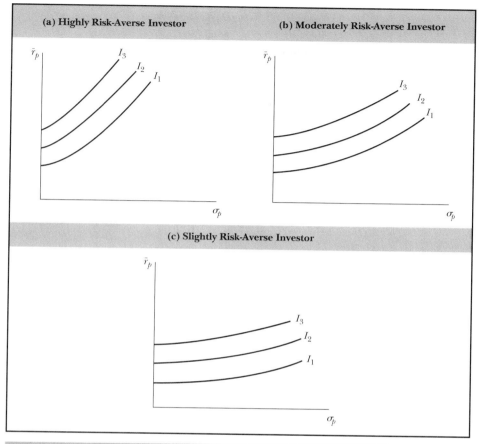

FIGURE 7.5 Indifference Curves for Three Types of Risk-Averse Investors

deviation of each security in the portfolio. The amount invested in each security is also important.

In order to show how the expected return on a portfolio depends on both the expected return on the individual securities and the amount invested in the securities, consider the three-security portfolio shown in Table 7.2(a). Assume that the investor has a one-year holding period and for this period the expected returns on Able, Baker, and Charlie stock are estimated to be 16.2%, 24.6%, and 22.8%, respectively. The investor has estimated the end-of-period values of these three stocks to be, respectively, $46.48 [= $40 × (1 + .162)], $43.61 [= $35 × (1 + .246)], and $76.14 [= $62 × (1 + .228)].[9] Furthermore, assume that this investor has initial wealth of $17,200.

Using End-of-Period Values

The expected return on this portfolio can be calculated in several ways, all of which give the same result. Consider the method shown in Table 7.2(b). This method involves calculating the expected end-of-period value of the portfolio and then using Equation (1.1) to calculate the return, as was shown earlier. First the initial portfolio value (W_0) is subtracted from the expected end-of-period value of the portfolio (W_1), and then

TABLE 7.2 Calculating the Expected Return on a Portfolio

(a) Security and Portfolio Values

Security Name	Number of Shares in Portfolio	Initial Market Price per Share	Total Investment	Proportion of Initial Market Value of Portfolio
Able Co.	100	$40	$4,000	$4,000/$17,200 = .2325
Baker Co.	200	35	7,000	7,000/$17,200 = .4070
Charlie Co.	100	62	6,200	6,200/$17,200 = .3605

Initial market value of portfolio = W_0 = $17,200   Sum of proportions = 1.0000

(b) Calculating the Expected Return for a Portfolio Using End-of-Period Values

Security Name	Number of Shares in Portfolio	Expected End-of-Period Value per Share	Aggregate Expected End-of-Period Value
Able Co.	100	$46.48	$46.48 × 100 = $4,648
Baker Co.	200	43.61	43.61 × 200 = 8,722
Charlie Co.	100	76.14	76.14 × 100 = 7,614

Expected end-of-period value of portfolio = W_1 = $20,984
Portfolio expected return = $\bar{r}_p$ = ($20,984 − $17,200)/$17,200 = 22.00%

(c) Calculating the Expected Return for a Portfolio Using Security Expected Returns

Security Name	Proportion of Initial Market Value of Portfolio	Security Expected Returns	Contribution to Portfolio Expected Return
Able Co.	.2325	16.2%	.2325 × 16.2% = 3.77%
Baker Co.	.4070	24.6	.4070 × 24.6 = 10.01
Charlie Co.	.3605	22.8	.3605 × 22.8 = 8.22

Portfolio expected return = $\bar{r}_p$ = 22.00%

this difference is divided by the initial portfolio value (W_0), the result of which is the portfolio's expected return. Although the example shown in Table 7.2(b) involves three securities, the procedure can be generalized to any number of securities.

Using Security Expected Returns

An alternative method for calculating the expected return on this portfolio is shown in Table 7.2(c). This procedure involves calculating the expected return on a portfolio as the weighted average of the expected returns on its component securities. The relative market values of the securities in the portfolio are used as weights. The general rule for calculating the expected return on a portfolio consisting of N securities is

$$\bar{r}_p = \sum_{i=1}^{N} X_i \bar{r}_i \tag{7.3a}$$

$$= X_1 \bar{r}_1 + X_2 \bar{r}_2 + \cdots + X_N \bar{r}_N \tag{7.3b}$$

where

$\bar{r}_p$ = the expected return of the portfolio

Σ = summation sign

X_i = the proportion of the portfolio's initial value invested in security i

$\bar{r}_i$ = the expected return of security i,

N = the number of securities in the portfolio[10]

expected return vector

An **expected return vector** can be used to calculate the expected return for any portfolio formed from the N securities. This vector consists of one column of numbers, where the entry in row i contains the expected return of security i. In the previous example, the expected return vector was estimated by the investor to be

$$\begin{matrix} Row\ 1 \\ Row\ 2 \\ Row\ 3 \end{matrix} \begin{bmatrix} 16.2\% \\ 24.6\% \\ 22.8\% \end{bmatrix}$$

where the entries in rows 1, 2, and 3 indicate the expected returns for securities Able, Baker, and Charlie, respectively.

Because a portfolio's expected return is a weighted average of the expected returns of its securities, the contribution of each security to the portfolio's expected return depends on its expected return and its proportionate share of the initial portfolio's market value. Nothing else is relevant. It follows from Equation (7.3a) that an investor who simply wants the greatest possible expected return should hold one security: the one he or she considers to have the greatest expected return. Very few investors do this, and very few investment advisers would counsel such an extreme policy. Instead, investors should diversify; their portfolios should include more than one security because diversification can reduce risk, as measured by standard deviation.

7.5.2 STANDARD DEVIATIONS

A useful measure of risk should somehow take into account the probabilities of various possible bad outcomes and their associated magnitudes. Instead of measuring the probability of a number of different possible outcomes, the measure of risk should somehow estimate the extent to which the actual outcome is likely to diverge from the expected outcome. Standard deviation is such a measure because it is an estimate of the likely divergence of an *actual* return from an *expected* return.

It may seem that any single measure of risk would provide at best a crude summary of bad possibilities. But in the common situation in which a portfolio's prospects are being assessed, standard deviation may be a good measure of the degree of uncertainty. The clearest example arises when the **probability distribution** for a portfolio's returns can be approximated by the familiar bell-shaped curve known as a **normal distribution.** This is often considered a plausible assumption for analyzing returns on diversified portfolios when the holding period being studied is relatively short (say, a quarter or less).

probability distribution
normal distribution

An obvious question about standard deviation as a measure of risk is, Why count "happy" surprises (those above the expected return) at all in a measure of risk? Why not just consider the deviations *below* the expected return? Measures that do so have merit. However, the results will be the same if the probability distribution is symmetric, as is the normal distribution. Why? Because the left side of a symmetric distribution is a mirror image of the right side. Thus, a list of portfolios ordered on the basis of "downside risk" will not differ from one ordered on the basis of standard deviation if returns are normally distributed.[11]

Formula for Standard Deviation

Just how is the standard deviation of a portfolio calculated? Unfortunately, it is not simply a weighted average of the standard deviations of the securities in the portfolio. Although it includes these standard deviations, it also takes into consideration how the various security returns tend to covary with each other, as will be explained shortly. For the three-security portfolio consisting of Able, Baker, and Charlie, the formula is

$$\sigma_p = \left[\sum_{i=1}^{3} \sum_{j=1}^{3} X_i X_j \sigma_{ij} \right]^{1/2} \tag{7.4}$$

covariance

where σ_{ij} denotes the **covariance** of the returns between security i and security j.

Covariance

Covariance is a statistical measure of the relationship between two random variables. That is, it is a measure of how two random variables, such as the returns on securities i and j, "move together." A positive value for covariance indicates that the securities' returns tend to move in the same direction; for example, a better-than-expected return for one security is likely to occur along with a better-than-expected return for the other. A negative covariance indicates a tendency for the returns to offset one another; for example, a better-than-expected return for one security is likely to occur along with a worse-than-expected return for the other. A relatively small or zero value for the covariance indicates that there is little or no relationship between the returns for the two securities.

Correlation

Closely related to covariance is the statistical measure known as correlation. In fact, the covariance between two random variables is equal to the correlation between the two random variables times the product of their standard deviations:

$$\sigma_{ij} = \rho_{ij} \sigma_i \sigma_j \tag{7.5}$$

correlation coefficient

where ρ_{ij} (the Greek letter *rho*) denotes the **correlation coefficient** between the return on security i and the return on security j. The correlation coefficient rescales the covariance to facilitate comparison with corresponding values for other pairs of random variables. Correlation coefficients always lie between -1 and $+1$. A value of -1 represents perfect negative correlation, and a value of $+1$ represents perfect positive correlation. Most cases lie between these two extreme values.

Figure 7.6(a) presents a scatter diagram for the returns on hypothetical securities A and B when the correlation between these two securities is perfectly positive. Note how all the points lie precisely on a straight upward-sloping line. This slope indicates that when one of the two securities has a relatively high return, so will the other. Similarly, when one of the two securities has a relatively low return, so will the other.

Alternatively, the returns on the two securities will have a perfectly negative correlation when the scatter diagram shows the points on a straight downward-sloping line, as in Figure 7.6(b). In such a case the returns on the two securities move opposite each other. When one security has a relatively high return, the other has a relatively low return.

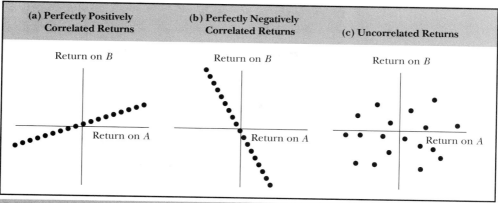

(a) Perfectly Positively Correlated Returns

Return on *B*

Return on *A*

(b) Perfectly Negatively Correlated Returns

Return on *B*

Return on *A*

(c) Uncorrelated Returns

Return on *B*

Return on *A*

FIGURE 7.6 Returns on Two Securities

A case of special importance arises when the scatter diagram of security returns shows a dispersion that cannot be represented even approximately by an upward-sloping or a downward-sloping line. In such an instance, the returns are uncorrelated; the correlation coefficient is zero. Figure 7.6(c) provides an example. In this situation, when one security has a relatively high return, the other can have a relatively high, low, or average return.

Double Summation

Given an understanding of covariance and correlation, it is important to understand how the *double summation* indicated in Equation (7.4) is computed. Although there are many ways of computing double summation, all of them lead to the same answer. However one method may be more intuitive than the others. It starts with the first summation and sets i at its initial value of 1. Then the second summation is performed for j going from 1 to 3. At this point, i in the first summation is increased by 1, so now $i = 2$. Again the second summation is performed by letting j go from 1 to 3, except that now $i = 2$. Continuing, i in the first summation is again increased by 1, so $i = 3$. Then the second summation is once again performed by letting j go from 1 to 3. At this point, note that i and j are each at their upper limits of 3; the double summation is finished. This process can be shown algebraically as follows:

$$\sigma_p = \left[\sum_{j=1}^{3} X_1 X_j \sigma_{1j} + \sum_{j=1}^{3} X_2 X_j \sigma_{2j} + \sum_{j=1}^{3} X_3 X_j \sigma_{3j} \right]^{1/2} \tag{7.6a}$$

$$= [X_1 X_1 \sigma_{11} + X_1 X_2 \sigma_{12} + X_1 X_3 \sigma_{13}$$
$$+ X_2 X_1 \sigma_{21} + X_2 X_2 \sigma_{22} + X_2 X_3 \sigma_{23} \tag{7.6b}$$
$$+ X_3 X_1 \sigma_{31} + X_3 X_2 \sigma_{32} + X_3 X_3 \sigma_{33}]^{1/2}$$

Each term in the double sum involves the product of the weights for two securities, X_i and X_j, and the covariance between these two securities. Note how there are nine terms to be added together in order to calculate the standard deviation of a portfolio consisting of three securities. It is no coincidence that the number of terms to be added together (9) equals the number of securities squared (3^2). In general, calculating the standard deviation for a portfolio consisting of N securities involves performing the double sum indicated in Equation (7.4) over N securities, thereby involving the addition of N^2 terms:

$$\sigma_p = \left[\sum_{i=1}^{N} \sum_{j=1}^{N} X_i X_j \sigma_{ij} \right]^{1/2} \tag{7.7}$$

An interesting feature of the double sum occurs when the subscripts i and j refer to the same security. In Equation (7.6), this occurs in the first $(X_1 X_1 \sigma_{11})$, fifth $(X_2 X_2 \sigma_{22})$, and ninth $(X_3 X_3 \sigma_{33})$ terms. What does it mean when the subscripts for covariance refer to the same security? For example, consider security 1 (Able) so that $i = j = 1$. Because σ_{11} denotes the covariance of security 1 (Able) with security 1 (Able), Equation (7.5) indicates that:

$$\sigma_{11} = \rho_{11} \sigma_1 \sigma_1 \tag{7.8}$$

Note the correlation of any security with itself, in this case ρ_{11}, is equal to $+1$.[12] Hence, Equation (7.8) reduces to

$$\sigma_{11} = 1 \times \sigma_1 \times \sigma_1$$
$$= \sigma_1^2$$

variance

which is the standard deviation of security 1 squared, known as the **variance** of security 1. Thus, the double sum involves both variance and covariance terms.

Variance–Covariance Matrix

variance–covariance matrix

As an example, consider the following **variance–covariance matrix** for the stocks of Able, Baker, and Charlie:

	Column 1	*Column 2*	*Column 3*
Row 1	146	187	145
Row 2	187	854	104
Row 3	145	104	289

Think of the matrix as the cells in a computer spreadsheet. Each cell is formed by the combination of a specific row and a specific column. The entry in cell (i,j) denotes the covariance between security i and security j. For example, the entry in $(1,3)$ denotes the covariance between the first and third securities, which in this case is 145. The entry in cell (i,i) denotes the variance of security i. For example, the variance of security 2 appears in cell $(2,2)$ and is equal to 854. Using this variance–covariance matrix along with Equation (7.6b), one can compute the standard deviation of any portfolio that consists of investments in Able, Baker, and Charlie. For example, consider the portfolio given in Table 7.2 that had proportions $X_1 = .2325$, $X_2 = .4070$, and $X_3 = .3605$:

$$\sigma_p = [X_1 X_1 \sigma_{11} + X_1 X_2 \sigma_{12} + X_1 X_3 \sigma_{13}$$
$$+ X_2 X_1 \sigma_{21} + X_2 X_2 \sigma_{22} + X_2 X_3 \sigma_{23}$$
$$+ X_3 X_1 \sigma_{31} + X_3 X_2 \sigma_{32} + X_3 X_3 \sigma_{33}]^{1/2}$$
$$= [(.2325 \times .2325 \times 146) + (.2325 \times .4070 \times 187) + (.2325 \times .3605 \times 145)$$
$$+ (.4070 \times .2325 \times 187) + (.4070 \times .4070 \times 854) + (.4070 \times .3605 \times 104)$$
$$+ (.3605 \times .2325 \times 145) + (.3605 \times .4070 \times 104) + (.3605 \times .3605 \times 289)]^{1/2}$$
$$= [277.13]^{1/2}$$
$$= 16.65\%$$

Several interesting features about variance–covariance matrices deserve mention.

1. Such matrices are square; the number of columns equals the number of rows, so that the total number of cells for N securities equals N^2.
2. The variances of the securities appear on the diagonal of the matrix, which are the cells that lie on a line going from the upper-left corner to the lower-right corner of the matrix. In the previous example, the variance of security 1 (146) appears in row 1, column 1. The variances of securities 2 and 3 appear in row 2, column 2 (854), and row 3, column 3 (289), respectively.
3. The matrix is symmetric; the number appearing in row i of column j also appears in row j of column i. That is, the elements in the cells above the diagonal also appear in the corresponding cells below the diagonal. In the previous example, note that the element in row 1 of column 2, 187, also appears in row 2 of column 1. Similarly, 145 appears in both row 1 of column 3 and row 3 of column 1, and 104 appears in both row 2 of column 3 and row 3 of column 2. The reason for this feature is quite simple—the covariance between two securities does not depend on the order in which the two securities are specified. For example, the covariance between the first and second securities is the same as the covariance between the second and first securities.[13]

Summary

1. The Markowitz approach to portfolio selection assumes that investors seek both maximum expected return for a given level of risk and minimum risk for a given level of expected return.
2. Expected return serves as the measure of potential reward associated with a portfolio. Standard deviation is the measure of a portfolio's risk.
3. The relationship between an investor's utility (satisfaction) and wealth is described by the investor's utility of wealth function. The assumption of nonsatiation requires the utility of wealth function to be upward sloping.
4. Risk-averse investors have diminishing marginal utility. Each extra unit of wealth provides the risk-averse investor with additional, but increasingly smaller, amounts of utility.
5. An indifference curve represents the various combinations of risk and return that the investor finds equally desirable.
6. Risk-averse investors are assumed to consider any portfolio lying on an indifference curve farther to the northwest as more desirable than any portfolio lying on an indifference curve that is not as far northwest.
7. The assumptions of investor nonsatiation and risk aversion cause indifference curves to be positively sloped and convex.
8. The expected return on a portfolio is a weighted average of the expected returns of its component securities, with the relative portfolio proportions of the component securities serving as weights.
9. Covariance and correlation measure the extent to which two random variables "move together."
10. The standard deviation of a portfolio depends on the standard deviations and proportions of the component securities as well as their covariances with one another.

Questions and Problems

1. Following are several portfolios and expected returns, standard deviations, and satisfaction amounts (measured in utils) these portfolios provide Arky Vaughn. Given this information, graph Arky's identifiable indifference curves.

Portfolio	Expected Return	Standard Deviation	Utility
1	5%	0%	10 utils
2	6	10	10
3	9	20	10
4	14	30	10
5	10	0	20
6	11	10	20
7	14	20	20
8	19	30	20
9	15	0	30
10	16	10	30
11	19	20	30
12	24	30	30

2. What does a set of convex indifference curves imply about an investor's trade off between risk and return as the amount of risk varies?

3. What is meant by the statement that "risk-averse investors exhibit diminishing marginal utility of wealth"? Why does diminishing marginal utility cause an investor to refuse to accept a "fair bet"?

4. Consider the following two sets of indifference curves for investors Hack Wilson and Kiki Cuyler. Determine whether Hack or Kiki

   a. Is more risk-averse
   b. Prefers investment A to investment B
   c. Prefers investment C to investment D
   Explain the reasons for your answers.

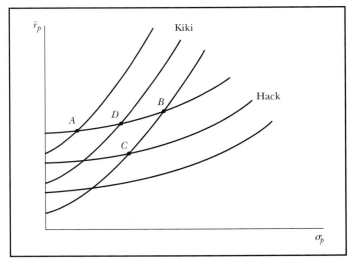

5. Consider four stocks with the following expected returns and standard deviations.

Stock	Expected Return	Standard Deviation
A	15%	12%
B	13	8
C	14	7
D	16	11

Are any of these stocks preferred over another by a risk-averse investor?

6. At the beginning of the year, Corns Bradley owned four securities in the following amounts and with the following current and expected end-of-year prices:

Security	Share Amount	Current Price	Expected Year-End Price
A	100	$ 50	$ 60
B	200	35	40
C	50	25	50
D	100	100	110

What is the expected return on Corns's portfolio for the year?

7. Given the following information about four stocks comprising a portfolio, calculate each stock's expected return. Then, using these individual securities' expected returns, calculate the portfolio's expected return.

Stock	Initial Investment Value	Expected End-of-Period Investment Value	Proportion of Portfolio Initial Market Value
A	$ 500	$ 700	19.2%
B	200	300	7.7
C	1,000	1,000	38.5
D	900	1,500	34.6

8. Both the covariance and the correlation coefficient measure the extent to which the returns on securities move together. What is the relationship between the two statistical measures? Why is the correlation coefficient a more convenient measure?

9. Given the following variance–covariance matrix for three securities, as well as the percentage of the portfolio for each security, calculate the portfolio's standard deviation.

	Security A	Security B	Security C
Security A	459		
Security B	–211	312	
Security C	112	215	179
	$X_A = .50$	$X_B = .30$	$X_C = .20$

10. If a portfolio's expected return is equal to the weighted average of the expected returns of the component securities, why is a portfolio's risk not generally equal to the weighted average of the component securities' standard deviations?

11. Consider two securities, A and B, with standard deviations of 30% and 40%, respectively. Calculate the standard deviation of a portfolio weighted equally between the two securities if their correlation is
   a. 0.9
   b. 0.0
   c. –0.9

12. Following are estimates of the standard deviations and correlation coefficients for three stocks.

Stock	Standard Deviation	Correlation with Stock		
		A	B	C
A	12%	1.00	–1.00	0.20
B	15	–1.00	1.00	–0.20
C	10	0.20	–0.20	1.00

a. If a portfolio is composed of 20% of stock *A* and 80% of stock *C*, what is the portfolio's standard deviation?

b. If a portfolio is composed of 40% of stock *A*, 20% of stock *B*, and 40% of stock *C*, what is the portfolio's standard deviation?

13. (Appendix Question) Squeaky Bluege has been considering an investment in Oakdale Merchandising. Squeaky has estimated the following probability distribution of returns for Oakdale stock:

Return	Probability
−10%	.10
0	.25
10	.40
20	.20
30	.05

Based on Squeaky's estimates, calculate the expected return and standard deviation of Oakdale stock.

14. (Appendix Question) Gibby Brock has estimated the following joint probability distribution of returns for investments in the stock of Lakeland Halfway Homes and Afton Brewery:

Lakeland	Afton	Probability
−10%	15%	.15
5	10	.20
10	5	.30
20	0	.35

On the basis of Gibby's estimates, calculate the covariance and correlation coefficient between the two investments.

15. (Appendix Question) Given the following joint probability distribution of returns for securities *A* and *B*, calculate the covariance between the two securities.

State	Security A	Security B	Probability
1	10%	20%	.10
2	12	25	.25
3	8	33	.35
4	14	27	.20
5	19	22	.10

APPENDIX A

Characteristics of Probability Distributions

This chapter introduces the concepts of expected return and risk for a portfolio of securities. Such a discussion presumes that the reader has some familiarity with probability distributions and the measures of central tendency and dispersion. This appendix is designed to provide a brief overview of these and other statistical concepts. Additional information can be obtained by consulting an introductory statistics textbook.

7A.1   Probability Distributions

A probability distribution describes the possible values that a random variable might take on and the associated probabilities of those values occurring. A discrete probability distribution displays a finite number of possible values that the random variable might assume. For example, in a classroom the possible amounts of money students might have in their pockets would constitute a discrete probability distribution because the smallest unit of currency that any student might hold is $.01. A continuous probability distribution, on the other hand, contains an infinite number of values for the random variable. For example, the distribution of temperatures that might occur during the day is described by a continuous probability distribution because temperature can be divided into smaller and smaller fractions of a degree.

Table 7.3 presents information regarding the probability distribution for Alpha Company's common stock returns, where there are assumed to be seven different "states of nature," or simply "states" [column (1)]. In this example, Alpha stock can produce seven different returns [column (2)] depending on the state that occurs. The probability of each state (and hence return) occurring is shown in column (3). Note that the sum of the probabilities is 1.0; there is a 100% chance that one of these seven returns will occur. The probability distribution of Alpha's stock returns is shown in Figure 7.7; typically distributions such as this are estimated (in reality, distributions of economic variables are almost never known precisely) using past data, intuition, or both.

TABLE 7.3   Estimating Alpha's Expected Return and Variance

(1) *State*	*(2)* *Alpha's Possible Returns*	*(3)* *Probability of State*	*(4)* *(2) × (3)*	*(5)* *Deviation from Expected Return*	*(6)* *Squared Deviation*	*(7)* *(3) × (6)*
1	−10%	.07	−.7%	−15.0%	225	15.8
2	−5	.10	−.5	−10.0	100	10.0
3	0	.18	0.0	−5.0	25	4.5
4	5	.30	1.5	0.0	0	0.0
5	10	.18	1.8	5.0	25	4.5
6	15	.10	1.5	10.0	100	10.0
7	20	.07	1.4	15.0	225	15.8
		Expected Return = 5.0%			Variance = 60.6%^{2}	

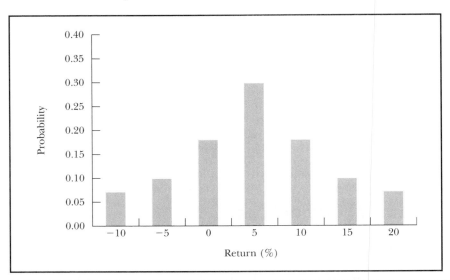

FIGURE 7.7 Probability Distribution of Alpha's Stock Returns

A probability distribution is characterized by a number of measures. Two of the most important characteristics are related to the central tendency and dispersion of the probability distribution.

7A.2 Central Tendency

median

mode

The center of a probability distribution is measured by several statistics. The **median** is the middle value of the distribution when the possible values of the random variable are arranged according to size. The **mode** is the most likely value. Finally, the expected value (or mean) is the weighted average value of the distribution, where all possible values are weighted by their respective probabilities of occurrence.

In Table 7.3, the median and the mode of Alpha Company stock both can quickly be identified as 5%. The expected value (or mean) is less obvious. It is calculated as the sum of the products of each of the possible values times their associated probabilities. That is,

$$EV = \sum_{i=1}^{N} p_i X_i$$

where

X_i = *i*th possible value for the random variable

p_i = probability of the *i*th value occurring

N = number of possible values that the random variable might take on (that is, the number of states)

The expected return on Alpha Company's stock is found by multiplying each possible return by its associated probability [column (4)]. The expected return for Alpha stock is

$$\bar{r}_{Alpha} = \sum_{i=1}^{7} p_i r_i$$

Table 7.3 displays the results of this calculation, with the expected return on Alpha's stock equal to 5%. (Note that the equality of the median, mode, and expected value is a feature of a random variable having a normal distribution.)

7A.3   Dispersion

The dispersion of possible values around the expected value is measured by the variance (or, equivalently, the standard deviation) of the probability distribution. The probability distributions of two random variables can have the same expected value, yet one can have a smaller variance than the other. This means that the values of the less dispersed random variable are less likely to stray from the expected value of its probability distribution than are the values of the random variable with the higher variance.

The variance of a random variable is calculated as the weighted average of the squared deviations from the expected value of the random variable. The weights assigned to those deviations are the probabilities of the particular values occurring. That is,

$$\sigma^2 = \sum_{i=1}^{N} p_i (X_i - EV)^2$$

Hence, the variance of returns of Alpha Company's stock is found by solving

$$\sigma_{Alpha}^2 = \sum_{i=1}^{7} p_i (r_i - \bar{r}_{Alpha})^2$$

The results of that calculation are shown in columns (5) through (7) of Table 7.3. The expected return of 5% is subtracted from each of the seven possible Alpha returns [column (5)]. The resulting value is squared [column (6)] and multiplied by the probability of that particular return occurring [column (7)]. Finally, the sum of the squared deviations is computed to arrive at a variance of 60.6%^{2}, or 60.6 "percent squared."

The variance is calculated in units that are different than those used to calculate the expected value of the random variable. Specifically, because the variance is an average squared deviation, these units are squared. Conceptually, this idea causes some difficulty for users attempting to interpret variance because the units of "return squared" or "percent return squared" are not readily understood by most people. The standard deviation addresses this problem by simply taking the square root of the variance and producing a statistic expressed in the same units as the expected value. That is,

$$\sigma_i = \sqrt{p_i (X_i - EV)^2}$$

Thus, taking the square root of the variance of returns for Alpha Company gives

$$\sigma_{Alpha} = \sqrt{\sigma_{Alpha}^2}$$
$$= \sqrt{60.6\%^2} = 7.8\%$$

Note that the units of measurement are "percent," just like the units used to measure Alpha's expected return.

7A.4   Comovement

Covariance measures the tendency for two random variables to move together (to covary). Instead of referring to the probability distribution for a single random variable, covariance considers the joint probability distribution of two random variables. That is, in a given state the two random variables take on particular values. The joint probability distribution describes what those pairs of values are for each possible state and the probabilities of those outcomes occurring. Covariance is found by computing the weighted average of the product of the deviations of two random variables from their respective expected values. The weights assigned to these joint deviations are the probabilities of the two random variables taking on their associated joint values:

$$\sigma_{XY} = \sum_{i=1}^{N} p_i(X_i - EV_X)(Y_i - EV_Y)$$

In the case of variance, the ith outcome refers to the value the random variable takes on when the ith state occurs. In the case of covariance, the ith outcome refers to the values that both random variables X and Y take on when the ith state occurs.

Continuing with the example of Alpha Company, consider now a second company's stock, that of Omega Company. Table 7.4 shows that corresponding to each of the seven possible returns on Alpha stock [column (2)], Omega stock has its own corresponding return [column (3)]. As an exercise, the reader can calculate the expected returns and standard deviation of returns for Omega Company (which are 11.8% and 5.9%, respectively). Computing the deviations of both Alpha and Omega's returns from their expected values for each of the seven possible states [columns (5) and (6)], taking the product of those two deviations for each possible states [column (7)], multiplying the product by the probability of the state [column (8)], and finally summing across all seven states gives the covariance between Alpha and Omega stock. That is,

$$\sigma_{Alpha,Omega} = \sum_{i=1}^{7} p_i(r_{Alpha,i} - \bar{r}_{Alpha})(r_{Omega,i} - \bar{r}_{Omega})$$

which, as shown in the table, equals $-41.5\%^2$. Note that the units of measurement here are "percent squared," just like the units used to measure variance.

TABLE 7.4   Estimating the Covariance between the Returns on Alpha and Omega

(1) State	(2) Alpha's Possible Returns	(3) Omega's Possible Returns	(4) Probability of State	(5) Alpha's Deviations	(6) Omega's Deviations	(7) (5) × (6) Deviation Products	(8) (4) × (7)
1	−10%	30%	.07	−15.0%	18.0%	−270.0	−18.9
2	−5	14	.10	−10.0	2.0	−20.0	−2.0
3	0	18	.18	−5.0	6.0	−30.0	−5.4
4	5	10	.30	0.0	−2.0	0.0	0.0
5	10	7	.18	5.0	−5.0	−25.0	−4.5
6	15	10	.10	10.0	−2.0	−20.0	−2.0
7	20	0	.07	15.0	−12.0	−180.0	−12.6
	Expected return of Alpha = 5.0%			Expected return of Omega = 11.8%			Covariance = −45.4%²

Once the covariance of Alpha and Omega's returns have been calculated, it is simple to compute the correlation between their returns. In general, this calculation is given by

$$\rho_{XY} = \frac{\sigma_{XY}}{\sigma_X \sigma_Y}$$

In the case of Alpha and Omega, the correlation is calculated as

$$\rho_{Alpha, Omega} = \frac{-45.4}{7.8 \times 5.9} = -.90$$

APPENDIX B

Risk-Neutral and Risk-Seeking Investors

Earlier, it was mentioned that the Markowitz approach assumes investors are risk-averse. Although this is a reasonable assumption to make, it is not necessary to do so. Alternatively, it can be assumed that investors are either risk-neutral or risk-seeking.

Consider the risk-seeking investor first. This investor, when faced with a fair gamble, wants to take the gamble. Furthermore, large gambles will be more desirable than small gambles because the utility (satisfaction) derived from winning is greater than the disutility (dissatisfaction) derived from losing. Because there is an equal chance of winning and losing, the risk-seeking investor will want to take the gamble. Such investors have utility functions that are upward-sloping and convex.

For example, in choosing between two portfolios with the same expected return but different standard deviations, the risk-seeking investor will choose the portfolio with the higher standard deviation. This choice suggests that the risk-seeking investor will have negatively sloped indifference curves.[14] In addition, risk-seeking investors prefer to be on the indifference curve that is farthest northeast. Figure 7.8 illustrates the indifference curves for a hypothetical risk-seeking investor. As shown in the figure, when choosing from *A, B, C,* and *D* (the same four portfolios shown in Figure 7.2), this investor will choose *B*.

FIGURE 7.8 Indifference Curves for a Risk-Seeking Investor

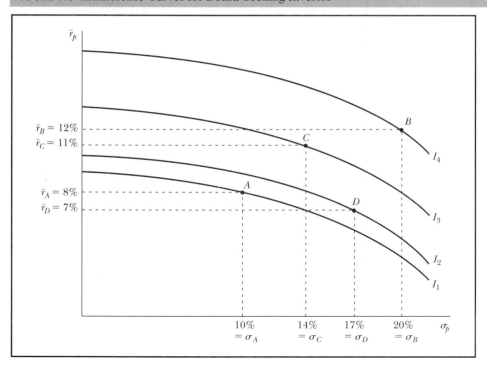

The risk-neutral case lies between the risk-seeking and risk-averse cases. Whereas the risk-averse investor does not want to take fair gambles and the risk-seeking investor does want to take such gambles, the risk-neutral investor does not care whether the gamble is taken. Risk, or more specifically, standard deviation, is unimportant to the risk-neutral investor in evaluating portfolios. Accordingly, the indifference curves for such investors are horizontal lines as shown in Figure 7.9. These investors prefer to be on the indifference curve that is farthest north. When faced with the choice of *A*, *B*, *C*, and *D*, such an investor will choose *B* because it has the highest expected return. Such investors have utility functions that are upward-sloping and straight.

Whereas investors can be either risk-seeking or risk-neutral, there is evidence to suggest that most are more accurately characterized as risk-averse. One piece of evidence is the observation that equities have historically had higher average returns than bonds, suggesting that investors must be induced with higher rewards to make riskier purchases.

FIGURE 7.9 Indifference Curves for a Risk-Neutral Investor

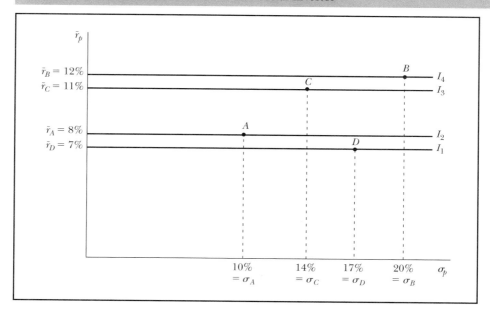

Endnotes

1. Markowitz recognized that investing was generally a multiperiod activity in which, at the end of each period, part of the investor's wealth was consumed and part was reinvested. Nevertheless, his one-period approach is optimal under a variety of reasonable circumstances. See Edwin J. Elton and Martin J. Gruber, *Finance as a Dynamic Process* (Upper Saddle River, NJ: Prentice Hall, 1975), particularly Chapter 5.

2. One portfolio that would not have an uncertain rate of return would involve the investor's putting all of his or her initial wealth in a pure-discount govern-

ment security that matures at $t = 1$. However, for almost all other portfolios the rate of return would be uncertain. See Chapter 9 for a discussion of this risk-free security.

3. A random variable's expected value is, in a sense, its "average" value. Thus, the expected value for the return of a portfolio can be thought of as its expected, or average, or mean, return. The standard deviation of a random variable is a measure of the dispersion (or "spread") of possible values that the random variable can take on. Accordingly, the standard deviation of a

portfolio is a measure of the dispersion of possible returns that could be earned on the portfolio. Sometimes variance is used as a measure of the dispersion instead of standard deviation. However, because variance is simply the squared value of the standard deviation of the random variable, this distinction is not of importance here. These concepts are discussed in more detail in Appendix A to this chapter.

4. Investors can also be **risk-seeking** or **risk-neutral.** Appendix B to this chapter discusses both risk-neutral and risk-seeking investors.

5. Equivalently, in order to determine U_r, one could calculate the utility of $100,000 and the utility of $110,000 and then take a weighted average of them where the weights correspond to the probabilities of the outcomes occurring, which in this case is .50 for each one of them. That is, the expected utility of the risky investment is equal to $U_r = [.5 \times U(\$100,000)] + [.5 \times U(\$110,000)]$.

6. For an alternative procedure, see Ralph O. Swalm, "Utility Theory: Insights into Risk Taking," *Harvard Business Review,* 44, no. 6 (November–December 1966): 123–136.

7. At some point the reader may wonder why an investor's preferences are based only on expected returns and standard deviations. For example, it may seem logical that the investor's preferences should be based on expected returns, standard deviations, and the probability that a portfolio will lose money. The assertion that an investor's preferences are not based on anything other than expected returns and standard deviations follows from some specific assumptions coupled with *utility theory.* See Gordon J. Alexander and Jack Clark Francis, *Portfolio Analysis* (Upper Saddle River, NJ: Prentice Hall, 1986), particularly Chapters 2 and 3, for more details. There is some dispute about the validity of using utility theory to describe people's behavior. Those holding the view that utility theory is not applicable are often referred to as behaviorists. For a discussion of their views, see the entire second part of the October 1986 issue of the *Journal of Business,* the entire November/December 1999 issue of the *Finanacial Analysts Journal,* and the Money Matters box in this chapter.

8. Convexity of indifference curves means that their slopes increase when moving from left to right along any particular curve. That is, each curve "bends upward." The underlying rationale for convexity lies in utility theory.

9. The figures given for the expected end-of-period values include both the expected prices and the expected dividends for the period. For example, Able has an expected end-of-period value of $46.48, which could consist of a hypothetical expected cash dividend of $2 and share price of $44.48. These expected returns and values are estimated by using security analysis, which is discussed in Chapter 15.

10. Security weights in a portfolio can be either positive (indicating a long position) or negative (indicating a short position). However, because of margin requirements, an investor does not have direct access to the proceeds of a short sale (see Chapter 2). As a result, the return on a stock sold short is not the opposite of the return on a stock held in a long position. This implies that a negative sign cannot simply be inserted into Equation (7.3a) to indicate a short position without adjusting the security's expected return for the effects of the short selling margin requirements.

11. If returns are not normally distributed, the use of standard deviation can still be justified in an approximate sense, provided the probabilities of extremely high and low returns are small. See H. Levy and H. M. Markowitz, "Approximating Expected Utility by a Function of Mean and Variance," *American Economic Review,* 69, no. 3 (June 1979): 308–317; and Yoram Kroll, Haim Levy, and Harry M. Markowitz, "Mean-Variance versus Direct Utility Maximization," *Journal of Finance,* 39, no. 1 (March 1984): 47–61. Some researchers have argued that the best model for a stock's returns is a mixture of normal distributions; for a discussion and references, see Richard Roll, "R^2," *Journal of Finance,* 43, no. 3 (July 1988): 541–566, particularly footnote 11 on p. 561.

12. Remember that correlation refers to how two random variables move together. If the two random variables are the same, then they move exactly together with each other. This movement can be visualized by graphing the values of the same random variable on both the X-axis and the Y-axis. In such a graph, all points lie on a straight 45-degree line passing through the origin implying a correlation of $+1$.

13. For any variance–covariance matrix there is an implied correlation matrix that can be determined by using the data in the variance–covariance matrix and Equation (7.5). Specifically, this equation can be used to show that the correlation between any two securities i and j is equal to $\sigma_{ij}/\sigma_i\sigma_j$. The values for σ_{ij}, σ_i, and σ_j can be obtained from the variance–covariance matrix. For example, $\rho_{12} = 187/(\sqrt{146} \times \sqrt{854}) = .53$.

14. For a risk-seeking investor, these indifference curves will be concave, meaning that their slopes decrease when moving from left to right along any particular one. The underlying rationale for concavity lies in utility theory.

C H A P T E R

Portfolio Analysis

The previous chapter introduced the portfolio selection problem that every investor faces. It also introduced the investment approach of Markowitz as a method of solving that problem. With this approach, an investor evaluates alternative portfolios on the basis of their expected returns and standard deviations by using indifference curves. A risk-averse investor would select for investment the portfolio with the indifference curve that is farthest northwest.

However, certain questions were left unanswered. In particular, how can Markowitz's approach be used once it is recognized that there are an infinite number of portfolios available for investment? What happens when the investor considers investing in a set of securities, one of which is riskless? What happens if the investor is allowed to buy securities on margin? This chapter and the next provide answers to those questions, beginning with the first one.

8.1 The Efficient Set Theorem

As mentioned earlier, an infinite number of portfolios can be formed from a set of N securities. Consider the situation with Able, Baker, and Charlie companies, where N is equal to 3. The investor could purchase just shares of Able, or just shares of Baker. Or, the investor could purchase a combination of shares of Able and Baker. For example, the investor could put 50% of his or her money in each company, or 25% in one company and 75% in the other, or 33% in one and 67% in the other, or any percentage (between 0% and 100%) in one company and the rest in the other. Without even considering investing in Charlie, there are already an infinite number of possible portfolios that could be purchased.[1]

Does the investor need to evaluate all these portfolios? Fortunately, the answer is no. The key to why the investor needs to look at only a subset of the available portfolios lies in the **efficient set theorem,** which states that

efficient set theorem

> An investor will choose his or her optimal portfolio from the set of portfolios that
>
> 1. Offers maximum expected return for varying levels of risk, and
> 2. Offers minimum risk for varying levels of expected return.

efficient set

The set of portfolios meeting these two conditions is known as the **efficient set** (also known as the efficient frontier).

8.1.1 THE FEASIBLE SET

feasible set

Figure 8.1 provides an illustration of the **feasible set** (also known as the opportunity set) from which the efficient set can be identified. The feasible set represents all portfolios that could be formed from a group of N securities. That is, all possible portfolios that could be formed from N securities lie either on or within the boundary of the feasible set. (The points, G, E, S, and H, in the figure are examples of such portfolios.) This set will usually have an umbrella-type shape similar to the one shown in the figure. Depending on the particular securities involved, it may be positioned further to the right or left, or higher or lower, or it may be fatter or skinnier than shown here. However, its shape will, except in perverse circumstances, look similar to what appears here.

8.1.2 THE EFFICIENT SET THEOREM APPLIED TO THE FEASIBLE SET

The efficient set can be located by applying the efficient set theorem to the feasible set. To begin with, the set of portfolios that meet the first condition of the efficient set theorem must be identified. Looking at Figure 8.1, portfolio E offers the least amount of risk because if a vertical line were drawn through E there would be no point in the feasible set that was to the left of the line. Portfolio H offers the most risk because if a vertical line were drawn through H there would be no point in the feasible set to the right of the line. Thus, the set of portfolios offering maximum expected return for varying levels of risk is that set on the northern boundary of the feasible set between points E and H.

Considering the second condition, there is no portfolio offering an expected return greater than portfolio S because no point in the feasible set lies above a horizontal line going through S. Conversely, there is no portfolio offering a lower expected return than portfolio G because no point in the feasible set lies below a horizontal line going through G. Thus, the set of portfolios offering minimum risk for varying levels of expected return is that set on the western boundary of the feasible set between points G and S.

FIGURE 8.1 Feasible and Efficient Sets

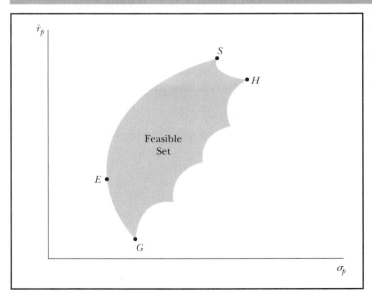

efficient portfolios

inefficient portfolios

optimal portfolio

Remember that both conditions have to be met in order to identify the efficient set. Only those portfolios lying on the northwest boundary between points *E* and *S* do so. Accordingly, these portfolios form the efficient set, and it is from this set of **efficient portfolios** that the risk-averse investor will find his or her optimal one.[2] All the other feasible portfolios are **inefficient portfolios** and can be ignored.

8.1.3 SELECTION OF THE OPTIMAL PORTFOLIO

How will the investor select an **optimal portfolio?** As shown in Figure 8.2, the investor should plot his or her indifference curves on the same figure as the efficient set and then choose the portfolio on the farthest northwest indifference curve. This portfolio will correspond to the point at which an indifference curve is just tangent to the efficient set. In the figure this is portfolio O^* on indifference curve I_2. Although the investor would prefer a portfolio on I_3, no such feasible portfolio exists. For I_1, there are several portfolios that the investor could choose (for example, O). However, portfolio O^* dominates such portfolios because it is on an indifference curve that is farther northwest. Figure 8.3 shows that the highly risk-averse investor will choose a portfolio close to *E*. Figure 8.4 shows that the investor who is only slightly risk-averse will choose a portfolio close to *S*.[3]

Upon reflection, the efficient set theorem is quite rational. According to the discussion in Chapter 7, an investor should select the portfolio that puts him or her on the indifference curve that is farthest northwest. The efficient set theorem, stating that the investor needs to be concerned only with portfolios that lie on the northwest boundary of the feasible set, is a logical consequence.

Indifference curves for the risk-averse investor were shown to be positively sloped and convex in Chapter 7. Now it will be shown that the efficient set is generally

FIGURE 8.2 Selecting an Optimal Portfolio

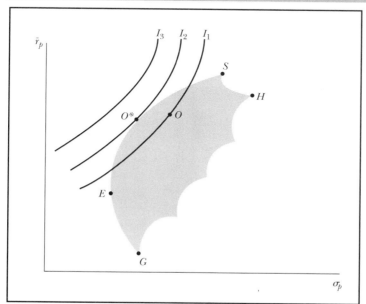

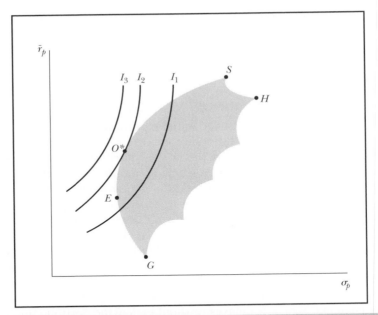

FIGURE 8.3 Portfolio Selection for a Highly Risk-Averse Investor

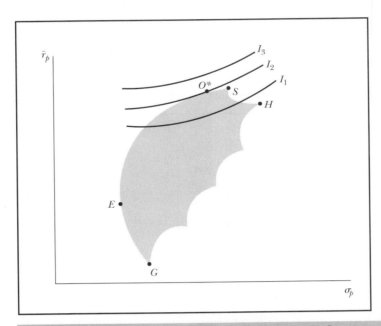

FIGURE 8.4 Portfolio Selection for a Slightly Risk-Averse Investor

positively sloped and concave, meaning that if a straight line is drawn between any two points on the efficient set, the straight line will lie below the efficient set. Consequently, there will be only one tangency point between the investor's indifference curves and the efficient set.

The Trouble with Optimizers

 Suppose the captain of a modern luxury liner chose not to use the ship's state-of-the-art navigational system (a system that employs computers to triangulate off geostationary-orbiting satellites, thereby estimating the ship's position accurately to within a few feet). Instead, the captain chose to rely on the old-fashioned method of navigating by the stars, an antiquated method fraught with problems and imprecision. Most people would view the captain's choice as, at best, eccentric and, at worst, highly dangerous.

When it comes to constructing portfolios, many investment managers make a choice analogous to that of the ship's captain. They reject computer-based portfolio construction methods in favor of traditional approaches. Are their decisions as foolhardy as the captain's? Or is there a method to their apparent madness?

As this chapter discusses, the concepts of the efficient set and the investor's optimal portfolio are central to modern investment theory. But how can an investor actually estimate the efficient set and select his or her optimal portfolio? Harry Markowitz first described the solution in the early 1950s. Using a mathematical technique called *quadratic programming,* investors can process estimates of expected returns, standard deviations, and covariances to calculate the efficient set. Given an estimate of their indifference curves (as reflected in their individual risk tolerances—see Chapter 17), they can then select a portfolio from the efficient set.

Simple, right? Certainly not in the 1950s. Given the data-processing facilities available to investors at that time, calculating the efficient set for even a few hundred securities was nearly impossible. However, with the advent of low-cost, high-speed computers and the development of sophisticated risk models (see Chapter 11), an efficient set can be created for thousands of securities in short order. The necessary computer hardware and software are available to institutional investors at a relatively low cost. In fact, the process has become so commonplace that it has acquired its own terminology. Using a computer to identify

the efficient set and select an optimal portfolio is known as using an "optimizer." Portfolios are "optimized," and investors are said to apply "optimization techniques."

Despite the technology's widespread availability, relatively few investment managers actually use an optimizer to build portfolios of individual securities (although optimizers are often used for allocating funds among major asset classes). Instead, they rely for the most part on a series of qualitative rules and judgments. Why do investment managers resist applying optimization techniques to portfolio building? Ignorance is not the answer. Most investment managers, having graduated from business schools where these ideas are discussed in detail, are well aware of Markowitz's portfolio selection concepts and the available technology. Instead, their resistance derives from two sources: territorial concerns and implementation inadequacies.

From a territorial perspective, many investment managers simply are not comfortable with a quantitative approach to investing. Their decision making emphasizes intuition and complex subjective judgments. The application of optimization techniques to portfolio construction imposes a systematic and formal decision-making structure. Security analysts are responsible for generating quantifiable expected return and risk forecasts. Portfolio managers must implement the decisions of a computer. As a result, the optimizer destroys the "artistry and grace" of investment management.

Further, with the introduction of an optimizer, a new breed of investment professional gains influence—the quantitative analyst (derisively called a "quant") who coordinates the collection and application of risk and return estimates. Authority gained by quantitative analysts diminishes the influence of traditional security analysts and portfolio managers, much to their consternation.

From the implementation perspective, serious problems have arisen with optimizers. In particular, they tend to produce counterintuitive, uninvestable portfolios. This situation is not so much a problem with optimizers as it is the fault of the human operators supplying inputs to the optimizers. Here the GIGO (garbage in, garbage out) paradigm rules.

By their design, optimizers are attracted to securities with high estimated expected returns, low estimated standard deviations, and low estimated covariances with other securities. Often this information is derived from historical databases covering thousands of securities. Unless the risk and return data are carefully checked, errors (for example, understating a security's standard deviation) can easily lead the optimizer to recommend purchases of securities for erroneous reasons. Even if the data are "clean," extreme historical values for some securities may lead the optimizer astray.

Optimizers also display a nasty habit of generating high turnover and recommending investments in relatively illiquid securities. *High turnover* refers to significant changes in portfolio composition from one period to the next. High turnover can result in unacceptably large transaction costs (see Chapter 3) and hinder portfolio performance. *Liquidity* refers to the ability to actually buy the securities selected by the optimizer. Selected securities may possess desirable risk–return characteristics but may not trade in sufficient volume to permit institutional investors to purchase them without incurring sizable transaction costs.

Solutions to these implementation problems do exist. They range from careful data checking to placing realistic limits (or "constraints") on maximum turnover or minimum liquidity allowed in the solution designed by the optimizer. In the end, however, nothing can substitute for skillful judgmental forecasts of security returns and risks, balanced by properly applied notions of market equilibrium.

Territorial and implementation problems have given investment managers convenient reasons to avoid optimizers and to stick to traditional portfolio construction methods. Nevertheless, the outlook for quantitative portfolio construction techniques is bright. The increasing efficiency of capital markets has forced institutional investment managers to process more information about more securities more rapidly than ever before. In response, they have generally increased their use of quantitative investment tools. Although most do not directly integrate optimizers into their portfolio construction procedures, virtually all have become more sensitive to the objective of creating diversified portfolios that display the highest levels of expected return at acceptable levels of risk.

8.2 Concavity of the Efficient Set

To understand why the efficient set is concave, consider the following two-security example. Security 1, the Ark Shipping Company, has an expected return of 5% and a standard deviation of 20%. Security 2, the Gold Jewelry Company, has an expected return of 15% and a standard deviation of 40%. Their locations are indicated by the letters A and G in Figure 8.5.

8.2.1 BOUNDS ON THE LOCATION OF PORTFOLIOS

Consider all the possible portfolios an investor could purchase with these two securities. Let X_1 denote the proportion of the investor's funds invested in Ark Shipping and X_2 ($= 1 - X_1$) the proportion invested in Gold Jewelry. If the investor purchased just Ark Shipping, then $X_1 = 1$ and $X_2 = 0$; but if the investor purchased just Gold Jewelry, then $X_1 = 0$ and $X_2 = 1$. A combination of .17 in Ark Shipping and .83 in Gold Jewelry is also possible, as are the combinations of .33 and .67, and .50 and .50. Although there are many other possibilities, only the following seven portfolios will be considered.

	Portfolio A	*Portfolio B*	*Portfolio C*	*Portfolio D*	*Portfolio E*	*Portfolio F*	*Portfolio G*
X_1	1.00	.83	.67	.50	.33	.17	.00
X_2	.00	.17	.33	.50	.67	.83	1.00

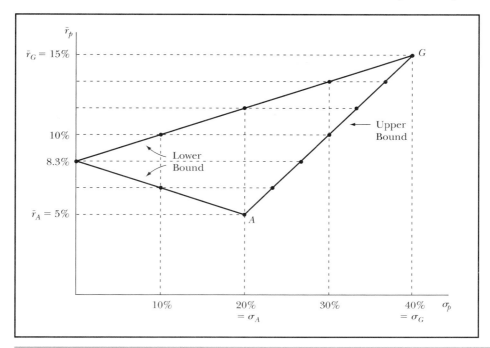

FIGURE 8.5 Upper and Lower Bounds of Combinations of Securities *A* and *G*

To consider these seven portfolios for possible investment, their expected returns and standard deviations must be calculated. All the necessary information to calculate the expected returns for these portfolios using Equation (7.3a) is available:

$$\bar{r}_p = \sum_{i=1}^{N} X_i \bar{r}_i \tag{7.3a}$$

$$= \sum_{i=1}^{2} X_i \bar{r}_i$$

$$= X_1 \bar{r}_1 + X_2 \bar{r}_2$$

$$= (X_1 \times 5\%) + (X_2 + 15\%)$$

For portfolios *A* and *G*, this calculation is trivial because the investor is purchasing shares of just one company. Thus their expected returns are 5% and 15%, respectively. For portfolios *B, C, D, E,* and *F,* the expected returns are

$$\bar{r}_B = (.83 \times 5\%) + (.17 \times 15\%)$$

$$= 6.70\%$$

$$\bar{r}_C = (.67 \times 5\%) + (.33 \times 15\%)$$

$$= 8.30\%$$

$$\bar{r}_D = (.50 \times 5\%) + (.50 \times 15\%)$$

$$= 10\%$$

$$\bar{r}_E = (.33 \times 5\%) + (.67 \times 15\%)$$

$$= 11.70\%$$

$$\bar{r}_F = (.17 \times 5\%) + (.83 \times 15\%)$$

$$= 13.30\%$$

In calculating the standard deviation of these seven portfolios, Equation (7.7) must be used:

$$\sigma_p = \left[\sum_{i=1}^{N} \sum_{j=1}^{N} X_i X_j \sigma_{ij} \right]^{1/2} \tag{7.7}$$

$$= \left[\sum_{i=1}^{2} \sum_{j=1}^{2} X_i X_j \sigma_{ij} \right]^{1/2}$$

$$= [X_1 X_1 \sigma_{11} + X_1 X_2 \sigma_{12} + X_2 X_1 \sigma_{21} + X_2 X_2 \sigma_{22}]^{1/2}$$

$$= [X_1^2 \sigma_1^2 + X_2^2 \sigma_2^2 + 2X_1 X_2 \sigma_{12}]^{1/2}$$

$$= [X_1^2 \times 20\%^2 + X_2^2 \times 40\%^2 + 2X_1 X_2 \sigma_{12}]^{1/2}$$

Again, for portfolios *A* and *G*, this calculation is trivial because the investor is purchasing shares of just one company. Thus, their standard deviations are 20% and 40%, respectively.

For portfolios *B*, *C*, *D*, *E*, and *F*, application of Equation (7.7) indicates that the standard deviations depend on the magnitude of the covariance between the two securities. As shown in Equation (7.5), this covariance term is equal to the correlation between the two securities multiplied by the product of their standard deviations:

$$\sigma_{ij} = \rho_{ij} \times \sigma_i \times \sigma_j \tag{7.5}$$

so letting $i = 1$ and $j = 2$,

$$\sigma_{12} = \rho_{12} \times \sigma_1 \times \sigma_2$$

$$= \rho_{12} \times 20\% \times 40\%$$

$$= 800\rho_{12}$$

Thus, the standard deviation of any portfolio consisting of Ark Shipping and Gold Jewelry can be expressed as

$$\sigma_p = [X_1^2 \times 20\%^2 + X_2^2 \times 40\%^2 + 2X_1 X_2 \times 800\rho_{12}]^{1/2} \tag{8.1}$$

$$= [400X_1^2 + 1,600X_2^2 + 1,600X_1 X_2 \rho_{12}]^{1/2}$$

Consider portfolio *D* first. The standard deviation of this portfolio is between 10% and 30%, the exact value depending on the size of the correlation coefficient. How were these bounds of 10% and 30% determined? First, for portfolio *D*, Equation (8.1) reduces to

$$\sigma_D = [(400 \times .25) + (1,600 \times .25) + (1,600 \times .5 \times .5\rho_{12})]^{1/2} \tag{8.2}$$

$$= [500 + 400\rho_{12}]^{1/2}$$

Equation (8.2) indicates that σ_D will be at a minimum when the correlation coefficient, ρ_{12}, is at a minimum. Recalling that the minimum value for any correlation coefficient is -1, the lower bound on σ_D is

$$\sigma_D = [500 + (400 \times -1)]^{1/2}$$

$$= [500 - 400]^{1/2}$$

$$= [100]^{1/2}$$

$$= 10\%$$

Similarly, Equation (8.2) indicates that σ_D will be at a maximum when the correlation coefficient is at a maximum, which is $+1$. Thus the upper bound on σ_D is

$$\sigma_D = [500 + (400 \times 1)]^{1/2}$$

$$= [500 + 400]^{1/2}$$

$$= [900]^{1/2}$$

$$= 30\%$$

In general, according to Equation (8.1), the lower and upper bounds will occur when the correlation between the two securities is -1 and $+1$, respectively. Applying the same analysis to the other portfolios reveals that their lower and upper bounds are

| | *Standard Deviation of Portfolio* | |
Portfolio	*Lower Bound*	*Upper Bound*
A	20.00%	20.00%
B	10.00	23.33
C	0.00	26.67
D	10.00	30.00
E	20.00	33.33
F	30.00	36.67
G	40.00	40.00

These values are shown in Figure 8.5.

Interestingly, the upper bounds all lie on a straight line connecting points A and G. Therefore, any portfolio consisting of these two securities cannot have a standard deviation that plots to the right of a straight line connecting the two securities. Instead, the standard deviation must lie on or to the left of the straight line. This observation suggests a motivation for diversifying a portfolio: *Diversification generally leads to risk reduction* because the standard deviation of a portfolio will generally be less than a weighted average of the standard deviations of the securities in the portfolio.

Also interesting is the observation that the lower bounds all lie on one of two line segments that go from point A to a point on the vertical axis corresponding to 8.30% and then to point G. Therefore, any portfolio consisting of these two securities cannot have a standard deviation that plots to the left of either of these two line segments. For example, portfolio B must lie on the horizontal line going through the vertical axis at 6.70% but bounded between the values of 10% and 23.33%. In sum, any portfolio consisting of two securities A and G will lie within or on the boundary of the triangle shown in Figure 8.5. Its actual location will depend on the magnitude of the correlation coefficient between the two securities and the weights in A and G.

8.2.2 ACTUAL LOCATIONS OF PORTFOLIOS

What would happen if the correlation were zero? In this case, Equation (8.1) reduces to

$$\sigma_p = [(400X_1^2) + (1,600X_2^2) + (1,600X_1X_2 \times 0)]^{1/2}$$

$$= [(400X_1^2) + (1,600X_2^2)]^{1/2}$$

Applying the appropriate weights for X_1 and X_2, the standard deviation for portfolios *B, C, D, E,* and *F* can be calculated as follows:

$$\sigma_B = [(400 \times .83^2) + (1,600 \times .17^2)]^{1/2}$$

$$= 17.94\%$$

$$\sigma_C = [(400 \times .67^2) + (1,600 \times .33^2)]^{1/2}$$

$$= 18.81\%$$

$$\sigma_D = [(400 \times .50^2) + (1,600 \times .50^2)]^{1/2}$$

$$= 22.36\%$$

$$\sigma_E = [(400 \times .33^2) + (1,600 \times .67^2)]^{1/2}$$

$$= 27.60\%$$

$$\sigma_F = [(400 \times .17^2) + (1,600 \times .83^2)]^{1/2}$$

$$= 33.37\%$$

Figure 8.6 indicates the location of these portfolios, along with the upper and lower bounds shown in Figure 8.5. These portfolios, as well as all other possible portfolios

FIGURE 8.6 Portfolios Formed by Combining Securities *A* and *G*

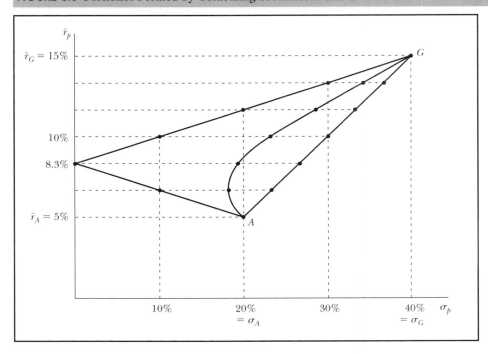

consisting of Ark Shipping and Gold Jewelry, lie on a line that is curved, or bowed, to the left. If the correlation were less than zero, the line would curve more to the left. If the correlation were greater than zero, it would not curve quite as much to the left. The important point about this figure is that as long as the correlation is less than $+1$ and greater than -1, the line representing the set of portfolios consisting of various combinations of the two securities will have some degree of curvature to the left. Furthermore, the northwest portion will be concave.

Similar analysis can be applied to a situation in which there are more than two securities under consideration. As long as the correlations are less than $+1$ and greater than -1, the northwest portion must be concave, just as it is in the two-security example.[4] Thus, in general, the efficient set will be concave.[5]

8.3   The Market Model

market model

Suppose that the return on a common stock during a given time period (say, a month) is related to the return during the same period that is earned on a market index such as the widely cited Standard and Poor's (S&P) 500.[6] If the index's value has gone up, then it is likely that the stock has gone up, and if the index's value has gone down, then it is likely that the stock has gone down. One way to capture this relationship is with the **market model:**

$$r_i = \alpha_{iI} + \beta_{iI} r_I + \varepsilon_{iI} \tag{8.3}$$

where

r_i = return on security i for some given period

r_I = return on market index I for the same period

α_{iI} = intercept term

β_{iI} = slope term

ε_{iI} = random error term

Assuming that the slope term β_{iI} is positive, Equation (8.3) indicates that the higher the return on the market index, the higher the return on the security is likely to be (note that the expected value of the random error term is zero). Consider stock A, for example, which has $\alpha_{iI} = 2\%$ and $\beta_{iI} = 1.2$. The market model for stock A is

$$r_A = 2\% + 1.2 r_I + \varepsilon_{AI} \tag{8.4}$$

so that if the market index has a return of 10%, the return on the security is expected to be 14% [$= 2\% + (1.2 \times 10\%)$]. If the market index's return is -5%, the return on security A is expected to be -4% [$= 2\% + (1.2 \times -5\%)$].

8.3.1   RANDOM ERROR TERMS

random error term

The term ε_{iI} in Equation (8.3), known as the **random error term,** shows that the market model does not explain security returns perfectly. When the market index goes up by 10% or down by 5%, the return on security A is not going to be exactly 14% or -4%, respectively. The difference between what the return actually is and what it is expected to be, given the return on the market index, is attributed to the effect of the random error term. Hence, if the security's return were 9% instead of 14%, the 5% difference would be attributed to the random error term (that is, $\varepsilon_{AI} = -5\%$; this example will be illustrated shortly in Figure 8.7). Similarly, if the security return were -2% instead of -4%, the 2% difference would be attributed to the random error term (that is, $\varepsilon_{AI} = +2\%$).

The random error term is a random variable that has a probability distribution with a mean of zero and a standard deviation denoted $\sigma_{\varepsilon i}$.[7] It can be viewed as the outcome that results from the spin of a special kind of roulette wheel. For example, security A might have a random error term corresponding to a roulette wheel with integer values on it that range from -10% to $+10\%$, with the values evenly spaced.[8] This wheel would have 21 possible outcomes, all of which have an equal probability of occurring. Given the range of numbers, the expected outcome of the random error term would be zero:

$$[-10 \times 1/21] + [-9 \times 1/21] + \cdots + [9 \times 1/21] + [10 \times 1/21] = 0$$

This calculation involves multiplying each outcome by its probability of occurring and then summing the resulting products. The standard deviation of this random error term equals 6.06%:

$$\{[(-10 - 0)^2 \times 1/21] + [(-9 - 0)^2 \times 1/21] + \cdots + [(9 - 0)^2 \times 1/21] +$$
$$[(10 - 0)^2 \times 1/21]\}^{1/2} = 6.06\%$$

This calculation involves subtracting the expected outcome from each possible outcome, then squaring each of those differences, multiplying each square by the probability of the corresponding outcome occurring, adding the products, and taking the square root of the resulting sum.[9]

Figure 8.7 illustrates the roulette wheel corresponding to this random error term. In general, securities will have random error terms whose corresponding roulette wheels have different ranges and different forms of uneven spacing. All of them will have an expected value of zero, but they will typically have different standard deviations. For example, security B may have a random error term whose standard deviation equals 4.76%.[10]

8.3.2 GRAPHICAL REPRESENTATION OF THE MARKET MODEL

The solid line in Figure 8.8(a) provides a graph of the market model for security A. This line corresponds to Equation (8.4), but without the random error term. Accordingly, the line that is graphed for security A is

$$r_A = 2\% + 1.2r_I \tag{8.5}$$

Here the vertical axis measures the return on the particular security (r_A), whereas the horizontal axis measures the return on the market index (r_I). The line goes through the point on the vertical axis corresponding to the value of α_{AI}, which in this case is 2%. The line has a slope equal to β_{AI}, or 1.2.

Panel (b) of Figure 8.8 presents the graph of the market model for security B. The corresponding line is

$$r_B = -1\% + .8r_I \tag{8.6}$$

This line goes through the point on the vertical axis corresponding to the value of α_{BI}, which in this case is -1%. Note that its slope is equal to β_{BI}, or .8.

8.3.3 BETA

The slope in a security's market model measures the sensitivity of the security's returns to the market index's returns. Both lines in Figure 8.8 have positive slopes, indicating that the higher the returns of the market index, the higher the expected returns of the two securities. However, the two securities have different slopes, indicating that they

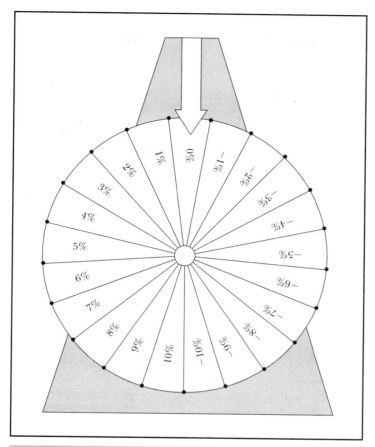

FIGURE 8.7 Security *A*'s Random Error Term

FIGURE 8.8 Market Model

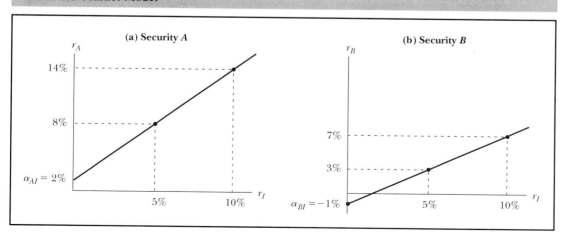

have different sensitivities to the returns of the market index. Specifically, *A* has a higher slope than *B*, indicating that the returns of *A* are more sensitive than the returns of *B* to the returns of the market index.

For example, assume that the market index's expected return is 5%. If the market index has an actual return of 10%, then it will have returned 5% more than expected. Figure 8.8(a) shows that security *A* should have a return that is 6% (= 14% − 8%) greater than initially expected. Similarly, Figure 8.8(b) shows that security *B* should have a return that is 4% (= 7% − 3%) greater than initially expected. The 2% (= 6% − 4%) difference in the two securities' actual returns is because security *A* has a higher slope than security *B*; that is, *A* is more sensitive than *B* to returns on the market index.

beta

The slope term in the market model is often referred to as **beta** and is equal to

$$\beta_{iI} = \frac{\sigma_{iI}}{\sigma_I^2} \tag{8.7}$$

aggressive stocks

defensive stocks

where σ_{iI} denotes the covariance of the returns on stock *i* and the market index, and σ_I^2 denotes the variance of returns on the market index. A stock that has a return that mirrors the return on the market index will have a beta equal to one (and an intercept of zero, resulting in a market model that is $r_i = r_I + \varepsilon_{iI}$). Stocks with betas greater than 1 (such as *A*) are more volatile than the market index and are known as **aggressive stocks.** In contrast, stocks with betas less than 1 (such as *B*) are less volatile than the market index and are known as **defensive stocks.**[11]

8.3.4   ACTUAL RETURNS

The random error term suggests that for a given return on the market index, the actual return on a security will usually lie off its market model line.[12] If the actual returns on securities *A* and *B* turn out to be 9% and 11%, respectively, and the market index's actual return turns out to be 10%, then the actual return on *A* and *B* would have the following three components:

	Security A	*Security B*
Intercept	2%	−1%
Actual return on the market index × beta	12% = 10% × 1.2	8% = 10% × .8
Random error outcome	−5% = 9% − (2% + 12%)	4% = 11% − (−1% + 8%)
Actual return	9%	11%

In this case, the roulette wheels for *A* and *B* were "spun," resulting in values (that is, random error outcomes) of −5% for *A* and +4% for *B*. These values are equal to the vertical distance by which each security's actual return was off its market model line, as shown in Figure 8.9.

8.4   Diversification

total risk

market risk

unique risk

According to the market model, the **total risk** of any security *i*, measured by its variance and denoted σ_i^2, consists of two parts: (1) **market** (or systematic) **risk** and (2) **unique** (or unsystematic or specific) **risk.** That is, σ_i^2 equals the following:

$$\sigma_i^2 = \beta_{iI}^2 \sigma_I^2 + \sigma_{\varepsilon i}^2 \tag{8.8}$$

where σ_I^2 denotes the variance of returns on the market index, $\beta_{iI}^2 \sigma_I^2$ denotes the market risk of security *i*, and $\sigma_{\varepsilon i}^2$ denotes the unique risk of security *i* as measured by the variance of the random error term, ε_{iI}, in Equation (8.3).

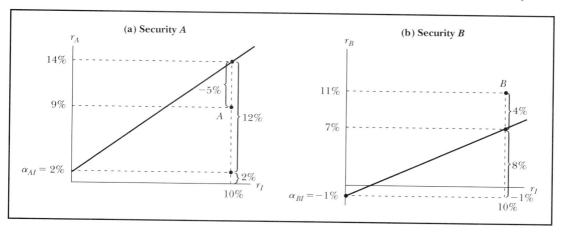

FIGURE 8.9 Market Model and Actual Returns

8.4.1   PORTFOLIO TOTAL RISK

When the return on every risky *security* in a portfolio is related to the return on the market index as specified by the market model, what can be said about the total risk of the *portfolio?* If the proportion of funds invested in security i for a given portfolio p is denoted X_i, then the return on this portfolio will be

$$r_p = \sum_{i=1}^{N} X_i r_i \tag{8.9}$$

Substituting the right-hand side of Equation (8.3) for r_i in Equation (8.9) results in the following market model for the portfolio:

$$r_p = \sum_{i=1}^{N} X_i(\alpha_{iI} + \beta_{iI} r_I + \varepsilon_{iI}) \tag{8.10a}$$

$$= \sum_{i=1}^{N} X_i \alpha_{iI} + \left(\sum_{i=1}^{N} X_i \beta_{iI}\right) r_I + \sum_{i=1}^{N} X_i \varepsilon_{iI}$$

$$= \alpha_{pI} + \beta_{pI} r_I + \varepsilon_{pI}$$

where

$$\alpha_{pI} = \sum_{i=1}^{N} X_i \alpha_{iI} \tag{8.10b}$$

$$\beta_{pI} = \sum_{i=1}^{N} X_i \beta_{iI} \tag{8.10c}$$

$$\varepsilon_{pI} = \sum_{i=1}^{N} X_i \varepsilon_{iI} \tag{8.10d}$$

In Equations (8.10b) and (8.10c), the portfolio's vertical intercept (α_{pI}) and beta (β_{pI}) are weighted averages of the intercepts and betas of the securities, respectively, using their relative proportions in the portfolio as weights. Similarly, in Equation (8.10d), the portfolio's random error term (ε_{pI}) is a weighted average of the random error terms of the securities, again using the relative proportions in the portfolio as weights. Thus, the portfolio's market model is a straightforward extension of the market model for individual securities given in Equation (8.3).[13]

From Equation (8.10a), it follows that the total risk of a portfolio, measured by the variance of the portfolio's returns and denoted σ_p^2, will be

$$\sigma_p^2 = \beta_{pI}^2 \sigma_I^2 + \sigma_{\varepsilon p}^2 \tag{8.11a}$$

where

$$\beta_{pI}^2 = \left[\sum_{i=1}^{N} X_i \beta_{iI} \right]^2 \tag{8.11b}$$

and, assuming the random error components of security returns are uncorrelated,

$$\sigma_{\varepsilon p}^2 = \sum_{i=1}^{N} X_i^2 \sigma_{\varepsilon i}^2 \tag{8.11c}$$

Equation (8.11a) shows that the total risk of any portfolio can be viewed as having two components similar to the two components of the total risk of an individual security. Accordingly, these components are also referred to as market risk ($\beta_{pI}^2 \sigma_I^2$) and unique risk ($\sigma_{\varepsilon p}^2$).

Next, it will be shown that increased diversification can lead to the reduction of a portfolio's total risk. Risk is reduced because the size of the portfolio's unique risk is reduced while the portfolio's market risk remains approximately the same size.

8.4.2 PORTFOLIO MARKET RISK

In general, the more diversified a portfolio (that is, the larger the number of securities in the portfolio), the smaller will be each proportion X_i. The portfolio's beta, β_{pI}, will neither decrease nor increase significantly unless a deliberate attempt is made to do so by adding either relatively low or high beta securities, respectively, to the portfolio. That is, because a portfolio's beta is an average of the betas of its securities, there is no reason to suspect that increasing the amount of diversification will cause the portfolio beta, and thus the market risk of the portfolio, to change in a particular direction. Accordingly,

Diversification leads to an *averaging* of market risk.

This concept makes sense because when prospects for the economy turn sour (or rosy), most securities will fall (or rise) in price. Regardless of the amount of diversification, portfolio returns will always be susceptible to marketwide influences.

8.4.3 PORTFOLIO UNIQUE RISK

The situation is entirely different for unique risk. In a portfolio, some securities will go up as a result of unexpected good news specific to the company that issued the securities (such as an unexpected approval of a patent). Other securities in the portfolio will go down as a result of unexpected company-specific bad news (such as an industrial accident). In the future, approximately as many companies will have good news as have bad news, so there will be little anticipated net impact on the return of a "well-diversified" portfolio. In other words, the more diversified a portfolio is, the smaller its unique risk will be and, in turn, its total risk.

This relation can be quantified precisely if the random error components of security returns are assumed to be uncorrelated, as in Equation (8.11c). Consider the following situation. If the amounts invested in all securities are equal, then the proportion X_i will equal $1/N$, and the level of unique risk, as shown in Equation (8.11c), will be equal to

$$\sigma_{\varepsilon p}^2 = \sum_{i=1}^{N} \left[\frac{1}{N} \right]^2 \sigma_{\varepsilon i}^2 \tag{8.12a}$$

$$= \frac{1}{N} \left[\frac{\sigma_{\varepsilon 1}^2 + \sigma_{\varepsilon 2}^2 + \cdots + \sigma_{\varepsilon N}^2}{N} \right] \tag{8.12b}$$

The value inside the square brackets in Equation (8.12b) is simply the average unique risk of the component securities. But the portfolio's unique risk is only one-Nth as large as this average unique risk because the term $1/N$ appears outside the square brackets. As the portfolio becomes more diversified, the number of securities in it (that is, N) becomes larger. In turn, $1/N$ will become smaller, and the portfolio will have less unique risk.[14] That is,

Diversification can substantially *reduce* unique risk.

Roughly speaking, a portfolio that has equal proportions of 30 or more randomly selected securities in it will have a relatively small amount of unique risk. Its total risk will be only slightly greater than the amount of market risk that is present. Such portfolios are well diversified. Figure 8.10 illustrates how diversification reduces unique risk and averages market risk.

FIGURE 8.10 Risk and Diversification

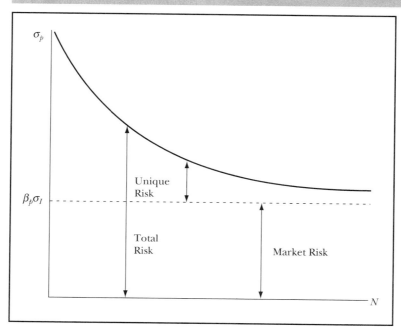

8.4.4   AN EXAMPLE

Consider the two securities, A and B, that were referred to earlier. These two securities had betas of 1.2 and .8, respectively. Given that the standard deviations of their random error terms were 6.06% and 4.76%, respectively, it follows that $\sigma_{\varepsilon A}^2 = 6.06^2 = 37$ and $\sigma_{\varepsilon B}^2 = 4.76^2 = 23$. Now assume that the standard deviation of the market index, σ_I, is 8%, which implies that the variance of the market index is $8^2 = 64$. Using Equation (8.8), the variances of securities A and B are as follows:

$$\sigma_A^2 = (1.2^2 \times 64) + 37$$
$$= 129$$
$$\sigma_B^2 = (.8^2 \times 64) + 23$$
$$= 64$$

A Two-Security Portfolio

Consider combining securities A and B into a portfolio that has equal amounts of the investor's money in each security (that is, $X_A = .5$ and $X_B = .5$). Because $\beta_{AI} = 1.2$ and $\beta_{BI} = .8$, the beta of this portfolio can be calculated using Equation (8.10c):

$$\beta_{pI} = (.5 \times 1.2) + (.5 \times .8)$$
$$= 1.0$$

Using Equation (8.11c), the variance of the portfolio's random error term, $\sigma_{\varepsilon p}^2$, equals

$$\sigma_{\varepsilon p}^2 = (.5^2 \times 37) + (.5^2 \times 23)$$
$$= 15$$

Based on Equation (8.11a), this portfolio will have the following variance:

$$\sigma_p^2 = (1.0^2 \times 64) + 15$$
$$= 79$$

which represents the total risk of the two-security portfolio.

A Three-Security Portfolio

Consider what would happen if a third security (C) was combined with the other two to form a three-security portfolio having $X_A = X_B = X_C = .33$. This third security has a beta of 1.0 and a random error term whose standard deviation ($\sigma_{\varepsilon C}$) is 5.50%. Thus, the variance of the random error term is $\sigma_{\varepsilon C}^2 = 5.5^2 = 30$, and the security's variance is

$$\sigma_C^2 = (1.0^2 \times 64) + 30$$
$$= 94$$

Note that the three-security portfolio has the same amount of market risk as the two-security portfolio because both portfolios have a beta of 1.0:

$$\beta_{pI} = (.33 \times 1.2) + (.33 \times .8) + (.33 \times 1.0)$$
$$= 1.0$$

Thus, increased diversification has not led to a change in the level of market risk. Instead it has led to an averaging of market risk.

Using Equation (8.11c), the variance of the portfolio's random error term equals

$$\sigma^2_{\varepsilon p} = (.33^2 \times 37) + (.33^2 \times 23) + (.33^2 \times 30)$$

$$= 10$$

Note that the variance of this three-security portfolio's random error term is less than the variance of the two-security portfolio's random error term $(10 < 15)$. Thus, in this example, increased diversification has indeed reduced unique risk. Based on Equation (8.11a), this three-security portfolio will have the following variance:

$$\sigma^2_p = (1.0^2 \times 64) + 10$$

$$= 74$$

which represents the total risk of the portfolio and is less than the total risk of the two-security portfolio $(74 < 79)$. Thus, increased diversification has led to a reduction in total risk.

8.4.5 RANDOM VERSUS EFFICIENT DIVERSIFICATION

random diversification

Equation (8.12b) demonstrates how adding randomly selected securities, and combining them in equal proportions, reduces a portfolio's unique risk. That analysis explicitly assumes that the random error components of the securities' returns are uncorrelated. In more general terms, this **random diversification** implicitly assumes that an investor has no knowledge of the standard deviations and correlations of the available securities. This situation contrasts with the Markowitz approach to portfolio construction. Using estimates of securities' risks allows an investor to make maximum use of the diversification potential of a group of securities, as is reflected in the efficient set, by explicitly considering their standard deviations and correlations. Diversifying a portfolio in this way is referred to as **efficient diversification.**

efficient diversification

Summary

1. The efficient set contains those portfolios that offer both maximum expected return for varying levels of risk and minimum risk for varying levels of expected return.
2. Investors are assumed to select their optimal portfolios from among the portfolios lying on the efficient set.
3. An investor's optimal portfolio is located at the tangency point between the investor's indifference curves and the efficient set.
4. The proposition that the efficient set is concave is based on the definition of a portfolio's standard deviation and the existence of assets whose returns are not perfectly correlated.
5. Diversification usually leads to risk reduction because the standard deviation of a portfolio generally will be less than a weighted average of the standard deviations of the component securities.
6. The relationship between the return on a security and the return on a market index is known as the market model.
7. The market index's return does not completely explain the return on a security. The unexplained elements are captured by the random error term of the market model.

8. The slope in a security's market model measures the sensitivity of the security's return to the market index's return. The slope term is known as the security's beta.

9. According to the market model, the total risk of a security consists of market risk and unique risk.

10. A portfolio's vertical intercept, beta, and random error term are weighted averages of the component securities' intercepts, betas, and random error terms, respectively, with the securities' relative proportions in the portfolio serving as weights.

11. Diversification leads to an averaging of market risk.

12. Diversification can substantially reduce unique risk.

Questions and Problems

1. Why would you expect individual securities to generally lie in the eastern portion of the feasible set, whereas only portfolios would lie in the northwestern portion?

2. Explain why most investors prefer to hold a diversified portfolio of securities as opposed to placing all of their wealth in a single asset. Use an illustration of the feasible and efficient sets to explain your answer.

3. Why would you expect most U.S. common stocks to have positive covariances? Give an example of two stocks that you would expect to have a very high positive covariance. Give an example of two stocks that you would expect to have a very low positive (or even negative) covariance.

4. Discuss why the concepts of covariance and diversification are closely related.

5. Mule Haas is a portfolio manager. On average, the expected returns on all securities that Mule is researching are positive. Under what conditions might Mule be willing to purchase a security with a negative expected return?

6. In terms of the Markowitz model, explain, using words and graphs, how an investor goes about identifying his or her optimal portfolio. What specific information does an investor need to identify this portfolio?

7. Dode Brinker owns a portfolio of two securities with the following expected returns, standard deviations, and weights:

Security	Expected Return	Standard Deviation	Weight
A	10%	20%	.35
B	15	25	.65

What correlation between the two securities produces the maximum portfolio standard deviation? What correlation between the two securities produces the minimum portfolio standard deviation. Show your calculations.

8. Leslie Nunamaker owns a portfolio whose market model is expressed as

$$r_p = 1.5\% + 0.90r_I + \varepsilon_{pI}$$

If the expected return on the market index is 12%, what is the expected return on Leslie's portfolio?

9. How is beta derived from a security's market model? Why are high beta securities termed "aggressive"? Why are low beta securities termed "defensive"?

10. The following table presents 10 years of return data for the stock of Glenwood City Properties and for a market index. Plot the returns of Glenwood City and the market index on a graph with the market index's returns on the horizontal axis and Glenwood City's returns on the vertical axis. Draw your best guess of the market model through these points. Examine the graph, and estimate the beta of Glenwood City stock.

Year	Glenwood City	Market Index
1	8.1%	8.0%
2	3.0	0.0
3	5.3	−4.9
4	1.0	5.0
5	−3.1	−4.1
6	−3.0	−8.9
7	5.0	10.1
8	3.2	5.0
9	1.2	1.5
10	1.3	2.4

11. The market model specifies a very simple relationship between a security's return and the return on the market index. Discuss some "real world" complexities that might diminish the predictive power of the market model.

12. Lyndon Station stock has a beta of 1.20. Over five years, the following returns were produced by Lyndon stock and a market index. Assuming a market model intercept term of 0%, calculate the standard deviation of the market model random error term over this period.

Year	Lyndon Return	Market Index
1	17.2%	14.0%
2	−3.1	−3.0
3	13.3	10.0
4	28.5	25.0
5	9.8	8.0

13. Why does diversification lead to a reduction in unique risk but not in market risk? Explain both intuitively and mathematically.

14. Siggy Boskie owns a portfolio composed of three securities with the following characteristics:

Security	Beta	Standard Deviation Random Error Term	Proportion
A	1.20	5%	.30
B	1.05	8	.50
C	0.90	2	.20

If the standard deviation of the market index is 18%, what is the total risk of Siggy's portfolio?

15. Consider two portfolios, one composed of 4 securities and the other of 10 securities. All the securities have a beta of 1 and unique risk of 30%. Each portfolio distributes weight equally among its component securities. If the standard deviation of the market index is 20%, calculate the total risk of both portfolios.

Endnotes

1. This fact can be seen by noting that there are an infinite number of points on the real number line between 0 and 100. If these numbers are thought of as representing the percentage of the investor's funds going into shares of Able, with 100 minus that percentage going into Baker, there are an infinite number of portfolios that could be formed from just the two securities. In this assertion, however, it is assumed that an investor can buy a fraction of a share. For example, the investor can buy not only one share of Able, but also 1.1 or 1.01 or 1.001 shares.

2. In order to determine the compositions of the portfolios on the efficient set, the investor must solve a quadratic programming problem. See Markowitz's book *Portfolio Selection,* particularly pages 176–185. (See reference 1 for Chapter 8 in the references at the end of this book.)

3. The risk-neutral investor will choose portfolio *S,* and the risk-seeking investor will choose either *S* or *H*. See Appendix B in Chapter 7.

4. This "curvature property" explains why the right side of the feasible set has the umbrella shape noted in Figure 8.1.

5. For an explanation of why there cannot be a convex region on the efficient set, see Gordon J. Alexander and Jack Clark Francis, *Portfolio Analysis* (Upper Saddle River, NJ: Prentice Hall, 1986): pp. 50–55.

6. This is an example of a single-factor model where the factor is the return on a market index (see Chapter 11 for more on factor models; see Chapters 18 and 26 for more on market indices). The model is actually more general than indicated here in that the return need not be that of a market index. It can be any variable that is believed to have a major influence on individual stock returns, such as the predicted rate of increase in industrial production or gross domestic product.

7. To be technically correct, the standard deviation of the random error term should be denoted $\sigma_{\varepsilon iI}$ because it is measured relative to market index *I*. The subscript *I* is not shown in the text for ease of exposition.

8. Because the range refers to the possible outcomes and the spacing refers to the probabilities of the various outcomes occurring, the roulette wheel is a convenient way of referring to the random error term's probability distribution. Typically, it is assumed that a random error term has a normal distribution with a mean of zero.

9. Appendix A of Chapter 7 discusses several basic statistical concepts, including expected value (or expected outcome) and standard deviation.

10. This would be the case if security *B* had a random error term whose roulette wheel had integers from −9% to +9% on it, but the spacing for each integer between −5% and +5% was twice as large as the spacing for each integer from −9% to −6% and from +6% to +9%. The probability that any specific integer between −5% and +5% will occur is equal to $\frac{2}{30}$, whereas the probability that any specific integer from −9% to −6% and from +6% to +9% occurring is equal to $\frac{1}{30}$.

11. Just how beta, the intercept term, and the standard deviation of the random error term are estimated is addressed in Chapter 13.

12. If the random error term takes on a value of zero, the security will lie *on* the line. However, the probability of this occurring is very small for most securities.

13. The market model can be used to estimate expected returns, variances, and covariances for the securities in the feasible set; with these estimates, one can determine the efficient set. See Appendix B in Chapter 7 of William F. Sharpe, Gordon J. Alexander, and Jeffery V. Bailey, *Investments* (Upper Saddle River, NJ: Prentice Hall, 1999).

14. Actually, all that is necessary for this reduction in unique risk to occur is for the maximum amount invested in any one security to continually decrease as *N* increases.

CHAPTER 9

Riskfree Lending and Borrowing

The previous two chapters focused on how an investor should determine what portfolio to select for investment. Markowitz's approach assumes that the investor has a certain amount of initial wealth (W_0) to invest for a given holding period. Of all the portfolios that are available, the optimal one corresponds to the point at which one of the investor's indifference curves is tangent to the efficient set. At the end of the holding period, the investor's initial wealth will have either increased or decreased depending on the portfolio's rate of return. The resulting end-of-period wealth (W_1) can then be completely reinvested, completely spent on consumption, or partially reinvested and partially consumed.

The Markowitz approach assumes that the assets considered for investment are individually risky; that is, each of the N risky assets is assumed to have an uncertain return during the investor's holding period. Because none of the assets has a perfectly negative correlation with any other asset, all the portfolios also have uncertain returns during the investor's holding period and thus are risky. Furthermore, the investor is not allowed to use borrowed money along with his or her initial wealth to purchase a portfolio of assets. This means that the investor cannot use financial leverage, or margin.

In this chapter, the Markowitz approach is expanded by first considering investments not only in risky assets but also in a riskfree asset. There are now N assets available for purchase consisting of $N - 1$ risky assets and 1 riskfree asset. And second, the investor is allowed to borrow money but has to pay a given rate of interest on the loan. The next section considers the effect of adding a riskfree asset to the set of risky assets.

9.1 Defining the Riskfree Asset

riskfree asset

What exactly is a **riskfree asset** in the context of Markowitz's approach? Because this approach involves investing for a single holding period, the return on the riskfree asset during that period is certain. An investor who purchases a riskfree asset at the beginning of a holding period knows exactly what the value of the asset will be at the end of the holding period. Because there is no uncertainty about the terminal value of the riskfree asset, the standard deviation of the riskfree asset is, by definition, zero.

In turn, the covariance between the rate of return on the riskfree asset and the rate of return on any risky asset is zero. Remember from Equation (7.5) that the covariance between the returns on any two assets i and j is equal to the product of the correlation coefficient between the assets and the standard deviations of the two assets: $\sigma_{ij} = \rho_{ij}\sigma_i\sigma_j$. Given that $\sigma_i = 0$ if i is the riskfree asset, it follows that $\sigma_{ij} = 0$.

169

Because a riskfree asset has by definition a certain return, it must be some type of fixed-income security with no possibility of default. In principle, all corporate securities have some chance of default, so the riskfree asset cannot be issued by a corporation. Instead it must be a security issued by the U.S. Treasury. However, not just any Treasury security qualifies as a riskfree security.

Consider an investor with a three-month holding period who purchases a Treasury security maturing in 20 years. This security is risky because the investor does not know what it will be worth at the end of the holding period. Because interest rates will likely change in an unpredictable manner during the investor's holding period, the market price of the security will likewise change in an unpredictable manner. The presence of such **interest-rate risk** (also known as *price risk*) makes the value of the Treasury security uncertain, disqualifying it as a riskfree asset. Indeed any Treasury security with a maturity date greater than the investor's holding period cannot be a riskfree asset.

interest-rate risk

Next, consider a Treasury security that matures before the end of the investor's holding period, such as a 30-day Treasury bill for the investor with the three-month holding period. In this situation, the investor does not know at the beginning of the holding period what interest rates will be in 30 days. As a result, the investor does not know the interest rate at which the proceeds from the maturing Treasury bill can be reinvested for the remainder of the holding period. The presence of such **reinvestment-rate risk** in all Treasury securities of a shorter maturity than the investor's holding period means that these securities are not riskfree assets.

reinvestment-rate risk

Only one type of Treasury security qualifies as a riskfree asset: a Treasury security with a maturity that matches the length of the investor's holding period. For example, the investor with the three-month holding period would find that a Treasury bill with a three-month maturity date had a certain return. Because this security matures at the end of the investor's holding period, it provides the investor with an amount of money at the end of the holding period that is known for certain at the beginning of the holding period when the investment decision is made.[1] Investing in the riskfree asset is often referred to as **riskfree lending** because such an investment involves the purchase of Treasury bills and thus involves a loan by the investor to the federal government.

riskfree lending

9.2   Allowing for Riskfree Lending

With the introduction of a riskfree asset, the investor can put part of his or her money in this asset and the remainder in any of the risky portfolios in Markowitz's feasible set. Adding these new opportunities expands the feasible set significantly and, more important, changes the location of a substantial part of Markowitz's efficient set. These changes should be analyzed because investors are concerned with selecting a portfolio from the efficient set. In this analysis, initial consideration is given to determining the expected return and standard deviation for a portfolio that consists of an investment in the riskfree asset combined with an investment in a single risky security.

9.2.1   INVESTING IN BOTH A RISKFREE ASSET AND A RISKY ASSET

In Chapter 7, the companies of Able, Baker, and Charlie were assumed to have expected returns, variances, and covariances as indicated in the following expected return vector and variance–covariance matrix:

$$
ER = \begin{bmatrix} 16.2 \\ 24.6 \\ 22.8 \end{bmatrix} \qquad VC = \begin{bmatrix} 146 & 187 & 145 \\ 187 & 854 & 104 \\ 145 & 104 & 289 \end{bmatrix}
$$

Defining the riskfree asset as security 4, consider all portfolios that involve investing in just the common stock of Able and the riskfree asset. Let X_1 denote the proportion of the investor's funds invested in Able and $X_4 = 1 - X_1$ denote the proportion invested in the riskfree asset. If the investor put all of his or her money in the riskfree asset, then $X_1 = 0$ and $X_4 = 1$, but if the investor could put all of his or her money in Able, then $X_1 = 1$ and $X_4 = 0$. A combination of .25 in Able and .75 in the riskfree asset is also possible, as are respective combinations of .50 and .50 or .75 and .25. Although there are many other possibilities, the focus here will be on these five portfolios:

	Portfolio A	*Portfolio B*	*Portfolio C*	*Portfolio D*	*Portfolio E*
X_1	.00	.25	.50	.75	1.00
X_4	1.00	.75	.50	.25	.00

Assuming the riskfree asset has a rate of return (often denoted r_f) of 4%, all the necessary information for calculating the expected returns and standard deviations for these five portfolios is available. Equation (7.3a) can be used to calculate the expected returns for these portfolios:

$$\bar{r}_p = \sum_{i=1}^{N} X_i \bar{r}_i \qquad \text{(7.3a)}$$

$$= \sum_{i=1}^{4} X_i \bar{r}_i$$

Portfolios A, B, C, D, and E do not involve investing in the second and third securities (that is, Baker and Charlie companies), meaning that $X_2 = 0$ and $X_3 = 0$ in these portfolios. So, the previous equation reduces to

$$\bar{r}_p = X_1 \bar{r}_1 + X_4 \bar{r}_4$$
$$= (X_1 \times 16.2\%) + (X_4 \times 4\%)$$

where the riskfree rate is now denoted $\bar{r}_4$.

For portfolios A and E the calculation is trivial because all the investor's funds are placed in just one security. Thus, their expected returns are 4% and 16.2%, respectively. For portfolios B, C, and D, the expected returns are, respectively,

$$\bar{r}_B = (.25 \times 16.2\%) + (.75 \times 4\%)$$
$$= 7.05\%$$
$$\bar{r}_C = (.50 \times 16.2\%) + (.50 \times 4\%)$$
$$= 10.10\%$$
$$\bar{r}_D = (.75 \times 16.2\%) + (.25 \times 4\%)$$
$$= 13.15\%$$

The standard deviations of portfolios A and E are simply the standard deviations of the riskfree asset and Able, or $\sigma_A = 0\%$ and $\sigma_E = 12.08\%$, respectively. In the calculation of the standard deviations of portfolios *B*, *C*, and *D*, Equation (7.7) must be used:

$$\sigma_p = \left[\sum_{i=1}^{N} \sum_{j=1}^{N} X_i X_j \sigma_{ij} \right]^{1/2} \tag{7.7}$$

$$= \left[\sum_{i=1}^{4} \sum_{j=1}^{4} X_i X_j \sigma_{ij} \right]^{1/2}$$

Because $X_2 = 0$ and $X_3 = 0$ in these portfolios, this equation reduces to

$$\sigma_p = [X_1 X_1 \sigma_{11} + X_1 X_4 \sigma_{14} + X_4 X_1 \sigma_{41} + X_4 X_4 \sigma_{44}]^{1/2}$$

$$= [X_1^2 \sigma_1^2 + X_4^2 \sigma_4^2 + 2 X_1 X_4 \sigma_{14}]^{1/2}$$

This equation can be reduced even further because security 4 is the riskfree security, which by definition, has $\sigma_4 = 0$ and $\sigma_{14} = 0$. Accordingly, it reduces to

$$\sigma_p = [X_1^2 \sigma_1^2]^{1/2}$$

$$= [X_1^2 \times 146]^{1/2}$$

$$= X_1 \times 12.08\%$$

Thus, the standard deviations of portfolios *B*, *C*, and *D* are

$$\sigma_B = .25 \times 12.08\%$$

$$= 3.02\%$$

$$\sigma_C = .50 \times 12.08\%$$

$$= 6.04\%$$

$$\sigma_D = .75 \times 12.08\%$$

$$= 9.06\%$$

In summary, the five portfolios have the following expected returns and standard deviations:

Portfolio	X_1	X_4	Expected Return	Standard Deviation
A	.00	1.00	4.00%	0.00%
B	.25	.75	7.05	3.02
C	.50	.50	10.10	6.04
D	.75	.25	13.15	9.06
E	1.00	.00	16.20	12.08

These portfolios are plotted in Figure 9.1. Note that they all lie on a straight line connecting the points representing the riskfree asset and Able. Although only five particular combinations of the riskfree asset and Able have been examined here, any combination of the riskfree asset and Able will lie somewhere on the straight line connecting them; the exact location depends on the relative proportions invested in these two assets. This observation can be generalized to combinations of the riskfree asset and any risky asset. Thus, any portfolio consisting of a combination of the riskfree asset and a risky asset will have an expected return and standard deviation that plots somewhere on a straight line connecting them.

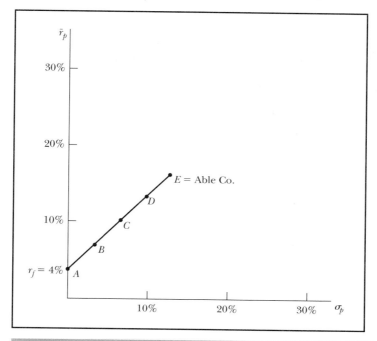

FIGURE 9.1 Combining Riskfree Lending with Investing in a Risky Asset

9.2.2   INVESTING IN BOTH THE RISKFREE ASSET AND A RISKY PORTFOLIO

Consider what happens when a portfolio consisting of more than one risky security is combined with the riskfree asset. For example, the risky portfolio *PAC* consists of Able and Charlie in proportions of .80 and .20, respectively. Its expected return (denoted $\bar{r}_{PAC}$) and standard deviation (denoted σ_{PAC}) are equal to

$$\bar{r}_{PAC} = (.80 \times 16.2\%) + (.20 \times 22.8\%)$$

$$= 17.52\%$$

$$\sigma_{PAC} = [(.80 \times .80 \times 146) + (.20 \times .20 \times 289) + (2 \times .80 \times .20 \times 145)]^{1/2}$$

$$= 12.30\%$$

Any portfolio that consists of an investment in both *PAC* and the riskfree asset will have an expected return and standard deviation that can be calculated the same way as for combinations of an individual asset and the riskfree asset. A portfolio that has the proportion X_{PAC} invested in the portfolio *PAC* and the proportion $X_4 = 1 - X_{PAC}$ in the riskfree asset will have an expected return and standard deviation that are equal to, respectively,

$$\bar{r}_{PAC} = (X_{PAC} \times 17.52\%) + (X_4 \times 4\%)$$

$$\sigma_{PAC} = X_{PAC} \times 12.30\%$$

For example, consider investing in a portfolio that consists of *PAC* and the riskfree asset in proportions of .25 and .75, respectively.[2] This portfolio will have an expected return of

$$\bar{r}_P = (.25 \times 17.52\%) + (.75 \times 4\%)$$
$$= 7.38\%$$

and a standard deviation of

$$\sigma_p = .25 \times 12.30\%$$
$$= 3.08\%$$

Figure 9.2 shows that this portfolio, indicated by point *P,* lies on a straight line connecting the riskfree asset and *PAC*. Other portfolios consisting of various combinations of *PAC* and the riskfree asset also lie on this line; their exact locations depend on the relative proportions invested in *PAC* and the riskfree asset. For example, a portfolio that involves investing a proportion of .50 in the riskfree asset and a proportion of .50 in *PAC* lies on this line exactly halfway between the two endpoints.

In summary, combining the riskfree asset with any risky portfolio is no different than combining the riskfree asset with an individual risky security. In both cases, the resulting portfolio has an expected return and standard deviation such that it lies somewhere on the straight line connecting the two endpoints.

9.2.3 THE EFFECT OF RISKFREE LENDING ON THE EFFICIENT SET

As mentioned earlier, the feasible set is changed significantly when riskfree lending is introduced. Figure 9.3 shows how riskfree lending changes the feasible set in the example. Here all risky assets and portfolios, not just Able and *PAC,* are considered in all

FIGURE 9.2 Combining Riskfree Lending with Investing in a Risky Portfolio

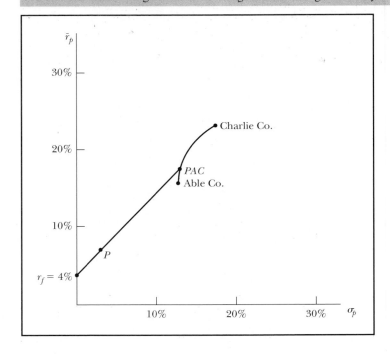

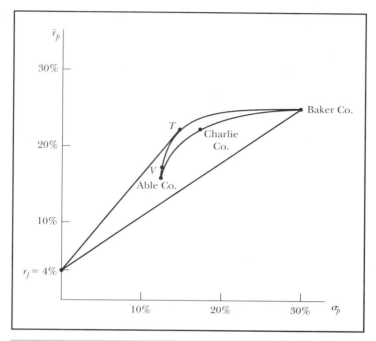

FIGURE 9.3 Feasible and Efficient Sets When Riskfree Lending Is Introduced

possible combinations with the riskfree asset. Note that there are two boundaries that are straight lines emanating from the riskfree asset. The bottom line connects the risk-free asset with Baker, and represents portfolios formed by combining Baker and the riskfree asset.

The other straight line emanating from the riskfree asset represents combinations of the riskfree asset and a particular risky portfolio on the efficient set of the Markowitz model. It is tangent to the efficient set with a tangency point *T*. This tangency point represents a risky portfolio consisting of Able, Baker, and Charlie in proportions equal to, respectively, .12, .19, and .69. Substituting these proportions into Equations (7.3a) and (7.7) gives the expected return and standard deviation of *T* as 22.4% and 15.2%, respectively.

Although other risky efficient portfolios from the Markowitz model can also be combined with the riskfree asset, portfolio *T* deserves special attention. Why? Because there is no other portfolio consisting purely of risky assets that, when connected by a straight line to the riskfree asset, lies northwest of it. In other words, of all the lines that can be drawn emanating from the riskfree asset and connecting with either a risky asset or a risky portfolio, none has a greater slope than the one that goes to *T*.

This fact is important because part of the efficient set of the Markowitz model is dominated by this line. Specifically, the portfolios on the Markowitz model efficient set going from the minimum-risk portfolio, denoted *V*, to *T* are no longer efficient when a riskfree asset is introduced. Instead, the efficient set now consists of a straight-line segment and a curved segment. The straight-line segment extends from the riskfree asset to *T* and consists of portfolios made up of various combinations of the riskfree asset and *T*. The curved segment consists of those portfolios to the northeast of *T* on the Markowitz model efficient set.

9.2.4 THE EFFECT OF RISKFREE LENDING
ON PORTFOLIO SELECTION

Figure 9.4 shows an optimal efficient portfolio with a riskfree asset in addition to a number of risky assets. If the investor's indifference curves look like those shown in Figure 9.4(a), the investor's optimal portfolio, O^*, will be invested partially in the riskfree asset and partially in T because his or her indifference curves are tangent to the efficient set between the riskfree asset and T.[3] However, if the investor is less risk-averse and has indifference curves that look like those shown in panel (b), then the investor's optimal portfolio, O^*, will not involve any riskfree lending; his or her indifference curves are tangent to the curved segment of the efficient set that lies to the northeast of T.

9.3 Allowing for Riskfree Borrowing

The analysis presented in the previous section can be expanded by allowing the investor to borrow money. This investor is no longer restricted to his or her initial wealth when it comes time to decide how much money to invest in risky assets.[4] However, if the investor borrows money, then interest must be paid on the loan. Because the interest rate is known and there is no uncertainty about repaying the loan, this practice is often referred to as **riskfree borrowing.** It will be assumed that the rate of interest charged on the loan is equal to the rate of interest that could be earned from investing in the riskfree asset.[5] The investor from the earlier example now not only has the opportunity to invest in a riskfree asset that earns a rate of return of 4% but also may borrow money at a rate of interest equal to 4%.

riskfree borrowing

Earlier the proportion invested in the riskfree asset was denoted X_4, and this proportion was constrained to be a number between 0 and 1. With the opportunity to borrow at the same rate, X_4 will no longer be so constrained. In the earlier example, the investor had initial wealth of $17,200. If the investor borrows money, then he or she will have in excess of $17,200 to invest in the risky securities of Able, Baker, and Charlie. For example, if the investor borrows $4,300, then he or she will have a total of $21,500 (= $17,200 + $4,300) to invest in these securities. In this situation, X_4 is equal to $-.25$ (=$-$4,300/$17,200). However, the sum of the proportions must still equal 1. If the investor borrows money, the sum of the proportions invested in risky assets would be greater than one. For example, borrowing $4,300 and investing $21,500 in Able means that the proportion in Able, X_1, equals 1.25 (= $21,500/$17,200). Note that in this case $X_1 + X_4 = 1.25 + (-.25) = 1$.

9.3.1 BORROWING AND INVESTING IN A RISKY SECURITY

The example presented in the previous section can be expanded to evaluate the effect that the introduction of riskfree borrowing has on the efficient set. In particular, consider portfolios *F, G, H,* and *I.* For these portfolios the investor will invest all the borrowed funds as well as his or her own funds in Able. Thus, the proportions for these portfolios can be summarized as follows:

	Portfolio F	*Portfolio G*	*Portfolio H*	*Portfolio I*
X_1	1.25	1.50	1.75	2.00
X_4	$-.25$	$-.50$	$-.75$	-1.00

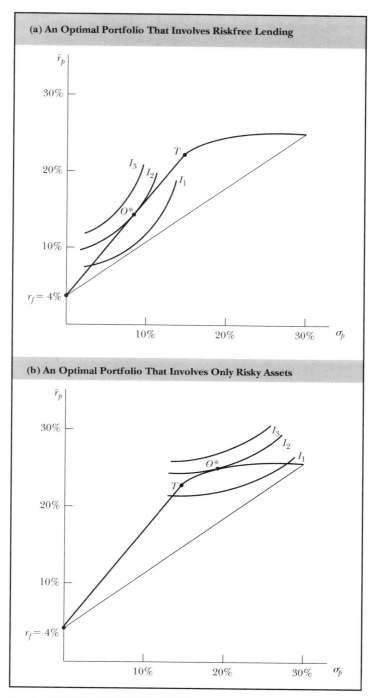

(a) An Optimal Portfolio That Involves Riskfree Lending

(b) An Optimal Portfolio That Involves Only Risky Assets

FIGURE 9.4 Portfolio Selection with Riskfree Lending

The expected returns of these portfolios are calculated in the same manner as was shown in the previous section. Equation (7.3a) is still used:

$$\bar{r}_p = \sum_{i=1}^{N} X_i \bar{r}_i \qquad \text{(7.3a)}$$

$$= \sum_{i=1}^{4} X_i \bar{r}_i$$

$$= X_1 \bar{r}_1 + X_4 \bar{r}_4$$

$$= (X_1 \times 16.2\%) + (X_4 \times 4\%)$$

Portfolios *F, G, H,* and *I* have the following expected returns:

$$\bar{r}_F = (1.25 \times 16.2\%) + (-.25 \times 4\%)$$
$$= 19.25\%$$
$$\bar{r}_G = (1.50 \times 16.2\%) + (-.50 \times 4\%)$$
$$= 22.30\%$$
$$\bar{r}_H = (1.75 \times 16.2\%) + (-.75 \times 4\%)$$
$$= 25.35\%$$
$$\bar{r}_I = (2.00 \times 16.2\%) + (-1.00 \times 4\%)$$
$$= 28.40\%$$

The standard deviations of these portfolios are calculated using Equation (7.7) as was done in the previous section:

$$\sigma_p = \left[\sum_{i=1}^{N} \sum_{j=1}^{N} X_i X_j \sigma_{ij} \right]^{1/2} \qquad \text{(7.7)}$$

$$= \left[\sum_{i=1}^{4} \sum_{j=1}^{4} X_i X_j \sigma_{ij} \right]^{1/2}$$

which was reduced to

$$\sigma_p = X_1 \times 12.08\%$$

The standard deviations of the four portfolios are

$$\sigma_F = 1.25 \times 12.08\%$$
$$= 15.10\%$$
$$\sigma_G = 1.50 \times 12.08\%$$
$$= 18.12\%$$
$$\sigma_H = 1.75 \times 12.08\%$$
$$= 21.14\%$$
$$\sigma_I = 2.00 \times 12.08\%$$
$$= 24.16\%$$

In summary, these four portfolios, as well as the five portfolios that involve risk-free lending, have the following expected returns and standard deviations:

Portfolio	X_1	X_4	Expected Return	Standard Deviation
A	.00	1.00	4.00%	0.00%
B	.25	.75	7.05	3.02
C	.50	.50	10.10	6.04
D	.75	.25	13.15	9.06
E	1.00	.00	16.20	12.08
F	1.25	−.25	19.25	15.10
G	1.50	−.50	22.30	18.12
H	1.75	−.75	25.35	21.14
I	2.00	−1.00	28.40	24.16

In Figure 9.5, the four portfolios that involve riskfree borrowing (*F, G, H,* and *I*) all lie on the same straight line that goes through the five portfolios that involve riskfree lending (*A, B, C, D,* and *E*). Furthermore, the larger the amount of borrowing, the farther out on the line the portfolio lies; equivalently, the smaller the value of X_4, the farther out on the line the portfolio lies.

Although only four particular combinations of borrowing and investing in Able have been examined here, any combination of borrowing and investing in Able will lie somewhere on this line, with the exact location depending on the amount of borrowing. Furthermore, this observation can be generalized to combinations of riskfree borrowing and an investment in any particular risky asset: Borrowing at the riskfree rate and investing all the borrowed money and the investor's own money in a risky asset will result in a portfolio that has an expected return and standard deviation such that it lies on the extension of the straight line connecting the riskfree rate and the risky asset.

FIGURE 9.5 Combining Riskfree Borrowing and Lending with Investing in a Risky Asset

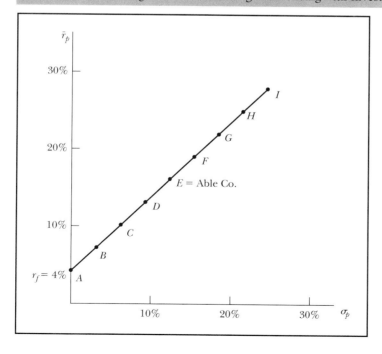

9.3.2 BORROWING AND INVESTING IN A RISKY PORTFOLIO

Next, consider what happens when a portfolio of more than one risky asset is purchased with both the investor's own funds and borrowed funds. Earlier it was shown that the portfolio having proportions invested in Able and Charlie equal to .80 and .20, respectively, had an expected return of 17.52% and a standard deviation of 12.30%. This portfolio was referred to as *PAC*. Any portfolio that involves borrowing money at the riskfree rate and investing these funds and the investor's own funds in *PAC* will have an expected return and standard deviation that can be calculated the same way as when borrowing was incurred and Able was purchased. A portfolio that involves borrowing the proportion X_4 and investing these funds and all the investor's own funds in *PAC* will have an expected return and standard deviation that are equal to, respectively,

$$\bar{r}_{PAC} = (X_{PAC} \times 17.52\%) + (X_4 \times 4\%)$$

$$\sigma_{PAC} = X_{PAC} \times 12.30\%$$

For example, consider borrowing an amount of money equal to 25% of the investor's initial wealth and then investing all the investor's own funds and these borrowed funds in *PAC*. Thus, $X_{PAC} = 1 - X_4 = 1 - (-.25) = 1.25$.[6] This portfolio will have an expected return of

$$\bar{r}_p = (1.25 \times 17.52\%) + (-.25 \times 4\%)$$

$$= 20.90\%$$

and a standard deviation of

$$\sigma_p = 1.25 \times 12.30\%$$

$$= 15.38\%$$

Figure 9.6 shows that this portfolio (denoted *P*) lies on the extension of the line that connects the riskfree rate with *PAC*. Other portfolios consisting of *PAC* and borrowing at the riskfree rate will also lie somewhere on this extension, with their exact location depending on the amount of the borrowing. Thus, borrowing to purchase a risky portfolio is no different than borrowing to purchase an individual risky asset. In both cases, the resulting portfolio lies on an extension of the line connecting the riskfree rate with the risky investment.

9.4 Allowing for Both Riskfree Borrowing and Lending

9.4.1 THE EFFECT OF RISKFREE BORROWING AND LENDING ON THE EFFICIENT SET

Figure 9.7 shows how the feasible set is changed when both borrowing and lending at the same riskfree rate are allowed. Here all risky assets and portfolios, not just Able and *PAC,* are considered. The feasible set is the entire area between the two lines emanating from the riskfree rate that go through the location of Baker and the portfolio denoted *T.* These two lines extend indefinitely to the right if it is assumed that there is no limit to the amount of borrowing that the investor can incur.

The straight line that goes through portfolio *T* is of special importance because it represents the efficient set, as is the set of feasible portfolios lying farthest northwest. Portfolio *T,* as was mentioned earlier, consists of investments in Able, Baker, and Charlie in proportions equal to .12, .19, and .69, respectively.[7]

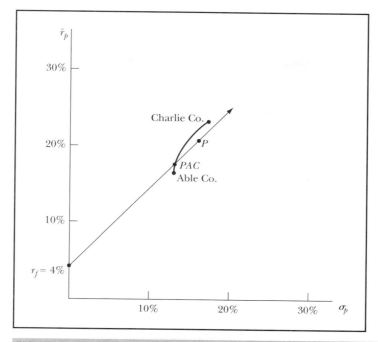

FIGURE 9.6 Combining Riskfree Borrowing and Lending with Investing in a Risky Portfolio

FIGURE 9.7 Feasible and Efficient Sets When Riskfree Borrowing
and Lending Are Introduced

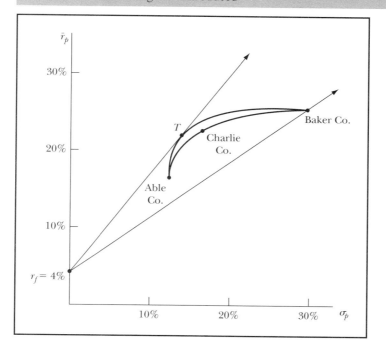

The Cost of Short-Term Borrowing

 The extension of the Markowitz model to incorporate borrowing and lending assumes that investors can borrow or lend at the riskfree rate. Certainly, every investor has the opportunity to lend at the riskfree rate by simply purchasing U.S. Treasury securities whose maturities correspond to the length of his or her investment holding period.

Borrowing at the riskfree rate is another matter. In reality, only one entity has the option to borrow at the riskfree rate: the U.S. Treasury. Other investors, be they individuals or institutional investors, must borrow at interest rates exceeding those paid by the Treasury. Just what level of interest rates do investors pay to borrow? To provide some perspective on this issue, we briefly survey some of the interest rates available in the market for short-term financial assets, known as the *money market.*

The standard of comparison for all money market interest rates is the rate paid on short-term U.S. Treasury securities called U.S. Treasury bills (see Chapter 1). The return on Treasury bills is completely certain over the short term because the federal government will never default on its obligations. It always has the option to print money or to raise taxes to pay off its debts. Other borrowers, no matter how strong their current financial position, run at least some risk of defaulting on their short-term debts. Largely owing to this fact, virtually all non-Treasury borrowers who issue taxable debt must pay interest rates exceeding those paid by the Treasury. The difference between what the Treasury pays to borrow money and what other borrowers pay is known as the *yield spread.* How large is the spread for non-Treasury borrowers?

If you as an individual investor wish to finance your investment in securities, you typically purchase them on margin from your broker. In such transactions the broker actually borrows money elsewhere in the money market (usually drawing down a line of credit at a bank and pledging securities as collateral). The interest rate paid by the broker is known as the *broker call money rate,* or broker call loan rate (see Chapter 3). Brokers add anywhere from 1% to 2% to the call money rate to determine the interest rate charged their margin purchase customers. Larger investors can usually negotiate more favorable borrowing terms than smaller investors.

During the 12-month period ending December 1998, the broker call money rate averaged roughly 7.08%. By comparison, the U.S. Treasury paid an average interest rate on 90-day Treasury bills of 4.86%. Thus, the broker call money spread was 2.22 percentage points. Assuming a 1 percentage point markup over the broker call money rate, margin investors faced an average spread over 90-day Treasuries of 3.22 percentage points during 1998.

Large, financially strong corporations usually borrow in the money market through an instrument known as *commercial paper.* Commercial paper represents negotiable, short-term, unsecured promissory notes of finance, industrial, utility, insurance, and bank holding companies. The financial strength of these corporations allows them to borrow at money market rates very near those of Treasury bills. During 1998, three-month commercial paper interest rates averaged 5.31%, a spread of .45 percentage points over similar-maturity 90-day Treasury bills.

Corporations without the size and financial strength to borrow in the commercial paper market usually obtain their short-term financing from banks. The interest rate officially quoted by banks on short-term unsecured loans to their best customers is known as the *prime rate.* The prime rate is not always an accurate measure of short-term borrowing costs because banks often discount from it on loans to their financially strong borrowers. Financially weaker clients, on the other hand, may be charged a premium above the prime rate. During 1998, the prime rate averaged 8.31%, a 3.45 percentage point spread over 90-day Treasuries.

Banks themselves borrow in the money market through large-denomination certificates of deposit (usually $1 million or larger). Although these loans are unsecured and do not carry federal deposit insurance, the strong financial standing of most banks requires them to pay little more than the government for short-term borrowing. During 1998, rates for large 3-month certificates of deposit averaged 5.44%, .58 percentage points above 90-day Treasuries.

From this brief money market survey, it is apparent that the Treasury bill rate is relevant to investor borrowing only as a base of comparison. Investors actually have to pay more, sometimes much more, to borrow in the money market, but then, of course, such borrowing is not considered riskfree, at least by the lenders.

The line going through *T* is just tangent to the Markowitz model efficient set. None of the portfolios, except for *T*, that were on the Markowitz model efficient set are efficient when riskfree borrowing and lending are introduced. Hence, every portfolio (except *T*) that lies on the Markowitz model efficient set is dominated by a portfolio on this straight line having the same standard deviation along with a higher expected return.

9.4.2 THE EFFECT OF RISKFREE BORROWING AND LENDING ON PORTFOLIO SELECTION

Given the opportunity to either borrow or lend at the riskfree rate, an investor would identify the optimal portfolio by plotting his or her indifference curves on this graph and noting where one of them is tangent to the linear efficient set. Figure 9.8 shows two alternative situations. If the investor's indifference curves look like the ones in panel (a), then the investor's optimal portfolio, *O**, will consist of investments in both the riskfree asset and *T*. Alternatively, if the investor is less risk averse and has indifference curves that look like those shown in panel (b), then the investor's optimal portfolio, *O**, will consist of borrowing at the riskfree rate and investing these funds as well as his or her own funds in *T*.[8]

Summary

1. The return on a riskfree asset is certain. The riskfree asset's standard deviation is zero as is its covariance with other assets.
2. The riskfree asset is a Treasury security with a maturity that matches the length of the investor's holding period.
3. In extending the Markowitz feasible set to include riskfree lending, investors are assumed to allocate their funds among a riskfree asset and a portfolio of risky assets.
4. With riskfree lending, the efficient set becomes a straight line from the riskfree rate to a point tangent to the curved Markowitz efficient set, in addition to the portion of the Markowitz efficient set that lies northeast of this tangency point.
5. Introducing riskfree borrowing permits an investor to engage in financial leverage. The investor may use all of his or her money, plus money borrowed at the riskfree rate, to purchase a portfolio of risky assets.
6. With riskfree lending and borrowing, the efficient set becomes a straight line from the riskfree rate through a point tangent to the curved Markowitz efficient set.
7. With riskfree lending and borrowing, the efficient set consists of combinations of a single risky portfolio and various proportions of riskfree lending or borrowing.
8. The investor's optimal portfolio is determined by plotting his or her indifference curves against the efficient set.

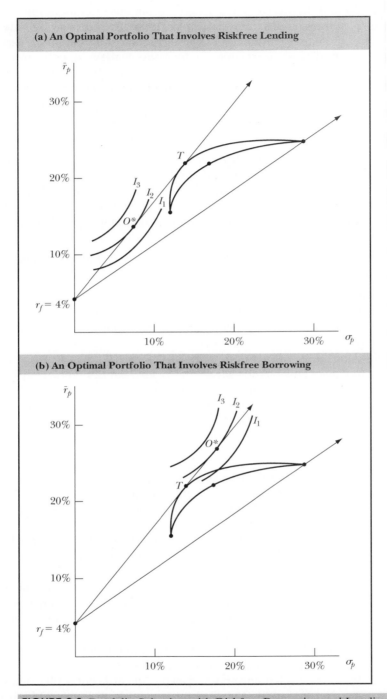

FIGURE 9.8 Portfolio Selection with Riskfree Borrowing and Lending

9. The investor's optimal portfolio includes an investment in the risky portfolio and either borrowing or lending at the riskfree rate.

10. Investors with higher levels of risk aversion will engage in less borrowing (or more lending) than investors with less risk aversion.

Questions and Problems

1. Why is a pure-discount government security (one that does not make coupon payments, pays interest at maturity, and sells at a discount from par) with no risk of default still risky to an investor whose holding period does not coincide with the maturity date of the security?

2. Lindsay Brown owns a risky portfolio with a 15% expected return. The riskfree return is 5%. What is the expected return on Lindsay's total portfolio if Lindsay invests the following proportions in the risky portfolio and the remainder in the riskfree asset?
   a. 120%
   b. 90%
   c. 75%

3. Consider a risky portfolio with an expected return of 18%. With a riskfree return of 5%, how could you create a portfolio with a 24% expected return?

4. Happy Buker owns a risky portfolio with a 20% standard deviation. If Happy invests the following proportions in the riskfree asset and the remainder in the risky portfolio, what is the standard deviation of Happy's total portfolio?
   a. −30%
   b. 10%
   c. 30%

5. Oyster Burns's portfolio is composed of an investment in a risky portfolio (with a 12% expected return and a 25% standard deviation) and a riskfree asset (with a 7% return). If Oyster's total portfolio has a 20% standard deviation, what is its expected return?

6. Hick Cady argues that buying a risky portfolio with riskfree borrowing is equivalent to a purchase of the risky portfolio on margin. Patsy Cahill contends that such an investment can be viewed as selling the riskfree asset short and using proceeds to invest in the risky portfolio. Who is correct? Explain.

7. How does the efficient set change when riskfree borrowing and lending are introduced into the Markowitz model? Explain with words and graphs.

8. Why does the efficient set with the Markowitz model extended to include riskfree borrowing and lending have only one point in common with the efficient set of the Markowitz model without riskfree borrowing and lending? Why are the other points on the "old" efficient set no longer desirable? Explain with words and graphs.

9. How does the feasible set change when riskfree borrowing and lending are introduced into the Markowitz model? Explain with words and graphs.

10. With the Markowitz model extended to include riskfree borrowing and lending, draw the indifference curves, efficient set, and optimal portfolio for an investor with high risk aversion and an investor with low risk aversion.

11. Given the following expected return vector and variance–covariance matrix for three assets:

$$ER = \begin{bmatrix} 10.1 \\ 7.8 \\ 5.0 \end{bmatrix} \qquad VC = \begin{bmatrix} 210 & 60 & 0 \\ 60 & 90 & 0 \\ 0 & 0 & 0 \end{bmatrix}$$

    and given the fact that Pie Traynor's risky portfolio is split 50:50 between the two risky assets,
    a. Which security of the three must be the riskfree asset? Why?
    b. Calculate the expected return and standard deviation of Pie's portfolio.
    c. If the riskfree asset makes up 25% of Pie's total portfolio, what are the total portfolio's expected return and standard deviation?

12. What does the efficient set look like if riskfree borrowing is permitted but no lending is allowed? Explain with words and graphs.

13. What will be the effect on total portfolio expected return and risk if you borrow money at the riskfree rate and invest in the optimal risky portfolio?

14. Suppose that your level of risk aversion decreased as you grew richer. In a world of riskfree borrowing and lending, how would your optimal portfolio change? Would the types of risky securities you hold change? Explain with words and graphs.

15. (Appendix Question) How does the efficient set change when the condition of borrowing and lending at the same riskfree rate is changed to borrowing at a rate greater than the rate at which riskfree lending can be conducted? Explain with words and graphs.

APPENDIX

Allowing for Different Borrowing and Lending Rates

In this chapter it was assumed that the investor could borrow funds at the same rate that could be earned on an investment in the riskfree asset. As a result, the feasible set became the area bounded by two straight lines emanating from the riskfree rate. The upper line represented the efficient set and had one portfolio in common with the curved efficient set of the Markowitz model. This portfolio was located where the straight line from the riskfree rate was tangent to the curved efficient set. Now consider what happens if the investor can borrow, but only at a rate greater than the rate that can be earned by an investment in the riskfree asset. The rate on the riskfree asset will be denoted r_{fL}, where L indicates lending, because, as mentioned earlier, an investment in the riskfree asset is equivalent to lending money to the U.S. Treasury. The rate at which the investor can borrow money will be denoted r_{fB} and is of a magnitude such that r_{fB} is greater than r_{fL}.

One way to understand the effect on the efficient set of assuming that these two rates are different is as follows.

1. Consider what the efficient set would look like if riskfree borrowing and lending were possible at the same rate, r_{fL}. The resulting efficient set would be the straight line shown in Figure 9.9 that goes through points r_{fL} and T_L.

2. Consider what the efficient set would look like if riskfree borrowing and lending were possible at the higher rate, r_{fB}. The resulting efficient set would be the straight line shown in Figure 9.9 that goes through the points r_{fB} and T_B. Note that portfolio T_B lies on Markowitz's efficient set above portfolio T_L because it corresponds to a tangency point associated with a higher riskfree rate.

FIGURE 9.9 Evaluating Different Riskfree Rates

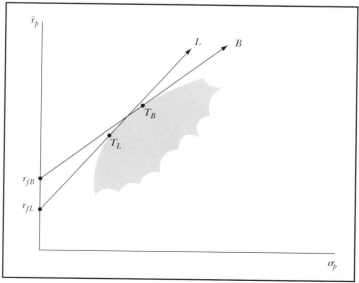

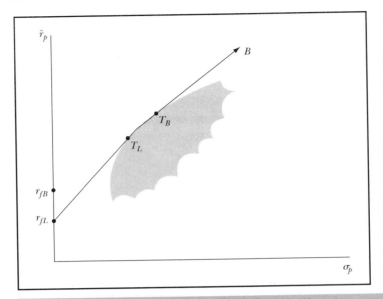

FIGURE 9.10 Efficient Set When the Riskfree Are Different

3. Because the investor cannot borrow at r_{fL}, that part of the line emanating from r_{fL} that extends to the right of T_L is not available to the investor and can be removed from consideration.

4. Because the investor cannot lend at the riskfree rate r_{fB}, the part of the line emanating from r_{fB} and going through T_B but lying to the left of T_B is not available to the investor and can be removed from consideration. The northwest boundary of what remains, shown in Figure 9.10, is the resulting efficient set.

This efficient set consists of three distinct but connected segments. The first segment is the straight line going from r_{fL} to T_L, which represents various amounts of riskfree lending combined with investing in the portfolio of risky assets, denoted T_L. The second segment is the curved line going from T_L to T_B, which represents various risky portfolios that were also on Markowitz's curved efficient set. The third segment is the straight line extending outward from T_B, which represents various amounts of borrowing combined with an investment in the risky portfolio denoted T_B.

The optimal portfolio for an investor will be, as before, the portfolio that corresponds to the point at which an indifference curve is tangent to the efficient set. Depending on the investor's indifference curves, this tangency point could be on any one of the three segments that define the efficient set. Highly risk-averse investors will tend to invest at least partly at the riskfree rate r_{fL} whereas slightly risk-averse investors will tend to borrow at the riskfree rate r_{fB}.

Endnotes

1. To be truly riskfree, the security must not provide the investor with any coupon payments during the holding period. Instead, it must provide the investor with only one cash inflow, and that inflow must occur at the end of the investor's holding period. Any intervening coupon payments would subject the investor to reinvestment-rate risk because he or she would not know at $t = 0$ the rate at which the coupon payments could be invested for the remainder of the holding period. It should also be noted that the discussion focuses on an asset that is riskfree in nominal terms because the presence of uncertain inflation means

that nearly all U.S. Treasury securities are risky in real terms (although the Treasury has recently begun to issue inflation-protected securities; see Chapter 19).

2. Note that investing the proportion .25 in portfolio *PAC* is equivalent to investing the proportion .20 (= .25 × .80) in Able and the proportion .05 (= .25 × .20) in Charlie.

3. A more risk-averse investor (meaning an investor whose indifference curves have greater slopes) would choose an optimal portfolio that is closer to the riskfree asset on the line that connects the riskfree asset to *T*. Only if the investor is infinitely risk-averse will the optimal portfolio consist of an investment in just the riskfree asset.

4. Borrowing gives the investor the opportunity to engage in margin purchases if he or she so desires. Thus, the investor can use financial leverage. Buying securities on margin is discussed in Chapter 2.

5. The appendix discusses what happens to the efficient set when the investor is able to borrow but at a rate that is greater than the rate that can be earned by investing in the riskfree asset.

6. Note that investing the proportion 1.25 in portfolio *PAC* is equivalent to investing the proportion 1.00 (= 1.25 × .80) in Able and the proportion .25 (= 1.25 × .20) in Charlie.

7. The composition of the tangency portfolio *T* can be found using commonly available mathematical algorithms. One such algorithm is available on the Internet at (www.wsharpe.com). Further, on a historical note, an early simple approach to determining the composition of *T* is presented in Edwin J. Elton, Martin J. Gruber, and Manfred D. Padberg, "Simple Criteria for Optimal Portfolio Selection," *Journal of Finance,* 31, no. 5 (December 1976): 1341–1357.

8. The less risk averse the investor is, the smaller the proportion invested in the riskfree rate and the larger the proportion invested in *T*.

The Capital Asset Pricing Model

Chapters 7, 8, and 9 presented a method for identifying an investor's optimal portfolio. With this method, the investor needs to estimate the expected returns and variances for all securities under consideration. Furthermore, all the covariances among these securities need to be estimated, and the riskfree rate needs to be determined. Once this is done, the investor can identify the composition of the tangency portfolio as well as its expected return and standard deviation. The investor can then identify the optimal portfolio by noting where one of his or her indifference curves touches but does not intersect the efficient set. This portfolio involves an investment in the tangency portfolio along with a certain amount of either riskfree borrowing or lending because the efficient set is linear (that is, a straight line).

normative economics
positive economics

Such an approach to investing is an exercise in **normative economics,** wherein investors are told what they should do. Thus, the approach is prescriptive in nature. This chapter enters the realm of **positive economics** by presenting a descriptive model of how assets are priced. The model assumes among other things that all investors use the approach to investing given in Chapters 7, 8, and 9. The major implication of the model is that the expected return of an asset is related to a measure of risk for that asset known as *beta*. The **capital asset pricing model (CAPM)** specifies the relationship between expected return and beta. This model provides the intellectual basis for a number of the current practices in the investment industry. Although many of these practices are based on various extensions and modifications of the CAPM, a sound understanding of the original version is necessary to understand these practices. Accordingly, this chapter presents the original version of the CAPM.[1]

capital asset pricing model (CAPM)

10.1 Assumptions

To understand how assets are priced, one must construct a model (that is, a theory). This process requires the model-builder to simplify a complex situation and focus only on the most important elements. This focus is achieved by making certain assumptions about the environment. The assumptions need to be simplistic in order to provide the degree of abstraction necessary for some success in building the model. The *reasonableness* of the assumptions (or lack thereof) is of little concern. Instead the test of a model is its ability to help one understand and predict the process being modeled. As Milton Friedman, recipient of the 1976 Nobel Memorial Prize in Economic Science, stated in a famous essay,

> [T]he relevant question to ask about the "assumptions" of a theory is not whether they are descriptively "realistic," for they never are, but whether

they are sufficiently good approximations for the purpose in hand. And this question can be answered only by seeing whether the theory works, which means whether it yields sufficiently accurate predictions.[2]

Some of the assumptions behind the CAPM are also behind the normative approach to investing described in the previous three chapters. These assumptions are as follows:

1. Investors evaluate portfolios by looking at the expected returns and standard deviations of the portfolios during a one-period horizon.
2. Investors are never satiated, so when given a choice between two portfolios with identical standard deviations, they will choose the one with the higher expected return.
3. Investors are risk-averse, so when given a choice between two portfolios with identical expected returns, they will choose the one with the lower standard deviation.
4. Individual assets are infinitely divisible, meaning that an investor can buy a fraction of a share if he or she so desires.
5. There is a riskfree rate at which an investor may either lend or borrow money.
6. Taxes and transaction costs are irrelevant.

To those assumptions the following ones are added:

7. All investors have the same one-period horizon.
8. The riskfree rate is the same for all investors.
9. Information is freely and instantly available to all investors.
10. Investors have **homogeneous expectations,** meaning that they have the same perceptions regarding the expected returns, standard deviations, and covariances of securities.

homogeneous expectations

The CAPM reduces the situation to an extreme case. Everyone has the same information and agrees about the future prospects for securities. Implicitly this means that investors analyze and process information in the same way. There are **perfect markets** for securities because potential impediments such as finite divisibility, taxes, transaction costs, and different riskfree borrowing and lending rates have been assumed away. This approach allows the focus to shift from how an individual should invest to what would happen to security prices if everyone invested in a similar manner. Examining the collective behavior of all investors in the marketplace enables one to develop the resulting equilibrium relationship between each security's risk and return.

perfect markets

10.2   The Capital Market Line

10.2.1   THE SEPARATION THEOREM

Having made these ten assumptions, the resulting implications can now be examined. First, investors would analyze securities and determine the composition of the tangency portfolio. In so doing, *everyone would obtain in equilibrium the same tangency portfolio.* This result is not surprising because there is complete agreement among investors on the estimates of the securities' expected returns, variances, and covariances, as well as on the level of the riskfree rate. Consequently, the linear efficient set (described in Chapter 9) is the same for all investors because it simply involves combinations of the agreed-on tangency portfolio and either riskfree borrowing or riskfree lending.

Because all investors face the same efficient set, the only reason they will choose dissimilar portfolios is that they have different preferences toward risk and return, resulting in distinct indifference curves. For example, the investor in Figure 9.8(a) will

**separation
theorem**

choose a different portfolio than the investor in Figure 9.8(b). Although the chosen portfolios will be different, *each investor will choose the same combination of risky securities,* denoted *T* in Figure 9.8. As a result, each investor will spread his or her funds among risky securities in the same relative proportions, adding riskfree borrowing or lending in order to achieve a personally preferred combination of risk and return. This feature of the CAPM is often referred to as the **separation theorem:**

> The optimal combination of risky assets for an investor can be determined without any knowledge of the investor's preferences toward risk and return.

In other words, the optimal combination of risky assets can be determined without any knowledge of the shape of an investor's indifference curves.

The reasoning behind the separation theorem involves a property of the linear efficient set introduced in Chapter 9. There it was shown that all portfolios located on the linear efficient set involved an investment in a tangency portfolio combined with varying degrees of riskfree borrowing or lending. With the CAPM everyone faces the same linear efficient set, meaning that each person invests in the same tangency portfolio in which everyone else is investing. (There will also be a certain amount of either riskfree borrowing or lending that depends on that person's indifference curves.) It follows that the risky portion of all investors' portfolios will be the same.

In the example from Chapter 9, three securities were considered, corresponding to the stocks of Able, Baker, and Charlie companies. With a riskfree rate of 4%, the tangency portfolio *T* consisted of investments in Able, Baker, and Charlie in proportions equal to .12, .19, and .69, respectively. If the 10 assumptions of the CAPM are made, the investor in Figure 9.8(a) will invest approximately half of his or her money in the riskfree asset and the remainder in *T*. The investor in Figure 9.8(b), on the other hand, will borrow an amount of money equal to approximately one-quarter the value of his or her initial wealth and invest these borrowed funds as well as his or her own funds in T.[3] The proportions invested in the three stocks for investors in Figure 9.8 would equal[4]

$$(.5) \times \begin{bmatrix} .12 \\ .19 \\ .69 \end{bmatrix} = \begin{bmatrix} .060 \\ .095 \\ .345 \end{bmatrix}$$

for the investor in panel (a) and

$$(1.25) \times \begin{bmatrix} .12 \\ .19 \\ .69 \end{bmatrix} = \begin{bmatrix} .150 \\ .238 \\ .862 \end{bmatrix}$$

for the investor in panel (b).

Although the proportions invested in each of these three risky securities for the Figure 9.8(a) investor (.060, .095, .345) are different in size from their values for the Figure 9.8(b) investor (.150, .238, .862), the relative proportions are the same, being equal to .12, .19, and .69, respectively.

10.2.2 THE MARKET PORTFOLIO

Another important feature of the CAPM is that in equilibrium each security must have a nonzero proportion in the composition of the tangency portfolio.[5] In equilibrium, no security can have a proportion in *T* that is zero. The reasoning behind this feature lies in the previously mentioned separation theorem, which asserts that the risky portion of every investor's portfolio is independent of the investor's risk–return preferences. The justification for the theorem was that the risky portion of each investor's portfolio is simply an investment in *T*. If every investor is purchasing *T* and *T* does not involve an investment in each security, then nobody is investing in those securities with zero proportions in *T*. Consequently, the prices of these zero-proportion securities must fall, thereby causing the expected returns of these securities to rise until the resulting tangency portfolio has a nonzero proportion associated with them.

In the previous example, Charlie had a current price of $62 and an expected end-of-period price of $76.14, so the expected return for Charlie was 22.8% $[= (\$76.14 - \$62)/\$62]$. Now imagine that the current price of Charlie is $72, not $62, and its expected return is therefore 5.8% $[= (\$76.14 - \$72)/\$72]$. If this were the case, the tangency portfolio associated with a riskfree rate of 4% would involve just Able and Baker in proportions of .90 and .10, respectively.[6] Because Charlie has a proportion of zero, nobody would want to hold shares of Charlie. Consequently, many orders to sell would be submitted with virtually no offsetting orders to buy being received. As a result, Charlie's price would fall as brokers tried to find buyers for the offered shares. As Charlie's price fell, its expected return would rise because the same end-of-period price ($76.14) would be forecast for Charlie as before and it would now cost less to buy one share. Eventually, as the price fell, investors would change their minds and want to buy shares of Charlie. Ultimately, at a price of $62 investors would want to hold enough shares of Charlie so that in aggregate the number of shares demanded would equal the number of shares outstanding. Thus, in equilibrium Charlie would have a nonzero proportion in the tangency portfolio.

Another interesting situation could also arise. What if each investor concludes that the tangency portfolio should involve a proportionate investment in the stock of Baker equal to .40, but at the current price of Baker there are not enough shares outstanding to meet the demand? In this situation orders to buy Baker will flood in, and brokers will raise the price in search of sellers. The higher price will cause the expected return of Baker to fall, making it less attractive and thereby reducing its proportion in the tangency portfolio to a level at which the number of shares demanded equals the number of shares outstanding.

Ultimately, everything balances out. When all the price adjusting stops, the market will be in equilibrium. First, each investor will want to hold a certain positive amount of each risky security. Second, the current market price of each security will be at a level where the number of shares demanded equals the number of shares outstanding.[7] Third, the riskfree rate will be at a level where the total amount of money borrowed equals the total amount of money lent. As a result, in equilibrium the proportions of the tangency portfolio will correspond to the proportions of the **market portfolio,** defined as follows:

market portfolio

> The market portfolio consists of all securities in which the proportion invested in each security corresponds to its relative market value. The relative market value of a security is equal to the aggregate market value of the security divided by the sum of the aggregate market values of all securities.[8]

The market portfolio plays a central role in the CAPM because the efficient set consists of an investment in the market portfolio, coupled with a desired amount of either riskfree borrowing or lending. The tangency portfolio is commonly referred to as the market portfolio and is denoted as *M* instead of *T*. In theory, *M* consists not only of common stocks but also of other kinds of investments such as bonds, preferred

The Elusive Market Portfolio

 The market portfolio holds a special place in modern investment theory and practice. It is central to the CAPM, which assumes that the market portfolio lies on the efficient set and that all investors hold the market portfolio in combination with a desired amount of riskfree borrowing and riskfree lending. Furthermore, the market portfolio represents the ultimate in diversification. Consequently, passive investors (or index fund managers, see Chapter 17), who do not bet on the performance of particular securities but desire broad diversification, seek to hold the market portfolio. The market portfolio also serves as a universal performance evaluation standard. Investment managers and their clients often compare the managers' results against the returns on surrogates for the market portfolio.

Despite its widespread application, the market portfolio is surprisingly ill defined. In theory, the composition of the market portfolio is simple: All assets are weighted in proportion to their respective market values. In reality, actually identifying the *true* market portfolio (or even a close approximation) is beyond the capability of any individual or organization. How might we specify the market portfolio? The process would involve two steps: enumerating the assets to be included and calculating the market values of those assets.

First, we must list the various types of assets that constitute the market portfolio. These days we should think globally by considering assets held by investors in the United States and foreign countries. Of course, we want to include all securities representing the assets of businesses, such as common stocks, preferred stocks, and corporate bonds. In that vein we should also consider the value of proprietorships and partnerships. How about government debt? It should be considered if the debt is backed by real assets such as buildings. (Because of deficit spending, much of the government's debt is actually backed by future taxes and thus does not represent current wealth—a technical matter often overlooked.) We should also include real estate, cash holdings,

monetary metals (primarily gold), and art. But we have not finished yet. We should also include consumer durable assets, such as autos, furniture, and major appliances. Last but certainly not least, we should include the largest asset of all, the training and education in which people have invested vast sums, called *human capital.*

Merely listing the composition of the market portfolio is a complex undertaking. Measuring its value is even more problematic. Given the sophistication of U.S. capital markets, the values of domestic publicly traded assets are relatively easy to collect. (We should be careful, however, to avoid double-counting—for example, when one corporation owns part of another corporation.) Data availability in foreign markets varies from country to country. In some markets, such as those in the United Kingdom and Japan, security data collection systems are just as sophisticated as those in the United States. In other markets, such as those in countries with "emerging" security markets, comprehensive security valuation data are difficult to acquire.

A similar situation exists for nonpublicly traded asset values. In some countries, such as the United States, the government attempts to make accurate estimates of myriad asset values from real estate to consumer durable goods. In other countries, little or no effort is made to compile these data. As far as estimating the value of human capital—well, good luck.

The difficulties involved in determining the composition and value of the *true* market portfolio have led to the use of market portfolio proxies. In dealing with common stocks, for example, most researchers and practitioners arbitrarily define the market portfolio to be a broad stock market index, such as the S&P 500, the Russell 3000, or the Wilshire 5000.

What are the ramifications of not knowing the market portfolio's true composition? From a theoretical perspective, the potential problems are significant. In two controversial articles (*Journal of Financial Economics,* March 1977; and *Journal of Finance,* September 1978), Richard

Roll argued that the ambiguity of the market portfolio leaves the CAPM untestable. He contended that only if one knows the true market portfolio can one test whether it actually lies on the efficient set. Considering that the CAPM linear relationship between expected return and beta depends on the efficiency of the market portfolio, Roll's argument should not be taken lightly. Furthermore, Roll argued that the practice of using proxies for the market portfolio is loaded with problems. Different proxies, even if their returns are highly correlated, could lead to different beta estimates for the same security. Roll's arguments, it should be noted, were strongly contested by prominent CAPM defenders.

From a practical perspective, investors have generally been willing to overlook the market portfolio's ambiguity. Passive managers typically segment the market into various asset classes, such as stocks and bonds, or into even finer subclasses, such as large and small stocks. They then construct portfolios to track the performance of the respective asset class market portfolios. Similarly, active managers frequently refer to a designated market index when they devise their investment strategies. Performance evaluators use market portfolio proxies in their CAPM risk-adjusted return calculations (see Chapter 18). For now, these practices appear to be the best approaches to managing and evaluating portfolios.

stocks, and real estate. However, in practice some people restrict *M* to just common stocks, which may give inappropriate results in some applications.

10.2.3 THE EFFICIENT SET

capital market line

In the CAPM it is simple to determine the relationship between risk and expected return for efficient portfolios (see Figure 10.1). Point *M* represents the market portfolio, and r_f represents the riskfree rate of return. Efficient portfolios, which plot along the line going from r_f through *M*, consist of alternative combinations of risk and expected return obtainable by combining the market portfolio with riskfree borrowing or lending. This linear efficient set of the CAPM is known as the **capital market line** (CML). All portfolios other than those using the market portfolio and riskfree borrowing or lending lie below the CML, although some might plot very close to it.

FIGURE 10.1 The Capital Market Line

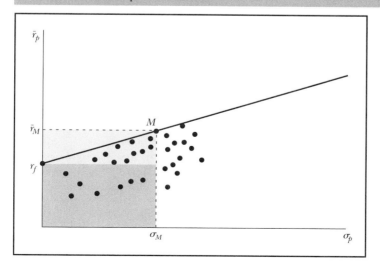

The slope of the CML is equal to the difference between the expected return of the market portfolio and that of the riskfree security $(\bar{r}_M - r_f)$ divided by the difference in their risks $(\sigma_M - 0)$, or $(\bar{r}_M - r_f)/(\sigma_M)$.[9] Because the vertical intercept of the CML is r_f, the straight line characterizing the CML has the following equation:

$$\bar{r}_p = r_f + \left[\frac{\bar{r}_M - r_f}{\sigma_M} \right] \sigma_p \tag{10.1}$$

where $\bar{r}_p$ and σ_p refer to the expected return and standard deviation of an efficient portfolio.[10] In the previous example, the market portfolio associated with a riskfree rate of 4% consisted of Able, Baker, and Charlie (these stocks are assumed to be the only ones that exist) in the proportions of .12, .19, and .69, respectively. It was shown in Chapter 9 that the expected return and standard deviation for this portfolio were 22.4% and 15.2%, respectively. The equation for the resulting CML is

$$\bar{r}_p = 4 + \left[\frac{22.4 - 4}{15.2} \right] \sigma_p = 4 + 1.21\sigma_p$$

Equilibrium in the security market can be characterized by two key numbers. The first is the vertical intercept of the CML (that is, the riskfree rate), which is often referred to as the *reward for waiting*. The second is the slope of the CML, which is often referred to as the *reward per unit of risk borne*. In essence, security markets provide a place where time and risk can be traded, with their prices determined by supply and demand. The intercept and slope of the CML can be thought of as the *price of time* and the *price of risk*, respectively. In the example, they are equal to 4% and 1.21, respectively.

10.3   The Security Market Line

10.3.1   IMPLICATIONS FOR INDIVIDUAL RISKY ASSETS

The capital market line represents the equilibrium relationship between the expected return and standard deviation for efficient portfolios. Individual risky securities will always plot below the line because a single risky security when held by itself is an inefficient portfolio. The CAPM does not imply any particular relationship between the expected return and the standard deviation (that is, total risk) of an individual security. To say more about the expected return of an individual security requires deeper analysis.

In Chapter 7 the following equation was given for calculating the standard deviation of any portfolio:

$$\sigma_p = \left[\sum_{i=1}^{N} \sum_{j=1}^{N} X_i X_j \sigma_{ij} \right]^{1/2} \tag{7.7}$$

where X_i and X_j denoted the proportions invested in securities i and j, and σ_{ij} denoted the covariance of returns between security i and j. Now consider using this equation to calculate the standard deviation of the market portfolio:

$$\sigma_M = \left[\sum_{i=1}^{N} \sum_{j=1}^{N} X_{iM} X_{jM} \sigma_{ij} \right]^{1/2} \tag{10.2}$$

where X_{iM} and X_{jM} denote the proportions invested in securities i and j in forming the market portfolio. Another way to write equation (10.2) is as follows:

$$\sigma_M = [X_{1M}\sigma_{1M} + X_{2M}\sigma_{2M} + X_{3M}\sigma_{3M} + \cdots + X_{NM}\sigma_{NM}]^{1/2} \qquad (10.3)$$

where σ_{1M} denotes the covariance of security 1 with the market portfolio, σ_{2M} denotes the covariance of security 2 with the market portfolio, and so on. Thus, the standard deviation of the market portfolio is equal to the square root of a weighted average of the covariances of all the securities with it, where the weights are equal to the proportions of the respective securities in the market portfolio.

Note this important point: Under the CAPM, each investor holds the market portfolio and is concerned with its standard deviation because this standard deviation affects the slope of the CML and hence the magnitude of his or her investment in the market portfolio. The contribution of each security to the standard deviation of the market portfolio in Equation (10.3) depends on the size of its covariance with the market portfolio. Accordingly each investor will note that *the relevant measure of risk for a security is its covariance with the market portfolio, σ_{iM}.* Securities with larger values of σ_{iM} contribute more to the risk of the market portfolio. However, securities with larger standard deviations do not necessarily add more risk to the market portfolio than securities with smaller standard deviations.[11] From this analysis it follows that securities with larger values for σ_{iM} have to provide proportionately larger expected returns to attract investors' interest in purchasing them. To see why, consider what would happen if such securities did not provide investors with proportionately larger levels of expected return. These securities would contribute to the risk of the market portfolio but do not contribute proportionately to the expected return of the market portfolio. Eliminating such securities from the market portfolio would cause the expected return of the market portfolio relative to its standard deviation to rise. Because investors would view this as a favorable change, the market portfolio would no longer be the optimal risky portfolio to hold, and security prices would be out of equilibrium.

The equilibrium relationship between risk and return can be expressed as follows:

$$\bar{r}_i = r_f + \left[\frac{\bar{r}_M - r_f}{\sigma_M^2} \right] \sigma_{iM} \qquad (10.4)$$

security market line

As illustrated in Figure 10.2(a), Equation (10.4) represents a straight line having a vertical intercept of r_f and a slope of $(\bar{r}_M - r_f)/\sigma_M^2$. Because the slope is positive, the equation indicates that securities with larger covariances with the market (σ_{iM}) will be priced so as to have larger expected returns ($\bar{r}_i$). This relationship between covariance and expected return is known as the **security market line** (SML).[12]

Interestingly, a risky security with $\sigma_{iM} = 0$ will have an expected return equal to the rate on the riskfree security, r_f. Why? Because this risky security, just like the riskfree security, will not affect the risk of the market portfolio when a marginal change is made in its weight. This is true even though the risky security has a positive standard deviation and the riskfree security has a standard deviation of zero.

It is even possible for some risky securities (meaning securities with positive standard deviations) to have expected returns less than the riskfree rate. According to the CAPM, this situation will occur if $\sigma_{iM} < 0$, thereby indicating that the securities contribute a negative amount of risk to the market portfolio (meaning that they cause the risk of the market portfolio to be lower than it would be if less money were invested

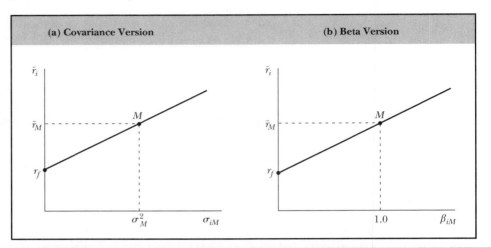

FIGURE 10.2 The Security Market Line

in them). Also of interest is the observation that a risky security with $\sigma_{iM} = \sigma_M^2$ will have an expected return equal to the expected return on the market portfolio, $\bar{r}_M$, because such a security contributes an average amount of risk to the market portfolio.

Another way of expressing the SML is as follows:

$$\bar{r}_i = r_f + (\bar{r}_M - r_f)\beta_{iM} \tag{10.5}$$

where the term β_{iM} is defined as

$$\beta_{iM} = \frac{\sigma_{iM}}{\sigma_M^2} \tag{10.6}$$

beta coefficient   The term β_{iM} is known as the **beta coefficient** (or simply the beta) for security i and is an alternative way of representing the covariance of a security. Equation (10.5) is a different version of the SML as can be seen in Figure 10.2(b). Although it has the same intercept as in Equation (10.4), r_f, it has a different slope. The slope of this version is $(\bar{r}_M - r_f)$, whereas the slope of the earlier version was $[(\bar{r}_M - r_f)/\sigma_M^2]$.

The beta of a portfolio is simply a weighted average of the betas of its component securities, where the proportions invested in the securities are the respective weights. That is, the beta of a portfolio can be calculated as

$$\beta_{pM} = \sum_{i=1}^{N} X_i \beta_{iM} \tag{10.7}$$

Previously it was shown that the expected return of a portfolio is a weighted average of the expected returns of its component securities, where the proportions invested in the securities are the weights. Therefore, every portfolio plots on the SML because every security plots on the SML. To put it more broadly, not only every security but also every portfolio must plot on an upward-sloping straight line in a diagram with expected return on the vertical axis and beta on the horizontal axis. Hence efficient portfolios plot on both the CML and the SML, but inefficient portfolios plot on the SML and below the CML.

The SML must go through the point representing the market portfolio itself. Its beta is 1 and its expected return is $\bar{r}_M$, so its coordinates are $(1, \bar{r}_M)$. Because riskfree securities have beta values of 0, the SML will also go through a point whose coordinates are $(0, r_f)$. As a result, the SML will have a vertical intercept equal to r_f and a slope equal to the vertical distance between these two points $(\bar{r}_M - r_f)$ divided by the horizontal distance between these two points $(1 - 0)$, or $(\bar{r}_M - r_f)/(1 - 0) = (\bar{r}_M - r_f)$. Thus, these two points fix the location of the SML.

The equilibrium relationship shown by the SML comes to exist through the combined effects of investors' adjustments in holdings and the resulting pressures on security prices (see Chapter 4). Given a set of security prices, investors calculate expected returns and covariances and then determine their optimal portfolios. If the number of shares of a security collectively desired differs from the number available, there will be upward or downward pressure on its price. Given a new set of prices, investors will reassess their desires for the various securities. The process continues until the number of shares collectively desired for each security equals the number available.

For the individual investor, security prices and prospects are fixed but the quantities held can be altered. For the market as a whole, the quantities are fixed (at least in the short run) and prices are variable. As in any competitive market, equilibrium requires the adjustment of each security's price until there is consistency between the quantity desired and the quantity available.

It may seem logical to examine historical returns on securities to determine whether securities have been priced in equilibrium as suggested by the CAPM. However, the issue of whether such testing of the CAPM can be done in a meaningful manner is controversial. For at least some purposes, affirmative test results may not be necessary to make practical use of the CAPM.

10.3.2 AN EXAMPLE

In the example that was used earlier, Able, Baker, and Charlie formed the market portfolio in proportions equal to .12, .19, and .69, respectively. With these proportions, the market portfolio had an expected return of 22.4% and a standard deviation of 15.2%. The riskfree rate in the example was 4%. For this example the SML as indicated in Equation (10.4) is

$$\bar{r}_i = r_f + \left[\frac{\bar{r}_M - r_f}{\sigma_M^2} \right] \sigma_{iM} \tag{10.4}$$

$$= 4 + \left[\frac{22.4 - 4}{(15.2)^2} \right] \sigma_{iM}$$

$$= 4 + .08\sigma_{iM} \tag{10.8}$$

The following expected return vector and variance–covariance matrix were used in this example:

$$ER = \begin{bmatrix} 16.2 \\ 24.6 \\ 22.8 \end{bmatrix} \qquad VC = \begin{bmatrix} 146 & 187 & 145 \\ 187 & 854 & 104 \\ 145 & 104 & 289 \end{bmatrix}$$

The covariance of a security with the market portfolio equals the weighted average of the covariances of that security with the other securities in the market portfolio. The weights applied to the covariances are the proportions of the respective securities in the market portfolio. As a result, the covariance of Able, Baker, and Charlie with the market portfolio can be shown to equal

$$\sigma_{1M} = \sum_{j=1}^{3} X_{jM}\sigma_{1j}$$

$$= (.12 \times 146) + (.19 \times 187) + (.69 \times 145)$$

$$= 153$$

$$\sigma_{2M} = \sum_{j=1}^{3} X_{jM}\sigma_{2j}$$

$$= (.12 \times 187) + (.19 \times 854) + (.69 \times 104)$$

$$= 257$$

$$\sigma_{3M} = \sum_{j=1}^{3} X_{jM}\sigma_{3j}$$

$$= (.12 \times 145) + (.19 \times 104) + (.69 \times 289)$$

$$= 236$$

The SML as given in Equation (10.8) indicates that the expected return for Able should be equal to $4 + (.08 \times 153) = 16.2\%$. The expected return for Baker should be $4 + (.08 \times 257) = 24.6\%$, and the expected return for Charlie should be $4 + (.08 \times 236) = 22.8\%$. Each of these expected returns corresponds to the respective value given in the expected return vector.

Equation (10.6) can be used to calculate the betas for the three companies, Able, Baker, and Charlie:

$$\beta_{1M} = \frac{\sigma_{1M}}{\sigma_M^2}$$

$$= \frac{153}{(15.2)^2}$$

$$= .66$$

$$\beta_{2M} = \frac{\sigma_{2M}}{\sigma_M^2}$$

$$= \frac{257}{(15.2)^2}$$

$$= 1.11$$

$$\beta_{3M} = \frac{\sigma_{3M}}{\sigma_M^2}$$

$$= \frac{236}{(15.2)^2}$$

$$= 1.02$$

Equation (10.5) indicated that the SML could be expressed in a form wherein the measure of risk for an asset was its beta. For the example under consideration, this reduces to

$$\bar{r}_i = r_f + (\bar{r}_M - r_f)\beta_{iM}$$
$$= 4 + (22.4 - 4)\beta_{iM}$$
$$= 4 + 18.4\beta_{iM} \tag{10.9}$$

The SML as given in this equation states that the expected return for Able should be equal to $4 + (18.4 \times .66) = 16.2\%$. Similarly, the expected return for Baker should be $4 + (18.4 \times 1.11) = 24.6\%$, and the expected return for Charlie should be $4 + (18.4 \times 1.02) = 22.8\%$. Each of these expected returns corresponds to the respective value given in the expected return vector.

It is important to realize that if any other portfolio is assumed to be the market portfolio, meaning that if any set of proportions other than .12, .19, and .69 is used, then such an equilibrium relationship between expected returns and betas (or covariances) will not hold. Consider a hypothetical market portfolio with equal proportions (that is, .333) invested in Able, Baker, and Charlie. Because this portfolio has an expected return of 21.2% and a standard deviation of 15.5%, the hypothetical SML would be as follows:

$$\bar{r}_i = r_f + \left[\frac{\bar{r}_M - r_f}{\sigma_M^2} \right] \sigma_{iM}$$

$$= r_f + \left[\frac{21.2 - 4}{(15.5)^2} \right] \sigma_{iM}$$

$$= 4 + .07\sigma_{iM}$$

Able has a covariance with this portfolio of

$$\sigma_{1M} = \sum_{j=1}^{3} X_{jM}\sigma_{1j}$$

$$= (.333 \times 146) + (.333 \times 187) + (.333 \times 145)$$

$$= 159$$

which means that Able's expected return according to the hypothetical SML should be equal to $15.1\% = 4 + (.07 \times 159)$. However, because this does not correspond to the 16.2% figure that appears in the expected return vector, a portfolio with equal proportions invested in Able, Baker, and Charlie cannot be the market portfolio.[13]

10.4 The Market Model

Chapter 8 introduced the market model, wherein the return on a common stock was assumed to be related to the return on a market index in the following manner:

$$r_i = \alpha_{iI} + \beta_{iI}r_I + \varepsilon_{iI} \tag{8.3}$$

where

r_i = return on security i for some given period
r_I = return on market index for the same period
α_{iI} = intercept term
β_{iI} = slope term
ε_{iI} = random error term

It is natural to think about the relationship between the market model and the CAPM. After all, both models have a slope of *beta,* and both models involve the market. However, there are two significant differences between the models.

First, the market model is a *factor model,* or, to be more specific, a single-factor model in which the factor is a market index (factor models are discussed in the next chapter). Unlike the CAPM, however, it is not an *equilibrium model* that describes how prices are set for securities.

Second, the market model uses a *market index* such as the S&P 500, whereas the CAPM involves the *market portfolio.* The market portfolio is a collection of all the securities in the marketplace, whereas a market index is based on a sample of the market broadly construed (for example, 500 in the case of the S&P 500). Therefore, conceptually the beta of a stock based on the market model, β_{iI}, differs from the beta of the stock according to the CAPM, β_{iM}, because the market model beta is measured relative to a market index whereas the CAPM beta is measured relative to the market portfolio. In practice, however, the composition of the market portfolio is not precisely known, so a market index must be used. Thus, although conceptually different, betas determined using a market index are often treated as if they were determined using the market portfolio. That is, β_{iI} is used as an estimate of β_{iM}.

In the example, only three securities existed: the common stocks of Able, Baker, and Charlie. Subsequent analysis indicated that the CAPM market portfolio consisted of these stocks in the proportions of .12, .19, and .69, respectively. It is against this portfolio that the betas of the securities should be measured. However, in practice they are likely to be measured against a market index (for example, one that is based on just the stocks of Able and Charlie in proportions of .20 and .80, respectively).

10.4.1 MARKET INDICES

One of the most widely known indices is the Standard & Poor's Stock Price Index (the S&P 500), a value-weighted average price of 500 large stocks. Complete coverage of the stocks listed on the NYSE is provided by the NYSE Composite Index. The National Association of Security Dealers (NASD) provides a similar index (the Nasdaq Composit) of stocks traded on the Nasdaq system. The Russell 3000 and Wilshire 5000 stock indices are the most comprehensive indices of U.S. common stock prices published regularly in the United States. Because they consist of both listed and Nasdaq stocks, they are closer than the others to representing the overall performance of U.S. stocks.[14]

Without question the most widely quoted market index is the Dow Jones Industrial Average (DJIA). Although it is based on the performance of only 30 stocks and uses a less satisfactory averaging procedure than the other indices use, the DJIA provides a fair idea of what is happening to stock prices.[15] Table 10.1 provides a listing of the 30 stocks whose prices are reflected in the DJIA.

10.4.2 MARKET AND UNIQUE RISK

In Chapter 8 it was shown that the total risk of a security, σ_i^2, could be partitioned into two components as follows:

$$\sigma_i^2 = \beta_{iI}^2 \sigma_I^2 + \sigma_{\varepsilon i}^2 \tag{8.8}$$

TABLE 10.1 Stocks in the DJIA

Allied Signal Inc.	International Business Machines Corp.
Alcoa, Inc.	Intel Corp.
American Express Co.	International Paper Co.
AT&T Corp.	J.P. Morgan & Co.
Boeing Co.	Johnson & Johnson
Caterpillar Inc.	McDonald's Corp.
Citigroup Inc.	Merck & Co.
Coca-Cola Co.	Microsoft Corp.
DuPont Co.	Minnesota Mining and Manufacturing Co.
Eastman Kodak Co.	Philip Morris Cos.
Exxon Corp.	Procter & Gamble Co.
General Electric Co.	SBC Communications Inc.
General Motors Corp.	United Technologies Corp.
Home Depot Inc.	Wal-Mart Stores Inc.
Hewlett-Packard Co.	Walt Disney Co.

Source: Web site <http://averages.dowjones.com/djia_cos.html>, November 14, 1999.

where

$$\beta_{iI}^2 \sigma_I^2 = \text{market risk}$$
$$\sigma_{\varepsilon i}^2 = \text{unique risk}$$

Because beta, or covariance, is the relevant measure of risk for a security according to the CAPM, it is appropriate to explore the relationship between it and the total risk of the security. The relationship is identical to that given in Equation (8.8) *except that the market portfolio is involved instead of a market index:*

$$\sigma_i^2 = \beta_{iM}^2 \sigma_M^2 + \sigma_{\varepsilon i}^2 \qquad \textbf{(10.10)}$$

market risk

nonmarket risk

As with the market model, the total risk of security *i*, measured by its variance and denoted σ_i^2, consists of two parts. The first component is related to moves of the market portfolio. It is equal to the product of the stock's beta squared and the market portfolio's variance, and is often referred to as the **market risk** of the security. The second component is not related to moves of the market portfolio. It is denoted $\sigma_{\varepsilon i}^2$ and can be considered **nonmarket risk.** Under the assumptions of the market model, it is unique to the security in question and is commonly referred to as *unique risk*. If β_{iI} is treated as an estimate of β_{iM}, the decomposition of σ_i^2 is the same in Equations (8.8) and (10.10).

10.4.3 AN EXAMPLE

From the earlier example, the betas of Able, Baker, and Charlie were calculated to be .66, 1.11, and 1.02, respectively. Because the standard deviation of the market portfolio was equal to 15.2%, the market risk of the three firms is equal to $(.66^2 \times 15.2^2) = 100$, $(1.11^2 \times 15.2^2) = 285$, and $(1.02^2 \times 15.2^2) = 240$, respectively.

The unique risk of any security can be calculated by solving Equation (10.10) for $\sigma_{\varepsilon i}^2$:

$$\sigma_{\varepsilon i}^2 = \sigma_i^2 - \beta_{iM}^2 \sigma_M^2 \qquad \textbf{(10.11)}$$

Equation (10.11) can be used to calculate the unique risk of Able, Baker, and Charlie, respectively:

$$\sigma_{\varepsilon 1}^2 = 146 - 100$$
$$= 46$$
$$\sigma_{\varepsilon 2}^2 = 854 - 285$$
$$= 569$$
$$\sigma_{\varepsilon 3}^2 = 289 - 240$$
$$= 49$$

Unique risk is sometimes expressed as a standard deviation. This is calculated by taking the square root of $\sigma_{\varepsilon i}^2$ and would be equal to $\sqrt{46} = 6.8\%$ for Able, $\sqrt{569} = 23.9\%$ for Baker, and $\sqrt{49} = 7\%$ for Charlie.

10.4.4 MOTIVATION FOR THE PARTITIONING OF RISK

At this point one may wonder, Why partition total risk into two parts? For the investor, it would seem that risk is risk—whatever its source. The answer lies in the domain of expected returns.

Market risk is related to the risk of the market portfolio and to the beta of the security in question. Securities with larger betas have larger amounts of market risk. In the CAPM, securities with larger betas have larger expected returns. These two relationships together imply that securities with larger market risks should have larger expected returns.

Unique risk is not related to beta. There is no reason securities with larger amounts of unique risks should have larger expected returns. Thus, investors are rewarded for bearing market risk but not for bearing unique risk.

Summary

1. The capital asset pricing model (CAPM) is based on a specific set of assumptions about investor behavior and the existence of perfect security markets.
2. Based on these assumptions, it can be stated that all investors will hold the same efficient portfolio of risky assets.
3. Investors will differ only in the amounts of riskfree borrowing or lending they undertake.
4. The risky portfolio held by all investors is known as the market portfolio.
5. The market portfolio consists of all securities, each weighted in proportion to its market value relative to the market value of all securities.
6. The linear efficient set of the CAPM is known as the capital market line (CML). The CML represents the equilibrium relationship between the expected return and standard deviation of efficient portfolios.
7. Under the CAPM the relevant measure of risk for determining a security's expected return is the covariance of its returns with those of the market portfolio.
8. The linear relationship between covariance and expected return is known as the security market line (SML).
9. The beta of a security is an alternative way of measuring the risk that a security adds to the market portfolio. Beta is a measure of the covariance between the returns of the security and those of the market portfolio relative to the market portfolio's variance.

10. The beta from the CAPM is similar in concept to the beta from the market model. However, unlike the CAPM, the market model is not an equilibrium model of security prices. Furthermore, the market model uses a market index, which is a subset of the CAPM's market portfolio.

11. Under the CAPM, the total risk of a security can be separated into market risk and nonmarket risk. Each security's nonmarket risk is unique to that security and, hence, is often called its unique risk.

Questions and Problems

1. Describe the key assumptions underlying the CAPM.
2. What is the separation theorem? What implications does it have for the optimal portfolio of risky assets held by investors?
3. Describe the price adjustment process that equilibrates the market's supply and demand for securities. What conditions will prevail under such an equilibrium?
4. Will an investor who owns the market portfolio have to buy and sell units of the component securities every time the relative prices of those securities change? Why?
5. Assume that two securities constitute the market portfolio. Those securities have the following expected returns, standard deviations, and proportions:

Security	Expected Return	Standard Deviation	Proportion
A	10%	20%	.4
B	15	28	.6

Based on this information, and given a correlation of .30 between the two securities and a riskfree rate of 5%, specify the equation for the capital market line.

6. The market portfolio is assumed to be composed of four securities. Their covariances with the market and their proportions follow.

Security	Covariance with Market	Proportion
A	242	.2
B	360	.3
C	155	.2
D	210	.3

Given these data, calculate the market portfolio's standard deviation.

7. Why should the expected return for a security be directly related to the security's covariance with the market portfolio?
8. The risk of a well-diversified portfolio to an investor is measured by the standard deviation of the portfolio's returns. Why shouldn't the risk of an individual security be calculated in the same manner?
9. Oil Smith, an investment student, argued, "A security with a positive standard deviation must have an expected return greater than the riskfree rate. Otherwise, why would anyone be willing to hold the security?" Based on the CAPM, is Oil's statement correct? Why?
10. The standard deviation of the market portfolio is 15%. Given the covariances with the market portfolio of the following securities, calculate their betas.

Security	Covariance
A	292
B	180
C	225

11. Kitty Bransfield owns a portfolio composed of three securities. The betas of those securities and their proportions in Kitty's portfolio are shown here. What is the beta of Kitty's portfolio?

Security	Beta	Proportion
A	.90	.3
B	1.30	.1
C	1.05	.6

12. Given that the expected return on the market portfolio is 10%, the riskfree rate of return is 6%, the beta of stock A is .85, and the beta of stock B is 1.20:
    a. Draw the SML.
    b. What is the equation for the SML?
    c. What are the equilibrium expected returns for stocks A and B?
    d. Plot the two risky securities on the SML.
13. The SML describes an equilibrium relationship between risk and expected return. Would you consider a security that plotted above the SML to be an attractive investment? Why?
14. The CAPM permits the standard deviation of a security to be segmented into market and nonmarket risk. Distinguish between the two types of risk.
15. Based on the risk and return relationships of the CAPM, supply values for the seven missing data in the following table.

Security	Expected Return	Beta	Standard Deviation	Nonmarket Risk $\sigma^2_{\varepsilon i}$
A	_____ %	0.8	_____ %	81
B	19.0	1.5	_____ %	36
C	15.0	_____	12	0
D	7.0	0	8	_____
E	16.6	_____	15	_____

Endnotes

1. Some extended versions of the CAPM are discussed in Gordon J. Alexander and Jack Clark Francis, *Portfolio Analysis* (Englewood Cliffs, NJ: Prentice Hall, 1986), Chapter 8; and Edwin J. Elton and Martin J. Gruber, *Modern Portfolio Theory and Investment Analysis* (New York: John Wiley, 1995), Chapter 14.
2. Milton Friedman, *Essays in the Theory of Positive Economics* (Chicago: University of Chicago Press, 1953), p. 15.
3. If the investor had initial wealth of $40,000, then he or she would borrow $10,000 and invest $50,000 (= $40,000 + $10,000) in T.
4. Note how the proportions in these three stocks sum to .5 for the panel (a) investor and 1.25 for the panel (b) investor. Because the respective proportions for the riskfree asset are .5 and −.25, the aggregate proportions for the stocks and riskfree asset sum to 1.0 for each investor.
5. Securities that have zero net amounts outstanding will not appear in the tangency portfolio. Options and futures, discussed in Chapters 24 and 25, are examples of such securities.
6. Although the expected return of Charlie has been changed, all the variances and covariances as well as the expected returns for Able and Baker are assumed to have the same values that were given in Chapters 7, 8, and 9. The singular change in the expected return of Charlie alters not only the composition of the tangency portfolio but also the location and shape of the efficient set.
7. In this situation the market for each security is said to have *cleared*.
8. The aggregate market value for the common stock of a company is equal to the current market price of the stock multiplied by the number of shares outstanding, and is known as the stock's market capitalization.
9. The slope of a straight line can be determined if the locations of two points on the line are known. It is determined by *rise over run*, meaning that it is determined by dividing the vertical distance between the two points by the horizontal distance between the two points. With the CML two points are known, the riskfree rate and the market portfolio, so its slope can be determined.

10. The equation of a straight line is $y = a + bx$, where a is the vertical intercept and b is the slope. Because the vertical intercept and slope of the CML are known, its equation can be written as shown in the text by making the appropriate substitutions for a and b.

11. More precisely, σ_{iM} is the relevant measure of a security's risk because $\partial\sigma_M/\partial X_{iM} = \sigma_{iM}/\sigma_M$. That is, a marginal change in the weight in security i will result in a marginal change in the variance of the market portfolio that is a linear function of the security's covariance with the market portfolio. Accordingly, the relevant measure of the security's risk is its covariance, σ_{iM}.

12. The original derivation of the SML is provided in William F. Sharpe, "Capital Asset Prices: A Theory of Market Equilibrium under Conditions of Risk," *Journal of Finance,* 19, no. 3 (September 1964): 425–442.

13. In this situation, Baker and Charlie have covariances with the market portfolio of 382 and 179, respectively, which means that their expected returns should be equal to 30.7% = 4 + (.07 × 382) and 16.5% = 4 + (.07 × 179). However, these figures do not correspond to the respective ones (24.6% and 22.8%) appearing in the expected return vector, indicating that there are discrepancies for all three securities. Although this example has used the covariance version of the SML, the analysis is similar for the beta version of SML that is shown in Equation (10.5).

14. Other indices of common stocks are commonly reported in the daily press. Many of these are components of the major indices mentioned here. For example, *The Wall Street Journal* reports on a daily basis not only the level of the S&P 500 but also the levels of four of its components: Standard & Poor's Industrials, Transportations, Utilities, and Financials. Their components, 500 stocks in total, make up the S&P 500; Standard & Poor's also reports, for example, the level of a 400 MidCap index based on the stock prices of middle-sized companies. See Chapters 18 and 26 for a thorough discussion of stock market indices.

15. Charles Dow created this index in 1884 by simply adding the prices of 11 companies and then dividing the sum by 11. In 1928 securities were added to bring the total number to 30. Since then the composition of these 30 has been changed periodically. Owing to corporate actions such as stock dividends and splits as well as changes in the index's companies, the divisor is no longer simply equal to the number of stocks in the index.

Factor Models

Modern investment theory provides a conceptually sound method for an investor to identify his or her optimal portfolio. First, the investor should estimate the expected return and standard deviation for each security under consideration for inclusion in the portfolio along with all the covariances between securities. Second, with these estimates the investor should derive the curved efficient set of Markowitz and then, for a given riskfree rate, determine the location of the linear efficient set. Finally, the investor should invest in the tangency portfolio and borrow or lend at the riskfree rate, with the amount of borrowing or lending depending on the investor's risk–return preferences.

Factor models fit into this framework in several ways. First, they can be used to estimate expected returns, standard deviations, and covariances of securities. Second, they can be used to tailor a portfolio's sensitivity to certain economic events. For example, an investor who is deeply concerned about an immediate increase in short-term interest rates might consider constructing a portfolio whose returns are not particularly sensitive to such an event. Third, factor models offer guidelines for diversification. This chapter introduces factor models and describes how they can be used.

11.1 Factor Models and Return-Generating Processes

return-generating process

The task of identifying the curved Markowitz efficient set can be simplified by introducing a **return-generating process.** A return-generating process is a statistical model that describes how the return on a security is produced. Chapter 8 presented a type of return-generating process known as the market model. In this model a security's return is a function of the return on a market index. However, there are many other types of return-generating processes for securities.

11.1.1 FACTOR MODELS

factor models

Factor models (or index models) assume that the return on a security is sensitive to the movements of various factors (or indices). The market model assumes that there is one factor—the return on a market index. However, in attempting to accurately estimate expected returns, variances, and covariances for securities, multiple-factor models are potentially more useful than the market model because security prices are sensitive to more than movements in a market index. That is, there probably is more than one pervasive factor in the economy that affects security returns.

As a return-generating process, a factor model attempts to capture the major economic forces that systematically move the prices of all securities. Implicit in the construction of a factor model is the assumption that the returns on two securities will be correlated only through common reactions to one or more of the factors specified in the model. Any aspect of a security's return unexplained by the factor model is assumed to be unique to the security and, therefore, uncorrelated with the unique elements of returns on other securities. As a result, a factor model is a powerful tool for portfolio management. It can supply the information needed to calculate expected returns, variances, and covariances for every security—a necessary condition for determining the curved Markowitz efficient set. It can also be used to characterize a portfolio's sensitivity to movements in the factors.

11.1.2   APPLICATION

All investors use factor models explicitly or implicitly. It is impossible to consider separately the interrelationship of every security with every other. Numerically, the problem of calculating covariances among securities rises exponentially as the number of securities analyzed increases. Conceptually, the tangled web of security variances and covariances becomes mind-boggling as the number of securities increases beyond just a few securities, let alone hundreds or thousands. Even the vast data processing capabilities of high-speed computers are strained when they are called on to construct efficient sets from a large number of securities.

Abstraction is therefore an essential step in identifying the curved Markowitz efficient set. Factor models supply the necessary level of abstraction. They provide investment managers with a framework to identify important factors in the economy and the marketplace and to assess the extent to which different securities and portfolios respond to changes in those factors.

If one or more factors influence security returns, a primary goal of security analysis should be to determine these factors and the sensitivities of security returns to movements in them. A formal statement of such a relationship is termed a *factor model of security returns*. The discussion begins with the simplest form of such a model, the one-factor model.

11.2   One-Factor Models

Some investors argue that the return-generating process for securities involves a single factor. For example, they may contend that the returns on securities respond to the growth rate in the gross domestic product (GDP). Table 11.1 and Figure 11.1 illustrate one way of providing substance for such statements.

11.2.1   AN EXAMPLE

The horizontal axis of Figure 11.1 is the growth rate in GDP, whereas the vertical axis measures the return on Widget's stock. Each point in the graph represents the combination of Widget's return and GDP growth rate for a particular year as reported in Table 11.1. A line has been statistically fitted to the data using *simple-linear regression analysis.* (*Simple* refers to the fact that there is one variable—GDP in this example—on the right-hand side of the equation).[1] This line has a positive slope of 2, indicating that there is a positive relationship between GDP growth rates and Widget's returns. Higher rates of GDP growth are associated with higher returns.[2]

In equation form, the relationship between GDP growth and Widget's return can be expressed as follows:

$$r_t = a + b\text{GDP}_t + e_t \qquad (11.1)$$

TABLE 11.1 Factor Model Data

Year	Growth Rate in GDP	Rate of Inflation	Return on Widget Stock
1	5.7%	1.1%	14.3%
2	6.4	4.4	19.2
3	7.9	4.4	23.4
4	7.0	4.6	15.6
5	5.1	6.1	9.2
6	2.9	3.1	13.0

where

r_t = the return on Widget in period t

a = the zero factor for GDP

b = sensitivity of Widget to GDP growth[3]

GDP_t = the rate of growth in GDP in period t

e_t = the unique return on Widget in period t

sensitivity

In Figure 11.1 the zero factor is 4% per period. This value would be the expected return for Widget if GDP growth equaled zero. The **sensitivity** of Widget to predicted GDP growth is 2 and is the same as the slope of the line in Figure 11.1. This value indicates that, in general, higher growth in GDP is associated with higher returns for Widget. If GDP growth equaled 5%, Widget should generate a return of 14% [= 4% + (2 × 5%)]. If GDP growth were 1% higher—that is, 6%—Widget's return should be 2% higher, or 16%.

In this example, GDP growth in year 6 was 2.9%, and Widget actually returned 13%. Therefore, Widget's unique return (given by e_t) in this particular year was +3.2%.

FIGURE 11.1 A One-Factor Model

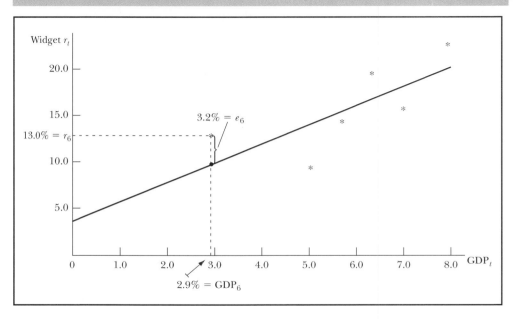

This amount was determined by subtracting Widget's expected return, given that GDP grew by 2.9%, from Widget's actual return of 13%. In this case, Widget was expected to return 9.8% [= 4 + (2 × 2.9%)], thereby resulting in a unique return of +3.2% (= 13% − 9.8%). Hence, the one-factor model presented in Figure 11.1 and Equation (11.1) attributes Widget's return in any particular period to three elements:

1. An effect common in any period (the term a)
2. An effect that differs across periods depending on the stock's sensitivity and the growth rate of GDP (the term $b\text{GDP}_t$)
3. An effect unique to the particular period observed that is not attributable to the factor (the term e_t)

11.2.2   GENERALIZING THE EXAMPLE

This example of a one-factor model can be generalized in equation form for any security i in period t:

$$r_{it} = a_i + b_i F_t + e_{it} \tag{11.2}$$

where F_t is the value of the factor in period t and b_i is the sensitivity of security i to this factor. If the value of the factor were zero, the return on the security would equal $a_i + e_{it}$. Note that e_{it} is a random error term like the one discussed in Chapter 8. Specifically, it is a random variable with an expected value of zero and a standard deviation σ_{ei}, whose actual outcome can be thought of as being determined by the spin of a roulette wheel as described in Chapter 8.

Expected Return

According to the one-factor model, the expected return on security i can be written as

$$\bar{r}_i = a_i + b_i \bar{F} \tag{11.3}$$

where $\bar{F}$ denotes the expected value of the factor. This equation can be used to estimate the expected return on the security. For example, if the expected growth rate in GDP is 3%, then the expected return for Widget equals 10% [= 4% + (2 × 3%)].

Variance

With the one-factor model, the variance of any security i equals

$$\sigma_i^2 = \beta_i^2 \sigma_F^2 + \sigma_{ei}^2 \tag{11.4}$$

where σ_F^2 is the variance of the factor F and σ_{ei}^2 is the variance of the random error term e_i. Thus if the variance of the factor σ_F^2 equals 3 and the residual variance σ_{ei}^2 equals 15.2, then according to this equation, Widget's variance equals

$$\sigma_i^2 = (2^2 \times 3) + 15.2$$
$$= 27.2$$

Covariance

With a one-factor model, the covariance between any two securities i and j equals

$$\sigma_{ij} = b_i b_j \sigma_F^2 \tag{11.5}$$

In the Widget example, Equation (11.5) can be used to estimate the covariance between Widget and another hypothetical security, such as the stock of Whatever Company.

Assuming that the factor sensitivity of Whatever is 4.0, the covariance between Widget and Whatever equals

$$\sigma_{ij} = 2 \times 4 \times 3$$
$$= 24$$

Assumptions

Equations (11.4) and (11.5) are based on two critical assumptions. The first is that the random error term and the factor are uncorrelated. This means that the outcome of the factor has no bearing on the outcome of the random error term. The second assumption is that the random error terms of any two securities are uncorrelated. This means that the outcome of the random error term of one security has no bearing on the outcome of the random error term of any other security. As a result, the returns of two securities will be correlated only through common responses to the factor. If either of these two assumptions is invalid, then the model is an approximation, and a different factor model (perhaps one with more factors) theoretically will be a more accurate representation of the return-generating process.

11.2.3 THE MARKET MODEL

The market model is an example of a one-factor model in which the factor is the return on a market index. In Chapter 8, the market model appeared as

$$r_i = \alpha_{iI} + \beta_{iI} r_I + \varepsilon_{iI} \qquad \textbf{(8.3)}$$

Equations (8.3) and (11.2) are similar. The intercept term α_{iI} from the market model equation corresponds to the zero factor term a_i in Equation (11.2). Furthermore, the slope term β_{iI} from the market model equates to the sensitivity term b_i in the generalized one-factor model. Each equation has a random error term of e_{it} in the factor model and ε_{iI} in the market model.[4] Finally, the market index return plays the role of the single factor. However, as mentioned earlier, the concept of a one-factor model does not restrict the investor to using a market index as the factor. Many other single factors are plausible. Macroeconomic variables such as growth in the economy, interest rates, and the inflation rate offer a fertile ground in the search for pervasive factors.

11.2.4 TWO IMPORTANT FEATURES OF ONE-FACTOR MODELS

Two features of one-factor models are of particular interest—the tangency portfolio and diversification.

The Tangency Portfolio

First, the assumption that the returns on all securities respond to a single common factor greatly simplifies the task of identifying the tangency portfolio. To determine the composition of the tangency portfolio, the investor needs to estimate all of the securities' expected returns, variances, and covariances. This task can be accomplished with a one-factor model by estimating a_i, b_i, and σ_{ei} for each of the N risky securities.

The expected value of the factor $\overline{F}$ and its standard deviation σ_F are also needed. With these estimates, Equations (11.3), (11.4), and (11.5) can be used to calculate expected returns, variances, and covariances for the securities, and thus allow the curved efficient set of Markowitz to be derived. Finally, the linear efficient set can be determined for a given riskfree rate.

The common responsiveness of securities to the factor eliminates the need to estimate directly the covariances between the securities. As indicated in Equation (11.5), those covariances are captured by the securities' sensitivities to the factor and the factor's variance.

Diversification

factor risk
nonfactor risk

The second interesting feature of one-factor models is diversification. Earlier it was shown that diversification leads to an averaging of market risk and a reduction in unique risk. This feature is true of any one-factor model except that instead of market and unique risk, the terms *factor risk* and *nonfactor risk* are used. In Equation (11.4) the first term on the right-hand side ($b_i^2 \sigma_F^2$) is the **factor risk** of the security, and the second term (σ_{ei}^2) is the **nonfactor** (or unique) **risk** of the security.

With a one-factor model, the variance of a portfolio is given by

$$\sigma_p^2 = b_p^2 \sigma_F^2 + \sigma_{ep}^2 \qquad (11.6a)$$

where

$$b_p = \sum_{i=1}^{N} X_i b_i \qquad (11.6b)$$

$$\sigma_{ep}^2 = \sum_{i=1}^{N} X_i^2 \sigma_{ei}^2 \qquad (11.6c)$$

Equation (11.6a) shows that the total risk of any portfolio has two components similar to the two components of the total risk of an individual security shown in Equation (11.4). In particular, the first and second terms on the right-hand side of Equation (11.6a) are the factor risk and nonfactor risk of the portfolio, respectively.

As a portfolio becomes more diversified (meaning that it contains more securities), each proportion X_i will become smaller. However, this change will not cause b_p to either decrease or increase significantly unless a deliberate attempt is made to do so by continually adding securities with values of b_i that are either relatively low or high, respectively. Equation (11.6b) shows that b_p is simply a weighted average of the sensitivities of the securities b_i, with the values of X_i serving as the weights. Thus, *diversification leads to an averaging of factor risk.*

As a portfolio becomes diversified, σ_{ep}^2, the nonfactor risk, will decrease. On the assumption that the same amount is invested in each security, Equation (11.6c) can be rewritten by substituting $1/N$ for X_i:

$$\sigma_{ep}^2 = \sum_{i=1}^{N} \left(\frac{1}{N}\right)^2 \sigma_{ei}^2$$

$$= \left(\frac{1}{N}\right)\left[\frac{\sigma_{e1}^2 + \sigma_{e2}^2 + \cdots + \sigma_{eN}^2}{N}\right]$$

The value inside the square brackets is the average nonfactor risk for the individual securities. But the portfolio's nonfactor risk is only one-Nth as large because the term $1/N$ appears outside the brackets. As the portfolio diversifies, the number of securities in it, N, increases. Consequently, $1/N$ becomes smaller, and the nonfactor risk of the portfolio is, in turn, reduced. Simply stated, *diversification reduces nonfactor risk.*[5]

11.3 Multiple-Factor Models

The health of the economy affects most firms. Thus, changes in expectations concerning the future of the economy have profound effects on the returns of most securities. However, the economy is not a simple, monolithic entity. Several common influences with pervasive effects might be identified.

1. The growth rate of gross domestic product
2. The level of interest rates on short-term Treasury securities
3. The yield spread between long-term and short-term Treasury securities
4. The yield spread between long-term corporate and Treasury securities
5. The inflation rate

11.3.1 Two-Factor Models

Instead of a one-factor model, a multiple-factor model for security returns that considers these various influences may be more accurate. Consider a multiple-factor model that assumes the return-generating process contains two factors. The equation for the two-factor model for period t is

$$r_{it} = a_i + b_{i1}F_{1t} + b_{i2}F_{2t} + e_{it} \tag{11.7}$$

where F_{1t} and F_{2t} are the two factors that have pervasive influences on security returns, and b_{i1} and b_{i2} are the sensitivities of security i to these two factors. As with the one-factor model, e_{it} is a random error term and a_i is the expected return on security i if each factor has a value of zero.

Figure 11.2 illustrates Widget Company's stock, whose returns are affected by expectations concerning both the growth rate in GDP and the rate of inflation. As with the one-factor example, each point in the figure corresponds to a particular year. (Plotting only one point avoids cluttering the figure.) This time, however, each point is a combination of Widget's return, the rate of inflation, and the growth in GDP in that year as given in Table 11.1. A two-dimensional plane is added to this scatter of points using the statistical technique of *multiple-regression analysis*. (*Multiple* refers to the fact that there is more than one variable on the right-hand side of the equation, in this case F_1 and F_2.) The plane for Widget is thus described by an adaptation of Equation (11.7):

$$r_t = a + b_1\text{GDP}_t + b_2\text{INF}_t + e_t$$

The slope of the plane in the GDP growth-rate direction (the term b_1) represents Widget's sensitivity to changes in GDP growth, assuming no change in inflation. The slope of the plane in the inflation rate direction (the term b_2) is Widget's sensitivity to changes in the inflation rate, assuming no change in GDP growth. Note that the sensitivities b_1 and b_2 in this example are positive and negative, respectively, having corresponding values of 2.2 and $-.7$.[6] This slope indicates that as GDP growth rises, Widget's return should increase, and as inflation rises, Widget's return should decrease.

The intercept term (the zero factor) in Figure 11.2 of 5.8% indicates Widget's expected return if both GDP growth and inflation are zero. Finally, in a given year the distance from Widget's actual point to the plane indicates its unique return (e_{it}), the portion of Widget's return not attributed to either GDP growth or inflation. For example, given that GDP grew by 2.9% and inflation was 3.1% in year 6, Widget's expected return equals 10% [$= 5.8\% + (2.2 \times 2.9\%) - (.7 \times 3.1\%)$]. Hence its unique return for that year is equal to $+3\%$ ($= 13\% - 10\%$).

Four parameters need to be estimated for each security with the two-factor model: a_i, b_{i1}, b_{i2}, and the standard deviation of the random error term, denoted σ_{ei}. For each

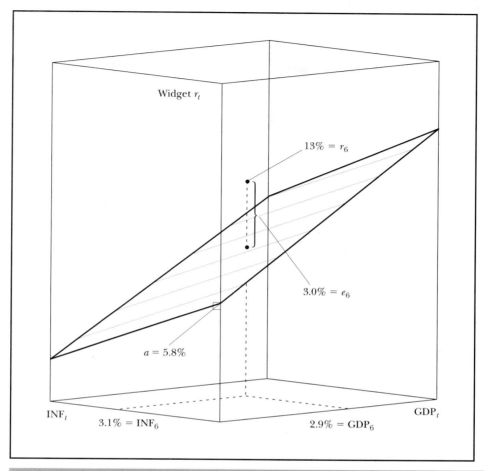

FIGURE 11.2 A Two-Factor Model

of the factors, two parameters need to be estimated. These parameters are the expected value of each factor ($\overline{F}_1$ and $\overline{F}_2$) and the variance of each factor (σ_{F1}^2 and σ_{F2}^2). Finally, the covariance between the factors $\text{COV}(F_1, F_2)$ needs to be estimated.

Expected Return

With these estimates, the expected return for any security i can be determined by specifying the expected values for the two factors in the following formula:

$$\overline{r}_i + a_i + b_{i1}\overline{F}_1 + b_{i2}\overline{F}_2 \tag{11.8}$$

For example, the expected return for Widget equals 8.9% [= 5.8% + (2.2 × 3%) − (.7 × 5%)] provided that the expected increases in GDP and inflation are 3% and 5%, respectively.

Variance

According to the two-factor model, the variance for any security i is

$$\sigma_i^2 = b_{i1}^2\sigma_{F1}^2 + b_{i2}^2\sigma_{F2}^2 + 2b_{i1}b_{i2}\text{COV}(F_1, F_2) + \sigma_{ei}^2 \tag{11.9}$$

If, in the example, the variances of the first (σ_{F1}^2) and second (σ_{F2}^2) factors are equal to 3 and 2.9, respectively, their covariance $[\text{COV}(F_1, F_2)]$ equals .65, and the random error term has a variance σ_{ei}^2 of 18.2, then the variance of Widget is 32.1 $[= (2.2^2 \times 3) + (-.7^2 \times 2.9) + (2 \times 2.2 \times -.7 \times .65) + 18.2]$ because its two sensitivities are 2.2 and $-.7$, respectively.

Covariance

Similarly, according to the two-factor model the covariance between any two securities i and j can be determined by

$$\sigma_{ij} = b_{i1}b_{j1}\sigma_{F1}^2 + b_{i2}b_{j2}\sigma_{F2}^2 + (b_{i1}b_{j2} + b_{i2}b_{j1})\,\text{COV}(F_1, F_2) \tag{11.10}$$

The covariance between Widget and Whatever is thus estimated to be 39.9 $\{= (2.2 \times 6 \times 3) + (-.7 \times -5 \times 2.9) + [(2.2 \times -5) + (-.7 \times 6)] \times .65\}$ because the sensitivities of Whatever to the two factors are 6 and -5, respectively.

The Tangency Portfolio

As with the one-factor model, once the expected returns, variances, and covariances have been determined using these equations, the investor can derive the curved efficient set of Markowitz. For a given riskfree rate, the tangency portfolio can then be identified, after which the investor can determine his or her optimal portfolio.

Diversification

Everything said earlier regarding one-factor models and the effects of diversification applies here as well.

1. Diversification leads to an averaging of factor risk.
2. Diversification can substantially reduce nonfactor risk.
3. For a *well-diversified portfolio*, nonfactor risk will be insignificant.

As with a one-factor model, the sensitivity of a portfolio to a particular factor in a multiple-factor model is a weighted average of the sensitivities of the securities where the weights are equal to the proportions invested in the securities. Recall that the return on a portfolio is a weighted average of the returns of its component securities:

$$r_{pt} = \sum_{i=1}^{N} X_i r_{it} \tag{11.11}$$

Substituting the right-hand side of Equation (11.7) for r_{it} on the right-hand side of Equation (11.11) results in

$$
\begin{aligned}
r_{pt} &= \sum_{i=1}^{N} X_i(a_i + b_{i1}F_{1t} + b_{i2}F_{2t} + e_{it}) \\
&= \left[\sum_{i=1}^{N} X_i a_i\right] + \left[\sum_{i=1}^{N} X_i b_{i1}F_{1t}\right] + \left[\sum_{i=1}^{N} X_i b_{i2}F_{2t}\right] + \left[\sum_{i=1}^{N} X_i e_{it}\right] \\
&= a_p + b_{p1}F_{1t} + b_{p2}F_{2t} + e_{pt}
\end{aligned}
\tag{11.12}
$$

where

$$a_p = \sum_{i=1}^{N} X_i a_i$$

$$b_{p1} = \sum_{i=1}^{N} X_i b_{i1}$$

$$b_{p2} = \sum_{i=1}^{N} X_i b_{i2}$$

$$e_{pt} = \sum_{i=1}^{N} X_i e_{it}$$

Note that the portfolio sensitivities b_{p1} and b_{p2} are weighted averages of the respective individual sensitivities b_{i1} and b_{i2}.

The Importance of Expectations

Security prices reflect investors' estimates of the present values of firms' future prospects. At any given time the price of Widget stock is likely to respond to the *projected* values of such factors as the growth rate of GDP or the rate of inflation, rather than depending on the *historical* values of those factors. If investors' projections of such fundamental economic conditions change, so too will the price of Widget. Because the return on a stock is influenced by changes in its price, stock returns are expected to be more highly correlated with changes in expected future values of fundamental economic variables than with the actual changes that occur contemporaneously.

For example, a large increase in inflation that was fully anticipated might have no effect on the stock price of a company whose earnings are highly sensitive to inflation. However, if the consensus expectation was for a low inflation rate, then the subsequent large unanticipated increase would have a significant effect on the company's stock price, particularly if investors believed that the unexpected increase was a harbinger of larger than previously anticipated future inflation.

For this reason, it is desirable to select factors that measure changes in expectations rather than realizations, as the latter typically include both changes that were anticipated and those that were not. One way to accomplish this goal is to rely on variables that involve changes in market prices. Thus, the difference in the returns on two portfolios—one consisting of stocks thought to be unaffected by inflation and the other consisting of stocks thought to be affected by inflation—can be used to measure revisions in inflation expectations.

11.3.2 EXTENDING THE MODEL

To extend the discussion to more than two factors requires the abandonment of diagrams because the analysis moves beyond three dimensions. Nevertheless, the concepts are the same. If there are k factors, the multiple-factor model can be written as

$$r_{it} = a_i + b_{i1}F_{1t} + b_{i2}F_{2t} + \cdots + b_{ik}F_{kt} + e_{it} \qquad \textbf{(11.13)}$$

where each security has k sensitivities, one for each of the k factors.[7]

The BARRA U.S. Equity Multiple-Factor Model

 For the quantitatively inclined investment professional, multiple-factor models are intuitively appealing tools. They capture the essence of the fundamental economic and financial forces that affect security returns in a concise and readily testable form. However, moving from abstract discussions to the development of factor models that are sufficiently comprehensive and robust to serve the varied needs of institutional investors is a difficult task. An overview of the BARRA U.S. equity multiple-factor model offers insights into the complex elements of factor-model implementation.

The BARRA model is based on the pioneering work of Barr Rosenberg, an econometrician and former finance professor. In the early 1970s, while at the University of California, Berkeley, he and Vinay Marathe formulated a sophisticated factor model. The model related common stock returns to a variety of factors derived primarily from the underlying companies' business operations.

Rosenberg is more than your typical ivory tower academic. Instead of being content to publish his results and receive the accolades of his colleagues, he recognized the commercial applications of his model. He formed a firm, now called BARRA, to enhance and sell the model to institutional investors. Both the model and the firm proved successful beyond anyone's imagination. BARRA has grown into a worldwide consulting organization with annual revenues exceeding $100 million. Its stock is publicly traded, and today has a market capitalization of more than $400 million. Although Rosenberg left the firm in 1985 to pursue personal investment management ambitions, BARRA has continued to leverage off of its factor-model expertise by designing additional factor models for the global equity market and various foreign stock markets. The firm has also built factor models for the U.S. and several foreign bond markets.

Rosenberg's original U.S. equity multiple-factor model underwent major revisions in 1982 and 1997 and is referred to by factor-model aficionados as the E3 model. Currently, hundreds of institutional investors (more than half of them outside of the United States) subscribe to the E3 model service (and its predecessor, the E2 model). These investors range from large investment managers to pension funds, and, in total, they manage more than $1 trillion of U.S. common stocks.

All factor models are based on the assumption that securities with similar exposures to specific factors exhibit similar investment behavior. The factor model–builder translates this basic concept into practice. The process of constructing factor models is far from an exact science. Although certain statistical tests can be applied to gauge the explanatory power of a particular factor model, the model–builder retains wide latitude to include or exclude potential factors.

It is instructive to review how BARRA developed the E3 model. The process is summarized in five steps.

1. Data collection and checking
2. Factor selection
3. Creation of composite factors
4. Estimation of factor returns and the factor variance–covariance matrix
5. Model testing

The E3 model's construction began with the collection of relevant security data. BARRA gathered monthly components of security returns, such as prices, dividends, and shares outstanding during an extended period of time for stocks that constitute the "estimation universe." This group included the largest 1,500 U.S. common stocks, with another roughly 400 stocks added to ensure adequate industry representation. BARRA also acquired a wide array of income and balance sheet information on the underlying companies. These financial data came mostly from the annual and quarterly financial statements issued by the companies. During the collection process, BARRA checked the data for quality. Although this task may seem mundane, it was a critical step because a small amount of bad data can have a disproportionately large impact on a factor model's accuracy.

The second step involved factor selection. Hundreds of potential factors were available for inclusion in the model. BARRA identified factors that had a pervasive influence on the returns and risks of individual securities. Using historical security return data, BARRA isolated 39 market-related, income statement, and balance sheet factors that demonstrated statistically significant relationships with security prices. The particular factors selected by BARRA ranged from the obvious to the novel. Examples included a company's beta, its consensus forecast earnings growth, its historical variability in earnings, the relative performance of its stock, its stock's book-to-price and earnings-to-price ratios, its debt to total assets, its earnings payout ratio, and the sensitivity of its stock to movements in foreign currency values.

The third step in the E3 model's construction entailed creating a set of composite fundamental factors from the individual factors. BARRA used 13 composite factors: volatility, momentum, size, size nonlinearity, trading activity, growth, earnings yield, value, earnings variability, leverage, currency sensitivity, dividend yield, and nonestimation universe estimator. The individual factors were assigned to and weighted within the composite factors on the basis of both judgment and statistical analyses. The weights of the factors may change over time as BARRA refits the model periodically. The purpose of creating these composite fundamental factors was largely statistical convenience. As the text describes, a factor model–builder estimates the variance of each factor and the covariances among all the factors. The number of variances and covariances grows exponentially as the number of factors increases. Therefore, instead of having to calculate variances and covariances for dozens of factors, BARRA's task was considerably reduced by combining the individual factors into a handful of composite factors.

To these 13 composite factors, BARRA added 13 sector-factors, each one representing a combination of a few industries. Like the composite fundamental factors, the sector-factors are composed of smaller items: 52 individual industries. (In the E3 model, a security can be assigned to as many as six industries, with total weights summing to 1, based on analysis of the company's sales, earnings, and assets. Although the defined sectors remain constant over time, the number and definitions of the industries evolve as eco-nomic forces dictate. For example, the computer software industry was unimportant in the 1970s but is a large industry today.) Thus, in its final form, the BARRA E3 factor model contains 26 fundamental and industry factors.

The fourth step involved estimating factor returns for each of the 26 factors and developing forecasts of nonfactor risk. Given return data on the model's estimation universe, BARRA effectively estimated for every month in its test period the returns on 26 portfolios that each had unit exposure to one particular factor and zero exposure to all other 25 factors. The returns to these unit-exposure portfolios represented the monthly returns to the respective factors. Using these factor returns, BARRA computed the factor variance–covariance matrix. Further, nonfactor returns were separated from the factor returns, and a nonfactor risk-forecasting model was estimated.

The last step involved testing the performance of the E3 model. BARRA was concerned with how effective its forecasts of security risk were outside the test period. Cutting through the statistical jargon, BARRA found that the model performed well.

The BARRA E3 model and its predecessors are applied by institutional investors in a variety of situations. Investment managers use the model to forecast the variability of their portfolios' returns, both in an absolute sense and relative to a benchmark. The model allows the managers to dissect this variability into factor and nonfactor components.

Managers can make informed judgments about the expected rewards offered by their particular portfolio strategies relative to the forecast risks. Managers and their clients also use the E3 model for analyzing portfolio performance. Here analysts use the model to calculate a portfolio's historical exposure to the various factors. Then, using BARRA's calculated factor returns, analysts compute the contribution of each of those exposures to the portfolio's total return. Finally, comparing the portfolio's exposures and the contributions of those exposures to the portfolio's performance against a relevant benchmark provides clues to the success or failure of the manager's strategies.

Institutional investors also use the E3 model to characterize the investment styles of their managers. Similar investment styles tend to exhibit similar E3 factor exposures. For example, large-capitalization growth managers typically have large size and growth exposures and low value exposures. By analyzing a series of past returns for various portfolios with the E3 model, a client can accurately identify the investment styles of its current and potential managers. This process aids in both manager selection and performance evaluation (see Chapter 18).

The BARRA U.S. equity multiple-factor model has contributed to the rigor and sophistication with which institutional investors approach the task of managing large pools of U.S. common stocks. Perhaps the most impressive testament to the model's utility and robustness is that, in the highly competitive and fickle world of investments, no alternative factor model has gained the widespread acceptance that the BARRA models have achieved.

11.4 Estimating Factor Models

Although many methods of estimating factor models are used, they can be grouped into three primary approaches:

1. Time-series approaches
2. Cross-sectional approaches
3. Factor-analytic approaches

11.4.1 TIME-SERIES APPROACHES

Time-series approaches are perhaps the most intuitive to investors.[8] The model–builder begins with the assumption that he or she knows in advance the factors that influence security returns. Identification of the relevant factors typically proceeds from an economic analysis of the firms involved. Aspects of macroeconomics, microeconomics, industrial organization, and fundamental security analysis play a major role in the process.

For example, as discussed earlier, certain macroeconomic variables might have a pervasive impact on security returns, including such things as growth in GDP, inflation, and interest rates. With these factors specified, the model–builder collects information concerning the historical values of the factors and security returns from period to period. Using these data, the model–builder calculates the sensitivities of the securities' returns to the factors, the securities' zero factors and unique returns, the standard deviations of the factors, and the correlations between factors. With this approach, accurate measurement of factor values is crucial, but in practice, it can be difficult.

An Example

Table 11.1 and Figure 11.2 present an example of the time-series approach to estimate a two-factor model. Returns on individual stocks such as Widget were related to two factors—GDP and inflation—by comparing over time each stock's returns with the values of the factors.

Fama and French conducted a study using a time-series approach to identify the factors that explain stock and bond returns.[9] They found that monthly stock returns were related to three factors: a market factor, a size factor, and a book-to-market equity factor. In equation form, their factor model for stocks is

$$r_{it} - r_{ft} = a_i + b_{i1}(r_{Mt} - r_{ft}) + b_{i2}\text{SMB}_t + b_{i3}\text{HML}_t + e_{it} \tag{11.14}$$

The first factor $(r_{Mt} - r_{ft})$ is simply the monthly return on a broad stock market index over and above the return on one-month Treasury bills. The size factor (SMB_t) is the difference in the monthly return on two stock indices: a small-stock index and a big-stock index. (Here a stock's size is measured by its market capitalization. The small-stock index consists of stocks whose market capitalizations are below the median NYSE size, and the big-stock index consists of stocks whose market capitalizations are above the median.) The book-to-market equity factor (HML_t) is also the difference in the monthly return on two stock indices: an index of stocks with high book-to-market equity ratios and an index of stocks with low book-to-market equity ratios. (Here book equity is stockholders' equity taken from the firm's balance sheet, and market equity is the same as the stock's size used in determining the previous factor. The high-ratio index consists of stocks that are in the top third, and the low-ratio index consists of stocks that are in the bottom third.)

Fama and French also identified two factors that seem to explain monthly bond returns. In equation form, their factor model for bonds is

$$r_{it} - r_{ft} = a_i + b_{i1}\text{TERM}_t + b_{i2}\text{DEF}_t + e_{it} \qquad \textbf{(11.15)}$$

These two factors are a term-structure factor and a default factor.[10] The term-structure factor (TERM_t) is simply the difference in the monthly returns on long-term Treasury bonds and one-month Treasury bills. The default factor (DEF_t) is the difference in the monthly returns on a portfolio of long-term corporate bonds and long-term Treasury bonds.[11]

Note that by creating factors using the return differences between two portfolios, Fama and French can indirectly capture investors' expectations. For example, when the DEF_t factor has a positive value, investors are expressing their optimistic expectations about the trend in corporate creditworthiness. They have bid up the price of securities exposed to default (corporate bonds) relative to securities free of default risk (Treasury bonds).

11.4.2   CROSS-SECTIONAL APPROACHES

Cross-sectional approaches are less intuitive than time-series approaches but can often be just as powerful a tool. The model–builder begins with estimates of securities' sensitivities to certain factors. Then in a particular time period, the values of the factors are estimated based on securities' returns and their sensitivities to the factors. This process is repeated over multiple time periods providing period-by-period estimates of the factors' values. These values can be used to estimate the factors' standard deviations and correlations.

The cross-sectional approach is entirely different from the time-series approach. With the time-series approach, the values of the factors are known and the sensitivities are estimated. Furthermore, the analysis is conducted for one security over multiple time periods, then another security, then another, and so on. With the cross-sectional approach, the sensitivities are known and the values of the factors are estimated. The sensitivities in the cross-sectional approach are sometimes referred to as *attributes*. In addition, the analysis is conducted over one time period for a group of securities, then another time period for the same group, then another, and so on. Examples of one-factor and two-factor models illustrate the cross-sectional approach.[12]

Figure 11.3 provides a hypothetical example of the relationship between the returns for a number of different stocks in a given time period and one security attribute—dividend yield—for each stock. Each point represents one particular stock, showing its return and dividend yield for the time period under evaluation. In this case, stocks with higher dividend yields tended to do better—that is, have higher returns—

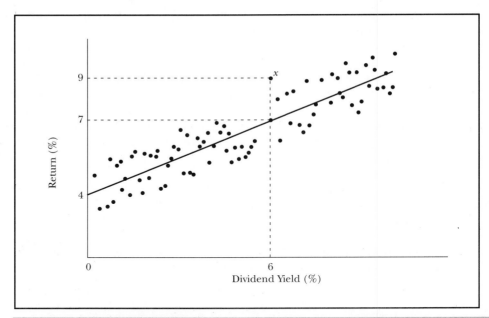

FIGURE 11.3 A Cross-Sectional One-Factor Model

than those with lower dividend yields. Whereas Figure 11.3 (an example of the cross-sectional approach) is based on many stocks for one time period, Figure 11.1 (an example of the time-series approach) is based on one stock for many time periods.

The relationship shown in Figure 11.3 was quantified by fitting a straight line to the diagram using the statistical technique of simple linear regression analysis. The equation of the line in Figure 11.3 is

$$\bar{r}_{it} = 4 + .5b_{it} \tag{11.16}$$

or, more generally,

$$\bar{r}_{it} = a_t + b_{it}F_t \tag{11.17}$$

where

$\bar{r}_{it}$ = the expected return on stock i in period t, given that the factor had an actual value of F_t

a_t = the zero factor in period t

b_{it} = the dividend yield of stock i in period t

F_t = the actual value of the factor in period t

The vertical intercept a_t indicates the expected return on a typical stock with a dividend yield of zero. It is called the zero factor as in Equation (11.1). In Figure 11.3 it is equal to 4%. The slope of .5 indicates the increase in expected return for each percent of dividend yield. It represents the actual value of the dividend yield factor (F_t) in this time period.

The cross-sectional approach uses sensitivities to provide estimates of the values of the factors. These factors are known as *empirical factors*. In comparison the time-series approach uses known values of factors to provide estimates of a security's sensitivities. These factors are known as *fundamental factors*.

The actual return on any given security may lie above or below the line shown in Figure 11.3 because of its nonfactor return. A complete description of the relationship for this one-factor model is

$$r_{it} = 4 + .5b_{it} + e_{it} \qquad (11.18)$$

where e_{it} denotes the nonfactor return during period t on security i. In Figure 11.3, security x had a dividend yield of 6%. Based on Equation (11.14), it had an expected return during this time period of 7% [= 4 + (.5 × 6)]. Because it actually had a return of 9%, its nonfactor return was +2% (= 9% − 7%).

In periods such as the one shown in Figure 11.3, high-yield stocks tend to outperform low-yield stocks, which indicates that the yield factor, F_t, is positive. In another time period low-yield stocks may outperform high-yield stocks. The regression line in the corresponding diagram would be downward-sloping, and the yield factor would be negative. In still other time periods, there will be no relationship between yield and return, resulting in a flat regression line and a yield factor of zero. The extension to more than one factor follows in a straightforward manner from what has been indicated in Equations (11.16) through (11.18).[13]

11.4.3   FACTOR-ANALYTIC APPROACHES

With factor-analytic approaches the model–builder knows neither the factor values nor the securities' sensitivities to those factors. A statistical technique called *factor analysis* is used to extract the number of factors and securities' sensitivities based simply on a set of securities' past returns. Factor analysis considers the returns, over many time periods, of a sample of securities and attempts to identify one or more statistically significant factors that could have generated the covariances of returns observed within the sample. In essence, the return data tell the model–builder about the structure of the factor model. Unfortunately, factor analysis does not specify what economic variables the factors represent.

11.4.4   LIMITATIONS

There is no reason to assume that a good factor model for one period will be a good one for the next period. Key factors—such as the effect of energy prices on security markets—change, as they did in the 1970s and during the 1991 war in the Persian Gulf. The risks and returns associated with various factors and the sensitivities of securities to factors can change over time.[14]

It would be convenient if neither the relevant factors nor their magnitudes were to change from period to period. If neither changed, mechanical procedures could be applied to security returns over an extended past period and the factor model inferred along with all the needed magnitudes. In reality, statistical estimation methods should be tempered with the judgment of the model–builder to account for the dynamic nature of the investment environment.

11.5   Factor Models and Equilibrium

Keep in mind that a factor model is not an equilibrium model of asset pricing. Compare, for example, the expected return on a stock using a one-factor model from Equation (11.3) with that of the CAPM from Equation (10.7):[15]

$$\bar{r}_i = a_i + b_i\bar{F} \qquad (11.3)$$

$$\bar{r}_i = r_f + (\bar{r}_M - f_f)\beta_{iM} \qquad (10.7)$$

Both equations show that the expected return on the stock is related to a characteristic of the stock, b_i or β_i. If the expected return on both the factor, $\overline{F}$, and the market risk premium, $(\overline{r}_M - r_f)$, are positive, the larger the size of the characteristic, the larger the security's expected return. Hence, at this point there seems to be little that differentiates these two equations of expected return.

The key is in the other term on the right-hand side of each equation: a_i and r_f. The only characteristic of the stock that determines its expected return according to the CAPM is β_i because r_f denotes the riskfree rate and is the same for all securities. However, with the factor model there is a second characteristic of the stock that needs to be estimated to determine the stock's expected return, namely, a_i. Because the size of a_i differs from one stock to another, it prevents the factor model from being an equilibrium model.

Stated differently, two stocks with the same value of b_i can have dramatically different expected returns according to a factor model. For example, if GDP is expected to rise 5%, then the expected return on Widget is 14% because a_i and b_i for Widget are 4 and 2 [14% = 4% + (2 × 5%)]. In comparison, even though another stock has the same sensitivity to GDP as Widget ($b_i = 2$), it can have an expected return of only 8% because its value of a_i is −2% [8% = −2% + (2 × 5%)].

In contrast, two stocks with the same value of β_i have the same expected return according to the equilibrium-based CAPM. If Widget and XYZ both have a beta of 1.2, then they both will have an expected return of 14% if the riskfree rate is 8% and the expected return on the market is 13% [14% = 8% + (13% − 8%) × 1.2].

Summary

1. A factor model is a return-generating process that relates returns on securities to the movement in one or more common factors.
2. Any aspect of a security's return unexplained by the factor model is assumed to be unique to the security and, therefore, is uncorrelated with the unique element of returns on other securities.
3. The market model is a specific example of a factor model where the factor is the return on a market index.
4. The assumption that the returns on securities respond to common factors simplifies the task of calculating the curved Markowitz efficient set.
5. The sensitivity of a portfolio to a factor is the weighted average of the sensitivities of the component securities in which the securities' proportions in the portfolio serve as the weights.
6. The total risk of a security is composed of factor risk and nonfactor risk.
7. Diversification leads to an averaging of factor risk.
8. Diversification reduces nonfactor risk.
9. Three basic methods are used to estimate factor models: the time-series approach, the cross-sectional approach, and the factor-analytic approach.
10. Unlike the CAPM, a factor model is not an equilibrium model of asset prices.

Questions and Problems

1. Expectations about growth in real GDP, real interest rates, and inflation are some of the factors that might be expected to influence security returns. For each factor, provide an example of an industry that is expected to have a high (either positive or negative) sensitivity to the factor.

2. Why do factor models greatly simplify the process of deriving the curved Markowitz efficient set?
3. What are two critical assumptions underlying any factor model? Cite hypothetical examples of violations of those assumptions.
4. Cupid Childs, a wise investment statistician, once said about factor models, "Similar stocks should display similar returns." What did Cupid mean by this statement?
5. Based on a one-factor model, consider a portfolio of two securities with the following characteristics:

Security	Factor Sensitivity	Nonfactor Risk (σ_{ei}^2)	Proportions
A	.2	49	.4
B	3.5	100	.6

   a. If the standard deviation of the factor is 15%, what is the factor risk of the portfolio?
   b. What is the nonfactor risk of the portfolio?
   c. What is the portfolio's standard deviation?

6. Based on a one-factor model, security A has a sensitivity of $-.50$, whereas security B has a sensitivity of 1.25. If the covariance between the two securities is -312.50, what is the standard deviation of the factor?
7. Based on a one-factor model, for two securities A and B,

$$r_{At} = 5\% + .8F_t + e_{At}$$

$$r_{Bt} = 7\% + 1.2F_t + e_{Bt}$$

$$\sigma_F = 18\%$$

$$\sigma_{eA} = 25\%$$

$$\sigma_{eB} = 15\%$$

calculate the standard deviation of each security.
8. Based on a one-factor model, if the average nonfactor risk (σ_{ei}^2) of all securities is 225, what is the nonfactor risk of a portfolio with equal weights assigned to its 10 securities? 100 securities? 1,000 securities?
9. With a five-factor model (assuming uncorrelated factors) and a 30-stock portfolio, how many parameters must be estimated to calculate the expected return and standard deviation of the portfolio? How many additional parameter estimates are required if the factors are correlated?
10. Beyond the factors discussed in the text, speculate about other factors that could reasonably be expected to pervasively affect security returns.
11. Based on a three-factor model, consider a portfolio composed of three securities with the following characteristics:

Security	Factor 1 Sensitivity	Factor 2 Sensitivity	Factor 3 Sensitivity	Proportion
A	−.2	3.6	.05	.6
B	.5	10.0	.75	.2
C	1.5	2.2	.30	.2

What are the sensitivities of the portfolio to factors 1, 2, and 3?
12. Smiler Murray, a quantitative security analyst, remarked, "The structure of any factor model concerns surprise, in particular the nature of correlations between surprises in different securities' returns." What does Smiler mean by this statement?

13. Based on a two-factor model, consider two securities with the following characteristics:

Characteristic	Security A	Security B
Factor 1 sensitivity	1.5	.7
Factor 2 sensitivity	2.6	1.2
Nonfactor risk (σ_{ei}^2)	25.0	16.0

The standard deviations of factors 1 and 2 are 20% and 15%, respectively, and the factors have a covariance of 225. What are the standard deviations of securities *A* and *B*? What is their covariance?

14. Compare and contrast the three approaches to estimating factor models.

15. Why are investor expectations about future factor values more relevant to security returns than are the historical value of the factors?

Endnotes

1. Only six data points are shown in the figure for ease of exposition. The standard statistical procedure of simple linear regression is discussed in Chapter 13 and in Mark Kritzman, ". . . About Regression," *Financial Analysts Journal,* 47, no. 3 (May/June 1991), 12–15. It can be found in most statistics books, such as James T. McClave and P. George Benson, *Statistics for Business and Economics* (New York: Macmillan, 1994), Chapter 10.

2. It is more appropriate to state that security returns respond to expectations (and deviations from those expectations) about the future values of factors such as GDP growth as opposed to merely the realized values of those factors. This subtle (but important) distinction will be addressed later in the chapter.

3. Sometimes *b* is referred to as the **factor loading** (or **attribute**) of the security.

4. The time subscript *t* was deleted from the market model simply for ease of exposition. Technically, the random error term should be written as ε_{iIt}.

5. Actually, all that is necessary for this reduction in nonfactor risk to occur is for the maximum amount invested in any one security to continually decrease as *N* increases. An example based on the market model is given in Chapter 8.

6. These values were arrived at by applying multiple regression (see McClave and Benson, *Statistics for Business and Economics,* Chapter 11) to the data given in Table 11.1.

7. As an alternative to equation (11.13), factor models can be written as $r_{it} = \bar{r}_{it} + c_{i1}FD_{1t} + c_{i2}FD_{2t} + \cdots + c_{ik}FD_{kt} + e_{it}$. Here $\bar{r}_{it}$ denotes the expected return of stock *i* in period *t* and the terms $FD_{1t}\ldots FD_{kt}$ denote the deviations of factors 1 through *k* from their expected values in period *t*. For example, in the case of the first factor, $FD_{1t} = F_{1t} - \bar{F}_{1t}$, which represents the difference between the actual value of the first factor and its expected value. Hence, if this factor is the rate

of inflation, then FD_{1t} would denote the unexpected rate of inflation because it is equivalent to the difference between the actual rate of inflation and the expected inflation rate. Lastly, the terms $c_{i1}\ldots c_{ik}$ denote the response coefficients in the rate of return of stock *i* to these factor deviations. The random error term, e_{it}, and the factor deviation terms, $FD_{1t}\ldots FD_{kt}$, all have expected values of zero.

8. The examples given earlier in the chapter based on Table 11.1 use this approach.

9. Eugene F. Fama and Kenneth R. French, "Common Risk Factors in the Returns on Stocks and Bonds," *Journal of Financial Economics,* 33, no. 1 (February 1993): 3–56. It should be noted that attempts to relate the Fama–French factor model to an asset pricing model of market equilibrium have been controversial. See, for example, A. Craig MacKinlay, "Multifactor Models Do Not Explain Deviations from the CAPM," *Journal of Financial Economics,* 38, no. 1 (May 1995): 3–28.

10. Speculative-grade bonds were found to be related to the three stock factors in addition to two bond factors.

11. Interestingly, Fama and French also found that the market factor ($r_{Mt} - r_{ft}$) was related to these two bond factors. Based on this finding, they constructed a revised market factor that consisted of the market factor less the influence of the two bond factors and the two other stock factors, and they found that stock returns were related to five factors: the revised market factor, SML_t, HML_t, $TERM_t$, and DEF_t. Investment-grade bond returns continued to be related to just the two bond factors.

12. In the time-series approach, a security's sensitivity to a factor is its "attribute," and the factor is a given macroeconomic variable. Hence the attribute's value is unknown and must be estimated, whereas the value of the factor is known. In the cross-sectional approach, a security's attribute is usually some micro-

economic variable measuring the security's exposure to the factor (a stock's dividend yield and market capitalization are examples of attributes). Hence the attribute's value is known whereas the factor's value is unknown and must be estimated.

13. One of the first studies to use the cross-sectional approach with more than two factors is by William F. Sharpe, "Factors in New York Stock Exchange Security Returns, 1931–1979," *Journal of Portfolio Management,* 8, no. 4 (Summer 1982): 5–19. A subsequent application is presented in Blake R. Grossman and William F. Sharpe, "Financial Implications of South African Divestment," *Financial Analysts Journal,* 42, no. 4 (July/August 1986): 15–29.

14. One study found that the factors that appear to explain security returns on even dates generally do not explain security returns on odd dates. See Dolores A. Conway and Marc R. Reinganum, "Stable Factors in Security Returns: Identification Using Cross Validation," *Journal of Business and Economic Statistics,* 6, no. 1 (January 1988): 1–15.

15. Time subscripts have been removed for ease of exposition.

Arbitrage Pricing Theory

The capital asset pricing model (CAPM) is an equilibrium model that asserts that securities have different expected returns because they have different betas. However, there exists an alternative model of asset pricing that was developed by Stephen Ross. It is known as **arbitrage pricing theory** (APT), and in some ways it is less complicated than the CAPM.

arbitrage pricing theory

The CAPM requires a number of assumptions, including those initially made by Markowitz when he developed the basic mean–variance model presented in Chapters 7 and 8. For example, each investor is assumed to choose his or her optimal portfolio using indifference curves based on portfolio expected returns and standard deviations. In contrast, APT makes different assumptions. One primary APT assumption is that each investor, when given the opportunity to increase the expected return of his or her portfolio without increasing its risk, will do so. The mechanism for doing so involves the use of arbitrage portfolios.

12.1 Factor Models

Arbitrage pricing theory starts with the assumption that security returns are related to an unknown number of unknown factors.[1] For ease of exposition, imagine that there is only one factor, and that factor is the rate of increase in industrial production. In this situation, security returns are related to the following one-factor model:

$$r_i = a_i + b_i F_1 + e_i \tag{12.1}$$

where

r_i = rate of return on security i

a_i = the zero factor

b_i = the sensitivity of security i to the factor

F_1 = the value of the factor, which in this case is the rate of growth in industrial production

e_i = random error term[2]

In this equation, b_i represents the sensitivity of security i to the factor. (It is also known as the factor loading for security i or the attribute of security i.)

Imagine that an investor owns three stocks, and the current market value of his or her holdings in each one is $4,000,000. Hence the investor's current investable wealth, W_0, is equal to $12,000,000. Everyone believes that these three stocks have the following expected returns and sensitivities:

	$\bar{r}_i$	b_i
Stock 1	15%	.9
Stock 2	21	3.0
Stock 3	12	1.8

Do these expected returns and factor sensitivities represent an equilibrium situation? If not, what will happen to stock prices and expected returns to restore equilibrium?

12.1.1 PRINCIPLE OF ARBITRAGE

In recent years, baseball card conventions have become commonplace events. Collectors gather to exchange baseball cards with one another at negotiated prices. Suppose that Ms. A attends such a gathering, where in one corner she finds S offering to sell a 1951 Mickey Mantle rookie card for $400. Exploring the convention further, she finds B trying to buy the same card for $500. Recognizing a financial opportunity, Ms. A agrees to sell the card to B, who gives her $500 in cash. She races back to give $400 to S, receives the card, and returns with it to B, who takes possession of the card. Ms. A pockets the $100 in profit from the two transactions and moves on in search of other opportunities. Ms. A has engaged in a form of arbitrage.

arbitrage   **Arbitrage** is the process of earning riskless profits by taking advantage of differential pricing for the same physical asset or security. As a widely applied investment tactic, arbitrage typically entails the sale of a security at a relatively high price and the simultaneous purchase of the same security (or its functional equivalent) at a relatively low price.

Arbitrage is a critical element of modern, efficient security markets. Because arbitrage profits are by definition riskless, all investors are motivated to take advantage of them whenever they are discovered. Granted, some investors have greater resources and are more inclined to engage in arbitrage than others. It only takes a few of these active investors to exploit arbitrage situations and, by their buying and selling actions, eliminate these profit opportunities.

The nature of arbitrage is clear when discussing different prices for an individual security. However, "almost arbitrage" opportunities involve "similar" securities or portfolios. The similarity can be defined in many ways, for example, in the exposure to pervasive factors that affect security prices.

A factor model implies that securities or portfolios with equal factor sensitivities will behave in the same way except for nonfactor risk. Therefore, securities or portfolios with the same factor sensitivities should offer the same expected returns. If they do not, then almost arbitrage opportunities exist. Investors will take advantage of these opportunities, thereby eliminating them. That is the essential logic underlying APT.

12.1.2 ARBITRAGE PORTFOLIOS

arbitrage portfolio   According to APT, an investor will explore the possibility of forming an **arbitrage portfolio** in order to increase the expected return of his or her current portfolio without increasing its risk. Just what is an arbitrage portfolio? There are three characteristics of an arbitrage portfolio:

1. It does not require any additional funds from the investor. If X_i denotes the *change* in the investor's holdings of security i (and hence the weight of security i in the arbitrage portfolio), this requirement of a three-security arbitrage portfolio can be written as

$$X_1 + X_2 + X_3 = 0 \qquad (12.2)$$

2. It has no sensitivity to any factor. (In the terminology of factor models, an arbitrage portfolio has "zero factor exposures.") Because the sensitivity of a portfolio to a factor is just a weighted average of the sensitivities of the securities in the portfolio to that factor, this requirement of a three-security arbitrage portfolio when there is one factor can be written as

$$b_1 X_1 + b_2 X_2 + b_3 X_3 = 0 \qquad (12.3a)$$

or, in the current example,

$$.9X_1 + 3.0X_2 + 1.8X_3 = 0 \qquad (12.3b)$$

Thus, in this example, an arbitrage portfolio has no sensitivity to the growth rate of industrial production.

3. It has a positive expected return. Mathematically, this third and last requirement for a three-security arbitrage portfolio is

$$X_1 \bar{r}_1 + X_2 \bar{r}_2 + X_3 \bar{r}_3 > 0 \qquad (12.4a)$$

or, for this example,

$$15X_1 + 21X_2 + 12X_3 > 0 \qquad (12.4b)$$

In the example, there are many potential arbitrage portfolios that meet the conditions given in Equations (12.2) and (12.3b). Note that there are three unknowns (X_1, X_2, and X_3) and two equations, which means that there is an infinite number of combinations of values for X_1, X_2, and X_3 that satisfy these two equations.[3] To find one combination, consider arbitrarily assigning a value of .1 to X_1. Doing so results in two equations and two unknowns:

$$.1 + X_2 + X_3 = 0 \qquad (12.5a)$$

$$.09 + 3.0X_2 + 1.8X_3 = 0 \qquad (12.5b)$$

The solution to Equations (12.5a) and (12.5b) is $X_2 = .075$ and $X_3 = -.175$. Hence one potential arbitrage portfolio has these weights. To ascertain that this portfolio is indeed an arbitrage portfolio, its expected return must be determined. If the return is positive, then an arbitrage portfolio has been identified.[4] Because the solution for this portfolio shows that its expected return is $(15\% \times .1) + (21\% \times .075) + (12\% \times -.175) = +.975\%$, an arbitrage portfolio has indeed been identified.

The arbitrage portfolio just identified involves buying $1,200,000 of stock 1 and $900,000 of stock 2. How were these dollar figures derived? The solution comes from taking the current market value of the portfolio ($W_0 = \$12,000,000$) and multiplying it by the weights for the arbitrage portfolio of $X_1 = .1$ and $X_2 = .075$. Where does the money come from to make these purchases? It comes from selling $2,100,000 of stock 3. (Note that $X_3 W_0 = -.175 \times \$12,000,000 = -\$2,100,000$.)

In summary, this arbitrage portfolio is potentially attractive to any investor who desires a higher return and is not concerned with nonfactor risk. It requires no additional dollar investment, it has no factor risk, yet it has a positive expected return.

12.1.3 THE INVESTOR'S POSITION

At this juncture the investor can evaluate his or her position from either one of two equivalent viewpoints: (1) holding both the old portfolio and the arbitrage portfolio or (2) holding a new portfolio. Consider, for example, the weight in stock 1. The old portfolio weight was .333 and the arbitrage portfolio weight was .10; the sum of these two weights equals .433. Note that the dollar value of the holdings of stock 1 in the new portfolio rises to $5,200,000 (= $4,000,000 + $1,200,000), so its weight is .433 (= $5,200,000/$12,000,000), equivalent to the sum of the old and arbitrage portfolio weights.

Similarly, the portfolio's expected return is equal to the sum of the expected returns of the old and arbitrage portfolios, or 16.975% (= 16% + .975%). The new portfolio's expected return is calculated using the new portfolio's weights and the expected returns of the stocks, or 16.975% [= (.433 × 15%) + (.408 × 21%) + (.158 × 12%)].

The sensitivity of the new portfolio is a weighted average of the securities' sensitivites, or 1.9 [= (.433 × .9) + (.408 × 3.0) + (.158 × 1.8)]. This value is equivalent to the sum of the sensitivities of the old and arbitrage portfolios (= 1.9 + 0.0).

What about the risk of the new portfolio? Assume that the standard deviation of the old portfolio was 11%. The variance of the arbitrage portfolio will be small because its only source of risk is nonfactor risk. Likewise, the variance of the new portfolio will differ from that of the old only as a result of changes in its nonfactor risk. Thus, it can be concluded that the risk of the new portfolio will be approximately 11%.[5] Table 12.1 summarizes these observations.

12.2 Pricing Effects

What are the consequences of buying stocks 1 and 2 and selling stock 3? Because everyone will be doing so, the stocks' prices will be affected and, accordingly, their expected returns will adjust. Specifically, the prices of stocks 1 and 2 will rise because of increased buying pressure. In turn, this will cause their expected returns to fall.

TABLE 12.1	How an Arbitrage Portfolio Affects an Investor's Position		
	Old Portfolio +	*Arbitrage Portfolio* =	*New Portfolio*
Weight			
X_1	.333	.100	.433
X_2	.333	.075	.408
X_3	.333	−.175	.158
Property			
$\bar{r}_p$	16.000%	.975%	16.975%
b_p	1.900	.000	1.900
σ_p	11.000	Small	Approx. 11.000

Conversely, the selling pressure put on stock 3 will cause its stock price to fall and its expected return to rise.

This outcome can be seen by examining the equation for estimating a stock's expected return:

$$\bar{r} = \frac{\overline{P}_1}{P_0} - 1 \tag{12.6}$$

where P_0 is the stock's current price and $\overline{P}_1$ is the stock's expected end-of-period price. Buying stock 1 or 2 will push up its current price, P_0, yet will have no impact on the stock's expected end-of-period price, $\overline{P}_1$. As a result, its expected return $\bar{r}$ will decline. Conversely, selling stock 3 will push down its current price and result in a rise in its expected return.

This buying-and-selling activity will continue until *all* arbitrage possibilities are significantly reduced or eliminated. That is, all possible portfolio adjustments that require no additional funds and that have zero factor exposures will have zero expected returns. At this point, an approximately linear relationship will exist between expected returns and sensitivities of the following sort:

$$\bar{r}_i = \lambda_0 + \lambda_1 b_i \tag{12.7}$$

where λ_0 and λ_1 are constants. This equation is the asset pricing equation of APT when returns are generated by one factor.[6] Note that it is the equation of a straight line, meaning that in equilibrium there will be a linear relationship between expected returns and sensitivities.

In the example, one possible equilibrium setting could have $\lambda_0 = 8$ and $\lambda_1 = 4$.[7] Consequently, the pricing equation is

$$\bar{r}_i = 8 + 4b_i \tag{12.8}$$

This relationship results in the following equilibrium levels of expected returns for stocks 1, 2, and 3:

$$\bar{r}_1 = 8 + (4 \times .9) = 11.6\%$$
$$\bar{r}_2 = 8 + (4 \times 3.0) = 20.0\%$$
$$\bar{r}_3 = 8 + (4 \times 1.8) = 15.2\%$$

As a result, the expected returns for stocks 1 and 2 fall from 15% and 21%, respectively, to 11.6% and 20% because of increased buying pressure. In contrast, increased selling pressure causes the expected return on stock 3 to rise from 12% to 15.2%. The bottom line is that the expected return on any security is, in equilibrium, a linear function of the security's sensitivity to the factor b_i.[8]

12.2.1 A GRAPHICAL ILLUSTRATION

Figure 12.1 illustrates the APT asset pricing line given in Equation (12.7). Any security that has a factor sensitivity and expected return that plots off the line will be mispriced according to the APT and will present investors with the opportunity of forming arbitrage portfolios. Security B is an example. An investor who buys security B and sells security S in equal dollar amounts will have formed an arbitrage portfolio.[9] How?

First, by selling an amount of security S to pay for the long position in security B, the investor will not have committed any new funds. Second, because securities B and S have the same sensitivity to the factor, the selling of security S and buying of secu-

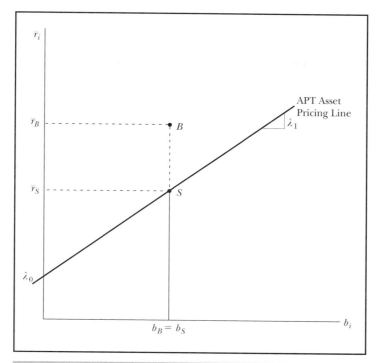

FIGURE 12.1 APT Asset Pricing Line

rity *B* will constitute a portfolio with no sensitivity to the factor. Finally, the arbitrage portfolio will have a positive expected return because the expected return of security *B* is greater than the expected return of security *S*.[10] As a result of investors buying security *B*, its price will rise and, in turn, its expected return will fall until it is located on the APT asset pricing line.[11]

In the three-security example presented earlier, the securities do not initially all lie on a straight line. Instead, any line that is drawn will have at least one of the securities lying above or below it. However, after the expected returns of stocks 1, 2, and 3 have adjusted from 15%, 21%, and 12% to 11.6%, 20%, and 15.2%, respectively, the three stocks will all lie on a straight line with a vertical intercept of 8% and with a slope of 4. This result will be shown next.

12.2.2   INTERPRETING THE APT PRICING EQUATION

How can the constants λ_0 and λ_1 that appear in Equation (12.7) be interpreted? Assuming there is a riskfree asset in existence, it will have a rate of return that is a constant. Therefore this asset will have no sensitivity to the factor, meaning $b_i = 0$. From Equation (12.7) it can be seen that $\bar{r}_i = \lambda_0$ for any asset with $b_i = 0$. For the riskfree asset, $\bar{r}_i = r_f$, implying that $\lambda_0 = r_f$. Because the value of λ_0 in Equation (12.7) must be r_f, this equation can be rewritten as

$$\bar{r}_i = r_f + \lambda_1 b_i \tag{12.9}$$

pure factor portfolio

The value of λ_1 can be determined by considering a **pure factor portfolio** (or pure factor play) denoted p^* that has unit sensitivity to the factor, meaning $b_{p^*} = 1$. (If there were other factors, the portfolio would be constructed with no sensitivity to them.) According to Equation (12.9), such a portfolio has the following expected return:

$$\bar{r}_{p*} = r_f + \lambda_1 \tag{12.10a}$$

This equation can be rewritten as

$$\bar{r}_{p*} - r_f = \lambda_1 \tag{12.10b}$$

factor risk premium

Thus λ_1 is the expected excess return (meaning the expected return over and above the riskfree rate) on a portfolio that has unit sensitivity to the factor. Accordingly, it is known as a **factor risk premium** (or factor-expected return premium). Letting δ_1 denote the expected return on a portfolio that has unit sensitivity to the factor, $\bar{r}_{p*}$ Equation (12.10b) can be rewritten as

$$\delta_1 - r_f = \lambda_1 \tag{12.10c}$$

Inserting the left-hand side of Equation (12.10c) for λ_1 in Equation (12.9) results in a second version of the APT pricing equation:

$$\bar{r}_i = r_f + (\delta_1 - r_f)b_i \tag{12.11}$$

In the example, because $r_f = 8\%$ and $\lambda_1 = \delta_1 - r_f = 4\%$, it follows that $\delta_1 = 12\%$. Therefore the expected return on a portfolio with unit sensitivity to the factor is 12%. This outcome is evident in the formation of a pure factor portfolio from securities 1 and 3. Because the securities have sensitivities of .9 and 1.8, respectively, their weights in the pure factor portfolio will be $\frac{8}{9}$ and $\frac{1}{9}$, respectively. [Note that $(.9 \times \frac{8}{9}) + (1.8 \times \frac{1}{9}) = 1$]. The portfolio's expected return will be 12% [$= (11.6\% \times \frac{8}{9}) + (15.2\% \times \frac{1}{9})$], as indicated earlier. Next, the pricing equation of APT is generalized by expanding the analysis to k factors, where $k > 1$.

12.3 Multiple-Factor Models

What happens to these APT pricing Equations (12.7) and (12.11) when returns are generated by a multiple-factor model where the number of factors k is greater than 1? It turns out that the basic pricing equations are expanded in a relatively straightforward manner.

In the case of k factors ($F_1, F_2, \ldots, F_k$) each security has k sensitivities ($b_{i1}, b_{i2},\ldots, b_{ik}$) in the following k-factor model:

$$r_i = a_i + b_{i1}F_1 + b_{i2}F_2 + \cdots + b_{ik}F_k + e_i \tag{12.12}$$

In turn, securities are priced by the following asset pricing equation, which is similar to Equation (12.7):

$$\bar{r}_i = \lambda_0 + \lambda_1 b_{i1} + \lambda_2 b_{i2} + \cdots + \lambda_k b_{ik} \tag{12.13}$$

As before, this is a linear equation, except now it is in $k + 1$ dimensions, with the dimensions being, $\bar{r}_i, b_{i1}, b_{i2},\ldots,$ and b_{ik}.

Extending the APT pricing relationship, Equation (12.11), to this situation is not complicated. As before, λ_0 is equal to the riskfree rate because the riskfree asset has no sensitivity to any factor. Each value of δ_j represents the expected return on a *pure factor portfolio* of stocks that has unit sensitivity to factor j and zero sensitivity to all the other factors. As a result, Equation (12.11) can be expanded as follows:

$$\bar{r}_i = r_f + (\delta_1 - r_f)b_{i1} + (\delta_2 - r_f)b_{i2} + \cdots + (\delta_k - r_f)b_{ik} \tag{12.14}$$

Hence a stock's expected return is equal to the riskfree rate plus k risk premiums based on the stock's sensitivities to the k factors.

Applying Arbitrage Pricing Theory

Since its inception in the mid-1970s, APT has provided researchers and practitioners with an intuitive and flexible framework through which to address important investment management issues. As opposed to the capital asset pricing model (CAPM), with its specific assumptions concerning investor preferences as well as the critical role played by the market portfolio, APT operates under relatively weaker assumptions. Because of its emphasis on multiple sources of systematic risk, APT has attracted considerable interest as a tool to better explain investment results and more effectively control portfolio risk.

Despite its attractive features, APT has not been widely applied by the investment community. The reason lies largely with APT's most significant drawback: the lack of specificity regarding the multiple factors that systematically affect security returns as well as the long-term return associated with each of these factors. Rightly or wrongly, the CAPM unambiguously asserts that a security's covariance with the market portfolio is the only systematic source of its investment risk within a well-diversified portfolio. Arbitrage pricing theory, conversely, is conspicuously silent regarding the particular systematic factors affecting a security's risk and return. Investors must fend for themselves in determining those factors.

Few investors actually use APT to manage assets. The most prominent organization that does use it is Roll & Ross Asset Management Corporation (R&R). Because Stephen Ross invented the APT, it is interesting to briefly review how R&R translates this theory into practice.

R&R begins with a statement of the systematic sources of risk (or factors) that it believes are *currently* relevant in the capital markets. Specifically, R&R has identified five factors that pervasively affect common stock returns:

- The business cycle
- Interest rates
- Investor confidence
- Short-term inflation
- Long-term inflationary expectations

R&R quantifies these factors by designating certain measurable macroeconomic variables as proxies. For example, the business-cycle factor is represented by real (inflation-adjusted) percentage changes in the index of industrial production, whereas short-term inflation is measured by monthly percentage changes in the consumer price index.

There are several assumptions at the heart of the R&R approach. First, each source of systematic risk has a certain current volatility and expected reward. Factor volatilities and expected rewards, and even the factors themselves, may change over time. Second, individual securities and portfolios have different sensitivities to each factor. These sensitivities may also vary over time. Third, a well-diversified portfolio's exposures to the factors will determine its expected return and total risk. Fourth, a portfolio should be constructed that offers the most attractive total expected reward-to-risk ratio, given the current expected rewards and volatilities exhibited by the factors.

R&R has developed a security database (updated monthly) that covers roughly 15,000 individual common stocks in 17 countries. For each country's stock market, R&R applies the database to create a pure factor portfolio (discussed in this chapter) for each of the five factors. R&R uses the historical returns on these pure factor portfolios not only to estimate the sensitivity of every security in its database to each of the factors but also to estimate factor standard deviations, correlations, and risk premiums as well as to calculate nonfactor returns and risk for every security.

Attention at this point turns to a client's benchmark. Typically, an investor in U.S. stocks selects a market index such as the S&P 500 as the benchmark. R&R's typical assignment is to devise a more efficient portfolio that exceeds the benchmark's expected return by a prespecified (reasonable) amount, yet maintains a similar standard deviation. R&R uses portfolio optimization techniques (see the Money Matters box in Chapter 8) that combine securities in a way that attempts to set portfolio standard deviation near that of the benchmark, reduce nonfactor risk to minimal levels, emphasize stocks with low market-to-book and price-to-earnings ratios as well as positive recent returns relative to other stocks, increase exposure to risk factors with attractive rewards-to-risk, and minimize buying and selling of securities (to control transaction costs). The process is repeated monthly to keep the portfolio properly aligned with the benchmark.

The R&R approach is highly quantitative and, intriguingly, involves no judgmental forecasts of factor returns or risks. Rather, historical data on the factors and securities' factor sensitivities are mechanically manipulated to determine the desired portfolio composition. This approach may prove effective if the future mimics the past, but it can produce disappointing results if past factor data display no stable relationship with future values.

R&R captured considerable U.S. institutional investor interest when it was organized in 1986, although it never has gained a large U.S. clientele. The firm has expanded to take on foreign partners who now apply its techniques abroad. Thus, R&R provides an interesting example of converting theoretical investment concepts into practical investment products.

12.4 Identifying the Factors

Left unanswered by APT are the number and identity of the factors that have values of lambda (λ) that are sufficiently positive or negative in magnitude that they need to be included when estimating expected returns. Several researchers have investigated stock returns and have estimated that anywhere from three to five factors are "priced." Various people attempted to identify those factors.[12] Nai-Fu Chen, Richard Roll, and Stephen Ross identify the following factors:

1. Growth rate in industrial production
2. Rate of inflation (both expected and unexpected)
3. Spread between long-term and short-term interest rates
4. Spread between low-grade and high-grade bonds[13]

Michael Berry, Edwin Burmeister, and Marjorie McElroy identify five factors: Three correspond closely to the last three identified by Chen, Roll, and Ross and the other two are the growth rate in aggregate sales in the economy and the rate of return on the S&P 500.[14]

Finally, consider the five factors used by Salomon Brothers (now Salomon Smith Barney) in their *fundamental factor model*. Only one factor, inflation, is the same as the factors identified by the others. The remaining factors are as follows:

1. Growth rate in gross national product
2. Rate of interest
3. Rate of change in oil prices
4. Rate of growth in defense spending[15]

It is interesting to note that the three sets of factors have some common characteristics. First, they contain some indication of aggregate economic activity (industrial production, aggregate sales, and GDP). Second, they include inflation. Third, they contain some type of interest rate factor (either spreads or a rate itself). Because stock prices are equal to the discounted value of future dividends, the factors make intuitive sense.[16] Future dividends are related to aggregate economic activity, and the discount rate used to determine present value is related to inflation and interest rates.

Summary

1. Arbitrage pricing theory (APT) is an equilibrium model of security prices, as is the capital asset pricing model (CAPM).
2. APT makes different assumptions than the CAPM does.
3. APT assumes that security returns are generated by a factor model but does not identify the factors.
4. An arbitrage portfolio includes long and short positions in securities. It must have a net market value of zero, no sensitivity to any factor, and a positive expected return.
5. Investors will invest in arbitrage portfolios, provided they exist, driving up the prices of the securities held in long positions and driving down the prices of securities held in short positions until all arbitrage possibilities have been eliminated.
6. When all arbitrage possibilities have been eliminated, the equilibrium expected return on a security will be a linear function of its sensitivities to the factors.
7. A factor-risk premium is the equilibrium return over the riskfree rate expected from a portfolio with a unit sensitivity to the factor and no sensitivity to any other factor.
8. APT does not specify the number or identity of the factors that affect expected returns or the magnitudes or signs of the risk premiums. Most research into factors has focused on indicators of aggregate economic activity, inflation, and interest rates.

Questions and Problems

1. In what significant ways does APT differ from the CAPM?
2. Why would an investor wish to form an arbitrage portfolio?
3. What three conditions define an arbitrage portfolio?
4. Assuming a one-factor model, consider a portfolio composed of three securities with the following factor sensivities:

Security	Factor Sensitivity
1	0.9
2	3.0
3	1.8

If the proportion of security 1 in the portfolio is increased by .2, how must the proportions of the other two securities change if the portfolio is to maintain the same factor sensitivity?

5. Assuming a one-factor model of the form:

$$r_i = 4\% + b_i F + e_i$$

consider three well-diversified portfolios (zero nonfactor risk). The expected value of the factor is 8%.

Portfolio	Factor Sensitivity	Expected Return
A	0.80	10.4%
B	1.00	10.0
C	1.20	13.6

Is one of the portfolio's expected return not in line with the factor model relationship? Which one? Can you construct a self-financing combination of the other two portfolios that has the same factor sensitivity as the "out-of-line" portfolio? What is the expected return of that combination? What action would you expect investors to take regarding these three portfolios?

6. Socks Seybold owns a portfolio with the following characteristics. (Assume that returns are generated by a one-factor model.)

Security	Factor Sensitivity	Proportion	Expected Return
A	2.0	.2	20%
B	3.5	.4	10
C	0.5	.4	5

Socks decides to create an arbitrage portfolio by increasing the holdings of security A by .2. (Hint: Remember, X_B must equal $-X_C - X_A$.
   a. What must be the weights of the other two securities in Socks's arbitrage portfolio?
   b. What is the expected return on the arbitrage portfolio?
   c. If everyone follows Socks's buy-and-sell decisions, what will be the effects on the prices of the three securities?

7. Assume that security returns are generated by a one-factor model. Hap Morse holds a portfolio whose component securities have the following characteristics:

Security	Factor Sensitivity	Proportion	Expected Return
A	.6	.4	12%
B	.3	.3	15
C	1.2	.3	8

Specify an arbitrage portfolio in which Hap might invest. (Remember that there are an infinite number of possibilities—choose one.) Demonstrate that this portfolio satisfies the conditions of an arbitrage portfolio.

8. Why is the concept of arbitrage central to the asset pricing mechanism of APT?

9. Based on a one-factor model, Wyeville Labs' stock has a factor sensitivity of 3. Given a riskfree rate of 5% and a factor risk premium of 7%, what is the equilibrium expected return on Wyeville stock?

10. According to APT, why must the relationship between a security's equilibrium return and its factor sensitivities be linear?

11. Based on a one-factor model, two portfolios, A and B, have equilibrium expected returns of 9.8% and 11.0%, respectively. If the factor sensitivity of portfolio A is 0.8 and that of portfolio B is 1.0, what must the riskfree rate be?

12. What is a pure factor portfolio? How is such a portfolio constructed?

13. Based on a one-factor model, assume that the riskfree rate is 6% and the expected return on a portfolio with unit sensitivity to the factor is 8.5%. Consider a portfolio of two securities with the following characteristics:

Security	Factor Sensitivity	Proportion
A	4.0	.3
B	2.6	.7

According to the APT, what is the portfolio's equilibrium expected return?

14. Some people have argued that the market portfolio can never be measured and that the CAPM, therefore, is untestable. Others have argued that APT specifies neither the number of factors nor their identity and, hence, is also untestable. If these views are correct, are the theories valueless? Explain.

15. Although APT does not specify the identity of the relevant factors, most empirical APT research has focused on certain types of factors. What are some of the common characteristics of those factors?

Endnotes

1. Factor models are discussed in detail in Chapter 11. The CAPM, while not requiring a factor model, can hold if returns are generated by a factor model. See the ninth set of Chapter 12 references at the end of the book for a comparison of APT and the CAPM.

2. As noted in footnote 7 of Chapter 11, there are other ways to write the equation for a factor model.

3. There will always be an infinite number of solutions whenever there are more unknowns than equations. For example, consider a situation in which there is one equation with two unknowns: $Y = 3X$. Note that there is an infinite number of paired values of X and Y that solve this equation, such as $(1, 3)$, $(2, 6)$, and $(3, 9)$.

4. If its expected return is negative, then changing the signs of the weights causes the expected return to become positive. Note that the new weights also sum to zero and still represent a portfolio that has zero sensitivity to the factor. Thus, the new weights represent an arbitrage portfolio.

5. Because the total risk of a portfolio σ_p^2 is equal to $b_p^2 \sigma_F^2 + \sigma_{ep}^2$ according to the one-factor model [see Equation (11.6a) in Chapter 11], and given that the arbitrage portfolio has no factor risk by design, meaning that $b_p^2 \sigma_F^2 = 0$ because $b_p = 0$, the arbitrage portfolio must be sufficiently diversified to have insignificant nonfactor risk and, consequently, insignificant total risk. This means that all but a small number of assets will be correctly priced. These securities will not necessarily be correctly priced because an arbitrage portfolio consisting of them will not have zero nonfactor risk. For ease of exposition, we assume here that an arbitrage portfolio consisting of three securities will have zero nonfactor risk.

6. Technically, this pricing equation may not apply to the small number of assets referred to in the previous endnote.

7. Why choose 8 and 4 for λ_0 and λ_1, respectively? The magnitudes of these two parameters in equilibrium depend on many things, such as investors' relative degrees of risk aversion, wealth, and time preferences.

8. To demonstrate that Equation (12.8) is indeed an equilibrium situation, the reader is encouraged to try setting various values for X_1, X_2, and X_3 and show that the resulting potential arbitrage portfolios all have expected returns of zero.

9. If B were to plot below the APT asset pricing line, then investors would do just the opposite of what is described here. They would buy S and sell B.

10. A simpler way of viewing this transaction is a stock swap of S for B. Because it is a swap, no new funds are needed. Furthermore, because B and S have the same factor sensitivity, the swap will not alter the sensitivity of the currently held portfolio. Finally, the replacement of S with B will increase the currently held portfolio's expected return because B has a higher level of expected return than S.

11. Technically, the APT asset pricing line would shift upward a bit because of the selling of S.

12. In Chapter 11 a three-factor model developed by Fama and French is described. In their model, the factors represent returns on (1) a general market index, (2) the difference between small and large stock indices, and (3) the difference between high and low book-to-market equity ratio stock indices. Fama and French argue that these factors are consistent with a three-factor APT. See Eugene F. Fama and Kenneth R. French, "Multi-Factor Explanations of Asset Pricing Anomalies," *Journal of Finance*, 51, no. 1 (March 1996): 55–83.

13. The third factor can be interpreted as a measure of the term structure of interest rates, and the fourth factor can be interpreted as a measure of the default risk premium that investors demand for holding risky corporate bonds instead of Treasury bonds.

14. Technically, they used the part of the rate of return of the S&P 500 that could not be attributed to the other four factors. Burmeister is now president of BIRR Portfolio Analysis, an investment consulting firm that uses APT in portfolio construction and evaluation.

15. Technically, the authors used inflation-adjusted figures for all the variables except the rate of interest.

16. Dividend discount models are discussed in depth in Chapter 15.

CHAPTER

Characteristics of Common Stocks

Common stocks are easier to describe than fixed-income securities such as bonds, but they are harder to analyze. Fixed-income securities almost always have a limited life and an upper dollar limit on cash payments to investors. Common stocks have neither. Although the basic principles of valuation apply to both, the role of uncertainty is larger for common stocks, so much so that it often dominates all other elements in their valuation.

common stock

  Common stock represents equity, or an ownership position in a corporation. It is a residual claim, in the sense that creditors and preferred stockholders must be paid as scheduled before common stockholders can receive any payments. In bankruptcy, common stockholders are in principle entitled to any value remaining after all other claimants have been satisfied. However, in practice, courts sometimes violate this principle.

limited liability

  The great advantage of the corporate form of organization is the **limited liability** of its owners. Common stocks are generally 'fully paid and nonassessable,' meaning that common stockholders may lose their initial investment but not more. If the corporation fails to meet its obligations, the stockholders cannot be forced to give the corporation the funds that are needed to pay off the obligations. However, as a result of such a failure, it is possible that the value of a corporation's shares will be negligible. This outcome will result in the stockholders' having lost an amount equal to the price paid to buy the shares.

13.1 The Corporate Form

charter

A corporation exists only when it has been granted a **charter,** or certificate of incorporation, by a state. This document specifies the rights and obligations of stockholders. It may be amended with the approval of the stockholders, perhaps by a majority or a two-thirds vote, wherein each share of stock generally entitles its owner to one vote. Both the initial terms of the charter and the terms of any amendment must also be approved by the state in which the corporation is chartered. The state of Delaware has captured a disproportionate number of corporate charters because it is particularly hospitable in this respect as well as in levying corporate taxes.

13.1.1 STOCK CERTIFICATES

The ownership of a firm's stock is usually represented by a single certificate, with the number of shares held by the particular investor noted on it. Such a stock certificate is registered, with the name, address, and holdings of the investor included on the corporation's books. Dividend payments, voting material, annual and quarterly reports, and other mailings are sent directly to the registered owner, taking into account the size of his or her holdings.

transfer agent

registrar

Shares of stock held by an investor may be transferred to a new owner with the assistance of either the issuing corporation or, more commonly, its designated **transfer agent.** The agent cancels the old stock certificate and issues a new one in its place, made out to the new owner. A **registrar** ensures that the canceling and issuing of certificates is done properly. Usually, banks and trust companies act as transfer agents and registrars. Many stockholders avoid these cumbersome procedures and use instead depository trust companies (discussed in Chapter 3), which substitute computerized records for embossed certificates. Furthermore, many investors have their stock holdings registered in street name (discussed in Chapter 2), where the legally registered owner is the investor's brokerage firm.

13.1.2 VOTING

proxy

Because a common shareholder is one of the owners of a corporation, he or she is entitled to vote on matters brought up at the corporation's annual meeting and to vote for the corporation's directors. Any owner may attend and vote in person, but most choose instead to vote by **proxy.** That is, the incumbent directors and senior management will typically solicit all the stockholders, asking each one to sign a proxy that, like a power of attorney, authorizes the designated party to cast all of the investor's votes on any matter brought up at the meeting. Occasionally, desired positions on specific issues are solicited on a proxy statement. However, most of the time the positions held by the incumbents are indicated on the statement. Because the majority of votes are controlled by the incumbents via proxies, the actual voting is perfunctory, leaving little if any controversy or excitement.[1]

13.1.3 PROXY FIGHT

proxy fight

Once in a while, however, a **proxy fight** develops. Insurgents from outside the corporation solicit proxies to vote against the incumbents, often in order to effect a takeover of some sort. Stockholders are deluged with literature and appeals for their proxies. The incumbents usually win, but the possibility of a loss in such a skirmish tends to curb activities clearly not in the stockholders' best interests.[2]

cumulative voting system

majority voting system

The number of votes given to an investor equals the number of shares held. Thus when a yes or no vote is called for, anyone controlling a majority of the shares can be sure that the outcome he or she favors receives a majority of the votes. When directors are to be elected, however, there are two types of voting systems that can be used. One is the **cumulative voting system,** which does not give a majority owner complete control of the outcome. The other is the **majority voting system** (or straight voting system), which does allow a majority owner to control the outcome completely. Under both systems, the winners of the election are those candidates who receive the highest vote totals. If six candidates were running for three directorships, the three receiving the greatest number of votes would be elected.

With both voting systems, the total number of votes a stockholder receives equals the number of directors to be elected times the number of shares owned. However, with the majority voting system, the stockholder may give any one candidate, as a maximum, only the number of votes equal to the number of shares owned. This feature means that in a situation where three directors are to be elected, a stockholder with 400 shares would have 1,200 votes but could give no more than 400 of these votes to any one candidate. Note that if there are a total of 1,000 shares outstanding and one stockholder owns, or has proxies for, 501 shares, then he or she can give 501 votes to each of the three candidates he or she favors. In doing so, this stockholder ensures that his or her choices are elected regardless of how the remaining 499 shares are voted. The majority shareholder's candidates each have 501 votes, whereas the most any other candidate could receive is 499 votes. Thus, with a majority voting system, a stockholder owning (or controlling with proxies) one share more than 50% is certain of electing all the candidates he or she favors.

The cumulative voting system differs from the majority voting system in that a stockholder can cast his or her votes in any manner. As a result, minority stockholders are sure to have some representation on the board of directors provided they own enough shares. In the previous example, the minority owner of the 400 shares could cast all of his or her 1,200 votes for one candidate. Imagine that this owner wanted to elect director *A*, but the majority owner of 501 shares wanted to elect candidates *B*, *C*, and *D*. In this situation, the minority stockholder could give all 1,200 votes to *A* and be certain that *A* would be one of the three directors elected regardless of what the majority stockholder did. Why? If the majority owner held the remaining 600 shares, he or she would have 1,800 votes. There is no way that candidate *A*, favored by the minority stockholder, can come in lower than second place in the vote totals; *A* will receive 1,200 votes, and there is no way that the 1,800 votes of the majority stockholder can be cast to give more than one of his or her favored candidates a vote total in excess of 1,200. Thus the minority stockholder is assured that *A* will be elected, whereas the majority stockholder is assured that only two of his or her favorites will be elected.

The voting system a corporation uses depends not only on the desires of the corporate founders but also on the state in which the firm is incorporated. Some states require cumulative voting systems. In Delaware, however, there is no cumulative voting unless it is specifically stated in the corporate charter.

13.1.4 TAKEOVERS

takeover
tender offer
bidder
target firm

Periodically, a firm or a wealthy individual, who is convinced that the management of a corporation is not fully exploiting its business opportunities, will attempt a **takeover.** This strategy is frequently implemented through a **tender offer** made by a **bidder** to a **target firm.**[3] Before the offer is announced, some of the target firm's shares are usually acquired by the bidder in the open market through brokers. (Once 5% of the stock is so acquired, the bidder has ten days to report the acquisition to the SEC in a 13d filing.) Then, in its quest to acquire more shares, the bidder announces the bid to the public. Advertisements to purchase shares (sometimes the bidder will offer its own shares instead of cash for the target's shares) are published in the financial press, and material describing the bid is mailed to the target's stockholders. The bidder generally offers to buy at a stated price some or all shares offered ("tendered") by the current stockholders of the target. The buying offer is usually contingent on the tender of a minimum number of shares by the target's stockholders by a fixed date. When the buying offer is first made, the offered price ("tender price") is generally set considerably above the current market price, although the offer itself usually leads to a subsequent price increase.

poison pill

Management of the target firm frequently responds to tender offers with its own advertisements, mailings, and the like, urging its stockholders to reject the bidder's offer. A defensive measure frequently taken by management to make the firm look less attractive to a bidder involves the use of **poison pills,** whereby the firm gives its shareholders certain rights that can be exercised only in the event of a subsequent takeover and that, once exercised, will be extremely onerous to the acquirer. Some observers argue that poison pills are used by management primarily for job security, while others argue that poison pills enhance management's bargaining position when entertaining a takeover offer. Thus, whether they are beneficial to shareholders is uncertain.

13.1.5 OWNERSHIP VERSUS CONTROL

Much has been written about the separation of ownership and control of the modern corporation.[4] This separation gives rise to a principal–agent problem. In particular, stockholders are viewed as principals who hire corporate managers to act as their agents. The agents make decisions that maximize shareholder wealth as reflected in the firm's stock price. There would be no problem if stockholders could monitor the managers costlessly because the stockholders would know whether managers acted in their best interests. However, monitoring is not costless, and complete monitoring of every decision is, practically speaking, impossible.[5] As a result, some, but not complete, monitoring is done, thereby giving managers considerable latitude in making decisions yet allowing the possibility that some decisions will not be in the stockholders' best interests.[6] However, the possibility of a proxy fight or tender offer provides some check on such decisions.

To align the interests of managers with their own, stockholders frequently offer certain incentives to management such as stock options. These options are given to high-level managers to purchase a specified number of shares at a stated price (typically at or above the market price when the options are initially issued) by a stated date. The options motivate managers to make decisions that will increase the stock price of the firm as much as possible because it is in the managers' own interest to do so. Given their relatively long life span (in comparison with listed options, discussed in Chapter 24), stock options implicitly exert pressure on management to take a long-term view in making decisions.

13.1.6 CORPORATE GOVERNANCE

corporate governance

Large institutional shareholders, such as pension, endowment, and mutual funds, now control significant proportions of most prominent U.S. corporations. The resources of these institutional investors have enabled them to actively oppose management decisions they feel diminish the value of their investments. **Corporate governance** has become a catchall description of institutional investors' efforts to influence the relationship between corporate management and the firm's shareholders. For example, the Council of Institutional Investors (CII), composed of more than 100 public and corporate pension funds controlling more than $1 trillion in assets, was organized for institutional investors to discuss and coordinate efforts to encourage enlightened shareholder rights policies by corporate management.

The CII and other shareholder rights organizations have become forces to be reckoned with on corporate governance issues. Under pressure from institutional investors, chief executives from large organizations such as General Motors, American Express, and Westinghouse were ousted. IBM restructured its board of directors to give more power to outsiders. Sears revamped its business strategy, eliminating unprofitable operations.

Many corporations have begun to negotiate directly with their large institutional shareholders. Although direct victories by institutional investors in proxy battles are rare, shareholder rights proponents are increasingly accomplishing their objectives away from the publicity of annual meetings. The mere threat of introducing corporate governance proposals at a company's annual meeting often is sufficient to force concessions from corporate management. In several cases, institutional investors have produced target lists of poorly performing companies and focused their reform efforts on those companies.

Institutional investors have been sufficiently encouraged by their successes to take their corporate governance proposals abroad. They have begun challenging corporate practices that disenfranchise shareholders and protect management in Europe and Japan. Further, in the United States, while shareholder rights activists continue to oppose blatant antishareholder takeover defenses, they also have begun to focus on subtler issues, such as executive compensation, independent boards of directors, and secret balloting in proxy fights. To what extent institutional investors should get involved with corporate business decision making remains a hotly contested subject, as does the issue of whether such activities actually enhance shareholder value.

13.1.7   STOCKHOLDERS' EQUITY
Par Value

par value

When a corporation is first chartered, it is authorized to issue up to a stated number of shares of common stock, with each typically carrying a specified **par value.** Legally, a corporation may be precluded from making payments to common stockholders if doing so would reduce the balance sheet value of stockholders' equity below the amount represented by the par value of outstanding stock. For this reason the par value is usually lower than the price for which the stock is initially sold. Some corporations issue no-par stock (in that case, a stated value must be recorded in place of the par value).

When stock is initially sold for more than its par value, the difference may be carried separately on the corporation's books under stockholders' equity. Frequently the entry is for "capital contributed in excess of par value" or "paid-in capital." The par value of the stock is carried in a separate account, generally titled "common stock," with an amount that is equal to the number of shares outstanding times the par value per share (for no-par stock, the stated value).

Book Value

book value of the equity

As time passes, a corporation will generate income, much of which is paid out to creditors (as interest) and to stockholders (as dividends). Any remainder is added to the amount shown as cumulative retained earnings on the corporation's books. The sum of the cumulative retained earnings and other entries (such as "common stock par value" and "capital contributed in excess of par") under stockholders' equity is the **book value of the equity:**

> Cumulative retained earnings
> + Capital contributed in excess of par
> + Common stock par value
> ―――――――――――――――――――
> = Book value of the equity

book value per share

The **book value per share** is obtained by dividing the book value of the equity by the number of shares outstanding.

Reserved and Treasury Stock

Corporations usually issue only part of their authorized stock. Some of the unissued stock may be reserved for outstanding options, convertible securities, and so on because the charter must be amended if a corporation wishes to issue new stock in excess of the amount originally authorized. Amending the charter requires approval by the state and the stockholders.

repurchase offer

treasury stock

Sometimes a corporation will issue a **repurchase offer** for some of its stock, where it buys some of its outstanding stock, either in the open market through a broker or with a tender offer. Afterward, this stock may be "held in the treasury." Such **treasury stock** does not carry voting rights or dividends and is equivalent economically (though not legally) to unissued stock.

A major study of more than 1,300 stock repurchases found that nearly 90% of the repurchases analyzed were executed in the open market, with the remainder being "self-tender offers."[7] Two types of self-tender offers occur with approximately equal frequency. The first is a "fixed-price" self-tender offer, in which the corporation offers to repurchase a stated number of shares at a set, predetermined price. The second is a "Dutch-auction" self-tender offer, in which the corporation offers to repurchase a stated number of shares but at a price determined by inviting existing shareholders to submit offers to sell. The ultimate repurchase price is the lowest offered price at which the previously stated number of shares can be repurchased from those shareholders who have submitted offers.[8]

Figure 13.1 shows the average stock price behavior for the three types of stock repurchases just mentioned. For each repurchase, the stock's "abnormal" return was determined by relating daily returns on the stock to the corresponding returns on a stock market index. This calculation was made for the 50-day period immediately prior to the repurchase announcement and the 50-day period immediately following it. These abnormal returns were averaged across firms for each day relative to the announcement and then cumulated across time. The figure shows that open-market repurchases are typically made after the stock price has had an abnormal decline. In contrast, fixed-

FIGURE 13.1 Abnormal Stock Price Behavior around Repurchase Announcements

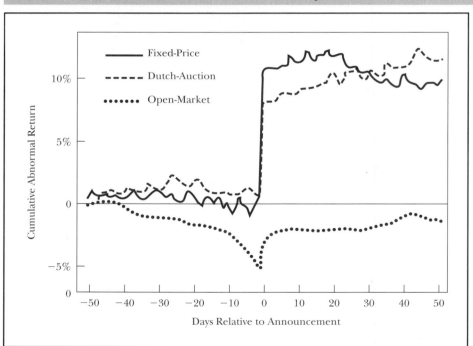

Source: Robert Comment and Gregg A. Jarrell, "The Relative Signalling Power of Dutch-Auction and Fixed-Price Self-Tender Offers and Open-Market Share Repurchases," *Journal of Finance*, 46, no. 4 (September 1991): 1254.

price and Dutch-auction repurchases are made after a period of fairly normal returns. Interestingly, the stock price jumped upward on the announcement of the repurchase offer for all three types. (The average size of the abnormal return on the announcement date was 11% for fixed-price, 8% for Dutch-auction, and 2% for open-market repurchases.) Finally, after the repurchase offer expired, the stock price did not fall back to its preannouncement level.

Two other studies found that investors could form profitable investment strategies to take advantage of the announcement of a stock repurchase. In one study the strategy involved fixed-price, self-tender offers where the stock was purchased by the investor in the open market shortly before the offer's expiration date if it was selling at least 3% below the repurchase price. Then the investor tenders the stock to the firm on the expiration date. If the repurchase was oversubscribed (meaning that more shares were submitted for repurchase than the corporation indicated it was to buy), then the number of the investor's shares that the corporation did not buy were sold in the marketplace shortly after the expiration date. The result was that for an investment of less than a week, this strategy generated an abnormal return of more than 9%.[9]

In the second study, investors who bought shares of a firm's stock on hearing of the firm's announcement of an open-market repurchase program would have made an abnormal return of about 12% during the next three years (or 4% per year). Furthermore, if these investors limited their purchases to those firms that had low book-value-to-market-value ratios, the abnormal returns were even higher, about 45% during three years (or about 15% per year).[10] Clearly, both of these studies uncovered investment strategies that appear to be inconsistent with the notion of efficient markets.

Why do firms repurchase their stock? One motive is to repel a takeover attempt; two other explanations have been offered. First, management may be attempting to send a *signal* to the shareholders (and the public) that the corporation's stock is undervalued in the marketplace. Second, management may want to alter its debt-to-equity ratio. Third, it may be beneficial taxwise to the current shareholders for the firm to use excess cash to repurchase stock instead of using it to pay a cash dividend.

For example, consider a shareholder who bought 10 shares of stock at $40 per share that are now worth $50 per share resulting in an unrealized capital gain of $10 per share, or $100 in total. The shareholder could receive a $10 per share cash dividend from the firm as part of a general disbursement of excess cash. As a result, the stock price will drop by roughly $10 per share, removing the capital gain, but all of this dividend will be taxable income to the shareholder. Alternatively, the corporation could spend the same amount to repurchase its stock. If the shareholder tenders his or her pro rata share, the investor will receive $100 for two shares of stock (= $100 cash dividend/$50 share price, assuming perfect markets) and will have to pay capital gains on only the amount of $100 that exceeds the $80 (= 2 shares × $40) cost of the two shares that were repurchased (if the shareholder does not tender any shares, then no taxes are owed). Hence the shareholder will pay capital gains taxes on only $20 of the $100 at that time but would have unrealized capital gains of $10 per share on the eight shares still owned (because the stock price will remain at $50 per share). Capital gains taxes will be paid at some later date when they are sold. The shareholder benefits taxwise from a repurchase in two ways: A *smaller* amount is taxed at a capital gains tax rate that is potentially *lower* than the ordinary income tax rate that is applicable to cash dividends.

Classified Stock

Some corporations issue two or more classes of common stock. For example, class *A* stock might have a preferred position for dividends but might not have any voting rights. In contrast, class *B* stock might have full voting rights but a lower position for dividends. Often issuing two classes of stock is similar to issuing preferred stock along with a normal class of common stock.

An interesting example involves the three classes of General Motors common stock that existed until the mid-1990s. These classes were referred to as $1\frac{2}{3}$ par value, class E, and class H stock (the E class no longer exists, but the other two still are outstanding). One share in each class had 1, $\frac{1}{4}$, and $\frac{1}{2}$ vote, respectively. In terms of dividends, class E and class H stocks received an amount that did not exceed the "adjusted earnings" of GM's Electronic Data Systems and Hughes Electronics subsidiaries, respectively. The $1\frac{2}{3}$ par value stock received dividends that did not exceed the remainder of GM's earnings. Such "tracking stocks" are becoming more popular at companies that have subsidiaries offering notably different products and services.

Another example involves Canadian corporations. Because of the Canada Income Tax Act of 1971, Canadian firms are now allowed to have class A and class B shares. The difference between the two classes is that class A shares receive cash dividends, whereas class B shares receive stock dividends. Owners of either class can swap their shares one-for-one for shares of the other class at any time.

Restricted Stock

restricted stock
letter stock

In the United States, security regulations require that most stock be registered with the SEC before it may be sold in a public offering. Under some conditions, unregistered stock may be sold directly to a purchaser through a private placement, but its subsequent sale is **restricted.** Such **letter stock** must be held for at least one year and can be sold during the next year only if ample information on the company is available and the amount sold is a relatively small percentage of the total amount outstanding. (Indeed, it is called letter stock because the purchaser must provide the SEC with a letter indicating that the shares will be held as an investment and will not be for resale.) However, under certain circumstances (defined by SEC Rule 144A), large institutional investors can trade nonpublic securities issued under this rule among themselves at any time after their issuance. (Rule 144A is discussed later in this chapter.)

13.2 Cash Dividends

dividends

date of record

Payments made in cash to stockholders are termed **dividends.** They are typically declared quarterly by the board of directors and are paid to current stockholders of record at a date specified by the board, known as the **date of record.** The dividends may be of almost any size, subject to certain restrictions such as those contained in the charter or in documents given to creditors. Thus, dividends could be even larger than the current earnings of the corporation, although they seldom are. (Such dividends are usually paid out of past earnings.)

Compiling a list of stockholders to receive the dividend is not as simple as it may seem because for many firms the list changes almost constantly as shares are bought and sold. Those stockholders who are to receive the dividend are identified by use of

ex dividend date

an **ex dividend date.** Because of the time required to record the transfer of ownership of common stock, major stock exchanges specify an ex dividend date that is two business days prior to the date of record. Investors purchasing shares before an ex dividend date are entitled to receive the dividend in question; those purchasing on or after the ex dividend date are not entitled to the dividend.

For example, a dividend may be declared on May 15 with a date of record of Friday, June 15, so that Wednesday, June 13, would be the ex dividend date. An investor who bought shares on Tuesday, June 12, would receive the cash dividend (unless the investor sold the shares later in the day on the 12th, in which case the new owner would receive the dividend). If the shares were bought on Wednesday, June 13, the investor would not receive the cash dividend. Besides a declaration date (May 15), an ex dividend date (June 13), and a date of record (June 15), there is also a fourth date, the "payment date." On this date (perhaps June 25) the checks for the cash dividends are mailed or deposited electronically in shareholder accounts at custodian banks. Summarizing the example:

May 15	$\longrightarrow$	June 13	$\longrightarrow$	June 15	$\longrightarrow$	June 25
Declaration date		Ex dividend date		Date of record		Payment date

13.3   Stock Dividends and Stock Splits

stock dividend

Occasionally, the board of directors forgoes a cash dividend and "pays" a **stock dividend** instead. For example, if a 5% stock dividend is declared, then the owner of 100 shares receives 5 additional shares that are issued for this occasion. The accounting treatment of a stock dividend is to increase the "common stock" and "capital contributed in excess of par" accounts by an amount equal to the market value of the stock at the time of the dividend times the number of new shares issued. (The "common stock" account would increase by an amount equal to the par value times the number of new shares. The remainder of the increase would go into the "capital contributed in excess of par" account.) The total book value of stockholders' equity remains the same by reducing the "retained earnings" account by an equivalent amount.

stock split

A **stock split** is similar to a stock dividend in that the stockholder owns more shares afterward. However, it is different in both magnitude and accounting treatment. With a stock split, all the old shares are destroyed and new ones are issued with a new par value. Afterward the number of new shares outstanding is usually greater than the previous number of old shares by 25% or more; the exact amount depends on the size of the split. In contrast, a stock dividend usually results in an increase of less than 25%. Whereas a stock dividend results in adjustments to the dollar amount in certain stockholders' equity, no adjustments are made for a split. For example, if a $1 par value stock is split two-for-one, the holder of 200 old shares receives 400 new $.50 par value shares, and none of the dollar amounts in stockholders' equity accounts (such as retained earnings) change.

reverse stock split

A **reverse stock split** reduces the number of shares and increases the par value per share. For example, in a reverse two-for-one split, the holder of 200 $1 par value shares exchanges them for 100 $2 par value shares. Again there is no change in the dollar figures in the stockholders' equity accounts.

Stock dividends and splits must be considered when following the price of a company's shares. For example, a fall in price per share may be due solely to a large stock split. To reduce confusion, most financial services provide data adjusted for at least some of these changes. Thus, if a stock split two-for-one on July 31, then prices prior to that date might be divided by 2 to facilitate comparison.

13.3.1   EX DISTRIBUTION DATES

ex distribution date

Similar to the process used to pay cash dividends, the corporation specifies three dates associated with either stock dividends or stock splits: a declaration date, a date of record, and a payment date. However, there is now an **ex distribution date** instead of an ex dividend date. For stock dividends less than 20%, the procedure is identical to the one described previously for cash dividends; the ex distribution date is two business days before the date of record, meaning that if you buy the stock on or after that date, you do not get the additional shares.

For larger stock dividends and all stock splits, the procedure is different because the ex distribution date is usually the business day after the payment date (which, in turn, is after the date of record). Hence if a 25% stock dividend is declared on May 15 with a date of record of June 15 and a payment date of June 25, then anyone buying the stock before June 26 will receive the stock dividend. However, those who wait until June 26 to buy the stock will not receive the stock dividend.[11]

13.3.2 REASONS FOR STOCK DIVIDENDS AND SPLITS

Why do corporations issue stock dividends and split their stocks? Nothing of importance seems to change because such actions do not increase revenues or reduce expenses. There is simply a change in the size of the units in which ownership may be bought and sold. Moreover, because the process involves administrative effort and costs something to execute, one wonders why it is done.

It is sometimes argued that stockholders respond positively to "tangible" evidence of the growth of their corporation. A related argument states that stock splits, like repurchases, are used by management to *signal* investors that they believe the firm's stock is undervalued in the marketplace. Another view holds that splits and stock dividends, by decreasing the price per share, may bring the stock's price into a more desirable trading range. This action is intended to increase the liquidity of the stock and subsequently its price. A related view contends that there is a desirable trading range for the stock based on the minimum tick size that is allowed (in 1999, $\frac{1}{16}$ for all NYSE stocks priced over $1). Lower prices result in larger spreads relative to the stock's price, thereby benefiting brokers and dealers but costing investors.[12] Figure 13.2 presents the average behavior of stock returns for 1,275 two-for-one stock splits.[13] For each split, the stock's "abnormal" return was determined by relating monthly returns on the stock to the corresponding returns in the stock market. This calculation was done for (1) the 12-month period before the split announcement month, (2) the five-day period running from two days before to two days after the split announcement, and (3) the three years after the split announcement. These abnormal returns were first averaged across firms for each day relative to the announcement of the firm's split and then were cumulated across time.

As the figure shows, the stocks tended to have a positive abnormal return of about 54% during the year before announcement of the split. Thus, it appears that unexpected positive developments (such as unexpected large increases in earnings) caused abnormal increases in the stock prices of these firms before they decided to split their stock. The announcement of the stock split seems to have triggered a boost in the firm's stock; it had an abnormal increase of a bit over 3% in the period from two days before to two days after the announcement. The behavior of the post-split prices indicates that during the following year investors continued to receive significantly positive abnormal returns of about 8%, following which no notable abnormal returns occurred.[14] Apparently the prices of firms whose stocks split did rise, but they did not rise to an equilibrium level on the announcement date. Such an underreaction to the announcement of a stock split can be interpreted as evidence of a market inefficiency. However, other studies, using different stocks and time periods, found slightly negative abnormal returns, no abnormal returns, or slightly positive abnormal returns after the split.[15]

The evidence also suggests that stock splits are associated with increased transactions costs. A study of pre-split and post-split behavior showed that after splits, trading

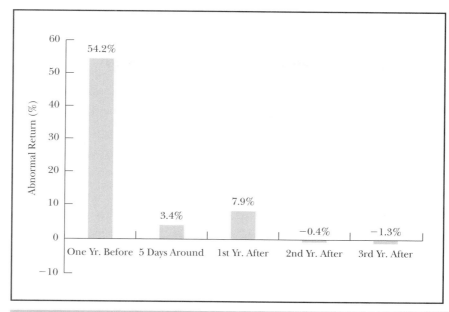

FIGURE 13.2 Average Abnormal Returns of Stocks around the Time of Stock Split Announcements

Source: Adapted from David Ikenberry, Graeme Rankine, and Earl K. Stice, "What Do Stock Splits Really Signal?" *Journal of Financial and Quantitative Analysis*, 31, no. 3 (September 1996): 360, 362, 367.

volume rose less than proportionately, and both commission costs and bid–ask spreads, expressed as a percentage of value, increased—hardly reactions that are favorable to stockholders.[16] For example, after a two-for-one stock split there will be twice as many shares outstanding, so it is reasonable to expect the daily number of shares that are traded to double. It is also reasonable to expect the commission for buying 200 shares after the split to be the same as the commission for buying 100 shares before the split. Instead, after the split the number of shares traded daily was less than twice as large and the commission costs per share traded were proportionately larger.

Another study of stock splits and stock dividends uncovered an apparent market inefficiency.[17] This study examined the performance of stocks around the "ex" dates associated with their stock splits and dividends. If an investor bought shares of a firm the day before its ex date and sold them the day after the ex date, then the investor made, on average, an abnormal return of roughly 2% for stock dividends and 1% for stock splits. This result seems to violate the notion of efficient markets because it suggests that an investor can make abnormal returns by trading stocks using a simple strategy based on publicly available information.

13.4 Preemptive Rights

preemptive rights

Under common law (and most state laws), a stockholder has an inherent right to maintain his or her proportionate ownership of the corporation. **Preemptive rights** give current stockholders the right of first refusal for the purchase of the new shares when new shares are to be sold.[18] Each current stockholder is issued a certificate that indicates the number of new shares he or she is authorized to purchase. This number is proportionate to the number of existing shares currently owned by the stockholder. Usually,

rights

the new shares are priced below the current market price of the stock, making such **rights** valuable. The stockholder can exercise the rights by purchasing his or her allotted amount of new shares, thereby maintaining his or her proportionate ownership in the firm, but at the cost of providing additional capital. Alternatively, the rights can be sold to someone else.[19]

rights offering
subscription price

For example, if a firm needs $10,000,000 for new equipment, it may decide to sell new shares in order to raise the capital. If the current market price of the stock is $60 per share, a **rights offering** may be used to raise the capital, where the **subscription price** is set at $50 per share.[20] Accordingly, 200,000 (= $10,000,000/$50) new shares are to be sold. If the firm has 4,000,000 shares outstanding, the owner of 1 share receives the right to buy $\frac{1}{20}$ (= 200,000/4,000,000) of a new share. Because the number of rights received is equal to the number of shares owned, 20 shares must be owned in order to buy 1 new share. Thus, a stockholder who owns 100 shares will receive 100 rights allowing him or her to buy 5 (= $100 \times \frac{1}{20}$) new shares. These rights are valuable because their owner can buy stock at $50 a share when the market price is significantly higher. The current owner of 100 shares can either use the 100 rights by coming up with cash equal to $250 (= $5 \times $50) or sell the 100 rights to someone else.

13.5 *Ex Ante* and *Ex Post* Values

Equilibrium theories, such as the CAPM and APT, imply that, in the opinion of well-informed investors, securities with different attributes have different expected returns.

ex ante
ex post

Thus the focus of these theories is on future, or ***ex ante*** (Latin for *before the fact*) returns. However, only historical, or ***ex post*** (Latin for *after the fact*), returns are subsequently observed. Because these historical returns are undoubtedly different from the expected returns, it is extremely difficult to tell whether security attributes and expected returns coincide as implied by either the CAPM or APT. Moreover, such theories do not reveal how a security's expected return and attributes might be estimated by examining historical returns.

To bridge this gap, investigators have sometimes used the average historical return of a security as an estimate of its expected return. This approach requires an assumption that the expected return did not change during some arbitrary time period and that the time period contains a sufficient number of historical returns to make a reasonably accurate estimate of the expected return. However, expectations almost certainly change over the time period needed to obtain a useful estimate of the expected return for any given security.[21] Despite this objection, it is worthwhile to examine historical returns to see how they might be used to come up with meaningful predictions about the future.[22] The next section explores the prediction of a firm's beta. It begins by discussing the estimation of the firm's historical beta using the market model.

13.6 Common Stock Betas

For purposes of portfolio management, the relevant risk of a security concerns its impact on the risk of a well-diversified portfolio. In the world of the CAPM, such portfolios are subject primarily to market risk. This fact suggests the importance of a security's beta, which measures the security's sensitivity to future market movements. In principle the possible sources of such movements should be considered when estimating beta. Then the reaction of the security's price to each of these sources should be estimated, along with the probability of each reaction. In the process, the economics of the relevant industry and firm, the impact of both operating and financial leverage on the firm, and other fundamental factors should be taken into account.

But what about investigating the extent to which the security's price moved with the market in the past? Such an approach ignores myriad possible differences between the past and the future. However, it is easily done and provides a useful starting point.

historical beta

As shown in Chapter 8, a security's beta is the slope of the market model. If this line were constant over time, the **historical beta** for a security could be estimated by examining the historical relationship between the returns on the security and on a market index. The statistical procedure used for making such estimates of *ex post* betas is simple linear regression, also known as ordinary least squares (OLS).[23]

As an example, consider estimating the *ex post* beta for Widget Manufacturing (WM) using a hypothetical market index. Table 13.1 presents the most recent 16 quarterly returns on both WM and the index and the calculations necessary to determine WM's *ex post* beta and alpha, as well as certain other statistical parameters. (Spreadsheets such as Excel can be utilized to make these calculations.) As can be seen, WM's beta and intercept term were .63 and .79%, respectively, during this period.[24]

Given these values, the market model for WM is

$$r_{WM} = .79\% + .63r_I + \varepsilon_{WM} \tag{13.1}$$

Figure 13.3 presents a scatter diagram of the returns on WM(r_{WM}) and the index r_I. Also shown in the figure is a graph of the market model except that the random error term is deleted; that is, the figure has a graph of the following line:

$$r_{WM} = .79\% + .63r_I \tag{13.2}$$

The vertical distance of each point in the scatter diagram from this line represents an estimate of the size of the random error term for the corresponding quarter. The exact distance can be found by rewriting Equation (13.1) as

$$r_{WM} - (.79\% + .63r_I) = \varepsilon_{WM} \tag{13.3}$$

For example, Table 13.1(a) shows that the returns on WM and the index were 7.55% and 2.66%, respectively, in quarter 14. The value of ε_{WM} for that quarter can be calculated using Equation (13.3) as follows:

$$7.55\% - [.79\% + (.63 \times 2.66\%)] = 5.08\%$$

standard deviation of the random error term

The values of ε_{WM} can be similarly calculated for the other 15 quarters of the estimation period. The standard deviation of the resulting set of 16 numbers is an estimate of the **standard deviation of the random error term** (or residual standard deviation) and in Table 13.1(b) is 6.67%. This number is an estimate of the historical unique risk of WM.

The market model for WM shown in Figure 13.3 corresponds to the regression line for the scatter diagram. Recall that a straight line is defined by its intercept and slope. There are no other values for the intercept term and beta that define a straight line that fits the scatter diagram any better than the regression line. This means that there is no line that could be drawn that would result in a smaller standard deviation of the random error term. Thus, the regression line is often referred to as the line of "best fit" because it has the smallest sum of squared values of the random error terms. That is, the 16 random error terms associated with the regression line can each be squared and then summed. This sum (the sum of squared errors) is smaller for the line of best fit than is the sum associated with any other line.

For example, if the intercept term equaled 1.5% and beta equaled .8, then the random error term, ε_{WM}, could be calculated for each of the 16 quarters using Equation

TABLE 13.1 Market Model for Widget Manufacturing

(a) Data

Year	Quarter	WM Returns = Y (1)	Index Returns = X (2)	Y^2 (3)	X^2 (4)	$Y \times X$ (5)
1	1	−13.38%	2.52%	178.92	6.35	−33.71
	2	16.79	5.45	282.00	29.71	91.54
	3	−1.67	0.76	2.77	0.57	−1.26
	4	−3.46	2.36	11.99	5.58	−8.18
2	5	10.22	8.56	104.53	73.36	87.57
	6	7.13	8.67	50.79	75.19	61.80
	7	6.71	10.80	45.07	116.59	72.49
	8	7.84	3.33	61.47	11.08	26.10
3	9	2.15	−5.07	4.62	25.66	−10.89
	10	7.95	7.10	63.22	50.42	56.46
	11	−8.05	−11.57	64.74	133.87	93.09
	12	7.68	4.65	58.97	21.58	35.67
4	13	4.75	14.59	22.55	212.97	69.29
	14	7.55	2.66	57.03	7.05	20.05
	15	−2.36	3.81	5.58	14.54	−9.01
	16	4.98	7.99	24.78	63.85	39.78
Sum (Σ) =		54.83%	66.61%	1039.03	848.37	590.79
		$= \Sigma Y$	$= \Sigma X$	$= \Sigma Y^2$	$= \Sigma X^2$	$= \Sigma XY$

(b) Calculations

1. Beta

$$\frac{(T \times \sum XY) - (\sum Y \times \sum X)}{(T \times \sum X^2) - (\sum X)^2} = \frac{(16 \times 590.79) - (54.83 \times 66.61)}{(16 \times 848.37) - (66.61)^2} = .63$$

2. Intercept term

$$[\sum Y/T] - [\text{Beta} \times (\sum X/T)] = [54.83/16] - [.63 \times (66.61/16)] = .79\%$$

3. Standard deviation of random error term

$$\{[\sum Y^2 - (\text{Alpha} \times \sum Y) - (\text{Beta} \times \sum XY)]/[T - 2]\}^{1/2}$$
$$= \{[1039.03 - (.79 \times 54.83) - (.63 \times 590.79)]/[16 - 2]\}^{1/2} = 6.67\%$$

4. Standard error of beta

Standard deviation of random error term$/\{\sum X^2 - [(\sum X^2)^2/T]\}^{1/2}$
$$= 6.67/\{848.37 - [(66.61)^2/16]\}^{1/2} = .28$$

5. Standard error of the intercept term

Standard deviation of random error term$/\{T - [(\sum X^2)^2/\sum X^2]\}^{1/2}$
$$= 6.67/\{16 - [(66.61)^2/848.37]\}^{1/2} = 2.03$$

6. Correlation coefficient

$$\frac{(T \times \sum XY) - (\sum Y \times \sum X)}{\{[(T \times \sum Y^2) - (\sum Y)^2] \times [(T \times \sum X^2) - (\sum X)^2]\}^{1/2}}$$

$$= \frac{(16 \times 590.79) - (54.83 \times 66.61)}{\{[(16 \times 1039.03) - (54.83)^2] \times [(16 \times 848.37) - (66.61)^2]\}^{1/2}} = .52$$

7. Coefficient of determination

$$(\text{Correlation coefficient})^2 = (.52)^2 = .27$$

8. Coefficient of nondetermination

$$1 - \text{Coefficient of determination} = 1 - .27 = .73$$

Note: All summations are carried out over *t*, where *t* goes from 1 to *T* (in this example, *t* = 1, 2,..., 16).

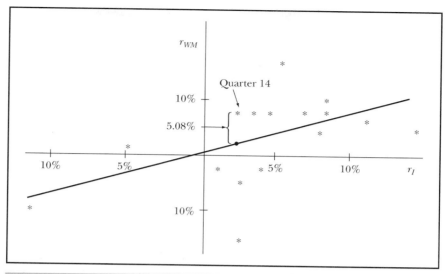

FIGURE 13.3 Market Model for WM

(13.3). With these 16 values, the standard deviation of the random error term could be calculated by squaring each value, summing the squared values, and dividing the sum by 14 [= (16 − 2)]. The standard deviation of the random error term would then be the square root of this number. However, it would be larger than 6.67%, which is the standard deviation of the random error term associated with the line of best fit—that is, the line with an intercept term of .79% and a beta of .63.

Remember that a security's "true" historical beta cannot be observed. All that can be done is to estimate its value. Even if a security's "true" beta remained the same forever, its estimated value, obtained as shown in Table 13.1, would still change from time to time because of mistakes (known as sampling errors) in estimating it. For example, if a different set of 16 quarters were examined, the resulting estimated beta for WM almost certainly would be different from .63, the estimated value for the set of 16 quarters given in Table 13.1. The **standard error of beta** shown in Table 13.1 attempts to indicate the extent of such estimation errors. Given a number of necessary assumptions (for example, the true beta did not change during the 16-quarter estimation period), the chances are roughly two out of three that the "true" beta is within a standard error, plus or minus, of the estimated beta. Thus, WM's true beta is likely to be larger than .35 (= .63 − .28) and smaller than .91 (= .63 + .28). Similarly, the **standard error of the intercept term,** provides an indication of the magnitude of the possible sampling error made in estimating the intercept term.

The **correlation coefficient** in Table 13.1 provides an indication of how closely the returns on WM were associated with the returns on the index. Because its range is between −1 and +1, the value for WM of .52 indicates a mildly strong positive relationship between WM and the index. This means that larger returns for WM seem to be associated with larger returns on the index.

The **coefficient of determination,** which equals the square of the correlation coefficient, represents the proportion of variation in the return on WM that is related to the variation in the return on the index. Accordingly, it shows how much of the movements in WM's returns can be explained by movements in the returns on the index. With a value of .27, movements in the index account for 27% of the movements in the return on WM during the 16-quarter estimation period.

standard error of beta

standard error of the intercept term

correlation coefficient

coefficient of determination

coefficient of nondetermination

Because the **coefficient of nondetermination** is 1 minus the coefficient of determination, it represents the proportion of movements in the return on WM that is not caused by movements in the return on the index. Thus, 73% of the movements in WM cannot be attributed to movements in the index.

Figure 13.4 is a page from a Security Risk Evaluation report prepared by Merrill Lynch, Pierce, Fenner & Smith Inc. Percentage price changes for many stocks, calculated for each of 60 months (when available), were compared by means of the corresponding percentage changes in the S&P 500 using the market model in Table 13.1. Seven of the resulting values from this analysis are of interest for each stock.

R-squared residual standard deviation

The values shown for Beta and Alpha indicate the slope and intercept, respectively, of the straight line that is the best fit for the scatter diagram of the percentage price changes for the stock and index. The value of **R-squared** (R-Sqr) is equivalent to the coefficient of determination shown in Table 13.1, whereas the value for **residual standard deviation** (Resid Std Dev-n) corresponds to the standard deviation of the random error term in Table 13.1.[25] The standard error of beta (Std. Err. of Beta) indicates that there is roughly a two out of three chance that the true beta is within one standard error, plus or minus, of the estimated beta. Standard error of alpha (Std. Err. of Alpha) can be interpreted similarly.

FIGURE 13.4 Sample Page from Security Risk Evaluation by Merrill Lynch, Pierce, Fenner & Smith Inc.

Ticker Symbol	Security Name	92/04 Close Price	Beta	Alpha	R-Sqr	Resid Std Dev-n	Std. Err. of Beta	Std. Err. of Alpha	Adjusted Beta	Number of Observ
AOI	AOI COAL CO	0.500	1.11	−1.79	0.07	19.23	0.49	2.51	1.07	60
APAT	APA OPTICS INC	4.875	0.60	0.80	0.08	9.66	0.25	1.26	0.73	60
APIE	API ENTERPRISES INC	0.688	1.00	2.51	0.02	26.90	0.69	3.51	1.00	60
ASKI	ASK COMPUTER SYS INC	14.875	1.65	−0.06	0.37	10.82	0.28	1.41	1.43	60
ATV	ARC INTL CORP	0.813	1.22	−1.38	0.07	20.71	0.53	2.70	1.15	60
ASTA	AST RESEARCH INC	16.750	1.47	1.66	0.16	16.75	0.43	2.19	1.31	60
ARX	ARX INC	1.875	1.02	−1.90	0.07	17.02	0.43	2.22	1.01	60
ASAA	ASA INTL LTD	1.875	0.79	−1.03	0.01	23.55	0.60	3.07	0.86	60
RCH	ARCO CHEM CO	45.375	1.33	0.03	0.47	7.35	0.19	1.00	1.22	55
ANB	ANB CORP	36.375	−0.02	1.80	0.10	1.90	0.13	0.56	0.32	12
ATCE	ATC ENVIRONMENTAL INC	2.813	−0.02	0.68	0.02	21.22	0.75	3.22	0.32	46
ATI	ATI MED INC	3.750	0.26	0.07	0.01	19.11	0.49	2.49	0.51	60
ATCIC	ATC INC	1.750	0.61	0.38	0.00	26.63	0.68	3.47	0.74	60
ATNN	ATNN INC	0.219	1.38	1.51	0.00	50.89	1.30	6.64	1.25	60
ATTNF	ATTN AVECA ENTERTAIN-MENT COR	1.750	2.81	0.39	0.05	42.49	1.59	6.97	2.20	39
AVSY	AVTR SYS INC	0.203	−0.54	6.23	0.06	55.49	3.33	14.41	−0.02	18
AWCSA	AW COMPUTER SYS INC CLASS A	5.875	1.23	7.08	0.01	71.41	1.85	9.29	1.15	60
ARON	AARON RENTS INC	13.125	0.92	−0.23	0.16	10.30	0.26	1.34	0.95	60
ABIX	ABATIX ENVIRONMENTAL CORP	1.750	0.00	0.36	0.03	17.54	0.67	2.96	0.34	37
ABT	ABBOTT LABS	66.000	0.87	0.87	0.51	4.31	0.11	0.56	0.92	60
ABERF	ABER RES LTD	0.969	1.53	3.52	0.02	29.18	1.11	4.93	1.35	37
AANB	ABIGAIL ADAMS NATL BANCORP I	11.000	−1.50	1.81	0.14	12.61	0.70	2.80	−0.66	24
ABBK	ABINGTON BANCORP INC	5.875	1.37	−0.15	0.09	20.09	0.51	2.62	1.24	60
ABD	ABIOMED INC	13.000	1.08	1.04	0.07	18.21	0.47	2.43	1.05	57
ABY	ABITIBI PRICE INC	12.625	0.65	−1.42	0.23	6.00	0.15	0.80	0.77	57
ABRI	ABRAMS INDS INC	4.313	1.28	1.90	0.07	20.91	0.53	2.73	1.18	60
ACAP	ACAP CORP	0.500	0.05	0.88	0.02	13.80	0.35	1.80	0.37	60
ACLE	ACCEL INTL CORP	6.750	1.12	−0.66	0.20	11.10	0.28	1.45	1.08	60
AKLM	ACCLAIM ENTHT INC	6.375	1.29	0.02	0.03	23.62	0.84	3.58	1.19	46
ACCU	ACCUHEALTH INC	5.438	0.53	0.60	0.00	13.47	0.49	2.17	0.69	41

Based on S&P 500 Index, Using Straight Regression   Page 3

Source: Reprinted by permission. Copyright © Merrill Lynch, Pierce, Fenner & Smith Incorporated.

adjusted beta   The seventh value in Figure 13.4 is the **adjusted beta,** representing an estimate of the *ex ante* (or future) beta of the firm's stock. Without any information at all it would be reasonable to estimate the *ex ante* beta of a stock to equal 1.0, the average size of beta. Given a chance to see how a stock moved in relation to a market index during some past time period, a modification of this prior *ex post* (or historical) estimate would seem appropriate. Such a modification would sensibly produce a final *ex ante* estimate of beta that would lie between the value of 1.0 and its initially estimated *ex post* value based purely on historical price changes. Typically, adjusted betas are obtained by simply taking a weighted average of the estimated *ex post* beta and 1.0. The weights used represent the importance that the analyst attaches to historical data. In Figure 13.4, the adjusted beta is found by (1) multiplying the *ex post* beta by .66, (2) multiplying 1.0 by .34, and (3) summing the two products. Thus, a firm with an *ex post* beta of 1.5 would have an adjusted beta of 1.33 [= (1.5 × .66) + (1.0 × .34)].

13.7   Growth versus Value

growth stocks
value stocks   Common stocks are often divided into two categories—**growth stocks** and **value stocks.** In general, growth stocks are stocks of companies that have experienced, or are expected to experience, rapid increases in earnings, whereas value stocks are stocks whose market price seems to be low relative to measures of their worth. Although there are no strict rules on how they are divided, and disagreement exists among investment professionals as to which category certain stocks belong, two financial measures are often used to distinguish growth stocks from value stocks: the book-value-to-market-value ratio (BV/MV) and the earnings-to-price ratio (E/P).[26]

13.7.1   BOOK-VALUE-TO-MARKET-VALUE RATIO

The book-value-to-market-value ratio is typically calculated as follows. First, the firm's book value of the equity (or simply "book value") is determined by using the most recent balance sheet data. Second, the market capitalization of the firm's common stock is determined by taking the most recent market price for the firm's common stock and multiplying it by the number of shares outstanding. Third, the book value is divided by the market capitalization to arrive at the BV/MV ratio. Relatively low values of this ratio characterize growth stocks, and relatively high values characterize value stocks.[27]

     An interesting question is whether there is a relationship between stock returns and the stocks' BV/MV ratios. Fama and French examined this issue and found that, on average, the larger the size of the BV/MV ratio, the larger the rate of return.[28] Table 13.2 presents their findings.

     Table 13.2(a) was constructed as follows. First, at the end of June 1963, the book value was determined for each stock on the NYSE, AMEX, and Nasdaq using the annual financial statements for the fiscal year ending in 1962. This value was divided by the market capitalization for each firm; the market capitalization was determined on the basis of the market price for each firm at the end of December 1962. Second, using these BV/MV ratios, the firms were ranked from smallest to largest, and formed into 12 portfolios. Third, the return on each portfolio was tracked monthly from July 1963 through June 1964. Fourth, the entire process was updated by a year so that returns were calculated from July 1964 to June 1965 on 12 BV/MV-ranked portfolios

TABLE 13.2 Growth versus Value Stocks

Portfolio Basis	Portfolio Number[a]											
	1	2	3	4	5	6	7	8	9	10	11	12
(a) BV/MV Ratio												
Return	.30	.67	.87	.97	1.04	1.17	1.30	1.44	1.50	1.59	1.92	1.83
BV/MV	.11	.22	.34	.47	.60	.73	.87	1.03	1.23	1.52	1.93	2.77
(b) E/P Ratio[b]												
Return	1.04	.93	.94	1.03	1.18	1.22	1.33	1.42	1.46	1.57	1.74	1.72
E/P	.01	.03	.05	.06	.08	.09	.11	.12	.14	.16	.20	.28
(c) Size												
Return	1.64	1.16	1.29	1.24	1.25	1.29	1.17	1.07	1.10	.95	.88	.90
1n(MV)[c]	1.98	3.18	3.63	4.10	4.50	4.89	5.30	5.73	6.24	6.82	7.39	8.44

[a]Portfolios formed on the basis of rankings of indicated financial measure for stocks from smallest (1) to largest (12); return indicates the average monthly return, in percent.

[b]The portfolio of stocks that had negative earnings had an average monthly return of 1.46.

[c]1n(MV) denotes the logarithmic value of the average stock's market value in the portfolio (expressed in millions of dollars).

Source: Eugene F. Fama and Kenneth R. French, "The Cross-Section of Expected Stock Returns," *Journal of Finance,* 47, no. 2 (June 1992): Tables 2 and 4.

created on the basis of data at the end of 1963. The process was repeated until a large set of monthly returns was available for each of the 12 portfolios.

Table 13.2(a) shows a clear relationship between average monthly return and the BV/MV ratio; higher values of the ratio are associated with higher average returns. Because growth stocks tend to have low BV/MV ratios and value stocks tend to have high BV/MV ratios, this result suggests that during the period analyzed, value stocks outperformed growth stocks.

13.7.2 EARNINGS-TO-PRICE RATIO

earnings yield

The earnings-to-price ratio, sometimes known as **earnings yield,** is typically calculated as follows. First, the accounting value of the firm's earnings per share is determined using the most recent income statement and dividing the firm's earnings after taxes by the number of shares outstanding. Second, the market price of the firm's common stock is determined from the most recent price at which the firm's common stock was traded. Third, the earnings per share figure is divided by the market price of the stock to arrive at the E/P ratio. Relatively low values of this ratio characterize growth stocks, and relatively high values characterize value stocks. (P/E ratios are simply the recipocal of E/P ratios. High and low P/E ratios characterize, respectively, growth and value stocks.)

Is there a relationship between stock returns and their E/P ratios? Fama and French examined this issue and found that on average, the larger the size of the E/P ratio, the larger the rate of return.[29] Their results are shown in Table 13.2(b), which was constructed in the same manner as part (a) except that here, at the end of each June, firms were ranked and assigned to portfolios on the basis of their E/P ratios. Except for portfolio 1, part (b) shows a clear relationship between average monthly return and the E/P ratio; higher values of the ratio are associated with higher average returns. Because growth stocks tend to have low E/P ratios and value stocks tend to have high E/P ratios, these data reinforce the conclusions drawn from the BV/MV data; namely, that value stocks tended to outperform growth stocks during the period analyzed.

There is one other interesting feature of this panel. When Fama and French assigned stocks to portfolios based on their E/P ratios, they assigned those stocks that had negative earnings and hence a negative E/P ratio to a separate portfolio. This portfolio had an average monthly return of 1.46%. Thus Fama and French found that if a portfolio with a negative E/P ratio is considered the lowest E/P portfolio (and thus a portfolio of growth stocks), then as E/P becomes larger, average returns decline at first and then rise. This finding led them to refer to the relationship between average returns and the E/P ratio as "U-shaped."

13.7.3 SIZE

Although firm size is not generally used as a criterion for distinguishing growth from value stocks, it is often used to sort stocks. Many investment professionals think of stocks in terms of two dimensions. Hence stocks could be classified as growth or value using the BV/MV ratio and as large or small using their size. Each stock could then be located in one of the four quadrants of a diagram like the one shown in Figure 13.5.

Typically a stock's market capitalization (the number of outstanding common shares times the current market price per share) is used as the measure of its size. Fama and French assigned stocks to 1 of 12 size portfolios after ranking them at the end of each June on the basis of market capitalization. Proceeding in a manner analogous to that discussed previously, they tracked the monthly returns for these 12 size-based portfolios. Table 13.2(c) displays the average returns and sizes of these portfolios.

In contrast to parts (a) and (b), there is a clear inverse relationship between size and average return so that stocks of smaller firms tend to have higher returns than stocks of larger firms. Even more notable is the average return for the smallest portfolio (1). This return is significantly higher than for the next smallest portfolio (2) or for any other. Hence when some observers refer to a **size effect** in stock returns, they are really referring to a "small firm effect."[30]

size effect

13.7.4 INTERRELATIONSHIPS

The existence of a relationship between any one of three financial variables (BV/MV ratio, E/P ratio, and firm size) and stock returns suggests that there is at least one missing factor that is needed to explain the differences in returns.[31] Therefore, it is of interest to

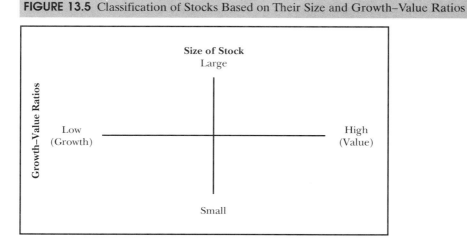

FIGURE 13.5 Classification of Stocks Based on Their Size and Growth–Value Ratios

examine the interrelationships between the BV/MV ratio, the E/P ratio, firm size, and average returns. The joint effect of E/P ratio and firm size on stock returns is examined next.

E/P, Size, and Average Returns

In order to examine the joint effect of the two financial variables, E/P and size, on stock returns, one study identified at each year-end the break points formed by sorting NYSE and AMEX stocks in quintiles based on just size and then on just the E/P ratio.[32] Then, using both of these sets of break points, the study assigned stocks to 1 of 25 size-E/P portfolios for the next year as follows. Each stock in the smallest size quintile was assigned to 1 of 5 E/P portfolios, then each stock in the next-to-smallest size quintile was assigned to 1 of 5 E/P portfolios, and so on until there were 25 (= 5 sizes $\times$ 5 E/P ratios) size-E/P portfolios. The process was repeated year after year until a set of daily returns was available for each of the 25 portfolios.

Comparison of the average returns for the 25 portfolios showed that there was a clear inverse relationship between size and average returns for any E/P quintile. For example, in the 5 size-ranked portfolios that were formed from the lowest E/P quintile, the larger the size, the smaller the average return. However, there was no clear relationship between E/P ratios and average returns for any size quintile. For example, in the case of the 5 E/P-ranked portfolios that were formed from the smallest size quintile, the largest average returns were associated with the lowest E/P portfolios. This result was contrary to previous observations of the relationship between E/P ratios and average returns. Consequently, it appears that there is a missing factor that is needed to explain differences in stock returns, and that this factor is more closely related to size than to the E/P ratio.[33]

BV/MV, Size, and Average Returns

Fama and French were interested in the joint effect of the BV/MV ratio and firm size on stock returns.[34] Accordingly, they formed 100 portfolios annually based on the rankings of stocks using size and BV/MV ratio. Monthly returns on these portfolios were then recorded.

Comparison of the average returns for the 100 portfolios showed that there was an inverse relationship between size and average return for almost every BV/MV decile. For example, for the 10 size-ranked portfolios that were formed from the largest BV/MV decile, in general the larger the size, the smaller the average return. The only exception was for the two smallest BV/MV deciles, where in each case there was no apparent relationship between size and return. Furthermore, there was a clear, direct relationship between BV/MV ratios and average returns for any size quintile. For example, in the comparison of the ten BV/MV-ranked portfolios that were formed from the smallest size decile, the larger the BV/MV ratio, the larger the average return. Fama and French concluded that there are at least two missing factors that are needed to explain differences in stock returns and that those factors are closely related to size and the BV/MV ratio.

13.8   Primary Markets

primary markets

This chapter and Chapter 21 focus on secondary markets for stocks and bonds, where these securities, having been initially issued at some previous point in time, are traded. The focus now shifts to **primary markets** for securities, where the initial issuance itself takes place. Some issuers deal directly with purchasers in this market, but many rely on

**investment
bankers**

investment bankers, who serve as intermediaries between issuers and the ultimate purchasers of their securities.

13.8.1   PRIVATE PLACEMENTS

private placements

Investment banking services are typically performed by brokerage firms and, to a lesser extent, by commercial banks. In some instances only a few large institutional investors are solicited, and the entire issue is sold to one or a few of them. Such **private placements** are often announced only after the fact, via advertisements in the financial press. As long as relatively few potential buyers are contacted, requirements for detailed disclosure, SEC registration, public notice, and so on may be waived, considerably reducing the cost of floating an issue. However, such investments are illiquid because the investor is typically prohibited from selling the security within one year of the purchase date. This restriction has resulted in relatively few equities being sold in this manner. Instead, most private placements involve fixed-income securities that are purchased by investors who are attracted by their coupon payments, not by the prospect of capital gains.

13.8.2   PUBLIC SALE

When public sale is contemplated, much more must be done than with private placements. Many firms may serve as intermediaries in the process. One, acting as the "lead" investment banker, puts together a syndicate (or purchase group) and a selling group.

**syndicate
underwrite
selling group**

The **syndicate** includes firms that purchase the securities from the issuing corporation and are said to **underwrite** the offering. The **selling group** includes firms that contact potential buyers and do the actual selling, usually on a commission basis.

**competitive
bidding**

The process begins with discussions between the issuing corporation and one or more investment bankers. Some issuers use **competitive bidding,** then select the investment banker offering the best terms. This procedure is used for many municipal bond issues and is required by law for securities issued by firms in certain regulated industries. However, many corporations maintain a continuing relationship with a single investment banker and negotiate the terms of each new offering with that firm. The investment banker is likely to be heavily involved in the planning of an offering, the terms involved, the amount to be offered, and so on, serving, in effect, as a financial consultant to the corporation.

**registration
statement
prospectus
red herring**

Once the basic characteristics of an offering have been established, a **registration statement** is filed with the SEC, and a preliminary **prospectus** disclosing material relevant to the prospective buyer is issued. (This prospectus is often referred to as a **red herring** because it has a disclaimer printed in red ink across the first page, which informs the reader that it is not an offer to sell.) The actual price of the security is not included in the preliminary prospectus, and no final sales may be made until the registration becomes effective and a final prospectus is issued, indicating the "offer" price at which the stock will be sold. The final prospectus may be issued as soon as the SEC determines there has been adequate disclosure and a reasonable waiting period has passed (usually 20 days). The commission does not take a position regarding the investment merits of an offering or the reasonableness of the price.

A security issue may be completely underwritten by an investment banker and the other members of the syndicate. If it is, the issuing corporation receives the public offering price less a stated percentage spread [although underwriters are occasionally compensated with some combination of shares and options to buy shares, known as warrants, perhaps in addition to a smaller spread]. The underwriters, in turn, sell the securities at the public offering price (or less) and may buy some of the securities themselves.

firm commitment

Underwriters who provide this sort of **firm commitment** bear all the risk because the public may not be willing to buy the entire issue.

Not all agreements are of this type. In the case of a rights offering (where the current stockholders are given the opportunity to buy the new shares first, as mentioned earlier), an underwriter may agree to purchase at a fixed price all securities not taken by current stockholders. This arrangement is termed a **standby agreement.** In the case of a nonrights offering (in which the shares are offered to the general public first), members of an investment banking group may serve as agents instead of dealers, agreeing to handle an offering only on a **best-efforts basis.**

standby agreement

best-efforts basis

During the period when new securities remain unsold, the investment banker is allowed to attempt to "stabilize" the price of the security in the secondary market by standing ready to make purchases at a particular price. There is a limit to the amount that can be purchased in this **pegging,** which is usually stated in the agreement under which the underwriting syndicate is formed because the members typically share the cost of such transactions. If pegging will occur, a statement to that effect must be included in the prospectus.

pegging

In any security transaction there may be explicit and implicit costs. In a primary distribution, the explicit cost is the underwriting spread, and the implicit cost is any difference between the public offering price and the price that might have been obtained otherwise. The spread provides the investment banking syndicate with compensation for selling the issue and bearing the risk that the issue may not be completely sold to the public, leaving it with ownership of unsold shares. The lower the public offering price, the smaller the risk that the issue will not be sold quickly at that price. If an issue is substantially underpriced, the syndicate is assured the securities will sell rapidly and requires little or no support in the secondary market. Because many corporations deal with only one investment banking firm and because the larger investment banking firms rely on one another for inclusion in syndicates, it has been alleged that issuers pay too much in spreads, given the prices at which their securities are offered. In other words, the returns to underwriters are alleged to be overly large relative to the risks involved because of ignorance on the part of issuers or the existence of an informal cartel among investment banking firms.

13.8.3 UNDERPRICING OF IPO'S

initial public offerings

unseasoned offerings

Regardless of whether returns to underwriting are overly large, many **initial public offerings** (IPOs) appear to be underpriced. An IPO is a company's first offering of shares to the public and is sometimes referred to as an **unseasoned offering.** The abnormal rates of return for a sample of IPOs are shown in Figure 13.6. Each one of the first 60 months after the initial offering is shown on the horizontal axis, and the corresponding average abnormal return (meaning the average return over and above that of stocks of equal risk) is shown on the vertical axis. The leftmost point indicates the average abnormal return obtained by an investor who purchased such a stock at its offering price and sold it for the bid price at the end of the month during which it was offered. The average abnormal return was substantial: 11.4%. The remaining points show the average abnormal returns that could have been obtained by an investor who purchased the security in the secondary market at the beginning of the month after its offering, which is indicated on the horizontal axis, and sold it at the end of that month. Some of these postoffering abnormal returns were positive, but most were negative.

A subsequent study found that the initial abnormal return, measured during the time period beginning with the offering and ending when the first closing price was reported, was 14.1%.[35] Although there is evidence that the average abnormal returns remained

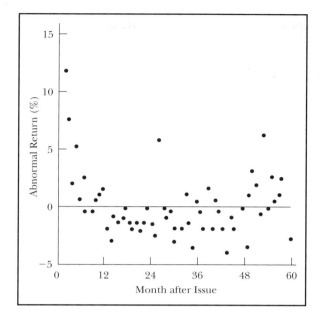

FIGURE 13.6 Average Abnormal Returns of Common Stock IPOs

Source: Roger G. Ibbotson, "Price Performance of Common Stock New Issues," *Journal of Financial Economics,* 2, no. 3 (September 1975): 252.

positive during the next two months, the average abnormal return over the three-year period after the first close was −37.4%. Three other interesting observations were made:

1. Offerings of smaller firms had lower three-year abnormal returns than those of larger firms
2. Firms that had the highest positive initial abnormal return had the worst performance during the subsequent three-year period
3. Younger firms going public had both higher initial abnormal returns and lower subsequent three-year abnormal returns than older firms going public.

Offerings of these unseasoned securities, it seems, are typically underpriced (and then overpriced). Investors purchasing a cross-section of such shares at their offering prices might expect better performance during the first two months than those holding other securities of equal risk. It is not surprising that such offerings are often rationed to "favored" customers by the members of the selling group. It is "not uncommon for underwriters to receive, prior to the effective date, 'public indication of interest' for five times the number of shares available."[36] Unfavored customers are presumably allowed to buy only the new issues that are not substantially underpriced. And, because costs may be incurred in becoming a favored customer, it is not clear that such an investor obtains abnormally large returns overall.

Whereas the initial return obtained by the purchaser of a new issue may be substantial *on average,* the amount may be very good or very bad in any particular instance, as Figure 13.7 shows. Although the odds may be in the purchaser's favor, a single investment of this type is far from a sure bet.

13.8.4 SEASONED OFFERINGS

The announcement of a seasoned stock offering seems to result in a decline of roughly 2% to 4% in the firm's stock price. This decline could be because managers tend to issue stock when they think it is overpriced in the marketplace. Thus the announcement of the offering causes investors to revise downward their assessment of the value of the

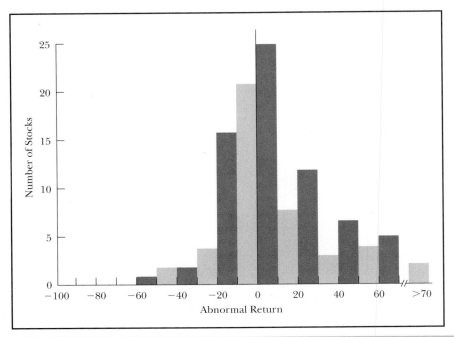

FIGURE 13.7 Average Abnormal Returns from Offering Date to End Month for Common Stock IPOs

Source: Roger G. Ibbotson, "Price Performance of Common Stock New Issus," *Journal of Financial Economics,* 2, no. 3 (September 1975): 248.

stock, leading to a price decline.[37] This decline is greater for stocks of industrial firms than for stocks of public utilities, probably because the typical utility issues seasoned offerings more often than the typical industrial firm.[38]

Figure 13.8 displays the average post-issue abnormal price performance of a sample of seasoned equity offerings.[39] In particular, it shows the average abnormal return during the six-month and one-year periods beginning with the first post-issue price recorded by the exchange on which the security was listed. Also shown are the average abnormal returns for the second, third, fourth, and fifth year after issuance. As the figure shows, for the first six months after a seasoned equity offering, nothing unusual happened to the typical firm's stock price. However, during the first year there was a −6.3% abnormal return, suggesting that the stocks performed poorly during the second six-month period after the offering. The second, third, fourth, and fifth years showed continued poor performance. Overall, the seasoned equity offerings had an abnormal return of roughly −8% per year for the five years after the offering. This trend presents a puzzle: Why do many firms issue equity when they ultimately provide investors with such low returns during the subsequent five years? Equivalently, why do investors buy such offerings? Indeed, these two questions can be asked not only about seasoned offerings but also about IPO's.

13.8.5 SHELF REGISTRATION

shelf registration

A 1982 change in regulations made it possible for large corporations to foster greater competition among underwriters when the SEC allowed firms to register securities prior to issuance under Rule 415. With such **shelf registration,** securities may be sold up to two years later. With securities "on the shelf," the corporation can require in-

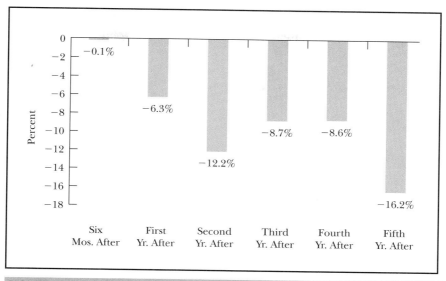

FIGURE 13.8   Average Abnormal Returns for Seasoned Equity Offerings

Source: Adapted from Tom Loughran and Jay R. Ritter, "The New Issues Puzzle," *Journal of Finance,* 50, no. 1 (March 1995): 33.

vestment bankers to bid competitively and can refuse to sell shares if desirable bids are not forthcoming. Thus, one purpose of the SEC in allowing shelf registration was to reduce the costs of issuing securities. The evidence seems to suggest that indeed such costs have been reduced.[40]

13.8.6   RULE 144A SECURITIES

Unregistered securities are issued via direct negotiations between issuers and investors. These securities are not registered with the SEC, and issuers do not have to satisfy stringent financial disclosure requirements. Before 1990 all investors had to wait two years (now one year) before being permitted to trade private placements, making such securities highly illiquid. In 1990 the SEC adopted Rule 144A, which permits privately placed securities issued under the provisions of the rule to be traded among large investors (those with assets in excess of $100 million who are primarily institutional investors) at any time after their initial purchase. By relaxing the time restriction for large investors, Rule 144A added liquidity to the private placement market and increased the attractiveness of these securities.

Historically, the private placement market has consisted predominantly of fixed-income securities. A large volume of high-yield bonds have been issued under Rule 144A. In fact, in 1996, for the first time, more high-yield debt was issued under the rule than through the traditional public process. However, Rule 144A also applies to common stocks. Foreign corporations, who in many cases cannot (or sometimes choose not to) meet the SEC's disclosure rules, have been the primary issuers of common stock under Rule 144A.

13.8.7   SECONDARY DISTRIBUTIONS

As mentioned earlier, an individual or institution wishing to sell a large block of stock can do so through a secondary distribution. An investment banking group buys the stock from the seller and offers the shares to the public. Typically, the shares are first

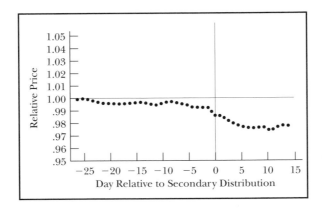

FIGURE 13.9 Price Performance for Secondary Distributions

Source: Myron S. Scholes, "The Market for Securities: Substitution versus Price Pressure and the Effects of Information on the Share Prices," *Journal of Business,* 45, no 2 (April 1972): 193.

offered after normal trading hours at the day's closing price. The buyer often pays no commission, and the original seller receives the total proceeds less an underwriting spread.

The SEC requires secondary distributions to be registered, with public announcements and disclosures and a 20-day waiting period, if the original seller has a "control relationship" with the issuer of the securities. Otherwise the distribution may be unregistered.

The impact of the sale of a large block on the market price of the stock provides information on the resiliency of the capital market. Figure 13.9 shows the average prices (adjusted for market changes) for 345 secondary distributions, with the price taken 25 days before the distribution as 1.0. The study showed that, on average, a secondary distribution leads to a 2% to 3% decline in price. Because there is no evidence of a subsequent price rebound, this decline was most likely due to the information conveyed by the fact that someone had decided to sell. Additional analysis of these results, as shown in Table 13.3, supports the assertion. The size of the decline was related to the identity of the seller, and it was greater for information-motivated sellers and smaller for liquidity-motivated sellers.[41]

TABLE 13.3   Average Price Decline versus Type of Seller for Secondary Distributions

Type of Seller	Percentage Change in Adjusted Price from 10 Days before the Distribution to 10 Days after the Distribution
Corporations and officers	2.9%
Investment companies and mutual funds	2.5
Individuals	1.1
Estates	.7
Banks and insurance companies	.3

Source: Myron S. Scholes, "The Market for Securities: Substitution versus Price Pressure and the Effects of Information on Share Prices," *Journal of Business,* 45, no. 2 (April 1972): 202.

How Firms in the People's Republic of China Raise Funds

Prepared by Ann E. Sherman

Companies in the communist People's Republic of China (PRC) are very different from those in capitalist countries. Most large firms are state-owned enterprises (SOEs), which traditionally had to return all reported "profits" to the government each year. However, losses could be covered by "loans" from the state-owned banks that did not have to be repaid and were counted as profits by the firm. Accounting methods varied by industry, and the accounting records were prepared by the firm itself, without the help of an independent auditor. Any revenue shortfall for the enterprise was offset by "loans," so managers and employees would not lose anything because of low output, but were not allowed to keep any of the profit from high output.

Reforming SOEs has been a top goal of the Chinese Communist Party since 1976. Many attempts have been made. In the early 1980s, managers were given some discretion and were allowed to keep part of any cost savings from greater efficiency. The cost savings could be used, for instance, to pay bonuses or to build better worker housing. In the mid-1980s, there was an attempt to make corporate taxes uniform across firms (at a rate of 55%). However, because managers had so much discretion in preparing accounting statements, they were easily able to avoid any taxable "profits." Beginning in 1987 target profit levels were set for each firm. Managers were allowed to keep profits above the target. Managers were given much more discretion than before, and they can now do almost anything except fire workers or raise outside funds (except with permission, which has been hard to obtain).

China has moved slowly in its reforms of SOEs, "groping for stones to cross the river." Although the government has resisted following outside examples, viewing its problems as uniquely Chinese, the problems are predictable by anyone with a basic knowledge of managerial incentives.

Despite the many reforms, managers of SOEs simply do not have an incentive to make companies profitable and efficient. They typically have no ownership stake, and their pay does not increase as corporate profits increase. One might guess that managing more efficiently would help them keep their jobs, but in fact, the opposite is often true. If a company is very profitable, then a Communist Party official may consider it easy to run and put a relative or friend in charge. The manager of a troubled firm is less likely to lose his or her job because no one else will want it.

Changes continue, however. In 1992, the Communist Party adopted the goal of a "socialist market economy," although it insisted that state ownership was still the backbone of the economy and that the market system was a temporary stage in its communist evolution. In 1993, a new business model was established that should allow greater separation of ownership and control. It became possible to privatize some companies, giving the state limited liability (as a shareholder), although the state usually maintains majority control of the shares. In 1997, the move toward freer markets continued when it was announced that roughly half (in terms of assets) of all state-owned firms would be privatized. While most SOEs should be privatized in the next few years, the largest firms will remain untouched, at least for now.

There are several popular ways a PRC firm can now raise funds. Joint ventures, although they usually involve forming a new corporation, allow an SOE to raise funds through a subsidiary that takes on a new project. Unfortunately, they do not transform existing SOEs. Another popular method is "back-door listing" on the Hong Kong market. PRC firms buy controlling interests in shell companies listed on the Stock Exchange of Hong Kong (SEHK). The companies picked are usually small and thinly traded (and thus cheap to purchase). The PRC parent can then issue new shares or debt through the subsidiary to raise funds. Funds are transferred through the sale of assets from parent to subsidiary or vice versa.

Back-door listings are a relatively painless method of raising capital because they do not require greater disclosure, reorganization, or the translation of the parent firm's accounting into international or Hong Kong standards. For that reason, however, they also do not improve the efficiency of the corporation, and they enable firms to transfer assets out of the PRC. Back-door listings are known as red chips (a play on the term *blue chips* because the companies are from "red," or communist, China). They typically sell at extremely low P/E ratios compared with other companies listed in Hong Kong because investors hope for future asset injections from the parent company.

Another way in which a PRC company can raise funds is through an A or B share listing on one of the country's two exchanges in Shanghai or Shenzhen. For a PRC company to be listed on any exchange (local or foreign), it must first become a stock company, which is defined as an enterprise with legal person status that divides its capital into equal shares. Enterprises in areas such as national defense or strategic resources are not allowed to organize as stock companies; enterprises in priority industries such as energy, transportation, and communication can become stock companies only if the state maintains a majority of the shares. Equity in a stock company must be divided into four categories: state shares (purchased with state assets by government departments), legal person shares (held by a PRC legal "person," or corporation), individual shares (purchased by a PRC citizen), and foreign investment shares (purchased by foreigners). The first two categories are known as C shares and usually are not tradable. Shares held by PRC citizens and purchased in Renminbi (the Chinese currency) are A shares, and shares held by foreign parties and denominated in U.S. dollars are B shares.

The fact that each type of share has a separate legal status means that there is a potential for discrimination; state shares may be treated better than individual shares, or A shareholders may be favored over B shareholders. Prices vary widely across the different share types, but it is virtually always true that B shares sell at a substantial discount to A shares. This relation reflects the fact that foreign investors have many choices, whereas PRC citizens have very few investment choices. The stock markets are still small relative to the amount of savings of PRC investors, but the government is trying to speed up listings. As a result of the huge excess demand for investments in the PRC, prices of A shares have been bid well above the prices of B shares in the same firms. With B shares selling at a substantial discount, PRC investors found ways to purchase them despite the fact that they are not legally allowed to do so. This practice increased prices above levels foreign investors were comfortable with, and now the B share market is primarily dominated by PRC investors. Occasionally, PRC officials threaten to crack down on the holding of B shares by PRC citizens. When the market takes these threats seriously, the prices of B shares fall dramatically, frightening regulators into backing off.

Listing standards and disclosure requirements for A and B shares on the Shanghai or Shenzhen exchanges are noticeably lower than for reputable foreign exchanges. For instance, B share firms have disclosed financial performance figures to analysts before revealing them to shareholders, failed to comply with disclosure obligations, failed to give adequate notice of shareholders' meetings, and failed to use funds in the manner specified in the prospectus. In direct contradiction to the plans outlined in prospectuses, a large portion of the funds raised so far have been used for property speculation.

A more prestigious funding choice for eligible firms is a foreign listing, for instance an H (Hong Kong) or N (New York) listing. H and N shares are Renminbi-denominated shares that may be purchased and traded in a foreign currency only by non-PRC residents. PRC firms are also seeking to list on the Singapore, Taiwan, and Vancouver exchanges. However, many adjustments are required for firms that want to list on an outside exchange. One problem is that many SOEs have several operating units, and it is difficult to decide which should be included in the public company. For instance, PRC firms in the past have been responsible for providing housing, medical care, education, and pensions to workers and their families. Thus, they often provide and run hospitals, schools, dormitories, child care centers, and even recreational facilities, which do not generate revenues and are not normally part of, say, a steel-making company. Changing accounting standards is another major adjustment. For example, PRC accounting methods do not recognize "prudence concepts" such as making provisions for bad debt or writing off obsolete inventory.

Finally, one of the biggest adjustments is in the attitude of managers toward stockholders. It is difficult to convince PRC managers that they have obligations to shareholders, such as deploying funds as they have promised. Of the first batch of H shares listed in Hong Kong in 1993, the most respected was Tsingtao Brewery. In its prospectus, Tsingtao stated that it would use the proceeds of its offering to build new breweries and to update equipment. When investors read the first annual report more than a year after the listing, they were shocked to learn that Tsingtao had simply lent most of the proceeds to other PRC firms.

Tsingtao calmly announced that it was planning a rights issue to raise more funds from stockholders because it still wanted to expand and update its breweries. From the perspective of the company managers, they were responding to profitable investment opportunities as they arose. The fact that investors wanted to invest in a brewery, rather than a bank, was of no concern to them. Although it was upsetting to investors to learn how their funds had been used, at least holders of H shares were able to find out where their money went. Issuers of A and B shares in the PRC are not required to tell investors how their funds have been used, and most firms choose not to make such disclosures.

Summary

1. Common stock represents an ownership position in a corporation. Common stockholders possess a residual claim on the corporation's earnings and assets. Their liability for the corporation's obligations is limited.
2. Common stockholders elect the corporation's directors through either a majority or a cumulative voting system.
3. Corporations may at times repurchase some of their outstanding stock either in the open market or through a tender offer. Such actions may involve an attempt to repel a takeover, a signal to shareholders that the stock is undervalued, or a tax-advantageous distribution of cash to shareholders.
4. Stock dividends and splits involve the issuance of additional shares of common stock to current stockholders, proportional to their ownership positions. No change in the total value of the corporation is caused by a stock dividend or split. Such actions may involve either an attempt to move the firm's stock price into a more desirable trading range or to signal favorable information to the firm's shareholders.
5. Preemptive rights give existing stockholders the right of first refusal to purchase new shares. Such shares are purchased in a rights offering.
6. A security's *ex post* beta can be estimated using historical return data for the security and a market index and can be adjusted to arrive at an estimate of the security's *ex ante* beta. The beta is the slope of the security's market model, calculated by using simple linear regression.
7. Firms that have either low BV/MV or low E/P ratios, or both, are generally referred to as growth stocks, whereas firms that have either high BV/MV or high E/P ratios, or both, are generally referred to as value stocks.
8. Firms that have high BV/MV ratios, high E/P ratios, or are of small firm size historically have higher stock returns than firms with low ratios or that are large.
9. When viewed jointly, stock returns seem to be related to both firm size and BV/MV ratio.
10. The primary market involves the initial issuance of securities.
11. Although some issuers deal directly with investors, most hire investment bankers to assist them in the sale of securities.

Questions and Problems

1. What is the significant advantage of the corporate form of business organization? Why would you expect that this advantage would be important to the success of a capitalist economy?
2. Fall Creek is conducting the annual election for its five-member board of directors. The firm has 1,500,000 shares of voting common stock outstanding.
   a. Under a majority voting system, how many shares must a stockholder own to ensure electing his or her choices to each of the five director seats?
   b. Under a cumulative voting system, how many shares must a stockholder own to ensure electing one of his or her choices as a director?
3. The issue of corporate ownership versus control has become quite controversial. Discuss the principal–agent problem as it concerns shareholder–management relations. Why is there a potential conflict between the two groups? What steps can be taken to mitigate this problem?
4. Why might a corporation wish to issue more than one class of common stock?
5. Theoretical arguments and empirical research support the case that stock dividends and splits do not enhance shareholder wealth. However, corporations continue to declare stock dividends and splits. Summarize the arguments for and against stock dividends and splits from the perspective of the shareholder.
6. Menomonie Publishing stock currently sells for $40 per share. The company has 1,200,000 shares outstanding. What would be the effect on the number of shares outstanding and on the stock price of the following:
   a. 15% stock dividend
   b. 4-for-3 stock split
   c. Reverse 3-for-1 stock split
7. Tomah Electronics' stock price at the end of several quarters, along with the market index value for the same periods, follows. Tomah pays no dividends. Calculate the beta of Tomah's stock during the eight quarters.

Quarter	Quarter-End Tomah Stock Price	Quarter-End Market Index Value
0	60.000	210.00
1	62.500	220.50
2	64.375	229.87
3	59.875	206.88
4	56.875	190.33
5	61.500	209.36
6	66.500	238.67
7	69.750	257.76
8	68.375	262.92

8. Using the data from problem 5 in Chapter 1, calculate the beta of the small stock portfolio during the 20-year period. Use the common stock returns from Table 1.1 as the returns on the market index.
9. Following are ten quarters of return data for Baraboo Associates stock, as well as return data during the same period for a broad stock market index. Using this information, calculate the following statistics for Baraboo Associates stock.
   a. Beta
   b. Alpha
   c. Standard deviation of random error term
   d. Coefficient of determination

Quarter	*Baraboo Return*	*Market Return*
1	3.8%	2.7%
2	5.3	3.1
3	–7.2	–4.9
4	10.1	9.9
5	1.0	2.7
6	2.5	1.2
7	6.4	3.8
8	4.8	4.0
9	6.0	5.5
10	2.2	2.0

10. Why are liquid and continuous secondary security markets important to the effective functioning of primary security markets?

11. Describe the role of an underwriting syndicate in a public security offering.

12. Why must companies that publicly issue securities file a prospectus with the SEC? What does the SEC's acceptance of the prospectus imply?

13. Discuss why IPOs appear to generate abnormal returns for investors. Are these returns a "sure thing"? What are the economic implications of these high returns for IPO issuers?

14. (Appendix Question) The empirical regularities cited in this chapter have potentially troubling implications for the capital asset pricing model and the concept of highly efficient markets. Discuss some of these implications.

15. (Appendix Question) Boileryard Clarke, an astute investment observer, wrote, "Testing for empirical regularities is conceptually difficult because it is really a two-hypothesis test. One test is related to the validity of the underlying asset pricing model, and the other test is related to the existence of the empirical regularity." What does Boileryard mean by this statement?

APPENDIX

Empirical Regularities in the Stock Market

empirical regularities

anomalies

Researchers have uncovered certain **empirical regularities** in common stocks. That is, certain cross-sectional differences among stock returns have been found to occur with regularity. Some regularities should occur according to certain asset pricing models. For example, the CAPM asserts that different stocks should have different returns because different stocks have different betas. The regularities that are discussed here are of special interest because they are not predicted by the traditional asset pricing models. Accordingly, they are sometimes referred to as **anomalies.**

As mentioned earlier, returns are related to a firm's size as well as to its BV/MV and E/P ratios. Although these relationships are often used as examples of anomalies, Fama and French argue that they can be explained by a three-factor APT model and should not be viewed as anomalies.[42] This appendix examines some calendar anomalies and presents some evidence on how they are related.[43]

13A.1 Seasonality in Stock Returns

January effect
day-of-the-week effect

The desire of individuals for liquidity may change from day to day and from month to month. If it does, there may be seasonal patterns in stock returns. One might presume that such patterns would be relatively unimportant. According to the notion of efficient markets, such patterns should be quite minor (if they exist at all) because they are not suggested by traditional asset pricing models. However, the evidence indicates that at least two are significant: the **January effect** and the **day-of-the-week effect.**[44]

A.1.1 JANUARY EFFECT

There is no obvious reason to expect stock returns to be higher in certain months than in others. However, in a study that examined average monthly returns on NYSE-listed common stocks, significant seasonalities were found.[45] In particular, the average return in January was higher than the average return in any other month. Table 13.4 indicates the average stock return in January and the other 11 months for various time periods. It seems that the average return in January is approximately 3% higher than the average monthly returns in February through December.[46]

TABLE 13.4 Seasonality in Stock Returns

Average Stock Return in January	Average Stock Return in Other Months	Difference in Returns
3.48%	.42%	3.06%

Source: Adapted from Michael S. Rozeff and William R. Kinney, Jr., "Capital Market Seasonality: The Case of Stock Returns," *Journal of Financial Economics,* 3, no. 4 (October 1976): 388.

TABLE 13.5	Analysis of Daily Returns				
	Monday	*Tuesday*	*Wednesday*	*Thursday*	*Friday*
French study	−.17%	.02%	.10%	.04%	.09%
Gibbons and Hess study	−.13	.00	.10	.03	.08

Source: Kenneth R. French, "Stock Returns and the Weekend Effect," *Journal of Financial Economics*, 8, no. 1 (March 1980): 58; and Michael R. Gibbons and Patrick Hess, "Day of the Week Effects and Asset Returns," *Journal of Business*, 54, no. 4 (October 1981): 582–583.

A.1.2 DAY-OF-THE-WEEK EFFECT

It is often assumed that the expected daily returns on stocks are the same for all days of the week. That is, the expected return on a given stock is the same for Monday as it is for the other trading days of the week. However, a number of studies have uncovered evidence that refutes this belief. Two studies examined the average daily return on NYSE-listed securities and found that the return on Monday was quite different from returns on other days.[47] In particular, the average return on Monday was much lower than the average return on any other day of the week. Furthermore, the average return on Monday was negative, whereas the other days of the week had positive average returns. Table 13.5 displays these findings.

The rate of return on a stock for a given day of the week is typically calculated by subtracting the closing price on the previous trading day from the closing price on that day, adding any dividends for that day to the difference, and dividing the resulting number by the closing price as of the previous trading day:

$$r_t = \frac{(P_t - P_{t-1}) + D_t}{P_{t-1}} \tag{13.4}$$

where P_t and P_{t-1} are the closing prices on days t and $t-1$, and D_t is the value of any dividends paid on day t. Therefore, the return for Monday uses the closing price on Monday as P_t and the closing price on Friday as P_{t-1} so that the change in the price of a stock for Monday $(P_t - P_{t-1})$ represents the change in price over the weekend, as well as during Monday. This observation has caused some people to refer to the day-of-the-week effect as the *weekend effect*. Other people use the *weekend effect* to refer to price behavior from Friday close to Monday open and the *Monday effect* to refer to price behavior from Monday open to Monday close.

A refinement of the day-of-the-week effect involved an examination of NYSE stock returns over 15-minute intervals during trading hours.[48] Figure 13.10 displays the results when these returns were cumulated and examined on a day-of-the-week basis. Several observations can be made. First, the negative returns during trading hours on Monday occurred within an hour of the opening. Afterward, the behavior of stock prices on Monday was similar to that on the other days of the week. Second, on Tuesdays through Fridays there was a notable upward movement in prices in the first hour of trading. Third, on all days of the week there was a notable upward movement in prices during the last hour of trading.[49] Hence most of the daily price movement in a stock typically comes near the open and close.

holiday effect   Somewhat related to the day-of-the-week effect is the **holiday effect.** A study of this effect found that average stock returns on trading days around federal holidays

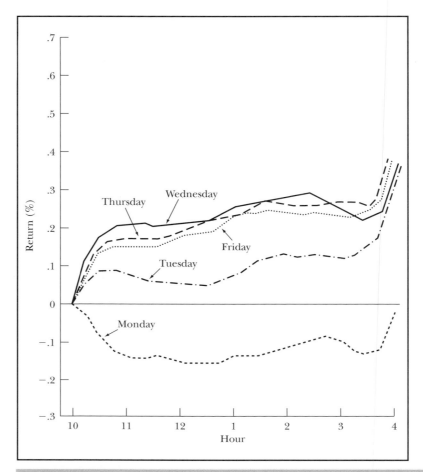

FIGURE 13.10 Cumulated 15-Minute Intraday Returns

Source: Lawrence Harris, "How to Profit from Intraday Stock Returns," *Journal of Portfolio Management,* 12, no. 2 (Winter 1986): 63.

(the market is closed on these holidays; there are eight each year) are 9 to 14 times higher than the average daily returns during the rest of the year.[50] Furthermore, this abnormally high return is spread out from the closing price two days before the holiday to the opening price on the day after the holiday. Tests indicate that it is unrelated to the size, January, or day-of-the-week effects.

13A.2   Interrelationship of Size and January Effects

Having observed that small firms have higher returns than large firms, and that returns are higher in January than in any other month of the year, one might wonder whether these two effects are somehow related. One study that examined this issue found that the two effects were strongly interrelated.[51] All NYSE-listed and AMEX-listed stocks were examined in this study. At the end of each year, each firm was ranked by market capitalization. Ten portfolios were formed based on size, with portfolio 1 containing the smallest 10% of the firms, portfolio 2 the next smallest 10%, and so on.

Abnormal returns were calculated for each portfolio on a monthly basis during the test period and averaged for each month. Figure 13.11, which displays the results, shows that the size effect was most pronounced in January because the line for this month slopes down sharply from left to right. The other 11 months of the year appear to be quite similar to each other. In general, each of these months displays a slight downward slope, indicating that the size effect also existed for these months, but only to a minor degree. Also of interest is the observation that large firms had a negative abnormal return in January. Thus, the January effect has been due primarily to the behavior of small firms, and the size effect has been concentrated mainly in the month of January.

Further examination of the interrelationship between the size effect and the January effect reveals that it has been concentrated in the first five trading days of January.[52] In particular, the difference in returns between the smallest-firm portfolio and the largest-firm portfolio during these five days was 8.0%, whereas during the entire year it was 30.4%. Thus, 26.3% $(= 8.0\%/30.4\%)$ of the annual size effect occurred during these five days. (If the size effect had been spread evenly over the year, then .4% of it would have been attributed to these five days.)

Attempts have been made to explain this interrelationship between the January effect and the size effect. One explanation that seems to have some merit has to do with "tax selling." This explanation argues that stocks that have declined during the year have downward pressure on their prices near year-end as investors sell them to realize capital losses in order to minimize tax payments. After the end of the year, the pressure is removed and the prices jump back to their "fair" values. A related argument asserts that some professional money managers sell those stocks that have performed poorly during the past year in order to eliminate them from year-end reports. Such activity is often referred to as "window dressing." (However, the notion of efficient markets would suggest that this behavior cannot happen because if investors sensed that stocks were becoming undervalued at year-end they would flood the market with buy orders, thereby preventing any substantive undervaluation from occurring.) Nevertheless, the

FIGURE 13.11 Relationship between the Size Effect and the January Effect

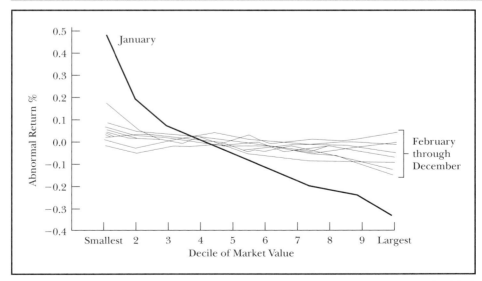

Source: Donald B. Keim, "Size-Related Anomalies and Stock Return Seasonality: Further Empirical Evidence," *Journal of Financial Economics*, 12, no. 1 (June 1983): 21.

arguments do appear to have some merit in that the stocks that declined during the previous year had the largest appreciation in January.[53] Unfortunately, this association between January returns and previous year stock-price declines does not appear to be attributable solely to such downward tax-selling price pressure because the biggest "losers" during a year appear to have abnormally high returns for as long as five Januaries thereafter. This finding contradicts tax-selling arguments because, according to them, the abnormal price rebound should occur only in the first subsequent January.[54]

Contradictory evidence is also provided by noting that the January effect exists in Japan, yet Japan has no capital gains tax and disallows any deduction for capital losses.[55] Rebutting this evidence, however, is the observation that the January effect apparently did not exist prior to the imposition of income taxes in the United States.[56]

A second possible explanation is that small stocks may be relatively riskier in January than during the rest of the year. If they are, then they should have a relatively higher average return in January. A study finding that the betas of small stocks tend to increase at the beginning of the year lends support to this explanation.[57]

13A.3 Summary of Empirical Regularities

What do these regularities suggest that the investor should do? First, investors who want to buy stocks should avoid doing so late on Friday or early on Monday. Conversely, investors who want to sell stocks should try to sell late on Friday or early on Monday. Second, if the stocks of small firms are to be purchased, they should be purchased in late December or somewhat earlier. If the stocks of small firms are to be sold, they should be sold in mid-January or somewhat later. Third, if the stocks of large firms are to be purchased, they should be purchased in early February or somewhat later. If the stocks of large firms are to be sold, they should be sold in late December or somewhat earlier.[58]

Two words of caution are in order here. First, none of these empirical regularities is of a sufficient magnitude to suggest that riches are to be made by exploiting them. Indeed, transaction costs would devour most if not all of any profits that might be made.[59] All they suggest is that if, for whatever reason, a buy or sell order is to be placed, there are some times when it may be more advantageous to do so. Second, although these regularities have been found to exist in the past, and in some instances for long periods of time and in several foreign markets, there is no guarantee that they will continue to exist in the future.[60] As more investors become aware of them and time their trades accordingly, such regularities may disappear.

Endnotes

1. For more information on proxies, see Paul Jessup and Mary Bochnak, "Exercising Your Rights: How to Use Proxy Material," *AAII Journal,* 14, no. 9 (October 1992): 8–11.

2. For an interesting discussion of proxy fights, see David Ikenberry and Josef Lakonishok, "Corporate Governance through the Proxy Contest: Evidence and Implications," *Journal of Business,* 66, no. 3 (July 1993): 405–435. In examining proxy contests that dealt with the election of directors, the authors found that such contests followed a period of below-average performance for both the firm's earnings and stock price. If management had its nominees elected, the firm's performance reverted to average. However, if the dissidents' nominees were elected, then the firm's performance continued its deterioration for another two years, with the deterioration being most acute if the dissidents took control of the board.

3. Another form of a takeover is a **merger.** A merger occurs when two firms combine their operations so that only one firm exists. Mergers usually are negotiated by the management of the two firms. Tender offers differ in that the management of the bidder makes a direct appeal to the stockholders of the target firm for their shares. Tender offers also differ in that afterward both firms still exist because most tender offers are

not for all the shares of the target. **Management buyouts** are a special kind of tender offer, where the current management of the firm uses borrowed funds to buy the company. (Hence they are a type of **leveraged buyout**, or LBO. LBOs can be executed by anyone, including incumbent management.)

4. See, for example, Michael C. Jensen and William H. Meckling, "Theory of the Firm: Managerial Behavior, Agency Costs and Ownership Structure," *Journal of Financial Economics*, 3, no. 4 (October 1976): 305–360; Eugene F. Fama, "Agency Problems and the Theory of the Firm," *Journal of Political Economy*, 88, no. 2 (April 1980): 288–307; Eugene F. Fama and Michael C. Jensen, "Separation of Ownership and Control," *Journal of Law and Economics*, 26 (June 1983): 301–325; Eugene F. Fama and Michael C. Jensen, "Agency Problems and Residual Claims," *Journal of Law and Economics*, 26 (June 1983): 327–349; the entire issues of vol. 11 (April 1983) and vol. 20 (January/March 1988) of the *Journal of Financial Economics;* Michael C. Jensen, "Eclipse of the Public Corporation," *Harvard Business Review*, 89, no. 5 (September–October 1989): 61–74; and John Byrd, Robert Parrino, and Gunnar Pritsch, "Stockholder-Manager Conflicts and Firm Value," *Financial Analysts Journal*, 54, no. 3 (May/June 1998): 14–30.

5. Having the firm's financial statements audited is an example of monitoring.

6. For example, management may decide to procure lavishly furnished offices and an executive jet when the conduct of business suggests that these actions are not merited. Furthermore, management may invest in negative net present value investment projects when the firm has "free cash flow" instead of paying it to the shareholders. See Michael C. Jensen, "Agency Costs of Free Cash Flow, Corporate Finance and Takeovers," *American Economic Review*, 76, no. 2 (May 1986): 323–329.

7. Robert Comment and Gregg A. Jarrell, "The Relative Signalling Power of Dutch-Auction and Fixed-Price Self-Tender Offers and Open-Market Share Repurchases," *Journal of Finance*, 46, no. 4 (September 1991): 1243–1271.

8. Although there were similar numbers of fixed-price and Dutch-auction tender offers in the study, the Dutch-auction method is becoming popular particularly among large corporations.

9. See Josef Lakonishok and Theo Vermaelen, "Anomalous Price Behavior around Repurchase Tender Offers," *Journal of Finance*, 45, no. 2 (June 1990): 455–477.

10. See David Ikenberry, Josef Lakonishok, and Theo Vermaelen, "Market Underreaction to Open Market Share Repurchases," *Journal of Financial Economics*, 29, nos. 2, 3 (October–November 1995): 181–208.

11. For more on "ex dates," see "Dividends and Interest: Who Gets Payments after a Trade?" *AAII Journal*, 12, no. 4 (April 1990): 8–11.

12. Some evidence in support of the optimal trading explanation is provided by Josef Lakonishok and Baruch Lev, "Stock Splits and Stock Dividends: Why, Who, and When," *Journal of Finance*, 42, no. 4 (September 1987): 913–932. The tick size explanation has been put forth by James J. Angel in "Tick Size, Share Prices, and Stock Splits," *Journal of Finance*, 52, no. 2 (June 1997): 655–681; and "Picking Your Tick: Toward a New Theory of Stock Splits," *Journal of Applied Corporate Finance*, 10, no. 3 (Fall 1997): 59–68.

13. David Ikenberry, Graeme Rankine, and Earl K. Stice, "What Do Stock Splits Really Signal?" *Journal of Financial and Quantitative Analysis*, 31, no. 3 (September 1996): 357–375.

14. Interestingly, a study of reverse stock splits found that for the typical firm (1) the stock had average performance before the announcement, (2) the announcement was associated with an abnormal return of about –6%, and (3) the stock continued to perform somewhat poorly after the announcement. See J. Randall Woolridge and Donald R. Chambers, "Reverse Splits and Shareholder Wealth," *Financial Management*, 12, no. 4 (Autumn 1983): 5–15.

15. See Eugene F. Fama, Lawrence Fisher, Michael C. Jensen, and Richard Roll, "The Adjustment of Stock Prices to New Information," *International Economic Review*, 10, no. 1 (February 1969): 1–21; Sasson Bar-Josef and Lawrence D. Brown, "A Re-Examination of Stock Splits Using Moving Betas," *Journal of Finance*, 32, no. 4 (September 1977): 1069–1080; and Guy Charest, "Split Information, Stock Returns and Market Efficiency: I," *Journal of Financial Economics*, 6, nos. 2, 3 (June/September 1978): 265–296.

16. See Thomas E. Copeland, "Liquidity Changes Following Stock Splits," *Journal of Finance*, 34, no. 1 (March 1979): 115–141; and Robert M. Conroy, Robert S. Harris, and Bruce A. Benet, "The Effects of Stock Splits on Bid–Ask Spreads," *Journal of Finance*, 45, no. 4 (September 1990): 1285–1295.

17. Mark S. Grinblatt, Ronald W. Masulis, and Sheridan Titman, "The Valuation Effects of Stock Splits and Stock Dividends," *Journal of Financial Economics*, 13, no. 4 (December 1984): 461–490.

18. Current stockholders may not be given this right if there is a provision in the charter denying it or if it is denied by the stockholders at the annual meeting.

19. The investor could simply let the rights expire, causing that investor's proportion in the corporation to decline as others are given ownership in the expanded firm in return for the provision of new capital. Sometimes an **oversubscription privilege** is given to the subscribing stockholders. Those stockholders who have

exercised their rights will be given an opportunity to buy the shares that were not purchased, which can become important if the rights are not transferable.

20. The subscription price is usually set at roughly 80% of the current market price of the stock.

21. It has been argued that roughly 300 months (25 years) of historical returns are needed for a simple averaging technique to produce useful estimates of expected returns, provided that the "true" but unobserved expected return is constant during this entire period. See J. D. Jobson and Bob Korkie, "Estimation for Markowitz Efficient Portfolios," *Journal of the American Statistical Association,* 75, no. 371 (September 1980): 544–554; and "Putting Markowitz Theory to Work," *Journal of Portfolio Management,* 7, no. 4 (Summer 1981): 70–74.

22. In doing so, a number of researchers have uncovered certain "empirical regularities" in common stocks; the appendix discusses a number of them. For a more detailed summary, see Donald B. Keim, "The CAPM and Equity Return Regularities," *Financial Analysts Journal,* 42, no. 3 (May/June 1986): 19–34; Douglas K. Pearce, "Challenges to the Concept of Market Efficiency," *Federal Reserve Bank of Kansas City Economic Review,* 72, no. 8 (September/October 1987): 16–33; and Robert A. Haugen and Josef Lakonishok, *The Incredible January Effect* (Homewood, IL: Dow Jones–Irwin, 1988).

23. For an introduction to regression, see Chapters 10 and 11 of James T. McClave and P. George Benson, *Statistics for Business and Economics* (New York: Macmillan, 1994); and Mark P. Kritzman, ". . . About Regressions," *Financial Analysts Journal,* 47, no. 3 (May/June 1991): 12–15. These calculations are easily made in a spreadsheet like Excel.

24. WM's beta and intercept term would have been .63 and .17%, respectively, if excess returns (that is, returns less the riskfree rate) had been used in the calculations instead of returns. Using returns or excess returns (as well as including or ignoring dividends in calculating returns) appears to make little difference in the estimated size of beta. However, there is a substantive difference in the estimated size of the intercept term. See William F. Sharpe and Guy M. Cooper, "Risk-Return Classes of New York Stock Exchange Common Stocks, 1931–1967," *Financial Analysts Journal,* 28, no. 2 (March/April 1972): 46–54.

25. *R* is often used to denote the correlation coefficient; sometimes (as in Chapter 8) the Greek letter rho (ρ) is used instead. Thus *R*-squared is equivalent to ρ-squared, or the square of the correlation coefficient.

26. Other ratios, such as dividend yield, are sometimes used in identifying these two types of stocks.

27. The S&P/BARRA Value Stock Index and the S&P/BARRA Growth Stock Index divide the S&P 500 stocks into two groups based on the size of their BV/MV ratios every six months. The stocks in each group are used to form these two market-capitalization-weighted indices. The construction of market indices is discussed in more detail in Chapter 18.

28. Eugene F. Fama and Kenneth R. French, "The Cross-Section of Expected Stock Returns," *Journal of Finance,* 47, no. 2 (June 1992): 427–465. Also see Barr Rosenberg, Kenneth Reid, and Ronald Lanstein, "Persuasive Evidence of Market Inefficiency," *Journal of Portfolio Management,* 11, no. 3 (Spring 1985): 9–16. The BV/MV ratio anomaly was found to exist in other countries, particularly France, Switzerland, and Japan, suggesting that value stocks have outperformed growth stocks outside the United States. See Carlo Capaul, Ian Rowley, and William F. Sharpe, "International Value and Growth Stock Returns," *Financial Analysts Journal,* 49, no. 1 (January/February 1993): 27–36.

29. Also see S. Basu, "Investment Performance of Common Stocks in Relation to Their Price-Earnings Ratios: A Test of the Efficient Market Hypothesis," *Journal of Finance,* 32, no. 3 (June 1977): 663–682; and "The Relationship between Earnings' Yield, Market Value and Return for NYSE Common Stocks: Further Evidence," *Journal of Financial Economics,* 12, no. 1 (June 1983): 129–156.

30. Other studies of the size effect include Rolf Banz, "The Relationship between Return and Market Value of Common Stocks," *Journal of Financial Economics,* 9, no. 1 (March 1981): 3–18; and Marc R. Reinganum, "Misspecification of Capital Asset Pricing: Empirical Anomalies Based on Earnings Yields and Market Values," *Journal of Financial Economics,* 9, no. 1 (March 1981): 19–46. One explanation of the size effect is that small firms have higher discount rates because they are riskier than large firms, thereby causing them to have higher average returns over long time periods; see Jonathan Berk, "Does Size Really Matter?" *Financial Analysts Journal,* 53, no. 5 (September/October 1997): 12–18; and "A Critique of Size-Related Anomalies," *Review of Financial Studies,* 8, no. 2 (Summer 1995): 275–286.

31. The missing variable apparently is not beta because the relationship between these variables and stock returns has been found to exist independent of differences in beta. See Fama and French, "The Cross-Section of Expected Stock Returns." Also see three papers by Fama and French: "Common Risk Factors in the Returns on Stocks and Bonds," *Journal of Financial Economics,* 33, no. 1 (February 1993): 3–56; "Size and Book-to-Market Factors in Earnings and Returns," *Journal of Finance,* 50, no. 1 (March 1995): 131–155; and "Multifactor Explanations of Asset Pricing Anomalies," *Journal of Finance,* 51, no. 1 (March 1996): 55–84.

32. Reinganum, "Misspecification of Capital Asset Pricing." Also see Rolf W. Banz and William J. Breen, "Sample Dependent Results Using Accounting and Market Data: Some Evidence," *Journal of Finance,* 41, no. 4 (September 1986): 779–793.

33. This view is not universally held. See Jeffrey Jaffe, Donald B. Keim, and Randolph Westerfield, "Earnings Yields, Market Values, and Stock Returns," *Journal of Finance,* 44, no. 1 (March 1989): 135–138; and Fama and French, "Multifactor Explanations of Asset Pricing Anomalies."

34. Fama and French, "The Cross-Section of Expected Stock Returns." Also see Peter J. Knez and Mark J. Ready, "On the Robustness of Size and Book-to-Market in Cross-Sectional Regressions," *Journal of Finance,* 52, no. 4 (September 1997): 1355–1382.

35. Investors who quickly sell their shares in order to capture this price spurt are known as "flippers." See Jay R. Ritter, "The Long-Run Performance of Initial Public Offerings," *Journal of Finance,* 46, no. 1 (March 1991): 3–27. Also, see Roger G. Ibbotson, Jody L. Sindelar, and Jay R. Ritter, "Initial Public Offerings," *Journal of Applied Corporate Finance,* 1, no. 2 (Summer 1988): 37–45. An interesting explanation for the initial underpricing is provided by Kevin Rock, "Why New Issues Are Underpriced," *Journal of Financial Economics,* 15, no. 1/2 (January/February 1986): 187–212.

36. Securities and Exchange Commission, *Report of Special Study on Security Markets,* 1973. Also see Roger G. Ibbotson, "Price Performance of Common Stock New Issues," *Journal of Financial Economics,* 2, no. 3 (September 1975): 235–272.

37. See Stewart C. Myers and Nicholas S. Majluf, "Corporate Financing and Investment Decisions When Firms Have Information That Investors Do Not Have," *Journal of Financial Economics,* 13, no. 2 (June 1984): 187–221; and Wayne H. Mikkelson and M. Megan Partch, "Valuation Effects of Security Offerings and the Issuance Process," *Journal of Financial Economics,* 15, no. 1/2 (January/February 1986): 31–60.

38. See Ronald W. Masulis and Ashok N. Korwar, "Seasoned Equity Offerings: An Empirical Investigation," *Journal of Financial Economics,* 15, no. 1/2 (January/February 1986): 91–118.

39. See Tim Loughran and Jay R. Ritter, "The New Issues Puzzle," *Journal of Finance,* 50, no. 1 (March 1995): 23–51. This study also looked at 4,753 IPOs and found that they too had significant negative abnormal returns during the five-year period after issuance. Also see D. Katherine Spiess and John Affleck-Graves, "Underperformance in Long-Run Stock Returns Following Seasoned Equity Offerings," *Journal of Financial Economics,* 38, no. 3 (July 1995): 243–267.

40. See Sanjai Bhagat, M. Wayne Marr, and G. Rodney Thompson, "The Rule 415 Experiment: Equity Markets," *Journal of Finance,* 40, no. 5 (December 1985): 1385–1401.

41. A later study has confirmed these findings. See Wayne H. Mikkelson and M. Megan Partch, "Stock Price Effects and Costs of Secondary Distributions," *Journal of Financial Economics,* 14, no. 2 (June 1985): 165–194.

42. See Fama and French, "Multifactor Explanations of Asset Pricing Anomalies." Another possible anomaly involves financial leverage because the stocks of firms with higher debt-to-equity ratios have had, on average, higher stock returns. See Laxmi Chand Bhandari, "Debt/Equity Ratio and Expected Common Stock Returns: Empirical Evidence," *Journal of Finance,* 43, no. 2 (June 1988): 507–528.

43. There is evidence that these anomalies also exist in other countries. See William F. Sharpe, Gordon J. Alexander, and Jeffery V. Bailey, *Investments* (Upper Saddle River, NJ: Prentice Hall, 1999), Appendix A to Chapter 16 for a summary. Also see Kiyoshi Kato and James S. Schallheim, "Seasonal and Size Anomalies in the Japanese Stock Market," *Journal of Financial and Quantitative Analysis,* 20, no. 2 (June 1985): 243–260; Yasushi Hamao, "Fifteen-Year Performance of Japanese Capital Markets," and Kiyoshi Kato, Sandra L. Schwartz, and William T. Ziemba, "Day of the Week Effects in Japanese Stocks," in Edwin J. Elton and Martin J. Gruber, (eds.), *Japanese Capital Markets* (New York: Ballinger, 1990), pp. 3–26 and 249–281, respectively; Mustafa N. Gultekin and N. Bulent Gultekin, "Stock Market Seasonality: International Evidence," *Journal of Financial Economics,* 12, no. 4 (December 1983): 469–481; Jeffrey Jaffe and Randolph Westerfield, "Patterns in Japanese Common Stock Returns: Day of the Week and Turn of the Year Effects," *Journal of Financial and Quantitative Analysis,* 20, no. 2 (June 1985): 261–272 and "The Weekend Effect in Common Stock Returns: The International Evidence," *Journal of Finance,* 40, no. 2 (June 1985): 433–454; and Eric C. Chang, J. Michael Pinegar, and R. Ravichandron, "International Evidence on the Robustness of the Day-of-the-Week Effect," *Journal of Financial and Quantitative Analysis,* 28, no. 4 (December 1993): 497–513; Jeffrey F. Jaffe, Randolph Westerfield, and Christopher Ma, "A Twist on the Monday Effect in Stock Prices: Evidence from the U.S. and Foreign Stock Markets," *Journal of Banking and Finance,* 13, no. 4/5 (September 1989): 641–650.

44. There is also evidence of a "weather effect" in that NYSE stock returns appear to be related to the amount of cloud cover in New York City, as the average daily return was .13% when the cloud cover was 0% to 20% and .02% when the the cloud cover was 100%. This difference has been interpreted to mean that investor psychology influences asset prices.

See Edward M. Saunders, Jr., "Stock Prices and Wall Street Weather," *American Economic Review*, 83, no. 5 (December 1993): 1337–1345.

45. Michael S. Rozeff and William R. Kinney, Jr., "Capital Market Seasonality: The Case of Stock Returns," *Journal of Financial Economics*, 3, no. 4 (October 1976): 379–402. For an argument that the market does not have a January effect, see Jay R. Ritter and Navin Chopra, "Portfolio Rebalancing and the Turn-of-the-Year Effect," *Journal of Finance*, 44, no. 1 (March 1989): 149–166.

46. Interestingly, it seems that the returns during the first half of any month (including the last day of the previous month) are significantly higher than the returns during the second half of the month. See Robert A. Ariel, "A Monthly Effect in Stock Returns," *Journal of Financial Economics*, 18, no. 1 (March 1987): 161–174. Another study found this effect to be concentrated in the first three trading days (plus the last trading day of the previous month) and labeled it the **turn-of-the-month effect.** See Josef Lakonishok and Seymour Smidt, "Are Seasonal Anomalies Real? A Ninety-Year Perspective," *Review of Financial Studies*, 1, no. 4 (Winter 1988): 403–425.

47. Kenneth R. French, "Stock Returns and the Weekend Effect," *Journal of Financial Economics*, 8, no. 1 (March 1980): 55–69; and Michael R. Gibbons and Patrick Hess, "Day of the Week Effects and Asset Returns," *Journal of Business*, 54, no. 4 (October 1981): 579–596. Apparently the weekend effect was actually first discovered in the late 1920s. See Edwin D. Maberly, "Eureka! Eureka! Discovery of the Monday Effect Belongs to the Ancient Scribes," *Financial Analysts Journal*, 51, no. 5 (September/October 1995): 10–11. For an argument that this effect disappeared in the mid-1970s, see Robert A. Connolly, "An Examination of the Robustness of the Weekend Effect," *Journal of Financial and Quantitative Analysis*, 24, no. 2 (June 1989): 133–169. It has been observed that NYSE trading volume is lower on Monday than on any other day of the week, but trading by individuals is highest on Mondays (and thus institutional trading is much lower), and individuals tend to be net sellers on Monday. This is offered as a possible explanation for the day-of-the-week effect; see Josef Lakonishok and Edwin Maberly, "The Weekend Effect: Trading Patterns of Individual and Institutional Investors," *Journal of Finance*, 45, no. 1 (March 1990): 231–243.

48. Lawrence Harris, "How to Profit from Intradaily Stock Returns," *Journal of Portfolio Management*, 12, no. 2 (Winter 1986): 61–64; and "A Transaction Data Study of Weekly and Intradaily Patterns in Stock Returns," *Journal of Financial Economics*, 16, no. 1 (May 1986): 99–117.

49. This rise in stock prices at the end of the day seems to be caused primarily by a large price rise between the next-to-last and last trades; this observation appears to be widespread over firms and days of the week. See Lawrence Harris, "A Day-End Transaction Price Anomaly," *Journal of Financial and Quantitative Analysis*, 24, no. 1 (March 1989): 29–45.

50. Robert A. Ariel, "High Stock Returns before Holidays: Existence and Evidence on Possible Causes," *Journal of Finance*, 45, no. 5 (December 1990): 1611–1626. Also see Paul Brockman, "A Review and Analysis of the Holiday Effect," *Financial Markets, Institutions & Instruments*, 4, no. 5 (1995): 37–58. The holiday effect also exists in Japan and the United Kingdom. See Chan-Wang Kim and Jinwoo Park, "Holiday Effects and Stock Returns: Further Evidence," *Journal of Financial and Quantitative Analysis*, 29, no. 1 (March 1994): 145–157.

51. Donald B. Keim, "Size-related Anomalies and Stock Return Seasonality: Further Empirical Evidence," *Journal of Financial Economics*, 12, no. 1 (June 1983): 13–32.

52. Rogalski also finds that the anomalous price behavior of stocks in January occurs mostly in the first five trading days. Roll has observed that the largest daily differences in the returns between small firms and large firms occur during the last trading day of the year and the first four trading days of the year. Furthermore, eight of the subsequent ten trading days also have notably large differences in returns. See Richard Rogalski, "New Findings Regarding Day-of-the-Week Returns over Trading and Non-Trading Periods: A Note," *Journal of Finance*, 39, no. 5 (December 1984): 1603–1614; and Richard Roll, "Vas ist das?" *Journal of Portfolio Management*, 9, no. 2 (Winter 1983): 18–28.

53. See Roll, "Vas Ist Das?"; Edward A. Dyl, "Capital Gains Taxation and Year-End Stock Market Behavior," *Journal of Finance*, 32, no. 1 (March 1977): 165–175; Ben Branch, "A Tax Loss Trading Rule," *Journal of Business*, 50, no. 2 (April 1977): 198–207; Dan Givoly and Arie Ovadia, "Year-End Tax-Induced Sales and Stock Market Seasonality," *Journal of Finance*, 38, no. 1 (March 1983): 171–185; Marc R. Reinganum, "The Anomalous Stock Market Behavior of Small Firms in January: Empirical Tests for Tax-Loss Selling Effects," *Journal of Financial Economics*, 12, no. 1 (June 1983): 89–104; Josef Lakonishok and Seymour Smidt, "Capital Gain Taxation and Volume of Trading," *Journal of Finance*, 41, no. 4 (September 1986): 951–974; Jay R. Ritter, "The Buying and Selling Behavior of Individual Investors at the Turn of the Year," *Journal of Finance*, 43, no. 3 (July 1988): 701–717; Joseph P. Ogden, "Turn-of-Month Evaluations of Liquid Profits and Stock Returns: A Common Explana-

tion for the Monthly and January Effects," *Journal of Finance,* 45, no. 4 (September 1990): 1259–1272; and Greggory A. Brauer and Eric C. Chang, "Return Seasonality in Stocks and Their Underlying Assets: Tax-Loss Selling versus Information Explanations," *Review of Financial Studies,* 3, no. 2 (1990): 255–280.

54. See K. C. Chan, "Can Tax-Loss Selling Explain the January Seasonal in Stock Returns?" *Journal of Finance,* 41, no. 5 (December 1986): 1115–1128; Werner F. M. DeBondt and Richard Thaler, "Does the Stock Market Overreact?" *Journal of Finance,* 40, no. 3 (July 1985), 793–805; and "Further Evidence on Investor Over-reaction and Stock Market Seasonality," *Journal of Finance,* 42, no. 3 (July 1987): 557–581.

55. A similar observation has been made regarding Canada. See Angel Berges, John J. McConnell, and Gary G. Schlarbaum, "The Turn-of-the-Year in Canada," *Journal of Finance,* 39, no. 1 (March 1984): 185–192.

56. See Steven L. Jones, Winson Lee, and Rudolf Apenbrink, "New Evidence on the January Effect before Personal Income Taxes," *Journal of Finance,* 46, no. 5 (December 1991): 1909–1924.

57. Richard J. Rogalski and Seha M. Tinic, "The January Size Effect: Anomaly or Risk Mismeasurement?" *Fi-nancial Analysts Journal,* 42, no. 6 (November/December 1986): 63–70. See also Avner Arbel, "Generic Stocks: An Old Product in a New Package," *Journal of Portfolio Management,* 11, no. 4 (Summer 1985): 4–13; and K. C. Chan and Nai-fu Chen, "Structural and Return Characteristics of Small and Large Firms," *Journal of Finance,* 46, no. 4 (September 1991): 1467–1484.

58. These recommendations are based on studies that typically involved exchange-listed stocks. For Nasdaq stocks, Richard D. Fortin and O. Maurice Joy ("Buying and Selling OTC Stock: Fine-Tuning Your Trade Date," *AAII Journal,* 15, no. 3 [March 1993]: 8–10) recommend (1) buying just before and selling just after the end of the month, (2) buying on Tuesday and selling on Friday, and (3) buying within two days on either side of a holiday and avoiding selling during this period.

59. See Donald B. Keim, "Trading Patterns, Bid–Ask Spreads, and Estimated Security Returns: The Case of Common Stocks at Calendar Turning Points," *Journal of Financial Economics,* 25, no. 1 (November 1989): 75–97.

60. The appendix to Chapter 22 discusses regularities in the bond market.

Financial Analysis of Common Stocks

In a broad sense, financial analysis involves determining the levels of risk and expected return of individual financial assets as well as groups of financial assets. For example, financial analysis involves both individual common stocks, such as IBM, and groups of common stocks, such as the computer industry or, on an even larger basis, the stock market itself. An alternative definition of financial analysis is more pragmatic: the *Financial Analyst's Handbook*[1] defines the term **financial analyst** as synonymous with security analyst or investment analyst—"one who analyzes securities and makes recommendations thereon."[2] According to this definition, financial analysis is the activity of providing inputs to the portfolio management process. This chapter (as well as Chapters 15 and 16) takes such a view in discussing the financial analysis of common stocks. Chapter 17 discusses how financial analysis can be used by **portfolio managers,** also known as investment or money managers.

financial analyst

portfolio manager

14.1 Professional Organizations

Around the world, individuals who belong to one of 87 local societies (64 in the United States) of financial analysts automatically belong to a national organization known as the Association for Investment Management and Research (AIMR). The local societies offer members the opportunity to meet as a group with corporate management, consultants, portfolio managers, and academics to discuss issues of relevance to the investment management business.

The AIMR organization acts as an advocate for the financial analyst profession, presenting unified positions before regulators and Congress. It also hosts conferences and workshops designed to enhance the investment knowledge of its members. In addition, AIMR publishes the *Financial Analysts Journal,* a major source of information on basic research conducted by analysts and by members of the academic community. In 1999 there were more than 36,000 members of AIMR.

In 1962 the Institute of Chartered Financial Analysts (ICFA) was formed by the Financial Analysts Federation (the precursor to AIMR) to award the professional designation of Chartered Financial Analyst (CFA). In 1999 more than 26,000 analysts (more than 70% of the AIMR membership) held the CFA designation. The CFA program is designed to establish a common set of investment knowledge and ethical standards for the various types of investment professionals. The ICFA attempts to accomplish the first objective by requiring that prospective CFAs pass three exams and attain several years of investment experience. It attempts to achieve the second objective by disseminating and enforcing a set of professional conduct guidelines. (The CFA program is discussed further in this chapter's Money Matters box.[3])

The Chartered Financial Analyst Program

 The investment profession encompasses a wide range of activities. Investment bankers, brokers, portfolio managers, traders, security analysts, salespeople, consultants, and pension fund administrators all fall under the rubric of investment professionals. These individuals, and the organizations for which they work, directly or indirectly affect the financial well-being of millions of people.

The Chartered Financial Analyst (CFA) program was born of a need to bring a common set of investment management concepts and standards of professional conduct to the diverse membership of the investment industry. From its modest beginnings in 1963, when 268 professionals were effectively "grandfathered" as chartered members, the CFA program has grown to a worldwide organization, with more than 26,000 CFA charters awarded and more than 70,000 candidates expected to take one of the CFA exams in 2000. Although the CFA charter is not a prerequisite for employment in the investment industry, many organizations are encouraging or even requiring new employees to participate in the CFA program.

From its inception, the Institute of Chartered Financial Analysts (ICFA), which administers the CFA program, has pursued three explicit objectives:

1. To compile a comprehensive set of currently accepted concepts and techniques relevant to the investment decision-making process (the CFA "Body of Knowledge")
2. To establish a uniform set of ethical standards to guide the activities of investment professionals
3. To ensure that CFA charter holders have demonstrated satisfactory understanding of the Body of Knowledge and that they adhere to the established ethical standards

Of course, like any other professional certification organization, the ICFA has multiple motives for promoting the CFA designation. By setting difficult hurdles for prospective members to clear, the CFA certification process enhances the monetary value of the charter to existing holders. Further, by demonstrating a responsible and comprehensive education and ethics program, the ICFA helps the investment industry ward off onerous government regulation and provides the industry with wide latitude to police itself.

To enroll in the CFA program, an individual must hold a bachelor's degree (or equivalent work experience), provide three acceptable character references, and pay the required registration fee. Once accepted into the program, to earn the CFA designation a candidate must (1) pass three exams; (2) possess three years of investment-related work experience; (3) be a member of (or have applied to) a constituent financial analyst society; (4) demonstrate a high level of professional conduct; and (5) abide by the Code of Ethics and Standards of Practice of the Association for Investment Management and Research.

The CFA course of study and examinations are the cornerstone of the CFA certification process. Candidates must pass three six-hour exams. The ICFA administers these exams once a year in June at over 100 locations around the world but primarily in the United States and Canada. Because candidates may take only one exam per year, a minimum of three years is required to complete the examination sequence.

The ICFA specifies review materials and assigned readings for candidates to use in preparation for the exams. The study program has evolved over the years as new concepts have been introduced into the exams. The ICFA estimates that candidates average 200 hours per exam in individual study time. Many candidates also participate in independently sponsored study groups.

The CFA examinations are designed in a progressive format. The exam levels become increasingly comprehensive, building on previous levels. The exams are divided into four major subject areas and several subtopics within each major subject:

1. Ethical and Professional Standards
   a. Applicable laws and regulations
   b. Professional standards of practice
   c. Ethical conduct and professional obligations
   d. International ethical and professional considerations

2. Tools for Inputs for Investment Valuation and Management
   a. Quantitative methods and statistics
   b. Macroeconomics
   c. Microeconomics
   d. Financial statements and accounting

3. Investment (Asset) Evaluation
   a. Overview of the valuation process
   b. Applying economic analysis in investment valuation
   c. Applying industry analysis in investment valuation
   d. Applying company analysis in investment valuation
   e. Equity securities
   f. Fixed-income securities
   g. Other investments
   h. Derivative securities

4. Portfolio Management
   a. Capital market theory
   b. Portfolio policies
   c. Expectational factors
   d. Asset allocation
   e. Fixed-income portfolio management
   f. Equity portfolio management
   g. Real estate portfolio management
   h. Specialized asset portfolio management
   i. Implementing the investment process
   j. Performance measurement

The CFA exams are rigorous and difficult. Many candidates fail at least one exam, although exams can be retaken. In 1998, more than 38,000 candidates sat for the exams. The pass rate was approximately 50% for each of the three exams.

The CFA program has experienced tremendous growth. The number of candidates sitting for the exams has increased more than 15-fold since 1980. Given this past success, where does the CFA program go from here?

Clearly, the ICFA wants to continue to enhance the prestige and uniqueness of its CFA certification. In recent years, however, the ICFA has also begun to strongly emphasize the continuing education aspect of its mission. Technological obsolescence is a serious problem in the rapidly changing investment industry. (For example, organized financial futures markets—see Chapter 25—did not even exist in 1980.) Many professionals who received the CFA designation just a decade ago might find it difficult to pass an exam now. Current charter holders are encouraged (although not yet required) to participate in a self-administered continuing education program. Further, to enhance the investment knowledge of its membership, the ICFA publishes conference proceedings and research monographs covering a wide range of topics.

The ICFA also sees a role for itself globally. With the investment industry becoming increasingly international in scope, the ICFA has moved to administer its program abroad. (One-third of the current CFA candidates reside outside of the United States.) It has also begun to join forces with analyst societies in other countries to develop means of jointly recognizing one another's certification programs. In fact, the CFA program has become the de facto global standard for investment education.

14.2 Reasons for Financial Analysis

There are two primary reasons for engaging in financial analysis. The first is to try to determine certain characteristics of securities. The second is to attempt to identify mispriced securities.[4]

14.2.1 DETERMINING SECURITY CHARACTERISTICS

According to capital market theory, a financial analyst should estimate a security's future sensitivity to major factors and unique risk to determine the risk (measured by standard deviation) of a portfolio. Perhaps the analyst will also want to estimate the dividend yield of a security during the next year to determine its suitability for portfolios in which dividend yield is relevant. Careful analysis of such matters as a company's dividend policy and likely future earnings and cash flows may lead to better estimates than can be obtained by simply extrapolating last year's values.

In many cases it is useful to know something about the sources of a security's risk and return. If a portfolio is managed for a person in the oil business, one might want to minimize the sensitivity of the portfolio's return to changes in oil prices because it is likely that if oil prices decline, the person's income from the oil business will also decline. If the portfolio were sensitive to oil prices (which would be the case if it contained a substantial investment in securities of businesses directly or indirectly involved in the energy sector), then it too would decline, furthering the deterioration of the person's financial position.[5]

fundamental analysis

14.2.2 ATTEMPTING TO IDENTIFY MISPRICED SECURITIES

The search for mispriced securities typically involves the use of **fundamental analysis.** This process entails identifying situations in which the financial analyst's estimates of such things as a firm's future earnings and dividends:

1. Differ substantially from consensus (that is, average) estimates of others
2. Are viewed as being closer to the correct values than the consensus estimates
3. Are not yet currently reflected in the market price of the firm's securities

Two different approaches may be taken in the search for mispriced securities using fundamental analysis. The first approach involves valuation, wherein the "intrinsic" or "true" value of a security is determined by discounting the cash flows the investor expects to receive from owning the asset (see Chapter 15). After this determination has been made, the intrinsic value is compared with the security's current market price. If the market price is substantially greater than the intrinsic value, then the security is *overpriced* or *overvalued.* If the market price is substantially less than the intrinsic value, then the security is *underpriced* or *undervalued.* Instead of comparing price with value, the analyst sometimes estimates a security's expected return over a specified period given its current market price and intrinsic value. This estimate is then compared with the "normal" or "fair" return for securities with similar attributes.

A security's intrinsic value may be determined in great detail using estimates of all major factors that influence security returns (for example, gross domestic product of the economy, industry sales, firm sales and expenses, and capitalization rates). Shortcuts may be taken whereby, for example, an estimate of earnings per share is multiplied by a "justified" or "normal" P/E ratio to determine the intrinsic value of a share of common stock. (See Chapter 15. To avoid complications arising when seeking the intrinsic value of a stock that has negative earnings per share, some analysts estimate sales or cash flow per share and multiply this figure by a "normal" price-sales or price-cash flow ratio.)

A second approach involves estimating only one or two financial variables and comparing these estimates directly with consensus estimates. For example, next year's earnings per share for a stock may be estimated. If the analyst's estimate substantially exceeds the consensus of other analysts' estimates, the stock may be an attractive investment because the analyst expects the actual earnings to provide a pleasant surprise for the market when announced. At that time, the stock's price is expected to increase, resulting in the investor's receiving a greater-than-normal return. Conversely, when an analyst's estimate of earnings per share is substantially below that of the other analysts, the analyst expects the market to receive an unpleasant surprise. The resulting decrease in the stock's price will lead to a smaller-than-normal return.

At an aggregate level, an analyst may be more optimistic about the economy than the consensus of other analysts. This view would suggest that a larger-than-normal investment in stocks be taken, offset perhaps by a smaller-than-normal investment in fixed-income securities. Conversely, a relatively pessimistic view would suggest a smaller-than-normal investment in stocks, offset perhaps by a larger-than-normal investment in fixed-income securities. The analyst might agree with the consensus view on both the economy and the individual characteristics of specific securities but feel that the consensus view of the prospects for a certain group of securities in a particular industry is in error. In this case, a larger-than-normal investment may be made in stocks from an industry that the analyst thinks has strong prospects. Conversely, a smaller-than-normal investment would be made in stocks from an industry that the analyst thinks has weak prospects.

The use of fundamental analysis to identify mispriced common stocks and fixed-income securities was briefly introduced in Chapter 1. This chapter discusses the subject in detail and, after introducing the method of technical analysis, compares the two methods of analysis. A strong warning should be conveyed at this point. Whenever the analyst feels a mispriced security has been identified, he or she should recognize that it is possible the security is correctly priced and that something has been overlooked in the analysis. Indeed, in an efficient market (see Chapter 4), this is precisely what will have happened.

14.2.3 CONVEYING ADVICE ON BEATING THE MARKET

Many books and articles have been written that allegedly explain how financial analysis can be used to "beat the market," meaning that they purport to show how to make abnormally high returns by investing in the stock market. It is interesting to ponder whether the advice will still be useful after becoming public. It seems logical that any such prescription in print for long is unlikely to allow the investor to continue to beat the market consistently. Just because someone *asserts* that an approach worked in the past does not mean, in fact, that it has worked. Moreover, even if it did work in the past, as more and more investors apply it, prices will be driven to levels at which the approach will not work in the future. Any system designed to beat the market, once known to more than a few people, carries the seeds of its own destruction.

There are two reasons for not including advice on "guaranteed" ways to beat the market in this book. First, to do so would make a successful system public and hence unsuccessful. Second, the authors know of no such system. Some apparent anomalies and possible inefficiencies have been described previously. But any book that purports to open the door to the *certainty* of making abnormally high returns for those who follow its advice should be regarded with the greatest skepticism.

This assertion does not mean that financial analysis is useless. Although individuals should be skeptical when others tell them how to use financial analysis to *beat* the market, individuals can try to *understand* the market using financial analysis.

14.2.4 FINANCIAL ANALYSIS AND MARKET EFFICIENCY

The concept of an efficient market (discussed in Chapter 4) may seem to be based on a paradox. Financial analysts carefully evaluate the prospects for companies, industries, and the economy in the search for mispriced securities. If an undervalued security is found, then it will be purchased. However, the act of purchasing the security tends to push its price up toward its intrinsic value, thereby making it no longer undervalued. Consequently, financial analysis tends to result in security prices that reflect intrinsic values, and hence it tends to make markets efficient. But if this is the case, why would anyone perform financial analysis in an attempt to identify mispriced securities?

There are two responses to that question. First, because there are costs associated with performing financial analysis, financial analysis is not conducted on all securities all the time. As a result, not all the prices of all securities reflect intrinsic values all the time. Pockets of opportunity may arise from time to time leading to the possibility of added benefits from financial analysis. The implication is that investors should engage in financial analysis only to the point where the added benefits cover the added costs.[6] Ultimately, in a highly competitive market, prices would be close enough to intrinsic values to make it worthwhile for only the most skillful analysts to search for mispriced securities because the market would be nearly, but not perfectly, efficient. Skilled investors can earn abnormally high gross returns, but after the costs of gathering and processing information and making the requisite trades are taken into consideration, their net return will not be abnormal.[7]

The other response to the question focuses on the first reason given earlier for engaging in financial analysis: to determine relevant characteristics of securities. This reason is appropriate even in a perfectly efficient market. Because investors differ in their circumstances (consider the person in the oil business), portfolios should be tailored to accommodate such differences. Success in this task generally requires estimation of certain securities' characteristics, thereby justifying the use of financial analysis.

14.2.5   NEEDED SKILLS

To understand and estimate the risk and return of individual securities as well as groups of securities (such as industries), one must understand financial markets and the principles of valuation. Much of the material required for this understanding is in this book. However, even more is required. Future prospects must be estimated and interrelationships assessed. This process requires the skills of an economist and an understanding of industrial organization. Some command of quantitative methods is needed, along with an understanding of the nuances of accounting to process relevant historical data.

This book cannot provide all the material needed to become a successful financial analyst. Knowledge of accounting, economics, industrial organization, and quantitative methods also is required. Instead, some techniques used by financial analysts are discussed, along with some of the pitfalls involved. In addition, sources of investment information are presented.

14.3   Technical Analysis

technical analysis

One of the major divisions among financial analysts is between those using fundamental analysis (known as fundamental analysts or fundamentalists) and those using **technical analysis** (known as technical analysts or technicians). The fundamentalist looks forward; the technician backward. The fundamentalist is concerned with future earnings and dividends, whereas the technician thinks little (if at all) about such matters.

> Technical analysis is the study of the internal stock exchange information as such. The word "technical" implies a study of the market itself and not of those external factors which are reflected in the market. . . . [A]ll the relevant factors, whatever they may be, can be reduced to the volume of the stock exchange transactions and the level of share prices; or more generally, to the sum of the statistical information produced by the market.[8]

Technicians usually attempt to predict short-term price movements and make recommendations concerning the *timing* of purchases and sales of either specific stocks, groups of stocks (such as industries), or stocks in general. It is sometimes said that fundamental analysis is designed to answer the question *what* and technical analysis to answer the question *when*.

The concept of technical analysis is completely at odds with the notion of efficient markets:

> The methodology of technical analysis . . . rests upon the assumption that history tends to repeat itself in the stock exchange. If a certain pattern of activity has in the past produced certain results nine times out of ten, one can assume a strong likelihood of the same outcome whenever this pattern appears in the future. *It should be emphasized, however, that a large part of the methodology of technical analysis lacks a strictly logical explanation.*[9] (Emphasis added.)

Technicians assert that the study of past patterns of variables such as prices and volumes allows investors to accurately identify times when specific stocks (or groups of stocks, or the market in general) are either overpriced or underpriced. Most (but not all) technical analysts rely on charts of stock prices and trading volumes. The appendix describes some of the more frequently used tools.

Early studies found little evidence showing that technical analysis was useful in enabling investors to "beat the market."[10] Many "proofs" of the ability of technical analysis to beat the market were offered, but most committed serious analytical errors that invalidated their results. However, several more recent studies have indicated that technical analysis may be useful to investors.[11] The evidence presented in these studies can be divided into two groups based on the strategies involved. The first group, consisting of momentum and contrarian strategies, simply examines the returns on stocks during a recent time period to identify candidates for purchase and sale. The second group, consisting of moving average and trading range breakout strategies, is based on the relationship of a security's price during a relatively short but recent time period to its price over a longer time period.

14.3.1 MOMENTUM AND CONTRARIAN STRATEGIES

Consider ranking a group of stocks on the basis of the size of their returns during some time period that just ended. *Momentum investors* seek stocks that have recently risen significantly in price. They believe that these stocks will continue to rise because of an upward shift in their demand curves. Conversely, those stocks that have recently fallen significantly in price are sold on the belief that their demand curves have shifted downward.

Investors who call themselves *contrarians* do just the opposite of what most other investors are doing in the market: They buy stocks that others have shunned and think of as losers, and they sell stocks that others have feverishly pursued and think of as winners. They believe investors tend to overreact to news. That is, stocks that have plunged in price because of some recent piece of bad news (such as weak earnings) are thought to have fallen too far in price. Hence such stocks are viewed as being ready for a price rebound as investors realize that they overreacted to the bad news and subsequently drive the price upward toward the stock's fundamental value. Similarly, stocks that have risen rapidly in price because of good news (such as strong earnings) are thought to have risen too far in price. Hence such stocks are viewed as being ready for a price drop as investors realize that they overreacted to the good news and subsequently drive the price downward toward the stock's fundamental value. Researchers have tested strategies of this type. Their overall test design is discussed next, followed by the results.

The Test Design

Consider the following investment strategy:

1. Identify those stocks listed on either the NYSE or National Market Issues of Nasdaq. This step focuses the technician's attention on established stocks.
2. Rank these stocks based on the size of their returns over a just-ended time period, referred to as the portfolio "formation period."
3. Assign some of the stocks with the lowest average return in the formation period to the "loser" portfolio and some of the stocks that have the highest average return in this period to the "winner" portfolio.
4. Determine the returns on the winner and loser portfolios over a just-started subsequent time period, the portfolio "test period."
5. Repeat the analysis, starting with step 1, but moving forward one time period. Stop after several repetitions.
6. Determine the abnormal returns on the winner portfolio by subtracting the returns on a benchmark portfolio having a comparable level of risk (see Chapter 18); calculate the average of these abnormal returns. Similarly, determine the average abnormal returns on the loser portfolio.

If a momentum strategy works, then the winner portfolio should have a significantly positive average abnormal return and the loser portfolio a significantly negative one. Conversely, if a contrarian strategy works, then the loser portfolio should have a significantly positive abnormal return and the winner portfolio a significantly negative one. However, if stocks are priced efficiently, then their past price behavior is useless in terms of its predictive value. Neither momentum nor contrarian strategies should "work"; winner portfolios should perform no differently than loser portfolios. Both portfolios should have average abnormal returns of approximately zero.

Test Results

Table 14.1 presents the test results of various momentum and contrarian strategies. In part (a), portfolios were formed on the basis of their returns during the past week. All stocks with an above-average return were put into a winner portfolio and those with a below-average return were put into a loser portfolio. The returns on these two portfolios were then tracked for the next week. When this process was repeated week by week, marked differences were found in the annualized average abnormal returns on the two portfolios. Specifically, the returns were nearly −25% for the winners and +90% for the losers, with both returns (as well as the other returns in the table) being, statistically speaking, significantly different from zero. A similar but not as extreme observation is apparent in part (b), where the time frame is one month instead of a week.[12] Overall, this evidence indicates that short-term contrarian strategies hold promise. Interestingly, the correction for the overreaction is asymmetric in part (a) because the losers rebound by a much larger percentage than the winners fall. Perhaps contrarians should concentrate on identifying losers than on identifying winners if they are going to focus on weekly returns.

In part (c) of Table 14.1, portfolios were formed on the basis of their returns during the past six months. The 10% of stocks with the highest returns were put in the winner portfolio, whereas the 10% with the lowest returns were put in the loser portfolio. Tracking their returns during the next six months revealed that the winners had

TABLE 14.1   Returns from Momentum and Contrarian Strategies

	Annualized Abnormal Returns	
Length of Portfolio Formation and Test Period	*Winner Portfolio*	*Loser Portfolio*
(a) Weekly		
Top 50% and bottom 50% of NYSE and AMEX stocks	−24.9%	89.8%
(b) Monthly		
Top 10% and bottom 10% of all NYSE and AMEX stocks	−11.6	12.1
(c) Semiannually		
Top 10% and bottom 10% of all NYSE and AMEX stocks	8.7	−3.5
(d) Annually		
Top 10% and bottom 10% of all NYSE and AMEX stocks[a]	5.0	−16.1
(e) Three years		
Top 35 and bottom 35 NYSE stocks	−1.7	6.5
(f) Five years		
Top 50 and bottom 50 NYSE stocks	−12.4	7.2

[a]Abnormal returns were measured during one month subsequent to the portfolio formation date.

Sources: Adapted from (a) Bruce N. Lehmann, "Fads, Martingales, and Market Efficiency," *Quarterly Journal of Economics,* 105, no. 1 (February 1990): 16. (b, d) Narasimhan Jegadeesh, "Evidence of Predictable Behavior of Security Returns," *Journal of Finance,* 45, no. 3 (July 1990): 890–891. (c) Narasimhan Jegadeesh and Sheridan Titman, "Returns to Buying Winners and Selling Losers: Implications for Stock Market Efficiency," *Journal of Finance,* 48, no. 1 (March 1993): 79. (e) Werner F. M. De Bondt and Richard Thaler, "Does the Stock Market Overreact?" *Journal of Finance,* 40, no. 3 (July 1985): 799. (f) Werner F. M. De Bondt and Richard Thaler, "Further Evidence on Investor Overreaction and Stock Market Seasonality," *Journal of Finance,* 42, no. 3 (July 1987): 561.

significantly positive abnormal returns and the losers had significantly negative abnormal returns. This result, which is in complete contrast to parts (a) and (b), suggests that momentum strategies have promise. Stocks that shot up in price during six months continued to rise during the next six months, whereas those that plunged during six months continued their fall. Although not quite as strong, similar results were observed when the top 10% and bottom 10% were identified on the basis of a full year's returns, as shown in part (d).[13]

Oddly, parts (e) and (f) show that the momentum strategy would not work if the winner and loser portfolios were formed on the basis of three-year stock returns. Instead, the contrarian strategy appears to have worked once again, as the average annual abnormal return on the loser portfolio was +6.5%, and the average annual abnormal return on the winner portfolio was −1.7%. Part (f) shows that similar results were obtained when portfolios were formed on the basis of returns during the previous five years.[14] As in part (a), the correction for the overreaction is asymmetric in that losers rebound by a much larger percentage than winners fall.

In summary, there does appear to be some merit to the contrarian strategy for both very short (a week or a month) and very long (three or five years) time periods.[15] Surprisingly, for intermediate periods such as six months and one year, an exact opposite strategy—momentum—seems to have merit. Unfortunately, both strategies involve a high degree of turnover because portfolios are reconstituted frequently—particularly for the weekly contrarian strategy.[16] The strategies would incur substantial transaction costs, so it remains to be seen whether they would be profitable after such costs were fully accounted for.

14.3.2 MOVING AVERAGE AND TRADING RANGE BREAKOUT STRATEGIES

Consider the following investment strategy:

1. Calculate the average closing price of a given stock during the past 200 trading days.
2. Take today's closing price and divide it by the 200-day average to form a short-to-long price ratio.
3. A ratio greater than 1 is a buy signal that indicates the stock is to be bought tomorrow. A ratio less than 1 is a sell signal that indicates the stock is to be sold tomorrow.
4. Tomorrow after closing, repeat the process.
5. At the end of a test period, calculate the average daily return during both the "buy" and "sell" days.

If the stock market is efficient, the average return during the buy days should be approximately the same as the average return during the sell days. That is, the difference in their returns should be approximately zero. However, technical analysis might have merit if they are significantly different.

A study examined this strategy using more than 25,000 trading days. The daily closing level of the Dow Jones Industrial Average (DJIA) was used instead of daily closing prices for individual stocks. As shown at the top of part (a) of Table 14.2, this strategy resulted in markedly different returns on buy and sell days. In particular, the annualized average return on buy days was 10.7%, whereas the return on sell days was −6.1%. The difference of 16.8% was, statistically speaking, significantly different from zero (as were the differences shown in the other parts of the table).

Because this strategy classifies every day as either a buy day or a sell day, thereby allowing a given stock to be bought on consecutive days, it is referred to as a variable-length moving average strategy. However, it can result in many trades during a year because an investor using it could be "whipsawed" into buying and selling repeatedly. The frequency of changing positions from buying to selling, or from selling to buying, can be reduced by modifying the strategy to make it a fixed-length moving average strategy. Buy signals would then be generated only when the ratio *changes* from less than 1 to greater than 1, and sell signals would be generated only when the ratio *changes* from greater than 1 to less than 1. Furthermore, when a buy signal is generated, the stock is

TABLE 14.2 Returns from Moving Average and Trading Range Breakout Strategies

	Annualized Average Returns		
	Buy Signal	*Sell Signal*	*Buy Return Less Sell Return*
(a) Moving average tests			
Variable length	10.7%	−6.1%	16.8%
Fixed length	13.8	−4.8	18.6
(b) Trading range breakout tests	11.8	−5.8	17.6

Source: Adapted from William Brock, Josef Lakonishok, and Blake LeBaron, "Simple Technical Trading Rules and the Stochastic Properties of Stock Returns," *Journal of Finance,* 47, no. 5 (December 1992): 1739, 1741, 1742. Based on 1-day short and 200-day long periods with no filter; annualized assuming that there are 260 trading days in a year and 26 ten-day trading periods in a year.

bought the next day and held for ten days. Similarly, when a sell signal is generated, the stock is sold and not bought for ten days. In either case, when the ten days are over, the investor starts looking again for a buy or a sell signal.

Part (a) of Table 14.2 shows that the fixed-length moving average strategy performed similarly to the variable-length one. The annualized average return on buy days was 13.8%, and on sell days it was −4.8%, resulting in a statistically significant difference of 18.6%.

The trading range breakout strategy is similar to the fixed-length moving average strategy. The high and low prices during the past 200 trading days are noted. A buy signal is generated on a given day only when that day's closing price is greater than the high, provided that the previous day's closing price was less than the high. Conversely, a sell signal arises when the closing price moves from above the low on one day to below the low on the next day. When a buy signal is generated, the stock is purchased the next day and held for ten days. Similarly, when a sell signal is generated, the stock is sold and not bought for ten days. In either case, when the ten days are over, the investor starts looking again for a buy or a sell signal.

Part (b) of Table 14.2 shows that the trading range breakout strategy performed similarly to the two moving average strategies. The annualized average returns on buy days was 11.8%, and on sell days it was −5.8%, with a significant difference of 17.6%.

14.3.3 THE BOTTOM LINE

What is the bottom line? The four strategies reported in Tables 14.1 and 14.2 have been rigorously tested to avoid procedural pitfalls that have tainted the results of many studies. Although not reported, slight variations among the strategies had only minor effects on their results. However, the usefulness of such technical strategies remains a subject for debate. Although the strategies seem to be profitable, even after transaction costs have been considered, it is possible that a more complete accounting of these costs (including the impact of bid–ask spreads) will reveal that the strategies are incapable of generating abnormal profits. Hence evaluating investment systems will not always provide unambiguous answers to their potential usefulness. In addition, it has been speculated that the commonplace usage of computerized trading programs designed to implement technical strategies will ultimately eliminate any potential such strategies have for generating abnormal profits.[17] Nevertheless, the apparent success of these strategies offers a challenge to those who contend the U.S. stock market is highly efficient.

14.4 Fundamental Analysis

The rest of this chapter is concerned with the principles of fundamental analysis of common stocks. Although technical analysis is used by many investors, fundamental analysis is far more prevalent. Furthermore, unlike technical analysis, it is an essential activity if capital markets are to be efficient.

14.4.1 TOP-DOWN VERSUS BOTTOM-UP FORECASTING

Fundamental analysts forecast, among other things, future levels of the economy's gross domestic product, future sales and earnings for a large number of industries, and future sales and earnings for a larger number of firms. Eventually such forecasts are converted to estimates of expected returns of specific stocks and, perhaps, certain industries and the stock market itself. In some cases the conversion is explicit. For example, an estimate of next year's earnings per share for a firm may be multiplied by a projected price-earnings ratio in order to estimate the expected price of the firm's stock in one year. Or an estimate of future dividends may be supplied to a dividend discount model. Both approaches allow the analyst to make a direct forecast of the stock's expected return. In other cases the conversion is implicit. For example, stocks with projected earnings substantially exceeding consensus estimates may be placed on an "approved" list.

**top-down
forecasting**

Some investment organizations that use financial analysts follow a sequential **top-down forecasting** approach. With this approach, the financial analysts are first involved in making forecasts for the economy, then for industries, and finally for companies. The industry forecasts are based on the forecasts for the economy and, in turn, a company's forecasts are based on the forecasts for both its industry and the economy.

**bottom-up
forecasting**

Other investment organizations begin with estimates of the prospects for companies and then build to estimates of the prospects for industries and ultimately the economy. Such **bottom-up forecasting** may unknowingly involve inconsistent assumptions. For example, one analyst may use one forecast of foreign exchange rates in projecting the foreign sales of company *A*, while another analyst may use a different forecast in projecting the foreign sales of company *B*. Top-down systems are less susceptible to this danger because all the analysts in the organization use the same forecast of exchange rates.

In practice, a combination of the two approaches is often used. For example, forecasts are made for the economy in a top-down manner. These forecasts then provide a setting within which financial analysts make bottom-up forecasts for individual companies. The sum of the individual forecasts should be consistent with the original economy-wide forecast.[18] If it is not, the process is repeated (perhaps with additional controls) to ensure consistency.

14.4.2 PROBABILISTIC FORECASTING

**probabilistic
forecasting**

Explicit **probabilistic forecasting** often focuses on economy-wide forecasts because uncertainty at this level is important in determining the risk and expected return of a well-diversified portfolio. Several alternative economic scenarios may be forecast, along with their respective probability of occurrence. Accompanying projections are made of the prospects for industries, companies, and stock prices. Such an exercise provides an idea of the likely sensitivities of different stocks to surprises concerning the economy and hence is sometimes referred to as "what-if" analysis. Risks may also be estimated by assigning probabilities to the different scenarios.

14.4.3 ECONOMETRIC MODELS

**econometric model
endogenous
variables
exogenous
variables**

An **econometric model** is a statistical model used to forecast the levels of certain variables, known as **endogenous variables.** In order to make these forecasts, the model relies on assumptions that have been made concerning the levels of certain other variables supplied by the model user, known as **exogenous variables.** For example, the level of next year's car sales may be specified by an econometric model to be related to next year's level of gross domestic product and interest rates. The values of next year's gross domestic product and interest rates, the exogenous variables, must be provided in order to forecast next year's car sales, the endogenous variable.

An econometric model may be extremely complex or it may be a simple formula that can be implemented with a calculator. In either case, it should involve a blend of economics and statistics, where first economics is used to suggest the forms of relevant relationships and then statistical procedures are applied to historical data to estimate the exact nature of the relationships involved.

Some investment organizations use large-scale econometric models to translate predictions about such factors as the federal budget, expected consumer spending, and planned business investment into predictions of future levels of gross domestic product, inflation, and unemployment. Several firms and nonprofit organizations maintain such models, selling either the forecasts or the computer program itself to investment organizations, corporate planners, public agencies, and others.

The developers of such large-scale models usually provide several "standard" predictions, based on different sets of assumptions about the exogenous variables. Some also assign probabilities to the alternative predictions. In some cases, users can substitute their own assumptions and subsequently examine the resulting predictions.

Large-scale econometric models of this type employ many equations that describe many important relationships. Although estimates of the magnitudes of such relationships are obtained from historical data, these estimates may or may not enable the model to work well in the future. When predictions are poor, it is sometimes said that there has been a structural change in the underlying economic relationships. However, the failure may result from the influence of factors omitted from the model. Either situation necessitates changes in either the magnitudes of the estimates or the basic form of the econometric model, or both. Rare indeed is the user who does not "fine-tune" (or completely overhaul) such a model from time to time as further experience is accumulated.

14.5 Financial Statement Analysis

For some, the image of a typical financial analyst is that of a gnome, fully equipped with green eyeshade, poring over financial statements in a back room. The physical description is rarely accurate, but many analysts do carefully study financial statements in an attempt to predict the future.

A company's financial statements can be regarded as the output of a model of the firm—a model designed by management, the company's accountants, and (indirectly) the tax authorities. Different companies use different models; they treat similar events in different ways because generally accepted accounting principles (GAAP) allow a certain degree of latitude in how to account for various events. Examples include the method of depreciating assets (straight-line or accelerated) and the method of valuing inventory (FIFO or LIFO).

To fully understand a company and to compare it with others that use different accounting procedures, the financial analyst must be a financial detective, looking for clues in footnotes and the accompanying text that discuss how the financial statements were prepared. Those who take bottom-line figures such as earnings per share on faith may be more surprised by future developments than those who try to look behind the accounting veil.

The ultimate goal of fundamental analysis is to determine the values of the outstanding claims on a firm's income (claimants include the firm's bondholders and stockholders). The firm's income must be projected, and then the possible distributions of that income among the claimants must be considered, with relevant probabilities assessed.

In practice, shortcut procedures are often used. Many analysts focus on reported accounting figures, even though such numbers may not adequately reflect true economic values. In addition, simple measures are often used to assess complex relationships. For example, some analysts attempt to estimate the probability that short-term creditors will be paid in full and on time by examining the ratio of liquid assets to the amount of short-term debt (known as the *quick ratio*). Similarly, the probability that interest will be paid to bondholders in a timely fashion may be estimated by examining the ratio of earnings before interest and taxes to the periodic amount of such interest payments (known as *times interest earned*). Often the value of a firm's common stock is estimated by examining the ratio of earnings after taxes to the book value of equity (known as *return on equity*).

Financial statement analysis can help an analyst understand a company's current situation, where it may be going, what factors affect it, and how these factors affect it. If such analysis is done well by others, it will be difficult for the analyst to find mispriced securities. However, it should be possible to identify firms likely to go bankrupt, firms with high or low betas, and firms with greater or lesser sensitivities to major factors. Increased understanding of such aspects provides ample rewards.

Analysts who regularly work with financial statements develop a keen sense of what items are important to their research. Those items vary depending on the type of security being examined (for example, the common stock of a company or its debt securities). Furthermore, the list of critical items varies from industry to industry and from company to company. Moreover, one analyst may approach the analysis of a particular company's financial statements differently than another analyst. Despite these differences, certain standard techniques are commonly applied and are discussed next. Understanding the analysis of financial statements is facilitated by applying the process to a specific example. In the following discussion, general steps and observations are presented with reference to Target Corporation, a large retailing company whose stock is both listed on the NYSE and is a constituent of the S&P 500.

14.5.1 COMPANY BACKGROUND

The analysis of a company's financial statements in a security analyst's research report typically begins with an overview of the company. Although the reporting analyst presumably knows the company well, the overview acquaints investors with the company. This discussion may include a short corporate history, a description of the company's lines of business, a listing of its primary competitors, a description of the key business challenges facing the company, a discussion of the quality of current management, and a summary of basic financial information.

Target Corporation

Target Corporation, formerly called Dayton Hudson Corporation, is one of the largest general merchandise retailers in the United States. The company has its roots in the department store business, even though today the vast majority of its sales and profits are derived from discount retailing. The J. L. Hudson Company was founded in Detroit in 1881 and the Dayton Department Store Company was established in 1902 in Minneapolis. Both companies were predominately department stores with long and storied traditions in their midwestern markets when they merged in 1969 to form the Dayton Hudson Corporation. In 1963 the Dayton Company opened its first Target store, an initial entrance into the low-margin merchandising business. In 1978, the Dayton Hudson Corporation acquired Mervyn's, a West Coast moderate-priced promotional department store chain. In 1990, the company purchased Chicago-based Marshall Field & Company, thereby establishing its dominance in the department store business in the upper Midwest.

Today, Target Corporation operates three lines of retailing business: Target Stores, Mervyn's, and Department Stores. Target Stores is an upscale discount retailer with a high-volume, low-margin orientation; it offers high-quality merchandise, convenience, and competitive prices. Mervyn's is a moderate-priced family department store, specializing in national brand and private-label clothing and other soft goods. Department Stores operate stores that emphasize fashion leadership and quality merchandise in the moderate to high price range supported by superior customer service.

Because of its multiline business, Target Corporation encounters different retail competitors. Target Stores competes primarily against Wal-Mart and Kmart on a national level. Mervyn's competes against J. C. Penney and Sears, Roebuck and Company, and, to a lesser extent, against Kohl's, a rapidly growing regional chain. Finally, in the Midwest, Department Stores faces Federated Department Stores, May Department Stores Company, and Nordstrom.

Dayton Hudson confronts a number of imposing business challenges, including:

- Can the company meet its goal of 15% long-run annual earnings growth in a highly competitive industry?
- Can it maintain the extraordinary growth of its Target Stores?
- Can sales growth at its Mervyn's and Department Stores be accelerated? Can earnings performance at those operations be improved and made more consistent?
- Can the multidivision corporation become better organized to take advantage of synergies between its operations and achieve increased economies of scale?

STATISTICAL ABSTRACT

Ticker/exchange	TGT/NYSE	Dividend	$0.40
Price (21-May-99)	$64.375	Dividend yield	0.62%
52-week price range	$31.4375–$64.500	Book value per share	$11.41
Earnings per share (1998) (diluted)	$1.98	Market capitalization	$28.5 billion
Sales (1998)	$31.0 billion	Net income (1998)	$935 million

14.5.2 REVIEW OF ACCOUNTING STATEMENTS

From an investment perspective, the analysis of a company's accounting statements is not an end in itself. Instead, it is a means to identify financial aspects of a company that may have direct relevance to understanding the intrinsic values and risks of the company's securities. The analyst will want to obtain access to a wide range of financial information about the company under review. Much of that information is found in the three primary accounting statements issued by the company in its annual report: the balance sheet, the income statement, and the statement of cash flows.

Balance Sheet

The balance sheet (also called the statement of financial position) presents a snapshot of the company's financial position at a point in time. It describes amounts or levels of various items. In particular, the balance sheet presents a listing of the company's *assets, liabilities,* and *stockholders' equity.*

Assets represent the company's economic resources. An asset is an item that has the potential to generate economic benefits (that is, cash inflows) for the company in the future. For example, plant and equipment can produce goods and services that can be sold to customers for cash. Liabilities are claims on the company's economic resources. These claims are usually of a specified amount and must be satisfied by a certain date in the future. Both assets and liabilities are classified on the balance sheet as either current or long-term. Current assets consist of cash or other assets, such as marketable securities, inventory, and accounts receivable, that are expected to be turned into cash in the near future. Current liabilities are expected to be (or are at risk of being) discharged shortly, usually within one year. Long-term assets are held and used for several years, whereas long-term liabilities are due more than a year in the future. Stockholders' equity (or *net worth*) is a residual claim of the owners of the company on the company's assets, after all liabilities have been extinguished. Thus, liabilities and stockholders' equity are the sources of funds used to procure the firm's assets.

The balance sheet does not show all of a company's assets and liabilities. For example, the capabilities of its management team are often the company's most valuable asset, yet the value of those capabilities does not appear on the balance sheet. On the liability side, the value of operating leases signed by the company may be large, yet are relegated to footnotes in the company's annual report.

Because the balance sheet represents the resources of the company and the claims on those resources, assets must equal liabilities plus stockholders' equity. In fact, a balance sheet is often presented with assets and their values listed on the left side and liabilities and stockholders' equity and their values listed on the right side. Balance sheet items are reported at their unadjusted or adjusted acquisition costs. For example, a building is carried on the balance sheet at its purchase price plus the value of any physical improvements less accumulated depreciation. Accounts receivable is reported as the actual amount of the account less an allowance for doubtful accounts.

Target Corporation

Table 14.3 presents the fiscal year-end consolidated balance sheets of Target Corporation from 1990 to 1998. A look at the company's balance sheets confirms that Target Corporation is a large company and is growing at a fairly rapid pace. The company's assets total more than $15 billion and have grown at 8% annual rate since 1990. Property and equipment, composed primarily of the company's stores and fixtures, represents the largest asset, making up 57% of 1998 total assets. Inventories, at 22% of 1998 total assets, are also a prominent asset. Somewhat surprisingly, accounts receivable, at 11% of 1998 total assets, have grown much more slowly than total assets. This slow growth is due in part to the company's policy of selling off a portion of its receivables to investors through a securitization process similar to that used to create mortgage-backed securities. (Asset-backed securities are discussed in Chapter 19.) It is also because of the increasing importance of Target Stores in the company's total financial picture; as a discount retailer, Target Stores tends to carry a relatively low level of receivables.

On the liability side, the company's long-term debt relative to total assets was about 28% in 1998. That debt has been declining as a proportion of total assets after reaching a high of 45% in 1991 following the 1990 acquisition of Marshall Field & Company. Stockholders' equity represents about 34% of total assets. Net working capital (current assets less current liabilities) is 6% of total assets, down from more than 14% in 1990. Again, this decline is because of the growth of Target Stores, which has a higher asset turnover than the other two operating divisions.

Income Statement

The income statement (also called the statement of earnings) indicates the *earnings* (or *profits* or *net income*) of the company. Instead of presenting levels at a point in time, the income statement presents flows that occur over a period of time. A company's net income is the difference between its sales (or revenues) and expenses. Sales measure the inflow of assets from selling goods and services to the company's customers. Expenses measure the outflow of assets (or the increase in liabilities) associated with generating sales. Ultimately, the success of a company is directly related to producing a sufficient surplus of sales over expenses.

TABLE 14.3 Target Corporation Consolidated Balance Sheets (millions)

	1990	1991	1992	1993	1994	1995	1996	1997	1998
Assets									
Cash & Equivalents	$ 92	$ 96	$ 117	$ 321	$ 147	$ 175	$ 201	$ 211	$ 255
Receivables	1,407	1,430	1,514	1,536	1,810	1,510	1,720	1,555	1,656
Inventories	2,016	2,381	2,618	2,497	2,777	3,018	3,031	3,251	3,475
Other	143	125	165	157	225	252	488	544	619
Total Current Assets	$3,658	$4,032	$ 4,414	$ 4,511	$ 4,959	$ 4,955	$ 5,440	$ 5,561	$ 6,005
Property & Equipment (net)	4,525	5,102	5,563	5,947	6,385	7,294	7,467	8,125	8,969
Other Assets	341	351	360	320	353	321	482	505	692
Total Assets	$8,524	$9,485	$10,337	$10,778	$11,697	$12,570	$13,389	$14,191	$15,666
Liabilities and Stockholders' Equity									
Short-Term Debt	$ 357	$ 453	$ 394	$ 373	$ 209	$ 182	$ 233	$ 273	$ 256
Accounts Payable	1,267	1,324	1,596	1,654	1,961	2,247	2,528	2,727	3,150
Accrued Liabilities	638	705	849	903	1,045	957	1,168	1,346	1,444
Taxes Payable	160	98	125	145	175	137	182	210	207
Total Current Liabilities	$2,422	$2,580	$ 2,964	$ 3,075	$ 3,390	$ 3,523	$ 4,111	$ 4,556	$ 5,057
Long-Term Debt	3,682	4,227	4,330	4,279	4,488	4,959	4,808	4,425	4,452
Deferred Taxes and Other	372	447	557	687	626	685	680	720	822
Total Liabilities	$6,476	$7,254	$ 7,851	$ 8,041	$ 8,504	$ 9,167	$ 9,599	$ 9,701	$10,331
Stockholders' Equity	$2,048	$2,231	$ 2,486	$ 2,737	$ 3,193	$ 3,403	$ 3,790	$ 4,490	$ 5,335
Total Liabilities and Stockholders' Equity	$8,524	$9,485	$10,337	$10,778	$11,967	$12,570	$13,389	$14,191	$15,666

The income statement provides a breakdown of the sources of sales and expenses for the company. Sales are reported net of returns and allowances. Expenses are divided into two groups. The first group are those expenses, such as (1) costs of goods sold; (2) selling, general, and administrative (SG&A) expenses; and (3) depreciation and amortization, directly associated with producing and selling the company's goods and services. These are called *operating expenses*. The second group are costs associated with financing and taxes on the company's income. These are called *nonoperating expenses*. Thus, the income statement has the following general format:

Sales

− Operating expenses

= Operating income (or earnings before interest and taxes, EBIT)

− Interest expense (net of any interest income)

= Pretax income (or earnings before taxes, EBT)

− Taxes

= Net income (or earnings after taxes, EAT)

The income statement is related to the beginning and end-of-period balance sheets. Net income that is not distributed to shareholders in the form of dividends increases retained earnings. On the balance sheet it increases the end-of-period stock-holders' equity and reflects an increase in one or more asset items and (or) decrease in one or more liability items.

Earnings are often presented on a "per share" basis. As Chapter 15 discusses, analysts commonly use the ratio of a stock's market price to the company's earnings per share as a measure of the stock's relative valuation. Earnings per share is calculated by dividing net income by the average number of common shares outstanding during the period. Comparisons with current numbers are made relevant by adjusting historical earnings per share for any stock splits or stock dividends that occurred after the earnings were originally reported. For example, if last year's income statement shows earnings per share of $6 and this year's of $4, it would be tempting to believe that the firm was less profitable this year. However, suppose that a two-for-one stock split took place right after the last year's earnings were announced. Hence, in this year's financial statements, last year's earnings per share would be reported as $3 $(= \$6/2)$, thereby revealing that the firm has actually been more, not less, profitable this year.

A company may issue securities, such as convertible bonds, convertible preferred stock, stock options, and warrants, that at some future date can be converted into common stock at the discretion of the company or the security holder, or sometimes both. Companies that issue these types of securities must calculate per share earnings on both a basic and a diluted basis. The basic earnings per share basis assumes no conversion of the securities into common shares; the diluted basis assumes full conversion. Because the existence of additional common shares "dilutes," or reduces, the net income available to existing common stockholders, diluted earnings per share will generally be less than or equal to basic earnings per share, with the difference depending on the existence and the terms of the dilutive securities.[19]

Sometimes a company will report nonrecurring (or one-time) expenses or income. Although these transactions may be intended to enhance the future operating profitability of the company, they are not expected to appear again on the company's income statement. The analyst generally will want to exclude these transactions in evaluating the company's operating performance.

Confusingly, some nonrecurring transactions are categorized as extraordinary items. Companies that incur these transactions must report them separately. The result is two sets of net income and earnings per share calculations: both before and after consideration of the extraordinary items. However, not all nonrecurring transactions are deemed extraordinary items. Nonrecurring transactions that are not deemed extraordinary enter the income statement as operating items, and consequently only one set of net income and earnings per share will be reported. In summary:

NONRECURRING ITEMS

Extraordinary	*Not extraordinary*
1. Reported separately	1. Not reported separately
2. Two sets of income figures	2. One set of income figures

Certain companies regularly report large transactions identified as nonrecurring. For example, from 1985 to 1994, AT&T reported four nonrecurring restructuring charges totaling $14.2 billion even though its total reported net income was only $10.3 billion. The high frequency of nonrecurring transactions at some companies has led analysts to question the reporting companies' motives and to wonder just how "nonrecurring" the transactions truly are.

Target Corporation

Table 14.4 shows the annual consolidated income statements for Target Corporation from 1990 to 1998. Target Corporation's revenues have grown at a 10% annual rate during the past eight years, whereas earnings increased at 11% per year. Actually, the earnings growth figure masks two distinct periods for the company. In the early and mid-1990s, the company's net income stagnated. In fact, in 1995 it was lower than in 1990. The primary explanation for the slow growth in earnings was the company's lack of pricing power to expand revenues relative to operating expenses as well as insufficiently tight controls over SG&A expenses. As a result, operating expenses grew from 93% of sales in 1990 to 96% of sales in 1995. However, from 1995 through 1998, earnings growth averaged 44% per year. Some of that extraordinary growth represents a rebound off a depressed base. Nevertheless, the company's rapid earnings expansion is in large part attributable to the strong growth in sales of its Target Stores, combined with a concerted cost control campaign and a more favorable pricing environment.

TABLE 14.4   Target Corporation Consolidated Income Statements (millions)

	1990	1991	1992	1993	1994	1995	1996	1997	1998
Revenues (Sales)	$14,739	$16,115	$17,927	$19,233	$21,311	$23,516	$25,371	$27,757	$30,951
Expenses									
Cost of Goods Sold	$10,652	$11,751	$13,129	$14,164	$15,636	$17,527	$18,628	$20,320	$22,634
SG&A Expenses	2,478	2,801	2,978	3,175	3,614	4,043	4,289	4,532	5,077
Depreciation and Amortization	369	410	459	498	548	594	650	693	780
Other Taxes	256	283	313	343	373	409	445	470	506
Nonrecurring Operating Expenses	0	0	0	0	0	0	134	0	0
Total Operating Expenses	$13,755	$15,245	$16,879	$18,180	$20,171	$22,573	$24,146	$26,015	$28,997
Operating Income (EBIT)	$ 984	$ 870	$ 1,048	$ 1,053	$ 1,140	$ 943	$ 1,225	$ 1,742	$ 1,954
Interest Expense	325	398	437	446	426	442	442	416	398
Pretax Income (EBT)	$ 659	$ 472	$ 611	$ 607	$ 714	$ 501	$ 783	$ 1,326	$ 1,556
Taxes	249	171	228	232	280	190	309	524	594
Net Income (EAT)	$ 410	$ 301	$ 383	$ 375	$ 434	$ 311	$ 474	$ 802	$ 962
Extraordinary Items	0	0	0	0	0	0	11	51	27
Net Income after Extraordinary Items	$ 410	$ 301	$ 383	$ 375	$ 434	$ 311	$ 463	$ 751	$ 935
Earnings per Share (diluted)	$ 0.85	$ 0.62	$ 0.80	$ 0.80	$ 0.92	$ 0.65	$ 1.00	$ 1.70	$ 2.04
Extraordinary Charges	0.00	0.00	0.00	0.00	0.00	0.00	(0.03)	(0.11)	(0.06)
Earnings per Share (diluted) after extraordinary charges	$ 0.85	$ 0.62	$ 0.80	$ 0.80	$ 0.92	$ 0.65	$ .97	$ 1.59	$ 1.98

Note that in 1996 through 1998, Target Corporation reported charges to earnings related to early redemption of long-term debt. Hence, in these years extraordinary charges were reported, resulting in two sets of net income and earnings per share figures. In addition, in 1996 the company reported a large nonrecurring operating expense related to the closing of stores in several states. This expense, however, was not classified as an extraordinary item.

Statement of Cash Flows

Analysts are concerned with the amount of cash that a company generates. In the long run, a company can afford to make payments to its security holders only if it produces surplus cash flow from its operations. Even profitable companies may find themselves facing cash shortages that, in the extreme, can lead to bankruptcy. In the short run, dwindling cash balances may be recharged by borrowing or through the sales of assets. However, those strategies may adversely affect the company's future profitability.

The statement of cash flows shows how a company's cash balance changed from one year to the next. It assists the analyst in evaluating the company's ability to meet its obligations for cash, its needs for future external financing, and the effectiveness of its financing and investing strategies. The statement of cash flows is divided into three parts:

1. Cash flow from operating activities
2. Cash flow from investing activities
3. Cash flow from financing activities

Construction of the statement of cash flows begins with a comparison of balance sheets from one period to another. Each activity of the corporation is classified into either operating, investing, or financing categories and identified as either an inflow or an outflow. For example, an increase in inventory constitutes an operating outflow of cash, whereas an increase in long-term debt represents an inflow of financing cash.

Cash flows from operating activities are obtained by adding the company's operating cash inflows to net income and subtracting the operating cash outflows from it. Cash from investing activities are primarily calculated from changes in the property, plant, and equipment accounts. Cash flows from financing are associated with raising or reducing capital through debt or equity offerings or refinancings and the payment of dividends.

Closely related to these measures of cash flows is a company's *free cash flow,* which takes two forms. First, there is *free cash flow to the firm,* determined as

$$
\begin{aligned}
&\text{After-tax operating income}\\
+\ &\text{Depreciation, amortization, and deferred taxes}\\
-\ &\text{Increase in working capital}\\
\underline{-\ &\text{Investment in fixed assets}}\\
=\ &\text{Free cash flow to the firm}
\end{aligned}
$$

After-tax operating earnings are equal to operating earnings times the quantity (1 minus the tax rate), that is, $EBIT(1 - t)$, or equivalently $EAT + tI$. The increase in working capital represents an increase in the amount of current assets relative to current liabilities and hence is short-term in nature. Investment in fixed assets is long-term because it involves spending on items such as property, plant, and equipment. Thus, free cash flow to the firm is the cash generated by the company's operations that is available to all of the company's debt and equity holders. Note that it is equivalent to the sum of cash flow from operating activities, cash flow from investing activities, and the after-tax cost of any interest and preferred stock dividend payments.

The second type of free cash flow is *free cash flow to equity,* defined as

Net income
+ Depreciation, amortization, and deferred taxes
− Increase in working capital
− Investment in fixed assets
− Principal repayments
+ New debt issued
= Free cash flow to equity

Free cash flow to equity represents cash flow generated by the company's operations that remains after the company has covered all its financial obligations, working capital needs, and fixed asset needs. It is what is left for the company to pay out as dividends, although most companies do not use the entire amount for this purpose. Note that it is equal to the sum of cash flow from operations, cash flow from investing, cash flow from financing, and dividends. It is also equal to free cash flow to the firm less principal repayments plus new debt issued.[20]

Target Corporation

Table 14.5 shows the annual consolidated statements of cash flows for Target Corporation from 1990 to 1998. Target Corporation needs cash to finance its capital expenditures program, a need that is primarily related to the rapid growth of its Target Stores and is indicated by its reported total investing cash flow figures. The company meets much of these cash requirements through its net income and noncash expenses (principally depreciation), as indicated by its total operating cash flow figures. Since 1992, cash from financing sources has generally been negative as indicated by its total financing cash flow figures, as the company has reduced its long-term debt outstanding as a proportion of total assets. Also interesting is the steady increase in aggregate dividends paid, whereas free cash flow to equity has been more volatile, being often above but sometimes below the amount of dividends paid.

Additional Financial Statement Information

The balance sheet, income statement, and statement of cash flows contain much of the financial statement information required by the analyst. However, considerable detail about the financial performance of the company also can be found in other parts of a company's annual report. Thus, as part of his or her research, the analyst will want to examine

- Notes to the financial statements
- Management discussion and analysis
- Auditor's report

The notes to the financial statements contain supplemental information regarding particular accounts, such as the company's method of valuing inventory and a list of its long-term debts outstanding. They present information regarding major acquisitions or divestitures, officer and employee retirement and stock option plans, leasing arrangements, legal proceedings, and changes in accounting procedures, among other issues.

Management discussion and analysis provide an interpretation by the company's senior officers of financial trends and significant events affecting the company, particularly as they affect the company's liquidity, financial resources, and results of operations.

TABLE 14.5 Target Corporation Consolidated Statements of Cash Flows (millions)

	1990	1991	1992	1993	1994	1995	1996	1997	1998
Cash from Operating Activities									
Net Income	$ 410	$ 301	$ 383	$ 375	$ 434	$ 311	$ 474	$ 802	$ 962
Depreciation and Amortization	372	410	459	498	548	594	650	693	780
Deferred Taxes and Other	(18)	60	59	89	(3)	46	(96)	(20)	59
Changes in Working Capital									
Receivables	(116)	(23)	(84)	(22)	(274)	300	(210)	165	(56)
Inventories	(36)	(365)	(237)	121	(280)	(241)	(13)	(220)	(198)
Accounts Payable	8	57	272	58	307	286	281	199	336
Accrued Liabilities	(15)	59	142	63	147	(88)	275	182	75
Income Taxes Payable	(13)	(62)	27	20	30	(38)	55	62	15
Other	33	0	(37)	17	(17)	(9)	42	(68)	(111)
Total Operating Cash Flow	$ 625	$ 437	$ 984	$1,219	$ 892	$ 1,161	$ 1,458	$ 1,795	$ 1,862
Cash from Investing Activities									
Capital Expenditures	$(1,732)	$(1,009)	$(918)	$ (969)	$(1,095)	$(1,522)	$(1,301)	$(1,354)	$(1,657)
Proceeds from Disposals, etc.	2	19	10	79	89	17	103	123	2
Total Investing Cash Flow	$(1,730)	$ (990)	$(908)	$ (890)	$(1,006)	$(1,505)	$(1,198)	$(1,231)	$(1,655)
Cash from Financing Activities									
Change in Notes Payable	$ (130)	$ 161	$(242)	$ (23)	$ 247	$ 501	$ (416)	$ (127)	$ (305)
Change in LT Debt	1,337	476	260	(53)	(199)	(60)	286	(315)	257
Equity Issuance	0	0	0	0	0	0	0	0	0
Dividends	(116)	(128)	(133)	(138)	(144)	(148)	(155)	(165)	(178)
Other	3	48	60	89	36	79	51	53	63
Total Financing Cash Flow	$ 1,094	$ 557	$ (55)	$ (125)	$ (60)	$ 372	$ (234)	$ (554)	$ (163)
Change in Cash	$ (11)	$ 4	$ 21	$ 204	$ (174)	$ 28	$ 26	$ 10	$ 44
Beginning Cash	$ 103	$ 92	$ 96	$ 117	$ 321	$ 147	$ 175	$ 201	$ 211
Ending Cash	$ 92	$ 96	$ 117	$ 321	$ 147	$ 175	$ 201	$ 211	$ 255
Free Cash Flow Analysis									
Total Operating Cash Flow	$ 625	$ 437	$ 984	$1,219	$ 892	$ 1,161	$ 1,458	$ 1,795	$ 1,862
Total Investing Cash Flow	(1,730)	(990)	(908)	(890)	(1,006)	(1,505)	(1,198)	(1,231)	(1,655)
Tax Rate × Interest Expense	123	144	163	170	167	168	174	164	151
Free Cash Flow to the Firm	$ (982)	$ (409)	$ 239	$ 499	$ 53	$ (176)	$ 434	$ 728	$ 358
Total Operating Cash Flow	$ 625	$ 437	$ 984	$1,219	$ 892	$ 1,161	$ 1,458	$ 1,795	$ 1,862
Total Investing Cash Flow	(1,730)	(990)	(908)	(890)	(1,006)	(1,505)	(1,198)	(1,231)	(1,655)
Total Financing Cash Flow	1,094	557	(55)	(125)	(60)	372	(234)	(554)	(163)
Dividends	116	128	133	138	144	148	155	165	178
Free Cash Flow to Equity	$ 105	$ 132	$ 154	$ 342	$ (30)	$ 176	$ 181	$ 175	$ 222

In preparing this report, corporate management of some firms are more forthcoming than others. Consequently, the value of the report to the analyst varies widely among companies.

The auditor's report presents the opinion of the company's independent auditor regarding the "fairness" of the company's financial statements. In the vast majority of cases, the auditor issues an unqualified opinion, stating that during the accounting period the company's financial statements fairly present, in all material respects, the financial position, results of operations, and the cash flows in conformance with generally accepted accounting principles (GAAP). A qualified opinion, indicating material departures from GAAP, is a rarity and may signal serious problems with the company's disclosures. The mere threat that the auditor might issue a qualified opinion is usually sufficient to prevent a company from releasing intentionally incorrect reports. Note, however, that an unqualified opinion is related merely to the fairness of the disclosures; it does not imply any endorsement on the part of the auditor as to the quality of the company's business operations or the value of the company's securities.

14.5.3   RATIO ANALYSIS

Ratio analysis is a technique commonly used by analysts examining a company's financial statements. Standing alone, the values of various financial statement items are difficult to interpret. They reveal more when they are considered in conjunction with one another. For example, a growing firm will generally increase the amount of its debt outstanding. Such increases are expected and appropriate. However, when that debt relative to total assets or stockholders' equity increases significantly, a red flag is raised for analysts. They will want to know the reasons for, and ramifications of, such an increase in leverage.

Ratios may be used in several ways. Some analysts apply absolute standards, on the grounds that a substandard ratio indicates a potential weakness that merits further analysis. Alternatively, ratios can be used as screening devices to identify stocks that deserve close scrutiny as possible buy recommendations. That is, only those firms whose ratios pass some absolute standards are analyzed in more detail. Other analysts compare a company's ratios with those of the "average" firm in the same industry to detect differences that may need further consideration. Others analyze trends in a company's ratios over time, perhaps in comparison with industry trends, hoping these past data will help them predict future changes. Still others combine ratios with technical analysis to arrive at investment decisions.

Ratio analysis can be very sophisticated, but it can also be overly simplistic. Routine extrapolation of a ratio (or its recent trend) may produce a poor estimate of its future value. (For example, there is no reason for a firm to maintain a constant ratio of inventory to sales.) Moreover, a series of simple projections may produce inconsistent financial statements. For example, projections of ratios imply predictions of the levels of various balance sheet items. However, it may be that when these levels are examined together, the resulting balance sheet does not balance. Furthermore, comparisons of one company's ratios with those of its competitors can be fraught with problems. In many industries, competitors' lines of business do not match precisely. Even very similar companies may use different accounting procedures. The result is often an apples and oranges situation that diminishes the value of peer comparisons.

The types of ratios considered depends on the purpose of the analysis. In general, analysts concerned with a company's equity securities look at ratios relating to the firm's return on equity. Analysts viewing the company from a creditor's perspective focus on measures of debt capacity and liquidity.

Equity Ratio Analysis

Stock prices are ultimately determined by expected growth in corporate earnings. Analysts, therefore, are naturally concerned with identifying the elements that cause a company's long-run earnings growth rate to increase or decrease. The long-run (or *sustainable*) growth rate (*g*) of a company's earnings depends on (1) the proportion of earnings that is retained ($1 - p$, where *p* is the proportion of earnings paid out as dividends) and (2) the average return on equity for the earnings that are retained (*r*):

$$g = r(1 - p) \qquad \qquad \textbf{(14.1)}$$

Thus, if Widget pays out 40% of its earnings and, in turn, receives a 10% return on the 60% of the earnings that are retained, then its earnings can be expected to grow by 6% [$= .10 \times (1 - .40)$] over the long run.

Ratio analysis is used to plumb the past return on equity for clues as to improvements or deterioration in the return on equity in the future. Ratio analysis breaks down the return on equity into its various components, which in turn are examined for trends and relative position versus competing companies. The simplest expression for return on equity (ROE) is to view it as the product of profit margin (net income divided by sales) and equity turnover (sales divided by stockholders' equity):[21]

$$\text{ROE} = \frac{\text{Net income}}{\text{Stockholders' equity}} = \frac{\text{Net income}}{\text{Sales}} \times \frac{\text{Sales}}{\text{Stockholders' equity}}$$

Although this expression aggregates considerable detail concerning the company's financial performance, it is only a useful starting point. A better understanding is gained by recognizing that the profit margin reflects not only the operating results of the company, but nonoperating factors as well. Disaggregating those two elements allows for a more intensive analysis. Similarly, equity turnover reflects not only the company's operating efficiency, but how it finances its operations.

Operating Results

Operating results measure the performance of the company's underlying business. That is, how profitable and efficient has the company been in producing (or acquiring) and selling its goods and services to its customers? A company's (pretax) return on assets (ROA) is expressed in a manner similar to its return on equity. That is, it is a function of operating margin (operating income divided by sales) and asset turnover (sales divided by total assets). However, in the definition of operating margin, operating income replaces net income and total assets replaces stockholders' equity:

$$\text{(Pretax) ROA} = \frac{\text{Operating income}}{\text{Total assets}} = \frac{\text{Operating income}}{\text{Sales}} \times \frac{\text{Sales}}{\text{Total assets}}$$

Operating margin can be further disaggregated. Operating expenses are composed of three primary components: cost of goods sold (primarily labor and materials); selling, general, and administrative (SG&A) expenses; and depreciation. The difference between sales and costs of goods sold is called gross income, and the ratio of gross income to sales is known as gross margin. Subtracting the other operating expenses from gross income yields operating income. An analyst considers the extent to which changes in operating margin are related to changes in the company's control over pricing (as reflected in gross margin) and its management of operating expenses.[22]

Asset turnover can likewise be further disaggregated. The analyst explores how the use of those assets relative to sales has changed over time and thus increased or decreased the ROA. The analyst also examines how the company's use of its assets compares with that of other similar companies.

Nonoperating Factors

Operating results translate into total financial performance through the interaction of two nonoperating factors: leverage and taxes. Whereas operating results measure how effective management is in producing and selling the goods and services of the company, another critical aspect of management policy is how the company finances its business activities. Common stock and long-term debt are the principal sources of financing for most businesses. Although leverage causes the return on equity to become more variable, effective use of debt financing can enhance shareholder returns. Return on equity (pretax) can be expressed as

$$\text{(Pretax) ROE} = \frac{\text{Pretax income}}{\text{Stockholders' equity}}$$

$$= \frac{\text{Operating income}}{\text{Total assets}} \times \frac{\text{Total assets}}{\text{Stockholders' equity}} - \frac{\text{Interest}}{\text{Stockholders' equity}}$$

Taxes reduce the return to shareholders. Multiplying the pretax return on equity by (1 minus the tax rate) yields the after-tax return on equity, ROE:

$$\frac{\text{Net income}}{\text{Stockholders' equity}} = \frac{\text{Pretax income}}{\text{Stockholders' equity}} \times (1 - \text{Tax rate})$$

Summarizing the relationship between the various financial ratios yields the expression for ROE:

$$\text{After-tax ROE} = \frac{\text{Net income}}{\text{Stockholders' equity}}$$

$$= \left[\frac{\text{Operating income}}{\text{Sales}} \times \frac{\text{Sales}}{\text{Total assets}} \times \frac{\text{Total assets}}{\text{Stockholders' equity}} - \frac{\text{Interest}}{\text{Stockholders' equity}} \right]$$

$$\times (1 - \text{Tax rate})$$

The company can influence its after-tax return on equity through three primary factors: (1) expenses relative to sales (operating margin), (2) sales relative to assets (asset turnover), and (3) the cost of debt used to support the company's capital structure (interest divided by stockholders' equity). The effect of these factors is magnified by financial leverage (total assets divided by stockholders' equity) and is reduced by taxes. The interaction of the various ratios to derive the after-tax return on equity is shown in Figure 14.1.

Target Corporation

Table 14.6 contains various relevant financial ratios for the Target Corporation from 1990 to 1998. From the company's income statement, the variability in the earnings per share is readily apparent. That variability is even more noticeable looking at the company's return on equity. Return on equity reached a high of 21.6% in 1990, declined to 9.4% in 1995, and rebounded to 19.6% in 1998. Examining the principal components of Target Corporation's return on equity reveals two observations. The first observation is that throughout the period the company's equity turnover (sales divided by stockholders' equity) steadily declined, from 7.8 times in 1990 to 6.3 times in 1998. This trend largely represents a deliberate effort by the company to reduce its debt-to-stockholders' equity ratio. The resulting relative increase in equity in its capital structure had the effect of reducing equity turnover. That this decline is not caused by a less efficient use of company resources is confirmed by noting that the company's asset

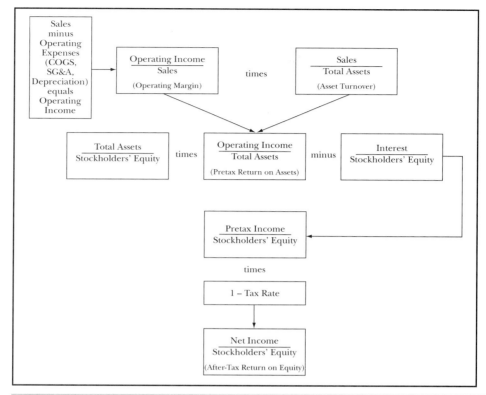

FIGURE 14.1 Interaction of Financial Ratios to Derive After-Tax Return on Equity

turnover shows a fairly constant value of roughly 1.9 times over the period and actually increased slightly in recent years. Presumably then, the equity turnover ratio will flatten out as the company approaches its desired debt level.

The second observation is that the profit margin (net income divided by sales) mirrored the up and down nature of the company's financial results. In 1990, Target Corporation's profit margin was 2.8%. In 1995, the profit margin fell to 1.3%, but it improved to 3.1% in 1998.

Target Corporation's operating margin (operating income divided by total assets) displayed less variability than the profit margin, as leverage tends to magnify the effects of variations in operating results on bottom line financial performance. Despite some interim fluctuations, the company's operating margin was lower in 1998 than it was in 1990. In part, this decline was because 1990 was an exceptional year for the company. Furthermore, the decline was also a result of the growing importance of Target Stores in Target Corporation's overall financial picture. (In fact, this increase inspired the company's recent name change from Dayton-Hudson Corporation to Target Corporation.) In 1990, Target Stores' sales represented 56% of the company's total sales. By 1998, that figure had increased to 75%. Because their discount retailing operations involve lower operating margins than either Mervyn's or particularly Department Stores, the increasing prominence of Target Stores reduces the company's total operating margin.

Breaking down the operating margin further, the ratios of costs of goods sold and SG&A expenses relative to sales were on an upward trend that peaked in 1995. Some of that increase is again related to the lower margin business of Target Stores. However,

TABLE 14.6 Target Corporation Selected Financial Ratios

	1990	1991	1992	1993	1994	1995	1996	1997	1998
Profit Margin	2.8%	1.9%	2.1%	2.0%	2.0%	1.3%	1.9%	2.9%	3.1%
Equity Turnover	7.8	7.5	7.6	7.4	7.2	7.1	7.0	6.7	6.3
Return on Equity	21.6%	14.1%	16.2%	14.4%	14.6%	9.4%	13.2%	19.4%	19.6%
Operating Margin	6.7%	5.4%	5.9%	5.5%	5.4%	4.0%	4.8%	6.3%	6.3%
Asset Turnover	1.9	1.8	1.8	1.8	1.9	1.9	2.0	2.0	2.1
Return on Operating Assets	12.9%	9.7%	10.6%	10.0%	10.1%	7.8%	9.4%	12.6%	13.1%
Cost of Goods Sold/Sales	72.3%	72.9%	73.2%	73.6%	73.4%	74.5%	73.4%	73.2%	73.1%
SG&A/Sales	16.8%	17.4%	16.6%	16.5%	17.0%	17.2%	16.9%	16.3%	16.4%
Depreciation/Sales	2.5%	2.5%	2.6%	2.6%	2.6%	2.5%	2.6%	2.5%	2.5%
Interest Expense/Sales	2.2%	2.5%	2.4%	2.3%	2.0%	1.9%	1.7%	1.5%	1.3%
Sales/Cash	151.2	171.4	168.3	87.8	91.1	146.1	135.0	134.7	132.8
Sales/Accounts Receivable	11.6	11.4	12.2	12.6	12.7	14.2	15.7	17.0	19.2
Sales/Inventories	7.7	7.3	7.2	7.5	8.1	8.1	8.4	8.8	9.2
Sales/Current Assets	4.4	4.2	4.3	4.3	4.5	4.7	4.9	5.1	5.4
Sales/Net Plant & Equipment	3.7	3.4	3.4	3.3	3.5	3.4	3.4	3.6	3.6
Total Assets/ Stockholders' Equity	4.0	4.2	4.2	4.0	3.8	3.7	3.6	3.3	3.0
Interest/Stockholders' Equity	17.1%	18.6%	18.5%	17.1%	14.4%	13.4%	12.3%	10.1%	8.1%
Pretax Income/ Stockholders' Equity	34.5%	22.1%	25.9%	23.2%	24.1%	15.2%	21.8%	32.0%	31.7%
Tax Rate	37.8%	36.2%	37.3%	38.2%	39.2%	37.9%	39.5%	39.5%	38.2%
Total Debt/Total Assets	.75	.76	.76	.75	.74	.73	.72	.70	.67
Current Assets/ Current Liabilities	1.47	1.54	1.52	1.48	1.46	1.43	1.36	1.27	1.20
Operating Income/ Interest Expense	3.03	2.19	2.40	2.36	2.68	2.13	2.77	4.2	4.9

the company still was able to control costs because operating expenses as a percent of sales declined from 94.3% in 1995 to 92.1% in 1998—a 2.2 percentage point improvement. Target Corporation's improved financial performance was due to a more favorable experience in terms of the company's gross margin (cost of goods sold divided by sales) and lower SG&A and interest expenses as a percent of sales. In terms of asset turnover, the key items of accounts receivable and inventories both demonstrated improved operating efficiency (higher sales to asset ratios), whereas the ratio of sales to net plant and equipment had little change.

Examining nonoperating factors, the company made a concerted effort, as discussed, to decrease leverage on its balance sheet. This change is evidenced by the decline in the company's debt-to-stockholders' equity ratio from 3.21 in 1991 to 2.04 in 1998. This reduced debt load decreased the company's relative interest expense, as interest payments relative to sales fell from 2.5% in 1991 to 1.3% in 1998. The reduction in leverage will ultimately lower the variability of the company's return on equity. However, it will also give less of a boost to net income in periods of high operating margins. In terms of taxes, the company's tax rate has remained fairly constant over the period at approximately 38%.

Being a national multiline retailer, Target Corporation faces a wide range of competitors. The diversity of its competition limits the validity of comparing its financial ratios with those of its competitors. Nevertheless, Table 14.7 lists various year-end 1998

TABLE 14.7 **Large U.S. Retailers versus Target Corporation 1998 Selected Financial Ratios**

	Wal-Mart	Kmart	Sears	J. C. Penney	Federated	Average	Target Corp.
Profit Margin	3.2%	1.5%	2.5%	1.9%	4.8%	2.7%	3.1%
Equity Turnover	6.4	5.0	5.6	4.2	2.9	4.8	6.3
Return on Equity	20.4%	7.7%	14.1%	8.2%	12.1%	12.5%	19.6%
Operating Margin	4.8%	3.3%	8.8%	4.8%	9.2%	6.2%	6.3%
Asset Turnover	2.9	2.4	1.1	1.3	1.2	1.8	2.1
Return on Assets	13.7%	8.0%	9.5%	6.3%	10.7%	9.7%	13.1%
Cost of Goods Sold/Sales	79.0%	78.2%	66.0%	73.5%	60.7%	71.5%	73.1%
SG&A/Sales	16.3%	18.6%	25.3%	21.7%	30.1%	22.4%	16.4%
Interest Expense/Sales	0.6%	0.9%	3.4%	2.2%	1.9%	1.8%	1.3%
Sales/Current Assets	6.8	4.4	1.4	2.7	2.6	3.6	5.4
Sales/Net Plant & Equipment	5.6	5.9	6.5	5.7	2.4	5.2	3.6
Total Assets/Stockholders' Equity	2.2	2.1	5.1	3.2	2.5	3.0	3.0
Interest/Stockholders' Equity	3.7%	4.4%	19.2%	9.1%	5.5%	8.4%	8.1%
Pretax Income/Stockholders' Equity	33.1%	11.2%	25.3%	13.2%	21.2%	20.8%	31.7%
Tax Rate	38.2%	30.8%	40.7%	37.8%	41.1%	37.7%	38.2%
Total Debt/Total Assets	.55	.52	.73	.81	.76	.67	.67
Current Assets/Current Liabilities	1.30	2.20	1.98	2.01	2.01	1.90	1.20
Operating Income/Interest Expense	8.21	3.79	4.03	2.55	3.08	4.33	4.91

ratios for five of the company's competitors: Wal-Mart, Kmart, Sears, J. C. Penney, and Federated Department Stores.

Wal-Mart is the largest U.S. retailer and has produced a higher return on equity than any of its competitors, including Target Corporation (see Table 14.7). Comparing Target Corporation's financial ratios with the five-company average shows both an above-average profit margin and a more efficient use of stockholders' equity, resulting in a considerably above-average return on equity. At the operating level, Target Corporation's operating margin and asset turnover interact to produce a comparatively strong return on assets. Operating expense relative to sales and sales relative to current assets both indicate superior performance by Target Corporation. Furthermore, the company has achieved these results while at the same time bringing its total debt-to-total assets ratio to that of its competitors.

In summary, through its improved gross margin and its cost-cutting efforts, Target Corporation increased its profit margin and continued to make efficient use of company assets. It also was able to continue its reduction in balance sheet leverage. These accomplishments put it in a strong financial position relative to its competitors. These improvements were associated with a 352% surge in the company's stock price from year-end 1995 to year-end 1998 as compared with a 95% average increase for its competitors. Target Corporation's challenge and the question confronting investors in its common stock is whether the company can continue its rapid revenue growth while maintaining and even building on the profit margin expansion of recent years.

Fixed-Income Ratio Analysis

Holders of a company's debt are primarily concerned with being paid their interest and principal in a full and timely manner. Some lenders want to know about the company's short-run ability to service its debt. For example, a banker making a short-term loan will want to examine financial ratios that indicate the company's liquidity.

Holders of the company's long-term debt, on the other hand, will place more emphasis on the company's long-run earnings power, somewhat akin to an equity analyst.

Liquidity ratios measure the company's ability to quickly discharge its near-term obligations. The most commonly used liquidity ratios are the *current ratio* (current assets divided by current liabilities) and the *quick ratio* (current assets less inventory, divided by current liabilities). The greater these liquidity ratios, the greater the company's capacity to generate cash that can be used to pay off its short-term obligations.

Leverage ratios indicate the extent to which the company's capital was financed through debt as opposed to equity. Higher leverage ratios indicate that more financing came from debt sources. As a result, more risk of the business is placed on creditors. Moreover, the higher the company's leverage, the more variable the company's earnings because a larger fixed expense (that is, interest payments) must be paid before earnings can flow through to the company's owners. The most widely recognized leverage ratio is the ratio of *total debt-to-stockholders' equity*. Coverage ratios, such as *times interest earned* (operating income divided by interest expense), measure the extent to which interest expense is covered by the company's operating income.

Target Corporation

As shown in Tables 14.6 and 14.7, Target Corporation's current ratio has remained fairly constant during the past eight years, and it is somewhat lower than that of its peers because of the company's previously mentioned program of selling off its accounts receivables to investors. Although this program has the effect of lowering its available liquidity, the company apparently believes that it can make more efficient use of those assets through investments in its capital projects and paying down debt. In fact, the company's current asset turnover (sales divided by current assets) has increased in recent years and is above most of its competitors. The increasing importance of Target Stores, which has high inventory turnover, is largely responsible for this result.

Target Corporation appears to be managing its debt effectively. As noted, it has brought down its total debt-to-stockholders' equity ratio considerably during the past several years and is now near the average of its competitors. Furthermore, the company's times interest earned ratio (operating income divided by interest expense) has also improved in recent years and is above that of its competitors.

14.6 Analysts' Recommendations and Stock Prices

When a security analyst decides that a stock is mispriced and informs certain clients, some of the clients may act on the information. As they do so, the price of the security may be affected. As news of the analyst's recommendation spreads, more investors may act, and the price may react even more. At some point, the analyst's information will be "fully reflected" in the stock price.

If the analyst decides that a stock is underpriced and clients subsequently purchase it, the stock's price tends to rise. Conversely, if the analyst decides that a stock is overpriced and clients subsequently sell it, the stock's price tends to decline. If the analyst's views were well-founded, no subsequent counterreaction in the stock's price would be expected. Otherwise, the price is likely to return to its prerecommendation level at some later time.

Table 14.8 summarizes six studies of publicly available analysts' recommendations. Two of the studies deal with recommendations that appeared in First Call and Zach's Investment Research, which maintain large computer databases that provide up-to-date records of analysts' recommendations from a number of different brokerage firms for a large number of securities.[23] The third study deals with recommendations that ap-

TABLE 14.8   Summary of Studies That Evaluate the Performance of Security Analysts

Source	Before Announcment		Around Announcement		After Announcement	
	Time Period	*Abnormal Return*	*Time Period*	*Abnormal Return*	*Time Period*	*Abnormal Return*
(a) Buy Recommendations						
First Call[1]	6 months	1.2%	−1 to +1	3.0%[a]	1 month	2.4%[a]
Zach's[2]	10 days	.7[a]	0 to +10	.9[a]	20 days	.6[a]
Barron's "Roundtable"[3]	25 days	2.7[b]	0	1.0[a]	25 days	.3
"Dartboard"[4]	25 days	.6	0 to +1	4.1[a]	24 days	−2.1
"Heard on the Street"[5]	28 days	.4	−2 to +1	2.1[a]	29 days	− .5
Value Line[6]	50 days	8.7[a]	0 to +2	2.4[a]	48 days	.7
(b) Sell Recommendations						
First Call[1]	6 months	−2.1%	−1 to +1	−4.7%[a]	6 months	−9.2%[a]
Zach's[2]	10 days	−1.1[a]	0 to +10	− .8[a]	20 days	− .3
Barron's "Roundtable"[3]	25 days	−1.8[b]	0	−1.2[a]	25 days	.1
"Heard on the Street"[5]	28 days	.4	−2 to +1	−3.6[a]	29 days	1.3
Value Line[6]	50 days	−7.0[a]	0 to −2	− .3[a]	48 days	−1.3[a]

[a]The number was found to be statistically significantly different from zero at the 5% level.

[b]A test of statistical significance was neither presented in the study nor could be conducted by an outside reader from the data provided.

Sources: The data are adapted from: (1) Kent L. Womack, "Do Brokerage Analysts' Recommendations Have Investment Value?" *Journal of Finance,* 51, no. 1 (March 1996): 148–149. (2) Scott E. Stickel, "The Anatomy of the Performance of Buy and Sell Recommendations," *Financial Analysts Journal,* 51, no. 5 (September/October 1995): 28. (3) Hemang Desai and Prem C. Jain, "An Analysis of the Recommendations of the 'Superstar' Money Managers at *Barron's* Annual Roundtable," *Journal of Finance,* 50, no. 4 (September 1995): 1264, 1270. (4) Brad M. Barber and Douglas Loeffler, "The 'Dartboard' Column: Second-Hand Information and Price Pressure," *Journal of Financial and Quantitative Analysis,* 28, no. 2 (June 1993): 276. (5) Messod D. Beneish, "Stock Prices and the Dissemination of Analysts' Recommendations," *Journal of Business,* 64, no. 3 (July 1991): 403, 406–407. (6) Scott E. Stickel, "The Effect of Value Line Investment Survey Rank Changes on Common Stock Prices," *Journal of Financial Economics,* 14, no. 1 (March 1985): 130–131.

peared annually in *Barron's,* a weekly publication, and involves eight to twelve prominent money managers who were invited to participate in their "Roundtable," referring to them as "Wall Street Superstars." The next two studies deal with recommendations that appeared in columns in *The Wall Street Journal.* One of these columns, "Heard on the Street," appears daily and involves a changing group of a variable number of analysts who discuss a variety of stocks.[24] The "Dartboard" is the second column; it appears monthly and presents "Pros' Picks," provided by a changing panel of four analysts who each recommend one stock. The last study involves recommendations made by Value Line analysts that appeared weekly in the *Value Line Investment Survey,* reputed to be the largest stock investment advisory service in the United States.[25]

In terms of how soon the analysts' recommendations appear publicly, First Call is the quickest because the brokerage firms generally send them in promptly. *Barron's* and *The Wall Street Journal* are probably the slowest; their featured analysts may have disclosed their recommendations to their clients at some point before publication (in the case of *Barron's,* the Roundtable meets about two weeks before publication). Zach's and Value Line are probably somewhere in the middle.

Although the recommendations in *The Wall Street Journal* and *Barron's* are simple recommendations to buy or sell, those in First Call, Zach's, and Value Line are more complicated. Often an analyst following a stock gives it a rating on a five-point scale, where 1 = strong buy, 2 = buy, 3 = hold, 4 = sell, and 5 = strong sell, or some similar metric. Thereafter, the rating will be either changed or confirmed at irregular intervals. In the First Call study, buy recommendations were defined as those recommendations that represented a rating upgrade to a 1, and sell recommendations were defined as a rating downgrade to a 5. In contrast, the Zach's study defined buys as those recommendations that were upgraded to a 1 or 2; sells were those recommendations that were downgraded to a 3, 4, or 5. In the Value Line study, the results shown in Table 14.8 focus on those stocks that were upgraded to a 1 and those that were downgraded to a 5.

Overall, the table reveals the following about analysts' recommendations:

1. The buy recommendations seem to be associated with a slight abnormal price rise in the period before the recommendations are widely published, perhaps because the recommendations are released early to certain clients or perhaps because analysts change their recommendations after a notable upward price movement by the stocks under analysis. Sell recommendations are associated with a slight abnormal price decline in the period before publication.

2. Around the time of the announcement (that is, day 0, with −1 and +1 referring to the day before and the day after the announcement) the buys jumped up in price and the sells slumped. This movement indicates that investors immediately acted on the recommendations when they were published.

3. There is mixed evidence regarding what happened after the announcement. The evidence that recommended buys keep rising for a month after First Call publishes a buy recommendation, and that their recommended sells keep falling for six months after publication is compelling because First Call has the "freshest" recommendations. These results seem to be inconsistent with the notion of efficient markets because they suggest that an investor might be able to earn abnormal returns by reacting promptly to First Call recommendations (note that because transaction costs have not been accounted for, it is entirely possible that these postannouncement abnormal returns are illusory). Nevertheless, at a minimum the absence of a subsequent correction to the announcement day's abnormal stock price movement for the other studies suggests that the recommendations in all of the studies contained information of value.[26]

4. Although not shown in the table, most of the recommendations were buys of large firms. One reason given for the predominance of buys is that there are several costs associated with sells, perhaps the biggest one being possible lost investment banking opportunities. That is, an analyst who issues a sell recommendation about a firm's stock may be fearful of annoying management of the firm to such an extent that they will not use the analyst's firm for any investment banking activities in the future. Hence, there is an incentive not to say anything negative about a firm's stock unless it is particularly obvious.

5. Also not shown in the table is the observation that analysts' recommendations are often made public around the same time earnings forecasts are released. Hence it is possible that one of these two pieces of information dominates the other by making the other valueless when both are provided to the investor. For example, a significant upward revision in a firm's earnings forecast by a prominent analyst might cause the firm's stock price to jump up, whereas the issuance of a buy recommendation two days later might not result in any notable price change. However, a study found that this is not the case; both announcements were found to be associated with notable stock price movements.[27] Furthermore, stock recommendations were found to be more valuable when they represented a change of position instead of a reiteration of a position.

TABLE 14.9 Analyst Following and Stock Returns				
Amount of Following	*All Stocks* *(1)*	*Small Firms* *(2)*	*Medium Firms* *(3)*	*Large Firms* *(4)*
High	7.5%	5.0%	7.4%	8.4%
Moderate	11.8	13.2	11.0	10.2
Low	15.4	15.8	13.9	15.3
Low minus high	7.9	10.8	6.5	6.9
Average return	11.0	13.5	10.7	9.8

Source: Adapted from Avner Arbel and Paul Strebel, "Pay Attention to Neglected Firms!" *Journal of Portfolio Management,* 9, no. 2 (Winter 1983): 39.

14.7 Analyst Following and Stock Returns

An interesting issue involves the relationship between the amount of attention devoted by analysts to individual stocks and the price behavior of those stocks. Do stocks that are intensively followed have significantly different returns from those stocks that are relatively neglected by analysts? One study examined all stocks in the S&P 500 to answer this question. Table 14.9 summarizes the results.

Column (1) shows that the stocks followed by the largest number of analysts had the lowest average returns and the stocks followed by the fewest analysts had the highest average returns, suggesting the presence of a **neglected-firm effect.** It is possible that this effect is simply a reflection of the size effect, because the average return on small-sized firms has been shown to be larger than the average return on larger firms.[28] The reason for this possibility is that the number of analysts following a stock is generally related to the size of the underlying firm. However, columns (2), (3), and (4) show that this effect is not simply another manifestation of the size effect.[29] The neglected-firm effect exists for all firm sizes and is most pronounced for small firms; note that the difference between the high and low categories is largest in column (2).

neglected-firm effect

What are the implications of the neglected-firm effect? First, the higher average return associated with neglected firms could be a reward for investing in securities that have less available information. Second, because the neglected-firm effect exists across all sizes of firms, large institutional investors that are prevented from investing in small firms can still take advantage of this effect because it also exists for medium and large firms (although it is notably less significant). Finally, whether such a simple rule will be useful in the future is debatable. Why? If investors increase their purchases of neglected firms, then such firms will no longer be neglected and hence will no longer provide abnormally high returns.

14.8 Insider Trading

insiders

The SEC requires the officers and directors of a corporation whose securities are traded on an organized exchange to report any transactions they have made in the firm's shares. Such a report, known as Form 4, must be filed within 10 days following the month in which the transaction takes place. This reporting requirement is also applicable to any stockholder who owns 10% or more of a firm's shares.[30] These stockholders, officers, and directors are referred to as **insiders.** The information they provide about their trading is subsequently reported in the SEC's monthly *Official Summary of Insider Transactions.*[31] For example, the summary of trades made in January (and reported by early

February) is published early in March. Thus, up to two months may elapse before knowledge of such trades becomes widespread.

The Securities Exchange Act of 1934 prohibits corporate insiders from short selling (discussed in Chapter 2). Furthermore, it requires them to return all short-term profits from security transactions in their own stocks to the corporation. For this purpose, short-term is defined as less than six months, meaning that the shares were both bought and sold within a six-month period.[32] As a result of this requirement, few insiders buy and sell within a six-month time period. Instead, most spread their buy-and-sell orders over longer periods so they do not have to return their profits.

In the United States it is illegal for anyone to enter into a security transaction if he or she has taken advantage of material "inside" information (that is, substantive nonpublic information) about the corporation that is unavailable to other people involved in the transaction. This proscription includes not only insiders but also those to whom they give such secret information. (The recipient of such a "tip" is the "tippee.")

Legally there are two types of nonpublic information: that which is "private" (that is, legal) and that which is "inside" (that is, possibly illegal). Unfortunately, the distinction between the two is ambiguous, causing continuous problems for security analysts.

Legal issues aside, two questions of relevance to outside investors may be posed: (1) Do insiders make unusual profits on transactions in their own stocks? and (2) if they do, can others profit by following their example as soon as it becomes public knowledge?

Insiders buy and sell their stock for many reasons. For example, some purchases result from the exercise of options, and some sales result from the need for cash. Moreover, it is not unusual to find some insiders purchasing a stock during a month in which other insiders are selling it. However, when a major piece of inside information suggests that a stock's value differs significantly from its current market price, it is reasonable to expect a preponderance of insider trades on one side of the market (that is, either purchases or sales). In this situation there is **asymmetric information** in the marketplace because insiders know more than others and are trading on the basis of this information.

asymmetric information

One way to search for such situations is to examine the *Official Summary* and count the number of days during a month that each insider traded his or her firm's stock (excluding the exercise of options).[33] If the number of days on which purchases were made exceeded those on which sales were made, the individual can be counted as a net purchaser during that month; if the converse held, the individual would be a net seller. Next the number of net purchasers and sellers of the firm's stock can be considered. If there were at least, say, three more net purchasers than net sellers, it might be inferred that, on balance, favorable insider information motivated the insider trades during the month. Conversely, if there were at least three more net sellers than net purchasers, it might be inferred that, on balance, unfavorable insider information motivated the insider trades. Different cutoff levels could be used in this process to reflect the intensity of insider trading. A cutoff of 1 would require a simple majority of trades of one type, whereas a cutoff of 5 would require a "supermajority" of trades of one type.

Such a procedure was used in a detailed study of insider transactions.[34] Table 14.10 summarizes the key results. The two columns on the right side of the table indicate the "abnormal" returns over an eight-month period on securities that exceeded the cutoff level for insider trading. For example, if an investor purchased every stock in the sample for which there were three or more net purchasers and sold every stock for which there were three or more net sellers during a month, more or less coincident with the transactions of the insiders themselves, then the investor would have earned, on average, an abnormal return of 5.07% during the subsequent eight months. If the transac-

TABLE 14.10 Abnormal Returns Associated with Insider Trading

Sample Cutoff (No. of Net Purchasers or Sellers)	No. of Cases	Average Abnormal Return (%) over Eight Months Following	
		Month of Transaction	Month Information Became Publicly Available
1	362	1.36	.70
3	861	5.07	4.94
4	293	5.14	4.12
5	157	4.48	4.08

Source: Jeffrey F. Jaffe, "Special Information and Insider Trading," *Journal of Business,* 47, no. 3 (July 1974): 421, 426. © 1974, The University of Chicago.

tions had been made instead at roughly the time the information was published in the *Official Summary,* an average abnormal return of 4.94% would have been earned during the next eight months.

As the first row in the table shows, a bare majority of insider trades does not appear to isolate possible effects of insider information. But a majority of 3, 4, or 5 does seem to do so. The figures shown are gross of any transaction costs; but even so, it appears that insiders can and do make money from special knowledge of their companies. This outcome is not surprising, because if anyone knows the true value of a firm, it should be the insiders. The information these insiders presumably are using is nonpublic in nature, so these findings suggest that markets are not strong-form efficient. (The notion of market efficiency was introduced in Chapter 4.)

On the other hand, the abnormal returns associated with transactions that could have been made by outsiders, using only publicly available information on insider trading, are quite surprising. After all, once the *Official Summary* is made public, for all practical purposes information is no longer asymmetric so investors should not be able to invest profitably based on its contents. Those abnormal returns associated with cutoffs of 3, 4, or 5 pass statistical tests designed to see if they might result simply from chance. After transaction costs, trades designed to capitalize on such information still appear to produce abnormal returns (although not highly so), suggesting that markets are not even semistrong-form efficient. However, later studies have found that outsiders cannot use the publicly available information about insider trading to make abnormal profits and thus support the notion that markets are semistrong-form efficient.[35] With such conflicting evidence it appears that whether insider trading information can be profitably used by outsiders remains an open question.

14.9 Sources of Investment Information

Because information affects the values of investments, the serious financial analyst must be well informed. There is a staggering array of "investment information"; some of it is published on paper and some of it appears in electronic form.

14.9.1 PUBLICATIONS

Every investor should read *The Wall Street Journal.* It provides extensive statistical data, financial news, and even a bit of humor. An alternative is the *Investors Business Daily* or the financial section of the *New York Times.* Most other daily newspapers contain financial information, but much less than the *Journal, Times,* and *Daily. Barron's* is a weekly publication with a wealth of statistical data (particularly in the "Market

Laboratory" section). Another weekly publication that contains reports prepared by security analysts at various brokerage firms is the *Wall Street Transcript.*

A useful source of daily stock price and volume figures is the *Daily Stock Price Record,* published by Standard & Poor's Corporation. Each issue covers one calendar quarter, and all values for a given stock are listed in a single column. Standard & Poor's also publishes forecasts of company earnings in the weekly *Earnings Forecaster* and dividend information in the *Dividend Record.* Furthermore, some brokerage houses provide their major clients with copies of Standard & Poor's monthly *Stock Guide* and *Bond Guide,* which are illustrated in Figures 14.2 and 14.3.

Standard & Poor's *Corporation Records* are a major reference source for the financial history of individual companies. They consist of six alphabetical volumes and are periodically updated. A second major reference source is provided by Moody's Investor Services, Inc. Their *Manuals* are published annually, with periodic updates, and cover various fields: *Bank & Finance, Industrial, International, Municipal & Government, OTC Industrial, OTC Unlisted, Public Utility,* and *Transportation* are the titles of various volumes. In addition, both Standard & Poor's and Moody's also provide other publications to subscribers.

FIGURE 14.2 Standard & Poor's *Stock Guide,* November 1999

6 S&P-ADF — Standard & Poor's

¶ S&P 500 · # MidCap 400 · ✣ SmallCap 600 · • Options

Index	Ticker	Name of Issue (Call Price of Pfd. Stocks)	Market	Com. Rank. & Pfd. Rating	Inst. Hold Cos	Inst. Hold Shs. (000)	Principal Business	Price Range 1971-97 High	1971-97 Low	1998 High	1998 Low	1999 High	1999 Low	Oct. Sales in 100s	October, 1999 Last Sale Or Bid High	Low	Last	%Div Yield	P-E Ratio	EPS 5 Yr Growth	% Annualized Total Return 12 Mo	36 Mo	60 Mo
1	SPSC	S&P Super Composite 1500 Index	IDX	....[51]	..	...	U.S. equity perform indicator	212.05	111.17	261.73	193.53	298.47	254.39	....	287.54	259.12	285.57	1.2	26	...	25.0	23.4	...
2•[1]	SPIC	S&P 500 Index	IDX	....[52]	..	...	Broad large-cap indicator	986.25	60.96	1244.93	912.83	1420.33	1205.46	....	1373.17	1233.70	1362.93	1.2	26	5	25.7	26.5	26.0
3•[1]	SPMC	S&P MidCap 400 Index	IDX	....[53]	..	...	Broad mid-cap indicator	340.40	119.43	392.31	268.65	428.66	352.35	....	401.07	366.05	399.62	1.2	21	7	21.1	19.7	19.5
4•[1]	SPYC	S&P SmallCap 600 Index	IDX	....[54]	..	...	Broad small-cap indicator	192.98	92.45	206.31	126.15	190.24	154.14	....	177.45	167.90	175.67	0.8	20	9	12.0	7.8	12.8
5•[2]	AAM	✓Aames Financial	NY,P	NR	61	4221	Mortgage brokerage svcs	40¾	1 15/16	15 11/16	1	3¾	11/16	48923	1 7/16	11/16	1⅜	...	d	Neg	−67.2	−63.8	−17.9
6	AAON	✓AAON Inc	NNM	B	9	1552	Mfr air-condition'g/heat'g eqp	16 9/16	7/16	11¾	6⅝	16⅜	8⅛	2385	14	12¼	13⅛	...	10	17	45.8	36.8	2.0
✣7•[3]	AIR	✓AAR Corp	NY,Ch,Ph	B+	202	22181	Mkts aviation parts/service	27	13/16	32 7/16	17 7/16	24	14⅜	15576	18 1/16	15 13/16	16 11/16	2.0	11	29	−26.6	−2.7	17.8
8	RNT	✓Aaron Rents	NY	A−	84	10504	Rents & sells furniture	20¼	3½	24 5/16	11⅛	22¼	12⅞	2246	17¾	15¼	15 13/16	0.3	13	16	7.4	5.3	20.6
9	RNT.A	✓ Cl 'A'	NY	A−	24	884		18½	1⅝	26	10 9/16	18 3/16	11⅝	421	15⅞	14¾	15B	0.3	12	16	9.4	1.4	20.2
10•[4]	AATT	✓Aavid Thermal Technologies	NNM	NR	74	4585	Thermal mgmt prds	38¼	6 3/16	36¾	8½	25	11⅜	6435	23⅜	21¾	22½	...	18	NM	50.0	36.4	...
11•[5]	ABDR	✓Abacus Direct	NNM	NR	198	7799	Direct mktg svcs	44¼	14	59¾	32⅞	147	41	30853	147	111¼	146½	...	..	49	201	77.4	...
12	ABAX	✓Abaxis Inc	NNM	NR	12	821	Dvlp stge:blood analyzer sys	17½	2 1/16	3¾	1⅛	5½	1 7/16	14017	5½	4¼	4⅞	...	d	36	162	9.4	−0.4
¶13•[6]	ABT	✓Abbott Laboratories	NY,B,C,Ch,P,Ph	A+	1668	774251	Diversified health care prod	34⅞	¼	50 1/16	32½	53 5/16	36 1/16	1156120	42⅞	36 1/16	40⅜	1.7	24	18	−12.9	18.6	23.3
14	ABCR	✓ABC-NACO Inc	NNM	NR	64	8725	Mfr orig'l&replace'mt rail prd	27⅝	12	20¼	8	21	8¾	12693	16⅛	8¾	10⅜	...	d	Neg	−23.2	−10.8	−13.5
#15•[7]	ANF	✓Abercrombie & Fitch Co'A'	NY,Ch,Ph	NR	564	88572	Retail casual apparel	18 1/16	6¼	36⅛	14 7/16	50¾	21	680568	39 15/16	21	27¼	...	21	67	37.3	35.3	...
16•[8]	ABY	✓Abitibi-Consolidated	NY,To,Mo,P,Vc	B−	126	89474	Newsprint,paper prods	28⅝	2 5/16	16 15/16	7⅝	13 13/16	7⅝	37773	12½	11¼	12 1/16	◆2.3	d	Neg	32.9	−1.5	0.7
✣17•[9]	ABM	✓ABM Industries Inc	NY,B,Ch,P,Ph	A+	145	14704	Janitorial & building maint	31½	¾	37	25	34½	21⅞	12196	25 9/16	22 13/16	23⅞	2.3	15	15	−13.2	12.7	20.3
18	ABN	✓ABN AMRO Holding ADS[58]	NY,Ph	NR	45	18172	Bank'g operations, Netherlands	24 7/16	18¼	27 9/16	14¼	25	19	8496	24¼	22 1/16	24⅛	2.2	15	10	29.3	...	...
19	BOUT	✓About.com Inc	NNM	NR	63	2213	Internet based news,info svcs	....	....	....	....	100	19½	80951	61½	45⅜	47¼	...	d	...	...	...	...
20	ABRI	✓Abrams Industries	NNM	B	17	567	Construct'n/mfg, real estate	8⅜	¾	8 13/16	4⅛	6⅞	3	311	5	4	4⅜	3.7	d	−25	−26.0	3.9	2.0
21	AKR	✓Acadia Realty Trust	NY,Ph,P	NR	26	4385	Real estate investment trust	20⅜	8¾	9 5/16	4¾	5¾	4 13/16	2402	5 3/16	4 13/16	5 1/16	9.5	d	Neg	−2.5	−18.4	−10.0
22	ANA	✓Acadiana Bancshares	AS	NR	12	254	Savings bank, Louisiana	24¾	11⅜	25¾	14¾	19⅞	17⅜	178	19⅞	18⅝	19⅝	2.6	13	...	17.3	15.1	...
23	ACLE	✓Accel Intl	NNM	C	12	806	Property & casualty insurance	14⅜	1 1/16	3½	2⅛	3⅜	½	6792	1 3/16	½	⅝	...	d	−18	−81.0	−43.2	−24.2
24	AIF	✓Acceptance Insur Cos	NY,B,Ch,P,Ph	B−	87	6128	Hldg co: prop & casualty insur	54 11/16	6	25¾	16¾	20 7/16	11⅝	7304	14 15/16	11⅝	14 7/16	...	72	−25	−26.4	−10.7	−2.5
25•[8]	AKLM	✓Acclaim Entertainment	NNM	†B−	147	29397	Dvlp video game cartridges	31¾	1 15/16	12 5/16	3⅝	13	5	160564	8 11/16	6¾	7⅛	...	13	−13	−10.9	13.0	−16.3
26	ACL	✓ACE Limited	NY,Ph	NR	377	177207	Provides liability insurance	33 11/16	6 15/16	43	24⅜	35¼	15½	226829	19⅞	15½	19 7/16	2.3	9	NM	−41.6	3.6	22.5
27	AK	✓Ackerley Group	NY	B−	65	6270	Brdcstg:pro basketball:adv	18½	⅝	24⅞	14⅜	20	11⅛	8896	16¾	11⅜	16 11/16	0.1	39	90	−17.3	11.0	38.5
28	ACME	Acme Communications	NNM	NR	5	554	Own,oper TV stations	....	....	....	....	36¼	23	48926	36¼	28	36	...	..	...	...	...	...
29	ACEE	✓Acme Electric	NNM,P	B−	28	856	Mfr pwr conversion eqp	38¾	⅜	6½	3 15/16	7⅛	4	3099	6⅜	5⅛	5⅞	...	10	NM	13.3	−9.3	−10.8
30	ACU	✓Acme United	AS,Ch	C	11	342	Medic eq:shears,scissors	19 9/16	1⅜	6½	1⅞	2½	15/16	970	1 3/16	15/16	1⅜	...	17	53	−50.0	−26.8	−17.0
#31•[10]	ART	✓ACNielsen Corp	NY	NR	355	51119	Marketing/info analysis	24⅝	14	29⅝	19⅛	32¾	19⅞	54474	23 15/16	19⅞	22	...	17	...	−17.8	12.7	...
32	ACRG	ACR Group	NSC	B−	2	316	Dstr heating & cooling equip	20 13/16	5/16	2 13/16	1	2⅜	1	3038	1⅝	1⅛	1¼	...	7	39	−13.0	−4.5	7.4
33	ACRO	Acrodyne Communications	NSC	NR	5	249	Dvlp,mfr transmitter equip	7¾	1⅞	5¾	2⅜	4 11/16	1¾	1858	2⅝	1¾	2	...	d	−44	−47.6	−19.8	...
34	AYS	✓ACSYS Inc	AS	NR	10	1072	Temporary staffing svcs	....	....	20½	2½	5⅝	1 11/16	6561	2⅝	1 11/16	1⅞	...	d	...	−80.8	...	...
35•[8]	ANET	✓ACT Networks	NNM	C	63	6632	Mfr data commun ntwk prd	48½	5¾	15¼	4¼	25⅝	4 15/16	110608	9	4 15/16	6½	...	d	Neg	−23.5	−42.5	...
36•[11]	ACTL	✓Actel Corp	NNM	NR	118	14534	Dvlp programmable gate arrays	29⅛	7¼	21½	7¼	22⅝	11	38877	19¼	16	18⅞	...	27	81	47.3	1.8	16.6
✣37	ACTN	✓Action Performance Cos	NNM	NR	236	15986	Motorsports replicas/merch	38½	1½	39¼	17	48¼	16¼	86570	25⅞	18⅝	20⅜	...	11	83	−31.9	10.7	52.1
38	IATV	✓ACTV Inc	NSC	C	40	5323	Interactive TV programming	9	⅝	4½	1⅜	25¼	3 13/16	117097	16⅝	13¼	15 13/16	...	d	−10	837	79.2	24.7
#39•[12]	ACN	✓Acuson Corp	NY,P	B−	127	13648	Medical ultrasound imaging	40	5	20 11/16	13 7/16	18 1/16	10¼	14602	12 15/16	10¼	10⅜	...	16	41	−31.1	−21.1	−10.8
40	ACX	✓ACX Technologies[62]	NY,Ch	NR	110	11069	Mfr packag'g ceramic,alum'n pd	31⅜	5⅜	25 13/16	9 9/16	16 11/16	7½	10512	10¼	7½	7 13/16	...	5	47	−45.7	−23.9	−14.8
#41	ACXM	✓Acxiom Corp	NNM	B	363	52845	Computer-based mkting svcs	25	1	31¼	16½	31	14 9/16	427910	23½	14 9/16	16½	...	20	−33	−34.3	−5.4	17.9
✣42•[10]	ADAC	✓ADAC Laboratories	NNM	B	129	12279	Nuclear medicine comput sys	82⅛	1½	31⅝	16⅞	24½	5⅝	28902	10	8¼	8 11/16	...	d	Neg	−70.7	−24.9	2.0
43	ADGO	✓Adams Golf	NNM	NR	18	370	Dgn/mfr golf clubs	....	....	18⅞	3	5 9/16	2	10553	3 9/16	2 9/16	2⅜	...	d	...	−48.6	...	...
44	AE	✓Adams Res & Energy	AS,B,Ch,Ph	B	17	774	Oil&gas explor,dev,prod'n	70½	1¾	14¾	5¼	11⅜	5 13/16	756	9½	7⅞	8 13/16	1.1	10	10	11.9	−11.3	3.4
¶45•[13]	ADPT	✓Adaptec Inc	NNM	B+	371	84591	Mfr computer data flow sys	54¼	9/16	39½	7⅞	45⅜	17 7/16	453558	45⅜	35¾	45	...	25	−40	178	14.0	31.1
✣46•[13]	ADAP	✓Adaptive Broadband	NNM	B	89	8994	Electr commun transmiss eq	39¾	¼	24¼	6¾	43⅞	8⅜	94204	43⅞	32½	36 15/16	...	32	NM	381	35.8	3.6
¶47•[14]	ADCT	✓ADC Telecommunications	NNM	B	465	99850	Telecommunications equip	45	1/64	42	15¾	53⅝	34⅜	446412	48 9/16	40	47 11/16	...	35	17	107	11.7	32.3
48	ADEX	✓ADE Corp	NNM	NR	36	5372	Mfr semiconductor mfg eqp	45½	8¼	21	6½	17	8 1/16	4404	15¼	12⅞	15	...	d	Neg	50.0	19.1	...
49	ABIZ	✓Adelphia Business Solutions'A'[63]	NNM	NR	76	7638	Telecommunication svcs	....	....	20⅛	3½	32¾	8⅜	42783	32¾	24⅛	28⅜	...	d	...	191	...	...
50•[15]	ADLAC	✓Adelphia Communic'A'	NNM	C	244	33106	Cable TV operations in U.S.	28½	4½	48⅛	16⅜	87	44⅞	302553	58⅞	47¼	54⅝	...	..	...	45.2	91.7	35.4
51	ADFC	✓AdForce Inc	NNM	NR	31	3791	Internet ad services	....	....	....	....	62¾	12 9/16	43549	28 9/16	22¾	27⅝	...	d	...	...	...	...

Uniform Footnote Explanations-See Page 1. Other: [1]CBOE. [2]CBOE:Cycle 3. [3]Ph:Cycle 1. [4]ASE,CBOE:Cycle 3. [5]Ph:Cycle 3. [6]Ph:Cycle 2. [7]CBOE,P:Cycle 2. [8]CBOE:Cycle 1. [9]P:Cycle 3. [10]ASE:Cycle 2. [11]P,Ph:Cycle 3. [12]P:Cycle 1. [13]ASE:Cycle 1. [14]P:Cycle 2. [15]CBOE,Ph:Cycle 1. [51]Inst. hold 54.99%(by $). [52]Inst. hold 54.53%(by $). [53]Inst. hold 60.33%(by $). [54]Inst. hold 57.03%(by $). [55]12 Mo Dec,'95. [56]12 Mo Dec'95. [57]Pfd in $M. [58]Ea ADS rep 1 ord 1.25NLG. [59]To be determined. [60]5 Mo Dec'96. [61]®$1.96,'96. [62]Plan spin-off Coors Ceramics Co. [63]Formerly Hyperion Telecommunications'A'. [64]Mar'98 & prior. [65]12 Mo Dec'98. [66]Fiscal Mar'98 & prior.

Source: Standard & Poor's *Stock Guide* (New York: Standard & Poor's, November 1999): p. 6.

26 **AAF-ADV** Standard & Poor's

Exchange / Individual Issue Statistics	Interest Dates	S&P Rating	Date of Last Rating Change	Prior Rating	Eligible	Bond Form	Redemption Provisions: Regular Price	Regular (Begins) Thru	Sinking Fund Price	Sinking Fund (Begins) Thru	Refund/Other Restriction Price	Refund/Other Restriction (Begins) Thru	Outst'g (Mil $)	Underwriting Firm	Underwriting Year	Price Range 1999 High	Price Range 1999 Low	Mo. End Price Sale(s) or Bid	Curr. Yield	Yield to Mat.
Title-Industry Code & Co. Finances (In Italics)	*Ind*	*Fixed Charge Coverage 1996*	*1997*	*1998*		*Year End*	*Million $ Cash & Equiv.*	*Curr. Assets*	*Curr. Liab.*	*Balance Sheet Date*	*L. Term Debt (Mil $)*		*Capital-ization (Mil $)*	*Total Debt % Capital*						
AAF-McQuay Inc	*42b*	*2.40*	*1.54*	*1.36*		*Je*	*9.85*	*368.0*	*330.0*	*3-31-99*	*138.0*		*472.0*	*56.7*						
Sr Nts[1] 8⅞s 2003	Fa15	B+			Y	R	NC	....	....	....	....	....	125	C4	'96	98	65	70	12.68	22.16
AAI.FosterGrant, Inc	*37*	*n/a*	*n/a*	*n/a*		*Dc*	*1.56*	*84.50*	*56.00*	*7-3-99*	*75.50*		*96.30*	*97.0*						
Sr Nts[2] 'B' 10¾s 2006	jJ15	CCC	3/99	B+	Y	BE	105.375	(7-15-02)	....	....	[3]Z110.75	7-15-01	75.0	Exch.	'98	95	35	35	....	....
Aames Financial	*25h*	*Δ2.01*	*Δ2.65*	*Δd4.47*		*Je*	*10.98*	*743.6*	*340.7*	*6-30-99*	*275.0*		*421.0*	*65.3*						
• Sr Nts 10½s 2002	[4]Feb	NR				R	■100	(2-1-00)	100	....	....	....	23.0	P2	'95	97	71	s77⅛	13.61	24.20
Sr Nts[2] 9⅛s 2003	mN	CCC+	11/98	B	Y	BE	104.562	(11-1-00)	....	....	....	....	150	B7	'96	75⅝	63	63¼	14.43	23.87
AAR Corp	*3a*	*Δ4.06*	*Δ4.53*	*Δ4.22*		*My*	*1.44*	*497.6*	*156.5*	*8-31-99*	*181.0*		*507.0*	*35.7*						
Nts[5] 9½s 2001	mN	BBB	7/97	BBB–	X	R	NC	....	....	....	....	....	65.0	G1	'89	108½	103¾	104	9.13	7.32
Nts 7¼s 2003	aO15	BBB	7/97	BBB–	X	R	NC	....	....	....	....	....	50.0	G1	'93	104¼	98⅜	99	7.32	7.55
Nts 6⅞s 2007	jD15	BBB			X	BE	NC	....	....	....	....	....	60.0	G1	'97	104⅛	93⅞	95¼	7.22	7.67
[6]Abbey Healthcare Group	*30a*	*2.06*	*d0.18*	*....*		*Dc*	*22.00*	*190.0*	*162.0*	*6-30-99*	*405.0*		*331.0*	*129.0*						
Sr[1]Sub Nts 9½s 2002	mN	B	11/98	B+	Y	R	102.375	10-31-00	....	....	....	....	200	D6	'93	101½	94	95⅝	9.93	11.26
Abbott Laboratories	*21a*	*29.11*	*22.84*	*21.26*		*Dc*	*401.7*	*5547*	*4170*	*6-30-99*	*1338*		*8760*	*26.5*						
Nts 5.60s 2003	aO	AAA			X	BE	NC	....	....	....	....	....	200	G1	'93	102⅛	96⅜	97	5.77	6.48
Nts 6.80s 2005	Mn15	AAA			X	BE	NC	....	....	....	....	....	150	G1	'95	108⅝	99¾	100¾	6.75	6.64
Nts 6.40s 2006	jD	AAA			X	BE	NC	....	....	....	....	....	250	G1	'96	107½	96⅜	97½	6.56	6.85
Nts 5.40s 2008	mS15	AAA			X	BE	NC	....	....	....	....	....	200	G1	'98	100¾	90	91¼	5.92	6.72
Accuride Corp	*8*	*n/a*	*n/a*	*1.40*		*Dc*	*22.60*	*159.0*	*81.70*	*6-30-99*	*455.0*		*429.0*	*108.0*						
Sr Sub[2]Nts[7] 'B' 9¼s 2008	Fa	B–			Y	BE	104.625	(2-1-03)	....	....	[8]Z109.25	2-1-03	200	Exch.	'98	102¼	90½	90½	10.22	11.03
ACME Television/Finance	*12c*	*n/a*	*n/a*	*n/a*		*Dc*	*1.62*	*22.00*	*59.60*	*6-30-99*	*162.0*		*284.0*	*73.6*						
Sr[9]Disc Nts[10] 'B' 10⅞s 2004	mS30	B–			Y	BE	105.438	(9-30-01)	....	....	[11]Z110.875	9-30-00	175	Exch.	'98	87¼	79¾	87¼	....	Flat
Adams Outdoor Advertising	*1*	*n/a*	*n/a*	*n/a*		*Dc*	*5.61*	*19.50*	*7.29*	*6-30-99*	*124.0*		*54.60*	*227.0*						
Sr Nts[2] 10¾s 2006	Ms15	B			Y	BE	105.375	(3-15-01)	....	....	....	....	105	Exch.	'96	110	101	102¾	10.46	10.15
Adelphia Communications	*12a*	*0.50*	*0.49*	*0.38*		*Mr*				*6-30-99*	*3527*		*2932*	*120.0*						
Sr Deb 11⅞s 2004	mS15	B+	9/98	B	Y	R	104.50	9-14-00	....	....	....	....	125	S1	'92	107½	104	104½	11.36	10.66
Sr Deb[12]'B' 9⅞s 2005	Ms	B+	9/98	B	Y	BE	NC	....	....	....	....	....	130	D6	'93	111½	101¼	101⅞	9.69	9.41
Sr Nts[13] 'B' 10¼s 2000	jJ15	B+	9/98	B	Y	R	NC	....	....	....	....	....	100	Exch.	'94	104½	100¼	101	10.15	8.73
Sr Nts[13] 'B' 9¼s 2002	aO	B+	9/98	B	Y	BE	NC	....	....	....	....	....	325	Exch.	'97	106½	100¼	100¼	9.23	9.15
Sr([14]PIK)Nts[13]'B' 9½s 2004	Fa15	B+	9/98	B	Y	R	103.56	2-14-00	....	....	....	....	[15]198	Exch.	'94	107⅛	100	100½	9.45	9.35
Sr Nts[13] 'B' 10½s 2004	jJ15	B+	11/98	NR	Y	BE	NC	....	....	....	....	....	150	Exch.	'97	114	103	104½	10.05	9.29
Sr Nts 'B' 9⅞s 2007	Ms	B+	9/98	B	X	BE	NC	....	....	....	....	....	350	Exch.	'97	112½	101¼	101¾	9.71	9.53
Sr Nts[2] 'B' 8⅜s 2008	Fa	B+	9/98	B	Y	BE	NC	....	....	....	....	....	150	Exch.	'98	105	93	94	8.91	9.43
ADT Operations	*63*	*Merged into Tyco Intl, see*																		
Sr Nts[2] 8¼s 2000	fA	A–	7/97	BBB–	X	R	NC	....	....	....	....	....	9.50	M2	'93	104	101¼	101¼	8.15	6.51
Advanced Accessory Sys	*42b*	*n/a*	*n/a*	*n/a*		*Dc*	*6.08*	*113.0*	*63.70*	*6-30-99*	*178.0*		*204.0*	*90.7*						
Sr Sub Nts[2] 'B' 9¾s 2007	aO	B–			Y	BE	104.875	(10-1-02)	....	....	[16]Z109.75	10-1-00	125	Exch.	'98	102	89¼	89¼	10.92	11.88
Advanced Micro Dev	*23h*	*d13.07*	*d1.23*	*d1.19*		*Dc*	*650.8*	*1297*	*783.1*	*6-27-99*	*1441*		*3595*	*47.9*						
Sr Sec Nts[2] 11s 2003	fA	B	4/98	BB–	Y	BE	105.50	(8-1-01)	....	....	....	....	400	D6	'96	106½	90¼	92	11.96	13.78
Advanced Radio Telecom	*67f*	*n/a*	*n/a*	*d1.53*		*Dc*	*53.80*	*72.68*	*101.6*	*6-30-99*	*118.0*		*236.0*	*82.2*						
Sr Nts[2] 14s 2007	Fa15	CCC	6/98	CCC+	Y	R	107	(2-15-02)	....	....	[17]Z114	2-14-00	135	M2	'97	93	66	90⅝	15.45	16.22
[18]Advanstar Communications	*63*	*n/a*	*n/a*	*n/a*		*Dc*	*39.30*	*53.10*	*72.70*	*3-31-99*	*408.0*		*579.0*	*72.4*						
Sr Sub Nts[19] 9¼s 2008	Mn	B–		B–	Y	BE	104.625	(5-1-03)	....	....	[20]Z109.75	5-1-01	150	Exch.	'98	104¼	93	93⅛	9.93	10.49
ADVANTA Corp	*25e*	*2.45*	*0.88*	*d0.28*		*Dc*				*6-30-99*	*1012*		*1579*	*64.1*						
M-T Nts[21]'C' 7⅝s 2000	aO16	BB–	2/98	BB	Y	BE	NC	....	....	....	....	....	25.0	B7	'97	97⅝	95⅛	96¼	7.66	11.59

Uniform Footnote Explanations-See Page 1. Other: [1] Co must offer repurch at 101 on Chge of Ctrl. [2] (HRO)On Chge of Ctrl at 101. [3] Max $26.25M red w/proceeds of Equity Off'g. [4] Int pd monthly. [5] (HRO)For Trigger Event at 100. [6] Now Apria Healthcare Group. [7] Co may repurch at 100&prem for Ctrl Chge. [8] Max $80M red w/proceeds of Eq Off'g. [9] (HRO)On Chge of Ctrl(Accreted Val). [10] Int accrues at 9-30-00. [11] Accreted:Max $61.3M red w/proceeds Eq Off'g. [12] Co must offer repurch at 100 on Chge of Ctrl. [13] (HRO)On Chge of Ctrl at 100. [14] Co may pay int in add'l nts to 2-15-99. [15] Incl disc. [16] Max $44M red w/proceeds of Pub Eq Off'g. [17] Max $33.8M red w/proceeds of Pub Eq Off'g. [18] Subsid & data of Advanstar Hldgs. [19] (HRO)On Chge of Ctrl at 100,to 5-01-03,101 aft. [20] Max $52M red w/proceeds of Equity Off'g. [21] Issued in min denom $100T.

FIGURE 14.3 Standard & Poor's *Bond Guide*, November 1999

Source: Standard & Poor's *Bond Guide* (New York: Standard & Poor's, November 1999): p. 26.

Historical data and analyses for approximately 1,700 stocks and most major industries can be found in the *Value Line Investment Survey.* Adjusted betas are also shown for the individual stocks in the *Survey.* The *Value Line Options* and *Convertibles* manuals, along with the *Survey,* offer estimates of the relative attractiveness of these investments.

Publications of major security analysts' societies include the *Financial Analysts Journal* (United States), *Analyse Financière* (France), and the *Professional Investor* (United Kingdom). Academic journals that contain articles on financial markets and various aspects of investing include the *Journal of Business,* the *Journal of Finance,* the *Journal of Financial and Quantitative Analysis,* the *Journal of Financial Economics,* the *Journal of Financial Intermediation,* the *Journal of Financial Markets,* and the *Review of Financial Studies.*

Anyone interested in the management of money for institutional or corporate investors (especially pension funds) should consider reading the *Journal of Portfolio Management,* the *Journal of Fixed Income,* the *Journal of Investing,* the *Journal of Futures Markets,* and the *Journal of Derivatives,* all of which publish the views of both practitioners and academicians. A biweekly periodical that covers current industry news and that is widely read by institutional investors and money managers is *Pensions and Investment Age. Institutional Investor,* a periodical full of feature stories on the investment industry, is published monthly. *Plan Sponsor* is a monthly publication directed at institutional investors managing pension funds. Individual investors will find the articles in the monthly issues of the *AAII Journal,* published by the Chicago-based American Association of Individual Investors, informative. Also of interest are *Business Week* (a weekly publication) and *Forbes* and *Fortune* (biweeklies).

Data on mutual funds is published in a number of places. Morningstar provides extensive information in both hard copy and computer-readable forms. Other sources include publications put out by Lipper Analytical Services, William E. Donoghue, American Association of Individual Investors, Value Line, Micropal, and CDA/Wiesenberger Financial Services.

Although a company's annual and quarterly reports provide useful information, the annual (10K) and quarterly (10Q) business and financial reports filed with the SEC usually include more details. Whereas the annual reports are audited, it should be noted that quarterly reports are unaudited.

A source of macroeconomic data such as monetary aggregates (like the money supply) and other monetary items is the *Federal Reserve Bulletin,* a monthly publication by the Board of Governors of the Federal Reserve System. The Department of the Treasury publishes quarterly the *Treasury Bulletin,* which contains data on government debt and interest rates. Data on national income and production are published monthly by the U.S. Department of Commerce in the *Survey of Current Business.* The Department of Commerce also publishes on a monthly basis the *Business Conditions Digest,* where various economic indicators can be found.

14.9.2 ELECTRONICALLY DELIVERED DATA

The rapid increase in the use of personal computers by those who invest money for others, as well as by those who invest for themselves, has led to a major expansion in the availability of computer-readable investment data. Large amounts of financial and economic data, such as common stock prices, mutual fund information, and financial statements, are provided on computer disks or over the Internet for a fee by Standard & Poor's Compustat Services, Value Line, Inc., Morningstar, and Lipper Analytical Services, among others.

The Internet has the potential to revolutionize the delivery of investment information. Nearly every organization involved in investment management maintains a Web site. In many cases, information that just a few years ago would have cost thousands of dollars to obtain is now available for free on demand over the Internet. The Internet simply is too dynamic to present an exhaustive list of attractive Web sites here. Nevertheless, students are encouraged to explore for themselves the immense investment resources now available to them on the Internet.[36] To help students, some of the more popular Web sites are listed in the chapter references at the end of the book and in various footnotes.

Summary

1. Financial analysts are investment professionals who evaluate securities and then make investment recommendations. Those recommendations may be used by portfolio managers or by certain clients of the analysts.
2. There are two primary reasons for engaging in financial analysis: to determine certain characteristics of securities and to attempt to identify mispriced securities.
3. To understand and estimate the risks and returns of individual securities as well as groups of securities, one must understand both financial markets and the principles of security valuation.
4. Technical analysis involves short-term predictions of security price movements based on past patterns of prices and trading volumes. Fundamental analysis con-

cerns estimates of the basic determinants of security values, such as future sales, expenses, and earnings for firms.

5. Many financial analysts focus their research efforts on analyzing company financial statements. Such research permits an analyst to better understand a company's business operations, its plans for future growth, what factors affect its profitability, and how those factors affect its profitability.

6. When prominent analysts publish favorable reports on a stock, its price tends to immediately rise by an abnormal amount. Conversely, when they publish unfavorable reports on a stock, its price tends to immediately fall. Neither of these price movements is subsequently reversed.

7. Stocks that are neglected by analysts tend to have abnormally high returns.

8. In the United States, trading on inside information is illegal in public security markets. However, defining inside information is difficult.

9. There are many printed sources of information about investing that are available to the public. However, the fastest-growing source is an electronic one—the Internet.

Questions and Problems

1. If security markets are highly efficient, what role is there for financial analysts?

2. If an analyst can correctly forecast a company's next year earnings, does that necessarily imply that the analyst can correctly forecast how the company's stock will perform? Why?

3. Despite the arguments and evidence offered by proponents of market efficiency, many investors pay attention to technical analysis in some form. Speculate as to why these investors use this kind of investment research.

4. Describe the types of behavior that must be exhibited by investors as a group if momentum and contrarian investment strategies are to be successful. In what ways do those behaviors run counter to how the efficient markets hypothesis assumes investors will act?

5. Last year both Hudson Homes and Baldwin Construction earned $1 million in net income. Both companies have assets of $10 million. Hudson generated a return on equity of 11.1%, whereas Baldwin produced a return on equity of 20.0%. What can explain the differences in return on equity between the two companies?

6. Last fiscal year, Afton Machinery had the following financial statement data:

Sales/Assets	2.10
Net Income/EBIT	0.65
EBIT/Sales	0.10
Assets/Equity	3.00

Calculate Afton's return on assets and return on equity.

7. Augusta Ironworks reported the following fiscal year-end financial data (in 000s).

Assets	$1,500
Liabilities	$900
Stockholders' Equity	$600
Net Income	$200
Dividends per Share	$0.50
Stock Price	$30.00
Average Shares Outstanding	100

Given this information, calculate Augusta's
a. Price-earnings ratio
b. Book value per share
c. Price-book ratio
d. Dividend yield
e. Payout ratio

8. Is it true that, when comparing the reported earnings of corporations, "a dollar is a dollar"?

9. Obtain an annual report for a corporation of your choosing. Using the financial statements contained in the report, compute the company's most recent year's return on equity by first calculating
   a. Operating margin
   b. Asset turnover
   c. Total assets-to-stockholders' equity
   d. Interest-to-stockholders' equity
   e. Tax rate

10. If Company *A* has a higher return on equity than Company *B,* does that necessarily mean that Company *A*'s earnings should grow faster than Company *B*'s earnings? Why?

11. Why does financial statement analysis typically rely heavily on examining financial ratios as opposed to absolute numbers (for example, net income-to-sales as opposed to just net income)?

12. What are some of the drawbacks of comparing a company's financial ratios to those of other companies within the same industry?

13. From the perspective of a proponent of market efficiency, why is it surprising that trades based on insider trading data found in the SEC's *Official Summary of Insider Transactions* appear to produce significant abnormal profits?

14. (Appendix Question) The closing, high, and low prices for Fort McCoy Packaging stock during a 10-day interval are shown below. Construct a bar chart for Fort McCoy Packaging stock for this period of time.

Fort McCoy Packaging

Day	Closing Price	High	Low
1	20	21	19
2	$20\frac{1}{4}$	$20\frac{1}{4}$	18
3	21	22	$20\frac{1}{2}$
4	$21\frac{1}{8}$	$22\frac{7}{8}$	$21\frac{1}{8}$
5	21	$23\frac{1}{4}$	20
6	$21\frac{3}{4}$	22	$20\frac{3}{4}$
7	22	$23\frac{1}{2}$	$20\frac{1}{8}$
8	$20\frac{1}{8}$	22	$19\frac{1}{4}$
9	$19\frac{1}{8}$	$21\frac{1}{2}$	19
10	$18\frac{1}{4}$	$21\frac{7}{8}$	$17\frac{1}{8}$

15. (Appendix Question) Calculate the relative strength of Fort McCoy Packaging stock versus the S&P 500 during the 10-day period in problem 14 given the following closing prices for the S&P 500:

	Day									
	1	*2*	*3*	*4*	*5*	*6*	*7*	*8*	*9*	*10*
S&P 500 Closing Price	300	302	306	310	320	315	330	325	325	330

APPENDIX

Technical Analysis

As mentioned earlier, most (but not all) technical analysts rely on charts of stock prices and trading volumes. Virtually all employ colorful, and sometimes even mystical, terminology. For example, a significant price rise on relatively large trading volume might be described as an *accumulation*. The stock is said to be moving from "weak hands" to "strong hands" because its rising price on large trading volume is viewed as a situation in which demand is stronger than supply. In contrast, a significant price decline on relatively large trading volume may be described as a *distribution*. The stock is said to be moving from "strong hands" to "weak hands" because its declining price on large trading volume is viewed as a situation in which supply is stronger than demand. In both situations, relatively large trading volume might be considered a sign of a sustainable change in the stock's price, whereas relatively small trading volume indicates a transitory change.

What if there is a period during which a stock's price does not move significantly? If the stock's price movements are within a narrow band, the stock is said to be in a *consolidation phase*. A price level that a stock has difficulty rising above is known as a *resistance level*, and a price level that a stock does not seem to fall below is known as a *support level*.

Such statements may sound meaningful, but a proponent of market efficiency would argue that they fail to pass the tests of simple logic. First, changes in a stock's price occur when the consensus opinion concerning its value changes. This observation means that large volume associated with a price change only reflects a substantial difference of opinion concerning the impact of new information on the stock's value; small volume reflects smaller differences of opinion. Second, if price or volume data could be used to predict future short-term price movements, investors would rush to exploit such information, moving prices rapidly enough to make the information useless. Although some evidence suggests that there may be some technical trading rules that have merit (see Tables 14.1 and 14.2), whether they will be useful after transaction costs are fully taken into account is difficult to determine. Even if they do pass muster with respect to transaction costs, it is uncertain whether they will be useful in the future.

14A.1 Charts

chartists

Chartists (technicians who rely on chart formations) believe that certain patterns carry great significance, although they often disagree among themselves on the significance of a pattern or even on the existence of a pattern. Three basic types of charts are used: bar charts, line charts, and point and figure charts.

On a *bar chart* the horizontal axis is a time line, and the vertical axis measures a particular stock's price. More specifically, corresponding to a given day on the horizontal axis will be a vertical line, the top and bottom of which represent the high and low price for that stock on that day. Somewhere on this vertical line will be a small horizontal line representing the closing price for the day. As an example, consider the following hypothetical stock, whose trading background during the past five days is as follows:

Day	High Price	Low Price	Closing Price	Volume
$t-5$	11	9	10	200
$t-4$	12	9	11	300
$t-3$	13	12	12	400
$t-2$	11	10	11	200
$t-1$	14	11	12	500

Figure 14.4(a) presents a bar chart for this stock. Figure 14.4(b) indicates how such a bar chart of prices can be augmented by adding trading volume at the bottom.

Figure 14.5(a) is a bar chart exhibiting a pattern known as "head and shoulders." As time passed, the stock's price initially rose, hit a peak at *A,* and then fell to a bottom at

FIGURE 14.4 Types of Charts

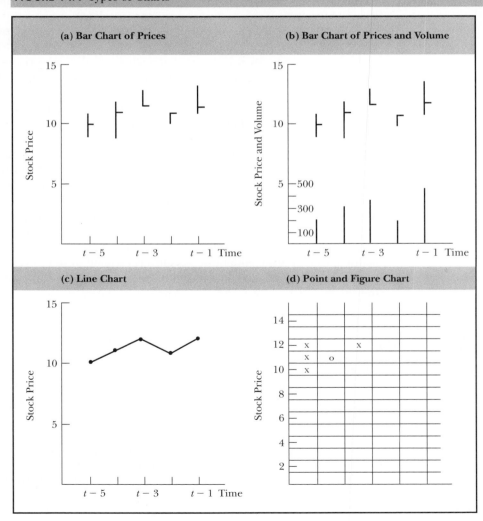

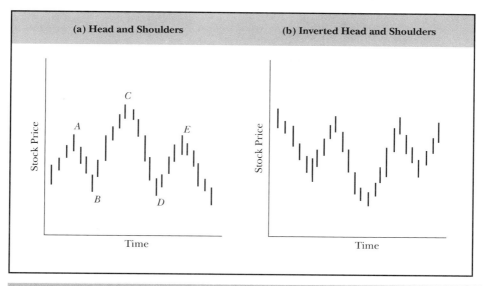

FIGURE 14.5 Bar Chart Patterns

B. Recovering from this fall, it went up to an even higher peak at *C*, but then fell again to a bottom at *D*. Next it rose to a peak at *E* that was not as high as the previous peak, *C*, and then it started to fall. As soon as the price went down past its previous low, *D*, a forecast was immediately made that the stock was going to plunge much lower (if the stock had not reached a level equal to *D*, no such forecast would have been made). Figure 14.5(b) shows a bar chart pattern known as "inverted head and shoulders," which results in a forecast that the stock is going to quickly rise by a substantial amount.[37]

On a *line chart*, the axes are the same as on a bar chart. However, only closing prices are presented, and they are connected to each other successively with straight lines, as illustrated in Figure 14.4(c). Although it is not shown, line charts are also frequently augmented with volume data similar to bar charts.

Methods of *point and figure chart* construction vary, but the idea is to plot closing prices that form a trend in a single column, moving to the next column only when the trend is reversed. For example, closing prices might be rounded to the nearest dollar and the chart begun by plotting a beginning rounded price on a certain day. As long as the (rounded) price does not change, nothing is done. When a different price is recorded, it is plotted on the chart. A price higher than the initial price is indicated with an X, with any gaps between the prices also marked with an X. A price below the initial price is marked with an O in a similar fashion. When a price is different from the last one recorded, it is plotted in the same column only if it is in the same direction. (In general, Xs denote advancing prices and Os denote declining prices.)

For example, if the first different price is above the beginning price, it is plotted above the beginning one. If another price is recorded that is above the second one, it is plotted in the same column, but if it is below the second one, it is plotted in a new column to the right of the first column. As long as new prices are in the same direction, they are plotted in the same column. Whenever there is a reversal, a new column is started (alternatively, a reversal is ignored and nothing is plotted unless it continues for a second day, at which point a new column is started). Figure 14.4(d) presents a point and figure chart for the same hypothetical stock used in the other panels.

Point and figure enthusiasts look for all sorts of patterns in their charts. As with all chartist techniques, the idea is to recognize a pattern early enough to profit from the ability to foresee the course of prices—a neat trick, if you can do it.

14A.2 Moving Averages

Many other procedures are used by technicians. Some construct moving averages to try to detect "intermediate" and "long-term" trends. With this procedure, a set number of the most recent closing prices on a security are averaged each day. (For example, daily closing prices during the previous 200 days may be used.) This process means that each day the oldest price is replaced with the most recent price in the set of closing prices that will be averaged. Frequently a line chart of these moving averages is plotted, along with a line chart of daily closing prices. Each day the charts are updated and examined for trends to see if there is a buy or a sell signal present somewhere.

Alternatively, a long-term moving average may be compared with a short-term moving average (the distinction between the two averages is that the long-term average uses a substantially larger set of closing prices in its calculations than the short-term average). When the short-term average crosses the long-term average, a "signal" is said to have been given. The action recommended depends on such things as whether the averages have been rising or falling, as well as the direction from which the short-term average crossed the long-term average (it may have been below and now is above, or it may have been above and now is below). A moving average trading rule was used to generate the returns shown in part (a) of Table 14.2.

Moving average techniques can also be applied to market indices in order to detect the direction of the stock market. In this case the signal tells the investor whether to devote more or less funds to stocks by altering his or her position in fixed-income securities.

14A.3 Relative Strength Measures

Another procedure used by technicians involves measuring relative strength. For example, a stock's price may be divided by a price index of its industry each day to indicate the stock's movement relative to its industry. Similarly, an industry index may be divided by a market index to indicate the industry's movement relative to the market, or a stock's price may be divided by a market index to indicate a stock's movement relative to the market. The idea is to examine changes in these relative strength measures with the hope of finding a pattern that can be used to accurately predict the future.

The momentum trading rules used in preparing Table 14.1 were based on the notion of relative strength in its simplest form. Stock returns over a just-ended holding period were calculated, and portfolios of winners and losers were formed. When semiannual or annual returns were used, the momentum trading rules seemed to have merit (at least before the consideration of transaction costs).

Some procedures of technical analysts focus on relationships among different indexes. For example, the Dow Theory requires that a pattern in the DJIA be "confirmed" by a certain movement in the Dow Jones Transportation Average before action be taken.[38] Another example involves computing the difference between the number of issues advancing and the number declining each day. A chart of the differences cumulated over time, known as the *advance–decline line,* may then be compared with a market index such as the Dow Jones Industrial Average.

14A.4 Contrary Opinion

Many technical procedures are based on the idea of contrary opinion (sometimes also known as *sentiment*). The idea is to determine the consensus opinion and then do the opposite. Two examples that were discussed earlier involved (1) buying stocks that had recently dropped in price and selling stocks that had recently risen in price and (2) buying stocks with low P/E ratios and selling stocks with high P/E ratios. For a third example, one might see whether the "odd-lotters" (those with trade orders involving less than 100 shares) are buying, and then sell any holdings of these stocks. If "the little investor is usually wrong," this procedure will usually be right. However, the basic premise about the little investor has yet to be factually established.

The widespread availability of personal computers and online services with data on stock prices and trading volumes has made it possible for individual investors to engage in technical analysis in the privacy of their own homes. Producers of software have been quick to provide programs to provide such analysis, complete with multicolored graphs. Online investors, particularly the infamous daytraders, appear to be heavy users of technical analysis.

Endnotes

1. Sumner N. Levine, ed., *Financial Analyst's Handbook I* (Homewood, IL: Dow Jones-Irwin, 1975).

2. William C. Norby, "Overview of Financial Analysis," in Levine, *Financial Analyst's Handbook I,* p. 3.

3. To obtain more information about becoming a CFA, contact the Institute of Chartered Financial Analysts. Their mailing address is P.O. Box 3668, Charlottesville, VA 22903, and their telephone number is (804) 980-3668. Information can also by obtained by contacting the AIMR Web site at <www.aimr.org>.

4. Some would add a third reason for conducting financial analysis: monitoring the firm's management in order to prevent managers from consuming an excessive amount of perquisites and making inappropriate decisions detrimental to the firm's shareholders. See Michael C. Jensen and William H. Meckling, "Theory of the Firm: Managerial Behavior, Agency Costs and Ownership Structure," *Journal of Financial Economics,* 3, no. 4 (October 1976): 305–360.

5. For a discussion regarding portfolio selection by an investor who has earned income (for example, from wages or from running a business), see Edward M. Miller, "Portfolio Selection in a Fluctuating Economy," *Financial Analysts Journal,* 34, no. 3 (May/June 1978): 77–83.

6. If the added benefits exceeded the added costs, then it would be profitable to perform more financial analysis because the incremental benefits from doing so would cover the associated costs. If the added costs exceeded the added benefits, then it would be profitable to cut back on the amount of financial analysis because costs would be reduced by an amount greater than benefits.

7. For an interesting argument on why the existence of trading costs results in some investors' performing financial analysis in an efficient market, see Sanford J. Grossman, "On the Efficiency of Competitive Stock Markets Where Traders Have Diverse Information," *Journal of Finance,* 31, no. 2 (May 1976): 573–585; Sanford J. Grossman and Joseph E. Stiglitz, "On the Impossibility of Informationally Efficient Markets," *American Economic Review,* 70, no. 3 (June 1980): 393–408; and Bradford Cornell and Richard Roll, "Strategies for Pairwise Competitions in Markets and Organizations," *Bell Journal of Economics,* 12, no. 1 (Spring 1981): 201–213.

8. Felix Rosenfeld, ed., *The Evaluation of Ordinary Shares,* is a summary of the proceedings of the Eighth Congress of the European Federation of Financial Analysts Societies (Paris: Dunod, 1975), p. 297.

9. Rosenfeld, *The Evaluation of Ordinary Shares,* pp. 297–298. For an argument that technical analysis is valuable in an efficient market, see David P. Brown and Robert H. Jennings, "On Technical Analysis," *Review of Financial Analysis,* 2, no. 4 (1989): 527–551. Also see Jack L. Treynor and Robert Ferguson, "In Defense of Technical Analysis," *Journal of Finance,* 40, no. 3 (July 1985): 757–773; and Lawrence Blume,

David Easley, and Maureen O'Hara, "Market Statistics and Technical Analysis: The Role of Volume," *Journal of Finance,* 49, no. 1 (March 1994): 153–181. A contrary view is offered by Hendrik Bessembinder and Kalok Chan, "Market Efficiency and the Returns to Technical Analysis," *Financial Management,* 27, no. 2 (Summer 1998): 5–17.

10. See, for example, Eugene F. Fama, "Efficient Capital Markets: A Review of Theory and Empirical Work," *Journal of Finance,* 25, no. 2 (May 1970): 383–417.

11. See, for example, Eugene F. Fama, "Efficient Capital Markets: II," *Journal of Finance,* 46, no. 5 (December 1991): 1575–1617.

12. Other studies present evidence that is consistent with these results. See, for example, Barr Rosenberg, Kenneth Reid, and Ronald Lanstein, "Persuasive Evidence of Market Inefficiency," *Journal of Portfolio Management,* 11, no. 3 (Spring 1985): 9–16; John S. Howe, "Evidence on Stock Market Overreaction," *Financial Analysts Journal,* 42, no. 4 (July/August 1986): 74–77; and Andrew W. Lo and A. Craig MacKinlay, "When Are Contrarian Profits Due to Stock Market Overreaction?" *Review of Financial Studies,* 3, no. 2 (1990): 175–205.

13. One explanation for these results that has been offered is that investors underreact to quarterly earnings announcements. See Chapter 16, particularly section 16.7, and Victor L. Bernard, Jacob K. Thomas, and Jeffery S. Abarbanell, "How Sophisticated Is the Market in Interpreting Earnings News?" *Journal of Applied Corporate Finance,* 6, no. 2 (Summer 1993): 54–63. Another related observation involving one-year formation periods concerns the Dow dividend strategy. This strategy requires buying the 10 highest dividend-yielding stocks in the DJIA and holding them for one year, at which point the portfolio is revised accordingly for another year. From 1973 through 1992 this strategy outperformed the DJIA by 5.15% per year, on average. Interestingly, it turns out that the stocks purchased in any year had a return that was 5.99% less than the DJIA the previous year, on average. Thus, the strategy actually involves buying last year's "losers" among the Dow Jones 30. See Dale L. Domian, David A. Louton, and Irene M. Seahawk, "The Dow Dividend Strategy: How It Works and Why," *AAII Journal,* 16, no. 4 (May 1994): 7–10.

14. A puzzling observation associated with part (f) was that 5% of the 7.2% abnormal return for the loser portfolio was earned during the Januaries that occurred during the test period. Conversely, −.8% of the −2.4% abnormal return for the winners was earned during Januaries. Hence the January anomaly (discussed in the appendix to Chapter 13) seems somehow to be intertwined with the long-term contrarian strategy.

15. Other studies have examined contrarian strategies and have been unable to confirm the usefulness of such strategies. In two of these studies it was argued that the benchmark portfolio returns were incorrectly determined. Thus, the abnormal returns were not calculated correctly because by definition they are equal to the difference between the returns on the portfolio and its benchmark. In a third study, the alleged cause of the overreaction—security analysts underpredicting earnings on losers and overpredicting earnings on winners—was contested. A fourth study suggested that the size effect (discussed in the appendix to Chapter 13) was largely responsible for the results because losers tend to be smaller than winners. Last, a fifth study argued that incorrect prices were used when the costs of buying and selling stocks were determined in arriving at the results reflected in parts (e) and (f) of Table 14.1. However, these studies have, in turn, been contested in a sixth study. Specifically, after their objections were taken into consideration, it was found that losers outperform winners by 5% to 10% per year, with the difference being the largest when only small firms were classified into winners and losers. The six studies are, respectively, K. C. Chan, "On the Contrarian Investment Strategy," *Journal of Business,* 61, no. 2 (April 1988): 147–163; Ray Ball and S. P. Kothari, "Nonstationary Expected Returns: Implications for Tests of Market Efficiency and Serial Correlations in Returns," *Journal of Financial Economics,* 25, no. 1 (November 1989): 51–74; April Klein, "A Direct Test of the Cognitive Bias Theory of Share Price Reversals," *Journal of Accounting and Economics,* 13, no. 2 (July 1990): 155–166; Paul Zarowin, "Size, Seasonality, and Stock Market Overreaction," *Journal of Financial and Quantitative Analysis,* 25, no. 1 (March 1990): 113–125; Jennifer Conrad and Gautam Kaul, "Long-Term Overreaction or Biases in Computed Returns?" *Journal of Finance,* 48, no. 1 (March 1993): 39–63; and Navin Chopra, Josef Lakonishok, and Jay R. Ritter, "Measuring Abnormal Performance: Do Stocks Overreact?" *Journal of Financial Economics,* 31, no. 2 (April 1992): 235–268.

Adding to the puzzle is the behavior of Canadian stocks. For one-year test periods the results were similar to those in the United States in that a momentum strategy seemed to work [as in part (d) of Table 14.1]. For three-year and five-year test periods, neither a momentum nor a contrarian strategy worked [unlike parts (e) and (f) of Table 14.1]. See Lawrence Kryzanowski and Hao Zhang, "The Contrarian Investment Strategy Does Not Work in Canadian Markets," *Journal of Financial and Quantitative Analysis,* 27, no. 3 (September 1992): 383–395.

16. Apparently significant returns can be earned from the weekly strategy if transaction costs are small (such as for large institutional investors). However, larger transaction costs result in negative net returns. See Bruce N. Lehmann, "Fads, Martingales, and Market Efficiency," *Quarterly Journal of Economics,* 105, no. 1 (February 1990): 1–28. For an argument that Lehmann has underestimated the size of transaction costs, see Jennifer Conrad, Mustafa N. Gultekin, and Gautam Kaul, "Profitability of Short-Term Contrarian Portfolio Strategies," unpublished paper, University of Michigan, 1991.

17. Lehmann, "Fads, Martingales, and Market Efficiency," p. 26.

18. Input–output analysis is sometimes used to ensure consistency between various industries and the economy in aggregate. This analysis is based on the notion that the output of certain industries (for example, the steel industry) is the input for certain other industries (for example, the household appliance industry).

19. In 1997, the Financial Accounting Standards Board adopted Rule 128, which affects how earnings per share are reported. The rule replaced *primary earnings per share,* which factored in some dilution for certain common stock equivalents, with an entirely undiluted measure of earnings per share called *basic earnings per share. Fully-diluted earnings per share* is calculated in almost the same manner as before but is now called *diluted earnings per share.* Financial analysts now have two distinct measures of earnings per share: one with no dilution and one with full dilution. For many companies, the change has been insignificant. For some companies, however, the change highlights the large impact that dilutive securities, such as warrants and employee stock options, can have on earnings per share.

20. For more on free cash flow and how it can be used to value a firm and its equity, see Aswath Damodaran, *Corporate Finance: Theory and Practice* (New York: Wiley, 1997), pp. 170–171, 634–646.

21. Analysts typically calculate an average value for balance sheet items used in financial ratios. This approach facilitates comparisons of point-in-time levels on the balance sheet with period flows on the income statement. In the Target Corporation example, the financial ratios were computed using the average of beginning-of-year and year-end values for balance sheet items.

22. In recent years analysts have increasingly come to view earnings before interest, taxes, depreciation, and amortization (EBITDA) relative to the total market value of the firm (its equity and debt) as a more effective measure of operating performance than pretax ROA. EBITDA is essentially a measure of the company's pretax cash flow.

23. Similar observations have been made regarding other studies of the recommendations made by major brokerage houses. See John C. Groth, Wilbur G. Lewellen, Gary G. Schlarbaum, and Ronald C. Lease, "An Analysis of Brokerage House Securities Recommendations," *Financial Analysts Journal,* 35, no. 1 (January/February 1979): 32–40; James H. Bjerring, Josef Lakonishok, and Theo Vermaelen, "Stock Prices and Financial Analysts' Recommendations," *Journal of Finance,* 38, no. 1 (March 1983): 187–204; and Philip Heitner, "Isn't It Time to Measure Analysts' Track Records?" *Financial Analysts Journal,* 47, no. 3 (May/June 1991): 5–6. For a comment on the first study, see the Letter to the Editor in the May/June 1980 issue by Clinton M. Bidwell, with a responding Letter to the Editor in the July/August 1980 issue by Wilbur G. Lewellen.

24. Two other studies of "Heard on the Street" recommendations reached similar conclusions. See Peter Lloyd-Davies and Michael Canes, "Stock Prices and the Publication of Second-Hand Information," *Journal of Business,* 51, no. 1 (January 1978): 43–56; and Pu Liu, Stanley D. Smith, and Azmat A. Syed, "Stock Price Reactions to *The Wall Street Journal*'s Securities Recommendations," *Journal of Financial and Quantitative Analysis,* 25, no. 3 (September 1990): 399–410. A former author of the "Heard on the Street" column, R. Foster Winans, was convicted of fraud and theft in 1985 for leaking the contents of his column to four brokers and subsequently sharing in the associated trading profits.

25. Value Line has a service called *Value Line Investment Survey for Windows,* to which investors can subscribe, that involves software and periodic updates of their rankings as well as other data. Besides its stock recommendations, Value Line also provides a measure of the risk of individual securities that is known as Safety Rank. This risk measure was found to be more highly correlated with subsequent returns than either beta or standard deviation, suggesting that it is a more useful measure of risk. See Russell J. Fuller and G. Wenchi Wong, "Traditional versus Theoretical Risk Measures," *Financial Analysts Journal,* 44, no. 2 (March/April 1988): 52–57, 67, and the Value Line Web site at <www.valueline.com>.

26. One study of Value Line recommendations found that most rank changes occur shortly after earnings announcements are made. Subsequent investigation revealed that Value Line's superior performance was attributable to the "post-earnings-announcement drift" (this phenomenon is discussed in Chapter 16). Hence the two anomalies seem to be related. See John Affleck-Graves and Richard R. Mendenhall, "The Relation between the Value Line Enigma and

Post-Earnings-Announcement Drift," *Journal of Financial Economics,* 31, no. 1 (February 1992): 75–96.

27. Jennifer Francis and Leonard Soffer, "The Relative Informativeness of Analysts' Stock Recommendations and Earnings Forecast Revisions," *Journal of Accounting Research,* 35, no. 2 (Autumn 1997): 193–211. Chapter 16 includes a discussion of analysts' forecasts of earnings.

28. See the appendix to Chapter 13 for a discussion of the size effect.

29. The presence of the size effect can be seen by noting that the average return for small firms of 13.5% is much larger than the average return for medium and large firms of 10.7% and 9.8%, respectively. It should be noted, however, that the existence of the neglected-firm effect has been contested; see Craig G. Beard and Richard W. Sias, "Is There a Neglected-Firm Effect?" *Financial Analysts Journal,* 53, no. 5 (September/October 1997): 19–23.

30. This reporting requirement should not be confused with SEC Rule 13d, which requires investors to disclose their holdings in a company once they are equal to 5% or more of the company's stock. Unlike Form 4 investors, Rule 13d investors are not viewed as insiders by the SEC, and they do not have to report every transaction they subsequently make.

31. The *Value Line Investment Survey* (published by Value Line, Inc., New York, NY) reports an "index of insider decisions" for each stock covered in its weekly service that is a cumulative index of the net number of purchasers (including those who exercise options) and sellers. The *Weekly Insider Report* (published by Vickers Stock Research Corp., Brookside, NJ) reports a ratio of total insider buying to total insider selling. For an article about what constitutes insider trading, see Gary L. Tidwell, "Here's a Tip—Know the Rules of Insider Trading," *Sloan Management Review,* 28, no. 4 (Summer 1987): 93–98.

32. If the insider bought the stock by exercising an option that was given to him or her as part of his or her compensation, then the six-month period is measured from the day the option was granted.

33. Examining 183 SEC cases, one study found that stock prices had an average abnormal return of 3.0% on each day that illegal insider buying took place and −3.5% on each day that illegal insider selling took place. See Lisa K. Meulbroek, "An Empirical Analysis of Illegal Insider Trading," *Journal of Finance,* 47, no. 5 (December 1992): 1661–1699.

34. Jeffrey F. Jaffe, "Special Information and Insider Trading," *Journal of Business,* 47, no. 3 (July 1974): 410–428. Also see Joseph E. Finnerty, "Insiders and Market Efficiency," *Journal of Finance,* 31, no. 4 (September 1976): 1141–1148; and Aaron B. Feigen, "Information Opportunities from Insider Trading Laws," *AAII Journal,* 11, no. 8 (September 1989): 12–15.

35. See Herbert S. Kerr, "The Battle of Insider Trading and Market Efficiency," *Journal of Portfolio Management,* 6, no. 4 (Summer 1980): 47–58; Wayne Y. Lee and Michael E. Solt, "Insider Trading: A Poor Guide to Market Timing," *Journal of Portfolio Management,* 12, no. 4 (Summer 1986): 65–71; H. Nejat Seyhun, "Insiders' Profits, Costs of Trading, and Market Efficiency," *Journal of Financial Economics,* 16, no. 2 (June 1986): 189–212; Michael S. Rozeff and Mir A. Zaman, "Market Efficiency and Insider Trading: New Evidence," *Journal of Business,* 61, no. 1 (January 1988): 25–44; and Ji-Chai Lin and John S. Howe, "Insider Trading in the OTC Market," *Journal of Finance,* 45, no. 4 (September 1990): 1273–1284.

36. Although such information can become quickly outdated, comprehensive lists of useful investment-related Web sites are found in Jean Henrich, "The Individual Investor's Guide to Investment Web Sites," *AAII Journal,* 19, no. 8 (September 1997): 15–23 and in almost every issue of *Computerized Investing* a bimonthly publication of the American Association of Individual Investors (see <www.aaii.com>). Also see the following three articles in the Fall/Winter 1996 issue (vol. 6, no. 2) of *Financial Practice and Education:* "An Introduction to Finance on the Internet" by Russ Ray; "A Guide to Locating Financial Information on the Internet" by James B. Pettijohn; and "The Ways in Which the Financial Engineer Can Use the Internet" by Anthony F. Herbst.

37. For details on other patterns, see Alan R. Shaw, "Technical Analysis," in Levine, *Financial Analyst's Handbook I,* pp. 944–988; Chapter 8 in Jerome B. Cohen, Edward D. Zinbarg, and Arthur Zeikel, *Investment Analysis and Portfolio Management* (Homewood, IL: Richard D. Irwin, 1987); and Richard L. Evans, "Chart Basics Using Bars, Point & Figure and Candlesticks," *AAII Journal,* 15, no. 4 (April 1993): 24–28.

38. For more on the Dow Theory, see Richard L. Evans, "Dow's Theory and the Averages: Relevant . . . or Relics?" *AAII Journal,* 15, no. 1 (January 1993): 27–29.

CHAPTER

15

CHAPTER

Dividend Discount Models

In Chapter 14 it was noted that one purpose of security analysis is to identify mispriced securities. Fundamental analysis was mentioned as one approach for conducting a search for such securities. With this approach the security analyst estimates such things as the firm's future earnings and dividends. If these estimates are substantially different from the average estimates of other analysts but seem more accurate, then from the viewpoint of the security analyst, a mispriced security has been identified. If it also seems that the market price of the security will adjust to reflect these more accurate estimates, then the security will be expected to produce an abnormal rate of return. Accordingly, the analyst will issue either a buy or sell recommendation depending on the direction of the anticipated price adjustment. Based on the capitalization of income method of valuation (also known as the *discounted cash flow* approach), dividend discount models have frequently been used by fundamental analysts as a means of identifying mispriced stocks.[1] This chapter discusses dividend discount models and how they are related to models based on price-earnings ratios.

15.1 Capitalization of Income Method of Valuation

capitalization of income method of valuation
discount rate

Many ways to implement fundamental analysis are directly or indirectly related to the **capitalization of income method of valuation.**[2] According to this method the "true," or "intrinsic," value of any asset is based on the cash flows that the investor expects to receive in the future from owning the asset. Because these cash flows are expected in the future, they are adjusted by a **discount rate** to reflect not only the time value of money but also the riskiness of the cash flows.

Algebraically, the intrinsic value, V, of an asset is equal to the sum of the present values of the asset's expected cash flows:

$$V = \frac{C_1}{(1+k)^1} + \frac{C_2}{(1+k)^2} + \frac{C_3}{(1+k)^3} + \cdots$$

$$= \sum_{t=1}^{\infty} \frac{C_t}{(1+k)^t} \tag{15.1}$$

where C_t denotes the expected cash flow associated with the asset at time t, and k represents the appropriate discount rate for cash flows of this degree of risk. In this equation the discount rate is assumed to be the same for all periods. Because the symbol ∞ above the summation sign in the equation denotes infinity, all expected cash flows, from immediately after making the investment until infinity, will be discounted at the same rate in determining V.[3]

15.1.1 NET PRESENT VALUE

net present value

For the sake of convenience, let the current moment in time be denoted as zero, or $t = 0$. If the cost of purchasing an asset at $t = 0$ is P, then its **net present value** (NPV) is equal to the difference between its intrinsic value and cost:

$$NPV = V - P$$

$$= \left[\sum_{t=1}^{\infty} \frac{C_t}{(1 + k)^t} \right] - P \qquad (15.2)$$

This NPV calculation is conceptually the same as the NPV calculation made for capital budgeting decisions that has long been advocated in introductory finance textbooks. Capital budgeting decisions involve deciding whether a given investment project should be undertaken (for example, whether a new machine should be purchased). In making this decision, the decision-maker focuses on the NPV of the project. Specifically, an investment project is viewed favorably if its NPV is positive and unfavorably if its NPV is negative. For a simple project involving a cash outflow now (at $t = 0$) and expected cash inflows in the future, a positive NPV means that the present value of all the expected cash inflows is greater than the cost of making the investment. Conversely, a negative NPV means that the present value of all the expected cash inflows is less than the cost of making the investment.

The same views about NPV apply when financial assets (such as a share of common stock), instead of real assets (such as a new machine), are considered for purchase.

underpriced

That is, a financial asset is viewed favorably and is said to be **underpriced** or undervalued if NPV > 0. Conversely, a financial asset is viewed unfavorably and is said to be

overpriced

overpriced or overvalued if NPV < 0. From Equation (15.2), this decision rule is equivalent to stating that a financial asset is underpriced if $V > P$:

$$\sum_{t=1}^{\infty} \frac{C_t}{(1 + k)^t} > P \qquad (15.3)$$

Conversely, the asset is overpriced if $V < P$:

$$\sum_{t=1}^{\infty} \frac{C_t}{(1 + k)^t} < P \qquad (15.4)$$

15.1.2 INTERNAL RATE OF RETURN

internal rate of return

Another way of making capital budgeting decisions similar to the NPV method involves calculating the **internal rate of return** (IRR) associated with the investment project. In computing the IRR, the NPV in Equation (15.2) is set equal to zero, and the discount rate becomes the unknown that must be calculated. That is, the IRR for a given investment is the discount rate that makes the NPV of the investment equal to zero. Algebraically, the procedure involves solving the following equation for the internal rate of return k^*:

$$0 = \sum_{t=1}^{\infty} \frac{C_t}{(1 + k^*)^t} - P \qquad (15.5)$$

Equivalently, Equation (15.5) can be rewritten as

$$P = \sum_{t=1}^{\infty} \frac{C_t}{(1 + k^*)^t} \tag{15.6}$$

The decision rule for IRR involves comparing the project's IRR, denoted by k^*, with the required rate of return for an investment of similar risk, denoted by k. Specifically, the investment is underpriced if $k^* > k$, and overpriced if $k^* < k$. As with NPV, the same decision rule applies if either a real asset or a financial asset is being considered for possible investment.[4]

Analysts should be aware that the use of either the IRR or NPV method can lead to erroneous decisions. A security that is identified as mispriced might actually be correctly priced because inaccurate forecasts of cash flows were used. Indeed, proponents of market efficiency (see Chapter 4) would argue that this is precisely what has happened. Hence, it is important to recognize that the usefulness of either method to identify mispriced securities depends on the analyst's forecasting ability.

15.1.3 APPLICATION TO COMMON STOCKS

dividend discount model

This chapter is concerned with using the capitalization of income method to determine the intrinsic value of common stocks. Because the cash flows associated with an investment in any particular common stock are the dividends that are expected to be paid throughout the future on the shares purchased, the models suggested by this method of valuation are often called **dividend discount models** (DDMs).[5] Accordingly, D_t is used instead of C_t to denote the expected cash flow in period t associated with a particular common stock, resulting in the following restatement of Equation (15.1):

$$V = \frac{D_1}{(1 + k)^1} + \frac{D_2}{(1 + k)^2} + \frac{D_3}{(1 + k)^3} + \cdots$$

$$= \sum_{t=1}^{\infty} \frac{D_t}{(1 + k)^t} \tag{15.7}$$

Usually the focus of DDMs is on determining the "fair," or "intrinsic," value of one share of a particular company's common stock, even if larger purchases are being contemplated because it is usually assumed that larger purchases can be made at a cost that is a simple multiple of the cost of one share. (For example, the cost of 1,000 shares is usually assumed to be 1,000 times the cost of one share.) Thus, the numerator in DDMs is the cash dividends per share that are expected in the future.

However, there is a complication in using Equation (15.7) to determine the intrinsic value of a share of common stock. In order to use this equation the investor must forecast *all* future dividends. Because a common stock does not have a fixed lifetime, a virtually infinite stream of dividends must be forecast. Although this may seem to be an impossible task, with the addition of certain assumptions, the equation can be made tractable (that is, usable).

These assumptions center on dividend growth rates (for ease of exposition, it is assumed that dividends are paid annually). Specifically, the dividend per share at any time t can be viewed as being equal to the dividend per share at time $t - 1$ times a dividend growth rate of g_t:

$$D_t = D_{t-1}(1 + g_t) \tag{15.8}$$

or, equivalently,

$$\frac{D_t - D_{t-1}}{D_{t-1}} = g_t \tag{15.9}$$

For example, if the dividend per share expected at $t = 2$ is \$4 and the dividend per share expected at $t = 3$ is \$4.20, then $g_3 = (\$4.20 - \$4)/\$4 = 5\%$. The different types of tractable DDMs reflect different sets of assumptions about dividend growth rates. The discussion begins with the simplest case, the zero-growth model.

15.2 The Zero-Growth Model

One assumption that could be made about future dividends is that they will remain at a fixed dollar amount. That is, the dollar amount of dividends per share paid during the past year D_0 will be paid during the next year D_1, and the year after that D_2, and the year after that D_3, and so on:

$$D_0 = D_1 = D_2 = D_3 = \cdots = D_\infty$$

This constant level of dividends assumes that all the dividend growth rates are zero because if $g_t = 0$, then $D_t = D_{t-1}$ in Equation (15.8). Consequently, this model is often **zero-growth model** referred to as the **zero-growth** (or no-growth) **model**.

15.2.1 NET PRESENT VALUE

The impact of this assumption on Equation (15.7) can be analyzed by noting what happens when D_t is replaced by D_0 in the numerator:

$$V = \sum_{t=1}^{\infty} \frac{D_0}{(1+k)^t} \tag{15.10}$$

Fortunately, Equation (15.10) can be simplified by noting that D_0 is a fixed dollar amount, which means that it can be written outside the summation sign:

$$V = D_0 \left[\sum_{t=1}^{\infty} \frac{1}{(1+k)^t} \right] \tag{15.11}$$

The next step involves using a property of infinite series from mathematics. If $k > 0$, then it can be shown that

$$\sum_{t=1}^{\infty} \frac{1}{(1+k)^t} = \frac{1}{k} \tag{15.12}$$

Applying this property to Equation (15.11) results in the following formula for the zero-growth model:

$$V = \frac{D_0}{k} \tag{15.13}$$

Because $D_0 = D_1$, Equation (15.13) is written sometimes as

$$V = \frac{D_1}{k} \tag{15.14}$$

An Example

Assume that Zinc Company is expected to pay cash dividends of $8 per share into the indefinite future and has a required rate of return of 10%. Using either Equation (15.13) or Equation (15.14), one can see that the value of a share of Zinc stock equals $80 (= $8/.10). With a current stock price of $65 per share, Equation (15.2) would suggest that the NPV per share is $15 (= $80 − $65). Equivalently, because $V = \$80 > P = \$65$, the stock is underpriced by $15 per share and would be a candidate for purchase.

15.2.2 INTERNAL RATE OF RETURN

Equation (15.13) can be reformulated to solve for the IRR on an investment in a zero-growth security. First, the security's current price P is substituted for V, and second, k^* is substituted for k. These changes result in

$$P = \frac{D_0}{k^*}$$

which can be rewritten as

$$k^* = \frac{D_0}{P} \tag{15.15a}$$

$$= \frac{D_1}{P} \tag{15.15b}$$

An Example

Applying this formula to the stock of Zinc indicates that $k^* = 12.3\%$ (= $8/$65). Because the IRR from an investment in Zinc exceeds the required rate of return on Zinc (12.3% > 10%), this method also indicates that Zinc is underpriced.[6]

15.2.3 APPLICATION

The zero-growth model may seem quite restrictive. After all, it seems unreasonable to assume that a given stock will pay a fixed dollar-size dividend forever. Although such a criticism has validity for common stock valuation, there is one particular situation in which this model is quite useful. Specifically, whenever the intrinsic value of a share of high-grade preferred stock is to be determined, the zero-growth DDM will often be appropriate because most preferred stock is nonparticipating. That is, it pays a fixed dollar dividend that will not change as earnings per share change. Furthermore, for high-grade preferred stock these dividends are expected to be paid regularly into the foreseeable future because preferred stock does not have a fixed lifetime. If the application of the zero-growth model is restricted to high-grade preferred stocks, the chance of a suspension of dividends is remote.[7] (Preferred stock is discussed in Chapter 19.)

15.3 The Constant-Growth Model

constant-growth model

The next type of DDM assumes that dividends grow from period to period at the same rate forever and is therefore known as the **constant growth model**.[8] Specifically, the dividends per share that were paid over the previous year D_0 are expected to grow at a given rate g, so that the dividends expected over the next year D_1 are expected to be equal to $D_0(1 + g)$. Dividends the year after that are again expected to grow by the same rate g, meaning that $D_2 = D_1(1 + g)$. Stating that $D_1 = D_0(1 + g)$ and that the growth rate is constant is equivalent to assuming that $D_2 = D_0(1 + g)^2$ and, in general,

$$D_t = D_{t-1}(1 + g) \tag{15.16a}$$

$$= D_0(1 + g)^t \tag{15.16b}$$

15.3.1 NET PRESENT VALUE

The impact of this assumption on Equation (15.7) can be analyzed by noting what happens when D_t is replaced by $D_0(1 + g)^t$ in the numerator:

$$V = \sum_{t=1}^{\infty} \frac{D_0(1 + g)^t}{(1 + k)^t} \tag{15.17}$$

Similar to the zero-growth model, Equation (15.17) can be simplified by noting that D_0 is a fixed dollar amount, so it can be written outside the summation sign:

$$V = D_0 \left[\sum_{t=1}^{\infty} \frac{(1 + g)^t}{(1 + k)^t} \right] \tag{15.18}$$

The next step involves using another mathematical property of infinite series. If $k > g$, then it can be shown that

$$\sum_{t=1}^{\infty} \frac{(1 + g)^t}{(1 + k)^t} = \frac{1 + g}{k - g} \tag{15.19}$$

Substituting Equation (15.19) into Equation (15.18) results in the valuation formula for the constant-growth model:

$$V = D_0 \left(\frac{1 + g}{k - g} \right) \tag{15.20}$$

Sometimes Equation (15.20) is rewritten as

$$V = \frac{D_1}{k - g} \tag{15.21}$$

because $D_1 = D_0(1 + g)$.

An Example

Assume that during the past year Copper Company paid dividends amounting to $1.80 per share. The forecast is that dividends on Copper stock will increase by 5% per year into the indefinite future. Thus, dividends during the next year are expected to equal $1.89 [= $1.80 \times (1 + .05)]$. Using Equation (15.20) and assuming a required rate of return, k, of 11% shows that the value of a share of Copper stock is equal to $31.50 [= $1.80 \times (1 + .05)/(.11 - .05) = $1.89/(.11 - .05)]$. With a current stock price of $40 per share, Equation (15.2) would suggest that the NPV per share is $-$8.50 (= $31.50 - $40). Equivalently, because $V = $31.50 < P = 40, the stock is overpriced by $8.50 per share and would be a candidate for sale if currently owned.

15.3.2   INTERNAL RATE OF RETURN

Equation (15.20) can be reformulated to solve for the IRR on an investment in a constant-growth security. First, the current price of the security P is substituted for V and then k^* is substituted for k. These changes result in

$$P = D_0 \left(\frac{1 + g}{k^* - g} \right) \tag{15.22}$$

which can be rewritten as

$$k^* = \frac{D_0(1 + g)}{P} + g \tag{15.23a}$$

$$= \frac{D_1}{P} + g \tag{15.23b}$$

An Example

Applying this formula to the stock of Copper indicates that $k^* = 9.72\%$ $\{= [\$1.80 \times (1 + .05)/\$40] + .05 = (\$1.89/\$40) + .05\}$. Because the required rate of return on Copper exceeds the IRR from an investment in Copper ($11\% > 9.72\%$), this method also indicates that Copper is overpriced.

15.3.3   RELATIONSHIP TO THE ZERO-GROWTH MODEL

The zero-growth model is a special case of the constant-growth model. If the growth rate, g, is assumed to be equal to zero, then dividends will be a fixed dollar amount forever, which is the same as saying that there will be zero growth. Letting $g = 0$ in Equations (15.20) and (15.23a) results in two equations that are identical to Equations (15.13) and (15.15a), respectively.

Even though the assumption of constant dividend growth may seem less restrictive than the assumption of zero dividend growth, it may still be viewed as unrealistic in many cases. However, the constant-growth model is important because it is embedded in the multiple-growth model, which is discussed next.

15.4   The Multiple-Growth Model

multiple-growth model

A more general DDM for valuing common stocks is the **multiple-growth model.** With this model, the focus is on a time in the future (denoted by T) after which dividends are expected to grow at a constant rate g. Although the investor is still concerned with forecasting dividends, these dividends do not need to have any specific pattern until time T, after which they will be assumed to have the specific pattern of constant growth. The dividends up to T ($D_1, D_2, D_3, ..., D_T$) are forecast individually by the investor. (The investor also forecasts when this time T will occur.) Thereafter dividends are assumed to grow by a constant rate g that the investor must also forecast, meaning that

$$D_{T+1} = D_T(1 + g)$$

$$D_{T+2} = D_{T+1}(1 + g) = D_T(1 + g)^2$$

$$D_{T+3} = D_{T+2}(1 + g) = D_T(1 + g)^3$$

and so on. Figure 15.1 presents a time line of dividends and growth rates associated with the multiple-growth model.

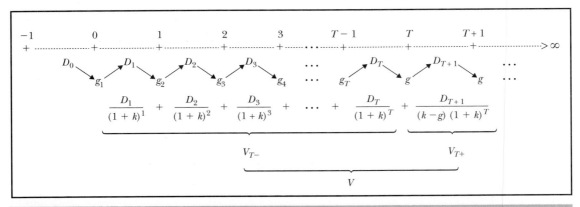

FIGURE 15.1 Time Line for Multiple-Growth Model

15.4.1 NET PRESENT VALUE

Valuing a share of common stock with the multiple-growth model requires that the present value of the forecast stream of dividends be determined. This process can be facilitated by dividing the expected dividend stream into two parts, finding the present value of each part, and then adding these two present values together.

The first part consists of finding the present value of all the forecast dividends that will be paid up to and including time T. Denoting this present value by V_{T-}, it is equal to

$$V_{T-} = \sum_{t=1}^{T} \frac{D_t}{(1+k)^t} \tag{15.24}$$

The second part consists of finding the present value of all the forecast dividends that will be paid after time T and involves the application of the constant-growth model. The application begins by imagining that the investor is not at time zero but is at time T and has not changed his or her forecast of dividends for the stock. As a result, the next period's dividend D_{T+1} and all those thereafter are expected to grow at the rate g. Because the investor would perceive the stock to have a constant growth rate, its value at time T, V_T, can be determined with the constant-growth model of Equation (15.21):

$$V_T = D_{T+1}\left(\frac{1}{k-g}\right) \tag{15.25}$$

One way to view V_T is that it represents a lump sum that is just as desirable as the stream of dividends after T. That is, an investor would find a lump sum of cash equal to V_T, received at time T, to be equally desirable as the stream of dividends $D_{T+1}, D_{T+2}, D_{T+3}$, and so on. If the investor is at time zero, not at time T, the present value at $t = 0$ of the lump sum V_T must be determined. This value is found simply by discounting V_T for T periods at the rate k, resulting in the following formula for finding the present value at time zero for all dividends after T, denoted V_{T+}:

$$V_{T+} = V_T\left[\frac{1}{(1+k)^T}\right]$$

$$= \frac{D_{T+1}}{(k-g)(1+k)^T} \tag{15.26}$$

Having found the present value of all dividends up to and including time T with Equation (15.24) and the present value of all dividends after time T with Equation (15.26), the investor can determine the value of the stock by summing these two amounts:

$$V = V_{T-} + V_{T+}$$

$$= \sum_{t=1}^{T} \frac{D_t}{(1+k)^t} + \frac{D_{T+1}}{(k-g)(1+k)^T} \tag{15.27}$$

Figure 15.1 illustrates the valuation procedure for the multiple-growth DDM given in Equation (15.27).

An Example

Assume that during the past year Magnesium Company paid dividends amounting to $.75 per share. During the next year, Magnesium is expected to pay dividends of $2 per share. Thus $g_1 = (D_1 - D_0)/D_0 = (\$2 - \$.75)/\$.75 = 167\%$. The year after that, dividends are expected to amount to $3 per share, indicating that $g_2 = (D_2 - D_1)/D_1 = (\$3 - \$2)/\$2 = 50\%$. At this time, the dividends are forecast to grow by 10% per year indefinitely, indicating that $T = 2$ and $g = 10\%$. Consequently, $D_{T+1} = D_3 = \$3(1 + .10) = \$3.30$. Given a required rate of return on Magnesium shares of 15%, the values of V_{T-} and V_{T+} can be calculated as follows:

$$V_{T-} = \frac{\$2}{(1 + .15)^1} + \frac{\$3}{(1 + .15)^2}$$

$$= \$4.01$$

$$V_{T+} = \frac{\$3.30}{(.15 - .10)(1 + .15)^2}$$

$$= \$49.91$$

Summing V_{T-} and V_{T+} results in a value for V of $4.01 + $49.91 = $53.92. With a current stock price of $55 per share, Magnesium seems fairly priced. That is, Magnesium is not significantly mispriced because V and P are nearly of equal size.

15.4.2   INTERNAL RATE OF RETURN

The zero-growth and constant-growth models have equations for V that can be reformulated to solve for IRR on an investment in a stock. Unfortunately, a convenient expression similar to Equations (15.15a), (15.15b), (15.23a), and (15.23b) is not available for the multiple-growth model. Note that the expression for IRR is derived by substituting P for V and k^* for k in Equation (15.27):

$$P = \sum_{t=1}^{T} \frac{D_t}{(1+k^*)^t} + \frac{D_{T+1}}{(k^* - g)(1+k^*)^T} \tag{15.28}$$

This equation cannot be rewritten with k^* isolated on the left-hand side, so a closed-form expression for IRR does not exist for the multiple-growth model.

However, all is not lost. It is still possible to calculate the IRR for an investment in a stock conforming to the multiple-growth model using an "educated" trial-and-error method. This method is based on the observation that the right-hand side of Equation (15.28) is simply equal to the present value of the dividend stream, where k^* is used as the discount rate. Hence the larger the value of k^*, the smaller the value of the right-hand side of Equation (15.28). The trial-and-error method proceeds by initially using an estimate for k^*. If the resulting value on the right-hand side of Equation (15.28) is larger than P, then a larger estimate of k^* is tried. Conversely, if the resulting value is smaller than P, then a smaller estimate of k^* is tried. Continuing this search process, the investor can home in on the value of k^* that makes the right-hand side equal P on the left-hand side. Fortunately, it is a relatively simple matter to program a computer to conduct the search for k^* in Equation (15.28). Most spreadsheets include a function that does so automatically.

An Example

Applying Equation (15.28) to Magnesium Company results in

$$\$55 = \frac{\$2}{(1 + k^*)^1} + \frac{\$3}{(1 + k^*)^2} + \frac{\$3.30}{(k^* - .10)(1 + k^*)^2} \qquad \textbf{(15.29)}$$

Initially a rate of 14% is used in attempting to solve this equation for k^*. Inserting 14% for k^* in the right-hand side of Equation (15.29) results in a value of $67.54. Earlier 15% was used in determining V and resulted in a value of $53.92. This means that k^* must have a value between 14% and 15% because $55 is between $67.54 and $53.92. If 14.5% is tried next, the resulting value is $59.97, suggesting that a higher rate should be tried. If 14.8% and 14.9% are subsequently tried, the respective resulting values are $56.18 and $55.03. Because $55.03 is the closest to P, the IRR associated with an investment in Magnesium is 14.9%. Given a required return of 15% and an IRR of approximately that amount, the stock of Magnesium seems fairly priced.

15.4.3 RELATIONSHIP TO THE CONSTANT-GROWTH MODEL

The constant-growth model is a special case of the multiple-growth model. If the time when constant growth is assumed to begin is set at zero, then

$$V_{T-} = \sum_{t=1}^{T} \frac{D_t}{(1 + k)^t} = 0$$

and

$$V_{T+} = \frac{D_{T+1}}{(k - g)(1 + k)^T} = \frac{D_1}{k - g}$$

because $T = 0$ and $(1 + k)^0 = 1$. Given that the multiple-growth model states that $V = V_{T-} + V_{T+}$, setting $T = 0$ results in $V = D_1/(k - g)$, a formula that is equivalent to the formula for the constant-growth model.

15.4.4 TWO-STAGE AND THREE-STAGE MODELS

Investors sometimes use two-stage and three-stage dividend discount models.[9] The two-stage model assumes that a constant growth rate g_1 exists only until some time T, when a different growth rate g_2 is assumed to begin and continue thereafter. The three-stage model assumes that a constant growth rate g_1 exists only until some time T_1, when a second growth rate is assumed to begin and last until a later time T_2, when a third growth rate is assumed to begin and last thereafter. Letting V_{T+} denote the present value of all dividends after the last growth rate has begun and V_{T-} denote the present value of all the preceding dividends indicates that these models are just special cases of the multiple-growth model.

In the application of the capitalization of income method of valuation to common stocks, it might seem appropriate to assume that a particular stock will be sold at some point in the future. In this case the expected cash flows consist of the dividends up to that point as well as the stock's expected selling price. Because dividends after the selling date are ignored, the use of a dividend discount model may seem improper. However, as will be shown next, it is not so.

15.5   Valuation Based on a Finite Holding Period

The capitalization of income method of valuation involves discounting all dividends that are expected throughout the future. Because the simplified models of zero growth, constant growth, and multiple growth are based on this method, they too involve a future stream of dividends. On reflection one may think that such models are relevant only for an investor who plans to hold a stock forever because only such an investor would expect to receive this stream of future dividends.

But what about an investor who plans to sell the stock in a year?[10] In such a situation, the cash flows that the investor expects to receive from purchasing a share of the stock are equal to the dividend expected to be paid one year from now (for ease of exposition, it is assumed that common stocks pay dividends annually) and the expected selling price of the stock. Thus, it would seem appropriate to determine the intrinsic value of the stock to the investor by discounting these two cash flows at the required rate of return as follows:

$$V = \frac{D_1 + P_1}{(1 + k)}$$

$$= \frac{D_1}{(1 + k)} + \frac{P_1}{(1 + k)} \qquad (15.30)$$

where D_1 and P_1 are the expected dividend and selling price at $t = 1$, respectively.

In order to use Equation (15.30), one must estimate the expected price of the stock at $t = 1$. The simplest approach assumes that the selling price will be based on the dividends that are expected to be paid after the selling date. Thus, the expected selling price at $t = 1$ is

$$P_1 = \frac{D_2}{(1 + k)^1} + \frac{D_3}{(1 + k)^2} + \frac{D_4}{(1 + k)^3} + \cdots$$

$$= \sum_{t=2}^{\infty} \frac{D_t}{(1 + k)^{t-1}} \qquad (15.31)$$

Substituting Equation (15.31) for P_1 in the right-hand side of Equation (15.30) results in

$$V = \frac{D_1}{(1 + k)^1} + \left[\frac{D_2}{(1 + k)^1} + \frac{D_3}{(1 + k)^2} + \frac{D_4}{(1 + k)^3} + \cdots \right] \left(\frac{1}{1 + k} \right)$$

$$= \frac{D_1}{(1 + k)^1} + \frac{D_2}{(1 + k)^2} + \frac{D_3}{(1 + k)^3} + \frac{D_4}{(1 + k)^4} + \cdots$$

$$= \sum_{t=1}^{\infty} \frac{D_t}{(1 + k)^t}$$

which is exactly the same as Equation (15.7). Thus, valuing a share of common stock by discounting its dividends up to some point in the future and its expected selling price at that time is equivalent to valuing stock by discounting all future dividends. The two are equivalent because the expected selling price is itself based on dividends to be paid after the selling date. Hence Equation (15.7), as well as the zero-growth, constant-growth, and multiple-growth models that are based on it, is appropriate for determining the intrinsic value of a share of common stock regardless of the length of the investor's planned holding period.

An Example

Reconsider the common stock of Copper Company. During the past year Copper paid dividends of $1.80 per share and the investor forecast that the dividends would grow by 5% per year forever. This assumption means that dividends during the next two years (D_1 and D_2) are forecast to be $1.89 [= $1.80 \times (1 + .05)$] for the first year and $1.985 [= $1.89 \times (1 + .05)$] for the second. If the investor plans to sell the stock after one year, the selling price can be estimated by noting that, at $t = 1$, the forecast of dividends for the forthcoming year will be D_2, or $1.985. Thus, the anticipated selling price at $t = 1$, denoted P_1, equals $33.08 [= $1.985/(.11 - .05)$]. Accordingly, the intrinsic value of Copper to such an investor would equal the present value of the expected cash flows, which are D_1 = $1.89 and P_1 = $33.08. Using Equation (15.30) and assuming a required rate of 11%, this value is equal to $31.50 [= ($1.89 + $33.08)/(1 + .11)$], which is the same amount that was calculated earlier when all the dividends from now to infinity were discounted using the constant-growth model: $V = D_1/(k - g) = $1.89/(.11 - .05) = $31.50.

15.6   Models Based on Price-Earnings Ratios

Despite the inherent sensibility of DDMs, many security analysts use a much simpler procedure to value common stocks. First, a stock's earnings per share during the forthcoming year E_1 are estimated, and then the analyst (or someone else) specifies a "normal" **price-earnings ratio** for the stock. The product of these two numbers gives the estimated future price P_1. Together with estimated dividends D_1 to be paid during the period and the current price P, the estimated return on the stock over the period can be determined:

price-earnings ratio

$$\text{Expected return} = \frac{(P_1 - P) + D_1}{P} \tag{15.32}$$

where $P_1 = (P_1/E_1) \times E_1$ (note that P_1/E_1 is the "normal" price-earnings ratio that is applicable to earnings per share over the forthcoming year).

Some security analysts expand this procedure, estimating earnings per share and price-earnings ratios for optimistic, most likely, and pessimistic scenarios to produce a rudimentary probability distribution of a security's return. Other analysts determine whether a stock is underpriced or overpriced by comparing the stock's actual price-earnings ratio with its "normal" price-earnings ratio, as is shown next.[11]

In order to make this comparison, Equation (15.7) must be rearranged and some new variables must be introduced. Earnings per share E_t are related to dividends per share D_t by the firm's **payout ratio** p_t:

payout ratio

$$D_t = p_t E_t \tag{15.33}$$

Thus, if an analyst has forecast earnings per share and payout ratios, then he or she has implicitly forecast dividends.

Equation (15.33) can be used to restate the various DDMs where the focus is on estimating what the stock's price-earnings ratio should be instead of on estimating the intrinsic value of the stock. In the restatement, $p_t E_t$ is substituted for D_t in the right-hand side of Equation (15.7), resulting in a general formula for determining a stock's intrinsic value that involves discounting earnings:

$$V = \frac{D_1}{(1+k)^1} + \frac{D_2}{(1+k)^2} + \frac{D_3}{(1+k)^3}$$

$$= \frac{p_1 E_1}{(1+k)^1} + \frac{p_2 E_2}{(1+k)^2} + \frac{p_3 E_3}{(1+k)^3} + \cdots$$

$$= \sum_{t=1}^{\infty} \frac{p_t E_t}{(1+k)^t} \tag{15.34}$$

Earlier it was noted that dividends in adjacent time periods could be viewed as being "linked" to each other by a dividend growth rate g_t. Similarly, earnings per share in any year t can be "linked" to earnings per share in the previous year $t-1$ by a growth rate in earnings per share, g_{et}:

$$E_t = E_{t-1}(1 + g_{et}) \tag{15.35}$$

This equation implies that

$$E_1 = E_0(1 + g_{e1})$$

$$E_2 = E_1(1 + g_{e2}) = E_0(1 + g_{e1})(1 + g_{e2})$$

$$E_3 = E_2(1 + g_{e3}) = E_0(1 + g_{e1})(1 + g_{e2})(1 + g_{e3})$$

and so on, where E_0 is the actual level of earnings per share during the past year, E_1 is the expected level of earnings per share during the forthcoming year, E_2 is the expected level of earnings per share for the year after E_1, and E_3 is the expected level of earnings per share for the year after E_2.

These equations relating expected future earnings per share to E_0 can be substituted into Equation (15.34), resulting in

$$V = \frac{p_1[E_0(1 + g_{e1})]}{(1+k)^1} + \frac{p_2[E_0(1 + g_{e1})(1 + g_{e2})]}{(1+k)^2}$$

$$+ \frac{p_3[E_0(1 + g_{e1})(1 + g_{e2})(1 + g_{e3})]}{(1+k)^3} + \cdots \tag{15.36}$$

Because V is the intrinsic value of a share of stock, it represents what the stock would be selling for if it were fairly priced. Both sides of Equation (15.36) can be divided by E_0 and the results simplified in the formula for determining the "normal" price-earnings ratio, V/E_0:

$$\frac{V}{E_0} = \frac{p_1(1 + g_{e1})}{(1+k)^1} + \frac{p_2(1 + g_{e1})(1 + g_{e2})}{(1+k)^2}$$

$$+ \frac{p_3(1 + g_{e1})(1 + g_{e2})(1 + g_{e3})}{(1+k)^3} + \cdots \tag{15.37}$$

This approach shows that, other things being equal, a stock's "normal" price-earnings ratio will be higher:

The *greater* the expected payout ratios ($p_1, p_2, p_3, \ldots$)

The *greater* the expected growth rates in earnings per share ($g_{e1}, g_{e2}, g_{e3}, \ldots$)

The *smaller* the required rate of return (k)

The qualifying phrase "other things being equal" should not be overlooked. For example, a firm cannot increase the value of its shares by simply making greater payouts. This will increase $p_1, p_2, p_3, \ldots$ but will decrease the expected growth rates in earnings per share $g_{e1}, g_{e2}, g_{e3}, \ldots$. If the firm's investment policy is not altered, the effects of the reduced growth in its earnings per share will just offset the effects of the increased payouts, leaving its share value unchanged.

Earlier it was noted that a stock was underpriced if $V > P$ and overpriced if $V < P$. Because dividing both sides of an inequality by a positive constant will not change the direction of the inequality, such a division can be done here to the two inequalities involving V and P, where the positive constant is E_0. The result is that a stock is underpriced if $V/E_0 > P/E_0$ and overpriced if $V/E_0 < P/E_0$. That is, a stock will be underpriced if its "normal" price-earnings ratio is greater than its actual price-earnings ratio, and it will be overpriced if its "normal" price-earnings ratio is less than its actual price-earnings ratio.

Unfortunately, Equation (15.37) is intractable; it cannot be used to estimate the normal price-earnings ratio for any stock. However, simplifying the assumptions can result in tractable formulas for estimating normal price-earnings ratios. These assumptions, along with the formulas, parallel those made previously regarding dividends.

15.6.1 THE ZERO-GROWTH MODEL

The zero-growth model assumed that dividends per share remain at a fixed dollar amount forever. This situation is most likely to occur if earnings per share remain at a fixed dollar amount forever, with the firm maintaining a 100% payout ratio. Why 100%? Because the assumption that a lesser amount was being paid out would mean that the firm was retaining part of its earnings. These retained earnings would be put to some use and would thus be expected to increase future earnings and hence dividends per share.

The zero-growth model assumes that $p_t = 1$ for all time periods and $E_0 = E_1 = E_2 = E_3$ and so on. Consequently, $D_0 = E_0 = D_1 = E_1 = D_2 = E_2$ and so on. Thus, the valuation Equation (15.13) can be restated as

$$V = \frac{E_0}{k} \tag{15.38}$$

Dividing Equation (15.38) by E_0 results in the formula for the normal price-earnings ratio for a stock having zero growth:

$$\frac{V}{E_0} = \frac{1}{k} \tag{15.39}$$

An Example

Earlier it was assumed that Zinc Company was a zero-growth firm paying dividends of $8 per share, selling for $65 a share, and having a required rate of return of 10%. Because Zinc is a zero-growth company, it is assumed that it has a 100% payout ratio, which means that $E_0 = \$8$. Equation (15.38) can be used to calculate a normal price-earnings ratio for Zinc of $1/.10 = 10$. Because Zinc has an actual price-earnings ratio of $\$65/\$8 = 8.1$, and because $V/E_0 = 10 > P/E_0 = 8.1$, Zinc stock is underpriced.

Note also that the expected price of Zinc one year from now, just before it pays an $8 dividend, is $80 (= 8×10). Therefore, the expected return during the forthcoming year on Zinc is 23.1% $[= (\$80 - \$65)/\$65]$, which is greater than its 10% required return and indicative of an underpriced stock.

15.6.2   THE CONSTANT-GROWTH MODEL

Previously it was noted that dividends in adjacent time periods can be connected to each other by a dividend growth rate g_t. It also was noted that earnings per share can be connected by an earnings growth rate g_{et}. The constant-growth model assumes that the growth rate in dividends per share will be the same throughout the future. An equivalent assumption is that earnings per share will grow at a constant rate g_e throughout the future, with the payout ratio remaining at a constant level p. These assumptions mean that

$$E_1 = E_0(1 + g_e) = E_0(1 + g_e)^1$$

$$E_2 = E_1(1 + g_e) = E_0(1 + g_e)(1 + g_e) = E_0(1 + g_e)^2$$

$$E_3 = E_2(1 + g_e) = E_0(1 + g_e)(1 + g_e)(1 + g_e) = E_0(1 + g_e)^3$$

and so on. In general, earnings in year t can be connected to E_0 as follows:

$$E_t = E_0(1 + g_e)^t \tag{15.40}$$

Substituting Equation (15.40) into the numerator of Equation (15.34) and recognizing that $p_t = p$ results in

$$V = \sum_{t=1}^{\infty} \frac{pE_0(1 + g_e)^t}{(1 + k)^t}$$

$$= pE_0 \left[\sum_{t=1}^{\infty} \frac{(1 + g_e)^t}{(1 + k)^t} \right] \tag{15.41}$$

The same mathematical property of infinite series given in Equation (15.19) can be applied to Equation (15.41), resulting in

$$V = pE_0 \left(\frac{1 + g_e}{k - g_e} \right) \tag{15.42}$$

The earnings-based, constant-growth model has a numerator that is identical to the numerator of the dividend-based, constant-growth model because $pE_0 = D_0$. Furthermore, the denominators of the two models are identical. Both assertions require the growth rates in earnings and dividends to be the same (that is, $g_e = g$). This equality can be seen by recalling that constant earnings growth means

$$E_t = E_{t-1}(1 + g_e)$$

When both sides of this equation are multiplied by the constant payout ratio, the result is

$$pE_t = pE_{t-1}(1 + g_e)$$

Because $pE_t = D_t$ and $pE_{t-1} = D_{t-1}$, this equation reduces to

$$D_t = D_{t-1}(1 + g_e)$$

which indicates that dividends in any period $t - 1$ will grow by the earnings growth rate g_e. Because the dividend-based, constant-growth model assumed that dividends in any period $t - 1$ would grow by the dividend growth rate g, the two growth rates must be equal for the two models to be equivalent.

Equation (15.42) can be restated by dividing each side by E_0, resulting in the following formula for determining the normal price-earnings ratio for a stock with constant growth:

$$\frac{V}{E_0} = p\left(\frac{1 + g_e}{k - g_e}\right) \tag{15.43}$$

An Example

Earlier it was assumed that Copper Company had paid dividends of $1.80 per share during the past year, with a forecast that dividends would grow by 5% per year forever. It also was assumed that the required rate of return on Copper was 11%, and the current stock price was $40 per share. Assuming that E_0 was $2.70, the payout ratio equals $66\frac{2}{3}\%$ (= $1.80/$2.70). Hence, the normal price-earnings ratio for Copper, according to Equation (15.43), equals 11.67 $[= .6667 \times (1 + .05)/(.11 - .05)]$. Because this is less than Copper's actual price-earnings ratio of 14.8 (= $40/$2.70), the stock of Copper Company is overpriced.

The expected price of Copper one year from now, just before it pays a $1.89 (= 1.80×1.05) dividend, is $33.075 (= $2.70 \times 1.05 \times 11.67$). Thus, the expected return during the forthcoming year on Copper is $-17.3\% = ($33.075 - $40)/$40$, which is less than the 11% required return and indicative of an overpriced stock.

15.6.3 THE MULTIPLE-GROWTH MODEL

Earlier it was noted that the most general DDM is the multiple-growth model, where dividends are allowed to grow at varying rates until some point in time T, after which they are assumed to grow at a constant rate. In this situation the present value of all the dividends is found by adding the present value of all dividends up to and including T, denoted by V_{T-}, and the present value of all dividends after T, denoted by V_{T+}:

$$V = V_{T-} + V_{T+}$$

$$= \sum_{t=1}^{T} \frac{D_t}{(1 + k)^t} + \frac{D_{T+1}}{(k - g)(1 + k)^T} \tag{15.27}$$

In general, earnings per share in any period t are equal to E_0 times the product of all the earnings growth rates from time zero to time t:

$$E_t = E_0(1 + g_{e1})(1 + g_{e2}) \cdots (1 + g_{et}) \tag{15.44}$$

Because dividends per share in any period t are equal to the payout ratio for that period times the earnings per share, it follows from Equation (15.44) that

$$D_t = p_t E_t$$
$$= p_t E_0(1 + g_{e1})(1 + g_{e2}) \cdots (1 + g_{et}) \tag{15.45}$$

Replacing the numerator in Equation (15.27) with the right-hand side of Equation (15.45) and dividing both sides by E_0 gives the following formula for determining a stock's normal price-earnings ratio with the multiple-growth model:

$$\frac{V}{E_0} = \frac{p_1(1 + g_{e1})}{(1 + k)^1} + \frac{p_2(1 + g_{e1})(1 + g_{e2})}{(1 + k)^2} + \cdots$$

$$+ \frac{p_T(1 + g_{e1})(1 + g_{e2}) \cdots (1 + g_{eT})}{(1 + k)^T}$$

$$+ \frac{p(1 + g_{e1})(1 + g_{e2}) \cdots (1 + g_{eT})(1 + g)}{(k - g)(1 + k)^T} \qquad \textbf{(15.46)}$$

An Example

Consider Magnesium Company again. Its share price is currently $55, and per share earnings and dividends during the past year were $3 and $.75, respectively. For the next two years, forecast earnings and dividends, along with the earnings growth rates and payout ratios, are

$$D_1 = \$2.00 \quad E_1 = \$5.00 \quad g_{e1} = 67\% \quad p_1 = 40\%$$

$$D_2 = \$3.00 \quad E_2 = \$6.00 \quad g_{e2} = 20\% \quad p_2 = 50\%$$

Constant growth in dividends and earnings of 10% per year is forecast to begin at $T = 2$, which means that $D_3 = \$3.30$, $E_3 = \$6.60$, $g = 10\%$, and $p = 50\%$.

Given a required return of 15%, Equation (15.46) can be used as follows to estimate a normal price-earnings ratio for Magnesium:

$$\frac{V}{E_0} = \frac{.40(1 + .67)}{(1 + .15)^1} + \frac{.50(1 + .67)(1 + .20)}{(1 + .15)^2} + \frac{.50(1 + .67)(1 + .20)(1 + .10)}{(.15 - .10)(1 + .15)^2}$$

$$= .58 + .76 + 16.67$$

$$= 18.01$$

Because the actual price-earnings ratio of 18.33 ($= \$55/\$3$) is close to the normal ratio of 18.01, the stock of Magnesium Company is fairly priced.

15.7 Sources of Earnings Growth

So far no explanation has been given as to why earnings or dividends are expected to grow in the future. One explanation uses the constant-growth model. Assuming that no new capital is obtained externally and no shares are repurchased (meaning that the number of shares outstanding does not increase or decrease), the portion of earnings not paid to stockholders as dividends will be used to pay for the firm's new investments. If p_t denotes the payout ratio in year t, then $(1 - p_t)$ will be the portion of earnings not paid out, known as the **retention ratio.** Furthermore, the firm's new investments, stated on a per share basis and denoted by I_t, will be

retention ratio

$$I_t = (1 - p_t)E_t \qquad \textbf{(15.47)}$$

If these new investments have an average return on equity of r_t in period t and every year thereafter, they will add $r_t I_t$ to earnings per share in year $t + 1$ and every year thereafter. If all previous investments also produce perpetual earnings at a constant rate of return, next year's earnings will equal this year's earnings plus the new earnings resulting from this year's new investments:

$$E_{t+1} = E_t + r_t I_t$$
$$= E_t + r_t(1 - p_t)E_t$$
$$= E_t[1 + r_t(1 - p_t)] \tag{15.48}$$

Because it was shown earlier that the growth rate in earnings per share is

$$E_t = E_{t-1}(1 + g_{et}) \tag{15.35}$$

it follows that

$$E_{t+1} = E_t(1 + g_{et+1}) \tag{15.49}$$

A comparison of Equations (15.48) and (15.49) indicates that

$$g_{et+1} = r_t(1 - p_t) \tag{15.50}$$

If the growth rate in earnings per share g_{et+1} is constant over time, then the average return on equity for new investments r_t and the payout ratio p_t must also be constant over time. In this situation Equation (15.50) can be simplified by removing the time subscripts:

$$g_e = r(1 - p) \tag{15.51a}$$

Because the growth rate in dividends per share g is equal to the growth rate in earnings per share g_e, Equation (15.51a) can be rewritten as

$$g = r(1 - p) \tag{15.51b}$$

From this equation it can be seen that the growth rate g depends on (1) the proportion of earnings retained, $1 - p$, and (2) the average return on equity for the earnings retained, r. Because it is expected to persist over the long term, g is sometimes referred to as the firm's rate of *sustainable growth*.

The constant-growth valuation formula given in Equation (15.20) can be modified by replacing g with the expression on the right-hand side of Equation (15.51b), resulting in

$$V = D_0\left(\frac{1 + g}{k - g}\right)$$
$$= D_0\left[\frac{1 + r(1 - p)}{k - r(1 - p)}\right]$$
$$= D_1\left[\frac{1}{k - r(1 - p)}\right] \tag{15.52}$$

Under these assumptions, a stock's value (and hence its price) should be greater, the greater its average return on equity for new investments, other things being equal.

An Example

Continuing with Copper Company, recall that $E_0 = \$2.70$ and $p = 66\frac{2}{3}\%$. This means that $33\frac{1}{3}\%$ of earnings per share during the past year were retained and reinvested, an amount equal to $\$.90 (= .3333 \times \$2.70)$. The earnings per share in the forthcoming year E_1 are expected to be \$2.835 [= \$2.70 × (1 + .05)] because the growth rate g for Copper is 5%.

The source of the increase in earnings per share of \$.135 (= \$2.835 − \$2.70) is the \$.90 per share that was reinvested at $t = 0$. The average return on equity for new investments r is 15% because \$.135/\$.90 = 15%. That is, the reinvested earnings of \$.90 per share has generated an annual increase in earnings per share of \$.135. This increase will occur not only at $t = 1$ but also at $t = 2$, $t = 3$, and so on. Equivalently, a \$.90 investment at $t = 0$ will generate a perpetual annual cash inflow of \$.135 beginning at $t = 1$.

Expected dividends at $t = 1$ can be calculated by multiplying the expected payout ratio p of $66\frac{2}{3}\%$ times the expected earnings per share E_1 of \$2.835, or .6667 × \$2.835 = \$1.89. They can also be calculated by multiplying 1 plus the growth rate g of 5% times the past amount of dividends per share D_0 of \$1.80, or 1.05 × \$1.80 = \$1.89. The growth rate in dividends per share of 5% is equal to the product of the retention rate ($33\frac{2}{3}\%$) and the average return on equity for new investments (15%), an amount equal to 5% (= .3333 × .15).

Two years from now ($t = 2$), earnings per share are anticipated to be \$2.977 [= \$2.835 × (1 + .05)], a further increase of \$.142 (= \$2.977 − \$2.835) due to the retention and reinvestment of \$.945 (= .3333 × \$2.835) per share at $t = 1$. This expected increase in earnings per share of \$.142 is the result of earning (15%) on the reinvestment (\$.945) because .15 × \$.945 = \$.142. The expected earnings per share at $t = 2$ can be viewed as having three components:

1. Earnings attributable to the assets held at $t = -1$, an amount equal to \$2.70.
2. Earnings attributable to the reinvestment of \$.90 at $t = 0$, earning \$.135.
3. Earnings attributable to the reinvestment of \$.945 at $t = 1$, earning \$.142.

These three components, when summed, equal E_2 = \$2.977 (= \$2.70 + \$.135 + \$.142).

Dividends at $t = 2$ are expected to be 5% greater than at $t = 1$, or \$1.985 (= 1.05 × \$1.89) per share, which corresponds to the amount calculated by multiplying the payout ratio by the expected earnings per share at $t = 2$, or \$1.985 (= .6667 × \$2.977). Figure 15.2 summarizes the example.

FIGURE 15.2 Growth in Earnings for Copper Company

−1 to 0	0 to 1	1 to 2	2 → ∞
E_0 = \$2.70	\$2.700	\$2.700	. . .
	\$.90 × .15 = .135	.135	. . .
	E_1 = \$2.835	\$.945 × .15 = .142	. . .
		E_2 = \$2.977	. . .
I_0 = \$ .90	I_1 = \$ .945	I_2 = \$ .992	. . .
D_0 = 1.80	D_1 = 1.890	D_2 = 1.985	. . .
E_0 = \$2.70	E_1 = \$2.835	E_2 = \$2.977	. . .

Applying Dividend Discount Models

Since the late 1960s, dividend discount models (DDMs) have been used by various professional common stock investors. Although few investment managers rely solely on DDMs to select stocks, many have integrated DDMs into their security valuation procedures.

There are two reasons why DDMs warrant consideration. First, DDMs are based on a simple, widely understood concept: The fair value of any security should equal the discounted value of the cash flows expected to be produced by that security. Second, the basic inputs for DDMs are standard outputs for many large investment management firms; that is, these firms employ security analysts who are responsible for projecting corporate earnings.

Valuing common stocks with a DDM technically requires an estimate of future dividends over an infinite time horizon. Given that accurately forecasting dividends three years from today, let alone 20 years into the future, is difficult, how do investment firms actually go about implementing DDMs? One approach uses constant or two-stage dividend growth models, as described in the text. Even though such models are relatively easy to apply, many professional investors find the assumed dividend growth assumptions are overly simplistic. Instead, these investors gen-

erally prefer three-stage models, believing that they provide the best combination of realism and ease of application.

Whereas many variations of the three-stage DDM exist, in general, the model is based on the assumption that companies evolve through three stages during their lifetimes. (See Figure 15.3.)

1. *Growth stage.* Characterized by rapidly expanding sales, high profit margins, and abnormally high growth in earnings per share. Because of highly profitable expected investment opportunities, the payout ratio is low. Competitors are attracted by the unusually high earnings, leading to a decline in the growth rate.

2. *Transition stage.* In later years, increased competition reduces profit margins and earnings growth slows. With fewer new investment opportunities, the company begins to pay out a larger percentage of earnings.

3. *Maturity (steady-state) stage.* Eventually the company reaches a position at which its new investment opportunities offer, on average, only slightly attractive returns on equity. At that time its earnings growth rate, payout ratio, and return on equity stabilize for the remainder of its life.

The forecasting process of the three-stage DDM involves specifying earnings and dividend growth rates in each stage. Although one cannot expect a security analyst to be omniscient in his or

FIGURE 15.3 The Three Stages of the Multible-Growth Model

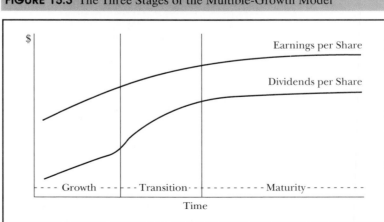

her growth forecast for a particular company, one can hope that the forecast pattern of growth (in terms of magnitude and duration) resembles that actually realized by the company, particularly in the short run.

Investment firms attempt to structure their DDMs to make maximum use of their analysts' forecasting capabilities. Thus the models emphasize specific forecasts in the near term, when it is realistic to expect security analysts to project earnings and dividends accurately. However, the models emphasize more general forecasts over the long term, when distinctions between companies' growth rates become less discernible. Typically, analysts are required to supply the following for their assigned companies:

1. Expected annual earnings and dividends for the next several years

2. After these specific annual forecasts end, earnings growth and the payout ratio forecasts until the end of the growth stage

3. The number of years until the transition stage is reached

4. The duration (in years) of the transition stage

Most three-stage DDMs assume that during the transition stage, earnings growth declines and payout ratios rise linearly to the maturity-stage, steady-state levels. (For example, if the transition stage is 10 years, earnings growth at the maturity

stage is 5% per year, and earnings growth at the end of the growth stage is 25%, then earnings growth declines 2% in each year of the transition stage.) Finally, most three-stage DDMs make standard assumptions that all companies in the maturity stage have the same growth rates, payout ratios, and return on equity.

With analysts' inputs, plus an appropriate required rate of return for each security, all the necessary information for the three-stage DDM is available. The last step involves merely calculating the discounted value of the estimated dividends to determine the stock's "fair" value.

The seeming simplicity of the three-stage DDM should not lead one to believe that it is without implementation problems. Investment firms must strive to achieve consistency across their analysts' forecasts. The long-term nature of the estimates involved, the substantial training required to make even short-term earnings forecasts accurately, and the coordination of a number of analysts covering many companies severely complicate the problem. Considerable discipline is required if the DDM valuations generated by a firm's analysts are to be sufficiently comparable and reliable to guide investment decisions. Despite these complexities, if successfully implemented, DDMs combine the creative insights of security analysts with the rigor and discipline of quantitative investment techniques.

15.8 Alpha and the Security Market Line

implied return

Sometimes the long-run internal rate of return k^* on a common stock, determined by using a dividend discount model, is referred to as the stock's **implied return.** After implied returns are estimated for a number of stocks, the associated beta for each stock can be estimated. Then for all the stocks analyzed, this information can be plotted on a graph that has implied returns on the vertical axis and estimated betas on the horizontal axis.

At this point there are alternative methods for estimating the security market line (SML).[12] One method involves determining a line of best fit for this graph by using simple linear regression (discussed in Chapter 13). That is, the values of an intercept term and a slope term are determined from the data, thereby indicating the location of the straight line that best describes the relationship between implied returns and betas.[13]

Figure 15.4 provides an example of the estimated SML. In this case the SML has an intercept of 8% and a slope of 4%, indicating that securities with higher betas are expected to have higher implied returns in the forthcoming period. Depending on the

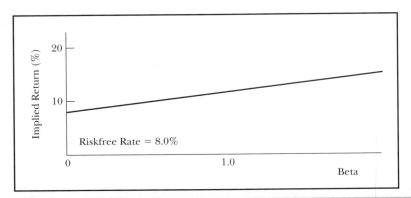

FIGURE 15.4 A Security Market Line Estimated from Implied Returns

sizes of the implied returns, such lines have steeper, or flatter, slopes or even negative slopes.

The second method of estimating the SML involves calculating the implied return for a portfolio of common stocks. This calculation is done by taking a value-weighted average of the implied returns of the stocks in the portfolio, with the resulting return being an estimate of the implied return on the "market" portfolio. Given this return and a beta of 1, the "market" portfolio can be plotted on a graph with implied returns on the vertical axis and betas on the horizontal axis. The riskfree rate, having a beta of zero, can be plotted on the same graph. The SML is determined by simply connecting these two points with a straight line.

Either of these SMLs can be used to determine the required return on a stock. However, they will likely result in different numbers because the two lines will likely have different intercepts and slopes. For example, in the first method the SML may not go through the riskfree rate, whereas the second method forces the SML to go through this rate.

15.8.1 REQUIRED RETURNS AND ALPHAS

Once a security's beta has been estimated, its required return can be determined from the estimated SML. For example, the equation for the SML shown in Figure 15.4 is

$$k_i = 8 + 4\beta_i$$

Thus if *ABC* has an estimated beta of 1.1, then it would have a required return equal to 12.4% [= $8 + (4 \times 1.1)$].

Once the required return on a stock has been determined, the difference between the stock's implied return (from the DDM) and the required return can be calculated. The difference is then viewed as an estimate of the stock's degree of mispricing. This value is referred to as the stock's abnormal return, or *alpha* (see Chapter 18). Positive alphas indicate underpriced securities and negative alphas indicate overpriced securities.[14] Because *ABC*'s implied and required returns were 14.8% and 12.4%, respectively, its estimated alpha would be 2.4% = 14.8% − 12.4%, indicating *ABC* is underpriced.

15.8.2 THE IMPLIED RETURN ON THE STOCK MARKET

The relative attractiveness of stocks and bonds can be assessed by comparing the implied return for a portfolio of stocks with the expected return on bonds. (The latter is typically represented by the current yield-to-maturity on long-term Treasury bonds.) Specifically, the difference between stock and bond returns can be used as an input for recommendations regarding the percentages of an investor's money that should go into stocks and bonds. For example, the greater the implied return on stocks relative to bonds, the larger the percentage of the investor's money that should be placed in common stocks.

15.9   Dividend Discount Models and Expected Returns

The procedures described here are similar to those used by a number of brokerage firms and portfolio managers.[15] A security's implied return, obtained from a DDM, is often treated as an expected return, which, in turn, can be divided into two components: the security's required return and alpha. However, the expected return on a stock during a given holding period may differ from its DDM-based implied return k^*. A simple set of examples shows why and when this difference exists.

Assume that a security analyst predicts that a stock will pay a dividend of $1.10 per year forever. In contrast, the consensus opinion of "the market" (that is, most other investors) is that the dividend will equal $1.00 per year forever. Thus, the analyst's prediction is a deviant, or nonconsensus, one.

Assume that both the analyst and other investors agree that the required rate of return for this stock is 10%. The formula for the zero-growth model indicates that the value of the stock is $D_1/.10 = 10D_1$, indicating the stock should sell for ten times its expected dividend. Because other investors expect to receive $1.00 per year, the stock has a current price P of $10 per share. The analyst thinks the stock has a value of $1.10/.10 = $11 and that it is underpriced by $11 - $10 = $1 per share.

In this situation the implied return according to the analyst is $1.10/$10 = 11%. If the analyst buys a share now, planning to sell it a year later, what rate of return might the analyst expect to earn? The answer depends on what assumption is made regarding the *rate of convergence of investors' predictions*—that is, the expected market reaction to the mispricing that the analyst believes currently exists.

The cases shown in Table 15.1 are based on an assumption that the analyst is confident that his or her forecast of future dividends is correct. In all of the cases, the analyst expects that at the end of the year, the stock will pay the predicted dividend of $1.10.

No Convergence

In column (A), other investors regard the higher dividend as a fluke and refuse to alter their projections of subsequent dividends from their initial estimate of $1.00. As a result, the security's price at $t = 1$ is expected to remain at $10 (= $1.00/.10). In this case the analyst's total return is expected to be 11% (= $1.10/$10), which is attributed entirely to dividends as no capital gains are expected. The 11% expected return consists of the required return of 10% plus an alpha of 1% that is equal to the portion of the dividend unanticipated by other investors, $.10/$10. Accordingly, if there is no convergence of predictions, then the expected return will be set at the implied rate of 11% and the alpha will be set at 1%.

Complete Convergence

Column (B) shows a very different situation. Here the other investors recognize their error and completely revise their predictions. At the end of the year, it is expected that they too will predict future dividends of $1.10 per year thereafter; thus, the stock

TABLE 15.1 Alpha and the Convergence of Predictions

	Expected Amount of Convergence		
	0% (A)	100% (B)	50% (C)
Dividend predictions D_2			
Consensus of other investors	1.00	1.10	1.05
Analyst	1.10	1.10	1.10
Expected stock price P_1	10.00	11.00	10.50
Expected return			
Dividend yield D_1/P	11%	11%	11%
Capital gain $(P_1 - P)/P$	0	10	5
Total expected return	11%	21%	16%
Less required return	10	10	10
Alpha	1%	11%	6%

Note: P_1 is equal to the consensus dividend prediction at $t = 1$ divided by the required return of 10%. The example assumes that the current stock price P is $10, and dividends are forecast by the consensus at $t = 0$ to remain constant at $1.00 per share, whereas the analyst forecasts the dividend at $t = 0$ to remain constant at $1.10 per share.

is expected to be selling for $11 $(= \$1.10/.10)$ at $t = 1$. Under these conditions, the analyst expects to achieve a total return of 21% by selling the stock at the end of the year for $11, obtaining 11% $(= \$1.10/\$10)$ in dividend yield and 10% $(= \$1/\$10)$ in capital gains. The 10% expected capital gains results directly from the expected repricing of the security because of the complete convergence of predictions. In this case the fruits of the analyst's superior prediction are expected to be obtained all in one year. Instead of an extra 1% per year forever, as in column (A), the analyst expects to obtain 1% $(= \$.10/\$10)$ in extra dividend yield plus 10% $(= \$1/\$10)$ in capital gains this year. If the analyst continues to hold the stock in subsequent years, he or she would expect to earn only the required return of 10% during those years. Accordingly, the expected return is 21% and the alpha is 11% for the forthcoming year when it is assumed that there is complete convergence of predictions.

Partial Convergence

Column (C) shows an intermediate case. Here the predictions of the other investors are expected to converge only halfway toward those of the analyst (that is, from $1.00 to $1.05 instead of to $1.10). Total return in the first year is expected to be 16%, consisting of 11% $(= \$1.10/\$10)$ in dividend yield plus 5% $(= \$.50/\$10)$ in capital gains.

Because the stock is expected to be selling for $10.50 $(= \$1.05/.10)$ at $t = 1$ but has an intrinsic value of $11 $(= \$1.10/.10)$ at that time, the analyst will still feel that it is underpriced. To obtain the remainder of the "extra return" owing to this underpricing, the investor would have to hold the stock past $t = 1$. Accordingly, the expected return then would be set at 16% and the alpha would be set at 6% for the forthcoming year when it is assumed that there is halfway convergence of predictions.

In general, a security's expected return and alpha will be larger as the assumed rate of convergence of predictions increases.[16] Many investors use the implied rate (that is, the internal rate of return k^*) as a surrogate for a relatively short-term (for example, one year) expected return, as in column (A). In doing so, they assume the dividend forecast is completely accurate but that there is no convergence. Alternatively, investors could assume that there is some degree of convergence, thereby raising their estimate of the security's expected return. Indeed, investors could further alter their estimate of the security's expected return by assuming that the security analyst's deviant prediction is less than perfectly accurate, as will be seen next.[17]

Summary

1. The capitalization of income method of valuation states that the intrinsic value of any asset is equal to the sum of the discounted cash flows investors expect to receive from that asset.
2. Dividend discount models (DDMs) are a specific application of the capitalization of income method of valuation to common stocks.
3. To use a DDM, the investor must implicitly or explicitly supply a forecast of all future dividends that are expected to be generated by a security.
4. Investors typically make certain simplifying assumptions about the growth of common stock dividends. For example, a common stock's dividends may be assumed to exhibit zero growth or growth at a constant rate. More complex assumptions allow for multiple growth rates over time.
5. Instead of applying DDMs, many security analysts use an alternative method of security valuation that involves estimating a stock's "normal" price-earnings ratio and comparing it with the stock's actual price-earnings ratio.
6. The growth rate in a firm's earnings and dividends depends on its earnings retention rate and its average return on equity for new investments.
7. Determining whether a security is mispriced using a DDM can be done in one of two ways. First, the discounted value of expected dividends can be compared with the stock's current price. Second, the discount rate that equates the stock's current price to the present value of forecast dividends can be compared with the required return for stocks of similar risk.
8. The rate of return that an analyst with nonconsensus dividend forecasts can expect to earn depends on both the analyst's accuracy and the rate of convergence of other investors' predictions to the predictions of the analyst.

Questions and Problems

1. Consider five annual cash flows (the first occurring one year from today):

Year	Cash Flow
1	$5
2	6
3	7
4	8
5	9

Given a discount rate of 10%, what is the present value of this stream of cash flows?

2. Alta Cohen is considering buying a machine to produce baseballs. The machine costs $10,000. With the machine, Alta expects to produce and sell 1,000 baseballs

per year for $3 per baseball, net of all costs. The machine's life is five years (with no salvage value). Based on these assumptions and an 8% discount rate, what is the net present value of Alta's investment?

3. Hub Collins has invested in a project that promised to pay $100, $200, and $300, respectively, at the end of the next three years. If Hub paid $513.04 for this investment, what is the project's internal rate of return?

4. Afton Products currently pays a dividend of $4 per share on its common stock.
   a. If Afton Products plans to increase its dividend at a rate of 5% per year indefinitely, what will be the dividend per share in 10 years?
   b. If Afton Products' dividend per share is expected to be $5.87 per share at the end of five years, at what annual rate is the dividend expected to grow?

5. Hammond Pipes has issued a preferred stock that pays $12 per share. The dividend is fixed and the stock has no expiration date. What is the intrinsic value of Hammond preferred stock, assuming a discount rate of 15%?

6. Milton Information Services currently pays a dividend of $4 per share on its common stock. The dividend is expected to grow at 4% per year forever. Stocks with similar risk currently are priced to provide a 12% expected return. What is the intrinsic value of Milton stock?

7. Spring Valley Bedding stock currently sells for $53 per share. The stock's dividend is expected to grow at 6% per year indefinitely. Spring Valley just paid a dividend of $3 per share. Given this information, calculate the stock's internal rate of return.

8. This year Monona Air Cleaners Inc. will pay a dividend on its stock of $6 per share. The following year the dividend is expected to be the same, increasing to $7 the year after. From that point on, the dividend is expected to grow at 4% per year indefinitely. Stocks with similar risk are currently priced to provide a 10% expected return. What is the intrinsic value of Monona stock?

9. Chief Medical Inc. is a little-known producer of heart pacemakers. The earnings and dividend growth prospects of the company are disputed by analysts. Albert Bender is forecasting 5% growth in dividends indefinitely. However, his brother John is predicting a 20% growth in dividends, but only for the next three years, after which the growth rate is expected to decline to 4% for the indefinite future. Chief dividends per share are currently $3. Stocks with similar risk are currently priced to provide a 14% expected return.
   a. What is the intrinsic value of Chief stock according to Albert?
   b. What is the intrinsic value of Chief stock according to John?
   c. Assume that Chief stock now sells for 39\frac{3}{4}$ per share. If the stock is fairly priced at the present time, what is the implied perpetual dividend growth rate? What is the implied P/E (price-earnings ratio) on next year's earnings, based on this perpetual dividend growth assumption and assuming a 25% payout ratio?

10. Elk Mound Candy Company currently pays a dividend of $3 per share. That dividend is expected to grow at a 6% rate indefinitely. Stocks with similar risk provide a 10% expected return. Calculate the intrinsic value of Elk Mound stock today using an interim computation based on the sale of the stock at its expected intrinsic value three years from now.

11. How would an increase in the perceived riskiness of a common stock's future cash flows affect its price-earnings ratio? Explain intuitively and mathematically.

12. Roberts Roofing currently earns $4 per share. Its return on equity is 20% and it retains 50% of its earnings (both figures are expected to be maintained indefinitely). Stocks of similar risk are priced to return 15%. What is the intrinsic value of Roberts' stock?

13. Osseo Operations recently paid an annual dividend of $4 per share. Earnings for the same year were $8 per share. The required return on stocks with similar risk is

11%. Dividends are expected to grow 6% per year indefinitely. Calculate Osseo's "normal" price-earnings ratio.

14. Reedsburg Associates is currently paying a dividend of $0.40 per share on earnings of $4 per share. Its stock is selling for $200 per share. Stocks of similar risk are priced to return 15%. What kind of return on equity could explain investors' willingness to pay a price equal to 50 times earnings on this stock?

15. Fay Thomas, a financial analyst, once remarked, "Even if your dividend estimates and discount rate are correct, dividend discount models identify stocks that will produce positive risk-adjusted returns only if other investors eventually come to agree with the DDM's valuation conclusions." Is Fay's statement correct? Why?

Endnotes

1. The usefulness of this method of valuation is shown in Steven N. Kaplan and Richard S. Ruback, "The Valuation of Cash Flow Forecasts: An Empirical Analysis," *Journal of Finance,* 50, no. 4 (September 1995): 1059–1093.

2. Some fundamental analysts use a model for identifying winners (that is, underpriced common stocks) that is not directly related to the capitalization of income method of valuation. Instead, stocks are identified as candidates for purchase if certain of their financial ratios exceed predetermined values. For example, the first screen might identify every stock whose price was less than $\frac{2}{3}$ of its net current asset value (that is, the per share value of current assets less total debt) and the second screen might identify stocks that also had a debt-to-equity ratio less than 1. Articles that discuss such screening methods include J. Ronald Hoffmeister and Edward A. Dyl, "Dividends and Share Value: Graham and Dodd Revisited," *Financial Analysts Journal,* 41, no. 3 (May/June 1985): 77–78; and Lewis D. Johnson, "Dividends and Share Value: Graham and Dodd Revisited, Again," *Financial Analysts Journal,* 41, no. 5 (September/October 1985): 79–80. For the most recent edition of the book, see Sidney Cottle, Roger F. Murray, and Frank E. Block, *Graham and Dodd's Security Analysis,* 5th ed. (New York: McGraw-Hill, 1988). For a brief discussion of their approach to investing, see Roger F. Murray, "Graham and Dodd: A Durable Discipline," *Financial Analysts Journal,* 40, no. 5 (September/October 1984): 18–23; Paul Blustein, "Ben Graham's Last Will and Testament," *Forbes,* August 1, 1977: 43–45; and James B. Rea, "Remembering Benjamin Graham—Teacher and Friend," *Journal of Portfolio Management,* 3, no. 4 (Summer 1977): 66–72; Henry R. Oppenheimer, "A Test of Ben Graham's Stock Selection Criteria," *Financial Analysts Journal,* 40, no. 5 (September/October 1984): 68–74; Henry R.

Oppenheimer, "Ben Graham's Net Current Asset Values: A Performance Update," *Financial Analysts Journal,* 42, no. 6 (November/December 1986): 40–47; and Marc R. Reinganum, "The Anatomy of Stock Market Winners," *Financial Analysts Journal,* 44, no. 2 (March/April 1988): 16–28.

3. Sometimes the expected cash flows after some time period will be equal to zero, meaning that the summation needs to be carried out only to that point. Even if they are never equal to zero, in many cases the denominator in Equation (15.1) will become so large as *t* gets large (for example, if *t* = 40 or more for a discount rate of 15%) that the present value of all expected cash flows past an arbitrary time in the future will be roughly zero and can be safely ignored. On a separate note, the discount rate may vary from period to period. It is assumed to be constant here for ease of exposition.

4. With complex cash flows (such as a mix of positive and negative cash flows), the IRR method can be misleading. However, this is not a problem when it is applied to securities such as stocks and bonds. For a discussion of potential problems in other contexts, see Richard A. Brealey and Stewart C. Myers, *Principles of Corporate Finance* (New York: McGraw-Hill, 1996), Chapter 5.

5. Because the focus of DDMs is on predicting dividends, there is a particular situation in which using DDMs to value common stocks is exceptionally difficult. This is the case where the firm has not paid dividends on its stock in the recent past, which results in a lack of historical record on which to base a prediction of dividends. Examples include valuing the stock of a firm being sold to the public for the first time (known as an *initial public offering,* or *IPO*), valuing the stock of a firm that has not paid dividends recently (perhaps the firm has never paid dividends, or perhaps it has suspended paying them), and valuing

the stock of a closely held firm. A more extensive discussion of DDMs is contained in the entire November/December 1985 issue of the *Financial Analysts Journal.* For articles that describe some of the current applications of DDMs, see Barbara Donnelly, "The Dividend Discount Model Comes into Its Own," *Institutional Investor,* 19, no. 3 (March 1985): 77–82; and Kent Hickman and Glen H. Petry, "A Comparison of Stock Price Predictions Using Court Accepted Formulas, Dividend Discount, and P/E Models," *Financial Management,* 19, no. 2 (Summer 1990): 76–87.

6. A share of common stock has a positive NPV if and only if it has an IRR greater than its required rate of return. Thus, there can never be inconsistent signals given by the two approaches. That is, there will never be a situation where one approach indicates that a stock is underpriced and the other approach indicates that it is overpriced. This is true not only for the zero-growth model, but for all DDMs.

7. The formula for valuing *consols* (these are bonds that make regular coupon payments but have no maturity date) is identical to Equation (15.13), where the numerator represents the annual coupon payment. Because it has been found that the price behavior of high-grade preferred stock is similar to that of bonds, it is not surprising that the zero-growth model can be used to value high-grade preferred stocks. See John S. Bildersee, "Some Aspects of the Performance of Non-Convertible Preferred Stocks," *Journal of Finance,* 28, no. 5 (December 1973): 1187–1201; and Enrico J. Ferreira, Michael F. Spivey, and Charles E. Edwards, "Pricing New-Issue and Seasoned Preferred Stock: A Comparison of Valuation Models," *Financial Management,* 21, no. 2 (Summer 1992): 52–62. For another method of valuing preferred stock, see Pradipkumar Ramanlal, "A Simple Algorithm for the Valuation of Preferred Stock," *Financial Practice and Education,* 7, no. 1 (Spring/Summer 1997): 11–19.

8. For an extension of this model that introduces capital gains taxes, see Raymond Chiang and Ricardo J. Rodriguez, "Personal Taxes, Holding Period, and the Valuation of Growth Stocks," *Journal of Economics and Business,* 42, no. 4 (November 1990): 303–309.

9. For a discussion of these models, see Russell J. Fuller and Chi-Cheng Hsia, "A Simplified Common Stock Valuation Model," *Financial Analysts Journal,* 40, no. 5 (September/October 1984): 49–56; Eric H. Sorensen and David A. Williamson, "Some Evidence on the Value of Dividend Discount Models," *Financial Analysts Journal,* 41, no. 6 (November/December 1985): 60–69; Richard W. Taylor, "A Three-Phase Quarterly Dividend Discount Model," *Financial Analysts Journal,* 44, no. 5 (September/October 1988): 79–80, and "A

Three-Phase Quarterly Earnings Model," *Financial Analysts Journal,* 45, no. 5 (September/October 1989): 79; and Michael S. Rozeff, "The Three-Phase Dividend Discount Model and the ROPE Model," *Journal of Portfolio Management,* 16, no. 2 (Winter 1990): 36–42.

10. The analysis is similar if it is assumed that the investor plans to sell the stock after some other length of time, such as six months or two years.

11. Alternatively, some analysts focus on the **earnings-price ratio,** which is the reciprocal of the price-earnings ratio. The formulas for a stock's "normal" earnings-price ratio can be found by simply taking the reciprocal of the forthcoming formulas for determining a stock's "normal" price-earnings ratio. In cases in which earnings are close to zero, the earnings-price ratio is computationally preferred by analysts to the price-earnings ratio because it approaches zero in such a situation, whereas the price-earnings ratio approaches infinity.

12. There are numerous methods besides those described here. Some of them are based on more complicated versions of the CAPM, whereas others are based on APT (discussed in Chapter 12).

13. There are ways of forcing the intercept of the line to go through the riskfree rate in order to agree with the implications of the traditional CAPM.

14. A subsequent procedure divides the estimated alpha by an estimate of the security's unique risk (that is, nonmarket or unsystematic risk) to obtain a standardized alpha. Based on the magnitude of the standardized alpha, the security is classified into one of ten "standardized alpha deciles." See also Marshall E. Blume, "The Use of 'Alphas' to Improve Performance," *Journal of Portfolio Management,* 11, no. 1 (Fall 1984): 86–92.

15. A similar procedure formerly used by Wells Fargo Investment Advisors is described by George Foster in *Financial Statement Analysis* (Englewood Cliffs, NJ: Prentice Hall, 1986), pp. 428–430.

16. In a perfectly efficient market (in the semistrong-form sense), these analysts would sometimes be right and sometimes be wrong, so, on balance, their predictions would be of no value. In such a situation, the expected return for any security would be its required return and the alpha would be zero.

17. As an example of how to estimate alpha if it is assumed that the analyst has less than perfect forecasting ability and there is less than 100% convergence, reconsider the example given in Table 15.1. First, assume that the forecast accuracy of the security analyst is 60%. Remember that the analyst's forecast of D_1 is $1.10, but the consensus forecast is $1.00, 60% accuracy means the forecast that should be used is

$1.06 [= $1.00 + .60 × ($1.10 − $1.00)]. Second, assume that there will be 50% convergence. This means that the security's price at $t = 1$ is expected to be $10.30 {= [$1.00 + .50 × ($1.06 − $1.00)]/.10}. Hence

the expected return under 60% forecast accuracy and 50% convergence is 13.6% {= [($10.30 − $10) + $1.06]/$10}, which translates into an alpha of 3.6% (= 13.6% − 10%).

Dividends and Earnings

Chapter 15 discussed how the intrinsic value of a share of common stock can be determined by discounting expected dividends per share at a rate of return that is appropriate for a security of similar risk. Alternatively, the implied return on a share of common stock can be determined by finding the discount rate that makes the present value of all the expected dividends equal to the current market price of the stock. In either case, a forecast of dividends per share is necessary. Because dividends per share are equal to earnings per share times a payout ratio, dividends can be forecast by forecasting earnings per share and payout ratios. There are numerous methods used by security analysts for forecasting either earnings or dividends. This chapter presents a discussion of some of the important features of dividends and earnings that the analyst should be aware of in making such forecasts. It begins with a discussion of the relationship among earnings, dividends, and investment.

16.1   Stock Valuation Based on Earnings

A continuing controversy in the investment community concerns the relevance of dividends versus earnings as the underlying source of value of a share of common stock. Clearly, earnings are important to stockholders because earnings provide the cash flow necessary for paying dividends.[1] However, dividends are also important because dividends are what stockholders actually receive from the firm, and they are the focus of the dividend discount models discussed in Chapter 15. Indeed, it would seem that if management increased the proportion of earnings per share paid out as dividends, they could make their stockholders wealthier, suggesting that the **dividend decision** (deciding on the amount of dividends to pay) is an important one.

dividend decision

Considerable light was shed on this controversy in 1961 when Merton Miller and Franco Modigliani (both are recipients of the Nobel Prize in Economic Science) published a seminal paper arguing that the underlying source of value of a share of common stock was earnings, not dividends. An implication of this conclusion is that the dividend decision is relatively unimportant to the stockholders because it will not affect the value of their investment in the firm.

In the course of a year, a firm generates revenues and incurs costs. With cash accounting, the difference between revenues and costs is termed *cash flow*. With accrual accounting, used by almost all firms, both revenues and costs are likely to include estimates made by accountants of the values of noncash items. Items such as depreciation charges are deducted from cash flow to obtain earnings. Moreover, each year some amount is invested in the business. Of the total (gross) investment, a portion is equal in value to the estimated depreciation of various real assets (such as machines and buildings); the rest is new (net) investment.

The dollar amount of new investment each year should be based on the investment opportunities that are available to the firm and should be unaffected by the dollar amount of dividends that are to be paid out. Any investment opportunity whose net present value (NPV) is positive should be undertaken. This assertion means that the future prospects of the firm can be described by a stream of expected earnings (E_1, E_2, E_3,...) and the expected net investment required to produce such earnings (I_1, I_2, I_3,...). When these two streams are taken as given, management can set the total dollar amount of current dividends (D_0) at any level without making the current stockholders either better or worse off.[2] This will be shown next.

16.1.1 EARNINGS, DIVIDENDS, AND INVESTMENT

Figure 16.1(a) shows one way a firm can use total earnings for the current year (E_0). In this situation, new investment (I_0) is financed out of earnings, and the firm uses the remainder of the earnings to pay dividends (D_0) to its stockholders. For example, if Plum Company has just earned $5,000 and has new investments that cost $3,000, then Plum could pay for these investments out of earnings and declare a dividend of $2,000.

Issuing Stock

Whereas earnings are exactly equal to dividends and investment ($E_0 = D_0 + I_0$) in Figure 16.1(a), this is not always the case. In the situation shown in Figure 16.1(b), earnings are less than dividends and investment ($E_0 < D_0 + I_0$). Because the amount of investment has been determined by the number of positive NPV projects available to the firm, this inequality results because the firm has decided to pay its current stockholders a higher dividend than was paid in Figure 16.1(a). However, in order for the higher dividend to be paid, additional funds must be obtained from outside the firm. Additional funds are obtained by a new sale of common stock (it is assumed that the flotation costs associated with a new sale of common stock are negligible).

The funds are obtained through a new sale of common stock instead of through a new sale of debt to avoid the confounding effects of a change in the firm's debt-equity ratio. If debt financing is allowed, then two things change at the same time: the amount of the dividend and the debt-equity ratio for the firm. If stockholders seem better off by a change in the amount of the dividend, their betterment may actually be a result of a change in the debt-equity ratio. If debt financing is prohibited, the debt-equity ratio will remain constant and only the amount of the dividend will change. That is, each

FIGURE 16.1 Earnings, Dividends, and Investment

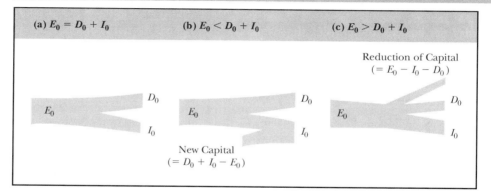

additional dollar in equity funds raised by issuing new stock is offset by a dollar in dividend payments. If stockholders seem better off, it has to be due to the change in the amount of the dividend because nothing else (specifically, the amount of investment and the debt-equity ratio) has changed.

Note that if investment is financed out of earnings, as in Figure 16.1(a), then it has been financed with equity obtained *internally*. In Figure 16.1(b), investment has also been financed with equity, but some of the equity has been obtained *externally*. As a result, the debt-equity ratio for the firm is the same in both situations.

In the case of Plum, instead of paying dividends amounting to $2,000, the firm could decide to pay dividends amounting to $3,000. Because investment is equal to $3,000, Plum will have a cash outflow of $6,000 (= $3,000 + $3,000), with earnings amounting to only $5,000. Hence, Plum will have to sell $1,000 (= $6,000 − $5,000) of new common stock.

Repurchasing Stock

In Figure 16.1(c), the situation is reversed from Figure 16.1(b); earnings are now greater than dividends and investment ($E_0 > D_0 + I_0$). If the amount of investment has been determined by the number of positive NPV projects available to the firm, then this inequality results because the firm decided to pay its stockholders a lower dividend than was paid in Figure 16.1(a). In paying this smaller dividend, the firm will be left with excess cash. It is assumed that the firm will use this cash to repurchase some of its outstanding shares in the marketplace (and that the transaction costs associated with such repurchases are negligible). The reason for this assumption is the desire to keep the situation comparable to the two earlier ones. Allowing the firm to keep the excess cash would be tantamount to letting the firm invest the cash, an investment decision that was not made in the two earlier cases and therefore does not have a positive NPV (remember that I_0 consists of all positive NPV projects). Allowing the firm to keep the excess cash would also mean that the firm has made a decision to lower its debt-equity ratio because retention of the excess cash would increase the amount of equity (through retained earnings) for the firm, thereby decreasing the amount of debt outstanding relative to the amount of equity.

The Plum Company could set dividends at $1,000 instead of $2,000 or $3,000. In this case, the firm would have a cash outflow for dividends and investment amounting to $4,000 (= $1,000 + $3,000). With earnings of $5,000 there would then be $1,000 (= $5,000 − $4,000) of cash left for the firm to use to repurchase its own stock.

The Dividend Decision

The firm has a decision to make regarding the size of its current dividends. The amount of current earnings E_0 and the amount of new investment I_0 have been determined. Dividends can be set equal to earnings less investment [as in Figure 16.1(a)], or greater than that amount [as in Figure 16.1(b)], or less than that amount [as in Figure 16.1(c)]. The question that remains to be answered is, Will one of these three levels of dividends make the current stockholders better off than the other two? That is, which level of dividends—$1,000, $2,000, or $3,000—will make the current stockholders better off?

The simplest way to answer that question is to consider a stockholder with 1% of the common stock of the firm who is determined to maintain this percentage ownership in the future.[3] If the firm follows a dividend policy as shown in Figure 16.1(a), then the stockholder's current dividends will equal $.01D_0$ or, equivalently, $.01(E_0 − I_0)$. Similarly, the stockholder's future dividends will be equal to $.01D_t$ or, equivalently, $.01(E_t − I_t)$. Because the stockholder wants to be certain of receiving this amount regardless of the level of current dividends, he or she will take whatever actions are necessary to maintain a 1% ownership position in the firm. When the situation is analyzed in this manner, there is only one variable that can affect the stockholder's current wealth—the amount of the current dividend.

If the firm follows a dividend policy as shown in Figure 16.1(b), the stockholder must invest additional funds in the firm's common stock to avoid a diminished proportional ownership position in the firm. Why? Because in this situation the firm must raise funds by selling additional shares to pay for the larger cash dividends. Because $E_0 < D_0 + I_0$, the total amount of funds the firm needs to raise is the amount F_0 such that

$$E_0 + F_0 = D_0 + I_0 \tag{16.1}$$

or

$$F_0 = D_0 + I_0 - E_0 \tag{16.2}$$

The amount of the additional investment that the stockholder needs to make to maintain a 1% position in the firm is $.01F_0$, which, from Equation (16.2), is equal to $.01(D_0 + I_0 - E_0)$. Because the stockholder receives 1% of the dividends, the net amount the stockholder receives at time zero is equal to $.01D_0 - .01F_0$, or

$$.01D_0 - .01(D_0 + I_0 - E_0) = .01E_0 - .01I_0 \tag{16.3}$$

Interestingly, the net amount the stockholder receives, $.01E_0 - .01I_0$, is the same as in the first situation. The amount of the extra cash dividend received is exactly offset by the amount the stockholder needs to spend to maintain his or her ownership position in the firm.

If the firm follows a dividend policy as shown in Figure 16.1(c), then the firm will repurchase shares. Accordingly, the stockholder must sell some shares back to the firm in order to avoid having an increased ownership position in the firm. Because $E_0 > D_0 + I_0$, the total amount of funds that the firm will spend on repurchasing its own shares is the amount R_0 such that

$$E_0 = D_0 + I_0 + R_0 \tag{16.4}$$

or

$$R_0 = E_0 - D_0 - I_0 \tag{16.5}$$

The amount of stock that the stockholder needs to sell back to the firm to maintain a 1% position in the firm is $.01R_0$, which, from Equation (16.5), is equal to $.01(E_0 - D_0 - I_0)$. Because the stockholder receives 1% of the dividends, the net amount the stockholder receives at time zero is equal to $.01D_0 + .01R_0$, or

$$.01D_0 + .01(E_0 - D_0 - I_0) = .01E_0 - .01I_0 \tag{16.6}$$

Again this net amount, $.01E_0 - .01I_0$, is the same as in the first situation. That is, in the third situation, the smaller amount of the cash dividend received by the stockholder is exactly made up for by the amount of cash received from the repurchase of shares by the firm.

In summary, no matter what the firm's dividend policy, a stockholder choosing to maintain a constant proportional ownership will be able to spend the same amount of money on consumption at time zero. This amount will be equal to the proportion times the quantity $E_0 - I_0$. This will also be true in the future. That is, in any year t the stockholder will be able to spend on consumption an amount that is equal to the proportion times the quantity $E_t - I_t$.

16.1.2 EARNINGS DETERMINE MARKET VALUE

In determining the value of 1% of the current shares outstanding, remember that the firm is about to declare and pay current dividends. Regardless of the magnitude of these dividends, the stockholder will be able to spend on consumption only an amount equal to $.01(E_0 - I_0)$. Furthermore, the stockholder will be able to spend on consumption an amount equal to $.01(E_t - I_t)$ in any future year t. Discounting these expected amounts by a (constant) rate k reveals that the value V of 1% of the current shares outstanding will be

$$.01V = \frac{.01(E_0 - I_0)}{(1+k)^0} + \frac{.01(E_1 - I_1)}{(1+k)^1} + \frac{.01(E_2 - I_2)}{(1+k)^2} + \cdots$$

Multiplying both sides of this equation by 100 results in the following expression for the total market value of all shares outstanding:

$$V = \frac{(E_0 - I_0)}{(1+k)^0} + \frac{(E_1 - I_1)}{(1+k)^1} + \frac{(E_2 - I_2)}{(1+k)^2} + \cdots \qquad (16.7)$$

Equation (16.7) shows that the aggregate market value of equity is equal to the present value of expected earnings net of investment. Note that the size of the dividends does not enter into the formula. As a result, the current market value of the stock is *independent* of the dividend decision made by the firm, meaning that the dividend decision is irrelevant to stock valuation. Instead, the market value of the firm is related to the earnings prospects of the firm, along with the required amounts of new investment needed to produce those earnings.[4] Hence, it is not surprising that many high-tech stocks have lofty price-earnings ratios even though they do not pay dividends.

Dividend Discount Models

Chapter 15 indicated that the value of a share of common stock was equal to the present value of all dividends expected in the future. Hence it is tempting to believe that, contrary to the assertion represented by Equation (16.7), the market value of a firm's stock is *dependent* on the dividend decision. However, there is nothing inconsistent between valuation based on dividend discount models and the irrelevancy of the dividend decision.

The dividend irrelevancy argument suggests that if the firm decides to increase its current dividend, then new shares will need to be sold. In turn, future dividends will be smaller because the aggregate amount of dividends will have to be divided among a greater number of shares outstanding. Consequently, the current stockholders will be neither better off nor worse off because the increased current dividend will be exactly offset by the decreased future dividends. Conversely, if the firm decides to decrease its current dividend, then shares will be repurchased and future dividends will be increased because there will be fewer shares outstanding. That is, the decreased current dividend will be exactly offset by the increased future dividends, again leaving current stockholders neither better off nor worse off.

An Example

These situations can be illustrated using the Plum Company example. Because Plum currently has reported earnings of $5,000 and investments totaling $3,000, if dividends amounting to $2,000 were paid, then the stockholder owning 1% of the firm would receive cash amounting to $20 (= .01 × $2,000).

Alternatively, if dividends amounting to $3,000 were paid, then Plum would have to raise $1,000 from the sale of new common stock. The stockholder would receive $30

(= .01 × $3,000) in dividends but would have to pay $10 (= .01 × $1,000) to purchase 1% of the new stock to maintain his or her 1% ownership position. Consequently, the net cash flow to the stockholder would be $20 (= $30 − $10), the same amount as in the previous situation.

Last, if dividends amounting to $1,000 were paid, then Plum would have cash amounting to $1,000 to repurchase common stock. The stockholder, in order to maintain a 1% position, would sell shares amounting to $10 (= .01 × $1,000). As a result, the stockholder would have a cash inflow totaling $20 (= $10 + $10), again the same amount as in the two previous situations.

Under all three situations, the 1% stockholder receives the same cash flow at the present time ($20) and has the same claim on the future earnings of Plum [= $.01(E_t − I_t)$]. In all three cases, the stockholder still owns 1% of Plum and receives the same amount of dividends in the future. Accordingly, the 1% stockholder (and all the others) would be neither better off nor worse off if Plum pays a dividend amounting to $1,000, $2,000, or $3,000. Thus, the dividend decision is a nonevent—whatever the level of dividends, current stockholders will be neither better off nor worse off. This result is sometimes referred to as the *dividend irrelevancy theorem.*

16.2 Determinants of Dividends

Few firms attempt to maintain a constant ratio of dividends to current earnings; doing so would result in a fluctuating dollar amount of dividends. The dividends fluctuate because earnings vary on a year-to-year basis. Instead, firms may attempt to maintain a desired ratio of dividends to earnings for some relatively long period, meaning that there is a target payout ratio of dividends to long-run or sustainable earnings. As a result, dividends are usually kept at a constant dollar amount and are increased only when management is confident that it will be able to pay an increased amount in the future.[5] Nonetheless, larger earnings are likely to be accompanied by some sort of increase in dividends, as Table 16.1 shows.

16.2.1 CHANGES IN EARNINGS AND DIVIDENDS

The first two lines of Table 16.1 indicate that 59.3% of the time the earnings of the firms examined rose, and 40.7% of the time earnings fell. The majority of the times current earnings rose, firms increased their current dividends. However, whenever current earnings fell, firms increased their current dividends as frequently as they decreased their current dividends (note that 42.8% ≅ 39.5%).

TABLE 16.1	**Earnings and Dividend Changes**				
Earnings Changes			**Percentage of Cases in Which Firms**		
Current Year	**Previous Year**	**Percentage of Cases**	**Increased Dividends**	**Did Not Change Dividends**	**Decreased Dividends**
+		59.3%	65.8%	13.9%	20.3%
−		40.7	42.8	17.9	39.5
+	+	33.4	74.8	11.4	13.8
+	−	25.9	54.1	17.2	28.7
−	+	24.7	49.7	16.9	33.4
−	−	16.0	31.8	19.4	48.8

Source: Eugene F. Fama and Harvey Babiak, "Dividend Policy: An Empirical Analysis," *Journal of the American Statistical Association,* 63, no. 324 (December 1968): 1134.

The next two lines of the table suggest that firms are more likely to increase current dividends if they have had two consecutive years of rising earnings than if they have had falling and then rising earnings (74.8% > 54.1%). The last two lines of the table suggest that firms are more likely to decrease current dividends if they have had two consecutive years of falling earnings than if they have had rising and then falling earnings (48.8% > 33.4%). Overall, the table shows that firms are more likely to increase dividends than to decrease them.

16.2.2 THE LINTNER MODEL

A formal representation of the kind of behavior implied by a constant long-run target payout ratio begins by assuming that the goal of the firm is to pay out $p*$ (for example, $p* = 60\%$) of long-run earnings. If this target ratio were maintained every year, total dividends paid in year t would be

$$D^*_t = p^*E_t \tag{16.8}$$

where D^*_t denotes the target amount for dividends to be paid in year t, and E_t is the amount of earnings in year t. The difference between target dividends in year t and the previous year's actual dividends is determined by subtracting D_{t-1} from both sides of Equation (16.8), resulting in

$$D^*_t - D_{t-1} = p^*E_t - D_{t-1} \tag{16.9}$$

Although firms would like to change their dividends from D_{t-1} to D^*_t, few (if any) firms would actually change their dividends by this amount. Instead, the actual change in dividends will be a proportion of the desired change:

$$D_t - D_{t-1} = a(D^*_t - D_{t-1}) \tag{16.10}$$

where a is a "speed of adjustment" coefficient, a number between 0 and 1.

For example, if a firm has just earned $5 million ($E_t$ = $5 million) and has a target payout ratio of 60%, then it would like to pay dividends amounting to $3 million (= .6 × $5 million). If it paid dividends of $2 million last year, this amount represents an increase of $1 million (= $3 million − $2 million). However, if a = 50%, then the firm will actually increase the dividends by $500,000 (= .5 × $1 million). Actual dividends will equal $2.5 million (= $2 million + $500,000), which is last year's dividends plus the change in dividends from last year to this year.

This model can be summarized by substituting p^*E_t for D^*_t in Equation (16.10) and then solving the resulting expression for D_t:

$$D_t = ap^*E_t + (1 - a)D_{t-1} \tag{16.11}$$

Equation (16.11) indicates that the amount of current dividends is based on the amount of current earnings and the amount of the last year's dividends.[6] In the previous example, a = 50%, $p*$ = 60%, E_t = $5 million, and D_{t-1} = $2 million. Thus, actual dividends D_t would be equal to $2.5 million [= (.5 × .6 × $5 million) + (1 − .5 × $2 million)].

Subtracting D_{t-1} from both sides of Equation (16.11), it can be seen that the change in dividends is equal to

$$D_t - D_{t-1} = ap^*E_t - aD_{t-1} \tag{16.12}$$

When written in this form, the model suggests that the size of the *change* in dividends will be positively related to the current amount of earnings (because $ap*$ is a positive

TABLE 16.2 Target Payout Ratios and Speed of Dividend Adjustment Factors

Speed of Adjustment Coefficient		Target Payout Ratio		Percentage of Variance Explained	
Value	*Percentage of Firms with Smaller Value*	*Value*	*Percentage of Firms with Smaller Value*	*Value*	*Percentage of Firms with Smaller Value*
.104	10%	.401	10%	11%	10%
.182	30	.525	30	32	30
.251	50	.584	50	42	50
.339	70	.660	70	54	70
.470	90	.779	90	72	90
Average .269		Average .591		Average 42	

Source: Eugene F. Fama, "The Empirical Relationship between the Dividend and Investment Decisions of Firms," *American Economic Review*, 64, no. 3 (June 1974): 310.

number) and negatively related to the amount of the previous period's dividends (because $-aD_{t-1}$ is a negative number). Thus, the larger current earnings are, the larger the change in dividends, but the larger the previous period's dividends, the smaller the change in dividends.

16.2.3 TEST RESULTS

Statistical analysis has been used to test how well this model describes the way a sample of firms set the amount of their dividends. Table 16.2 summarizes some of the values obtained in one such study. The average firm had a target payout ratio of 59.1% and adjusted dividends 26.9% of the way toward its target each year. However, most firms' dividends varied substantially from the pattern implied by their targets and adjustment factors. Somewhat less than half (42%) of the annual variance in the typical firm's dividends could be explained in this manner. This result means that the model, although explaining a portion of the changes in dividends that occurred, leaves a substantial portion unexplained.

A refinement of the model presented in Equation (16.12) uses an alternative definition of earnings. Specifically, the term E_t in Equation (16.8) can be defined as the *permanent* earnings of the firm in year t instead of total earnings. Here total earnings can be thought of as having two components: permanent earnings, which are likely to be repeated, and transitory earnings, which are not likely to be repeated. Accordingly, the refinement is based on the idea that management ignores the transitory component of earnings in arriving at its target amount of dividends. The target amount is based on the permanent earnings of the firm, not on the total earnings, and the change in dividends shown in equation (16.12) is related to the past level of dividends and permanent earnings. A test of this model found that it described changes in dividends better than the previously described model that was based on total earnings.[7] An implication is that a firm's intrinsic value will be based on investors' forecasts of the firm's permanent earnings.

16.3 The Information Content of Dividends

Management usually has more information about the future earnings of the firm than the public (including its own stockholders). This situation of asymmetric information suggests that managers will convey the information to the public if they have an incentive to do so. Assuming they have such an incentive, one way of conveying information is to announce a change in the amount of the firm's dividends. When used in this manner, dividend announcements are said to be a signaling device.[8]

16.3.1 SIGNALING

A relatively simple view of dividend changes is that an announced increase in dividends is a signal that management has increased its assessment of the firm's future earnings. The announced increase in dividends is therefore good news and will, in turn, cause investors to raise their expectations regarding the firm's future earnings. Conversely, an announced decrease in dividends is a signal that management has decreased its assessment of the firm's future earnings. The announced decrease in dividends is therefore bad news and will, in turn, cause investors to lower their expectations regarding the firm's future earnings. Thus, an announced increase in dividends should cause the firm's stock price to rise, and an announced decrease should cause it to fall.

This simple model of dividend changes is a special case of the model given in Equation (16.12), where the speed of adjustment, *a*, is zero. With this model, the expected change in dividends, $D_t - D_{t-1}$, is zero, suggesting that an increase in dividends is good news and a decrease in dividends is bad news.

One way to test whether dividend changes convey information to the public is to see how stock prices react to announcements of changes in dividends. However, care must be exercised because the firm's announcement of dividends is often made at the same time as the firm announces its earnings. When such announcements are made at the same time, any price change in the firm's common stock may be attributable to either (or both) announcements.

One study attempted to avoid such contamination by looking only at cases in which the announcement of earnings was at least 11 trading days apart from the announcement of dividends. Figure 16.2 illustrates the average abnormal return (that is, the return in excess of the return required on securities of similar risk) associated with a firm's dividend announcement for firms that announced their dividends 11 or more days after they announced their earnings. (Similar results were obtained when the authors of the study examined cases in which dividend announcements preceded earnings announcements). When firms announced an increase in their dividends, there was a significant positive reaction in their stock prices. Conversely, for firms announcing a decrease in their dividends, there was a significant negative reaction in their stock prices. These findings strongly support the **information content of dividends hypothesis,** which asserts that dividend announcements are asserted to contain inside information about the firm's future prospects.

information content of dividends hypothesis

There is nothing inconsistent with dividends being used as a signal and with the dividend irrelevancy argument of Miller and Modigliani that was made earlier. Stockholders will be neither better off nor worse off if the *level* of dividends, relative to earnings, is high or low. *Changes* in dividends, however, may be important because they convey information to the public about the future earnings prospects for the firm.

16.3.2 DIVIDEND INITIATIONS AND OMISSIONS

One study looked at the relationship between dividend changes and past, current, and future changes in earnings.[9] It focused on the most dramatic dividend announcements possible—dividend initiations and omissions—because the information conveyed in these announcements is unambiguous. If the information content of dividends hypoth-

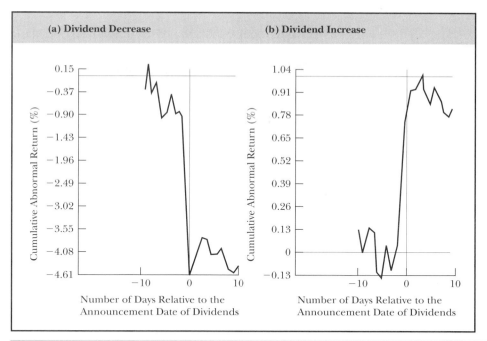

FIGURE 16.2 Cumulative Abnormal Returns Starting Ten Days before a Dividend Announcement

Source: Joseph Aharony and Itzhak Swary, "Quarterly Dividend and Earnings Announcements and Stockholders' Returns: An Empirical Analysis," *Journal of Finance,* 35, no. 1 (March 1980): 8.

esis is correct, then firms that start to pay dividends for the first time in at least 10 years must be signaling that they believe earnings have recently increased to a permanently higher level and that earnings may increase even more in the near future. The question to be addressed is, Have firms actually experienced notably higher earnings around the time of such initiations and afterward? In contrast, firms that have paid dividends for at least ten years and that suddenly stop paying any dividends must believe that their earnings have recently decreased to a permanently lower level and that earnings may decrease even more in the future. For them the question is, Have firms actually experienced notably lower earnings around the time of such omissions and afterward?

After examining 131 dividend-initiating stocks and 172 dividend-omitting stocks on the NYSE and AMEX, support was found for the information content of dividends hypothesis. The study found that earnings tended to increase for at least one year leading up to dividend initiations and to decrease for up to two years leading up to dividend omissions. Furthermore, earnings continued to increase for at least one year after initiations and to decrease for one year after omissions, and such changes seem permanent. Interestingly, the larger the change in the firm's stock price when the dividend initiation or omission was announced, the larger the change in the firm's earnings in both the year of the announcement and the year thereafter. Thus, it seems that dividends convey information about earnings.

A second study also focused on the stock price movements of firms around the time that they either initiated or omitted dividends.[10] In this study, which examined a sample of firms listed on the NYSE and the AMEX, 887 occurrences of dividend omissions and 561 initiations were analyzed. The following observations were made:

1. The stocks of firms that initiated dividends had an average abnormal return of 15.1% during the year up to the time of the dividend announcement. The corresponding figure for firms that omitted dividends was −31.8%. Hence, firms that initiated dividends seem to have been prior "winners," whereas firms that omitted dividends seem to have been prior "losers."
2. During the three-day period centered on the announcement of an initiating dividend, the stocks of these firms had an average abnormal return of 3.4%. The corresponding figure for omissions was −7.0%.
3. The average stock of firms that initiated a dividend had an abnormal return of 24.8% in the 3 years afterward, whereas the average stock price of firms that omitted a dividend had an abnormal return of –15.0% during the subsequent 2 years, and thereafter had normal returns. Because of this lagged response to dividend initiations and omissions, it seems that the market underreacts to these dividend announcements, implying a market inefficiency.
4. The average dividend yield at the time a dividend was initiated was .9%; the average dividend yield just before an omission was 6.7%.

16.3.3 DIVIDENDS AND LOSSES

It is interesting to examine situations in which firms that have had a string of at least 10 years of positive earnings and dividend payments suddenly experience negative earnings. In particular, do dividends in such a situation convey information about future earnings?

One study examined firms that had at least 1 year of negative earnings during a 6-year period but previously had at least 10 consecutive years of positive earnings and dividend payments; 167 "loss" firms were uncovered that met these criteria.[11] A comparison sample of 440 "nonloss" firms with 6 straight years of positive earnings as well as during a previous 10-year period was also formed.

Approximately half the loss firms reduced or omitted their dividends in the four subsequent quarters after the fiscal year-end of the loss. In comparison, fewer than 1% of the nonloss firms either reduced or omitted their dividends during the 6-year period. Further examination revealed that

1. The loss firms that did not reduce their dividends were likely to have unusual income items, indicating that their earnings problems were more likely to be temporary.
2. The loss firms that reduced their dividends had deeper losses than the loss firms that did not reduce their dividends.
3. The loss firms that reduced their dividends were more likely to have negative earnings in the next two years than the nonreducing loss firms.

Hence knowing what happened to dividends for a loss firm tends to make it easier to predict its future earnings, thereby indicating that dividends have information content when a firm suddenly has negative earnings.

16.4 Accounting Earnings versus Economic Earnings

Because the prediction of earnings is of critical importance in security analysis and investment research, a review of what is known about earnings and the relationship between earnings and security prices is essential. At a fundamental level, just what is meant by "earnings" and how does its meaning affect the valuation process?

16.4.1 ACCOUNTING EARNINGS

accounting earnings

A firm's accountants operate under constraints and guidelines imposed by regulatory authorities and professional organizations such as the SEC and the Financial Accounting Standards Board (FASB).[12] In cooperation with management, accountants produce, on a quarterly basis, financial statements for the firm that includes a figure for the firm's **accounting earnings** (or reported earnings). In a broad sense, such earnings represent the difference between revenues and expenses, including the expenses associated with nonequity sources of funds (such as debt). This difference, the "total earnings available for common stock," is divided by the number of shares outstanding to calculate **earnings per share** (EPS). It may also be divided by the book value per share to calculate the **return on equity** (ROE).

earnings per share
return on equity

A basic principle of accounting makes the book value of a firm's equity at the end of a period (such as a quarter or a year) equal to (1) its value at the end of the previous period plus (2) the portion of accounting earnings for the period that is retained by the firm (here it is assumed that there has been no change in the number of shares outstanding during the period).[13] Letting B_t denote the book value of the equity at the end of period t, E_t^a denote the accounting earnings for period t, and D_t denote the dividends paid during period t, this relationship can be expressed algebraically as

$$B_t = B_{t-1} + E_t^a - D_t \qquad (16.13)$$

Based on Equation (16.13), it can be seen that accounting earnings equal the change in book value of the equity plus dividends paid:

$$E_t^a = B_t - B_{t-1} + D_t \qquad (16.14)$$

Equivalently, accounting earnings are equal to the change in retained earnings plus dividends paid.

16.4.2 ECONOMIC EARNINGS

economic earnings
economic value of the firm

Economic earnings (E_t^e) are defined as the amount that would be obtained in Equation (16.14) if the change in the book value of the firm equaled the change in the **economic value of the firm**:

$$E_t^e = V_t - V_{t-1} + D_t \qquad (16.15)$$

Here the change in the economic value of the firm during period t, $V_t - V_{t-1}$, is defined as the change in the market value of the firm's common stock (assuming that there is no change in the market value of the firm's other securities).[14]

Reported book values and market values (that is, economic values) of stocks are often considerably different. Figure 16.3 shows the ratio of (1) the year-end market price per share for Standard & Poor's Industrial Stock Index to (2) the corresponding year-end book value per share. That ratio is typically greater than 1.0 and has fluctuated considerably from year to year.

Figure 16.3 indicates that there can be sizable differences between market and book values. Because Equations (16.14) and (16.15) show that accounting and economic earnings will be equal only if market and book values are equal, the evidence suggests that accounting and economic earnings differ by varying amounts for different firms.

As Chapter 15 discussed, investors sometimes estimate the value of a firm's common stock by directly applying a formula to the firm's current and past accounting earnings.[15] Such a belief may tempt a firm's managers to try to "manage" such earnings in

FIGURE 16.3 Ratio of Market Price to Book Value: Standard & Poor's Industrial Stock Index, 1946–1997

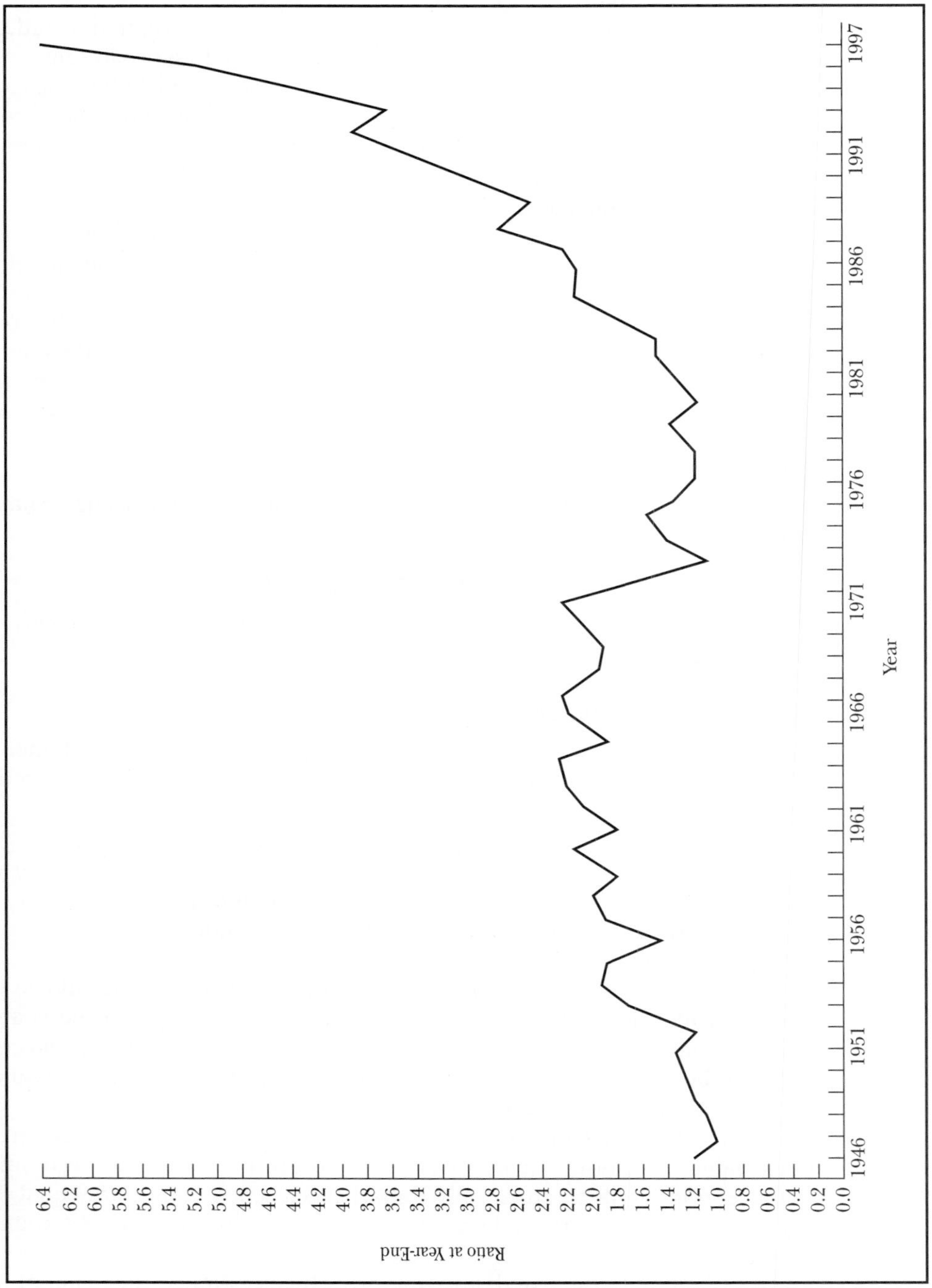

Source: Standard & Poor's *Statistical Service: Current Statistics,* various issues.

generally accepted accounting principles

order to make a firm appear more valuable than it is, thereby fooling investors, at least temporarily. This "managing" is possible because the **generally accepted accounting principles** (GAAP) set by the regulatory authorities (such as FASB) allow discretion in how certain items are accounted for (examples include methods for depreciation and inventory valuation). As a result, management may pressure accountants to use principles that maximize the level of reported earnings, or that result in a high growth rate of reported earnings, or that "smooth" earnings by reducing the year-to-year variability of earnings around a growth rate.[16] Some of these activities can be continued for only a limited number of years; others can go on indefinitely.

To obtain a truly independent estimate of value, analysts must dissect reported earnings. To avoid being fooled by accounting illusions, they should unravel any manipulations that may have been made by the accountants at management's request.[17] Anyone who estimates value by applying a formula (no matter how complex) to reported earnings is not producing an estimate that is completely free from all possible manipulations by management. This is not to say that reported earnings are irrelevant for security valuation. Instead, they should be viewed as one source of information about the future prospects of a firm.

16.5 Relative Growth Rates of Firms' Earnings

Because security analysis typically involves forecasting earnings per share, it is useful to examine the historical record to see how earnings per share have changed over time. An interesting question about growth rates in earnings over time focuses on "growth stocks" (growth stocks are discussed in Chapter 13). The very idea of a growth stock suggests that increases in some firms' earnings will exceed the average increase of all firms' earnings in most years, whereas other firms' earnings will increase less than the average.

16.5.1 EARNINGS GROWTH RATES

The results of a study of the earnings growth rates are shown in Table 16.3. For every year, each sampled firm's earnings were compared with its earnings in the previous year, and the percentage change was calculated. The year was counted as "good" for the firm if its percentage change was in the top half of the changes for all firms that year and as "bad" if it was in the bottom half. Fairly long runs of good years should occur for firms that experience above-average earnings growth rates. Conversely, fairly long runs of bad years should occur for firms that experience below-average earnings growth rates.

The middle two columns of Table 16.3 indicate the actual number of runs of various lengths. The right column shows the number that would be expected if there were a 50:50 chance of either a good year or a bad year. The three columns are remarkably similar. Above-average earnings growth in the past does not appear to indicate above-average growth in the future, and below-average growth in the past does not appear to indicate below-average growth in the future. Flipping a coin seems to be as reliable a predictor of future growth as looking at past growth rates.

A study using longer time periods for measuring growth reached similar conclusions.[18] For each sampled firm with positive earnings each year during the 20-year sample period, average growth rates were computed for the first and second 10-year periods. Differences among firms' earnings growth rates in the first period accounted for less than 1% of the variation in the differences among their earnings growth rates in the second period.

TABLE 16.3 Earnings Growth Rates

Length of Run	Actual Number of Good Runs	Actual Number of Bad Runs	Number of Good or Bad Runs Expected If the Odds Each Year Were 50:50 Regardless of Past Performance
1	1,152	1,102	1,068
2	562	590	534
3	266	300	267
4	114	120	133
5	55	63	67
6	24	20	33
7	23	12	17
8	5	6	8
9	3	3	4
10	6	0	2
11	2	0	1
12	1	0	1
13	0	0	0
14	0	1	0

Source: Richard A. Brealey, *An Introduction to Risk and Return from Common Stocks* (Cambridge, MA: MIT Press, 1983), p. 89.

16.5.2 ANNUAL EARNINGS

random walk model

The results of these and other studies suggest that *annual reported earnings* follow a **random walk model** where annual earnings for the forthcoming year (E_t) are equal to annual earnings during the past year (E_{t-1}) plus a random error term. Accordingly, next year's earnings can be described by the following statistical model:

$$E_t = E_{t-1} + \varepsilon_t \qquad (16.16)$$

where ε_t is the random error term. With this model, the best estimate of next year's earnings is simply the past year's earnings, E_{t-1}. Another way to view a random walk model for earnings is to consider the change in earnings to be independent and identically distributed:

$$E_t - E_{t-1} = \varepsilon_t \qquad (16.17)$$

This means that the change in earnings, $E_t - E_{t-1}$, is unrelated to past changes in earnings and can be thought of as the outcome resulting from a spin of a roulette wheel that is, perhaps, unique to the firm but, more importantly, is used year after year. Because the expected outcome from a spin of the roulette wheel is zero, the expected change in earnings is zero. This relation implies that the expected level of earnings is equal to the past year's earnings, as was suggested earlier.[19]

16.5.3 QUARTERLY EARNINGS

In terms of *quarterly reported earnings,* there is typically a seasonal component to a firm's earnings (for example, many retailing firms have high earnings during the quarter that includes Christmas). As a result, a slightly different model would be best for forecasting purposes. This model forecasts the growth in earnings for the forthcoming quarter relative to the same quarter one year ago, a quantity denoted $QE_t - QE_{t-4}$. It relates this growth to the growth during the most recent quarter relative to the comparable quarter one year before it, $QE_{t-1} - QE_{t-5}$. Formally, the model for the "seasonally differenced series" of quarterly earnings is known as an *autoregressive model of order one:*

$$QE_t - QE_{t-4} = a(QE_{t-1} - QE_{t-5}) + b + e_t \qquad \textbf{(16.18)}$$

where a and b are constants and e_t is a random error term.

Alternatively, the model can be rewritten by moving the term QE_{t-4} to the right-hand side:

$$QE_t = QE_{t-4} + a(QE_{t-1} - QE_{t-5}) + b + e_t \qquad \textbf{(16.19)}$$

When the constants a and b are estimated, this model can be used to forecast quarterly earnings.[20] For example, assuming estimates for a and b of .4 and .05, respectively, the forecast of a firm's earnings for the next quarter would be equal to $QE_{t-4} + .4(QE_{t-1} - QE_{t-5}) + \$.05$. Thus, if a firm had earnings per share for the last quarter $(t-1)$ of \$3, for four quarters ago $(t-4)$ of \$2, and for five quarters ago $(t-5)$ of \$2.60, then its forecast earnings for the forthcoming quarter would be equal to \$2.21 [$= \$2 + .4(\$3 - \$2.60) + \$.05$]. Note that the forecast consists of three components: (1) a component equal to last quarter's earnings (\$2); (2) a component that considers the year-to-year quarterly growth in earnings [$\$.16 = .4(\$3 - \$2.60)$]; and (3) a component that is a constant (\$.05).[21]

16.6   Earnings Announcements and Price Changes

A number of studies have shown large price changes for stocks of companies that report earnings that differ substantially from consensus expectations. One study looked at three groups of 50 stocks.[22] The first group consisted of the 50 stocks listed on the NYSE that experienced the greatest price rise during a sampled year. The second group consisted of 50 stocks chosen randomly from all those listed on the NYSE during the year. The third group consisted of the 50 stocks listed on the NYSE that experienced the greatest price decline during the year. As shown in Figure 16.4, the median changes in the prices of the stocks in the top, random, and bottom groups were 48.4%, −3.2%, and −56.7%, respectively.

Next, the study looked at the actual change in earnings per share from the previous year for each stock in each group. As shown in Figure 16.4, the median changes in earnings per share for the top, random, and bottom groups were 21.4%, −10.5%, and −83.0%, respectively.

Last, the study determined the forecast change in earnings per share at the beginning of the year for each stock in each group. The investigators used the predictions contained in Standard & Poor's *Earnings Forecaster,* which reports estimates made by several investment research organizations. The median forecast changes in earnings per share for the top, random, and bottom groups are shown in Figure 16.4 to be 7.7%, 5.8%, and 15.3%, respectively.

Interestingly, the forecasts of earnings per share hardly correspond to the price movements of the stocks. In fact, the earnings of the stocks in the bottom group were expected to increase more than the earnings of the stocks in the top group (15.3%, compared with 7.7%). However, the prediction for the bottom group was disastrously wrong, with a median earnings per share decline of 83.0%. And, as Figure 16.4 shows, prices definitely followed suit. Overall, it appears that unexpected changes in earnings do affect security prices.[23]

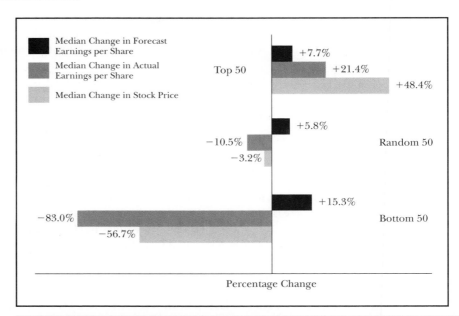

FIGURE 16.4 Earnings and Stock Price Changes

Source: Victor Niederhoffer and Patrick J. Regan, "Earnings Changes, Analysts' Forecasts, and Stock Prices," *Financial Analysts Journal,* 28, no. 3 (May/June 1972): 67.

But do earnings surprises affect prices before or after their announcement? In a completely efficient market, such information would be reflected in prices as soon as it had been disseminated to a few major market participants. The reaction of security prices around the time of earnings announcements has been examined by a number of authors and is discussed next.

16.6.1   DEVIATIONS FROM TIME-SERIES MODELS OF EARNINGS

A comprehensive study provided evidence concerning the response speed of security prices to earnings announcements.[24] For each sampled company, an expected earnings figure was computed for each quarter using the model of the time-series behavior of earnings shown in Equation (16.19). With this model, the expected earnings for a firm during period t was equal to $QE_{t-4} + a(QE_{t-1} - QE_{t-5}) + b$. For example, the earnings expected for the firm in the second quarter of a test year would equal (1) the firm's earnings in the second quarter of the previous year, plus (2) the change in earnings from the first quarter of the previous year to the first quarter of the test year times the parameter a, plus (3) the parameter b. The values of a and b are determined by analyzing the behavior of earnings prior to the second quarter of the test year.

Given actual earnings and an estimate of expected earnings, a forecast error (FE_t) can be computed for the firm:

$$FE_t = QE_t - \overline{QE}_t \qquad \textbf{(16.20)}$$

where QE_t is the actual earnings for quarter t and $\overline{QE}_t$ are the expected earnings for quarter t, forecast at time $t - 1$. Equation (16.20) indicates that the forecast error for a quarter is the difference between actual earnings for that quarter and expected earnings.

The forecast error provides a measure of the "surprise" in the quarterly earnings announcement, but it fails to differentiate between stocks for which large forecast errors are routine and those for which they are rare. Important surprises are associated with forecast errors that are large by historical standards. Surprises are accounted for by relating a forecast error to previous errors to obtain a measure of **standardized unexpected earnings** (SUE):

standardized unexpected earnings

$$\text{SUE}_t = \frac{FE_t}{\sigma_{FE_t}} \tag{16.21}$$

where σ_{FE_t} is the standard deviation of forecast errors over the 20 quarterly earnings of the firm prior to t. (That is, forecast errors are determined for each one of the 20 quarters before t, then the standard deviation for this set of 20 errors is estimated.)

For example, a firm with a forecast of earnings per share of $3 that subsequently reports actual earnings of $5 will have a forecast error of $2 (= $5 − $3), thereby surprising investors by $2. If the standard deviation of past errors is $.80, this surprise is notable because the standardized unexpected earnings (SUE) equals 2.50 (= $2/$.80).[25] However, if the standard deviation is $4, then this surprise is minor because SUE equals .50 (= $2/$4). Thus, a large positive value for SUE indicates that the earnings announcement contained significant good news, whereas a large negative SUE indicates that the earnings announcement contained significant bad news.

In the study, the SUEs associated with all the earnings announcements for all the sampled firms were ranked from smallest to largest. Then they were divided into 10 equal-sized groups based on the ranking. Group 1 consisted of those announcements resulting in the most negative SUEs, and group 10 consisted of those with the most positive SUEs. After these 10 groups were formed, the stock returns for each firm in each group were measured for the period from 60 days before its earnings announcement through 60 days after its announcement. Figure 16.5 shows the abnormal return for the average firm in each of the ten groups for three different time periods:

1. Figure 16.5(a) shows the average abnormal return for the period from 60 days before the earnings announcement through the day the announcement appeared in *The Wall Street Journal*. This period is denoted (–60, 0).

2. Figure 16.5(b) shows the average abnormal return for the two-day period consisting of the day before the announcement appeared in *The Wall Street Journal* and the day the announcement appeared, a period denoted (−1, 0). Because day 0 is the day the announcement appeared in *The Wall Street Journal*, day −1 is the day the announcement was made to the public. If the announcement was made after trading hours on day −1, investors could not have bought or sold the stock until the next day, day 0. If the announcement was made during trading hours on day −1, then investors could have acted on that day. Because the hour of the announcement could not be pinpointed, the return during the two-day period was examined to see the immediate impact of the announcement on the price of the security.

3. Figure 16.5(c) shows the average abnormal return for the period from the day after the announcement through 60 days after the announcement. This period is denoted (1, 60).

Figure 16.5(a) shows that prices of firms that announced unexpectedly high earnings (such as SUE group 10) tended to increase *before* the announcement (day 0), suggesting that information relevant to the earnings announcement was available to the market before the actual announcement. In contrast, prices of firms that announced

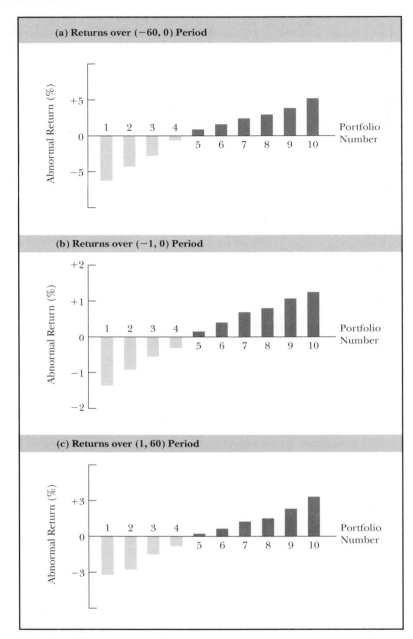

FIGURE 16.5 Security Returns in Periods Surrounding Earnings Announcements

Source: George Foster, Chris Olsen, and Terry Shevlin, "Earnings Releases, Anomalies, and the Behavior of Security Returns," *Accounting Review,* 59, no. 4 (October 1984): 587.

unexpectedly low earnings (such as SUE group 1) tended to decrease *before* the announcement, undoubtedly for the same reason. In general, there seems to be a strong direct correspondence between the size of the unexpected earnings and the size of the abnormal return. Note that an investor who knew what earnings were going to be 60 days before the announcement then could exploit this information by either buying the stock if the firm was going to announce unexpectedly large earnings or short selling the stock if the firm was going to announce unexpectedly low earnings. However, because investors typically do not have prior access to earnings, such exploitation is rarely possible. Thus the existence of abnormal returns before the announcement date does not necessarily indicate a market inefficiency.

Figure 16.5(b) shows that the larger the size of the unexpected earnings, the larger the price movement during the two-day period surrounding the announcement. For example, firms in SUE group 1 had an abnormal return of -1.34%, whereas those in SUE group 10 had an abnormal return of 1.26%. As in Figure 16.5(a), there is a direct relationship between the size of the unexpected earnings and the abnormal stock return.[26] Thus it seems that the market reacted in a predictable fashion, pushing up the stock prices of those firms announcing good news and pushing down the stock prices of those firms announcing bad news.

As shown in Figure 16.5(c), the changes in stock prices after the announcement dates are remarkable because they seem to suggest a market inefficiency. Prices of stocks of firms announcing unexpectedly high earnings tended to *increase for many days after* the announcement (the average abnormal return during the 60-day period after the announcement was 3.23% for SUE group 10). Conversely, the prices of firms announcing unexpectedly low earnings tended to *decrease for many days after* the announcement (the average abnormal return during the 60-day period subsequent to the announcement was -3.08% for SUE group 1). Thus, an investor apparently could make abnormal returns by simply looking at quarterly earnings announcements and, based on the magnitude and sign of the unexpected component, by acting appropriately. If the firm announces earnings notably above expectations, the investor should immediately purchase some of the firm's stock. If the announced earnings are notably below expectations, the investor should immediately sell any holdings and perhaps even short sell the firm's stock; announcements of earnings that are reasonably close to expectations will not motivate either a buy or a sell order. This "post-earnings-announcement drift" can be viewed as an empirical anomaly that is inconsistent with the notion of semistrong efficient markets.[27]

16.6.2 UNEXPECTED EARNINGS AND ABNORMAL RETURNS

One possible explanation for the abnormal returns associated with large SUEs, which is inconsistent with the notion of efficient markets, concerns the cost of information transfer. "New news" must reach a large number of investors before the appropriate new equilibrium price is completely established. (In an efficient market, investors immediately exploit the mispricing, causing it to rapidly disappear.) Although large institutional investors can obtain news quickly, it may take some time before it reaches smaller institutional investors and individuals. Thus after an earnings announcement there can be a period of abnormal price movement that is related in sign and magnitude to the nature of the announcement.

Perhaps the measurement of "abnormal" returns is in error, because it is based on a determination of a "normal" return, which is difficult. That is, the estimated abnormal returns could be caused by measurement errors, leaving the possibility that a more accurate measure of normal return would have resulted in no significant abnormal returns.

Nevertheless, there seem to be striking differences in subsequent stock returns for firms with different SUEs. Although the magnitudes of the return differences may be too small to warrant extensive trading, they do suggest the consideration of such things as SUE values and forecast revisions when money must be invested or a portion of an existing portfolio must be liquidated.

16.6.3 SECURITY ANALYSTS' FORECASTS OF FUTURE EARNINGS

It was mentioned earlier that, when only the historical record of past earnings is used to forecast future earnings, an autoregressive model of order one, as shown in Equation (16.19), seems to work as well as any other model. However, security analysts do not restrict themselves to past earnings when developing their forecasts. Instead, they look at many different pieces of information. How well can analysts forecast earnings? And do their forecasts actually incorporate information other than that contained in past earnings? The results of two studies that provide some answers to those questions are shown in Tables 16.4 and 16.5.

Forecasts of Analysts

In one study, summarized in Table 16.4, two sets of forecasts were examined for the quarterly earnings of 50 firms.[28] The first set was obtained by applying mechanical models to each firm's previous earnings history [such as the autoregressive model of Equation (16.19)]. The second set was obtained from the earnings forecasts of security analysts as reported in the *Value Line Investment Survey*.[29] The results suggest that the analysts outperformed the mechanical model. For example, 63.5% of the analysts' forecasts were within 25% of the actual earnings values, whereas only 54.4% of the forecasts made by means of mechanical models came as close. Analysts seem to base their forecasts on both past earnings and other information, and the latter seems to help.

In another study, forecasts of annual earnings made by security analysts approximately 240, 180, 120, and 60 days before the announcement date of actual annual earnings were examined.[30] Typically these days correspond to dates in each of the year's fiscal quarters before the announcement date. Hence, 240 days falls roughly between last year's earnings announcement and this year's first-quarter earnings announcement; 180 days falls roughly between the first-quarter and second-quarter earnings announcement, and so on. These forecasts, made by analysts at brokerage firms, were obtained from the Institutional Brokers Estimate System (I/B/E/S) database developed by the brokerage firm of Lynch, Jones, & Ryan.

Table 16.5 presents a comparison of the accuracy of four forecasts. The first forecast is the annual forecast generated using a model like the random walk model of

TABLE 16.4 Accuracy of Mechanical and Judgmental Earnings Forecasts		
Earnings Forecast Error as a Percentage of Actual Earnings	*Percentage of Forecasts with a Smaller Error*	
	Mechanical Model	*Analysts' Forecasts*
5%	15.0%	18.0%
10	26.5	32.0
25	54.5	63.5
50	81.0	86.5
75	87.5	90.5
100	89.5	92.0

Source: Lawrence D. Brown and Michael S. Rozeff, "The Superiority of Analyst Forecasts as Measures of Expectations: Evidence from Earnings," *Journal of Finance,* 33, no. 1 (March 1978): 7–8.

TABLE 16.5	Earnings Forecast Errors of Time-Series Models and Security Analysts			
	Number of Days before Annual Announcement Date			
Model	*240*	*180*	*120*	*60*
Random walk	$.963	$.781	$.620	$.363
Autoregressive	.975	.780	.592	.350
Average analyst	.747	.645	.516	.395
Current analyst	.742	.610	.468	.342

Source: Adapted from Patricia C. O'Brien, "Analysts' Forecasts as Earnings Expectations," *Journal of Accounting and Economics,* 10, no. 1 (January 1988): Table 4.

Equation (16.16). The second is the annual forecast produced by using an autoregressive model like the one shown in Equation (16.19). The third is the average forecast published by I/B/E/S, and the fourth is the single most current individual forecast published by I/B/E/S. Forecast accuracy for a particular model and firm is measured by absolute forecast error (*FE*):

$$FE = |A - F| \qquad \textbf{(16.22)}$$

where *F* denotes the forecast and *A* denotes the subsequent actual earnings of the firm.

There are several interesting observations to be made from Table 16.5. First, as the announcement date gets closer, all of the forecasting models become more accurate. This result is hardly surprising because more information is available as the announcement date approaches. Second, for long horizons both the average and most current forecasts are more accurate than either of the time-series models. Third, the current forecast is more accurate than any of the other models. However, subsequent examination of the forecasts indicates that the average forecast was more accurate than the most current forecast, provided that none of the individual forecasts used to determine the average was "stale" (that is, more than roughly a week old). Such averaging reduces the forecast error by allowing individual forecast errors to offset each other (that is, positive errors will offset negative errors, resulting in a smaller error for the average forecast). In summary, analysts seem to be better forecasters of earnings than mechanical models.[31]

Another interesting observation is that security analysts' forecasts tend to be too optimistic, meaning that they tend to have an upward bias (more on this shortly). Hence most of the typical analysts' revisions are downward. One interpretation of this observation is that many of the analysts work for brokerage firms and find it in their employers' best interest (and thus their own) to avoid antagonizing any corporation that is or might become an investment banking client.[32] However, some analysts have recently begun to publicly release revised earnings forecasts that are below their actual forecasts while providing favored investors (typically large institutional investors) with the actual forecasts, known as "whisper" numbers. This practice has emerged in the apparent belief that the company will have a better chance of exceeding the publicly released forecast and thus will be more likely to experience a jump in its stock price. (This practice has become especially common for high-tech stocks.) Recent evidence suggests such whispered forecasts are more accurate than average published forecasts even though they typically exceed actual subsequent earnings.[33]

16.6.4 MANAGEMENT FORECASTS OF FUTURE EARNINGS

Often management itself will discuss and make a forecast of next year's earnings for the firm (sometimes by having conference calls, usually with analysts and money managers). In general, the forecasts of security analysts are not as accurate as the forecasts of management when the two sets of forecasts are made at about the same time, as shown in Table 16.6.[34] Average security analysts' forecasts, as reported weekly by Zacks Investment Research's Icarus Service, were compared with corresponding management forecasts.[35] The objective was to determine who was the more accurate forecaster. Forecast errors (*FE*) were calculated for both sets of forecasts as:

$$FE = |(F - A)/A| \qquad (16.24)$$

TABLE 16.6 Security Analyst and Management Forecast Errors

Week	Average Analyst Forecast Error	Average Analyst Forecast Error – Average Management Forecast Error[a]
−12	.224	.074
−11	.222	.072
−10	.221	.071
−9	.221	.071
−8	.214	.064
−7	.221	.071
−6	.222	.072
−5	.216	.066
−4	.210	.060
−3	.208	.058
−2	.211	.061
−1	.209	.059
0	.195	.045
+1	.186	.036
+2	.177	.027
+3	.174	.024
+4	.171	.021
+5	.166	.016
+6	.160	.010
+7	.153	.003
+8	.150	.000
+9	.141	−.009
+10	.133	−.017
+11	.129	−.021
+12	.124	−.026

[a]The size of the average management forecast error was .150.

Source: Adapted from John M. Hassell and Robert H. Jennings, "Relative Forecast Accuracy and the Timing of Earnings Forecast Announcements," *Accounting Review,* 61, no. 1 (January 1986): Tables 2 and 3.

where F is the earnings forecast, and A is the actual earnings subsequently reported by the firm. Hence an earnings forecast of \$3 per share that subsequently turned out to be \$4 would have $FE = |(\$3 - \$4)/\$4| = .25$ or 25%.

Letting $t = 0$ denote the date that the management forecast was released, analysts' forecasts were collected weekly from 12 weeks before to 12 weeks after $t = 0$. Table 16.6 shows the average forecast error for management was .150, while analyst forecast errors ranged from .224 at week -12 (meaning 12 weeks prior to the date of the management forecast) to .124 at week $+12$. Hence, analysts' forecasts became more accurate as the date the actual earnings were announced came closer because the size of the average forecast error decreases fairly steadily from $t = -12$ to $t = +12$.

Most important, however, is the observation that management forecasts were more accurate than analyst forecasts from $t = -12$ to $t = +8$ (the difference was found to be statistically significant through $t = +4$). That is, forecasts issued by analysts before, co-incident to, or up to four months after management's forecast were less accurate. This observation is not surprising up to $t = 0$ because management has private information about the firm that is not available to the analysts. However, it is surprising that management forecasts were statistically superior from $t = +1$ through $t = +4$ because it suggests that analysts could have improved their accuracy simply by using management's previously released forecast. After $t = +4$, the analysts' forecasts were more accurate (the difference was statistically significant beginning nine weeks after the release date of the management forecast), not a surprising finding because the analysts probably had access to more timely information on which to base their forecasts.

These results leave three questions: Why does management occasionally produce an earnings forecast for the firm? Is it to reduce *information asymmetry* in the marketplace? Does management want to tell investors about the firm's prospects when it feels the prevailing view of the investing public is in serious error? One way to examine this issue is to look at the firm's bid–ask spread. In Chapter 3 it was noted that specialists tend to widen the bid–ask spread if they sense an increase in information asymmetry because they tend to sustain losses from trading with informed investors. One study examined the bid–ask spreads of firms whose management issued forecasts and a matching sample of firms whose management did not issue forecasts.[36] The study found that the firms whose management issued forecasts had significantly wider spreads than those that did not issue forecasts in the period before the forecasts were made. Afterward the spreads of the two were equivalent. Thus, it appears that the management tends to issue forecasts when it senses an increased level of information asymmetry, and that the forecast reduces the amount of asymmetry.

16.6.5 SOURCES OF ERRORS IN FORECASTING

Because security analysts' forecasts are not perfect, it is interesting to consider the major source of their errors. One study examined the I/B/E/S database and attempted to break down the forecast errors into three components: (1) errors from misjudgments about the economy, (2) errors from misjudgments about the firm's particular industry, and (3) errors from misjudgments about the firm.[37] The results indicated the following: Less than 3% of the typical error was because of misjudgments about the economy; roughly 30% of the typical error was because of misjudgments about the industry; and more than 65% of the typical error was because of misjudgments about the firm. In light of the last observation, it is not surprising that security analysts spend time evaluating the quality of corporate management.

Consensus Earnings Expectations

 Reference is frequently made in the financial press to "market" or "consensus" expectations. We may read that the "market" expects inflation to remain stable or that the "market" expects the Fed to raise interest rates. If the market is the amalgam of a large, diverse group of investors, then how does anyone determine what it really expects?

Of course, the most important market expectations are established and published daily—that is, the expected values of corporate assets as reflected in security prices. But what about market expectations regarding economic and financial variables that underlie security prices? In general, these expectations are reported anecdotally, perhaps through interviews with prominent investors or through surveys.

Investing based on such ambiguous information is problematic. Abnormal returns can be earned only by staking out positions based on expectations contrary to those of the market. Superior investors will consistently identify securities for which market expectations are somehow in error. But unless these investors can correctly gauge the market's expectations, they will not know whether their expectations are significantly different than those of the market.

As discussed in the text, earnings expectations are the most important determinant of common stock prices. An investor who can identify companies for which the market is under- or overestimating future earnings can appropriately buy and sell those stocks to produce portfolio returns superior to those of the market on a risk-adjusted basis.

Many organizations publish earnings estimates, including Standard & Poor's, Value Line, and brokerage houses. However, individually these estimates do not represent market expectations; they are merely the opinions of specific analysts. What is needed is a means to collect the earnings estimates of many analysts following a particular company. That need has been satisfied for more than 25 years by a firm called I/B/E/S International.

Although I/B/E/S is not the only company collecting earnings expectations data (Zacks Investment Research and First Call are prominent competitors), it was the first and it remains a leader in the field. I/B/E/S was formed in 1971. Its initial objectives were modest: to collect timely earnings estimates from brokerage firms on several hundred large, well-followed companies. These estimates were then compiled and the distributions of earnings estimates (high, low, median, measure of dispersion) were periodically reported to subscribers.

For example, suppose that an institutional investment firm was estimating earnings next year of $2.50 per share for *XYZ* company and $3.30 per share for *ABC* company. Through I/B/E/S, the institutional investor might find that the consensus earnings estimates for *XYZ* and *ABC* were currently $1.50 and $3.50, respectively. In addition, the coefficient of variation (standard deviation divided by mean—a measure of the estimates' relative dispersion) was .20 for *XYZ* and .80 for *ABC*. If the institutional investor has confidence in its own estimates, then it should expect *XYZ* stock to perform relatively well. The market's earnings expectations are clustered tightly around the $1.50 level, which is $1.00 less than the investor's estimate. If the market comes to realize that $2.50 is the actual level of *XYZ* earnings, it will likely bid the company's stock price up.

ABC stock is less attractive. The institutional investor's estimate is less than the consensus by $0.20, so it might wish to sell *ABC* out of its portfolio if it owns the stock or perhaps even short sell the stock. However, the relatively high dispersion of estimates around the median indicates that the market's expectations are not firm. If *ABC*'s earnings actually come in at $3.30, the result may not be a particularly unpleasant surprise for the market, and, therefore, may have little impact on *ABC*'s stock price.

The advantages of using consensus earnings expectations in common stock analysis attracted institutional investors. Today, I/B/E/S receives, compiles, and distributes earnings estimates from more than 7,100 equity analysts in over 800 research departments in more than 50 countries. Although by far the most intense analyst earnings coverage is for U.S. companies, the contributing I/B/E/S analysts now cover more than 18,000 companies in 60 equity markets around the world. Even companies in emerging equity markets such as Estonia and the Czech Republic have attracted institutional analysts' coverage and have been included in the I/B/E/S service.

I/B/E/S collects earnings estimates in a number of ways, primarily through direct electronic feeds that are supplemented by e-mail, faxes, telephone calls, and printed reports. On receipt of analysts' earnings estimates, I/B/E/S staffers perform quality checks to ensure the integrity of the data and then enter the estimates into the firm's database. Summary consensus numbers are updated daily and made available to I/B/E/S subscribers.

The original I/B/E/S reports were simply printed books containing summary data on indi-vidual company earnings estimates. Although the original printed format is still available, I/B/E/S now provides data through its own electronic services as well as a variety of third-party vendors. Customers can now receive I/B/E/S data diced and sliced in a number of ways. The firm makes available to subscribers analyst-by-analyst data, daily alerts of analyst changes, and custom-designed reports. The firm also provides commentaries and analyses of market trends it discovers from the earnings estimate data.

The systematic collection of earnings estimates is an excellent example of the forces that have been increasing the efficiency of security markets. Before I/B/E/S collected such data, consensus earnings estimates were difficult to obtain and highly ambiguous. Now those estimates are rigorously quantified and widely distributed, decreasing the likelihood of investors' acting on incomplete or erroneous information.

Summary

1. Assuming that a firm undertakes positive NPV projects and maintains a constant debt-equity ratio, shareholders will be indifferent to the level of dividends.

2. If dividends and new investment are greater than earnings, the firm may issue new equity. If dividends and new investment are less than earnings, the firm may repurchase equity. In either case, a stockholder maintaining constant proportional ownership will be able to spend the same amount on consumption, regardless of the level of dividends.

3. Earnings, not dividends, are the source of a firm's value.

4. Few firms attempt to maintain a constant ratio of dividends to current earnings. Instead firms tend to establish a long-run payout ratio and adjust current actual dividends based on the difference between current target dividends and the last period's actual dividends.

5. Corporate management may use dividend changes as a signaling device, raising or lowering dividends based on its assessment of the firm's future earnings.

6. A firm has considerable discretion in calculating its accounting earnings. These accounting earnings may differ substantially from the firm's economic earnings. Similarly, a firm's book value may differ considerably from its market value.

7. Firms initiate paying dividends after a period during which their stock price has risen by an abnormally large amount and earnings have increased. The announcement of the initiation is typically associated with an abnormal increase in the stock's price, with earnings and price continuing to move up afterward.

8. Firms omit paying dividends after a period during which their stock price has fallen by an abnormally large amount and earnings have decreased. The announcement of the omission is typically associated with an abnormal decrease in the stock's price, with earnings and price continuing to move down afterward.

9. Stocks with the highest returns typically have earnings that are substantially greater than expected, whereas those with the lowest returns have earnings substantially below expectations.

10. Stock prices tend to correctly anticipate earnings announcements by moving in the appropriate direction beforehand.

11. Stock prices tend to react correctly but not fully to earnings announcements immediately afterward.

12. Stock prices continue to move in a direction similar to their initial reaction for several months afterward. This observation is known as post-earnings-announcement drift.

13. Analysts appear to forecast earnings better than sophisticated mechanical models.

14. Analysts tend to overestimate when forecasting earnings per share.

15. Management's earnings forecasts are generally more accurate than analysts' forecasts.

Questions and Problems

1. For a given level of earnings (E), net new investment (I), and dividends (D), explain why a firm must issue new stock if $E < D + I$ and it desires to maintain a constant debt-equity ratio. Why must it repurchase shares if $E > D + I$ and it desires to maintain a constant debt-equity ratio?

2. Merrillan Motors had earnings of $8 million last year. It made $5 million of investments in projects with positive net present values. Pat Collins owns 20% of the firm's common stock. Assume that Pat desires no change in proportional ownership of Merrillan and the firm wishes to maintain a constant debt-equity ratio. What will be Pat's action in response to
   a. Merrillan's paying out dividends of $5 million?
   b. Merrillan's paying out dividends of $1 million?
   c. Merrillan's paying out dividends of $3 million?

3. Why is an individual stockholder indifferent about whether the firm retains $1 of earnings or pays out the $1 of earnings as a dividend, assuming that the firm and the stockholder maintain a constant debt-equity ratio and a constant proportional ownership position, respectively?

4. If the dividend decision is irrelevant to the valuation of a firm, then are not dividend discount models irrelevant to valuing a share of common stock? Why?

5. Why do most corporations not maintain a constant payout ratio? What payout strategy do most firms pursue?

6. Hixton Farms has a target payout ratio of 50%. Dividends paid last year amounted to $10 million. Its earnings were $20 million. Hixton's "speed of adjustment" factor for dividends is 60%. What will be its dividend payments over the next five years if its earnings display the following path:

Year	Earnings
1	$30 million
2	35 million
3	30 million
4	25 million
5	30 million

Draw a graph of Hixton's actual dividends paid versus the desired dividend payments during this five-year period.

7. Rockton Plastics has made changes to its dividends during the past 14 years. Based on a target payout ratio of 30%, according to the Lintner Model, the firm would have preferred to make a different set of dividend changes. Both the actual and preferred dividend changes are shown in the following table. What "speed of adjust-

ment" factor is implied by these two dividend change series? (Use of a regression program, such as one provided with a computer spreadsheet, is recommended.)

Year	Actual Change in Dividends	Preferred Change in Dividends
1	$–0.28	$–0.47
2	–0.09	–0.16
3	–0.05	–0.08
4	–0.01	–0.02
5	0.01	0.02
6	0.04	0.07
7	0.01	0.01
8	0.03	0.05
9	0.03	0.05
10	0.01	0.02
11	0.04	0.07
12	0.03	0.06
13	0.03	0.05

8. How are dividends used as a signaling device by corporate management? To the extent that dividends are a signaling device, how are dividend changes related to stock prices?

9. The price per share of the Dells Deli Corporation is less than its book value. Does this difference indicate that the firm's present shareholders have lost money in the past? Does it indicate that they are likely to lose money in the future? Does it indicate that Dells Deli should not undertake any further capital investment? Explain your answers.

10. Why might a steady trend in a firm's reported earnings from year to year suggest that the figures do not represent the firm's economic earnings?

11. Reported earnings typically differ, sometimes considerably, from economic earnings. Nevertheless, it is often argued that reported earnings are intended simply to provide a "source of information" to investors about the value of the firm. If that is true, might there not be many alternative accounting procedures of equal use to investors? How might one go about evaluating the usefulness of such procedures?

12. Harlond Clift once wrote in a market newsletter, "I focus my research on consensus earnings forecasts. Those companies that the consensus believes will produce the largest earnings increases next year are most likely to produce the best returns." Is Harlond's opinion consistent with empirical evidence? Explain why or why not.

13. Calculate the relationship between the following series of quarterly earnings using an autoregressive model of order one (use of a computer regression program is recommended). What is your forecast for earnings in quarter 21?

Quarter	Earnings	Quarter	Earnings
1	$4.00	11	$4.25
2	4.10	12	4.49
3	3.95	13	4.59
4	4.20	14	4.58
5	4.30	15	4.39
6	4.29	16	4.63
7	4.11	17	4.73
8	4.35	18	4.72
9	4.44	19	4.54
10	4.43	20	4.78

14. Oakdale Orchards has produced the following earnings during the past nine quarters:

Quarter	Earnings per Share
1	$2.00
2	1.95
3	2.05
4	2.10
5	2.40
6	2.24
7	2.67
8	2.84
9	2.64

The expected earnings for the current quarter are based on the equation $QE_t = QE_{t-4} - .75(QE_{t-1} - QE_{t-5})$. Calculate the standardized unexpected earnings in each of the past four quarters, given a standard deviation of $.35.

15. Why might the price of a stock react only partially to an "earnings surprise" on the first day or two after the earnings announcement?

Endnotes

1. Although earnings and cash flow are typically highly correlated, they are not perfectly correlated because there can be instances in which earnings rise and cash flow falls. Hence, earnings do not always provide the cash flow necessary for paying dividends. For more on cash flow analysis, see Chapter 14.

2. In Chapter 15, D_0 denotes the *per-share* dividends that had been paid during the past year. Now D_0 denotes the *aggregate* amount of dividends that are about to be paid. Similarly, the quantities of earnings (E_t) and new investment (I_t) are measured for the firm on an aggregate basis, not a per-share basis. Note that dividends cannot be set at an arbitrarily high value relative to earnings (for example, earnings of $10 million and dividends of $100 million) because the firm would then find it practically impossible to obtain the necessary funds to pay the dividends.

3. The use of such a stockholder is for ease of exposition. The same answer would be obtained if other types of stockholders (such as those who are not interested in maintaining a constant proportional ownership position in the firm in the future) are considered.

4. It has been argued that if the tax rate on dividends is greater than the tax rate on capital gains, then stockholders will earn more on an after-tax basis if the firm has a relatively low payout ratio. An additional benefit to stockholders if the firm has a low payout ratio is that capital gains taxes are paid only when the stock is sold and can, therefore, be deferred. Thus, it appears that stockholders will be better off if the firm has a relatively low payout ratio. For a more detailed discussion of the issue, along with the relevant citations, see pp. 128–135 of Gordon J. Alexander and Jack

Clark Francis, *Portfolio Analysis* (Upper Saddle River, NJ: Prentice Hall, 1986). Also see James S. Ang, David W. Blackwell, and William L. Megginson, "The Effect of Taxes on the Relative Valuation of Dividends and Capital Gains: Evidence from Dual-Class British Investment Trusts," *Journal of Finance,* 46, no. 1 (March 1991): 383–399.

5. In addition to a regular dividend, on rare occassions a firm will declare a "special" or "extra" dividend, usually at year-end. By calling it a special dividend, the firm is conveying a message to its stockholders that such a dividend is a one-time event.

6. Looking backward in time, current dividends, D_t, are a linear function of past earnings, $E_{t-1}, E_{t-2}, E_{t-3}$, and so on. More specifically,

$$D_t = ap^*[(1-a)^0 E_{t-0} + (1-a)^1 E_{t-1} + (1-a)^2 E_{t-2} + (1-a)^3 E_{t-3} + \cdots]$$

Because the quantity $(1-a)$ is a positive fraction (for example, $\frac{1}{3}$), when it is raised to a power it becomes smaller in value, with larger powers resulting in values closer to zero. Thus, current dividends depend more on recent past earnings than on distant past earnings, and the equation can be approximated by using an arbitrary number of past earnings (the accuracy of the approximation depends on the number used).

7. See Bong-Soo Lee, "Time Series Implications of Aggregate Dividend Behavior," *Review of Financial Studies,* 9, no. 2 (Summer 1996): 589–618.

8. Other signaling devices include changes in the firm's capital structure (for example, announcing an issuance

of debt with the proceeds being used to repurchase stock). It has been argued that in order for the signal to be useful to the public, (1) management must have an incentive to send a truthful signal, (2) the signal cannot be imitated by competitors in different financial positions, and (3) there cannot be a cheaper means of conveying the same information. See Stephen A. Ross, "The Determination of Financial Structure: The Incentive Signalling Approach," *Bell Journal of Economics,* 8, no. 1 (Spring 1977): 23–40.

9. Paul M. Healy and Krishna G. Palepu, "Earnings Information Conveyed by Dividend Initiations and Omissions," *Journal of Financial Economics,* 21, no. 2 (September 1988): 149–175.

10. See Roni Michaely, Richard H. Thaler, and Kent L. Womack, "Price Reactions to Dividend Initiations and Omissions: Overreaction or Drift?" *Journal of Finance,* 50, no. 2 (June 1995): 573–608.

11. Harry DeAngelo, Linda DeAngelo, and Douglas J. Skinner, "Dividends and Losses," *Journal of Finance,* 47, no. 5 (December 1992): 1837–1863. Also see Harry DeAngelo and Linda DeAngelo, "Dividend Policy and Financial Distress: An Empirical Investigation of Troubled NYSE Firms," *Journal of Finance,* 45, no. 5 (December 1990): 1415–1431 and the August 1998 issue of *Financial Management,* which is devoted to dividends.

12. The Securities Exchange Act of 1934 gives the SEC the authority to set accounting standards for firms that must register with it. The SEC has delegated this responsibility to FASB while retaining final authority if any disagreements arise. See Robert Van Riper, *Setting Standards for Financial Reporting: FASB and the Struggle for Control of a Critical Process* (Westport, CT: Quorum Books, 1994) for more on the history of FASB and its relationship to the SEC.

13. Book value of the equity is also called stockholders' equity, particularly when the discussion refers to a company's balance sheet. Stockholders' equity is discussed in Chapter 14.

14. Sir John R. Hicks, winner in 1972 of the Nobel Prize in Economic Science, defined the weekly economic income of an individual as "the maximum value which he can consume during a week and still be as well off at the end of the week as he was at the beginning" (*Value and Capital,* London: Oxford University Press, 1946, p. 172). The definition of the economic earnings of a firm given in Equation (16.15) is an extension of Hicks's definition for an individual.

15. Two assertions that have been made regarding what investors look at when valuing stocks are known as the *mechanistic hypothesis* and the *myopic hypothesis.* The former asserts that investors look only at reported earnings, and the latter asserts that investors look only at the short-term future. Both assertions

seem invalid when data are analyzed. For an in-depth discussion, see George Foster, *Financial Statement Analysis* (Upper Saddle River, NJ: Prentice Hall, 1986), pp. 443–445.

16. For a discussion of related issues, see Ross Watts, "Does It Pay to Manipulate EPS?" in *Issues in Corporate Finance* (New York: Stern Stewart Putnam & Macklis, 1983).

17. There is evidence that investors in publicly held firms are not fooled by such manipulations. See, for example, John R. M. Hand and Patricia Hughes, "The Motives and Consequences of Debt–Equity Swaps and Defeasances: More Evidence That It Does Not Pay to Manipulate Earnings," *Journal of Applied Corporate Finance,* 3, no. 3 (Fall 1990): 77–81.

18. John Lintner and Robert Glauber, "Higgledy Piggledy Growth in America," in James Lorie and Richard Brealey, eds., *Modern Developments in Investment Management* (Hinsdale, IL: Dryden Press, 1978). However, a more recent study came to a different conclusion concerning the predictability of earnings changes. This study divided a large number of companies into five groups based on their earnings-to-price (E/P) ratios, and found that lower E/P stock groups exhibited consistently higher long-term earnings growth rates. See two articles by Russell J. Fuller, Lex C. Huberts, and Michael Levinson, "It's Not Higgledy-Piggledy Growth!" *Journal of Portfolio Management,* 18, no. 2 (Winter 1992): 38–45, and "Predictability Bias in the U.S. Equity Market," *Financial Analysts Journal,* 51, no. 2 (March/April 1995): 12–28. Also see H. Bradlee Perry, "Analyzing Growth Stocks: What's a Good Growth Rate?" *AAII Journal,* 13, no. 9 (October 1991): 7–10.

19. Some people [for example, Jane Ou and Stephen H. Penman, "Financial Statement Analysis and the Prediction of Stock Returns," *Journal of Accounting and Economics,* 11, no. 4 (November 1989): 295–329] think that a "random walk with drift" model as follows is more accurate:

$$E_t - E_{t-1} = \delta + \varepsilon_t$$

where δ is a positive constant that represents the "drift" term. With this model, the expected change in earnings is equal to δ. The random walk model given in Equation (16.17) is a special case where $\delta = 0$.

20. This model also can be used to forecast annual earnings by working forward one quarter at a time and then adding up the forecasts for the forthcoming four quarters. Doing so would result in a forecast of annual earnings (E_t) equal to $E_{t-1} + c(QE_{t-1} - QE_{t-5}) + d$, where $c = a^1 + a^2 + a^3 + a^4$ and $d = 4b + 3ab + 2a^2b + a^3b$. The random walk model is a special case where a and b are equal to zero, thereby making c and d equal to zero.

21. It has been argued that an improvement can be made in this model by either (1) adding the term $k(QE_{t-4} - QE_{t-8})$ to the right-hand side where k is a constant or (2) multiplying the constant b term by the random error term that occurred four quarters ago (e_{t-4}). See P. A. Griffin, "The Time-Series Behavior of Quarterly Earnings: Preliminary Evidence," *Journal of Accounting Research,* 15, no. 1 (Spring 1977): 71–83; Lawrence D. Brown and Michael S. Rozeff, "Univariate Time-Series Models of Quarterly Accounting Earnings per Share: A Proposed Model," *Journal of Accounting Research,* 17, no. 1 (Spring 1979): 179–189; and Allen W. Bathke, Jr. and Kenneth S. Lorek, "The Relationship between Time Series Models and the Security Market's Expectations of Quarterly Earnings," *Accounting Review,* 59, no. 2 (April 1984): 163–176.

22. One of the original studies was Victor Niederhoffer and Patrick J. Regan, "Earnings Changes, Analysts' Forecasts, and Stock Prices," *Financial Analysts Journal,* 28, no. 3 (May/June 1972): 65–71. Also the entire June/September 1992 issue of the *Journal of Accounting and Economics* is devoted to an examination of how stock prices are related to earnings and other financial statement information.

23. Another study that sampled a different year reached similar conclusions. That is, the top 50 stocks had forecast and actual earnings growth rates of 14.3% and 31.3%, respectively. For the bottom 50 stocks the respective rates were 17.4% and −10.3%. See Gary A. Benesh and Pamela P. Peterson, "On the Relation between Earnings Changes, Analysts' Forecasts and Stock Price Fluctuations," *Financial Analysts Journal,* 42, no. 6 (November/December 1986): 29–39, 55.

24. George Foster, Chris Olsen, and Terry Shevlin, "Earnings Releases, Anomalies, and the Behavior of Security Returns," *Accounting Review,* 59, no. 4 (October 1984): 574–603. For a related paper, see Roger Kormendi and Robert Lipe, "Earnings Innovations, Earnings Persistence, and Stock Returns," *Journal of Business,* 60, no. 3 (July 1987): 323–345.

25. Assume that a firm's earnings are normally distributed and that this distribution remains unchanged over time. Accordingly, 67% of the actual earnings should fall within one standard deviation of the firm's expected earnings, implying 67% of the SUEs should fall between +1 and −1. Similarly, 95% of the SUEs should fall between +2 and −2. One study has argued that most forecast errors are too large for the forecast to be useful; see David N. Dreman and Michael A. Berry, "Analyst Forecasting Errors and Their Implications for Security Analysis," *Financial Analysts Journal,* 51, no. 3 (May/June 1995): 30–41. For a refutation, see Lawrence D. Brown, "Analyst Forecasting Errors and Their Implications for Security Analysis: An Al-

ternative Perspective," *Financial Analysts Journal,* 52, no. 16 (January/February 1996): 40–47.

26. Studies have shown that earnings announcements containing good news are often made earlier than expected, whereas those containing bad news are often made later than expected. These studies also show that the "timeliness" (defined as the difference between the actual announcement date and the expected announcement date) affects the size of the abnormal return. Interestingly, around the time of earnings announcements there appears to be both increased trading volume and increased variability in security returns. See George Foster, *Financial Statement Analysis* (Upper Saddle River, NJ: Prentice Hall, 1986): 377–386; and V. V. Chari, Ravi Jagannathan, and Aharon Ofer, "Seasonalities in Security Returns: The Case of Earnings Announcements," *Journal of Financial Economics,* 21, no. 1 (May 1988): 101–121.

27. One article argues that the post-earnings-announcement drift should be listed with the set of empirical regularities described in the appendix to Chapter 13. See Charles P. Jones and Bruce Bublitz, "The CAPM and Equity Return Regularities: An Extension," *Financial Analysts Journal,* 43, no. 3 (May/June 1987): 77–79.

28. Lawrence D. Brown and Michael S. Rozeff, "The Superiority of Analyst Forecasts as Measures of Expectations: Evidence from Earnings," *Journal of Finance,* 33, no. 1 (March 1978): 1–16.

29. Value Line also ranks stocks in terms of their relative attractiveness as investments. For a discussion of the usefulness of the Value Line rankings, see Table 14.8 and the references for Chapter 14.

30. Patricia C. O'Brien, "Analysts' Forecasts as Earnings Expectations," *Journal of Accounting and Economics,* 10, no. 1 (January 1988): 53–83.

31. In one study it was found that sophisticated investors (such as big institutional investors) placed more weight on analysts' forecasts than on mechanical models in forming their expectations about earnings. See Beverly R. Walther, "Investor Sophistication and Market Earnings Expectations," *Journal of Accounting Research,* 35, no. 2 (Autumn 1997): 157–179.

32. The observation that analysts (1) tend to be too optimistic in their EPS forecasts, (2) tend to revise these forecasts downward, and (3) issue far more buy than sell recommendations has been documented in several places. See, for example, the studies cited in Table 14.8 of Chapter 14 as well as John C. Groth, Wilbur G. Lewellen, Gary Schlarbaum, and Ronald C. Lease, "An Analysis of Brokerage House Recommendations," *Financial Analysts Journal,* 35, no. 1 (January/February 1979): 32–40; and Werner F. De Bondt and Richard H. Thaler, "Do Security Analysts Overreact?" *American Economic Review,* 80, no. 2 (May 1990): 52–57. For a counterview, see Michael P. Keane

and David E. Runkle, "Are Financial Analysts' Forecasts of Corporate Profits Rational?" *Journal of Political Economy,* 106, no. 4 (August 1998): 768–805. One study found that analysts tend to give more favorable investment recommendations for stocks that their firm is underwriting than analysts who are not affiliated with the underwriting; see Hsiou-wei Lin and Maureen F. McNichols, "Underwriting Relationships, Analysts' Earnings Forecasts and Investment Recommendations," *Journal of Accounting and Economics,* 25, no. 1 (February 1998): 101–127.

33. Mark Bagnoli, Messod D. Beneish, and Susan Watts, "Whisper Forecasts of Quarterly Earnings per Share," *Journal of Accounting and Economics,* 28, no. 1 (November 1999): 27–50.

34. John M. Hassell and Robert H. Jennings, "Relative Forecast Accuracy and the Timing of Earnings Forecast Announcements," *Accounting Review,* 61, no. 1 (January 1986): 58–75.

35. Similar to I/B/E/S, Zacks Investment Research provides weekly summaries of earnings forecasts for thousands of firms that are provided by analysts at roughly 50 brokerage firms. Whereas Zacks dates forecasts based on the date of issuance by the analysts' employers, I/B/E/S dates forecasts based on when they receive them.

36. Maribeth Collier and Teri Lombardi Yohn, "Management Forecasts and Information Asymmetry: An Examination of Bid–Ask Spreads," *Journal of Accounting Research,* 35, no. 2 (Autumn 1997): 181–191.

37. Edwin J. Elton, Martin J. Gruber, and Mustafa N. Gultekin, "Professional Expectations: Accuracy and Diagnosis of Errors," *Journal of Financial and Quantitative Analysis,* 19, no. 4 (December 1984): 351–363.

Investment Management

Investment management, also known as portfolio management, is the process of managing money. It may (1) be active or passive, (2) use explicit or implicit procedures, and (3) have a risk level that is relatively controlled or uncontrolled. The trend is toward highly controlled operations consistent with the notion that capital markets are relatively efficient. However, approaches to investment management vary widely. This chapter discusses investment management and in doing so presents various types of investment styles.

17.1 Traditional Investment Management Organizations

Few people or organizations like to be called "traditional." However, some investment management organizations follow procedures that have changed little over time and thus deserve the title. Figure 17.1 shows the major characteristics of a traditional investment management organization.

Projections concerning the economy and the financial markets are made by economists, technicians, fundamentalists, or other market experts within or outside the organization. The projected economic environment is communicated through briefings and written reports—usually in an implicit and qualitative manner—to the organization's security analysts. Each analyst is responsible for a group of securities in one or more industries (in some organizations, analysts are called industry specialists). A group of analysts may report to a senior analyst responsible for a sector of the economy or market.

The analysts, often drawing heavily on reports of others (for example, "street analysts" in brokerage houses), make predictions about the securities for which they are responsible. These predictions generally are conditional on the assumed economic and market environments, although the relationship is typically quite loose. Analysts' predictions seldom specify an expected rate of return or the time over which predicted performance will take place. Instead, an analyst's thoughts on a security may be summarized by assigning it a relative ranking whereby, for example, a 1 represents a buy and a 5 represents a sell, as indicated in Figure 17.1.[1] In many organizations, a simple buy-hold-sell designation is given.

These security codings and various written reports constitute the information formally transmitted to an **investment committee,** which typically includes the senior management of the organization. In addition, analysts occasionally brief the investment committee about various securities. The investment committee's primary formal out-

investment committee

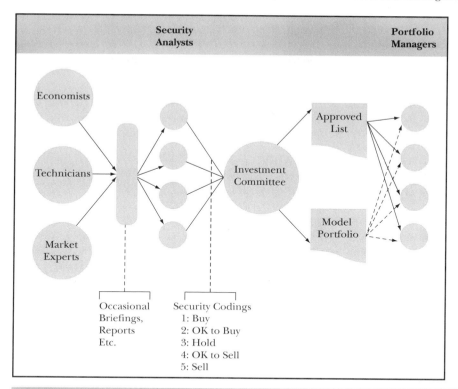

FIGURE 17.1 A Traditional Investment Management Organization

approved list

put is often an **approved list,** which consists of the securities deemed worthy of accumulation in a given portfolio. The rules of the organization typically specify that any security on the list may be bought, whereas those not on the list should be either held or sold, barring special circumstances.

The presence or absence of a security on the approved list constitutes the major

portfolio manager

information transmitted explicitly from the investment committee to a **portfolio manager** (or investment manager or money manager). In some organizations, senior management supervises a "model portfolio" (for example, a bank's major commingled equity fund), the composition of which indicates to portfolio managers the relative intensity of senior management's assessment of different securities.

In many ways, this description is a caricature of an investment organization—even one run along traditional lines. Nevertheless, most of these attributes can be observed in practice in one form or another. More recently, specialty investment firms have gained considerable popularity. As opposed to traditional investment firms that invest in a broad spectrum of securities, these organizations concentrate their investment efforts on a particular asset class, such as stocks or bonds. They often specialize even further, focusing on a narrow segment of a particular asset class, such as the stocks of high-tech companies.

Although these specialty investment firms may follow many of the procedures of the traditional investment organizations, they usually employ few security analysts. Often the portfolio managers serve jointly as analysts. Furthermore, their decision-making processes are typically more streamlined, often avoiding investment committee structures entirely, thereby permitting portfolio managers considerable discretion in researching securities and constructing portfolios. Whether this less hierarchical approach to investing actually produces superior results is open to question.

17.2 Investment Management Functions

In Chapter 1 a five-step procedure was outlined for making investment decisions. These steps should be viewed as functions of investment management, and they must be undertaken for each client whose money is being managed. They are as follows:

1. *Set investment policy.* Identify the client's investment objectives, particularly regarding his or her attitude toward the trade-off between expected return and risk.
2. *Perform security analysis.* Scrutinize individual securities or sectors of securities in order to identify mispriced situations.
3. *Construct a portfolio.* Identify specific securities in which to invest, along with the proportion of investable wealth to be put into each security.
4. *Revise the portfolio.* Determine which securities in the current portfolio are to be sold and which securities are to be purchased to replace them.
5. *Evaluate the performance of the portfolio.* Determine the actual performance of a portfolio in terms of risk and return, and compare the performance with that of an appropriate "benchmark" portfolio.

The remainder of this chapter considers how an investment management organization performs the first four functions; the next chapter deals with the fifth function.

17.3 Setting Investment Policy

An investment manager who is in charge of a client's entire portfolio must be concerned with the client's risk–return preferences. Investors who use more than one manager can select one to help in this important phase, or they may use the services of a consultant or financial planner. In any event, one of the key characteristics that differentiates clients from one another concerns their investment objectives. These objectives usually reflect the client's attitude toward risk and expected return (there might be other objectives having to do with issues such as mimimizing taxes and producing at least a certain amount of cash flow, but these are ignored here). As discussed in Chapter 7, specifying indifference curves is one method of describing these objectives, but doing so is not a simple task. In practice, it can be done in an indirect and approximate fashion

risk tolerance   by estimating the client's level of **risk tolerance,** defined as the largest amount of risk that the client is willing to accept for a given increase in expected return.

17.3.1 ESTIMATING RISK TOLERANCE

The starting point in estimating a client's level of risk tolerance is to provide the client with a set of risks and expected returns for different combinations of two hypothetical portfolios. For example, imagine that the client is told that the expected return on a stock portfolio is 12%, whereas the return on a riskfree portfolio consisting of Treasury bills is 7.5% (that is, $\bar{r}_s = 12\%$ and $r_f = 7.5\%$). The client is also told that the standard deviation of the stock portfolio is 15%, whereas the standard deviation of the riskfree portfolio is, by definition, 0% (that is, $\sigma_s = 15\%$ and $\sigma_f = 0\%$).[2] In addition, the client is told that all combinations of these two portfolios lie on a straight line that connects them. (The reason is that the covariance between these two portfolios is 0, meaning that $\sigma_{sf} = 0$.) Some combinations of these two portfolios are shown in Table 17.1.

TABLE 17.1   Combinations of Stock and Riskfree Treasury Bill Portfolios

Proportion in		Expected Return	Standard Deviation	Implied Level of Risk Tolerance
Stock	Bills			
0%	100%	7.50%	0.0%	0
10	90	7.95	1.5	10
20	80	8.40	3.0	20
30	70	8.85	4.5	30
40	60	9.30	6.0	40
50	50	9.75	7.5	50
60	40	10.20	9.0	60
70	30	10.65	10.5	70
80	20	11.10	12.0	80
90	10	11.55	13.5	90
100	0	12.00	15.0	100
110	−10	12.45	16.5	110
120	−20	12.90	18.0	120
130	−30	13.35	19.5	130
140	−40	13.80	21.0	140
150	−50	14.25	22.5	150

Equivalently, the client is presented with the efficient set that arises when there is a set of stocks and a riskfree borrowing and lending rate. As shown in Chapter 9, the efficient set is linear, meaning that it is a straight line that emanates at the riskfree rate and goes through a tangency portfolio that consists of a certain combination of securities. (In this case those securities are common stocks.) Hence negative percentages in Treasury bills (shown at the bottom of Table 17.1) represent riskfree borrowing in order to purchase greater amounts of stocks.

Next, the client is asked to identify the most desirable combination in terms of expected return and standard deviation. Note that asking the client to identify the most desirable combination is equivalent to asking the client to locate where one of his or her indifference curves is tangent to the linear efficient set; this point represents the client's most desirable portfolio.[3]

After the client selects the best mix of stocks and Treasury bills, what can be said about his or her risk tolerance? One would, of course, like to identify all the indifference curves that represent a client's attitude toward risk and expected return. However, in practice a more modest goal is usually adopted: to obtain a reasonable representation of the shape of such curves in the region of risk and expected return within which the client's optimal choices will most likely fall.

The points in Figure 17.2 plot the alternative mixes presented to the client that were given in Table 17.1. Curve *fCS* shows the risk–return characteristics of all possible mixes, and point *C* identifies the attributes of the mix chosen by the client. In this figure expected return is measured on the vertical axis and *variance* on the horizontal axis. Although the combinations available to the client plot on a straight line when standard deviation is measured on the horizontal axis, the combinations plot on a concave curve when variance is used.

If all the possible mixes have been presented to the client and point *C* has been chosen, it could be inferred that the slope of the client's indifference curve going

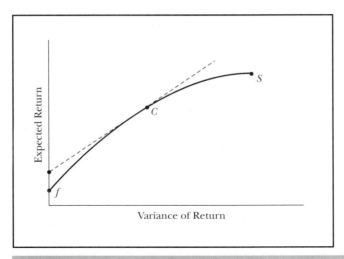

FIGURE 17.2 Inferring Client Risk Tolerance

through C is precisely equal to that of curve fCS at this point. As mentioned earlier, this inference is derived from the observation that the portfolio on the efficient set that a client identifies as being the "best" corresponds to the one where the client's indifference curves are just tangent to the efficient set.

17.3.2 CONSTANT RISK TOLERANCE

In principle, the choice of a mix provides information about the slope of an indifference curve at only one point. To go beyond this inference, the analysts must make an assumption about the general shape of the client's indifference curves. An assumption commonly made is that the client has constant risk tolerance over a range of alternative portfolios near the point originally chosen. Figure 17.3 shows the nature of this assumption. As shown in panel (a), indifference curves in a diagram with variance on the horizontal axis are linear when it is assumed that the client has *constant risk tolerance*. This means that the equation for the indifference curve for such an investor is equivalent to the equation for a straight line where the variable on the horizontal axis is variance (σ_p^2) and the variable on the vertical axis is expected return ($\bar{r}_p$). Because the equation of a straight line is $Y = a + bX$, where a is the vertical intercept and b is the slope, the equation for an indifference curve is

$$\bar{r}_p = a + b\sigma_p^2$$

or

$$\bar{r}_p = u_i + \frac{1}{\tau}\,\sigma_p^2 \tag{17.1}$$

where u_i is the vertical intercept for indifference curve i and the slope of the indifference curve is $1/\tau$.[4] Any two indifference curves for a client differ from one another only by the value of the vertical intercept because the indifference curves are parallel, meaning that they have the same slope, $1/\tau$.

Figure 17.3(b) plots the same indifference curves with *standard deviation* on the horizontal axis. Note that the curves indicate that the client requires more return to

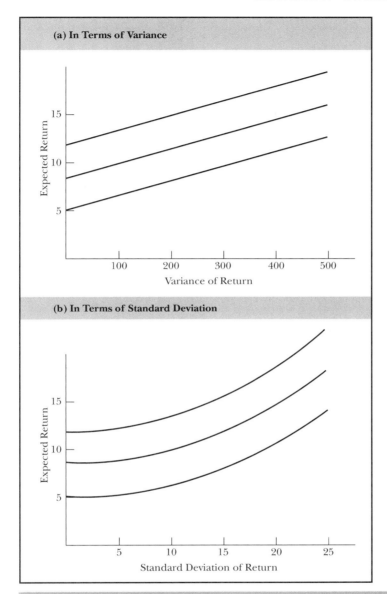

FIGURE 17.3 Constant Risk Tolerance

compensate for an additional unit of standard deviation as the risk of the portfolio increases. That is, the curves are *convex* when standard deviation is measured on the horizontal axis.

In the estimation of the client's level of risk tolerance τ, the slope of the indifference curve, $1/\tau$, is equal to the slope of the efficient set at the location of the portfolio that was selected, denoted portfolio C. Hence, the following formula can be used to estimate τ:

$$\tau = \frac{2[(\bar{r}_C - r_f)\sigma_S^2]}{(\bar{r}_S - r_f)^2} \tag{17.2}$$

where $\bar{r}_C$ denotes the expected return of the portfolio that the client selected, $\bar{r}_S$ and r_f denote the expected return of the stock portfolio and riskfree rate, respectively, and σ_S^2 denotes the variance of the stock portfolio.[5]

In the example, the client was given a choice between S, f, and various combinations of S and f where $\bar{r}_S = 12\%$, $r_f = 7.5\%$, and $\sigma_S^2 = 15^2 = 225$. Using Equation (17.2), the client's level of risk tolerance τ inferred from the choice of portfolio C equals:

$$\tau = \frac{2[(\bar{r}_C - 7.5)225]}{(12 - 7.5)^2} \tag{17.3}$$

$$= 22.22\bar{r}_C - 166.67$$

Assuming the choice of a portfolio with an expected return of 9.75%, Equation (17.3) can be used to determine the value of τ, resulting in a value of 50 [$= (22.22 \times 9.75) - 166.67$]. This means that the client will accept up to an additional 50 units of variance (or up to a 7% ($= \sqrt{50}$) standard deviation) in order to receive an extra 1% in expected return. Thus, the client's indifference curves are estimated to have the form of

$$\bar{r}_p = u_i + \frac{1}{50}\,\sigma_p^2 \tag{17.4}$$

Table 17.1 shows the inferred level of risk tolerance for various portfolios that could have been chosen by the client [these levels were determined by substituting the appropriate values for $\bar{r}_C$ into the right-hand side of Equation (17.3) and then solving for τ]. Note that the level of risk tolerance is lower if the selected portfolio is more conservative (that is, when the selected level of expected return and standard deviation is lower). Thus, more conservative risk-averse clients will have lower levels of risk tolerance (and thus steeper indifference curves) than less conservative risk-averse clients.

Recall from Chapter 7 that the objective of investment management is to identify the portfolio that lies on the indifference curve farthest to the northwest. Such a portfolio offers the client the level of expected return and risk that is preferable to all the other portfolios. Identifying this portfolio is the same as identifying the portfolio that lies on the indifference curve that has the highest vertical intercept, u_i. This equivalence can be seen graphically in both panels of Figure 17.3, where the indifference curves have been extended to the vertical axis.

17.3.3   CERTAINTY EQUIVALENT RETURN

certainty equivalent

The term u_i in Equation (17.1) is the return on the **certainty equivalent** for any portfolio that lies on indifference curve i.[6] Thus, portfolio C in Figure 17.2 is as desirable for this particular client as a hypothetical portfolio with an expected return of u_i and no risk—that is, one providing a return of u_i with certainty. In essence, the portfolio manager's job is to identify the portfolio with the highest certainty equivalent return for a client's given level of risk tolerance. In the example, the investor selected the portfolio with $\bar{r}_p = 9.75\%$ and $\sigma_p^2 = 56.25$ ($= 7.5^2$), and thus a certainty equivalent return of 8.625% [$= 9.75 - (56.25/50)$]. When the certainty equivalent return for any other portfolio shown in Table 17.1 is calculated (assuming the client's risk tolerance is 50), it will have a lower value {for example, the 80/20 portfolio has a certainty equivalent return of 8.22% [$= 11.1 - (144/50)$]}.

17.4   Security Analysis and Portfolio Construction

17.4.1   PASSIVE AND ACTIVE MANAGEMENT

passive management
active management

index fund

Buy Hold

In the investment industry, a distinction is often made between **passive management** —holding securities for relatively long periods with small and infrequent changes—and **active management.** Passive managers generally act as if the security markets are relatively efficient. Put somewhat differently, their decisions are consistent with the acceptance of consensus estimates of risk and return. The portfolios they hold may be surrogates for the market portfolio that are known as **index funds,** or they may be portfolios that are tailored to suit clients with preferences and circumstances that differ from those of the average investor.[7] In either case, passive portfolio managers do not try to outperform their designated benchmarks.

For example, a passive manager might only have to choose the appropriate mixture of Treasury bills and an index fund designed to match the return on a selected market index, such as the S&P 500. The best mixture would depend on the shape and location of the client's indifference curves. Figure 17.4 provides an illustration. Point *f* plots the riskfree return offered by Treasury bills, and point *M* plots the risk and expected return of the market index, using consensus forecasts. Mixtures of the two investments plot along line *fM*. The client's attitude toward risk and return is shown by the set of indifference curves, and the optimal mixture of *f* and *M* lies at the point *O** where an indifference curve is tangent to line *fM*. In this example, the best mixture uses both Treasury bills and the index fund. In other situations, the index fund might be "levered up" by borrowing (that is, money might be borrowed and added to the client's own investable funds, with the total being used to purchase the index fund).

FIGURE 17.4 Passive Investment Management

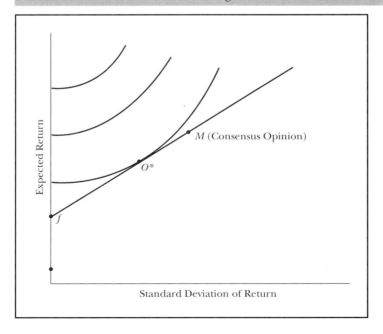

When management is passive, the optimal mixture is altered only when

- The client's preferences change
- The riskfree rate changes
- The consensus forecast about the risk and expected return of the benchmark portfolio changes

The manager must continue to monitor the last two variables and keep in touch with the client concerning the first one. No additional activity is required.

Active managers believe that from time to time there are mispriced securities or sectors of securities. They do not act as if they believe that security markets are efficient. Put somewhat differently, they use deviant predictions; that is, their forecasts of risks and expected returns differ from consensus opinions. Whereas some managers may be more bullish than average about a security, others may be more bearish. The former will hold "more-than-normal" proportions of the security; the latter will hold "less-than-normal" proportions.

It is useful to think of a portfolio as having two components: (1) a benchmark portfolio and (2) deviations designed to take advantage of security mispricing. For example, a portfolio can be broken down as follows:

Name of Security (Col. 1)	Proportion in Actual Portfolio (Col. 2)	Proportion in Benchmark Portfolio (Col. 3)	Active Position (Col. 4)
S1	.30	.45	−.15
S2	.20	.25	−.05
S3	.50	.30	+.20
	1.00	1.00	.00

active position

The second column shows the actual proportions in the actively managed portfolio. The third column shows the percentages in a benchmark portfolio. The **active positions** are represented by the differences between the proportions in the actual and benchmark portfolios. Such differences arise because active managers disagree with the consensus forecast about expected returns or risks. When expressed as differences of this sort, the actual portfolio is an investment in the benchmark portfolio with a series of *bets* placed on certain securities (such as S3) and against certain other securities (such as S1 and S2). Note that the bets are "balanced"; the amount of the negative bets exactly counters the amount of the positive bets.

17.4.2 SECURITY SELECTION, ASSET ALLOCATION, AND MARKET TIMING

Security Selection

security selection

In principle, the investment manager should make forecasts of expected returns, standard deviations, and covariances for all available securities. These forecasts allow an efficient set to be generated, on which the indifference curves of the client can be plotted. The investment manager should invest in those securities that form the optimal portfolio (that is, the portfolio indicated by the point at which an indifference curve is tangent to the efficient set) for the client in question. This one-stage **security selection** process is illustrated in Figure 17.5(a). In practice, this process is rarely (if ever) used. Excessive costs would be incurred to obtain detailed forecasts of the expected returns, standard deviations, and covariances for all the individual securities under consideration. Instead, deciding which securities to purchase is done in two or more stages.

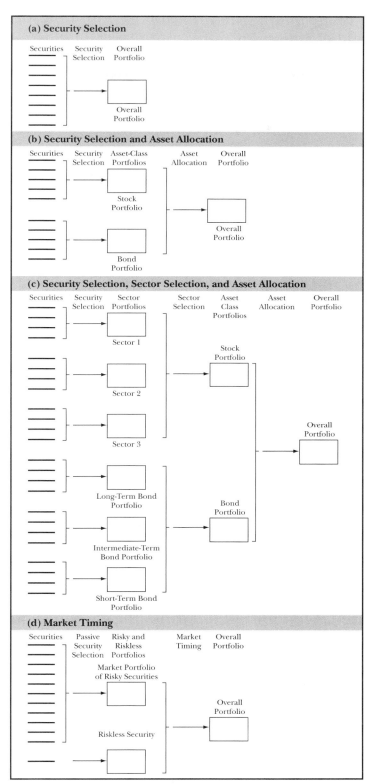

FIGURE 17.5 Investment Styles

Figure 17.5(b) illustrates a two-stage procedure in which the investment manager has decided to consider investing in common stocks and corporate bonds for a client. In the first stage, the expected returns, standard deviations, and covariances are forecast for all common stocks under consideration. Then, on the basis of just these common stocks, the efficient set is formed and the optimal stock portfolio identified. Next the same analysis is performed for all corporate bonds under consideration to identify the optimal bond portfolio. The security selection process used in each of these two **asset class**   **asset classes** can be described as myopic; covariances between the individual common stocks and corporate bonds have not been considered in the identification of the two optimal portfolios.

Although this example has only two asset classes—stocks and bonds—the number of asset classes can be relatively large. Other asset classes that are often used consist of money market securities ("cash"), foreign stocks, foreign bonds, venture capital, and real estate.

Asset Allocation

asset allocation   The second stage of the process divides the client's funds among two (or more) asset class portfolios and is known as **asset allocation.**[8] In this stage, forecasts of the expected return and standard deviation are needed for both the optimal stock portfolio and the optimal bond portfolio, along with the covariance between the two portfolios. With this information, the expected return and standard deviation can be determined for all combinations of the two portfolios. Finally, after the efficient set has been generated, the indifference curves of the client are used to determine which portfolio should be chosen.[9]

Some people refer to two types of asset allocation. *Strategic asset allocation* refers to how a portfolio's funds would be divided, given the portfolio manager's long-term forecasts of expected returns, variances, and covariances, whereas *tactical asset allocation* refers to how these funds are to be divided at any particular moment, given the investor's short-term forecasts. Hence the former reflects what the portfolio manager would do for the long term, and the latter reflects what he or she would do under current market conditions.

For example, the first stage might have indicated that the investor should hold the proportions of stocks $S1$, $S2$, and $S3$ given earlier (that is, the optimal stock portfolio has proportions of .30, .20, and .50, respectively). Similarly, the first stage might have indicated that the investor should hold a proportion of .35 in bond $B1$ and .65 in bond $B2$. Then under tactical asset allocation, the second stage might indicate that the client's funds should be split so that 60% goes into stocks and 40% goes into bonds because of current market conditions (whereas under strategic asset allocation these percentages might have been 70% and 30%, respectively). This decision translates into individual investments of the following magnitudes:

Stocks
$S1$	$.60 \times .30 = .18$
$S2$	$.60 \times .20 = .12$
$S3$	$.60 \times .50 = .30$

Bonds
$B1$	$.40 \times .35 = .14$
$B2$	$.40 \times .65 = \underline{.26}$
	1.00

The two-stage process can be extended by introducing *sectors*. Figure 17.5(c) illustrates a three-stage process. In the first stage, known as security selection, the investment manager exercises discretion in identifying sectors of securities in each asset class and determines the optimal portfolio within each sector. For example, within the asset class of common stocks, the investment manager might identify all industrial stocks as the first sector, all utility stocks as the second sector, and all transportation stocks as the third sector. (An increasingly popular division of stocks into sectors involves classifying them based on market capitalization and growth-value status. For example, there could be four sectors: large-cap value stocks, large-cap growth stocks, small-cap value stocks, and small-cap growth stocks.) Within the asset class of bonds, sectors of long-term, intermediate-term, and short-term bonds have been identified. Then, the investment manager would select securities to create an optimal portfolio within each of the six sectors.

sector selection

In the second stage, known as **sector selection** (or sector rotation), the investment manager determines the appropriate combination of the sectors within each asset class. For example, the manager may decide that the appropriate combination of stock sectors is 70% industrials, 10% utilities, and 20% transportation stocks, while the appropriate combination of bond sectors is 100% in long-term, with nothing in either intermediate-term or short-term bonds. Thus, in this stage the manager determines the composition of an optimal stock portfolio and an optimal bond portfolio but will not know how much to allocate to each one.

The third and final stage makes this allocation and, as noted previously, is referred to as asset allocation. It is identical to the second stage of the two-stage procedure illustrated in Figure 17.5(b).

Active or passive management may be used in any stage. For example, *active bets* might be placed on individual securities but with funds allocated among asset classes on the basis of consensus long-term forecasts of expected returns for such classes. That is, the investment manager may decide to stick to a long-term mix of 70% stocks and 30% bonds. However, the choice of individual stocks and bonds in which to invest will change with time on the basis of the manager's forecasts.

Alternatively, passive portfolios of individual stocks might be constructed with deviant predictions of sector returns used to allocate funds actively among the stock sectors. For example, the investment manager may decide to always hold transportation stocks in the same relative proportions they have in the transportation sector. However, the proportion of funds invested in the transportation sector will change at the start of every period on the basis of the overall prognosis for the various sectors. Thus, during one period the manager may have as much as 100% of the client's funds in transportation stocks, strongly believing that the transportation sector is going to rise rapidly in the near future. During another period the manager may have as much as 100% of the client's funds in the utilities sector, strongly believing that the transportation sector will soon decline sharply.

Market Timing

market timing

Figure 17.5(d) portrays one example of a manager following an investment style known as **market timing.** The only active decision concerns the appropriate allocation of funds between a surrogate market portfolio (usually consisting of either stocks or long-term bonds) and a riskfree asset (such as Treasury bills). An investment organization following this style changes its mixture of risky and riskfree assets on the basis of its own forecasts of the risk and expected return of "the market" relative to the riskfree rate, even if there is no change in consensus forecasts or in the client's attitude toward risk and return.

Investment organizations that engage in the type of management that places active bets on individual securities are said to have a *security selection style*. Those that engage in the type of management that places active bets on asset classes are said to have an *asset allocation style,* with market timing as one specific example. Last, investment organizations that place active bets on certain sectors of securities are said to use

investment style

a *sector rotation style.* Some organizations use relatively pure **investment styles,** meaning that they use primarily one of the three styles mentioned. Others employ various combinations, making it difficult to classify them into categories.

Although these styles have been described in terms of modern investment theory, other procedures could be used to implement them. For example, based on theory an optimal stock portfolio [as in Figure 17.5(b)] is identified using forecasted expected returns, standard deviations, and covariances in conjunction with indifference curves. Once it has been identified, the portfolio manager determines the appropriate relative investments in individual common stocks. However, such a determination often is done on a less formal and more qualitative basis. Expectations concerning security returns may involve simple rankings (for example, using a five-point scale). Covariances between securities and security standard deviations may not be considered explicitly or even implicitly. Risk may be controlled through various limits on the proportions of the portfolio invested in individual securities and sectors.

17.4.3 INTERNATIONAL INVESTING

An interesting extension of the previous discussion of investment styles involves international investing (which is the subject of Chapter 26). Consider security selection first. This style, when applied internationally, involves determining the efficient set associated with a number of stocks found around the world. Alternatively, a security selection style could be combined with an asset allocation style. For example, the portfolio manager could first determine the optimal portfolios associated with just Japanese stocks, just U.S. stocks, and just German stocks. Then, using these three optimal portfolios, the manager decides how much to allocate to each of the countries.

Imagine that the optimal Japanese portfolio consisted of two stocks, J_1 and J_2, in proportions of 70% and 30%, respectively, and half of the portfolio's funds were to be devoted to Japanese stocks. As a result, 35% (= .50 × 70%) would be invested in J_1 and 15% (= .50 × 30%) in J_2. Similar calculations could be done for the sets of U.S. and German stocks.

Analogous procedures to those previously described could be followed for the security selection, sector rotation, asset allocation, and market timing styles in an international setting. However, the issue of foreign currency risk adds a confounding element to this comparison.[10]

17.5 Portfolio Revision

With the passage of time, a previously purchased portfolio that is currently held will often be viewed as suboptimal by the investment manager, meaning that the portfolio is no longer considered to be the best one for the client. Either the weights in the different securities have changed as their market prices have changed, or the client's attitude toward risk and return has changed, or, more likely, the manager's forecasts have changed. In response, the manager could identify a new optimal portfolio and make the necessary revisions to the current portfolio. However, this process is not as straightforward as it might seem at first because transaction costs have to be paid when any revisions are made. Such costs must be compared with the perceived benefits associated with the revision in order to determine what course of action to take.

Evaluating Investment Systems

 Investors are constantly in search of the holy grail: an investment system that can produce high returns with low risk and without the expense of retaining a team of skilled analysts. This search has led down many and varied paths. Over the years, numerous individuals and organizations have claimed to have developed mechanical investment systems that use only available historical data and objective analytical procedures to produce results superior to passive management. Some mechanical systems simply provide predictions of how the market will behave; others prescribe a complete set of instructions for investing in individual securities. Almost all of them present impressive statistics based on tests using data from some past evaluation period.

Advocates of such mechanical investment systems may sincerely believe that they have found the path to instant affluence. However, their proofs often rest on shaky ground. In the evaluation of any system, it is imperative that several possible errors be avoided.

Failure to Adjust for Risk

Any investment system that results in the selection of high-beta stocks is likely to produce above-average returns in bull markets and below-average returns in bear markets. Because the stock market over the long-term has trended upward, on balance such a system tends to produce above-average returns over the long run (as do systems that involve purchasing either small-capitalization stocks or stocks with high book-to-market ratios; see Chapter 13). Therefore, an evaluation of the performance of any investment system should involve not only measuring the resulting average return but also determining the amount of risk incurred. Then the average return from a passive management benchmark of similar risk can be computed for comparison. Techniques for making such comparisons are presented in Chapter 18.

Failure to Consider Transaction Costs

Systems that rely on frequent, high-volume trading may produce *gross* returns that exceed

those of a similar risk, passive management benchmark. However, if transaction costs have not been included in the analysis, the results may be invalid. *Net* returns are calculated by adding transaction costs to the purchase price of an investment and deducting them from the investment's selling price. After inclusion of realistic transaction costs, most high-turnover investment systems produce negative risk-adjusted performance.

Failure to Consider Dividends

When the performance of a mechanical system is compared with that of a passive management benchmark, dividends (and interest payments) are often ignored. Failure to consider dividends may seriously bias the results. For example, a system may be advocated that, in effect, selects low-yield stocks. The prices of such stocks should increase at a faster rate than those of high-yield stocks with the same amount of risk because a stock's return consists of both dividends and capital appreciation. Two stocks with the same risk should have the same return, meaning that the stock with a smaller yield will have a larger capital appreciation. Thus if just capital appreciation is examined, a system that selects low-yield stocks would tend to show a more rapid rate of capital appreciation than a passive management benchmark involving a well-diversified portfolio consisting of both low- and high-yield stocks. Consequently, when yields of systems differ significantly from average yields, it is important to examine *total* returns, not just the rate of capital appreciation.

Nonoperational Systems

Although obvious, it still must be mentioned: To be useful, a system must not require knowledge about the future. For example, many systems require action after some time-series of values (such as a stock's price) has reached a "peak" or a "trough." But it is rarely apparent until well afterward that in fact a peak or trough has been reached. Hence such a system is nonoperational. Similarly, an investigator might use a database prepared in 2000 with stock price data relating to the period from 1989 through 1999. The stocks included in the database may have been chosen because they existed and were important in 2000 (for example, they may have been considered important because they were listed on the NYSE in 2000). A superior investment system based on an analysis of this database is a type of nonoperational system involving *ex post* **selection bias** (or survivorship bias) because it was based on an analysis of those stocks that were certain to be alive and important in 2000. However, this system requires knowledge in 1989 of which stocks will exist in 2000.

Spurious Fits

When a set of data from a past period is used, it is not difficult to discover an investment system that works quite well when tested on the same data. One simply has to test enough systems. However, this process is not necessarily useful to the investor. If 100 seemingly irrelevant systems are tried with a set of data, according to the laws of probability, one of them is likely to give results that are "statistically significant at the 1% level." This result should not cause undue excitement because it would not necessarily have any notable predictive power in the future. For example, stock prices in the United States have been shown to be correlated with both sunspot activity and the length of skirts. However, these correlations are unlikely to demonstrate actual causal relationships. Instead, they are likely to have been "spurious," meaning that they were probably coincidental. Without solid reasons to believe that a relationship is caused by underlying forces, it would be unwise to predict its continuation in the future.

Reliance on Misleading Visual Comparisons

Occasionally the proponent of a system will produce a graph that plots both the level of an indicator intended to predict market moves and the levels of the market itself. Visual comparison of the two curves may suggest that the indicator does indeed predict changes in the market (this conclusion is made easier when the proponent chooses the beginning and, to a lesser extent, the ending dates). However, the eye cannot easily differentiate between a situation in which changes in a market predictor *lead* the market and one in which the changes *lag* behind the market. This distinction is crucial because only a leading indicator can bring superior investment performance.

Failure to Use Out-of-Sample Data

Can any evidence concerning a system's ability to beat the market be persuasive? Probably not according to those who believe in perfect market efficiency. But there are appropriate tests that can be undertaken. The search for a system should be conducted using one set of data, and the test of the system's predictive ability should be performed using an entirely different set of data. The latter set of data is sometimes known as **out-of-sample data** or a holdout sample. To be complete, such a test should involve the (simulated) management of a portfolio and be designed so that each investment decision is based solely on information available at the time the decision is made. Finally, the performance of the system should be evaluated in the same way one would evaluate the performance of any investment manager (discussed in Chapter 18). This evaluation involves, among other things, determining the probability that the investment outcome resulted from chance rather than skill.

Despite the increasing popularity of passive management, the search for successful investment systems will continue. As always the most useful advice to investors considering such systems is *caveat emptor* (buyer beware). Checking for these errors will make for more intelligent evaluations of prospective investment systems.

17.5.1 COST-BENEFIT ANALYSIS

Transaction costs were discussed in Chapter 3. They include brokerage commissions, price impacts, and bid–ask spreads. A security would have to increase in value by a certain amount to compensate for these costs so that the investor is neither better nor worse off. This necessary increase in value may exceed 1% for many securities and can range as high as 5% to 10% or more for other securities, particularly small, illiquid stocks.

Transaction costs complicate the job of investment managers, and the more active the manager, the greater the complications. The hoped-for advantage of any revision must be weighed against the cost of making that revision. That is, a revision may bring certain benefits: It may increase the expected return of the portfolio; it may reduce the standard deviation of the portfolio; or it may do both. The transaction costs that will be incurred must be weighed against the benefits. Some of the revisions in the holdings of individual securities that the manager may initially want to make will be dropped from consideration because of the transaction costs involved. The goal of the manager is to identify the set of individual revisions that collectively maximizes the improvement, after transaction costs, in the risk–return characteristics of the current portfolio.

Identifying the appropriate set of individual revisions requires sophisticated methods to compare the relevant costs and benefits. Fortunately, improvements in measurement procedures and dramatic decreases in computing costs have made such approaches economically feasible for many investment managers.

In some situations investors may find it economically more attractive to revise their portfolios by transacting in entire asset classes instead of individual securities. Buying or selling futures contracts (see Chapter 25) on stock market indices or Treasury bonds is one such approach.[11] A potentially more flexible strategy uses the swaps market.

17.5.2 SWAPS

Consider a situation in which a portfolio manager wants to make major changes in the proportions of funds that are invested in different asset classes. He or she recognizes that substantial transaction costs will be incurred if the traditional method of selling certain securities and replacing them with others is used to make the changes. Indeed, these costs can be so large that most of the changes, if conducted in this manner, should not be made. One relatively new method that has become popular in allowing such changes to be made at relatively low transaction costs involves the use of swaps.[12]

Although the unique features of swaps can become complicated, their general nature is quite simple. Such "plain vanilla" swaps are contracts that typically involve two parties (in the language of swaps the two parties are referred to as *counterparties*) exchanging sets of cash flows over a predetermined period of time.[13] Two types of swaps—equity and interest rate—are considered here.

Equity Swaps

equity swap

With an **equity swap,** one counterparty agrees to pay a second counterparty a stream of variable-size cash payments that is typically based on the rate of return of an agreed-on stock market index. In return, the second counterparty agrees to pay the first counterparty a stream of fixed cash payments that is based on current interest rates. Both sets of payments are to be made for a given time period and are based on a certain percentage (the percentage is variable for one counterparty and fixed for the other) of an underlying *notional principal*. Through an equity swap the first counterparty has, in essence, sold stocks and bought bonds, whereas the second counterparty has sold bonds and bought stocks. Both of them have effectively restructured their portfolios without paying transaction costs, other than a relatively small fee to a **swap**

swap bank

bank (usually a commercial or investment bank) that set up the contract.

Consider the example shown in Figure 17.6(a). Ms. Bright, a pension fund manager, thinks the stock market will move up in the next three years. In contrast, Mr. Gloom, who also runs a pension fund, thinks the stock market will move downward in the next

(a) The Contract

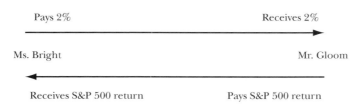

Pays 2%   Receives 2%

Ms. Bright   Mr. Gloom

Receives S&P 500 return   Pays S&P 500 return

(b) The Cash Flows

Quarter	S&P 500 Return	Ms. Bright's Cash Flows*			Mr. Gloom's Cash Flows*		
		Payment from Gloom	Payment to Gloom	Net	Payment from Bright	Payment to Bright	Net
First	3%	$3	$2	$1	$2	$3	−$1
Second	−4	−4	2	−6	2	−4	6
Third	1	1	2	−1	2	1	1
Fourth	5	5	2	3	2	5	−3

*All cash flows are in millions because the notional principal is $100 million.

FIGURE 17.6 Equity Swap

three years. Ms. Bright is considering selling $100 million of bonds and investing the proceeds in common stocks whereas Mr. Gloom is thinking of selling $100 million of common stocks and using the proceeds to purchase bonds. Both portfolio managers realize that such changes will involve the payment of substantial transaction costs. Consequently, both of them contact a swap bank.

The swap bank sets up the following contract for Ms. Bright and Mr. Gloom. Shortly after the end of each quarter Mr. Gloom is to pay Ms. Bright an amount equal to the rate of return on the S&P 500 for the quarter times the notional principal. At the same time, Ms. Bright is to pay Mr. Gloom an amount equal to 2% of the notional principal. Both Ms. Bright and Mr. Gloom agree that the notional principal will be equal to $100 million and that the contract will last for three years. Each pays the swap bank a small fee for setting up the contract.

Imagine that the quarterly rates of return on the S&P 500 during the first year of the swap contract are equal to 3%, −4%, 1%, and 5%, as shown in Figure 17.6(b). Ms. Bright must pay $2 million (= .02 × $100 million) to Mr. Gloom each quarter; in return Mr. Gloom must pay Ms. Bright the following amounts:

First quarter:	.03 × $100 million =	$3 million
Second quarter:	−.04 × $100 million =	−$4 million
Third quarter:	.01 × $100 million =	$1 million
Fourth quarter:	.05 × $100 million =	$5 million

It appears that in the first quarter Ms. Bright pays $2 million to Mr. Gloom and in return Mr. Gloom pays $3 million to Ms. Bright. However, the way the contract is structured, only the net amount is paid; in this case, Mr. Gloom pays $1 million (= $3 million − $2 million) to Ms. Bright. In the second quarter it appears that Mr. Gloom must pay −$4 million to Ms. Bright. However, the minus sign means Ms. Bright actually must pay Mr. Gloom $4 million plus the fixed payment of $2 million, for a total payment of $6 million. In the third period, Ms. Bright must pay Mr. Gloom $1 million (= $2 million −

$1 million), and in the fourth quarter Mr. Gloom must pay Ms. Bright $3 million (= $5 million − $2 million). In summary, the net payments are

First quarter:	Mr. Gloom pays $1 million to Ms. Bright
Second quarter:	Ms. Bright pays $6 million to Mr. Gloom
Third quarter:	Ms. Bright pays $1 million to Mr. Gloom
Fourth quarter:	Mr. Gloom pays $3 million to Ms. Bright

These amounts reflect what would have happened (roughly) if Mr. Gloom had sold stocks and bought bonds and Ms. Bright had sold bonds and bought stocks, and both had incurred relatively low transaction costs. Consider the first quarter. If Mr. Gloom sold the stocks and replaced them with 8% coupon (2% per quarter) bonds, he would have earned $2 million. Instead, he kept the stocks and earned $3 million on them (remember that the S&P 500 went up 3%) but had to pay Ms. Bright a net amount of $1 million, leaving him with $2 million, the same amount.[14]

There are many ways that equity swaps can be modified. For example, a foreign stock market index such as the Nikkei 225 could be used instead of the S&P 500, allowing one counterparty to cheaply achieve the benefits of international diversification. Alternatively, the swap could involve two stock market indices, say, a large stock index such as the S&P 500 and a small stock index such as the Russell 2000. There are other variations, limited only by investors' imaginations and their ability to periodically determine the value of the swaps.

Interest Rate Swaps

interest rate swap

With an **interest rate swap,** one counterparty agrees to pay a second party a stream of cash payments, the size of which is reset regularly based on the current level of a highly visible interest rate. A popular one is the London Interbank Offered Rate (LIBOR), which is an interest rate set daily in London that applies to short-term loans made among large international banks. In return, the second counterparty agrees to pay the first counterparty a stream of fixed cash payments based on the level of interest rates in existence at the time the contract is signed. As in equity swaps, both sets of payments are made for a certain number of years and are based on a certain percentage of an underlying notional principal. (The percentage is variable—or "floating"— for one counterparty and usually fixed for the other.) Through the interest rate swap the first counterparty has, in essence, sold short-term fixed-income securities and bought long-term bonds, whereas the second counterparty has sold these bonds and bought the short-term fixed-income securities. As in equity swaps, both of them have effectively restructured their portfolios without having to pay any transaction costs other than a relatively small fee to a swap bank that set up the contract.

Consider the example shown in Figure 17.7(a). Ms. Uppe, a fixed-income mutual fund manager, thinks interest rates will rise in the near future. In contrast, Mr. Downe, who also runs a fixed-income mutual fund, thinks interest will decline. Consequently, Ms. Uppe is considering selling $100 million of long-term bonds and investing the proceeds in money market securities, whereas Mr. Downe is thinking of selling $100 million of money market securities and using the proceeds to purchase long-term bonds.[15] As with the case of an equity swap, both of them contact a swap bank to help them make such changes without the payment of substantial transaction costs.

The swap bank sets up the following contract for the two of them. Shortly after the end of each quarter Mr. Downe is to pay Ms. Uppe an amount equal to the end-of-quarter three-month LIBOR times the notional principal. At the same time Ms. Uppe

(a) The Contract

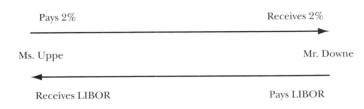

Pays 2%   Receives 2%

Ms. Uppe   Mr. Downe

Receives LIBOR   Pays LIBOR

(b) The Cash Flows

Quarter	LIBOR	Ms. Uppe's Cash Flows*			Mr. Downe's Cash Flows*		
		Payment from Downe	Payment to Downe	Net	Payment from Uppe	Payment to Uppe	Net
First	1.5%	$1.5	$2	−$.5	$2	$1.5	$.5
Second	1.8	1.8	2	−.2	2	1.8	.2
Third	2.1	2.1	2	.1	2	2.1	−.1
Fourth	2.4	2.4	2	.4	2	2.4	−.4

*All cash flows are in millions as the notional principal is $100 million.

FIGURE 17.7 Interest Rate Swap

is to pay Mr. Downe an amount equal to 2% of the notional principal. Both Ms. Uppe and Mr. Downe agree that the notional principal will be equal to $100 million and that the contract will last for five years. Each pays the swap bank a fee for setting up the contract.

Imagine that the three-month LIBOR at the end of each of the next four quarters equals, successively, 1.5%, 1.8%, 2.1%, and 2.4%. This means that the following amounts are to be paid by Mr. Downe to Ms. Uppe:

First quarter:	$.015 \times \$100$ million = $1.5 million
Second quarter:	$.018 \times \$100$ million = $1.8 million
Third quarter:	$.021 \times \$100$ million = $2.1 million
Fourth quarter:	$.024 \times \$100$ million = $2.4 million

In return, Ms. Uppe must pay $2 million (= $.02 \times \$100$ million) to Mr. Downe each quarter.

Because the payments from Ms. Uppe and Mr. Downe are netted against each other, the net payments are

First quarter:	Ms. Uppe pays $.5 million to Mr. Downe
Second quarter:	Ms. Uppe pays $.2 million to Mr. Downe
Third quarter:	Mr. Downe pays $.1 million to Ms. Uppe
Fourth quarter:	Mr. Downe pays $.4 million to Ms. Uppe

These amounts reflect what would have happened (roughly) if Ms. Uppe had sold bonds and bought money market securities and Mr. Downe had sold money market securities and bought bonds, and both had incurred relatively low transaction costs. Consider the first quarter. If Ms. Uppe had sold the bonds and replaced them with money market securities yielding roughly LIBOR, she would have earned $1.5 million in interest. Instead, she kept the bonds and earned $2 million on them but had to pay Mr. Downe a net amount of $.5 million, leaving her with $1.5 million, the same amount.[16]

As with equity swaps, there are many variations on this plain vanilla interest rate swap. For example, the notional principal could change over time. Or one variable-rate stream of cash flows based on one interest rate (such as LIBOR) could be swapped for a variable rate stream of cash flows based on another interest rate (such as Treasury bills). In addition, there can be caps or floors or collars on the size of the variable payments.

Swaps Market

The swaps market is an unregulated market in that no governmental agency has oversight responsibilities. As a consequence, there has been a high degree of innovation in the types of swap contracts that have been created.[17] Furthermore, there is privacy for all parties involved because no reporting requirements exist other than those imposed by accountants. In addition, anyone involved in a swap must be concerned with *counterparty risk*. That is, each counterparty to a swap must pay close attention to the creditworthiness of the other counterparty to reduce the risk that the other counterparty will default in making his or her required payments under the terms of the contract. As a consequence, swaps are most often used by large, well-established companies and financial institutions

At the heart of the swaps market are swap banks. These "banks" facilitate the creation of swaps for their clients, and they often will take the other side of the contract if another counterparty is not available at the moment. In such situations they act as *swap dealers,* and they use various techniques (such as taking positions in futures or contacting other swap banks) to hedge their exposure to financial risk. In such a situation no fee is typically charged to the counterparty. Instead, the terms of the swap are set in the swap dealer's favor, thereby allowing the dealer to make a profit after hedging his or her position.

What happens if at some point during the life of the swap one counterparty wants to get out of the contract? In such a situation the counterparty has a choice of contacting either the other counterparty or a swap bank. In the first case, it is possible that the swap contract can be canceled if a mutually acceptable cash payment is made from one counterparty to the other. In the interest rate swap example, if interest rates have risen high enough (as in the third and fourth quarter), then Ms. Uppe will be in a favorable position because the swap's net cash flows will be going from Mr. Downe to her. Hence, regardless of who wants to get out of the swap, Ms. Uppe would want to be compensated for the loss of the anticipated future cash flows. This means that Mr. Downe would give her a lump sum payment when the contract is canceled.

Similarly, if a swap bank is contacted, then either it will assume the counterparty's position in the contract or it will search for someone else to do so. (Note that the counterparty that wants to get out of the contract can conduct such a search without using a swap bank.) In the previous example, if Ms. Uppe wants to get out of the contract, then the swap bank will pay her a lump sum. Conversely, if Mr. Downe wants to get out, then he will have to pay a lump sum to the swap bank. In either case, the contract remains in force afterward for the other counterparty.

Alternatively, the swap bank may arrange for the party that wants to get out to agree to a second swap contract that effectively cancels the first one. For example, if after one year Ms. Uppe wants to get out of the contract where she "pays fixed and receives floating," then the swap bank could construct a four-year swap with a different counterparty where she "pays floating and receives fixed" for the same amount of notional principal. With the first contract she pays 2% and receives LIBOR, and with the second contract she will pay LIBOR and receive 2.3%. The fixed rate is higher with the second contract (2.3% > 2%) because interest rates have risen since the first contract was signed. Now

Ms. Uppe both receives and pays LIBOR, so those two cash streams effectively cancel each other out. She also pays 2% and receives 2.3%, meaning that, on balance, she receives .3%, or $300,000 (= .003 × $100 million) quarterly for the next four years.

17.6 Manager–Client Relations

The larger the amount of money being managed, the more communication there is likely to be between investment managers and clients. Not surprisingly, corporate, union, and government officials responsible for pension funds spend a great deal of time with those who manage their money. Such officials are also concerned with a number of questions: Who should manage the money? How should it be managed? How should the managers be instructed and constrained?

split-funding

Many of the aspects of manager–client relations can be characterized as responses to a difference of opinion concerning the manager's abilities to make "good bets." Often clients divide their funds among two or more managers. There are two reasons for this type of **split-funding.** First, it allows access to managers with different skills or different styles. Second, the impact of erroneous "bets" is reduced by diversifying among managers because the managers are the "bettors." However, if a client were to broadly diversify among managers without regard to the managers' investment abilities, the overall portfolio would likely produce results similar to those of the market portfolio. Thus excessive use of split-funding is like explicitly investing in a passive fund but at considerably greater cost to the client because of the expenses associated with transaction costs and fees charged by the investment managers.[18]

Institutional investors (for example, pension and endowment funds) often use more than one investment manager and provide each with objectives and constraints on allowed divergences from specified target positions.[19] Individual investors who use investment managers tend to give such instructions only implicitly, if at all. This timidity may reflect less sophistication, a less formal relationship with the manager, or the fact that the management fee for a small account is not large enough to cover the cost of dealing with a series of client-specific objectives and constraints.

Summary

1. Investment decisions are made using a five-step procedure: (1) set investment policy; (2) perform security analysis; (3) construct a portfolio; (4) revise the portfolio; and (5) evaluate the performance of the portfolio.

2. To set investment policy, an investor should specify his or her risk tolerance—that is, the maximum amount of additional risk that the investor will accept for a given increase in expected return.

3. One means of establishing an investor's risk tolerance is for the investor to identify the most desirable portfolio from a set of portfolios. Once this identification has been made, the slope of the investor's indifference curve, and hence the investor's attitude toward risk and expected return, can be estimated.

4. Passive management rests on the belief that markets are efficient and typically involves investing in an index fund. Active management, conversely, involves a belief that mispriced situations occur and can be identified with reasonable consistency.

5. There are many forms of active management. They can involve security selection, sector selection, asset allocation, and market timing.

6. Portfolio revision involves both realizing that the currently held portfolio is not optimal and specifying another portfolio to hold with superior risk–return characteristics. The investor must balance the costs of moving to the new portfolio against the benefits of the revision.

7. Swaps often provide a low-cost method of restructuring a portfolio's funds across various asset classes.

8. Most large investors use split-funding to spread their investments across various managers with different styles and to protect themselves against incorrect active management decisions by a single manager.

Questions and Problems

1. Describe the functioning of a "traditional" investment management organization. Much of the decision making in these organizations is "qualitative" in nature. What types of "quantitative" decision-making techniques might be introduced?

2. Technological changes have decreased the cost and increased the speed of information dissemination in security markets. Why might one suspect that firms following a "traditional" approach to investment management would find it increasingly difficult to generate "positive alphas" (that is, to identify and acquire underpriced securities) in this environment?

3. Consider Table 17.1. If your investment advisor presented you with these data, which stock–Treasury bill combination would you choose? Describe your thought process in making this choice.

4. Consider a portfolio whose asset mix varies between stocks and Treasury bills. Given the historical returns on these two assets that is provided in Chapter 1, describe the distribution of possible portfolio returns as the proportion of the portfolio invested in stocks increases and that invested in Treasury bills decreases. What causes the distribution to change as the asset mix changes?

5. Explain the meaning of the slope of an investor's indifference curve at any particular point. For a "typical" risk-averse investor, describe how the investor's risk–return tradeoff changes at different points along one of his or her indifference curves.

6. Assume that the expected return on stocks is 12%, the standard deviation of stocks is 18%, and the riskfree rate is 5%. Given this information, an investor selects a portfolio with a 70% allocation to stocks and a 30% allocation to the riskfree asset. According to the derivation of risk tolerance found in Equation (17.2), what risk tolerance is indicated by this choice? In words, describe what this value means.

7. Should an "overpriced" stock definitely be excluded from an investor's portfolio? Why or why not?

8. Studies that simulate the value of an investment portfolio under alternative mixes of stocks and bonds invariably demonstrate that higher stock allocations produce higher returns, particularly as the holding period increases. If you, as an investor, have a time horizon that is reasonably long, say 10 years or more, and you have no current income needs, could you justify holding any bonds in your portfolio?

9. Dee Cousineau can earn a riskfree return of 6%. Dee expects the stock market to return 15% and exhibit a standard deviation of 20%. If Dee chooses a portfolio of 60% stocks and 40% riskfree asset, calculate Dee's certainty equivalent return.

10. Despite its obvious simplicity and potential benefits, common-stock passive management is a relatively new investment tool. Yet in the past 25 years, assets under passive management have grown from essentially zero to hundreds of billions of dollars. What are some possible reasons for the tremendous growth in passive management?

11. It is often argued (especially by active managers) that passive management implies settling for "mediocre" performance. Explain whether or not this statement is true.

12. Why is the one-stage approach to security selection theoretically superior to the two-stage approach? Why is the two-stage approach preferred by most investment managers?

13. Dude Blake has entered into a one-year equity swap with Smily Bischooff. The terms of the swap call for Smiley to deliver Dude the returns on the Trout Stock Index, whereas Dude must deliver to Smiley the returns on LIBOR. The notational principal of the swap is $50 million. Payment is made quarterly. Over the next four quarters, the Trout index and LIBOR return the following:

Quarter	Trout Index	LIBOR
1	+5%	+1.5%
2	−1%	+1.4%
3	+2%	+1.3%
4	+1%	+1.6%

Calculate the cash flows that will take place between Dude and Smiley (on a net basis) over this one-year period.

14. A typical money management firm, particularly one specializing in stocks or bonds, invests in essentially the same portfolio for all of its clients, regardless of the clients' individual risk–return preferences. Speculate as to why money managers often operate in this manner. What can clients do to ensure that their portfolios reflect their own specific risk–return preferences?

15. Many investment management clients split their assets among a number of managers. Two rationales for this approach have been described as "diversification of judgment" and "diversification of style." Explain the meaning of these two terms.

Endnotes

1. One study found that a firm's stock price tended to move upward when analysts upgraded its coding and downward when analysts downgraded its coding. See Edwin J. Elton, Martin J. Gruber, and Seth Grossman, "Discrete Expectational Data and Portfolio Performance," *Journal of Finance,* 41, no. 3 (July 1986): 699–713.

2. This example is taken from William F. Sharpe, *Asset Allocation Tools* (Redwood City, CA: Scientific Press, 1987), p. 38.

3. If such a decision is made on behalf of the client (for example, by a trustee for one or more beneficiaries), the task is much more difficult, but a decision is still required.

4. Note that the reciprocal of risk tolerance, $1/\tau$, appears in Equation (17.1). This is necessitated by having risk on the horizontal axis in Figure 17.3. That is, the slope of a line is "rise over run" or the change in the Y-axis value for a given change in the X-axis value. Because the variable τ indicates variance per unit of expected return, its reciprocal must be used to indicate the slope of the indifference curve.

5. For more on estimating risk tolerance, see William F. Sharpe, *Asset Allocation Tools* (Redwood City, CA: Scientific Press, 1987): 33–39; also see the appendix to Chapter 23 of William F. Sharpe, Gordon J. Alexander, and Jeffery V. Bailey, *Investments* (Upper Saddle River, NJ: Prentice Hall, 1999).

6. The term u_i is also known as the expected utility of indifference curve i. It represents the level of satisfaction associated with all portfolios plotting on indifference curve i. For more about utility theory, indifference curves, and certainty equivalent returns, see Mark Kritzman, "...About Utility," *Financial Analysts Journal,* 48, no. 3 (May/June 1992): 17–20. In considering an investor's utility of wealth function, Chapter 7 discusses a closely related concept, the certainty equivalent of wealth.

7. An example of a tailored portfolio would be one consisting of stocks with high dividend yields. Such a portfolio might be purchased for a corporate investor because 80% of all dividends received by a corporate investor are exempt from corporate income tax.

8. For evidence suggesting that asset allocation is the most important decision an investor has to make, see Gary P. Brinson, L. Randolph Hood, and Gilbert L. Beebower, "Determinants of Portfolio Performance," *Financial Analysts Journal,* 42, no. 4 (July/August 1986): 39–44; and Gary P. Brinson, Brian D. Singer, and Gilbert L. Beebower, "Determinants of Portfolio

Performance II: An Update," *Financial Analysts Journal,* 47, no. 3 (May/June 1991): 40–48.

9. One study examined four prominent sources who provided recommendations for how investors should allocate their money and found that all of them recommended that the ratio of bonds to stocks should be higher for conservative investors relative to more aggressive investors. According to the separation theorem (see Chapter 10), this ratio should not change because, according to capital market theory, investors should purchase the market portfolio, which is a fixed blend of stocks and bonds, and then either invest or borrow money at the riskfree rate. Consequently, they refer to this as the "asset allocation puzzle." See Niko Canner, N. Gregory Mankiw, and David N. Weil, "An Asset Allocation Puzzle," *American Economic Review,* 87, no. 1 (March 1997): 181–191.

10. An intriguing description of how to use equilibrium models (like the CAPM, discussed in Chapter 10) and portfolio optimization techniques to make asset allocation decisions in a global setting is presented in Fischer Black and Robert Litterman, "Global Portfolio Optimization," *Financial Analysts Journal,* 48, no. 5 (September/October 1992): 28–43. Black and Litterman's model includes foreign currencies as one of the assets; see Chapter 26 for a discussion of foreign currencies and their risks.

11. The AMEX has available for purchase and sale two securities known as Standard & Poor's Depository Receipts (or "spiders") and Diamonds. These two securities are designed to represent ownership in the S&P 500 and the DJIA, respectively. Hence, they allow an investor to "buy" and "sell" either index, with the investor's gain or loss closely tracking the index's gain or loss. Similar securities exist for other U.S. stock market indices and the Morgan Stanley Capital International indices on various foreign countries. For more information on these unique securities, see the AMEX home page at <www.nasdaq-amex.com/mktofmkts/AMEX.stm>.

12. The discussion of swaps should not be confused with the discussion of bond swaps in Chapter 22.

13. For a discussion of many of the complicating features present in swaps, see Robert H. Litzenberger, "Swaps: Plain and Fanciful," *Journal of Finance,* 47, no. 3 (July 1992): 831–850. He notes that more than $\frac{2}{3}$ of swaps are of the "plain vanilla" variety and that the first major swap took place in 1981. The International Swaps and Derivatives Association (an industry association for participants in swaps and other privately negotiated derivatives transactions) reports on its Web site <www.isda.org>, that at June 30, 1999, the notional amount of swaps outstanding were $52.7 trillion.

14. Swaps can be compared to a series of forward contracts (forward contracts are discussed in Chapter 20). In this case, Ms. Bright has a swap position equivalent to having long positions in a series of equity forward contracts, whereas Mr. Gloom has short positions in these contracts. Consider the swap contract's first quarterly payment. Imagine that instead of the swap contract Ms. Bright had taken a long position in a forward contract. In general, forward contracts involve the exchange of a stated amount of cash for a given asset at a specified future date. Ms. Bright has agreed to pay $2 million one quarter later for delivery of an asset that can be thought of as shares in an S&P 500 index fund (the number of shares will be determined on the delivery date and will equal $100 million times the quarterly return on the S&P 500 divided by the fund's net asset value at the end of the quarter).

15. By convention, the counterparty that makes the fixed payments (Ms. Uppe) is known as the *swap buyer,* and the counterparty that makes the variable payments (Mr. Downe) is known as the *swap seller.* Hence the swap buyer "pays fixed and receives floating," and the swap seller "pays floating and receives fixed."

16. In this case, Ms. Uppe has a swap position equivalent to having long positions in a series of money market forward contracts, whereas Mr. Downe has short positions in these contracts. For example, the first quarterly payment is identical to what would happen if Ms. Uppe signed a forward contract agreeing to pay $2 million in exchange for the delivery of shares in a money market mutual fund (the number of shares will be determined on the delivery date and will equal $100 million times the LIBOR divided by the fund's net asset value at the end of the quarter). See endnote 14.

17. One interesting innovation is the *swaption,* a contract that combines an option (see Chapter 24) with an interest rate swap (or some other kind of swap). Call swaptions involve the right to "pay fixed and receive floating," and put swaptions involve the right to "pay floating and receive fixed." The notional principal, fixed rate, source of the floating rate, and swap life are all set when the swaption is created, as is the life of the swaption itself. If the owner of either type of swaption decides to exercise the option, then the writer (usually a swap bank) becomes the other counterparty to the swap. In return for this right, the owner pays the writer a premium. Owners of calls exercise their options if interest rates rise because then the fixed payment cash outflows will be less than the floating rate cash inflows. Conversely, put owners will exercise their options if interest rates fall. See David R. Smith, "A Simple Method for Pricing Interest Rate Swaptions," *Financial Analysts Journal,* 47, no. 3 (May/June 1991): 72–76.

18. Whether or not split funding is used, a client who feels a manager is "betting" too much may place limits on the manager's holdings in individual securities. There are other kinds of restrictions frequently imposed on managers, such as limits on the holdings of bonds versus stocks, or on the amount invested in a single industry. Many times these restrictions are stated relative to the manager's assigned benchmark.

19. Sometimes these objectives and constraints are stated vaguely; in other cases they are specified precisely.

CHAPTER

Portfolio Performance Evaluation

An investor who pays someone to actively manage his or her portfolio has every right to know how the investments are performing. This information can be used to alter the constraints placed on the manager, the investment objectives given to the manager, or the amount of money allocated to the manager. Perhaps more important, by evaluating performance in specified ways, a client can forcefully communicate his or her interests to the investment manager and possibly affect the way in which his or her portfolio is managed in the future. Moreover, an investment manager, by evaluating his or her own performance, can identify sources of strengths or weaknesses. Although the previous chapter indicated that portfolio performance evaluation was the last stage of the investment management process, it is actually part of a continuing operation, serving as a feedback and control mechanism that makes the process more effective.

Superior performance in the past may have resulted from good luck, in which case such performance should not be expected to continue in the future. On the other hand, such performance may have resulted from the actions of a highly skilled investment manager and hence can be expected to continue in the future. In comparison, inferior performance in the past may have been the result of bad luck, but it may also have resulted from excessive turnover, high management fees, or other costs associated with an unskilled investment manager. These possibilities suggest that the first task in performance evaluation is to try to determine whether past performance was superior or inferior. The second task is to try to determine whether such performance was because of skill or luck. Unfortunately, there are difficulties associated with carrying out both of these tasks. Accordingly, this chapter presents certain methods that have been advocated and used for evaluating portfolio performance and a discussion of the difficulties encountered with their use.

18.1 Measures of Return

Portfolio performance is frequently evaluated over at least four years, with returns measured for a number of periods within the interval—typically monthly or quarterly. This approach provides a fairly adequate sample size for statistical evaluation (for example, if returns are measured quarterly for four years, there will be 16 observations). Sometimes, however, a shorter time interval must be used to avoid examining a portfolio's returns that were earned by a different investment manager. The examples that follow involve 16 quarterly observations for tractability. In practice, one would prefer monthly observations if only four years were to be analyzed.

In the simplest situation, the client neither deposits nor withdraws money from the portfolio during a time period. As a result, calculation of the portfolio's periodic return is straightforward. All that is required is that the market value of the portfolio be known at two points in time—the beginning and the end of the period. In general, the market value of a portfolio at a point in time is determined by adding the market values of all the securities held at that particular time. For example, the value of a common stock portfolio at the beginning of a period is calculated by (1) noting the market price per share of each stock held in the portfolio at that time, (2) multiplying each of these stock prices by the corresponding number of shares held, and (3) adding up the resulting products. The market value of the portfolio at the end of the period is calculated in the same way, only using end-of-period prices and shares.

With the beginning and ending portfolio values in hand, the return on the portfolio (r) can be calculated by subtracting the beginning value (V_b) from the ending value (V_e) and then dividing the difference by the beginning value:

$$r = \frac{V_e - V_b}{V_b} \qquad\qquad \textbf{(18.1)}$$

For example, if a portfolio has a market value of $40 million at the beginning of a quarter and a market value of $46 million at the end of the quarter, then the return on this portfolio for the quarter would be 15% [= ($46 million − $40 million)/$40 million].

Measurement of portfolio returns is complicated by the fact that the client may add to or withdraw money from the portfolio. If the client does either, the percentage change in the market value of the portfolio during a period will not be an accurate measurement of the portfolio's return during that period. Note that dividends and interest payments to the portfolio do not cause any difficulties in using Equation (18.1). However, if these payments are made directly to the client and do not remain in the portfolio, then they are like withdrawals, necessitating the use of a different method of measuring returns.

For example, consider a portfolio that at the beginning of a quarter has a market value of $100 million. Just before the end of the quarter the client deposits $5 million with the investment manager; at the end of the quarter the market value of the portfolio is $103 million. If the quarterly return was measured without consideration of the $5 million deposit, the reported return would be 3% [= ($103 million − $100 million)/ $100 million]. However, this return would be incorrect because $5 million of the ending $103 million market value did not result from the investment actions of the manager. An accurate measure of the quarterly return that takes into account the deposit would be −2% {= [($103 million − $5 million) − $100 million]/$100 million}.

Identification of exactly *when* deposits or withdrawals occur is important in accurately measuring portfolio returns. If a deposit or withdrawal occurs just *before* the end of the period, then the return on the portfolio should be calculated by adjusting the ending market value of the portfolio. In the case of a deposit, the ending value should be reduced by the dollar amount (as was done in the previous example). In the case of a withdrawal, the ending value should be increased by the dollar amount.

If a deposit or withdrawal occurs just *after* the start of the period, then the return on the portfolio should be calculated by adjusting the beginning market value of the portfolio. In the case of a deposit, the beginning value should be increased by the dollar amount. In the case of a withdrawal, the beginning value should be decreased by the dollar amount. For example, if the $5 million deposit in the earlier example had been received just after the start of the quarter, the return for the quarter should be calculated as −1.90% {= [$103 million − ($100 million + $5 million)]/($100 million + $5 million)}.

18.1.1   DOLLAR-WEIGHTED RETURNS

dollar-weighted return

When deposits or withdrawals occur *between* the beginning and end of the period, the calculations are more difficult. One method that has been used for calculating a portfolio's return in this situation is the **dollar-weighted return,** which is similar to the internal rate of return method used in Chapter 15 to value common stocks. In general, the beginning-of-period value of the portfolio is set equal to the discounted value of all cash flows associated with the portfolio as well as the end-of-period value. The resulting equation is solved for the discount rate, which is known as the dollar-weighted return. For example, if the $5 million deposit in the earlier example was made in the middle of the quarter, the dollar-weighted return would be calculated by solving the following equation for r:

$$\$100 \text{ million} = \frac{-\$5 \text{ million}}{(1+r)} + \frac{\$103 \text{ million}}{(1+r)^2} \tag{18.2}$$

The solution to this equation, $r = -.98\%$, is a semiquarterly rate of return. It can be converted into a quarterly rate of return by adding 1 to it, squaring this value, and subtracting 1 from the square, resulting in a quarterly return of -1.95% $\{= [1 + (-.0098)]^2 - 1\}$.[1]

18.1.2   TIME-WEIGHTED RETURNS

time-weighted return

Alternatively, the **time-weighted return** on a portfolio can be calculated when cash flows occur between the beginning and end of the period. This method uses the market value of the portfolio just before each cash flow occurs. In the earlier example, assume that in the middle of the quarter the portfolio had a market value of $96 million, so that right after the $5 million deposit the market value was $101 million (= $96 million + $5 million). In this case, the return for the first half of the quarter would be -4% $[= (\$96 \text{ million} - \$100 \text{ million})/\$100 \text{ million}]$, and the return for the second half of the quarter would be 1.98% $[= (\$103 \text{ million} - \$101 \text{ million})/\$101 \text{ million}]$. These two semiquarterly returns can be converted into a quarterly return by adding 1 to each return, multiplying the sums, and subtracting 1 from the product. In the example, this procedure results in a quarterly return of -2.1% $\{= [(1 - .04) \times (1 + .0198)] - 1\}$.

18.1.3   COMPARING DOLLAR-WEIGHTED AND TIME-WEIGHTED RETURNS

Which method is preferable for calculating the return on a portfolio? In the example given here, the dollar-weighted return was -1.95%, whereas the time-weighted return was -2.1%, suggesting that the difference between the two methods may not be important. Although this may be true in certain situations, the differences can be quite large, in which case the time-weighted return method usually is preferable.

Consider a hypothetical portfolio that starts a quarter with a market value of $50 million. In the middle of the quarter, the portfolio's market value falls to $25 million, at which point the client deposits $25 million with the investment manager. At the end of the quarter the portfolio has a market value of $100 million. The semiquarterly dollar-weighted return for this portfolio is equal to the value of r in the following equation:

$$\$50 \text{ million} = \frac{-\$25 \text{ million}}{(1+r)} + \frac{\$100 \text{ million}}{(1+r)^2} \tag{18.3}$$

Solving this equation for r results in a value of 18.6%, which equals a quarterly dollar-weighted return of 40.66% $[= (1.186)^2 - 1]$. However, its quarterly time-weighted return is 0% because its return for the first half of the quarter was −50% and its return for the second half of the quarter was 100% [note that $(1 - .5) \times (1 + 1) - 1 = 0\%$].

Comparing these two returns—40.66% and 0%—indicates that a sizable difference exists. However, the time-weighted return of 0% is more meaningful for performance evaluation than the dollar-weighted return of 40.66%. The reason can be seen by considering the return during the entire quarter on each dollar that was in the portfolio at the start of the quarter. Each dollar lost half of its value during the first half of the quarter, but then the remaining half-dollar doubled its value during the second half. Consequently, a dollar at the beginning was worth a dollar at the end, suggesting that a return of 0% on the portfolio is a more accurate measure of the investment manager's performance than the 40.66% figure.

In general, the dollar-weighted return method of measuring a portfolio's return for purposes of evaluation is inappropriate because the return is strongly influenced by the size and timing of the cash flows (namely, deposits and withdrawals), over which the investment manager typically has no control. In the example, the dollar-weighted return was 40.66% because the client fortuitously made a big deposit just before the portfolio appreciated rapidly in value. Thus, the 40.66% return figure results at least partly from the actions of the client, not of the manager.

18.1.4 ANNUALIZING RETURNS

The previous discussion focused on calculating quarterly returns. Such returns may be added or multiplied to obtain an annual measure of return. For example, if the returns in the first, second, third, and fourth quarters of a given year are denoted r_1, r_2, r_3, and r_4, respectively, then the annual return can be calculated by adding the four figures:

$$\text{Annual return} = r_1 + r_2 + r_3 + r_4 \qquad \textbf{(18.4)}$$

Alternatively, the annual return also could be calculated by adding 1 to each quarterly return, then multiplying the four figures, and finally subtracting 1 from the resulting product:

$$\text{Annual return} = [(1 + r_1)(1 + r_2)(1 + r_3)(1 + r_4)] - 1 \qquad \textbf{(18.5)}$$

This method is more accurate because it reflects the value that one dollar would have at the end of the year if it were invested at the beginning of the year and grew *with compounding* at the rate of r_1 for the first quarter, r_2 for the second quarter, r_3 for the third quarter, and r_4 for the fourth quarter. That is, it assumes reinvestment of both the dollar and any earnings at the end of each quarter.

18.2 Making Relevant Comparisons

The essential idea behind performance evaluation is to compare the returns obtained by the investment manager through active management with the returns that could have been obtained for the client if one or more appropriate alternative portfolios had been chosen for investment. The reason for this comparison is straightforward: Performance should be evaluated on a relative basis, not on an absolute basis.

As an example, consider a client who is told that his or her portfolio, invested in a diversified common stock portfolio of average risk, had a return of 20% last year. Does this return suggest superior or inferior performance? If a broad stock market index (such as the Wilshire 5000) went up by 10% last year, then the return on the portfolio suggests superior performance and is good news. However, if the index went up by 30% last year, then the return on the portfolio suggests inferior performance and is bad news. The returns on "similar" portfolios are needed for comparison in order to infer whether the manager's performance is superior or inferior.

benchmark portfolios

Such comparison portfolios are often referred to as **benchmark portfolios.** In selecting them, the client should be certain that they are relevant, feasible, and known in advance, meaning that they should represent alternative portfolios that could have been chosen for investment instead of the portfolio being evaluated. That is, the benchmark should reflect the objectives of the client. Hence, if the objective is to earn superior returns by investing in small stocks, then the S&P 500 would be an inappropriate benchmark. Instead, an index such as the Russell 2000 would be more suitable. *Return* is a key aspect of performance, of course, but the portfolio's exposure to *risk* must also be taken into account. The choice of benchmark portfolios should be restricted to portfolios perceived to have similar levels of risk, thereby allowing a direct comparison of returns.

Figure 18.1 illustrates a comparison for a hypothetical common stock (or "equity") portfolio referred to as Fund 07632. Fund 07632's performance for each year is represented by a diamond. The hypothetical comparison portfolios are other common stock portfolios that are represented by the box surrounding the diamond (hence such a representation is known as a *box plot* or a *floating bar chart*). The top and bottom lines of the box indicate the returns of the 5th and 95th percentile comparison portfolios, respectively. Similarly, the top and bottom dashed lines represent the 25th and 75th percentiles, respectively. The solid line in the middle represents the median (that is, the 50th

FIGURE 18.1 Comparing Returns of Equity Portfolios

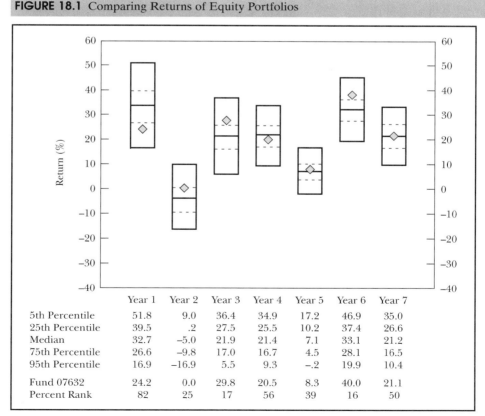

	Year 1	Year 2	Year 3	Year 4	Year 5	Year 6	Year 7
5th Percentile	51.8	9.0	36.4	34.9	17.2	46.9	35.0
25th Percentile	39.5	.2	27.5	25.5	10.2	37.4	26.6
Median	32.7	−5.0	21.9	21.4	7.1	33.1	21.2
75th Percentile	26.6	−9.8	17.0	16.7	4.5	28.1	16.5
95th Percentile	16.9	−16.9	5.5	9.3	−.2	19.9	10.4
Fund 07632	24.2	0.0	29.8	20.5	8.3	40.0	21.1
Percent Rank	82	25	17	56	39	16	50

Source: Adapted from SEI, *Funds Evaluation Service.*

percentile) portfolio. This particular evaluation technique presumes that the comparison portfolios exhibit risk similar to Fund 07632 and that they represent feasible alternatives for Fund 07632's owner. Failing to meet these conditions (as is often the case in such peer group comparisons) will generally invalidate the performance evaluation.

Alternatively, risk may be incorporated into the analysis so that a single measure of performance takes both return and risk into account. This method allows benchmark portfolios of varying degrees of risk to be compared with the portfolio being evaluated. One such approach compares the portfolio with a market index that is constructed from the same set of securities that the portfolio manager evaluates in making investments. Hence, it is useful to understand just how market indices are constructed, which is discussed next.

18.3   Market Indices

market index

What did the market do yesterday? How much would an unmanaged common stock portfolio have returned last year? Such questions are often answered by examining the performance of a **market index.** Figure 18.2 shows stock market indices that are commonly referenced. These indices differ from one another with respect to (1) the securities included in the index and (2) the method used in calculating the value of the index.[2]

In order to understand how some of the most popular indices are computed, consider a simple example in which the market index is based on two stocks, referred to as *A* and *B*. At the end of day 0, their closing prices are, respectively, $10 and $20 per share. At this time *A* has 1,500 shares outstanding and *B* has 2,000 shares outstanding.

18.3.1   PRICE WEIGHTING

price weighting

There are three weighting methods that are most often used in computing a market index. The first method, involving **price weighting,** begins by summing the prices of the stocks that are included in the index and ends by dividing this sum by a constant (the "divisor") in order to calculate an average price. If the index includes only stocks *A* and *B* and was started on day 0, the divisor equals the number of stocks in the average, 2. Thus, on day 0 the average price would be 15 $[= (10 + 20)/2]$, which denotes the level of the index. The divisor is adjusted thereafter whenever there is a stock split in order to avoid giving misleading indications of the "market's" direction (it is also adjusted in a similar manner whenever the composition of the index changes, meaning whenever one stock is substituted for another).

For example, assume that on day 1, *B* splits two-for-one and closes at $11 per share, while *A* closes at $13. In this situation, it is clear that the market has risen because both stocks have a higher price than on day 0 after adjusting *B* for the split. If nothing were done in computing the index, its value on day 1 would be 12 $[= (13 + 11)/2]$, a drop of 20% $[= (12 - 15)/15]$ from day 0 that incorrectly suggests that the market went down on day 1. In reality, the index went up to 17.5 $\{= [13 + (11 \times 2)]/2\}$, a gain of 16.67% $[= (17.5 - 15)/15]$.

A stock split is accounted for in a price-weighted index by adjusting the divisor whenever a split takes place. In the example, the divisor is adjusted by examining the index on day 1, the day of the split. More specifically, the following equation would be solved for the unknown divisor *d:*

$$\frac{13 + 11}{d} = 17.5 \tag{18.6}$$

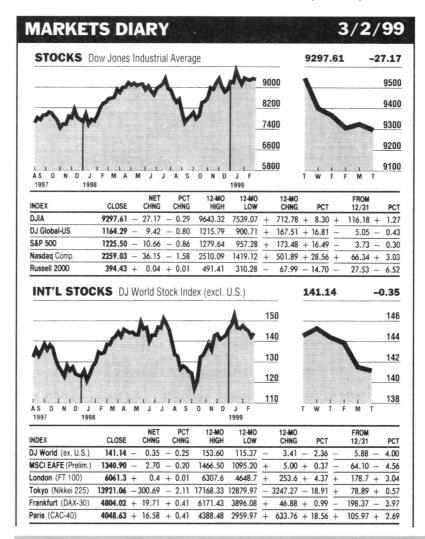

FIGURE 18.2 Stock Market Indices Published in *The Wall Street Journal,* March 3, 1999

Source: Reprinted by permission of *The Wall Street Journal,* Dow Jones & Company, Inc., March 3, 1999, pp. C1, C2. All rights reserved worldwide.

The value of *d* that solves this equation is 1.37. The new divisor continues in use after day 1 until there is another split or index composition change, when it will again be recalculated.

If it is desired to have the index begin at a given level, such as 100 on day 0, then updating it is straightforward. First, the percentage change in average price is calculated. In the example, this percentage change was 16.67%. Second the percentage change is multiplied by the previous day's index value to determine the change in the index. In the example, the index level on day 0 was 100, so the change from day 0 to day 1 would be 16.67 (= 16.67% × 100), resulting in a level on day 1 of 116.67. This step is equivalent to dividing the average price on day 1 ($17.50) by the average price on

STOCK MARKET DATA BANK 3/2/99

MAJOR INDEXES

| — †12-MO — | | | DAILY | | | NET | | †12-MO | | FROM | |
HIGH	LOW		HIGH	LOW	CLOSE	CHG	% CHG	CHG	% CHG	12/31	% CHG
DOW JONES AVERAGES											
9643.32	7539.07	30 Industrials	9421.22	9268.00	9297.61	− 27.17	− 0.29	+ 712.78	+ 8.30	+ 116.18	+ 1.27
3686.02	2345.00	20 Transportation	3301.37	3226.01	x3279.06	+ 53.20	+ 1.65	− 166.26	− 4.83	+ 129.75	+ 4.12
320.51	271.67	15 Utilities	293.93	290.13	290.72	− 0.30	− 0.10	+ 18.25	+ 6.70	− 21.58	− 6.91
2995.83	2411.00	65 Composite	2915.89	2875.14	x2883.14	+ 4.84	+ 0.17	+ 109.88	+ 3.96	+ 12.31	+ 0.43
1215.79	900.71	DJ Global-US	1185.70	1160.87	1164.29	− 9.42	− 0.80	+ 167.51	+ 16.81	− 5.05	− 0.43
NEW YORK STOCK EXCHANGE											
611.06	477.20	Composite	591.07	581.34	582.94	− 2.49	− 0.43	+ 36.05	+ 6.59	− 12.87	− 2.16
761.48	593.49	Industrials	733.09	720.89	722.97	− 3.19	− 0.44	+ 44.17	+ 6.51	− 20.68	− 2.78
460.50	348.81	Utilities	434.95	425.69	426.40	− 5.22	− 1.21	+ 74.50	+ 21.17	− 19.54	− 4.38
537.19	351.13	Transportation	480.19	474.46	477.18	+ 2.52	+ 0.53	− 11.68	− 2.39	− 5.20	− 1.08
599.15	399.19	Finance	535.28	527.99	529.62	+ 0.22	+ 0.04	+ 5.00	+ 0.95	+ 8.20	+ 1.57
STANDARD & POOR'S INDEXES											
1279.64	957.28	500 Index	1248.31	1221.87	1225.50	− 10.66	− 0.86	+ 173.48	+ 16.49	− 3.73	− 0.30
1551.65	1134.73	Industrials	1496.08	1462.77	1466.86	− 15.45	− 1.04	+ 240.81	+ 19.64	− 12.30	− 0.83
267.38	229.71	Utilities	238.44	235.22	235.73	+ 0.09	+ 0.04	+ 2.61	+ 1.12	− 23.89	− 9.20
395.13	275.93	400 MidCap	363.01	357.81	359.82	+ 2.01	+ 0.56	+ 5.29	+ 1.49	− 32.49	− 8.28
206.18	128.70	600 SmallCap	162.36	160.47	160.74	+ 0.27	+ 0.17	− 33.47	− 17.23	− 16.63	− 9.38
268.68	200.77	1500 Index	261.41	256.16	256.88	− 1.89	− 0.73	+ 31.08	+ 13.76	− 3.17	− 1.22
NASDAQ STOCK MARKET											
2510.09	1419.12	Composite	2317.57	2257.07	2259.03	− 36.15	− 1.58	+ 501.89	+ 28.56	+ 66.34	+ 3.03
2130.93	1126.83	Nasdaq 100	1953.83	1886.36	1888.66	− 49.04	− 2.53	+ 712.94	+ 60.64	+ 52.65	+ 2.87
1408.56	882.40	Industrials	1330.15	1304.30	1305.49	− 4.68	− 0.36	+ 0.93	+ 0.07	+ 1.24	+ 0.10
1945.34	1346.58	Insurance	1836.54	1806.37	1820.09	+ 13.46	+ 0.75	− 36.70	− 1.98	+ 23.30	+ 1.30
2297.71	1486.32	Banks	1789.45	1779.69	1780.95	− 0.15	− 0.01	− 352.24	− 16.51	− 57.05	− 3.10
1374.84	690.19	Computer	1210.00	1162.51	1164.77	− 35.22	− 2.94	+ 418.69	+ 56.12	+ 30.58	+ 2.70
586.92	310.74	Telecommunications	573.32	562.37	562.45	− 3.07	− 0.54	+ 203.42	+ 56.66	+ 61.54	+ 12.29
OTHERS											
753.67	563.75	Amex Composite	703.97	698.29	699.21	+ 0.92	+ 0.13	− 9.76	− 1.38	+ 10.22	+ 1.48
665.64	494.35	Russell 1000	649.76	636.59	638.30	− 4.90	− 0.76	+ 84.08	+ 15.17	− 4.57	− 0.71
491.41	310.28	Russell 2000	398.30	394.01	394.43	+ 0.04	+ 0.01	− 67.99	− 14.70	− 27.53	− 6.52
687.11	509.20	Russell 3000	667.96	654.90	656.57	− 4.67	− 0.71	+ 71.89	+ 12.30	− 7.70	− 1.16
508.39	346.66	Value-Line(geom.)	410.03	405.33	406.01	− 0.80	− 0.20	− 76.42	− 15.84	− 31.14	− 7.12
11724.83	8620.80	Wilshire 5000	...	...	11212.49	− 65.09	− 0.58	+ 1187.34	+ 11.84	− 105.10	− 0.93

†-Based on comparable trading day in preceding year.

FIGURE 18.2 Continued

the beginning date ($15) and then multiplying the result by the index's level on the beginning day (100). Mathematically the formula is

$$I_t = I_0 \times \frac{AP_t}{AP_0} \tag{18.7}$$

where AP_t denotes the average price on day t and I_t denotes the index level on day t.

The Dow Jones Industrial Average (DJIA), one of the most widely followed indices, is a price-weighted index of 30 stocks that generally represent large mature firms. Other Dow Jones Averages, for example one involving 20 transportation stocks and another involving 15 utility stocks, are similarly calculated. Historical data on the Averages, including quarterly dividends and earnings figures, are published from time to time in *Barron's* and other periodicals. It should be noted that Dow Jones also calculates stock market indices for various countries and regions of the world. However, these are value-weighted indices, which are discussed next.

18.3.2   VALUE WEIGHTING

value weighting

A second weighting method is known as **value weighting** or capitalization weighting. In this method, the prices of the stocks in the index are multiplied by their respective number of shares outstanding and then added to arrive at a figure equal to the aggregate market value for that day. This figure is then divided by the corresponding figure for the day the index was started, with the resulting value multiplied by an arbitrarily determined beginning index value.

Continuing with the example, assume that the start-up day for the index is day 0 and that the index will be assigned a beginning value of 100. First, note that the aggregate market value on day 0 is equal to $55,000 [= ($10 × 1,500) + ($20 × 2,000)]. Next, note that the aggregate market value on day 1 is equal to $63,500 [= ($13 × 1,500) + ($11 × 4,000)]. Dividing $63,500 by $55,000 and then multiplying the result by 100 gives the index value for day 1 of 115.45 [= ($63,500/$55,000) × 100]. Thus, the market would be reported as having risen by 15.45% [= (115.45 − 100)/100] from day 0 to day 1. No special procedures are needed to handle stock splits because the resulting increased number of shares for a company is automatically used after a split in calculating its market value. In general, the total market value of the securities in the index on day t (MV_t) is divided by the total market value on the beginning date (MV_0) and then multiplied by the index's level on the beginning day in order to get its value on day t. Mathematically the formula is

$$I_t = I_0 \times \frac{MV_t}{MV_0} \tag{18.8}$$

The Standard & Poor's 500 (the S&P 500), widely used by institutional investors, is a value-weighted average of 500 large-sized stocks. Standard & Poor's also computes value-weighted indices for industrial, transportation, utility, and financial stocks as well as other size-based indices. Industry indices are also calculated. Values for all indices, along with quarterly data on dividends, earnings, and sales, may be found in Standard & Poor's *Analysts' Handbook* (annual), *Trade and Securities Statistics* (annual), and *Analysts' Handbook Supplement* (monthly).

More comprehensive value-weighted indices for U.S. stocks are computed by other organizations. The NYSE publishes a composite index of all stocks listed on that exchange, as well as four subindices (industrials, utilities, transportation, and finance). The AMEX computes an index of its stocks. The National Association of Securities Dealers (NASD) computes the Nasdaq Composite Index based on the market value of more than 5,000 Nasdaq-listed stocks. In addition to this composite index, NASD calculates indices for various economic sectors such as industrials, banks, transportation, and utilities. NASD also publishes indices that are based on just those stocks in their National Market System (the previously mentioned NASD indices are based on both NMS and non-NMS stocks). One of the most popular NASD indices is the Nasdaq 100, which is based on 100 of the largest nonfinancial NMS stocks.

The broadest value-weighted index is calculated by Wilshire Associates. Their index, known as the Wilshire 5000 Equity Index, is based on all stocks listed on the New York and American Stock Exchanges plus those "actively traded over-the-counter." The Russell 1000, 2000, and 3000 are also broad value-weighted indices, covering the largest 1,000 U.S. stocks; the next 2,000; and the sum of the two. Various value-weighted U.S. stock indices are also produced to represent certain investment styles, as were discussed in Chapter 13. For example, the S&P 500 is split into a value stock index and a growth stock index. Stocks in the S&P 500 are first ordered by their book-value-to-market-value (BV/MV) ratios. The index is then divided into two segments with equal aggregate market value; the low BV/MV stocks constitute the S&P/BARRA 500 Growth Index, and the high BV/MV stocks constitute the S&P/BARRA 500 Value Index. A similar procedure is used to construct growth and value indices for Standard & Poor's middle-capitalization stocks (the S&P 400) and small-capitalization stocks (the S&P 600).

In terms of international indices, *Morgan Stanley Capital International Perspective* publishes value-weighted indices using various combinations of more than 1,000 stocks from many different countries, resulting in a "world market index" (these, and other international indices, are discussed in Chapter 26). Dow Jones calculates various value-weighted indices of more than 30 countries, various regions of the world, and a world index. Levels of many of these indices are published weekly in *Barron's* and daily in *The Wall Street Journal.*

18.3.3 EQUAL WEIGHTING

equal weighting

price relatives

The third method of weighting is known as **equal weighting.** This index is computed daily by multiplying the level of the index on the previous day by the arithmetic mean of the daily **price relatives** (today's price divided by yesterday's price) of the relevant stocks in the index. For example, the value of the index consisting of A and B on day 1 would be calculated by first determining the price relatives to be equal to 1.3 $(= \frac{13}{10})$ for A and 1.1 $[= (11 \times 2)/20]$ for B. Note that an adjustment was made in calculating the price relative for B because of its stock split; the post-split price of 11 was multiplied by 2, the split ratio.

Once the price relatives have been determined, their arithmetic mean can be calculated as

$$(1.3 + 1.1)/2 = 1.20$$

If the value of the index on day 0 was 100, then the value on day 1 would be reported as 120 $(= 100 \times 1.20)$, an increase of 20% $(= 1.20 - 1)$. (When the index is created, its value on that day can be set at any arbitrary starting value, such as 100.) The Value Line Composite (Arithmetic) Index, based on more than 1,500 stocks, is prepared in this manner.

18.3.4 GEOMETRIC MEAN

Value Line also prepares a popular index that does not involve price weighting, value weighting, or equal weighting. This index is computed daily by multiplying the previous day's index by the *geometric mean* of the daily price relatives of the relevant stocks in the index. It is referred to as the Value Line Composite (Geometric) Index and is based on the same stocks that are used in the arithmetic version of the index.

In the example, the geometric index for day 1 is calculated in the following manner. First, the geometric mean of the daily price relatives of stocks A and B is calculated:

$$(1.3 \times 1.1)^{1/2} = 1.1958$$

Second, given that the value of the index on the previous day (day 0) was 100, then the value on day 1 would be reported as 119.58 $(= 100 \times 1.1958)$, an increase of 19.58% $(= 1.1958 - 1)$. More generally, if there are N stocks in the index, then the geometric index is calculated by multiplying their price relatives, taking the Nth root of the resulting product, and multiplying the level of the index on the previous day by this root.

In summary, four types of indices have been presented. Investors often use these indices interchangeably when they refer to how "the market" has done. However, the indices can give notably different answers. In the example, the market was calculated to have risen by either 16.67%, 15.45%, 20%, or 19.58%, depending on the index used. In practice, most professional money managers use a value-weighted index such as the S&P 500 as the barometer of the stock market because such an index, by weighting larger companies more heavily than smaller companies, represents the performance of the average dollar invested in the part of the market being analyzed.

18.4 Risk-Adjusted Measures of Performance

Once the periodic returns for a portfolio during a time interval (say, quarterly returns for four years) have been measured, the next step is to determine whether these returns represent superior or inferior performance. This step requires an estimate of the portfolio's risk level during the time interval. Two kinds of risk can be estimated: (1) the portfolio's market (or systematic) risk, measured by its beta; and (2) the portfolio's total risk, measured by its standard deviation.

It is important to analyze risk appropriately. The key issue is to determine the impact of the portfolio on the client's overall level of risk. If the client has many other assets, then the market risk of the portfolio provides the relevant measure of the portfolio's impact on the client's overall level of risk. If, however, the portfolio provides the client's sole support, then its total risk is the relevant measure of risk. Risk-adjusted performance evaluation is generally based on one of these two viewpoints, taking either market risk or total risk into consideration.

Assume that there are T time periods in the time interval (for example, $T = 16$ when there are four years of quarterly data), and let r_{pt} denote the return on the portfolio during period t. The average return on the portfolio, denoted ar_p, is simply

$$ar_p = \frac{\sum_{t=1}^{T} r_{pt}}{T} \tag{18.9}$$

Once ar_p, has been calculated, the *ex post* (that is, "after the fact," or historical) standard deviation σ_p can be calculated as

$$\sigma_p = \left[\frac{\sum_{t=1}^{T} (r_{pt} - ar_p)^2}{T - 1} \right]^{1/2} \tag{18.10}$$

This estimate of the portfolio's standard deviation indicates the amount of total risk that the portfolio had during the time interval.[3] It can be compared directly with the standard deviations of other portfolios, as illustrated in Figure 18.3. (This figure is to be interpreted in the same manner as Figure 18.1.)

The returns of a portfolio may also be compared with those of a substitute for the market portfolio, such as the S&P 500, to determine the portfolio's *ex post* beta during
excess return   the time interval. With the **excess return** on the portfolio during period t denoted as

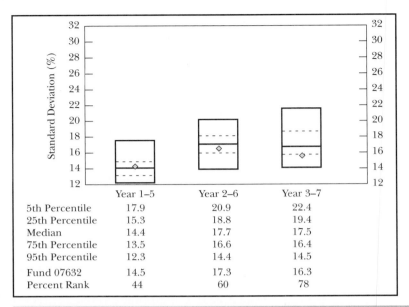

	Year 1–5	Year 2–6	Year 3–7
5th Percentile	17.9	20.9	22.4
25th Percentile	15.3	18.8	19.4
Median	14.4	17.7	17.5
75th Percentile	13.5	16.6	16.4
95th Percentile	12.3	14.4	14.5
Fund 07632	14.5	17.3	16.3
Percent Rank	44	60	78

FIGURE 18.3 Comparing Standard Deviations of Equity Portfolios

Source: Adapted from SEI, *Funds Evaluation Service.*

$er_{pt} = r_{pt} - r_{ft}$ and the excess return on the S&P 500 (or some other market index) during period t denoted as $er_{Mt} = r_{Mt} - r_{ft}$, this beta can be estimated as follows:

$$\beta_p = \frac{\left(T \sum_{t=1}^{T} er_{Mt} er_{pt} \right) - \left(\sum_{t=1}^{T} er_{pt} \sum_{t=1}^{T} er_{Mt} \right)}{\left(T \sum_{t=1}^{T} er_{Mt}^2 \right) - \left(\sum_{t=1}^{T} er_{Mt} \right)^2} \tag{18.11}$$

This estimate of the portfolio's beta indicates the amount of market risk that the portfolio had during the time interval.[4] It can be compared directly with the betas of other portfolios, as illustrated in Figure 18.4. (This figure is to be interpreted in the same manner as Figures 18.1 and 18.3.)

Although a portfolio's return and a measure of its risk can be compared individually with those of other portfolios, as in Figures 18.1, 18.3, and 18.4, it is often not clear how the portfolio performed on a risk-adjusted basis relative to the other portfolios. For the fund shown in the figures, the average percentile rank for the portfolio's return during years 3 through 7 is 36 $[= (17 + 56 + 39 + 16 + 50)/5]$. During the same period, its standard deviation put it in the 78th percentile rank. How would a client who is concerned with total risk interpret these percentile ranks? In the case of the return, the portfolio was slightly above average. In terms of standard deviation, it was less risky than approximately three-quarters of the other portfolios. Overall, this result suggests that the portfolio did better on a risk-adjusted basis than the others, but it does not give the client a clear and precise sense of how much better.

Such a sense can be conveyed by certain CAPM-based measures of portfolio performance. Each one of these measures provides an estimate of a portfolio's risk-adjusted performance, thereby allowing the client to see how the portfolio performed relative to other portfolios and relative to the market. They are presented next.

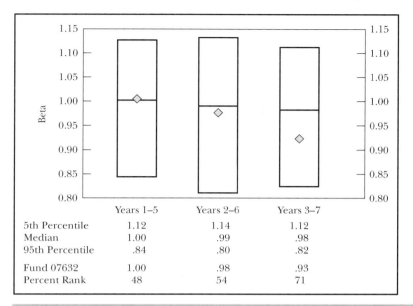

	Years 1–5	Years 2–6	Years 3–7
5th Percentile	1.12	1.14	1.12
Median	1.00	.99	.98
95th Percentile	.84	.80	.82
Fund 07632	1.00	.98	.93
Percent Rank	48	54	71

FIGURE 18.4 Comparing Betas of Equity Portfolios

Source: Adapted from SEI, *Funds Evaluation Service.*

18.4.1   *EX POST* CHARACTERISTIC LINES

Over a time interval, an *ex post* security market line (SML) can be estimated by determining the average riskfree rate and market return:

$$ar_f = \frac{\sum_{t=1}^{T} r_{ft}}{T} \tag{18.12}$$

$$ar_M = \frac{\sum_{t=1}^{T} r_{Mt}}{T} \tag{18.13}$$

Once these averages have been calculated, the *ex post* SML is simply the equation of the line going through the points $(0, ar_f)$ and $(1, ar_M)$. The return given by the *ex post* SML for a portfolio with a beta of β_p can be used as a benchmark return, ar_{bp}, for that portfolio:

$$ar_{bp} = ar_f + (ar_M - ar_f)\beta_p \tag{18.14}$$

Panel (a) of Table 18.1 presents an example using the quarterly returns for the S&P 500 during a 16-quarter time interval, along with corresponding returns on 90-day Treasury bills. Equations (18.12) and (18.13) show that the average riskfree return and market return were, respectively, 2.23% and 4.88%. These values can be inserted into Equation (18.14) to obtain the *ex post* SML for this time interval:

$$ar_{bp} = 2.23\% + (4.88\% - 2.23\%)\beta_p \tag{18.15}$$

$$= 2.23\% + 2.65\%\beta_p$$

Thus, after a portfolio's *ex post* beta has been estimated and this value entered on the right-hand side of Equation (18.15), a benchmark return for the portfolio can be

TABLE 18.1   The *Ex Post* Characteristic Line for the First Fund

(a) DATA

Quarter	Treasury Bill Return	First Fund Return	First Fund Excess Return	S&P 500 Return	S&P 500 Excess Return
1	2.97%	−8.77%	−11.74%	−5.86%	−8.83%
2	3.06	−6.03	−9.09	−2.94	−6.00
3	2.85	14.14	11.29	13.77	10.92
4	1.88	24.96	23.08	14.82	12.94
5	1.90	3.71	1.81	11.91	10.01
6	2.00	10.65	8.65	11.55	9.55
7	2.22	−.22	−2.44	−.78	−3.00
8	2.11	.27	−1.84	.02	−2.09
9	2.16	−3.08	−5.24	−2.52	−4.68
10	2.34	−6.72	−9.06	−1.85	−4.19
11	2.44	8.58	6.14	8.73	6.29
12	2.40	1.15	−1.25	1.63	−.77
13	1.89	7.87	5.98	10.82	8.93
14	1.94	5.92	3.98	7.24	5.30
15	1.72	−3.10	−4.82	−2.78	−4.50
16	1.75	13.61	11.86	14.36	12.61

(b) CALCULATIONS[a]

Quarter	First Fund Excess Returns Y (1)	S&P 500 Excess Returns X (2)	Y^2 (3)	X^2 (4)	$Y \times X$ (5)
1	−11.74%	−8.83%	137.83	77.93	103.66
2	−9.09	−6.00	82.63	36.05	54.54
3	11.29	10.92	127.46	119.26	123.29
4	23.08	12.94	532.69	167.53	298.66
5	1.81	10.01	3.28	100.11	18.12
6	8.65	9.55	74.82	91.28	82.61
7	−2.44	−3.00	5.95	8.97	7.32
8	−1.84	−2.09	3.39	4.35	3.85
9	−5.24	−4.68	27.46	21.94	24.52
10	−9.06	−4.19	82.08	17.54	37.96
11	6.14	6.29	37.70	39.53	38.62
12	−1.25	−.77	1.56	.60	.96
13	5.98	8.93	35.76	79.82	53.40
14	3.98	5.30	15.84	28.07	21.09
15	−4.82	−4.50	23.23	20.25	21.69
16	11.86	12.61	140.66	158.93	149.56
Sum (S)	27.31	42.49	1,332.34	972.16	1,039.85
	$= \sum Y$	$= \sum X$	$= \sum Y^2$	$= \sum X^2$	$= \sum XY$

[a]All summations are to be carried out over t, where t goes from 1 to T (in this example, $t = 1, \ldots, 16$).

TABLE 18.1   (cont.)

(b) CALCULATIONS

1. Beta

$$\frac{(T \times \sum XY) - (\sum Y \times \sum X)}{(T \times \sum X^2) - (\sum X)^2} = \frac{(16 \times 1,039.85) - (27.31 \times 42.49)}{(16 \times 972.16) - (42.49)^2} = 1.13$$

2. Alpha

$$[\sum Y/T] - [\text{Beta} \times (\sum X/T)] = [42.49/16] - [1.13 \times (42.49/16)] = -1.29$$

3. Standard deviation of random error term

$$\{[\sum Y^2 - (\text{Alpha} \times \sum Y) - (\text{Beta} \times \sum XY)]/(T - 2)\}^{1/2}$$
$$= \{[1,332.34 - (-1.29 \times 27.31) - (1.13 \times 1,039.85)]/(16 - 2)\}^{1/2} = 3.675$$

4. Standard error of beta

Standard deviation of random error term$/\{\sum X^2 - [(\sum X)^2/T]\}^{1/2}$
$$= 3.75/\{972.16 - [(42.49)^2/16]\}^{1/2} = .13$$

5. Standard error of alpha

Standard deviation of random error term$/\{T - [(\sum X)^2/\sum X^2]\}^{1/2}$
$$= 3.75/\{16 - [(42.49)^2/972.16]\}^{1/2} = 1.00$$

6. Correlation coefficient

$$\frac{(T \times \sum XY) - (\sum Y \times \sum X)}{\{[(T \times \sum Y^2) - (\sum Y)^2] \times [(T \times \sum X^2) - (\sum X)^2]\}^{1/2}}$$
$$= \frac{(16 \times 1,039.85) - (27.31 \times 42.49)}{\{[(16 \times 1,332.34) - (27.31)^2] \times [(16 \times 972.16) - (42.49)^2]\}^{1/2}} = .92$$

7. Coefficient of determination

$$(\text{Correlation coefficient})^2 = (.92)^2 = .85$$

8. Coefficient of nondetermination

$$1 - \text{Coefficient of determination} = 1 - .85 = .15$$

determined. For example, a portfolio with a beta of .8 during the 16-quarter time interval has a benchmark return of 4.35% [= 2.23 + (2.65 × .8)]. Figure 18.5 presents a graph of the *ex post* SML given by Equation (18.15).

One measure of a portfolio's risk-adjusted performance is the difference between its average return (ar_p) and the return on its corresponding benchmark portfolio, denoted ar_{bp}. This difference is generally referred to as the portfolio's ***ex post* alpha** (or differential return) and is denoted α_p:

ex post alpha

$$\alpha_p = ar_p - ar_{bp} \tag{18.16}$$

A positive value of α_p for a portfolio indicates that the portfolio had an average return greater than the benchmark return, suggesting that its performance was superior. On the other hand, a negative value of α_p indicates that the portfolio had an average return less than the benchmark return, suggesting that its performance was inferior.

By substituting the right-hand side of Equation (18.14) for ar_{bp} in Equation (18.16), one can see that a portfolio's *ex post* alpha based on the *ex post* SML is equal to[5]

$$\alpha_p = ar_p - [ar_f + (ar_M - ar_f)\beta_p] \tag{18.17}$$

After the values for α_p and β_p for a portfolio have been determined, the *ex post* **characteristic line** for the portfolio can be written as

characteristic line

$$r_p - r_f = \alpha_p + \beta_p(r_M - r_f) \tag{18.18}$$

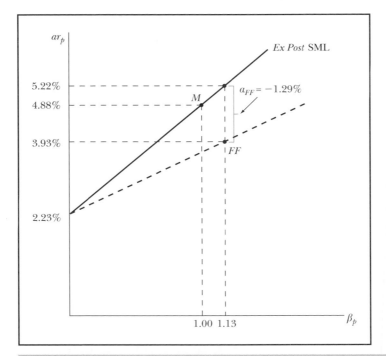

FIGURE 18.5 Performance Evaluation Using the *Ex Post* SML

The characteristic line is similar to the market model (introduced in Chapter 8) except that the portfolio's returns and the market index's returns are expressed in excess of the riskfree return. Graphically, the characteristic line formulation is the equation of a straight line where $(r_M - r_f)$ is measured on the horizontal axis and $(r_p - r_f)$ is measured on the vertical axis; the line has a vertical intercept of α_p and a slope of β_p.

As an example, consider the performance of the hypothetical portfolio First Fund, indicated in panel (a) of Table 18.1 for the given 16-quarter time interval. During this interval, First Fund had an average quarterly return of 3.93%. Based on Equation (18.11) First Fund had a beta of 1.13. Having an average beta for the 16 quarters that is greater than the market portfolio's beta of 1 indicates that First Fund was relatively aggressive (if its average beta had been less than 1, it would have been relatively defensive).

Given these values for its beta and average return, in Figure 18.5 First Fund is represented by the point with coordinates (1.13, 3.93), denoted *FF*. The exact vertical distance from *FF* to the *ex post* SML can be calculated using Equation (18.17):

$$\alpha_p = ar_p - [ar_f + (ar_M + ar_f)\beta_p]$$
$$= 3.93\% - [2.23\% + (4.88\% - 2.23\%)1.13]$$
$$= -1.29\%$$

Because *FF* lies below the *ex post* SML, its *ex post* alpha is negative, and its performance would be viewed as inferior.[6] Using Equation (18.18), the *ex post* characteristic line for First Fund would be

$$r_p - r_f = -1.29\% + 1.13(r_M - r_f)$$

Figure 18.6 provides an illustration of this line.[7]

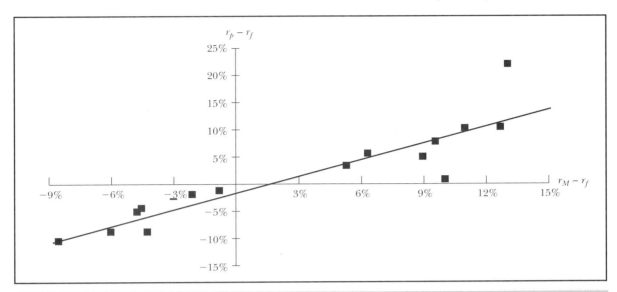

FIGURE 18.6 *Ex Post* Characteristic Line for First Fund

The method for determining a portfolio's *ex post* alpha, beta, and characteristic line suggests the use of a five-step procedure:

1. Determine the periodic rates of return for the portfolio and market index over the time interval, as well as the corresponding riskfree rates.
2. Determine the average market return and riskfree rate using the formulas in Equations (18.12) and (18.13).
3. Determine the portfolio's *ex post* beta using the formula in Equation (18.11).
4. Determine the portfolio's *ex post* alpha using the formula in Equation (18.17).
5. Insert these values for alpha and beta in Equation (18.18) to determine the portfolio's *ex post* characteristic line.

However, there is a simpler method for determining a portfolio's *ex post* alpha, beta, and characteristic line that also provides other pieces of information relating to the portfolio's performance. This method uses simple linear regression, and corresponds to the method presented in Chapters 8 and 13 for estimating the market model for an individual security.

With this method, the excess return on portfolio *p* in a given period *t* has three components. The first component is the portfolio's alpha; the second component is a risk premium equal to the excess return on the market times the portfolio's beta; and the third component is a random error term.[8] These three components are on the right-hand side of the following equation:

$$r_{pt} - r_{ft} = \alpha_p + \beta_p(r_{Mt} - r_{ft}) + \varepsilon_{pt} \tag{18.19}$$

Because α_p and β_p are assumed to be constant during the time interval, Equation (18.19) can be viewed as a regression equation. Accordingly, there are standard formulas for estimating α_p, β_p, and a number of other statistical parameters associated with the regression equation.

The legend below panel (b) of Table 18.1 presents these formulas using First Fund as an example. The formulas indicate that First Fund's *ex post* alpha and beta were equal to -1.29 and 1.13, respectively, for the 16-quarter time interval. These values are the same as those derived from Equations (18.11) and (18.17). Indeed, they will always result in the same values.

Figure 18.6 presents a scatter diagram of the excess returns on First Fund and the S&P 500. Based on Equation (18.19), the regression equation for First Fund is

$$r_{FF} - r_f = -1.29\% + 1.13(r_M - r_f) + \varepsilon_{FF} \qquad (18.20)$$

where -1.29 and 1.13 are the estimated *ex post* alpha and beta for First Fund during the 16-quarter time interval. Also shown in the figure is the *ex post* characteristic line for First Fund, a line that is derived using simple linear regression:

$$r_{FF} - r_f = -1.29\% + 1.13(r_M - r_f) \qquad (18.21)$$

The vertical distance between each point in the scatter diagram and the regression line represents an estimate of the size of the random error term for the corresponding quarter. The exact distance can be found by rewriting Equation (18.20) as

$$\varepsilon_{FF} = (r_{FF} - r_f) - [-1.29\% + 1.13(r_M - r_f)] \qquad (18.22)$$

For example, in the 11th quarter the excess returns on First Fund and the S&P 500 were 6.14% and 6.29%, respectively. The value of ε_{FF} for that quarter can be calculated using Equation (18.22) as follows:

$$\varepsilon_{FF} = (6.14\%) - [-1.29\% + 1.13(6.29\%)]$$

$$= .32\%$$

The value of ε_{FF} can be calculated similarly for the other 15 quarters of the time interval. The standard deviation of the resulting 16 numbers is an estimate of the standard deviation of the random error term (also known as the residual standard deviation) and in panel (b) of Table 18.1 equals 3.75%. This number can be viewed as an estimate of the *ex post* unique (or unsystematic or nonmarket) risk of First Fund.

The regression line for First Fund shown in Figure 18.6 is the line of best fit for the scatter diagram and corresponds to First Fund's *ex post* characteristic line. What is meant by "best fit"? Given that a straight line is defined by its intercept and slope, it means that there are no other values for alpha and beta that fit the scatter diagram any better than this one. In terms of simple linear regression, this means that there is no line that could be drawn such that the resulting standard deviation of the random error term would be smaller than the one of best fit.

A portfolio's "true" *ex post* beta cannot be observed; only an estimate of its true value can be obtained. Even if a portfolio's true beta remained the same forever, its estimated value, obtained as illustrated in Table 18.1 and Figure 18.6, would change from time to time because of errors (known as sampling errors) in estimating it. For example, if a different set of 16 quarters were examined, with the first quarter being replaced by a more recent quarter, the resulting estimated beta for First Fund would almost certainly be different than 1.13.

The standard error of beta shown in Table 18.1 attempts to indicate the extent of such estimation errors. Given a number of necessary assumptions (for example, the "true" beta did not change during the 16-quarter estimation period), the chances are roughly two out of three that the true beta is within one standard error, plus or minus, of the estimated beta. Thus, First Fund's true beta is likely to be between the values of $1.00 (= 1.13 - .13)$ and $1.26 (= 1.13 + .13)$. Similarly, the value under standard error of alpha provides an indication of the magnitude of the possible sampling error that has been made in estimating the portfolio's alpha.

The value under correlation coefficient provides an indication of how closely the excess returns on First Fund were associated with the excess returns on the S&P 500. Because its range is between -1 and $+1$, the value for First Fund of .92 indicates a strong positive relationship between First Fund and the S&P 500. That is, larger excess returns for First Fund seem to have been closely associated with larger excess returns for the S&P 500.

The coefficient of determination is equal to the squared value of the correlation coefficient; it represents the proportion of variation in the excess return on First Fund that is related to the variation in the excess return on the S&P 500. That is, it shows how much of the movement in First Fund's excess returns can be explained by movements in the excess returns on the S&P 500. The value of .85 shows that 85% of the movement in the excess return on First Fund during the 16 quarters can be attributed to movement in the excess return on the S&P 500.

Because the coefficient of nondetermination is 1 minus the coefficient of determination, it represents the proportion of movement in the excess return on First Fund that does not result from movement in the excess return on the S&P 500. Thus 15% of the movement in First Fund cannot be attributed to movement in the S&P 500.

Although Table 18.1 shows the formulas for calculating all these values, it should be pointed out that there are many software packages that can quickly carry out these calculations. The only substantive effort involves gathering all the return data shown in panel (a) of Table 18.1 and entering it into a computer spreadsheet.

18.4.2 THE REWARD-TO-VOLATILITY RATIO

reward-to-volatility ratio

Closely related to the *ex post* alpha measure of portfolio performance is a measure known as the **reward-to-volatility ratio.**[9] This measure, denoted $RVOL_p$, also uses the *ex post* security market line to form a benchmark for performance evaluation but in a different manner. The calculation of the reward-to-volatility ratio for a portfolio involves dividing its average excess return by its market risk as follows:

$$RVOL_p = \frac{ar_p - ar_f}{\beta_p} \qquad (18.23)$$

Here the beta of the portfolio can be determined using Equation (18.11).

In the example of First Fund, the average return for the 16-quarter time interval was 3.93% and the average Treasury bill rate was 2.23%. Thus, the average excess return for First Fund was 1.70% $(= 3.93\% - 2.23\%)$ and, given a beta of 1.13, its reward-to-volatility ratio was 1.50% $(= 1.70\%/1.13)$.

The reward-to-volatility ratio corresponds to the slope of a line originating at the average riskfree rate and going through the point (β_p, ar_p). This correspondence can be seen by noting that the slope of a line is easily determined if two points on the line are known; it is simply the vertical distance between the two points ("rise") divided by the horizontal distance between the two points ("run"). In this case, the vertical distance is $ar_p - ar_f$ and the horizontal distance is $\beta_p - 0$, so the slope is $(ar_p - ar_f)/\beta_p$ and thus corresponds to the formula for $RVOL_p$ in Equation (18.23). Because the value measured on the horizontal axis is β_p and the value measured on the vertical axis is ar_p, the line can be drawn on the same diagram as the *ex post* SML.

In the First Fund example, the *ex post* SML for the 16-quarter time interval is the solid line in Figure 18.5. Also appearing in this figure is the point denoted *FF,* corresponding to $(\beta_p, ar_p) = (1.13, 3.93\%)$ for First Fund. The dashed line in this figure originates from the point $(0, ar_f) = (0, 2.23\%)$, goes through *FF,* and has a slope of 1.50% $[= (3.93\% - 2.23\%)/1.13]$ corresponding to the value for $RVOL_p$.

The benchmark for comparison with this measure of performance is the slope of the *ex post* SML. Because this line goes through the points $(0, ar_f)$ and $(1, ar_M)$, its slope is $(ar_M - ar_f)/(1 - 0) = (ar_M - ar_f)$. If $RVOL_p$ is greater than this value, then the portfolio lies above the *ex post* SML, indicating that it has outperformed the market. However, if $RVOL_p$ is less than this value, then the portfolio lies below the *ex post* SML, indicating that it has not performed as well as the market.

In the case of First Fund, the benchmark is 2.65% $[= (ar_M - ar_f) = (4.88\% - 2.23\%)]$. Because $RVOL_p$ is less than the benchmark ($1.50\% < 2.65\%$), according to this measure of portfolio performance, First Fund did not perform as well as the market.

In comparing the two measures of performance that are based on the *ex post* SML, α_p and $RVOL_p$, it should be noted that they will *always* give the same assessment of a portfolio's performance relative to the market portfolio. That is, if one measure indicates that the portfolio outperformed the market, then so will the other; if one measure indicates that the portfolio did not perform as well as the market, the other measure will show the same thing. Why is this so? Any portfolio with a positive *ex post* alpha (an indication of superior performance) lies *above* the *ex post* SML and thus must have a slope *greater* than the slope of the *ex post* SML (also an indication of superior performance). Similarly, any portfolio with a negative *ex post* alpha (an indication of inferior performance) lies *below* the *ex post* SML and thus must have a slope *less* than the slope of the *ex post* SML (also an indication of inferior performance).

However, it is possible for the two measures to *rank* portfolios differently on the basis of performance simply because the calculations are different. For example, if Second Fund had a beta of 1.5 and an average return of 4.86%, its *ex post* alpha would be -1.34% $\{= 4.86\% - [2.23 + (4.88 - 2.23) \times 1.5]\}$. Thus, its performance appears to be worse than that of First Fund because it has a smaller *ex post* alpha ($-1.34\% < -1.29\%$). However, its reward-to-volatility ratio of 1.75% $[= (4.86\% - 2.23\%)/1.5]$ is larger than the reward-to-volatility of 1.50% for First Fund, suggesting that its performance was better than First Fund's.

18.4.3 THE SHARPE RATIO

Sharpe ratio

Both the *ex post* alpha and reward-to-volatility ratio use benchmarks based on the *ex post* security market line (SML) and therefore measure returns relative to the market risk of the portfolio. In contrast, the **Sharpe ratio** (or reward-to-variability ratio) is a measure of risk-adjusted performance that uses a benchmark based on the *ex post* capital market line (CML).[10] It measures returns relative to the total risk of the portfolio, where total risk is the standard deviation of portfolio returns.

In order to use the Sharpe ratio (SR_p), one must determine the location of the *ex post* CML. This line goes through two points on a graph that measures average return on the vertical axis and standard deviation on the horizontal axis. The first point is the vertical intercept of the line and corresponds to the average riskfree rate during the 16-quarter time interval. The second point corresponds to the location of the market portfolio, meaning that its coordinates are the average return and standard deviation of return for the market portfolio during the evaluation interval, or (σ_M, ar_M). Because the *ex post* CML goes through these two points, its slope is calculated as the vertical distance between the two points divided by the horizontal distance between the two points, or $(ar_M - ar_f)/(\sigma_M - 0) = (ar_M - ar_f)/\sigma_M$. The return given by the *ex post* CML for a portfolio with a total risk σ_p can be used as a benchmark return, ar_{bp}, for that portfolio:

$$ar_{bp} = ar_f + \frac{ar_M - ar_f}{\sigma_M} \sigma_p \qquad (18.24)$$

In the example shown in Table 18.1, the average return and standard deviation for the S&P 500, calculated using Equations (18.9) and (18.10), were 4.88% and 7.39%, respectively, and the average return on Treasury bills was 2.23%. Hence, the *ex post* CML during these 16 quarters was

$$ar_{bp} = 2.23\% + \frac{4.88\% - 2.23\%}{7.39\%} \sigma_p \qquad (18.25)$$

$$= 2.23\% + .36\sigma_p$$

Once the location of the *ex post* CML has been determined, the average return and standard deviation of the portfolio being evaluated can be calculated using Equations (18.9) and (18.10). When these values are known, the portfolio can be located on the same graph as the *ex post* CML. In the case of First Fund, its average return and standard deviation were 3.93% and 9.08%, respectively. In Figure 18.7 its location corresponds to the point with coordinates (9.08%, 3.93%), which is denoted *FF*.

The calculation of the Sharpe ratio, SR_p, is analogous to the calculation of the reward-to-volatility ratio $RVOL_p$ described earlier. Whereas $RVOL_p$ involves dividing the portfolio's average excess return by its beta, SR_p involves dividing the portfolio's average excess return by its standard deviation:

$$SR_p = \frac{ar_p - ar_f}{\sigma_p} \qquad (18.26)$$

Note that SR_p corresponds to the slope of a line originating at the average riskfree rate and going through a point with coordinates of (σ_p, ar_p). The slope of this line is simply the vertical distance between the two points divided by the horizontal distance

FIGURE 18.7 Performance Evaluation Using the *Ex Post* CML

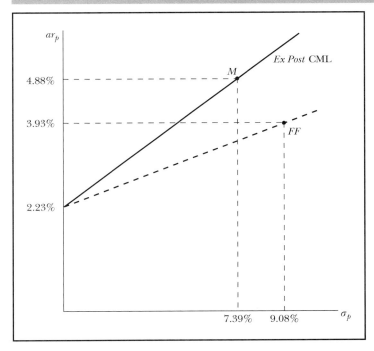

between the two points, or $(ar_p - ar_f)/(\sigma_p - 0) = (ar_p - ar_f)/\sigma_p$, which corresponds to the formula for SR_p given in Equation (18.26).

In the First Fund example, the *ex post* CML is shown by the solid line in Figure 18.7. Also appearing in this figure is the point denoted *FF*, corresponding to $(\sigma_p, ar_p) = (9.08\%, 3.93\%)$ for First Fund. The dashed line in this figure originates from the point $(0, ar_f) = (0, 2.23\%)$ and goes through *FF*, and has a slope of .19 $[= (3.93 - 2.23)/9.08]$.

Because the *ex post* CML represents various combinations of riskfree lending or borrowing with investing in the market portfolio, it can be used to provide a benchmark for the Sharpe ratio similar to the SML-based benchmark for the reward-to-volatility ratio. As noted earlier, the slope of the *ex post* CML is $(ar_M - ar_f)/\sigma_M$. If SR_p is greater than this value, then the portfolio lies above the *ex post* CML, indicating that it has outperformed the market. However, if SR_p is less than this value, then the portfolio lies below the *ex post* CML, indicating that it has not performed as well as the market.

In the case of First Fund, the benchmark is .36 $[= (4.88 - 2.23)/7.39]$. Because SR_p is less than the benchmark (.19 < .36), First Fund did not perform as well as the market according to this risk-adjusted measure of portfolio performance.

18.4.4 M^2

M-squared

The measure **M-squared** (M^2) uses standard deviation as the relevant measure of risk.[11] Thus, like the Sharpe ratio, it is based on the *ex post* CML. This measure simply takes a portfolio's average return and determines what it would have been if the portfolio had had the same degree of total risk as the market portfolio (typically the S&P 500). Consider a line that goes through the average riskfree rate and the average return on the portfolio, where standard deviation is used as the measure of risk, such as the line going through the average riskfree rate of 2.23% and First Fund (*FF*) in Figure 18.7. The following equation describes such a line:

$$ar_i = ar_f + \left(\frac{ar_p - ar_f}{\sigma_p}\right)\sigma_i \tag{18.27}$$

because the line has a vertical intercept of ar_f and a slope of $(ar_p - ar_f)/\sigma_p$. This equation indicates the average return, ar_i, that would have been earned by investing in portfolio p and either investing or borrowing at the riskfree rate to such a degree that the resulting standard deviation was σ_i. The risk-adjusted return, M_p^2, is the average return that would have been earned if the amount of riskfree investing or lending had resulted in the standard deviation of the portfolio being equal to that of the market portfolio. Hence, setting σ_i equal to σ_M in Equation (18.27) results in the value of M_p^2 for portfolio p:

$$M_p^2 = ar_f + \left(\frac{ar_p - ar_f}{\sigma_p}\right)\sigma_M \tag{18.28}$$

Accordingly, M_p^2 measures the return an investor would have earned if the portfolio had been altered using the riskfree rate through borrowing or lending in order to match the market portfolio's standard deviation.[12]

For example, First Fund had, on a quarterly basis, an average return of 3.93% and a standard deviation of 9.08%. Because the average riskfree rate was 2.23%, the equation describing the dashed line in Figure 18.7 can be determined using Equation (18.27):

$$ar_i = 2.23 + \left(\frac{3.93 - 2.23}{9.08}\right)\sigma_i$$

$$= 2.23 + .19\sigma_i \tag{18.29}$$

The standard deviation of the market portfolio (estimated using the S&P 500) was 7.39%, resulting in M_p^2 for the First Fund of 3.61% ($= 2.23 + .19 \times 7.39$). That is, by investing $7.39/9.08 = 81.4\%$ in First Fund and 18.6% in the riskfree rate, the investor would have had a portfolio with the same standard deviation as the market portfolio. In this example, M^2 effectively "de-levers" First Fund's return to bring its risk level down to that of the market portfolio and then proportionately reduces First Fund's return by the degree of de-leveraging. If the market portfolio's standard deviation had been greater than that of First Fund, then M^2 would have leveraged First Fund's return by borrowing at the riskfree rate to increase its standard deviation to that of the market portfolio. This action would have proportionately increased First Fund's return by the degree of leveraging.

M_p^2 can be compared directly with the average return on the market portfolio, ar_M, to determine whether the portfolio outperformed or underperformed the market portfolio on a risk-adjusted basis. In the case of First Fund, the market portfolio had an average return of 4.88%, suggesting underperformance on the fund's part because $M_{FF}^2 = 3.61\% < 4.88\% = ar_M$.

When the two measures of risk-adjusted performance that are based on the *ex post* CML, SR_p and M_p^2, are compared, they will always give the same assessment of a portfolio's performance relative to the market portfolio.[13] Hence, it is impossible for one measure to indicate that a portfolio performed better than the market and the other to indicate that it performed worse. If a portfolio plots below the *ex post* CML, then (1) the slope of the line going through the portfolio (SR_p) will be less than the slope of the *ex post* CML and (2) M_p^2 will lie on the line going through the portfolio at a point directly below the market portfolio on the *ex post* CML. The converse is true if the portfolio plots above the *ex post* CML.

Furthermore, the two measures will rank a set of portfolios exactly the same because comparing slopes of lines that all go through the average riskfree rate will rank portfolios exactly the same as comparing the average returns on all of these lines at a given level of standard deviation. Equations (18.26) and (18.28) can be combined to show that

$$M_p^2 = ar_f + SR_p\sigma_M \qquad (18.30)$$

Thus, the value of M_p^2 for any portfolio is simply equal to a positive constant plus the portfolio's Sharpe ratio multiplied by another positive constant. Because these two constants are the same for all portfolios, the ranking for M_p^2 will be exactly the same as the ranking for SR_p.

18.4.5 COMPARING THE RISK-ADJUSTED MEASURES OF PERFORMANCE

The measures of performance that are based on the *ex post* SML, α_p and $RVOL_p$, can be compared with just the measure of performance that is based on the *ex post* CML, SR_p. There is no need for comparing them with the *ex post* CML-based measure M_p^2 because M_p^2 evaluates portfolios exactly the same as SR_p.

Importantly, $RVOL_p$ and SR_p give different assessments of a portfolio's performance relative to the market portfolio in certain situations. (The comparison also applies to α_p and SR_p.) If $RVOL_p$ indicates the portfolio outperformed the market, then SR_p may indicate that the portfolio did not perform as well as the market if the portfolio has a relatively large amount of unique risk. Such risk would not be a factor in determining the value of $RVOL_p$ because only *market risk* is in the denominator. However, such risk would be included in the denominator of SR_p because this measure is based on *total risk* (that is, both market and unique risk). Thus, a portfolio with a low amount of market risk could have a high amount of total risk, resulting in a relatively high $RVOL_p$ (because of the low amount of market risk) and a low SR_p (because of the high amount of total risk). Accordingly, $RVOL_p$ could indicate that the portfolio outperformed the market at the same time that SR_p indicated that it did not perform as well as the market.[14]

As an example, consider Third Fund, with an average return of 4.5%, a beta of .8, and a standard deviation of 18%. Using the same riskfree return as in the First Fund example, $RVOL_{TF} = 2.71\%$ $[= (4.5\% - 2.23\%)/.8]$, indicating that Third Fund outperformed the market portfolio because the benchmark was 2.65% $[= (4.88\% - 2.23\%)/1.0]$. However, $SR_{TF} = .12$ $[= (4.5\% - 2.23\%)/18\%]$, indicating that Third Fund did not perform as well as the market portfolio because the benchmark is .36 $[= (4.88\% - 2.23\%)/7.39\%]$. The difference is a result of Third Fund's low beta relative to the market $(.8 < 1.0)$ but high standard deviation relative to the market $(18\% > 7.39\%)$. This outcome suggests that Third Fund had a relatively high level of unique risk.

It also follows that $RVOL_p$ and SR_p may rank two or more portfolios differently on the basis of their performance because these two measures of risk-adjusted performance use different types of risk. Recall that First Fund had an average return of 3.93%, a beta of 1.13, and a standard deviation of 9.08%. Thus, $RVOL_{FF} = 1.50\%$ $[= (3.93\% - 2.23\%)/1.13]$, which is less than $RVOL_{TF} = 2.65\%$, thereby indicating that First Fund ranked lower than Third Fund. However, $SR_{FF} = .13$ $[= (3.93\% - 2.23\%)/9.08\%]$, which is greater than $SR_{TF} = .12$, thereby indicating that First Fund ranked higher than Third Fund.

Did Third Fund do better or worse than the market on a risk-adjusted basis? And did Third Fund perform better or worse than First Fund? The answer to those two questions lies in identifying the appropriate measure of risk for the client. If the client has many other assets, then beta is the relevant measure of risk, and performance should be based on $RVOL_p$. For such a client, Third Fund should be viewed as a superior performer relative to both the market and First Fund. However, if the client has few other assets, then standard deviation is the relevant measure of risk, and performance should be based on SR_p. For such a client, Third Fund should be viewed as an inferior performer relative to both the market and First Fund.

18.5 Market Timing

A market timer structures a portfolio to have a relatively high beta when he or she expects the market to rise and a relatively low beta when a market drop is anticipated. Why? Because the expected return on a portfolio is a linear function of its beta:

$$\bar{r}_p = \alpha_p + r_f + (\bar{r}_M - r_f)\beta_p \qquad \textbf{(18.31)}$$

This relationship means that the market timer wants a high-beta portfolio when he or she expects the market to have a higher return than the riskfree rate because such a portfolio will have a higher expected return than a low-beta portfolio. Conversely, the market timer wants a low-beta portfolio when he or she expects the market to have a lower return than the riskfree rate because it will have a higher expected return than a high-beta portfolio. Simply put, the market timer will want to

1. Hold a high-beta portfolio when $\bar{r}_M > r_f$
2. Hold a low-beta portfolio when $\bar{r}_M < r_f$

If the timer is accurate in his or her forecasts of the expected return on the market, then his or her portfolio will outperform a benchmark portfolio with a constant beta equal to the average beta of the timer's portfolio.

For example, if the market timer set the portfolio beta at 0.0 when $\bar{r}_M < r_f$ and at 2.0 when $\bar{r}_M > r_f$, the return on the portfolio will be higher than the return on a portfolio having a beta constantly equal to 1.0, provided the timer is accurate in forecasting $\bar{r}_M$. Unfortunately, if the market timer's forecasts are inaccurate and consequently the portfolio's beta is altered in ways unrelated to subsequent market moves, then the timer's portfolio will not perform as well as a constant-beta portfolio. For example, if the timer sometimes sets the portfolio's beta equal to 0 when the market is forecast to fall but actually rises, and at other times sets the beta equal to 2 when the market is forecast to rise but actually falls, then the portfolio will have an average return less than what a portfolio with a constant beta of 1 would have earned.

To "time the market," one must change either the average beta of the risky securities held in the portfolio or the relative amounts invested in the riskfree asset and risky securities. For example, the beta of a portfolio could be increased by selling bonds or low-beta stocks and using the proceeds to purchase high-beta stocks. Alternatively, Treasury bills in the portfolio could be sold (or the amount of borrowing increased), with the resulting proceeds invested in stocks. (Because of the relative ease of buying and selling stock derivative instruments, such as index futures, most investment organizations specializing in market timing prefer using them.)

In Figure 18.8, the excess returns of two hypothetical portfolios are measured on the vertical axis and those of a market index are on the horizontal axis. Straight lines derived from standard regression methods reveal positive *ex post* alpha values in each case. However, the scatter diagrams tell a different story.

The scatter diagram for the portfolio shown in panel (a) seems to indicate that the relationship between the portfolio's excess returns and the market's excess returns was linear because the points cluster close to the regression line. This result suggests that the portfolio beta was roughly the same at all times. Because the *ex post* alpha was positive, it appears that the investment manager successfully identified and invested in some underpriced securities.

The scatter diagram for the portfolio shown in panel (b) seems to indicate that the relationship between this portfolio's excess returns and the market's excess returns was not linear because the points in the middle lie below the regression line and those at the

FIGURE 18.8 Superior Fund Performance

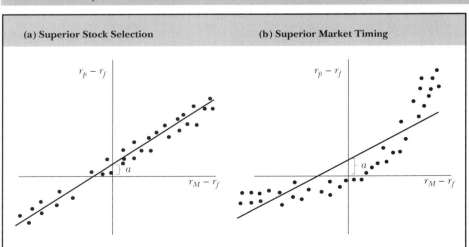

ends lie above the regression line. This diagram suggests that the portfolio consisted of high-beta securities during periods when the market return was high and low-beta securities during periods when the market return was low. It appears that the portfolio has a positive *ex post* alpha because of successful market timing by the investment manager.

18.5.1 QUADRATIC REGRESSION

Measuring the ability of an investment manager to successfully time the market requires that something more complex than a straight line be "fit" to scatter diagrams such as those shown in Figure 18.8. One procedure fits a curve to the data using statistical methods to estimate the parameters *a, b,* and *c* in the following *quadratic regression equation:*

$$r_{pt} - r_{ft} = a + b(r_{Mt} - r_{ft}) + c[(r_{Mt} - r_{ft})^2] + \varepsilon_{pt} \tag{18.32}$$

where ε_{pt} is the random error term.

The *ex post characteristic curve* shown in Figure 18.9(a) represents the following quadratic function, where the values of *a, b,* and *c* for the portfolio have been estimated by standard regression methods:

$$r_{pt} - r_{ft} = a + b(r_{Mt} - r_{ft}) + c[(r_{Mt} - r_{ft})^2] \tag{18.33}$$

If the estimated value of *c* is positive [as it is for the portfolio depicted in Figure 18.9(a)], the slope of the curve will increase as one moves to the right. This change in slope indicates that the portfolio manager successfully timed the market. Note that this equation corresponds to the equation for the *ex post* characteristic line if *c* is approximately equal to zero. In such a situation, *a* and *b* would correspond to the portfolio's *ex post* alpha and beta, respectively.[15]

18.5.2 DUMMY VARIABLE REGRESSION

An alternative procedure fits two *ex post* characteristic lines to the scatter diagram, as shown in Figure 18.9(b). Periods when risky securities outperform riskfree securities (that is, when $r_{Mt} > r_{ft}$) can be called *up markets*. Periods when risky securities do not perform as well as riskfree securities (that is, when $r_{Mt} < r_{ft}$) can be called *down mar-*

FIGURE 18.9 *Ex Post* Characteristic Curve and Line

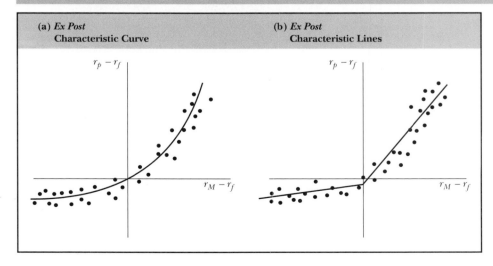

(a) *Ex Post* Characteristic Curve

(b) *Ex Post* Characteristic Lines

kets. A successful market timer would select a high up-market beta and a low down-market beta. Graphically, the slope of the *ex post* characteristic line for positive excess market returns (up markets) is greater than the slope of the *ex post* characteristic line for negative excess market returns (down markets).

Such a relationship can be estimated using standard regression methods to determine the parameters *a*, *b*, and *c* in the following *dummy variable regression equation:*

$$r_{pt} - r_{ft} = a + b(r_{Mt} - r_{ft}) + c[D_t(r_{Mt} - r_{ft})] + \varepsilon_{pt} \tag{18.34}$$

Here, ε_{pt} is the random error term, and D_t is a "dummy variable" assigned a value of zero for any past time period t when $r_{Mt} > r_{ft}$ and a value of minus one for any past time period t when $r_{Mt} < r_{ft}$. To see how this procedure works, consider the effective equations for different values of $r_{Mt} - r_{ft}$:

Value of $r_{Mt} - r_{ft}$	Equation
> 0	$r_{pt} - r_{ft} = a + b(r_{Mt} - r_{ft}) + \varepsilon_{pt}$
$= 0$	$r_{pt} - r_{ft} = a + \varepsilon_{pt}$
< 0	$r_{pt} - r_{ft} = a + (b - c)(r_{Mt} - r_{ft}) + \varepsilon_{pt}$

The parameter b corresponds to the portfolio's up-market beta, whereas $(b - c)$ corresponds to the portfolio's down-market beta. Thus, the parameter c indicates the difference between the two betas and will be positive for the successful market timer.

For the portfolio shown in Figure 18.9(b), the *ex post* characteristic line on the right side of the graph corresponds to the equation:

$$r_{pt} - r_{ft} = a + b(r_{Mt} - r_{ft}) \tag{18.35a}$$

whereas the *ex post* characteristic line shown on the left side of the graph corresponds to the equation:

$$r_{pt} - r_{ft} = a + (b - c)(r_{Mt} - r_{ft}) \tag{18.35b}$$

In this example, the investment manager has successfully engaged in market timing because the slope of the line on the right side (that is, b) is greater than the slope of the line on the left side (that is, $b - c$).

In either regression Equation (18.32) or (18.34), the value of the parameter a provides an estimate of the investment manager's ability to identify mispriced securities (that is, security selection ability), and the value of the parameter c provides an estimate of the manager's market timing ability. The difference between the two equations is that the quadratic equation indicates that the portfolio's beta fluctuated over many values, depending on the size of the market's excess returns. This fluctuation can be seen graphically by noting that the slope of the quadratic curve continually increases when moving from left to right in Figure 18.9(a). In comparison, the dummy variable equation indicates that the portfolio's beta fluctuated between just two values, depending on whether r_{Mt} was less than or greater than r_{ft}; the slope of the equation increases from one value (that is, $b - c$) to a second value (that is, b) when moving from left to right in Figure 18.9(b).

As an example, again consider First Fund. Table 18.2 presents the results from applying regression Equations (18.32) and (18.34) to this portfolio during the 16-quarter time interval. The table indicates that the portfolio manager has neither selectivity nor market timing ability because the parameter a is negative whereas the parameter c is near zero.[16] Further evidence reveals the lack of market timing ability because the correlation coefficient is higher for the *ex post* characteristic line than for either of the other equations.

TABLE 18.2 Market Timing Test Results for First Fund

Parameter Being Estimated[a]	*Ex Post Characteristic Line*	*Quadratic Equation*	*Dummy Variable Equation*
a	−1.29%	−2.12%	−1.33%
	(1.00)	(1.65)	(2.54)
b	1.13	1.03	1.13
	(.13)	(.20)	(.28)
c	—	.02	.02
	—	(.03)	(.78)
Correlation[b]	.92	.91	.91

[a]Standard errors are in parentheses below the respective parameters.

[b]The correlation coefficient for the quadratic and dummy variable equations has been adjusted for the number of independent variables.

18.6 Criticisms of Risk-Adjusted Performance Measures

The previously mentioned risk-adjusted measures of portfolio performance have been criticized on several grounds. Some of the major criticisms are described in this section.[17]

18.6.1 USE OF A MARKET INDEX

Because all of the measures other than the Sharpe ratio and M^2 require the identification of a surrogate for the market portfolio, whatever index is used can be criticized as inadequate. Indeed, it has been shown that when a slightly different index is used, the performance rankings of a set of portfolios can be completely reversed (that is, the top-ranked portfolio with one index could be the bottom-ranked portfolio if a slightly different index were used). However, when commonly used NYSE-based indices are involved, such as the DJIA, the S&P 500, and an index comparable to the NYSE Composite, the performance rankings of common stock portfolios seem similar.[18]

A related criticism of using a market index such as the S&P 500 to determine the benchmark portfolio's return is that it is nearly impossible for an investor to form a portfolio whose returns replicate those on such an index over time. Transaction costs are encountered in initially forming the portfolio, in restructuring the portfolio when stocks are replaced in the index, and in purchasing more shares of the stocks when cash dividends are received.[19] Hence it has been argued that the returns on an index overstate the returns that a passive investor could earn, meaning that the returns on the benchmark portfolio are too high.[20]

18.6.2 DISTINGUISHING SKILL FROM LUCK

A very long time interval is needed to obtain a measure of performance that distinguishes skill from luck on the part of the investment manager. That is, it would be useful to know if an apparently successful manager was skilled or just lucky because skill will have a favorable impact on the portfolio's performance in the future, whereas luck may not continue. Unfortunately, too many years' worth of data are generally needed to make such a determination.[21] (This issue is discussed further in this chapter's Money Matters box.)

Assessing Manager Skill

Perhaps no issue elicits more frustration among investors than the evaluation of manager investment skill. The problem stems from the inherent uncertainty of manager investment performance. Even the most talented managers can underperform their benchmarks during any given quarter, year, or even multiyear period. Conversely, ineffective managers at times may make correct decisions and outperform their benchmarks simply by good fortune.

The odds that a "skillful" manager will underperform his or her benchmark for what most observers would consider to be acceptably long evaluation intervals are surprisingly high (under reasonable assumptions about expected return and return volatility, roughly one out of four during a three-year evaluation period). The chances that an "unskillful" manager will outperform his or her benchmark are likewise considerable (roughly one out of three during a three-year evaluation period). Even when we extend the evaluation period to five years (an eternity in the investment management business), the possibility of confusing skillful with unskillful managers decreases only slightly.

Let us step back for a moment and define the term investment skill. It is the ability to outperform a passive risk-adjusted benchmark consistently over time. In other words, the skillful manager is capable of generating a statistically significant alpha. Because no manager is omniscient, every manager's alpha, regardless of skill, will be positive in some periods and negative in others. Nevertheless, a skillful manager will produce a larger alpha more frequently than his or her less talented peers.

Note that a skillful manager may produce a small alpha very frequently or a larger alpha less frequently. It is the magnitude of the alpha relative to the volatility around that alpha value that determines a manager's skill (the ratio of these two variables is a form of the Sharpe ratio discussed in the text). Yet when investors evaluate their portfolio managers, most focus solely on the level of alpha produced, ignoring volatility around the alpha. As a result, superior managers may be terminated (or not hired) and inferior managers may be retained (or hired) on the basis of statistically questionable performance data.

Attempting to evaluate manager skill strictly by consulting past performance data is a problem in statistical inference. Essentially, we want to test whether the manager's alpha is positive enough not to be considered a result of mere chance. To undertake this analysis, we must make three key assumptions concerning the shape and dispersion of the manager's returns around his or her benchmark. Somewhat paradoxically, we first assume that the manager has no investment skill. That is, we begin with a *null hypothesis* that the manager's alpha is zero on average over time. It is actually this assumption of no skill that we want to test. Second, we assume that the manager's alpha is normally distributed around the average (or mean) value of zero (that is, the alpha distribution is in the form of the familiar bell-shaped curve, with zero as its center). Third, we assume that the volatility of the manager's returns around the benchmark in the future will be the same as occurred in the past. That is, we will assume that the standard deviation of the manager's alpha is constant over time. (Recall that a normally distributed random variable has two-thirds of its outcomes within one standard deviation from the mean.)

Statistical inference by its nature can be a baffling exercise in double negatives. For example, we do not accept the null hypothesis. Rather, we fail to reject it. Conversely, although we may reject the null hypothesis, that does not necessarily mean we accept an alternative hypothesis. Nevertheless, the equivocal nature of this type of analysis is well suited to the world of investments where luck often masquerades as skill and skill is frequently overwhelmed by random events.

Consider a manager whose alpha exhibits an annual standard deviation of 4.0%. Assuming a normal distribution and a mean alpha of 0, the expected distribution of the manager's alpha during a three-year period should look like the accompanying graph. (Note that as time passes the normal distribution will become tighter around the mean of zero because the longer the evaluation period the more likely the manager's random positive and negative alphas will offset one another, gradually converging on the mean value. Specifically, the three-year annualized standard deviation is 2.3% or $1/\sqrt{3}$ times the one-year standard deviation of 4.0%.) Now suppose, based on monthly observations, the manager actually produced an alpha of 3% per year during the three years. What can be said about that outcome? If our null hypothesis of no skill is correct, then there is only a 10-in-100 chance that this result would have occurred by luck. It is up to us to decide whether we believe that luck was the cause of this outcome or whether we should reject the null hypothesis. That is, do we believe that the manager actually is skillful and that his or her true expected alpha is not zero but some positive number? This would make the 3% realized alpha seem much more plausible.

Unfortunately, it is the rare manager who demonstrates sufficiently strong results to allow us to comfortably reject the null hypothesis. Most managers live in a statistical netherworld, producing neither sufficiently large positive nor sufficiently large negative alphas to warrant definitive conclusions. For example, few U.S. common stock managers can hope to outperform their benchmarks by more than 1% per year on average after accounting for all fees and expenses. With an alpha standard deviation of 4%, it would take more than 40 years before our statistical test would indicate that there is less than a 5-in-100 chance that such an outcome was because of luck.

As a result of these nebulous statistical answers, it should not be surprising that investors turn to various qualitative decision rules to help them identify manager skill. For example, they may intensively examine the manager's process for selecting securities and want to understand the pedigree of the firm's portfolio managers. Whether such investigations actually help to uncover skillful managers is highly debatable.

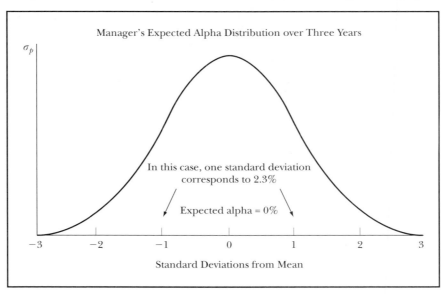

Manager's Expected Alpha Distribution over Three Years

σ_p

In this case, one standard deviation corresponds to 2.3%

Expected alpha = 0%

Standard Deviations from Mean

18.6.3 MEASURING THE RISKFREE RATE

The use of Treasury bills for measuring the riskfree rate in determining benchmark portfolios based on either the *ex post* SML or CML can be criticized. Consider a benchmark portfolio that includes an investment in both Treasury bills and the market portfolio. Such a benchmark portfolio can be criticized for having too low a rate of return, making it easier for a portfolio to show superior performance because Treasury bills may provide excessively low returns to compensate for their high degree of liquidity. If a higher riskfree rate (such as the commercial paper rate) is used, then any benchmark portfolio that lies between this riskfree rate and the market portfolio on either the *ex post* SML or *ex post* CML will have a higher rate of return and thus will represent a higher but more appropriate standard.

Furthermore, consider a benchmark portfolio that involves leveraging a positive investment in the market portfolio by borrowing at the riskfree rate. Using the Treasury bill rate can be criticized because realistic borrowing alternatives typically involve a higher rate and are thus less attractive. Accordingly, benchmarks that involve borrowing at the Treasury bill rate have too high a rate of return, making it more difficult for a portfolio to show superior performance. If a higher riskfree borrowing rate (such as the call money rate plus a small premium) is used, then any benchmark portfolio involving riskfree borrowing will have a lower rate of return and therefore will represent a lower but more appropriate standard.

In summary, measures of portfolio performance based on either the *ex post* SML or *ex post* CML that use Treasury bills to determine the riskfree rate are alleged to discriminate in favor of conservative portfolios and against aggressive ones.

18.6.4 VALIDITY OF THE CAPM

The measures of portfolio performance that involve beta (namely, the *ex post* alpha and reward-to-volatility measures) are based on the CAPM, yet the CAPM may not be the correct asset pricing model. Assets may be priced according to some other model and if they are, the use of beta-based performance measures may be inappropriate.

Interestingly, a measure analogous to *ex post* alpha has been presented as a meaningful gauge of performance if arbitrage pricing theory's (APT) model of asset pricing is believed to be more appropriate.[22] In such a situation, APT is used to estimate the benchmark portfolio's return ar_{bp} used in Equation (18.16) to calculate α_p. The Sharpe ratio cannot be considered inappropriate on these grounds because it uses standard deviation as a measure of risk and does not rely on the validity of either the CAPM or APT.

Summary

1. Performance measurement is an integral part of the investment management process. It is a feedback and control mechanism that can make this process more effective.
2. In evaluating performance, there are two major tasks: Determine whether the performance is superior or inferior, and determine whether the performance is because of luck or skill.
3. Without intraperiod contributions or withdrawals, measurement of periodic portfolio returns is simple: the difference between ending and beginning portfolio values divided by beginning portfolio value.
4. Intraperiod cash flows complicate the calculation of periodic portfolio returns. Two methods have been developed to calculate returns when these cash flows occur: dollar-weighted and time-weighted returns.
5. The dollar-weighted return is influenced by the size and timing of cash flows, whereas the time-weighted return is not. As a result, the time-weighted return is generally the preferred method when evaluating portfolio performance.
6. The essential idea behind performance evaluation is to compare an actively managed portfolio's returns against the returns of an alternative benchmark portfolio.

An appropriate benchmark should be relevant and feasible, and it should exhibit risk similar to that of the actively managed portfolio.

7. Risk-adjusted performance measures involve both a portfolio's *ex post* return and its *ex post* risk.
8. *Ex post* alpha (differential return) and the reward-to-volatility ratio involve analysis of a portfolio's excess return and systematic risk. The Sharpe ratio and M^2 involve analysis of a portfolio's excess return and total risk.
9. Successful equity market timers hold portfolios with relatively high betas during market rises and relatively low betas during market declines. Quadratic regression and dummy variable regression are two methods designed to measure market timing ability.
10. Risk-adjusted measures of performance have been criticized for using a market surrogate instead of the "true" market portfolio; being unable to statistically distinguish luck from skill except over very long periods of time; using an inappropriate riskfree rate; and relying on the validity of the CAPM.

Questions and Problems

1. Crungy Patrick owns a portfolio of three stocks. Crungy's holdings and the prices of the stocks at the end of Year 1 and Year 2 follow. Assuming no contributions, withdrawals, or dividends paid, what is the return on Crungy's portfolio in Year 2?

Stock	Shares Owned	Year 1 Price	Year 2 Price
A	100	$10	$15
B	300	5	4
C	250	12	14

2. New Lisbon Laundry's pension fund was worth $30 million at the end of Year 1. On the first day of Year 2 the firm made a $2 million contribution to the fund. At the end of Year 2, the pension fund was valued at $38 million. What was the return on the New Lisbon pension fund during Year 2?
3. At the beginning of the year, Con Daily's portfolio was worth $9,000. At the end of each of the next four quarters, Con received a gift of $500, which was invested in the portfolio. At the end of each quarter, Con's portfolio was worth, respectively, $9,800, $10,800, $11,200, and $12,000. What is the time-weighted rate of return on Con's portfolio during the year?
4. Dell Darling's portfolio is worth $12,000 at the beginning of a 30-day month. On day 10 of the month, Dell received a contribution to the portfolio of $800. At the end of the month, Dell's portfolio is worth $13,977.71. What was the dollar-weighted return on Dell's portfolio for the month?
5. Distinguish between time-weighted and dollar-weighted rates of return. Under what performance measurement circumstances might the dollar-weighted return be preferred to the time-weighted?
6. At the beginning of a 30-day month, Buttercup Dickerson owned a portfolio valued at $5,000. On day 10, Buttercup's portfolio was worth $7,300 after a $2,000 contribution had been made on that day. At the end of the month, the portfolio was worth $9,690.18. Calculate both the time-weighted and dollar-weighted returns on Buttercup's portfolio for the month. Why do the two returns differ so substantially?
7. It is common practice for performance evaluation services to compare the returns on a common stock portfolio to a distribution of returns obtained from a large sample of other common stock portfolios. What are potential problems with this sort of analysis?

8. Consider a price-weighted market index composed of two securities, A and B, with prices of $16 and $30, respectively. The index divisor is currently 2.0. Calculate the value of the divisor if
   a. Stock A issues a 5% stock dividend
   b. Stock B undergoes a 3-for-1 stock split
   c. Stock A undergoes a 4-for-1 stock split
9. Consider three stocks, X, Y, and Z, with the following closing prices on two particular dates:

Stock	Date 1	Date 2
X	$16	$22
Y	5	4
Z	24	30

   On date 1 there are 100 shares of stock X, 200 shares of stock Y, and 100 shares of stock Z outstanding.
   a. Construct a price-weighted market index using the three stocks, X, Y, and Z. What is the index's value on date 1?
   b. What is the price-weighted index's value on date 2?
   c. Assume that, on date 2, stock X splits 4-for-1. What is the price-weighted index's value on that date?
   d. Construct a value-weighted index using the three stocks. Assign the value-weighted index a value of 100 on date 1. What is the index's value on date 2?
10. According to Ferris Fain, "The success of a stock market index depends on its ability to measure the performance of stocks not included in the index." Explain what Ferris means.
11. Consider an equal-weighted market index composed of three securities. The market prices of those securities on three dates follow.

	Market Prices		
Security	Date 1	Date 2	Date 3
A	$50	$55	$60
B	30	28	30
C	70	75	73

   a. What is the return on the index from date 1 to date 2?
   b. What is the return on the index from date 2 to date 3?
12. Pickles Dillhoefer owns a portfolio that during the past five years produced a 16.8% annual return. During that time the portfolio produced a 1.10 beta; the risk-free return and market return averaged 7.4% and 15.2% per year, respectively. What was the *ex post* alpha on Pickles's portfolio during this time period? Draw the *ex post* SML and the position of Pickles's portfolio.
13. The performance of the Venus Fund, a common stock mutual fund, compared with that of the S&P 500 during a ten-year period follows:

	Venus Fund	S&P 500
Average quarterly excess return	0.6%	0.5%
Standard deviation of quarterly excess returns	9.9	6.6
Beta	1.10	1.00

   Dazzy Vance is considering investing in either the Venus Fund or another mutual fund whose objective is to track the performance of the S&P 500. Assuming that your decision is based solely on past performance, which fund would you recommend that

Dazzy select? Justify your answer using various measures of risk-adjusted performance.

14. Why is the Sharpe ratio a more appropriate measure of performance than the *ex post* alpha if the portfolio being assessed represents the entire wealth of the portfolio's owner?

15. Consider the following annual returns produced by a MiniFund, a mutual fund investing in small stocks:

1971	16.50%	1976	57.38%	1981	13.88%	1986	6.85%
1972	4.43	1977	25.38	1982	28.01	1987	−9.30
1973	−30.90	1978	23.46	1983	39.67	1988	22.87
1974	−19.95	1979	43.46	1984	−6.67	1989	10.18
1975	52.82	1980	39.88	1985	24.66	1990	−21.56

Referring to Table 1.1, use the Treasury bill returns as the riskfree return and the common stock returns as the market return, and calculate the following risk-adjusted return measures for the small stock mutual fund:

a. *Ex post* alpha
b. Reward-to-volatility ratio
c. Sharpe ratio

Comment on the mutual fund's risk-adjusted performance. What problems are associated with using a large capitalization index such as the S&P 500 (the source of the common stock returns) as the benchmark in evaluating this small company mutual fund?

Endnotes

1. This procedure provides a quarterly return with "quarterly compounding." Alternatively, the semiquarterly return could be doubled, resulting in a quarterly return with "semiquarterly compounding" of -1.96% ($= -.98\% \times 2$).

2. For more on the construction of market indices, see Mary M. Cutler, "Market Indices: A Learning Exercise Using Warsaw Stock Exchange Prices," *Financial Practice and Education,* 5, no. 2 (Fall/Winter 1995): 99–106.

3. Sometimes the excess return for a portfolio, which is equal to its return minus the riskfree rate ($= r_{pt} - r_{ft}$), is used instead of r_{pt} in Equation (18.9) to determine the average excess return (denoted aer_p). Then, the summation in the numerator of Equation (18.10) is carried out using $[(r_{pt} - r_{ft}) - aer_p]^2$ instead of $(r_{pt} - ar_p)^2$. The resulting number is the standard deviation of excess returns, which is sometimes used as an estimate of the total risk of the portfolio. Typically, the two standard deviations are quite similar in numerical value.

4. Equation (18.11) corresponds to the formula for estimating the slope term in a simple regression model where the independent variable is er_{Mt} and the dependent variable is er_{pt}. Sometimes returns are used in Equation (18.11), where er_{Mt} is replaced by r_{Mt} and er_{pt} is replaced by r_{pt}. In this situation, the beta corresponds to the slope term in the market model for the

portfolio (as discussed in Chapter 8). Typically, the two betas are quite similar in numerical value.

5. This measure of performance is sometimes known as the *Jensen coefficient* (or *Jensen alpha*) because it was developed by Michael C. Jensen in "The Performance of Mutual Funds in the Period 1945–1964," *Journal of Finance,* 23, no. 2 (May 1968): 389–416.

6. Alternatively, if *FF*'s average return had been 6%, then its coordinates would have been (1.13, 6.00), placing it above the *ex post* SML. In this situation, *FF*'s *ex post* alpha would have been .78%, and its performance would have been viewed as superior.

7. An alternative measure of performance involves dividing the *ex post* alpha by an estimate of the *ex post* unique (or unsystematic) risk of the portfolio. This measure, known as the *appraisal* (or *information*) *ratio*, would be equal to $-.34$ ($= -1.29/3.75$) for First Fund. Comparisons can be made with the value of the appraisal ratio for the market portfolio (its value is defined to be zero) and other portfolios. Note that a positive value indicates superior performance, and that the larger the value, the better the performance. See Jack L. Treynor and Fischer Black, "How to Use Security Analysis to Improve Portfolio Selection," *Journal of Business,* 46, no. 1 (January 1973): 66–86.

8. The random error term is similar to a number that arises from a spin of a roulette wheel, where the num-

bers on the wheel are symmetrically distributed around zero so that the expected outcome from a spin of the roulette wheel is zero. The standard deviation associated with the wheel is denoted σ_{ep}.

9. This measure of performance is sometimes known as the *Treynor ratio* because it was developed by Jack L. Treynor in "How to Rate Management of Investment Funds," *Harvard Business Review*, 43, no. 1 (January/February 1965): 63–75.

10. This measure of performance is known as the Sharpe ratio because it was developed by William F. Sharpe in "Mutual Fund Performance," *Journal of Business,* 39, no. 1 (January 1966): 119–138. It is used by Morningstar, Inc. in its evaluation of mutual fund performance, as will be discussed in Chapter 23.

11. The popular use of M^2 to refer to this measure of performance can be attributed to the fact that the measure was put forth by Nobel laureate Franco Modigliani and his granddaughter, Leah Modigliani, in "Risk-Adjusted Performance," *Journal of Portfolio Management*, 23, no. 2 (Winter 1997): 45–54.

12. Similarly, a version of M_p^2 can be calculated using beta as a measure of risk, resulting in $ar_f + (ar_p - ar_f)/\beta_p$, which would then be compared to the average return on the market to assess the portfolio's performance. This measure simply involves adding the riskfree rate to $RVOL_p$.

13. There is a third measure of portfolio performance that is based on the *ex post* CML. This measure, called the *ex post total risk alpha*, is simply the vertical distance the portfolio lies above or below the *ex post* CML. It is similar to the measure referred to earlier as *ex post* alpha, except that it is based on a different risk measure (total risk instead of market risk) and uses a different benchmark (the *ex post* CML instead of the *ex post* SML). It also gives the same assessment of a portfolio's performance relative to the market as the Sharpe ratio and M^2, but it can lead to a different ranking for the portfolio.

14. The market portfolio does not have any unique risk. If $RVOL_p$ indicates that a portfolio did not perform as well as the market, then SR_p must also indicate that the portfolio did not perform as well as the market because a portfolio with a relatively high amount of market risk also has a relatively high amount of total risk.

15. The quadratic regression equation (18.32), originally suggested by Treynor and Mazuy, has been refined by Sudipto Bhattacharya and Paul Pfleiderer in a 1983 Stanford University unpublished paper (Technical Report 714), the principal results of which are described in T. Daniel Coggin, Frank J. Fabozzi, and Shafiqur Rahman, "The Investment Performance of U.S. Equity Pension Fund Managers: An Empirical Investigation," *Journal of Finance*, 48, no. 3 (July 1993): 1040–1043.

16. The size of parameter c (as well as the parameters a and b) should be judged relative to its standard error. In both of the equations shown here, it is quite small relative to both zero and the respective standard errors. Most standard statistical textbooks have an introductory discussion of the regression procedures that are used here. See, for example, Chapters 10 and 11 in James T. McClave and P. George Benson, *Statistics for Business and Economics,* 6th ed. (New York: Macmillan College Publishing, 1994).

17. One criticism is that the methods presented do not indicate *why* a portfolio performed as given by one of the measures described earlier in the chapter. Both *style analysis* and *performance attribution* are methods of making such a determination. The basic idea behind these methods is to examine a portfolio's returns in order to determine what types of stocks and other securities have been purchased by the portfolio manager instead of relying on his or her description. Two of the pioneering papers in this area are William F. Sharpe, "Major Investment Styles," *Journal of Portfolio Management,* 4, no. 2 (Winter 1978): 68–74; and Eugene F. Fama, "Components of Investment Performance," *Journal of Finance,* 27, no. 3 (June 1972): 551–567. For more on style analysis, see the fifth set of references in Chapter 17 as well as William F. Sharpe, "Determining a Fund's Effective Asset Mix," *Investment Management Review* (December 1988): 59–69; Angelo Lobosco and Dan diBartolomeo, "Approximating the Confidence Intervals for Sharpe Style Weights," *Financial Analysts Journal,* 53, no. 4 (July/August 1997): 80–85; and Dan diBartolomeo and Erik Witkowski, "Mutual Fund Misclassification: Evidence Based on Style Analysis," *Financial Analysts Journal,* 53, no. 5 (September/October 1997): 32–43. For more on performance attribution, see H. Russell Fogler, "Common Stock Management in the 1990s," *Journal of Portfolio Management,* 16, no. 2 (Winter 1990): 26–35; Ernest M. Ankrim, "Risk-Adjusted Performance Attribution," *Financial Analysts Journal,* 48, no. 2 (March/April 1991): 74–82; Peter J. Higgs and Stephen Goode, "Target Active Returns and Attribution Analysis," *Financial Analysts Journal,* 49, no. 3 (May/June 1993): 77–80; Ernest M. Ankrim and Chris R. Hensel, "Multicurrency Performance Attribution," *Financial Analysts Journal,* 50, no. 2 (May/June 1994): 29–35; and Brian D. Singer and Denis S. Karnosky, "The General Framework for Global Investment Management and Performance Attribution," *Journal of Portfolio Management,* 21, no. 2 (Winter 1995): 84–92.

18. See Richard Roll, "Ambiguity When Performance Is Measured by the Security Market Line," *Journal of Finance,* 33, no. 4 (September 1978): 1051–1069; David Peterson and Michael L. Rice, "A Note on Ambiguity

in Portfolio Performance Measures," *Journal of Finance,* 35, no. 5 (December 1980): 1251–1256; and Heinz Zimmermann and Claudia Zogg-Wetter, "On Detecting Selection and Timing Ability: The Case of Stock Market Indexes," *Financial Analysts Journal,* 48, no. 1 (January/February 1992): 80–83.

19. The problem is much more severe when the index is equal-weighted because periodically part of the holdings of those stocks that had risen the most would have to be sold and the proceeds invested in additional shares of those stocks that had risen the least in order to keep equal weights in each stock.

20. With the widespread use of index funds and index futures (discussed in Chapters 17 and 25, respectively), this criticism has lost much of its validity.

21. See Dan W. French and Glenn V. Henderson Jr., "How Well Does Performance Evaluation Perform?" *Journal of Portfolio Management,* 11, no. 2 (Winter 1985): 15–18.

22. Under APT (discussed in Chapter 12), there is another measure of portfolio performance that is analogous to the CAPM-based *appraisal ratio* mentioned in endnote 7. It involves dividing the APT-based *ex post* alpha by the *ex post* standard deviation of the APT-based random error term.

CHAPTER 19

Types of Fixed-Income Securities

This chapter surveys the major types of fixed-income securities, with an emphasis on those currently popular in the United States. Such a survey cannot be exhaustive. A security is, after all, a contract giving the investor certain rights to the future prospects of the issuer. Because the rights given to the investor can differ from one security to another, and because the future prospects of issuers can differ substantially, the number of different types of fixed-income securities is quite large (and growing), making a complete survey virtually impossible.

pure-discount security

coupon payments
maturity date
principal

The term *fixed-income* is commonly used to cover the types of securities discussed in this chapter, but it is a bit misleading. Typically, these securities promise the investor that he or she will receive specified cash flows at specified times in the future. It may be one cash flow, in which case the security is known as a **pure-discount security** (or zero-coupon security). Alternatively, it may involve multiple cash flows. If all of these cash flows (except for the last one) are of the same size, they are generally referred to as **coupon payments.** The specified date beyond which the investor will no longer receive cash flows is known as the **maturity date.** On this date, the investor receives the **principal** (also known as the par value or face value) associated with the security along with the last coupon payment. However, all these cash flows are *promised* but may not be received because in many cases there is at least some risk that a promised payment will not be made in full and on time.

19.1 Money Market Instruments

Certain types of short-term (meaning, arbitrarily, one year or less), highly marketable loans play a major role in the investment and borrowing activities of both financial and nonfinancial corporations. Individual investors with substantial funds may invest in such money market instruments directly, but most do so indirectly via money market accounts at various financial institutions.[1]

Some money market instruments are negotiable and are traded in active secondary dealer markets; others are not. Some may be purchased by anyone with adequate funds; others only by particular types of institutions. Many are sold on a discount basis. For example, a 90-day note with a face value of $100,000 might be sold for $98,000, where $100,000 is paid to the investor at maturity. The difference of $2,000 represents interest income.

bank discount basis

Interest rates on such money market instruments are often reported on a **bank discount basis.** The note in the example is described in the media as having a discount of

2% per quarter, or 8% per year. However, the discount does not represent the true interest rate on the note. In such a situation, the true interest rate is higher; in this case it equals $2,000/\$98,000 = 2.04\%$ per quarter, or the equivalent of 8.16% per year (with quarterly compounding, it would equal $8.41\% = 1.0204^4 - 1$).

The Wall Street Journal publishes on a daily basis a list of the current interest rates on a number of money market instruments (see Figure 19.1). Some of the money market instruments listed are described next.

19.1.1 COMMERCIAL PAPER

commercial paper

Commercial paper is an unsecured short-term promissory note. Instruments of this type are issued by both financial and nonfinancial companies. The dollar amount of commercial paper outstanding exceeds the amount of any other type of money market instrument except for Treasury bills, with the majority being issued by financial companies such as bank holding companies as well as companies involved in sales and personal finance, insurance, and leasing. Such notes are often issued by large firms that have unused lines of credit at banks, making it highly likely that the loan will be paid off when it becomes due. The interest rates on commercial paper reflect this small risk by being relatively low in comparison with the interest rates on other corporate fixed-income securities.

FIGURE 19.1 Interest Rates on Money Market Instruments

MONEY RATES

Monday, March 1, 1999

The key U.S. and foreign annual interest rates below are a guide to general levels but don't always represent actual transactions.

PRIME RATE: 7.75% (effective 11/18/98). The base rate on corporate loans posted by at least 75% of the nation's 30 largest banks.

DISCOUNT RATE: 4.50% (effective 11/17/98). The charge on loans to depository institutions by the Federal Reserve Banks.

FEDERAL FUNDS: 5 1/2% high, 4 3/4% low, 4 7/8% near closing bid, 5% offered. Reserves traded among commercial banks for overnight use in amounts of $1 million or more. Source: Prebon Yamane (U.S.A.) Inc.

CALL MONEY: 6.50% (effective 11/18/98). The charge on loans to brokers on stock exchange collateral. Source: Telerate.

COMMERCIAL PAPER placed directly by General Electric Capital Corp.: 4.82% 30 to 35 days; 4.86% 36 to 126 days; 4.88% 127 to 270 days.

EURO COMMERCIAL PAPER placed directly by General Electric Capital Corp.: 3.07% 30 days; 3.06% two months; 3.05% three months; 3.00% four months; 2.99% five months; 2.98% six months.

DEALER COMMERCIAL PAPER: High-grade unsecured notes sold through dealers by major corporations: 4.87% 30 days; 4.87% 60 days; 4.85% 90 days.

CERTIFICATES OF DEPOSIT: 4.60% one month; 4.66% two months; 4.73% three months; 4.98% six months; 5.13% one year. Average of top rates paid by major New York banks on primary new issues of negotiable C.D.s, usually on amounts of $1 million and more. The minimum unit is $100,000. Typical rates in the secondary market: 4.91% one month; 4.94% three months; 5.05% six months.

BANKERS ACCEPTANCES: 4.81% 30 days; 4.82% 60 days; 4.84% 90 days; 4.84% 120 days; 4.84% 150 days; 4.84% 180 days. Offered rates of negotiable, bank-backed business credit instruments typically financing an import order.

LONDON LATE EURODOLLARS: 4 31/32% - 4 27/32% one month; 5% - 4 7/8% two months; 5 1/32% - 4 29/32% three months; 5 1/16 % - 4 15/16% four months; 5 3/32% - 4 31/32% five months; 5 1/8% - 5% six months.

LONDON INTERBANK OFFERED RATES (LIBOR): 4.96500% one month; 5.02750% three months; 5.12250% six months; 5.38000% one year. British Bankers' Association average of interbank offered rates for dollar deposits in the London market based on quotations at 16 major banks. Effective rate for contracts entered into two days from date appearing at top of this column.

EURO LIBOR: 3.12313% one month; 3.1000% three months; 3.05938% six months; 3.07563% one year. British Bankers' Association average of interbank offered rates for euro deposits in the London market based on quotations at 16 major banks. Effective rate for contracts entered into two days from date appearing at top of this column.

EURO INTERBANK OFFERED RATES (EURIBOR): 3.122% one month; 3.099% three months; 3.059% six months; 3.079% one year. European Banking Federation-sponsored rate among 57 Euro zone banks.

FOREIGN PRIME RATES: Canada 6.75%; Germany 3.099 %(eff. 3/1/99); Japan 1.500%; Switzerland 3.25%; Britain 5.50%. These rate indications aren't directly comparable; lending practices vary widely by location.

TREASURY BILLS: Results of the Monday, March 1, 1999, auction of short-term U.S. government bills, sold at a discount from face value in units of $10,000 to $1 million: 4.57% 13 weeks; 4.585% 26 weeks.

OVERNIGHT REPURCHASE RATE: 4.98%. Dealer financing rate for overnight sale and repurchase of Treasury securities. Source: Telerate.

FEDERAL HOME LOAN MORTGAGE CORP. (Freddie Mac): Posted yields on 30-year mortgage commitments. Delivery within 30 days 7.08%, 60 days 7.13%, standard conventional fixed-rate mortgages; 5.625%, 2% rate capped one-year adjustable rate mortgages. Source: Telerate.

FEDERAL NATIONAL MORTGAGE ASSOCIATION (Fannie Mae): Posted yields on 30 year mortgage commitments (priced at par) for delivery within 30 days 7.16%, 60 days 7.21%, standard conventional fixed rate-mortgages; 5.95%, 6/2 rate capped one-year adjustable rate mortgages. Source: Telerate.

MERRILL LYNCH READY ASSETS TRUST: 4.48%. Annualized average rate of return after expenses for the past 30 days; not a forecast of future returns.

CONSUMER PRICE INDEX: January, 164.3, up 1.7% from a year ago. Bureau of Labor Statistics.

Commercial paper is usually sold in denominations of $100,000 or more, with maturities of up to 270 days (the maximum allowed without requiring registration of the issue with the Securities and Exchange Commission) to large institutional investors such as money market mutual funds. Typically these investors hold onto the paper until maturity, resulting in a very small secondary market.

19.1.2   CERTIFICATES OF DEPOSIT

certificates of deposit

Certificates of deposit represent a type of interest-bearing deposit at commercial banks or savings and loan associations. Large-denomination (or jumbo) CDs are issued in amounts of $100,000 or more, have a specified maturity, and generally are negotiable, meaning that they can be sold by one investor to another. In most cases, all interest is paid, along with principal, at maturity. Such certificates are insured by the Federal Deposit Insurance Corporation (FDIC) or the National Credit Union Administration (NCUA), but only up to a maximum of $100,000 (in 1999).[2] Interestingly, foreign banks that have branches in the United States also offer dollar-denominated CDs to investors. These CDs have been dubbed Yankee CDs by the media. The top part of Figure 19.2 shows average yields of CDs with various maturities issued by major banks, as published each Wednesday in *The Wall Street Journal*.[3]

19.1.3   BANKERS ACCEPTANCES

Historically, bankers acceptances were created to finance goods in transit; currently, they are generally used to finance foreign trade. For example, the buyer of the goods may issue a written promise to the seller to pay a given sum within a short period of time (for example, 180 days or less). A bank then "accepts" this promise, obligating itself to pay the amount when requested, and obtains in return a claim on the goods as collateral. The written promise becomes a liability of both the bank and the buyer of

bankers acceptance

the goods and is known as a **bankers acceptance.**

The seller of the goods, having received the written promise from the buyer that the bank has "accepted," need not wait until the promise is due in order to receive payment. Instead, the acceptance can be sold to someone else at a price that is less than the amount of the promised payment to be made in the future. Thus, such instruments are pure-discount securities.

19.1.4   EURODOLLARS

Eurodollar CDs

Eurodollar deposits

In the world of international finance, large, short-term CDs denominated in dollars and issued by banks outside the United States (most often in London) are known as **Eurodollar CDs** (or simply Euro CDs). Also available for investment are dollar-denominated time deposits in banks outside the United States, known as **Eurodollar deposits.** A key distinction between Euro CDs and Eurodollar deposits is that Euro CDs are negotiable, meaning that they can be traded whereas Eurodollar deposits are nonnegotiable, meaning that they cannot be traded.

The demand and supply conditions for such instruments may differ from the conditions for other U.S. money market instruments because of restrictions imposed (or likely to be imposed) by the United States and other governments. However, enough commonality exists to keep interest rates from diverging too much from rates available on domestic alternatives. One difference between CDs issued by U.S. banks and Euro CDs is that the Euro CDs do not have federal deposit insurance.

BANXQUOTE® MONEY MARKETS

Tuesday, March 2, 1999

AVERAGE YIELDS OF MAJOR BANKS

	MMI*	One Month	Two Months	Three Months	Six Months	One Year	Two Years	Five Years
NEW YORK								
Savings	2.05%			3.95%	3.97%	3.99%	4.07%	4.25%
Jumbos	3.33%	3.37%	3.37%	4.12%	4.19%	4.25%	4.58%	4.73%
CALIFORNIA								
Savings	2.48%			4.04%	4.17%	4.23%	4.24%	4.36%
Jumbos	3.11%	4.39%	4.39%	4.49%	4.56%	4.69%	4.83%	5.01%
PENNSYLVANIA								
Savings	2.66%			2.76%	3.09%	3.49%	4.05%	4.39%
Jumbos	3.77%	4.64%	4.53%	3.92%	4.18%	4.25%	4.50%	4.88%
ILLINOIS								
Savings	2.33%			3.99%	4.16%	4.25%	4.30%	4.54%
Jumbos	3.51%	4.33%	4.33%	4.35%	4.47%	4.57%	4.64%	4.87%
TEXAS								
Savings	3.38%			3.24%	3.83%	3.88%	4.00%	4.27%
Jumbos	3.80%	4.13%	4.13%	4.22%	4.23%	4.32%	4.48%	4.67%
FLORIDA								
Savings	2.50%			3.07%	3.38%	3.55%	3.75%	4.10%
Jumbos	4.17%	3.89%	3.97%	4.20%	4.32%	4.28%	4.43%	4.47%
U.S. BANK AVERAGE								
Savings	2.93			3.56	4.00	4.13	4.22	4.40
Jumbos	3.61	3.93	3.97	4.13	4.34	4.44	4.46	4.60
WEEKLY CHANGE (in percentage points)								
Savings	−0.04			−0.03	−0.01	−0.01	....	....
Jumbos	−0.04	....	....	+0.01	+0.01	+0.04	+0.03	+0.03

SAVINGS CD YIELDS OFFERED THROUGH LEADING BROKERS

	Three Months	Six Months	One Year	Two Years	Five Years
BROKER AVERAGE	4.65%	4.81%	5.10%	5.34%	5.57%
WEEKLY CHANGE	−0.06	−0.02	+0.10	+0.14	+0.17

*Money Market Investments include MMDA, NOW, savings deposits, passbook and other liquid accounts.

Each depositor is insured by the Federal Deposit Insurance Corp. (FDIC) up to $100,000 per issuing institution.

COMPOUND METHODS: c-Continuously. d-Daily. w-Wkly. m-Mthly. q-Qrtly. s-Semi-annually. a-Annually.

SIMPLE INTEREST: si-Paid Monthly. e-Paid Semi-annually. y-Paid at Maturity.

OTHER SYMBOLS: APY-Annual percentage yield. F-Floating rate P-Prime CD. T-T-Bill CD.

BD-Broker-Dealer. pp-Priced below par.

Day BASIS: A-Actual/Actual. B-30/360. C-Actual/360.

The information included in this table has been obtained directly from broker-dealers, banks and savings institutions, but the accuracy and validity cannot be guaranteed. Rates are subject to change. Yields, terms and capital adequacy should be verified before investing. Only well capitalized or adequately capitalized depository institutions are quoted.

z-Unavailable.

HIGH YIELD SAVINGS

Small minimum balance/opening deposit, generally $500 to $25,000

Money Market Investments*	Rate		APY	Six Months CDs	Rate		APY
USAccess Bank, Louisville KY	5.18%	mA	5.30	NeT.B@Nk, Alpharetta GA	5.12%	dA	5.25
Advanta Natl, Wilmingtn DE	5.05%	dA	5.18	USAccess Bank, Louisville KY	5.10%	qA	5.20
BankFirst, Sioux Falls SD	5.05%	mA	5.17	Telebank, Arlington VA	5.05%	dA	5.18
NeT.B@Nk, Alpharetta GA	5.00%	dA	5.13	Providian National, Tilton NH	5.04%	dA	5.17
Chase Manhttn USA, Wilmgtn DE	4.93%	dA	5.05	Providian Bk, Salt Lake Cty UT	5.04%	dA	5.17
One Month CDs	**Rate**		**APY**	**One Year CDs**	**Rate**		**APY**
New South FSB, Birmingham AL	4.95%	siA	5.06	Telebank, Arlington VA	5.31%	dA	5.45
Southn Pac Bk, Los Angeles CA	4.72%	dA	4.83	USAccess Bank, Louisville KY	5.29%	qA	5.40
Bluebonnet Savings, Dallas TX	4.70%	siA	4.80	NeT.B@Nk, Alpharetta GA	5.21%	dA	5.35
Pacific Crest, San Diego CA	4.64%	dA	4.75	Providian National, Tilton NH	5.18%	dA	5.32
Safra National, New York NY	4.16%	dA	4.25	Providian Bk, Salt Lake Cty UT	5.18%	dA	5.32
Two Months CDs	**Rate**		**APY**	**Two Years CDs**	**Rate**		**APY**
New South FSB, Birmingham AL	4.95%	siA	5.05	Telebank, Arlington VA	5.50%	dA	5.65
Southn Pac Bk, Los Angeles CA	4.77%	dA	4.89	Capital One FSB, Glen Allen VA	5.46%	dA	5.61
Bluebonnet Savings, Dallas TX	4.75%	siA	4.85	Keybank USA, Albany NY	5.45%	dA	5.60
Pacific Crest, San Diego CA	4.64%	dA	4.75	EAB, Uniondale NY	5.35%	dA	5.50
Safra National, New York NY	4.40%	dA	4.50	Providian National, Tilton NH	5.34%	dA	5.48
Three Months CDs	**Rate**		**APY**	**Five Years CDs**	**Rate**		**APY**
New South FSB, Birmingham AL	5.05%	siA	5.15	Capital One FSB, Glen Allen VA	5.69%	dA	5.85
Telebank, Arlington VA	4.97%	dA	5.10	Telebank, Arlington VA	5.69%	dA	5.85
Keybank USA, Albany NY	4.90%	dA	5.02	Providian National, Tilton NH	5.66%	dA	5.82
Southn Pac Bk, Los Angeles CA	4.82%	dA	4.94	Providian Bk, Salt Lake Cty UT	5.66%	dA	5.82
Bluebonnet Savings, Dallas TX	4.80%	siA	4.89	Keybank USA, Albany NY	5.60%	dA	5.76

HIGH YIELD JUMBOS

Large minimum balance/opening deposit, generally $95,000 to $100,000

Money Market Investments*	Rate		APY	Six Months Jumbo CDs	Rate		APY
USAccess Bank, Louisville KY	5.18%	mA	5.30	NeT.B@Nk, Alpharetta GA	5.12%	dA	5.25
Advanta Natl, Wilmingtn DE	5.15%	dA	5.28	Providian National, Tilton NH	5.05%	dA	5.18
BankFirst, Sioux Falls SD	5.05%	mA	5.17	Providian Bk, Salt Lake Cty UT	5.05%	dA	5.18
First Signature, Portsmouth NH	5.01%	dA	5.14	Advanta Natl, Wilmingtn DE	5.05%	siA	5.11
NeT.B@Nk, Alpharetta GA	5.00%	dA	5.13	Acacia Bank, Laguna Hills CA	4.97%	dA	5.10
One Month Jumbo CDs	**Rate**		**APY**	**One Year Jumbo CDs**	**Rate**		**APY**
New South FSB, Birmingham AL	4.95%	siA	5.06	NeT.B@Nk, Alpharetta GA	5.21%	dA	5.35
LaSalle Natl, Chicago IL	4.75%	yC	4.92	EAB, Uniondale NY	5.21%	dA	5.35
Heritage Bank, Holstein IA	4.79%	yA	4.90	Providian National, Tilton NH	5.19%	dA	5.33
Advanta Natl, Wilmingtn DE	4.79%	dA	4.85	Providian Bk, Salt Lake Cty UT	5.19%	dA	5.33
EAB, Uniondale NY	4.74%	dA	4.85	Capital One FSB, Glen Allen VA	5.19%	dA	5.33
Two Months Jumbo CDs	**Rate**		**APY**	**Two Years Jumbo CDs**	**Rate**		**APY**
New South FSB, Birmingham AL	4.95%	siA	5.05	Capital One FSB, Glen Allen VA	5.47%	dA	5.62
EAB, Uniondale NY	4.86%	dA	4.98	Keybank USA, Albany NY	5.45%	dA	5.60
Advanta Natl, Wilmingtn DE	4.85%	siA	4.95	Providian National, Tilton NH	5.36%	dA	5.51
LaSalle Natl, Chicago IL	4.75%	yC	4.91	Providian Bk, Salt Lake Cty UT	5.36%	dA	5.51
Equitable Federal, Wheaton MD	4.75%	siA	4.85	Advanta Natl, Wilmingtn DE	5.35%	siA	5.35
Three Months Jumbo CDs	**Rate**		**APY**	**Five Years Jumbo CDs**	**Rate**		**APY**
New South FSB, Birmingham AL	5.05%	siA	5.15	Capital One FSB, Glen Allen VA	5.70%	dA	5.87
Advanta Natl, Wilmington DE	4.95%	siA	5.04	Providian National, Tilton NH	5.67%	dA	5.83
Providian National, Tilton NH	4.91%	dA	5.03	Providian Bk, Salt Lake Cty UT	5.67%	dA	5.83
EAB, Uniondale NY	4.91%	dA	5.03	Keybank USA, Albany NY	5.60%	dA	5.76
Keybank USA, Albany NY	4.90%	dA	5.02	MBNA America, Wilmingtn DE	5.50%	dA	5.65

Additional information on deposits and loans for all 50 states is available in the **BanxQuote® Banking Center** in The Wall Street Journal Interactive Edition at http://wsj.com

WSJ.com

For BanxQuote® Dealer Market and Institutional CDs see Telerate pages 22300-99.

Source: BanxQuote Inc., N.Y. N.Y. Tel. 212-499-9100.

454

FIGURE 19.2 Yields on Certificates of Deposit

Source: Reprinted by permission of *The Wall Street Journal,* Dow Jones & Company, Inc., March 3, 1999, p. C24. All rights reserved worldwide.

19.1.5 REPURCHASE AGREEMENTS

repurchase agreement

Often one investor (usually a financial institution) will sell another investor (usually another financial institution) a money market instrument and agree to repurchase it for an agreed-on price at a later date. For example, investor *A* might sell investor *B* a number of Treasury bills that mature in 180 days for a price of $10 million. As part of the sale, investor *A* signs a **repurchase agreement** (or "repo") with investor *B*. (From the perspective of the purchaser, investor *B*, the agreement is referred to as a "reverse repo".) This agreement specifies that after 30 days, investor *A* will repurchase these Treasury bills for $10.1 million. Thus, investor *A* will have paid investor *B* $100,000 in interest to use $10 million for 30 days. Investor *B* has, in essence, purchased a money market instrument that matures in 30 days. The annualized interest rate is known as the

repo rate

repo rate, which in this case is equal to 12% $[= (\$100{,}000/\$10{,}000{,}000) \times (360/30)]$.

Note how this repurchase agreement is like a collateralized loan from *B* to *A*, with the Treasury bills serving as the collateral. Such loans involve little risk to the lender (*B*) because the money market instruments typically used in repurchase agreements are of high quality.

19.2 U.S. Government Securities

It should come as no surprise that the U.S. government relies heavily on debt financing. Despite recent budget surpluses, since the 1960s revenues have seldom covered expenses, and the differences have been financed primarily by issuing debt instruments. Moreover, new debt must be issued to acquire the necessary funds to pay off old debt that comes

debt refunding

due. Such **debt refunding** sometimes allows the holders of the maturing debt to exchange it directly for new debt, and in the process receive beneficial treatment for tax purposes.

Some idea of the magnitude and ownership structure of U.S. Treasury debt can be gained by examining Table 19.1. Through the U.S. Treasury, federal agencies, and various trust funds, the federal government itself is a large holder, as is the Federal Reserve System. However, a large amount is held by state and local governments as well as private investors of one sort or another. For example, these securities are a major factor in the portfolios of commercial banks and other financial institutions. To a lesser extent, business corporations also invest in them, primarily as outlets for relatively short-term excess working capital. The amount held by individual households is also substantial, with more than half of their investment in U.S. government securities being in savings bonds and notes. Last, holdings by foreigners have become quite large in recent years.

About two-thirds of the public debt is *marketable,* meaning that it is represented by securities that can be sold at any time by the original purchaser through government security dealers.[4] The major *nonmarketable* issues are held by U.S. government agencies, foreign governments, state and local governments, and individuals (the latter in the form of U.S. Savings Bonds). Marketable issues include Treasury bills, notes, and bonds. Table 19.2 shows the amounts of interest-bearing U.S. public debt at the end of 1998. (There was an additional $8.8 billion of non-interest-bearing U.S. public debt outstanding at that time, so total U.S. public debt amounted to $5,614.2 billion.)

term-to-maturity

The relative maturity dates for U.S. government debt are influenced by a number of factors. As time passes, of course, the **term-to-maturity** (that is, the remaining time until maturity) of an outstanding issue decreases. Moreover, the Treasury has considerable latitude in selecting maturities for new issues and can also engage in refunding operations. From time to time, congressional limits on amounts issued or interest paid on certain types of instruments may force reliance on other types of instruments. Debt operations may also be used as a conscious instrument of government economic policy in an attempt to influence the current interest rates for securities of various maturities.

TABLE 19.1 Ownership of Outstanding Public Debt of U.S. Treasury, End of 1998

Held By		Dollar Amount (billions)	Percentage of Total Amount
U.S. Treasury, federal agencies, and trust funds		$1,497.2	28.2%
Federal Reserve banks		410.9	7.7
Private investors:			
Commercial banks	$ 261.7		4.9%
Money market funds	91.6		1.7
Insurance companies	235.9		4.4
Other companies	258.5		4.9
State and local treasuries	358.0		6.7
Individuals	356.6		6.7
Foreign and international	1,131.8		21.3
Other miscellaneous	717.1		13.5
Total private investors		3,411.2	64.1
Total gross public debt[a]		$5,319.3	100.0%

[a]According to the Federal Reserve Bulletin, the components do not necessarily sum to the total because of rounding.

Source: Federal Reserve Bulletin, May 1999, p. A27.

TABLE 19.2 Interest-Bearing U.S. Public Debt, End of 1998

Category	Amount (billions)	
Nonmarketable		
Government account series	$1,840.0	
U.S. Savings Bonds and notes	180.3	
Foreign issues	34.3	
State and local government series	165.3	
Other	30.0	
Total nonmarketable debt		$2,249.9
Marketable		
Bills	$ 691.0	
Notes	1,960.7	
Bonds	621.2	
Inflation-indexed notes and bonds	50.6	
Total marketable debt		3,355.5
Total debt[a]		$5,605.4

[a]According to the Federal Reserve Bulletin, the components do not necessarily sum to the total because of rounding.

Source: Federal Reserve Bulletin, April 1999, p. A27.

Figure 19.3 shows that the maturity structure of marketable, interest-bearing U.S. public debt held by private investors was not long in December 1998. For example, about 33% was short-term debt, maturing in less than one year. About 72% had a maturity date within five years. The total amount of the debt covered by the figure is $2.9 trillion, which is less than the $3.4 trillion shown in the bottom of Table 19.2 because some of the $3.4 trillion was not held by private investors but by others such as the Federal Reserve banks.

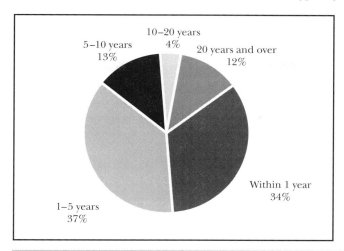

FIGURE 19.3 Maturity Structure of Marketable Interest-Bearing U.S. Public Debt Held by Private Investors, December 1998

Source: Treasury Bulletin, September 1999, p. 26.

Many types of debt have been issued by the U.S. government as well as by U.S. government agencies and organizations sponsored by the federal government. Figure 19.4 presents a list of price quotations for certain types of debt securities that have been issued by the U.S. Treasury. These securities are discussed next.

19.2.1   U.S. TREASURY BILLS

Treasury bills

Treasury bills are issued on a discount basis, with maturities of up to 52 weeks and in denominations of $1,000 or more. (Before August 1998, the minimum denomination was $10,000.) All are issued in book-entry form; the buyer receives a receipt at the time of purchase that indicates the bill's face value at maturity. Although Treasury bills are sold at discount, their dollar yield (that is, the difference between the purchase price and the face value if the bill is held to maturity) is treated as interest income for tax purposes.

Offerings of 13-week and 26-week bills are usually made once each week; 52-week bills are usually offered every fourth week. All are sold using a *multiple price auction* held on Mondays. Bids may be entered on either a competitive or a noncompetitive basis. With a competitive bid, the investor states a price that he or she is willing to pay (which can be converted to the interest rate that would be earned if the bid is accepted). For example, an investor might enter a bid for a stated number of 13-week bills at a price of 98.512. If the bid is accepted, the investor will pay $985.12 for each $1,000 of face value, meaning that an investment of $985.12 will generate a receipt of $1,000 if held to maturity 13 weeks later. With a noncompetitive bid, the investor agrees to pay the average price of all bids that will be accepted by the Treasury.

Before each auction, the Treasury announces the total face value and the maturities of all bills that it plans to issue. At the auction itself, having received the bids, the Treasury accepts all noncompetitive bids. For example, if $6 billion of 13-week bills are issued, perhaps $2 billion of noncompetitive bids will have been received by the time of the auction. Because all these bids will be accepted, the Treasury will accept only $4 billion of competitive bids, taking the highest prices offered by competitive-bidding investors. The average price on the accepted competitive bids will be charged to the

TREASURY BONDS, NOTES & BILLS

Tuesday, March 2, 1999

Representative and Indicative Over-the-Counter quotations based on $1 million or more.

Treasury bond, note and bill quotes are as of mid-afternoon. Colons in bond and note bid-and-asked quotes represent 32nds; 101:01 means 101 1/32. Net changes in 32nds. Treasury bill quotes in hundredths, quoted in terms of a rate discount. Days to maturity calculated from settlement date. All yields are to maturity and based on the asked quote. Most recently auctioned treasury bonds and notes, and current 13-week and 26-week bills are boldfaced. For bonds callable prior to maturity, yields are computed to the earliest call date for issues quoted above par and to the maturity date for issues quoted below par. n-Treasury note. i-Inflation-indexed. wi-When issued. iw-Inflation-indexed when issued; daily change is expressed in basis points.

Source: Dow Jones/Cantor Fitzgerald.

U.S. Treasury strips as of 3 p.m. Eastern time, also based on transactions of $1 million or more. Colons in bid-and-asked quotes represent 32nds; 99:01 means 99 1/32. Net changes in 32nds. Yields calculated on the asked quotation. ci-stripped coupon interest. bp-Treasury bond, stripped principal. np-Treasury note, stripped principal. For bonds callable prior to maturity, yields are computed to the earliest call date for issues quoted above par and to the maturity date for issues below par.

Source: Bear, Stearns & Co. via Street Software Technology Inc.

GOVT. BONDS & NOTES

Rate	Maturity Mo./Yr.	Bid	Asked	Chg.	Ask Yld.
5 7/8	Mar 99n	100:02	100:04	....	4.14
6 1/4	Mar 99n	100:02	100:04	....	4.50
7	Apr 99n	100:07	100:09	....	4.49
6 3/8	Apr 99n	100:07	100:09	....	4.51
6 1/2	Apr 99n	100:07	100:09	....	4.63
6 3/8	May 99n	100:09	100:11	....	4.57
9 1/8	May 99n	100:26	100:28	....	4.62
6 1/4	May 99n	100:09	100:11	-1	4.75
6 3/4	May 99n	100:13	100:15	....	4.73
6	Jun 99n	100:12	100:14	....	4.60
6 3/4	Jun 99n	100:19	100:21	....	4.67
6 3/8	Jul 99n	100:18	100:20	....	4.62
5 7/8	Jul 99n	100:12	100:14	....	4.77
6 7/8	Jul 99n	100:25	100:27	....	4.77
6	Aug 99n	100:15	100:17	....	4.80
8	Aug 99n	101:12	101:14	....	4.76
5 7/8	Aug 99n	100:15	100:17	+ 1	4.77
6 7/8	Aug 99n	100:30	101:00	....	4.79
5 3/4	Sep 99n	100:15	100:17	+ 1	4.80
7 1/8	Sep 99n	101:07	101:09	....	4.84
6	Oct 99n	100:20	100:22	....	4.85
5 5/8	Oct 99n	100:13	100:15	+ 1	4.88
7 1/2	Oct 99n	101:19	101:21	....	4.90
5 7/8	Nov 99n	100:20	100:22	+ 1	4.85
7 7/8	Nov 99n	101:31	102:01	+ 1	4.88
5 5/8	Nov 99n	100:15	100:17	+ 1	4.88
7 3/4	Nov 99n	102:00	102:02	....	4.88
4 1/2	Jan 01n	98:23	98:24	+ 1	5.19
5 1/4	Jan 01n	100:02	100:04	+ 2	5.18
5 3/8	Feb 01n	100:10	100:12	+ 2	5.17
7 3/4	Feb 01n	104:21	104:23	+ 2	5.18
11 3/4	Feb 01	111:30	112:02	+ 1	5.19
5	**Feb 01n**	**99:22**	**99:23**	**+ 2**	**5.15**
5 5/8	Feb 01n	100:25	100:27	+ 2	5.17
6 3/8	Mar 01n	102:08	102:10	+ 2	5.18
6 1/4	Apr 01n	102:02	102:04	+ 2	5.19
5 5/8	May 01n	100:27	100:29	+ 2	5.18
8	May 01n	105:21	105:23	+ 2	5.21
13 1/8	May 01	116:05	116:09	+ 2	5.19
6 1/2	May 01n	102:21	102:23	+ 3	5.20
6 5/8	Jun 01n	102:31	103:01	+ 2	5.22
6 5/8	Jul 01n	103:03	103:05	+ 3	5.21
7 7/8	Aug 01n	105:30	106:00	+ 2	5.24
13 3/8	Aug 01	118:15	118:19	+ 2	5.22
6 1/2	Aug 01n	102:28	102:30	+ 2	5.23
6 3/8	Sep 01n	102:21	102:23	+ 3	5.23
6 1/4	Oct 01n	102:13	102:15	+ 2	5.24
7 1/2	Nov 01n	105:17	105:19	+ 3	5.25
15 3/4	Nov 01	126:00	126:06	+ 3	5.22
5 7/8	Nov 01n	101:18	101:20	+ 3	5.23
6 1/8	Dec 01n	102:07	102:09	+ 3	5.24
6 1/4	Jan 02n	102:18	102:20	+ 2	5.26
14 1/4	Feb 02	124:03	124:09	+ 1	5.28
6 1/4	**Feb 02n**	**102:19**	**102:21**	**+ 2**	**5.28**
6 5/8	Mar 02n	103:23	103:25	+ 3	5.28
6 5/8	Apr 02n	103:24	103:26	+ 2	5.30
7 1/2	May 02n	106:11	106:13	+ 3	5.29
6 1/2	May 02n	103:15	103:17	+ 3	5.30
6 1/4	Jun 02n	102:26	102:28	+ 4	5.29
3 5/8	Jul 02i	99:11	99:12	-1	3.82
6	Jul 02n	102:03	102:05	+ 4	5.30
6 3/8	Aug 02n	103:06	103:08	+ 3	5.33
6 1/4	Aug 02n	102:27	102:29	+ 4	5.33
5 7/8	Sep 02n	101:23	101:25	+ 3	5.32
5 3/4	Oct 02n	101:10	101:12	+ 4	5.33
11 5/8	Nov 02	120:18	120:24	+ 4	5.36
5 3/4	Nov 02n	101:10	101:12	+ 4	5.34
5 5/8	Dec 02n	100:31	101:01	+ 6	5.32
5 1/2	Jan 03n	100:16	100:18	+ 5	5.34
6 1/4	Feb 03n	103:05	103:07	+ 5	5.34
10 3/4	Feb 03	118:25	118:29	+ 5	5.38
5 1/2	Feb 03n	100:16	100:18	+ 5	5.34
5 1/2	Mar 03n	100:16	100:18	+ 5	5.34
5 3/4	Apr 03n	101:14	101:16	+ 6	5.34
10 3/4	May 03	119:25	119:29	+ 5	5.39
5 1/2	May 03n	100:16	100:18	+ 5	5.35
5 3/8	Jun 03n	100:03	100:05	+ 5	5.33
5 1/4	Aug 03n	99:21	99:23	+ 6	5.32
5 3/4	Aug 03n	101:17	101:19	+ 7	5.34
11 1/8	Aug 03	122:08	122:14	+ 5	5.39
4 1/4	Nov 03n	95:21	95:22	+ 4	5.30
11 7/8	Nov 03	126:08	126:14	+ 7	5.42
4 3/4	Feb 04n	97:24	97:25	+ 6	5.26
5 7/8	**Feb 04n**	**102:11**	**102:13**	**+ 7**	**5.32**
7 1/4	May 04n	108:12	108:14	+ 8	5.37
12 3/8	May 04	130:28	131:02	+ 7	5.43
7 1/4	Aug 04n	108:18	108:20	+ 6	5.40
13 3/4	Aug 04	138:16	138:22	+ 8	5.46
7 7/8	Nov 04n	111:25	111:29	+ 6	5.42
11 5/8	Nov 04	129:24	129:30	+ 8	5.44
7 1/2	Feb 05n	110:10	110:14	+ 7	5.43
6 1/2	May 05n	105:17	105:19	+ 7	5.42
8 1/4	May 00-05	103:09	103:11	+ 4	5.33
12	May 05	133:26	134:00	+ 8	5.46
6 1/2	Aug 05n	105:19	105:21	+ 8	5.45
10 3/4	Aug 05	128:05	128:11	+ 7	5.48
5 7/8	Nov 05n	102:08	102:10	+ 8	5.46
5 5/8	Feb 06n	100:31	101:01	+ 8	5.44
9 3/8	Feb 06	122:09	122:15	+ 8	5.45
6 7/8	May 06n	108:07	108:09	+ 8	5.47
7	Jul 06n	109:03	109:05	+ 10	5.47
6 1/2	Oct 06n	106:07	106:09	+ 9	5.48
3 3/8	Jan 07i	96:16	96:17	+ 1	3.89
6 1/4	Feb 07n	104:26	104:28	+ 9	5.49
7 5/8	Feb 02-07	105:26	105:28	+ 4	5.45
6 5/8	May 07n	107:11	107:13	+ 9	5.49
6 1/8	Aug 07n	104:06	104:08	+ 9	5.49
7 7/8	Nov 02-07	107:30	108:00	+ 6	5.46
3 5/8	Jan 08i	97:30	97:31	....	3.90
5 1/2	Feb 08n	100:18	100:20	+ 9	5.41
5 5/8	May 08n	101:11	101:12	+ 10	5.43
8 3/8	Aug 03-08	111:11	111:15	+ 5	5.44
4 3/4	**Nov 08n**	**95:16**	**95:17**	**+ 10**	**5.35**
8 3/4	Nov 03-08	112:29	113:01	+ 6	5.56
3 7/8	Jan 09i	100:00	100:01	-1	3.87
9 1/8	May 04-09	115:23	115:27	+ 6	5.57
10 3/8	Nov 04-09	123:00	123:06	+ 7	5.57
11 3/4	Feb 05-10	130:23	130:29	+ 8	5.58
10	May 05-10	122:22	122:28	+ 8	5.58
12 3/4	Nov 05-10	139:13	139:19	+ 9	5.58
13 7/8	May 06-11	148:07	148:13	+ 10	5.61
14	Nov 06-11	151:18	151:24	+ 11	5.62
10 3/8	Nov 07-12	131:22	131:28	+ 12	5.68
12	Aug 08-13	145:14	145:20	+ 13	5.70
13 1/4	May 09-14	157:18	157:24	+ 16	5.70
12 1/2	Aug 09-14	152:22	152:28	+ 15	5.72
11 3/4	Nov 09-14	147:25	147:31	+ 19	5.70
11 1/4	Feb 15	156:03	156:09	+ 30	5.80

U.S. TREASURY STRIPS

Mat.	Type	Bid	Asked	Chg.	Ask Yld.
May 99	ci	99:02	99:02	....	4.74
May 99	np	99:02	99:02	....	4.79
Aug 99	ci	97:28	97:28	+ 1	4.80
Aug 99	np	97:26	97:27	+ 1	4.90
Nov 99	ci	96:22	96:23	+ 2	4.84
Nov 99	np	96:21	96:22	+ 2	4.89
Feb 00	ci	95:12	95:13	+ 1	5.01
Feb 00	np	95:12	95:13	+ 1	5.00
May 00	ci	94:07	94:08	+ 2	5.01
May 00	np	94:03	94:03	+ 2	5.13
Aug 00	ci	92:29	92:29	+ 2	5.12
Aug 00	np	92:27	92:28	+ 2	5.16
Nov 00	ci	91:22	91:23	+ 2	5.15
Nov 00	np	91:20	91:21	+ 2	5.20
Feb 01	ci	90:14	90:15	+ 2	5.19
Feb 01	np	90:14	90:15	+ 2	5.20
May 01	ci	89:09	89:11	+ 2	5.20
May 01	np	89:08	89:09	+ 2	5.22
Aug 01	ci	88:04	88:05	+ 3	5.21
Aug 01	np	88:02	88:03	+ 3	5.24
Nov 01	ci	86:30	86:31	+ 3	5.24
Nov 01	np	86:28	86:30	+ 3	5.26
Feb 02	ci	85:21	85:23	+ 4	5.29
May 02	ci	84:17	84:18	+ 4	5.31
May 02	np	84:14	84:16	+ 4	5.34
Aug 02	ci	83:12	83:14	+ 4	5.31
Aug 02	np	83:09	83:11	+ 4	5.35
Nov 02	ci	82:23	82:26	+ 4	5.16
Feb 03	ci	81:03	81:06	+ 3	5.34
Feb 03	np	81:03	81:06	+ 3	5.34
May 03	ci	80:01	80:04	+ 4	5.35
Aug 03	ci	79:03	79:06	+ 4	5.31
Aug 03	np	78:30	79:02	+ 4	5.35
Nov 03	ci	78:03	78:06	+ 2	5.30
Feb 04	ci	76:28	76:31	+ 5	5.35
Feb 04	np	77:00	77:04	+ 5	5.31
May 04	ci	75:24	75:27	+ 5	5.39
May 04	np	75:27	75:30	+ 5	5.36
Aug 04	ci	75:02	75:06	+ 5	5.30
Aug 04	np	74:22	74:26	+ 5	5.39
Nov 04	ci	73:19	73:23	+ 6	5.43
Nov 04	bp	73:13	73:16	+ 6	5.47
Nov 04	np	73:19	73:23	+ 6	5.42
Feb 05	ci	72:16	72:20	+ 7	5.45
Feb 05	np	72:17	72:21	+ 7	5.44
May 05	ci	71:14	71:19	+ 7	5.47
May 05	bp	71:10	71:14	+ 7	5.50
May 05	np	71:21	71:25	+ 7	5.42
Aug 05	ci	70:14	70:19	+ 7	5.47
Aug 05	bp	70:07	70:12	+ 7	5.52
Aug 05	np	70:18	70:22	+ 7	5.45
Nov 05	ci	69:19	69:24	+ 8	5.45
Nov 05	np	69:18	69:23	+ 8	5.46
Feb 06	ci	68:13	68:17	+ 8	5.51
Feb 06	bp	68:13	68:18	+ 8	5.51
Feb 06	np	68:21	68:26	+ 8	5.45
May 06	ci	67:16	67:20	+ 8	5.51
Aug 06	ci	66:21	66:26	+ 8	5.49
Nov 06	ci	65:30	66:03	+ 8	5.45
Feb 07	ci	64:18	64:22	+ 9	5.55
May 07	ci	63:23	63:28	+ 9	5.55
Aug 07	ci	62:25	62:30	+ 9	5.55
Nov 07	ci	62:07	62:13	+ 9	5.50
Feb 08	ci	60:26	60:31	+ 10	5.60
May 08	ci	59:28	60:01	+ 10	5.63
Aug 08	ci	59:00	59:05	+ 10	5.63
Nov 08	ci	58:02	58:07	+ 10	5.66
Feb 09	ci	57:06	57:12	+ 10	5.66
May 09	ci	56:09	56:15	+ 10	5.68
Aug 09	ci	55:12	55:17	+ 10	5.71
Nov 09	ci	54:15	54:20	+ 10	5.73
Nov 09	bp	53:29	54:02	+ 10	5.83
Feb 10	ci	53:19	53:25	+ 10	5.74
May 10	ci	52:22	52:28	+ 10	5.77
Aug 10	ci	51:27	52:01	+ 10	5.79
Nov 10	ci	51:01	51:07	+ 10	5.80
Feb 11	ci	50:09	50:15	+ 12	5.80
May 11	ci	49:16	49:22	+ 12	5.82
Aug 11	ci	48:22	48:28	+ 12	5.83
Nov 11	ci	47:30	48:03	+ 12	5.85
Feb 12	ci	47:06	47:12	+ 12	5.85
May 12	ci	46:14	46:19	+ 12	5.87
Aug 12	ci	45:22	45:27	+ 13	5.88
Nov 12	ci	44:31	45:05	+ 13	5.89
Feb 13	ci	44:07	44:13	+ 12	5.90
May 13	ci	43:17	43:22	+ 13	5.92
Aug 13	ci	42:26	42:31	+ 12	5.93
Nov 13	ci	42:04	42:10	+ 12	5.94
Feb 14	ci	41:14	41:20	+ 12	5.95
May 14	ci	40:25	40:31	+ 12	5.96
Aug 14	ci	40:04	40:10	+ 12	5.97
Nov 14	ci	39:15	39:21	+ 12	5.98
Feb 15	ci	38:26	39:00	+ 12	5.99
Feb 15	bp	39:04	39:10	+ 13	5.94
May 15	ci	38:07	38:12	+ 12	6.00
Aug 15	ci	37:18	37:24	+ 12	6.01
Aug 15	bp	37:21	37:27	+ 12	5.99
Nov 15	ci	36:31	37:05	+ 12	6.02
Nov 15	bp	37:04	37:10	+ 12	5.99
Feb 16	ci	36:15	36:20	+ 13	6.01
Feb 16	bp	36:18	36:24	+ 13	5.99
May 16	ci	35:29	36:03	+ 13	6.02
May 16	bp	36:08	36:14	+ 13	5.96
Aug 16	ci	35:11	35:16	+ 13	6.02
Nov 16	ci	34:25	34:31	+ 13	6.03
Nov 16	bp	35:03	35:09	+ 13	5.98
Feb 17	ci	34:10	34:16	+ 13	6.02
May 17	ci	33:26	34:00	+ 13	6.02
May 17	bp	33:30	34:04	+ 13	6.00
Aug 17	ci	33:09	33:14	+ 13	6.02
Aug 17	bp	33:14	33:20	+ 13	5.99
Nov 17	ci	32:26	33:00	+ 13	6.02
Feb 18	ci	32:12	32:18	+ 13	6.01
May 18	ci	31:28	32:02	+ 13	6.01
May 18	bp	32:00	32:06	+ 13	5.99
Aug 18	ci	31:15	31:21	+ 13	6.00
Nov 18	ci	30:30	31:04	+ 13	6.01
Nov 18	bp	31:02	31:08	+ 13	5.99
Feb 19	ci	30:14	30:20	+ 12	6.02
Feb 19	bp	30:19	30:24	+ 12	6.00
Feb 25	ci	22:11	22:16	+ 12	5.83
Feb 25	bp	22:15	22:20	+ 12	5.81
May 25	ci	22:01	22:06	+ 11	5.83
Aug 25	ci	21:23	21:29	+ 11	5.82
Aug 25	bp	21:28	22:01	+ 12	5.80
Nov 25	ci	21:14	21:20	+ 12	5.82
Feb 26	ci	21:04	21:09	+ 11	5.82
Feb 26	bp	21:15	21:20	+ 12	5.76
May 26	ci	20:27	21:00	+ 11	5.82
Aug 26	ci	20:18	20:24	+ 11	5.81
Aug 26	bp	20:24	20:29	+ 12	5.78
Nov 26	ci	20:11	20:16	+ 11	5.80
Nov 26	bp	20:17	20:22	+ 11	5.77
Feb 27	ci	20:07	20:12	+ 11	5.77
Feb 27	bp	20:11	20:16	+ 11	5.75
May 27	ci	19:23	19:28	+ 11	5.81
Aug 27	ci	19:23	19:28	+ 11	5.76
Aug 27	bp	19:25	19:30	+ 11	5.75
Nov 27	ci	19:18	19:23	+ 11	5.74
Nov 27	bp	19:23	19:29	+ 11	5.71

TREASURY BILLS

Maturity	Days to Mat.	Bid	Asked	Chg.	Ask Yld.
Mar 04 '99	1	4.73	4.65	+0.23	4.72
Mar 11 '99	8	4.67	4.59	+0.15	4.66
Mar 18 '99	15	4.55	4.47	+0.05	4.54
Mar 25 '99	22	4.30	4.22	+0.11	4.29
Apr 01 '99	29	4.51	4.43	−0.04	4.51
Apr 08 '99	36	4.48	4.44	−0.01	4.52
Apr 15 '99	43	4.51	4.47	−0.02	4.56
Apr 22 '99	50	4.82	4.78	+0.02	4.88
Apr 29 '99	57	4.66	4.62	....	4.72
May 06 '99	64	4.61	4.59	+0.04	4.69
May 13 '99	71	4.60	4.58	+0.03	4.69
May 20 '99	78	4.60	4.58	+0.03	4.69
May 27 '99	85	4.61	4.59	+0.01	4.70
Jun 03 '99	**92**	**4.59**	**4.58**	**+0.01**	**4.70**
Jun 10 '99	99	4.57	4.55	+0.01	4.67
Jun 17 '99	106	4.56	4.54	+0.02	4.67
Jun 24 '99	113	4.56	4.54	+0.02	4.67
Jul 01 '99	120	4.53	4.51	....	4.64
Jul 08 '99	127	4.52	4.50	+0.01	4.64
Jul 15 '99	134	4.49	4.47	....	4.61
Jul 22 '99	141	4.53	4.51	+0.02	4.65
Jul 29 '99	148	4.45	4.43	−0.02	4.57
Aug 05 '99	155	4.54	4.52	−0.01	4.67
Aug 12 '99	162	4.54	4.52	−0.01	4.68
Aug 19 '99	169	4.56	4.54	−0.01	4.70
Aug 26 '99	176	4.52	4.50	−0.03	4.67
Sep 02 '99	**183**	**4.54**	**4.53**	**....**	**4.70**
Sep 16 '99	197	4.53	4.51	−0.03	4.68
Oct 14 '99	225	4.57	4.55	−0.03	4.73
Nov 12 '99	254	4.60	4.58	−0.03	4.77
Dec 09 '99	281	4.59	4.57	−0.03	4.77
Jan 06 '00	309	4.58	4.56	−0.02	4.77
Feb 03 '00	337	4.64	4.63	−0.02	4.85
Mar 02 '00	365	4.67	4.66	−0.05	4.90

INFLATION-INDEXED TREASURY SECURITIES

Rate	Mat.	Bid/Asked	Chg.	*Yld.	Accr. Prin.
3.625	07/02	99-11/12	− 01	3.802	1024
3.375	01/07	96-16/17	+ 01	3.885	1035
3.625	01/08	97-30/31	....	3.889	1015
3.875	01/09	100-00/01	− 01	3.863	1000
3.625	04/28	97-06/07	....	3.779	1014

*-Yld. to maturity on accrued principal.

FIGURE 19.4 Price Quotations for U.S. Treasury Securities (excerpts)

Source: Reprinted by permission of *The Wall Street Journal,* Dow Jones & Company, Inc., March 3, 1999, p. C15. All rights reserved worldwide.

on-the-run issues

noncompetitive bidders. Once the auction is completed, the newly offered Treasury securities are referred to as **on-the-run issues,** meaning that they are the most recently issued ones. Typically, on-the-run issues have more liquidity than "off-the-run" issues, which are issues offered at previous auctions.

Each Tuesday *The Wall Street Journal* publishes the results of the auction from the previous day. Figure 19.5 presents the results of the auction that took place on March 2, 1999. Individuals may purchase new issues of Treasury bills directly from one of the 12 Federal Reserve banks, or over the Internet, or by telephone. They can also be bought indirectly via a bank or broker. Government security dealers maintain an active secondary market in bills, and it is a simple matter to buy or sell a bill prior to maturity (especially if the original purchase was through a bank or a broker). Terms offered by government security dealers are reported daily in the financial press, stated on a "bank discount" basis. To determine the actual dollar prices, an investor needs to "undo" the bank discount computation.

For example, a bill with 120 days left to maturity might be listed as "7.48% bid, 7.19% ask." Both of these discounts were obtained by multiplying the actual discount by 360/120 (the inverse of the portion of a 360-day year involved). Thus, to find the actual discount associated with the 7.48% bid, multiply 7.48% by 120/360, which results in 2.493%. This means that the dealer is bidding 97.507% (= 100% − 2.493%) of face value, or $975.07 for this $1,000 Treasury bill.

dealer's spread

Similarly, the dealer offers to sell such a bill at a discount of 2.397% {= 100% − [7.19% × (120/360)]}, or $976.03 [= $1,000 × (100% − 2.397%)]. The difference between the prices—$.96 (= $976.03 − $975.07)—is known as the **dealer's spread,** and it serves as compensation for carrying inventories of bills, taking associated risks, and bearing the clerical and other costs associated with being a market-maker.

equivalent yield

In addition to the bid and asked discounts, *The Wall Street Journal* and other media provide an **equivalent yield** based on the asked price. In the example, the equivalent yield would be calculated by determining the dollar discount on the security ($1,000 − $976.03 = $23.97) and then dividing this figure by the purchase price ($23.97/$976.03 = 2.455%) to arrive at the rate of return associated with purchasing the security. This rate of return would be annualized by multiplying it by 360 divided by the number of days until maturity. The resulting figure would be the equivalent yield. In the example, the equivalent yield would be 7.37% [= 2.455% × (360/120)].[5]

Here are the details of yesterday's 52-week Treasury bill auction. All bids are awarded at a single price at the market-clearing yield. Rates are determined by the difference between that price and face value.

	52-Week Bills
Applications	$30,605,391,000
Accepted bids	$10,007,191,000
Accepted noncompetitively	$1,020,904,000
Auction price (Rate)	95.283 (4.665%)
Coupon equivalent	4.918%
Bids at market yield	12%
Cusip number	912795DK4

The bills are dated March 4 and mature March 2, 2000.

Here are the details of yesterday's Treasury cash management 12-day bill auction. All bids are awarded at a single price at the market-clearing yield. Rates are determined by the difference between that price and the face value.

	12-Day Bills
Applications	$46,945,000,000
Accepted bids	$19,041,000,000
Accepted noncompetitively	$0
Auction price (rate)	99.840 (4.79%)
Coupon equivalent	4.89%
Bids at market yield	47%
Cusip number	912795EN7

The bills are dated March 3 and mature March 15.

FIGURE 19.5 Treasury Bill Auction Results for March 2, 1999

Source: Reprinted by permission of *The Wall Street Journal,* Dow Jones & Company, Inc., March 3, 1999, p. C19. All rights reserved worldwide.

19.2.2 U.S. TREASURY NOTES

Treasury notes

Treasury notes are issued with maturities from 1 to 10 years and generally make coupon payments semiannually. Some, issued before 1983, were in *bearer* form with coupons attached; the owner simply submitted each coupon on its specified date to receive payment for the stated amount (hence the phrase, "clipping coupons"). Beginning in 1983, the Treasury ceased the issuance of bearer notes (and bonds). All issues since then are in *registered* form; the current owner is registered with the Treasury, which sends him or her each coupon payment when due and the principal value at maturity. When a registered note is sold, the new owner's name and address are substituted for those of the old owner on the Treasury's books.

Treasury notes are issued in denominations of $1,000 or more. Coupon payments are set at an amount so that the notes initially sell close to par value. In most cases a *single price auction* is held monthly when 2- and 5-year notes are sold with both competitive and noncompetitive bids being submitted. As in a Treasury bill multiple price auction, all noncompetitive bids are accepted first, and then the competitive bids offering the highest prices (and thus the lowest yields) are accepted until the entire offering has been fully allocated. However, unlike the practice in the multiple price auction, in a single price auction all of the accepted noncompetitive and competitive bids pay the lowest price that was accepted. Every quarter the Treasury also sells 3- and 10-year notes but uses a multiple price auction to allocate them.

Treasury notes are traded in an active secondary market made by dealers in U.S. government securities. For example, consider the following quotation from Figure 19.4:

Rate	Maturity	Bid	Asked	Change	Ask Yield
7	July 06n	109:03	109:05	+10	5.47

The quotation indicates that a note (n), maturing in July 2006, carried a coupon rate of 7%. It could be sold to a dealer for $109\frac{03}{32}\%$ of par value, which is equivalent to $1,090.9375 per $1,000 of par value. Alternatively, it could be purchased from a dealer for $109\frac{05}{32}\%$ of par value, which is equivalent to $1,091.5625 per $1,000 of par value. Thus, the dealer's spread equals $.625 (= $1,091.5625 − $1,090.9375). Lastly, the bid price was $\frac{10}{32}$ more than it had been on the previous trading day, resulting in a reported change (Chg.) of +10 (note that numbers are expressed in 32nds, reflecting an old tradition). The effective yield-to-maturity at the time, based on the asked price, was approximately 5.47% per year.[6]

accrued interest

In practice, the situation facing a potential buyer (or seller) is a little more complicated. The buyer is generally expected to pay the dealer not only the stated price ($1,091.5625) but also any **accrued interest.** For example, if 122 days have elapsed since the last coupon payment and 61 days remain, then an amount equal to $\frac{2}{3}[= 122/(122 + 61)]$ of the semiannual coupon ($\frac{2}{3} \times \frac{1}{2} \times \$70 = \$23.3333$) is added to the stated purchase price to determine the total payment required (in this case, $23.3333 + $1,091.5625 = $1,114.8958). If an investor were to sell a note to the dealer, the dealer would pay the investor the stated bid price plus accrued interest (in this case, $1,090.9375 + $23.3333 = $1,114.2708). This procedure is commonly followed with both government and corporate bonds.[7]

In 1997 the Treasury began to issue 5- and 10-year inflation-indexed Treasury notes, followed by 30-year bonds in 1998. (See Chapter 6 for a description of how these securities provide the investor with a known real return but an uncertain nominal return; they are sold using a single-price auction.) These securities make a coupon payment every six months that is determined by multiplying one-half of the coupon rate times an inflation-adjusted amount of principal that is equal to $1,000 multiplied by the inflation rate from the date the note was first issued to the coupon date. (Technically, there is a three-month lag in which, for example, the first coupon payment reflects the rate of inflation over the six-month period beginning three months before the note was issued.) Hence, if the coupon rate was 4% and the rate of inflation during the first six months was 3%, then the principal would be increased to $1,030 (= $1,000 × 1.03). Consequently, the coupon payment would be $20.60 (= $1,030 × .04/2). At the end of the life of the note, the investor would receive not only the final coupon payment but also the inflation-adjusted principal. Furthermore, the Treasury guarantees a minimum of $1,000 so that in a period of deflation (that is, falling prices) when the inflation-adjusted principal is less than $1,000, the investor would nevertheless receive $1,000. Given the record of U.S. inflation during the past 50 years, however, it seems unlikely that this guarantee would ever come into play.

19.2.3 U.S. TREASURY BONDS

Treasury bonds

call provisions

Treasury bonds have maturities greater than 10 years at the time of issuance. Those issued before 1983 may be in either bearer or registered form; subsequent issues are all in registered form. Denominations range from $1,000 upward. Unlike Treasury notes, some Treasury bond issues have **call provisions** allowing them to be "called" during a specified period (usually the period begins 5 to 10 years before maturity and ends at the maturity date); at any scheduled coupon payment date during this period, the Treasury has the right to force the investor to sell the bonds back to the government at par value. Callable issues can be identified in Figure 19.4 by noting which issues have a range of years given as the maturity date (this "range of years" indicates the call period). For example, the $7\frac{5}{8}$ bonds of Feb 02-07 mature in 2007 but may be called beginning in 2002 (the "$7\frac{5}{8}$" indicates that the bonds have a coupon rate of $7\frac{5}{8}$%, paid semiannually, just like the Treasury notes discussed previously).

For callable issues, the yield-to-maturity is calculated using the asked price. If this price is greater than par, then the yield-to-maturity is based on an assumption that the bond will be called at the earliest allowable date. Otherwise, Treasury bonds are comparable to Treasury notes, with dealers' bid and asked quotations stated in the same form. Thirty-year bonds are sold semiannually using a multiple-price auction.

19.2.4 U.S. SAVINGS BONDS

Nonmarketable U.S. Savings Bonds are offered only to individuals and select organizations. No more than a specified amount—currently $15,000 of issue price, which corresponds to a total face amount of $30,000 (the bonds are sold at half of their face amount)—may be purchased by any person in a single year. Three types are available. Series EE bonds are essentially pure-discount bonds, meaning that no interest is paid on them in the form of coupon payments before maturity. The term-to-maturity at the date of issuance varies from time to time. For bonds issued in 1999, it was 17 years. However, they may continue to be held as long as an additional 13 years before they must be either redeemed or exchanged for an HH bond (if held, they will continue to earn interest during these additional years just as they did for the first 17 years). Series HH bonds mature in 20 years and pay interest semiannually but can be redeemed for their purchase price at any time. Both types are registered.

Series EE bonds are available in small denominations (the smallest has a face amount of $50) and may be purchased from commercial banks and other financial institutions. Some employers even allow employees to obtain them through payroll savings plans. Series HH bonds are available only in exchange for eligible Series EE bonds (that is, a Series EE bond must be purchased first and held for a minimum of six months before it can be exchanged) and can be obtained only from the Treasury or one of the 12 Federal Reserve banks.

Series EE bonds use a floating market-based rate that is determined every six months (on May 1 and November 1) and is applicable for the next six months. This rate is equal to 90% of the average market yield during the previous six months on 5-year Treasury securities. The Treasury guarantees that these securities will be worth their face amount after 17 years. Thus, if an EE savings bond that was bought for $500 grows to be worth $900 after 17 years, the Treasury would step in and change its value to $1,000. This $1,000 could then be either redeemed for cash, swapped for a $1,000 HH savings bond, or kept in the EE bond, where interest would initially be based on the $1,000 value instead of the $900 (subsequent interest would be based on the ever increasing value). Should the savings bond be held for 17 years, the investor will be paid the higher of (1) the floating rates in existence since the bond was purchased or (2) 4.16% $\left[= (\$1,000/\$500)^{1/17} - 1\right]$, because $500 growing annually at 4.16% will be worth $1,000 after 17 years. Should the bond be held for less than five years, the investor forfeits the last three months worth of interest.

Unlike the taxation on interest of most other discount bonds, taxes are not paid on the interest as it accumulates monthly on the Series EE bonds. Only when these bonds are redeemed is the interest subject to federal income tax. In addition, no state or local income taxes are assessed.[8] Thus, a $15,000 investment that grows to $25,000 in 12 years will create a tax obligation only at the end of the 12th year, provided it is redeemed at that time. If a Series EE bond is exchanged for a Series HH bond, the tax obligation on the interest earned on the Series EE bond can be deferred until the Series HH bond is redeemed. However, the HH bond interest is subject to federal income tax annually. Hence, the tax obligation on the $30,000 would be deferred if the EE bond were exchanged for an HH bond, but the $1,800 (= .06 × $30,000, assuming a 6% interest rate) annual HH interest would be taxable each year after the exchange.

Series I bonds are a relatively new type of savings bond. These bonds earn interest at a composite rate that is set on each May 1 and November 1. There are two components to the composite rate, the first being a fixed rate that remains the same throughout the life of the bond. The second component is a variable rate equal to the inflation rate during the previous six months as measured by the Consumer Price Index (see Chapter 6). Otherwise, the bonds are treated similarly to the Series EE bonds.

The terms on which savings bonds are offered have been revised from time to time. (The terms previously described apply only to newly issued savings bonds at the time of this book's writing.) In some cases, improved terms have been offered to holders of outstanding bonds. Terms may be inferior to those available on less well-known or less accessible instruments with similar characteristics. At such times, the Treasury department sells savings bonds by appealing to patriotism rather than to the desire for high returns.

19.2.5 ZERO-COUPON TREASURY SECURITY RECEIPTS

coupon stripping

A noncallable Treasury note or bond is, in effect, a portfolio of pure-discount bonds (or, equivalently, a portfolio of zero-coupon bonds). Each coupon payment, as well as the principal, can be viewed as a bond unto itself; the investor who owns the bond effectively holds a number of individual pure-discount bonds. In 1982, several brokerage firms began separating these components, using a process known as **coupon stripping.**

With this process, Treasury bonds of a given issue are purchased and placed in trust with a custodian (for example, a bank). Sets of *receipts* are then issued, one set for each coupon date. For example, an August 15, 2005, receipt might entitle its holder to receive $1,000 on that date (and nothing on any other date). The amount required to meet the payments on all the August 15, 2005, receipts would exactly equal the total amount received on that date from coupon payments on the Treasury securities held in the trust account.

In addition to issuing sets of receipts corresponding to the particular Treasury bond issue's coupon dates, another set of receipts would be issued that mature on the date the principal of the securities held in trust is due. Thus, holders of these receipts share in the principal payment.[9]

Noting the favorable market reaction to the offering of these stripped securities, in 1985 the Treasury introduced a program for investors called Separate Trading of Registered Interest and Principal Securities (STRIPS). This program, which has been very successful, allows purchasers of certain coupon-bearing Treasury securities to keep whatever cash payments they want and to sell the rest. The prices at which such pure-discount securities sold on March 2, 1999, are shown in Figure 19.4.

Figure 19.6 shows typical market prices for a set of stripped Treasury securities, where price is expressed as a percentage of maturity value. As the figure shows, the longer the investor has to wait until maturity, the lower the price of the security.

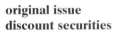

The Internal Revenue Service requires that taxes be paid annually on the accrued interest earned on such securities. That is, such securities are treated for tax purposes as **original issue discount securities,** also known as OID debt instruments. They are securities that were issued at a discount from par because of their relatively small (or nonexistent) coupon payments.[10]

For example, a STRIP that matures in two years for $1,000 might be purchased currently for $900. The investor would therefore earn $100 in interest for two years, realizing it when the STRIP matures. However, the IRS would make the investor pay taxes on a portion of the $100 each year. The amount to be recognized must be calculated using the *constant interest method,* which reflects the actual economic accrual of interest. Using this method, the investor does not report $50 $(= \$100/2)$ per year as interest income. Instead, the annual yield is calculated, which in this case is 5.4% $[= (\$1,000/\$900)^{1/2} - 1]$. In turn, the implied value of the STRIP at the end of the first

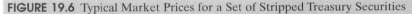

FIGURE 19.6 Typical Market Prices for a Set of Stripped Treasury Securities

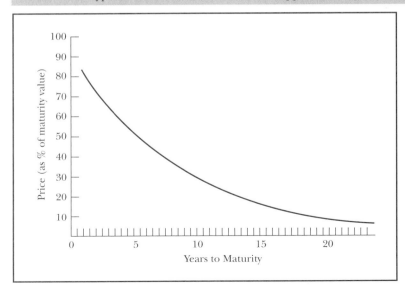

year would be $948.60 (= $900 × 1.054). The amount of interest income reported in the first year would thus be $48.60 (= $948.60 − $900). The amount of interest income reported in the second year, assuming that the STRIP is held to maturity, will be $51.40 (= $1,000 − $948.60; note that $1,000 = $948.60 × 1.054). Unfortunately, the taxable investor has a cash outflow not only when purchasing the STRIP, but also every year until it matures. Only then does the investor experience a cash inflow. As a result, such securities are attractive primarily for tax-exempt investors and for investors in low tax brackets. (For example, some people purchase them as investments held in the names of their children.)

19.3 Federal Agency Securities

Although much of the federal government's activity is financed directly, via taxes and debt issued by the Treasury, a substantial amount is financed in other ways. In some situations, various government departments provide explicit or implicit backing for the securities of quasi-governmental agencies. In other situations, the federal government has guaranteed both the principal and coupon payments on bonds issued by certain private organizations. In both cases, some of the arrangements are so convoluted that cynics suggest that the original legislative intent was to obscure the nature and extent of government backing. In any event, a wide range of bonds with different degrees of government backing has been created. Many of the bonds are considered second in safety only to the debt obligations of the U.S. government itself.

Table 19.3 lists the issuers of these securities and the amounts outstanding at the end of 1998. A partial list of typical price quotations is shown in Figure 19.7; these quotations can be interpreted in a manner similar to that used for Treasury security quotations.

TABLE 19.3 Debt Outstanding of Federal and Federally Sponsored Agencies, End of 1998

Federal Agencies	*Amount (millions)*
Defense Department: Family Housing and Homeowner's Assistance	$ 6
Export–Import Bank	552
Federal Housing Administration	102
Tennessee Valley Authority	27,786
Total debt of federal agencies	$28,446

Federally Sponsored Agencies	*Amount (millions)*
Federal Home Loan Banks	$313,919
Federal National Mortgage Association	369,774
Federal Home Loan Mortgage Corporation	169,200
Student Loan Marketing Association	37,717
Farm Credit Banks	63,517
Financing Corporation	8,170
Farm Credit Financial Assistance Corporation	1,261
Resolution Funding Corporation	29,996
Total debt of federally sponsored agencies	$994,817

Source: Federal Reserve Bulletin, December 1999, p. A30.

GOVERNMENT AGENCY & SIMILAR ISSUES

Tuesday, March 2, 1999

Over-the-Counter mid-afternoon quotations based on large transactions, usually $1 million or more. Colons in bid-and-asked quotes represent 32nds; 101:01 means 101 1/32.

All yields are calculated to maturity, and based on the asked quote. * -- Callable issue, maturity date shown. For issues callable prior to maturity, yields are computed to the earliest call date for issues quoted above par, or 100, and to the maturity date for issues below par.

Source: Bear, Stearns & Co. via Street Software Technology Inc.

FNMA Issues

Rate	Mat.	Bid	Asked	Yld.
5.55	3-99	100:00	100:03	0.61
6.00	3-99	100:08	100:11	0.36
5.65	5-99	100:02	100:05	4.81
6.60	6-99	100:12	100:15	4.93
8.45	7-99	101:06	101:09	4.77
5.86	7-99	100:02	100:05	5.44
6.35	8-99	100:18	100:21	4.82
5.47	8-99	100:00	100:03	5.21
8.55	8-99	101:18	101:21	5.04
5.81	10-99	100:00	100:03	5.61
5.73	10-99	100:02	100:05	5.48
6.07	10-99	100:18	100:21	5.00
8.35	11-99	102:03	102:06	5.03
5.78	11-99	100:01	100:04	5.59
5.83	12-99	100:02	100:05	5.58
5.34	1-00	99:22	99:25	5.59
6.10	2-00	100:08	100:11	5.71
9.05	4-00	103:12	103:15	5.74
5.58	4-00	99:29	100:00	5.57
5.65	4-00	100:00	100:03	5.56
6.41	5-00	101:08	101:11	5.25
5.79	6-00*	100:01	100:04	5.19
5.80	6-00*	100:00	100:03	5.71
5.75	6-00*	99:30	100:01	5.70
8.90	6-00	103:23	103:26	5.74
6.20	6-00	101:01	101:04	5.29
5.90	7-00	100:20	100:23	5.32
5.56	7-00	99:28	99:31	5.57
5.97	7-00	100:28	100:31	5.23
5.69	8-00*	100:01	100:04	5.38
5.49	8-00	99:18	99:21	5.73
9.20	9-00	105:07	105:10	5.50
5.20	9-00	99:08	99:11	5.66
5.97	10-00	100:26	100:29	5.35
5.83	10-00	100:04	100:07	5.67
6.03	10-00	100:31	101:02	5.34
4.90	11-00*	98:14	98:17	5.85
5.86	11-00	100:20	100:23	5.39
5.05	11-00*	98:20	98:23	5.85
8.25	12-00	104:10	104:13	5.61
5.72	1-01	100:16	100:19	5.37
5.55	1-01	99:30	100:02	5.50
5.44	1-01	100:02	100:06	5.34
5.78	1-01*	100:02	100:06	5.31
5.50	2-01	100:04	100:08	5.37
5.37	2-01	99:01	99:05	5.84
5.41	2-01	98:08	98:12	6.30
5.36	2-01	99:00	99:04	5.84
5.63	3-01	100:11	100:15	5.38
6.16	4-01	100:26	100:30	5.66
6.63	4-01	101:24	101:28	5.66
6.45	4-01	102:03	102:07	5.33
6.00	4-01*	100:02	100:06	4.79
6.74	5-01*	100:26	100:30	1.34
7.00	5-01*	100:25	100:29	2.00
6.59	5-01	101:24	101:28	5.67
5.95	7-01*	100:01	100:05	4.40
6.67	8-01	102:05	102:09	5.64
6.69	8-01	102:07	102:11	5.64
6.70	8-01*	100:08	100:12	5.75
6.38	8-01	101:14	101:18	5.67
5.43	9-01*	98:08	98:12	6.12
6.58	10-01	102:14	102:18	5.49
4.63	10-01	97:30	98:02	5.43
5.00	11-01*	98:15	98:19	5.57
5.00	11-01*	98:14	98:18	5.58
5.26	11-01*	98:20	98:24	5.76
6.44	11-01*	98:26	98:30	6.87
6.38	1-02	102:10	102:14	5.45
6.41	2-02	101:30	102:02	5.63
7.50	2-02	104:14	104:18	5.79
6.23	3-02	101:14	101:18	5.66
6.49	3-02	102:12	102:16	5.58
7.12	4-02*	100:04	100:08	4.97
7.55	4-02	105:08	105:12	5.64
6.82	4-02	103:10	103:14	5.61
6.70	5-02	102:30	103:02	5.63
6.61	5-02	102:18	102:22	5.68
6.59	5-02	102:18	102:22	5.66
6.22	7-02	101:16	101:20	5.68
6.23	7-02	101:16	101:20	5.69
6.26	7-02	101:18	101:22	5.71
6.54	9-02*	102:22	102:26	4.62
6.09	9-02	101:07	101:11	5.67
6.48	10-02*	100:10	100:14	5.68
6.06	10-02	100:16	100:20	5.86
5.90	10-02	100:16	100:20	5.70
6.40	10-02*	100:18	100:22	5.94
6.21	10-02	101:12	101:16	5.74
5.89	11-02	100:20	100:24	5.66
7.05	11-02	104:08	104:14	5.70
6.00	11-02	101:03	101:09	5.61
6.32	12-02*	100:01	100:07	6.02
6.80	1-03	104:00	104:06	5.57
6.06	1-03*	99:31	100:05	6.01
6.01	1-03*	99:24	99:30	6.03
5.25	1-03	98:21	98:27	5.59
6.15	1-03*	99:23	99:29	6.18
5.99	2-03*	98:21	98:27	6.33
5.78	2-03*	99:18	99:24	5.86
6.14	3-03*	100:00	100:06	5.23
5.75	4-03	100:12	100:18	5.60
5.96	4-03*	100:11	100:17	5.69
6.00	4-03*	100:08	100:14	5.78
6.19	4-03*	100:10	100:16	5.74
6.10	4-03*	100:08	100:14	5.71
6.16	5-03*	100:04	100:10	5.88
6.06	5-03*	100:08	100:14	5.83
6.71	5-03	104:09	104:15	5.50
6.20	5-03*	100:05	100:11	5.89
6.03	6-03*	100:06	100:12	5.84
6.16	6-03*	100:06	100:12	5.86
6.20	6-03*	100:00	100:06	6.15
5.89	7-03*	100:00	100:06	5.84
5.94	8-03*	100:02	100:08	5.82
6.09	8-03*	99:11	99:17	6.21
5.86	8-03*	99:20	99:26	5.91
5.91	8-03*	99:16	99:22	5.99
5.50	9-03*	96:24	96:30	6.28
5.26	10-03*	96:06	96:12	6.18
5.45	10-03	98:28	99:02	5.68
5.43	11-03*	97:08	97:14	6.06
5.46	11-03*	97:25	97:31	5.96
4.75	11-03	96:10	96:16	5.61
5.53	12-03*	97:08	97:14	6.16
5.80	12-03	100:14	100:20	5.64
6.85	4-04	104:12	104:18	5.80
6.79	6-04	105:15	105:21	5.53
7.55	6-04*	100:20	100:26	4.39
7.40	7-04	106:02	106:08	6.01
7.70	8-04*	101:18	101:24	3.58
7.85	9-04*	101:16	101:22	4.49
8.25	10-04*	101:08	101:14	5.75
8.40	10-04*	101:15	101:21	5.71
8.63	11-04*	103:19	103:25	2.97
6.00	1-05*	99:13	99:19	6.08
8.50	2-05*	102:16	102:22	5.42
7.88	2-05	111:02	111:08	5.63
6.25	2-05*	99:26	100:00	6.25
7.65	3-05	109:04	109:10	5.80
6.35	5-05*	102:28	103:02	4.87
6.35	6-05	101:25	101:31	5.97
5.75	6-05	100:02	100:08	5.70
6.55	9-05	104:14	104:20	5.69
6.85	9-05*	100:31	101:05	6.04
6.40	9-05	103:14	103:20	5.73
6.70	11-05*	100:22	100:28	6.14
5.94	12-05	101:00	101:06	5.72
5.88	2-06	99:19	99:25	5.91
6.41	3-06	103:14	103:20	5.77
6.22	3-06	102:15	102:21	5.76
6.89	4-06	106:01	106:07	5.81
7.90	6-06*	100:14	100:20	5.76
7.07	7-06	106:10	106:16	5.97
7.93	9-06*	101:00	101:06	5.64
7.59	10-06*	101:22	101:28	4.29
7.50	11-06*	100:24	100:30	6.11
6.88	11-06*	101:14	101:20	6.21
6.96	4-07	105:28	106:02	6.00
6.64	7-07	103:19	103:25	6.05
6.99	7-07*	100:26	101:00	6.64
6.52	7-07	104:30	105:04	5.74
6.54	9-07	104:31	105:05	5.76
7.13	9-07*	100:23	100:29	6.49
6.59	9-07	103:04	103:10	6.09
6.39	9-07	103:18	103:24	5.82
6.87	10-07	101:04	101:10	6.67
6.83	10-07*	101:00	101:06	6.05
6.34	10-07	103:12	103:18	5.80
6.94	10-07*	100:21	100:27	6.38
6.97	10-07*	100:22	100:28	6.41
6.65	11-07*	100:10	100:16	6.31
6.15	12-07	102:11	102:17	5.78
6.56	12-07*	100:12	100:18	6.39
6.16	12-07	102:10	102:18	5.78
6.48	12-07*	101:20	101:28	5.91
6.40	12-07*	100:14	100:22	6.20
6.17	1-08*	99:18	99:26	6.19
6.41	1-08*	95:30	96:06	6.99
6.29	1-08*	97:04	97:12	6.68
6.24	1-08*	100:05	100:13	6.12
6.27	2-08*	99:00	99:08	6.38
6.43	2-08*	96:19	96:27	6.91
6.42	2-08*	100:06	100:14	6.18
5.75	2-08	99:05	99:13	5.84
6.38	2-08*	100:02	100:10	6.20
6.58	5-08*	100:02	100:10	6.42
6.00	5-08	100:20	100:28	5.88
6.22	8-08*	100:03	100:11	6.13
6.20	8-08*	99:22	99:30	6.21
6.14	9-08*	97:22	97:30	6.43
6.00	9-08*	95:08	95:16	6.64
6.00	11-08*	95:28	96:04	6.55
6.01	11-08*	99:22	99:30	6.01
0.00	7-14	39:08	39:16	6.15
10.35	12-15	140:02	140:10	6.39
8.20	3-16	121:12	121:20	6.13
8.95	2-18	127:25	128:01	6.38
8.10	8-19	121:18	121:26	6.20
0.00	10-19	28:08	28:16	6.19
7.13	4-26	113:21	113:27	6.08
6.09	9-27	95:01	95:09	6.45
6.03	10-27	98:16	98:24	6.12
6.75	2-28*	100:06	100:14	6.62
5.63	4-28	92:28	93:04	6.14

Federal Home Loan Bank

Rate	Mat.	Bid	Asked	Yld.
6.44	4-99	100:06	100:09	3.92
8.60	6-99	101:02	101:05	4.72
6.11	6-99	100:04	100:07	5.31
8.45	7-99	101:10	101:13	4.78
6.26	8-99	100:14	100:17	4.98
8.60	8-99	101:18	101:21	4.99
5.87	10-99	100:03	100:06	5.55
8.38	10-99	101:30	102:01	5.11
5.00	10-99*	99:28	99:31	5.01
5.80	11-99	100:01	100:04	5.60
8.60	1-00	102:18	102:21	5.49
5.53	2-00	99:27	99:30	5.59
5.78	5-00*	100:00	100:03	5.70
4.49	11-00	98:04	98:07	5.63
5.62	1-01	100:10	100:13	5.37
5.20	9-01	98:24	98:28	5.67
4.86	10-01	98:00	98:04	5.64
4.63	10-01	97:18	97:22	5.60
4.66	10-01	97:18	97:22	5.63
4.64	10-02	95:30	96:02	5.87
4.68	10-02	100:10	100:14	4.55
6.18	10-02	101:08	101:12	5.76
5.66	1-03	99:28	100:02	5.64
5.37	1-03	98:10	98:16	5.81
6.25	1-03*	99:26	100:00	6.25
5.42	1-03	99:08	99:14	5.58
6.07	1-03*	99:17	99:23	6.14
6.05	2-03*	99:16	99:22	6.14
6.03	5-03*	100:10	100:16	5.77
5.76	6-03	100:09	100:15	5.63
5.57	9-03	98:28	99:02	5.82
5.63	9-03	99:24	99:30	5.65
5.13	9-03	97:24	97:30	5.65
4.78	10-03	95:14	95:20	5.87
5.06	10-03*	99:27	100:01	5.05
6.02	10-03*	96:13	96:19	6.89
9.50	2-04	117:07	117:13	5.46
6.00	5-04*	96:04	96:10	6.85
7.00	7-07*	100:24	100:30	6.29
7.00	8-07*	100:30	101:04	6.17
5.80	9-08	99:00	99:08	5.90

World Bank Bonds

Rate	Mat.	Bid	Asked	Yld.
8.38	10-99	101:22	101:25	5.14
8.13	3-01	105:08	105:12	5.24
6.38	5-01	101:29	102:01	5.39
6.75	1-02	102:16	102:20	5.75
12.38	10-02	119:28	120:02	6.10
5.25	9-03	99:00	99:06	5.45
6.38	7-05	104:00	104:06	5.58
6.63	8-06	105:28	106:04	5.61
8.25	9-16	121:14	121:22	6.20
8.63	10-16	125:11	125:19	6.21
9.25	7-17	132:27	133:03	6.20
7.63	1-23	119:08	119:16	6.07
8.88	3-26	133:05	133:13	6.29

Financing Corporation

Rate	Mat.	Bid	Asked	Yld.
10.70	10-17	143:27	144:03	6.56
9.80	11-17	140:09	140:17	6.13
9.40	2-18	130:15	130:23	6.55
9.80	4-18	139:09	139:17	6.23
10.00	5-18	141:01	141:09	6.27
10.35	8-18	144:24	145:00	6.30
9.65	11-18	138:02	138:10	6.24
9.90	12-18	140:12	140:20	6.28
9.60	12-18	137:02	137:10	6.28
9.65	3-19	138:00	138:08	6.27
9.70	4-19	138:10	138:18	6.29
9.00	6-19	129:23	129:31	6.35
8.60	9-19	125:20	125:28	6.33

Inter-Amer. Devel. Bank

Rate	Mat.	Bid	Asked	Yld.
7.13	9-99	100:28	100:31	5.37
8.50	5-01	106:28	107:00	5.04
6.13	3-06	102:20	102:26	5.63
6.63	3-07	105:22	105:28	5.70
12.25	12-08	144:18	144:26	6.10
8.88	6-09	120:30	121:06	6.07
8.40	9-09	118:06	118:14	6.00
8.50	3-11	119:14	119:22	6.16
7.13	3-23*	99:06	99:14	7.17
7.00	6-25	109:00	109:08	6.28
6.80	10-25	106:20	106:28	6.26

GNMA Mtge. Issues Mar99

Rate	Mat.	Bid	Asked	Yld.
5.50	30Yr	93:27	93:29	6.40
6.00	30Yr	96:17	96:19	6.59
6.50	30Yr	99:00	99:02	6.72
7.00	30Yr	101:02	101:04	6.82
7.50	30Yr	102:21	102:23	6.74
8.00	30Yr	104:04	104:06	6.54
8.50	30Yr	105:28	105:30	6.37
9.00	30Yr	106:24	106:26	6.66
9.50	30Yr	107:20	107:22	6.91

Tennessee Valley Authority

Rate	Mat.	Bid	Asked	Yld.
8.38	10-99	101:10	101:13	5.83
6.00	11-00	100:09	100:12	5.75
6.50	8-01	101:24	101:28	5.68
6.38	6-05	102:04	102:10	5.93
3.38	1-07	95:19	95:25	4.01
8.05	7-24*	97:10	97:18	8.28
6.75	11-25	105:06	105:14	6.32
8.63	11-29*	97:22	97:30	8.82
8.25	9-34*	97:02	97:10	8.49
8.25	4-42*	109:04	109:12	7.40
7.25	7-43*	97:19	97:27	7.42
6.88	12-43*	103:10	103:18	6.62

Farm Credit Fin. Asst. Corp.

Rate	Mat.	Bid	Asked	Yld.
9.38	7-03	113:18	113:24	5.78
8.80	6-05	116:20	116:26	5.58
9.20	9-05*	107:22	107:28	3.96

Resolution Funding Corp.

Rate	Mat.	Bid	Asked	Yld.
8.13	10-19	124:02	124:10	6.05
8.88	7-20	133:23	133:31	6.03
9.38	10-20	134:24	135:00	6.37
8.63	1-21	130:31	131:07	6.03
8.63	1-30	127:22	127:30	6.51
8.88	4-30	140:16	140:24	5.97

Federal Farm Credit Bank

Rate	Mat.	Bid	Asked	Yld.
5.60	5-99	100:09	100:12	3.24
5.55	7-99	100:02	100:05	5.06
8.65	10-99	101:23	101:26	5.39
6.28	6-01	101:20	101:24	5.45
6.10	9-01	101:14	101:18	5.43
5.70	6-03	99:24	99:30	5.71
6.75	6-07	106:20	106:26	5.70

Student Loan Marketing

Rate	Mat.	Bid	Asked	Yld.
5.52	6-99	100:02	100:05	4.86
5.66	2-00*	99:28	99:31	5.67
5.56	3-00*	99:24	99:27	5.72
7.50	3-00	101:23	101:26	5.63
6.05	9-00	100:26	100:29	5.41
7.00	12-02	104:00	104:06	5.73
7.30	8-12	112:12	112:20	5.92
0.00	10-22	21:25	22:01	6.52

FIGURE 19.7 Price Quotations for Government Agency Issues

Source: Reprinted by permission of *The Wall Street Journal,* Dow Jones & Company, Inc., March 3, 1999, p. C15.

19.3.1   BONDS OF FEDERAL AGENCIES

Bonds issued by federal agencies provide funds to support such activities as housing (through either direct loans or the purchase of existing mortgages); export and import activities (via loans, credit guarantees, and insurance); the postal service; and the activities of the Tennessee Valley Authority. Many issues are guaranteed by the full faith and credit of the U.S. government, but some (for example, those of the Tennessee Valley Authority) are not.

19.3.2   BONDS OF FEDERALLY SPONSORED AGENCIES

federally sponsored agencies

Federally sponsored agencies are privately owned agencies that issue securities and use the proceeds to support the granting of certain types of loans to farmers, students, homeowners, and others. A common procedure involves the creation of a series of governmental "banks" to buy securities issued by private organizations that grant the loans in the first instance. Some or all of the initial capital for these banks may be provided by the government, but subsequent amounts typically come from bonds issued by the banks.

Although the debts of agencies of this type are usually not guaranteed by the federal government, governmental control is designed to ensure that each debt issue is backed by extremely safe assets (for example, mortgages insured by another quasi-governmental agency). Moreover, it is generally presumed that governmental assistance of one sort or another would be provided if there were any danger of default on such debt.

As shown in Table 19.3, there are eight federally sponsored agencies. Federal Home Loan Banks make loans to thrift institutions, primarily savings and loan associations. The Federal National Mortgage Association (FNMA, or "Fannie Mae") purchases and sells real estate mortgages—not only those insured by the Federal Housing Administration or guaranteed by the Veterans Administration but also conventional mortgages. The Federal Home Loan Mortgage Corporation (FHLMC, or "Freddie Mac") deals only in conventional mortgages. The Student Loan Marketing Association (SLMA, or "Sallie Mae") purchases federally guaranteed loans made to students by other lenders, such as commercial banks, and may make direct student loans under special circumstances. The Farm Credit Banks lend to farmers as well as farm associations and cooperatives, and the Farm Credit Financial Assistance Corporation supports the Farm Credit Bank System. The Financing Corporation recapitalized the Federal Savings and Loan Insurance Corporation (FSLIC). Last, the Resolution Funding Corporation assisted in the recovery of the thrift industry, mainly by assisting bankrupt or near-bankrupt savings and loans.

19.3.3   PARTICIPATION CERTIFICATES

participation certificates securitization

To support credit for home purchases, the government has authorized the issuance of **participation certificates** (or *pass-throughs*). In a process known as **securitization,** a group of assets (for example, mortgages) is placed in a pool, and certificates representing ownership of those assets are issued to pay for them. The holders of the certificates receive the interest and principal payments as they are made by homeowners, minus a small service charge. The most important certificates of this type are those issued by the Government National Mortgage Association (GNMA, or "Ginnie Mae") and are known as GNMA Modified Pass-Through Securities. These securities are guaranteed by GNMA and are backed by the full faith and credit of the U.S. government.

GNMA pass-through securities are created by certain private organizations such as savings and loans and mortgage bankers that bundle a package of similar (in terms of maturity date and interest rate) mortgages together. These mortgages must be individually guaranteed by either the Federal Housing Administration or the Veterans Administration (thereby making them free from default risk) and have, in aggregate, a principal amount of at least $1 million. After these mortgages have been bundled together, an application is made to GNMA for a guarantee on the pass-through securities. Typically, each security represents $25,000 worth of principal. Once the guarantee is received, the securities are sold to the public through brokers. The interest rate paid on the securities is .5% less than the interest rate paid on the mortgages, with GNMA keeping .1% and the creator .4%.

Unlike most bonds, GNMA pass-through securities pay investors on a monthly basis an amount of money that represents both a pro rata return of principal and interest on the underlying mortgages. For example, the holder of a $25,000 certificate from a $1 million pool would indirectly "own" $2\frac{1}{2}$% of every mortgage in the pool. Each month the homeowners make mortgage payments that consist of part principal and part interest. In turn, each month the investor receives $2\frac{1}{2}$% of the aggregate amount paid by the homeowners. Because the mortgages are free from default risk, there is no default risk on the pass-through securities. (If homeowner payments are late, GNMA will either use excess cash or borrow money from the Treasury to ensure investors are paid in a timely fashion.)

Prepayment Risk

There is one particular risk to investors, however, that arises because homeowners are allowed to prepay their mortgages. As a result of the prepayment provision, typical pass-through securities may have shorter lives than their initially stated lives of 30 years. If interest rates have fallen since the time the pass-through security was created, homeowners may start to prepay their mortgages. If the investor bought an existing pass-through that was selling at a premium and homeowners prepay, then the investor will receive par value on the security shortly after having paid a premium for it. Therefore, the investor will incur a loss. In addition, the investor will be faced with the problem of reinvesting the proceeds of the prepayments because similar risk securities will now yield a lower interest rate than had been paid by the pass-through security.

Consider a pass-through security of $25,000, initially issued with a stated interest rate of 12%. Suppose that afterward interest rates unexpectedly fall so that new pass-throughs carry a stated rate of 10%. At this time the older pass-through security has $20,000 of principal outstanding, but as a consequence of the fall in interest rates it is selling at a premium, perhaps for $22,000. Now suppose interest rates unexpectedly fall again, this time to 8%. At this point many homeowners prepay their mortgages in order to refinance them at the current rate of 8%. As a result an investor who purchased the older pass-through security for $22,000 ends up shortly thereafter receiving $20,000, thereby quickly losing $2,000.[11] Furthermore, the $20,000 can now be reinvested only in similar risk securities yielding 8% instead of 10%, resulting in an opportunity loss in income of $400 [= $20,000 × (.10 − .08)] per year.

Innovations

The interest the investing public has shown in GNMA pass-through securities has caused a number of similar securities to be created. One, typically issued in denominations of $100,000 or more, is the "guaranteed mortgage certificate" sold by the Federal Home Loan Mortgage Corporation, a federally sponsored agency previously mentioned. Some banks have offered similar pass-through mortgage certificates backed by private insurance companies. Other financial institutions have repackaged the cash flows that are paid by the homeowners so investors receive something other than a pro rata share of them. A broad class of such securities, called collateralized mortgage obligations, are discussed next.

19.3.4 COLLATERALIZED MORTGAGE OBLIGATIONS

collateralized mortgage obligations

Collateralized mortgage obligations (CMOs) are a means to allocate a mortgage pool's principal and interest payments among investors in accordance with their preferences for prepayment risk. A CMO originator (or "sponsor") transforms a traditional mortgage pool into a set of securities, called CMO *tranches* (French for "slices"), that have different priority claims on the interest and principal paid by the mortgages underlying the CMO. Sponsors of CMOs may be government agencies, such as GNMA or FNMA, or they may be private entities, such as brokerage firms.

Although there is no standard form of CMO, consider an example of a simple "sequential-pay" CMO structure that involves three tranches: *A*, *B*, and *C*. The tranches were formed from a pool of mortgages with a total principal value of $250 million. The mortgages in the pool all carry an interest rate of 8%. As shown in Table 19.4, each tranche is initially allocated a specific proportion of the underlying mortgage pool's principal: $150 million for tranche *A*, $25 million for tranche *B*, and $75 million for tranche *C*. Interest payments, as with any bond, are paid as a percentage of the outstanding principal corresponding to each tranche. (The example assumes that interest and principal are paid annually. In practice, those payments occur monthly.)

TABLE 19.4   Three-Tranche Sequential-Pay CMO

	Tranche A			Tranche B		
Year	Year-End Balance	Principal	Interest	Year-End Balance	Principal	Interest
0	$150,000,000			$25,000,000		
1	132,742,627	$17,257,372	$12,000,000	25,000,000	0	$2,000,000
2	114,104,665	18,637,962	10,619,410	25,000,000	0	2,000,000
3	93,975,667	20,128,999	9,128,373	25,000,000	0	2,000,000
4	72,236,348	21,739,319	7,518,053	25,000,000	0	2,000,000
5	48,757,884	23,478,464	5,778,908	25,000,000	0	2,000,000
6	23,401,142	25,356,741	3,900,631	25,000,000	0	2,000,000
7	0	23,401,142	1,872,091	21,015,862	$3,984,138	2,000,000
8	0	0	0	0	21,015,862	1,681,294
9	0	0	0	0	0	0
10	0	0	0	0	0	0

	Tranche C			Mortgage Pool		
Year	Year-End Balance	Principal	Interest	Year-End Balance	Principal	Interest
0	$75,000,000			$250,000,000		
1	75,000,000	0	$6,000,000	232,742,628	$17,257,372	$20,000,000
2	75,000,000	0	6,000,000	214,104,666	18,637,962	18,619,410
3	75,000,000	0	6,000,000	193,975,667	20,128,999	17,128,373
4	75,000,000	0	6,000,000	172,236,348	21,739,319	15,518,053
5	75,000,000	0	6,000,000	148,757,884	23,478,464	13,778,908
6	75,000,000	0	6,000,000	123,401,142	25,356,741	11,900,631
7	75,000,000	0	6,000,000	96,015,862	27,385,281	9,872,091
8	66,439,758	$8,560,242	6,000,000	66,439,758	29,576,103	7,681,269
9	34,497,567	31,942,192	5,315,181	34,497,567	31,942,192	5,315,181
10	0	34,497,567	2,759,805	0	34,497,567	2,759,805

In this example, the three tranches earn the same interest rate on their principal. However, they differ in terms of how they are retired (that is, how principal payments are allocated among them). All principal payments (both scheduled and prepaid) made by the pool are funneled to the *A* tranche until its outstanding principal has been extinguished. The *B* and *C* tranches receive only interest payments as long as the *A* tranche has not been fully paid off. Once it has, the *B* tranche receives all principal payments until it is retired; afterward, principal payments go to the *C* tranche. For example, in year 1, each tranche receives an 8% interest payment on its principal balance at the beginning of the year. Furthermore, in year 1 the pool's mortgages make a combined principal payment of $17,257,372, which is assigned in full to tranche *A*. Its principal balance falls by the amount of the payment, leaving $132,742,627 in outstanding principal to begin the second year. In year 2, tranche *A*'s interest payment is smaller because its beginning-of-year principal balance has been reduced by $17,257,372. The interest payments to tranches *B* and *C* remain the same, however, because their principal balances have not yet been reduced. By the end of year 6 the outstanding principal of tranche *A* has been completely extinguished, and it receives no further interest or principal payments. Tranche *B* is now the recipient of all principal payments, with tranches *B* and *C* (the two remaining tranches) earning interest based on their outstanding principal. Because of its small size, the *B* tranche is quickly retired. By year 8, only the *C* tranche is still in existence. It now receives all of the pool's interest and principal payments. By the end of year 10 it too has been retired because all of the mortgages in the pool have paid off their principal balances.

The primary purpose of dividing a mortgage pass-through pool's principal and income flows into various tranches is to create a set of securities with varying levels of interest rate and prepayment risk. Investors can match their risk preferences and predictions with the appropriate securities. The CMO originator expects that investors will pay a premium for this flexibility, with the sum of the parts being worth more than the whole.

Considerably more complex CMO structures than that involved in the simple sequential-pay CMO example are common. Greater complexity provides greater fine-tuning of risk. Note that in the sequential-pay CMO example, investors seeking shorter maturity, mortgage-backed securities generally will hold the faster pay tranches, whereas investors desiring longer maturity, mortgage-backed securities will hold the slower pay tranches. Nevertheless, both types of investors are still exposed to considerable prepayment risk. If interest rates fall, then prepayments will increase, shortening the maturities of all three tranches, but if interest rates rise, then prepayments will decline, increasing the effective maturities of all three tranches.

Solutions to this problem involve creating tranches whose interest and principal payments respond in various ways to movements in market interest rates and the prepayment tendencies of the pool's mortgages. Some CMO structures contain dozens of tranches. Instead of fixed interest rates, certain tranches may have interest rates that vary directly with the movement of short-term interest rates. These securities are called "floaters." They are paired with "inverse floaters," whose interest payments move in the opposite direction of short-term interest rates. Other tranches, called planned amortization classes (PACs), make fixed principal and interest payments for a specified period, similar to a standard coupon bond. They are matched with support (or companion) bonds, which are exposed to high levels of prepayment risk. The seemingly endless list of CMO variations is limited only by the imaginations of CMO sponsors and the appetite of investors for different cash flow patterns and different levels of prepayment risk.

Although the risk of principal prepayments can be allocated among various tranches, in the final analysis the prepayment risk of the mortgage pool cannot be reduced. Evaluating prepayment risk can be extremely difficult, particularly in complex

CMO structures. Various organizations have developed prepayment models designed to simulate the behavior of mortgage prepayments under specified interest rate scenarios. These models allow CMO investors to better evaluate the riskiness and, hence, the appropriate yields of the available CMO tranches.

19.4 State and Local Government Securities

The 1997 Census of Governments showed that there were 85,005 governmental units in the United States in addition to the federal government itself.[12] These nonfederal governmental units consist of

State government		50
Local government		
County	3,043	
Municipal	19,372	
Township and town	16,629	
School district	13,726	
Special district	34,683	
Total local governmental units		87,453
Total governmental units		87,503

municipal bonds   Many of these units borrow money; their securities are called **municipal bonds** or simply "municipals" or "muni's." (Only the securities of the U.S. government are referred to as "governments.") Figure 19.8 provides estimates of the amounts of various types of fixed-income securities outstanding at the end of 1998; it shows there are nearly $1.5 trillion in outstanding municipal securities—a sizable category of securities that clearly warrants attention.

19.4.1 ISSUING AGENCIES

Figure 19.9 shows the dollar values of municipal bonds issued in 1998 by various agencies, and Figure 19.10 shows the purposes for the issuance of such debt. States gener-

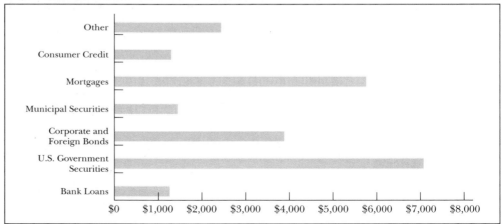

FIGURE 19.8 Estimated Amounts of Various Fixed-Income Securities Outstanding, Year-End 1998 (in billions)

Source: Federal Reserve Bulletin, April 1999, p. A40.

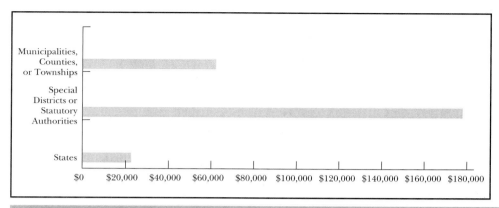

FIGURE 19.9 New Security Issues of State and Local Governments in 1998, Classified by Issues (in millions)

Source: Federal Reserve Bulletin, April 1999, p. A31.

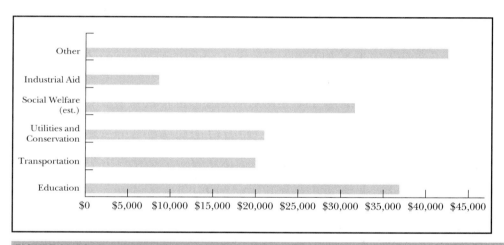

FIGURE 19.10 New Security Issues of State and Local Governments in 1998, Classified by Purpose (in millions)

Source: Federal Reserve Bulletin, April 1999, p. A31.

ally issue debt to finance capital expenditures, primarily for highways, housing, and education.[13] The concept behind the issuance of such debt is that the revenue generated by the resulting facilities will be used to make the required debt payments. In some cases, the link is direct (for example, tolls may be used to pay for a bridge). In other cases it is somewhat indirect (for example, gasoline taxes may be used to pay for highway construction) or very indirect (for example, state sales taxes or income taxes may be used to pay for the construction of new government buildings).

States cannot be sued without their consent. Because bondholders may have no legal recourse in the event of default, state-issued bonds that are dependent on particular revenues from some capital project may involve considerable risk. However, bonds backed by the "full faith and credit" of a state government are generally considered quite safe despite the inability of the bondholders to sue. It is anticipated that state legislatures will do whatever is necessary to see that such bonds are paid off in a timely manner.

Unlike state governments, local governments can be sued against their will, making it possible for bondholders to force officials to collect whatever amount is needed in order to meet required debt payments. In many cases, only revenues from specific projects may be used (for example, the tolls collected on a particular highway). In other cases, collections from a particular tax may be used, although possibly only up to some statutory limit.

Some local governments (for example, Cleveland in 1978–1979) have defaulted on their debts, and others (for example, New York City in 1975 and Orange County, California, in 1996) have restructured their debt, giving current bondholders new certificates offering lower or deferred interest and longer maturities in exchange for currently outstanding certificates. Thus, the right of bondholders to sue does not always mean that they will be able to collect what they are owed in a timely fashion.

Counties and municipalities are familiar to most people, but other forms of local government also exist. Examples include school districts as well as other districts and authorities created to finance and operate seaports or airports. All are established by state charter and may be granted monopoly powers as well as rights to collect certain types of taxes. However, limits are often placed on the amount of taxes collected, the tax rate charged, and the amount (or type) of debt issued.

The primary source of funding for such agencies is the property tax. Because a given property may be liable for taxes levied by several agencies (such as a city, a county, a school district, a port authority, and a sewer district), the risk of an agency's bonds may depend on both the value of property subject to its taxes and the amount of other debt dependent on the same property.

19.4.2 TYPES OF MUNICIPAL BONDS

In 1998, new municipal bonds with a par value of $262.3 billion were issued. Of this total, $87.0 billion were general obligation bonds (GOs) and $175.3 billion were revenue bonds.[14]

general obligation bonds

General obligation bonds are backed by the full faith and credit (and thus the full taxing power) of the issuing agency. Most are issued by agencies with unlimited taxing power, although in a minority of cases the issuer is subject to limits on the amount of taxes or on the tax rate (or both).

revenue bonds

Revenue bonds are backed by revenues from a designated project, authority, or agency, or by the proceeds from a specific tax. In many cases, such bonds are issued by agencies that hope to sell their services, pay the required expenses, and have enough left over to meet required payments on outstanding debt. Except for the possible granting of monopoly powers, the authorizing state and local government may provide no further assistance to the issuer. Such bonds are only as creditworthy as the enterprise associated with the issuer.

Many revenue bonds are issued to finance capital expenditures for publicly owned utilities (for example, water, electricity, or gas). Others are issued to finance quasi-utility operations (for example, public transportation). Some are financed by special assessments levied on properties benefiting from the original expenditure (for example,

industrial development bonds

properties connected to a new sewer system). Industrial development bonds (IDBs) are used to finance the purchase or construction of industrial facilities that are to be leased to firms on a favorable basis. In effect, such bonds provide cheap financing to businesses choosing to locate in the geographical area of the issuer.

Although most municipal financing involves the issuance of long-term securities, a number of short-term securities have been issued to meet short-term demands for cash. Examples include tax anticipation notes (TANs), revenue anticipation notes (RANs), grant anticipation notes (GANs), and tax and revenue anticipation notes (TRANs). In each case, the name of the security refers to the source of repayment. Thus some can be classified as general obligation securities and others as revenue securities.

More recently, municipalities have begun issuing two other kinds of short-term securities. Tax-exempt commercial paper is similar to corporate commercial paper, having a fixed interest rate and a maturity typically within 270 days. Variable-rate demand obligations have an interest rate that changes periodically (perhaps weekly) as some prespecified market interest rate changes. Furthermore, they can be redeemed at the desire of the investor within a prespecified number of days after the investor has given notice to the issuer (for example, 7 days after notification of intent).

19.4.3   TAX TREATMENT

Through a reciprocal arrangement with the federal government, coupon payments on state and local government securities are exempt from federal taxation, and coupon payments on Treasury and agency (except FNMA) securities are exempt from state and local taxation (for more on reciprocal taxation arrangements, see Chapter 5). Similar tax treatment is accorded to the price appreciation on short-term and long-term issues that are original issue discount securities. (As mentioned earlier, OID securities are securities that were issued for a below-par price.)

market discount bonds

However, a different tax treatment is generally given to coupon-bearing securities issued at par value but subsequently bought at a discount (that is, below par value) in the marketplace. Such securities, known as **market discount bonds,** provide the investor with income not only from the coupons but also from the difference between the purchase price and the par value. Unlike the coupons, which are tax-exempt, this difference is treated as taxable interest income.

Another interesting tax feature of municipals is that an investor who resides in the state of the issuer is generally exempt not only from paying federal taxes on the coupon payments but also from paying state taxes. Furthermore, an investor who resides in a city that has an income tax and who purchases municipals issued by the city usually is exempt from paying city taxes on the coupon payments. Thus, a resident of New York City who purchases a municipal security issued by the city (or one of its political subdivisions) will not have to pay federal, state, or city income taxes on the coupon payments. However, if the New York City resident were to purchase a California municipal bond, then both New York State and New York City income taxes would have to be paid on the coupon payments. This feature tends to make local issues more advantageous from an after-tax return viewpoint (an advantage that is offset to a certain degree by the resulting lack of diversification).

The avoidance of federal income tax on interest earned on a municipal bond makes such a security attractive to individual investors in high tax brackets as well as corporate investors. As shown in Figure 19.11, the lack of federal taxation has resulted in municipal securities having yields that are often considerably lower than those on taxable securities.[15] Consequently, the cost of financing to municipal issuers is lower, suggesting that a federal subsidy has been provided to the issuers.

taxable municipals

Over the years, this subsidy has been used to support activities deemed worthy of encouragement (even though the encouragement may be hidden). For example, private universities may issue tax-exempt bonds to finance certain improvements, and private firms may do so to finance certain pollution-reducing activities. Such bonds are generally backed only by the resources of the issuer, with government involvement limited to the granting of favorable tax treatment. The Tax Reform Act of 1986 greatly restricted the granting of such tax treatment, leading to the emergence of **taxable municipals,**

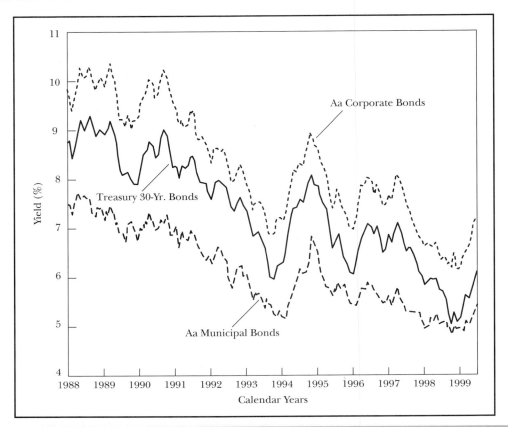

FIGURE 19.11 Average Yields of Long-Term, Fixed-Income Securities (monthly average)

Source: Treasury Bulletin, September 1999, p. 55.

which are typically issued to finance projects that are not viewed as essential under the tax law.

19.4.4 THE MARKET FOR MUNICIPAL BONDS

serial bonds

term bonds

Municipals are usually issued as **serial bonds;** one prespecified group matures a year after issue, another two years after issue, another three years after, and so on. Alternatively, **term bonds** (that is, bonds that all mature on the same date) or a mixture of serial and term bonds may be issued. The overall package is generally offered by the issuer on a competitive basis to various underwriters. The winning bidder then reoffers the individual bonds to investors at a higher price.

Unlike corporate bonds, municipal bonds do not need to be registered with the SEC before public issuance.[16] Indeed, the federal government leaves most regulation in this market to state and local authorities and the Municipal Securities Rulemaking Board.

sinking fund

Municipal bonds may be callable at specified dates and prices. Occasionally, the issuing authority is obligated to make designated payments into a **sinking fund,** which is used to buy similar bonds (or perhaps even its own bonds). As the issuing authority's bonds mature, the money for paying them off comes from having the sinking fund sell some of its holdings.

A secondary market in municipal bonds is made by various dealers. Standard & Poor's Corporation publishes on a daily basis a listing of municipal bond quotations by various dealers in the *Blue List*. In addition, the *Bond Buyer* has an electronic system that provides dealer quotations. However, the relatively small amounts of particular issues and maturities outstanding limit the size of the market. Many individuals who invest in municipals simply buy new issues and hold them to maturity. Nevertheless, the Municipal Securities Rulemaking Board has recently introduced a Daily Transaction Report that reports individual transaction information for issues that trade four or more times on a given day, giving municipal bond investors information to assist them in making investment decisions.

19.4.5 MUNICIPAL BOND INSURANCE

An investor concerned about possible default of a municipal bond can purchase an insurance policy to cover any losses that would be incurred if coupons or principal were not paid in full and on time. That is, an investor can contract with a company to have a specific portfolio of bonds insured. The issuer of the bonds also can purchase such insurance from one of the firms that specialize in issuing this type of insurance. The cost of this insurance is generally more than offset by the lower interest rate that the issuer has to pay as a result of insuring its bonds. Regardless of whether the investor or the issuer purchases the insurance, the cost of the insurance depends on the bonds included and their ratings.

19.5 Corporate Bonds

Corporate bonds are similar to other kinds of fixed-income securities in that they promise to make specified payments at specified times and provide legal remedies in the event of default. Restrictions are often placed on the activities of the issuing corporation in order to provide additional protection for bondholders (for example, there may be restrictions on the amount of additional bonds that can be issued in the future).

19.5.1 TAX TREATMENT

Corporate bonds that are original issue discount securities generally have the discount taxed as ordinary income by the federal government. The constant interest method is used to determine the portion of the discount that must be reported as taxable interest each year. (This method was described earlier with stripped Treasury bonds.) Using this method a portion of the discount must be recognized as income each year that the security is held, and the investor must pay taxes on that amount.

Corporate bonds carrying coupon payments have the coupon taxed as income each year. Furthermore, if the bond was originally sold at par but was later bought at a discount in the marketplace (as mentioned earlier, such bonds are known as market discount bonds), then the investor generally will have to pay ordinary income taxes on both the coupon payments and the discount. Using either the constant interest method or the straight-line method, wherein the discount is spread out evenly over the remaining life of the bond, the investor can recognize a portion of the discount as interest income each year that the bond is held and pay taxes on it. Alternatively, the investor can wait until the bond is sold and recognize the market discount as taxable interest income at that time.[17]

From the viewpoint of the issuing corporation, debt differs from equity in two crucial respects. First, principal and interest payments are obligatory. Failure to make any payment in full and on time can expose the issuer to expensive, time-consuming, and potentially disruptive legal actions. Second, unlike dividend payments, interest payments are considered expenses to the corporation and hence can be deducted from earnings before calculating the corporation's income tax liability. As a result, each dollar paid in interest reduces earnings before taxes by a dollar, thereby reducing corporate taxes by 35 cents for a firm in the 35% marginal tax bracket. This reduction leads to less than a dollar decline in earnings after taxes (in the 35% tax bracket example, the decline in earnings is 65 cents).

19.5.2 THE INDENTURE

indenture
trustee

An issue of bonds is generally covered by an **indenture,** in which the issuing corporation promises a specified **trustee** that it will comply with stated provisions. Chief among these provisions is the timely payment of required coupons and principal on the issue. Other terms are often included to control the sale of pledged property, the issuance of other bonds, and the like.

The trustee for a bond issue, usually a bank or a trust company, acts on behalf of the bondholders. Some actions may be required by the indenture; others, such as acting in response to a request from specific bondholders, may be done at the trustee's discretion.

If the corporation defaults on an interest payment, then after a relatively short period of time (perhaps one to six months) the entire principal typically becomes due and payable—a procedure designed to enhance the bondholders' status in any forthcoming bankruptcy or related legal proceedings.

19.5.3 TYPES OF BONDS

An exhaustive list of the names used to describe bonds would be intolerably long. Different names are often used for the same type of bond, and occasionally the same name will be used for two different bonds. A few major types do predominate, however, with relatively standard nomenclature.

Mortgage Bonds

mortgage bonds

Mortgage bonds represent debt that is secured by the pledge of specific property. In the event of default, the bondholders are entitled to obtain the property in question and to sell it to satisfy their claims on the firm. In addition to the property itself, the holders of mortgage bonds have an unsecured claim on the corporation.

Mortgage bondholders are usually protected by terms included in the bond indenture. The corporation may be constrained from pledging the property for other bonds (or such bonds, if issued, must be "junior" or "second" mortgages, with a claim on the property only after the first mortgage is satisfied). Certain property acquired by the corporation after the bonds were issued may also be pledged to support the bonds.

Debentures

debentures

Debentures are general obligations of the issuing corporation and thus represent unsecured credit. To protect the holders of such bonds, the indenture will usually limit the future issuance of secured debt as well as any additional unsecured debt.

Subordinated Debentures

subordinated
debentures

When more than one issue of debenture is outstanding, a hierarchy may be specified. For example, **subordinated debentures** are junior to unsubordinated debentures, meaning that in the event of bankruptcy, junior claims are to be considered only after senior claims have been fully satisfied.

Asset-Backed Securities

Asset-backed securities are much like the participation securities that were described earlier. However, instead of mortgages being pooled and pieces of ownership in the pool being sold, debt obligations such as credit card revolving loans, automobile loans, student loans, and equipment loans are pooled to serve as collateral backing the securities. The basic concept, known as securitization, is the same, however. Originators of these loans pool them and sell securities that represent part ownership of the pool. A servicing company collects the payments made by the debtors over a period of time, such as a month, and then pays each owner the appropriate percentage of the aggregate amount received. As for investors in participation certificates associated with mortgages, two concerns for investors in asset-backed securities are default risk and prepayment risk.

19.5.4 CALL PROVISIONS

Management would like to have the right to pay off the corporation's bonds at par at any time prior to maturity. This ability would provide management with flexibility because debt could be reduced or its maturity altered via refunding. Most important, expensive high-coupon debt that was issued during a time of high interest rates could be replaced with cheaper, low-coupon debt if rates decline.

Not surprisingly, investors hold quite a different opinion on the matter. The issuer's ability to redeem an issue at par at any time virtually precludes a substantive rise in price over par and robs the holder of potential gains from price appreciation associated with declining interest rates. Moreover, it introduces a new form of uncertainty. A bond with such a feature will almost certainly sell for less than one without it.

Despite the cost of obtaining this sort of flexibility, many corporations include call provisions in their bond indentures that give the corporation the option to call some or all of the bonds from their holders at stated prices during specified periods before maturity. In a sense, the firm sells a bond and simultaneously buys an option from the holders. The net price of the bond becomes the difference between the value of the bond and the option.

call premium

call price

The indenture usually gives investors two kinds of call protection. First, during the first few years after being issued, a bond may not be callable. Second, a **call premium** may be specified in the call provision. Such a premium indicates that if the issue is called, the issuer must pay the bondholders a **call price** that is a stated amount above par. Often, the amount above par becomes smaller as time passes and the maturity date approaches. An entire issue may be called, or only specific bonds that are chosen randomly by the trustee may be called. In either case, a notice of redemption will appear in advance in the financial press.

putable bonds

Putable bonds, in contrast, give holders the option to exchange their bonds for cash equal to the bonds' face value. Generally, this option may be exercised over a brief period of time after a stated number of years has elapsed since the bond's issuance.[18] In a sense, the firm sells a bond and an option simultaneously to the owners. (Putable bonds are discussed more fully in Chapter 21.)

19.5.5 SINKING FUNDS

A bond indenture will often require the issuing corporation to make annual payments into a sinking fund. The idea is to pay part of the principal of the debt (as well as the interest) each year, thereby reducing the amount outstanding at maturity.

Sinking funds operate by having the corporation transmit cash to the trustee, who can then purchase bonds in the open market. Alternatively, the corporation may obtain the bonds itself, by either purchase or call, and deposit them with the trustee. Call prices for sinking fund purchases may differ from those specified when the entire issue is to be repaid prior to maturity.

Required contributions to a sinking fund may not be the same each year. In some cases, the required amount may depend on earnings, output, and so on; in others, the goal is to make the total paid for interest and principal the same each year.

19.5.6 PRIVATE PLACEMENTS

private placements

Bonds intended for eventual public sale are usually issued in denominations of $1,000 each. Often, however, a single investor or small group of investors will buy an entire issue. Such an offering, known as a **private placement,** does not involve a prospectus and is not required to be registered with the SEC provided certain conditions are met. The two most important ones prohibit general advertising and solicitation of interest and restrict the sale to investors who are deemed "sophisticated" as evidenced by their wealth and income. Subsequent trading after a lapse of one year from the offering date is allowed, but Rule 144A allows trading before the one year is up provided the purchaser is a qualified institutional buyer, which is an institution with assets of at least $100 million, dubbed a "QIB" (for more on Rule 144A, see Chapter 13).

19.5.7 BANKRUPTCY

When a corporation fails to make a scheduled coupon or principal payment on a bond, the corporation is said to be in default on that obligation. If the payment is not made within a relatively short period, some sort of litigation almost inevitably follows.

A corporation unable to meet its obligatory debt payments is said to be technically insolvent (or insolvent in the equity sense). If the value of the firm's assets falls below its liabilities, it is said to be insolvent (or insolvent in the bankruptcy sense). Behind these definitions lie much legislation, many court cases, and varied legal opinions. Although the details differ, the usual situation begins with a default on one or more required coupon payments. Failure to obtain voluntary agreements with creditors usually leads to a filing of bankruptcy by the corporation itself. Subsequent developments involve courts, court-appointed officials, representatives of the firm's creditors, and the management of the firm, among others.

Liquidation

A question that arises in most bankruptcy cases is whether the firm's assets should be liquidated (that is, sold) and the proceeds divided among the creditors. Such action is taken only if the court feels that the resulting value would exceed that likely to be obtained if the firm continued in operation (perhaps after substantial reorganization).

When the firm's assets are liquidated in a "straight bankruptcy," secured creditors receive either the property pledged for their loans or the proceeds from the sale of the secured property. If this amount falls short of their claims, the difference is considered an unsecured debt of the firm; in contrast, any excess amount is made available for other creditors. Next, assets are used to pay the claims of priority creditors to the extent possible. These include claims for such items as administrative expenses, wages (up to a stated limit per person), uninsured pension claims, taxes, and rents. Anything left over is used to pay unsecured creditors in proportion to their claims on the firm.

Reorganization

If the value of a firm's assets when used as part of a "going concern" appears to exceed the value of the assets in liquidation, a reorganization of the firm and its liabilities may be undertaken. Such proceedings, conducted under the provisions of the Federal Bankruptcy Act, may be voluntary (initiated by the firm) or involuntary (initiated by three or more creditors). Several parties must concur in the proposed reorganization, including the holders of two-thirds of the value in each general class of creditor that is affected by the reorganization.

Among the goals of reorganization are "fair and equitable" treatment of various classes of securities, and the elimination of "burdensome" debt obligations. Typically, creditors are given new claims on the reorganized firm, with the amounts of the new claims intended to be at least equal in value to the amounts that the creditors would have received in liquidation. For example, holders of debentures might receive bonds of longer maturity, holders of subordinated debentures might become stockholders, and stockholders might be left without any claims on the firm.

Arrangements

A third procedure is available to financially distressed corporations. The Federal Bankruptcy Act authorizes *arrangements,* in which debts may be extended (to longer maturities) or reduced.

Some Financial Aspects of Bankruptcy

Although the subject is far too complex for detailed treatment here, two aspects of bankruptcy deserve some discussion. First, the choice between continuation of a firm and liquidation of its assets should be unrelated to considerations of bankruptcy. If an asset can be sold for more than the present value of its future earnings, it should be liquidated. Management may have to be taken to court to be forced to sell, but the issue is not really one of solvency or lack thereof.

Second, the definition of insolvency is rather vague. Assume, for the sake of argument, that assets can be adequately assessed at the larger of either the liquidating value or the going-concern value. A firm is said to be insolvent if this value is less than that of the firm's liabilities. But how should the liabilities be valued? Their current market value will inevitably be less than the value of the assets, whereas their book value can be greater than the value of the assets.

19.5.8 TRADING IN CORPORATE BONDS

Although most of the trading in corporate bonds takes place through dealers in the over-the-counter market, many corporates, as well as Treasuries, agencies, and municipals, are listed on the NYSE's Fixed Income Market (a notably smaller number are listed on the AMEX). However, trading in corporate bonds on the NYSE is done differently than the way common stocks are traded because neither specialists nor trading posts are involved. Instead, bonds that are listed on the NYSE are traded through a computer system known as the **Automated Bond System** (ABS). With this system, subscribers (ABS is available for a fee) enter their bid or asked prices, along with the quantities, into computer termi-

Automated Bond System

Distressed Securities

 Investments in fixed-income securities have traditionally encompassed investment-grade bonds—securities rated Baa (or BBB) or higher by the major credit rating agencies. In the 1980s, the universe of popular fixed-income investments expanded to include below-investment-grade bonds, called high-yield bonds. As interest rates fell in the early and mid-1990s, high-yield bonds became increasingly inviting to portfolio managers seeking to maintain attractive interest payouts to their clients.

Even in prosperous times, a surprisingly large percentage of high-yield bond issuers (1% to 3% annually) default on their debt. Although the high-yield bond category technically includes securities whose issuers have defaulted on their debt, high-yield bond portfolio managers in practice do not usually purchase bonds already in default. Rather, they focus their efforts on issuers who they anticipate can avoid default and therefore make the high yields paid on the issuers' bonds attractive relative to alternative fixed-income investments.

The securities of firms that have defaulted on their debt and who either (1) have filed for legal bankruptcy protection or (2) are negotiating out of court with creditors in the hope of avoiding bankruptcy are called *distressed securities*. These securities include publicly traded bonds as well as privately traded debt owed to commercial banks (known as bank debt) or suppliers of goods and services to the distressed companies (called trade debt). In addition, distressed securities can also include common stock because one likely resolution to a bankruptcy is for holders of the company's debt to be compensated, in part, with newly issued equity.

Most companies that restructure their debt do so out of court. Those that do enter legal bankruptcy either reorganize their debt under Chapter 11 of the U.S. Bankruptcy Code or liquidate under Chapter 7. Investors in distressed securities often prefer a Chapter 11 reorganization as opposed to an out-of-court restructuring because the reorganized company must file considerable financial information with the court. This disclosure makes an evaluation of the company's debt easier.

For those companies that do enter bankruptcy, each situation is unique. Nevertheless, there are common aspects of most bankruptcies. Figure 19.12 provides an overview of the bankruptcy process from a company's initial financial problems to its ultimate reorganization.

It is often argued that distressed securities represent a more inefficient sector of the fixed-income market than either investment-grade or high-yield bonds. The reasoning is several-fold. First, there may be a market segmentation effect. Many institutional investors are prohibited from owning bankrupt securities. Thus, when a company enters bankruptcy, these investors are forced to sell their holdings, potentially driving down the price of the company's debt excessively. Second, the process of bankruptcy is time-consuming and unpredictable. Debtholders of a company near, or in, bankruptcy may wish to avoid these complications and sell their holdings cheaply to investors willing to see the process through to reorganization. Third, there is a lack of research coverage on bankrupt companies. Analysts at major brokerage firms typically suspend their coverage when a company becomes bankrupt, leaving investors to secure their own information about the company's financial condition. Finally, there is the issue of limited liquidity. The reluctance of most organizations to make a market in distressed securities results in wider bid–ask spreads.

Investors use different strategies to invest in distressed securities. Some follow a nonparticipatory approach in which they do not attempt to influence the bankruptcy proceedings. They simply purchase the debt of bankrupt companies that they view to be attractively priced and hold that debt until, hopefully, it can be sold at a higher price later in the bankruptcy process. Other investors follow a proactive approach, serving on creditors committees that are charged with negotiating the terms of the company's reorganization. Through these committees, they hope to secure outcomes favorable to the value of their holdings.

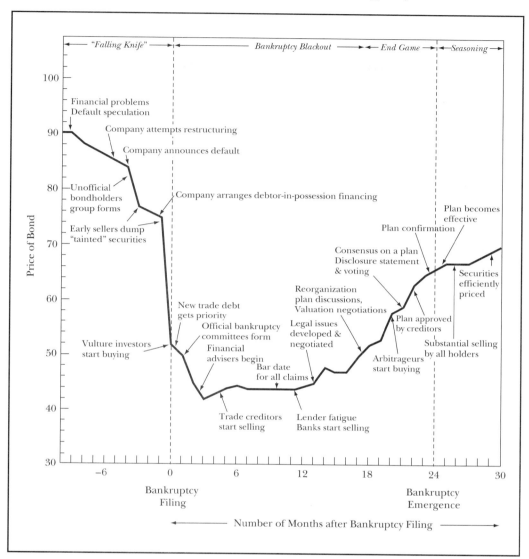

FIGURE 19.12 Time Line of the Bankruptcy Process

Source: Provided by T. Rowe Price Associates, 1998.

At the most aggressive end of the spectrum are investors who attempt to impose their solutions on other creditors by acquiring "blocking" positions in certain classes of a bankrupt company's debt. Because two-thirds of each class of debt must concur with the bankruptcy settlement, holding at least a one-third position in a strategically located debt class gives an investor effective veto power over a settlement. Applied appropriately, this power can be translated into an outcome that favors the holders of the position.

Some investors prefer to own the most senior debt in a bankrupt company's financial structure. Their reasoning is that bankruptcy rules require that creditors be paid in order of seniority (although in practice this rule is not always followed to the letter). Thus, owning senior debt provides more of a valuation cushion in the event that the company's value in reorganization turns out to be worth less than originally expected. Other investors prefer to own junior claims. Their logic is that junior debt is the most likely to appreciate significantly in value if a successful reorganization plan can be developed and implemented. In the reorganization, senior claims tend to receive more cash and newly issued debt whereas junior claims tend to receive more common stock.

The bankruptcy court is responsible for assigning a value to the company's assets and allocating that value among the creditors. The court's assigned value may not necessarily equal the value of the company's assets after the reorganization. Therefore, holders of junior claims will benefit more if the bankruptcy court assigns a greater value to the company's assets because their claim is largely a residual. Holders of senior claims prefer a lower assigned asset value because that will leave more of the company's assets in their hands and reduce the proportion of assets allocated to junior claims.

A successful distressed-securities investor possesses a blend of skills. First, the ability to ac-curately estimate the value of the company's assets that the bankruptcy court will assign is critical to determining an appropriate price to pay for different classes of the company's debt. Second, the investor must have a thorough knowledge of the bankruptcy process. Many intricate aspects of that process can easily trip up an inexperienced investor. Third, the investor must be a skillful negotiator. He or she must be able to strike deals with a disparate group of creditors who may have financial agendas quite different from the investor's. Negotiations that become stalemated can quickly drag down returns while the investor's capital remains tied up in unproductive assets. Finally, the investor must be a savvy trader who understands the market for the company's debt and maintains access to sources of liquidity, both in initiating positions in the company's debt and in exiting those positions.

---

nals. Other subscribers can see these orders at display terminals and can respond by entering an order at a terminal. Thus, ABS not only provides subscribers with quotes, it also provides them with execution capability.

Because some corporate bonds are traded on the NYSE, the prices at which such trades are made are found in the financial press, summarized daily as shown in Figure 19.13. Consider the following entry:

Bonds	Current Yield	Volume	Close	Net Change
ATT 7S05	6.7	20	$104\frac{5}{8}$	$-\frac{1}{4}$

current yield
Fixed Income Pricing System

This entry indicates that AT&T bonds carrying a 7% coupon (paid semiannually) and maturing in 2005 last traded at $104\frac{5}{8}$. Because these bonds have a par value of $1,000, the last trade was at $1,046.25. The **current yield,** meaning the annual coupon rate divided by the current closing price, was approximately 6.7% (= $70/$1,046.25). In all, 20 bonds traded hands on the exchange during the day, and the closing price was down $\frac{1}{4}$ (= $2.50) from that of the previous trading day.

In a sense, the NYSE is the "odd lot" market for bonds, even though at the end of 1998 it had nearly 2,000 different bond issues available for trading, with one-half of them being U.S. corporate debt issues having an aggregate par value of one-quarter of a trillion dollars.[19] Major trades of bonds are generally negotiated elsewhere by dealers and institutional investors, either directly or through brokers. Reported prices on the NYSE may be poor guides to values associated with large transactions (the same can be said for quotes that are publicly supplied by bond dealers) but may be reasonable for small transactions.

A second bond market run by the Nasdaq Stock Market is known as the **Fixed Income Pricing System** (FIPS). Unlike ABS, this market is devoted to trading high-yield

NEW YORK EXCHANGE BONDS

Quotations as of 4 p.m. Eastern Time
Tuesday, March 2, 1999

Volume $16,201,000

	Domestic		All Issues	
Issues Traded	Tue	Mon	Tue	Mon
Issues Traded	202	215	210	225
Advances	77	61	80	65
Declines	86	114	90	119
Unchanged	39	40	40	41
New highs	3	1	3	2
New lows	14	9	14	9

SALES SINCE JANUARY 1
(000 omitted)

1999	1998	1997
$559,392	$722,221	$1,114,170

Dow Jones Bond Averages

—1998—		—1999—			—1999—			—1998—	
High	Low	High	Low		Close	Chg.	%Yld	Close	Chg.
107.17	104.42	106.88	104.13	20 Bonds	104.30	−0.11	6.80	105.11	+0.07
104.71	101.88	104.72	102.03	10 Utilities	102.15	−0.18	6.82	102.26	−0.03
109.81	106.48	109.44	106.23	10 Industrials	106.44	−0.05	6.79	107.95	+0.17

CORPORATION BONDS
Volume, $16,062,000

[Detailed bond quotation listings for Corporation Bonds, Foreign Bonds, AMEX Bonds, and NASDAQ Convertible Debentures follow in multiple columns.]

FOREIGN BONDS
Volume, $102,000

AMEX BONDS
Volume $651,000

SALES SINCE JANUARY 1

1999	1998	1997
$27,103,000	$56,624,000	$69,928,000

	Tue.	Mon.	Fri.	Thu.
Issues Traded	14	10	17	14
Advances	1	1	7	2
Declines	8	3	5	9
Unchanged	5	6	5	3
New highs	0	0	0	1
New lows	0	1	1	1

NASDAQ
Convertible Debentures
Monday, March 1, 1999

EXPLANATORY NOTES
(For New York and American Bonds)
Yield is Current yield.
cv-Convertible bond. cf-Certificates. cld-Called. dc-Deep discount. ec-European currency units. f-Dealt in flat. il-Italian lire. kd-Danish kroner. m-Matured bonds, negotiability impaired by maturity. na-No accrual. r-Registered. rp-Reduced principal. st, sd-Stamped. t-Floating rate. wd-When distributed. ww-With warrants. x-Ex interest. xw-Without warrants. zr-Zero coupon.
vj-In bankruptcy or receivership or being reorganized under the Bankruptcy Act. or securities assumed by such companies.

FIGURE 19.13 Price Quotations for Corporate Bonds

bonds, which are defined as bonds that are less than investment grade (bond grades are discussed in more detail in Chapter 22), meaning they are speculative and have a reasonable chance of default. All members of the NASD that consider themselves dealers or brokers in high-yield bonds are required to use FIPS. However, because FIPS lists only liquid high-yield debt, brokers and dealers in less liquid issues are not required to use FIPS. Quotes are entered on FIPS by dealers and must be at least one-sided (that is, either a bid or asked quote must be given); trades are made by contacting a dealer, typically by telephone, and depending on the bond, may have to be reported within five minutes of execution. All quotations and trade reports are disseminated by Nasdaq and other market data vendors on an hourly basis for the 50 most liquid issues. These bonds are identified every six months and are known as *mandatory bonds.*

19.6 Foreign Bonds

The foreign bond market refers to bonds issued and denominated in the currency of a country other than the one in which the issuer is primarily located. For example, Inco (a Canadian firm) has issued bonds that are denominated in U.S. dollars, mature in 2016, and carry a $7\frac{3}{4}$% coupon rate. Although some foreign bonds (such as Inco's) appear daily at the end of the "New York Exchange Bonds" quotations section in *The Wall Street Journal,* as shown in Figure 19.13, the amount of trading is often so small that only the total volume is reported. Foreign bonds that are issued in the United States and are denominated in U.S. dollars are referred to as Yankee bonds.

In issuing foreign bonds, the issuer must abide by the rules and regulations imposed by the government of the country in which the bonds are issued. Compliance may be relatively easy or difficult depending on the country involved.

One of the main advantages of purchasing foreign bonds is the opportunity to diversify internationally the default risk of a bond portfolio while not having to be concerned about foreign exchange fluctuations. For example, a U.S. investor might be able to buy a Toyota bond in Japan that is denominated in yen but, in doing so, would have to worry about the yen–dollar exchange rate because the coupon payments and ultimately the principal would be paid to the investor in yen. The yen then would have to be converted into dollars at a currently unknown exchange rate. Investors can avoid such worries by purchasing a Toyota bond that is denominated in U.S. dollars.

19.7 Eurobonds

Eurobond

Owing in part to government restrictions on investment in foreign securities, some borrowers have found it advantageous to sell securities in other countries. The term **Eurobond** is loosely applied to bonds that are offered outside the country of the borrower and outside the country in whose currency the securities are denominated.[20] Thus, a bond issued by a U.S. corporation, denominated in Japanese yen (or U.S. dollars), and sold in Europe would be a Eurobond.

As the Eurobond market is neither regulated nor taxed, it offers substantial advantages for many issuers and buyers of bonds. For example, a foreign subsidiary of a U.S. corporation may issue a Eurobond in "bearer" form. No tax will be withheld by the corporation, and the tax (if any) paid by the purchaser will depend on his or her country of residence. For tax reasons, interest rates on Eurobonds tend to be somewhat lower than those on domestic bonds denominated in the same currency.

19.8 Preferred Stock

preferred stock

In some respects, **preferred stock** is like a perpetual bond. A given dollar amount is paid each year by the issuer to the investor. This amount may be stated as a percent of the stock's par value (for example, 8% of $100, meaning $8 per year) or directly as a dollar figure (for example, $2.75 per year). Because the security is a "stock," the payments are called dividends instead of interest and hence do not qualify as a tax-deductible expense for the issuing corporation. Furthermore, failure to make the payments does not constitute grounds for bankruptcy proceedings.

A recent innovation is adjustable rate preferred stock (ARPS), where the dividend is reset periodically in terms of an applicable rate. For example, the annualized "percent of par" for the dividend might be reset every three months to be equal to the largest of the rates on (1) three-month Treasury bills, (2) 10-year Treasury bonds, and (3) 20-year Treasury bonds. Related to ARPS are Dutch auction rate preferred stocks (DARPS), where the dividend is reset periodically (more often than for ARPS) at a level determined by bidding from current and potential owners.[21] Preferred stock generally receives preferential treatment when it comes to dividends. Specified payments must be made on the preferred stock before any dividends are paid to holders of the firm's common stock. Failure to pay a preferred dividend in full does not constitute default, but unpaid dividends are usually **cumulative;** that is, all previously unpaid preferred stock dividends must be paid (but seldom with interest) before any dividends may be paid on the common stock.

cumulative dividends

No indenture is provided with a preferred stock issue. However, various provisions protecting the preferred stockholders against potentially harmful actions may be written into the corporation's charter. For example, one provision may limit the dollar amount of senior securities that can be issued in the future. Although preferred stockholders typically do not have voting rights, there may be another provision that gives them voting rights when the corporation is in arrears on its preferred dividends.

Many issues of preferred stock are callable at a stated redemption price. *Participating preferred stock* entitles the holder to receive extra dividends when earnings permit. *Convertible preferred stock* may, at the option of the holder, be converted into another security (usually the firm's common stock) on stated terms. Some firms issue more than one class of preferred stock, with preference accorded the various classes in a specified order.

In the event of the dissolution of a firm, preferred stock often receives preferential treatment as to assets in liquidation. Preferred stockholders are generally entitled to receive the stock's par value before any payment is made to common stockholders.

As indicated in Chapter 5, interest income from bonds held by a corporate investor is subject to the corporate income tax, but 80% of any dividend income received is exempt from taxation.[22] For a corporate investor this exemption makes the effective tax rate on dividends from preferred stock approximately 7% (= .35 × .20), compared with 35% for interest received on bonds. For this reason, preferred stocks tend to sell at prices that give lower before-tax returns than long-term bonds, even though bonds may be considerably lower in risk. As a result, preferred stocks are generally unattractive holdings for noncorporate investors, such as individuals and tax-exempt investors.

Because preferred stock has many features of a bond but is without the substantial tax advantage that bonds give to the issuer, it is used less often than debt. A recent innovation that blurs the distinction between debt and preferred stock involves the use of *trust preferred stock*. From the issuer's perspective, the distinguishing feature of this security is that it is structured so that its dividend payments are treated as tax-deductible interest by the issuer. From the corporate investor's perspective, trust preferred stock is treated as traditional preferred stock with one exception: All of a trust preferred's dividends are taxable income where, as previously mentioned, up to 80% of a traditional preferred's dividends are exempt from taxes.[23]

Just how such securities are structured is quite clever, as the following example shows. Big Widget, Inc., sets up a wholly owned subsidiary, Little Widget, Inc., which issues 10 shares of trust preferred stock, carrying an 8% dividend yield, to the public for $100 per share. The $1,000 in proceeds received by Little Widget is used to buy an 8% $1,000 bond issued by Big Widget. After one year, Big Widget makes a tax-deductible interest payment of $80 {thus costing Big Widget only $52 [= $80 × (1 − .35)] after taxes} to Little Widget, which, in turn, pays $8 to each of the 10 trust preferred stockholders. Note that Little Widget receives $80 and pays out $80. Because Little Widget is organized as a limited liability corporation, it pays no taxes on the $80 received from Big Widget.[24]

Many preferred stocks are traded on major exchanges in a manner similar to common stocks. Typically, they are assigned to the same specialist that is responsible for the firm's common stock. Trading prices are reported in the financial press in the same format used for common stocks.

Summary

1. Highly marketable short-term securities are referred to as money market instruments. These securities include commercial paper, large-denomination certificates of deposit, bankers' acceptances, repurchase agreements, and Eurodollar CDs.

2. The U.S. Treasury issues debt securities to finance the government's borrowing needs. These securities are issued in various maturities—short-term (Treasury bills), intermediate-term (Treasury notes), and long-term (Treasury bonds). The Treasury also issues savings bonds to individual investors.

3. Treasury notes or bonds can be converted into a set of pure-discount bonds by issuing marketable receipts entitling the holder to a specific coupon payment or the bond's principal payment. Separating a bond into its component payments is known as coupon stripping.

4. Federal agencies also issue securities to finance their operations. In some cases this debt is explicitly backed by the U.S. Treasury. In other cases the government guarantee is implicit.

5. Participation certificates (pass-throughs) represent ownership of a pool of mortgages. The holders receive cash flows from the pool's mortgages in proportion to their ownership in the pool.

6. Collateralized mortgage obligations (CMOs) are classes of securities that have different claims on the payments received from a pool of mortgages.

7. State and local governments issue a wide variety of fixed-income securities. These securities may be backed solely by the full faith and credit of the issuer or by a specific revenue source.

8. Because municipal securities are generally exempt from federal taxation, they usually offer lower yields than taxable securities.

9. Some types of corporate bonds, such as mortgage bonds, are backed by specific assets. Other types, such as debentures, may represent general obligations of the issuing corporations.

10. Corporate bonds (and some federal government and municipal bonds) may contain call provisions, giving the issuer the right to redeem the security prior to maturity under specified terms.

11. Corporations entering bankruptcy may undergo liquidation or reorganization or enter into arrangements.

12. Preferred stock dividends are generally fixed but do not represent legal obligations of the issuers. Most preferred stock dividends are cumulative, requiring payment of all unpaid preferred dividends before common stock dividends can be paid.

Questions and Problems

1. Consider a 13-week Treasury bill, issued today, which is selling for $9,675. (Its face value is $10,000.)
   a. What is the annual discount based on the selling price of the security?
   b. What is the annual equivalent yield of the security?
2. If a three-month Treasury bill sells for a price of 98, whereas a six-month Treasury bill sells for 96, is the equivalent yield (unannualized) for the six-month bill twice that of the three-month bill? Why?
3. Rank the various money market instruments discussed in the text in terms of default risk. Explain the reasoning behind your rankings. Find the latest interest rates for these securities. Do they correspond with your default-risk rankings?
4. Describe the standard practice by which sellers of government and corporate bonds are compensated for accrued interest.
5. What is the rationale for including a call provision in the indenture of a bond issue? How do bond investors typically respond to the inclusion of a call provision?
6. Consider a 10-year zero-coupon Treasury security selling for a price of $300, with a face value of $1,000. What is the before-tax annual rate of return to an investor who buys and holds this security to maturity?
7. Why does the IRS treat the difference between the price of a bond purchased at a discount and its face value as ordinary income to the investor, as opposed to treating it as a capital gain?
8. What is a mortgage participation certificate? What is the primary risk that such securities present to investors?
9. Cozy Dolan, an amateur investor, said, "I prefer investing in GNMA pass-through securities. Their government guarantee gives me a riskfree return." Comment on Cozy's remark.
10. Pigeon Falls Airlines was having financial difficulties because of ongoing recession and labor problems. To this point the firm had issued no debt, but management believed that borrowing in the bond market was the only way to get through the tough times. Because of its poor financial condition, Pigeon Falls's investment bankers advised management that a debenture issue would not be well received. What other bond issuance options might Pigeon Falls pursue?
11. A callable bond is sometimes described as a combination of a noncallable bond and an option. Explain why this description is appropriate, and explain how these two features affect the price of a callable bond.
12. Muddy Ruel is considering purchasing one of two bonds: a corporate bond with a 9% coupon interest rate, selling at par, or a tax-free municipal bond with a 6% coupon interest rate, selling at par. Given that Muddy is in the 30% tax bracket, and assuming that all other relevant factors are the same between the two bonds, which bond should Muddy select?
13. Is it true that most corporations that default on their debt eventually enter bankruptcy and see their assets liquidated to repay creditors? Explain.
14. In trying to explain the concept of preferred stock to a novice investor, Patsy Donovan referred to it as a "hybrid" security. What did Patsy mean by this term?
15. The preferred stock of Clinton Foods carries a dividend of $8 per share. The stock currently sells for $50. If one year from today the Clinton preferred stock's price remains unchanged, what is the return from holding the stock for
   a. A corporation in the 35% tax bracket?
   b. An individual in the 35% tax bracket?

Endnotes

1. Short-term obligations of the U.S. government and its agencies are also considered money market instruments; they are described in the next section.

2. One recent innovation is the issuance of "equity-linked CDs," which provide the investor with a return based on the performance of a given market index, coupled with a guarantee that the investor will not experience a loss (some even guarantee the investor some minimal interest rate if the market index performs poorly). See Michael D. Joehnk, "Short-Term Investing: Socking It Away in CDs," *AAII Journal*, 12, no. 8 (September 1990): 7–9. See also Jeffrey Cohn and Michael E. Edieson, "Banking on the Market: Equity-Linked CDs," *AAII Journal*, 15, no. 3 (March 1993): 11–15.

3. Many insurance companies sell large denomination *guaranteed investment contracts* (GICs) that are similar to CDs in that they typically pay a stated interest rate for a given number of years. Other types of financial institutions offer contracts similar to GICs. See Robert T. Kleiman and Anandi P. Sahu, "The ABCs of GICs for Retirement Plan Investing," *AAII Journal*, 14, no. 3 (March 1992): 7–10.

4. For more on trading Treasuries, see Jay Goldinger, "Trading Treasuries: Know the Risks before You Invest," *AAII Journal*, 11, no. 10 (November 1989): 12–15.

5. This approach to calculating equivalent yields for Treasury bills is applicable only if the maturity is six months or less; a more complicated approach is necessary for T-bills with longer lives. See Richard J. Kish, "Discrepancy in Treasury Bill Yield Calculations," *Financial Practice and Education*, 2, no. 1 (Spring/Summer 1992): 41–45.

6. The yield-to-maturity on a bond is the discount rate that makes the present value of the future coupon payments and par value equal to its current market price (which in this case is the asked price). Chapter 21 discusses yields more thoroughly.

7. The procedure for calculating accrued interest on corporate bonds is different because it is based on an assumption that there are 30 days in each month and 180 days in each semiannual period. Specifically, (1) the number of complete months left until the next coupon payment is determined and multiplied by 30; (2) the number of days left in the current month is determined and added to the previous figure; (3) the resulting figure is subtracted from 180, thereby giving the number of days that have elapsed since the last coupon payment; (4) this figure is divided by 180, giving the fraction of the period that has elapsed; and (5) this fraction is multiplied by the semiannual coupon, resulting in the amount of accrued interest. See "Dividends and Inter-est: Who Gets Payments after a Trade?" *AAII Journal*, 12, no. 4 (April 1990): 8–11.

8. If the bonds are used to pay for certain educational expenses, the interest may be completely tax-free. For more on savings bonds, see Paul F. Jessup, "The Purloined Investment: EE Savings Bonds Make Sense," *AAII Journal*, 12, no. 8 (September 1990): 10–13; and Phillip R. Daves and Robert A. Kunkel, "After the Fall: Savings Bonds Are Still Attractive Short Term," *AAII Journal*, 15, no. 4 (April 1993): 11–12.

9. If the underlying Treasury security is callable, this set of receipts provides holders with all coupon payments received after the date of first call as well as the principal.

10. OID securities can have either no coupons (in which case they are pure-discount securities) or small coupons. The key distinguishing feature of an OID security is that, at issuance, it was sold for a significant discount from par value. *De minimus rules* indicate that, for tax purposes, small discounts can be ignored until the security is sold or matures.

11. Determining an appropriate price for a pass-through security is complicated. For an analysis, see Richard J. Kish and James Greenleaf, "Teaching How Mortgage Pass-Through Securities Are Priced," *Financial Practice and Education*, 3, no. 1 (Spring/Summer 1993): 85–94.

12. This census is conducted every five years. The data reported here are from the *1998 Statistical Abstract of the United States* (Washington, DC: GPO, 1998), Table 496, p. 305; it can also be found at <http://www.census.gov/prod/3/98pubs/98statab/sasec9.pdf>.

13. In some cases no capital expenditure is involved. (For example, the proceeds from the debt issue may be used to refund an outstanding debt issue.)

14. *Federal Reserve Bulletin*, April 1999, p. A31.

15. As noted in Chapter 5, the yields on municipal bonds have historically been 20% to 40% below the yields on similar taxable bonds.

16. However, municipal bonds that are unregistered with respect to ownership cannot be issued (this prohibition began July 1, 1983). See Hildy Richelson, "Municipal Bonds: A Guide to the Various Forms of Ownership," *AAII Journal*, 13, no. 4 (April 1991): 13–16.

17. This practice assumes that the bond was purchased on or after May 1, 1993. For more on the taxation of bonds, see Chapter 5, or Clark Blackman II and Donald Laubacher, "The Basics of Bond Discounts and Premiums," *AAII Journal*, 15, no. 3 (March 1993): 24–27, or IRS Publications 550 and 1212. The taxation of securities in general and bonds in particular is a complex matter, with many exceptions and alternative procedures. Any investor would be well advised

to check carefully beforehand to be certain of the method of taxation involved for any security being considered for purchase.

18. It has been reported that 1996 was the first year that putable bond volume exceeded callable bond volume. See Leland E. Crabbe and Panos Nikoulis, "The Putable Bond Market: Structure, Historical Experience, and Strategies," *Journal of Fixed Income,* 7, no. 3 (December 1997): 47–60.

19. *New York Stock Exchange Fact Book 1998 Data* (New York Stock Exchange, 1999), p. 84.

20. There are also fixed-income securities of this nature that have shorter lives; they are sometimes referred to as Euronotes or Euro-commercial paper. The market where they (and Eurobonds) are issued and traded is known as the Eurocredit market.

21. For a discussion of ARPS and DARPS, see Michael J. Alderson, Keith C. Brown, and Scott L. Lummer, "Dutch Auction Rate Preferred Stock," *Financial Management,* 16, no. 2 (Summer 1987), 68–73. See also Michael J. Alderson and Donald R. Fraser, "Financial

Innovations and Excesses Revisited: The Case of Auction Rate Preferred Stock," *Financial Management,* 22, no. 2 (Summer 1993): 61–75.

22. This proportion is based on the assumption that the corporate investor owns between 20% and 80% of the firm's common stock. If less than 20% is owned, then only 70% of the dividend is exempt from taxation, whereas if more than 80% is owned, then all of the dividend is exempt.

23. It has been reported that trust preferred stocks have recently "largely replaced traditional preferred stock as a source of capital"; see Ellen Engel, Merle Erickson, and Edward Maydew, "Debt–Equity Hybrid Securities," unpublished paper, University of Chicago, Graduate School of Business, August 1997, p. 2.

24. Trust preferred stock is only one example of many financial innovations that have been created in recent years to avoid taxes. These securities may satisfy the legal letter of the law, but critics view them as devious attempts to thwart the intent of the tax code.

CHAPTER

Fundamentals of Bond Valuation

A useful first step in understanding bond valuation is to consider riskless securities, which are those fixed-income securities that are certain of making their promised payments in full and on time. The obvious candidates for consideration as riskless securities are the securities that represent the debt of the federal government. Because the government can print money whenever it chooses, the promised payments on such securities are virtually certain to be made on schedule. However, there is a degree of uncertainty as to the purchasing power of the promised payments. Although government bonds may be riskless in terms of their nominal payments, they may be quite risky in terms of their real (or inflation-adjusted) payments, as noted in Chapter 6.

Despite the concern with inflation risk, it will be assumed that there are fixed-income securities whose nominal and real payments are certain. Specifically, it will be assumed that the magnitude of inflation can be accurately predicted. Such an assumption makes it possible to focus on the impact of *time* on bond valuation. The influences of other attributes on bond valuation can be considered afterward.

20.1 Yield-to-Maturity

There are many ways that interest rates can be calculated. One such method results in an interest rate that is known as the yield-to-maturity, and another results in an interest rate known as the spot rate. The yield-to-maturity is discussed first, followed by the spot rate.

In describing yields-to-maturity and spot rates, three hypothetical Treasury securities that are available to the public for investment will be considered. Treasury securities are widely believed to be free from default risk, meaning that investors have no doubts about being paid fully and on time. Thus, the impact of differing degrees of default risk on yields-to-maturity and spot rates is removed.

The three Treasury securities to be considered will be referred to as bonds A, B, and C. Bonds A and B are called pure-discount or zero-coupon bonds because they make no interim interest (or "coupon") payments prior to maturity. Any investor who purchases this kind of bond pays a market-determined price and in return receives the principal (or "face") value of the bond at maturity. In this case, bond A matures in a year, at which time the investor will receive $1,000. Similarly, bond B matures in two years, at which time the investor will receive $1,000. However, bond C is a coupon bond

Almost Riskfree Securities

 Riskfree securities play a central role in modern financial theory, providing the baseline against which to evaluate risky investment alternatives. It is, perhaps, surprising that no riskfree financial asset has historically been available to U.S. investors. Recent developments in the U.S. Treasury bond market, however, have made important strides toward bringing that deficiency to an end.

A riskless security provides an investor with a guaranteed (certain) return over the investor's time horizon. As the investor is ultimately interested in the purchasing power of his or her investments, the riskless security's return should be certain, not just on a nominal but on a real (or inflation-adjusted) basis.

Although U.S. Treasury securities have zero risk of default, even they have not traditionally provided riskless real returns. Their principal and interest payments are not adjusted for inflation over the securities' lives. As a result, unexpected inflation may produce real returns quite different from those expected at the time the securities were purchased.

Assume for the moment that U.S. inflation remains low and fairly predictable so that we can effectively ignore inflation risk. Will Treasury securities provide investors with riskless returns? The answer is generally no.

An investor's time horizon usually will not coincide with the life of a particular Treasury security. If the investor's time horizon is longer than the security's life, then the investor must purchase another Treasury security when the first security matures. However, if interest rates have changed in the interim, then the investor will earn a different return than he or she originally anticipated. (This risk is known as reinvestment-rate risk; see Chapter 9.)

If the Treasury security's life exceeds the investor's time horizon, then the investor will have to sell the security before it matures. However, if interest rates change before the sale, then the price of the security will change causing the investor to earn a different return from the one originally anticipated. (This risk is known as interest-rate or price risk; see Chapter 9.)

Even if the Treasury security's life matches the investor's time horizon, it generally will not provide a riskless return. With the exception of Treasury bills and STRIPS, all Treasury securities make periodic interest payments (see Chapter 19), which the investor must reinvest. If interest rates change during the security's life, then the investor's reinvestment rate will change, causing the investor's return to differ from that originally anticipated at the time the security was purchased.

Clearly, what investors need are Treasury securities that make only one payment (which includes principal and all interest) when those securities mature. Investors could then select a security whose life matched their investment time horizons. These securities would be truly riskless, at least on a nominal basis.

A fixed-income security that makes only one payment at maturity is called a zero-coupon (or pure-discount) bond. Until the 1980s, however, zero-coupon Treasury bonds did not exist, except for Treasury bills (which have a maximum maturity of one year). However, a coupon-bearing Treasury security can be viewed as a *portfolio* of zero-coupon bonds, with each interest payment, as well as the principal, considered a separate bond. In 1982, several brokerage firms came to a novel realization: A Treasury security's payments could be segregated and sold piecemeal through a process known as coupon stripping (see Chapter 19).

For example, brokerage firm *XYZ* purchases a newly issued 20-year Treasury bond and deposits the bond with a custodian bank. Assuming semiannual interest payments, *XYZ* creates 41 separate zero-coupon bonds (40 interest payments plus 1 principal repayment). Naturally, *XYZ* can create larger zero-coupon bonds by buying and depositing more securities of the same Treasury issue. These zero-coupon bonds, in turn, are sold to investors (for a fee, of course). As the Treasury makes its required payments on the bond, the custodian bank remits the payments to the zero-coupon bondholders of the appropriate maturity and effectively retires that particular bond. The process continues until all interest and principal payments have been made and all of the zero-coupon bonds associated with this Treasury bond have been extinguished.

Brokerage firms and investors benefit from coupon stripping. The brokerage firms found that the sum of the parts was worth more than the whole because the zero-coupon bonds could be sold to investors at a higher combined price than could the source Treasury security. Investors benefited from the creation of a liquid market in riskless securities.

The U.S. Treasury belatedly recognized the popularity of stripped Treasury securities. In 1985, the Treasury introduced the STRIPS (Separate Trading of Registered Interest and Principal Securities) program, which allows purchasers of certain interest-bearing Treasury securities to keep whatever cash payments they want and to sell the rest. The stripped bonds are "held" in the Federal Reserve System's computer (called the book entry system), and payments on the bonds are made electronically. Any financial institution registered on the Federal Reserve System's computer may participate in the STRIPS program. Brokerage firms soon found that it was less expensive to create zero-coupon bonds through STRIPS than to use bank custody accounts. They subsequently switched virtually all of their activity to that program.

The introduction of stripped Treasuries still did not solve the inflation risk problem faced by investors seeking a truly riskfree security. Finally, in 1997 the U.S. Treasury offered the first U.S. securities whose principal and interest payments were indexed to inflation, officially named Treasury Inflation Indexed Securities (the Treasury recently began to offer Series I Savings Bonds that are similarly indexed to inflation; see Chapters 6 and 19). With the introduction of these securities, the United States joined Australia, Canada, Israel, New Zealand, Sweden, and the United Kingdom in issuing debt that is indexed to the rate of inflation.

To date, the Treasury has issued three maturities (for 5, 10, and 30 years). The principal amounts of these "indexed" bonds are adjusted semiannually based on the cumulative change in the CPI since issuance of the bonds. A fixed rate of interest, determined at the time of the bonds' issuance, is paid on the adjusted principal, producing inflation-adjusted interest payments as well. Coupon stripping is allowed so that investors can purchase zero-coupon inflation-protected U.S. bonds—seemingly the real McCoy of riskfree securities.

Only a nitpicker would note several flaws in this arrangement. The bonds' issuer (the U.S. government) controls the definition and calculation of the CPI. In light of concerns over whether the CPI accurately measures inflation, there is some risk that the government might change the index in ways detrimental to inflation-indexed security holders (although the Treasury could adjust the bond terms to compensate for such an adverse change). Additionally, the adjustments to the bonds' principal values are taxable income, reducing (perhaps significantly, depending on the investor's tax rate) the inflation protection provided by the bonds for taxable investors. Despite these complications, the Treasury has finally introduced a security that can truly claim the title of (almost) riskfree.

that pays the investor $50 one year from now and matures two years from now, paying the investor $1,050 at that time. The prices at which these bonds are currently being sold in the market are

Bond *A* (the one-year pure-discount bond): $934.58

Bond *B* (the two-year pure-discount bond): $857.34

Bond *C* (the two-year coupon bond): $946.93

yield-to-maturity   The **yield-to-maturity** (or yield) on any fixed-income security is the single interest rate (with interest compounded at some specified interval) that, if paid by a bank on the amount invested, would enable the investor to obtain all the payments promised by the security in question. It is simple to determine the yield-to-maturity on a one-year pure-discount security such as bond A. Because an investment of $934.58 will pay $1,000 one year later, the yield-to-maturity on this bond is the interest rate r_A that a bank would have to pay on a deposit of $934.58 in order for the account to have a balance of $1,000 after one year. Thus, the yield-to-maturity on bond A is the rate r_A that solves the following equation:

$$(1 + r_A) \times \$934.58 = \$1,000 \tag{20.1}$$

which is 7%.

In the case of bond B, assuming annual compounding at a rate r_B, an account with $857.34 invested initially (the cost of B) would grow to $(1 + r_B) \times \$857.34$ in one year. If this total is left intact, the account will grow to $(1 + r_B) \times [(1 + r_B) \times \$857.34]$ by the end of the second year. The yield-to-maturity is the rate r_B that makes this amount equal to $1,000. In other words, the yield-to-maturity on bond B is the rate r_B that solves the following equation:

$$(1 + r_B) \times [(1 + r_B) \times \$857.34] = \$1,000 \tag{20.2}$$

which is 8%.

For bond C, consider investing $946.93 in a bank account. At the end of one year, the account would grow in value to $(1 + r_C) \times \$946.93$. Then the investor would remove $50, leaving a balance of $[(1 + r_C) \times \$946.93] - \$50$. At the end of the second year this balance would have grown to an amount equal to $(1 + r_C) \times \{[(1 + r_C) \times \$946.93] - \$50\}$. The yield-to-maturity on bond C is the rate r_C that makes this amount equal to $1,050:

$$(1 + r_C) \times \{[(1 + r_C) \times \$946.93] - \$50\} = \$1,050 \tag{20.3}$$

which is 7.975%.

Equivalently, yield-to-maturity is the discount rate that makes the present value of the promised future cash flows equal in sum to the current market price of the bond.[1] When viewed in this manner, yield-to-maturity is analogous to internal rate of return, a concept used in Chapter 15 to value common stocks. This equivalence can be seen for bond A by dividing both sides of Equation (20.1) by $(1 + r_A)$, resulting in

$$\$934.58 = \frac{\$1,000}{(1 + r_A)} \tag{20.4}$$

Similarly, for bond B both sides of Equation (20.2) can be divided by $(1 + r_B)^2$, resulting in

$$\$857.34 = \frac{\$1,000}{(1 + r_B)^2} \tag{20.5}$$

whereas for bond C both sides of Equation (20.3) can be divided by $(1 + r_C)^2$:

$$\$946.93 - \frac{\$50}{(1 + r_C)} = \frac{\$1,050}{(1 + r_C)^2}$$

or

$$\$946.93 = \frac{\$50}{(1 + r_C)} + \frac{\$1,050}{(1 + r_C)^2} \tag{20.6}$$

Because Equations (20.4), (20.5), and (20.6) are equivalent to Equations (20.1), (20.2), and (20.3), respectively, the solutions must be the same as before, with $r_A = 7\%$, $r_B = 8\%$, and $r_C = 7.975\%$.

For coupon-bearing bonds, the procedure for determining yield-to-maturity involves trial and error. In the case of bond C, a discount rate of 10% could be tried initially, resulting in a value for the right-hand side of Equation (20.6) of $913.22, a value that is too low. This result indicates that the number in the denominator is too high, so a lower discount rate is used next, say 6%. In this case, the value on the right-hand side is $981.67, which is too high and indicates that 6% is too low. The solution is somewhere between 6% and 10%, and the search could continue until the answer, 7.975%, is found. Fortunately, computers are good at trial-and-error calculations. One can enter a complex series of cash flows into a spreadsheet or hand calculator and instantly find the yield-to-maturity.

20.2 Spot Rates

A **spot rate** is measured at a given point in time by the yield-to-maturity on a pure-discount security. It can be thought of as the interest rate specified in a spot contract. Such a contract, when signed, involves the immediate loan of money from one party to another. The loan, along with interest, is to be repaid in its entirety at a specific time in the future.

Bonds A and B in the previous example were pure-discount securities. An investor who purchased either one would expect to receive only one cash payment from the issuer. Accordingly, in this example the one-year spot rate is 7% and the two-year spot rate is 8%. In general, the t-year spot rate s_t is the solution to the following equation:

$$P_t = \frac{M_t}{(1 + s_t)^t} \tag{20.7}$$

where P_t is the current market price of a pure-discount bond that matures in t years and has a maturity value of M_t. For example, the values of P_t and M_t for bond B would be $857.34 and $1,000, respectively, with $t = 2$.

Spot rates can also be determined in another manner if only coupon-bearing Treasury bonds are available for longer maturities using a procedure known as *bootstrapping*. The one-year spot rate (s_1) generally is known because there typically is a one-year pure-discount Treasury security available for making this calculation. However, it may be that no two-year pure-discount Treasury security exists. Instead, only a two-year coupon-bearing bond may be available for investment, having a current market price of P_2, a maturity value of M_2, and a coupon payment one year from now equal to C_1. In this situation, the two-year spot rate (s_2) is the solution to the following equation:

$$P_2 = \frac{C_1}{(1 + s_1)} + \frac{M_2}{(1 + s_2)^2} \tag{20.8}$$

Once the two-year spot rate has been calculated, then it and the one-year spot rate can be used in a similar manner to determine the three-year spot rate by examining a three-year coupon-bearing bond. Applying this procedure iteratively in a similar fashion over and over again, one can calculate an entire set of spot rates from a set of coupon-bearing bonds.

For example, assume that only bonds A and C exist where the one-year spot rate, s_1, is 7%. Equation (20.8) can be used to determine the two-year spot rate, s_2, where $P_2 = \$946.93$, $C_1 = \$50$, and $M_2 = \$1,050$:

$$\$946.93 = \frac{\$50}{(1 + .07)} + \frac{\$1,050}{(1 + s_2)^2}$$

The solution to this equation is $s_2 = .08 = 8\%$. Thus, the two-year spot rate is the same in this example regardless of whether it is calculated directly by analyzing pure-discount bond B or indirectly by analyzing coupon-bearing bond C in conjunction with bond A. Although the rate may not always be the same in both calculations when actual bond prices are examined, typically the differences are insignificant.

20.3   Discount Factors

discount factors

Once a set of spot rates has been determined, it is a straightforward matter to determine the corresponding set of **discount factors.** A discount factor d_t is equivalent to the present value of $1 to be received t years in the future from a Treasury security, and is equal to

$$d_t = \frac{1}{(1 + s_t)^t} \qquad \textbf{(20.9)}$$

market discount function

The set of these factors is sometimes referred to as the **market discount function,** and it changes from day to day as spot rates change. In the example, $d_1 = 1/(1 + .07)^1 = .9346$; and $d_2 = 1/(1 + .08)^2 = .8573$.

Once the market discount function has been determined, it is fairly easy to find the present value of any Treasury security (or, for that matter, any default-free security). Let C_t denote the cash payment to be made to the investor at year t by the security being evaluated. The multiplication of C_t by d_t is termed **discounting:** It converts the given future value into an equivalent present value. The latter is equivalent in the sense that P present dollars can be converted into C_t dollars in year t via available investment instruments, given the currently prevailing spot rates. An investment paying C_t dollars in year t with certainty should sell for $P = d_t C_t$ dollars today. If it sells for more, it is overpriced; if it sells for less, it is underpriced. These statements rely on comparisons with equivalent opportunities in the marketplace. Valuation of default-free investments thus requires no assessment of individual preferences.

discounting

The simplest and, in a sense, most fundamental characterization of the market structure for default-free bonds is given by the current set of discount factors (or spot rates), referred to earlier as the market discount function. With this set of factors, it is simple to evaluate a default-free bond that provides more than one payment, for it is, in effect, a package of bonds, each of which provides a single payment. Each amount is multiplied by the appropriate discount factor and the resultant present values are summed.

For example, assume that the Treasury is preparing to offer for sale a two-year coupon-bearing security that will pay $70 in one year and $1,070 in two years. What is a fair price for such a security? It is the present value of $70 and $1,070. How can this value be determined? By multiplying the $70 and $1,070 by the one-year and two-year discount factors, respectively. Doing so results in ($70 × .9346) + ($1,070 × .8573), which equals $982.73.

No matter how complex the pattern of payments, this procedure can be used to determine the value of any default-free bond of this type. The general formula for a bond's present value (*PV*) is

$$PV = \sum_{t=1}^{n} d_t C_t \tag{20.10}$$

where the bond has promised cash payments C_t for each year from year 1 through year n.

At this point, it has been shown how spot rates and, in turn, discount factors can be calculated. However, no link between different spot rates (or different discount factors) has been established. For example, it has yet to be shown how the one-year spot rate of 7% is related to the two-year spot rate of 8%. The concept of forward rates makes that link.

20.4 Forward Rates

In the example, the one-year spot rate was determined to be 7%. This value means that the market determined that the present value of $1 to be paid by the U.S. Treasury in one year is $1/1.07, or $.9346. Because, as was also noted, the two-year spot rate was 8%, the present value of $1 to be paid by the Treasury in two years is $1/1.08^2$, or $.8573.

As an alternative, $1 paid in two years can be discounted in two steps. The first step determines its equivalent one-year value. That is, $1 to be received in two years is equivalent to $1/(1 + f_{1,2})$ to be received in one year. The second step determines the present value of this equivalent one-year amount by discounting it at the one-year spot rate of 7%:

$$\frac{\$1/(1 + f_{1,2})}{(1 + .07)}$$

This value must be equal to $.8573 according to the two-year spot rate because $.8573 is the present value of $1 to be paid in two years. That is,

$$\frac{\$1/(1 + f_{1,2})}{(1 + .07)} = \$.8573 \tag{20.11}$$

forward rate

which has a solution for $f_{1,2}$ of 9.01%.

The discount rate $f_{1,2}$ is known as the **forward rate** from year 1 to year 2. That is, it is the discount rate for determining the equivalent value one year from now of a dollar that is to be received two years from now. In the example, $1 to be received two years from now is equivalent in value to $1/1.0901 = \$.9174 to be received one year from now (in turn, note that the present value of $.9174 is $.9174/1.07 = \$.8573).

The link between the one-year spot rate, two-year spot rate, and one-year forward rate is

$$\frac{\$1/(1 + f_{1,2})}{(1 + s_1)} = \frac{\$1}{(1 + s_2)^2} \tag{20.12}$$

which can be rewritten as

$$(1 + f_{1,2}) = \frac{(1 + s_2)^2}{(1 + s_1)} \tag{20.13}$$

or

$$(1 + s_1)(1 + f_{1,2}) = (1 + s_2)^2 \tag{20.14}$$

Figure 20.1 illustrates this relation by referring to the example and then generalizing from it. More generally, for year $t - 1$ and year t spot rates, the link to the forward rate between years $t - 1$ and t is

$$(1 + f_{t-1,t}) = \frac{(1 + s_t)^t}{(1 + s_{t-1})^{t-1}} \tag{20.15}$$

or

$$(1 + s_{t-1})^{t-1} \times (1 + f_{t-1,t}) = (1 + s_t)^t \tag{20.16}$$

forward contract   Another interpretation can be given to forward rates. Consider a **forward contract** made now wherein money will be loaned a year from now and paid back two years from now. The interest rate specified on the one-year loan (note that the interest will be paid when the loan matures in two years) is known as the forward rate. It is important to distinguish this rate from the rate for one-year loans that will prevail for deals made a year from now (the spot rate at that time). A forward rate applies to contracts made now but relating to a period "forward" in time. By the nature of the contract the terms are certain now, even though the actual transaction will occur later. If instead one were to wait until next year and sign a contract to borrow money in the spot market at that time, the terms might turn out to be better or worse than today's forward rate because the future spot rate is not perfectly predictable.

In the example, the marketplace has priced Treasury securities such that a representative investor making a two-year loan to the government would demand an interest rate equal to the two-year spot rate, 8%. Equivalently, the investor would be willing to simultaneously (1) make a one-year loan to the government at an interest rate equal to the one-year spot rate, 7%, and (2) sign a forward contract with the government to

FIGURE 20.1 Spot and Forward Rates

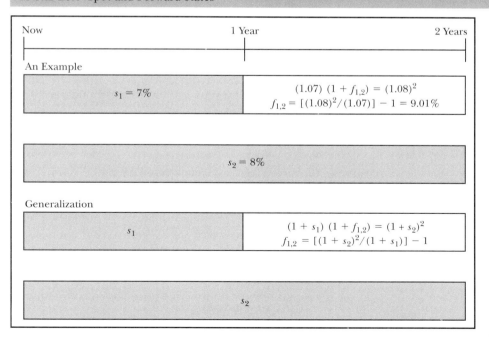

loan the government money one year from now, being repaid two years from now with the interest rate to be paid being the forward rate, 9.01%.

When viewed in this manner, forward contracts are implicit. However, they are sometimes made explicitly. For example, a contractor might obtain a commitment from a bank for a one-year construction loan a year hence at a fixed rate of interest. Financial futures (discussed in Chapter 25) are standardized forward contracts of this type. For example, in September an investor could contract to pay approximately $970 in December to purchase a 90-day Treasury bill that would pay $1,000 the following March.

20.5 Forward Rates and Discount Factors

In Equation (20.9) it was shown that a discount factor for t years could be calculated by adding 1 to the t-year spot rate, raising this sum to the power t, and then taking the reciprocal of the result. For example, the two-year discount factor associated with the two-year spot rate of 8% was equal to $1/(1 + .08)^2 = .8573$.

Equation (20.14) suggests an equivalent method for calculating discount factors. In the case of the two-year factor, this method involves multiplying (1 plus the one-year spot rate) by (1 plus the forward rate) and taking the reciprocal of the result:

$$d_2 = \frac{1}{(1 + s_1) \times (1 + f_{1,2})} \qquad (20.17)$$

which in the example is

$$d_2 = \frac{1}{(1 + .07) \times (1 + .0901)}$$
$$= .8573$$

More generally, the discount factor for year t that is shown in Equation (20.9) can be restated as follows:

$$d_t = \frac{1}{(1 + s_{t-1})^{t-1} \times (1 + f_{t-1,t})} \qquad (20.18)$$

Thus, given a set of spot rates, one can determine the market discount function in either of two ways, both of which will provide the same figures. First, the spot rates can be used in Equation (20.9) to arrive at a set of discount factors. Alternatively, the spot rates can be used to determine a set of forward rates, and then the spot rates and forward rates can be used in Equation (20.18) to arrive at a set of discount factors.

20.6 Compounding

Thus far, the discussion has concentrated on annual interest rates by assuming that cash flows are compounded (or discounted) annually. This assumption is often appropriate, but for more precise calculations a shorter period may be more desirable. Moreover, some lenders explicitly compound funds more often than once each year.

compounding

Compounding is the payment of "interest on interest." At the end of each compounding interval, interest is computed and added to principal. This sum becomes the principal on which interest is computed at the end of the next interval. The process continues until the end of the final compounding interval is reached.

It is easy to adapt the previous formulas to compounding intervals other than a year. The simplest procedure is to count in units of the chosen interval. For example, yield-to-maturity can be calculated using any chosen compounding interval. If payment of P dollars now will result in the receipt of F dollars 10 years from now, the yield-to-maturity can be calculated using annual compounding by finding a value r_a that satisfies the equation:

$$P(1 + r_a)^{10} = F \qquad (20.19)$$

because F will be received 10 annual periods from now. The result, r_a, will be expressed as an annual rate with annual compounding.

Alternatively, yield-to-maturity can be calculated using semiannual compounding by finding a value r_s that satisfies the equation:

$$P(1 + r_s)^{20} = F \qquad (20.20)$$

because F will be received 20 semiannual periods from now. The result, r_s, will be expressed as a semiannual rate with semiannual compounding. It can be doubled to give an annual rate with semiannual compounding. However, the annual rate with annual compounding can be computed for a given value of r_s by using the following equation:

$$1 + r_a = (1 + r_s)^2 \qquad (20.21)$$

For example, consider an investment costing \$2,315.97 that will pay \$5,000 ten years later. Applying Equations (20.19) and (20.20) to this security results in, respectively,

$$\$2,315.97(1 + r_a)^{10} = \$5,000$$

and

$$\$2,315.97(1 + r_s)^{20} = \$5,000$$

where the solutions are $r_a = 8\%$ and $r_s = 3.923\%$. Thus, this security has an annual rate with annual compounding of 8%, a semiannual rate with semiannual compounding of 3.923%, and an annual rate with semiannual compounding of 7.846% ($= 2 \times 3.923\%$).[2]

Semiannual compounding is commonly used to determine the yield-to-maturity for bonds because coupon payments are usually made twice each year. Most preprogrammed calculators and spreadsheets use this approach.[3]

20.7 The Bank Discount Method

One time-honored method to summarize interest rates is the *bank discount method.* If someone "borrows" \$100 from a bank, to be repaid a year later, the bank may subtract the interest payment of, for instance, \$8, and give the borrower \$92. According to the bank discount method, the interest rate is 8%. However, this method understates the effective annual interest rate that the borrower pays. The true interest rate must be based on the money the borrower actually gets to use, which in this case is \$92, making the true interest rate 8.70% ($= \$8/\$92$).

It is simple to convert an interest rate quoted on the bank discount method to a true interest rate. (In this situation, the true interest rate is often called the bond equivalent yield.) If the bank discount rate is denoted *BDR,* the true rate is simply $BDR/(1 - BDR)$. Because $BDR > 0$, the bank discount rate understates the true cost of borrowing [note that $BDR < BDR/(1 - BDR)$]. The previous example provides an illustration: $8.70\% = .08/(1 - .08)$, indicating the bank discount rate of 8% understates the true cost of borrowing by .70%.

20.8 Yield Curves

At any point in time, Treasury securities are priced approximately in accord with the existing set of spot rates and the associated discount factors. Although there have been times when all the spot rates are roughly equal in size, usually they have different values. Often the one-year spot rate is less than the two-year spot rate, which in turn is less than the three-year spot rate, and so on (that is, s_t increases as t increases). At other times, the one-year spot rate is greater than the two-year spot rate, which in turn is greater than the three-year spot rate, and so on (that is, s_t decreases as t increases). It is wise for the security analyst to know which situation currently prevails, as this is a useful starting point in valuing fixed-income securities.

Unfortunately, specifying the current situation is easier said than done. Only U.S. government bonds are clearly free from default risk. However, U.S. government bonds differ in tax treatment, as well as in callability, liquidity, and other features. Despite these issues, a summary of the approximate relationship between yields-to-maturity on Treasury securities of various terms-to-maturity is presented in each issue of the *Treasury Bulletin*. This summary is given in the form of a graph illustrating the current yield curve as presented in Figure 20.2.

FIGURE 20.2 Yield Curve of Treasury Securities, December 1, 1999 (based on constant maturities)

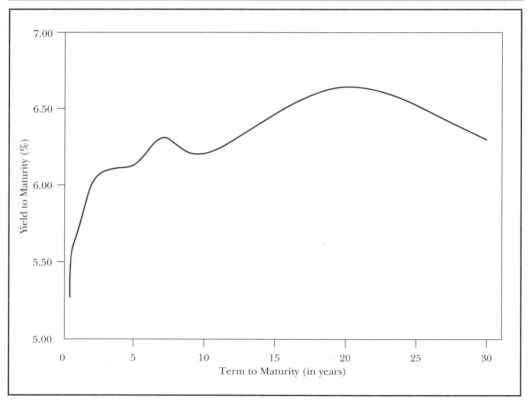

Note: The curve is based only on the most actively traded issues. Market yields on coupon issues due in less than three months are excluded.

Source: Federal Reserve System Board of Governors Web site: <www.bog.frb.fed.us/releases/H15/19991206>, December 1, 1999.

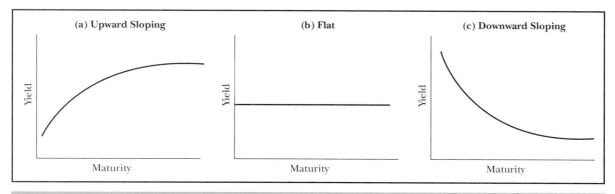

FIGURE 20.3 Typical Yield Curve Shapes

yield curve

term structure

A **yield curve** is a graph that shows the yields-to-maturity (on the vertical axis) for Treasury securities of various maturities (on the horizontal axis) as of a particular date. This graph provides an estimate of the current **term structure** of interest rates, and will change daily as yields-to-maturity change. Figure 20.3 illustrates some of the commonly observed shapes that the yield curve has taken in the past.[4]

Although not shown in Figures 20.2 and 20.3, the relationship between yields and maturities is not perfect because not all Treasury securities lie exactly on the yield curve. Part of this variation is because of the previously mentioned differences in tax treatment, callability, liquidity, and the like. Part is because the yield-to-maturity on a coupon-bearing security is not clearly linked to the set of spot rates currently in existence. Because the set of spot rates is a fundamental determinant of the price of any Treasury security, there is no reason to expect yields to lie exactly on the curve. Indeed, a more meaningful graph would be one in which spot rates instead of yields-to-maturity are measured on the vertical axis. With this caveat in mind, consider three interesting questions:

1. Why do the spot rates differ in magnitude?
2. Why do the differences in these rates change over time?
3. Why are long-term spot rates usually greater than short-term spot rates?

Attempts to answer such questions can be found in various term structure theories.

20.9   Term Structure Theories

Four primary theories are used to explain the term structure of interest rates. In discussing them, the focus will be on the term structure of spot rates because these rates (not yields-to-maturity) are critically important in determining the price of any Treasury security.

20.9.1   THE UNBIASED EXPECTATIONS THEORY

unbiased expectations theory

According to the **unbiased expectations theory** (or pure expectations theory, as it is sometimes called), the forward rate represents the average opinion regarding the level of the expected future spot rate for the period in question. A set of rising spot rates can be explained by arguing that the marketplace (that is, the general opinion of investors) believes that spot rates will rise in the future. Conversely, a set of decreasing spot rates is explained by arguing that the marketplace expects spot rates to fall in the future.[5]

Upward-Sloping Yield Curves

In order to understand this theory more fully, consider the example in which the one-year spot rate was 7% and the two-year spot rate was 8%. The basic question is, Why are these two spot rates different? Equivalently, why is the yield curve upward sloping?

Consider an investor with $1 to invest for two years (for ease of exposition, it will be assumed that any amount of money can be invested at the prevailing spot rates). This investor could follow a "maturity strategy," investing the money now for the full two years at the two-year spot rate of 8%. With this strategy, at the end of two years the dollar will have grown in value to $1.1664 (= $1 × 1.08 × 1.08). Alternatively, the investor could invest the dollar now for one year at the one-year spot rate of 7%, so that the investor knows that one year from now he or she will have $1.07 (= $1 × 1.07) to reinvest for one more year. Although the investor does not know what the one-year spot rate will be one year from now, the investor has an *expectation* about what it will be (this expected future spot rate will hereafter be denoted $es_{1,2}$). If the investor thinks that it will be 10%, then his or her $1 investment has an expected value two years from now of $1.177 (= $1 × 1.07 × 1.10). In this case, the investor would choose a "rollover strategy" and invest in a one-year security at 7% rather than in the two-year security because he or she expects to have more money at the end of two years by doing so (note that $1.177 > $1.1664).

However, an expected future spot rate of 10% cannot represent the general view in the marketplace. If it did, people would not be willing to invest money at the two-year spot rate because a higher return would be expected from investing money at the one-year rate and using the rollover strategy. Thus, the two-year spot rate would quickly rise as the supply of funds for two-year loans at 8% would be less than the demand. Conversely, the supply of funds for one year at 7% would be more than the demand, causing the one-year rate to fall quickly. Thus, a one-year spot rate of 7%, a two-year spot rate of 8%, and an expected future spot rate of 10% cannot represent an equilibrium situation.

What if the expected future spot rate is 6% instead of 10%? In this case, according to the rollover strategy, the investor would expect $1 to be worth $1.1342 (= $1 × 1.07 × 1.06) at the end of two years. This value is less than the value the dollar will have if the maturity strategy is followed (note that $1.1342 < $1.664), so the investor would choose the maturity strategy. Again, however, an expected future spot rate of 6% cannot represent the general view in the marketplace because if it did, people would not be willing to invest money at the one-year spot rate.

Earlier, it was shown that the forward rate in the example was 9.01%. What if the expected future spot rate was of this magnitude? At the end of two years the value of $1 with the rollover strategy would be $1.1664 (= $1 × 1.07 × 1.0901), the same as the value of $1 with the maturity strategy. In this case, equilibrium would exist because the two strategies would be perceived by the market to have the same expected return. Accordingly, investors with a two-year holding period would not have an incentive to choose one strategy over the other.

Note that an investor with a one-year holding period could follow a maturity strategy by investing $1 in the one-year security and receiving $1.07 after one year. Alternatively, a "naive strategy" could be followed where a two-year security could be purchased now and sold after one year. If that were done, the expected selling price would be $1.07 (= $1.1664/1.0901), for a return of 7% (the security would have a maturity value of $1.1664(= $1 × 1.08 × 1.08), but because the spot rate is expected to be 9.01% in a year, its expected selling price is just the discounted value of its maturity value). Because the maturity and naive strategies have the same expected return, investors with a one-year holding period would not have an incentive to choose one strategy over the other.

Thus, the unbiased expectations theory asserts that the expected future spot rate is equal in magnitude to the forward rate. In the example, the current one-year spot rate is 7%, and, according to this theory, the general opinion is that it will rise to a rate of 9.01% in one year. This expected rise in the one-year spot rate is the reason behind the upward-sloping term structure where the two-year spot rate (8%) is greater than the one-year spot rate (7%).

Equilibrium

In equation form, the unbiased expectations theory states that in equilibrium the expected future spot rate is equal to the forward rate:

$$es_{1,2} = f_{1,2} \tag{20.22}$$

Thus, Equation (20.14) can be restated with $es_{1,2}$ substituted for $f_{1,2}$ as follows:

$$(1 + s_1)(1 + es_{1,2}) = (1 + s_2)^2 \tag{20.23}$$

which can be conveniently interpreted to mean that the expected return from a maturity strategy must equal the expected return on a rollover strategy.[6]

The previous example dealt with an upward-sloping term structure; the longer the term, the higher the spot rate. It is straightforward to deal with a downward-sloping term structure where the longer the term, the lower the spot rate. Whereas the explanation for an upward-sloping term structure was that investors expect spot rates to rise in the future, the reason for the downward-sloping curve is that investors expect spot rates to fall in the future.

Changing Spot Rates and Inflation

Why do investors expect spot rates to change, either rising or falling, in the future? A possible answer is that spot rates observed in the marketplace are nominal rates. That is, they are a reflection of the underlying real rate and the expected inflation rate.[7] If either (or both) of these rates is expected to change in the future, then the spot rate will be expected to change.

For example, assume a constant real rate of 3%. Because the current one-year spot rate is 7%, a constant real rate of 3% means that the general opinion in the marketplace is that the expected rate of inflation during the next year is approximately 4% [the nominal rate is approximately equal to the sum of the real rate and the expected inflation rate; see Equation (6.5)]. According to the unbiased expectations theory, the expected future spot rate is 9.01%, an increase of 2.01% from the current one-year spot rate of 7%. Assuming a constant real rate, this increase can be attributed to investors, on average, expecting the inflation rate to rise by about 2%. That is, the expected inflation rate during the next 12 months is approximately 4%, and during the following 12 months it is expected to be higher, at approximately 6.01%.

To recapitulate, the two-year spot rate (8%) is greater than the one-year spot rate (7%) because investors expect the future one-year spot rate to be greater than the current one-year spot rate. They expect it to be greater because of an anticipated rise in the rate of inflation, from approximately 4% to approximately 6%.

In general, when current economic conditions make short-term spot rates abnormally high (owing, say, to a relatively high current rate of inflation), according to the unbiased expectations theory, the term structure should be downward sloping because inflation would be expected to abate in the future. Conversely, when current conditions make short-term rates abnormally low (owing, say, to a relatively low current rate of inflation), the term structure should be upward sloping because inflation would be expected to rise in the future. Examination of historical term structures suggests that this is what has actually happened because the term structure has been upward-sloping in periods of lower interest rates and downward-sloping in periods of higher interest rates.

However, examining historical term structures uncovers a problem. In particular, it is logical to expect that over time there will be roughly as many occurrences of investors expecting spot rates to rise as there are occurrences of investors expecting spot rates to fall. Therefore, the unbiased expectations theory should imply that there will be as many instances of upward-sloping term structures as downward-sloping term structures. In reality, upward-sloping term structures occur much more frequently than downward-sloping term structures. The unbiased expectations theory would have to explain this phenomenon by suggesting that the majority of the time investors expect spot rates to rise. The liquidity preference theory (also known as the liquidity premium theory) provides a more plausible explanation for the observed prevalence of upward-sloping term structures.

20.9.2   THE LIQUIDITY PREFERENCE THEORY

liquidity preference theory

The **liquidity preference theory** starts with the notion that investors are primarily interested in purchasing short-term securities. Even though some investors may have longer holding periods, there is a tendency for them to prefer short-term securities. These investors realize that they may need their funds sooner than anticipated and recognize that they face less "price risk" (that is, "interest rate risk") if they invest in shorter term securities.

Price Risk

For example, an investor with a two-year holding period would tend to prefer the rollover strategy because he or she would be certain of having a known amount of cash at the end of one year when it may be needed. An investor who followed a maturity strategy would have to sell the two-year security after one year if cash were needed. However, the price that investor would get for the two-year security in one year is unknown at this time. Thus, there is an extra element of risk associated with the maturity strategy that is absent from the rollover strategy.[8]

The upshot is that investors with a two-year holding period will not choose the maturity strategy if it has the same expected return as the rollover strategy because it is riskier. Investors will follow the maturity strategy and buy the two-year securities only if the expected return is higher. That is, borrowers will have to pay the investors a risk premium in the form of a greater expected return in order to get them to purchase two-year securities.

Will borrowers be inclined to pay such a premium when issuing two-year securities? Yes, they will, according to the liquidity preference theory. First, frequent refinancing may be costly in terms of registration, advertising, and paperwork. These costs are reduced by issuing longer term securities. Second, some borrowers will realize that longer term bonds are a less risky source of funds than shorter term bonds because borrowers who use them are not concerned about the possibility of refinancing in the future at higher interest rates. Thus, borrowers may be willing to pay more (via higher expected interest costs) for longer term funds.

In the example, the one-year spot rate was 7% and the two-year spot rate was 8%. According to the liquidity preference theory, investors will agree to follow a maturity strategy only if the expected return from doing so is higher than the expected return from following the rollover strategy. So the expected future spot rate must be *less* than the forward rate of 9.01%; perhaps it is 8.6%. At 8.6% the value of a $1 investment in two years is expected to be $1.1620 (= $1 × 1.07 × 1.086) if the rollover strategy is followed. Because the value of a $1 investment with the maturity strategy is $1.1664 (= $1 × 1.08 × 1.08), the maturity strategy has a higher expected return for the two-year period (note that $1.1664 > $1.1620), which can be attributed to its greater degree of price risk.

Liquidity Premium

liquidity premium

The difference between the forward rate and the expected future spot rate is known as the **liquidity premium.**[9] It is the "extra" return given investors to entice them to purchase the riskier longer maturity two-year security. In the example, it is equal to .41% (= 9.01% − 8.6%). More generally,

$$f_{1,2} = es_{1,2} + L_{1,2} \qquad (20.24)$$

where $L_{1,2}$ is the liquidity premium for the period starting one year from now and ending two years from now.[10]

How does the liquidity preference theory explain the slope of the term structure? In order to answer this question, note that with the rollover strategy the expected value of a dollar at the end of two years is $1 × (1 + s_1) × (1 + es_{1,2})$. Alternatively, with the maturity strategy, the expected value of a dollar at the end of two years is $1 × (1 + s_2)^2$. According to the liquidity preference theory, there is more risk with the maturity strategy, which in turn means that it must have a higher expected return so that the following inequality holds:

$$\$1(1 + s_1)(1 + es_{1,2}) < \$1(1 + s_2)^2 \qquad (20.25)$$

or

$$(1 + s_1)(1 + es_{1,2}) < (1 + s_2)^2 \qquad (20.26)$$

This inequality is the key to understanding how the liquidity preference theory explains the term structure.[11]

Downward-Sloping Yield Curves

Consider the downward-sloping case first, where $s_1 > s_2$. The previous inequality will hold in this situation only if the expected future spot rate ($es_{1,2}$) is substantially lower than the current one-year spot rate (s_1).[12] Thus, a downward-sloping yield curve will be observed only when the marketplace believes that interest rates are going to decline substantially.

As an example, assume that the one-year spot rate (s_1) is 7% and the two-year spot rate (s_2) is 6%. Because 7% is greater than 6%, the term structure is downward sloping. According to the liquidity preference theory, Equation (20.26) indicates that

$$(1 + .07)(1 + es_{1,2}) < (1.06)^2$$

which can be true only if the expected future spot rate ($es_{1,2}$) is substantially less than 7%. Given the one-year and two-year spot rates, the forward rate ($f_{1,2}$) is equal to 5.01%. Assuming the liquidity premium ($L_{1,2}$) is .41%, then according to Equation (20.24), $es_{1,2}$ must be 4.6% (= 5.01% − .41%). Thus, the term structure is downward sloping because the current one-year spot rate of 7% is expected to decline to 4.6% in the future.

In comparison, the unbiased expectations theory also would explain the term structure by saying it was downward sloping because the one-year spot rate was expected to decline in the future. However, the unbiased expectations theory would expect the spot rate only to decline to 5.01%, not to 4.6%.

Flat Yield Curves

Consider next the case of a flat yield curve, where $s_1 = s_2$. Equation (20.26) will be true in this situation only if $es_{1,2}$ is less than s_1. Thus, a flat term structure will occur only when the marketplace expects interest rates to decline. Indeed, if $s_1 = s_2 = 7\%$ and $L_{1,2} = .41\%$, then $f_{1,2} = 7\%$, and according to Equation (20.24), the expected future spot rate is 6.59% (= 7% − .41%), a decline from the current one-year spot rate of 7%. This outcome is in contrast to the unbiased expectations theory, which would interpret a flat term structure to mean that the marketplace expected interest rates to remain at the same level.

Upward-Sloping Yield Curves

The last case is an upward-sloping yield curve where $s_1 < s_2$. A slightly upward-sloping curve may be consistent with the expectation that interest rates will decline in the future. For example, if $s_1 = 7\%$ and $s_2 = 7.1\%$, then the forward rate is 7.2%. In turn, if the liquidity premium is .41%, then the expected future spot rate is 6.79% (= 7.2% − .41%), a decline from the current one-year spot rate of 7%. Thus, the reason for the slight upward slope to the term structure is because the marketplace expects a small decline in the spot rate. In contrast, the unbiased expectations theory would argue that the reason for the slight upward slope is because of the expectation of a small increase in the spot rate.

If the term structure is more steeply sloped, the marketplace probably expects interest rates to rise in the future. For example, if $s_1 = 7\%$ and $s_2 = 7.3\%$, then the forward rate is 7.6%. Assuming a liquidity premium of .41%, Equation (20.24) indicates that the marketplace expects the one-year spot rate to rise from 7% to 7.19% (= 7.6% − .41%). The unbiased expectations theory also would explain this steep slope by saying that the spot rate was expected to rise in the future, but by a larger amount. In particular, the unbiased expectations theory would state that the spot rate was expected to rise to 7.6%, not to 7.19%.

In summary, with the liquidity preference theory, downward-sloping term structures are indicative of an expected decline in the spot rate, whereas upward-sloping term structures may indicate either an expected rise or a decline depending on how steep the slope is. In general, the steeper the slope, the more likely it is that the marketplace expects spot rates to rise. If roughly half the time investors expect spot rates to rise and half the time investors expect spot rates to decline, then the liquidity preference theory suggests that there should be more occurrences of upward-sloping term structures than downward-sloping ones. As mentioned earlier, this outcome is indeed what has been observed.

20.9.3 THE MARKET SEGMENTATION THEORY

market segmentation theory

A third explanation for the determination of the term structure rests on the assumption that there is market segmentation. Various investors and borrowers are thought to be restricted by law, preference, or custom to certain maturities. Perhaps there is a market for short-term securities, another for intermediate-term securities, and a third for long-term securities. According to the **market segmentation theory,** spot rates are determined by supply and demand conditions in each market. In the theory's most restrictive form, investors and borrowers will not leave their market and enter a different one even when the current rates suggest to them that there is a substantially higher expected return available if they make such a move.

With this theory, an upward-sloping term structure exists when the intersection of the supply and demand curves for shorter term funds is at a lower interest rate than the intersection for longer term funds. This situation could be caused by either a relatively greater demand for longer term funds by borrowers or a relatively greater supply of shorter term funds by investors, or some combination of the two. Conversely, a downward-sloping term structure would exist when the intersection for shorter term funds was at a higher interest rate than the intersection for longer term funds.

20.9.4 THE PREFERRED HABITAT THEORY

preferred habitat theory

A more moderate and realistic version of the market segmentation theory is the **preferred habitat theory.** According to this theory, investors and borrowers have segments of the market in which they prefer to operate, similar to the market segmentation theory. However, they are willing to leave their desired maturity segments if there are significant differences in yields between the various segments. These yield differences are determined by the supply and demand for funds within the segments (the supply and demand for funds are, in turn, determined by the state of the economy—for example, unemployment and inflation rates, Federal Reserve policy regarding the money supply, balance of payments, and so on). Consequently, as under the liquidity preference theory, the term structure under the preferred habitat theory reflects both expectations of future spot rates and a risk premium. Unlike the risk premium according to the liquidity preference theory, however, the risk premium under the preferred habitat theory does not necessarily rise directly with maturity. Instead, it is a function of the extra yield required to induce borrowers and investors to shift out of their preferred habitats. The risk premium may, therefore, be positive or negative in the various segments.

20.9.5 EMPIRICAL EVIDENCE ON THE THEORIES

Empirical evidence provides some insight into the determinants of the term structure, but it is difficult to precisely assess the relative importance of these four theories with a high degree of precision.

The market segmentation theory receives relatively slight empirical validation. This is understandable when it is realized that the theory will not hold if there are some investors and borrowers who are flexible enough to move into whatever segment has the highest expected return. By their actions, these investors and borrowers give the term structure a continuity that is linked to expectations of future interest rates.

There does appear to be some evidence that the term structure conveys information about expected future spot rates, as hypothesized by the unbiased expectations, preferred habitat, and liquidity preference theories. The evidence tends to favor the liquidity preference theory because liquidity premiums also appear to exist.[13] In particular, there seems to be liquidity premiums of increasing size associated with Treasury securities of up to roughly one year in maturity (meaning that, for example, $L_{.5,.75} < L_{.75,1}$), but the premiums beyond one year do not seem to be much larger than those for one-year periods. That is, investors must be paid a premium to get them to purchase a one-year security instead of, say, a 6-month security. However, the premium needed to get them to purchase an 18-month security (even though the 18-month security has more price risk than a one-year security) may be no larger than the premium needed to get them to purchase the one-year security (meaning that $L_{.5,1} = L_{1,1.5}$).

A word of caution is in order here regarding estimating the size of liquidity premiums. Undoubtedly these premiums (if they exist) change in size over time. Hence trying to estimate their average size accurately is difficult, and any observations must be made cautiously.

Examining the term structure of interest rates is important for determining the current set of spot rates, which can be used as a basis for valuing any fixed-income security. Such an examination is also important because it provides some information about what the marketplace expects regarding the level of future interest rates.

Summary

1. A convenient starting point for understanding how bonds are valued in the marketplace is to examine those fixed-income securities that are free from default risk—namely, Treasury securities.
2. The yield-to-maturity of a security is the discount rate that makes the present value of the security's promised future cash flows equal to the current market price of the security.
3. The spot rate is the yield-to-maturity on a pure-discount Treasury security.
4. Once spot rates (each one associated with a different maturity) have been calculated, they can be used, for example, to value coupon-bearing Treasury securities.
5. A forward rate is the interest rate, established today, that will be paid on money to be borrowed at some specific date in the future, and to be repaid at a specific but even more distant date in the future.
6. Compounding is the payment of interest on interest.
7. Increasing the number of compounding intervals within a year will increase the effective annual interest rate (see the appendix).
8. A yield curve shows the relationship between yield-to-maturity and term-to-maturity for Treasury securities. This relationship is also known as the term structure of interest rates.
9. Four theories have generally been used to explain the term structure of interest rates: the unbiased expectations theory, the liquidity preference theory, the market segmentation theory, and the preferred habitat theory.
10. The unbiased expectations theory states that forward rates represent the consensus opinion about what spot rates will be in the future.
11. The liquidity preference theory states that forward rates overstate the consensus opinion about future spot rates by an amount necessary to compensate investors for the risk involved in holding longer maturity securities.
12. The market segmentation theory states that different spot rates have different values because of the interaction of supply and demand for funds in markets that are separated from each other by maturity.
13. The preferred habitat theory states that different spot rates occur because investors and borrowers at times must be induced to leave their preferred maturity segments (or habitats).
14. Evidence tends to favor the liquidity preference theory, at least for maturities up to roughly one year.

Questions and Problems

1. Consider two bonds, each with a $1,000 face value and each with three years remaining to maturity.
   a. The first bond is a pure-discount bond that currently sells for $816.30. What is its yield-to-maturity?
   b. The second bond currently sells for $949.37 and makes annual coupon payments at a rate of 7% (that is, it pays $70 in interest each year). The first interest payment is due one year from today. What is this bond's yield-to-maturity?

2. Camp Douglas Dirigibles has a bond outstanding with four years to maturity, a face value of $1,000, and an annual coupon payment of $100. What is the price of the Camp Douglas bond if its yield-to-maturity is 12%? If its yield-to-maturity is 8%?

3. Patsy Dougherty bought a $1,000-face-value bond with a 9% annual coupon and three years to maturity that makes its first interest payment one year from today. Patsy bought the bond for $975.13. What is the bond's yield-to-maturity?

4. Consider three pure-discount bonds with maturities of one, two, and three years and prices of $930.23, $923.79, and $919.54, respectively. Each bond has a $1,000 face value. Based on this information, what are the one-year, two-year, and three-year spot rates?

5. What are the discount factors associated with three-year, four-year, and five-year $1,000 face-value pure-discount bonds that sell for $810.60, $730.96, and $649.93, respectively?

6. Given the following spot rates for various periods of time from today, calculate forward rates from years one to two, two to three, and three to four.

Years from Today	Spot Rate
1	5.0%
2	5.5
3	6.5
4	7.0

7. Given the following forward rates, calculate the one-, two-, three-, and four-year spot rates.

Forward Time Period	Forward Rate
$f_{0,1}$	10.0%
$f_{1,2}$	9.5
$f_{2,3}$	9.0
$f_{3,4}$	8.5

8. Assume that the government has issued three bonds. The first, which pays $1,000 one year from today, is now selling for $909.09. The second, which pays $100 one year from today and $1,100 one year later, is now selling for $991.81. The third, which pays $100 one year from today, $100 one year later, and $1,100 one year after that, is now selling for $997.18.
   a. What are the current discount factors for dollars paid one, two, and three years from today?
   b. What are the forward rates?
   c. Honus Wagner, a friend, offers to pay you $500 one year from today, $600 two years from today, and $700 three years from today in return for a loan today. Assuming that Honus will not default on the loan, how much should you be willing to loan?

9. Mercury National Bank offers a passbook savings account that pays interest at a stated annual rate of 6%. Calculate the effective annual interest rate paid by Mercury National if it compounds interest
   a. Semiannually
   b. Daily (365 days in a year)

10. A finance company offers you a loan of $8,000 for two years. Interest of $1,500 on the loan is subtracted from the loan proceeds immediately. What is the bank discount rate on the loan? What is the true interest rate?

11. Turn to the table in *The Wall Street Journal* entitled "Treasury Bonds, Notes & Bills." Find the yield-to-maturity for Treasury securities maturing in one month, three months, 1 year, 5 years, 10 years, and 20 years. With this information, construct the yield curve as of the paper's publication date.

12. Is it true that an observed downward-sloping yield curve is inconsistent with the liquidity preference theory of the term structure of interest rates? Explain.

13. Assume that the current spot rates are as follows:

Years from Today	Spot Rate
1	8%
2	9
3	10

If the unbiased expectations theory holds, what should be the yields-to-maturity on one- and two-year pure-discount bonds one year from today?

14. The one-year spot rate is 9% while the two-year spot rate is 7%. If the one-year spot rate expected in one year is 4.5%, according to the liquidity preference theory, what must be the one-year liquidity premium commencing one year from now?

15. (Appendix Question) Recalculate your answers to question 9 assuming interest compounds continuously.

APPENDIX

Continuous Compounding

In the computation of an investment's return, the compounding interval makes a difference. For example, regulations may limit a savings institution to paying a fixed rate of interest but make no specifications about the compounding interval. This was the situation in early 1975, when the legal limit on interest paid by savings and loan companies on deposits committed from 6 to 10 years was 7.75% per year. Initially, most savings and loans paid "simple interest." Thus, $1 deposited at the beginning of the year would grow to $1.0775 by the end of the year. Later, in an attempt to attract depositors, some enterprising savings and loans announced that they would pay 7.75% per year, compounded semiannually at a rate of 3.875% (= 7.75%/2). As a result, $1 deposited at the beginning of the year would grow to $1.03875 at the end of six months, and this total would then grow to $1.079 (= $1.03875 × 1.03875) by the end of the year, for an effective annual interest rate of 7.9%. This procedure was considered within the letter, if not the spirit, of the law.

Before long, other competitors offered 7.75% per year compounded quarterly (that is, 7.75%/4 = 1.938% per quarter), giving an effective annual interest rate of 7.978%. Then others offered to compound the 7.75% rate on a monthly basis (at 7.75%/12 = .646% per month) for an effective annual interest rate of 8.031%. The end was reached when one company offered continuous compounding of the 7.75% annual rate. This rather abstract procedure represents the limit as interest is compounded more and more frequently. If r equals the annual rate of interest (in this case, 7.75%) and n the number of times compounding takes place each year, the effective annual rate, r_e, is given by

$$\left(1 + \frac{r}{n}\right)^n = 1 + r_e \tag{20.27}$$

Thus, with semiannual compounding of 7.75%,

$$\left(1 + \frac{.0775}{2}\right)^2 = (1 + .03875)^2 = 1.079$$

and with quarterly compounding,

$$\left(1 + \frac{.0775}{4}\right)^4 = (1 + .0938)^4 = 1.07978$$

and so on. Note that as the compounding interval grows shorter, the number of times compounding takes place, n, grows larger and the effective interest rate, r_e, becomes higher.

Mathematicians can prove that as n grows larger, the quantity $[1 + (r/n)]^n$ becomes increasingly close to e^r where e is 2.71828 (rounded to five-place accuracy). In this case, $e^{.0775} = 1.0806$, indicating an effective annual rate of 8.06%. (Tables of natural logarithms may be used for such calculations, although most hand calculators and computer spreadsheets have a natural logarithm function key. The natural logarithm of 1.0806 is .0775, and the antilogarithm of .0775 is 1.0806.)

A more general formula for continuous compounding can also be derived. At an annual rate of *r*, with continuous compounding, *P* dollars will grow to F_t dollars *t* years from now, where the relationship between *P*, *r*, and F_t is

$$Pe^{rt} = F_t \qquad\qquad\qquad (20.28)$$

The present value of F_t dollars received *t* years later at an annual rate of *r* that is continuously compounded will be

$$P = \frac{F_t}{e^{rt}} \qquad\qquad\qquad (20.29)$$

Thus if spot rates are expressed as annual rates with continuous compounding, then the discount factors d_t can be calculated as

$$d_t = \frac{1}{e^{rt}} \qquad\qquad\qquad (20.30)$$

These last three formulas can be used for any value of *t*, including fractional amounts (for example, if F_t is to be received in $2\frac{1}{2}$ years, then $t = 2.5$).

Endnotes

1. This calculation assumes that the bond will not be called before maturity. If it is assumed that the bond will be called as soon as possible, then the discount rate that makes the present value of the corresponding cash flows equal to the current market price of the bond is known as the bond's yield-to-call.

2. Note how, when Equation (20.21) is used, $r_a = (1.03923)^2 - 1 = 8\%$, a solution that is the same as the one provided by Equation (20.19).

3. Consider what would happen if the number of compounding intervals in a year became arbitrarily large so that each interval was very small. In the limit there would be an infinite number of infinitely small intervals; such a situation involves *continuous compounding*, which is discussed in the chapter appendix.

4. Occasionally, the yield curve will be "humped." It rises for a short while and then declines, perhaps leveling off for intermediate to long-term maturities. For more on yield curves and term structure, see Carol Lancaster and Jerry L. Stevens, "Debt Term Structures: Beyond Yield to Maturity Assumptions," *Financial Practice and Education*, 5, no. 2 (Fall/Winter 1995): 125–137.

5. Recently, a "modern" expectations theory has been developed that is economically more logical than the "unbiased" expectations theory. However, it provides approximately the same empirical implications and explanations of the term structure as those given by the unbiased expectations theory. Thus, given the similarities of the two theories, only the unbiased expectations theory is presented.

6. Equation (20.22) can be expressed more generally as $es_{t-1,t} = f_{t-1,t}$. Using Equation (20.16), the unbi-

ased expectations theory states that, in general, $(1 + s_{t-1})^{t-1} \times (1 + es_{t-1,t}) = (1 + s_t)^t$.

7. See Chapter 6 for a discussion of the nature of the relationship between nominal rates, real rates, and expected inflation rates.

8. Unfortunately, this risk is often referred to as "liquidity risk" when it would be more appropriate to call it "price risk" because it is the price volatility associated with longer term securities that is of concern to investors. Partially offsetting this price risk is a risk that is present in the rollover strategy and absent from the maturity strategy—namely, the risk associated with the uncertainty of the reinvestment rate at the end of the first year when the rollover strategy is chosen. The liquidity preference theory assumes that this risk is of relatively little concern to investors.

9. Sometimes the difference is referred to as the *term premium*. See Bradford Cornell, "Measuring the Term Premium: An Empirical Note," *Journal of Economics and Business*, 42, no. 1 (February 1990): 89–92.

10. Although the forward rate can be determined, neither the expected future spot rate nor the liquidity premium can be observed. Hence, their values must be estimated.

11. Equation (20.24) can be expressed more generally as $f_{t-1,t} = es_{t-1,t} + L_{t-1,t}$. Using Equation (20.16), the liquidity preference theory states that

$$(1 + s_{t-1})^{t-1} \times (1 + es_{t-1,t} + L_{t-1,t}) = (1 + s_t)^t$$

Because $L_{t-1,t} > 0$, it follows that, in general,

$$(1 + s_{t-1})^{t-1} \times (1 + es_{t-1,t}) < (1 + s_t)^t$$

12. If $es_{1,2}$ were equal to or greater than s_1, then the inequality would not hold in the correct direction because it was assumed that $s_1 > s_2$.

13. The empirical evidence is not without dispute. Fama has argued that the evidence is inconsistent with both the unbiased expectations and liquidity preference theories, whereas McCulloch refutes Fama's findings and argues in favor of the latter theory. See Eugene F. Fama, "Term Premiums in Bond Returns," *Journal of Financial Economics,* 13, no. 4 (December 1984): 529–546; and J. Huston McCulloch, "The Monotonicity of the Term Premium: A Closer Look," *Journal of Financial Economics,* 18, no. 1 (March 1987): 185–192, and "An Estimate of the Liquidity Premium," *Journal of Political Economy,* 83, no. 1 (February 1975): 95–119. McCulloch's findings are supported by Matthew Richardson, Paul Richardson, and Tom Smith in "The Monotonicity of the Term Premium: Another Look," *Journal of Financial Economics,* 31, no. 1 (February 1992): 97–105.

Bond Analysis

Consider an investor who believes that there are situations in which public information can be used to identify mispriced bonds, which are bonds that are not selling for their "fair" values. To translate that belief into action about which bonds to buy and sell, the investor needs an analytical procedure. One procedure involves comparing a bond's yield-to-maturity with a yield-to-maturity that the investor feels is appropriate, based on the characteristics of the bond as well as on current market conditions. If the yield-to-maturity is higher than the appropriate yield-to-maturity, then the bond is said to be underpriced (or undervalued), and it is a candidate for buying. Conversely, if the yield-to-maturity is lower than the appropriate yield-to-maturity, then the bond is said to be overpriced (or overvalued), and it is a candidate for selling (or even short-selling).

Instead of examining yields, the investor could estimate the bond's "true" or "intrinsic" value and compare it with the bond's current market price. If the current market price is less than the bond's intrinsic value, then the bond is underpriced, and if it is greater, then the bond is overpriced. Both procedures for analyzing bonds are based on the capitalization of income method of valuation.[1] The first procedure involving yields is analogous to the internal rate of return (IRR) method, and the second procedure involving intrinsic value is analogous to the net present value method (NPV); both of these methods were discussed with respect to valuing common stocks in Chapter 15.[2]

21.1 Applying the Capitalization of Income Method to Bonds

capitalization of income method of valuation

The **capitalization of income method of valuation** states that the intrinsic value of any asset is based on the discounted value of the cash flows that the investor expects to receive in the future from owning the asset. As mentioned earlier, one way this method has been applied to bond valuation is by comparing the bond's yield-to-maturity, y, with the appropriate yield-to-maturity, y^*. Specifically, if $y > y^*$, then the bond is underpriced, and if $y < y^*$, then the bond is overpriced. If $y = y^*$, then the bond is said to be fairly priced.

21.1.1 PROMISED YIELD-TO-MATURITY

promised yield-to-maturity

Letting P denote the current market price of a bond with a remaining life of n years and promising cash flows to the investor of C_1 in year 1, C_2 in year 2, and so on, the yield-to-maturity (more specifically, the **promised yield-to-maturity**) of the bond is the value of y that solves the following equation:

$$P = \frac{C_1}{(1+y)^1} + \frac{C_2}{(1+y)^2} + \frac{C_3}{(1+y)^3} + \cdots + \frac{C_n}{(1+y)^n}$$

With summation notation, this equation can be rewritten as

$$P = \sum_{t=1}^{n} \frac{C_t}{(1+y)^t} \qquad (21.1)$$

For example, consider a bond that is currently selling for $900 and has a remaining life of three years. For ease of exposition, assume that it makes annual coupon payments of $60 per year and has a par value of $1,000; that is, $C_1 = \$60$, $C_2 = \$60$, and $C_3 = \$1,060$ (= $1,000 + $60). Using Equation (21.1), the yield-to-maturity on this bond is the value of y that solves the following equation:

$$P = \frac{\$60}{(1+y)^1} + \frac{\$60}{(1+y)^2} + \frac{\$1,060}{(1+y)^3}$$

which is $y = 10.02\%$. If subsequent analysis indicates that the yield-to-maturity should be 9.00%, then this bond is underpriced because $y = 10.02\% > y^* = 9.00\%$.

21.1.2   INTRINSIC VALUE

The intrinsic value of a bond can be calculated using the following formula:

$$V = \frac{C_1}{(1+y^*)^1} + \frac{C_2}{(1+y^*)^2} + \frac{C_3}{(1+y^*)^3} + \cdots + \frac{C_n}{(1+y^*)^n}$$

or, using summation notation,

$$V = \sum_{t=1}^{n} \frac{C_t}{(1+y^*)^t} \qquad (21.2)$$

After V has been estimated, it should be compared with the bond's market price P to see whether $V > P$, in which case the bond is underpriced, or whether $V < P$, in which case the bond is overpriced.

net present value   Alternatively, the **net present value** (NPV) of the bond can be calculated as the difference between the value of the bond and the purchase price:

$$NPV = V - P = \sum_{t=1}^{n} \frac{C_t}{(1+y^*)^t} - P \qquad (21.3)$$

The NPV of the bond in the previous example is the solution to the following equation:

$$NPV = \frac{\$60}{(1+.09)^1} + \frac{\$60}{(1+.09)^2} + \frac{\$1,060}{(1+.09)^3} - \$900$$

$$= \$24.06$$

Because this bond has a positive NPV, it is underpriced. A bond will always have a positive NPV when it has a yield-to-maturity that is higher than the appropriate one. (Earlier it was shown that this bond's yield-to-maturity was 10.02%, which is more than 9.00%, the appropriate yield-to-maturity.) That is, in general, any bond with $y > y^*$ will always have a positive NPV and vice versa, so that under either method it would be underpriced.[3]

If the investor had determined that y^* was equal to 11.00%, then the bond's NPV would have been $-$22.19. This value suggests that the bond was overpriced, just as would have been noted when the yield-to-maturity of 10.02% was compared with 11.00%. In general, a bond with $y < y^*$ will always have a negative NPV and vice versa, so that under either method it would be found to be overpriced.

If the investor had determined that y^* had a value of approximately the same magnitude as the bond's yield-to-maturity of 10%, then the NPV of the bond would be approximately zero. In such a situation the bond is fairly priced.

Note that in order for the capitalization of income method of valuation to be used, the values of C_t, P, and y^* must be determined. It is generally easy to determine the values for C_t and P because they are the bond's promised cash flows and current market price, respectively. However, determining the value of y^* is difficult because it depends on the investor's subjective evaluation of certain characteristics of the bond and current market conditions. Given that the key ingredient in bond analysis is determining the appropriate value of y^*, the next section discusses the attributes that should be considered in making such a determination.

21.2 Bond Attributes

Six primary attributes of a bond are of significant importance in bond valuation:

- Length of time until maturity
- Coupon rate
- Call provisions
- Tax status
- Marketability
- Likelihood of default

yield structure

term structure

risk structure

At any time the structure of market prices for bonds differing in those dimensions can be examined and described in terms of yields-to-maturity. This overall structure is sometimes referred to as the **yield structure.** Often attention is confined to differences along a single dimension, holding the other attributes constant. For example, the set of yields of bonds of different maturities constitutes the **term structure** (discussed in Chapter 20), and the set of yields of bonds of different default risk is referred to as the **risk structure.**

Most bond analysts consider the yields-to-maturity for default-free bonds to form the term structure. "Risk differentials" are then added to obtain the relevant yields-to-maturity for bonds of lower quality. Although subject to some criticism, this procedure makes it possible to think about a complicated set of relationships sequentially.

yield spread

basis point

The differential between the yields of two bonds is usually called a **yield spread.** Most often it involves the bond that is under analysis and a comparable default-free bond (that is, a Treasury security of similar maturity and coupon rate). Yield spreads are sometimes measured in basis points, where 1 **basis point** equals .01%. If the yield-to-maturity for one bond is 11.50% and that of another is 11.90%, the yield spread is 40 basis points.

21.2.1 COUPON RATE AND LENGTH OF TIME UNTIL MATURITY

The coupon rate and length of time to maturity are important attributes of a bond because they determine the size and timing of the cash flows promised to the bondholder by the issuer. If a bond's current market price is known, these attributes can be used to determine the bond's yield-to-maturity, which will subsequently be compared with what the investor thinks it should be. More specifically, if the market for Treasury securities is viewed as being efficient, then the yield-to-maturity on a Treasury security similar to the bond being evaluated can form a starting point in the analysis of the bond.

Consider the previously mentioned bond selling for $900 with promised cash flows during the next three years of $60, $60, and $1,060, which generates a yield-to-maturity of 10.02%. In this case, perhaps a Treasury security with a cash flow during the next three years of $50, $50, and $1,050 that is currently selling for $910.61 would be the starting point of the analysis. Because the yield-to-maturity on this Treasury security is 8.5%, the yield spread between the bond and the Treasury security is 10.02% − 8.50% = 1.52%, or 152 basis points. Figure 21.1 illustrates the yield spread between an index of long-term Aaa-rated corporate bonds and U.S. Treasury bonds, and shows that it has recently been over 100 basis points.

21.2.2 CALL PROVISIONS

There are times when, by historical standards, yields-to-maturity are relatively high. Bonds issued during such times may, at first glance, appear to be unusually attractive investments. However, deeper analysis indicates that this perception is not necessarily correct. Why? Because most corporate bonds have a call provision (discussed in Chapter 19) that enables the issuer to redeem the bonds prior to maturity, usually for a price somewhat above par.[4] This price is known as the call price, and the difference between

FIGURE 21.1 Yield Spreads on High-Grade Corporate Bonds

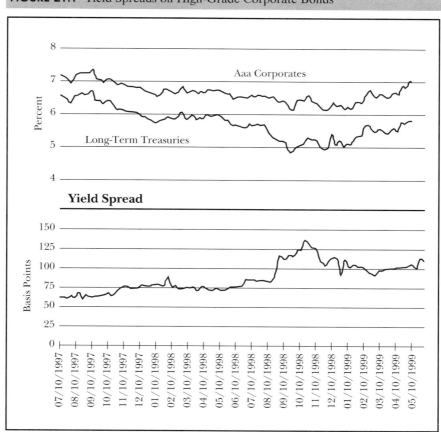

Source: Moody's Bond Record, June 1999, p. 1117.

it and the par value of the bond is known as the call premium. An issuer often finds it financially advantageous to call the existing bonds if yields drop substantially after the bonds were initially sold because the issuer can replace them with lower yielding securities that are less costly.[5]

For example, consider a 10-year bond issued at par ($1,000) that has a coupon rate of 12% and is callable at $1,050 any time after it has been outstanding for 5 years.[6] If, after 5 years, yields on similar 5-year bonds were 8%, the bond would probably be called. An investor who had planned on receiving annual coupon payments of $120 for 10 years would instead actually receive $120 annual coupon payments for 5 years and the call price of $1,050 after 5 years. At this time the investor could take the $1,050 and reinvest it in the 8% bonds, thereby receiving $84 per year in coupon payments over the remaining 5 years and $1,050 at the end of the 10th year as a return of principal (it is assumed here that the investor can purchase a fraction of a bond, so that the full $1,050 can be invested in the 8% bonds). With this pattern of cash flows, the bond's actual yield-to-maturity (otherwise known as the *realized return*) over the 10 years would be 10.96% instead of the 12% that would have been its actual yield if it had not been called.

This example suggests that the higher the coupon rate of a callable bond, the greater is the likely divergence between actual and promised yields. This relation is borne out by experience. Figure 21.2 plots the coupon rate, set at the time of issue, on the horizontal axis. Because most bonds are initially sold at (or very close to) par, the coupon rate is also a measure of the yield-to-maturity that an investor may have thought was obtainable by purchasing one of the newly issued bonds.

The vertical axis in this figure plots the subsequent actual yields-to-maturity obtained up to the original maturity date by an investor, assuming that the payments received in the event of a call were reinvested in noncallable bonds with appropriate maturities. The curve is based on experience for a group of callable bonds issued by utility companies during a period of fluctuating interest rates. As can be seen, the coupon rate and actual yield are quite similar in magnitude until the coupon rate nears

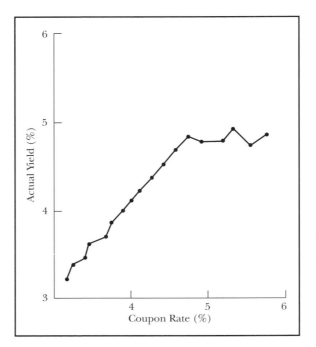

FIGURE 21.2 Promised and Actual Yields of Callable Aa Utility Bonds

Source: Frank C. Jen and James E. Wert, "The Effect of Call Risk on Corporate Bond Yields," *Journal of Finance,* 22, no. 4 (December 1967): p. 646.

5%. At that point, higher coupon rates are no longer associated with higher actual yields because these coupon rates were relatively high during the time period examined. As a consequence, most of the bonds with coupon rates above 5% were ultimately called.

The upshot is that a bond with a greater likelihood of being called should have a higher yield-to-maturity; that is, the higher the coupon rate or the lower the call premium, the higher the yield-to-maturity should be. Equivalently, callable bonds with higher coupon rates or lower call premiums will have lower intrinsic values, keeping everything else equal.

putable bonds

A relatively new innovation in the issuance of bonds is the use of *put provisions.* Bonds with put provisions, known as **putable bonds,** allow the investor to return the bond to the issuer before maturity and receive the par value in return. Similar to call provisions, typically the put provision does not allow the bond to be "put" with the issuer until several years (for example, five) have elapsed after the issuance of the bond. Although call provisions are valuable to the issuer and potentially detrimental to investors, resulting in callable bonds having a higher yield-to-maturity than noncallable bonds, the opposite occurs with putable bonds. The put provision is a benefit to investors and costly to issuers because it allows investors to receive the par value of the bond after the waiting period has elapsed (unlike call provision, the put provision will typically allow the put to be exercised only for a brief time at the end of the waiting period, not for the rest of the bond's life). Thus, if interest rates rise, an investor can turn in the bond and use the proceeds to invest in a higher yielding bond, thereby forcing the issuer to issue new bonds at a higher rate. Consequently, put provisions are likely to be used when interest rates rise, whereas call provisions are likely to be used when interest rates fall. Because put provisions are potentially beneficial to investors, the result is that a putable bond will have a lower yield than a nonputable bond, when all other features of the bonds are similar.

21.2.3 TAX STATUS

In Chapter 5 it was noted that tax-exempt municipal bonds have had yields-to-maturity that were typically 20% to 40% lower than the yields-to-maturity on similar taxable bonds because the coupon payments on muni's are exempt from federal income taxation. However, taxation can also affect bond prices and yields in other ways. For example, any low-coupon taxable bond selling at a discount provides return in two forms: coupon payments and gains from price appreciation. In the United States both are taxable as ordinary income, but taxes on the latter may be deferred until the bond either is sold or matures if the bond was initially sold at par.[7] Such *market discount bonds* seem to have a tax advantage because of this deferral. As a result, they should have slightly lower before-tax yields than high-coupon taxable bonds, other things being equal—that is, such low-coupon bonds will have a slightly higher intrinsic value than will high-coupon bonds.

21.2.4 MARKETABILITY

Marketability (sometimes also referred to as *liquidity*) refers to the ability of an investor to sell an asset quickly without having to make a substantial price concession. An example of an illiquid asset would be a collectible, such as a piece of artwork. An investor who owns a van Gogh painting may have to settle for a relatively low price if the painting must be sold within an hour. If the sale is postponed long enough for a public auction to be set up, undoubtedly a much higher price could be obtained. Alternatively, an investor who must sell $1,000,000 worth of IBM common stock within an hour will probably be able to receive a price close to the price that other sellers of IBM stock recently received. Furthermore, it is unlikely that waiting would increase the selling price of such a security.

Because most bonds are bought and sold in dealer markets, one measure of a bond's marketability is the bid–ask spread that dealers quote on the bond. Bonds that are actively traded tend to have lower bid–ask spreads than bonds that are inactive because the dealer is more exposed to risk when making a market in an inactive security than when making a market in an active security. One source of this risk is that interest rates in general may move in a way that causes the dealer to lose money on his or her inventory. Accordingly, a bond that is actively traded should have a lower yield-to-maturity and higher intrinsic value than a bond that is inactive, all else being equal.

21.2.5 LIKELIHOOD OF DEFAULT

bond ratings

Currently several corporations—the two largest being Standard & Poor's Corporation and Moody's Investors Service, Inc.—provide ratings of the creditworthiness of thousands of corporate and municipal bonds. Such **bond ratings** are often interpreted as an indication of the likelihood of default by the issuer. Figure 21.3 provides details on the ratings assigned by Standard & Poor's, and Figure 21.4 provides similar details for Moody's.[8]

FIGURE 21.3 Standard & Poor's Rating Definitions

'AAA' An obligation rated 'AAA' has the highest rating assigned by Standard & Poor's. The obligor's capacity to meet its financial commitment on the obligation is extremely strong.

'AA' An obligation rated 'AA' differs from the highest rated obligations only in small degree. The obligor's capacity to meet its financial commitment on the obligation is very strong.

'A' An obligation rated 'A' is somewhat more susceptible to the adverse effects of changes in circumstances and economic conditions than obligations in higher rated categories. However, the obligor's capacity to meet its financial commitment on the obligation is still strong.

'BBB' An obligation rated 'BBB' exhibits adequate protection parameters. However, adverse economic conditions or changing circumstances are more likely to lead to a weakened capacity of the obligor to meet its financial commitment on the obligation. Obligations rated 'BB', 'B', 'CCC', 'CC', and 'C' are regarded as having significant speculative characteristics. 'BB' indicates the least degree of speculation and **'C'** the highest. While such obligations will likely have some quality and protective characteristics, these may be outweighed by large uncertainties or major exposures to adverse conditions.

'BB' An obligation rated 'BB' is less vulnerable to nonpayment than speculative issues. However, it faces major ongoing uncertainties or exposure to adverse business, financial, or economic conditions which could lead to the obligor's inadequate capacity to meet its financial commitment on the obligation.

'B' An obligation rated 'B' is more vulnerable to nonpayment than obligations rated 'BB', but the obligor currently has the capacity to meet its financial commitment on the obligation. Adverse business, financial, or economic conditions will likely impair the obligor's capacity or willingness to meet its financial commitment on the obligation.

'CCC' An obligation rated 'CCC' is currently vulnerable to nonpayment, and is dependent upon favorable business, financial, and economic conditions for the obligor to meet its financial commitment on the obligation. In the event of adverse business, financial, or economic conditions, the obligor is not likely to have the capacity to meet its financial commitment on the obligation.

'CC' An obligation rated 'CC' is currently highly vulnerable to nonpayment.

'C' The 'C' rating may be used to cover a situation where a bankruptcy petition has been filed or similar action has been taken, but payments on this obligation are being continued.

'D' An obligation rated 'D' is in payment default. The 'D' rating category is used when payments on an obligation are not made on the date due even if the applicable grace period has not expired, unless Standard & Poor's believes that such payments will be made during such grace period. The 'D' rating also will be used upon the filing of a bankruptcy petition or the taking of a similar action if payments on an obligation are jeopardized.

Source: Standard & Poor's Bond Guide, June 1999, p. 12.

Aaa

Bonds which are rated **Aaa** are judged to be of the best quality. They carry the smallest degree of investment risk and are generally referred to as "gilt edged." Interest payments are protected by a large or by an exceptionally stable margin and principal is secure. While the various protective elements are likely to change, such changes as can be visualized are most unlikely to impair the fundamentally strong position of such issues.

Aa

Bonds which are rated **Aa** are judged to be of high quality by all standards. Together with the **Aaa** group they comprise what are generally known as high grade bonds. They are rated lower than the best bonds because margins of protection may not be as large as in **Aaa** securities or fluctuation of protective elements may be of greater amplitude or there may be other elements present which make the long-term risk appear somewhat larger than the **Aaa** securities.

A

Bonds which are rated **A** possess many favorable investment attributes and are to be considered as upper-medium-grade obligations. Factors giving security to principal and interest are considered adequate, but elements may be present which suggest a susceptibility to impairment some time in the future.

Baa

Bonds which are rated **Baa** are considered as medium-grade obligations, (i.e., they are neither highly protected nor poorly secured). Interest payments and principal security appear adequate for the present but certain protective elements may be lacking or may be characteristically unreliable over any great length of time. Such bonds lack outstanding investment characteristics and in fact have speculative characteristics as well.

Ba

Bonds which are rated **Ba** are judged to have speculative elements; their future cannot be considered as well-assured. Often the protection of interest and principal payments may be very moderate, and thereby not well safeguarded during both good and bad times over the future. Uncertainty of position characterizes bonds in this class.

B

Bonds which are rated **B** generally lack characteristics of the desirable investment. Assurance of interest and principal payments or of maintenance of other terms of the contract over any long period of time may be small.

Caa

Bonds which are rated **Caa** are of poor standing. Such issues may be in default or there may be present elements of danger with respect to principal or interest.

Ca

Bonds which are rated **Ca** represent obligations which are speculative in a high degree. Such issues are often in default or have other marked shortcomings.

C

Bonds which are rated **C** are the lowest rated class of bonds, and issues so rated can be regarded as having extremely poor prospects of ever attaining any real investment standing.

FIGURE 21.4 Moody's Rating Definitions

Source: Moody's Bond Record, June 1999, pp. 3–4.

investment-grade bonds
speculative-grade bonds

high-yield bonds
junk bonds
fallen angels

A broader set of categories is often used, with bonds classified as either **investment-grade** or **speculative-grade.** Typically, investment-grade bonds have been assigned to one of the top four ratings (AAA through BBB by Standard & Poor's; Aaa through Baa by Moody's), whereas speculative-grade bonds have been assigned to one of the lower ratings (BB and below by Standard & Poor's; Ba and below by Moody's). Sometimes these low-rated securities are called **high-yield bonds** or, derisively, **junk bonds.**[9] Furthermore, if the high-yield bonds were of investment grade when originally issued, they are often called **fallen angels.**

At times certain regulated financial institutions, such as banks, savings and loans, and insurance companies, have been prohibited from purchasing bonds that were not of investment grade. As a consequence, investment-grade bonds are sometimes thought to command "superpremium" prices and, hence, disproportionately low yields. However, a major disparity in yields could attract a great many new issuers, who would increase the supply of such bonds, thereby causing bond prices to fall and yields to rise. For a significant superpremium to persist, substantial market segmentation on both the buying and the selling sides would be required. As there is no clear evidence that such segmentation exists, it seems more likely that the differences in yields between investment-grade bonds and speculative-grade bonds are roughly proportional to differences in default risk.

According to Moody's, ratings are designed to provide "investors with a simple system of gradation by which the relative investment qualities of bonds may be noted."[10] Moreover:

> Since ratings involve judgments about the future, on the one hand, and since they are used by investors as a means of protection, on the other, the effort is made when assigning ratings to look at "worst" potentialities in the "visible" future, rather than solely at the past record and the status of the present. Therefore, investors using the ratings should not expect to find in them a reflection of statistical factors alone, since they are an appraisal of long-term risks, including the recognition of many non-statistical factors.[11]

Despite this disclaimer, the influence of "statistical factors" on the ratings is apparently significant. Several studies have investigated the relationship between historical measures of a firm's performance and the ratings assigned its bonds. Many of the differences in the ratings accorded various bonds can in fact be attributed to differences in the issuers' financial situations, measured in traditional ways. For corporate bonds, better ratings are generally associated with the following:

1. *Lower financial leverage.* For example, a smaller debt-to-total-assets (or debt-to-equity) ratio and a larger current (or quick) ratio (that is, current assets divided by current liabilities or, in the case of the quick ratio, current assets except inventory divided by current liabilities)
2. *Larger firm size.* For example, a larger amount of total assets
3. *Larger and steadier profits.* For example, a consistently high rate of return on equity or rate of return on total assets (often earnings before interest and taxes is used as the numerator in such ratios when evaluating a firm's debt) and coverage ratio, such as times interest earned (measured by dividing earnings before interest and taxes by interest)
4. *Larger cash flow.* For example, a large cash flow to debt ratio
5. *Lack of subordination to other debt issues*

These observations are used, among other things, in the development of models for predicting the initial ratings that will be given to forthcoming bond issues as well as for predicting changes in the ratings of outstanding bonds.

Default Premiums

Because common stocks do not "promise" any cash flows to the investor, they are not subject to default. To assess the investment prospects for a common stock, one might consider all possible holding-period returns. Multiplying each return by its perceived probability of occurrence and then adding the products yields an estimate of the expected holding-period return.

A similar procedure that focuses on yield-to-maturity can be used with bonds. Formally, all possible yields are considered with their respective probabilities, and a weighted average is computed to determine the **expected yield-to-maturity.** As long as there is any possibility of default or late payment, the expected yield will fall below the promised yield. In general, the greater the risk of default and the greater the amount of loss in the event of default, the greater will be this disparity in yields.

expected yield-to-maturity

MONEY MATTERS

Taking Advantage of the Bond Rating Process

"Your bond rating: Don't try to issue debt without it," might read the motto of U.S. bond rating agencies. Receiving a bond rating has long been a prerequisite for any U.S. debt issuer desiring easy access to the domestic bond market. Without such a rating, debt issuers are often forced to seek financing from more expensive sources, such as banks or the market for privately placed debt.

Once they have acquired a bond rating, debt issuers strive to maintain that rating or even to improve it. The benefits of an improved rating (and the costs of a lower rating) can be substantial. The difference in yields between the highest and lowest rated investment-grade bonds fluctuates over time, but it is often well over a full percentage point (as is illustrated in Figure 21.5). Yield differences between investment-grade and below-investment-grade bonds typically are even greater. As U.S. corporations have increased the amount of debt on their balance sheets in recent decades, the financial ramifications of bond rating changes have increased commensurately.

Most institutional bond investors focus their efforts on forecasting changes in interest rates

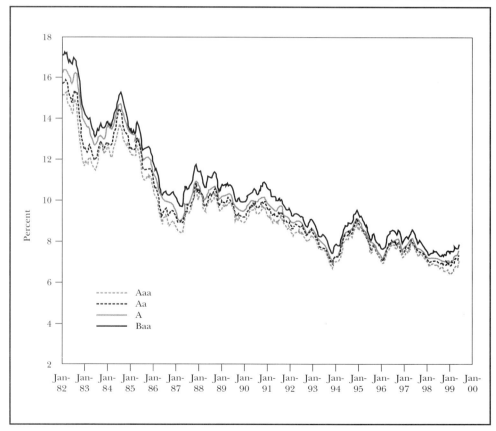

FIGURE 21.5 Corporate Bonds Yields by Ratings, Long-Term Monthly Averages

Source: Moody's Bond Record, June 1999, p. 1110.

and structuring their portfolios to benefit from those expected movements. However, the emphasis placed by the bond market on both a debt issue's initial rating and subsequent changes in that rating present insightful investors with another approach to bond management: searching for bonds whose "true" credit quality is different from their assigned ratings. In discussing those opportunities, we first consider some additional information on the bond rating process.

Two companies dominate the bond rating business: Standard & Poor's and Moody's. Virtually every corporate debt security that comes to the public market is rated by at least one of these organizations. More than 2,000 debt issuers submit financial data to these organizations. For all practical purposes, no bond can be considered an investment-grade security without the acquiescence of S&P's or Moody's.

In addition, a relatively small market exists for "third opinions." Three other firms—Fitch Investors; Duff & Phelps; and McCarthy, Crisanti & Maffei—provide ratings on a portion of the bonds that are rated by the two big firms. Although their ratings rarely differ significantly from S&P's and Moody's, in some situations investors and issuers are comforted by a confirmation of the two big firms' ratings. They may also believe that the smaller rating agencies will uncover aspects of the debt issuers' financial conditions overlooked by S&P's and Moody's.

The text describes many of the financial factors that rating agencies use in assigning bond ratings, including the issuers' leverage, earnings variability, and profitability. Research has shown that such factors systematically "explain" a large portion of bond rating differences among debt issues, implying that there is a significant "mechanical" aspect to the rating process.

Despite this dominant formulistic element of bond ratings, qualitative judgments by the rating agencies still appear to play an important role in rating assignments. Interestingly, as corporations have increased the leverage on their balance sheets, a firm's ability to generate future cash flow to meet its interest expenses has come to play a major role in setting bond ratings. However, evaluating the prospective, rather than contemporaneous, cash flow strength of an issuer is an uncertain process and requires more subjective interpretations of the financial data on the part of the rating agencies.

Some institutional bond investors attempt to take advantage of the uncertainty surrounding a bond's rating. They recognize that, all other factors being equal, a bond with a lower rating will sell for a lower price (equivalently, a higher yield) than a bond with a higher rating. If bonds are discovered whose credit quality supports a higher rating, then these bonds will offer premium yields relative to bonds with the same "actual" credit quality. Conversely, bonds that deserve a lower rating will provide yields below those with the same "actual" credit quality. Thus, an investor who purchases underrated bonds and avoids overrated bonds can construct a portfolio that will outperform a passively managed portfolio of similar risk.

Owners of underrated bonds may benefit even further if their bonds are subsequently upgraded by the rating agencies. Such upgrades are usually associated with substantial price increases, although those increases usually occur before rating changes rather than after them.

Why do such institutional bond investors expect to beat the ratings game? They believe that with intensive security analysis they can understand a debt issuer's financial condition more accurately and on a more timely basis than can the rating agencies. Essentially, these investors make their moves and wait for the market and the rating agencies to catch up to them.

Security analysis of this type is similar to fundamental stock analysis (see Chapters 14 and 15), although less emphasis is placed on an issuer's long-term growth prospects and more attention is paid to the issuer's ability to cover near- and medium-term obligations. Nevertheless, an interpretation of a debt issuer's "true" financial condition is based on a wide range of disparate variables, from the quality of the debt issuer's management to the market for its products.

To a certain extent, these bond investors play a numbers game with the rating agencies. S&P and Moody's each employ less than 100 analysts (the smaller rating agencies employ far fewer). Thus, the rating agencies cannot cover all debt issuers at all times. Further, they devote the majority of their resources to evaluating new debt offerings. It is true that significant positive or negative news about an issuer may cause the rating agencies to immediately reevaluate their bond ratings. However, at other times a debt issuer's financial condition may change slowly, without full recognition by the market and the rating agencies.

Of course, as with successful common stock analysis, identifying incorrectly rated bonds consistently and accurately requires skills possessed by few investors in an efficient market. However, as with common stock analysis, the potential profits to bond investors who correctly diverge from the current consensus can be great.

This relationship is illustrated in Figure 21.6 for a hypothetical risky bond. Its promised yield-to-maturity is 12%, but because of a high default risk, the expected yield is only 9%. The 3% difference between promised and expected yields is the **default premium.** Any bond having some probability of default should offer such a premium, and the greater the probability of default, the greater the premium should be.

default premium

Just how large should a bond's default premium be? According to one model, the answer depends on both the probability of default and the likely financial loss to the bondholder in the event of default.[12] Consider a bond that is perceived to be equally likely to default in each year (given that it did not default in the previous year), with the probability that it will default in any given year denoted by p_d. Assume that if the bond does default, a payment of $(1 - \lambda)$ times its market price a year earlier will be made to the owner of each bond. According to this model, a bond will be fairly priced if its promised yield-to-maturity, y, is

$$y = \frac{\bar{y} + \lambda p_d}{1 - p_d} \qquad (21.4)$$

where $\bar{y}$ denotes the bond's expected yield-to-maturity. The difference, d, between a bond's promised yield-to-maturity, y, and its expected yield-to-maturity, $\bar{y}$, was referred to earlier as the bond's default premium. In Equation (21.4), this difference for a fairly priced bond will be equal to

$$d = y - \bar{y} \qquad (21.5a)$$

FIGURE 21.6 Yield-to-Maturity for a Risky Bond

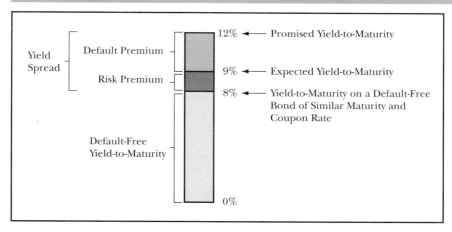

which, after solving Equation (21.4) for $\bar{y}$ and inserting the result in Equation (21.5a), equals

$$d = p_d(y + \lambda) \tag{21.5b}$$

As an example, consider the bond illustrated in Figure 21.6. Assume that this bond has a 6% annual default probability, and that it is estimated that if the bond does default, each bondholder will receive an amount equal to 60% of the bond's market price a year earlier (thus, $1 - \lambda = .60$, which in turn means that $\lambda = .40$). Equation (21.5b) can be used to determine that this bond would be fairly priced if its default premium were equal to

$$d = .06(.09 + .40)$$
$$= .0294$$

or 2.94%. Because the actual default premium was estimated to be 3%, the two figures are similar. This similarity suggests that the actual default premium is appropriate according to this model.

What sort of default experience might the long-run bond investor anticipate, and how is this experience likely to be related to the ratings of the bonds held? Edward Altman examined the default experience of corporate bonds.[13] For each bond in his sample, he noted its rating when it was originally issued and then how many years later it went into default (if at all). From this information he compiled "mortality tables," such as Table 21.1, which shows the percentage of bond issues that went into default within various years after issuance.

Several interesting observations can be made on inspection of this table. First, in looking down any particular column, one can see that the cumulative rate of default increases as one moves farther from the date of issuance. Second, except for those bonds originally rated AA, lower rated bonds had higher default rates. Third, the default rates for the speculative grades of bonds are strikingly high. This result raises a question of whether such bonds make good investments; their higher yields might not make up for their higher default rates.[14] That issue will be addressed shortly.

TABLE 21.1   Default Rates of U.S. Bonds

Number of Years After Issuance	Original Rating						
	AAA	*AA*	*A*	*BBB*	*BB*	*B*	*CCC*
1	.00%	.00%	.00%	.03%	.00%	.87%	1.31%
2	.00	.00	.30	.57	.93	3.22	4.00
3	.00	1.11	.60	.85	1.36	9.41	19.72
4	.00	1.42	.65	1.34	3.98	16.37	36.67
5	.00	1.70	.65	1.54	5.93	20.87	38.08
6	.14	1.70	.73	1.81	7.38	26.48	40.58
7	.19	1.91	.87	2.70	10.91	29.62	NA
8	.19	1.93	.94	2.83	10.91	31.74	NA
9	.19	2.01	1.28	2.99	10.91	39.38	NA
10	.19	2.11	1.28	3.85	13.86	40.86	NA

Source: Edward I. Altman, "Defaults and Returns on High-Yield Bonds through the First Half of 1991," *Financial Analysts Journal,* 47, no. 6 (November/December 1991): Table X, pp. 74–75.

Risk Premiums

It is useful to compare the expected return of a risky security with the certain return of a default-free security. In an efficient market, the difference in these returns is related to the relevant systematic (or nondiversifiable) risk of the security. Consider an investor in common stocks who has a holding period of one year or less. In this situation the expected return on a share is typically compared with the yield of a Treasury bill having a maturity date corresponding to the end of the holding period. (Note that the yield on such a Treasury bill is equal to its holding period return.)

Traditionally, a risky bond's expected yield-to-maturity is compared with that of a default-free bond of similar maturity and coupon rate. The difference between these yields is known as the bond's risk premium. In the example shown in Figure 21.6, default-free bonds of similar maturity and coupon rate offer a certain 8% yield-to-maturity. Because the risky bond's expected yield-to-maturity is 9%, its risk premium is 1% (that is, 100 basis points).

Every bond that might default offers a default premium. But the risk premium is another matter. Any security's expected return should be related only to its systematic risk, for it is this risk that measures its contribution to the risk of a well-diversified portfolio; its total risk is not directly relevant. For example, if a group of companies all faced the possibility of bankruptcy, but from totally unrelated causes, a portfolio that included all of their bonds would subsequently provide an actual return very close to its expected return. The default premiums earned on the bonds that did not default would offset the losses incurred from the bonds that did default. Consequently, there should be little reason for this expected return to differ significantly from that of a default-free bond because there is little doubt concerning what its actual return will be. Accordingly, each bond should be priced to offer little or no risk premium (but each bond should have a substantive default premium).

The risks associated with bonds are not unrelated, however. The ratio of the par value of corporate bonds defaulting during the year to the par value of bonds outstanding at the start of the year was found, over a period of time, to peak during periods of economic distress.[15] When the economy is bad, most firms are affected. The market value of a firm's common stock declines when an economic downturn is anticipated. If the likelihood of default on its debt also increases, the market value of its outstanding bonds will follow suit. Thus, the holding-period return on a bond may be correlated with the returns of other bonds and with those of stocks. Most important, a risky bond's holding-period return is likely to be correlated, at least to some extent, with the return on a widely diversified "market portfolio" that includes both corporate bonds and stocks. It is this part of the risk of a bond that is known as systematic risk and causes a bond to have a risk premium in the form of an expected return that is greater than the default-free rate because it is not diversifiable.

Bonds with a greater likelihood of default have greater potential sensitivity to market declines, which, in turn, represents lowered assessments of prospects for the economy as a whole. This relation is illustrated in Table 21.2, which summarizes the investment performance of three portfolios of bonds, known as bond funds, in the Keystone group.[16] All values shown in the table are based on annual returns earned during a 24-year period by each portfolio. As might be anticipated, the bond portfolio with the lowest rated bonds (fund B4) had the highest average return and highest standard deviation, whereas the bond portfolio with the highest rated bonds (fund B1) had the lowest average return and lowest standard deviation.

Each portfolio's returns were compared with those of the S&P 500 to estimate each portfolio's sensitivity to changes in stock prices. Specifically, a beta was calculated

TABLE 21.2 Risk and Return of Keystone Bond Funds			
	Fund B1: Conservative Bonds	*Fund B2: Investment-Grade Bonds*	*Fund B4: Discount Bonds*
Average return (% per year)	7.84	8.53	8.64
Standard deviation of return (% per year)	8.27	9.35	13.68
Beta value, relative to S&P 500	.26	.38	.54
Proportion of variance explained by S&P 500	.28	.45	.42

for each portfolio to measure the sensitivity of each portfolio to swings in the stock market. As can be seen in the table, the lower the bond rating of the portfolio, the higher the estimated beta, indicating that lower-rated bonds were more sensitive to stock price movements and thus should have had higher average returns.

The final row in the table shows the proportion of the year-to-year variation in bond portfolio returns that was associated with stock market swings. More of the B2 and B4 portfolios' variation was associated with the stock market than was the case with the B1 portfolio. Thus, for higher-rated bonds, interest-rate risk appears to have been more important than stock market risk.[17]

21.3   The Risk Structure of Interest Rates

The greater a bond's risk of default, the greater its default premium. This fact alone will cause a bond with a higher default risk to offer a higher promised yield-to-maturity. If it is also true that the greater a bond's risk of default, the greater its risk premium, then the promised yield-to-maturity will have to be even higher. As a result, bonds with lower credit ratings should have higher promised yields-to-maturity if such ratings really do reflect the risk of default.

Figure 21.5 shows that this is indeed the case. Each of the curves plots the promised yield-to-maturity for a group of corporate bonds assigned the same ratings by Moody's. This figure shows not only that bonds are priced so that higher promised yields go with lower ratings, but also that the differences between the yields in the rating categories vary considerably over time. This result suggests that credit ratings indicate *relative* levels of risk instead of *absolute* levels of risk.

If an absolute level of risk were indicated by a rating classification, then each classification would be associated with a particular probability of default (or, more accurately, a range of probabilities of default). Consequently, as the economy became more uncertain in terms of such factors as the near-term level of gross domestic product, bonds would be reclassified, with most moving to lower ratings. In this situation, yield spreads between classifications would change only slightly because each classification would still reflect bonds having the same probability of default. However, Figure 21.5 shows that these spreads change over time, an observation that can be interpreted as evidence that the ratings do not reflect absolute levels of risk. Further evidence is provided in Table 21.3, which shows the historical difference in the returns on high-yield bonds and U.S. Treasuries for various holding periods. As shown in the table, sometimes these differences are positive and other times they are negative. (For example, the average annual differences for 1978 through 1983 and 1984 through 1991 are +5.82% and −2.31%, respectively.)

TABLE 21.3 Historical Return Differences between High-Yield Bonds and U.S. Treasuries

Base Period (Jan. 1)	Terminal Period (December 31)													
	1978	1979	1980	1981	1982	1983	1984	1985	1986	1987	1988	1989	1990	1991
1978	8.68%	6.60%	5.01%	5.51%	3.17%	5.82%	4.13%	2.70%	1.59%	2.22%	2.41%	0.98%	(0.04%)	1.37%
1979		4.55	3.23	4.48	1.71	5.22	3.32	1.77	0.62	1.44	1.73	0.23	(0.82)	0.74
1980			1.96	4.45	0.67	5.39	3.05	1.24	(0.02)	1.01	1.38	(0.25)	(1.35)	0.37
1981				7.08	(0.13)	6.74	3.36	1.07	(0.42)	0.85	1.29	(0.54)	(1.73)	0.19
1982					(9.63)	6.49	1.93	(0.69)	(2.16)	(0.33)	0.36	(1.60)	(2.80)	(0.60)
1983						19.57	6.62	1.84	(0.56)	1.22	1.74	(0.65)	(2.11)	0.26
1984							(6.32)	(7.60)	(7.73)	(3.48)	(1.89)	(4.06)	(5.19)	(2.31)
1985								(9.03)	(8.50)	(2.50)	(0.76)	(3.60)	(5.00)	(1.70)
1986									(7.99)	0.34	1.64	(2.41)	(4.30)	(0.54)
1987										7.34	5.89	0.76	(3.49)	0.93
1988											4.27	(5.16)	(7.31)	(1.04)
1989												(14.37)	(12.76)	(3.11)
1990													(11.24)	4.34
1991[a]														19.01

[a]First six months of 1991.

Source: Edward I. Altman, "Defaults and Returns on High-Yield Bonds through the First Half of 1991," *Financial Analysts Journal,* 47, no. 6 (November/December 1991): Table XIV, p. 77.

Rating agencies prefer to avoid making a large number of rating changes as the economy becomes more uncertain. Instead, they prefer to use the classifications to indicate relative levels of risk, so that an overall increase in economic uncertainty would not result in a significant number of reclassifications. Thus, the probability of default associated with bonds in a given rating classification would be greatest at times of economic uncertainty. In turn, the yield spreads between classifications of corporate bonds and the yield spreads between corporate and government bonds would increase at such times. Indeed, there is considerable evidence that the spread between the promised yields of bonds of different rating classifications increases when the degree of uncertainty about the economy increases.

Some models have attempted to take advantage of this observation in order to predict the amount of economic uncertainty. In particular, these models use the size of the yield spread between, say, bonds rated AAA and those rated BBB by Standard & Poor's as an indication of the degree of economic uncertainty. For example, widening of this spread might indicate that the near-term future of the economy was becoming more uncertain. There are other models that look not at yield spreads but at differences in the holding-period returns of AAA and BBB bonds.

21.4 Determinants of Yield Spreads

As mentioned previously, when bond analysts refer to a corporate bond's yield spread, they are typically referring to the difference between the corporate bond's promised yield-to-maturity and that of another bond (often a Treasury security) having a similar maturity and coupon rate. The greater the risk of default, the greater this spread should be. Moreover, bonds that have less marketability might also command a greater spread. Given a large enough sample of bonds, one should be able to see whether these relationships really do exist.

One seminal study of corporate bond prices dealt with this matter.[18] Four measures were used to assess the probability of default:

1. The extent to which the firm's net income varied during the preceding nine years (measured by the coefficient of variation of earnings—that is, the ratio of standard deviation of earnings to average earnings)
2. The length of time the firm had operated without forcing any of its creditors to take a loss
3. The ratio of the market value of the firm's equity to the par value of its debt
4. The market value of the firm's outstanding debt (an indication of marketability)

First, these measures were calculated, along with the yield spread, for each of 366 bonds. Second, the logarithm of every yield spread and measure was calculated. Third, statistical methods were used to analyze the relationship between a bond's yield spread and these measures. The one that was found to most accurately describe this relationship was

$$\text{Yield spread} = 1.987 + (.307 \times \text{earnings variability}) - (.253 \times \text{time without default})$$
$$- (.537 \times \text{equity/debt ratio}) - (.275 \times \text{market value of debt}) \quad \textbf{(21.6)}$$

This form of the relationship accounted for roughly 75% of the variation in the bonds' yield spreads.

The advantage of an equation such as this is that the coefficients can be easily interpreted. Because all yield spreads and values were converted to logarithms, each coefficient indicates the percentage change in a bond's yield spread likely to accompany a 1% change in the associated measure. Thus, a 1% increase in a bond's earnings variability can be expected to bring about an increase of .307% in the bond's yield spread, other things being equal. Similarly, a 1% increase in a bond's time without default can be expected to cause a decrease of approximately .253% in the bond's yield spread, and so on. Because every measure was found to be related in the expected direction to the yield spread, the study provides substantial support for the notion that bonds with higher default risk and less marketability have higher yield spreads.

21.5 Financial Ratios as Predictors of Default

For years, security analysts have used accounting ratios to indicate the probability that a firm will fail to meet its financial obligations. Specific procedures have been developed to predict default with such ratios. Univariate analysis attempts to find the best single predictor for this purpose, whereas multivariate analysis searches for the best combination of two or more predictors.

21.5.1 UNIVARIATE METHODS

Cash inflows are contributions to the firm's cash balance, whereas cash outflows are drains on that balance. When the balance falls below zero, default is likely to occur. The probability of default will be greater for the firm when (1) the existing cash balance is smaller, (2) the expected net cash flow (measured before payments to creditors and stockholders) is smaller, and (3) the net cash flow is more variable.

In an examination of various measures used to assess these factors, it was found that the ratio of net cash flow (income before depreciation, depletion, and amortization charges) to total debt was particularly useful.[19] Figure 21.7(a) shows the mean value of this ratio for a group of firms that defaulted on a promised payment and for a companion group that did not. As early as five years before default the two groups' ratios diverged, and the spread widened as the year of default approached.

This changing spread suggests that the probability of default may not be constant through time. Instead, warning signals may indicate an increase in the probability, which should, in turn, cause a fall in the market price of the firm's bonds along with a fall in the market price of its common stock. Figure 21.7(b) shows that such signals are indeed recognized in the marketplace. The median market value of common stock in the firms that did not default went up, while that of the firms that subsequently defaulted went down as the date of default approached.

21.5.2 MULTIVARIATE METHODS

Combinations of certain financial ratios and cash flow variables have been considered as possible predictors of default. In one of the first studies, statistical analysis indicated that the most accurate method of predicting default involved calculating a firm's default-risk rating, known as its *Z-score,* from some of its financial ratios as follows:

$$Z = 1.2X_1 + 1.4X_2 + 3.3X_3 + .6X_4 + .99X_5 \qquad \textbf{(21.7)}$$

where the following five ratios were calculated from information contained in the firm's most recent income statement and balance sheet:

X_1 = (current assets − current liabilities)/total assets
X_2 = retained earnings/total assets
X_3 = earnings before interest and taxes/total assets
X_4 = market value of equity/book value of total debt
X_5 = sales/total assets

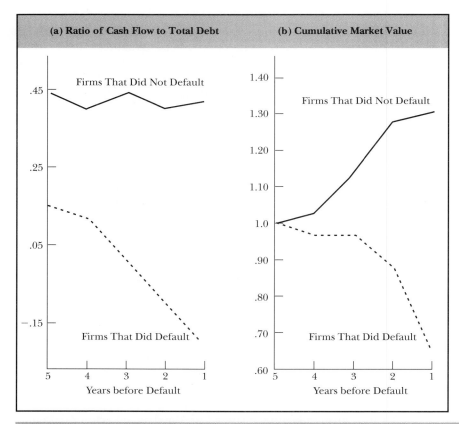

FIGURE 21.7 Financial Ratios and Market Prices for Firms That Defaulted and Those That Did Not

Source: William H. Beaver, "Market Prices, Financial Ratios and the Prediction of Failure," *Journal of Accounting Research,* 6, no. 2 (Autumn 1968): 182, 185.

Any firm with a Z-score below 1.8 was considered a likely candidate for default, and the lower the score, the greater the likelihood.[20] Firms with Z-scores between 1.81 and 2.99 were in the "gray area" whereas those above 2.99 were considered to be unlikely to default.

21.5.3 INVESTMENT IMPLICATIONS

Should the securities of firms whose ratio of cash flow to total debt or Z-score has declined be avoided? Hardly. Remember that the firms represented by the dashed lines in Figure 21.7 were chosen because they eventually defaulted. Had all firms with declining ratios been selected, corresponding decreases in their market prices would undoubtedly have been observed, reflecting the increased probability of future default. However, only some of these firms would have ultimately defaulted; the others would have recovered. Consequently, the gains on the firms that recovered might have offset the losses on the firms that defaulted. The net result from purchasing a portfolio of stocks with declining ratios or Z-scores could easily have been the achievement of an average return.

What about purchasing bonds of companies that have just had their ratings increased, and selling (or avoiding) bonds of companies that have just had their ratings decreased? After all, such changes in ratings should be related to a change in the default risk of the issuer. In a study that looked at the behavior of bond prices around the time of ratings changes, some evidence was found that the bond price adjustment to a rating change occurred in the period from eighteen to seven months *before* the rating change. Little or no evidence of a substantive price change was found either during the month of the rating change or in the period from six months before to six months after the rating change.[21] These findings are consistent with the notion that the bond market is semistrong-form efficient, because bond ratings are at least partly predictable from publicly available information.

The study previously mentioned examined primarily ratings changes within investment-grade categories. Another study also looked at what happened around the time of ratings changes for bonds that (1) were not investment grade and were downgraded or (2) were investment grade and were downgraded to no longer be investment grade.[22] Care was taken to ensure that there were no other announcements related to the bond issuers and that the downgrades were issued at the same time by both Moody's and Standard & Poor's. In both cases, there was a strong negative price reaction during the month of the downgrade and during the previous six months. The reaction before the downgrade is consistent with semistrong-form market efficiency, but the reaction during the month of the downgrade might not be; it is unclear whether the reaction occurred, at least in part, on or after the day of the downgrade. A significant negative price reaction after the day of the downgrade would be evidence of an inefficiency because investors could short sell such bonds on the announcement date and make abnormal profits. However, if most of the reaction was before the announcement, then there would not be any way to profit from trading after the announcement was made.

Summary

1. The capitalization of income method of valuation is a commonly used approach to identify mispriced bonds. It is based on the discounted value of the cash flows that the investor expects to receive from owning a bond.
2. Given the bond's current market price and promised cash flows, the investor can calculate the bond's promised yield-to-maturity and compare it with an appropriate discount rate.
3. Alternatively, the investor can use an appropriate discount rate to discount the bond's promised cash flows. The sum of the present value of these cash flows, the bond's intrinsic value, is compared with the bond's market price.
4. Six primary attributes are of significance in bond valuation: length of time to maturity, coupon rate, call and put provisions, tax status, marketability, and likelihood of default.
5. Time to maturity, call provisions, tax status, and likelihood of default tend to be directly related to promised yield-to-maturity. Coupon rate, put provisions, and marketability tend to be inversely related to promised yield-to-maturity.
6. Several organizations provide ratings of the creditworthiness of thousands of corporate and municipal bonds. These ratings are often interpreted as an indication of the issuer's likelihood of default.
7. Bond ratings indicate relative levels of risk instead of absolute levels of risk.
8. A bond's promised yield-to-maturity can be decomposed into a default-free yield-to-maturity and a yield spread. Furthermore, the yield spread can be decomposed into a risk premium and a default premium.
9. Various statistical models have been developed to predict the probability that a bond issuer will default. These models typically use financial ratios derived from the issuer's balance sheet and income statement.

Questions and Problems

1. Grapefruit Yeargin is considering purchasing a 10-year Treasury STRIP with a $10,000 par value. If the Treasury yield curve indicates that 6% is the appropriate yield for such bonds, what is the fair market value of this bond? (Assume annual compounding.)

2. Bones Ely owns a $1,000 face-value bond with three years to maturity. The bond makes annual interest payments of $75, the first to be made one year from today. The bond is currently priced at $975.48. Given an appropriate discount rate of 10%, should Bones hold or sell the bond?

3. Patsy Tebeau is considering investing in a bond currently selling for $8,785.07. The bond has four years to maturity, a $10,000 face value, and an 8% coupon rate. The next annual interest payment is due one year from today. The appropriate discount rate for investments of similar risk is 10%.
   a. Calculate the intrinsic value of the bond. Based on this calculation, should Patsy purchase the bond?
   b. Calculate the yield-to-maturity of the bond. Based on this calculation, should Patsy purchase the bond?

4. Consider two bonds with $1,000 face values that carry coupon rates of 8%, make annual coupon payments, and exhibit similar risk characteristics. The first bond has 5 years to maturity whereas the second has 10 years to maturity. The appropriate discount rate for investments of similar risk is 8%. If this discount rate rises by two percentage points, what will be the respective percentage price changes of the two bonds?

5. Why is it convenient to use Treasury securities as a starting point for analyzing bond yields?

6. Bond *A*'s yield-to-maturity is 9.80%; bond *B*'s yield-to-maturity is 8.73%. What is the difference in yields stated in basis points?

7. Bibb Falk recently purchased a bond with a $1,000 face value, a 10% coupon rate, and four years to maturity. The bond makes annual interest payments, the first to be received one year from today. Bibb paid $1,032.40 for the bond.
   a. What is the bond's yield-to-maturity?
   b. If the bond can be called two years from now at a price of $1,100, what is its yield-to-call?

8. Burleigh Grimes purchased at par a bond with a face value of $1,000. The bond had five years to maturity and a 10% coupon rate. The bond was called two years later for a price of $1,200, after making its second annual interest payment. Burleigh then reinvested the proceeds in a bond selling at its face value of $1,000, with three years to maturity and a 7% coupon rate. What was Burleigh's actual yield-to-maturity over the five-year period?

9. Nellie Fox acquired at par a bond for $1,000 that offered a 9% coupon rate. At the time of purchase, the bond had four years to maturity. Assuming annual interest payments, calculate Nellie's actual yield-to-maturity if all the interest payments were reinvested in an investment earning 15% per year. What would Nellie's actual yield-to-maturity be if all interest payments were spent immediately on receipt?

10. What is the primary purpose of bond ratings? Given the importance attached to bond ratings by bond investors, why don't common stock investors focus on quality ratings of entire companies in making their investment decisions?

11. According to Lave Cross, "Agency ratings indicate *relative* levels of risk instead of *absolute* levels of risk." Explain the meaning of Lave's statement.

12. Based on the default premium model presented in the text, what is the fair value default premium for a bond with an expected yield-to-maturity of 8.5%, a 10% annual default probability, and an expected loss as a percent of market value of 60%?

13. Corporate default seems to be an event specific to an individual company. Yet despite the apparent diversifiable nature of corporate default (meaning that rela-

tively few bonds would default in a well-diversified portfolio), the bond market systematically adds default premiums when valuing corporate bonds. Explain why.

14. Examine Equation (21.6), and explain the rationale underlying the observed relationship (positive or negative) between each of the variables and the yield spread.

15. Urban Shocker has noted that the spread between the yield-to-maturity on BBB-rated bonds and that on AAA-rated bonds has recently widened considerably. Explain to Urban what this change might indicate.

Endnotes

1. The capitalization of income approach to valuation is also known as the discounted cash flow approach; its usefulness is discussed in Steven N. Kaplan and Richard S. Ruback, "The Valuation of Cash Flow Forecasts: An Empirical Analysis," *Journal of Finance,* 50, no. 4 (September 1995): 1059–1093.

2. While complex cash flows (such as a mix of positive and negative cash flows) can cause problems with the IRR and NPV methods, such problems do not occur when it is applied to either stocks or bonds. For a discussion of potential problems in other contexts, see Richard A. Brealey and Stewart C. Myers, *Principles of Corporate Finance* (New York: McGraw-Hill, 2000), Chapter 5.

3. A more accurate method of determining a bond's intrinsic value involves the use of spot rates. In the example, the investor might have determined that the relevant spot rates for the one-year, two-year, and three-year cash flows are 8.24%, 8.69%, and 9.03%, respectively. Using these values, the investor would find that the bond's intrinsic value equals $924.06 \{= [\$60/(1.0824)] + [\$60/(1.0869)^2] + [\$1,060/(1.0903)^3]\}$. Although V is the same in this example when either spot rates or y^* is used in the calculations, this result need not always be the case.

4. Many corporate bonds have, in addition to a call provision, a provision for a sinking fund where each year the issuer retires a prespecified portion of the original bond issue.

5. The investor may be able to avoid having his or her bonds called if either Treasury securities or discounted corporate bonds are purchased. However, because these securities have less "call risk," they are likely to have lower yields-to-maturity than similar bonds with higher levels of "call risk." Call risk is analyzed by Duane Stock in "Par Coupon Yield Curves for Callable Bonds and Amortizing Instruments," *Financial Practice and Education,* 6, no. 2 (Fall/Winter 1996): 49–59.

6. In this example, the **yield-to-call** (or, to be more specific, the yield-to-first-call) is 12.78%. That is, 12.78% is the discount rate that makes the present value of $120 received after each of the first four years and $1,170 (= $1,050 + $120) at the end of five years equal to the issue price of the bond, $1,000. Note that the

yield-to-call is greater than the bond's 12% promised yield-to-maturity at the time of issue.

7. Any gains from price appreciation realized by an investor in municipal bonds is taxable as ordinary income. For more on the taxation of fixed-income securities, see Chapter 5 or Clark Blackman II and Donald Laubacher, "The Basics of Amortizing Bond Premiums and Discounts," *AAII Journal,* 15, no. 3 (March 1993): 24–27.

8. Both rating agencies actually use finer gradations than those shown in the figures. Standard & Poor's sometimes places a + or a − next to its letter rating if a bond is in a category ranging from AA to CCC. Similarly, Moody's may place a 1, 2, or 3 next to its letter rating if a bond is in a category ranging from Aa down to B. Both agencies also rate certain types of short-term debt instruments. In addition, these agencies apply the same rating scale to the debt of more than 50 foreign governments; see Richard Cantor and Frank Packer, "Determinants and Impact of Sovereign Credit Ratings," *Journal of Fixed Income,* 6, no. 3 (December 1996): 76–91. Furthermore, preferred stock is also rated; see Lea V. Carty, "Moody's Preferred Stock Ratings and Dividend Impairment," *Journal of Fixed Income,* 5, no. 3 (December 1995): 95–103.

9. For a primer on high-yield bonds, see Stanley Block, "High-Yielding Securities: How Appropriate Are They?" *AAII Journal,* 11, no. 10 (November 1989): 7–11; and Glenn E. Atkins and Ben Branch, "A Qualitative Look at High-Yield Bond Analysis," *AAII Journal,* 13, no. 12 (October 1991): 12–15. Also see the articles cited in endnotes 13 and 14.

10. *Moody's Bond Record* (New York: Moody's Investors Service, June 1999): p. 3.

11. Ibid.

12. The model was developed by Gordon Pye in "Gauging the Default Premium," *Financial Analysts Journal,* 30, no. 1 (January/February 1974): 49–52.

13. Edward I. Altman, "Defaults and Returns on High-Yield Bonds through the First Half of 1991," *Financial Analysts Journal,* 47, no. 6 (November/December 1991): 67–77. For two of the first studies in this area, see W. Braddock Hickman, *Corporate Bond Quality and Investor Experience* (Princeton, NJ: Princeton University Press, 1958); and Harold G. Fraine and

Robert H. Mills, "The Effect of Defaults and Credit Deterioration on Yields of Corporate Bonds," *Journal of Finance,* 16, no. 3 (September 1961): 423–434. Although the Fraine and Mills work may seem dated, the "work holds up extremely well a generation or so after its publication," according to Martin S. Fridson, "Fraine's Neglected Findings: Was Hickman Wrong?" *Financial Analysts Journal,* 50, no. 5 (September/October 1994): 52.

14. Interestingly, one study found that investors who purchased the equity of B-rated firms at the time that they issued debt subsequently received relatively poor returns during the next three years, whereas those who bought the equity of Ba or higher rated firms received a normal return. See Jeff Jewell and Miles Livingston, "The Long-Run Performance of Firms Issuing Debt," *Journal of Fixed Income,* 7, no. 2 (September 1997): 61–66.

15. See Marshall E. Blume and Donald B. Keim, "Realized Returns and Defaults on Low-Grade Bonds: The Cohort of 1977 and 1978," *Financial Analysts Journal,* 47, no. 2 (March/April 1991): 63–72; Marshall E. Blume, Donald B. Keim, and Sandeep A. Patel, "Returns and Volatility of Low-Grade Bonds, 1977–1989," *Journal of Finance,* 46, no. 1 (March 1991): 49–74; and Marshall E. Blume and Donald B. Keim, "The Risk and Return of Low-Grade Bonds: An Update," *Financial Analysts Journal,* 47, no. 5 (September/October 1991). Similar observations have been made for municipal bonds. See George H. Hempel, *The Postwar Quality of State and Local Debt* (New York: Columbia University Press, 1971).

16. For an in-depth analysis of such bond portfolios, see Bradford Cornell and Kevin Greene, "The Investment Performance of Low-Grade Bond Funds," *Journal of Finance,* 46, no. 1 (March 1991): 29–48; and Bradford Cornell, "Liquidity and the Pricing of Low-Grade Bonds," *Financial Analysts Journal,* 48, no. 1 (January/February 1992): 63–67, 74.

17. In a study of preferred stocks, the price movements of low-rated preferred stocks were found to be related more to the price movements of common stocks than to the price movements of bonds; for high-rated preferred stocks, the findings were just the opposite. See John S. Bildersee, "Some Aspects of the Performance of Non-Convertible Preferred Stocks," *Journal of Finance,* 28, no. 5 (December 1973): 1187–1201.

18. Lawrence Fisher, "Determinants of Risk Premiums on Corporate Bonds," *Journal of Political Economy,* 67, no. 3 (June 1959): 217–237.

19. William H. Beaver, "Market Prices, Financial Ratios and the Prediction of Failure," *Journal of Accounting Research,* 6, no. 2 (Autumn 1968): 179–192.

20. Edward I. Altman, "Financial Ratios, Discriminant Analysis and the Prediction of Corporate Bankruptcy," *Journal of Finance,* 23, no. 4 (September 1968): 589–609.

21. Mark I. Weinstein, "The Effect of a Rating Change Announcement on Bond Price," *Journal of Financial Economics,* 5, no. 3 (December 1977): 329–350. Another study that examined rating change announcements that were "noncontaminated" by other news releases found a small but statistically significant upward movement in daily bond prices around upgrades; downgrades produced no significant movements. See John R. M. Hand, Robert W. Holthausen, and Richard W. Leftwich, "The Effect of Bond Rating Agency Announcements on Bond and Stock Prices," *Journal of Finance,* 47, no. 2 (June 1992): 733–752.

22. Gailen Hite and Arthur Warga, "The Effect of Bond-Rating Changes on Bond Price Performance," *Financial Analysts Journal,* 53, no. 3 (May/June 1997): 35–51. The authors looked at other rating change scenarios in addition to the two mentioned here.

CHAPTER 22

Bond Portfolio Management

The methods currently in use for managing bond portfolios can be divided into two general categories: passive and active. Methods in the passive category are based on the assumption that bond markets are semistrong-form efficient. That is, current bond prices are viewed as accurately reflecting all publicly available information and are thus felt to be priced fairly in the marketplace, providing a return commensurate with the risk involved. In addition to believing that individual bonds are not mispriced, passive investors believe that attempting to predict interest rates is, in general, futile. In summary, passive management rests on the belief that attempts at both security selection (that is, identifying mispriced bonds) and market timing (for example, buying long-term bonds when interest rates are predicted to fall and replacing them with short-term bonds when interest rates are predicted to rise) will be unsuccessful in providing the investor with above-average returns.

Active methods of bond portfolio management are based on the assumption that the bond market is not so efficient, thereby giving some investors the opportunity to earn above-average returns. That is, active management is based on the belief that the portfolio manager can either identify mispriced bonds or "time" the bond market by accurately predicting interest rates.

This chapter discusses these two general approaches to bond portfolio management. It begins by reviewing some of the findings regarding the efficiency of the bond market.

22.1 Bond Market Efficiency

In the assessment of bond market efficiency, only a few of the major studies will be mentioned. In general, their conclusion is that bond markets are highly, but not perfectly, semistrong-form efficient where bond prices tend to reflect almost all publicly available information. Not surprisingly, this impression is similar to the one obtained from studies of the efficiency of stock markets.

22.1.1 PRICE BEHAVIOR OF TREASURY BILLS

An early study of bond market efficiency focused on the price behavior of Treasury bills. In particular, the prices of Treasury bills were analyzed on a weekly basis for 796 weeks. The study found that knowledge of past price changes in Treasury bills was of little use in predicting how they would change in the future. Consequently, the results from this study are consistent with the notion that the market for Treasury bills is weak-form efficient.[1]

22.1.2 EXPERT PREDICTIONS OF INTEREST RATES

Bond market efficiency has also been studied by examining the accuracy of interest-rate predictions that have been made by experts. These people use a wide range of techniques and many different sources of information. It is reasonable to assume that their information is publicly available, so such studies can be viewed as tests of semistrong-form efficiency.

One way these tests have been conducted involves the building of statistical models based on what the experts say about how interest rates should be predicted. Once these models have been constructed, their predictive accuracy can be evaluated. In one study six models were constructed, and their one-month-ahead predictions were tested during a two-year period. Consistent with the notion of efficient markets, it was found that all six models were less accurate than a simple model of "no change"—that is, a model that forecasts no change from the current level of interest rates.[2]

Another way these tests were conducted involves comparing a set of explicit predictions with what subsequently occurred. One source of such predictions is the quarterly survey of interest-rate expectations that appears in the *Goldsmith-Nagan Bond and Money Market Newsletter,* published by Goldsmith-Nagan, Inc. Specifically, this survey reports the predictions made by roughly 50 "money market professionals" regarding three-month-ahead and six-month-ahead levels of 10 interest rates. In one study, 14 sets of quarterly predictions were compared with those of a no-change model.[3] Interestingly, the professionals seemed to forecast better than the no-change model for short-term interest rates (such as forecasting what the three-month Treasury bill rate will be three months in the future) but did worse than the no-change model for longer term interest rates (such as forecasting what the intermediate-term Treasury note rate will be three months in the future).

A subsequent study examined the 39 Goldsmith-Nagan predictions of three-month Treasury bill rates six months in the future.[4] These predictions were compared with those of three "simple" models, the first one being the no-change model. The second model was based on the liquidity preference theory of the term structure of interest rates (discussed in Chapter 20). According to this theory, the forward rate implicit in current market rates should be equal to the expected future interest rate plus a liquidity premium. Thus, a forecast of the expected future rate can be obtained by subtracting an estimate of the liquidity premium from the forward rate. The third model was what statisticians refer to as an *autoregressive model,* in which a forecast of the future Treasury bill rate was formed from the current Treasury bill rate as well as what the Treasury bill rate was one, two, three, and six quarters ago. The study found that the professionals were more accurate than both the no-change model and the liquidity premium model, but less accurate than the autoregressive model.

Another study evaluated the six-month-ahead predictions of three-month Treasury bill rates that were made by nine economists and reported semiannually in *The Wall Street Journal.* Evaluation of the forecasts showed that the no-change model was the most accurate.[5] An update of this study examined six-month-ahead predictions of three-month Treasury bill and 30-year Treasury bond yields made by economists in surveys conducted by *The Wall Street Journal.* Yields moved in the opposite direction of the economists' consensus prediction 53% of the time for the Treasury bill forecasts and 67% of the time for the Treasury bond forecasts. Furthermore, a no-change model produced smaller forecast errors. Last, no evidence was uncovered that the best forecasters in one period were able to demonstrate superior forecasting ability in the next period.[6]

In summary, it appears from this evidence that the no-change model sometimes provides the most accurate forecasts of future interest rates, whereas at other times the experts are more accurate. On balance, a reasonable interpretation of these results is that the bond market is nearly semistrong-form efficient. Although the bond market may not be perfectly efficient, the evidence clearly suggests that it is hard to forecast interest rates consistently with greater accuracy than a no-change model.[7]

22.1.3 PRICE REACTION TO BOND RATING CHANGES

A different test of market efficiency concerned the reaction of bond prices to rating changes. If ratings are based on public information, then any rating change will follow the release of such information. This fact suggests that in a semistrong-form efficient market, a bond's price will react to the release of the public information rather than to the subsequent announcement of the rating change. Thus, an announcement of a rating change should not trigger a subsequent adjustment in the associated bond's price.

In a study that examined 100 rating changes, no significant changes in bond prices were detected in the period from 6 months before through 6 months after the announcement of the change. However, a significant change was observed in the period from 18 months through 7 months before the announcement. Specifically, rating increases were preceded by price increases, and rating decreases were preceded by price decreases.[8]

In a second study that looked at downgrades to a below-investment-grade rating, it was found that there was a large abnormal downward price movement in the bond during the 6-month period before the downgrade. Furthermore, there was a smaller but still significant abnormal downward price movement during the month of the downgrade.[9] However, it is unknown whether this downward price movement occurred during the days before or after the day of the downgrade.

22.1.4 MONEY SUPPLY ANNOUNCEMENTS

Every week, generally on Thursdays, the Federal Reserve Board announces the current size of the money supply in the economy. It is known that interest rates are related to, among other things, the availability of credit, and that the money supply affects this availability. As a result, if the money supply figures are surprisingly high or low, then the announcement should trigger adjustments in the levels of various interest rates.[10] Such adjustments should take place rapidly in a semistrong-form efficient market. Studies indicate that such adjustments are rapid, generally taking place within a day after the announcement, and are thus consistent with the notion of a semistrong-form efficient market.[11]

22.1.5 PERFORMANCE OF BOND PORTFOLIO MANAGERS

Perhaps the best test of bond market efficiency is to examine the performance record of those professionals who manage bond portfolios. After all, if these people who make their living by investing other people's money in fixed-income securities cannot, on average, generate abnormal returns for their clients, then it would be difficult to argue that these markets are not highly efficient. One study that examined the performance of 41 bond funds found that, depending on the model of performance used, between 27 (66%) and 33 (80%) of the funds had negative abnormal returns with the underperformance ranging from −.023% to −.069% per month (or −.3% to −.8% per year).

Despite the evidence that the average fund was not able to generate positive abnormal returns, it is still possible that some of the managers were consistently able to do so. One way of testing their investment skills is to examine whether the top performing funds in one time period continued as top performers in the next period. More specifically, the managers were ranked based on their funds' performance during a five-year period and then ranked again based on their performance during the next five-year period. If the top managers had a special talent for "beating the market," then these rankings would have been highly correlated. However, depending on the model used to generate the rankings, the correlations ranged from .234 to −.111; none were statistically significantly different from zero.

The issue of bond market efficiency was slightly clouded in a study that analyzed 223 bond funds. The average fund had negative abnormal returns of from −.077% to −.107% per month (or −.9% to −1.3% per year), a finding that is supportive of market efficiency. However, the performance rankings from a three-year period had a significantly positive correlation ranging from .212 to .451 with the rankings for the following two years, suggesting a persistence in relative performance.[12]

22.1.6 SUMMARY

The evidence on the efficiency of the bond market is consistent with the notion that it is highly, but not perfectly, semistrong-form efficient.[13] Statistical tests of past prices of Treasury bills suggest that the bond market is efficient. It appears that corporate bonds reflect the information leading to a rating change in a timely fashion, and that interest rates change rapidly when there is a surprise in the announced size of the money supply—observations that are also consistent with the notion of efficiency. Furthermore, professional bond portfolio managers appear, on average, to be unable to consistently generate abnormally high returns.

However, some evidence suggests that certain professionals occasionally forecast interest rates accurately, and some bond portfolio managers consistently rank above average in terms of performance relative to their peers. With this in mind, one should not be surprised to find that some bond managers follow a passive approach to investing whereas others have decided to be more active in their approach. These two approaches are presented next, beginning with a discussion of some bond pricing theorems. In turn, these theorems will be related to a concept known as duration, which is the basis for one method of passively managing a bond portfolio.

22.2 Bond Pricing Theorems

Bond pricing theorems deal with how bond prices move in response to changes in the bonds' yields-to-maturity. Before the theorems are presented, a brief review of some terms associated with bonds is provided.

The typical bond is characterized by a promise to pay the investor two types of cash flows. The first involves the payment of a fixed dollar amount periodically (usually every six months), with the last payment being on a stated date. The second type of cash flow involves the payment of a lump sum on this stated date. The periodic payments are known as **coupon payments,** and the lump-sum payment is known as the bond's principal (or par value or face value). A bond's **coupon rate** is calculated by taking the dollar amount of the coupon payments a bondholder will receive over the course of a year and dividing this total by the par value of the bond. Finally, the amount of time left until the last promised payment is made is known as the bond's term-to-maturity, and the discount rate that makes the present value of all the cash flows equal to the market price of the bond is known as the bond's yield-to-maturity (or, simply, yield).

Note that if a bond has a market price that is equal to its par value, then its yield-to-maturity equals its coupon rate. However, if the market price is less than par value

coupon payments
coupon rate

(a situation in which the bond is said to be selling at a *discount*), then the bond has a yield-to-maturity that is greater than the coupon rate. Conversely, if the market price is greater than par value (a situation in which the bond is said to be selling at a *premium*), then the bond has a yield-to-maturity that is less than the coupon rate. In short,

Discount:	Market price < Par value	Yield-to-maturity > Coupon rate
Par:	Market price = Par value	Yield-to-maturity = Coupon rate
Premium:	Market price > Par value	Yield-to-maturity < Coupon rate

Five theorems that deal with bond pricing have been derived on the basis of these relations.[14] For ease of exposition, it is assumed that there is one coupon payment per year (that is, coupon payments are made every 12 months), although the theorems hold in the more common case of two coupon payments per year. The theorems are as follows:

1. *If a bond's market price increases, then its yield must decrease; conversely, if a bond's market price decreases, then its yield must increase.*

    As an example, consider bond *A,* which has a life of five years, a par value of $1,000, and pays coupons annually of $80. Its yield is 8% because it is currently selling for $1,000. However, if its price increases to $1,100, then its yield will fall to 5.76%. Conversely, if its price falls to $900, then its yield will rise to 10.68%.

2. *If a bond's yield does not change during its life, then the size of its discount or premium will decrease as its life gets shorter.*

    This relation can be seen by examining Figure 22.1. Note how the price of a bond that is selling at either a premium or a discount today will converge over time to its par value. Ultimately the premium or discount will completely disappear at the maturity date.

    As an example, consider bond *B,* which has a life of five years, a par value of $1,000, and pays coupons annually of $60. Its current market price is $883.31, indicating that it has a yield of 9%. After one year, if it still has a yield of 9%, it will sell for $902.81. Thus, its discount has decreased from $116.69 (= $1,000 − $883.31) to $97.19 (= $1,000 − $902.81), for a change of $19.50 (= $116.69 − $97.19).

    Another interpretation of this theorem is that if two bonds have the same coupon rate, par value, and yield, then the one with the shorter life will sell for a smaller discount or premium. Consider two bonds, one with a life of five years and the other with a life of four years. Both bonds have a par value of $1,000, pay annual coupons of $60, and yield 9%. In this situation, the bond with a five-year life has a discount of $116.69, whereas the bond with a four-year life has a smaller discount of $97.19.

3. *If a bond's yield does not change during its life, then the size of its discount or premium will decrease at an increasing rate as its life gets shorter.*

    Figure 22.1 also illustrates this theorem. Note how the size of the premium or discount does not change much as time passes from today to tomorrow. In contrast, the size changes more notably as time passes just before the maturity date.

    As an example, consider bond *B* again. After two years, if it still has a yield of 9%, then it will sell for $924.06. Thus, its discount decreased to $75.94 (= $1,000 − $924.06), so the amount of the change in the discount from five years to four years is $19.50 (= $116.69 − $97.19). However, the amount of the change from four years to three years is larger, going from $97.19 to $75.94 for a dollar change of $21.25.

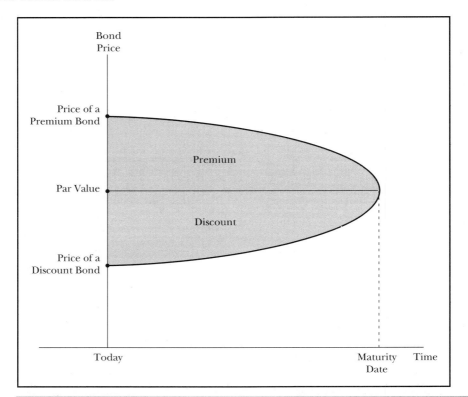

FIGURE 22.1   Changes in a Bond's Price over Its Life*

*Assuming that the bond's yield-to-maturity remains constant through time.

4. *A decrease in a bond's yield will raise the bond's price by an amount that is greater in size than the corresponding fall in the bond's price that would occur if there were an equal-sized increase in the bond's yield.*

   As an example, consider bond *C*, which has a life of five years and a coupon rate of 7%. Because it is currently selling at its par value of $1,000, its yield is 7%. If its yield rises by 1% to 8%, then it will sell for $960.07, a change of $39.93. Alternatively, if its yield falls by 1% to 6%, then it will sell for $1,042.12, a change of $42.12, which is of greater magnitude than the $39.93 associated with the 1% rise in the bond's yield.

5. *The percentage change in a bond's price associated with a change in its yield will be smaller if its coupon rate is higher.* (Note: This theorem assumes that there is at least one coupon payment besides the one at maturity remaining to be paid. It does not apply to bonds with a life of one year or to bonds that have no maturity date, known as consols or perpetuities.)

   As an example, compare bond *D* with bond *C*. Bond *D* has a coupon rate of 9%, which is 2% larger than *C*'s. However, bond *D* has the same life (five years) and yield (7%) as *C*. Thus, *D*'s current market price is $1,082.00. If the yield on both *C* and *D* increases to 8%, then their prices will be $960.07 and $1,039.93, respectively. This represents a decrease in the price of *C* of $39.93 (= $1,000 − $960.07), or 3.993% (= $39.93/$1,000). For *D*, the decrease in price is $42.07 (= $1,082 − $1,039.93), or

3.889% (= \$42.07/\$1,082). Because D had the higher coupon rate, it has the smaller percentage change in price.

Bond analysts must understand these properties of bond prices thoroughly because they are valuable in forecasting how bond prices respond to changes in interest rates.

22.3 Convexity

convexity

The first and fourth bond pricing theorems have led to the concept in bond valuation known as **convexity.** Consider what happens to the price of a bond if its yield increases or decreases. According to Theorem 1, bond prices and yields are inversely related. However, this relationship is not linear, according to Theorem 4. The amount of the increase in a bond's price associated with a given decrease in its yield is greater than the drop in the bond's price for a similar-sized increase in the bond's yield.

This relationship can be seen by examining Figure 22.2. The price and the current yield-to-maturity for the bond are denoted by P and y, respectively. Consider what would happen to the bond's price if the yield increased or decreased by a fixed amount (for example, 1%), denoted y^+ and y^-. The associated bond prices are denoted by P^- and P^+, respectively.

Two observations can be made by examining this figure. First, an increase in the yield to y^+ is associated with a drop in the bond's price to P^-, and a decrease in the yield to y^- is associated with a rise in the bond's price to P^+. This movement is in accord with the first bond theorem. (Hence the symbols + and − are paired inversely so

FIGURE 22.2 Bond Convexity

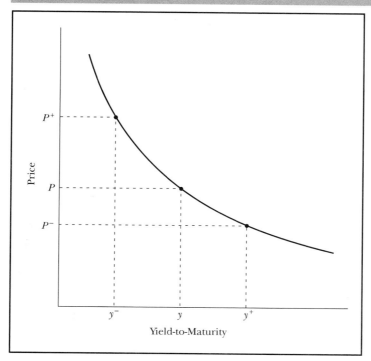

that, for example, y^+ is associated with P^-.) Second, the amount of the rise in the bond's price $(P^+ - P)$ is greater than the amount of the drop in the bond's price $(P - P^-)$. This relation is in accord with the fourth bond theorem.

The curved line in the figure shows that the relationship between bond prices and yields is convex because it opens upward. Accordingly, the relationship is frequently referred to as convexity. Although this relationship is true for standard types of bonds, the degree of curvature (or convexity) is not the same for all bonds. Instead, it depends on, among other things, the size of the coupon payments, the life of the bond, and its current market price. Furthermore, if the bond has a call provision, then the convexity disappears at sufficiently low yields because such a drop in yields triggers a call, limiting the rise in the bond's price to its call price.

22.4   Duration

duration

Duration is a measure of the "average maturity" of the stream of payments associated with a bond. More specifically, it is a weighted average of the lengths of time until the remaining payments are made. Consider, for example, a bond with annual coupon payments of $80, a remaining life of three years, and a par value of $1,000. Because it has a current market price of $950.25, it has a yield-to-maturity of 10.00%. As shown in Table 22.1, its duration is 2.78 years. Note that this is calculated by taking the present value of the cash flows, multiplying each one by the respective amount of time until it is received, summing the resulting figures, and then dividing this sum ($2,639.17) by the market price of the bond ($950.25).

22.4.1   THE FORMULA

The formula for calculating a bond's duration D is

$$D = \frac{\sum_{t=1}^{T} PV(C_t) \times t}{P_0} \tag{22.1}$$

where $PV(C_t)$ denotes the present value of the cash flow to be received at time t; P_0 denotes the current market price of the bond; and T denotes the bond's remaining life. Sometimes D is referred to as *Macaulay duration,* after its originator.[15] Although $PV(C_t)$ can be calculated using the appropriate current spot rates as the discount rates, it is common practice to use the bond's yield-to-maturity (which is used hereafter).

Why is duration the "average maturity of the stream of payments associated with a bond"? The reason can be seen by realizing that the current market price of the bond,

TABLE 22.1 Calculation of Duration

Time until Receipt of Cash Flow	Amount of Cash Flow	Discount Factor	Present Value of Cash Flow	Present Value of Cash Flow × Time
1	$ 80	.9091	$ 72.73	$ 72.73
2	80	.8264	66.12	132.23
3	1,080	.7513	811.40	2,434.21
			$950.25	$2,639.17

Duration = $2,639.17/$950.25 = 2.78 years

P_0, equals the sum of the present values of the cash flows, $PV(C_t)$, where the discount rate is the bond's yield-to-maturity. That is,

$$P_0 = \sum_{t=1}^{T} PV(C_t) \qquad (22.2)$$

Thus, there is an equivalent method for calculating a bond's duration that can be seen by rewriting Equation (22.1) in a slightly different manner:

$$D = \sum_{t=1}^{T} \left[\frac{PV(C_t)}{P_0} \times t \right] \qquad (22.3)$$

First, the present value of each cash flow, $PV(C_t)$, is expressed as a proportion of the market price P_0. Second, these proportions are multiplied by the respective amount of time until the cash flows are received. Third, these figures are summed, with the sum being equal to the bond's duration.

In the example shown in Table 22.1, note that .07653 (= \$72.73/\$950.25) of the bond's market price will be received in one year; .06958 (= \$66.12/\$950.25) will be received in two years; and .85388 (= \$811.40/\$950.25) will be received in three years. These proportions sum to 1, so they can be interpreted as weights in calculating a weighted average. Thus, the average maturity of the payments associated with a bond is calculated by multiplying each weight by the respective amount of time until the corresponding cash flow is received and then summing the products: $(1 \times .07653) + (2 \times .06958) + (3 \times .85388) = 2.78$ years.

Note that a zero-coupon bond has a duration equal to its remaining life, T, because there is only one cash flow associated with such a bond. That is, because $P_0 = PV(C_T)$ for such bonds, Equation (22.3) reduces to:

$$D = \frac{PV(C_T)}{P_0} \times T$$
$$= 1 \times T$$
$$= T$$

For any coupon-bearing bond, duration will always be less than the amount of time to its maturity date T. Again, examination of Equation (22.3) indicates why. Because the largest value that t can have is T, and each value of t is multiplied by a weight equal to $PV(C_t)/P_0$, it follows that D must be less than T.

22.4.2   RELATIONSHIP TO BOND PRICE CHANGES

One implication of Theorem 5 is that bonds having the same maturity date but different coupon sizes may react differently to a given change in interest rates. That is, the prices of these bonds may adjust by notably different amounts when there is a given change in interest rates. However, bonds with the same duration will react similarly because duration considers the effect a change in interest rates has on the value of not only a bond's maturity date cash flow but also its coupon payments. Thus, duration can be thought of as a measure of the *price risk* of a bond. Specifically, the percentage change in a bond's price is related to its duration as follows:

Percentage change in price $\cong -D \times$ Percentage change in (1 + the bond's yield)   **(22.4a)**

where the symbol $\cong$ means "is approximately equal to." This formula implies that when the yields of two bonds having the same duration change by the same percentage, then the prices of the two bonds will change by approximately equal percentages. Equation (22.4a) can also be written as:

$$\frac{\Delta P}{P} \cong -D\left(\frac{\Delta y}{1 + y}\right) \tag{22.4b}$$

where ΔP denotes the change in the bond's price, P is the bond's initial price, Δy is the change in the bond's yield-to-maturity, and y is the bond's initial yield-to-maturity.

As an example, consider a bond that is currently selling for $1,000 with a yield-to-maturity of 8%. If the bond has a duration of 10 years, then by how much will the bond's price change if its yield increases to 9%? Equation (22.4b) shows that $\Delta y = 9\% - 8\% = 1\% = .01$, so that $\Delta y/(1 + y) = .01/1.08 = .00926 = .926\%$ and $-D[\Delta y/(1 + y)] = -10[.926\%] = -9.26\%$. Hence the one-percentage-point rise in the yield causes approximately a 9.26% drop in the bond's price to $907.40 [= $1,000 − (.0926 × $1,000)].

Equation (22.4b) can be rewritten by rearranging terms, resulting in

$$\frac{\Delta P}{P} \cong -\left[\frac{D}{(1 + y)}\right] \times \Delta y \tag{22.4c}$$

modified duration The quantity $D/(1 + y)$ is sometimes referred to as a bond's **modified duration** (D_m); it reflects the bond's percentage change in price for a one percent change in its yield, and hence is a better measure of the price risk of a bond than Macaulay's duration, D. Thus, the link between these two measures of duration is

$$D_m = \frac{D}{(1 + y)} \tag{22.4d}$$

As an illustration of why some people prefer D_m over D as the measure of a bond's price risk, consider the previous example. Because the bond's duration is 10 years, its modified duration is $10/(1 + .08) = 9.26$ years. Thus, a 1% change in yields causes the bond's price to change in an opposite direction [note the minus sign in Equation (22.4c)] by approximately 9.26%, as stated earlier:

$$+.01 \times (-9.26) = -.0926$$

or, equivalently,

$$+1\% \times (-9.26) = -9.26\%$$

An important assumption has been made in presenting Equations (22.4a) through (22.4d). These equations reflect the price risk of a bond only when the yield curve is horizontal and any shifts up or down in it are parallel. Hence, in the example the current yield curve is assumed initially to be flat at 8%, and then to shift either up to 9% or down to 7% so that it remains horizontal afterward. Yield curves are seldom horizontal and infrequently shift in a parallel manner, so these equations are approximations. There are other reasons they are approximations, as is discussed next.

22.4.3   RELATIONSHIP BETWEEN CONVEXITY AND DURATION

At this point it is useful to consider how the concepts of convexity and duration are related to each other. After all, both have something to do with measuring the association of the change in a bond's price with a change in the bond's yield-to-maturity. Figure 22.3 shows the nature of the relationship. Like Figure 22.2, this figure represents a bond that is currently selling for P and has a yield-to-maturity of y. Note the straight line that is tangent to the curve at the point associated with the current price and yield.

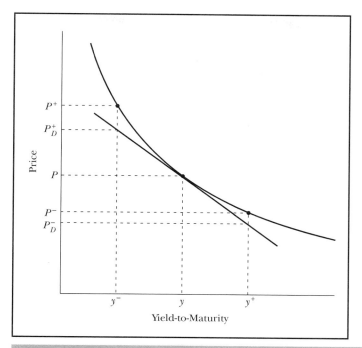

FIGURE 22.3 Bond Convexity and Duration

If the bond's yield increases to y^+, then the associated price of the bond will fall to P^-. Conversely, if the bond's yield decreases to y^-, then the associated price of the bond will rise to P^+. However, Equation (22.4b) shows that if the yield decreases to y^-, the estimated price will be P_D^+, and if the yield increases to y^+ the estimated price will be P_D^-. The reason is that the relationship between the bond's price, yield, and duration, as mentioned earlier, is not exact. Instead, it is an approximation that assumes the percentage change in the bond's price is a linear function of its duration. Hence the equation approximates the new price in a linear fashion represented by the straight line and leading to an error that is a consequence of convexity. [In the example, the sizes of the respective errors are $(P^- - P_D^-)$ and $(P^+ - P_D^+)$.] That is, because the relationship between yield changes and bond price changes is convex, not linear, Equation (22.4b) will underestimate the new price associated with either an increase or a decrease in the bond's yield.[16] However, for small changes in yields the error is relatively small, and thus, as an approximation, Equation (22.4b) works reasonably well. Its usefulness can be seen by observing in Figure 22.3 that the size of the pricing error becomes smaller as the size of the yield change gets smaller. (Note that the distance between the linear approximating line and the convex curve will be smaller for smaller changes in yields from y.)

22.4.4   CHANGES IN THE TERM STRUCTURE

As mentioned earlier, when yields change, most bond prices also change, but some react more than others. Even bonds with the same maturity date can react differently to a given change in yields. However, it was shown in Equations (22.4a) and (22.4b) that the percentage change in a bond's price is related to its duration. Hence the prices of two bonds that have the same duration will react similarly to a given change in yields.

For example, the bond shown in Table 22.1 has a duration of 2.78 and a yield of 10%. If its yield changes to 11%, then the percentage change in (1 + the bond's yield) is .91% $[= (1.11 - 1.10)/1.10]$. Thus, its price should change by approximately -2.53% $(= -2.78 \times .91\%)$. With a discount rate of 11%, its price can be calculated to equal $926.69, for an actual price change of $-\$23.56 (= \$926.69 - \$950.25)$ and a percentage change of $-2.48\% (= -\$23.56/\$950.25)$. Any other bond having a duration of 2.78 years will experience a similar price change if it has a similar percentage change in its yield. Equivalently, any other bond having a modified duration of 2.53 $(= 2.78/1.10)$ will experience a similar price change for a similar change in its yield.

Consider a bond with a maturity of 4 years that also has a duration of 2.78 years. When there is a shift in interest rates, and the yields on the 3-year and 4-year bonds change by the same amount, their prices will change similarly. For example, if the yield on the 4-year bond goes from 10.8% to 11.81% at the same time the yield on the 3-year bond is going from 10% to 11%, then the percentage change in the present value of the 4-year bond will be approximately -2.53% $[= -2.78 \times (1.1181 - 1.108)/1.108 = -2.78 \times .91\%]$, which is the same percentage as the 3-year bond. Here the difference in the two bonds' modified durations $(2.53 = 2.78/1.10$ for the 3-year bond; $2.51 = 2.78/1.108$ for the 4-year bond) is exactly offset by the different changes in yield (1% for the 3-year bond; 1.01% for the 4-year bond).

What if the "percentage change in (1 + the bond's yield)" is different? That is, what happens if the term structure shifts so that "the percentage change in (1 + the bond's yield)" is not the same for all bonds? Perhaps when the 3-year bond goes from a yield of 10% to a yield of 11% [a percentage change of .91% $= (1.11 - 1.10)/1.10$], the 4-year bond will go from a yield of 10.8% to a yield of 11.5% [a percentage change of .63% $= (1.115 - 1.108)/1.108$]. In this case the percentage change in price for the 4-year bond will be approximately -1.75% $[= -2.78 \times (1.115 - 1.108)/1.108]$, which is a smaller change than the -2.53% associated with the 3-year bond. Accordingly, even though the two bonds have the same duration or modified duration, it does not automatically follow that their prices will react identically to *any* change in the yield curve because the associated yield changes can be different for two bonds having the same duration.

22.5   Immunization

immunization

The introduction of the concept of duration led to the development of the technique of bond portfolio management known as **immunization.** This technique purportedly allows a bond portfolio manager to be relatively certain of meeting a given promised stream of cash outflows. Thus, once the portfolio has been formed, it is "immunized" from any adverse effects associated with future changes in interest rates.

22.5.1   HOW IMMUNIZATION IS ACCOMPLISHED

Immunization is accomplished simply by calculating the duration of the promised outflows and then investing in a portfolio of bonds that has an identical duration. In doing so, this technique takes advantage of the observation that *the duration of a portfolio of bonds is equal to the weighted average of the durations of the individual bonds in the portfolio.* For example, if a portfolio has one-third of its funds invested in bonds having a duration of six years and two-thirds in bonds having a duration of three years, then the portfolio itself has a duration of four years $[= (\frac{1}{3} \times 6) + (\frac{2}{3} \times 3)]$.

Consider a simple situation in which a portfolio manager has one and only one cash outflow to make from a portfolio—an amount equal to $1,000,000, which is to be paid in two years.[17] Because there is only one cash outflow, its duration is simply two years. Now the bond portfolio manager is considering investing in two different bond issues. The first issue is the one shown in Table 22.1, with bonds that have a maturity of three years. The second issue involves a set of bonds that mature in one year, providing the holder of each bond with a single payment of $1,070 (consisting of a single coupon payment of $70 and a par value of $1,000). Because these bonds are currently selling for $972.73, their yield-to-maturity is 10%.

Consider the choices available to the portfolio manager. All of the portfolio's funds could be invested in the one-year bonds, with the intention of reinvesting the proceeds from the maturing bonds one year from now in another one-year issue. However, doing so would involve risks. If interest rates declined during the next year, then the funds from the maturing one-year bonds would have to be reinvested at a lower rate than the currently available 10%. Thus, the portfolio manager faces reinvestment-rate risk because of the possibility that the funds one year from now might have to be reinvested at a lower rate.[18]

A second alternative would be for the portfolio manager to invest all of the funds in the three-year issue. However, this choice also entails risks. The three-year bonds will have to be sold after two years in order to come up with the $1,000,000. The risk is that interest rates will have risen before then, meaning that bond prices, in general, will have fallen and the bonds will not have a selling price that is at least $1,000,000. Thus, the portfolio manager faces interest-rate risk with this strategy.

One proposed solution is to invest part of the portfolio's funds in the one-year bonds and the rest in the three-year bonds. How much should be placed in each issue? If immunization is used, the solution can be found by solving simultaneously a set of two equations involving two unknowns:

$$W_1 + W_3 = 1 \tag{22.5}$$

$$(W_1 \times 1) + (W_3 \times 2.78) = 2 \tag{22.6}$$

Here W_1 and W_3 denote the weights (or proportions) of the portfolio's funds that are to be invested in the bonds with maturities of one and three years, respectively. Note that Equation (22.5) states that the sum of the weights must equal 1, whereas Equation (22.6) states that the weighted average of the durations of the bonds in the portfolio must equal the duration of the cash outflow, which is two years.

The solution to these two equations is easily found. First, Equation (22.5) is rewritten as

$$W_1 = 1 - W_3 \tag{22.7}$$

Then $1 - W_3$ is substituted for W_1 in Equation (22.6), resulting in

$$[(1 - W_3) \times 1] + (W_3 \times 2.78) = 2 \tag{22.8}$$

Because this is one equation with one unknown, W_3, it can be solved easily. Doing so results in $W_3 = .5618$. Inserting this value into Equation (22.7) indicates that $W_1 = .4382$. Thus, the portfolio manager should put 43.82% of the portfolio's funds in the one-year bonds and 56.18% in the three-year bonds.

In this case, the portfolio manager would need $826,446 $[= \$1,000,000/(1.10)^2]$ in order to purchase bonds that would create a fully immunized portfolio. With this money, $362,149 $(= .4382 \times \$826,446)$ would be used to buy one-year bonds and $464,297 $(= .5618 \times \$826,446)$ would be used to buy three-year bonds. Because the current market prices of the one-year and three-year bonds are $972.73 and $950.25, respectively, this means that 372 one-year bonds (= \$362,149/\$972.73) and 489 three-year bonds (= \$464,297/\$950.25) would be purchased.

What does immunization accomplish? According to the theory, if yields rise, then the portfolio's losses caused by the selling of the three-year bonds at a discount after two years will be exactly offset by the gains from reinvesting the maturing one-year bonds (and first-year coupons on the three-year bonds) at the higher rate. Alternatively, if yields fall, then the loss from being able to reinvest the maturing one-year bonds (and first-year coupons on the three-year bonds) at a lower rate will be exactly offset by being able to sell the three-year bonds after two years at a premium. Thus the portfolio is *immunized* from the effect of any movements in interest rates in the future.

Table 22.2 shows what would happen to the portfolio. The second column shows what it would be worth at the end of two years if yields remained at 10% over the next two years. As can be seen, the value of the portfolio of one-year and three-year bonds would be approximately equal to the promised cash outflow of \$1,000,000. Alternatively, if yields fell to 9% or rose to 11% before one year had passed and remained at the new level, then the value of the portfolio would be slightly more than the needed \$1,000,000.[19]

22.5.2 PROBLEMS WITH IMMUNIZATION

The preceding section described what immunization purports to accomplish. What can cause it to work less than perfectly? Underlying this issue is another question: Why might duration fail to measure the interest-rate risk of a bond accurately? In terms of the example, what can cause the value of the portfolio to be less than \$1,000,000 at the end of two years?

Default and Call Risk

Immunization (and duration) are based on the assumptions that the bonds will not default and will not be called before maturity. That is, the bonds are assumed to be free from both call risk and default risk so that they will pay their promised cash flows in full and on time. Consequently, if a bond in the portfolio either enters into default or is called, the portfolio will not be immunized.

effective duration
Because of problems with the use of the traditional measure of duration in forming immunized portfolios, an alternative measure known as **effective duration** has been introduced.[20] Specifically, this measure is of use in evaluating any bond that contains

TABLE 22.2 Example of an Immunized Portfolio			
	Yield-to-Maturity at the End of One Year		
	9%	*10%*	*11%*
Value at $t = 2$ from reinvesting one-year bond proceeds			
[\$1,070 × 372.3 × (1 + y)] =	\$ 434,213	\$438,197	\$ 442,181
Value at $t = 2$ from reinvesting coupons received at $t = 1$ on three-year bonds			
[\$80 × 488.6 × (1 + y)] =	42,606	42,997	43,388
Coupons received at $t = 2$			
[\$80 × 488.6] =	39,088	39,088	39,088
Selling price at $t = 2$			
[\$1,080 × 488.6/(1 + y)] =	484,117	479,716	475,395
Aggregate portfolio value at $t = 2$	\$1,000,024	\$999,998	\$1,000,052

embedded options, meaning that either the bond issuer or the bondholder has the ability to cause the actual stream of cash payments to differ from that which would be received if the bond were paid off as promised over its entire life. Examples of embedded options include the option of the issuer to go into default or to prepay the bond before maturity by exercising the bond's call provision, and the option of bondholders of putable bonds to force the issuer to pay them off before maturity.

The formula for calculating a bond's effective duration D_e is

$$D_e = \frac{P^+ - P^-}{2P\Delta y} \tag{22.9}$$

where P^+ and P^- denote the bond's price if its yield decreases or increases by a given amount Δy (say, 1%), such as is shown in Figure 22.2. For example, consider a default-free bond with a 7% coupon paid annually that has 15 years left until maturity but can be called at any time for $1,050. The bond is currently selling for par, so if its yield increases by 1% to 8%, the bond's price will be $914.41 because no embedded options will be exercised. However, if its yield drops by 1% to 6%, the call option likely will be exercised so the value of the bond will be $1,050 instead of $1,097.12. Thus, the effective duration for this bond can be approximated using Equation (22.9) and will be $(\$1,050 - \$914.41)/(2 \times \$1,000 \times .01) = 6.8$ years, in contrast to the traditional duration and modified duration measures of 9.75 years and 9.11 years, respectively.

Multiple Nonparallel Shifts in a Nonhorizontal Yield Curve

Immunization (and duration) are also based on the assumption that the yield curve is horizontal and that any shifts in it will be parallel and will occur before any payments are received from the bonds that were purchased. In the example, the one-year and the three-year bonds had the same 10% yield-to-maturity at the start, and the shift of 1% in yields was assumed to be the same for both bond issues. Furthermore, this shift was assumed to occur sometime before one year had passed.

In reality, the yield curve will not be horizontal at the start, and shifts in it are not likely to be either parallel or restricted when they occur. Perhaps the one-year and the three-year bonds will have initial yields of 10% and 10.5%, respectively, with the yields on the one-year and three-year bonds falling by 1% and .8%, respectively, after one year. Indeed, there is evidence of greater volatility in yields of shorter term securities. If these kinds of shifts occur, then it is possible that the portfolio will not be immunized.[21]

cash matching

If the bond portfolio manager followed a special kind of immunization known as **cash matching,** then frequent nonparallel shifts in a nonhorizontal yield curve would have no adverse effect on the portfolio. The reason is that cash matching involves the purchase of bonds so that the cash received each period from the bonds is identical in size to the promised cash outflow for that period. Such a cash-matched portfolio of bonds is

dedicated portfolio

often referred to as a **dedicated portfolio.** Note that there is no need to reinvest any cash inflows with a dedicated portfolio, so there is no reinvestment-rate risk. Furthermore, because bonds do not have to be sold before maturity, there is also no interest-rate risk.

In the simplest situation with one promised cash outflow, the dedicated portfolio would consist of zero-coupon bonds, with each bond having a life corresponding to the date of the promised cash outflow. In the previous example, where there was a promised cash outflow of $1,000,000 after two years, this goal would be accomplished by purchasing the requisite number of zero-coupon bonds having a maturity of two years.

However, cash matching often is not so easily accomplished because the promised cash outflows may involve an uneven stream of payments for which no zero-coupon bonds exist. The growth in the stripped Treasury bond market has facilitated cash matching, but it still can be difficult and expensive to exactly match cash inflows with promised outflows.

Another potential way around the problem of nonhorizontal yield curves that experience nonparallel shifts is to use one of a variety of more complicated immunization models. These models involve various assumptions about the current shape of the yield curve and how it will shift in the future. No single model can be said to work best in all situations. Consequently, the bond portfolio manager should choose the model he or she perceives is most accurate. Interestingly, various studies have found that despite the inconsistency of its assumptions with actual movements in yields, simple immunization through duration matching works quite well in many cases. Thus, some researchers argue that the portfolio manager interested in immunization would be well advised to use the simple version.[22]

An implication is that regardless of the model used, the bond portfolio manager must recognize that a risk is incurred—the risk that the yield curve will shift in a way that does not correspond with the shift assumed by the model. For example, if the model presented here is used, then the bond portfolio faces the risk that the yield curve will not shift in a parallel manner. As a result, some people have argued that none of the immunization models are useful.[23] Others have argued that there are ways to use immunization in the presence of such risk, which has been called **stochastic process risk.**[24]

stochastic process risk

Rebalancing

Another problem with the use of immunization is the effect of the passage of time on the duration of the bonds held and on the duration of the promised cash outflows. As time passes and yields change, these durations can change at different rates such that the portfolio is no longer immunized. Consequently, the portfolio may need to be rebalanced fairly often.

Here *rebalancing* refers to selling some bonds currently held and replacing them with others so that afterward the duration of the portfolio matches the duration of the promised cash outflows. However, because rebalancing causes the portfolio manager to incur transaction costs, the manager might not want to rebalance whenever the durations do not match; the costs might outweigh the perceived gains from rebalancing. Ultimately, the bond portfolio manager has to decide how frequently to rebalance the portfolio considering the risk of being unbalanced and the transaction costs associated with rebalancing.

Many Candidates

Finally, there are usually many portfolios that have a duration of the requisite length. Which one should the bond portfolio manager choose? In the example, imagine that in addition to the one-year and three-year bonds, there is a zero-coupon bond with a life of four years (thus, its duration is also four years) that the manager is considering. The manager faces a choice of which portfolio to hold; there are many that have the requisite duration of two years. In addition to the one previously described that consisted of just one-year and three-year bonds, there is also one in which two-thirds and one-third of the portfolio's funds are invested in one-year bonds and four-year bonds, respectively. [Note that the duration of this portfolio is also two years: $\left(\frac{2}{3} \times 1\right) + \left(\frac{1}{3} \times 4\right) = 2$.] Furthermore, there are other candidate portfolios.

One possible solution is to choose the portfolio having the highest average yield-to-maturity (or, alternatively, the lowest cost). Here the yield of each issue is multiplied by the percentage of the portfolio's funds invested in that issue. Another possible solution is to choose the portfolio that most closely resembles a "bullet" portfolio because such a portfolio has less stochastic process risk than any other. Such a portfolio is one in which all the bonds have durations (or, alternatively, terms-to-maturity) that closely match the duration of the promised outflows. In the example, the portfolio consisting of just one-year and three-year bonds would be more focused than the one consisting of the one-year and four-year bonds.

22.6 Active Management

As mentioned earlier, active management of a bond portfolio is based on the belief that the bond market is not perfectly efficient. Such management can involve security selection where the portfolio manager tries to identify mispriced bonds. Alternatively, it can involve market timing where the portfolio manager tries to forecast general movements in interest rates. It is also possible for an active portfolio manager to be involved in both security selection and market timing. Although there are many methods of actively managing a bond portfolio, some general types of active management can be described.

22.6.1 HORIZON ANALYSIS

The return on a bond during any given holding period, sometimes referred to as the bond's *realized return* (or holding period return), depends on its price at the beginning of the period and its price at the end of the period, as well as on its coupon rate. Thus, the return on a bond during a one-year holding period depends on the yield structure at the beginning of the year and the yield structure at the end of the year because the price of the bond at those two points in time depends on those structures. It follows that possible subsequent changes to the beginning-of-period yield structure must be analyzed to estimate possible bond returns during a given holding period. Bond portfolio managers who believe that they are able to identify such changes will want to translate their beliefs into action.

horizon analysis One method, known as **horizon analysis,** involves both a single holding period for analysis and consideration of possible yield structures at the end of the period (that is, at the "horizon"). The possible returns for two bonds—one currently held and one candidate to replace it—are then analyzed; neither bond is assumed to default up to the horizon date. In the process of the analysis, the sensitivities of the returns to changes in key assumptions regarding yields are estimated, allowing at least a rough assessment of some of the relevant risks.

Horizon analysis is another way of implementing the capitalization-of-income method of valuation discussed in Chapter 21. By focusing on the estimated end-of-period price of a bond, it seeks to determine whether the current market price is relatively high or low. That is, for a given estimated end-of-period price, a bond will have a relatively high expected return if its current price is relatively low. Conversely, a bond will have a relatively low expected return if its current price is relatively high.

Figure 22.4 represents a page from a standard yield book for bonds with a 4% coupon. As indicated, a 4% bond with 10 years remaining to maturity that is currently priced at $67.48 (for ease of exposition, a par value of $100 is used here) will have a 9% promised annual yield-to-maturity (or 4.5% semiannually). Five years into the future, such a bond's term-to-maturity will have decreased, and the relevant promised yield-to-maturity will probably have changed. Thus, as time passes, the bond might follow a particular path "through the table" as indicated by the dashed line. If it does follow that path, then it will end up at a price of $83.78 at the *horizon* (5 years hence) with an 8% promised annual yield-to-maturity (or 4% semiannually).

During any holding period, a bond's return will typically be affected by both the passage of time and a change in yield. Horizon analysis explicitly breaks this return into those two parts: one owing solely to the passage of time, whereby the bond's price moves toward the par value to be paid at maturity (assuming no change in yield), and the other owing solely to a change in yield (assuming no passage of time). These effects are illustrated in Figure 22.4. The total price change from \$67.48 to \$83.78 (or \$16.30) is broken into a change from \$67.48 to \$80.22 (or \$12.74), followed by an instantaneous change from \$80.22 to \$83.78 (or \$3.56). The intermediate value of \$80.22 is the price the bond would have commanded at the horizon if its promised yield-to-maturity had remained unchanged at its initial level of 9%. The actual price of \$83.78 is that which the bond commands at its actual yield-to-maturity of 8%. In summary, the total price change can be broken into two parts, representing the two effects:

$$\text{Price change} = \text{Time effect} + \text{Yield change effect} \quad \textbf{(22.10)}$$

Thus far no account has been taken of the coupon payments to be received before the horizon date. In principle, one should consider all possible uses of such cash flows or at least analyze possible alternative yield structures during the period to determine likely reinvestment opportunities. In practice, this analysis is rarely done. Instead, a single reinvestment rate is assumed, and the future value of all coupon payments at the horizon date is determined by compounding each one using this rate.[25]

For example, if \$2 is received every six months (as in Figure 22.4), with the first payment occurring six months from now and the last payment occurring five years from now, and if each payment is reinvested at 4.25% per six months, then the value at the end of five years will be approximately \$24.29. Of this amount, \$20 can be considered interest (coupon payments of \$2 for ten six-month periods), with the remaining \$4.29 being "interest on interest."

FIGURE 22.4 The Effect of Time and Yield Change on a 4% Coupon Bond

		YEARS TO MATURITY							
	Yield to Maturity (%)	10 Yrs.	9 Yrs.	. . .	5 Yrs.		. . .	1 Yr.	0 Yrs.
	7.00	78.68	80.22		87.53			97.15	100.00
	7.50	75.68	77.39		85.63			96.69	100.00
y_H	(8.00)	72.82	74.68		(83.78)	P_H		96.23	100.00
	8.50	70.09	72.09		81.98	Yield Change Effect		95.77	100.00
		Actual Price Pattern Over Time							
y_0	(9.00)	P_0 (67.48)	69.60		(80.22)	P_A		95.32	100.00
		Time Effect							
	9.50	64.99	67.22		78.51			94.87	100.00
	10.00	62.61	64.92	. . .	76.83		. . .	94.42	100.00
	10.50	60.34	62.74		75.21			93.98	100.00
	11.00	58.17	60.64		73.62			93.54	100.00

Note: y_0 and P_0 denote the bond's annual yield-to-maturity and price at the beginning of the period; y_H and P_H denote the bond's annual yield-to-maturity and price at the horizon (the end of the period); P_A denotes the bond's price at the horizon if its annual yield had remained at $y_0 = 9\%$; yields are compounded semiannually.

Source: Martin L. Leibowitz, "Horizon Analysis for Managed Bond Portfolio," *Journal of Portfolio Management,* 1, no. 3 (Spring 1975): 26.

In summary, a bond's overall dollar return has four components; the time effect, the yield change effect, the coupons, and the interest from reinvesting the coupons. In the example, the overall dollar return is

Overall dollar return = Time effect + Yield change effect + Coupons + Interest on coupons

$$= (\$80.22 - \$67.48) + (\$83.78 - \$80.22) + \$20.00 + \$4.29$$

$$= \$12.74 + \$3.56 + \$20.00 + \$4.29$$

$$= \$40.59$$

This overall dollar return can be converted into an overall rate of return by dividing it by the market price of the bond at the beginning of the period, $67.48. Thus, the bond's overall rate of return consists of four components:

$$\text{Overall rate of return} = \frac{\$12.74}{\$67.48} + \frac{\$3.56}{\$67.48} + \frac{\$20.00}{\$67.48} + \frac{\$4.29}{\$67.48}$$

$$= .1888 + .0528 + .2964 + .0635$$

$$= .6015 \quad \text{or} \quad 60.15\%$$

The first term is caused by the passage of time; the second term is based on yield change; the third term is the coupon return; and the fourth term is from the reinvestment of the coupon payments.

Because the second term is uncertain, it is important to analyze it further. In the example, a change in yield from 9.0% to 8.0% results in a change in the market price from $80.22 to $83.78. If 8.0% was the expected yield at the horizon, then the expected overall rate of return is 60.15%, as indicated. Using different end-of-period yields enables one to calculate different overall rates of return. Estimates of the probabilities of these yields occurring provide a sense of the bond's risk. Indeed, it can now be seen why bond portfolio managers devote a great deal of attention to making predictions of future yields.

22.6.2   BOND SWAPS

Given a set of predictions about future bond yields, a portfolio manager can estimate holding-period returns over one or more horizons for one or more bonds. The goal of **bond swapping** is to actively manage a portfolio by exchanging bonds to take advantage of any superior ability to predict such yields.[26] In making a swap, the portfolio manager believes that an overpriced bond is being exchanged for an underpriced bond. Some swaps are based on the belief that the market will correct for its mispricing in a short period of time, whereas other types of swaps are based on a belief that corrections either will never take place or will take place, but over a long period of time.

There are several categories for classifying swaps, and the distinctions between the categories are often blurry. Nevertheless, many bond swaps can be placed in one of four general categories:

bond swapping

1. *Substitution swap.*   Ideally, this swap is an exchange of a bond for a perfect substitute or "twin" bond. The motivation here is temporary price advantage, presumably resulting from an imbalance in the relative supply and demand conditions in the marketplace.

substitution swap

2. *Intermarket spread swap.*   This swap involves a movement out of one market component and into another with the intention of exploiting a currently advantageous yield relationship. The idea is to benefit from a forecasted changing relationship between the two market components. Although such swaps will almost always have

intermarket spread swap

some sensitivity to the direction of the overall market, the idealized focus of this swap is the spread relationship itself.

rate anticipation
swap

pure yield pickup
swap

3. *Rate anticipation swap.* This swap is geared toward profiting from an anticipated movement in overall market rates.

4. *Pure yield pickup swap.* This swap is oriented toward yield improvements over the long term, with little heed for interim price movements in either the respective market components or the market as a whole.[27]

Consider a hypothetical portfolio manager who holds some of a 30-year AA utility bond issue that has a 7% coupon rate. These bonds are currently selling at par, so their yield-to-maturity is 7%. Now imagine that there is another 30-year AA utility bond issue with a 7% coupon rate that is available to the manager at a price that provides a yield-to-maturity of 7.10%. In a substitution swap the manager would exchange a given dollar amount of the currently held bonds for an equivalent dollar amount of the second bond issue, thereby picking up 10 basis points in yield.

Alternatively, the manager might note that there is a 10-year AA utility bond issue outstanding that carries a 6% coupon and a yield of 6%, because it is priced at par. In this case there is a 100-basis-point yield spread between the currently held 30-year bonds and the 10-year bonds. If the manager feels that this spread is too low, then an intermarket spread swap might be used; some of the 30-year bonds would be exchanged for an equivalent dollar amount of the 10-year bonds. Because the manager expects the spread to increase in the future, the yield on the 10-year bonds is expected to fall. It follows that the price on these bonds is expected to rise by an abnormal amount, resulting in an abnormally high holding-period return.

Another possibility is that the manager feels that yields in general are going to rise. In such a situation, the manager will recognize that the currently held portfolio is in a very risky position: Longer term bonds generally move downward further in price for a given rise in yields than do shorter term bonds because they generally have a longer duration. Accordingly, the manager might use a rate anticipation swap to exchange a given dollar amount of the 30-year bonds for an equivalent amount of short-term bonds.

Finally, the manager might not want to make any predictions about future yields or yield spreads. Instead, it might simply be noted that some 30-year AA industrial bonds are currently priced to yield 8%. In this case the manager might want to enter a pure yield pickup swap, in which some of the 7% utility bonds would be exchanged for an equivalent dollar amount of the 8% industrial bonds, the motivation being to earn the extra 100 basis points in yield from the industrials.

22.6.3 CONTINGENT IMMUNIZATION

contingent
immunization

One method of bond portfolio management that has both passive and active elements is **contingent immunization.** In the simplest form of contingent immunization, the portfolio is actively managed as long as favorable results are obtained. However, if unfavorable results occur, then the portfolio will be immunized immediately.

As an illustration, consider the earlier example in which the portfolio manager had to come up with $1,000,000 at the end of two years and the current yield curve was horizontal at 10%. The portfolio manager could immunize the portfolio by investing $826,446 in one-year and three-year bonds. However, the portfolio manager might convince the client that the portfolio should be *contingently* immunized with $841,680. In this case, the portfolio manager must be certain that the portfolio will be worth at least $1,000,000 at the end of the two years, with any excess going to the client and the manager being compensated accordingly. Equivalently, the portfolio manager must earn a minimum average return of 9% (note that $841,680 \times 1.09^2 = $1,000,000$) during the two years. Here, the client is willing to settle for a return as low as 9% but hopes that the portfolio manager will be able to exceed the 10% return that could have been locked in with an immunized portfolio.

In this situation the manager would proceed to actively manage the portfolio by engaging in either selectivity or timing, or both. Perhaps the arrangement with the client is that the status of the portfolio will be reviewed weekly, and yields that are currently available will be determined.

Consider how the review would be conducted after one year has elapsed and the yield curve is still horizontal but now is at 11%. First, it is noted that $900,901 ($= \$1,000,000/1.11$) is needed to immunize the portfolio at this point in time. Second, the market value of the current portfolio is determined to be $930,000. In this example, the arrangement between the client and the portfolio manager is that the manager can continue to actively manage the portfolio as long as it is worth at least $10,000 more than the amount needed for immunization. Because it is worth $930,000, an amount greater than $910,901 ($= \$900,901 + \$10,000$), the portfolio manager can continue being active. However, if the portfolio had been worth less than $910,901, then, according to the agreement, the manager would immediately immunize the portfolio.

22.6.4   RIDING THE YIELD CURVE

Riding the yield curve is a method of bond portfolio management that is sometimes used by portfolio managers who, having liquidity as a primary objective, invest in short-term fixed-income securities. One way of investing is to simply purchase these securities, hold them until they mature, and then reinvest the proceeds. An alternative is to ride the yield curve, provided certain conditions exist.

One condition is that the yield curve be upward sloping, indicating that longer-term securities have higher yields. Another condition is that the investor believe that the yield curve will remain upward sloping. Given these two conditions, the investor who is riding the yield curve will purchase securities that have a somewhat longer term-to-maturity than desired and then will sell them before they mature, thereby capturing some capital gains.

For example, consider an investor who prefers investing in 90-day Treasury bills. Currently such bills are selling for $98.25 per $100 of face value, indicating that they have a yield of 7.00% [note that $\$98.25 = \$100 - (7.00 \times 90/360)$]. However, 180-day Treasury bills are currently selling for $96.00, indicating that they have a higher yield of 8.00% [note that $\$96 = \$100 - (8.00 \times 180/360)$]. If, as this investor believes, the yield curve remains upward-sloping during the next three months, riding the yield curve will result in a higher return than simply buying and holding the 90-day Treasury bills.

If the investor buys and holds the 90-day Treasury bills, then the resulting annualized rate of return will be

$$\frac{\$100 - \$98.25}{\$98.25} \times \frac{365}{90} = 7.22\%$$

Alternatively, if the investor buys the 180-day Treasury bills and subsequently sells them after 90 days, then the expected selling price will be $98.25. (Note that this is the same as the current price of 90-day bills because it is assumed that the yield curve will not have changed after 90 days have elapsed.) In this case, the expected return is

$$\frac{\$98.25 - \$96.00}{\$96.00} \times \frac{365}{90} = 9.50\%$$

In comparison, the expected return from riding the yield curve is higher. The reason is that the investor expects to benefit from a decline in yield, a decline that does not result from a shift in the yield curve but is attributable to the shortening of the maturity of the 180-day Treasury bills that were initially purchased.

Keep in mind that if the yield curve does change, then "riding it" might be detrimental to the investor's return.[28] That is, riding the yield curve has more risk than simply buying securities that mature at the appropriate time. Furthermore, two transactions are necessary (buying and then selling the security) when riding the yield curve, whereas a maturity strategy has only one transaction (buying the security). Thus, there will be larger transaction costs associated with riding the yield curve.

22.7   Passive Management

The previous discussion of active management assumes that there are inefficiencies in the market that can be exploited. Examples include the ability to find mispriced bonds and the ability to discern when certain market sectors are likely to outperform others (for example, when short-term Treasuries are likely to outperform long-term Treasuries and vice versa). However, if one believes that bond markets are highly efficient, then a passive approach to investing in bonds is in order.

The most common passive approach involves *indexing*. With this approach, an investor selects a bond index that is consistent with his or her risk-return preferences. The objective of indexing is to invest in a portfolio of bonds whose performance tracks (that is, closely follows) that of the index.[29] Three broad-based indices commonly used by investors creating indexed bond portfolios are

1. Lehman Brothers Aggregate Index
2. Merrill Lynch Domestic Market Index
3. Salomon Brothers Broad Investment-Grade Bond Index

Each of these indices is based on more than 5,000 bonds that have maturities of greater than one year and are rated BBB or above. In addition, Lehman Brothers, Merrill Lynch, and Salomon Brothers as well as other organizations, such as Morgan Stanley and First Boston, publish narrower market indices (more on bond indices in the next section).[30]

Investing in a portfolio of bonds whose performance tracks that of a given index is not simple. Indeed, it is quite challenging. Why? First of all, buying all the bonds in the index is impractical because, as mentioned earlier, there are thousands of bonds in each of the broad-based indices. Indeed, even the narrower bond indices are typically composed of many bonds. Second, transactions costs are not reflected in the performance of a bond index but will be incurred in buying and selling bonds in an attempt to manage a portfolio whose performance tracks the index. Third, each of the bonds held will provide the investor with coupon payments periodically that need to be reinvested. However, it is impractical to take, say, $3,000 of coupon payments received during a given week and invest these coupons in all the bonds that are currently held in the portfolio.

As a consequence, most approaches to constructing indexed bond portfolios involve sampling techniques. That is, a subset of all the bonds in the index (plus, possibly, some bonds that are outside the index) is selected for investment such that the portfolio's rate of return is expected to produce minimal deviations from the return on the bond index.[31]

22.8   Bond Portfolio Performance Evaluation

The performance of portfolios of bonds and other types of fixed-income securities is often evaluated by comparing their total returns (consisting of coupon payments plus capital gains or losses) with those of an index representing a comparable class of securities over some interval of time. Hence a portfolio that invested in investment-grade

Modified Duration and Key Rate Durations

Issues concerning the term structure of interest rates stand at the top of most bond managers' decision-making hierarchies. Shifts in, and changes in the shape of, the yield curve affect the value of investment-grade bond portfolios to a far greater extent than do other factors. Controlling interest rate risk is of paramount importance whether bond managers follow strategies to actively benefit from interest rate changes or whether they simply want to neutralize the impact of those changes on their portfolios.

If we were to poll bond managers and ask them what single measure best indicates their interest rate risk exposure, they would be nearly unanimous in answering modified duration. As the text discusses, modified duration gauges the sensitivity of the market value of a bond (or a portfolio of bonds) to changes in the level of interest rates. Modified duration represents the approximate percentage change in a bond's price caused by a 100-basis-point change in the bond's yield. Thus, for example, if you own a bond with a modified duration of four years and its yield rises by 100 basis points, your bond's price should fall by roughly 4%.

An active bond manager attempting to outperform an assigned benchmark may adjust his or her portfolio's modified duration in anticipation of changes in interest rates. Expectations of falling interest rates call for maintaining a modified duration greater than that of the benchmark. Conversely, a bond manager anticipating rising interest rates will want to hold his or her portfolio's modified duration to less than that of the benchmark. A passive bond manager also pays close attention to modified duration. If the manager lets the portfolio's modified duration differ significantly from that of the index, the portfolio's returns likely will fail to track the index's returns adequately. Other passive bond management strategies, such as immunization, also rely on matching a portfolio's modified duration with that of a target.

Despite its importance to bond portfolio management, modified duration does have certain practical limitations that restrict its ability to accurately measure how a bond's price will respond to a change in yields. Those limitations are related to the underlying assumptions made in calculating a bond's duration. Of particular consequence is the assumption that interest rate changes take the form of parallel shifts along a flat yield curve. In actuality, such shifts are unusual. Various segments of the yield curve usually move by different amounts. In some instances one or more segments may move in the opposite direction of other segments. When these nonparallel shifts occur, two bonds with the same durations may respond quite differently, depending on the pattern of their cash flows. As a simple example, if long-term interest rates rise and short-term interest rates fall (referred to as a yield curve *steepening*), then a portfolio holding a single zero-coupon bond with a 5-year modified duration may respond quite differently than a portfolio with an equal weighting in two zero-coupon bonds, one with a 2-year and the other with an 8-year modified duration, even though the modified durations of the two portfolios are the same. Alternative measures of interest rate risk are needed that can account for the valuation effect of more complex changes in the yield curve. One such tool is known as *key rate durations*.

Essentially, key rate durations are a means of breaking apart a bond's modified duration. Instead of one number summarizing the bond's interest rate sensitivity, key rate durations are a set of numbers identifying the sensitivity of the bond to interest rate changes at various points along the yield curve. As the name implies, key rate durations entail specifying certain key rates and associated terms on the yield curve. Thus, a bond manager might select four key rates at 90 days, 1 year, 5 years, and 30 years. (In practice, more are usually chosen. Regardless of the number chosen, the key rates must extend across the entire yield curve—effectively from zero to 30 years. Further, the larger the number of key rates, the greater the ability of the key rate analysis to capture the diverse nature of yield curve shifts, but the more complex the analysis becomes.) The shape of a yield curve shift is indicated by measuring the yield change at each key rate and linearly interpolating the change in between key rates.

At each key rate, the sensitivity of a bond's value to a small shift in the yield curve is estimated. That is, the modified duration of the bond at that point is calculated. For example, if the yield curve at one year were to move by .01 percentage point (1 basis point) and the bond's value changed in the opposite direction by .02%, then the bond's 1-year key rate duration would be 2. Carrying out this calculation at all key rates provides a *profile* of the bond's sensitivity to changes in the yield curve.

By construction, the sum of all key rate durations equals the modified duration of the entire bond. Further, key rate durations combine in a portfolio of bonds in the same way that modified duration does. That is, the key rate duration of a bond portfolio at a particular term is the weighted average of the individual bonds' key rate durations at that term, where the weights are the proportion of the portfolio invested in each bond.

Key rate durations enhance the ability of bond managers to fine tune interest-rate risk in their portfolios. For example, *XYZ* Financial Management is an active bond manager who attempts to outperform a bond market index benchmark while keeping tight control over interest rate risk. *XYZ* maintains a modified duration of 4.69 that is close to that of the index's 4.49 years. However, the manager is willing to place small interest rate "bets" at various points along the yield curve. The following table shows how a portfolio managed by *XYZ* compares with the index in terms of key rate durations.

The portfolio's key rate durations are greater than those of the benchmark at the long end of the yield curve. For example, at the 30-year term, the portfolio's key rate duration is .40 years versus the benchmark's .14 years. A 100-basis-point decline in the 30-year rate would cause the portfolio to outperform the benchmark by .26% [= (.40 − .14) × 100]. The portfolio is also tilted in favor of rates declining at the 10-year term. Because *XYZ* maintains a modified duration near that of the benchmark, the key rate duration bets at the long end of the yield curve and at the 10-year term must be largely offset by opposite bets at other key rates along the yield curve. This is the case, particularly at the 3-, 7-, and 20-year terms.

Use of key rate durations is not limited to active bond managers. By constructing an indexed portfolio whose key rate durations match those of the assigned index, a bond index fund manager can have greater confidence that yield curve shifts will not result in unacceptable levels of tracking error.

Key rate durations as an analytical tool are not without deficiencies. Because they involve a set of numbers, their application is more complex than is modified duration with its single summary statistic. Key rate durations also ignore potentially valuable information about the covariance of different segments of the yield curve by assuming that all the segments move independently. Nevertheless, key rate durations are a valuable additional arrow in the quiver of bond managers seeking to effectively control interest rate risk.

	Key Rate Durations											*Modified Duration*
	.25	**1**	**2**	**3**	**5**	**7**	**10**	**15**	**20**	**25**	**30**	
Portfolio	.02	.11	.33	.43	.69	.56	.99	.43	.31	.43	.40	4.69
Benchmark	.02	.15	.31	.52	.66	.71	.71	.46	.46	.34	.14	4.49
Gap	.00	(.04)	.02	(.09)	.03	(.15)	.27	(.04)	(.15)	.09	.26	0.20

long-term corporate bonds would be compared with an investment-grade long-term corporate bond index; a portfolio that invested in mortgage-backed securities would be compared with a mortgage-backed securities index; and a high-yield bond fund would be compared with a high-yield bond index.

22.8.1 BOND INDICES

Bond indices typically represent either the average total return or the average price on a portfolio of bonds that have certain similar characteristics. Figure 22.5 presents various bond indices that are published daily in *The Wall Street Journal*.[32] The Lehman

Brothers Long Treasury Bond Index is typical of many bond market indices. This index is a total return index, reflecting interest income and changes in prices from one day to the next of nearly all Treasury securities with maturities between 10 and 30 years. It is value-weighted in that price changes and interest income for each bond in the index are weighted by the bond's issue size relative to the combined size of all the securities in the index. It was set at a level of 1,000 at year-end 1980, and each day since then it has changed by the average total return measured from the previous day. Note that the way this index is constructed so that it is easy to determine the return on long-term Treasuries during any time period by simply looking up the value of the index on the previous date. For example, Figure 22.5 indicates that on March 3, 1999, the index was at 8285.49. A year before then the index was at 7631.97 (= 8285.49 − 653.52; elsewhere in *The Wall Street Journal* readers are given the change in the value of the index from a year earlier), so the annual return was 8.56% [= (8285.49 − 7631.97)/7631.97].

There is a yield figure of 5.84% also presented for the Lehman Brothers Long Treasury Bond Index. In the calculation of this index, the annual interest payments for each bond are divided by its current market price, and these interest yields are averaged using value weighting. Hence it is an index of *current yields*.

The second index shown in Figure 22.5 is the Dow Jones 20 Bond Index, where the prices of 20 bonds (10 utilities and 10 industrials) are simply added together and then divided by 20. Similarly, the yield on this index is an average of the yields on the 20 bonds. The figure reveals this index was at 104.30 on March 3, 1999, indicating that the average bond was selling at a 4.30% premium with a yield of 6.80%.

The third index is the Merrill Lynch mortgage-backed bond index. It is based on conventional mortgage pass-through securities as well as those issued by GNMA, FHLMC, FNMA, and FHA. Like the Lehman Brothers Long Treasury Bond Index, it is a total return index standardized to equal 100 at year-end 1979.

The fourth index is the Bond Buyer municipal bond index. It is based on a set of long-term investment-grade general obligation and revenue bonds whose prices and yields are averaged in a manner similar to those of the Dow Jones 20 Bond Index.

FIGURE 22.5 Bond Indices Published in *The Wall Street Journal*, March 3, 1999

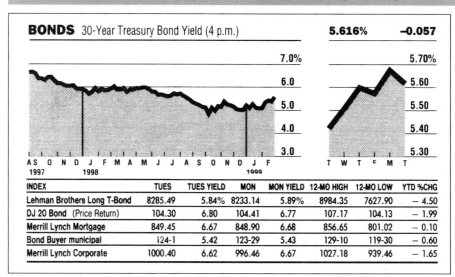

INDEX	TUES	TUES YIELD	MON	MON YIELD	12-MO HIGH	12-MO LOW	YTD %CHG
Lehman Brothers Long T-Bond	8285.49	5.84%	8233.14	5.89%	8984.35	7627.90	− 4.50
DJ 20 Bond (Price Return)	104.30	6.80	104.41	6.77	107.17	104.13	− 1.99
Merrill Lynch Mortgage	849.45	6.67	848.90	6.68	856.65	801.02	− 0.10
Bond Buyer municipal	124-1	5.42	123-29	5.43	129-10	119-30	− 0.60
Merrill Lynch Corporate	1000.40	6.62	996.46	6.67	1027.18	939.46	− 1.65

The fifth index is the Merrill Lynch corporate bond index. It is based on a set of corporate bonds, including industrial, utility, financial, and transportation bonds, of all maturities. It is a value-weighted total return index, like the Lehman Brothers Long Treasury Bond Index, except that its base of 100 was set at year-end 1972.

22.8.2 TIME-SERIES AND CROSS-SECTIONAL COMPARISONS

Figure 22.6 illustrates two ways of evaluating the returns on a bond portfolio by comparing them with the returns on a bond index during a time interval. In part (a), a time-series comparison is made; the bond portfolio's quarterly returns (for example, the past 16 quarters) during the time interval are graphed along with those of a comparable bond index.

In part (b), a cross-sectional comparison is made in a manner similar to the equity performance measures that were based on the *ex post* CML. Here the bond portfolio's average return and standard deviation are graphed and compared with a line that goes through the average riskfree rate and the average return and standard deviation of the bond index (instead of a common stock index), based on quarterly returns during the time interval.

FIGURE 22.6 Bond Portfolio Performance Evaluation

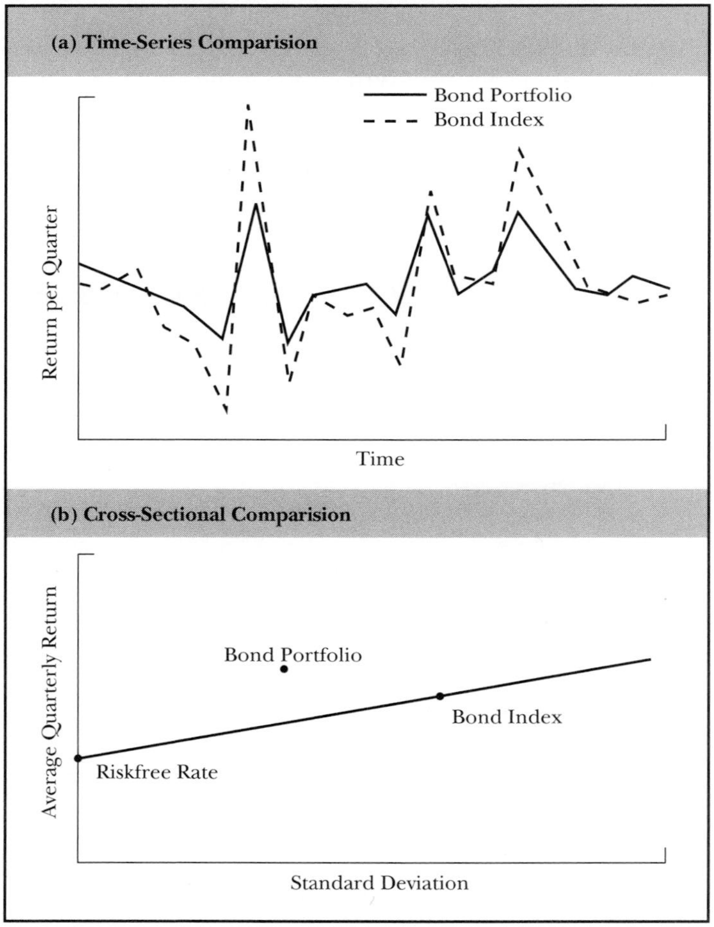

A variation of this procedure involves estimating the bond portfolio's *ex post* alpha using the *ex post* characteristic line approach described in Chapter 18. That is, a figure similar to Figure 18.6 would be prepared, but now the excess returns on a bond portfolio would be measured on the vertical axis and the excess returns on a bond index would be measured on the horizontal axis.[33] Many analysts use as the market index the returns on the Lehman Government/Corporate bond index, which is a value-weighted index of government and corporate investment-grade bonds that have more than one year remaining until maturity. Others use the returns on a bond index that most closely fits with the investment objectives and policies of the portfolio under scrutiny. In either case, an *ex post* alpha would be calculated and used as a measure of portfolio performance.[34]

22.9 Bonds versus Stocks

asset allocation

Bonds and stocks are different kinds of securities, with quite different characteristics. Making an investment decision between them should not be based on some simple one-dimensional comparison. In many cases this decision, known as **asset allocation,** involves investing in both bonds and stocks.[35]

Although historical relationships may not be useful for predicting future relationships accurately, it is instructive to examine the average values, standard deviations, and correlations of past stock and bond returns. These statistics are presented in Table 22.3, based on annual excess returns (that is, returns over Treasury bills) during a 100-year period, 1899 to 1998, and two subperiods, a 50-year period, 1949 to 1998, and a 25-year period, 1974 to 1998. (The returns were published by Global Financial Data; see Figure 1.1 and Table 1.1 in Chapter 1.)

Based on average returns, stocks appear to have a substantial advantage for the investor with a reasonably long horizon.[36] However, there is good reason to believe that the average returns on long-term bonds are not representative of investors' expectations for future returns. The returns show the results obtained by purchasing a long-term government bond, holding it for a period of time, then replacing it with another long-term government bond. The total returns include both income and capital gains or losses. During the postwar subperiod, bond price changes were frequently negative,

TABLE 22.3 Historical Relationships between Bonds and Stocks			
	Stocks	*Bonds*	*Correlation*
A. 100 years: 1899–1998			
Average annual excess return	7.71%	.81%	
Standard deviation	20.00	7.82	
Correlation			.25
B. 50 years: 1949–1998			
Average annual excess return	9.31%	1.10%	
Standard deviation	17.07	10.30	
Correlation			.27
C. 25 years: 1974–1998			
Average annual excess return	8.93%	3.02%	
Standard deviation	16.70	13.59	
Correlation			.42

Source: Adapted from Meir Statman and Neal L. Ushman, "Bonds versus Stocks: Another Look," *Journal of Portfolio Management,* 13, no. 2 (Winter 1987): pp. 33–38, using data from Global Financial Data <globalfindata.com>.

averaging roughly $-.7\%$ per year.[37] A better estimate of investors' expectations might be obtained by assuming that the price would be as likely to increase as to decrease (that is, the expected price change is zero). Expected future returns on bonds might then have been roughly .7% per year greater than shown in the table.

Bond returns were less variable than stock returns in both the full period and the two subperiods. However, the standard deviation of bonds in the 25-year subperiod was nearly double that of the entire 100-year period. It is likely that the increased uncertainty concerning the rate of inflation during this recent subperiod increased the variability of bond returns.

The correlation between stock and bond returns has been low, and during various multiyear subperiods it has even had negative values. This low correlation indicates that portfolios combining both stocks and bonds benefited considerably from diversification. More recently, correlations have been considerably more positive than in the past, in part because of common reactions to changes in inflationary expectations. Consequently, the gains from diversification have been reduced substantially in recent years. Nevertheless, from the historical record it would be reasonable to expect that, in the future, bonds will still offer diversification benefits.

Summary

1. Similar to the U.S. common stock market, the U.S. bond market seems to be highly, but not perfectly, semistrong-form efficient.
2. For a typical bond making periodic interest payments and a final principal repayment on a stated date, five bond pricing theorems apply:
   a. If a bond's market price increases, then its yield must decrease; conversely, if a bond's market price decreases, then its yield must increase.
   b. If a bond's yield does not change during its life, then the size of its discount or premium will decrease as its life gets shorter.
   c. If a bond's yield does not change during its life, then the size of its discount or premium will decrease at an increasing rate as its life gets shorter.
   d. A decrease in a bond's yield will raise the bond's price by an amount that is greater in size than the corresponding fall in the bond's price that would occur if there were an equal-sized increase in the bond's yield. (That is, the price–yield relationship is convex.)
   e. The percentage change in a bond's price caused by a change in its yield will be smaller if its coupon rate is higher.
3. Duration is a measure of the "average maturity" of the stream of payments associated with a bond. It is a weighted average of the length of time until the bond's remaining payments are made, with the weights equal to the present value of each cash flow relative to the price of the bond.
4. The duration of a portfolio of bonds is equal to the weighted average of the durations of the individual bonds in the portfolio.
5. A bond portfolio manager can be fairly confident in meeting a given promised stream of cash outflows by creating a bond portfolio with a duration equal to the liabilities. This procedure is known as immunization.
6. Problems with immunization include default and call risk, multiple nonparallel shifts in a nonhorizontal yield curve, costly rebalancings, and choosing from a wide range of candidate bond portfolios.
7. Active bond management may involve security selection, market timing (where attempts are made to forecast general movements in interest rates), or combinations of the two.

8. Active management strategies include horizon analysis, bond swaps, contingent immunization, and riding the yield curve.
9. The most common passive management strategy is indexing, where a portfolio is formed whose performance tracks that of a chosen index.
10. Bond portfolio performance is usually evaluated by comparing the portfolio's returns with those of a comparable bond index.
11. Portfolios consisting of both stocks and bonds benefit from the resulting diversification because of the relatively low correlation of returns between the two asset classes.

Questions and Problems

1. A $10,000 face-value bond with a 10-year term-to-maturity and an 8% coupon rate currently sells at a price that produces an 8% yield-to-maturity. What is the bond's price? Calculate the bond's price if its yield rises to 10%; if its yield falls to 5%.
2. Bonds *A* and *B* both have $10,000 face values, 10% coupon rates, and sell with yields-to-maturity of 9%. However, bond *A* has a 20-year term-to-maturity, whereas bond *B* has a 5-year term-to-maturity. Calculate the prices of the two bonds. Despite having the same yields, why is one bond's price different from the other's?
3. Consider a 5-year term-to-maturity bond with a $1,000 face value and $100 annual coupon interest payments. The bond sells at par. What is the bond's percentage price change if the yield-to-maturity rises to 12%; if it falls to 8%?
4. Consider two bonds, one with 5 years to maturity and the other with 20 years to maturity. Both have $1,000 face values and 8% coupon rates (with annual interest payments), and both sell at par. Assume that the yields of both bonds fall to 6%. Calculate the dollar increases in the bonds' prices. What percentage of this increase in each case comes from a change in the present value of the bonds' principals, and what percentage comes from a change in the present value of the bonds' interest payments?
5. Bonds *A* and *B* both have $10,000 face values, 8% yields-to-maturity, and 10-year terms-to-maturity. However, bond *A* has a 10% coupon rate, whereas bond *B* sells at par. (Both make annual interest payments.) If the yields on both bonds decline to 6%, calculate the percentage price changes of the two bonds.
6. Consider a bond selling at its par value of $1,000, with three years to maturity and a 7% coupon rate (with annual interest payments). Calculate the bond's duration.
7. What is the modified duration of the bond in Problem 6?
8. Liz Funk owns a portfolio of four bonds with the following durations and proportions:

Bond	Duration	Proportion
A	4.5 years	.20
B	3.0	.25
C	3.5	.25
D	2.8	.30

What is the duration of Liz's bond portfolio?

9. Rank order the following bonds in terms of duration. Explain the rationale behind your rankings. (You do not have to calculate the bonds' durations. Logical reasoning will suffice.)

Bond	Term-to-Maturity	Coupon Rate	Yield-to-Maturity
1	30 years	10%	10%
2	30	0	10
3	30	10	7
4	5	10	10

10. Consider a bond with a 3.5-year duration. If its yield-to-maturity increases from 8.0% to 8.3%, what is the expected percentage change in the price of the bond?

11. The price–yield relationship for a typical bond is convex, opening upward as shown in Figure 22.2. Investment professionals often describe the price–yield relationship of mortgage pass-through securities (described in Chapter 20) as being "negatively convex"—that is, a graph of the relationship opens downward. What features of these securities could produce such a relationship?

12. Explain why immunization permits a bond investor to be confident of meeting a given liability on a predetermined future date.

13. Old True Blue Richardson is planning to offset a single-payment liability with an immunized bond portfolio. Old True Blue is considering buying either bonds with durations close to that of the liability (a "bullet" strategy) or bonds with durations considerably above and below that of the liability (a "barbell" strategy). Why is the bullet strategy a lower risk strategy for Old True Blue? What are its disadvantages relative to the barbell strategy?

14. Consider a bond with a $1,000 face value, 10 years to maturity, and $80 annual coupon interest payments. The bond sells at a price that produces a 10% yield-to-maturity. That yield is expected to decline to 9% at the end of 4 years. Interest income is assumed to be invested at 9.5%. Calculate the bond's 4-year holding period return and the four components of that return.

15. Compare contingent immunization with the strategy of using stop orders (discussed in Chapter 2) to protect a portfolio's value.

APPENDIX

Empirical Regularities in the Bond Market

Certain empirical regularities in the stock market are well known among investment professionals.[38] Because these regularities cannot be explained by any of the currently known asset pricing models, they are referred to as anomalies. An interesting question to ponder is: Do such regularities also exist in the bond market? One study looked at this question by examining the daily performance of the Dow Jones 20 Bond Index.[39]

22A.1 The January Effect

Table 22.4 presents evidence that, as with common stocks, there is a January effect in bonds because, on average, corporate bonds have a notably higher return during the month of January than during the other 11 months of the year. Furthermore, this table also shows that this observation was true for all investment-grade (Aaa to Baa) and two speculative-grade (Ba and B) risk classes. Interestingly, the effect is extremely pronounced for the speculative classes.

22A.2 The Day-Of-The-Week Effect

Table 22.5 presents the average daily returns for each business day of the week. As with common stocks, the average return on Monday is negative. However, it is also negative for every day except Thursday, and the average returns for all five days are not statistically significantly different from one another.[40] Hence in contrast to common stocks, the day-of-the-week effect does not seem to exist for corporate bonds.

TABLE 22.4 Seasonality in Bond Returns

	Average Return in January	*Average Monthy Return in Other Months*
(a) 1963–1986[a]	4.34%	−.56%
(b) 1963–1979[b]	1.15%	.22%
Aaa	1.21	.29
Aa	1.18	.30
Baa	1.55	.30
Ba	3.32	.27
B	5.09	.36

[a]*Source:* Susan D. Jordan and Bradford D. Jordan, "Seasonality in Daily Bond Returns," *Journal of Financial and Quantitative Analysis,* 26, no. 2 (June 1991): Table 5, p. 281

[b]*Source:* Eric C. Chang and Roger D. Huang, "Time-Varying Return and Risk in the Corporate Bond Market," *Journal of Financial and Quantitative Analysis,* 25, no. 3 (September 1990): Table 1, p. 331

TABLE 22.5	Analysis of Daily Return
Day of Week	*Average Daily Return*
Monday	−.20%
Tuesday	−.93
Wednesday	−.00
Thursday	.44
Friday	−.00

Source: Susan D. Jordan and Bradford D. Jordan, "Seasonality in Daily Bond Returns," *Journal of Financial and Quantitative Analysis* 26, no. 2 (June 1991): Table 5, p. 281

Endnotes

1. For details, see Richard Roll, *The Behavior of Interest Rates* (New York: Basic Books, 1970). Interestingly, this study also produced evidence rejecting the unbiased expectations theory of the term structure of interest rates (see Chapter 20 for a discussion of this theory). Also of interest is that U.S. Treasury bonds appear to have been mispriced in May and June of 1986. See Bradford Cornell and Alan C. Shapiro, "The Mispricing of U.S. Treasury Bonds: A Case Study," *Review of Financial Studies,* 2, no. 3 (1989): 297–310.

2. J. Walter Elliott and Jerome R. Baier, "Econometric Models and Current Interest Rates: How Well Do They Predict Future Rates?" *Journal of Finance,* 34, no. 4 (September 1979): 975–986. The models used by major economic forecasting firms tend to have similar amounts of accuracy. See Stephen K. McNees, "Forecasting Accuracy of Alternative Techniques: A Comparison of U.S. Macroeconomic Forecasts," *Journal of Business & Economic Statistics,* 4, no. 1 (January 1986): 5–15, particularly Table 6, where 90-day Treasury bill rate forecasts are evaluated; and Dean Croushore, "Introducing: The Survey of Professional Forecasters," *Federal Reserve Bank of Philadelphia Business Review* (November–December 1993): 3–15.

3. Michael J. Prell, "How Well Do the Experts Forecast Interest Rates?" *Federal Reserve Bank of Kansas City Monthly Review* (September–October 1973): 3–13.

4. Adrian W. Throop, "Interest Rate Forecast and Market Efficiency," *Federal Reserve Bank of San Francisco Economic Review* (Spring 1981): 29–43. This article contains a useful reference list of other studies concerning the prediction of interest rates.

5. Forecasts implicit in the futures market (discussed in Chapter 25) for Treasury bills were also found to be more accurate than those of the economists, but less accurate than those of the no-change model during this time period. For a longer time period, the futures market and no-change model forecasts were of comparable accuracy; see Michael T. Belognia, "Predicting Interest Rates: A Comparison of Professional and Market-Based Forecasts," *Federal Reserve Bank of St. Louis Review,* 69, no. 3 (March 1987): 9–15.

6. See Kevin Stephenson, "Just How Bad Are Economists at Predicting Interest Rates? (And What Are the Implications for Investors?)," *Journal of Investing,* 6, no. 2 (Summer 1997): 8–10.

7. The reported accuracy of macroeconomic forecasters in regard to Treasury bill rates (see the Early Quarter results for a two-quarter horizon in Table 6 of McNees, "Forecast Accuracy of Alternative Techniques") can be compared with the reported accuracy of the no-change model (see Table 1 of Belognia, "Predicting Interest Rates"). Although such a comparison should be done with caution, it does suggest that the no-change model is of similar, and in some cases superior, accuracy. It also appears that the record of the experts in predicting the level of the stock market seems to be of little value. See Werner F. De Bondt, "What Do Economists Know about the Stock Market?" *Journal of Portfolio Management,* 17, no. 2 (Winter 1991): 84–91.

8. See Mark I. Weinstein, "The Effect of a Rating Change Announcement on Bond Price," *Journal of Financial Economics,* 5, no. 3 (December 1977): 329–350. A study of the prices of the common stocks associated with bonds that had rating changes reported similar results—stock prices tended to change several months prior to the announcement dates of the rating changes. See George E. Pinches and J. Clay Singleton, "The Adjustment of Stock Prices to Bond Rating Changes," *Journal of Finance,* 33, no. 1 (March 1978): 29–44. Another study that examined rating change announcements that were "uncontaminated" by other news releases found a small but statistically

significant upward movement in daily bond prices around upgrades; downgrades produced no significant movements. Oddly, these findings were reversed when stock prices were examined in that no significant movements were found around upgrades but marginally significant downward movements were observed around downgrades. See John R. M. Hand, Robert W. Holthausen, and Richard W. Leftwich, "The Effect of Bond Rating Agency Announcements on Bond and Stock Prices," *Journal of Finance,* 47, no. 2 (June 1992): 733–752. Further analysis revealed that one type of downgrade—namely, "downgrades associated with deteriorating financial prospects"—resulted in a significant downward movement in the price of the associated firm's stock. See Jeremy C. Goh and Louis H. Ederington, "Is a Bond Downgrade Bad News, Good News, or No News for Stockholders?" *Journal of Finance,* 48, no. 5 (December 1993): 2001–2008.

9. Gailen Hite and Arthur Warga, "The Effect of Bond-Rating Changes on Bond Price Performance," *Financial Analysts Journal,* 53, no. 3 (May/June 1997): 35–51. The authors looked at other rating change scenarios in addition to the downgrades mentioned here.

10. For an explanation and empirical investigation of this adjustment process, see Richard G. Sheehan, "Weekly Money Announcements: New Information and Its Effects," *Federal Reserve Bank of St. Louis Review,* 67, no. 7 (August/September 1985): 25–34; and Anthony M. Santomero, "Money Supply Announcements: A Retrospective," *Journal of Economics and Business,* 43, no. 1 (February 1991): 1–23.

11. See, for example, Thomas Urich and Paul Wachtel, "Market Response to Weekly Money Supply Announcements in the 1970s," *Journal of Finance,* 36, no. 5 (December 1981): 1063–1072, and "The Effects of Inflation and Money Supply Announcements on Interest Rates," *Journal of Finance,* 39, no. 4 (September 1984): 1177–1188; and Bradford Cornell, "Money Supply Announcements and Interest Rates: Another View," *Journal of Business,* 56, no. 1 (January 1983): 1–23.

12. See Christopher R. Blake, Edwin J. Elton, and Martin J. Gruber, "The Performance of Mutual Bond Funds," *Journal of Business,* 66, no. 3 (July 1993): 371–403.

13. Like the stock market, the bond market has some anomalies. However, they are fewer in number and less pronounced. These anomalies are briefly discussed in the appendix.

14. Burton G. Malkiel, "Expectations, Bond Prices, and the Term Structure of Interest Rates," *Quarterly Journal of Economics,* 76, no. 2 (May 1962): 197–218.

15. See Frederick R. Macaulay, *Some Theoretical Problems Suggested by the Movement of Interest Rates, Bond Yields, and Stock Prices in the United States Since 1856* (New York: National Bureau of Economic Research, 1938).

16. It follows that if there are two bonds that are identical in all aspects except that one has "more convexity," then the one with more convexity would be more desirable. If yields rise, its price will drop by a smaller amount than the price of the other bond. Conversely, if yields drop, its price will rise by a larger amount than the price of the other bonds. In either case, the investor is better off owning the bond having more convexity.

17. To accomplish immunization when there is more than one promised outflow, additional conditions must be met; see Frank J. Fabozzi, *Bond Market Analysis and Strategies* (Upper Saddle River, NJ: Prentice Hall, 1996): 544–545.

18. If there were two-year coupon-bearing bonds available for investment, then there would be no reinvestment-rate risk associated with the principal. However, the investor would still face reinvestment-rate risk in terms of the coupon payments received after one year. Such risk seems relatively minor in this example, but it becomes more substantial in situations involving promised cash outflows that are more than two years into the future.

19. The value is more than $1,000,000 because of the convexity property of bonds, discussed previously.

20. The concept of *effective convexity* has also been introduced to take into consideration such issues as default and call risk when measuring a bond's convexity. See, for example, Fabozzi, *Bond Markets, Analysis and Strategies,* pp. 344–345, 358.

21. See Jeffrey Nelson and Stephen Schaefer, "The Dynamics of the Term Structure and Alternative Portfolio Immunization Strategies," pp. 61–101; and Jonathan E. Ingersoll, Jr., "Is Immunization Feasible? Evidence from the CRSP Data," pp. 163–182 in George G. Kaufman, G. O. Bierwag, and Alden Toevs, eds., *Innovations in Bond Portfolio Management: Duration Analysis and Immunization* (Greenwich, CT: JAI Press 1983); and Robert R. Reitano, "Non-Parallel Yield Curve Shifts and Spread Leverage," *Journal of Portfolio Management,* 17, no. 3 (Spring 1991): 82–87.

22. For a summary and set of references, see G. O. Bierwag, George G. Kaufman, Robert Schweitzer, and Alden Toevs, "The Art of Risk Management in Bond Portfolios," *Journal of Portfolio Management,* 7, no. 3 (Spring 1981): 27–36; G. O. Bierwag, George G. Kaufman, and Alden Toevs, "Duration: Its Development and Use in Bond Portfolio Management," *Financial Analysts Journal,* 39, no. 4 (July/August 1983): 15–35; and Stephen M. Schaefer, "Immunization and Duration: A Review of Theory, Performance and Applications," *Midland Corporate Finance Journal,* 2, no. 3 (Fall 1984): 41–58.

23. See N. Bulent Gultekin and Richard J. Rogalski, "Alternative Duration Specifications and the Measure-

ment of Basis Risk," *Journal of Business,* 57, no. 2 (April 1984): 241–264. For rebuttals and responses, see G. O. Bierwag, George G. Kaufman, Cynthia M. Latta, and Gordon S. Roberts, "Duration: Response to Critics," *Journal of Portfolio Management,* 13, no. 2 (Winter 1987): 48–52; N. Bulent Gultekin and Richard J. Rogalski, "Duration: Response to Critics: Comment," *Journal of Portfolio Management,* 15, no. 3 (Spring 1989): 83–87; G. O. Bierwag, George G. Kaufman, Cynthia M. Latta, and Gordon S. Roberts, "Duration as a Measure of Basis Risk: The Wrong Answer at Low Cost—Rejoinder," *Journal of Portfolio Management,* 15, no. 4 (Summer 1989): 82–85; and N. Bulent Gultekin and Richard J. Rogalski, "Duration as a Measure of Basis Risk: The Wrong Answer at Low Cost—Answer to Rejoinder," *Journal of Portfolio Management,* 15, no. 4 (Summer 1989): 86–87.

24. G. O. Bierwag, George G. Kaufman, and Alden Toevs, "Bond Portfolio Immunization and Stochastic Process Risk:" *Journal of Bank Research,* 13 (Winter 1983): 282–291; and G. O. Bierwag, George G. Kaufman, and Cynthia M. Latta, "Duration Models: A Taxonomy," *Journal of Portfolio Management,* 15, no. 1 (Fall 1988): 50–54.

25. The longer the horizon, the greater the importance of the size of the reinvestment rate in determining a bond's return. Thus, if the investor's horizon is greater than, say, ten years, alternative reinvestment rates should be considered. See Richard W. McEnally, "Rethinking Our Thinking about Interest Rates," *Financial Analysts Journal,* 41, no. 2 (March/April 1985): 62–67.

26. Bond swaps should not be confused with interest-rate swaps, wherein two issuers of debt keep the respective amounts raised but make each other's coupon payments. That is, issuer *A* makes the coupon payments on issuer *B*'s debt, and issuer *B* makes the coupon payments on issuer *A*'s debt, perhaps because *A* has fixed-rate debt and *B* has floating-rate debt. See, for example, Stuart M. Turnbull, "Swaps: A Zero Sum Game?" *Financial Management,* 16, no. 1 (Spring 1987): 15–21; Clifford W. Smith, Jr., Charles W. Smithson, and D. Sykes Wilford, *Managing Financial Risk* (New York: Harper & Row, 1990), Chapters 9–12; John F. Marshall and Kenneth R. Kapner, *The Swaps Market* (Miami: Kolb Publishing, 1993); and Bernadette A. Minton, "An Empirical Examination of Basic Valuation Models for Plain Vanilla U.S. Interest Rate Swaps," *Journal of Financial Economics,* 44, no. 2 (May 1997): 251–277. Interest rate swaps are discussed in Chapter 17.

27. Martin L. Leibowitz, "Horizon Analysis for Managed Bond Portfolios," *Journal of Portfolio Management,* 1, no. 3 (Spring 1975): 32–33.

28. According to the unbiased expectations theory (discussed in Chapter 20), the yield curve would be expected to shift in such a manner that the expected

return of the two strategies (in the example, buy and hold the 90-day T-bills versus buy and sell 90 days later the 180-day T-bills) would be the same.

29. A hybrid approach is known as enhanced indexing. It involves managing a portfolio with the objective of earning a return that is at least equal to and sometimes slightly better than the return on a chosen index. See Fabozzi, *Bond Markets, Analysis and Strategies,* pp. 423–424.

30. For more information on bond market indices, see Frank K. Reilly, G. Wenchi Kao, and David J. Wright, "Alternative Bond Market Indices," *Financial Analysts Journal,* 48, no. 3 (May/June 1992): 44–58.

31. For more on passive management in general and sampling in particular, see Fabozzi, *Bond Markets, Analysis and Strategies,* Chapter 18.

32. Like the equity indices described in Chapter 18, many of these bond indices as well as others are published in *Barron's* and *The Wall Street Journal.* For more on bond indices, see John Markese, "The Complexities of Bond Market Indicators," *AAII Journal,* 14, no. 9 (October 1992): 34–36.

33. As will be discussed in Chapter 23, this method is used by Morningstar, Inc. in evaluating bond mutual fund performance. It is also used by Christopher R. Blake, Edwin J. Elton, and Martin J. Gruber in "The Performance of Bond Mutual Funds," *Journal of Business,* 66, no. 3 (July 1993): 371–403. These authors also used multiple regression where the excess returns on more than one bond index were the explanatory variables.

34. Bond portfolio performance evaluation is also discussed in Peter O. Dietz and Jeanette R. Kirschman, "Evaluating Portfolio Performance," in John L. Maginn and Donald L. Tuttle (eds.) *Managing Investment Portfolios: A Dynamic Process* (Boston: Warren, Gorham & Lamont, 1990), Chapter 14.

35. Chapter 17 presents a discussion of some methods for making the asset allocation decision. For a model on how to measure the interest-rate sensitivity of a portfolio consisting of both stocks and bonds, see Martin L. Leibowitz, "Total Portfolio Duration: A New Perspective on Asset Allocation," *Financial Analysts Journal,* 42, no. 5 (September/October 1986): 18–29.

36. Another study involving simulation found that, based on historical returns, an investor with a 20-year horizon had about a 5% probability of earning less when investing in a common stock index than when investing in a long-term Treasury bond index. For a ten-year horizon the probability was 11%. See Kirt C. Butler and Dale L. Domian, "Risk, Diversification, and the Investment Horizon," *Journal of Portfolio Management,* 17, no. 3 (Spring 1991): 41–47.

37. More recent data since 1982 indicate that bond price changes have more often been positive than negative, averaging a positive 4.5% per year.

38. Some of these anomalies are discussed in the appendix to Chapter 13.

39. Susan D. Jordan and Bradford D. Jordan, "Seasonality in Daily Bond Returns," *Journal of Financial and Quantitative Analysis*, 26, no. 2 (June 1991): 269–285. This study did not examine the bond market in order to see whether the "size effect" (observed for common stocks) was present. Hence only two of the anomalies discussed in the appendix to Chapter 16 are discussed here.

40. The returns on Wednesday and Friday are zero but only because of rounding; they are actually slightly negative.

CHAPTER

Investment Companies

investment companies

Investment companies are a type of financial intermediary. They obtain money from investors and use it to purchase financial assets such as stocks and bonds. In return, the investors receive certain rights regarding the financial assets that the investment company has bought and any earnings that the company may generate. In the simplest and most common situation, the investment company has only one type of investor—stockholders. These stockholders own the investment company directly and thus own indirectly the financial assets that the company itself owns.

For an individual there are two advantages to investing in such companies instead of investing directly in the financial assets that these companies own. The advantages arise from (1) economies of scale and (2) professional management. Consider an individual with moderate financial resources who wishes to invest in the stock market. In terms of economies of scale, the individual could buy stocks in odd lots to build a diversified portfolio. However, the brokerage commissions on odd lot transactions are relatively high. Alternatively, the individual could purchase round lots, but would be able to afford only a few different securities. Unfortunately the individual would then give up the benefits of owning a well-diversified portfolio. In order to receive the benefits of both diversification and substantially reduced brokerage commissions, the individual could invest in the shares of an investment company. Economies of scale make it possible for an investment company to provide diversification at a lower cost per dollar of investment than would be incurred by a small individual investor.

In terms of professional management, the individual investing directly in the stock market would have to go through all the details of investing, including making all buying and selling decisions as well as keeping records of all transactions for tax purposes. In doing so, the individual would have to be continually on the lookout for mispriced securities in an attempt to find underpriced ones for purchase, while selling any that were found to be overpriced. Simultaneously, the individual would have to keep track of the overall risk level of the portfolio so that it did not deviate from some desired level. However, by purchasing shares of an investment company, the individual can turn over all of these tasks to a professional money manager.

Many of these managers hope to identify areas of mispricing in the market, exploit them, and share the resultant abnormal gains with investors by charging them for a portion of the gains. However, it seems that most managers cannot find mispriced situations frequently enough to recoup more than the additional costs they have incurred, costs that take the form of increased operating expenses and transaction costs from the continual buying and selling of securities. Nevertheless, other potential advantages to be gained from investing in an investment company may still outweigh the disadvantages, particularly for smaller investors.

Investment companies differ in many ways, and classification of them is difficult. Common practice will be followed here, where the term *investment company* will be restricted to financial intermediaries that do not obtain money from "depositors." Thus the traditional operations of savings and loan companies and commercial banks, for example, will be excluded. However, the process of deregulation is rapidly breaking down barriers that previously prevented financial intermediaries from competing with traditional investment companies. The future will likely find many different types of organizations offering investment company services.

23.1 Net Asset Value

net asset value

An important concept in understanding how investment companies operate is **net asset value** (NAV). If an investment company has assets consisting of various securities, it is often (but not always) easy to determine the market value of all the assets held by the investment company at the end of each business day. For example, an investment company that holds various common stocks traded on the NYSE, the AMEX, and Nasdaq could easily find out what the closing prices of those stocks were at the end of the day and then simply multiply these prices by the number of shares that it owns. After adding the figures, the investment company subtracts any liabilities it has outstanding. Dividing the resulting difference by the number of outstanding shares of the investment company produces its net asset value:

$$NAV_t = \frac{MVA_t - LIAB_t}{NSO_t} \tag{23.1}$$

where MVA_t, $LIAB_t$, and NSO_t denote the market value of the investment company's assets, the dollar amount of the investment company's liabilities, and the number of shares the investment company has outstanding, respectively, as of the end of day t.

As an example, consider an investment company with 4,000,000 shares outstanding whose assets consisted of common stocks with an aggregate market value of $102,000,000 and whose liabilities amounted to $2,000,000 as of November 15. This company would report a net asset value on that date of $25 $[= (\$102,000,000 - \$2,000,000)/4,000,000]$ per share. This amount changes every day because the values of MVA_t, $LIAB_t$, or NSO_t (or of some combination of them) will typically change daily.

Investors should note that calculating NAV_t can be difficult if some of the assets do not trade frequently or if they include foreign securities that trade in vastly different time zones. In such situations, estimates of their fair market value are often used. Continuing with the previous example, what if, on November 16 there were still 4,000,000 shares outstanding, the liabilities were still $2,000,000, but the common stocks had not been traded on any market since November 15? In this situation MVA_t is often calculated using the last bid prices for the stocks on November 16, which in this example is assumed to result in a value for MVA_t of $106,000,000.[1] Hence the net asset value on November 16 is $26 $[= (\$106,000,000 - \$2,000,000)/4,000,000]$.

23.2 Major Types of Investment Companies

The Investment Company Act of 1940 classifies investment companies as follows[2]:

1. Unit investment trusts
2. Managed investment companies
   a. Closed-end investment companies
   b. Open-end investment companies

These types of investment companies are discussed next.

23.2.1   UNIT INVESTMENT TRUSTS

**unit investment
trust**

A **unit investment trust** is an investment company that owns a fixed set of securities for the life of the company.[3] That is, the investment company rarely alters the composition of its portfolio during the life of the company.

Formation

To form a unit investment trust, a sponsor (often a brokerage firm) purchases a specific set of securities and deposits them with a trustee (such as a bank). Then a number of shares known as redeemable trust certificates are sold to the public. These certificates provide their owners with proportional interests in the securities that were previously deposited with the trustee. All income received by the trustee on these securities is subsequently paid to the certificate holders, as are any repayments of principal. Changes in the original set of securities (that is, selling some of them and buying different ones) are made only under exceptional circumstances. Because there is no active management of a unit investment trust, the annual fees charged by the sponsor are correspondingly low (perhaps .15% of the net asset value per year).

Most unit investment trusts hold fixed-income securities and expire after the last one has matured (or, possibly, been sold). Life spans range from six months for unit investment trusts of money market instruments to more than 20 years for trusts of bond market instruments. Unit investment trusts usually specialize in certain types of securities. Some trusts include only federal government bonds, others only corporate bonds, others only municipal bonds, and so on.

Not surprisingly, the sponsor of a unit investment trust seeks compensation for the effort and risk involved in setting up the trust. This remuneration is accomplished by setting a selling price for the shares that exceeds the cost of the underlying assets. For example, a brokerage firm might purchase $10,000,000 worth of bonds, place them in a unit investment trust, and issue 10,000 shares. Each share might be offered to the public for $1,035. When all the shares have been sold, the sponsor will have received $10,350,000 (= $1,035 × 10,000). This amount is enough to cover the $10,000,000 cost of the bonds, leaving $350,000 for selling expenses and profit. Markups (or load charges) of this sort range from less than 1% for short-term trusts to 3.5% for long-term trusts.

Secondary Market

Typically an investor who purchases shares of a unit investment trust is not required to hold the shares for the entire life of the trust. Instead the shares usually can be sold back to the trust at net asset value, calculated on the basis of bid prices for the assets in the portfolio; that is, the market value of the securities in the portfolio is determined, using dealers' bid quotations. Because unit investment trusts have no liabilities, this amount is divided by the number of shares outstanding to obtain the net asset value per share. Having determined the per share price, the trustee may sell one or more securities to raise the required cash for the repurchase.

Alternatively, it is possible that a secondary market is maintained by the sponsor of the trust. In this situation investors can sell their shares back to the sponsor. Afterward other investors (including those who did not participate in the initial sale) can purchase these shares. Typically the sponsor's selling price in the secondary market is equal to the net asset value of the securities in the portfolio (based on the dealers' asked prices) plus a markup charge equal to that in effect at the time the trust was created.

23.2.2 MANAGED COMPANIES

managed
investment
company

Whereas a unit investment trust has no board of directors and no portfolio manager, a **managed investment company** has both. Because it is typically organized as either a corporation or a trust (a few have been limited partnerships), a managed investment company has a board of directors or trustees that is elected by its shareholders. In turn, the board will commonly hire a firm—the management company—to manage the company's assets for an annual fee that is typically based on the total market value of the assets.

This management company may be an independent firm, an investment adviser, a firm associated with brokers, or an insurance company. Often the management company is the business entity (for example, a subsidiary of a brokerage firm) that started and promoted the investment company. A management company may have contracts to manage a number of investment companies, each of which is a separate organization with its own board of directors or trustees. However, it is often the case that the boards are the same for several of the investment companies. That is, if funds F1 and F2 both employ the same management company, their boards often consist of the same individuals.

Annual management fees (also known as advisory fees) usually range from .50% to 1% of the average market value of the investment company's total assets, with the percentage sliding downward as the dollar value of the assets increases. Some funds provide "incentive compensation," where the better the fund's investment performance, the higher the fee paid to the management company.

In addition to the fee paid by an investment company to its management company, there are administrative expenses that cover record keeping and services to shareholders. (Sometimes these are embedded in the management fee.) Such annual expenses usually range from .20% to .40% of the average market value of total assets.

Last, there are other operating expenses that the investment company incurs annually for such things as state and local taxes, legal and auditing expenses, and directors' fees. These annual expenses usually range from .10% to .30% of the average market value of total assets. Some funds also charge investors distribution fees (also known as 12b-1 fees, which are discussed later) that are used to pay for certain services as well as advertising. The combination of these fees and expenses results in total annual operating expenses typically ranging from .80% to 1.70% of the average total assets.[4] This figure is referred to as a fund's **operating expense ratio.** During 1998 the average bond and equity fund had an operating expense ratio of 1.13% and 1.59%, respectively.[5]

operating expense
ratio

Closed-End Investment Companies

closed-end
investment
company

Unlike unit investment trusts, a **closed-end investment company** (or closed-end fund) does not stand ready to purchase its own shares whenever one of its owners decides to sell them. Instead its shares are typically traded either on an organized exchange or in the Nasdaq market. Thus, an investor who wants to buy or sell shares of a closed-end fund simply places an order with a broker, just as if the investor wanted to buy or sell shares of IBM.

Most closed-end funds have unlimited lives. Dividends and interest received by a closed-end fund from the securities in its portfolio are paid to its shareholders, as are any net realized capital gains. However, most funds allow (and encourage) the reinvestment of such payments in which the fund keeps the money and sends the investor additional shares based on the lower of net asset value or market price per share at that time. For example, consider a closed-end fund whose shares are selling for $20 that has just declared a dividend of $1 per share. If its net asset value were $15 per share, a holder of 30 shares would have a choice of receiving either $30 (= 30 × $1) or 2 shares

(= $30/$15). However, if the shares were selling for $10, then the choice would be between $30 and 3 shares.

Being a corporation, a closed-end fund can issue new shares through reinvestment plans or with public stock offerings, but it rarely does either one. Hence the fund's capitalization is "closed" most of the time. Furthermore, the fund's capitalization will have little or no interest-bearing debt because of restrictions imposed by the Investment Company Act of 1940.

Typically, a closed-end fund's shares are initially offered to the public at a price that is nearly 10% above its net asset value because of investment banking fees charged to the fund. This practice suggests that the shares are overpriced because most funds' shares sell for a price below their net asset value in the aftermarket. Evidence indicates that there are no unusual movements in the price of a typical fund on the offering day, but, in the 100 days thereafter, its price declines relative to the market to the point at which it sells for roughly 10% below its net asset value. This movement is in sharp contrast to the price behavior of nonfund IPOs, where the stocks, on average, experience a substantial price jump on the offering day of about 14% and no notable price movements in the following 100 or so days.[6] Left unanswered is why an investor would want to be involved in the IPO of a closed-end fund.[7]

Most closed-end funds can repurchase their own shares in the open market, although they seldom do. Whenever a fund's market price falls substantially below its net asset value, a repurchase will increase the fund's net asset value per share. For example, if the net asset value were $20 per share at a time when the fund's shares could be purchased in the open market (say, on the NYSE) for $16 per share, the managers of the fund could sell $20 worth of securities from the fund's portfolio, buy back one of the fund's outstanding shares, and have $4 left over. If the $4 were used to buy securities for the fund, the net asset value per share would increase, with the size of the increase depending on the number of remaining shares, the number of shares repurchased, and their repurchase price.

Quotations

The market prices of the shares of closed-end funds are published daily in the financial press, provided that the funds are listed on an exchange or traded actively on Nasdaq. However, their net asset values are published only weekly, on the basis of closing market prices for securities in their portfolios as of the previous Friday. Figure 23.1 provides an example. The first column indicates where a fund's shares are traded (N = NYSE, A = AMEX, O = Nasdaq, C = Chicago Stock Exchange, T = Toronto Stock Exchange; the "club" symbol next to the exchange indicates a free annual or semiannual report can be obtained by calling 800/965-2929).

Both the net asset value and the last price at which the fund's shares traded on the day in question are shown next, followed by the percentage of net asset value that the difference between the two figures represents. If this percentage is positive (meaning that the stock price is greater than the net asset value), then the fund's shares are said to be selling at a *premium*. Conversely, if this difference is negative (meaning that the stock price is less than the net asset value), then the fund's shares are said to be selling at a *discount*. For example, Figure 23.1 indicates that the India Growth Fund was selling at a 25.3% discount, whereas the Indonesia Fund was selling for a 33.3% premium. (These two investment companies are known as "country funds," as they specialize in Indian and Indonesian stocks, respectively.) Most closed-end funds that invest in stocks (other than a few country funds) sell at a discount.[8] The last column in the figure shows

Fund Name (Symbol)	Stock Exch	NAV	Market Price	Prem /Disc	52 week Market Return
Friday, July 16, 1999					
General Equity Funds					
Adams Express (ADX)	♣N	36.68	30 1/8	− 17.9	16.9
Alliance All-Mkt (AMO)-f	N	50.76	43 7/8	− 13.6	1.4
Avalon Capital (MIST)	O	18.61	16 1/4	− 12.7	− 16.7
Baker Fentress (BKF)	♣N	21.90	19 9/16	− 10.7	14.6
Bergstrom Cap (BEM)	A	228.92	199	− 13.1	37.6
Blue Chip Value (BLU)-a	♣N	10.61	10 1/4	− 3.4	− 4.0
Brantley Capital Corp (BBDC)	O	NA	8	NA	− 14.6
Central Secs (CET)	A	33.73	27 7/16	− 18.7	7.8
Corp Renaissance (CREN)-c	O	12.14	10	− 17.6	58.4
Engex (EGX)	A	10.53	9	− 14.5	− 14.3
Equus II (EQS)	♣N	23.16	16 1/2	− 28.8	− 32.2
Gabelli Equity (GAB)-a	N	12.09	12 1/16	− 0.3	17.2
General American (GAM)	♣N	37.31	32 5/8	− 12.5	19.8
Librty AllStr Eq (USA)	♣N	14.94	13 9/16	− 9.2	6.4
Librty AllStr Gr (ASG)	♣N	13.07	11 5/16	− 13.5	− 2.6
MFS Special Val (MFV)-a	N	16.28	17 1/4	+ 6.0	0.5
Morgan FunShares (MFUN)-c	O	NA	7 1/4	NA	− 3.3
Morgan Gr Sm Cap (MGC)	♣N	12.74	11	− 13.7	0.2
NAIC Growth (GRF)-c	C	13.57	12 1/8	− 10.7	− 3.8
Royce Focus Trust (FUND)	O	6.31	5 3/16	− 17.8	− 8.7
Royce Micro-Cap (OTCM)	O	10.45	8 17/32	− 18.4	− 15.5
Royce Value (RVT)	N	15.90	13 11/16	− 13.9	− 7.3
Salomon SBF (SBF)	N	21.54	20 7/16	− 5.1	30.6
Source Capital (SOR)	N	54.36	50	− 8.0	0.5
Tri-Continental (TY)	♣N	37.78	31 3/8	− 16.9	20.7
Zweig (ZF)	♣N	12.25	11 1/2	− 6.1	0.3
Specialized Equity Funds					
ASA Limited (ASA)-cv	N	17.17	15 5/8	− 9.0	− 15.7
BGR Prec Metals (DPM.A)-cy	T	12.80	9	− 29.7	− 13.9
C&S Realty (RIF)	♣A	7.53	9	+ 19.5	8.1
C&S Total Rtn (RFI)-a	♣N	12.29	12 3/8	+ 0.7	− 2.3
Centrl Fd Canada (CEF)-c	♣A	3.65	3 7/16	− 5.8	− 9.5
Duff&Ph Util Inc (DNP)	N	9.87	10 9/16	+ 7.0	6.1
First Financial (FF)	N	10.02	8 13/16	− 12.1	− 35.9
GABELLI UTILITY FUND (N/A)	z	7.54	7 7/8	+ 4.5	NS
Gabelli Gl Media (GGT)	N	17.72	15	− 15.4	47.2
H&Q Health Inv (HQH)	♣N	20.25	15 15/16	− 21.3	− 3.0
H&Q Life Sci Inv (HQL)	♣N	16.58	14 9/16	− 12.2	9.9
INVESCO Gl Hlth (GHS)-j	♣N	18.68	16 3/8	− 12.3	− 2.4
J Han Bank (BTO)	♣N	11.64	9 13/16	− 15.7	− 7.3
Petroleum & Res (PEO)	♣N	42.38	36	− 15.1	1.1
SthEastrn Thrift (STBF)	♣O	24.07	19 1/4	− 20.0	− 13.9
Thermo Opprtunty (TMF)	A	9.99	7 15/16	− 20.5	− 15.3
Income & Preferred Stock Funds					
Chartwell D & I (CWF)-a	♣N	13.84	13 1/8	− 5.1	− 8.0
Delaware Gr Div (DDF)-a	N	15.30	14 7/8	− 2.8	− 5.5
Delaware Grp Gl (DGF)-a	N	15.54	14 1/4	− 8.3	− 5.5
J Han Pat Globl (PGD)	♣N	14.25	11 9/16	− 18.9	− 5.7
J Han Pat Pref (PPF)	♣N	13.49	11 5/8	− 13.8	− 14.0
J Han Pat Prm (PDF)-a	♣N	10.39	8 15/16	− 14.0	− 1.3
J Han Pat Prm II (PDT)	♣N	12.79	10 3/4	− 16.0	− 3.0
J Han Pat Sel (DIV)	♣N	16.09	13 13/16	− 14.2	− 2.6
Preferred Inc Op (PFO)	♣N	12.38	11 7/16	− 7.6	− 0.1
Preferred IncMgt (PFM)	♣N	14.85	11 5/8	− 21.7	− 9.7
Preferred Income (PFD)	♣N	15.34	13 3/4	− 10.4	− 3.0
Putnam Divd Inc (PDI)-a	N	11.19	9 9/16	− 14.6	− 2.5
Convertible Sec's. Funds					
Bancroft Conv (BCV)	♣A	28.73	23 1/2	− 18.2	− 3.5
Castle Conv (CVF)	A	27.13	22 5/8	− 16.6	− 3.9
Ellsworth Conv (ECF)	♣A	12.18	9 13/16	− 19.5	− 0.5
Gabelli Conv Sec (GCV)	N	12.34	11 1/4	− 8.8	13.2
Lincoln Conv (LNV)-c	♣N	17.99	14 3/8	− 20.1	− 11.9
Putnam Conv Opp (PCV)-a	N	23.99	21 1/4	− 11.4	− 5.6
Putnam Hi Inc Cv (PCF)-a	N	8.57	9 11/16	+ 13.1	0.5
Ren Cap G&I III (RENN)	O	12.42	8 15/16	− 28.0	9.2
TCW Conv Secs (CVT)	♣N	10.38	10	− 3.7	13.9
VK Conv Sec (VXS)	N	27.61	21 7/8	− 20.8	2.8
World Equity Funds					
AIM Eastern Euro (GTF)	N	8.88	8 5/16	− 6.4	− 14.8
Argentina (AF)	N	14.13	10 11/16	− 24.4	− 9.1
Asia Pacific (APB)	N	NA	9 1/4	NA	46.4
Asia Tigers (GRR)	N	11.07	9 1/8	− 17.5	39.3
Austria (OST)	♣N	11.63	9 5/8	− 17.2	− 10.1
Brazil (BZF)	N	16.71	13 7/8	− 16.9	− 18.4
Herzfeld Caribb (CUBA)	O	5.86	5 11/16	− 2.9	8.9
India Fund (IFN)	N	14.82	11 1/2	− 22.4	61.4
India Growth (IGF)-d	N	14.57	10 7/8	− 25.3	38.2
Indonesia (IF)	♣N	5.02	6 11/16	+ 33.3	64.7
Irish Inv (IRL)	N	20.20	16 3/8	− 18.9	− 27.0
Italy (ITA)	N	17.63	15 1/16	− 14.6	4.2
Jakarta Growth (JGF)	N	3.34	3 5/8	+ 8.7	35.1
Japan Equity (JEQ)	♣N	8.22	9 7/8	+ 20.2	29.6
Japan OTC Equity (JOF)	N	11.30	12 3/16	+ 7.9	121.6
Jardine Fl China (JFC)	♣N	9.31	7 11/16	− 17.4	20.6
Jardine Fl India (JFI)-c	♣N	10.95	7 13/16	− 28.7	38.8
Korea (KF)	N	18.65	16 3/16	− 13.2	105.6
Korea Equity (KEF)	N	6.85	5 11/16	− 16.9	97.9
Korean Inv (KIF)	N	9.83	8 5/16	− 15.5	155.7
Latin Amer Disc (LDF)	N	11.26	9 1/16	− 19.5	− 13.6
Latin Amer Eq (LAQ)	♣N	13.61	10 3/16	− 25.1	− 11.0
Latin Amer Inv (LAM)	♣N	14.51	10 7/8	− 25.0	− 9.4
MSDW E Europe (RNE)	N	17.59	15 1/2	− 11.9	− 20.8
Malaysia (MF)	N	5.19	6 15/16	+ 33.7	12.2
Mexico (MXF)-cl	♣N	23.17	16 15/16	− 26.9	7.1
Mexico Eqty&Inc (MXE)-c	N	9.62	7 7/8	− 18.1	6.0
Morgan St Africa (AFF)	N	13.02	10 1/16	− 22.7	− 14.3
Morgan St Asia (APF)	N	12.29	10	− 18.6	35.6
Morgan St Em (MSF)	N	15.04	12 1/16	− 19.8	10.3
Morgan St India (IIF)	N	15.04	11 1/8	− 26.0	61.9
Pakistan Inv (PKF)	N	2.75	2 5/16	− 16.0	6.9
Portugal (PGF)	♣N	15.04	13 15/16	− 7.3	− 13.2
ROC Taiwan (ROC)	N	8.24	7 5/8	− 7.4	7.4
Scudder New Asia (SAF)	N	17.77	14 5/8	− 17.7	48.2
Scudder New Eur (NEF)	N	22.81	21 5/16	− 6.6	5.6
Singapore (SGF)-c	♣N	10.79	9 13/16	− 9.1	46.9
Southern Africa (SOA)	N	14.78	11 5/8	− 21.3	− 5.3
Spain (SNF)	N	16.08	15	− 6.7	3.5
Swiss Helvetia (SWZ)	♣N	16.85	14 1/16	− 16.6	− 11.2
Taiwan (TWN)-c	N	20.36	18 1/16	− 11.3	30.4
Taiwan Equity (TYW)-c	♣N	14.51	12 1/4	− 15.6	24.8
Templeton China (TCH)-c	N	10.70	8 5/16	− 22.3	27.3
Templeton Dragon (TDF)	N	12.70	10 3/16	− 19.8	27.6
Templeton Em App (TEA)-c	N	13.89	11 13/16	− 15.0	19.6
Templeton Em Mkt (EMF)	N	12.79	14 1/2	+ 13.4	21.0
Templeton Russia (TRF)-c	N	14.90	17 3/16	+ 15.4	− 29.1
Templeton Vietnm (TVF)	N	12.78	10 3/8	− 18.8	71.2
Thai (TTF)	N	5.26	10 1/2	+ 99.6	44.8
Thai Capital (TC)	♣N	3.87	6 9/16	+ 69.5	49.9
Third Canadian (THD)-cy	T	20.31	15 3/4	− 22.5	− 14.8
Turkish Inv (TKF)	N	8.82	7 9/16	− 14.3	− 7.6
United Corps Ltd (UNC)-cy	T	68.14	45 1/4	− 33.6	− 13.9
United Kingdom (UKM)	N	NA	NA	NA	NA
Z-Seven (ZSEV)	O	7.70	7 11/16	− 0.1	− 5.4

Fund Name (Symbol)	Stock Exch	NAV	Market Price	Prem Disc	12 Mo Yield 6/30/99
U.S. Gov't. Bond Funds					
ACM Govt Inc (ACG)	N	8.04	8 5/8	+ 7.3	11.6
ACM Govt Oppty (AOF)	N	7.87	7 5/16	− 7.1	9.5
ACM Govt Secs (GSF)	N	7.99	8 3/16	+ 2.5	12.2
ACM Govt Spec (SI)	N	6.62	5 13/16	− 12.2	10.1
Excelsior Income (EIS)-c	♣N	18.39	15 1/2	− 15.7	6.8
Kemper Int Govt (KGT)-a	♣N	7.41	7	− 5.5	8.5
MFS Govt Mkts (MGF)-a	N	7.11	6 3/16	− 12.9	7.2
MSDW Govt Inc (GVT)	♣N	9.20	8 1/4	− 10.3	5.8
U.S. Mortgage Bond Funds					
2002 Target Term (TTR)-ac	N	14.69	14	− 4.7	6.1
Amer Sel Port (SLA)-c	N	12.83	11 5/8	− 9.2	8.9
Amer Str Inc II (BSP)-c	N	12.79	11	− 7.1	8.7
Amer Str Inc III (CSP)-c	N	12.16	11 1/2	− 5.4	8.8
Amer Str Income (ASP)-c	N	12.60	11 11/16	− 7.2	8.4
BlckRk 1999 Term (BNN)-c	N	10.11	9 15/16	− 1.7	4.4

FIGURE 23.1 Closed-End Funds (excerpts)

Source: Reprinted by permission of *Barron's*, Dow Jones & Company, Inc., July 19, 1999, p. MW64. All rights reserved worldwide.

the rate of return during the past 12 months for funds investing primarily in stocks and the past 12-month yield for funds investing primarily in fixed-income securities.

Open-End Investment Companies

**open-end
investment
company
mutual funds**

An investment company that stands ready at all times to purchase its own shares at or near their net asset value is termed an **open-end investment company** (or open-end fund). Most of these companies, commonly known as **mutual funds,** also continuously offer new shares to the public for a price at or near their net asset values. Because their capitalization is "open," the number of shares outstanding changes on a daily basis.

There are two methods used by mutual funds to sell their shares to the public: direct marketing and the use of a sales force. With direct marketing the mutual fund sells shares directly to investors without using a sales organization. These open-end companies, known as **no-load funds,** sell their shares at a price equal to their net asset value. The other method of selling shares involves a sales force that is paid a commission based on the number of shares it sells. This sales force often involves brokers, financial planners, and employees of insurance companies and banks. Open-end companies that use this method are known as **load funds** because the commission involves adding a percentage **load charge** to the net asset value.

no-load funds

**load funds
load charge**

The percentage load charge by law cannot exceed 8.5% of the amount invested. For example, a selling organization receiving $1,000 to be invested in a fund might retain as much as $85, leaving $915 to purchase the fund's shares at the current net asset value per share. Although this expense is usually described as a load charge of 8.5%, it actually equals 9.3% (= $85/$915) of the amount ultimately invested. Load charges of this magnitude are levied by some funds for small purchases, but typically they are reduced for larger purchases. Some funds have loads of less than 3.5% for purchases of all sizes and are hence dubbed **low-load funds.**[9]

low-load funds

With either load or no-load mutual funds, an investor must be provided with a copy of the fund's *prospectus* either before he or she buys shares of the fund or with the confirmation notice that indicates he or she has just purchased shares of the fund. The prospectus provides information to an investor, describing the fund's fees and expenses, investment objectives, strategies to meet those objectives, risks, past performance, and how to buy and sell shares. After purchasing shares, the investor receives copies of the fund's annual and semiannual reports describing the fund's performance, holdings, and financial statements.

When mutual fund shareholders want to sell their shares, they usually receive an amount equal to the fund's net asset value times the number of shares sold. However, a few funds charge a **redemption fee,** which usually is no more than 1% of the fund's net asset value and typically is not levied if the investor has owned the shares for more than a specified time, such as one year. By discouraging such in-and-out trading, the fund avoids the transaction costs associated with having to sell securities frequently to satisfy some investors' desires to buy and sell their mutual fund shares rapidly.[10]

redemption fee

distribution fee

In addition, mutual funds may charge current shareholders a **distribution fee** annually. This 12b-1 fee (named for an SEC ruling involving a section of the Investment Company Act of 1940) is legally not allowed to exceed 1% of the average market value of the total assets. It pays for advertising, promoting, and selling the fund to prospective buyers as well as for providing certain services to existing investors.[11] Sometimes the fee is coupled with a load charge that is paid when shares are initially purchased. One alleged benefit of the 12b-1 fee to current owners of the fund is that the resulting increased size of the portfolio brings greater economies of scale.

contingent
deferred sales
charge

Some mutual funds have different classes of stock. In such a situation an investor can choose the class he or she wants to purchase. For example, class *A* stock might have a 5% load charge but no annual 12b-1 fee, whereas class *B* stock might not have a load charge. Instead class *B* might have a 12b-1 fee of .5% per year plus a **contingent deferred sales charge** (paid when the investor sells shares) that starts at 5% if the investor sells his or her shares within a year of purchase and declines thereafter by 1% a year for each year the stock is held, reaching zero after the fifth year. In addition, the class *B* shares might be set up so that they convert to class *A* shares after five years (when the contingent deferred sales charge has declined to zero). This feature allows investors who initially bought class *B* shares to avoid 12b-1 fees after five years. There might also be class *C* stock for which the investor pays an annual 12b-1 fee of 1% for as long as the shares are held.

In summary, there are many different methods mutual funds use to get the cash needed to pay for sales commissions and other selling costs. Some methods (such as the class *C* stock) are more attractive to investors who plan to hold their investment only for the short term. Others (such as the class *B* stock) are more attractive to investors who plan to hold their investment for the long term.

As will be discussed later, the investment performance of no-load funds as a whole does not differ in any notable way from that of load funds. This fact is not surprising. The load charge (roughly 30% to 50% of which goes to the individual who sold the shares, with the selling organization keeping the rest) represents the cost of advertising, education, and persuasion. Mail-order firms often sell items for less than stores charge. Sales representatives who work in stores and those who sell mutual funds provide a service and require compensation. Buyers who consider such services worth less than their cost can and should avoid paying for them.

Quotations

Figure 23.2 shows a portion of the quotations for mutual funds provided in *The Wall Street Journal.* Funds listed under a name in boldface type have a common management company associated with that name. For example, note all the funds that are listed under AARP Invst. (AARP Invst stands for *AARP Investment Program from Scudder,* an investment program sponsored by the American Association of Retired People that involves mutual funds and is run by the management company of Scudder, Stevens & Clark.) After the abbreviated name of a mutual fund comes its net asset value, based on closing prices for the fund's securities on the day in question. The third column displays the change in net asset value from the close of the previous trading day, and the fourth column indicates the fund's rate of return for the year so far.

Once a month, *The Wall Street Journal* presents more detailed information on mutual funds. Besides presenting net asset value, its change from the previous day, and the year-to-date return for each fund, the following information is presented in a separate section:

1. Investment objective
2. Monthly return
3. Total return for the past year, three years, and five years, along with an indication of the fund's pentile rank relative to other funds with the same investment objective (top 20% = *A*, next 20% = *B*, middle 20% = *C*, next 20% = *D*, bottom 20% = *E*) for each of these time periods
4. Front-end load charge
5. Operating expense ratio

Figure 23.3 shows the weekly quotations that appear for a special type of mutual fund known as a money market fund. These funds invest in short-term, fixed-income

LIPPER INDEXES

Thursday, March 4, 1999

Equity Indexes	Prelim. Close	Percentage chg. since Prev.	Wk ago	Dec. 31
Capital Appreciation ...	2248.86	+ 1.16	+ 0.12	+ 0.36
Growth Fund	7983.48	+ 1.24	+ 0.06	+ 1.36
Small Cap Fund	578.92	+ 0.53	- 0.22	- 7.08
Growth & Income	6820.45	+ 1.28	+ 0.50	- 0.47
Equity Income Fd	3586.56	+ 1.20	+ 0.51	- 1.27
Science and Tech Fd ...	742.82	+ 1.09	- 3.65	+ 0.93
International Fund	656.45	+ 0.18	- 2.64	- 3.87
Gold Fund	69.43	+ 1.01	+ 0.85	- 2.24
Balanced Fund	4215.98	+ 0.75	- 0.02	- 0.67
Emerging Markets	59.06	+ 0.08	+ 0.55	- 2.69
Bond Indexes				
Corp A-Rated Debt	788.64	- 0.13	- 0.35	- 1.94
US Government	298.74	- 0.15	- 0.34	- 2.14
GNMA	324.52	- 0.14	- 0.31	- 0.50
High Current Yield	774.03	- 0.04	- 0.55	+ 0.92
Intmdt Inv Grade	218.18	- 0.12	- 0.33	- 1.67
Short Inv Grade	199.05	- 0.04	+ 0.01	+ 0.11
General Muni Debt	574.49	- 0.12	- 0.44	- 0.03
High Yield Municipal ..	279.11	- 0.08	- 0.29	+ 0.17
Short Municipal	121.94	- 0.09	- 0.15	+ 0.47
Global Income	205.25	- 0.30	- 1.22	- 3.36
International Income ...	135.67	- 0.44	- 1.88	- 4.83

Indexes are based on the largest funds within the same investment objective and do not include multiple share classes of similar funds. The Yardsticks table, appearing with Friday's listings, includes all funds with the same objective.

Source: Lipper Inc. The Lipper Funds Inc. are not affiliated with Lipper Inc.

Ranges for investment companies, with daily price data supplied by the National Association of Securities Dealers and performance and cost calculations by Lipper Inc. The NASD requires a mutual fund to have at least 1,000 shareholders or net assets of $25 million before being listed. NAV-Net Asset Value. Detailed explanatory notes appear elsewhere on this page.

Name	NAV	Net Chg	YTD %ret
AAL Mutual A:			
Balance p	11.74	+0.09	+ 1.0
Bond p	9.87	-0.02	- 1.8
CGrowth p	33.71	+0.53	+ 3.0
EqInc p	13.85	+0.20	- 0.2
HiYBdA	8.87	...	- 0.8
Intl p	10.44	-0.05	- 2.4
MidCap p	13.28	+0.09	- 4.9
MuniBd p	11.44	-0.01	- 0.1
SmCap p	10.71	+0.07	- 9.1
AAL Mutual B:			
Balance †	11.69	+0.09	+ 0.9
CGrowth p	33.21	+0.53	+ 2.8
EqInc p	13.82	+0.20	- 0.4
HiYBdB p	8.87	...	- 0.9
Intl p	10.34	-0.05	- 2.6
MidCap	13.07	+0.09	- 5.1
SmCap p	10.57	+0.07	- 9.3
AARP Invst:			
BalS&B	19.60	+0.11	- 1.9
BdInc	14.70	-0.02	- 1.4
CaGr	58.35	+0.76	+ 1.2
DivGr	17.50	+0.11	- 2.5
DivInc	15.98	+0.03	- 1.1
GiniM	14.98	-0.03	- 0.6
GlblGr	18.01	+0.07	- 6.1
GthInc	48.57	+0.51	- 1.8
HQSTBd	16.01	-0.01	- 0.4
IntlG&I	16.36	+0.01	- 9.8
SmCoStk	16.63	+0.10	- 10.9
TxFBd	18.54	-0.04	+ 0.2
USStkI	23.54	+0.38	+ 1.6
ABN AMRO Funds:			
AsiaTCm	6.56	-0.01	- 2.5
Bal Cm	11.69	+0.09	- 0.9
FixIncCm	10.07	-0.01	- 2.0
Gwth Cm	16.91	+0.23	- 1.1
IntFxCm	10.10	-0.01	- 1.3
IntlEqCm	18.09	+0.03	- 4.6
IntlFICm	10.02	-0.08	- 7.4
LatinAm	7.16	+0.26	- 11.7
SmCpGrCm	10.83	+0.09	- 11.3
TE FICm	10.46	-0.02	0.0
ValueCm	12.52	+0.14	+ 1.8
AFBA Equity	11.39	+0.07	- 1.0
AHA Funds:			
Balan	13.21	+0.04	- 2.3
DivrEq	19.73	+0.17	- 0.1
Full	10.03	-0.01	- 1.8
Lim	10.23	...	0.0
AIM Funds A:			
AdvFlex p	19.81	+0.16	- 1.2
AdvIntV p	15.68	-0.06	- 5.4
AdvLgCp p	24.78	+0.20	- 1.7
AdvMulF p	12.64	+0.03	- 6.0
AdvRlEst p	10.89	+0.01	- 5.0
Agrsv p	43.40	+0.21	- 9.8
AsianGr p	7.58	-0.04	- 3.7
Bal p	27.76	+0.18	- 1.7
BasicVal p	17.97	+0.13	- 0.9
BlChp p	41.99	+0.60	+ 1.2
CapDev p	13.43	+0.07	- 10.5
Chart p	15.25	+0.24	+ 2.3
Const p	29.04	+0.34	- 4.8
DevMkt p	7.47	+0.06	- 2.7
EmMkDt p	7.92	+0.04	- 1.1
Euro p	15.22	-0.09	- 2.9
EuroDev p	13.88	-0.11	- 2.7
GlAgGr	16.81	...	- 5.1
GlGr p	19.48	+0.12	- 1.2
GlGrInc p	8.12	+0.02	- 3.1
GlGvInc p	8.61	-0.03	- 4.8
GlInc p	10.35	-0.02	- 2.0
GlTrend p	11.48	+0.12	+ 0.2
GlUtil p	20.31	+0.08	- 2.9
HiIncMuA p	9.98	...	- 0.2
HYld p	8.64	-0.02	+ 0.3

Name	NAV	Net Chg	YTD %ret
Acorn Funds:			
AcornInt	20.52	-0.01	- 1.4
Acorn40	11.40	-0.02	+ 3.6
AcornF	15.88	-0.01	- 5.8
Acorn20	10.84	+0.15	+ 1.2
AcornUS	13.39	+0.01	- 9.5
AdsnCa p	28.43	+0.31	- 2.8
Advance Capital I:			
Balanc p	16.84	+0.14	- 1.2
Equity p	19.59	+0.30	- 2.3
RetInc p	10.27	-0.01	- 1.6
Advantus Fds:			
BondA	9.99	-0.01	- 2.2
BondB p	10.02	-0.01	- 2.3
CStoneA	15.37	+0.16	- 3.3
CStoneB p	15.18	+0.17	- 3.4
EnterpA	13.26	-0.01	- 9.2
EnterpB p	12.71	-0.01	- 9.3
HorznA	25.49	+0.36	- 2.5
HorznB p	24.33	+0.35	- 2.6
Idx500A p	16.66	+0.26	+ 1.3
Idx500B p	16.57	+0.25	+ 1.0
IntBalA	10.69	+0.04	- 4.7
MtgSecA	10.52	-0.02	0.0
SpectmA	17.46	+0.15	- 2.5
SpectmB p	17.36	+0.15	- 2.6
VentureA	9.78	+0.01	- 12.9
Aetna Class A:			
Balanced †	NA	...	NA
Bond †	10.25	-0.01	- 1.2
Grow †	19.64	+0.23	+ 1.8
GrInc †	NA	...	NA
Intl †	11.47	-0.06	- 1.8
SmCo †	10.33	+0.03	- 7.9
Aetna Class I:			
Ascent	NA	...	NA
Balanced	NA	...	NA
Bond	10.25	-0.01	- 1.2
Crossrds	NA	...	NA
Grwth	19.96	+0.23	+ 1.9
GrwIncm	NA	...	NA
IndPlLgCpI	15.77	+0.23	+ 2.0
Intl	11.48	-0.06	- 1.8
Legacy	NA	...	NA
SmCo	10.60	+0.03	- 7.8
Alger Funds A:			
CapApr	11.29	+0.17	+ 9.1
Growth	13.92	+0.21	+ 4.9
MidCpGr	21.97	+0.33	- 1.2
SmCap	9.60	+0.10	+ 1.2
Alger Funds B:			
Balncd p	18.63	+0.17	+ 3.9
CapApr †	11.08	+0.16	+ 8.9
Growth †	13.64	+0.20	+ 4.7
MidCpGr †	21.55	+0.33	- 1.2
SmCap †	9.41	+0.10	+ 1.0
Alger Retirement Fds:			
CapAppr	12.82	+0.19	+ 11.7
Growth	15.68	+0.22	+ 4.7
MidCpGr	10.73	+0.13	- 0.9
SmCap	21.07	+0.23	+ 2.8
Alleghany/Chicago Tr:			
Balanced p	12.51	+0.12	+ 1.1
Bond	10.01	-0.01	- 1.4
Gro&Inc	25.43	+0.44	+ 2.8
SmCpVal p	9.24	-0.01	NA
Talon p	12.79	+0.15	- 8.2
Alleghany/Montag:			
Balanced I	18.59	+0.18	NA
Balanced N	18.58	+0.18	+ 1.2
Growth N	30.66	+0.46	+ 3.4
Alliance Advisor Cl:			
GrIncAdv	3.45	+0.06	0.0
GwthAdv	51.24	+0.62	NA
IntlAdv	15.00	-0.04	- 6.5
PrGrAdv	32.11	+0.37	+ 5.2
QusarAdv	22.78	-0.17	- 9.4
TechAdv	77.68	+0.82	- 0.4

Name	NAV	Net Chg	YTD %ret
LabGIC p	11.37	+0.12	+ 0.3
LabGIX p	11.38	+0.12	+ 0.3
MarCpGrA p	12.31	+0.11	+ 3.8
MarCpGrB p	12.28	+0.10	+ 3.7
MarCpGrC p	12.27	+0.11	+ 3.7
MarCpGrX p	12.27	+0.11	+ 3.7
OppLgCpGB p	11.99	+0.13	NA
OppLgCpGX p	11.96	+0.13	- 3.9
TotRtBdB p	10.22	-0.01	- 3.4
TotRtBdX p	10.22	-0.01	- 3.5
TRInEqX †	9.75	-0.03	- 5.6
TRSmCVA	8.41	+0.05	- 8.9
TRSmCVB p	8.37	+0.04	- 9.0
TRSmCVC p	8.37	+0.04	- 9.0
TRSmCVX	8.37	+0.05	- 8.9
AmanaGrowth	8.75	+0.07	+ 0.9
AmanaIncome	18.86	+0.22	- 4.0
AmUtlFd	29.37	+0.35	- 5.6
Amer AAdvant Inst:			
BalInst	13.01	+0.10	- 2.3
GrInInst	18.76	+0.25	- 2.3
IntBdInst	9.89	-0.01	- 2.4
IntlInst	16.22	+0.01	- 4.9
S&PInst	17.04	+0.26	+ 1.5
StBndInst	9.40	-0.01	- 0.4
Amer AAdvant Plan:			
BalPlan	12.82	+0.09	- 2.4
GrInPlan	18.52	+0.24	- 2.4
IntlPlan	16.06	...	- 4.9
Amer Century:			
Balanced	18.20	+0.11	- 1.5
EqGro	22.37	+0.24	- 1.5
EqInc	5.98	+0.04	- 5.2
GlGold	5.33	+0.08	- 3.4
IncGro	29.19	+0.38	- 0.2
NatRes	10.19	+0.22	- 3.7
Real	12.27	+0.02	- 3.9
SmCpQ p	4.44	+0.02	- 11.6
SmCpVal p	4.69	+0.02	- 8.4
StrAgg	6.44	+0.04	- 2.6
StrConv	5.36	+0.02	- 2.5
StrMod	6.05	+0.03	- 2.6
Util	15.48	+0.21	- 3.0
Value	5.68	+0.07	- 6.1
Amer Century Benham:			
AZIntMu	10.70	-0.02	0.0
Bond	9.43	-0.01	- 2.3
CaHYMu	9.76	-0.01	+ 0.2
CaInsTF	10.45	-0.01	- 0.1
CaIntTF	11.21	-0.02	+ 0.1
CaLgTF	11.51	-0.02	- 0.1
CaLtdTF	10.43	-0.01	+ 0.4
FlIntMu	10.58	-0.02	+ 0.1
GNMA	10.58	-0.01	0.0
HighYld	9.00	-0.04	+ 1.0
HiYldMu	10.14	...	+ 0.3
Int TF	10.50	-0.01	0.0
IntlBnd	11.57	-0.06	- 7.0
IntTrBd	9.93	-0.01	- 1.3
ITreas	10.37	-0.01	- 2.3
Lg TF	10.64	-0.01	- 0.2
LtdBnd	9.87	...	- 0.1
Ltd TF	10.18	-0.02	+ 0.3
LTreas	10.05	-0.03	- 5.3
PrmBnd	10.02	-0.02	- 1.6
SGov	9.43	...	- 0.3
STreas	9.81	...	- 0.2
Tg2000	94.00	-0.02	- 0.3
Tg2005	72.88	-0.12	- 4.2
Tg2010	56.59	-0.27	- 6.8
Tg2015	44.92	-0.25	- 7.8
Tg2020	32.65	-0.27	- 9.4
Tg2025	27.85	-0.19	- 10.5
Amer Century 20th:			
EmgMkI	3.31	-0.01	- 2.4
Gift	18.57	+0.15	- 8.3
Gl Grwth	5.51	+0.03	+ 1.5
Grwth	27.52	+0.37	+ 1.3
Heritage	11.09	+0.09	- 3.2
IntDisc	9.64	-0.02	+ 0.7
Intl Gr	9.32	+0.01	- 2.7
New Opp	5.50	+0.01	- 7.6
Select	48.80	+0.83	+ 3.0
Ultra	34.90	+0.56	+ 4.5
Vista	10.24	+0.14	- 3.8
AmerDivrGlbl p	15.58	+0.15	- 0.5
Amer Express IDS A:			
BluCpA	11.58	+0.19	+ 2.0
BondA	4.98	-0.01	- 1.4
CalA	5.35	...	+ 0.1
DEIA	9.32	+0.15	+ 0.4
DiscvA	10.06	+0.13	- 10.3
EmgMkA	3.63	-0.03	- 1.5
EqSelA	14.20	+0.17	- 3.3
EqValA	11.14	+0.19	+ 0.9
ExtlA	3.98	...	+ 3.2
FdInA	4.97	-0.01	- 0.6
GlBal	6.17	+0.02	- 2.0
GlBdA	5.94	-0.03	- 4.3
GloGrA	8.33	+0.06	0.0
GwthA	38.56	+0.70	+ 4.0
HiYdA	4.64	...	+ 0.3
InsrA	5.60	-0.01	- 0.1
IntlA	11.31	+0.08	- 2.3
MassA	5.53	-0.01	- 0.1
MgdAllA	10.38	+0.08	- 0.4
MichA	5.52	-0.01	0.0
MinnA	5.40	...	+ 0.4
MutlA	13.05	+0.14	+ 0.2
NYA	5.29	-0.01	0.0
NwDA	29.29	+0.43	+ 1.6
OhioA	5.49	-0.01	+ 0.1
PreMtA	5.51	+0.05	- 3.9
ProgA	7.28	+0.09	- 6.3
RschOpA	7.52	+0.13	+ 1.7
SelectA	9.03	-0.02	- 1.7
SmColA	5.64	+0.05	- 9.0
StockA	26.43	+0.34	- 0.8
StrAgA	21.53	+0.25	- 5.3
TE BdA	4.12	-0.01	- 0.3
UtilInA	9.07	+0.09	- 3.9
Amer Express IDS B:			
BluCpB †	11.48	+0.19	+ 1.9

Name	NAV	Net Chg	YTD %ret
ARCH Funds Trust:			
Balance	11.87	+0.09	- 1.2
BdIdx	10.08	-0.02	- 1.8
EqIdx	15.38	+0.23	+ 1.5
EqInc	7.74	+0.11	- 5.1
GrInc	18.34	+0.25	- 1.0
GroEq	19.83	+0.30	+ 2.0
GvtCorpBd	10.24	-0.01	- 1.8
Intl	12.67	+0.01	- 3.0
IntmCorBd	9.96	-0.01	- 2.1
MOTF	11.96	-0.01	0.0
NatlMuBd	10.03	-0.03	- 0.3
ShIntmMu	10.21	-0.01	+ 0.3
SmCap	11.69	+0.09	- 9.5
USGvtSec	10.57	-0.01	- 0.7
ARMADA FUNDS:			
BalALLI p	10.43	+0.07	- 0.7
Bond I p	10.08	-0.01	- 1.8
CorEqI p	13.11	+0.22	+ 0.8
EnhIncI p	9.99	...	- 0.1
EqGroA p	24.56	+0.35	+ 1.6
EqGroI p	24.60	+0.34	+ 1.6
EqIdxI p	10.83	+0.17	+ 1.6
EqInI p	17.19	+0.22	- 1.2
GNMA I p	10.19	-0.01	- 0.2
IntEqI p	10.56	+0.02	- 4.7
IntmBdI p	10.47	-0.01	- 1.6
NtlTxE I p	10.06	-0.02	+ 0.2
OH TE I p	11.13	-0.02	+ 0.1
PA MuI p	10.49	-0.02	+ 0.1
SmCapGrI	9.65	+0.02	- 15.1
SCapVIn p	12.06	+0.05	- 7.9
TotAdvI p	10.12	-0.01	- 2.4
TxMgdI p	12.19	+0.18	+ 1.9
Ariel Mutual Funds:			
Apprec p	35.32	+0.28	- 1.0
BondInst	10.17	-0.01	- 1.1
Growth p	37.15	-0.14	- 7.0
AristataBd	9.86	-0.01	- 1.3
AristataEq	10.01	+0.11	- 3.0
Amstng	12.40	+0.16	+ 1.7
Artisan Funds:			
Intl	17.06	+0.20	+ 5.8
MidCap	13.94	+0.17	- 2.9
SCapVal	8.68	-0.01	- 5.0
SmCap	9.86	+0.03	- 11.6
Atlas Funds:			
BalancA p	14.28	+0.08	- 1.3
CaMuniA p	11.41	-0.01	+ 0.1
EmgGrA p	12.19	+0.03	- 11.3
GlbGroA p	14.27	+0.10	- 2.0
GvtScA p	10.03	-0.01	- 0.3
GroIncA p	22.70	+0.25	+ 2.8
GroIncB †	22.57	+0.24	+ 2.6
NaMuniA p	11.46	-0.01	- 0.1
StrGroA p	16.84	+0.03	- 1.6
StrGroB †	16.64	+0.04	- 1.6
StrIncA p	4.81	-0.01	- 2.1
BB&T:			
BalA p	13.84	+0.10	- 4.2
BalB †	13.76	+0.09	- 4.3
BalT	13.81	+0.10	- 4.2
GroIncA p	19.66	+0.21	- 5.0
GroIncB p	19.59	+0.22	- 5.0
GroIncT	19.71	+0.22	- 4.9
IntGovT	9.97	-0.01	- 2.3
IntlEqT	10.69	-0.03	- 5.6
LgCoGrT	11.39	+0.16	+ 0.3
NCIntT	10.30	-0.02	- 0.3
SIGovT	9.79	-0.01	- 0.7
SmGrA p	19.99	+0.25	- 6.5
SmGrB p	19.50	+0.23	- 6.7
SmGrT	20.23	+0.25	- 6.5
BEA Instl Funds:			
EmgMktEq	11.43	+0.03	+ 0.3
HighYld	15.70	-0.01	+ 0.8
IntlEq	21.19	-0.02	- 5.7
MuniBd	14.84	-0.03	- 0.2
SelValue	17.85	+0.33	NA
StGlFxIn	15.02	-0.10	- 5.2
USCFxIn	15.34	-0.02	- 1.2
USCorEq	18.61	+0.37	+ 1.3
BT Index Funds:			
EAFE In	10.99	-0.01	- 5.2
Eq500	158.33	+2.41	+ 1.5
Eq500 In	159.13	+2.42	+ 1.5
SmCap In	9.04	+0.05	- 6.6
USBnd In	10.20	-0.01	- 1.7
BT Institutional Fds:			
InstAstMg	12.91	+0.10	+ 0.1
IntlEq I	12.86	-0.04	- 7.2
IntlEqII	12.96	-0.04	- 7.2
PPlus In	10.00	...	+ 0.9
PPlus IS	10.00	...	+ 0.9
BT Investment Funds:			
CapAppr	12.81	+0.10	+ 0.2
EqtyAppr	17.60	+0.15	0.0
GloHiYld	NA	...	NA
IntlEqty	22.42	-0.07	- 7.3
IntTaxFr	10.81	-0.02	0.0
LatAmEq	NA	...	NA
LfcyLong	12.38	+0.10	0.0
LfcyMid	10.49	+0.06	- 0.6
LfcyShort	10.20	+0.02	- 1.6
SmCap	18.14	+0.08	- 5.6
Babson Group:			
Bond L	1.56	...	- 1.0
Bond S	9.77	-0.01	- 0.4
Enterp2	20.24	+0.12	- 10.9
Enterp	12.61	-0.01	- 11.6
Gwth	19.92	+0.35	- 3.5
Intl	17.82	+0.02	- 6.8
Shadw	10.74	+0.01	- 7.4
TaxFrL	9.18	-0.02	0.0
TaxFrS	10.77	-0.01	+ 0.3
Value	45.37	+0.58	- 1.1
BkBayTR A	9.87	-0.01	- 1.8
Bailard Biehl&Kaiser:			
Diversa	13.07	+0.05	- 1.8
IntlEq	6.17	-0.02	- 4.6
IntlBd	7.86	-0.03	- 3.2
Baird Funds Group:			
AdjInc	8.67	...	NA

FIGURE 23.2 Mutual Funds (excerpts)

Source: Reprinted by permission of *The Wall Street Journal,* Dow Jones & Company, Inc., March 5, 1999, p. C21.

The following quotations, collected by the National Association of Securities Dealers Inc., represent the average of annualized yields and dollar-weighted portfolio maturities ending Wednesday, March 3, 1999. Yields don't include capital gains or losses.

Fund	Avg. Mat.	7 Day Yield	Assets	Fund	Avg. Mat.	7 Day Yield	Assets
AAL Mny	59	4.20	294	ChVistaFed	84	4.24	516
AARP HQ	33	4.16	568	ChVistaFedInst	84	4.68	252
AAdMileP	45	4.06	149	ChVistaFedPre	84	4.44	303
AAdvGovP	21	3.92	89	ChVistaGovtPr	58	4.54	1105
AAdvMMPlat	45	4.18	832	ChVistaGovt	58	4.40	3298
ABN AMROGovl	60	4.33	84	ChVistaGovtInst	58	4.73	3123
ABN AMRO Gvt	60	4.65	402	ChVistaPrmPr	52	4.66	848
ABN AMROInv	60	4.37	223	ChVistaTrPlus	47	3.99	1525
ABN AMRO MM	60	4.73	1131	ChVistaTrPre	47	4.13	208
ABN AMRO Trs	34	4.39	305	ChVistaPrmInst	52	4.85	6728
AFD ExRsv A	19	3.95	200	ChVistaTrPlIn	47	4.33	1159
AFD ExResB	19	3.44	181	ChicagoTr	31	4.43	296
AFD ExResC p	19	3.69	98	ChchCsh	58	4.53	114
AIM MMCshRes	23	3.97	1205	CitiFndPUST	57	4.02	300
ARKGvtA	42	4.38	75	CitFInsCashRs	48	4.74	336
ARK Gvln II	42	4.54	174	CitFCashRs	86	4.40	2603
ARK MMln II	49	4.56	188	CitFInstLiq	86	4.90	4986
ARKMM A	49	4.63	438	CitFUSTr	57	4.22	207
ARKMM A	49	4.40	218	CitFPrmLq	86	4.70	823
ARKUSG A	42	4.61	1733	CitFUSTrs	57	3.77	328
ARKUST A	77	4.15	278	ColnIGvMMA	39	4.40	172
ARKUST A	77	3.92	20	ColnIGvMMB	39	3.66	97
ARKUST C	77	4.08	151	ColDIn f	39	4.39	1095
AZMunCTIns	45	2.49	31	CG CapGov	70	4.28	336
AccUSGov	53	4.39	222	CortldGn	56	4.05	636
ActAsGv	60	4.28	1001	CortldUS	40	3.85	57
ActAsMny	74	4.53	15841	CW MoneyMk	57	4.60	32
Advantus a	62	3.26	50	CW STGvt	55	3.86	105
AetnaAdvs	62	4.67	180	CW InstGvt	44	4.62	51
Aetna Sel	62	4.67	279	CrestCshTr	63	4.45	1060
AlexBwn	46	4.56	3727	CrestCshInvA	63	4.44	197
AlxBTr	46	3.94	815	CrestUST Tr	21	4.16	749
AlgerMM	21	4.18	386	DlyPasp	47	4.10	7646
AlliaGenMu	22	2.09	53	DavisGvtA	45	4.20	539
AlliaGov	66	4.12	49	DelaCashA	60	4.12	599
AlliMMass	45	2.08	44	DryBasic	76	4.66	1838
AlliaPrime	69	4.13	730	DryBasGov	82	4.55	1179
Alli TrResv	55	3.62	754	DryResInv	76	4.44	355
AliaCpRs	74	4.15	9570	DryUSTI	52	4.20	97
AliaGvR	61	4.05	5745	Drv100 US	88	4.05	1108
AlliMny	.76	4.11	1489	DryGvt	63	4.21	435
AmAAdGvl	21	4.72	30	DryInG	71	4.15	68
AmAAdMMI	45	4.89	1297	DryInst	77	4.51	609
AmPerCsh	41	4.46	485	DryfLA	86	4.35	5708
AmPerTrs	30	4.12	391	DryMM	76	4.17	111
AmAAdGvP	21	4.38	107	DryResR	76	4.66	291
AmAAdMMP	45	4.60	358	DryWld	87	4.40	1582
AmAAdGvM	21	4.29	32	DryInstGv1	47	4.47	287
AmAAdMMM	45	4.51	127	DryInstPrm1	52	4.65	528
AmSthInstPri	20	4.66	87	DryInstUST1	49	4.32	576
AmSouthPrC	66	4.22	137	DryUSTR	52	4.40	583
AmSouthPrP	66	4.32	552	EatVCsh	37	4.08	91
AmSouthUSP	51	3.95	314	ElfunMM	50	4.72	205
AonMMktY	38	4.72	807	EnterpriseA p	37	4.39	151
ArchMMInst	46	4.23	43	EnterpriseB p	37	4.39	12
ArchMMInvA	46	4.23	228	EurPrimeT	44	4.54	175
ArchMM Tr	46	4.23	649	EurUSTrOblT	51	4.36	122
ArchMMTrII	46	4.48	637	EvgrnMM A	64	4.35	5937
ArchTreaTr	41	3.70	209	EvgrnMM B	64	3.65	77
ArchTreaTrII	41	3.95	93	EvgrnMM Y	64	4.65	1718
ArchUSTrInvA	41	3.70	24	EvgrnNJMuA	6	2.15	114
ArmadaGvR A	45	4.40	570	EvgrnPaA	14	2.52	95
Armada Gvl	45	4.55	902	EvgSelMktI	65	4.99	2938
Armada MMI	42	4.58	2355	EvgSelMktIS	65	4.73	2256
Armada MMRA	42	4.43	1273	EvgSelMu I	7	2.82	141
ArmadaTrA p	47	3.95	78	EvgSelMu IS	7	3.07	867
Armada Trsyl	47	4.10	288	EvgSelTrsyI	52	4.72	2068
AMF MM Pt	4	4.77	90	EvgSelTrsyIS	52	4.48	1453
Atlas USTrs	53	3.75	56	EvgSelUSTrI	74	4.44	543
AutCsh	56	4.52	1804	EvgrTreasA	51	4.17	3263
AutGvt	46	4.30	2249	EvgrTreasY	51	4.47	1113
AuGvSvc	49	4.34	754	ExcelsiorGvt	24	4.61	646
AutCshCII	56	4.35	755	ExcelsiorMny	54	4.58	1074
AutTreasC	48	3.97	267	ExcelsrMM	86	4.86	173
BB&T PrimTr	65	4.53	66	ExcelsiorTry	32	4.15	495
BB&T UST Tr	54	4.23	266	ExpMM	50	4.34	192
BNYHam TrHm	46	4.59	194	ExpMMInst	50	4.59	80
BNYHmltTrPr	46	4.35	570	FThirdComP A	45	4.25	60
BNY Hmltn	53	4.76	1449	FThirdComP I	45	4.50	372
BNY HmltnPr	53	4.51	652	FThirdGov A	50	4.17	476
BT InstCash	50	4.74	2686	FThirdGov I	50	4.37	270
BT InstCshRv	50	4.79	2950	FThirdTO	39	4.47	926
BT Inst Trsv	34	4.59	1896	FFTW	84	4.89	26
BT InvCash	50	4.22	258	FIMMDom I	44	4.85	2518
BT InvTrsv	34	4.10	321	FIMMDomII p	44	4.70	437
BT InvMMkt	50	4.62	415	FIMMDomIII	44	4.59	582
BT LqdAsst	49	4.83	3495	F!MMGov I	54	4.80	4919
Babson	39	4.05	41	FIMMGovII	54	4.65	375
BearST Prime	49	4.84	292	FIMMGovIII	54	4.55	735

FIGURE 23.3 Money Market Mutual Funds (excerpts)

Source: Reprinted by permission of *The Wall Street Journal,* Dow Jones & Company, Inc., March 4, 1999, p. C20. All rights reserved worldwide.

securities, such as Treasury bills, commercial paper, and bank certificates of deposit. Next to the name of each fund are presented the average maturity of its holdings, the annual yield based on what was earned over the past seven days, and the aggregate market value of its assets. Not shown, but an important factor in selecting a money market fund, is the degree of safety (that is, default risk) associated with the assets held by each fund.

An Example

In order to highlight the differences in purchasing shares of closed-end funds, no-load funds, and load funds, consider the following example. An investor has $1,000 to use in purchasing shares of a fund and is considering the following funds, all of which have the same NAV of $10 per share.

Closed-end fund E is selling for a market price that equals its NAV, whereas closed-end fund D is selling at a 20% discount, or $8 (= $10 × .80). The broker charges a commission of 2% of the market price for each share purchased. Mutual fund N is a no-load fund, whereas mutual fund L charges an $8\frac{1}{2}$% load. How many shares does the investor end up with in each case?

Closed-end fund E:	Cost per share = $10 + $.20 commission = $10.20
	Number of shares = $1,000/$10.20 = 98.04
Closed-end fund D:	Cost per share = $8 + $.16 commission = $8.16
	Number of shares = $1,000/$8.16 = 122.55
Mutual fund N:	Cost per share = $10
	Number of shares = $1,000/$10 = 100
Mutual fund L:	Cost per share = $10 + $.93 load = $10.93
	(*Note:* 8.5% × $10.93 = $.93)
	Number of shares = $1,000/$10.93 = 91.50

Thus, the largest number of shares would be received when buying the shares of discounted closed-end fund D; the fewest shares would be received when buying the shares of load fund L.

23.3   Investment Policies

Different investment companies have different investment objectives (also termed investment styles). Some companies are designed as substitutes for their shareholders' entire portfolio; others expect their shareholders to own other securities. Some restrict their domain or selection methods severely; others give their managers wide latitude. Many engage in highly active management, with substantial portfolio changes designed to exploit perceived superior investment predictions. Others are more passive, concentrating instead on tailoring a portfolio to serve the interests of a particular clientele.

Although categorization is difficult, broad classes of investment objectives are often defined. As mentioned earlier, money market funds hold short-term (typically less than one year) fixed-income instruments, such as bank CDs, commercial paper, and Treasury bills. The fund manager extracts an annual fee for this service, usually between .25% and 1% of the average value of total assets. There are usually no load charges, and investors may add or remove money from their accounts at almost any time. Dividends are usually declared daily. Arrangements with a cooperating bank often allow investors to write checks on an account, where the bank obtains the amount involved by redeeming "shares" in the fund when the check clears.

Bond funds invest in fixed-income securities. Some go further, specifying that only particular types will be purchased. There are corporate bond funds, U.S. government bond funds, GNMA (or Ginnie Mae) funds, convertible bond funds, and so on. Some are organized as open-end investment companies, others as closed-end investment companies.

As indicated earlier, the predominant type of unit investment trust in the United States is the bond unit investment trust. Some purchase only government issues, others purchase only corporate issues, and still others specialize to a greater extent. Municipal bond unit investment trusts make it easier for those in high tax brackets to obtain diversification and liquidity while taking advantage of the exemption of such securities from personal income taxation. Bond unit investment trusts typically hold securities with different coupon payment schedules and pay roughly equal-size dividends every month.

Many open-end companies consider themselves managers for the bulk of the investment assets of their clientele. Those that hold both equity and fixed-income securities particularly fit this description. CDA/Wiesenberger Investment Companies Service refers to such companies as *balanced funds,* provided at least 25% of their portfolios are invested in bonds. These funds seek to "minimize investment risks without unduly sacrificing possibilities for long-term growth and current income."[12] Whereas balanced funds typically hold relatively constant mixes of bonds, preferred stock, convertible bonds, and common stocks, *asset allocation funds* often alter the proportions periodically in attempts to "time the market."[13]

A diversified common stock fund invests most of its assets in common stocks, although some short-term money market instruments may be held to accommodate irregular cash flows or to engage in market timing. CDA/Wiesenberger classifies the majority of diversified common stock funds as having one of three types of objectives: (1) *capital gain,* (2) *growth,* or (3) *growth and income.*[14] Two factors appear to be involved in this classification: the relative importance of dividend income versus capital gains and the overall level of risk taken. The classifications are arranged in decreasing order of emphasis the funds place on capital appreciation but in increasing order of emphasis the funds place on current income and relative price stability. Because high-dividend portfolios are generally less risky than portfolios with low dividends, relatively few major conflicts arise, although two rather different criteria are involved. There is also another class, *equity income funds,* that CDA/Wiesenberger describes as seeking to generate a stream of current income by investing in stocks with sizable dividend yields.

Borderline cases exist in which the difference between a capital gain fund and a growth fund is a matter of degree, which, in some cases, can be small. Similarly, the differences between a growth fund and a growth-income fund also can be small. Classification is difficult because the official statement of investment objectives in a fund's prospectus is often fuzzy and also because the fund's manager may change the types of stocks held in the fund's portfolio over time.

A few specialized investment companies concentrate on the securities of firms in a particular industry or sector; these are known as *sector funds* (or specialized funds). For example, there are chemical funds, aerospace funds, technology funds, and gold funds. Others deal in securities of a particular type; examples include funds that hold growth or value stocks and funds that invest in the stocks of small companies. Still others provide a convenient means for holding the securities of firms in a particular country, such as the previously mentioned India and Indonesia funds. There are also investment companies that, by design, invest internationally, purchasing stocks and bonds from a variety of countries. (From the U.S. viewpoint there are two types of *international funds: foreign funds* invest in non-U.S. securities, whereas *global funds* invest in both U.S. and non-U.S. securities.[15])

Although municipal bond unit investment trusts have been available for many years, open-end municipal bond funds were first offered in 1976. Some municipal bond funds hold long-term issues from many states. Others specialize in the long-term issues of governmental units in one state ("single-state" funds) in order to provide an investment vehicle for residents of that state who wish to avoid paying state taxes (as well as federal taxes) on the income. Still others buy short-term municipal securities, with some specializing in the short-term issues of governmental units in one state.

An index fund attempts to provide results similar or identical to those computed for a specified market index. For example, the Vanguard Index 500 Trust, a no-load open-end investment company, provides a vehicle for investors who wish to obtain results matching those of the S&P 500 stock index, less operating expenses. Similarly, a number of banks have established commingled index funds, and corporations and other organizations have set up index funds for their own employee retirement trust funds.

Table 23.1 provides an indication of the number of mutual funds pursuing various kinds of investment objectives, along with the amount of assets under their control. In total there were slightly more than 7,300 mutual funds in existence at year-end 1998. At that time these funds had roughly $5.5 trillion invested in a variety of financial assets.

TABLE 23.1 Mutual Fund Classifications as of Year-End 1998

Classification	*Number of Funds*	*Total Net Assets (billions)*
A. Classification by assets		
Equity	3,513	$2,978
Hybrid	525	365
Bond and income	2,250	831
Taxable money market	685	1,163
Tax-exempt money market	341	188
Total	7,314	$5,525
B. Classification by investment objective		
Aggressive growth		$ 394
Growth		890
Sector		121
World equity		391
Growth and income		1,033
Income equity		149
Total equity funds		$2,978
Asset allocation		40
Balanced		168
Flexible portfolio		86
Income—mixed		71
Total hybrid funds		$ 365
Corporate bond		143
High-yield bond		118
World bond		25
Government bond		144
Strategic income		102
State municipal		140
National municipal		159
Total bond funds		$ 831
Taxable money market		1,163
Tax-exempt money market		188
Total money market		$1,351
Total		$5,525

Source: Adapted from *1999 Mutual Fund Fact Book* (Washington, DC: Investment Company Institute, 1999): pp. 67, 69, 71. Used with permission of the Investment Company Institute.

Both the number of funds and the dollars invested in them have continued to rise rapidly as investors, ranging from individuals to large institutions, have come to appreciate the advantages of investing through mutual funds.

23.4 Mutual Fund Taxation

The U.S. Internal Revenue Code allows an investment company to avoid corporate income taxation, provided it meets certain standards and pays at least 90% of its net income to its stockholders. However, its stockholders must pay taxes on the income that they receive. Most investment companies choose to distribute their net income by making two kinds of cash payments to their shareholders—one for income (from dividends and interest that the fund has received) and one for net realized capital gains. These two payments are then taxed at the shareholder level as ordinary income and capital gains, respectively.

This practice creates a potential problem for investors near the end of the year that can best be seen with an example. Imagine an investor makes a $10,000 investment on December 15 in a no-load fund whose shares are selling for $20, thus receiving 500 shares. On December 16 the fund declares and pays a dividend of $2 per share, thereby lowering its net asset value by $2 per share to $18. When the new year arrives, the investor must report $1,000 of taxable income because he or she received a dividend check for $1,000 (= $2 × 500), even if the shares are still selling for $18 at the end of the year. Thus, the investor must seen his or her investment increase in value but still owes income taxes on the investment. Consequently, most financial advisers suggest that investors avoid investing in a taxable mutual fund near year-end. (Investors who buy mutual funds with their tax-exempt accounts such as IRAs would escape such taxation at this time, as mentioned in Chapter 5.)

23.5 Mutual Fund Performance

Mutual funds are required to compute and publicize their net asset values daily. Because their income and their capital gain distributions are also publicized, they are ideal candidates for studies of the performance of professionally managed portfolios. Thus, it is hardly surprising that mutual funds have frequently been the subject of extensive study.

23.5.1 CALCULATING RETURNS

In studies of performance, the rate of return on a mutual fund for period t is calculated by adding the change in net asset value to the amount of income and capital gains distributions made during the period, denoted by I_t and G_t, respectively, and dividing this total by the net asset value at the beginning of the period:

$$r_t = \frac{(NAV_t - NAV_{t-1}) + I_t + G_t}{NAV_{t-1}} \qquad (23.2)$$

For example, a mutual fund that had a net asset value of $10 at the beginning of month t, made income and capital gain distributions of, respectively, $.05 and $.04 per share during the month, and then ended the month with a net asset value of $10.03 would have a monthly return of

$$r_t = \frac{(\$10.03 - \$10.00) + \$.05 + \$.04}{\$10.00}$$

$$= 1.20\%$$

Variable Annuities

Variable annuities have become one of the hottest products to hit the investment market in the 1990s. Despite the rather incongruous name, assets invested in variable annuities have grown to more than $500 billion.

What is a variable annuity? To start, perhaps a better question is: What is an annuity? In the world of financial services, an annuity is a tax-advantaged form of investment made through an insurance company. The insurer makes certain promises about how the proceeds of the investment will be returned to the investor (or the investor's beneficiaries). There are two types of annuities: fixed and variable. Familiarity with fixed annuities is helpful to understanding variable annuities.

With a fixed annuity, you as the investor enter into a contract with an insurance company, agreeing to pay a stated amount known as the *premium,* which represents the cost of the annuity. This premium is usually paid in a lump sum. In exchange for the premium, the insurance company sets an interest rate that is used to determine an amount to credit your investment with during a specified *guarantee period* of time. You choose the length of the guarantee period, with rates usually higher for longer periods. At the end of the guarantee period, the insurance company establishes new rates and you choose another guarantee period.

The commitment involved in a fixed annuity is a two-way street. In the early years of your contract, withdrawing more than a small proportion (usually up to 10%) of your investment annually invokes a *surrender penalty.* Over several years, the size of the penalty declines to zero. Further, if at the end of a rate guarantee period, the newly offered rate is materially lower (as defined by the annuity contract) than the previous rate, you can withdraw from the contract penalty-free and move the balance to another annuity provider.

Fixed annuities are similar in many respects to bank certificates of deposit (CDs). There are several distinctions however. Most important, your investment accumulates interest on a tax-deferred basis. Only when you withdraw from the annuity must you pay tax on the earned interest. With a CD, you pay taxes annually on your earnings. In exchange for this tax advantage, however, you cannot withdraw funds from your annuity until age $59\frac{1}{2}$ (unless you transfer to another annuity) without being assessed a 10% penalty by the IRS.

Fixed annuities are also different from CDs in that you have the option to "annuitize" the distribution of your accumulated investment. There are many different annuity variations. Payments are typically monthly or quarterly. You can receive payments for a specified period of time, or you can have the payments continue for your entire life, ending only when you die. You can even have your payments go to your beneficiary after you die. The size of your annuity payments depends on the selected payout option.

Variable annuities are really not much more complicated than fixed annuities. Essentially the word *variable* refers to the rate of return earned on the premiums that you invest with the insurance company. Instead of offering a fixed interest rate guaranteed for a specified period of time, the annuity provider offers you a set of investment options into which your premiums can be invested, such as a portfolio of growth stocks. You make the decision as to where to place your investment and if, and when, to switch those choices. The value of your accumulated earnings responds commensurately (up or down) with the returns on your investment selection.

Variable annuities are different from fixed annuities in two other key ways. First, you can add funds to a variable annuity at any time before starting to receive annuitized distributions. With fixed-rate annuities, adding additional funds requires purchasing a new contract at possibly a different interest rate. Second, the insurance company promises your beneficiaries a "death benefit" if you die before starting to receive distributions that is equal to the greater of your paid premiums (less any withdrawals) or the value of your investments. Thus, variable annuities offer an insured "floor" on the value of your investments. (Because of the guaranteed interest rate, fixed-rate annuities have no need for such a provision.)

The remainder of the variable annuity contract is essentially no different from the fixed annuity contract. Your earnings compound on a tax-deferred basis. Withdrawals are subject to surrender penalties depending on the terms of your contract. IRS penalties are charged on withdrawals before age $59\frac{1}{2}$. And when you move from the accumulation phase to the distribution phase, you can annuitize your distributions in similar ways.

Variable annuities have existed since the early 1950s. The explosion in variable annuity popularity came in recent years when the federal government vastly reduced the ability of investors to shelter investment income from taxes. Especially for people without access to employer-sponsored 401(k) retirement plans or for those who make contributions to either IRAs or Keogh Plans that are capped by law (see Chapter 5), variable annuities offer the only means to easily make large tax-deferred investments.

Traditionally, insurance companies offered their variable annuity customers only investment options managed by the insurance companies themselves. Today, many insurance companies make arrangements with mutual fund providers to offer versions of the mutual funds to variable annuity investors, with the insurers handling the death benefits. Although variable annuity investments must be kept in legally separate portfolios (known as "separate accounts"), mutual fund providers in many cases create "clone" versions of their popular funds specifically for variable annuity clients. More recently, an increasing number of mutual fund companies have turned the tables on the insurance companies by offering their own variable annuity products and making arrangements with insurance companies to provide the death benefits.

Should you invest in mutual funds on a taxable basis or in variable annuities on a tax-deferred basis? The answer is not as clear-cut as many proponents of variable annuities might contend. Certainly if you are under age $59\frac{1}{2}$ and may need access to your funds soon, you should factor in the IRS 10% withdrawal penalty and any insurance company surrender charges into your calculations.

Suppose though that you are investing for the long haul. The tax-deferred benefits of variable annuities appear attractive compared with the alternative of paying taxes annually on distributed income and realized capital gains that investors in taxable mutual funds must pay. However, the tax benefits may be overwhelmed by two adverse aspects of variable annuities. The first is cost. Variable annuity investors not only pay standard management and administrative expense fees similar to those paid by mutual fund shareholders, but they also pay a fee to cover the death benefit. That fee typically runs in the range of 1% to 1.5% per year. Only you can decide whether the option to redeem your investment at its original value is worth this expense. (It is true that variable annuities do not involve explicit sales commissions, but an informed mutual fund investor generally should not purchase a load fund.)

Further, when assets are ultimately withdrawn from a variable annuity, the investor pays taxes at ordinary income tax rates. The mutual fund investor, on the other hand, has annually been paying taxes, primarily on realized capital gains at capital gains tax rates, which are currently much lower than ordinary income tax rates (see Chapter 5). Depending on how quickly capital gains in the taxable mutual funds are realized and the amount of dividend and interest income earned, it is possible that the combination of no death-benefit expenses and lower taxes paid at capital gains tax rates may be better than deferring ordinary income taxes until distribution. In general, the longer your investment horizon, the more the tax-deferred aspects of variable annuities are able to overcome their higher costs relative to taxable mutual funds.

If you are an investor who likes to move among funds (for example, between stock and bond funds) within a family of funds, variable annuities offer a significant advantage over taxable mutual funds in rising markets. Within a variable annuity's fund family, switches occur without triggering a taxable event. With taxable mutual funds, a switch among funds requires payment of capital gains taxes on any appreciation in fund share values, regardless of whether the funds belong to a family of funds.

Finally, in terms of estate planning, variable annuities are at a disadvantage compared with taxable mutual funds. The death proceeds from a variable annuity bypass probate, easing administration of your estate. However, those proceeds are taxable to your beneficiaries as ordinary income. Conversely, the cost basis of taxable mutual funds is increased to their market value at the time of your death—potentially a huge tax benefit.

Returns calculated in this manner can be used to evaluate the performance of the portfolio manager of a mutual fund because this method reflects the results of the manager's investment decisions. However, it does not necessarily indicate the return earned by the shareholders in the fund because a load charge may have been involved. In the example, perhaps the investor paid $10.50 at the beginning of the month for one share of this fund, with $.50 being a front-end load. If this were the case, the investor's return for this month is calculated using Equation (23.2), where NAV_{t-1} is $10.50, not $10.00:

$$r_t = \frac{(\$10.03 - \$10.50) + \$.05 + \$.04}{\$10.50}$$

$$= -3.62\%$$

Thus, the return for the investor who bought one share at the beginning of the month and paid a $.50 per share load charge at that time would be -3.62%. However, the portfolio manager was only given $10.00 per share to invest because the load charge was paid to certain people who were responsible for getting the investor to buy the share. Accordingly, the portfolio manager should be evaluated on the basis of the return provided on the $10.00, which in this example was 1.20%.

Data on professionally managed pension funds and bank commingled funds has become more widely available in recent years. The performance of the managers of such funds appears to be similar to that of mutual fund managers: They do reasonably well tailoring portfolios to meet clients' objectives, but few seem to be able to consistently "beat the market." Although the following sections deal only with U.S. mutual funds, many of the results apply to other investment companies, both in the United States and in other countries. A detailed discussion of certain risk-adjusted measures of performance and their application to mutual funds is presented in Chapter 18.

23.5.2 AVERAGE RETURN

Some organizations have established indices based on the net asset values of mutual funds that have similar investment objectives. For example, one index may include funds that invest in a particular type of common stocks, such as small capitalization stocks, whereas another index may include funds that invest in a particular type of fixed-income security, such as corporate A-rated debt. As shown in Figure 23.2, these two indices are published every day (and, more extensively, every month) in *The Wall Street Journal*, where mutual fund indices prepared by Lipper Analytical Services are provided.

Many studies have compared the performance of investment companies that have invested primarily in common stocks with the performance of a benchmark portfolio that generally consisted of a combination of (1) a market index, such as the S&P 500 stock index; (2) a riskfree asset, such as Treasury bills; and sometimes other indices, such as (3) an index to account for the difference in performance between large and small capitalization stocks; and (4) an index to account for the difference in performance between high and low book value-to-market value stocks. Each combination was chosen so that the benchmark portfolio had a risk level equal to that of the investment company. Thus, an investment company that had a beta of .80 would be compared with a benchmark portfolio that had 80% invested in the market index and 20% in the riskfree asset (provided these were the only indices used to construct the benchmark portfolio).[16] Alternatively, sometimes *style analysis* is used to arrive at the appropriate benchmark. With this approach, a fund's returns are matched with those of a set of indices, such as the Standard & Poor's/BARRA Value and Growth indices, the Wilshire 4500 index (for small-cap stocks), and various others to arrive at a combination of the indices that seems to best describe the investment style of the fund.

One common way of determining whether or not a mutual fund has had superior performance is to subtract the average return on the benchmark portfolio from the average return of the mutual fund. As discussed in Chapter 18, this abnormal return is known as the fund's *ex post* alpha:

$$\alpha_p = ar_p - ar_{bp} \tag{23.3}$$

where ar_p is the average return on portfolio p and ar_{bp} is the average return on the benchmark portfolio associated with portfolio p. Note that if $\alpha_p > 0$, then the portfolio has performed well because it has earned positive risk-adjusted returns. Conversely, if $\alpha_p < 0$, then the portfolio has earned inferior returns.

In addition to examining portfolio performance to see if some group of mutual funds has earned abnormally high (or low) returns, it is also important to examine the persistence of funds' performance. That is, do the funds that have had the highest returns (or abnormal returns) during some time period continue to have the highest returns (or abnormal returns) during a succeeding time period? Do poor performers in one time period continue to be poor performers in the next time period? Alternatively, does a fund's performance in one time period provide any indication of how it will perform in the next time period? The next two sections examine portfolio performance and persistence of performance for equity funds and bond funds.

23.5.3 EQUITY FUNDS

A major study published in 1997 examined the 32-year performance of 1,892 diversified equity funds.[17] This study first sorted funds on January 1 of each year by their returns the previous year and then put the top 10% into portfolio 1, the next 10% into portfolio 2, and so on through portfolio 10, which consisted of the 10% worst performers the previous year. The portfolio's returns were then tracked during the next year. Thus, there is a 32-year series of monthly returns for each of the 10 portfolios.

The top part of Figure 23.4 shows the average monthly excess return (that is, the average monthly return over the monthly Treasury bill rate) on the 10 portfolios formed by sorting them on their previous year's returns. The returns clearly decrease with the ranking: Portfolio 1 has the highest average excess return of .68% per month, and portfolio 10, at .01%, has the lowest.

The bottom part of Figure 23.4 shows the average monthly *abnormal* returns earned by the 10 portfolios *subsequent* to their formation. Three observations can be made. First, note that all of the abnormal returns are negative. This result appears to be consistent with the argument that the typical mutual fund cannot beat the market. Second, there is still dispersion in the returns: portfolios 1 and 2 have the highest, and portfolio 10 has the lowest abnormal return. Third, the bottom decile portfolio stands out for having by far the lowest abnormal return.[18]

Each fund's abnormal return was related to certain fund characteristics to determine if an explanation could be found for the different levels of abnormal returns. Measures of the following fund characteristics were used:

portfolio turnover rates

1. Operating expense ratio
2. Portfolio turnover rate (a fund's **portfolio turnover rate** is the ratio of the smaller of purchases or sales during a time period divided by the average total asset value during the period and hence is a measure of how much trading was done during that period)
3. Maximum load charge
4. Average total net assets

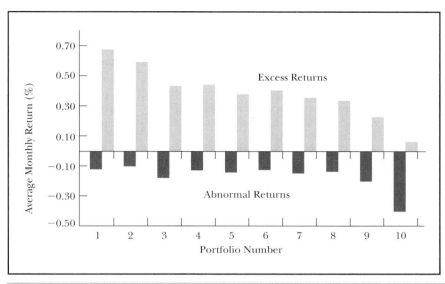

FIGURE 23.4 Average Monthly Returns of Mutual Fund Portfolios Based on Previous One-Year Returns

Source: Adapted from Mark M. Cathcart, "On Persistence in Mutual Fund Performance," *Journal of Finance,* 52, no. 1 (March 1997): p. 64.

The results indicated that there was a strong negative relationship between abnormal return and the first two of these characteristics.[19] That is, funds with higher operating expense ratios and portfolio turnover rates had lower abnormal returns. Although a negative relationship between load charges and abnormal returns was observed, load funds tend to have higher portfolio turnover rates, and the existence of higher loads does not, by itself, lead to lower performance. Larger funds tended to have slightly lower abnormal returns, but the relationship was not statistically significant. There is also evidence that transaction costs are inversely related to fund performance because funds with lower abnormal returns tend to hold more illiquid stocks that cost more to trade.

One reasonable explanation for these observations is that, in an efficient market, higher expense ratios and more frequent revisions cause a fund to incur more costs without consistently earning gains from the purchase of underpriced securities as an offset. Furthermore, whereas revisions in a fund's portfolio may be desirable to maintain a desired risk level or dividend yield, the evidence indicates that revisions intended to exploit supposed market inefficiencies generally prove unproductive because of the associated transaction costs.

Aside from concluding that the evidence suggests that stock markets are highly efficient, the study provides three rules of thumb for the investor:

1. Do not purchase funds that have persistently poor performance.
2. Expect funds with high returns during the past year to have, at most, high returns only in the next year.
3. Expect high expense ratios, load fees, and transaction costs to hinder fund performance.

In summary, these results suggest that the average equity mutual fund has not significantly outperformed an equal-risk passive alternative during any extended period.[20] This outcome is not surprising. After all, the market's performance is itself an average of the performance of all investors. If, on average, mutual funds had beaten the market, then some other group of investors would have "lost" to the market. With the substantial amount of professional management in today's stock market, it is difficult to think of a likely group of victims.

23.5.4 BOND FUNDS

All of the results reported so far focus on mutual funds that have at least a large part of their assets invested in common stocks. This leaves open the question of bond mutual fund managers: Is their performance similar to that of stock fund managers? One study looked at a sample of 41 bond funds over a 20-year period.[21]

A variety of models were used to produce benchmark returns. The average abnormal return ranged from −.023% to −.069% per month. Furthermore, regardless of the model, at least two-thirds of the funds had negative abnormal returns. Expanding the sample to cover 223 bond funds but over a shorter 5-year period produced similar results. It was determined that there was an inverse relationship between the size of a fund's expense ratio and its performance; that is, higher expenses tended to be associated with worse performance. In summary, the results regarding stock funds also seem to be applicable to bond funds.

A more recent study of 123 bond funds (excluding high-yield funds) during a 6-year period revealed that no matter which one of four methods was used to estimate benchmark returns, the average bond fund had a negative abnormal return, and in three of the cases it was significantly negative. Specifically, the four average abnormal returns were −.12%, −.06%, −.10%, and −.08% per month. Average abnormal returns calculated using gross returns were −.04%, .02%, −.02%, and .00% per month, with none of these values being significantly different from zero.[22] Thus, apparently the average fund approximately matches the returns on a similar-risk benchmark, but, because of expenses, it underperforms its benchmark. This outcome suggests that investors in bond mutual funds should choose low-expense funds, unless they are confident in the forecasting ability of a particular fund's manager.

23.6 Evaluating Mutual Funds

Along with the rapid growth in money invested in mutual funds in recent years has come a corresponding increase in the number and diversity of mutual funds offered to investors. Not surprisingly then, various organizations have created businesses devoted to evaluating mutual funds. One of the most prominent of these organizations is Morningstar, Inc., located in Chicago. Besides providing a wealth of information on a given fund, it also provides an in-depth analysis of past returns.

The best way to understand the breadth of Morningstar's mutual fund evaluations is to consider an analysis of a specific fund. Morningstar assigns each mutual fund to an *investment class* based broadly on the securities the fund holds in its portfolio. Figure 23.5 provides an example involving the Fidelity Magellan Fund, classified as a domestic equity fund. The analysis is also applied to funds belonging to another investment class, domestic taxable bond funds, where they differ.

23.6.1 PERFORMANCE

On the left side of Figure 23.5 is a section with the heading "Performance." Displayed here are, first, the quarterly returns during the past 5 years and, second, the average returns earned by the fund during various time periods ending September 30, 1999, rang-

Performance 09-30-99

	1st Qtr	2nd Qtr	3rd Qtr	4th Qtr	Total
1995	8.44	15.77	10.60	-1.46	36.82
1996	1.79	1.00	1.67	6.85	11.69
1997	-0.56	16.55	9.67	-0.40	26.59
1998	14.22	3.37	-11.05	27.22	33.63
1999	7.39	5.93	-5.97	—	—

Trailing	Total Return%	+/- S&P 500	+/-Wil Top 750	% Rank All	Cat	Growth of $10,000
3 Mo	-5.97	0.27	0.59	77	39	9,403
6 Mo	-0.40	-0.77	0.03	58	66	9,960
1 Yr	36.08	8.29	8.36	15	8	13,608
3 Yr Avg	24.58	-0.51	-0.05	5	14	19,333
5 Yr Avg	22.33	-2.69	-2.22	7	32	27,399
10 Yr Avg	17.06	0.25	0.82	6	7	48,319
15 Yr Avg	19.70	1.73	2.22	3	1	148,409

Tax Analysis	Tax-Adj Ret %	% Rank Cat	% Pretax Ret	% Rank Cat
3 Yr Avg	22.58	18	91.9	32
5 Yr Avg	19.49	35	87.3	54
10 Yr Avg	13.85	22	81.2	57

Potential Capital Gain Exposure: 39% of assets

Historical Profile

Return	Above Avg
Risk	Average
Rating	★★★★★
	Highest

Risk Analysis

Time Period	Load-Adj Return %	Risk % Rank[1] All	Cat	Morningstar Return	Morningstar Risk	Morningstar Risk-Adj Rating
1 Yr	32.00					
3 Yr	23.32	66	57	1.98	0.88	★★★★
5 Yr	21.59	73	84	1.48	0.94	★★★★
10 Yr	16.71	71	72	1.62	0.94	★★★★★

Average Historical Rating (166 months): 4.7★s

[1]1=low, 100=high

Category Rating (3 Yr)

2 3 4
1 5
Worst — Best

Return	Above Avg
Risk	Average

Other Measures	Standard Index S&P 500	Best Fit Index S&P 500
Alpha	-0.6	-0.6
Beta	1.02	1.02
R-Squared	94	94
Standard Deviation		21.72
Mean		24.58
Sharpe Ratio		1.01

Current Investment Style

Style: Value Blnd Growth — Size: Large Med Small

	Stock Port Avg	Relative S&P 500 Current	Hist	Rel Cat
Price/Earnings Ratio	36.6	1.02	1.15	1.11
Price/Book Ratio	8.6	0.96	1.12	1.12
Price/Cash Flow	25.1	1.04	0.99	1.11
3 Yr Earnings Growth	20.7	1.27	1.41	1.17
1 Yr Earnings Est %	20.6	1.13	—	1.18
Med Mkt Cap $ mil	70.670	1.0	1.3	1.55

FIGURE 23.5 Performance and Risk Analysis of the Magellan Fund (excerpts)

Source: Excerpts from *Morningstar Mutual Funds,* Morningstar, Inc., 225 W. Wacker Dr., Chicago, IL 60606, 312-696-6000, October 21, 1999, p. 121.

ing from the past three months to the past 15 years. These returns are calculated net of operating expenses and 12b-1 fees, although load charges are ignored. Thus, the average returns reflect what an investor would have earned after having bought the fund's shares.[23] Next to each average return is an indication of how it compares with the average return on the S&P 500 and Wilshire 750 indices during the same time period. For fixed-income funds these indices are replaced by the Lehman Brothers Aggregate Bond Index and another fixed-income bond index that best matches the fund's holdings.

In the fourth and fifth columns from the left are the percentile ranks of the fund's average return relative to all mutual funds in the same investment class (for Magellan, all domestic equity funds) and relative to those funds identified by Morningstar as being in the same *category.* (Just how Morningstar divides funds within an investment class into categories will be shown shortly; Magellan currently is in the large-cap blended fund category.[24]) Here a rank of 1 places a fund at the top, and a rank of 100 places a fund at the bottom. The sixth column shows the amount a $10,000 investment in the fund would have grown to during the applicable time period (ignoring taxes and load charges).

Over the three months ending September 30, 1999, Magellan had a return of -5.97%, which was 0.27% higher than the S&P 500 and .59% higher than the Wilshire 750. This return caused the fund to be ranked at the 77th percentile of all funds and the 39th percentile of funds in the same category. The Magellan Fund did substantially better than both indices during the past 15 years, placing it in the third percentile among domestic equity funds and in the first percentile among funds in its category. Note how a $10,000 investment in the Magellan Fund made on September 30, 1984, would have grown to $148,409 on September 30, 1999, 15 years later.

23.6.2 RATINGS

In the "Risk Analysis" section of Figure 23.5 are columns labeled Load-Adj Return, Risk % Rank: All and Cat, Morningstar Return and Risk, and Morningstar Risk-Adj Rating. The three columns labeled Load-Adj Return, Morningstar Return, and Morningstar Risk need to be explained first. It is easiest to focus on the 10-year row, as the other rows are straightforward extensions of it. First, the average return for Magellan is determined for the past 10 years. The return is adjusted for any load charges that the fund levies on investors, producing a return of 16.71% in the Load-Adj Return column. Second, the average 10-year returns for all funds in the same investment class are averaged. Third, Magellan's average return is divided by this overall average so that a return measure greater than 1 means that the fund did better than average, whereas a return measure less than 1 indicates that the fund did worse than average. In Magellan's case the Morningstar Return measure of 1.62 indicates that its average return was 62% better than the overall average.

For the 10-year Morningstar Risk entry, the appropriate monthly Treasury bill return is subtracted from each of the previous 120 monthly net returns to calculate the fund's excess returns. Then only the negative excess returns are summed, and the absolute value is divided by 120 to provide a measure of the fund's downside risk.

For example, imagine that this risk measure is calculated for 6 months instead of 120 months and that the following returns are observed:

Month	Fund Return	T-bill Return	Fund Return less T-bill Return
1	4.0%	.5%	3.5%
2	−2.0	.5	−2.5
3	.4	.6	−0.2
4	5.0	.6	4.4
5	−3.0	.6	−3.6
6	1.0	.7	.3

The three negative excess returns of −2.5%, −.2%, and −3.6% sum to −6.3%. Dividing the absolute value of this sum by 6, the total number of months, results in a downside risk measure of 1.05 (= 6.3/6).

Downside risk measures are calculated by Morningstar for funds in the same investment class, and an overall average for these funds is determined. Then the fund's downside risk measure is divided by this overall measure; the result is Morningstar's measure of the fund's risk. In the case of Magellan, it is .94, indicating that it had 6% less downside risk than the average domestic equity fund over the 10-year period.

Under the heading "Risk % Rank" are the percentile rankings for a fund's downside risk measured against all funds in the same investment class (All) and funds in the same category (Cat). Here a percentile rank of 1 indicates that the fund had the least risk, whereas a rank of 100 indicates that the fund had the most risk. In the case of Magellan, its ranks of 71 and 72 for 10 years indicate that it had more risk than 71% of the other domestic equity funds and 72% of the other funds in the same category.

Morningstar's rating system has five ranks, as follows:

Stars	Percentile	Return Rating	Risk Rating
*****	1–10	Highest or high	Lowest or low
****	11–32.5	Above average	Below average
***	33.5–67.5	Average	Average
**	68.5–90	Below average	Above average
*	91–100	Lowest or low	Highest or high

Hence the percentile rank determines how many stars the fund is given and the category in which it is placed.[25]

The Morningstar Risk-Adj Rating is determined by subtracting the fund's downside risk measure from its return measure. In the case of Magellan, its 10-year risk-adjusted measure is .68 (= 1.62 − .94). This measure is also determined for all the other funds in the same investment class, and then percentile ranks are determined. Magellan ranked somewhere between 1 and 10, resulting in it receiving a five-star rating.[26]

23.6.3 HISTORICAL PROFILE

Summary performance measures are contained in the Historical Profile in Figure 23.5. Consider the return measure first. The previously described fund-return measures for 3, 5, and 10 years are averaged using weights of 20%, 30%, and 50% to arrive at a weighted-average return. After this calculation has been made for each of the other funds in the same investment class, the fund is given a percentile rank and then a rating, as indicated before. Magellan's percentile rank was somewhere between 11 and 32.5, giving it a four-star *above average* ranking. Similar weighted-average calculations are made for the fund's downside risk measure and risk-adjusted measure, resulting in Magellan's receiving a three-star *average* risk rating and a five-star *highest* risk-adjusted rating.

23.6.4 CATEGORY RATING AND OTHER MEASURES

Just below the "Risk Analysis" section of the figure is a gauge that can point to one of five numbers based on the fund's returns during the past three years. This measure indicates the overall performance of the fund during the past three years but uses a gauge instead of the star-based system described earlier. Thus, during the past three years Fidelity Magellan received a rating of 4, the second highest overall rating. This rating is the result of receiving a rating of *above average* for its three-year return, and a rating of *average* for its level of risk during the past three years, as indicated directly below the gauge. These two ratings are the equivalent of four and three stars, respectively, and are based on Magellan's performance relative to other funds in the same category.

Next to the "Category Rating" section in Figure 23.5 is the section that Morningstar refers to as "Other Measures." The top section gives values for alpha, beta, and R-squared. They correspond to the statistics related to a portfolio's *ex post* characteristic line, which is a simple linear regression model.[27] Hence Morningstar reports the results from regressing the previous 36 monthly excess returns of the mutual fund (that is, the fund's net returns less the corresponding Treasury bill rates) on the corresponding 36 monthly excess returns of the S&P 500 (that is, the index's returns less the corresponding Treasury bill rates). As a result, the fund's *ex post* alpha and beta are estimated. Similarly, R-squared is the coefficient of determination (multiplied by 100) calculated when the 36 excess returns of the fund are compared with those of the S&P 500. Morningstar also reports the regression results for the index that produced the highest R-squared from a set of indices. For example, if the R-squared of a fund is higher with the Russell 2000 than with the S&P 500, this result suggests that the fund follows an investment objective of investing in small companies and would be reported in the right column under Best Fit Index.

Magellan had a beta of 1.02 when regressed against the S&P 500, which also was the index with the highest R-squared. Its *ex post* alpha of −0.6% indicates that it did much worse than the S&P 500 during the past 36 months on a risk-adjusted basis. The R-squared value of 94 means that roughly 94% of the variation in the excess returns of the fund could be attributed to variations in the excess returns on the S&P 500.

The second part of this section provides values for standard deviation, mean, and Sharpe ratio. These three values are also based on the previous 36 monthly rates of return on the fund. Standard deviation and mean are the standard deviation and the average return (annualized) for the portfolio, which for Magellan are 21.72% and 24.58%, respectively. The Sharpe ratio, discussed in Chapter 18, gives a risk-adjusted measure of performance. Morningstar takes the fund's average excess return during the previous 12 months and divides it by the fund's standard deviation for the previous 36 months. Hence it is the ratio of excess return to risk, which for Magellan equals 1.01.

23.6.5 INVESTMENT STYLE

The "Current Investment Style" section appears in the lower right part of Figure 23.5. On the right are six descriptive measures of the average stock held by the fund using the most recently available data. For example, the average price-earnings ratio of the stocks held in the Magellan Fund was 36.6 as of September 30, 1999. This number is divided by the average price-earnings ratio of the stocks in the S&P 500, indicating a value of 1.02, or 2% more than the average ratio in the index. Furthermore, the average price-earnings ratio for the past three years for the stocks in the fund's portfolio, relative to the average for the stocks in the S&P 500, was 1.15. Last, the current value of the ratio, when divided by the average for all funds in the same category, was 1.11, indicating that the ratio was 11% more than the average price-earnings ratio for similar funds. The ratios are weighted averages, in which the weight for each security is based on the relative proportion of the fund invested in the security. If a fund invests in fixed-income securities, then these measures are replaced by measures such as duration, maturity, credit quality, coupon interest rate, and price.

Also in this part of Figure 23.5 is a 3-by-3 matrix, which Morningstar calls a *style box.* The three rows of the style box are based on the current size of the stocks held by the fund, where size is measured by the market capitalization of the typical stock in the fund relative to the 5,000 largest domestic stocks in Morningstar's database. If this figure is less than the size of the 1,000 largest stocks, then the fund's size is *small,* and if it is within the largest 250, then the fund's size is *large;* if it is between these two, then the fund's size is *medium.* Because the typical size of Magellan's holdings is $70.670 billion, the fund is categorized as *large.*

The two outer columns of the style box represent the investment styles of value and growth; the middle column represents a blend of the two. A fund's style is determined by analyzing the current price-earnings and price-book value ratios of the fund's holdings. Morningstar has decided that if these two ratios are relatively low, then the fund follows a *value* style because these are characteristics of value stocks. On the other hand, if they are relatively large, then the fund follows a *growth* style because these are characteristics of growth stocks. Ratios between these two extremes indicate that the fund follows a *blended* style, investing in stocks that in aggregate have no distinct style. Magellan currently follows a blended style because its holdings have price-earnings and price-book value ratios that, on average, are neither relatively high nor low.

In Chapter 13 it was mentioned that stocks can be classified along the two dimensions of value-growth and size. Now it can be seen that investment companies investing primarily in stocks can be similarly classified. Morningstar does this by use of the style box, thereby allowing investors to quickly understand a fund's investment style. Nine combinations of the three levels of value-growth and size are possible. Morningstar indicates its classification of a fund by shading one of the nine sections of the style box. In the case of Magellan the upper center box is shaded, indicating that its investment style currently involves purchases of large value and growth stocks.

In the case of fixed-income funds, the columns of the style box are based on the average duration of the securities in the fund, and hence the style box focuses on the fund's interest rate sensitivity. The column headings are Short Term (if the average duration is between 1 and 3.5 years), Intermediate Term (if the average duration is between 3.5 and 6 years), and Long Term (if the average duration is greater than 6 years). The rows are based on the average credit quality of the securities in the fund, and hence measure default risk. The credit quality row headings are High (if the average bond rating is at least AA), Average (if the average is between BBB and AA), and Low (if the average is less than BBB); federal government securities are treated as AAA.

In general, when Morningstar assigns a stock or bond fund to a category, the category is based on where in the style box the fund is located most often over the past three years. Hence, there are nine categories of stock funds and nine categories of bond funds for the two style boxes. In addition, there are special categories for sector and international stock funds as well as for municipal and international bond funds.[28]

23.6.6 CAVEATS

Morningstar's performance measures are useful in giving an investor a quick reading of how a mutual fund has performed in the past relative to other funds. However, keep several things in mind.

1. Performance comparisons are made with the S&P 500 and Lehman Brothers Aggregate Bond Index for all equity and bond funds, respectively, but these indices may not be appropriate for certain funds. For example, a fund that invests primarily in small-cap stocks might appropriately be compared with an index composed of just small-cap stocks. Morningstar attempts to overcome this problem by making performance comparisons within categories composed of funds with similar investment objectives.

2. As discussed in Chapter 17, portfolio managers attempt to earn abnormal returns by trying to (1) buy underpriced securities and then profit from their subsequent abnormal price appreciation; or (2) if a stock fund, shift assets out of the stock market just before it goes down and then back into the stock market just before it rises or, if a bond fund, shift assets between long-term and short-term bonds depending on the forecast for interest rates; or (3) do both. Morningstar's performance measures do not indicate which approach the fund is using in its quest for abnormal returns.

3. The use of peer group comparisons to evaluate performance has several serious conceptual and practical shortcomings. For example, the set of similar funds may not be entirely appropriate (even though they may be the best match that Morningstar can provide), causing the ratings to be misleading. One fund may be restricted to buying just NYSE-listed common stocks whereas another is free to purchase stocks that are listed on the NYSE, AMEX, or Nasdaq. Furthermore, similar funds may differ considerably in the amount of risk that they assume. Morningstar has attempted to minimize this problem by using narrowly defined categories for comparison purposes, but such categorization is far from perfect.

4. Finally, *survivorship bias* (the tendency for poorly performing funds to go out of business and hence leave the peer group) hampers comparisons with similar funds.

23.7 Closed-End Fund Premiums and Discounts

Several studies have shown that the performance of diversified closed-end investment company managers in the United States is similar to that of open-end investment company managers.[29] When returns are measured by changes in net asset values (plus all distributions), closed-end investment companies appear to be neither better nor worse than open-end ones. There is little evidence that portfolio managers can, on average, either select underpriced securities or time the market successfully.

23.7.1 PRICING OF SHARES

There is more to be said about closed-end funds. Except for operating expenses, load charges, and 12b-1 fees, the performance of the *management* of an open-end fund, based on net asset values, corresponds exactly to the returns provided to the *shareholders*. This situation is not the same for closed-end investment companies because investors buy and sell shares of investment companies at prices determined on the open (secondary) market. As mentioned earlier, few closed-end companies have share prices that are above their net asset values (such shares are said to sell at a *premium*), but many have share prices below their net asset values (such shares are said to sell at a *discount*).

This situation has resulted in several puzzles concerning the typical pricing of closed-end fund shares. Three of the most prominent are as follows:

1. As mentioned earlier, the shares sell at a premium of roughly 10% of their net asset value when initially sold and fall to a discount of roughly 10% of their net asset value shortly thereafter. Why would investors buy such shares when they are initially offered for sale, knowing that their price is going to fall substantially afterward?

2. The size of this discount fluctuates widely over time.[30] Figure 23.6 shows the price behavior of a sample of 16 closed-end funds. Note that the average fund sold at a

FIGURE 23.6 Closed-End Fund Performance

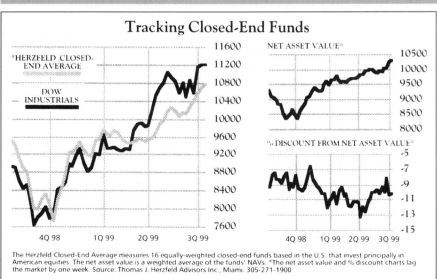

The Herzfeld Closed-End Average measures 16 equally-weighted closed-end funds based in the U.S. that invest principally in American equities. The net asset value is a weighted average of the funds' NAVs. *The net asset value and % discount charts lag the market by one week. Source: Thomas J. Herzfeld Advisors Inc., Miami, 305-271-1900

Source: Reprinted by permission of *Barron's,* Dow Jones & Company, Inc., July 19, 1999, p. MW64. All rights reserved worldwide.

discount that ranged from roughly 7% to 13% during the previous four quarters. What causes these fluctuations?

3. It appears possible to earn abnormally high returns by purchasing funds with the biggest discounts. One study that examined closed-end funds found that buying a portfolio of roughly seven funds with the biggest discounts and holding them until their relative discounts shrank resulted in an inexplicable average abnormal monthly return of .8% (or about 10% per year).[31] How can such a simple investment strategy exist in an efficient market?

23.7.2   INVESTING IN FUND SHARES

The fact that the share price of a closed-end investment company differs from its net asset value, with the magnitude of the difference varying over time, introduces an added source of risk and potential return to investors. By purchasing shares at a discount, an investor may be able to earn more than just the change in the company's net asset value. Even if the company's discount remains constant, the effective dividend yield is greater than that of an otherwise similar no-load, open-end investment company because the purchase price is less. If the discount is substantial when the shares are purchased, it may subsequently narrow and the return will be even greater.[32] On the other hand, if the discount increases, the investor's overall return may be less than that of an otherwise comparable open-end investment company.

Consider a closed-end fund at the beginning of the year that has a net asset value of $10 per share but is selling at a 10% discount for $9 per share. During the year it receives cash dividends amounting to $.50 per share, which it distributes to its shareholders. Hence its dividend yield is 5.6% $(= \$.50/\$9.00)$, which is larger than the 5% yield $(= \$.50/\$10)$ that it would pay if it were an open-end fund. Furthermore, if its net asset value at year-end remains at $10 per share but its discount shrinks to 4% so that it is selling at $9.60 per share, then its annual return of 12.2% $[= (\$.60 + \$.50)/\$9]$ will be notably larger than the 5% return of its open-end counterpart. Of course, if its discount widened to 20% so that it was selling at $8 per share, then its annual return of -5.6% $[= (-\$1 + \$.50)/\$9]$ would be notably lower than the counterpart's 5% return.

Some of the risk associated with varying discounts can be reduced by holding a portfolio of shares in several closed-end investment companies. Discounts on different companies move together, but not perfectly. For example, past data suggest that the standard deviation of the percentage change in the ratio of market price to net asset value for a *portfolio* of 10 to 12 closed-end investment companies is likely to be approximately half that of a typical investment in the shares of a *single* closed-end investment company.[33]

23.7.3   OPEN-ENDING CLOSED-END FUNDS

Explaining the puzzling behavior of prices of closed-end investment companies is a challenge for anyone who believes that capital markets are highly efficient. For anyone not firmly committed to such a view, the purchase of shares of closed-end investment companies at prices sufficiently below net asset values may provide an opportunity for superior returns.[34] One way of realizing superior returns is for the closed-end investment company to convert to an open-end one.[35] If the company converts, the discount on the shares will have to disappear because conversion will result in the investment company's offering its shareholders the right to redeem their shares for their net asset value.

In one study, a sample of 138 closed-end funds was examined to determine the amount of concentrated ownership in each fund. Shareholdings of officers and directors as well as others who owned 5% or more of a fund's shares were identified and aggregated for each fund in the sample. After eight funds in which at least some share-holders were actively involved in attempting to open up the fund had been discarded, the remaining funds were analyzed. Those with blockholdings sold at an average discount of 14.2%, whereas those without blockholdings sold at a discount of only 4.1%. Subsequent analysis revealed that the larger the size of the blockholdings, the larger the discount. One explanation is that the funds with blockholdings were less likely to be opened up. Large investors in such funds were receiving a variety of private benefits (for example, being involved with firms that execute the fund's trades, or being involved with the management firm that receives the fund's management fees, or being able to find employment at the fund for close friends and relatives) that were not available to small investors. Given their voting power, these large investors apparently gain more from these benefits than they would gain from opening up the fund and hence vote against any effort to do so.[36] Needless to say, this finding leaves open the question of why small investors hold shares in such funds.

Summary

1. Investment companies are financial intermediaries that obtain money from investors to purchase financial assets.
2. Investment companies offer investors the advantages of economies of scale and professional management.
3. The net asset value (NAV) of an investment company is the difference between the market value of its assets and its liabilities divided by the number of outstanding shares.
4. The operating expense ratio of an investment company represents the annual percentage of total assets that are spent in operating the fund. Typically these expenses consist of fees paid to the management company as well as administrative and other operating expenses.
5. The three major types of investment companies are unit investment trusts, closed-end investment companies, and open-end investment companies.
6. Unit investment trusts typically make a set of initial investments in fixed-income securities and hold those securities until they mature.
7. Closed-end investment companies issue shares initially to capitalize the fund. After that, new shares are rarely issued nor are outstanding shares repurchased. Closed-end investment company shares trade on organized exchanges or on Nasdaq at prices determined by the market.
8. Open-end investment companies have a variable capitalization, standing ready to issue new shares or to repurchase existing shares daily at prices based on their net asset values.
9. Different investment companies follow different investment policies. These policies determine such characteristics as the asset classes in which the investment companies invest, the degree of active management (if any), and the emphasis on income as opposed to capital appreciation.
10. Because of data availability, mutual funds have been the subject of many performance studies. The results show that the typical fund has not been able to produce superior rates of return consistently.
11. There is evidence that the superior results of the top performing and the inferior results of the bottom performing mutual funds persist over time, largely because of differences in operating expenses. However, this evidence is not strong for equity funds, indicating that many top and bottom performers subsequently become middle-of-the-pack performers.

12. Closed-end investment companies typically sell at premiums to their NAV at their initial offerings. Later they typically sell at discounts to their NAV, and these discounts tend to vary over time. Why investors buy IPOs of closed-end investment companies, why the discounts of these companies vary over time, and why an investment strategy that involves buying a portfolio of roughly seven or eight funds with the deepest discounts produces abnormally high returns, are puzzles for proponents of market efficiency.

Questions and Problems

1. The Neptune Value Fund has sold 150,000 shares to investors. Currently the fund has accrued investment management fee obligations of $50,000. The fund's portfolio is shown below. Calculate the fund's net asset value.

Stock	Shares	Price/Share
A	50,000	$10
B	20,000	7
C	35,000	30
D	10,000	100

2. Using a recent *Wall Street Journal,* find the NAV for the following funds:
   a. The Magellan Fund (Fidelity Investments)
   b. The Wellington Fund (Vanguard Funds)
   c. The New Horizons Fund (Price Funds)
   What is the percentage change in each fund's NAV from the previous day? Calculate each fund's load as a percentage of its NAV.

3. Wildfire Schulter, a veteran mutual fund investor, argued, "I can compute the monthly rate of return on a mutual fund by calculating the percentage change in the fund's NAV from the beginning to the end of the month (assuming no distributions to shareholders)." Is Wildfire correct? Why?

4. The *X* Fund, a closed-end investment company, has a portfolio of assets worth $500 million. It has liabilities of $2 million. It also has 40 million shares outstanding.
   a. What is the fund's NAV?
   b. If the fund trades at an 8% discount from its NAV, what is the market price of the fund's shares?

5. Assume that you placed a $1,000 investment with a mutual fund that charged an 8.5% load. Management and other fees charged by the fund total 1.10% per annum. Ignoring other costs, during five years, what annual return would the fund have to produce to equal the value that your initial investment would have earned in a savings account paying 5% interest? (Assume annual compounding of income and no taxes.)

6. There are literally thousands of mutual funds available for purchase. Describe what criteria you might use in selecting from among these many funds.

7. At the beginning of the year, the Saturn Fund's NAV was $18.50. At the end of the year its NAV was $16.90. At year-end the fund paid out $1.25 in income and capital gains. What was the return to an investor in the Saturn Fund during the year?

8. During the past three years, the Pluto Fund produced the following per share financial results. Calculate the annual returns on an investment in the Pluto Fund during this period.

	Year 1	Year 2	Year 3
NAV at beginning of year	$13.89	$14.40	$15.95
NAV at end of year	14.40	15.95	15.20
Income distribution	0.29	0.33	0.36
Capital gains distribution	0.12	0.25	0.05

9. Lip Pike is attempting to select a superior-performing mutual fund. Based on the evidence presented in the text, discuss how much importance Lip should attach to the past performance of mutual funds in making decisions.

10. What is the purpose of Rule 12b-1? Does it seem designed to serve the interests of existing shareholders? Explain.

11. Why do the stated percentage load charges of mutual funds not fully reflect the percentage costs of these sales fees?

12. If most investment managers are unable to "beat the market" on a risk-adjusted basis, should an investor still consider investing in investment companies? Why?

13. Consider three individuals: a young, well-educated woman beginning a career with high expected future earnings; a middle-aged man with a young family who has a secure job but modest expected future earnings growth; a widow in her 70s, living comfortably, but not richly, off a pension. Referring to Table 23.1, prescribe and explain an investment strategy for these persons involving investments in the various funds listed. (Feel free to introduce other assumptions regarding such things as the individuals' risk tolerances and consumption preferences.)

14. Assuming certain conditions are satisfied, an investment company does not have to pay federal tax on the income it earns. Why?

15. Why do the market prices of closed-end investment company shares represent a "mystery" to proponents of market efficiency?

Endnotes

1. As mentioned in Chapter 3, dealers in securities generally quote both bid and asked prices. The bid price is the amount the dealer will pay for a security; the asked price is the amount at which the dealer will sell a security.

2. Another classification covers certain companies that issue "face-amount certificates" promising specific payments. This type of company is rare and is not discussed here.

3. In some countries (such as the United Kingdom), the term *unit trust* refers to an open-end investment company.

4. Many investment companies require their management companies to cover all expenses over a specified amount, effectively limiting total expenses. All of these fees are discussed extensively in Chapter 10 of John Bogle, *Bogle on Mutual Funds* (Burr Ridge, IL: Richard D. Irwin, 1994).

5. CDA/Wiesenberger Investment Companies Service, *Investment Companies Yearbook 1999* (Rockville, MD: CDA Investment Technologies, 1998), p. 22. The percentages include distribution fees, also known as 12b-1 fees, which are discussed later. In general, larger funds have smaller operating expense ratios. Hence, the average *dollar* invested in bond or equity funds will pay a slightly lower percentage than those indicated here.

6. See Jay R. Ritter, "The Long-Run Performance of Initial Public Offerings," *Journal of Finance,* 46, no. 1 (March 1991): 3–27. During the three years following the initial offering date, nonfund IPOs underperformed a matching sample of firms by roughly 27%.

7. Closed-end funds that have received permission from foreign governments to invest in local securities do not show the type of price behavior described here and hence may be initially attractive to investors. See John W. Peavey, III, "Returns on Initial Public Offerings of Closed-End Funds," *Review of Financial Studies,* 3, no. 4 (1990): 695–708. For more information about closed-end investment companies, see Albert J. Fredman and George Cole Scott, "Analyzing and Finding Data on Closed-End Funds," *AAII Journal,* 13, no. 8 (September 1991): 15–19 and "Guidelines for Handling Closed-End Fund Transactions," *AAII Journal,* 14, no. 5 (June 1992): 18–22, and Albert J. Fredman, "What You Need to Know about Investing in Closed-End Funds," *AAII Journal,* 22, no. 1 (January 2000): 2–7.

8. **Real estate investment trusts (REITs),** although not classified as investment companies for legal purposes, are similar to closed-end funds because they serve as a conduit for earnings on investments in real estate or loans secured by real estate, passing earnings on to their shareholders and avoiding corporate taxation. For more on REITS, see Steven D. Kapplin and Arthur L. Schwartz, Jr., "Investing in REITs: Are They All They're Cracked Up to Be?" *AAII Journal,* 13, no. 5 (May 1991): 7–11; and Joseph Gyourko and Donald B. Keim, "Risk and Return in Real Estate: Evidence from a Real Estate Stock Portfolio," *Financial Analysts Journal,* 49, no. 5 (September/October 1993): 39–46.

9. Investing in a **wrap account** is similar to investing in a mutual fund. This type of account is sponsored by a

brokerage firm and involves brokers helping investors identify suitable money managers (or mutual funds) that will manage some of the investors' wealth. All of the fees for financial planning, investment management, and securities trading are "wrapped up" into one annual fee that typically amounts to 3% of assets. See John Bogle, *Bogle on Mutual Funds,* p. 54, for a discussion of the analogy between wrap accounts and mutual funds.

10. For more on mutual fund load charges and redemption fees, see Tarun Chordia, "The Structure of Mutual Fund Charges," *Journal of Financial Economics,* 41, no. 1 (May 1996): 3–39. Typically, redemption fees are paid to the fund, not to the fund's manager. Thus, departing shareholders effectively compensate remaining shareholders for the costs of liquidating a portfolio of the fund's assets.

11. To be precise, the limit is .75% for advertising, promoting, and selling the fund and .25% for servicing existing investors.

12. CDA/Wiesenberger, *Investment Companies Yearbook 1999,* p. 26.

13. CDA/Wiesenberger, *Investment Companies Yearbook 1999,* p. 26.

14. Sometimes the capital gain category is referred to as "maximum capital gain" or "aggressive growth." A fourth category ("specialized") consists of funds that, by design, are not highly diversified. One interesting kind of fund (typically organized as a limited partnership) is a hedge fund, where the manager will often engage in short selling and margin purchases of securities. CDA/Wiesenberger, *Investment Companies Yearbook 1999,* pp. 25–26.

15. CDA/Wiesenberger, *Investment Companies Yearbook 2000,* p. 26. For more information about mutual funds that specialize in investing in foreign stocks, see Ken Gregory, "Traveling Overseas Via No-Load Mutual Funds," *AAII Journal,* 13, no. 9 (October 1991): 22–25. It should be noted that the Investment Company Institute agrees with this definition of a global fund but defines an international fund as one that invests in non-U.S. securities; see *1999 Mutual Fund Fact Book* (Washington, DC: Investment Company Institute, 1999), p. 13.

16. Benchmarks can be calculated in many different ways. For example, the benchmark may be based on the investment company's standard deviation relative to that of a market index, such as the S&P 500. Thus, if the investment company's standard deviation is 60% of the index's standard deviation, then the mix would consist of 60% invested in the index and 40% invested in the riskfree asset. The results from evaluating mutual fund performance using this type of benchmark are similar to the results when beta-based benchmarks

are used. See, for example, Hany A. Shawky, "An Update on Mutual Funds: Better Grades," *Journal of Portfolio Management,* 8, no. 2 (Winter 1982): 29–34. Portfolio performance evaluation and benchmarks are discussed in detail in Chapter 18.

17. See Mark M. Carhart, "On Persistence in Mutual Fund Performance," *Journal of Finance,* 51, no. 1 (March 1997): 57–82. Sector, balanced, and international equity funds were excluded from the sample.

18. Similar results were observed when the ten portfolios were formed based on the abnormal returns of the funds during the previous three years.

19. Similar results were reported in Edwin J. Elton, Martin J. Gruber, Sanjiv Das, and Matthew Hlavka, "Efficiency with Costly Information: A Reinterpretation of Evidence from Managed Portfolios," *Review of Financial Studies,* 6, no. 1 (1993): 1–22.

20. Similar conclusions can be drawn regarding pension and endowment funds. See Eugene F. Fama, "Efficient Capital Markets: II," *Journal of Finance,* 46, no. 5 (December 1991): 1575–1617, particularly pp. 1605–1607; and Josef Lakonishok, Andrei Shleifer, and Robert W. Vishny, "The Structure and Performance of the Money Management Industry," *Brookings Papers on Economic Activity: Microeconomics 1992* (Washington, DC: Brookings Institute, 1992), pp. 339–379. Also see T. Daniel Coggin, Frank J. Fabozzi, and Shafiqur Rahman, "The Investment Performance of U.S. Equity Pension Fund Managers: An Empirical Investigation," *Journal of Finance,* 48, no. 3 (July 1993): 1039–1055.

21. Christopher R. Blake, Edwin J. Elton, and Martin J. Gruber, "The Performance of Bond Mutual Funds," *Journal of Business,* 66, no. 3 (July 1993): 371–403.

22. Edwin J. Elton, Martin J. Gruber, and Christopher R. Blake, "Fundamental Economic Variables, Expected Returns, and Bond Fund Performance," *Journal of Finance,* 50, no. 4 (September 1995): 1229–1256, particularly pages 1251–1252. Also see William Reichenstein, "Bond Fund Returns and Expenses: A Study of Bond Market Efficiency," *Journal of Investing,* 8, no. 4 (Winter 1999): 8–16, who reports finding a strong negative relationship between bond fund returns and expenses that, in turn, results in persistence of performance. It should be noted that all of these studies finding persistence have been challenged by other investigators on methodological grounds.

23. Morningstar's average return referred to here and elsewhere is calculated using compounding. For example, the one-year return is calculated by compounding the four previous quarterly returns and; the three-year average return is calculated by compounding the 12 previous quarterly returns.

24. Since 1996, Morningstar has defined its own set of investment objectives that it calls *categories.* These are

different from the CDA/Weisenberger investment objectives discussed earlier. Morningstar determines a fund's investment objective based on a set of variables related to the composition of the fund's portfolio. For domestic equity funds, these variables include the market value and the price-earnings and price-book value ratios of the fund's holdings. For taxable bond funds, these variables include the duration and credit quality of the fund's holdings. The Morningstar approach is more complex than the CDA/Weisenberger approach, but it allows an investor to better differentiate among funds. Interestingly, Lipper Analytical Services had traditionally classified mutual funds in a manner similar to CDA/Weisenberger but has recently switched to a classification scheme similar to Morningstar's.

25. Similar ratings are provided in *The Individual Investor's Guide to No-Load Mutual Funds* (Chicago: American Association of Individual Investors, 1999).

26. For more on Morningstar's risk-adjusted ratings, see William F. Sharpe, "Morningstar's Risk-Adjusted Ratings," *Financial Analysts Journal,* 54, no. 4 (July/August 1998): 21–33.

27. The *ex post* characteristic line is discussed more fully in Chapter 18.

28. For more on mutual fund styles, see Stephen J. Brown and William N. Goetzmann, "Mutual Fund Styles," *Journal of Financial Economics,* 43, no. 3 (March 1997): 373–399.

29. See, for example, William F. Sharpe and Howard B. Sosin, "Closed-End Investment Companies in the United States: Risk and Return," *Proceedings, 1974 Meeting of the European Finance Association,* ed. B. Jacquillat (Amsterdam: North-Holland Publishing, 1975): 37–63; Antonio Vives, "Analysis of Forecasting Ability of Closed-End Fund's Management" (unpublished working paper, Carnegie-Mellon University, September 1975), and "Discounts and Premiums on Closed-End Funds: A Theoretical and Empirical Analysis" (unpublished Ph.D. thesis, Carnegie-Mellon University, 1975).

30. These two puzzles are investigated in Charles M. C. Lee, Andrei Shleifer, and Richard H. Thaler, "Investor Sentiment and the Closed-End Fund Puzzle," *Journal of Finance,* 46, no. 1 (March 1991): 75–109. In the June 1991 issue of *Journal of Finance* there is a contentious debate about their findings. For a comparison of the volatility of closed-end fund share prices and the volatility of the underlying securities in their portfolios, see Jeffrey Pontiff, "Excess Volatility

and Closed-End Funds," *American Economic Review,* 87, no. 1 (March 1997): 155–169.

31. See Jeffrey Pontiff, "Closed-End Fund Premia and Returns: Implications for Financial Market Equilibrium," *Journal of Financial Economics,* 37, no. 3 (March 1995): 341–370, especially the appendix. Also see Rex Thompson, "The Information Content of Discounts and Premiums on Closed-End Fund Shares," *Journal of Financial Economics,* 6, no. 2/3 (June/September 1978): 151–186.

32. There is evidence that this is what happens to funds with the greatest discounts; see Pontiff, "Closed-End Fund Premia and Returns." There is also some evidence that discounts narrow during down markets and widen during up markets, and that the size of discounts and premiums increases as interest rates increase. See R. Malcolm Richards, Donald R. Fraser, and John C. Groth, "Premiums, Discounts, and the Volatility of Closed-End Mutual Funds," *Financial Review* (Fall 1979): 26–33, and "The Attractions of Closed-End Bond Funds," *Journal of Portfolio Management,* 8, no. 2 (Winter 1982): 56–61; and Jeffrey Pontiff, "Costly Arbitrage: Evidence from Closed-End Funds," *Quarterly Journal of Economics,* 111, no. 4 (November 1996): 1135–1151.

33. Sharpe and Sosin, "Closed-End Investment Companies in the United States."

34. Burton G. Malkiel advocated such an investment strategy in the 1973, 1975, and 1981 editions of *A Random Walk down Wall Street* (New York: W. W. Norton) but not in recent editions. The basis for his initial advocacy can be found in two studies: Burton Malkiel, "The Valuation of Closed-End Investment Company Shares," *Journal of Finance,* 32, no. 3 (June 1977): 847–859; and Thompson, "The Information Content of Discounts and Premiums on Closed-End Fund Shares." Pontiff's recent study supports these two earlier studies; see Pontiff, "Closed-End Fund Premia and Returns."

35. For an analysis of the "open-ending" of closed-end investment companies, see Greggory A. Brauer, "'Open-Ending' Closed-End Funds," *Journal of Financial Economics,* 13, no. 4 (December 1984): 491–507.

36. See Michael Barclay, Clifford Holderness, and Jeffrey Pontiff, "Concentrated Ownership and Discounts on Closed-End Funds," *Journal of Applied Corporate Finance,* 8, no. 1 (Spring 1995): 32–42 (an expanded version of this paper appears in the June 1993 issue of the *Journal of Financial Economics*).

24

Options

option

In the world of investments, an **option** is a type of contract between two people wherein one person grants the other person the right to buy a specific asset at a specific price within a specific time period. Alternatively, the contract may grant the other person the right to sell a specific asset at a specific price within a specific time period. The person who has received the right and thus has a decision to make is known as the option buyer because he or she must pay for this right. The person who has sold the right and thus must respond to the buyer's decision is known as the option writer.

Options have become a popular type of investment because the potential returns from taking positions in options are much larger than those associated with long and short positions in the underlying asset. Perhaps the biggest difference is that the amount of leverage associated with options is greater than what can be achieved by taking a position in the underlying asset. As a result, the risks associated with positions in options are also larger than those associated with long and short positions in the underlying asset.

The variety of contracts containing an option feature is enormous. Even within the domain of publicly traded securities, many types can be found. Traditionally only certain instruments are referred to as options; the others, though similar in nature, are designated differently. This chapter introduces the institutional features of option contracts along with some basic information about how they are valued, their risks and potential returns, and how they are used in the marketplace.

24.1 Types of Option Contracts

The two most basic types of option contracts are known as calls and puts. Such contracts are traded on many exchanges around the world and many are created privately (that is, "off exchange" or "over the counter"). Privately created calls and puts typically involve financial institutions or investment banking firms and their clients.

24.1.1 CALL OPTIONS

call option

The most prominent type of option contract is the **call option** for stocks. It gives the buyer the right to buy ("call away") a specific number of shares of a specific company from the option writer at a specific purchase price at any time up to and including a specific date. The contract specifies four items:

1. The company whose shares can be bought
2. The number of shares that can be bought

exercise price
3. The purchase price for those shares, known as the **exercise price** (or strike price)

expiration date
4. The date when the right to buy expires, known as the **expiration date**

605

Example

Consider a simple hypothetical example in which investors *B* and *W* are thinking about signing a call option contract. This contract allows *B* to buy 100 shares of Widget from *W* for $50 per share at any time during the next six months. Currently Widget is selling for $45 per share on an organized exchange. Investor *B*, the potential option buyer, believes that the price of Widget's common stock will rise substantially during the next six months. Investor *W*, the potential option writer, has a different opinion about Widget, believing that its stock price will not rise above $50 during this time period.

Will investor *W* be willing to sign this contract without receiving something in return from investor *B*? No. *W* is running a risk by signing the contract and will demand compensation for doing so. The risk is that Widget's stock price will rise above $50 per share, in which case *W* will have to buy the shares at the market price and then turn them over to *B* for only $50 per share. Perhaps the stock will rise to $60, costing *W* $6,000 (= $60 × 100 shares) to buy the stock. Then *W* will give the 100 shares to *B* and receive in return $5,000 (= $50 × 100 shares). Consequently, *W* will have lost $1,000 (= $6,000 − $5,000).

premium

The point is that the buyer of a call option has to pay the writer something to get the writer to sign the contract. The amount paid is known as the **premium**, although option price is a more appropriate term. In the example, perhaps the premium is $3 per share, meaning that investor *B* will pay $300 (= $3 × 100 shares) to investor *W* to induce *W* to sign the contract. Because investor *B* expects Widget's stock price to rise in the future, *B* would expect to make money if he or she purchased shares of Widget today at $45 per share. However, the attraction of purchasing call options instead of shares is that investor *B* can apply a high degree of leverage because only $3 per share needs to be spent to purchase the option.

At some point in time after investors *B* and *W* have signed the call option contract, investor *W* might like to get out of the contract, but breaching the contract is illegal. Investor *W* could buy the contract back from investor *B* for a negotiated amount of money and then destroy the document. If Widget rises in one month to $55 per share, perhaps the amount will be $7 per share [or, in total, $700 (= $7 × 100 shares)]. In this case, *W* will have lost $400 (= $300 − $700) and *B* will have made $400. Alternatively, if Widget falls to $40 per share, perhaps the amount will be $.50 per share [or, in total, $50 (= $.50 × 100 shares)], in which case *W* will have made $250 (= $300 − $50) and *B* will have lost $250.

Another way that *W* can get out of the contract is to find someone else to take his or her position in the contract (assuming that the contract has a provision that allows for this transfer). For example, if Widget has risen to $55 per share after one month, perhaps investor *W* will find an investor, denoted *WW*, who is willing to become the option writer if *W* will pay him or her $7 per share (or $700 in total). If they agree, the contract will be amended so that *WW* is now the option writer, with *W* no longer being a party in the contract.

What if investor *B* wants to get out of the contract? Analogous to *W*'s actions, *B* could try to find someone who is willing to pay an agreed-on sum of money to possess the right to buy Widget stock under the terms of the contract; that is, *B* could try to sell the contract to someone else. Perhaps investor *B* will find another investor, denoted *BB*, who is willing to pay *B* $7 per share (or $700 in total) in return for the right to buy Widget under the terms of the call option contract. If *B* agrees, the call option contract will be sold to *BB* and amended, making *BB* the option buyer.

In this example, both of the original parties, *W* and *B*, "closed out" (or "offset" or "unwound") their positions and are no longer involved in the call option contract. However, the example suggests that the original writer and buyer must meet face to face to create the terms of the contract. It also suggests that if either the original writer or the original buyer wants to get out of the contract, then he or she must reach an agreeable price with the other original party or, alternatively, find a third investor to whom he or she can transfer the position in the contract. Thus, it seems that there is a great amount of effort involved if an investor wants to deal in options.

Role of Exchanges

Fortunately this effort is not necessary in the United States because of the introduction of *standardized contracts* and the maintenance by organized exchanges of a relatively liquid marketplace for listed options.[1] The Options Clearing Corporation (OCC), a company jointly owned by several exchanges, greatly facilitates trading in these options. It does so by maintaining a computer system that keeps track of all of the contracts, recording the position of each investor in each contract. Although the mechanics are complex, the principles are simple enough. As soon as a buyer and a writer decide to trade a particular option contract and the buyer pays the agreed-on premium, the OCC steps in, becoming the effective writer as far as the buyer is concerned and the effective buyer as far as the writer is concerned. Thus, at this time all direct links between original buyer and writer are severed. If a buyer chooses to exercise an option, the OCC will randomly choose a writer who has not closed his or her position and assign the exercise notice accordingly. The OCC also guarantees delivery of stock if the writer is unable to come up with the shares.

The OCC makes it possible for buyers and writers to close out their positions at any time. If a buyer subsequently becomes a writer of the same contract, meaning that the buyer later "sells" the contract to someone else, the OCC notes the offsetting positions in this investor's account and simply cancels both entries. Consider an investor who buys a contract on Monday and then sells it on Tuesday. The OCC notes that the investor's net position is zero and removes both entries. The second trade is a **closing sale** because it closes out the investor's position from the earlier trade. Closing sales thus allow buyers to sell options rather than exercise them.

closing sale

A similar procedure allows a writer to pay to be relieved of the potential obligation to deliver stock. Consider an investor who writes a contract on Wednesday and buys an identical one on Thursday. The latter is a **closing purchase** and, analogous to a closing sale, closes out the investor's position from the earlier trade.

closing purchase

Stock Split and Dividend Protection

Call options are protected against stock splits and stock dividends on the underlying stock. In the example of the option on 100 shares of Widget stock with an exercise price of $50, a two-for-one stock split would cause the terms of the contract to be altered to 200 shares at $25 per share. The reason for this protection has to do with the effect that stock splits and stock dividends have on the share price of the firm. Because either of these events will cause the share price to fall below what it otherwise would have been, they work to the disadvantage of the call option buyer and to the advantage of the call option writer if no adjustments were made.

In terms of cash dividends, there is no protection for listed call options.[2] That is, the exercise price and the number of shares are unaffected by the payment of cash dividends. For example, the terms of the Widget call option would remain the same if Widget declared and paid a $4 per share cash dividend.

24.1.2 PUT OPTIONS

put option

A second type of option contract for stocks is the **put option.** It gives the buyer the right to sell ("to put away") a specific number of shares of a specific company to the option writer at a specific selling price at any time up to and including a specific date. The contract specifies four items that are analogous to those for call options:

1. The company whose shares can be sold
2. The number of shares that can be sold
3. The selling price for those shares, known as the exercise price (or strike price)
4. The date when the right to sell expires, known as the expiration date

An Example

Consider an example in which investors B and W are thinking about signing a put option contract. This contract will allow B to sell 100 shares of XYZ Company to W for $30 per share at any time during the next six months. Currently XYZ is selling for $35 per share on an organized exchange. Investor B, the potential option buyer, believes that the price of XYZ's common stock will fall substantially during the next six months. Investor W, the potential option writer, has a different opinion about XYZ, believing that its stock price will not fall below $30 during this time period.

As with the call option on Widget, investor W would be running a risk by signing the contract and would demand compensation for doing so. The risk is that XYZ's stock price will subsequently fall below $30 per share, in which case W will have to buy the shares at $30 per share from B when they are not worth that much in the marketplace. Perhaps XYZ will fall to $20, costing W $3,000 (= $30 × 100 shares) to buy stock that is worth only $2,000 (= $20 × 100 shares). Consequently, W would have lost $1,000 (= $3,000 − $2,000). In this case B would make $1,000, purchasing XYZ in the marketplace for $2,000 and then selling the shares to W for $3,000.

As with a call option, the buyer of a put option has to pay the writer an amount of money known as a premium to get the writer to sign the contract and assume this risk. Also as with call options, the buyer and writer may close out (or offset or unwind) their positions at any time by simply entering an offsetting transaction. As with calls, this is easily done for listed put options in the United States because these contracts are standardized.

Again, the OCC facilitates trading in listed puts because these contracts exist only in the memory of its computer system. As with calls, as soon as a buyer and a writer decide to trade a particular put option contract and the buyer pays the agreed-on premium, the OCC steps in, becoming the effective writer as far as the buyer is concerned and the effective buyer as far as the writer is concerned. If a buyer chooses to exercise an option, the OCC randomly chooses a writer who has not closed his or her position and assigns the exercise notice accordingly. The OCC also guarantees delivery of the exercise price if the writer is unable to come up with the necessary cash.

Like calls, puts are protected against stock splits and stock dividends on the underlying stock. In the example of the option on 100 shares of XYZ stock with an exercise price of $30, a two-for-one stock split would cause the contract to be altered to 200 shares at $15 per share. In terms of cash dividends, there is no protection for listed puts.

24.2 Option Trading

Exchanges begin trading a new set of options on a given stock every three months. The newly created options have roughly nine months before they expire.[3] For example, options on Widget might be introduced in January, April, July, and October, with expiration dates in, September, December, March, and June, respectively. Furthermore, the exchange might decide to introduce long-term options on Widget, dubbed *LEAPS* by the exchanges for *long-term equity anticipation securities,* that expire as far into the future as two years. They might also allow the creation of customized options on Widget, dubbed *FLEX* options for *flexible exchange options,* that have exercise prices and expiration dates of the investor's choice.

In general, two call options on a stock are introduced at the same time. The two options are identical in all respects except for the exercise price. If the stock is selling for $200 or less at the time the options are to be introduced, then two exercise prices will be set at $5 intervals bracketing the stock price.[4] Furthermore, a pair of put option contracts may also be introduced at the same time. For example, if Widget is selling for $43 in January, then two September call options may be introduced that have exercise prices of $40 and $45. Similarly, two September put options with exercise prices of $40 and $45 may also be introduced.

After an option has been introduced, new options with the same terms as the existing ones but with different exercise prices may be introduced when the stock price of the company moves up or down so much that it is substantially outside of the initial bracket. In terms of Widget, if its stock price rises in the next month to $49, perhaps September put and call options having a $50 exercise price will be introduced.

Once listed, an option remains listed until its expiration date. Specifically, listed options on common stocks generally expire on the third Friday of the specified month.

24.2.1   TRADING ACTIVITY

Common stock options are currently traded on the Chicago Board Options Exchange (CBOE) and on the American, Pacific, and Philadelphia stock exchanges; many options are traded on more than one exchange. Figure 24.1 shows a portion of the daily listing of the trading activity on the CBOE. The first column lists the name of the company and, indented below it, the closing price on its common stock. The next column lists the exercise price for the option contracts on the company, followed by a column giving the expiration date. The next two columns give the trading volume and last trade premium for call options with the exercise price and expiration date shown on the left. The last two columns give the trading volume and last trade premium for the matching put option.

For example, AT&T common stock closed at 84\frac{7}{16}$ on March 4, 1999. By the end of that day, 595 AT&T call option contracts having an exercise price of $90 per share that expire on the third Friday of July of 1999 had been traded. The closing trade that day took place at 5\frac{1}{2}$ per share (or $550 per contract). Similarly, two AT&T put option contracts with the same exercise price ($90) and expiration date (July 1999) had been traded. The closing trade was at 10\frac{1}{8}$ per share (or $1,012.50 per contract).

Some options are not traded during a given day, which is indicated by three periods ". . .". Others, although included because of the format of the report, have not been introduced and are therefore unavailable for trading. These contracts are also indicated by the three periods. Hence when nothing is reported (see, for example, Abbott Labs puts in Figure 24.1), it cannot be determined whether there was no trading or the contracts simply did not exist at the time.

Although not shown in Figure 24.1, the total volume (the number of contracts traded) and the open interest (that is, the number of contracts outstanding) for calls and puts are displayed at the bottom of the listings for each exchange and overall.

Thursday, March 4, 1999

Composite volume and close for actively traded equity and LEAPS, or long-term options, with results for the corresponding put or call contract. Volume figures are unofficial. Open interest is total outstanding for all exchanges and reflects previous trading day. Close when possible is shown for the underlying stock on primary market. **CB**-Chicago Board Options Exchange. **AM**-American Stock Exchange. **PB**-Philadelphia Stock Exchange. **PC**-Pacific Stock Exchange. **NY**-New York Stock Exchange. **XC**-Composite. **p**-Put.

			–Call–		–Put–	
Option/Strike		Exp.	Vol.	Last	Vol.	Last
A M R	55	May	5	6 1/2	525	3 1/2
A S A	17 1/2	Mar	22	5/16	300	3/4
AT&T	85	Mar	2016	2 1/4	94	2 1/2
84 7/16	85	Apr	358	3 3/4	101	4 1/4
84 7/16	90	Mar	571	5/8	5	5 3/4
84 7/16	90	Apr	652	2	6	7 5/8
84 7/16	90	Jul	595	5 1/2	2	10 1/8
AbacusDir	50	Mar	300	13 3/4	...	...
65 1/8	60	Apr	500	8 3/8	...	...
Abbt L	47 1/2	May	324	3	...	...
48 7/16	50	Mar	570	1/2	...	...
48 7/16	50	May	354	2 1/16	...	...
AbleTel	5	Mar	1105	1 7/8	...	...
6 15/16	5	Jun	1000	2 1/2	...	...
AdobeS	40	Mar	532	5	64	1/2
A M D	15	Apr	600	3 3/4	15	9/16
18 1/4	20	Mar	226	3/8	15	2 1/4
AdvRdio	10	Mar	530	3/8	...	...
AirbFr	35	Mar	501	2 11/16	...	...
AirTran	5	Jun	403	1/2	...	...
Albtsn	60	Mar	45	1/4	250	4 1/8
Alcatl	25	Mar	288	15/16	20	1 1/2
Alcoa	37 1/2	Apr	...	...	328	1 5/8
39 1/8	40	Mar	154	11/16	515	2 11/16
39 1/8	40	Apr	295	1 11/16	77	2 3/4
Allste	35	Apr	31	2 5/16	400	1 1/4
Amazon	80	Jul	20	48 1/4	545	8 3/4
120 1/8	90	Mar	31	30 1/4	372	1
120 1/8	100	Mar	42	19 7/8	637	1 3/4
120 1/8	110	Mar	141	14	1097	4 1/4
120 1/8	120	Mar	937	9	862	7 3/4
120 1/8	130	Mar	1429	4 1/8	114	14 3/4
120 1/8	140	Mar	508	2 3/8	46	24
120 1/8	150	Mar	290	1 1/8	1	32
AmeriTrde	40	Mar	7	7 5/8	507	1 7/16
46 1/2	50	Mar	249	2 1/4	30	6
AmOnline	50	Apr	54	36 1/8	1144	3/8
86 7/16	60	Apr	84	26	760	15/16
86 7/16	67 1/2	Mar	50	19	285	5/16
86 7/16	70	Mar	342	16	63	1/2
86 7/16	70	Apr	328	18 1/8	109	2
86 7/16	75	Mar	123	11 1/8	709	5/8
86 7/16	75	Apr	358	14	122	3 1/8
86 7/16	75	Jul	27	20 1/4	332	7 7/8
86 7/16	77 1/2	Mar	21	9 3/4	257	1 3/16
86 7/16	80	Mar	566	8	548	1 3/8
86 7/16	82 1/2	Mar	127	6 1/8	451	2 7/16
86 7/16	85	Mar	1132	4 1/2	2825	2 7/8
86 7/16	85	Apr	651	8 1/4	116	6 3/4
86 7/16	87 1/2	Mar	2906	3 1/8	361	4 3/8
86 7/16	90	Mar	3668	2 5/16	195	5 3/4
86 7/16	90	Apr	835	6 1/4	324	10
86 7/16	90	Jul	322	12 7/8	5	15 1/4
86 7/16	92 1/2	Mar	382	1 1/2	27	7 1/2
86 7/16	95	Mar	1063	15/16	84	9 1/4
86 7/16	95	Apr	479	4 3/8	...	...
86 7/16	95	Jul	304	10 7/8	...	...
86 7/16	95	Oct	235	15 1/8	221	21 1/2
86 7/16	97 1/2	Mar	238	5/8	5	12 1/2
86 7/16	100	Mar	1059	7/16	12	14
86 7/16	100	Apr	356	3	12	16
86 7/16	100	Jul	232	9 1/2	20	21 5/8
AmBankrs	45	Mar	254	4 1/4	...	...
48	50	Mar	1265	1 7/16	...	...
48	50	Apr	603	2 5/8	...	...
48	55	Mar	640	3/8	...	...
48	55	Apr	300	5/8	...	...
AEagleOt	75	May	811	6 7/8	...	...
AmExpr	100	Apr	260	12 3/8	118	1 1/2
113	110	Mar	287	5	135	2 3/16
113	110	Apr	453	7 1/8	1054	5 1/2
113	115	Apr	1147	4 7/8	5	7 1/8
Am Hom	50	Apr	30	11	327	7/16
60 13/16	55	Mar	250	5 7/8	6	5/16
60 13/16	60	Apr	999	3 1/4	...	...
60 13/16	60	Jul	310	5 7/8	...	...
AmIntG	95	May	...	...	400	1 3/4
115 7/16	100	May	...	...	400	2 3/4
115 7/16	105	May	...	...	2000	4 1/4
115 7/16	110	May	2019	11	...	...
115 7/16	115	Mar	2188	3 7/8	13	4 1/2
115 7/16	120	Mar	353	1 1/2	...	...
Amgen	60	Mar	264	4 3/4	59	5/8
64 11/16	62 1/2	Mar	610	3	98	1 1/2
64 11/16	65	Mar	504	1 7/16	50	2 5/8
64 11/16	67 1/2	Mar	234	5/8	...	...
Amresco	5	Mar	...	...	1000	1/8
9 1/8	10	Mar	601	5/8	...	...
9 1/8	12 1/2	Mar	282	5/16	...	...
AmSouth	50	Mar	1516	1 1/4	5	2 5/8
AppleC	32 1/2	Mar	50	2 1/8	328	1 3/16
33 7/16	35	Apr	286	2 1/2	97	4 5/8
33 7/16	37 1/2	Mar	260	7/16	100	3 3/4
33 7/16	37 1/2	Jul	405	4 1/2	...	...
33 7/16	40	Oct	1006	4 1/8	...	...
33 7/16	45	Apr	385	3/8	10	11 3/4
AplMat	55	Mar	297	4 3/8	363	2
57 9/16	60	Mar	570	1 7/8	198	4 1/2
57 9/16	65	Mar	680	11/16	4	6 3/4
57 9/16	70	Mar	238	3/8	2	11 3/8
57 9/16	80	Oct	521	5 1/2	...	...
AscendC	65	Apr	...	...	500	2 1/8
76 7/8	80	Mar	241	1 7/8	47	4 7/8
AtHome	115	Mar	272	5 1/2	18	8
AtwdOcn	20	Apr	250	1 3/8	...	...
Aviall	15	Mar	235	3/4	...	...
Aviron	20	May	250	3 1/2	...	...
21 5/8	22 1/2	May	...	...	250	3 1/4
Avnet	40	Apr	...	2 13/16	570	2 13/16
BB&T	40	Sep	300	2 5/8	...	...
BEA Sys	15	Jun	225	3 3/8	...	...
16 7/8	20	Jun	702	1 3/4	...	...
BMC Sft	40	Mar	101	1 3/8	449	2 5/8
BakrHu	17 1/2	Apr	355	3 1/2	...	...
20 3/8	20	Mar	1255	1	...	...
20 3/8	20	Apr	251	1 3/4	27	1 1/2
BancOne	50	May	300	6 3/8	7	2
BankAm	50	May	...	...	530	1/2
66 1/2	55	May	...	...	580	1
66 1/2	60	May	805	9	...	...
66 1/2	60	Aug	580	11 3/8	51	3 7/8
66 1/2	70	Mar	496	1/2	...	...
BkrsTr	80	Jul	400	10 3/4	22	3 3/4
87 1/16	85	Jul	700	6 5/8	...	...
BarNbl	35	Apr	172	5/8	483	7 5/8
BarickG	17 1/2	Mar	228	1 1/16	10	7/16
BattlM	5	Jul	260	1/4	...	...
BedBth	30	Apr	250	3	...	...
Beth S	7 1/2	Jul	12	1 7/8	225	11/16
Biogen	85	Mar	2	20 1/8	260	1/8
105	95	Mar	277	10	10	1 1/4
105	105	Apr	1003	7 1/2	1050	7 1/2
Boeing	30	Mar	500	5	50	3/16
34 15/16	35	Mar	648	15/16	35	7/8
Borders	20	Mar	275	1/16	...	...
BostSc	25	Mar	335	5 3/8	...	...
30 1/16	30	Mar	354	1 5/16	10	1 3/8
30 1/16	30	Aug	1104	4 1/8	...	...
30 1/16	37 1/2	May	345	13/16	...	...
BrMSq	62 1/2	Mar	405	3 3/8	43	3/4
65 3/16	65	Mar	737	1 5/8	163	2 1/8
brdc.com	45	Oct	...	...	325	7 5/8
87 3/4	70	Oct	...	...	333	19 7/8
87 3/4	85	Mar	67	8 3/4	312	6 1/2
87 3/4	95	Mar	228	4 5/8	...	...
Broadcom	55	Mar	382	1 11/16	60	6 1/8
50 1/16	65	Mar	272	1/4	2	15 1/2
BwnFer	30	Mar	710	4 1/8	56	9/16
33 3/4	30	Apr	469	4 3/8	175	1 3/16
33 3/4	35	Mar	2381	1 1/2	...	...
33 3/4	35	Apr	1493	2 1/2	75	3 1/4
33 3/4	35	Sep	501	3 1/2	...	...
BudgetGp	10	Apr	300	2 9/16	...	...
ConsCap	10	May	528	7 1/2	430	2
16 3/4	20	May	485	3/4	435	9 1/2
CBS Cp	22 1/2	Apr	2650	14 1/2	...	...
36 15/16	35	Apr	1019	3 1/4	8	1
CHS Elec	7 1/2	Mar	358	9/16	10	7/8
CMGI Inc	145	Mar	354	8 3/4	24	16 1/4
139 3/8	150	Mar	524	6 3/4	34	17
139 3/8	160	Mar	341	4 5/8	...	...
139 3/8	165	Mar	468	3 5/8	...	...
CNET	130	Mar	226	19 1/2	302	10 3/4
139 3/4	140	Mar	419	15	57	15 5/8
Cabltrn	10	Apr	235	3/8	25	2 3/8
CallGolf	10	Aug	240	2 5/16	15	1 1/8
Caterp	45	Mar	1345	3 1/4	178	5/8
47 15/16	50	May	1675	2 1/4	1750	4 5/8

FIGURE 24.1 Listed Options Quotations (excerpts)

Source: Reprinted by permission of *The Wall Street Journal,* Dow Jones & Company, Inc., March 5, 1999, p. C24. All rights reserved worldwide.

24.2.2 MOST ACTIVE OPTIONS

Additional information besides the trading activity for options that is shown in Figure 24.1 is provided every day for the "most active" options. Figure 24.2 provides an example of the most active options on March 4, 1999. After the name of the company and the contract specifications come the trading volume on the contract on that day, the exchange on which the option is traded, the closing price on the contract, the change this represents from the previous day's closing price, the closing price on the underlying stock, and the open interest in that contract.

For example, Dell Computer March 85 calls that are traded on the American Stock Exchange ("AM") were the most active issue on March 4, 1999. On that day, 8,645 of

MOST ACTIVE CONTRACTS

Option/Strike				Vol	Exch	Last	Net Chg	a-Close	Open Int
DellCptr	Mar	85		8,645	AM	2 1/2	− 1/4	81 7/8	26,576
DellCptr	Mar	90		8,065	AM	1 1/4	− 1/16	81 7/8	29,192
VLSI	Apr	17 1/2		5,796	XC	1 1/2	+ 7/16	18 5/16	6,454
VLSI	Mar	15		5,750	XC	3 1/2	+ 5/8	18 5/16	23,806
Halbtn	Mar	30		4,858	CB	2 1/4	+ 3/4	32	5,306
DellCptr	Mar	80		4,809	AM	4 7/8	...	81 7/8	19,183
TelBrasH	Mar	70		4,756	XC	1 7/8	+ 15/16	66 13/16	31,134
I B M	Mar	170	p	4,394	XC	4 1/8	− 2 3/8	170 5/8	5,633
3Com	Apr	27 1/2		3,809	PC	1 1/2	+ 1/8	25	1,845
Compaq	Jan 00	35		3,807	XC	6 7/8	− 3/8	33 5/16	21,307
Intel	Mar	110	p	3,741	AM	3 1/8	+ 3/8	113 3/8	10,972
Citigroup	Jun	60		3,685	XC	5 1/4	+ 7/8	60 5/16	14,618
I B M	Mar	180		3,680	XC	1 5/8	+ 11/16	170 5/8	6,697
AmOnline	Mar	90		3,668	XC	2 5/16	− 5/16	86 7/16	43,758
I B M	Mar	175		3,618	XC	2 15/16	+ 1 1/16	170 5/8	4,055
Iomega	May	7 1/2	p	3,513	XC	2 1/4	+ 1/8	5 5/8	218,616
Citigroup	Jun	60	p	3,510	XC	4 1/2	− 1 3/8	60 5/16	2,322
Slumb	Mar	55		3,390	XC	2 1/2	+ 1 7/8	56 3/8	3,184
Compaq	Mar	35		3,361	XC	13/16	− 1/4	33 5/16	14,045
Intel	Mar	120		3,217	AM	2 1/16	− 11/16	113 3/8	12,548
TelBrasH	Apr	70		3,217	XC	4 1/8	+ 1 5/8	66 13/16	14,814
Intel	Mar	115		3,187	AM	3 3/4	− 1 1/8	113 3/8	6,680
Intel	Mar	110		3,057	AM	6 7/8	− 5/8	113 3/8	2,603
MerrLyn	Mar	80		3,051	XC	5 5/8	+ 3 3/8	84 1/2	13,266
Tex In	Mar	100	p	3,039	CB	8	− 2 1/8	93 7/16	6,098
Micsft	Mar	155		2,933	PC	3 1/4	+ 1/2	152 1/4	7,998
AmOnline	Mar	87 1/2		2,906	XC	3 1/8	− 1/2	86 7/16	44,151
Cisco	Mar	105		2,882	XC	1 1/4	+ 1/2	98 1/4	37,772
Cisco	Mar	95	p	2,874	XC	2 3/16	− 1 9/16	98 1/4	15,948
AmOnline	Mar	85	p	2,825	XC	2 7/8	− 1/4	86 7/16	61,050
TelSv.com	Mar	12 1/2		2,825	XC	3/16	+ 1/16	8 31/32	7,752
Citigroup	Mar	60		2,788	XC	2	+ 7/8	60 5/16	41,494
Cisco	Mar	90		2,783	XC	9 1/4	+ 2 1/8	98 1/4	5,792
CBS Cp	Apr	22 1/2		2,650	AM	14 1/2	+ 2 3/8	36 15/16	5,283
CBS	Jan 00	25		2,650	AM	13 7/8	− 5/8	36 15/16	1,814
DellCptr	Mar	80	p	2,628	AM	3	− 1/2	81 7/8	20,780
Slumb	Aug	60		2,604	XC	5 1/8	+ 2 1/8	56 3/8	849
Intel	Mar	125		2,597	AM	15/16	− 5/16	113 3/8	11,236
MerrLyn	Mar	85		2,563	XC	2 5/8	+ 1 3/4	84 1/2	6,786
Maxtor	Apr	10		2,496	XC	13/16	− 1/16	8 5/16	2,976

FIGURE 24.2 Most Active Options Quotations

Source: Reprinted by permission of *The Wall Street Journal,* Dow Jones & Company, Inc., March 5, 1999, p. C24. All rights reserved worldwide.

these contracts were traded. The premium on the last trade was $\$2\frac{1}{2}$ per share (or \$250.00 per contract). This represents a decrease of $\$\frac{1}{4}$ from the last trade premium on the previous trading day. On March 4, 1999, the closing price on the common stock of Dell Computer was $\$81\frac{7}{8}$ per share.

Investors may place the same kinds of orders for options as for stocks; market, limit, stop, and stop limit orders. (These orders were discussed in Chapter 2.) However, the way that the orders for options are executed on the exchanges is, in some cases, different from the way that orders for stocks are executed.

24.2.3 TRADING ON EXCHANGES

There are two types of exchange-based mechanisms in the United States for trading option contracts. The focal point for trading involves either specialists or market-makers, whose procedures for handling orders involving options are similar to the procedures used for orders involving shares of stock. However, many options are created and traded in the over-the-counter market where the terms are negotiated between the buyer and writer, who are typically financial institutions, corporations, and large institutional investors. The possibility that the writer of one of these off-exchange options may default on his or her obligation is referred to as **counterparty risk.**

counterparty risk

Like the organized stock exchanges in the United States, all option exchanges are continuous markets, meaning that orders can be executed any time while the exchanges are open. However, actual trading in options is, on occasion, far from continuous. In the financial press it is not unusual to find prices for various options that appear to be out of line with one another or with the price of the underlying stock. Remember that each listed price is that of the last trade of the day and that these trades may have taken place at different times. Apparent price disparities may simply reflect trades that occurred before and after major news, rather than concurrent values at which obviously profitable trades could have been made.

24.2.4 COMMISSIONS

Although a commission must be paid to a stockbroker whenever an option is either written, bought, or sold, the size of the commission has been reduced substantially since options began to be traded on organized exchanges in 1973. However, the investor

Open Outcry

Is it a scene from a Fellini movie? Or perhaps the crowd at a 90%-off sale at Bloomingdale's? No, it is simply the members of the Chicago Board Options Exchange (CBOE) participating in the time-honored tradition of open outcry.

As the text describes, at the CBOE and other option exchanges (as well as futures exchanges; see Chapter 25), members come together in various trading pits to conduct transactions in specific option contracts. Like the trading posts of the NYSE (see Chapter 3), the CBOE trading pits serve as central locations where market-clearing prices for option contracts are continuously determined through an auction process. Unlike the NYSE trading posts, however, the CBOE and most other option exchanges do not use a specialist system. No one individual acts as a monopolistic dealer and auctioneer, ensuring the setting of market-clearing prices. Instead, those prices are established through *open outcry,* a public auction method involving verbal bids and offers initiated by the exchange members in the pit. Open outcry is a raucous and colorful trading mechanism that combines the mental gymnastics of rapid-fire decision making with a set of physical skills ranging from strategic positioning in the trading pit to shouting instructions to frenetic hand signaling.

To describe the open outcry system as "the pits" is no exaggeration. The process begins in the trading pits, large depressions in the exchange floor surrounded by several levels of stairs on which the members stand. Although no formal rules are involved, traders generally behave territorially in the pit. Floor traders usually have certain market-makers with whom they prefer to trade, and these individuals position themselves to make convenient contact with one another. Further, the most senior and important traders take positions in the pit where they have most efficient access to their counterparts. Junior members must stand in less desirable positions where they are less likely to catch the attention of other traders.

The trading pits are often crowded, noisy, and uncomfortable. Members may jostle each other for position. Hence, attributes such as voice strength and physical endurance are important. The pits are dominated by men, and the disadvantages endured by women in this physical environment are not lost on critics of the open outcry system.

Members deliver their trading intentions using a system of verbal orders and, to a lesser extent, hand signals. For example, a floor broker may enter the IBM trading pit and verbally announce his or her intention to purchase June IBM call option contracts at a specified price. At the same time, he or she may repeat the buy order and desired price using hand signals. A market-maker who wishes to sell at that price will shout out the desired quantity and possibly confirm those intentions by hand.

Hand signals, formerly a distinguishing feature of open outcry in the trading pits, are no longer used as widely as they once were. The number of traders in the pits has declined over the years, making verbal communication more effective, particularly in the individual stock pits. However, in the index option pits, in which many more traders congregate, hand signals are still used to convey trading intentions.

To the uninitiated, the hand gestures used by members seem wild and unintelligible. In actuality, the signals are simple and efficient. Buy and sell orders are indicated by the position of the trader's palms. If the trader's palms are facing him or her, a buy is signaled. The trader signals a sell with palms pointed outward.

The trader indicates the bid or asked price by holding his or her hand in a vertical position and using fingers to indicate the fraction of a dollar involved. For example, one finger indicates an eighth of a dollar, and a closed fist indicates a full dollar.

Traders likewise display their quantity intentions with their hands. Fingers pointed vertically indicate 1 through 5 contracts, whereas fingers pointed horizontally indicate 6 through 9 contracts. One finger to the forehead indicates 10 contracts.

At any given time, members in the pit may be trading in different option contracts, shouting in an attempt to make their voices heard above the din, and flailing their arms about to signal their trading intentions. Floor brokers are parading around wearing radio headsets, and market-makers are using handheld devices to conduct trades in stocks on the NYSE. Add to this scene runners milling about the edge of the pit, time and sale clerks, price reporters, order book officials keeping track of transactions, and persons situated away from the pit signaling orders to the floor brokers, and pandemonium hardly seems an adequate description of the trading process.

Open outcry is a controversial trading mechanism. It has been criticized as an archaic method designed primarily to perpetuate control over lucrative option trading by the exchanges' members. In an age of advanced electronics, there are readily available computer systems that could facilitate electronic auctions and allow wider access to the auction process. (For example, the three

major U.S. futures exchanges operate electronic after-hours trading systems. Volume on those systems has been growing more rapidly than has regular hours trading volume. Further, the major European futures exchanges are rapidly moving toward all-electronic trading.) The benefits of such electronic auction systems seem to be lower trading costs and greater liquidity.

Defenders of the open outcry system claim that it is the most efficient method of price discovery. They believe that the system's face-to-face contact permits traders to better ascertain the "true" intentions of buyers and sellers. Moreover, the defenders contend that price manipulation is less likely in an open environment. Regardless of the system's merits, the Chicago-based options (and futures) exchanges are coming to recognize that they must move away from open outcry or lose considerable business to rival systems using electronic trading. It is reasonable to expect that within only a few years, open outcry will be considered a quaint anachronism from a bygone era.

should be aware that exercising an option usually results in the buyer paying a commission equivalent to the commission that would be paid if the stock itself were being bought or sold.[5]

24.3 Margin

Any buyer of an option would like some assurance that the writer can deliver as required if the option is exercised. Specifically, the buyer of a call option would like some assurance that the writer is capable of delivering the requisite shares, and the buyer of a put option would like some assurance that the writer is capable of delivering the necessary cash. Because all option contracts are with the OCC, it is actually the OCC that is concerned with the ability of the writer to fulfill the terms of the contract.

To relieve the OCC of this concern, the exchanges where the options are traded have set margin requirements. However, brokerage firms are allowed to impose even stricter requirements if they desire because they are ultimately liable to the OCC for the actions of their investors.

In the case of a call, shares are to be delivered by the writer in return for the exercise price. In the case of a put, cash is to be delivered in return for shares. In either case the net cost to the option writer is the absolute difference between the exercise price and the stock's market value at the time of exercise. The OCC is at risk if the writer is unable to bear this cost, so it is not surprising that the OCC has a system in place to protect itself from the actions of the writers. This system is known as margin, and it is similar to the notion of margin associated with stock purchases and short sales discussed in Chapter 2.[6]

24.4   Valuation of Options

24.4.1   VALUATION AT EXPIRATION

The value of an option is related to the value of the underlying security. That relationship is most evident just before the option's expiration date (which, for simplicity, will be referred to as "at expiration"). Figure 24.3(a) relates the value of a call option with an exercise price of $100 to the price of the underlying stock at expiration. If the stock price is below $100, the option will be worthless when it expires. If the price is above $100, the option can be exercised for $100 to obtain a security with a greater value, resulting in a net gain to the option buyer that will equal the difference between the security's market price and the $100 exercise price. However, there is no need for the option buyer to actually exercise the option. Instead, the option writer can simply pay the buyer the difference between the security price and the $100 exercise price, thereby allowing both parties to avoid the inconvenience of exercise. This practice is commonly used for listed options (by using the services of the OCC), although a minority of investors do exercise their options, possibly for tax purposes.

Figure 24.3(b) shows the value at expiration of a put option with an exercise price of $100. If the stock price is above $100, the option will be worthless when it expires. If the price is below $100, the option can be exercised to obtain $100 for stock having a lower value, resulting in a net gain to the option buyer that will equal the difference between the $100 exercise price and the stock's market price. As with a call option, neither the put option buyer nor the writer need actually deal in the stock. Instead, the writer of any put option that is worth exercising at expiration can simply pay the buyer of the option the difference between the stock price and the $100 exercise price.

In both panels of Figure 24.3, the lines indicating the value of a call and a put at expiration can be interpreted as the *exercise value* of a call or a put, meaning it is the option's value at the moment it is exercised, no matter when that occurs during the life of the option. In particular, for calls the kinked line connecting points 0, *E,* and *Z* is known as the **intrinsic value** of the call. Similarly, for puts, the kinked line connecting points *Z, E,* and $200 is known as the intrinsic value of the put. The kinked lines representing the intrinsic values of calls and puts such as those shown in Figure 24.3 can be expressed as IV_c and IV_p, respectively, as follows:

intrinsic value

$$IV_c = \max \{0, P_s - E\} \tag{24.1a}$$

$$IV_p = \max \{0, E - P_s\} \tag{24.1b}$$

where P_s denotes the market price of the underlying stock and E denotes the exercise price of the option. (Here "max" means to use the larger of the two values in braces.)

Consider the call option in Figure 24.3(a). Its intrinsic value, according to Equation (24.1a), is $\max \{0, P_s - \$100\}$ because its exercise price is $100. Note that for any market price of the stock below $100, such as $50, the intrinsic value of the call option is $0 = \max \{0, \$50 - \$100\}$. Hence $IV_c = 0$ in such situations. Next imagine that the market price of the stock is above $100, for example, $150. In this situation the call option's intrinsic value is $\$50 = \max \{0, \$150 - \$100\}$. Hence $IV_c = \$50$. Thus, the kinked intrinsic value line has its kink at E because two components meet there: a horizontal line going through the origin out to the value E and a 45-degree line (which has a slope of one) going northeast from E. The kinked intrinsic value line for the put also has its kink at $E,$ as shown in Figure 24.3(b).

Calls and puts will not sell for less than their intrinsic values because of the actions of shrewd investors. If an option sold for less than its intrinsic value, then such investors could instantly make riskless profits. For example, if the stock price was $150 and the call

FIGURE 24.3 Values of Options at Expiration

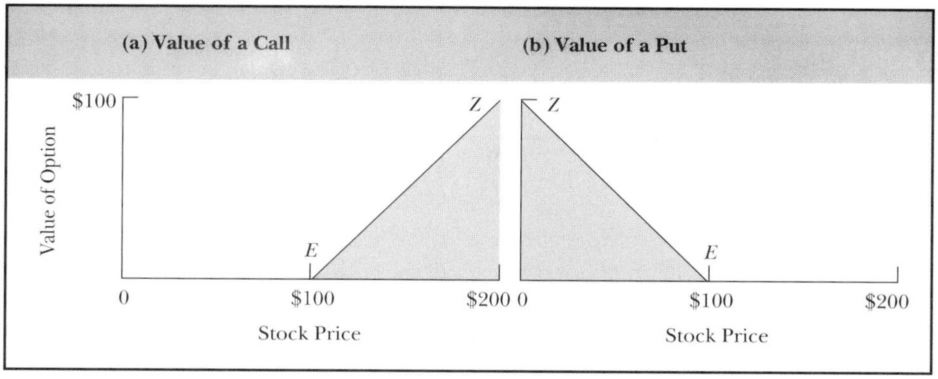

was selling for $40, which is $10 less than its intrinsic value of $50, then these investors would simultaneously buy these calls, exercise them, and sell the shares received from the writers. In doing so they would spend a total of $140 on each call ($40) and exercise price ($100) and get $150 in return for each share sold, resulting in a net riskless profit of $10 per call. As a consequence, the call will not sell for less than $50 if the stock price is $150.

24.4.2   PROFITS AND LOSSES ON CALLS AND PUTS

Figure 24.3 shows the values of call and put options at expiration. However, to determine profits and losses from buying or writing these options, one must consider the premiums involved.[7] Figure 24.4 accounts for premiums in some of the more complicated option strategies. Each strategy assumes that the underlying stock is selling for $100 when an option is initially bought or written. It also assumes that closing transactions are made just before the expiration date for the option being considered. Outcomes are shown for each of ten strategies. Because the profit obtained by a buyer is the writer's loss and vice versa, each diagram in the figure has a corresponding mirror image.

Panels (a) and (b) in Figure 24.4 show the profits and losses associated with buying and writing a call, respectively. Similarly, panels (c) and (d) show the profits and losses associated with buying and writing a put, respectively.

Consider panels (a) and (c) first. The kinked lines representing profits and losses in these two panels are simply graphs of the intrinsic value equations, Equations (24.1a) and (24.1b), shown in Figure 24.3, less the premiums on the options. Thus, they are graphs of the following equations:

$$\pi_c = \mathrm{IV}_c - P_c$$
$$= \max\{0, P_s - E\} - P_c$$
$$= \max\{-P_c, P_s - E - P_c\} \qquad \textbf{(24.2a)}$$

$$\pi_p = \mathrm{IV}_p - P_p$$
$$= \max\{0, E - P_s\} - P_p$$
$$= \max\{-P_p, E - P_s - P_p\} \qquad \textbf{(24.2b)}$$

where π_c and π_p denote the profits associated with buying a call and a put, and P_c and P_p denote the premiums on the call and the put, respectively. Taking into account option

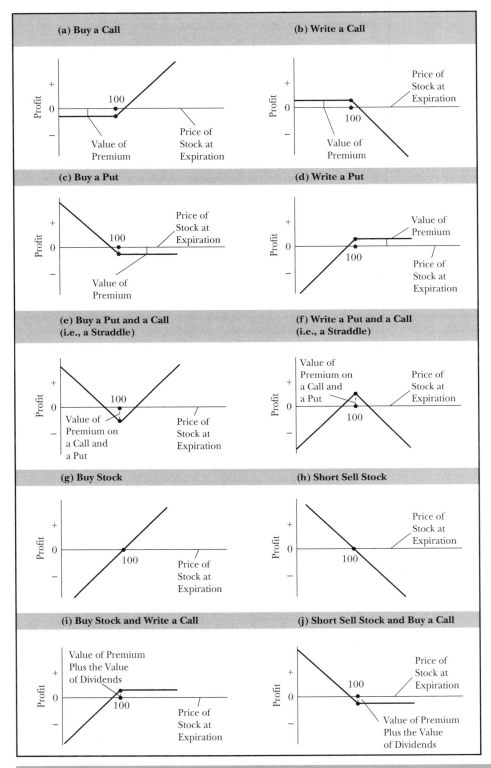

FIGURE 24.4 Profits and Losses from Various Strategies

premiums, the kinked profit line for the call is the same kinked line for the call's intrinsic value but lowered by an amount equal to the call premium P_c. Similarly, the kinked profit line for the put is the kinked intrinsic value line for the put, lowered by an amount equal to the put premium P_p. In both cases the premium is subtracted from the option's intrinsic value because the buyer had to pay the premium.

If the premium on the call and put options shown in Figure 24.3 were $5, then their profit lines would be graphs of the following two equations:

$$\pi_p = \max\left\{-\$5, P_s - \$100 - \$5\right\}$$
$$= \max\left\{-\$5, P_s - \$105\right\}$$
$$\pi_p = \max\left\{-\$5, \$100 - P_s - \$5\right\}$$
$$= \max\left\{-\$5, \$95 - P_s\right\}$$

Therefore the kinked line for the call would be horizontal, intersecting the vertical axis at −$5, and it would have a kink at a stock price of $100, where it would angle upward to intersect the horizontal axis at $105. This graph indicates that the call buyer would not make a profit unless the stock price was above the breakeven point of $105 at expiration. Each dollar that the stock price is above $105 represents an additional dollar of profit. (Hence a price of $108 would represent a profit of $3 because the call buyer pays a premium of $5 and an exercise price of $100 to procure a share of stock that is worth $108.)

Similarly, the kinked line for the put would be a downward-sloping line with a kink at a stock price of $100 after intersecting the horizontal axis at $95. At the kink the line would become horizontal so that if this part of the line were extended leftward to the vertical axis, it would intersect it at −$5. This graph indicates that the put buyer would not make a profit unless the stock price was below the breakeven point of $95 at expiration. Each dollar that the stock price is below $95 represents an additional dollar of profit. (Hence a price of $92 would represent a profit of $3 because the put buyer pays a premium of $5 and gives up a share of stock worth $92 in order to receive $100 in return.)

Panels (b) and (d) of Figure 24.4 are mirror images of panels (a) and (c), respectively, because options are zero-sum games, where the profits to one party occur at the expense of the other party. Hence if the stock price is at $108 so that the call buyer has a $3 profit, then the call writer has a $3 loss (because the writer receives the $5 premium and $100 exercise price but must give up a share of stock worth $108). Similarly, if the put buyer has a $3 profit, then the put writer has a loss of $3. Panel (b) corresponds to what is known as **naked call writing** and panel (d) to **naked put writing.** The term "naked" indicates that the option writer does not own the stock on which the option is written. In both cases the premium is added to the option's intrinsic value because the writer receives the premium.

naked call writing
naked put writing

24.4.3 PROFITS AND LOSSES FROM SOME OPTION STRATEGIES

straddle

Panels (e) and (f) of Figure 24.4 illustrate a more complicated options strategy known as a **straddle.** This strategy involves buying (or writing) both a call and a put on the same stock, with the options having the same exercise price and expiration date.[8] Note that panel (e) is derived by adding the profits and losses shown in panels (a) and (c), whereas panel (f) can be derived by adding the profits and losses shown in panels (b) and (d). Panels (e) and (f) are mirror images of each other, again reflecting the fact that the profits to buyers equal the losses to writers and vice versa. In panel (e), an investor profits if the stock price moves sharply up or down from $100, but loses if the price remains at about $100. In contrast, in panel (f), the investor profits if the stock price remains at about $100, but loses if it moves sharply up or down.

Panel (g) of Figure 24.4 shows the profit or loss made by an investor who avoids options entirely but buys a share of the underlying stock (at $100) at the same time that others buy or write options and sells the stock when the options expire. If no dividends are paid in the interim, the relationship is that shown by the solid line.[9] Similarly, panel (h) shows the profit or loss obtained by an investor who short sells the stock at the initial date and then buys it back at the expiration date.

covered call writing

Panel (i) of Figure 24.4 shows the results obtained by an investor who buys one share of stock and simultaneously writes a call on it, a strategy known as **covered call writing.** These results are derived by adding the profits and losses shown in panels (b) and (g). Note how the investor's gains are capped, but the losses can get quite large.

Panel (j) of Figure 24.4 shows the results obtained by an investor who short sells one share of stock and simultaneously buys a call option. It is derived by adding the profits and losses in panels (a) and (h). This panel is the mirror image of panel (i). Note how the investor's losses are capped, but the gains can get quite large.

Comparison of the diagrams in Figure 24.4 suggests that similar results can be obtained via alternative strategies. Panels (c) and (j) are similar, as are (d) and (i). Neither the premiums involved nor the initial investments required need be equal in every case. Nonetheless, the similarity of the results obtained with different "packages" of securities suggests that the total market values of the packages will be similar.

Now that the value of options (and option-based strategies) when they expire have been discussed, it is appropriate to discuss the value of options before they expire. Specifically, what is the fair (or true) value of an option today if it expires at some future date? A method using the binomial option pricing model can be used to answer such a question.

24.5 The Binomial Option Pricing Model

The binomial option pricing model (BOPM) can be used to estimate the fair value of a call or put option. It is best presented using an example in which it is assumed that the options are **European options,** meaning that they can be exercised only on their expiration dates. In addition, it is assumed that the underlying stock does not pay any dividends during the life of the option. The model can be modified to value **American options,** which are options that can be exercised at any time during their life and can also be used to value options on stocks that pay dividends during the life of the option.

European options

American options

24.5.1 CALL OPTIONS

Assume that the price of Widget stock today ($t = 0$) is $100, and that after one year ($t = T$) its stock sells for either $125 or $80, meaning that the stock will either rise by 25% or fall by 20% during the year. In addition, the annual riskfree rate is 8% compounded continuously. Investors can either lend (by purchasing these 8% bonds) or borrow (by short selling the bonds) at this rate.

Now consider a call option on Widget that has an exercise price of $100 and an expiration date of one year from now. On the expiration date the call will have a value of either $25 (if Widget is at $125) or $0 (if Widget is at $80). Panel (a) of Figure 24.5 illustrates the situation using a "price tree," which has two branches that represent prices at the expiration date, thus making the term "binomial" an appropriate title for the model.

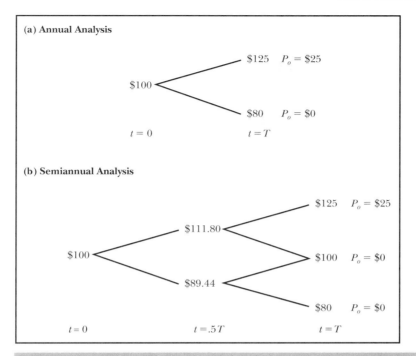

(a) Annual Analysis

$100 $\rightarrow$ $125 $P_o = 25

$100 $\rightarrow$ $80 $P_o = 0

$t = 0$ $t = T$

(b) Semiannual Analysis

$100 $\rightarrow$ $111.80 $\rightarrow$ $125 $P_o = 25

$111.80 $\rightarrow$ $100 $P_o = 0

$100 $\rightarrow$ $89.44 $\rightarrow$ $100 $P_o = 0

$89.44 $\rightarrow$ $80 $P_o = 0

$t = 0$ $t = .5T$ $t = T$

FIGURE 24.5 Binomial Model of Prices for Widget

Valuation

The question that arises is this: What is a fair value for the call at time 0? The binomial option pricing model is designed to answer that question.

Three investments are of interest here: the stock, the option, and a riskfree bond. The prices and payoffs for the stock and option are known. It is also known that $100 invested in a riskfree bond will grow to approximately $108.33 if interest is continuously compounded at an annual rate of 8%.[10] What is to be determined is a fair price that the option should sell for now.

The key to understanding the situation is the observation that there are two possible future *states of nature*. The stock's price may go up or down. For simplicity, these two states are called the "up state" and the "down state," respectively. This essential information is summarized as follows:

Security	Payoff in Up State	Payoff in Down State	Current Price
Stock	$125.00	$ 80.00	$100.00
Bond	108.33	108.33	100.00
Call	25.00	0.00	???

Note that at this juncture the current price of the call is unknown.

Replicating Portfolios

Although the Widget call option may seem exotic, its characteristics can in fact be replicated with an appropriate combination of the Widget stock and the riskfree bond. Moreover, the cost of this *replicating portfolio* constitutes the fair value of the option. Why? Because otherwise there would be an *arbitrage opportunity;* an investor could buy the cheaper of the two alternatives and sell the more expensive one, thereby achieving a guaranteed profit. (Just how this transaction is done is revealed shortly.)

The composition of a portfolio that precisely replicates the payoffs of the Widget call option needs to be determined. Consider a portfolio with N_s shares of Widget stock and N_b riskfree bonds. In the up state such a portfolio has a payoff of $125N_s + \$108.33N_b$, whereas in the down state it has a payoff of $\$80N_s + \$108.33N_b$. Because the call option is worth \$25 in the up state, N_s and N_b need to have values so that

$$\$125N_s + \$108.33N_b = \$25 \tag{24.3a}$$

And because the call option is worthless in the down state, N_s and N_b need to have values so that

$$\$80N_s + \$108.33N_b = \$0 \tag{24.3b}$$

These two linear equations, (24.3a) and (24.3b), have two unknowns and can be solved easily. Subtracting the second equation from the first gives

$$(\$125 - \$80)N_s = \$25 \tag{24.3c}$$

so that N_s equals .5556. Substituting this value in either Equation (24.3a) or Equation (24.3b) gives the remainder of the solution, $N_b = -.4103$.

What does this mean in financial terms? It means that an investor can replicate the payoffs from the call by *short selling* \$41.03 of the riskfree bonds (note that investing $-.4103$ in \$100 bonds is equivalent to short selling \$41.03 of the bonds or borrowing \$41.03 at the riskfree rate) and *purchasing* .5556 shares of Widget stock. This is indeed the case, as can be seen here:

Portfolio Component	*Payoff in Up State*	*Payoff in Down State*
Stock investment	.5556 × \$125 = \$69.45	.5556 × \$80 = \$44.45
Loan repayment	−\$41.03 × 1.0833 = −\$44.45	−\$41.03 × 1.0833 = −\$44.45
Net payoff	\$25.00	\$0.00

Because the replicating portfolio provides the same payoffs as the call, only its cost needs to be calculated to find the fair value of the option. To obtain the portfolio, the investor must spend \$55.56 to purchase .5556 shares of Widget stock (at \$100 per share). However, \$41.03 of this amount is provided by the proceeds from the short sale of the bond, which is equivalent to borrowing \$41.03. Thus, only \$14.53 (\$55.56 − \$41.03) of the investor's own funds must be spent. Accordingly, this is the fair value of the call option.

More generally, the value of the call option will be

$$V_o = N_s P_s + N_b P_b \tag{24.4}$$

where V_o represents the value of the option, P_s is the price of the stock, P_b is the price of a riskfree bond, and N_s and N_b are the number of shares and riskfree bonds required to replicate the option's payoffs.

Overpricing

To see that equilibrium will be attained if the call sells for \$14.53, consider what a shrewd investor would do if the call were selling for either more or less than this amount. Imagine that the call is selling for \$20, so it is overpriced. In this case the investor would consider writing one call, buying .5556 shares, and borrowing $41.03. The net cash flow when this is done (that is, at $t = 0$) would be $5.47 [= $20 − (.5556 × $100) + $41.03], indicating that the investor has a net cash inflow. At the end of the year (that is, at $t = T$) the investor's net cash flow will be as follows:

Portfolio Component	Payoff in Up State	Payoff in Down State
Written call	−$25.00	$0.00
Stock investment	.5556 × $125 = $69.45	.5556 × $80 =$44.45
Loan repayment	−$41.03 × 1.0833 = −$44.45	−$41.03 × 1.0833 = −$44.45
Net payoff	$0.00	$0.00

Because the net aggregate value is zero regardless of the ending stock price, the investor has no risk of loss from this strategy. Thus, the investor currently has a means for generating free cash as long as the call is priced at $20 because the investment strategy does not require any cash from the investor later on. This situation cannot represent equilibrium, because anyone can get free cash by investing similarly.

Underpricing

Next imagine that the call is selling for $10 instead of $20, so it is underpriced. In this case the investor would consider buying one call, short selling .5556 shares, and investing $41.03 at the riskfree rate. The net cash (that is, at $t = 0$) would be $4.53 [= −$10 + (.5556 × $100) − $41.03], indicating that the investor has a net cash inflow. At the end of the year (that is, at $t = T$) the investor's net cash flow will be as follows:

Portfolio Component	Payoff in Up State	Payoff in Down State
Call investment	$25.00	$0.00
Repay shorted stock	−.5556 × $125 = −$69.45	−.5556 × $80 = −$44.45
Riskfree investment	$41.03 × 1.0833 = $44.45	$41.03 × 1.0833 = $44.45
Net payoff	$0.00	$0.00

Once again, the net aggregate value is zero regardless of the ending stock price, indicating that the investor has no risk of loss from this strategy. Hence the investor currently has a means for generating free cash as long as the call is priced at $10. This situation cannot represent equilibrium, however, because anyone can get free cash by investing similarly.

The Hedge Ratio

To replicate the Widget call option, imagine borrowing $41.03 and purchasing .5556 shares of Widget stock. Consider the effect of a change in the price of the stock tomorrow (not a year from now) on the value of the replicating portfolio. Because .5556 shares of stock are included in the portfolio, the value of the portfolio will change by $.5556 for every $1 change in the price of Widget stock. But because the call option and the portfolio should sell for the same price, it follows that the price of the call should also change by $.5556 for every $1 change in the price of the stock. This relationship is

hedge ratio

defined as the option's **hedge ratio,** denoted h. It equals the value N_s that was determined in Equation (24.3c).

In the case of the Widget call option, the hedge ratio was .5556, which equals the value of ($25 − $0)/($125 − $80). Note that the numerator equals the difference between the option's payoffs in the up and down states, and the denominator equals the difference between the stock's payoffs in the two states. More generally, in the binomial model the hedge ratio is

$$h = \frac{P_{ou} - P_{od}}{P_{su} - P_{sd}} \tag{24.5}$$

where P represents the end-of-period price and the subscripts indicate the instrument (o for option, s for stock) and the state of nature (u for up, d for down).

To replicate a call option in a binomial world, an investor must purchase h shares of stock and risklessly borrow an amount B by short selling bonds. The amount to be borrowed is

$$B = PV(hP_{sd} - P_{od}) \tag{24.6}$$

where PV refers to the present value of the figure calculated in the following parentheses. (Note that the figure in parentheses is the value of the bond at the end of the period.[11])

To summarize, the value of a call option is

$$V_o = hP_s - B \tag{24.7}$$

where h and B are the hedge ratio and the current value of a short bond position in a portfolio that replicates the payoffs of the call and that are calculated using Equations (24.5) and (24.6).

More Than Two Prices

It is reasonable to wonder about the accuracy of the BOPM if it is based on an assumption that the price of Widget stock can assume only one of two values at the end of a year. Realistically, Widget stock can assume any one of a great number of prices at year-end. This added complexity is not a problem because the model can be extended in a straightforward manner.

In the case of Widget, divide the year into two six-month periods. In the first period, assume that Widget can go up to $111.80 (an 11.80% increase) or down to $89.44 (a 10.56% decrease). For the second six-month period, the price of Widget can again go either up by 11.80% or down by 10.56%. Hence the price of Widget will follow one of the paths of the price tree shown in Figure 24.5(b) during the forthcoming year. Note that Widget can now assume one of three prices at year-end: $125, $100, or $80. The associated value of the call option is also given in the figure for each of these stock prices.

How can the value of the Widget call option at time 0 be calculated from the information given in the figure? The answer is remarkably simple. By breaking the problem into three parts, each is solved in a manner similar to that shown earlier when panel (a) was discussed. The three parts must be approached sequentially by working backward in time.

First, imagine that six months have passed and the price of Widget stock is $111.80. What is the value of the call option at this node in the price tree? The hedge ratio h is calculated to be 1.0 [= ($25 − $0)/($125 − $100)], and the amount of the borrowing B is calculated to be $96.08 [= (1 × $100 − $0)/1.0408]. (The 8% riskfree rate compounded continuously corresponds to a discrete discount rate of 4.08% for the six-month period.) Using Equation (24.7), the value of the call is $15.72 (= $1 \times \$111.80 - \$96.08$).

Second, again imagine that six months have passed, but the price of Widget is $89.44. Equations (24.5), (24.6), and (24.7) could be used to determine the value of the call at this node in the price tree, but intuition gives the answer in this example more quickly: The call has to be selling for $0. In six months the price of Widget will be either $100 or $80, and regardless of which it is, the call will still be worthless. That is, investors will realize that the call will be worthless at the end of the year if the stock price is at $89.44 after six months, so they will be unwilling to pay anything for the call option.

Third, imagine that no time has elapsed, so that it is time 0. In this case the price tree can be simplified to

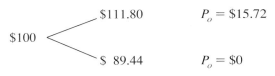

Applying Equations (24.5) and (24.6) reveals that the hedge ratio, h, is equal to .7030 $[= (\$15.72 - \$0)/(\$111.80 - \$89.44)]$, and the amount of borrowing B is equal to $60.41 $[= (.7030 \times \$89.44 - \$0)/1.0408]$. Applying Equation (24.7) results in a value for the call at $t = 0$ of $9.89 $[= (.7030 \times \$100) - \$60.41]$.

There is no need to stop here. Instead of analyzing 2 six-month periods, 4 quarterly periods can be analyzed, or 12 monthly periods. Note that the number of year-end stock prices for Widget is equal to one more than the number of periods in a year. Hence, when annual periods were used in Figure 24.5(a), there were two year-end prices, and when semiannual prices were used, there were 3 year-end prices. It follows that if quarterly or monthly periods had been used, then there would have been 5 or 13 year-end prices, respectively.

24.5.2 PUT OPTIONS

Can the BOPM be used to value puts? Because the formulas cover any set of payoffs, they can be applied directly. Consider Widget, where the put option has an exercise price of $100 and an expiration date of one year. Its price tree will be

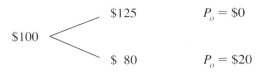

Applying Equation (24.5) gives the hedge ratio for the put option as $-.4444$ $[= (\$0 - \$20)/(\$125 - \$80)]$. This value is a negative number, indicating that Widget stock is to be sold short and that a rise in the price of the stock will lower the price of the put.

Applying Equation (24.6) shows that B equals $-\$51.28$, which is the present value of the year-end value of $-\$55.55$. Because these are negative numbers, they denote the amount of bonds to be purchased (that is, the negative value of a short position should be interpreted as the value of a long position).

To replicate the put option, then, one *sells short* .4444 shares of Widget and *lends* (that is, invests in the riskfree bond) $51.28. As the short sale will generate $44.44, whereas the bond purchase will cost $51.28, the net cost of the replicating portfolio will be $6.84 (= $51.28 − $44.44). Accordingly, this amount is the fair value of the put, which is the same value that is obtained when Equation (24.7) is used: $6.84 [= −.4444 × $100 − (−$51.28)], where $h = −.4444$, $B = −$51.28$, and $P_s = 100. Hence Equations (24.5), (24.6), and (24.7) can be used to value not only calls but also puts. Furthermore, the procedure for extending the valuation of puts to the situation in which there are two or more periods between now and the expiration date is analogous to the one given for calls.

24.5.3 PUT-CALL PARITY

Earlier it was shown that the call on Widget had a hedge ratio of .5556. Note that .5556 − 1 = −.4444, the hedge ratio for the put. This relationship is not a coincidence. The hedge ratios of a European put and call having the same exercise price and expiration date are related in the following manner:

$$h_c - 1 = h_p \tag{24.8}$$

where h_c and h_p denote the hedge ratios for the call and the put, respectively.

The relationship between the market prices of a call and a put on a given stock with the same exercise price and expiration date is of even greater interest. Again consider the example involving Widget options that have an exercise price of $100 and an expiration date of one year. Two investment strategies are compared. Strategy *A* involves buying a put and a share of stock. (This strategy is sometimes known as a "protective put" or a "married put.") Strategy *B* involves buying a call and investing an amount of money in the riskfree asset equal to the present value of the exercise price.

At the expiration date the values of these two investment strategies can be calculated under two scenarios: the price of Widget being below its exercise price of $100, and the price of Widget being above its exercise price. Table 24.1 shows the calculations for both scenarios. Note that if the stock of Widget is selling for less than the $100 exercise price on the expiration date, both strategies have a payoff of $100 in cash. Alternatively, if the price of Widget stock is above $100, then the two strategies result in the investor's having possession of a share of stock. Hence, because both strategies have the same payoffs, they must cost the same amount in equilibrium:

$$P_p + P_s = P_c + E/e^{RT} \tag{24.9}$$

where P_p and P_c denote the current market prices of the put and the call, respectively.

put-call parity

This equation represents what is known as **put-call parity.** According to Table 24.1, the cost of each strategy is $106.84, just as was suggested previously by the calculations using Equations (24.5), (24.6), and (24.7).

TABLE 24.1   Put-Call Parity Involving Widget

Strategy	Initial Cost	Value at Expiration Date	
		$P_s < E = 100	$P_s > E = 100
A: Buy put Buy share of stock	$P_p + P_s$ = $6.84 + $100 = $106.84	Exercise put, get $100	Throw away put, have stock worth P_s
B: Buy call Invest present value of *E* in riskfree asset	$P_c + E/e^{RT}$ = $14.53 + $92.31 = $106.84	Throw away call, get $100 from riskfree asset	Exercise call, get stock worth P_s

24.6   The Black–Scholes Model for Call Options

Consider what would happen with the binomial option pricing model if the number of periods before the expiration date were allowed to increase. For example, with Widget's option for which the expiration date was a year in the future, there could be a price tree with periods for each one of the approximately 250 trading days in a year. Hence there would be 251 possible year-end prices for Widget stock. Needless to say, the fair value of any call associated with such a tree would require a computer to perform calculations such as those shown earlier for Widget. If the number of periods were larger, with each one representing a specific hour of each trading day, then there would be about 1,750 (= 7 × 250) hourly periods (and 1,751 possible year-end prices). Note that the number of periods in a year gets larger as the length of each period gets shorter. In the end there will be an infinite number of infinitely small periods (and, consequently, an infinite number of possible year-end prices). In this situation the BOPM given in Equation (24.7) reduces to the Black–Scholes model, so named in honor of its originators.[12]

24.6.1   THE FORMULA

In a world not bothered by taxes and transaction costs, the fair value of a call option can be estimated using the valuation formula developed by Black and Scholes. It has been widely used by those who deal with options to search for situations in which the market price of an option differs substantially from its fair value. A call option found to be selling for substantially less than its Black–Scholes value is a candidate for purchase, whereas one that is found to be selling for substantially more is a candidate for writing. The Black–Scholes formula for estimating the fair value of a call option V_c is

$$V_c = N(d_1)P_s - \frac{E}{e^{RT}} N(d_2) \tag{24.10}$$

where

$$d_1 = \frac{\ln(P_s/E) + (R + .5\sigma^2)T}{\sigma\sqrt{T}} \tag{24.11}$$

$$d_2 = \frac{\ln(P_s/E) + (R - .5\sigma^2)T}{\sigma\sqrt{T}} \tag{24.12a}$$

$$= d_1 - \sigma\sqrt{T} \tag{24.12b}$$

and where

P_s = current market price of the underlying stock

E = exercise price of the option

R = continuously compounded riskfree rate of return, expressed on an annual basis

T = time remaining before expiration, expressed as a fraction of a year

σ = risk of the underlying common stock, measured by the standard deviation of the continuously compounded annual rate of return on the stock and commonly referred to as **volatility**

volatility

Note that E/e^{RT} is the present value of the exercise price where a continuous discount rate is used. The quantity $\ln(P_s/E)$ is the natural logarithm of P_s/E. Finally, $N(d_1)$ and

$N(d_2)$ denote the probabilities that outcomes of less than d_1 and d_2, respectively, will occur in a normal distribution that has a mean of 0 and a standard deviation of 1.

Table 24.2 provides values of $N(d_1)$ for various levels of d_1.[13] Only this table and a pocket calculator are needed to use the Black–Scholes formula for valuing a call option. It should be noted that with this formula the interest rate R and the stock volatility σ are assumed to be constant over the life of the option. (More recently, formulas have been developed where these assumptions are relaxed.)

For example, consider a call option that expires in three months and has an exercise price of \$40 (thus $T = .25$ and $E = \$40$). Furthermore, the current price and the volatility of the underlying common stock are \$36 and 50%, respectively, whereas the riskfree rate is 5% (thus $P_s = \$36$, $R = .05$, and $\sigma = .50$). Solving Equations (24.11) and (24.12b) provides the following values for d_1 and d_2:

$$d_1 = \frac{\ln(36/40) + [.05 + .5(.50)^2].25}{.50\sqrt{.25}} = -.25$$

$$d_2 = -.25 - .50\sqrt{.25} = -.50$$

Table 24.2 can be used to find the corresponding values of $N(d_1)$ and $N(d_2)$:

$$N(d_1) = N(-.25) = .4013$$

$$N(d_2) = N(-.50) = .3085$$

Finally, Equation (24.10) can be used to estimate the fair value of this call option:

$$V_c = (.4013 \times \$36) - \left(\frac{\$40}{e^{.05 \times .25}} \times .3085\right)$$

$$= \$14.45 - \$12.19 = \$2.26$$

If this call option is currently selling for \$5, the investor should consider writing some of them because they are overpriced according to the Black–Scholes model, suggesting that their price will fall in the near future. Thus, the writer would receive a premium of \$5 and would expect to be able to enter a closing buy order later for a lower price, making a profit on the difference. Conversely, if the call option were selling for \$1, the investor should consider buying some of them because they are underpriced and can be expected to rise in value in the future.

24.6.2 COMPARISON WITH THE BINOMIAL OPTION PRICING MODEL

At this juncture the BOPM formula [given in Equation (24.7) where V_o is denoted V_c] can be compared with the Black–Scholes option pricing formula [given in Equation (24.10)]:

$$V_c = hP_s - B \tag{24.7}$$

$$V_c = N(d_1)P_s - \frac{E}{e^{RT}}N(d_2) \tag{24.10}$$

Comparison of the two equations shows the quantity $N(d_1)$ in Equation (24.10) corresponds to h in Equation (24.7). Recall that h is the hedge ratio, so the quantity $N(d_1)$ in the Black–Scholes formula can be interpreted in a similar manner. That is, it corresponds to the number of shares that an investor would need to purchase in executing an investment strategy designed to have the same payoffs as a call option. Similarly, the quantity $EN(d_2)/e^{RT}$ corresponds to B, the amount of money the investor borrows as the other part of the strategy. Consequently, the quantity $EN(d_2)$ corresponds to the face

TABLE 24.2 Values of N(d) for Selected Values of d

d	N(d)	d	N(d)	d	N(d)
		−1.00	.1587	1.00	.8413
−2.95	.0016	−.95	.1711	1.05	.8531
−2.90	.0019	−.90	.1841	1.10	.8643
−2.85	.0022	−.85	.1977	1.15	.8749
−2.80	.0026	−.80	.2119	1.20	.8849
−2.75	.0030	−.75	.2266	1.25	.8944
−2.70	.0035	−.70	.2420	1.30	.9032
−2.65	.0040	−.65	.2578	1.35	.9115
−2.60	.0047	−.60	.2743	1.40	.9192
−2.55	.0054	−.55	.2912	1.45	.9265
−2.50	.0062	−.50	.3085	1.50	.9332
−2.45	.0071	−.45	.3264	1.55	.9394
−2.40	.0082	−.40	.3446	1.60	.9452
−2.35	.0094	−.35	.3632	1.65	.9505
−2.30	.0107	−.30	.3821	1.70	.9554
−2.25	.0122	−.25	.4013	1.75	.9599
−2.20	.0139	−.20	.4207	1.80	.9641
−2.15	.0158	−.15	.4404	1.85	.9678
−2.10	.0179	−.10	.4602	1.90	.9713
−2.05	.0202	−.05	.4801	1.95	.9744
−2.00	.0228	.00	.5000	2.00	.9773
−1.95	.0256	.05	.5199	2.05	.9798
−1.90	.0287	.10	.5398	2.10	.9821
−1.85	.0322	.15	.5596	2.15	.9842
−1.80	.0359	.20	.5793	2.20	.9861
−1.75	.0401	.25	.5987	2.25	.9878
−1.70	.0446	.30	.6179	2.30	.9893
−1.65	.0495	.35	.6368	2.35	.9906
−1.60	.0548	.40	.6554	2.40	.9918
−1.55	.0606	.45	.6736	2.45	.9929
−1.50	.0668	.50	.6915	2.50	.9938
−1.45	.0735	.55	.7088	2.55	.9946
−1.40	.0808	.60	.7257	2.60	.9953
−1.35	.0885	.65	.7422	2.65	.9960
−1.30	.0968	.70	.7580	2.70	.9965
−1.25	.1057	.75	.7734	2.75	.9970
−1.20	.1151	.80	.7881	2.80	.9974
−1.15	.1251	.85	.8023	2.85	.9978
−1.20	.1357	.90	.8159	2.90	.9981
−1.05	.1469	.95	.8289	2.95	.9984

Source: Derived using the NORMSDIST command in Excel.

amount of the loan because it is the amount that must be paid back to the lender at time T, the expiration date. Hence e^{RT} is the discount (or present value) factor, indicating that the interest rate on the loan is R per period and that the loan is for T periods. Thus the seemingly complex Black–Scholes formula has an intuitive interpretation. It simply involves calculating the cost of a buy-stock-and-borrow-money investment strategy that has the same payoffs at T as a call option.

In the example, $N(d_1)$ was equal to .4013 and $EN(d_2)/e^{RT}$ was equal to $12.19. As a result, an investment strategy that involves buying .4013 shares and borrowing $12.19 at time 0 will have payoffs exactly equal to those associated with buying the call.[14] Because this strategy costs $2.26, it follows that in equilibrium the market price of the call must also be $2.26.

24.6.3   STATIC ANALYSIS

Close scrutiny of the Black–Scholes formula reveals some interesting features of European call option pricing. In particular, the fair value of a call option is dependent on five inputs—the market price of the common stock P_s, the exercise price of the option E, the length of time until the expiration date T, the riskfree rate R, and the volatility of the common stock σ. What happens to the fair value of a call option when one of these inputs is changed and the other four remain the same?

1. The higher the price of the underlying stock P_s, the higher the value of the call option.
2. The higher the exercise price E, the lower the value of the call option.
3. The longer the time to the expiration date T, the higher the value of the call option.
4. The higher the riskfree rate R, the higher the value of the call option.
5. The greater the volatility σ of the common stock, the higher the value of the call option.

Of these five factors, the first three (P_s, E, and T) are readily determined. The fourth factor, the riskfree rate R, is often estimated by using the yield-to-maturity on a Treasury bill having a maturity date close to the expiration date of the option. The fifth factor, the volatility of the underlying stock σ, is not readily observed; consequently various methods for estimating it have been proposed. Two of these methods are presented next.

24.6.4   ESTIMATING A STOCK'S VOLATILITY
FROM HISTORICAL PRICES

One method for estimating the volatility of the underlying common stock involves analyzing historical prices of the stock. Initially a set of $n + 1$ market prices on the underlying stock must be obtained from either financial publications or a computer database. These prices are then used to calculate a set of n continuously compounded returns as follows:

$$r_t = \ln\left(\frac{P_{st}}{P_{st-1}}\right) \tag{24.13}$$

where P_{st} and P_{st-1} denote the market price of the underlying stock at times t and $t - 1$, respectively. Here, ln denotes taking the natural logarithm of the quantity P_{st}/P_{st-1}, which thus results in a continuously compounded return.

For example, the set of market prices for the stock might consist of the closing price at the end of each of 53 weeks. If the price at the end of one week is $105, and the price at the end of the next week is $107, then the continuously compounded return for the week r_t equals 1.886% $[= \ln(107/105)]$. Similar calculations will result in a set of 52 weekly returns.

Once a set of n returns on the stock have been calculated, the next step involves using them to estimate the stock's average return:

$$r_{ave} = \frac{1}{n} \sum_{t=1}^{n} r_t \qquad (24.14)$$

The average return is used to estimate the per-period variance, which is the square of the per-period standard deviation:

$$s^2 = \frac{1}{n-1} \sum_{t=1}^{n} (r_t - r_{ave})^2 \qquad (24.15)$$

This value is called the per-period variance because its size depends on the length of time during which each return is measured. In the example, weekly returns were calculated and would lead to the estimation of a weekly variance. Alternatively, daily returns could have been used, leading to a daily variance that would be of smaller magnitude than the weekly variance. However, an annual variance, not a weekly or a daily variance, is needed. This value is obtained by multiplying the per period variance by the number of periods in a year. Thus, an estimated weekly variance is multiplied by 52 to estimate the annual variance σ^2 (that is, $\sigma^2 = 52s^2$).[15]

Alternative methods of estimating a stock's volatility exist. One method involves subjectively estimating possible future stock prices, the corresponding returns, and their probabilities of occurring (see Appendix A to Chapter 7). For any estimate of future uncertainty, historical data are likely to prove more helpful than definitive. And because recent data may prove more helpful than older data, some analysts study daily or weekly price changes for the most recent 6 to 12 months, sometimes giving more weight to more recent data than to earlier ones.

24.6.5 THE MARKET CONSENSUS OF A STOCK'S VOLATILITY

Another way to estimate a stock's volatility is based on the assumption that a currently outstanding call option is fairly priced in the marketplace. Because this means that $P_c = V_c$, the current market price of the call P_c can be entered on the left-hand side of Equation (24.10) in place of the fair value of the call V_c. Next, all the other factors except for σ are entered on the right-hand side, and a value for σ, the only unknown variable, is found that satisfies the equation. The solution for σ can be interpreted as representing a consensus opinion in the marketplace on the size of the stock's volatil-

implied volatility ity, and it is sometimes known as the stock's **implied volatility.**[16]

For example, assume that the riskfree rate is 6% and that a six-month call option with an exercise price of $40 sells for $4 when the price of the underlying stock is $36. Different estimates of σ can be "plugged into" the right-hand side of Equation (24.10) until a value of $4 for this side of the equation is obtained. In this example an estimated value of .40 (that is, 40%) for σ results in a number for the right-hand side of Equation (24.10) equal to $4, the current market price of the call option on the left-hand side. The procedure can be modified by applying it to several call or put options on the same stock having different exercise prices or expiration dates. The resulting estimates for σ can be averaged and, in turn, used to determine the fair value of another call option on the same stock having another exercise price but a similar expiration date.[17] It should be remembered, however, that all of these methods assume that volatility remains constant over the life of the option—an assumption that can be challenged.

In the example, σ can be estimated not only for a six-month option having an exercise price of $40, but also for a six-month option having an exercise price of $50. The two estimates of σ can be averaged to produce a best estimate of σ used to value a six-month $45 option on the same stock.

24.6.6 MORE ON HEDGE RATIOS

The slope of the Black–Scholes curve at any point represents the expected change in the value of the option for each dollar change in the price of the underlying common stock. This amount corresponds to the hedge ratio of the call option and is equal to $N(d_1)$ in Equation (24.10). As Figure 24.6 shows (assuming that the market price of the call is equal to its Black–Scholes value), the slope (that is, the hedge ratio) of the curve is always positive. Note that if the stock has a relatively low market price, the slope will be near zero. For higher stock prices the slope increases, ultimately approaching a value of one for relatively high prices.

Because the hedge ratio is less than 1, a $1 increase in the stock price typically results in an increase in a call option's value of less than $1. However, the percentage change in the value of the call option will generally be greater than the percentage change in the price of the stock. It is this relationship that leads people to say that options offer high leverage.

The reason for referring to the slope of the Black–Scholes curve as the hedge ratio is that a "hedge" portfolio, meaning a nearly riskfree portfolio, can be formed by simultaneously writing one call option and purchasing a number of shares equal to the hedge ratio, $N(d_1)$. For example, assume that the hedge ratio is .5, indicating that the hedge portfolio consists of writing one call and buying .5 shares of stock. If the stock price rises by $1, the value of the call option will rise by approximately $.50. This relationship means that the hedge portfolio will lose approximately $.50 on the written call option but gain $.50 from the rise in the stock's price. Conversely, a $1 decrease in the stock's price results in a $.50 gain on the written call option but a loss of $.50 on the half-share of stock. Overall, the hedge portfolio neither gains nor loses value when the price of the underlying common stock changes by a relatively small amount.[18]

FIGURE 24.6 Option Terminology for Calls

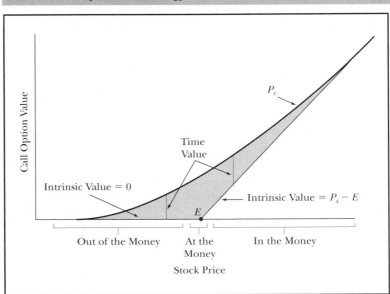

CHAPTER 24 *Options*   **631**

Even if the Black–Scholes model is valid and all the inputs have been correctly specified, risk is not permanently eliminated in the hedge portfolio when the portfolio is first formed (or, for that matter, at any time). There will still be risk because the hedge ratio changes as the stock price changes and as the life of the option decreases with the passage of time. To eliminate risk from the hedge portfolio, the investor has to alter its composition continuously. Altering it less often reduces but does not completely eliminate risk.

24.6.7   LIMITATIONS ON THE USE OF THE BLACK–SCHOLES MODEL

At first the Black–Scholes model might seem to have limited use because almost all options in the United States are American options that can be exercised at any time up to their expiration date, whereas the Black–Scholes model applies only to European options. Furthermore, the model is applicable only to options on stocks that will not pay dividends during the life of the option. However, most of the common stocks on which options are written do, in fact, pay dividends.

The first drawback of the Black–Scholes model—that it is applicable only to European options—can be dispensed with rather easily when the option is a call and the underlying stock does not pay dividends because it is unwise for an investor holding an American call option on a non-dividend-paying stock to exercise it before maturity.[19] If there is no reason for exercising such an option before maturity, then the opportunity to do so is worthless. Consequently, there will be no difference in the values of an American and a European call option. In turn, the Black–Scholes model can be used to estimate the fair value of American call options on non-dividend-paying stocks.

at the money

out of the money
in the money

The reason can be seen in Figure 24.6, but first some terminology must be introduced. A call option is said to be **at the money** if the underlying stock has a market price roughly equal to the call's exercise price. If the stock's market price is below the exercise price, the call is said to be **out of the money,** and if the market price is above the exercise price, the call is said to be **in the money.** Occasionally, finer gradations are invoked, and one hears of "near the money," "deep in the money," or "far out of the money."

time value

As mentioned earlier, the value of an option if it were exercised immediately is known as its intrinsic value. This value is equal to zero if the option is out of the money. However, it is equal to the difference between the stock price and the exercise price if the option is in the money. The excess of the option's price over its intrinsic value is the option's **time value** (or time premium). As shown in Figure 24.3(a), for call options at expiration, the time value is zero. However, before then the time value is positive because no matter how low the stock's current price is, there is some positive probability that the price will rise enough to cause the call option to be in the money before the option reaches expiration. Note that a call option's premium is simply the sum of its intrinsic and time values.

An investor considering exercising a call option on a non-dividend-paying stock before its expiration date will always find it cheaper to sell the call option and purchase the stock in the marketplace. Exercising the call results in the investor's losing the time value of the option (hence the expression that call options are "worth more alive than dead").

For example, consider a stock that has a current price of $110. If this stock has a call option with an exercise price of $100 that is selling for $14, then the intrinsic and time values of this option are $10 (= $110 − $100) and $4 (= $14 − $10), respectively. An investor who owns one of these calls could exercise it by spending an additional $100. However, it would be cheaper for the investor to get the share of stock by selling the call option and buying the share of stock in the marketplace because the additional cost would be only $96 (= $110 − $14).

The second drawback of the Black–Scholes model—that it is applicable only to non-dividend-paying stocks—cannot be easily dismissed because many call options are written on stocks that pay dividends during the life of the option. Some procedures have been suggested for amending this formula to value call options on such stocks.[20] As will be seen shortly, European options on dividend-paying stocks can generally be valued using the Black–Scholes formula by making one simple alteration, but American options are more problematic.[21]

24.6.8 ADJUSTMENTS FOR DIVIDENDS

Thus far the issue of dividend payments on the underlying stock during the life of an option has been avoided. Other things being equal, the greater the amount of the dividends to be paid during the life of a call option, the lower the value of the call option because the greater the dividend a firm declares, the lower its stock price will be. Options are not "dividend-protected," so the lower stock price results in a lower value for the call option (and a higher value for put options).

The simplest case is valuing European call options on dividend-paying stocks when the future dividends can be accurately forecast, both in size and date. An accurate forecast is often possible because most options have an expiration date within nine months. In such cases, all that is done in valuing European call options is to take the current stock price, subtract from it the discounted value of the dividends (using the *ex dividend* date and the riskfree rate for discounting), and insert the resulting adjusted price in the Black–Scholes call option formula along with the other inputs. The reason is quite straightforward. The current stock price can be viewed as consisting of two components: the present value of the known dividends that will be paid during the life of the option and the present value of all the dividends thereafter (see the discussion of dividend discount models in Chapter 15). Because the option is exercisable only at expiration, it is applicable only to the second component, whose current value is just the adjusted price. Thus, if the stock previously discussed that is currently priced at $36 will pay a dividend in six months of $1, its adjusted price is $35.025 given a riskfree rate of 5% [$35.025 = $36 − ($1/$e^{.05 \times .5}$)]. Consequently, any European calls that expire in more than six months but before the next *ex dividend* date associated with a second dividend can be valued using the Black–Scholes call option formula and a current price of $35.025.

24.7   The Valuation of Put Options

Similar to a call option, a put option is said to be *at the money* if the underlying stock has a market price roughly equal to the put's exercise price. However, the terms *out of the money* and *in the money* have, in one sense, opposite meanings for puts and calls. A put option is out of the money if the underlying stock has a market price above the exercise price and is in the money if the market price is below the exercise price. Figure 24.7 provides an illustration of how these terms apply to a put option. An option's intrinsic value equals zero if the option is out of the money, and it equals the difference between the exercise price and the stock price if the stock is in the money.

As mentioned previously, the excess of the price of a call or a put over this intrinsic value is the option's time value (or time premium). For calls and puts in panels (a) and (b) of Figure 24.3, respectively, the time value is zero at expiration. However, Figures 24.6 and 24.7 show that the time value is generally positive before expiration. Like calls, a put's premium is simply the sum of its intrinsic value and its time value.

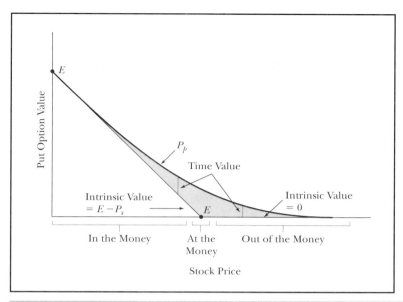

FIGURE 24.7 Option Terminology for Puts

24.7.1   PUT-CALL PARITY

Consider a put and a call on the same underlying stock that have the same exercise price and expiration date. Earlier it was shown in Equation (24.9) that their market prices should be related, with the nature of the relationship known as put-call parity. However, this relationship is valid only for European options on non-dividend-paying stocks. Equation (24.9) can be rearranged in the following manner to estimate the value of European put options:

$$P_p = P_c + \frac{E}{e^{RT}} - P_s \tag{24.16}$$

Thus the value of a put can be estimated by using either the BOPM or the Black–Scholes formula to estimate the value of a matching call option, then adding an amount equal to the present value of the exercise price to this estimate, and finally subtracting from this sum an amount equal to the current market price of the underlying common stock.

For example, consider a put option that expires in three months and has an exercise price of $40, whereas the current market price and the volatility of the underlying common stock are $36 and 50%, respectively. It was shown earlier that if the riskfree rate is 5%, then the Black–Scholes estimate of the value for a matching call option is $2.26. Because the 5% riskfree rate is a continuously compounded rate, the present value of the exercise price equals $39.50 $\left[= \$40/(e^{.05 \times .25}) \right]$. At this point, because it has been determined that $P_c = \$2.26$, $E/e^{RT} = \$39.50$, and $P_s = \$36$, Equation (24.16) can be used to estimate the value of the put option as equal to $5.76 (= $2.26 + $39.50 − $36).

Alternatively, the Black–Scholes formula for estimating the value of a call given in Equation (24.10) can be substituted for P_c in Equation (24.16). After this substitution, the resulting equation can be used directly to estimate the value of a put:

$$P_p = \frac{E}{e^{RT}} N(-d_2) - P_s N(-d_1) \tag{24.17}$$

where d_1 and d_2 are given in Equations (24.11) and (24.12a), respectively.

In the previous example, $d_1 = -.25$ and $d_2 = -.50$; thus $N(-d_1) = N(.25) = .5987$ and $N(-d_2) = N(.50) = .6915$. With the application of Equation (24.17), the value of this put can be estimated directly:

$$P_p = \left(\frac{\$40}{e^{.05 \times .25}} \times .6915 \right) - (\$36 \times .5987)$$

$$= \$27.31 - \$21.55 = \$5.76$$

which is the same estimated value indicated earlier when Equation (24.16) was used.

24.7.2 STATIC ANALYSIS

Close scrutiny of the put-call parity equation reveals some interesting features of European put option pricing. In particular, the value of a put option depends on the values of the same five inputs used for call valuation: the market price of the common stock P_s, the exercise price of the option E, the length of time until the expiration date T, the riskfree rate R, and the volatility of the common stock σ. What happens to the value of a put option when one of these inputs is changed while the other four remain the same?

1. The higher the price of the underlying stock P_s, the lower the value of the put option.
2. The higher the exercise price E, the higher the value of the put option.
3. In general, but not always, the longer the time to the expiration date T, the higher the value of the put option.
4. The higher the riskfree rate R, the lower the value of the put option.
5. The greater the volatility σ of the common stock, the higher the value of the put option.

The relationships for the underlying stock price P_s, exercise price E, and riskfree rate R are in the opposite direction from those shown earlier for call options; the relationships for the time to the expiration date T and volatility σ are in the same direction. Exceptions can occur with T when the put is deep in the money. In such a situation a longer time to expiration could actually decrease the value of the put.

24.7.3 EARLY EXERCISE AND DIVIDENDS

Equations (24.16) and (24.17) apply to a European put on a stock that will not pay dividends before the option's expiration. As with call options, it is straightforward to handle European puts if there are dividends that will be paid on the underlying common stock during the option's life, provided they can be accurately forecast. All that needs to be done is to follow the same procedure described earlier for calls: Reduce the current stock price by the present value of the dividends that are to be paid during the option's life, and use this adjusted price in the Black–Scholes put option formula along with the other inputs. However, complications arise when put options are American because they can be exercised before expiration. Dividends on the underlying common stock that will be paid before the expiration date further complicate matters.[22] Thus, the uncertainty of when to exercise makes American puts difficult to value regardless of whether the underlying stock pays dividends. Nevertheless, as is the case for calls, the BOPM can be modified to handle such situations.

24.8   Index Options

Not all options are written on individual issues of common stock.[23] In recent years many new options have been created that have as an underlying asset something other than the stock of a particular company. One of them—index options—is introduced here. The discussion begins by presenting the concept of *cash settlement*, which is a standard feature of index options.

24.8.1   CASH SETTLEMENT

A call option on General Motors stock is a relatively simple instrument. On exercise, the call buyer literally calls away 100 shares of GM stock. The call writer is expected to physically deliver the shares. In practice, both the buyer and the writer may find it advantageous to close their positions to avoid the costs associated with the physical transfer of shares. In this event the buyer may expect a gain (and the seller a loss) approximately equal to the difference between the current market price of the security and the option's exercise price, with a net gain equal to this amount less the premium paid to purchase the call.

It would be entirely feasible to use only a "cash settlement" procedure on expiration for any option contract. The call writer would be required to pay the buyer an amount equal to the call's intrinsic value, which is the difference between the current price of the security and the option's exercise price (provided the current price is larger than the exercise price). Similarly for puts, the writer could be expected to pay the buyer an amount equal to the put's intrinsic value, which is the difference between the option's exercise price and the current market price (provided the exercise price is larger than the current price). Although listed options on individual securities involve the obligation to deliver, the realization that cash settlement can serve as a substitute has allowed the creation of index options.

24.8.2   THE CONTRACT

An index option is based on the level of an index of stock prices and thus allows investors to take positions in the market that the index represents. Some indices are designed to reflect movements in the stock market, broadly construed. Other "specialized" indices are intended to capture changes in the fortunes of particular industries or sectors. Figure 24.8 presents two of the major indices on which options were offered in 1999, along with their quotations. Some indices are highly specialized, consisting of only a few stocks. Others are broadly representative of major portions of the stock market. Roughly one-half are European and the other half are American. In general, the options expire within a few months, but a few last up to two years.

Contracts for index options are not stated in terms of numbers of shares. Instead, the size of a contract is determined by multiplying the level of the index by a *multiplier* specified by the exchange on which the option is traded. The premium (price) of an index option times the applicable multiplier indicates the total amount paid.

Consider, for example, the Dow Jones Industrial Average (DJX) index call option traded on the CBOE with an exercise price of 88 expiring in June 1999. Because the DJX contracts are based on $\frac{1}{100}$ of the value of the Dow, this exercise price corresponds to a value for the Dow of 8,800. Note that the option had an indicated premium of $9\frac{1}{2}$ on March 4, 1999. Because the multiplier for these contracts is 100, an investor would have to pay $950 (= $9.50 \times 100) for this contract (plus a commission).

Thursday, March 4, 1999

Volume, last, net change and open interest for all contracts. Volume figures are unofficial. Open interest reflects previous trading day. p–Put c–Call

CHICAGO

Strike		Vol.	Last	Net Chg.	Open Int.
DJ INDUS AVG(DJX)					
Mar	72 p	8	1/16	...	2,162
Jun	72 c	5	23 3/4	− 1 1/4	10
Mar	80 p	5	1/8	+ 1/16	11,131
Jun	80 p	16	1 7/16	− 1/16	6,579
Mar	84 c	3	10 1/4	+ 1 3/8	438
Mar	84 p	625	1/4	− 3/16	6,455
Apr	84 c	25	11 3/8	+ 1 1/8	6
Apr	84 p	10	15/16	− 1/16	684
Jun	84 c	1	12 7/8	+ 1 1/8	462
Jun	84 p	547	2 3/16	− 3/16	1,665
Apr	85 p	50	1	− 1/4	215
Mar	86 c	5	8 1/2	+ 3/8	25
Mar	88 c	32	7	+ 1 3/8	1,413
Mar	88 p	951	5/16	− 5/16	8,917
Apr	88 c	1	8	+ 7/8	400
Apr	88 p	357	1 1/4	− 1/2	1,978
Jun	88 c	13	9 1/2	+ 7/8	883
Jun	88 p	14	3 1/8	− 1/4	2,898
Sep	88 p	11	4 1/2	− 3/8	154
Mar	89 c	6	5 1/2	+ 1/8	39
Mar	89 p	16	7/16	− 7/16	1,980
Apr	89 c	6	6 7/8	...	1
Apr	89 p	161	1 1/2	− 11/16	76
Mar	90 c	3	5 3/8	+ 1 1/8	4,376
Mar	90 p	161	9/16	− 1/2	6,467
Apr	90 p	413	1 3/4	− 5/8	1,055
Jun	90 p	220	3 3/8	− 5/8	1,680
Sep	90 p	120	4 3/4	− 3/4	335
Mar	91 c	55	3 7/8	+ 3/4	355
Mar	91 p	6	1	− 1/4	1,579
Apr	91 p	26	2 3/16	− 9/16	23
Mar	92 c	180	3 5/8	+ 1 3/8	4,562
Mar	92 p	1,373	15/16	− 5/8	5,404
Apr	92 c	3	5 1/4	+ 1 1/4	295
Apr	92 p	194	2 1/8	− 1 1/8	1,232
Jun	92 c	6	6 1/2	+ 5/8	923
Jun	92 p	48	4 1/4	− 5/8	6,035
Sep	92 p	26	5 1/4	− 3/4	1,039
Mar	93 c	41	3	+ 1 1/4	2,602
Mar	93 p	158	1 3/16	− 3/4	4,827
Apr	93 c	12	3 7/8	+ 5/8	318
Apr	93 p	187	2 1/2	− 1 1/8	484
Mar	94 c	164	2 1/4	+ 1 1/8	6,591
Mar	94 p	501	1 1/2	− 7/8	8,293
Apr	94 c	23	3 1/4	+ 3/8	422
Apr	94 p	60	2 13/16	− 1 1/16	411
Mar	95 c	604	1 9/16	+ 11/16	7,331
Mar	95 p	160	2 1/16	− 1 7/16	7,359
Apr	95 c	12	2 7/8	+ 7/16	2,223
Apr	95 p	26	3 1/8	− 1 3/8	2,083
Mar	96 c	594	1 3/16	+ 11/16	7,614
Mar	96 p	320	2 1/4	− 1 3/4	2,012
Apr	96 c	23	2 1/4	− 1/16	753
Apr	96 p	29	3 3/4	− 1 1/4	706
Jun	96 p	20	5 5/8	− 7/8	892
Sep	96 p	18	6 3/4	− 1/2	600
Mar	97 c	19	9/16	...	243
Mar	97 p	23	3 5/8	− 1	148
Mar	98 p	76	3 7/8	− 1 1/4	95
Apr	98 p	25	5 1/8	− 5/8	5
Mar	99 p	40	4 1/2	− 2 1/4	305
Apr	99 c	10	1 1/8	− 3/8	8
Apr	99 p	3	5 1/8	...	...
Mar	100 c	1,130	1/8	+ 1/16	6,329
Mar	100 p	67	6 1/8	− 1 3/8	6,811
Apr	100 p	11	6 3/8	− 1 1/8	222
Jun	100 p	108	7 1/4	− 1/2	1,207
Jun	104 c	20	1 3/8	− 9/16	1,700
Jun	110 c	22	1/2	− 5/16	26

Call Vol. ....3,026 Open Int......91,573
Put Vol. ....7,621 Open Int. ...167,424

Strike		Vol.	Last	Net Chg.	Open Int.
S & P 100 INDEX(OEX)					
Mar	460 p	145	1/16	...	3,181
Mar	470 p	151	1/8	...	1,059
Mar	480 c	1	144	− 13 1/8	2
Mar	480 p	225	1/8	...	1,944
Mar	490 p	131	3/16	...	3,157
Mar	510 p	455	3/16	− 5/16	8,659
Jun	510 c	9	125	...	...
Jun	510 p	81	6 7/8	− 1 5/8	2,022
Mar	520 p	638	1/4	− 3/8	5,847
Apr	520 c	4	109	+ 15 1/2	47
Apr	520 p	652	2 1/2	− 5/8	3,011
Mar	530 c	110	94 3/4	+ 6 3/4	785
Mar	530 p	218	7/16	− 1/4	5,456
Apr	530 p	65	2 5/8	− 1 5/8	1,247
Mar	540 c	8	79	+ 8 1/8	38
Mar	540 p	1,262	7/16	− 1/2	4,709
Apr	540 p	11	3 3/4	− 1 3/8	2,407
Mar	550 c	321	75	+ 10	1,150
Mar	550 p	522	11/16	− 9/16	7,985
Apr	550 p	294	5 1/8	− 1 1/2	4,015
May	550 p	10	8 7/8	− 2 5/8	1,419
Mar	560 c	110	62	+ 10	1,204
Mar	560 p	1,942	1 1/8	− 1	12,293
Apr	560 c	15	69 1/2	+ 5 1/8	30
Apr	560 p	51	6 5/8	− 1 7/8	955
Jun	560 c	13	78 3/8	− 5 5/8	248
Jun	560 p	1	14 3/8	+ 1/4	1,940
Mar	570 p	1,959	1 5/8	− 1 1/4	6,868
Apr	570 p	21	7 3/8	− 3 7/8	4,125
May	570 c	10	66	+ 8	45
May	570 p	12	12 5/8	− 3 1/8	875
Mar	575 p	569	1 7/8	− 1 7/8	2,868
Apr	575 p	2	8 1/4	− 2 1/2	121
Mar	580 c	312	46	+ 12 1/2	1,407
Mar	580 p	1,448	2 1/4	− 2	6,063
Apr	580 c	5	54 1/2	+ 11	171
Apr	580 p	137	9 3/4	− 3 7/8	869
May	580 p	6	17	− 1/2	861
Jun	580 p	7	18 1/4	− 4 3/8	1,071
Mar	585 p	537	2 15/16	− 1 15/16	2,333
Apr	585 p	106	10 1/2	− 2 1/2	253
Mar	590 c	333	37 3/8	+ 8 7/8	2,479
Mar	590 p	2,571	3 1/2	− 2 3/4	5,970
Apr	590 p	612	10 5/8	− 3 1/8	748
Jun	590 p	1	20 5/8	− 2 3/8	932
Mar	595 c	105	33 1/2	+ 8 1/2	1,615
Mar	595 p	2,164	4	− 3 1/8	4,307

FIGURE 24.8 Index Options Quotations (excerpts)

Source: Reprinted by permission of *The Wall Street Journal,* Dow Jones & Company, Inc., March 5, 1999, p. C24. All rights reserved worldwide.

After purchasing this contract, the investor could later sell it or exercise it for its cash settlement value. In May 1999 the Dow was at 11,000, so its value for the option contract was 110 (= 11,000/100). At this time the investor could have exercised the call, receiving its intrinsic value of $1,200 [= (110 − 88) × $100] for doing so. Alternatively, the investor could have simply sold the call on the exchange. In doing so, the investor would have received an amount greater than $1,200 because the call would sell for an amount equal to the sum of its intrinsic and time values (see Figure 24.6).

Summary

1. An option is a contract between two investors that grants one investor the right (but not the obligation) to sell to or buy from the other investor a specific asset at a specific price within a specific time period.

2. A call option for a stock gives the buyer the right to buy a specific number of shares of a specific company from the option writer at a specific price at any time up to and including a specific date.

3. A put option for a stock gives the buyer the right to sell a specific number of shares of a specific company to the option writer at a specific price at any time up to and including a specific date.

4. Option trading is facilitated by standardized contracts traded on organized exchanges. These exchanges use the services of a clearing corporation, which maintains records of all trades and acts as a buyer from all option writers and a writer to all option buyers.

5. Option writers are required to deposit margin to ensure performance of their obligations. The amount and form of the margin depends on the particular option strategy involved.

6. The intrinsic value of a call option equals the difference between the stock's price and the option's exercise price, if this difference is positive. Otherwise, the option's intrinsic value is zero.

7. The intrinsic value of a put option equals the difference between its exercise price and the stock's price, if this difference is positive. Otherwise, the option's intrinsic value is zero.

8. Calls and puts will not sell for less than their intrinsic values. However, they may sell for more than their intrinsic values because of their time values.

9. The binomial option pricing model can be used to determine the fair value of an option based on the assumption that the underlying asset will attain one of two possible known prices at the end of each of a finite number of periods, given its price at the start of each period.

10. An option's hedge ratio indicates the change in the option's value resulting from a one dollar change in the value of the underlying asset.

11. The Black–Scholes option valuation model shows that the fair value of an option is determined by five factors: the market price of the stock, the exercise price, the life of the option, the riskfree rate, and the volatility of the common stock. It assumes that the riskfree rate and common stock volatility are constant for the option's life.

12. Put-call parity states that buying both a put option on a stock and a share of the stock will produce the same payoff as buying both a call option on the stock and a riskfree bond (assuming that both options have the same exercise price and expiration date).

13. In addition to put and call options on individual common stocks, options on other assets are traded, including stock indices.

Questions and Problems

1. How do organized options exchanges permit option buyers and writers to open and close positions without having to contact one another directly?

2. From the latest two consecutive issues of *The Wall Street Journal,* find the price of the General Motors call option with the nearest expiration date and the exercise price closest to the current price of GM stock. What is the premium on the call option? What is the percentage change in the option's price from the previous day? From another part of the *Journal,* calculate the percentage change in the price of

GM stock from the previous day. Compare this number with the option's percentage price change.

3. Draw a profit-loss graph for the following option strategies:
   a. Buy a put, $2 premium, $70 exercise price
   b. Write a call, $3 premium, $40 exercise price
   c. Buy a stock for $80 and buy a put on the same stock, $1 premium, $70 exercise price

4. What is the time value of an option? Why does an option's time value decline as the option approaches expiration?

5. Shorewood Systems stock currently sells for $50 per share. One year from today the stock will be worth either $58.09 or $43.04. The continuously compounded risk-free rate is 5.13% for one year. Based on the binomial option pricing model, what is the fair value for a call option on Shorewood stock with one year to expiration and a $50 exercise price?

6. Hopkins Pharmaceuticals stock is currently priced at $40 per share. Six months from now its price will be either $44.21 or $36.19. If the price rises to $44.21, then six months later the price will be either $48.86 or $40. If, however, the price initially falls to $36.19, then six months later the price will be either $40 or $32.75. The risk-free rate (continuously compounded) is 3.05% for each six-month period. Use the binomial option pricing model to determine the fair value of a one-year call option on Hopkins stock.

7. Given the following information, calculate the three-month price of a call that is consistent with the Black–Scholes model:

$$P_s = \$47, \quad E = \$45, \quad R = .05, \quad \sigma = .40$$

8. If the premium on a call option has recently declined, does this decline indicate that the option is a better buy than it was previously? Why?

9. List the variables needed to estimate the value of a call option. Describe how a change in the value of these variables affects the value of a call option.

10. Using the Black–Scholes model, calculate the implied volatility of a stock with a three-month call option currently selling for $8.54 and

$$P_s = \$83, \quad E = \$80, \quad R = .05$$

11. Blondy Ryan owns 20,000 shares of Merrimac Monitoring Equipment stock. This stock makes up the bulk of Blondy's wealth. Concerned about the stock's near-term prospects, Blondy wishes to fully hedge the risk of the stock. Given a hedge ratio of .37 and a premium of $2.50 for the near Merrimac put option, how many put options should Blondy buy?

12. Given the following information, calculate the three-month price of a put that is consistent with the Black–Scholes model:

$$P_s = \$32, \quad E = \$45, \quad R = .06, \quad \sigma = .35$$

13. Explain why call options on nondividend-paying stocks are "worth more alive than dead."

14. In February Gid Gardner sold a September 55 call on Dane Corporation stock for $4.375 per share and simultaneously bought a September 55 put on the same stock for $6 per share. At the time, Treasury bills coming due in September were priced to yield 12.6%, and Dane stock sold for $53 per share.
    a. What value would put-call parity suggest was appropriate for the Dane put?
    b. Dane was expected to make three dividend payments between February and September. Could that account for the discrepancy between your answer to part (a) and the actual price of the put? Why or why not?

15. Why does a stock index option sell at a lower price than the cost of a portfolio of options on the constituent stocks? (Assume that the index call option and the portfolio of call options control the same dollar value of stocks.)

Endnotes

1. Prior to 1973, options were traded over the counter through dealers and brokers in a relatively illiquid market. These dealers and brokers brought buyers and writers together, arranged terms, helped with the paperwork, and charged fees for their efforts.

2. However, there is protection for any cash dividend that is formally designated a "return of capital." Furthermore, options that are traded over the counter typically are protected from any type of cash dividend. In both cases the protection is in the form of a reduction in the exercise price.

3. For some active stocks, options may also be introduced that have only one or two months to expiration.

4. If the stock sells for less than $25, the interval may be $2.50 (for example, at $15 and $17.50 for a stock selling at $16). If the stock sells for more than $200, the interval will be for $10 (or perhaps even $20). Exchange officials have discretion in setting the terms of the options.

5. For more on commissions, see John C. Hull, *Options, Futures and Other Derivatives* (Upper Saddle River, NJ: Prentice Hall, 2000), pp. 159–160.

6. A call or put buyer is not allowed to use margin. Instead, the option buyer is required to pay 100% of the option's purchase price. In contrast, the stock buyer can use margin, where part of the cost of purchasing the stock is borrowed. For the specifics on margin requirements, see the option textbooks cited in the references for this chapter.

7. Because the premium is paid by the buyer to the writer at the time the option is created, its value should be compounded to the expiration date using an appropriate rate of interest when calculating profits and losses.

8. *Strips* and *straps* are option strategies similar to a straddle. The former involves combining two puts with one call, and the latter involves combining two calls with one put. Another strategy is known as a *spread,* where one call is bought while another is written on the same underlying security. Specifically, a price spread involves two calls having the same expiration date but different exercise prices. A time spread involves two calls having the same exercise price but different expiration dates.

9. If there are dividends, they should be expressed as a compounded value at the expiration date associated with the options (as they would have been previously received) and added to the line, thereby shifting it upward.

10. In general, $1 will grow to 1e^{RT}$ at the end of T periods if it is continuously compounded at a rate of R per period. Here e represents the base of the natural logarithm, which is equal to approximately 2.71828. For a more detailed discussion, see the appendix to Chapter 20.

11. Equations (24.5) and (24.6) can be derived by solving the set of Equations (24.3a) and (24.3b) using symbols instead of numbers.

12. Fischer Black and Myron Scholes, "The Pricing of Options and Corporate Liabilities," *Journal of Political Economy,* 81, no. 3 (May/June 1973): 637–654. Also see Fischer Black, "How We Came Up with the Option Formula," *Journal of Portfolio Management,* 15, no. 2 (Winter 1989): 4–8, and "How to Use the Holes in Black–Scholes," *Journal of Applied Corporate Finance,* 1, no. 4 (Winter 1989): 67–73. For an intuitive explanation of the Black–Scholes formula, see Dwight Grant, Gautam Vora, and David Weeks, "Teaching Option Valuation: From Simple Discrete Distributions to Black/Scholes Via Monte Carlo Simulation," *Financial Practice and Education,* 5, no. 2 (Fall/Winter 1995): 149–155. Scholes and Robert Merton were the co-recipients of the 1997 Nobel Memorial Prize in Economic Science, largely for their contributions in this area. Undoubtedly, Black would have shared the Prize with them had he not suffered an untimely death.

13. Table 24.2 is an abbreviated version of a standard cumulative normal distribution table. More detailed versions can be found in most statistics textbooks or by using a spreadsheet such as Excel.

14. The investment strategy is more complicated than it might appear because the number of shares that are held will change over time as the stock price changes and the expiration date gets closer. Similarly, the amount of the loan will also change over time. Hence it is a *dynamic strategy.*

15. If daily data are used, it is best to multiply the daily variance by 250 instead of 365 because there are about 250 trading days in a year. See Mark Kritzman, "About Estimating Volatility: Part I," *Financial Analysts Journal,* 47, no. 4 (July/August 1991): 22–25, and "About Estimating Volatility: Part II," *Financial Analysts Journal,* 47, no. 5 (September/October 1991): 10–11. For a method of estimating σ that uses high, low, opening, and closing prices as well as trading volume, see Mark B. Garman and Michael J. Klass, "On the Estimation of Security Price Volatilities from Historical Data," *Journal of Business,* 53, no. 1 (January 1980): 67–78.

16. Alternatively, Equation (24.10) could be solved for the interest rate $R;$ doing so gives an estimate of the *implied interest rate.* See Menachem Brenner and Dan Galai, "Implied Interest Rates," *Journal of Business,* 59, no. 3 (July 1986): 493–507.

17. For further discussion of these methods, see any of the options textbooks cited in the references for this

chapter or see Menachem Brenner and Marti Subrahmanyam, "A Simple Formula to Compute the Implied Standard Deviation," *Financial Analysts Journal*, 44, no. 5 (September/October 1988): 80–83; and Charles J. Corrado and Thomas W. Miller, Jr., "A Note on a Simple Accurate Formula to Compute Implied Standard Deviations," *Journal of Banking and Finance*, 20, no. 3 (April 1996): 595–603.

18. This explanation of a hedge ratio follows from the BOPM-based interpretation of the Black–Scholes formula given earlier. That is, if a call's payoffs can be duplicated by buying stock and borrowing at the risk-free rate, it follows that buying stock and writing a call will duplicate investing in the riskfree asset.

19. See Robert C. Merton, "Theory of Rational Option Pricing," *Bell Journal of Economics and Management Science*, 4, no. 1 (Spring 1973): 141–183.

20. These procedures are reviewed in the options textbooks cited in the references for this chapter.

21. See the options textbooks cited in the references for this chapter for valuing American options on dividend-paying stocks. Also see Thomas J. Finucane, "An Empirical Analysis of Common Stock Call Exercise: A Note," *Journal of Banking and Finance*, 21, no. 4 (April 1997): 563–571.

22. See Robert Geske and Kuldeep Shastri, "The Early Exercise of American Puts," *Journal of Banking and Finance*, 9, no. 2 (June 1985): 207–219, and the options textbooks cited in the references for this chapter.

23. There are two other securities that are options on individual shares, *rights* (discussed in Chapter 13) and *warrants*, which are like rights in many respects except that they have a life of several years when they are originally issued, and allow an investor to buy, in general, one or more shares for each warrant held. Both rights and warrants differ from calls because they are issued by the firm and their exercise affects the firm by increasing its cash balance and the number of shares outstanding. Firms issue other securities that have option-like characteristics. *Convertible bonds* (mentioned in Chapter 19) give investors the option of exchanging them for shares of common stock. *Call and put provisions* (discussed in Chapter 21) also involve options, with call provisions giving the firm the option of paying off the bond before it matures and put provisions giving the investor the option of asking to be paid off before the bond matures. For more, see, for example, Richard A. Brealey and Stewart C. Myers, *Principles of Corporate Finance* (New York: McGraw-Hill, 2000), Chapters 22 and 24, and Stephen A. Ross, Randolph W. Westerfield, and Jeffrey Jaffe, *Corporate Finance* (Boston: Irwin McGraw-Hill, 1996), Chapters 20 and 22.

Futures

Consider a contract that involves the delivery of some specific asset by a seller to a buyer at an agreed-on future date. Such a contract also specifies the purchase price, but the asset will not be paid for until the delivery date. However, the buyer and the seller will both be requested to make a security deposit when the contract is signed to protect each person from experiencing losses should the other person renege on the contract. Hence the size of the deposit is checked daily to see that it provides sufficient protection. If it is insufficient, it must be increased. If it is more than sufficient, the excess can be withdrawn.

futures

These contracts are often referred to as **futures** (short for futures contract), and in the United States they involve assets such as agricultural goods (for example, wheat), natural resources (for example, copper), foreign currencies (for example, Swiss francs), fixed-income securities (for example, Treasury bonds), and market indices (for example, the S&P 500).[1] As with options, standardization of the terms in these contracts makes it easy for anyone to create and subsequently trade the contracts.

25.1 Hedgers and Speculators

speculators

There are two types of people who deal in futures (and options): speculators and hedgers. **Speculators** buy and sell futures for the sole purpose of making a profit by closing out their positions at a price that is better than the initial price (or so they hope). They neither produce nor use the asset in the ordinary course of business. In contrast, **hedgers** buy and sell futures to offset an otherwise risky position in the spot market. In the ordinary course of business, they either produce or use the asset.

hedgers

25.1.1 AN EXAMPLE OF HEDGING

For example, consider wheat futures. A farmer might note today that the market price for a wheat futures contract with delivery around harvest time is $4 per bushel, a price that is high enough to ensure a profitable year. The farmer could sell wheat futures today. Alternatively, the farmer could wait until harvest and at that time sell the wheat on the **spot market** (which involves the immediate exchange of an asset for cash). However, waiting until harvest involves risk because the **spot price** (the purchase price of an asset) of wheat could fall by then, perhaps to $3 per bushel. Such a fall could bring financial ruin to the farmer. In contrast, selling wheat futures today allows the farmer to "lock in" a $4 per bushel selling price. Doing so removes an element of risk from the farmer's primary business of growing wheat. Thus, a farmer who sells futures is known as a hedger or, more specifically, a **short hedger.**

spot market
spot price

short hedger

Perhaps the buyer of the farmer's futures contract is a baker who uses wheat to make bread. Currently the baker has enough wheat in inventory to last until harvest season. In anticipation of the need to replenish the inventory at that time, the baker could buy a wheat futures contract today at $4 per bushel. Alternatively, the baker could simply wait until the inventory runs low and then buy wheat in the spot market. However, there is a chance that the spot price will be $5 per bushel at that time. If it were, the baker would have to raise the selling price of bread and perhaps lose sales in doing so. By purchasing wheat futures, the baker can "lock in" a $4 per bushel purchase price, thereby removing an element of risk from the bread business. Thus, a baker who buys futures is also known as a hedger or, more specifically, a **long hedger.**

long hedger

25.1.2 AN EXAMPLE OF SPECULATING

The farmer and the baker can be compared to a speculator—a person who buys and sells wheat futures, based on the forecast price of wheat, in the pursuit of short-term profits. As mentioned earlier, such a person neither produces nor uses the asset in the ordinary course of business.

reversing trade

A speculator who thinks that the price of wheat is going to rise substantially will buy wheat futures. Later this person will enter a **reversing trade** by selling wheat futures. Assuming the forecast was accurate, the increase in the wheat futures price will prove profitable.

For example, consider a speculator expecting at least a $1 per bushel rise in the spot price of wheat (which is currently $4 per bushel). This person could buy wheat, store it, and plan to sell it later at the anticipated higher price, but it would be easier and more profitable to buy a wheat futures contract today at $4 per bushel. Later, if the spot price of wheat did rise by $1, the speculator would enter a reversing trade by selling the wheat futures contract for perhaps $5 per bushel. (A $1 rise in the spot price of wheat will cause the futures price to rise by about $1.) Thus, the speculator will make a profit of $1 per bushel, or $5,000 in total, because these contracts are for 5,000 bushels. As will be shown later, the speculator might need to make a security deposit of $1,000 at the time the wheat futures contract is bought. The deposit is returned when the reversing trade is made, so the speculator's rate of return is quite high (500%) relative to the percentage rise in the price of wheat (25%).

If a speculator forecasts a substantial price decline, then initially wheat futures would be sold. Later the speculator would enter a reversing trade by purchasing wheat futures. Assuming the forecast was accurate, the decrease in the wheat futures price will prove profitable. In the example, the speculator would sell a wheat futures contract today at $4 per bushel. When the spot price of wheat later falls by $1 per bushel, the speculator would then buy a wheat futures contract for perhaps $3 per bushel, resulting in a $5,000 profit.

25.2 The Futures Contract

Futures contracts are standardized in terms of delivery as well as the type of asset allowed for delivery. For example, the Chicago Board of Trade specifies the following requirements for its July wheat contract:

1. The seller agrees to deliver 5,000 bushels of either no. 2 soft red wheat, no. 2 hard red winter wheat, no. 2 dark northern spring wheat, or no. 1 northern spring wheat at the agreed-on price. Alternatively, a number of other grades can be delivered at specified premiums or discounts from the agreed-on price. In any case, the seller is allowed to decide which grade shall be delivered.

2. The grain will be delivered by registered warehouse receipts issued by approved warehouses in Chicago or Toledo, Ohio. (Toledo deliveries are discounted $.02 per bushel.)

3. Delivery will take place during the month of July; the seller decides the actual date.
4. On delivery of the warehouse receipt from the seller to the buyer, the latter will pay the former the agreed-on price in cash.

After an organized exchange has set all the terms of a futures contract except for its price, the exchange will authorize trading in the contract.[2] Buyers and sellers (or their representatives) meet at a specific place on the floor of the exchange and try to agree on a price at which to trade. If they reach an agreement, one or more contracts will be created, with all the standard terms plus an additional one—the price. Prices are normally stated on a per unit basis. Thus, if a buyer and a seller agree to a price of $4 per bushel for a contract of 5,000 bushels of wheat, the amount of money involved is $20,000.

Figure 25.1 shows a set of daily quotations giving the prices at which some popular futures contracts were traded and the total volume of sales for each type of contract. Such listings of active futures markets are published regularly in the financial press. Each item for delivery (such as corn) has a heading that indicates the number of units per contract (5,000 bushels) and the terms on which prices are stated (cents per bushel).

Below the heading for the asset are details for each type of contract. In Figure 25.1, the first column shows the delivery dates for the contracts. For example, there are eight futures contracts for corn, each one involving the same item but having different delivery dates. In the next column, the term *open* denotes the price at which the first transaction was made on that day; *high* and *low* represent the highest and lowest prices during the day; and **settle** (short for settlement price) is a representative price (for example, the average of the high and low prices) during the "closing period" designated by the exchange in question (for example, the last two minutes of trading). After *change* from the previous day's settlement price come the highest and lowest prices recorded during the lifetime of the contract. The last column on the right shows the **open interest** (the number of outstanding contracts) on the previous day.

For each futures contract, summary figures are given below the figures for the last delivery date. (In the case of corn, these summary figures are below the December 2000 delivery date figures.) They indicate the total volume (that is, the number of contracts) traded on that day and on the previous trading day ("Mn" is Monday) as well as the total open interest in such contracts on that day and the change in total open interest from the previous day.

settle

open interest

25.3 Futures Markets

The futures contracts shown in Figure 25.1 are traded on various organized exchanges. The Chicago Board of Trade (CBT) was the first, founded in 1848, and currently is the largest futures exchange in the world. Other futures exchanges are listed in the lower right corner of Figure 25.1.

The method of trading futures on organized exchanges is in some ways similar to and in other ways different from the way stocks and options are traded. As with stocks and options, customers can place market, limit, and stop orders with a **futures commission merchant** (FCM), which is simply a firm that carries out orders for futures (much as a brokerage firm carries out orders for stocks; often brokerage firms are also FCMs). Furthermore, once an order is transmitted to an exchange floor, it must be taken to a designated spot for execution by a member of the exchange, just as is done for stocks and options. This spot is known as the *pit* because of its shape, which is circular with a set of interior descending steps on which members stand. What happens in the pit is what distinguishes trading in futures from trading in stocks.

futures commission merchant

Tuesday, March 2, 1999

Open Interest Reflects Previous Trading Day.

GRAINS AND OILSEEDS

CORN (CBT) 5,000 bu.; cents per bu.

	Open	High	Low	Settle	Change	Lifetime High	Lifetime Low	Open Interest
Mar	206	210¾	205	210¼	+ 4	305	204	22,268
May	211¼	216½	211¼	215¾	+ 4½	299	210	142,038
July	216¾	223	216¾	222¼	+ 5	312	215½	105,321
Sept	224¼	229¾	224¼	228¾	+ 4½	280	224	24,785
Dec	234	239½	234	238¼	+ 4¼	291½	233½	64,948
Mr00	241¾	246¾	241¾	246	+ 4¼	270	241	7,216
July	251½	254½	251½	254½	+ 4¼	278½	250½	1,953
Dec	251	254½	251	252	+ 3	279½	249	1,828

Est vol 69,000; vol Mn 72,700; open int 370,888, +981.

OATS (CBT) 5,000 bu.; cents per bu.

	Open	High	Low	Settle	Change	Lifetime High	Lifetime Low	Open Interest
Mar	108	108	106	106	− 1½	166½	99¾	538
May	106½	107	105	105¼	− 1	161	103¼	6,942
July	109¼	109¼	107½	107¾	− ¾	150	106	3,922
Sept	111½	112	111	111	− ¾	140	109	1,104
Dec	115½	115½	114¾	115	+ ¼	147	113¾	2,345

Est vol 2,000; vol Mn 2,594; open int 14,867, −162.

SOYBEANS (CBT) 5,000 bu.; cents per bu.

	Open	High	Low	Settle	Change	Lifetime High	Lifetime Low	Open Interest
Mar	454½	464½	454½	462½	+ 8	694	449	7,560
May	463	473½	462¾	471½	+ 8½	671	457	60,796
July	471¼	481¾	471¼	480	+ 8¾	728	465½	44,475
Aug	476	485	475½	483½	+ 8¾	618¼	469½	14,033
Sept	479½	487	477½	486	+ 9¼	616½	472	4,982
Nov	486½	495	484¾	493¾	+ 7½	680	480	25,043
Ja00	497	504	495	504	+ 7¼	632	490½	1,054
Mar	507	513½	506½	513½	+ 6¾	594	501	298

Est vol 55,000; vol Mn 54,073; open int 159,416, +189.

METALS AND PETROLEUM

COPPER-HIGH (Cmx.Div.NYM)-25,000 lbs.; cents per lb.

	Open	High	Low	Settle	Change	Lifetime High	Lifetime Low	Open Interest
Mar	61.50	62.35	61.30	62.15	+ .55	98.20	61.15	3,964
Apr	62.05	62.70	62.05	62.55	+ .50	96.00	61.70	3,671
May	62.50	63.20	61.90	63.00	+ .60	98.50	61.90	41,220
June	63.40	63.40	63.30	63.45	+ .60	91.00	62.50	1,694
July	62.90	63.75	62.80	63.75	+ .60	95.75	62.80	9,581
Aug	64.00	64.00	64.00	64.10	+ .60	90.50	63.40	1,415
Sept	63.60	64.50	63.50	64.50	+ .60	94.60	63.50	4,783
Oct	•	....	....	64.80	+ .60	90.00	64.35	1,081
Nov		....	....	65.70	+ .60	86.90	64.70	963
Dec	64.80	65.50	64.50	65.40	+ .60	86.00	64.50	5,847
Ja00		....	....	65.70	+ .60	83.80	65.75	315
Feb		....	....	65.90	+ .60	79.50	66.00	480
Mar	65.50	66.20	65.50	66.15	+ .60	83.00	65.50	950
Apr	66.00	66.00	66.00	66.40	+ .60	80.50	66.00	200
May		....	....	66.60	+ .60	77.70	66.80	302
June		....	....	66.90	+ .60	77.50	67.00	245
July		....	....	67.05	+ .60	78.10	67.00	619
Sept		....	....	67.55	+ .60	78.60	68.15	461
Oct		....	....	67.85	+ .60	71.95	71.95	119
Dec	68.25	68.25	68.25	68.35	+ .60	74.00	68.25	573

Est vol 9,000; vol Mn 6,881 ; open int 78,666, +111.

GOLD (Cmx.Div.NYM)-100 troy oz.; $ per troy oz.

	Open	High	Low	Settle	Change	Lifetime High	Lifetime Low	Open Interest
Mar	285.00	285.00	285.00	286.90	....	294.00	284.50	0
Apr	288.00	290.50	287.40	288.00	+ .30	351.20	280.00	108,626
June	289.60	292.50	289.00	289.80	+ .30	520.00	282.00	24,636
Aug	293.70	293.70	292.60	291.80	+ .30	327.00	288.40	7,194
Oct		....	....	293.70	+ .30	308.40	287.00	2,886
Dec	295.90	297.50	295.90	295.60	+ .30	506.00	286.50	12,884
Fb00		....	....	297.00	+ .30	312.00	294.00	7,288
Apr		....	....	299.00	+ .30	311.00	298.00	1,120
June		....	....	301.00	+ .30	473.50	290.50	10,113
Dec		....	....	306.70	+ .30	474.50	299.00	6,749
Ju01		....	....	312.50	+ .30	447.00	319.00	2,231
Dec		....	....	318.30	+ .30	429.50	316.00	4,620
Ju02		....	....	324.60	+ .30	385.00	325.00	1,614
Dec		....	....	330.20	+ .30	327.40	327.40	1,351
Ju03		....	....	336.10	+ .30	....	....	643

CRUDE OIL, Light Sweet (NYM) 1,000 bbls.; $ per bbl.

	Open	High	Low	Settle	Change	Lifetime High	Lifetime Low	Open Interest
Apr	12.24	12.55	12.18	12.51	+ 0.27	20.27	11.35	117,780
May	12.40	12.67	12.36	12.64	+ 0.24	20.29	11.53	73,604
June	12.60	12.78	12.59	12.75	+ 0.23	20.47	11.48	55,881
July	12.71	12.90	12.70	12.86	+ 0.22	20.14	11.90	27,859
Aug	12.80	12.95	12.80	12.96	+ 0.21	19.47	12.01	19,642
Sept	13.00	13.05	12.95	13.06	+ 0.21	20.10	12.20	13,913
Oct	13.02	13.08	13.02	13.16	+ 0.21	20.14	12.34	11,936
Nov	13.15	13.20	13.15	13.26	+ 0.21	19.90	12.48	19,481
Dec	13.25	13.35	13.25	13.36	+ 0.20	20.75	12.55	52,056
Ja00	13.36	13.36	13.36	13.44	+ 0.19	19.15	12.76	18,073
Feb	13.50	13.50	13.50	13.53	+ 0.19	20.16	12.90	10,051
Mar	13.60	13.60	13.60	13.60	+ 0.17	20.10	12.97	15,774
Apr	....	....	....	13.68	+ 0.17	19.16	13.03	5,443
May	13.65	13.65	13.65	13.75	+ 0.17	19.16	13.65	1,997
June	13.80	13.80	13.80	13.82	+ 0.17	20.10	13.26	12,320
July	....	....	....	13.90	+ 0.17	17.88	13.70	1,680
Aug	....	....	....	14.00	+ 0.18	17.47	13.78	3,251
Sept	....	....	....	14.07	+ 0.18	17.70	14.40	2,917
Oct	....	....	....	14.15	+ 0.18	17.55	15.53	1,228
Nov	....	....	....	14.23	+ 0.19	17.68	15.63	3,210
Dec	....	....	....	14.31	+ 0.20	20.75	13.85	18,331
Ja01	14.30	14.30	14.30	14.37	+ 0.19	17.18	14.25	472
Feb	....	....	....	14.43	+ 0.18	17.15	14.30	302
June	....	....	....	14.67	+ 0.17	18.13	14.30	3,384
Dec	....	....	....	15.04	+ 0.16	20.98	14.70	17,295
Dc02	....	....	....	15.62	+ 0.16	21.38	15.50	6,702
Dc03	....	....	....	16.05	+ 0.16	22.00	15.92	4,925
Dc04	....	....	....	16.46	+ 0.16	19.27	16.35	4,107

Est vol 93,855; vol Mon 96,948; open int 524,884, −4,526.

INTEREST RATE

TREASURY BONDS (CBT)-$100,000; pts. 32nds of 100%

	Open	High	Low	Settle	Change	Lifetime High	Lifetime Low	Open Interest
Mar	120-16	121-14	120-11	121-03	+ 16	134-26	103-04	210,210
June	120-00	120-30	119-25	120-19	+ 17	134-02	110-07	512,421
Sept	120-10	120-15	120-00	120-05	+ 16	131-06	115-11	9,501
Dec	119-19	119-21	119-16	119-21	+ 17	128-28	118-07	3,355

Est vol 490,000; vol Mn 599,510; open int 735,487, +3,720.

TREASURY BONDS (MCE)-$50,000; pts. 32nds of 100%

	Open	High	Low	Settle	Change	Lifetime High	Lifetime Low	Open Interest
Mar	120-22	121-14	120-22	121-09	+ 26	134-28	120-03	5,909

Est vol 5,000; vol Mn 5,747; open int 10,278, +561.

TREASURY NOTES (CBT)-$100,000; pts. 32nds of 100%

	Open	High	Low	Settle	Change	Lifetime High	Lifetime Low	Open Interest
Mar	113-30	114-16	113-30	114-10	+ 8	123-22	112-04	215,848
June	114-02	114-16	114-01	114-09	+ 8	120-21	113-18	363,098

Est vol 175,000; vol Mn 239,348; open int 581,891, −7,879.

5 YR TREAS NOTES (CBT)-$100,000; pts. 32nds of 100%

	Open	High	Low	Settle	Change	Lifetime High	Lifetime Low	Open Interest
Mar	110-18	10-205	10-095	10-115	+ 4.5	116-15	109-30	92,286
June	10-205	110-29	10-195	10-225	+ 4.5	116-08	110-11	167,990

Est vol 90,000; vol Mn 92,271; open int 260,283, +236.

2 YR TREAS NOTES (CBT)-$200,000, pts. 32nds of 100%

	Open	High	Low	Settle	Change	Lifetime High	Lifetime Low	Open Interest
Mar	104-19	104-24	104-19	04-197	+ .5	106-30	04-175	9,048

Est vol 6,000; vol Mn 5,192; open int 41,699, −87.

30-DAY FEDERAL FUNDS (CBT)-$5 million; pts. of 100%

	Open	High	Low	Settle	Change	Lifetime High	Lifetime Low	Open Interest
Mar	95.210	95.220	0.215	95.220	+ .010	95.780	0.215	5,200
Apr	95.17	95.20	95.17	95.20	+ .02	95.76	94.43	2,659
May	95.15	95.18	95.15	95.17	+ .01	95.82	94.61	1,728
June	95.11	95.14	95.11	95.12	+ .02	95.60	0.12	1,152

Est vol 4,567; vol Mn 3,470; open int 11,576, −5,109.

MUNI BOND INDEX (CBT)-$1,000; times Bond Buyer MBI

	Open	High	Low	Settle	Change	Lifetime High	Lifetime Low	Open Interest
Mar	123-22	124-11	123-22	124-03	+ 9	129-27	122-25	21,220
June	122-21	123-10	122-21	123-01	+ 11	125-06	122-16	8,475

Est vol 3,300; vol Mn 6,273; open int 29,697, +662.
The index: Close 124-01; Yield 5.42.

TREASURY BILLS (CME)-$1 mil.; pts. of 100%

	Open	High	Low	Settle	Chg	Discount Settle	Discount Chg	Open Interest
Mar	95.45	95.46	95.45	95.46	....	4.54	....	2,328
June	95.43	95.46	95.43	95.45	+ .01	4.55	− .01	1,328

Est vol 461; vol Mon 48; open int 3,656, −23.

LIBOR-1 MO. (CME)-$3,000,000; points of 100%

	Open	High	Low	Settle	Chg	Discount Settle	Discount Chg	Open Interest
Mar	95.01	95.02	95.01	95.02	+ .01	4.98	− .01	5,136
Apr	94.99	95.00	94.99	95.00	+ .01	5.00	− .01	4,417
May	94.96	94.97	94.96	94.97	+ .01	5.03	− .01	3,269
June	94.91	94.93	94.91	94.92	+ .01	5.08	− .01	490
July	....	....	....	94.87	+ .02	5.13	− .02	279
Aug	....	....	....	94.82	+ .02	5.18	− .02	112

Est vol 3,820; vol Mon 2,290; open int 14,216, +500.

EURODOLLAR (CME)-$1 million; pts of 100%

	Open	High	Low	Settle	Chg	Yield Settle	Yield Chg	Open Interest
Mar	94.94	94.95	94.94	94.95	....	5.05	....	443,043
Apr	94.90	94.92	94.90	94.90	+ .01	5.10	− .01	5,378
May	....	....	....	94.86	+ .01	5.14	− .01	1,984
June	94.78	94.83	94.76	94.81	+ .02	5.19	− .02	500,032
Sept	94.60	94.68	94.58	94.63	+ .03	5.37	− .03	468,405
Dec	94.20	94.26	94.19	94.22	+ .02	5.78	− .02	305,581
Mr00	94.28	94.35	94.27	94.30	+ .02	5.70	− .02	277,456
June	94.19	94.28	94.19	94.23	+ .02	5.77	− .02	184,046
Sept	94.15	94.24	94.15	94.18	+ .02	5.82	− .02	143,756
Dec	94.05	94.12	94.05	94.07	+ .02	5.93	− .02	119,235
Mr01	94.09	94.16	94.09	94.11	+ .02	5.89	− .02	106,338
June	94.06	94.13	94.06	94.09	+ .02	5.91	− .02	81,151
Sept	94.04	94.11	94.04	94.07	+ .02	5.93	− .02	70,835
Dec	93.98	94.05	93.98	94.00	+ .02	6.00	− .02	56,024
Mr02	94.02	94.06	94.01	94.03	+ .02	5.97	− .02	53,234
June	93.99	94.04	93.99	94.00	+ .02	6.00	− .02	50,502
Sept	93.97	94.02	93.96	93.98	+ .02	6.02	− .02	44,970
Dec	93.89	93.94	93.89	93.90	+ .02	6.10	− .02	38,272
Mr03	93.90	93.95	93.90	93.91	+ .02	6.09	− .02	31,400
June	93.87	93.91	93.87	93.88	+ .02	6.12	− .02	29,840
Sept	93.84	93.89	93.84	93.85	+ .02	6.15	− .02	32,909
Dec	93.76	93.80	93.75	93.77	+ .02	6.23	− .02	18,900
Mr04	93.77	93.80	93.77	93.78	+ .03	6.22	− .03	17,654
June	....	....	....	93.75	+ .03	6.25	− .03	13,986
Sept	....	....	....	93.72	+ .03	6.28	− .03	13,086
Dec	....	....	....	93.61	+ .03	6.39	− .03	11,460
Mr05	....	....	....	93.62	+ .03	6.38	− .03	11,383
June	....	....	....	93.59	+ .03	6.41	− .03	9,683
Sept	....	....	....	93.56	+ .03	6.44	− .03	9,401
Dec	93.42	93.48	93.42	93.45	+ .03	6.55	− .03	6,675
Mr06	....	....	....	93.46	+ .03	6.54	− .03	6,217
June	....	....	....	93.43	+ .04	6.57	− .04	5,083
Sept	....	....	....	93.40	+ .04	6.60	− .04	5,868
Dec	....	....	....	93.29	+ .04	6.71	− .04	5,666
Mr07	....	....	....	93.30	+ .04	6.70	− .04	5,038
June	....	....	....	93.26	+ .04	6.74	− .04	4,671
Sept	....	....	....	93.22	+ .04	6.78	− .04	4,188
Dec	93.11	93.12	93.08	93.10	+ .04	6.90	− .04	4,761
Mr08	93.12	93.13	93.09	93.11	+ .04	6.89	− .04	4,204
June	93.08	93.09	93.05	93.07	+ .04	6.93	− .04	4,444
Sept	93.04	93.05	93.01	93.03	+ .04	6.97	− .04	3,694

Est vol 595,724; vol Mon 494,968; open int 3,212,696, +19,-157.

INDEX

DJ INDUSTRIAL AVERAGE (CBOT)-$10 times average

	Open	High	Low	Settle	Chg	High	Low	Open Interest
Mar	9336	9430	9280	9330	− 10	9760	7220	16,229
June	9400	9505	9365	9408	− 11	9810	7670	1,848
Sept	9480	9490	9470	9489	− 12	9891	7875	881
Dec		....	....	9574	− 12	9974	7987	923
Dc00		....	....	9960	− 14	10300	8100	45

Est vol 13,000; vol Mon 12,502; open int 19,926, +127.
Idx prl: High 9421.22; Low 9268.00; Close 9297.61 −27.17

S&P 500 INDEX (CME)-$250 times index

	Open	High	Low	Settle	Chg	High	Low	Open Interest
Mar	124000	125100	122110	122950	− 9.50	129420	902.85	342,179
June	125450	126300	123400	124140	− 9.50	130250	914.85	59,473
Sept		....	....	125320	− 9.70	131370	927.35	2,983
Dec		....	....	126570	− 9.70	132520	960.70	2,261
Mr00		....	....	127870	− 9.80	133850	970.00	269
June	130250	131400	128350	129270	− 9.80	135200	980.00	499
Dec		....	....	131770	− 9.80	137750	126650	683

Est vol 120,067; vol Mon 110,129; open int 408,347, −3,784.
Idx prl: High 1248.31; Low 1221.87; Close 1225.50 −10.66

MINI S&P 500 (CME)-$50 times index

	Open	High	Low	Settle	Chg	High	Low	Open Interest
Mar	123925	125125	123250	1229.50	− 9.50	129425	939.50	20,921

Vol Mon 31,172; open int 21,200, −143.

S&P MIDCAP 400 (CME)-$500 times index

	Open	High	Low	Settle	Chg	High	Low	Open Interest
Mar	360.00	364.25	358.50	360.00	+ .50	398.90	274.30	14,202
June	363.00	366.50	363.00	363.45	+ .50	402.25	278.95	1,539

Est vol 1,130; vol Mon 2,084; open int 15,741, −44.
Idx prl: High 363.01; Low 357.85; Close 359.82 +2.01

NIKKEI 225 STOCK AVERAGE (CME)-$5 times index

	Open	High	Low	Settle	Chg	High	Low	Open Interest
Mar	13950.	13990.	13925.	13975.	− 310	17150.	12690.	21,529
June	13950.	13970.	13910.	13935.	− 310	16755.	12640.	1,316

Est vol 1,952; vol Mon 1,652; open int 22,851, −487.
Idx prl: High 14306.01; Low 13921.06; Close 13921.06 −300.69

NASDAQ 100 (CME)-$100 times index

	Open	High	Low	Settle	Chg	High	Low	Open Interest
Mar	194150	196200	188500	189650	− 45.00	216500	109000	15,154
June	196950	198300	191700	191900	− 45.50	218600	110800	242

Est vol 6,346; vol Mon 4,853; open int 15,434, +50.
Idx prl: High 1953.83; Low 1886.36; Close 1888.66 −49.04

GSCI (CME)-$250 times nearby index

	Open	High	Low	Settle	Chg	High	Low	Open Interest
Mar	131.40	132.70	131.40	132.60	+ 1.30	160.70	129.20	26,735

Est vol 266; vol Mon 291; open int 26,775, −30.
Idx prl: High 132.67; Low 131.16; Close 132.62 +1.51

RUSSELL 2000 (CME)-$500 times index

	Open	High	Low	Settle	Chg	High	Low	Open Interest
Mar	397.00	400.00	393.15	393.50	− 3.00	514.75	310.00	14,076

Est vol 1,366; vol Mon 1,469; open int 14,295, +216.
Idx prl: High 398.30; Low 394.01; Close 394.43 +.04

CURRENCY

JAPAN YEN (CME)-12.5 million yen; $ per yen (.00)

	Open	High	Low	Settle	Change	Lifetime High	Lifetime Low	Open Interest
Mar	.8367	.8369	.8286	.8323	− .0044	.9319	.6997	82,110
June	.8445	.8445	.8390	.8424	− .0045	.9430	.7086	11,107
Sept	.8530	.8530	.8530	.8531	− .0046	.9500	.7680	1,511
Dec	....	....	....	.8638	− .0047	.9600	.8520	424

Est vol 18,288; vol Mon 16,417; open int 95,152, +4,363.

DEUTSCHEMARK (CME)-125,000 marks; $ per mark

	Open	High	Low	Settle	Change	Lifetime High	Lifetime Low	Open Interest
Mar	.5571	.5596	.5556	.5586	+ .0016	.6347	.5540	56,434
June	.5597	.5624	.5589	.5612	+ .0015	.6285	.5530	2,569
Sept	....	....	....	.5643	+ .0015	.6300	.5670	183

Est vol 18,438; vol Mon 14,136; open int 59,254, +852.

CANADIAN DOLLAR (CME)-100,000 dlrs.; $ per Can $

	Open	High	Low	Settle	Change	Lifetime High	Lifetime Low	Open Interest
Mar	.6570	.6585	.6539	.6577	+ .0008	.7247	.6290	61,102
June	.6563	.6587	.6546	.6577	+ .0008	.7172	.6300	6,684
Sept	.6569	.6586	.6565	.6578	+ .0007	.7080	.6310	1,446
Dec	.6568	.6586	.6568	.6581	+ .0007	.6785	.6320	1,214

Est vol 5,669; vol Mon 16,622; open int 70,694, −4,106.

BRITISH POUND (CME)-62,500 pds.; $ per pound

	Open	High	Low	Settle	Change	Lifetime High	Lifetime Low	Open Interest
Mar	1.6086	1.6160	1.6040	1.6138	+ .0054	1.7150	1.5940	67,625
June	1.5980	1.6148	1.5980	1.6128	+ .0056	1.7060	1.5880	7,176
Sept		....	....	1.6134	+ .0056	1.6980	1.5940	235

Est vol 6,219; vol Mon 11,930; open int 75,066, +4,092.

SWISS FRANC (CME)-125,000 francs; $ per franc

	Open	High	Low	Settle	Change	Lifetime High	Lifetime Low	Open Interest
Mar	.6843	.6876	.6830	.6869	+ .0024	.7890	.6635	56,411
June	.6915	.6938	.6913	.6932	+ .0024	.7930	.6695	6,093
Sept	....	....	....	.6998	+ .0024	.7831	.6980	322

Est vol 8,426; vol Mon 16,134; open int 62,832, +2,001.

AUSTRALIAN DOLLAR (CME)-100,000 dlrs.; $ per A.$

	Open	High	Low	Settle	Change	Lifetime High	Lifetime Low	Open Interest
Mar	.6191	.6226	.6191	.6220	+ .0028	.6545	.5710	23,609

Est vol 892; vol Mon 3,529; open int 24,594, −1,690.

MEXICAN PESO (CME)-500,000 new Mex. peso, $ per MP

	Open	High	Low	Settle	Change	Lifetime High	Lifetime Low	Open Interest
Mar	.10000	.10000	.09910	.09965	− 00125	.10565	.07500	12,018
June	.09410	.09470	.09380	.09433	− 00200	.10230	.06900	9,377
Sept	.08930	.08980	.08930	.08968	− 00125	.09510	.06350	627
Dec	.08480	.08550	.08480	.08568	− 00175	.84345	.06700	686

Est vol 4,470; vol Mon 7,294; open int 22,998, +42.

EXCHANGE ABBREVIATIONS
(for commodity futures and futures options)

CBT-Chicago Board of Trade; CME-Chicago Mercantile Exchange; CSCE-Coffee, Sugar & Cocoa Exchange, New York; CMX-COMEX (Div. of New York Mercantile Exchange); CTN-New York Cotton Exchange; EUREX-European Exchange; FINEX-Financial Exchange (Div. of New York Cotton Exchange; IPE-International Petroleum Exchange; KC-Kansas City Board of Trade; LIFFE-London International Financial Futures Exchange; MATIF-Marche a Terme International de France; ME-Montreal Exchange; MCE-MidAmerica Commodity Exchange; MPLS-Minneapolis Grain Exchange; NYFE-New York Futures Exchange (Sub. of New York Cotton Exchange); NYM-New York Mercantile Exchange; SIMEX-Singapore International Monetary Exchange Ltd.; SFE-Sydney Futures Exchange; TFE-Toronto Futures Exchange; WPG-Winnipeg CommodityExchange. CBT, CME, NYMX/CMX, CTN, FINEX, NYFE reflect overnight trading.

FIGURE 25.1 Quotations for Futures Prices (excerpts)

Source: Reprinted by permission of *The Wall Street Journal,* Dow Jones & Company, Inc., March 3, 1999, p. C16.

First, there are no specialists or market-makers on futures exchanges. Instead, members can be floor brokers, meaning that they execute customers' orders. In doing so, they (or their phone clerks) each keep a file of any stop or limit orders that cannot be immediately executed. Alternatively, members can be floor traders (those with very short holding periods, of less than a day, are known as **locals** or scalpers), meaning that they execute orders for their own personal accounts in an attempt to make profits by buying low and selling high. Floor traders are similar to market-makers because a floor trader may have an inventory of futures contracts and may act as a dealer. However, unlike a market-maker, a floor trader is not required to do so.

locals

Second, all futures orders must be announced by "open outcry," meaning that any member wishing to buy or sell any futures contract must verbally announce the order and a price at which the member is willing to trade. In this way, the order is exposed to everyone in the pit, thereby enabling an auction to take place that will lead to the order being filled at the best possible price.

25.3.1   THE CLEARINGHOUSE

Each futures exchange has an associated clearinghouse that becomes the "seller's buyer" and the "buyer's seller" as soon as a trade is concluded. The procedure is similar to that used for options which is not surprising because the first market in listed options was organized by people associated with a futures exchange. (Specifically, the Chicago Board Options Exchange was set up by the Chicago Board of Trade.)

In order to understand how a clearinghouse operates, consider the futures market for wheat. Assume that on the first day of trading in July wheat, buyer *B* agrees to purchase 5,000 bushels (one contract) from seller *S* for $4 per bushel, or $20,000 in total. (Actually, a floor broker working for *B*'s brokerage firm and a floor broker working for *S*'s brokerage firm meet in the wheat pit and agree on a price.) In this situation, *B* might believe that the price of wheat is going to rise, whereas *S* might believe that it is going to fall.

After *B* and *S* reach their agreement, the clearinghouse immediately steps in and breaks the transaction apart; that is, *B* and *S* no longer deal directly with each other. It is the obligation of the clearinghouse to deliver the wheat to *B* and to accept delivery from *S*. At this point there is an open interest of one contract (5,000 bushels) in July wheat because only one contract exists at this time. (Technically there are two because the clearinghouse has separate contracts with *B* and *S*.) Figure 25.2 illustrates the creation of this contract.

It is important to realize that if nothing else is done at this point, the clearinghouse is in a potentially risky position. For example, if the price of wheat rises to $5 per bushel by July, what happens if *S* does not deliver the wheat? The clearinghouse will have to buy the wheat on the spot market for $25,000 (= 5,000 × $5) and then deliver it to *B*. Because the clearinghouse will receive the selling price of $20,000 (= 5,000 × $4) from *B* in return, it will have lost $5,000. Even though the clearinghouse has a claim on *S* for the $5,000, it faces protracted legal battles in trying to recover this amount and may end up with little or nothing from *S*.

Alternatively, if the price of wheat falls to $3 per bushel by July, then *B* will pay $20,000 for wheat that is worth only $15,000 (= 5,000 × $3) on the spot market. What happens if *B* refuses to make payment? In this case the clearinghouse will not deliver the wheat it receives from *S*. Instead, it will sell the wheat for $15,000 on the spot market. Because the clearinghouse paid $20,000 to *S* for the wheat, it will have lost $5,000. Again, although the clearinghouse has a claim on *B* for the $5,000, it may end up with little or nothing from *B*.

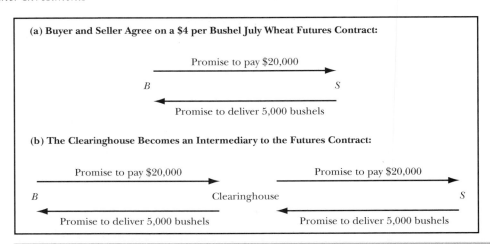

FIGURE 25.2 Creating a Futures Contract

Procedures that protect the clearinghouse from such potential losses include the following:

- Brokers impose initial margin requirements on both buyers and sellers
- They mark to market the accounts of buyers and sellers every day
- They impose daily maintenance margin requirements on both buyers and sellers

25.3.2 INITIAL MARGIN

performance margin

In order to buy and sell futures, an investor must open a futures account with a brokerage firm. This type of account must be kept separate from other accounts (such as a cash account or a margin account) the investor might have. Whenever a futures contract is signed, both buyer and seller are required to post initial margin. That is, both buyer and seller are required to make security deposits to guarantee they will fulfill their obligations; accordingly, initial margin is often referred to as **performance margin.** The amount of this margin is roughly 5% to 15% of the total purchase price of the futures contract. However, it is often stated as a given dollar amount regardless of the purchase price.[3]

For example, a July wheat futures contract for 5,000 bushels at $4 per bushel would have a total purchase price of $20,000 (= 5,000 × $4). With a 5% initial margin requirement, buyer B and seller S would each have to make a deposit of $1,000 (= .05 × $20,000). This deposit can be made in the form of cash, cash equivalents (such as Treasury bills), or a bank line of credit, and it forms the equity in the account on the first day.

Initial margin provides some protection to the clearinghouse, but it does not provide complete protection. As indicated earlier, if the futures price of wheat rises to $5 per bushel by July, the clearinghouse faces a potential loss of $5,000, only $1,000 of which can be quickly recovered from the margin deposit. However, the use of marking to market, coupled with a maintenance margin requirement, provides the requisite amount of additional protection. It should be noted that this process does not always provide complete protection; there are circumstances in which the clearinghouse will still be exposed to a loss (more on this later).

25.3.3 MARKING TO MARKET

In order to understand marking to market, consider the previous example in which *B* and *S* were, respectively, a buyer and a seller of a 5,000-bushel wheat futures contract at $4 per bushel. Assume that on the second day of trading the settlement price of July wheat is $4.10 per bushel. In this situation, *S* has "lost" $500 because of the rise in the price of wheat from $4 to $4.10 per bushel, whereas *B* has "made" $500 (= $.10 × 5,000). Thus the equity in the account of *S* is reduced by $500, and the equity in the account of *B* is increased by $500. Because the initial equity was equal to the initial margin requirement of $1,000, *S* now has equity of $500, whereas *B* has equity of $1,500. This process of adjusting the equity in an investor's account in order to reflect the change in the settlement price of the futures contract is known as **marking to market.** As part of the marking-to-market process, the clearinghouse every day replaces each existing futures contract with a new one that has as the purchase price the settlement price as reported in the financial press.

marking to market

In general, the equity in either a buyer or a seller's account is the initial margin deposit and the sum of all daily gains, less losses, on open positions in futures. Because the amount of the gains (less losses) changes every day, the amount of equity changes every day.

In the example, if the settlement price of the July wheat futures contract had fallen to $3.95 per bushel the third day (that is, the day after rising to $4.10), then *B* would have lost $750 [= 5,000 × ($4.10 − $3.95)], whereas *S* would have made $750 on that day. When their accounts were marked to market at the end of the day, the equity in *B*'s account would have dropped from $1,500 to $750, whereas *S*'s equity would have risen from $500 to $1,250.

25.3.4 MAINTENANCE MARGIN

Another key concept is maintenance margin. According to the maintenance margin requirement, the investor must keep the account's equity equal to or greater than a certain percentage of the amount deposited as initial margin. Because this percentage is roughly 75%, the investor must have equity equal to or greater than 75% of the initial margin. If this requirement is not met, then the investor will receive a margin call from his or her broker for an additional deposit of cash (nothing else can be deposited for this purpose) known as **variation margin** to bring the equity up to the initial margin level. If the investor does not (or cannot) respond, then the broker will close out the investor's position by entering a reversing trade in the investor's account.

variation margin

For example, reconsider investors *B* and *S,* who had, respectively, bought and sold a July wheat futures contract at $4 per bushel. Each investor made a deposit of $1,000 to meet the initial margin requirement. The next day the price of the wheat futures contract rose to $4.10 per bushel, or $20,500. Thus, the equity of *B* increased to $1,500, whereas the equity of *S* decreased to $500. If the maintenance margin requirement is 75% of initial margin, both *B* and *S* are required to have equity of at least $750 (= .75 × $1,000) in their accounts every day. Because the actual level of equity for *B* clearly exceeds that amount, *B* does not need to do anything. Indeed, *B* may withdraw an amount of cash equal to the amount by which the equity exceeds the initial margin; in this example, *B* can withdraw cash of $500.

However, *S* is undermargined and will be asked to make a cash deposit of at least $500 to increase the equity from $500 to $1,000, the level of the initial margin. If *S* refuses to make this deposit, then the broker will enter a reversing trade for *S* by purchasing a July wheat futures contract. The result is that *S* will simply receive an amount of money approximately equal to the account's equity, $500, and the account will be closed. Because *S* initially deposited $1,000, *S* will have sustained a loss of $500.

On the third day the price of the July wheat futures contract is assumed to settle at $3.95 per bushel, representing a $750 loss for *B* and a $750 gain for *S* (see Table 25.1). As a consequence, *B* is now undermargined and will be asked to deposit $750 so the equity in *B*'s account is $1,000. (This example assumes that *B* had withdrawn the $500 in excess margin that had accumulated from the previous day's price change.) Conversely, *S* can withdraw $750, because the equity in *S*'s account is more than the $1,000 initial margin requirement by that amount. (Remember that *S* had added $500 to bring the account's equity up to $1,000 at the end of the previous day.)

25.3.5 REVERSING TRADES

Suppose that on the next day *B* finds that people are paying $4.15 per bushel for July wheat. This represents a daily profit to *B* of $.20 per bushel because the price was $3.95 the previous day. If *B* believes the price of July wheat will not go any higher, then *B* might sell a July wheat futures contract for $4.15 to someone else. (Conversely, *S* might buy a July wheat futures contract because *S*'s equity has been reduced to zero.) In this situation *B* has made a reversing trade, because *B* now has offsetting positions with respect to July wheat. (Equivalently, *B* is said to have *unwound* or *closed out* or *offset* his or her position in July wheat.)

At this point the benefit to *B* of having a clearinghouse involved is evident. Nominally, *B* is obligated to deliver 5,000 bushels of wheat to the clearinghouse in July, which in turn is obligated to deliver it back to *B*. Why? Because *B* is involved in two July wheat contracts, one as a seller and one as a buyer. However, the clearinghouse will note that *B* has offsetting positions in July wheat, and it will immediately cancel

TABLE 25.1   Margin Requirements for a Futures Contract

Day	Price of Wheat	Event	Buyer B Amount	Buyer B Equity in Account	Seller S Amount	Seller S Equity in Account
(a) If Maintenance Margin Were Not Required						
1	$4	Deposit initial margin	$1,000	$1,000	$1,000	$1,000
2	$4.10	Mark to market	+500	1,500	−500	500
3	$3.95	Mark to market	−750	750	+750	1,250
4	$4.15	Mark to market	+1,000	1,750	−1,000	250
(b) With Required Maintenance Margin						
1	$4	Deposit initial margin	$1,000	$1,000	$1,000	$1,000
2	$4.10	Mark to market:	+500	1,500	−500	500
		Buyer withdraws cash	−500	1,000	—	—
		Seller deposits cash	—	—	+500	1,000
3	$3.95	Mark to market:	−750	250	+750	1,750
		Buyer withdraws cash	+750	1,000	—	—
		Seller deposits cash	—	—	−750	1,000
4	$4.15	Mark to market:	+1,000	2,000	−1,000	0
		Reversing trade and withdrawal of cash	−2,000	0	—	—

both of them. Furthermore, once the reversing trade has been made, *B* will be able to withdraw $2,000, consisting of

- The initial margin of $1,000
- A variation margin deposit because of the daily marking to market of $250 [= 5,000 × ($4 − $3.95)]
- The $750 [= 5,000 × ($4.15 − $4)] net profit that has been made

Table 25.1 illustrates the effect these events have on the equity in the account of *B* (and that of *S*). In effect, a futures contract is replaced every day by adjusting the equity in the investor's account and drawing up a new contract that has a purchase price equal to the current settlement price. The daily marking-to-market procedure, coupled with margin requirements, results in the clearinghouse's always having a security deposit of sufficient size to protect it from losses caused by the actions of the individual investors.[4]

These rather complex arrangements make it possible for futures traders to think in simple terms. In the example, *B* bought a contract of July wheat at $4 and sold it on day 4 for $4.15, making a profit of $.15 per bushel. If *S*, having initially sold a contract of July wheat at $4, later made a reversing trade for $4.25, then *S*'s position is also simple; *S* sold July wheat for $4 and later bought it back for $4.25, suffering a loss of $.25 per bushel in the process. Although not mentioned, both the buyer and seller have to pay commissions to have their orders executed. Hence, consideration of these costs indicates that profits will be a bit less and losses will be a bit larger than shown here.

25.3.6 FUTURES POSITIONS

In the previous example, *B* was the person who initially bought a July wheat futures contract. Accordingly, *B* has a long position and is said to be *long* one contract of July wheat. In contrast, *S*, having initially sold a July wheat futures contract, has a short position and is said to be *short* one contract of July wheat.

The process of marking to market every day means that changes in the settlement price are realized as soon as they occur. When the settlement price rises, investors with long positions realize profits and those who are short realize losses. Conversely, when the settlement price falls, those with long positions realize losses, whereas those with short positions realize profits. In either event, total profits always equal total losses. Thus, either the buyer gains and the seller loses, or the seller gains and the buyer loses because both parties are involved in a "zero-sum game" (as was also the case with buyers and writers of options, discussed in Chapter 24).

25.3.7 OPEN INTEREST

When trading is first allowed in a contract, there is no open interest because no contracts are outstanding. As people begin to make transactions, the open interest grows. At any time open interest equals the amount that those with short positions (the sellers) are currently obligated to deliver. It also equals the amount that those with long positions (the buyers) are obligated to receive.

Open interest figures are typically shown with futures prices in the financial press. For example, Figure 25.1 indicates that on March 2, 1999, a total of 142,038 contracts in May 1999 corn were outstanding on the CBT. Note the substantial differences in the open interest figures for the other corn contracts on the CBT on that day. This disparity is typical. Figure 25.3 shows why. Open interest for a December corn contract is shown for every month from January until the contract expired at the end of the delivery month, December. From January until the end of October, more trades were

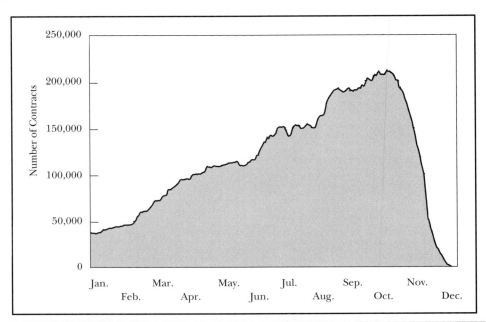

FIGURE 25.3 Open Interest, December 1997 Chicago Board of Trade Corn Futures Contract: January 2, 1997 through December 29, 1997

generally made to open new positions than to reverse old ones, and open interest continued to increase. As the delivery month approached, reversing trades began to outnumber trades intended to open new positions, and the open interest began to decline.[5] The amount remaining at the beginning of December was the number of bushels of corn that would have been delivered against futures contracts at that time, but most of these contracts were also settled by reversing trades instead of delivery.

Relatively few futures positions—less than 3% of the total—end in actual delivery of the asset involved.[6] However, the fact that delivery is a possibility makes a contract's value in the delivery month differ only slightly, if at all, from the spot price (that is, the current market price) of the asset.

If not reversed, most futures contracts require delivery of the corresponding asset. Notable exceptions are market index futures; they do not require delivery of the set of securities for the corresponding index. Instead, *cash settlement* is required; an amount equal to the difference between the level of the index and the purchase price must be paid in cash on the delivery date. Nevertheless, similar to other types of futures, most positions in market index futures are closed out with reversing trades before the date at which delivery (in cash) is required.

25.3.8 PRICE LIMITS

Commodity Futures Trading Commission

The futures exchanges place dollar limits on the extent to which futures prices can vary from day to day, subject to approval by the **Commodity Futures Trading Commission** (the CFTC is the federal agency that regulates trading in futures). For example, if July wheat closed at $4 on the previous day and the daily price limit is $.20, then on the following day contracts at prices outside the range from $3.80 to $4.20 would not be allowed to be traded on the exchange. If a major piece of news during the day led traders to consider $4.25 a reasonable price for the contract, they would have the following options:

1. Trade privately, forgoing the advantages offered by the exchange
2. Trade on the exchange at the limit price of $4.20
3. Let the contract settle at $4.20 and wait until the next day, when the range of acceptable prices would be from $4 to $4.40

One result of the "limit move" to $4.20 is that no contracts may be traded at all on that day. Nobody will want to sell these wheat contracts for a below-market price of $4.20, preferring to wait until the next day when the range of acceptable prices is raised. Indeed, if the news is important enough (such as a massive freeze in Florida, destroying many orange trees and dramatically affecting orange juice futures), there can be limit moves for successive days, with no trading taking place for several days.

The futures exchanges impose price limits on futures because of a belief that traders may overreact to news, and they should be "protected" from voluntarily entering into agreements under such conditions. Interestingly, initial margins are usually set at an amount roughly equal to the price limit times the size of the contract. In the case of wheat with a $.20 price limit and a contract for 5,000 bushels, the initial margin is usually about $1,000 (= $.20 × 5,000). Thus, if the price of wheat moves up the limit of $.20, then only the initial margin of $1,000 will be lost by the seller on the day of the adverse limit move. In a sense, the price limit "protects" the investor (and the clearinghouse) from losing more than $1,000 on that day. However, it is possible that the investor cannot enter a reversing trade as soon as prices have moved the limit, meaning that much larger losses can be incurred later (as in the case of the Florida freeze and orange juice futures).

25.4 Basis

basis

The difference between the current spot price on an asset (that is, the price of the asset for immediate delivery) and the corresponding futures price (that is, the purchase price stated in the futures contract) is known as the **basis** for the futures:

$$\text{Basis} = \text{Current spot price} - \text{Futures price} \qquad (25.1)$$

25.4.1 SPECULATING ON THE BASIS

Because the futures price equals the spot price on the delivery date, the basis ultimately narrows and disappears on the delivery date. Prior to the delivery date, it can widen or narrow, providing opportunities for profitable investing if changes in the basis can be accurately forecast. Typically, depending on whether the basis is positive or negative and on whether the basis is forecasted to widen or narrow, an investor who is confident of accurately forecasting the basis will want to be either (1) short in the futures contract and long in the underlying deliverable asset or (2) long in the futures contract and short in the underlying deliverable asset. The risk that the basis will narrow or widen, causing gains or losses to these investors, is known as **basis risk.** The only type of uncertainty they face concerns the difference between the spot price of the deliverable asset and the price of the futures contract. Such a person is said to be *speculating on the basis.*[7]

basis risk

25.4.2 SPREADS

It is possible to take a long position in a futures contract and a short position in another futures contract in the same asset but with a different delivery date. The person who does this is speculating on changes in the difference between the prices of the two contracts.

Others attempt to profit from temporary imbalances among the prices of futures contracts on different but related assets. For example, one might take a long position in soybeans and a short position in soybean meal. Another possibility would be a position in wheat with an offsetting position in corn, which can be substituted for wheat in many applications.

Such people are known as *spreaders,* and, like those who speculate on the basis, they reduce or eliminate the risk associated with general price moves. Instead, they take on the risk associated with changes in price *differences,* hoping that their alleged superior knowledge will enable them to consistently make profits from such changes.

25.5 Returns on Futures

Over a 27-year period, a portfolio made up of positions in 23 different commodity futures contracts was compared with a diversified portfolio of common stocks.[8] The average rates of return and risk levels of the two portfolios were found to be of similar magnitude:

Portfolio	Average Annual Return	Standard Deviation
Futures	13.83%	22.43%
Common stocks	13.05%	18.95%

Given these results, an investor might view the two alternatives as equally desirable. Better yet, a combination of the two portfolios was found to be more desirable than either portfolio by itself. The returns of the commodity futures and stock portfolios were negatively correlated, suggesting that the return on a combined portfolio would have had considerably less variation than the return on either portfolio separately. Specifically, the correlation coefficient was $-.24$, resulting in the following standard deviations for portfolios with different combinations:

Percent in Stocks	Percent in Futures	Average Annual Return	Standard Deviation
0%	100%	13.83%	22.43%
20	80	13.67	17.43
40	60	13.52	13.77
60	40	13.36	12.68
80	20	13.20	14.74
100	0	13.05	18.95

Whereas there was little difference in the average returns of the various portfolios, there was a noticeable difference in their risks. In particular, the portfolio with roughly 60% in stocks and 40% in futures seems to have had much less risk than the others.

Also of interest was the observation that commodity futures have been at least a partial hedge against inflation. During the 27-year period, the returns on the portfolio of 23 futures were positively correlated with changes in the CPI, having a correlation coefficient of .58. In contrast, the returns on the portfolio of common stocks were negatively correlated with changes in the CPI, having a correlation coefficient of $-.43$.

At this point it is appropriate to discuss the pricing of futures contracts. Specifically, what is the relationship between the futures price and investors' expectations of what the spot price will be on the delivery date? And what is the relationship between

Transportable Alpha

 Years ago trustees of the multi-billion dollar General Mills pension fund adopted a disciplined approach to allocating assets among various broad categories by establishing specific long-run allocation targets: 60% to common stocks and 40% to fixed-income securities. The trustees believe that this *policy asset allocation* provides an optimal balance of expected return and risk, given their collective tolerance for possible adverse outcomes. The trustees expect the fund's staff, which handles the fund's day-to-day investment operations, to stick closely to this policy asset allocation. In turn, the staff follows a procedure of reducing exposure to any asset category that has appreciated in relative value and increasing exposure to any asset category that has depreciated in relative value.

To manage the pension fund's assets, the staff had retained what the trustees considered to be a superior group of domestic common stock managers. Over a 10-year period, those managers, in aggregate, had outperformed the S&P 500 by 1.5% annually (after all fees and expenses)—an exceptional amount by the standards of the investment management business. The trustees and staff expected such superior performance to continue in the future.

More recently the trustees found themselves facing a dilemma: The trustees would have liked to have assigned more than 60% of the fund's assets to the common stock managers. However, the trustees were also committed to the discipline of their asset allocation process. Could the trustees have their proverbial cake and eat it too? The answer was yes, through a concept called *transportable alpha.*

Consider three strategies through which General Mills could have maintained its policy asset allocation yet taken advantage of its common stock managers' skills. Each strategy involves allocating more than 60% of the pension fund's assets to the common stock managers, while simultaneously reducing the pension fund's common stock exposure and increasing its fixed-income exposure in order to comply with the fund's asset allocation targets.

1. *Long–short strategy.* The managers, in aggregate, purchase long positions in stocks as they typically would with their assigned assets. However, they also short sell stocks (see Chapter 2) equal in value to the pension fund's overweighting of domestic equity assets. The cash generated by these short sales is used to buy fixed-income securities that are held as margin but nevertheless provide returns through interest income and price changes. The particular long–short transactions result from the managers' investment research, which identifies under- and overpriced securities.

2. *Futures strategy.* The managers purchase long stock positions with their assigned assets. At the same time the pension fund's staff sells futures contracts on a stock market index and buys futures contracts on Treasury bonds in sufficient amounts to compensate for the over- and underweighting of common stocks and fixed-income securities, respectively.

3. *Swap strategy.* The managers purchase long stock positions with their assigned assets. Through a financial intermediary (such as a bank or a broker) the pension fund "swaps" (exchanges) with another institutional investor the return on a common stock index in order to receive the return on a fixed-income index. These swaps (see Chapter 17) are based on dollar amounts equal to the over- and underweightings of the common stocks and fixed-income securities, respectively.

In general, these strategies can be characterized as allowing the pension fund to earn (1) the total return generated by a 40% allocation to fixed-income securities, (2) the total return produced by a 60% allocation to common stocks (that is, the normal plus abnormal returns of the common stock managers), and (3) the abnormal returns earned by the common stock managers associated with the allocation in excess of 60% to common stocks. The common stock managers' abnormal returns (known as *alphas*) are effectively "transported" to the fixed-income asset category.

In the final analysis, General Mills chose to implement the second strategy. The pension fund's staff believed that listed futures contracts provided the cheapest and administratively least cumbersome means of carrying out its alpha transport program. Nevertheless, the ability to customize the other strategies to specific situations may make those strategies attractive at times to certain institutional investors.

These strategies highlight fundamental changes in the financial markets that began in the 1980s and have rapidly gathered momentum in the 1990s. Through the development of derivative financial instruments (options, futures, and swaps) and the technological advancements in communications and computing power, financial markets have become highly integrated and fungible. Investors are increasingly able to exploit perceived profit opportunities and simultaneously maintain desired risk positions.

Transportable alpha involves investors capturing inefficiencies in certain markets while maintaining desired exposure to markets beyond those in which the superior performance is earned. Transportable alpha is not a free lunch. Investors must pay commissions on their trades in stocks, options, futures, and swaps either directly or through bid–ask spreads. Real-world frictions such as collateral requirements and even custodial accounting difficulties still complicate the smooth implementation of the alpha transport strategies. Further, investors must take active management risk in order to earn their alphas. For example, General Mills's common stock managers, in aggregate, may underperform the stock market. However, institutional investors applying the transportable alpha concept believe that their active management investment strategies possess sufficiently positive expected returns that more than compensate for the additional risk assumed.

the futures price and the current spot price of the deliverable asset? The next two sections explore these relationships.

25.6 Futures Prices and Expected Spot Prices

25.6.1 CERTAINTY

If future spot prices could be predicted with certainty, there would be no reason for anyone to be either a buyer or a seller of a futures contract. To understand why, imagine what a futures contract would look like in a world of certainty. First, the purchase price of the futures contract would simply equal the (perfectly predictable) expected spot price on the delivery date. Neither buyers nor sellers would make profits from the existence of futures. Second, the purchase price would not change as the delivery date got closer.[9] Finally, no margin would be necessary because there would not be any unexpected "adverse" price movements.

25.6.2 UNCERTAINTY

Although it is useful to know something about the way futures prices and expected spot prices are related to each other in a world of certainty where forecasting is completely accurate, the real world is uncertain. Consequently, how are futures prices related to expected spot prices? There are several possible explanations, but no definitive answer has been provided.

Expectations Hypothesis

expectations hypothesis

One possible explanation is given by the **expectations hypothesis:** The current purchase price of a futures contract equals the consensus expectation of the spot price on the delivery date. In symbols:

$$P_f = \overline{P}_s$$

where P_f is the current purchase price of the futures contract and $\overline{P}_s$ is the expected spot price of the asset on the delivery date. Thus, if a July wheat futures contract is currently selling for \$4 per bushel in March, then it can be inferred that the consensus opinion in March is that in July the spot price of wheat will be \$4.

If the expectations hypothesis is correct, a speculator should not expect either to either win or lose from a position in the futures market, be it long or short. Neglecting margin requirements, a speculator who takes a long position in futures agrees to pay P_f at the delivery date for an asset that is expected to be worth $\overline{P}_s$ at that time. Thus, the long speculator's expected profit is $\overline{P}_s - P_f$, which equals zero. Conversely, a speculator with a short position will have sold an asset at a price of P_f and will expect to enter a reversing trade at $\overline{P}_s$ on the delivery date, resulting in an expected profit of $P_f - \overline{P}_s$, which also equals zero.

The expectations hypothesis is often defended on the grounds that speculators are indifferent to risk and are thus willing to accommodate hedgers without any compensation in the form of the risk premium. Their indifference is based on the belief that the impact of a specific futures position on the risk of a diversified portfolio will be very small. As a result, speculators holding diversified portfolios may be willing to take over some risk from hedgers with little (if any) compensation in the form of a risk premium. Figure 25.4 shows the pattern of futures prices implied by the expectations hypothesis, given that the expected spot price $\overline{P}_s$ does not change during the life of the contract.

Normal Backwardation

The famous economist John Maynard Keynes felt that the expectations hypothesis did not correctly explain futures prices.[10] He argued that, on balance, hedgers want to be short in futures, and therefore they will have to entice the speculators to be long in futures. Because there are risks associated with being long, Keynes hypothesized that the hedgers would have to entice the speculators by making the expected return from a long position greater than the riskfree rate. Doing so requires the futures price to be less than the expected spot price:

$$P_f < \overline{P}_s$$

FIGURE 25.4 Price of a Futures Contract When the Spot Price Expected at the Time of Delivery Does Not Change

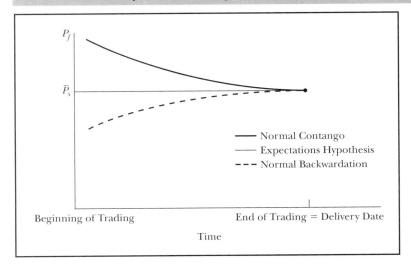

normal backwardation

Thus, a speculator who bought a futures contract at a price P_f would expect to be able to sell it on (or near) the delivery date at a higher price, $\overline{P}_s$. This relationship between the futures price and the expected spot price has been referred to as **normal backwardation,** and implies that the price of a futures contract will rise during its life, as shown in Figure 25.4.

Normal Contango

A contrary hypothesis holds that, on balance, hedgers want to be long in futures and therefore they will have to entice speculators to be short in futures. Because there are risks associated with being short, the hedgers will have to entice the speculators by making the expected return from a short position greater than the riskfree rate. Doing so requires the futures price to be greater than the expected spot price:

$$P_f - \overline{P}_s$$

normal contango

Thus, a speculator who short sold a futures contract at a price P_f would expect to be able to buy it back on (or near) the delivery date at a lower price, $\overline{P}_s$. This relationship between the futures price and the expected spot price has been referred to as **normal contango,** and implies that the price of a futures contract will fall during its life, as shown in Figure 25.4.[11]

25.7 Futures Prices and Current Spot Prices

The previous section discussed the relationship between the futures price associated with an asset and the expected spot price of the asset on the delivery date given in the futures contract. What about the relationship between the futures price and the current spot price of the asset? In general, they will be different, but is there an explanation for why these prices are different? Is there a model that can be used to forecast how the size of the difference will change over time? This section attempts to answer those questions.[12]

25.7.1 INTRODUCING THE PROBLEM

Consider the owner of a circa 1910 Honus Wagner baseball card who is ready to sell the card. The owner knows that the card's current market price is $100,000 because there are very few (reputedly fewer than five) of these cards available. (One actually sold for $451,000 in 1990.) Furthermore, an investor has offered to buy it but wants to pay for it a year from now. The buyer is willing to take delivery of the card then and wants to sign the contract for sale today. More specifically, he or she wants to sign a futures contract with the owner in which the delivery date is one year from now.

25.7.2 NO COSTS OR BENEFITS OF OWNERSHIP

What price should the owner ask for in the futures contract? Assume that there is no risk that either party will default on the contract and that there are no benefits (such as from showing the card) or costs (such as insurance) associated with owning the card. If the current one-year interest rate is 4%, then the owner could sell the card today on the spot market for $100,000, put the proceeds in the bank to earn 4%, and have $104,000 in one year. Hence the owner would not be willing to sign the futures contract for any futures price that is less than $104,000. The buyer, on the other hand, is unwilling to pay more than $104,000 because he or she could pay $100,000 now and get the card immediately but forgo $4,000 of interest that would have been paid had the $100,000 been left in the bank where it earned 4%. Because the seller wants to receive at least $104,000 and the buyer will pay no more than $104,000, they will settle at a futures price of $104,000.

To generalize, let P_s denote the current spot price of the asset (in this case, $100,000) and I the dollar amount of interest corresponding to the period of time from the present to the delivery date (in this case, $4,000). If P_f denotes the futures price, then:

$$P_f = P_s + I \qquad (25.2)$$

This equation shows that the futures price will be greater than the spot price by the amount of the interest that the owner forgoes by holding on to the asset, provided there are no costs or benefits associated with ownership.

25.7.3 BENEFITS FROM OWNERSHIP

To complicate the model, imagine that a baseball card exhibition will be held in 12 months, just before the delivery date. The exhibitor is willing to pay the card owner $1,000 to have the card displayed at the exhibition. How will this benefit of ownership affect the futures price?

As mentioned earlier, if the owner sells the card now, then he or she will receive $100,000 immediately, which could be invested right away and be worth $104,000 in 12 months. Alternatively, the owner could hold on to the card and receive the $1,000 exhibitor fee as well as the futures price. Hence the futures price must be at least $103,000 for the owner to benefit as much financially by selling the card using a futures contract as by selling it immediately in the spot market. On the other side, the buyer will agree to a futures price of no more than $103,000 because he or she could buy the card on the spot market for $100,000, forgo $4,000 of interest, but receive the $1,000 exhibitor fee. Consequently, the futures price will be $103,000; this is the only price that is agreeable to both buyer and seller.

What if the exhibition were held in 6 months instead of one year? In that case the owner of the card would receive the $1,000 exhibitor fee in 6 months and would be able to invest it risklessly at 2% for the remaining 6 months until the delivery date. Thus the $1,000 in 6 months would be equivalent to $1,020 in 12 months, and the futures price would be $102,980 (= $100,000 + $4,000 − $1,020).

Let B denote the value of the benefits of ownership (sometimes known as the *convenience yield* of the asset) as of the delivery date (in this case, $1,020). When such benefits are present, the futures price can be calculated as

$$P_f = P_s + I - B \qquad (25.3)$$

This equation shows that the futures price can be greater or less than the spot price, depending on whether the net amount of interest forgone less benefits received is positive or negative and provided there are no costs associated with ownership of the asset.

25.7.4 COSTS OF OWNERSHIP

What if the owner of the baseball card decides that it must be insured at an annual cost of $100? How will insuring the card affect the futures price? Costs of ownership such as insurance and storage are the opposite of benefits of ownership because the benefits of ownership result in cash inflows to the owner, whereas the costs of ownership result in cash outflows. Hence the previously calculated futures price of $102,980 would have to be increased by the $100 cost of insurance (assuming the insurance is paid in 12 months) to $103,080. If C denotes the costs of ownership (in this example, $100), then the futures price will be

$$P_f = P_s + I - B + C \qquad (25.4)$$

cost of carry

The total value of interest less benefits received plus cost of ownership, $I - B + C$, is known as the **cost of carry** associated with the futures contract. Note that the futures price can be greater or less than the spot price, depending on whether the cost of carry is positive or negative.

25.8 Financial Futures

Until the 1970s, futures contracts were limited to agricultural goods and natural resources. Since then, financial futures based on foreign currencies, fixed-income securities, and market indices have been introduced on major exchanges. Indeed, in terms of trading volume, they are now far more important than both the underlying assets and traditional futures contracts. Unlike other types of futures that permit delivery any time during a given month, most financial futures have a specific delivery date. (The exceptions involve some fixed-income futures.)

25.8.1 FOREIGN CURRENCY FUTURES

Anyone who has crossed a national border knows that there is an active spot market for foreign currency and that the rate at which one currency is exchanged for another varies over time. At any particular point in time, however, all such rates must be in conformance or else a riskless profit-making situation may arise. For example, it is usually possible to exchange U.S. dollars for British pounds, then exchange the British pounds for Swiss francs, and, finally, exchange the Swiss francs for U.S. dollars. If all three exchange rates were not in line, an investor might end up with more dollars at the end of this chain of transactions than at the beginning. Such an opportunity would attract large amounts of money, placing pressure on exchange rates and rapidly restoring balance. Although transaction costs and exchange restrictions might limit the ability of people to exploit such imbalances among exchange rates, they would nevertheless force the rates to be closely aligned.

The familiar market in foreign currency operated by banks, travel agents, and others is, in effect, a spot market because both the agreement on terms and the actual exchange of currencies occur at the same time. There are also markets for agreements involving the future delivery of foreign currency. The largest market is operated by banks and specialized brokers that maintain close communications with each other throughout the world. Corporations, institutions, and some individuals deal in this market via large banks. Substantial amounts of money are involved, and every agreement is negotiated separately. Typical rates are quoted daily in the financial press, as shown in Figure 25.5. This network of large institutions is generally called the *market for forward exchange* because there is no marking to market. Furthermore, because the contracts are not standardized, no organized secondary market for them exists. However, there is a market that deals in standardized futures contracts for foreign currency.[13] Procedures are similar to those used for commodity futures.

For example, one of the currency futures contracts traded on the International Monetary Market (IMM) of the Chicago Mercantile Exchange requires the seller to deliver 12,500,000 Japanese yen to the buyer on a specific date for a number of U.S. dollars agreed on in advance. Only the price of the transaction (expressed in both dollars per yen and yen per dollar) is negotiated by the parties involved; all other terms are standard. Clearing procedures allow positions to be covered by reversing trades, and few contracts result in the actual delivery of foreign currency. As shown in Figure 25.1, prices and volumes for such contracts are quoted daily in the financial press along with those for other futures.

CURRENCY TRADING

Tuesday, March 2, 1999

EXCHANGE RATES

The New York foreign exchange mid-range rates below apply to trading among banks in amounts of $1 million and more, as quoted at 4 p.m. Eastern time by Telerate and other sources. Retail transactions provide fewer units of foreign currency per dollar. Rates for the 11 Euro currency countries are derived from the latest dollar-euro rate using the exchange ratios set 1/1/99.

Country	U.S. $ equiv. Tue	Mon	Currency per U.S. $ Tue	Mon
Argentina (Peso)	1.0002	1.0002	.9998	.9998
Australia (Dollar)	.6227	.6192	1.6060	1.6151
Austria (Schilling)	.07947	.07916	12.584	12.632
Bahrain (Dinar)	2.6386	2.6525	.3790	.3770
Belgium (Franc)	.02711	.02700	36.891	37.033
Brazil (Real)	.4630	.4695	2.1600	2.1300
Britain (Pound)	1.6160	1.6088	.6188	.6216
1-month forward	1.6152	1.6079	.6191	.6219
3-months forward	1.6146	1.6073	.6193	.6222
6-months forward	1.6151	1.6073	.6192	.6222
Canada (Dollar)	.6570	.6572	1.5220	1.5215
1-month forward	.6570	.6572	1.5222	1.5217
3-months forward	.6569	.6571	1.5223	1.5217
6-months forward	.6567	.6572	1.5226	1.5216
Chile (Peso)	.001989	.001991	502.65	502.35
China (Renminbi)	.1208	.1208	8.2789	8.2792
Colombia (Peso)	.0006409	.0006376	1560.40	1568.30
Czech. Rep. (Koruna) .				
Commercial rate	.02906	.02902	34.414	34.457
Denmark (Krone)	.1471	.1465	6.7995	6.8275
Ecuador (Sucre)				
Floating rate	.0001002	.0001066	9984.50	9380.00
Finland (Markka)	.1839	.1832	5.4373	5.4583
France (Franc)	.1667	.1661	5.9987	6.0218
1-month forward	.1670	.1663	5.9889	6.0120
3-months forward	.1675	.1668	5.9702	5.9947
6-months forward	.1684	.1677	5.9382	5.9613
Germany (Mark)	.5591	.5569	1.7886	1.7955
1-month forward	.5600	.5578	1.7856	1.7928
3-months forward	.5618	.5594	1.7801	1.7876
6-months forward	.5648	.5618	1.7705	1.7800
Greece (Drachma)	.003396	.003385	294.51	295.45
Hong Kong (Dollar)	.1291	.1291	7.7477	7.7473
Hungary (Forint)	.004330	.004309	230.96	232.05
India (Rupee)	.02352	.02353	42.515	42.500
Indonesia (Rupiah)	.0001127	.0001131	8870.00	8845.00
Ireland (Punt)	1.3885	1.3831	.7202	.7230
Israel (Shekel)	.2470	.2467	4.0488	4.0540
Italy (Lira)	.0005647	.0005626	1770.71	1777.54

Country	U.S. $ equiv. Tue	Mon	Currency per U.S. $ Tue	Mon
Japan (Yen)	.008317	.008345	120.23	119.83
1-month forward	.008352	.008381	119.73	119.32
3-months forward	.008419	.008447	118.78	118.39
6-months forward	.008532	.008555	117.21	116.89
Jordan (Dinar)	1.4045	1.4045	.7120	.7120
Kuwait (Dinar)	3.2819	3.2819	.3047	.3047
Lebanon (Pound)	.0006616	.0006616	1511.50	1511.50
Malaysia (Ringgit-b)	.2632	.2632	3.8000	3.8000
Malta (Lira)	2.5419	2.5368	.3934	.3942
Mexico (Peso)				
Floating rate	.1005	.1007	9.9490	9.9300
Netherland (Guilder)	.4962	.4943	2.0153	2.0231
New Zealand (Dollar)	.5291	.5264	1.8900	1.8997
Norway (Krone)	.1264	.1259	7.9108	7.9458
Pakistan (Rupee)	.01952	.01948	51.235	51.335
Peru (new Sol)	.2948	.2951	3.3925	3.3890
Philippines (Peso)	.02561	.02567	39.050	38.950
Poland (Zloty)	.2521	.2551	3.9670	3.9200
Portugal (Escudo)	.005454	.005433	183.34	184.05
Russia (Ruble) (a)	.04369	.04369	22.890	22.890
Saudi Arabia (Riyal)	.2666	.2666	3.7506	3.7510
Singapore (Dollar)	.5771	.5788	1.7328	1.7277
Slovak Rep. (Koruna)	.02499	.02489	40.010	40.176
South Africa (Rand)	.1602	.1604	6.2430	6.2350
South Korea (Won)	.0008168	.0008200	1224.35	1219.50
Spain (Peseta)	.006572	.006547	152.16	152.75
Sweden (Krona)	.1213	.1211	8.2440	8.2583
Switzerland (Franc)	.6866	.6839	1.4565	1.4623
1-month forward	.6888	.6862	1.4517	1.4573
3-months forward	.6929	.6902	1.4431	1.4489
6-months forward	.6996	.6838	1.4293	1.4624
Taiwan (Dollar)	.03023	.03030	33.075	33.000
Thailand (Baht)	.02664	.02677	37.535	37.350
Turkey (Lira)	.00000281	.00000281	356480.00	356380.00
United Arab (Dirham)	.2700	.2700	3.7040	3.7040
Uruguay (New Peso) ..				
Financial	.09095	.09095	10.995	10.995
Venezuela (Bolivar) ...	.001736	.001738	576.00	575.25
SDR	1.3592	1.3658	.7357	.7322
Euro	1.0935	1.0893	.9145	.9180

Special Drawing Rights (SDR) are based on exchange rates for the U.S., German, British, French, and Japanese currencies. Source: International Monetary Fund.
a-Russian Central Bank rate. Trading band lowered on 8/17/98. b-Government rate.
The Wall Street Journal daily foreign exchange data from 1996 forward may be purchased through the Readers' Reference Service (413) 592-3600.

FIGURE 25.5 Quotations for Foreign Exchange

Source: Reprinted by permission of *The Wall Street Journal,* Dow Jones & Company, Inc., March 3, 1999, p. C17. All rights reserved worldwide.

Markets for foreign currency futures attract both hedgers and speculators. Hedgers wish to reduce or eliminate the risk associated with planned future transfers of funds from one country to another.

An Example

For example, an American importer might know on March 2, 1999, that he or she will have to make a payment of 50 million yen to a Japanese exporter in June 1999. Figure 25.5 shows that the current exchange rate is $.008317 per yen (or 120.23 yen per dollar), so the anticipated dollar size of the payment is $415,850 (= $.008317 × 50,000,000). The risk the importer faces by simply waiting until June to make this payment is that the exchange rate will change in an unfavorable manner—perhaps rising to $.01 per yen, in which case the dollar cost to the importer will have risen to $500,000 (= $.01 × 50,000,000). The importer can hedge this risk by purchasing four (= 50,000,000/12,500,000) June futures contracts for yen. Figure 25.1 indicates that the settlement price on March 2, 1999, for these contracts was $.008424, meaning that the dollar cost of one contract is $421,200 (= $.008424 × 50,000,000). Thus, the importer can remove the risk of the yen's appreciating by more than $.000107 (= $.008424 − $.008317) against the dollar before the payment date by purchasing the four yen futures contracts.

Speculators are attracted to the foreign currency futures market when they believe that the current price of the futures contract is substantially different from what they expect the spot rate to be on the delivery date. For example, a speculator might believe that the price of the June futures contract for Japanese yen is too high. Perhaps a speculator might believe that when June comes around, the exchange rate will be $.008 per yen (or, equivalently, 125 yen per dollar). By selling (that is, short selling) a June futures contract for yen, the speculator is selling yen for $.008424, the settlement price on March 2, 1999. When delivery has to be made, the speculator believes that yen can be bought on the spot market for $.008, thereby profiting on the difference between the selling and buying prices.[14] Specifically, the speculator expects to make a profit of $5,300 [= ($.008424 − $.008) × 12,500,000] per futures contract.

25.8.2 INTEREST RATE FUTURES

Futures involving fixed-income securities are often referred to as interest rate futures because their prices are influenced by the current and forecast interest rates. More specifically, their pricing is related to the term structure of interest rates, which in turn is related to the concept of forward rates.[15] Like other futures contracts, they can be used for either speculation or hedging, in this case on the movement of interest rates. For example, a firm that forecasts it will need to borrow money in six months could simply wait until six months have passed and then borrow in the marketplace. The risk of doing this, however, is that interest rates might have increased by then, resulting in the firm having to pay a higher interest rate. The firm hedges this risk by shorting an interest rate futures contract. In essence, the firm reaches an agreement with a lender on the terms of a loan that will be executed in six months.

An Example

Just how the pricing of interest rate futures is related to the concept of forward rates can be illustrated with an example. Consider the futures market for Treasury bonds, which is the most popular long-term interest rate futures contract in the United States. As Figure 25.1 indicates, on March 2, 1999, any seller of a futures contract calling for delivery in June 1999 of a $100,000 face-value Treasury bond would have received a settlement price of 120-19, meaning $120\frac{19}{32}$ of par, or $120,593.75, from the purchaser.[16] However, the actual amount that the seller would receive equals the settlement price times a *conversion factor,* plus accrued interest. The conversion factor varies depending on which Treasury bond is delivered by the purchaser to satisfy the contract because the contract calls for delivery of a Treasury bond that either (1) if not callable, has a maturity of at least 15 years from December 1 or (2) if callable, has a first call date of at least 15 years after December 1.[17] The conversion factor is the proportion of par the delivered Treasury bond would be selling for on the first day of the delivery month if it had a yield-to-maturity of 8%. Thus, deliverable bonds with coupons less than 8% have a conversion factor less than 1 (because they sell at a discount), and those with coupons greater than 8% have conversion factors greater than 1 (because they sell at a premium).

As an example, a noncallable 7% coupon Treasury bond that matures 20 years after the delivery month would sell for $90.10 per $100 of par value (= $20.83 + $69.27 = the present value of the $100 par value of the bond plus the present value of a stream of 40 semiannual coupon interest payments of $3.50 each). Thus, the conversion value for this bond is .9010 (= $90.10/$100). If there is no accrued interest on this bond on the delivery date, then the purchaser of the futures would pay $108,654.97 (= $120,593.75 × .9010) to the seller for this Treasury bond on the June delivery date. This price corresponds with a 6.33% yield-to-maturity. If the market yield on this bond on the delivery date is greater than 6.33%, then the seller of the futures will make a profit because his or her purchase price is less than the spot price of the bond. If the seller has to pay $100,000 to buy the 7% bond in the market on the delivery date because of a rise in interest rates, then the seller profits by $8,654.94 (= $108,654.94 − $100,000) from the futures contract. In turn, this profit offsets the higher interest the seller will incur in borrowing the needed funds at that time in the spot market.

As with commodity futures, neither the buyers nor the sellers of such contracts must maintain their positions until the delivery date. Reversing trades can be made at any time, and relatively few contracts result in actual delivery.

Actively traded interest rate futures involve underlying securities ranging from short-term (such as 90-day Treasury bills) to intermediate-term (such as 10-year Treasury notes) to long-term (such as the 20-year Treasury bonds just described). Prices are generally stated in terms of percentages of par values for the corresponding securities. Yields-to-maturity (or discounts) associated with the settlement prices are also given.

25.8.3 MARKET INDEX FUTURES

Figure 25.1 shows a set of quotations for futures contracts on the S&P 500 market index. This contract involves the payment of *cash* on the delivery date of an amount equal to a *multiplier* times the difference between the value of the index at the close of the last trading day of the contract and the purchase price of the futures contract. If the index is above the futures price, those with short positions pay those with long positions. If the index is below the futures price, those with long positions pay those with short positions.

In practice, a clearinghouse is used, and all contracts are marked to market every day. The delivery day differs from other days in only one respect; all open positions are marked to market for the last time and then closed.

Cash settlement provides results similar to those associated with the delivery of all the securities in the index. It avoids the effort and transaction costs associated with (1) the purchase of securities by people who have taken short futures positions; (2) the delivery of these securities to people who have taken long futures positions; and (3) the subsequent sale of the securities by those who receive them.

Major Contracts

Several U.S. stock market index futures were available in 1999, with the most popular one in terms of both trading volume and open interest being the S&P 500. This contract is traded on the Chicago Mercantile Exchange (CME). Also of note are futures contracts on the DJIA, which is traded on the Chicago Board of Trade.

For the S&P 500, the multiplier is $250 and for the DJIA it is $10. Thus, the purchase of an S&P 500 contract when the settlement price is 1,200 would cost $300,000 (= $250 × 1,200). The subsequent sale of this contract when the settlement price is 1,220 would result in proceeds of $305,000 (= $250 × 1,220) and a profit of $5,000 (= $305,000 − $300,000). Similarly, if the settlement price is at 9,500, a DJIA futures contract would cost $95,000 (= $10 × 9,500). If the investor later executed a reversing trade with the settlement price at 9,600, the resulting profit would be $1,000 [= $10 × (9,600 − 9,500)].

Trading Volume

The volume of trading in futures contracts is large. Its relative size can be assessed by multiplying the number of contracts by the total dollar value represented by one contract. As shown in Figure 25.1, the estimated volume on March 2, 1999, for S&P 500 futures was 120,067 contracts. At a value of $1,229.50 for the lowest-priced S&P 500 contract, the total dollar value of all S&P 500 contracts is in excess of $36 billion (= 120,067 × 1,229.50 × $250). In comparison, the average daily dollar value of all trades of shares on the NYSE during 1998 was approximately $29 billion per day—a figure that is much lower than the dollar size of the S&P futures on March 2, 1999. This situation is not unusual. On many days the dollar value involved in trades of S&P 500 futures exceeds that of all trades of individual stocks.

Hedging

What accounts for the popularity of market index futures in general and the S&P 500 in particular? Simply stated, they provide relatively inexpensive and highly liquid positions similar to diversified stock portfolios.

For example, instead of purchasing these 500 stocks in anticipation of a market advance, one can invest an equivalent amount of money in Treasury bills and take a long position in S&P 500 futures. Alternatively, instead of trying to take short positions in these 500 stocks in anticipation of a market decline, one can take a short position in S&P these 500 futures using Treasury bills as margin.

Market index futures can also be used by broker–dealers to hedge the market risk associated with the temporary positions they often take in the course of their business.[18] This hedging ultimately benefits investors by providing them with greater liquidity than they would have otherwise.

For example, consider an investor who wants to sell a large block of stock. A broker–dealer might agree to purchase the stock immediately at an agreed-on price and then spend time "lining up" buyers. In the interim, however, economic news might cause the market to fall, and with it the price of the stock. The broker–dealer would experience a loss because the broker–dealer owns the stock during the period between purchasing it from the investor and lining up the buyers. One traditional way broker–dealers protect themselves (at least partially) from this risk is by paying the investor a relatively low price for the stock. However, the broker–dealer can now hedge this risk (at least partially) by short selling S&P 500 futures when the stock is bought from the investor and later reversing this position when the buyers are found. Because of competition among broker–dealers, the availability of S&P 500 futures leads them to provide higher bid prices and lower asked prices. Because of this reduced bid–ask spread, the existence of S&P 500 futures has the effect of providing the associated spot market for stocks with greater liquidity.

It should be pointed out that the use of S&P 500 futures (or any index futures) in such situations does not remove all risk from the position of the broker–dealer. All it removes is market risk because these futures contracts involve a broad market index, not an individual stock. Thus, it is possible for the broker–dealer to experience a loss even if an appropriate position has been taken in futures. Specifically, the individual stock with which the broker–dealer is involved may move up or down in price while the S&P 500 is stable, or the S&P 500 may move up or down while the individual stock is stable. In either case, the broker–dealer who has hedged with S&P 500 futures may still experience a loss. The possibility of this happening is substantial when the broker–dealer has little diversification, with the greatest possibility associated with a one-stock portfolio.

Index Arbitrage

When stock index futures were first proposed, a number of people predicted that at long last there would be an indicator of investors' expectations about the future course of the stock market. It was said that the market price of such a futures contract would indicate the consensus opinion of investors concerning the future level of the associated index. In times of optimism, the futures price might be much higher than the current level of the market, whereas in times of pessimism, the futures price might be much lower.

arbitrageurs

Such predictions were quite off the mark because the price of a futures contract on an asset will not diverge by more than the cost of carry from the spot price of the asset. Should a relatively large divergence occur, clever investors known as **arbitrageurs** can be expected to make trades designed to capture riskless (that is, "arbitrage") profits.

What effect does the presence of these arbitrageurs have on the pricing of stock index futures? Their actions force the price of a stock index futures contract to stay close to an "appropriate" relationship with the current level of the associated index. To find out just what is meant by appropriate, consider a hypothetical example. Today is a day in June when the S&P 500 is at 1,000 and a December S&P 500 futures contract is selling for $1,100. The following investment strategies will be compared:

1. Purchase the stocks in the S&P 500, hold them until December, and then sell them on the delivery date of the December S&P 500 contract.
2. Purchase a December S&P 500 futures contract along with Treasury bills that mature in December. Hold them until the delivery date of the futures contract in December.

Strategy 1 would cost $1,000 (in "index terms") at the outset. In return, it would provide the investor with (1) an amount of money equal to the value of the S&P 500 on the delivery date and (2) dividends on those stocks that went *ex dividend* before the delivery date. By denoting the level the S&P 500 will have on the delivery date by P_d and assuming that the dividend yield during the six-month time period from June to December is 3%, the investor following strategy 1 will receive in December a net cash inflow equal to $P_d + $30 [that is, $P_d + (.03 \times $1,000)].[19]

Assume that $1,000 is invested in Treasury bills in strategy 2. Because Treasury bills can be used as margin on futures, the total cost of strategy 2 is $1,000, which is the same as the cost of strategy 1. In return, strategy 2 would provide the investor with (1) an amount of money equal to the difference between the value of the S&P 500 and $1,100 on the delivery date and (2) the face value of the Treasury bills on the delivery date. By assuming the six-month yield on the Treasury bills is 5%, the investor following strategy 2 will receive in December a net cash inflow equal to $P_d - $50 [that is, $(P_d - $1,100) + (1.05 \times $1,000)].

By design, the two strategies require the same initial outlay of $1,000. Furthermore, both strategies are subject to precisely the same uncertainty: the unknown level of the S&P 500 on the future delivery date, P_d. However, the December net cash inflows are

index arbitrage

not equal, indicating that an opportunity exists for **index arbitrage.**[20]

In this example, an investor who engages in index arbitrage would go "long" strategy 1 and "short" strategy 2. Why? Because strategy 1 has a higher payoff than strategy 2 (note that $P_d + $30 > P_d - $50). Going long strategy 1 means the investor does exactly what was indicated earlier—purchase the stocks in the S&P 500 and hold them until the December delivery date. Going short strategy 2 means doing exactly the opposite of what was indicated earlier. Specifically, the investor is to short (that is, sell) a December S&P 500 futures contract and sell Treasury bills that mature in December. (It is assumed that the investor has these in his or her current portfolio.) The net cash outflow of going long strategy 1 and short strategy 2 is zero; $1,000 is spent buying the stocks in going long strategy 1, which is obtained by selling $1,000 worth of December Treasury bills when the investor goes short strategy 2. The margin necessary for being short the futures contract is met by having purchased the underlying stocks. Thus, no additional cash needs to be committed to engage in index arbitrage; the investor simply must own Treasury bills that mature in December.

Next, consider the investor's position on the delivery date in December. First of all, the investor "bought" the individual stocks in the S&P 500 at $1,000 and "sold" them at $1,100 by being short the S&P 500 futures contract. Thus, the investor has made $100 by being long the individual stocks and short the futures on the index. Second, the investor will have received dividends totaling $30 (= .03 × $1,000) from owning the stocks from June to December. Third, the investor will have given up $50 (= .05 × $1,000) in interest that would have been earned on the December Treasury bills. This interest is forgone because the investor sold $1,000 of these Treasury bills in June to get the requisite cash to buy the individual stocks. Overall, the investor has increased the dollar return that would have been made on the Treasury bills by $80 (= $100 + $30 − $50). Furthermore, this increase is certain, meaning that it will be received regardless of what happens to the level of the S&P 500. Thus, by going long strategy 1 and short strategy 2 the investor will not have increased the risk of his or her portfolio but will have increased the dollar return.

Earlier it was mentioned that an investor going long strategy 1 would receive cash of P_d + $30 in December, whereas an investor going long strategy 2 would receive cash of P_d − $50. It can now be seen that going long strategy 1 and short strategy 2 provides a net dollar return of $80 [that is, ($P_d$ + $30) − ($P_d$ − $50)], just as was shown in the previous paragraph. However, if enough investors do this, the opportunity for making the $80 profit will disappear because (1) going long will push the prices of the individual stocks up, thereby raising the current level of the S&P 500 from 1,000, and (2) going short the S&P 500 futures will push the price of the futures down from 1,100. These two adjustments will continue until it is no longer profitable to go long strategy 1 and short strategy 2.

What if the price of the S&P 500 December futures contract is $900 instead of $1,100? The net cash inflow from being long strategy 1 is still equal to P_d + $30. However, the net cash inflow from being long strategy 2 will be different. In particular, purchasing Treasury bills and the futures contract will provide the investor with P_d + $150 [that is, ($P_d$ − $900) + (1.05 × $1,000)] on the delivery date. Because these two inflows are not equal, again there is an opportunity for index arbitrage. However, it would involve the investor going short strategy 1 and long strategy 2. Why? Because strategy 1 has a lower payoff than strategy 2 (note that P_d + $30 < P_d + $150). By making these transactions, the investor will, without risk, earn $120 [that is, ($P_d$ + $150) − ($P_d$ + $30)]. Furthermore, being short the individual stocks and long the futures will push the current level of the S&P 500 down from 1,000 and the price of the futures up from 900.

In equilibrium, because these two strategies cost the same to implement, prices will adjust so that their net cash inflows are equal. Letting y denote the dividend yield on the stocks in the index, P_f the current price of the futures contract on the index, and P_s the current spot price of the index (that is, P_s denotes the current level of the index), the net cash inflow from strategy 1 is

$$P_d + yP_s$$

Letting R denote the interest rate on Treasury bills, the net cash inflow from strategy 2 is

$$(P_d - P_f) + [(1 + R) \times P_s]$$

Setting these two inflows equal to each other results in

$$P_d + yP_s = (P_d - P_f) + [(1 + R) \times P_s] \tag{25.5}$$

Simplifying this equation results in

$$P_f - P_s = (R - y)P_s \tag{25.6}$$

or

$$P_f = P_s + RP_s - yP_s \qquad (25.7)$$

Equation (25.6) indicates that the difference between the price of the futures contract and the current level of the index should depend only on (1) the current level of the index P_s and (2) the difference between the interest rate on Treasury bills and the dividend yield on the index $R - y$. As the delivery date nears, the difference between the interest rate and the dividend yield diminishes, converging to zero on the delivery date. Hence the futures price P_f should converge to the current spot price P_s.

Equation (25.7) shows that index futures are priced according to the cost of carry model given earlier in Equation (25.4), where the costs of ownership C are zero. Here the interest forgone by ownership I is equal to RP_s, whereas the benefit of ownership B is the dividend yield yP_s. Hence the cost of carry is

$$RP_s - yP_s \qquad (25.8)$$

which will be positive as long as the riskfree interest rate R is greater than the dividend yield on the index y—a situation that exists nearly all the time.

In the example the interest rate was 5%, the dividend yield was 3%, and the current level of the S&P 500 was 1,000. Therefore, the difference between the S&P 500 December futures contract and the current level of the S&P 500 should be 20 [= (.05 − .03) × 1,000]. Equivalently, the equilibrium price of the futures contract when the S&P 500 is 1,000 would be 1,020 because the cost of carry is 20. Note that when three of the six months have passed, the interest rate and the dividend yield will be about 2.5% (= 5%/2) and 1.5% (= 3%/2), respectively. Thus, the difference should be about 10 [= (.025 − .015) × 1,000], assuming that the S&P 500 is still at 1,000 at that time.

In practice, the situation is not this simple for a number of reasons. Positions in futures, stocks, and Treasury bills involve transaction costs.[21] Consequently, arbitrage will not take place unless the difference diverges far enough from the amount shown in Equation (25.6) to warrant incurring such costs. The futures price, and hence the difference, can be expected to move within a band around the "theoretical value," with the width of the band determined by the costs of those who engage in transactions most efficiently.

To add to the complexity, both the dividend yield and the relevant interest rate on Treasury bills are subject to some uncertainty. Neither the dividends to be declared nor their timing can be specified completely in advance. Furthermore, because futures positions must be marked to market daily, the amount of cash required for strategy 2 may have to be varied by means of additional borrowing (if short this strategy) or lending (if long this strategy). Also, on occasion market prices may be reported with a substantial time lag, making the current level and the futures price of the index seem out of line when they actually are not. (An extreme example of this situation occurred during the market crash of October 1987.) Thus, an investor may enter into the transactions necessary for index arbitrage when actual prices are in equilibrium, thereby incurring useless transaction costs. Nevertheless, index arbitrage is still actively pursued, most notably by brokerage firms, as shown in Figure 25.6.

Stock index futures are also used extensively by other professional money managers. As a result, prices of such contracts are likely to track their underlying indices closely, taking into account both dividends and current interest rates.[22] It is unlikely that a private investor will be able to exploit "mispricing" of such a contract by engaging in index arbitrage. Nevertheless, stock index futures can provide inexpensive ways to take positions in the stock market or to hedge portions of the risk associated with other positions. Furthermore, their use can lower transaction costs by reducing the size

PROGRAM TRADING

NEW YORK — Program trading for the week ended Feb. 26 accounted for 21%, or an average 159.6 million daily shares, of New York Stock Exchange volume.

Brokerage firms executed an additional 51 million daily shares of program trading away from the Big Board, mostly on foreign markets. Program trading is the simultaneous purchase or sale of at least 15 different stocks with a total value of $1 million or more.

Of the program total on the Big Board, 17.2% involved stock-index arbitrage, unchanged from the prior week. In this strategy, traders dart between stocks and stock-index options and futures to capture fleeting price differences.

About 63.4% of program trading was executed by firms for their customers, while 31.5% was done for their own accounts, or principal trading. An additional 5.1% was designated as customer facilitation, in which firms use principal positions to facilitate customer trades.

The report includes a special profile of trading whenever the Dow Jones Industrial Average rises or falls more than 180 points from its previous close during any one-hour period. The exchange implemented a new rule Feb. 16 that increased the trading collar to 180 points from 50 points. The trigger levels will be revised each quarter as 2% of the exchange average. There were no such periods during the week.

Of the five most-active firms, BNP Securities, Morgan Stanley Dean Witter, Deutsche Bank Securities and Bear Stearns executed all or most of their program activity for customers as agent, while Credit Suisse First Boston executed most of its program activity as principal for its own accounts.

NYSE PROGRAM TRADING
Volume (in millions of shares) for the week ended February 26, 1999

Top 15 Firms	Index Arbitrage	Derivative-Related*	Other Strategies	Total
BNP Securities	....	....	93.2	93.2
Morgan Stanley Dean Wttr	2.8	0.3	82.1	85.2
CS First Boston	4.3	....	73.3	77.6
Deutsche Bank Securities	19.4	....	48.6	68.0
Bear Stearns	....	....	66.6	66.6
CIBC Wood Gundy	21.5	....	24.4	45.9
Salomon Smith Barney	0.1	....	44.5	44.6
TLW Securities LLC	3.6	2.0	32.0	37.6
RBC Dominion	32.6	....	4.6	37.2
Lehman Brothers	....	4.5	32.1	36.6
W&D Securities	....	....	34.2	34.2
Nomura Securities	21.5	....	4.3	25.8
Merrill Lynch	9.6	....	12.2	21.8
Goldman Sachs	....	....	21.0	21.0
Interactive Brokers	....	....	18.4	18.4
OVERALL TOTAL	137.6	6.8	653.8	798.2

*Other derivative-related strategies besides index arbitrage
Source: New York Stock Exchange

FIGURE 25.6 Index Arbitrage as a Form of Program Trading

Source: Reprinted by permission of *The Wall Street Journal,* Dow Jones & Company, Inc., March 5, 1999, p. C5. All rights reserved worldwide.

of the bid–ask spread in individual securities, thereby benefiting investors who may never take direct positions in futures contracts.

25.9 Futures versus Options

People occasionally make the mistake of confusing a futures contract with an options contract.[23] With an options contract there is the possibility that both parties involved will have nothing to do at the end of the life of the contract. In particular, if the option is out of the money on the expiration date, then the options contract will be worthless and can be thrown away. However, with a futures contract, both parties must do something at the end of the life of the contract. They are obligated to complete the transaction either by a reversing trade or by actual delivery.

Figure 25.7 contrasts the payoffs for the buyer and seller of a call option with the payoffs for the buyer and seller of a futures contract. These payoffs are shown at the last possible moment—the expiration date for the option and the delivery date for the futures contract.

As shown in Figure 25.7(a), no matter what the price of the underlying stock, an option buyer cannot lose and an option seller cannot gain on the expiration date. Op-

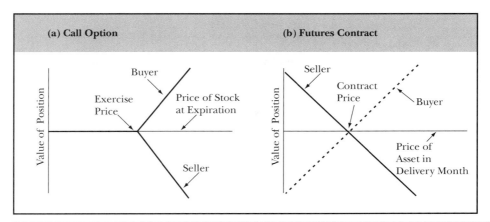

FIGURE 25.7 Terminal Values of Positions in Calls and Futures

tion buyers compensate sellers for putting sellers in this position by paying them a premium when the contract is signed.

The situation is quite different with a futures contract. As shown in Figure 25.7(b), the buyer may gain or lose, depending on the price of the asset in the delivery month. Whatever the buyer gains or loses, an exactly offsetting loss or gain will be registered by the seller. The higher the contract price (that is, the price of the futures contract when the buyer purchased it from the seller), the greater the likelihood that the buyer will lose and the seller will gain. The lower the contract price, the greater the likelihood that the seller will lose and the buyer will gain.

Summary

1. A futures contract involves the delivery of a specific type of asset at a specific location at a given future date.
2. People who buy and sell futures can be classified as either hedgers or speculators. Hedgers transact in futures primarily to reduce risk because they either produce or use the asset in their ordinary course of business. Speculators transact in futures in pursuit of relatively short-term profits.
3. Futures are bought and sold on organized exchanges. Futures are standardized in terms of the type of asset, time of delivery, and place of delivery.
4. Each futures exchange has an associated clearinghouse that becomes the "seller's buyer" and the "buyer's seller" as soon as the trade is concluded.
5. A futures investor is required to deposit initial margin in order to guarantee fulfillment of his or her obligations.
6. A futures investor's account is marked to market daily, with the equity in the investor's account adjusted to reflect the change in the futures contract's settlement price.
7. A futures investor must maintain his or her account's equity equal to or greater than a certain percentage of the amount deposited as initial margin. If this requirement is not met, the investor will be requested to deposit variation margin in the account.
8. The basis for futures is the difference between the current spot price of the asset and the corresponding futures price.

9. There are three possible relationships between the current futures price and the expected spot price: the expectations hypothesis (futures price equal to expected spot price), normal backwardation (futures price less than expected spot price), and normal contango (futures price greater than expected spot price).

10. The current futures price should equal the current spot price plus the cost of carry. The cost of carry equals (1) the amount of interest that the owner forgoes by holding onto the asset, less (2) the benefits of owning the asset, plus (3) the costs of owning the asset.

11. If the price of a futures contract becomes too far removed from the current spot price of the asset plus the cost of carry, arbitrageurs enter into transactions that generate riskless profits from the perceived price discrepancy. Their actions cause prices to adjust until the opportunity to make such profits disappears.

Questions and Problems

1. Distinguish between a speculator and a hedger. Give an example of a short hedger and a long hedger.

2. How do organized futures exchanges ensure that obligations incurred as various parties enter into futures contracts are ultimately satisfied?

3. Zack Wheat has just bought four September 5,000-bushel corn futures contracts at $1.75 per bushel. The initial margin requirement is 3%. The maintenance margin requirement is 80% of the initial margin requirement.
   a. How many dollars in initial margin must Zack put up?
   b. If the September price of corn rises to $1.85, how much equity is in Zack's commodity account?
   c. If the September price of corn falls to $1.70, how much equity is in Zack's commodity account? Will Zack receive a margin call?

4. How does a futures contract differ from a forward contract?

5. Do exchange-imposed price limits protect futures traders from losses that would result in the absence of such limits? Explain.

6. Consider a futures contract on mangoes that calls for the delivery of 2,000 pounds of the fruit three months from now. The spot price of mangoes is $2 per pound. The three-month riskfree rate is 2%. It costs $.10 per pound to store mangoes for three months. What should be the price of this futures contract?

7. Byrd Lynn owns a famous Renoir painting that has a current market value of $5,000,000. It costs Byrd $200,000 annually to insure the painting, payable at the start of the year. Byrd is able to loan the painting to a local art gallery for $300,000 per year, paid at the end of the year. Byrd is considering selling the painting under a futures contract arrangement that calls for delivery one year from today. If the one-year riskfree rate is 5%, what is the fair value of the futures contract?

8. Tuck Turner is planning a trip to Germany in six months, where Tuck intends to purchase a BMW for 80,000 German marks (DM). Using a recent copy of *The Wall Street Journal,* calculate how much the purchase would cost in U.S. dollars at the current exchange rate. Given the recent settlement price of a six-month DM futures contract, how much would Tuck have to pay to hedge the cost of the BMW purchase?

9. Estel Crabtree believes that the spread between long-term interest rates and short-term interest rates will narrow in the next few months but does not know in which direction interest rates will move. What financial futures position would permit Estel to profit from this forecast if it is correct?

10. Swats Swacina, a futures investor who has lost considerable sums in futures investments, said, "Even though I don't directly borrow to invest in futures, the performance of my investments acts as if I were highly leveraged." Is Swats correct? Why?

11. Sleeper Sullivan bought 10 December S&P 500 index futures contracts at 310. If the index rises to 318, what is Sleeper's dollar profit?

12. Why does hedging a common stock portfolio using stock index futures work best if the portfolio being hedged is similar to the underlying stock index of the futures contract?

13. Assume that a stock market index currently has a value of 200. The dividend yield on the underlying stocks in the index is expected to be 4% during the next six months. New-issue six-month Treasury bills now sell for a six-month yield of 6%.
    a. What is the theoretical value of a six-month futures contract on the index?
    b. What potential problems are inherent in this calculation?

14. In each of the following situations, discuss how Hippo Vaughn might use stock index futures to protect a well-diversified stock portfolio:
    a. Hippo expects to receive a sizable bonus check next month and would like to invest in stocks, believing that current stock market prices are extremely attractive (but realizing they may not remain so for long).
    b. Hippo expects the stock market to decline dramatically very soon and realizes that selling a stock portfolio quickly would result in significant transaction costs.
    c. Hippo has a large, unrealized gain and for tax purposes would like to defer the gain until the next tax year, which is several weeks away.

15. Does the fair value of a stock index futures contract depend on investors' expectations about the future value of the underlying stock index? Why?

Endnotes

1. The term *commodity futures* is often used to refer to futures on agricultural goods and natural resources. The term *financial futures* is typically used in reference to futures on financial instruments such as Treasury bonds, foreign currencies, and stock market indices.

2. For a description of the terms for many exchange-traded futures contracts, see the *Commodity Trading Manual* (Chicago Board of Trade, 1989); and Malcolm J. Robertson, *Directory of World Futures and Options* (Upper Saddle River, NJ: Prentice Hall, 1990). These two books also contain descriptions of various futures exchanges.

3. Since Black Monday and Terrible Tuesday (October 19 and 20, 1987), a number of people have advocated an increase in the size of the initial margin deposit for certain futures contracts (particularly stock index futures, which are discussed later). The levels of initial and maintenance margins are set by each exchange, and brokers are allowed to set them higher. Typically, higher amounts of margin are required on futures contracts that have greater price volatility because the clearinghouse faces larger potential losses on such contracts.

4. Actually, only brokerage firms belong to a clearinghouse, and it is *their* accounts that are settled by the clearinghouse at the end of every day. Each brokerage firm acts in turn as a clearinghouse for its own clients. For more information on clearing procedures, see Chapter 6 of the *Commodity Trading Manual*.

5. Interestingly, the volatility of the futures price seems to increase as the contract approaches its delivery date. This phenomenon is known as the "Samuelson hypothesis"; see Paul A. Samuelson, "Proof That Properly Anticipated Prices Fluctuate Randomly," *Industrial Management Review,* 6, no. 2 (Spring 1965): 41–49. Also see Hendrik Bessembinder, Jay F. Coughenour, Paul J. Seguin, and Margaret Monroe Smoller, "Is There a Term Structure of Futures Volatilities? Reevaluating the Samuelson Hypothesis," *Journal of Derivatives,* 4, no. 2 (Winter 1996): 45–58.

6. Merrill Lynch, Pierce, Fenner & Smith, Inc., *Speculating on Inflation: Futures Trading in Interest Rates, Foreign Currencies and Precious Metals,* July 1979.

7. For more on the relationship between spot and futures prices as reflected in the basis, see the *Commodity Trading Manual,* Chapter 8. It should be noted that sometimes basis is defined as the futures price less the current spot price—the reverse of Equation (25.1).

8. The futures contracts consisted of agricultural goods and natural resources. See Zvi Bodie and Victor Rosansky, "Risk and Return in Commodity Futures," *Financial Analysts Journal,* 36, no. 3 (May/June 1980): 27–39. Similar conclusions were reached by Cheng F. Lee, Raymond M. Leuthold, and Jean E. Cordier, "The Stock Market and the Commodity Futures Market: Diversification and Arbitrage Potential," *Financial Analysts Journal,* 41, no. 4 (July/August 1985): 53–60.

9. The first two points do not mean that the current spot price will not change as time passes. For futures involving a seasonal commodity (such as wheat), the spot price will sometimes be greater than and sometimes be less than the futures price during the life of

the contract. Furthermore, sometimes a futures contract involving a more distant delivery date will sell for more than one with a nearer delivery date, whereas at other times it will sell for less.

10. J. M. Keynes, *Treatise on Money*, vol. 2 (London: Macmillan, 1930), 142–144.

11. There are other hypotheses regarding the relationship between futures prices and expected spot prices. See, for example, Paul H. Cootner, "Speculation and Hedging," Stanford University, *Food Research Institute Studies*, Supplement, 1967.

12. This section and the next one borrow from Kenneth R. French, "Pricing Financial Futures Contracts: An Introduction," *Journal of Applied Corporate Finance*, 1, no. 4 (Winter 1989): 59–66. It ignores the apparently minor effect that daily marking to market has on the futures price that is stated in futures contracts (see page 65 and footnotes 5 and 6 in French's paper).

13. The prices of foreign currency forward and futures contracts seem similar. See Bradford Cornell and Marc Reinganum, "Forward and Futures Prices: Evidence from the Foreign Exchange Market," *Journal of Finance*, 36, no. 5 (December 1981): 1035–1045. Their findings are challenged by Michael A. Polakoff and Paul C. Grier, "A Comparison of Foreign Exchange Forward and Futures Prices," *Journal of Banking and Finance*, 15, no. 6 (December 1991): 1057–1079, but they are supported by Carolyn W. Chang and Jack S. K. Chang, "Forward and Futures Prices: Evidence from the Foreign Exchange Markets," *Journal of Finance*, 45, no. 4 (September 1990): 1333–1336. See Kenneth R. French, "A Comparison of Futures and Forward Prices," *Journal of Financial Economics*, 12, no. 3 (November 1983): 311–342 for a discussion of the difficulties of testing whether the prices of forward and futures contracts are similar.

14. Actually the typical speculator will plan to realize this profit by entering a reversing trade instead of buying yen on the spot market and then making delivery. Similarly, the previously mentioned hedging importer will typically plan to enter a reversing trade.

15. See Chapter 20 for a discussion of term structure and forward rates.

16. Delivery on Treasury bond futures can take place on any business day in the delivery month even though trading ceases when there are seven business days left in the month.

17. For this and certain other interest-rate futures contracts there is flexibility in just what the seller has to deliver, known as the *quality option*. The short position in the contract usually decides on the *cheapest-to-deliver* Treasury bond and delivers it to the long position. Sometimes there is flexibility regarding when during a business day an intention to deliver must be announced, known as the *wild card option*.

18. Similarly, interest rate futures are often used by financial institutions to hedge interest rate risk to which they may be exposed—that is, when a large movement in interest rates would cause a large loss, these institutions seek protection by either buying or selling interest rate futures.

19. The 3% dividend yield is actually the accumulated December value of the dividends divided by the purchase price of the stocks. Hence the dividends might be received in three months and amount to 2.93% of the purchase price of the index. Putting them in a risk-free asset that returns 2.47% for the last three months results in a yield of 3%, or $3, in December.

20. Index arbitrage is one of the major forms of program trading; another form is known as portfolio insurance. For a discussion and example of how futures can be used to procure portfolio insurance, see Stephen R. King and Eli M. Remolona, "The Pricing and Hedging of Market Index Deposits," *Federal Reserve Bank of New York Quarterly Review*, 12, no. 2 (Summer 1987): 9–20; or Thomas J. O'Brien, *How Option Replicating Portfolio Insurance Works: Expanded Details*, Monograph Series in Finance and Economics #1988-4 (New York University Salomon Center, Leonard N. Stern School of Business, 1988).

21. People involved in index arbitrage must quickly make a large number of transactions in individual stocks. In order to do this, they often have their computers send their orders through the SuperDOT system (discussed in Chapter 3). For a discussion of some of the complications involved in successfully executing index arbitrage strategies, see David M. Modest, "On the Pricing of Stock Index Futures," *Journal of Portfolio Management*, 10, no. 4 (Summer 1984): 51–57.

22. The near-simultaneous quarterly expiration of (1) options on individual stocks and market indices, (2) futures on market indices, and (3) options on market index futures (see endnote 23) is referred to as the **triple witching hour.** When it occurs, the stock market is allegedly roiled, particularly in the latter part of the day. See Hans R. Stoll and Robert E. Whaley, "Program Trading and Expiration Day Effects," *Financial Analysts Journal*, 43, no. 2 (March/April 1987): 16–28; Arnold Kling, "How the Stock Market Can Learn to Live with Index Futures and Options," *Financial Analysts Journal*, 43, no. 5 (September/October 1987): 33–39; and G. J. Santoni, "Has Programmed Trading Made Stock Prices More Volatile?" *Federal Reserve Bank of St. Louis Review*, 69, no. 5 (May 1987): 18–29.

23. Adding to the confusion is the existence of a contract known as a **futures option,** which is an option that has a futures contract instead of a stock as its underlying asset. The commonly given reason futures options exist when options also exist is because it is easier to make or take delivery of a futures contract on the

asset as required by the futures options contract than to make or take delivery in the asset itself as required by the options contract. In addition, there also may be more timely price information on the deliverable asset for the futures option contract (namely, price information on the futures contract) than on the deliverable asset for the options contract (namely, price information in the spot market). For more on futures options, see Chapter 12 of the *Commodity Trading Manual*. For a computer program that can be used to determine the "true" value of these complex contracts, see Chapter 8 of Stuart M. Turnbull, *Option Valuation* (Holt, Rinehart and Winston of Canada, 1987). The seminal paper on the pricing of futures options is Fischer Black, "The Pricing of Commodity Contracts," *Journal of Financial Economics,* 3, nos. 1/2 (January/March 1976): 167–179.

International Investing

One of the major themes of modern portfolio theory concerns the merits of diversification: In an efficient capital market, sensible investment strategies will include holdings of many different assets. Previous chapters considered traditional domestic securities, such as stocks and bonds, and some less traditional ones, such as options and futures. However, an investor should also consider holding foreign securities to diversify his or her portfolio internationally.[1]

If the world were under one political jurisdiction, with one currency and complete freedom of trade, then "the market portfolio" could be considered to include all securities in the world, each in proportion to its market value. In such a situation, limiting one's investments to securities representing firms located in only one part of the world would likely result in a relatively low rate of return per unit of risk. After all, few people would advocate that Californians own only securities issued by California-based firms. Similarly, in a world without political boundaries, few people would advocate that Americans own only securities issued by American firms.

Unfortunately, there are political boundaries, different currencies, varying disclosure rules and accounting procedures, and restrictions on trade and currency exchange. Such irritants diminish, but do not destroy, the advantages gained from international investment. This chapter discusses international investing, giving consideration to these "irritants" in the process.

26.1 The Total Investable Capital Market Portfolio

Figure 26.1 provides a 1998 year-end estimate of $58.1 trillion for the size of the total investable capital market portfolio in the world, which can be thought of as representing the set of investments that are available to U.S. portfolio managers. Many problems are encountered in the construction of such a portfolio. It is almost impossible to adequately represent *all* security markets because undoubtedly certain classes of assets are omitted (such as foreign real estate) and double counting occurs when some firms own parts of other firms.[2]

The figure indicates that non-U.S. bond and equity markets amount to $28.2 trillion (= $2.4 + $9.0 + $0.7 + $0.9 + $10.4 + $4.8) and constitute almost one-half the value of the entire $58.1 trillion world portfolio (there are six foreign categories—Japan Equity, Other Equity, Emerging Market Equity, Emerging Market Debt, Other Bonds, and Japan Bonds). Also of interest is the observation that fixed-income securities amount to $30.9 trillion (= $11.4 + $0.6 + $0.9 + $2.8 + $10.4 + $4.8) and make up slightly more than one-half of the portfolio's value.[3] About one-half of this total is non-U.S. fixed-income securities. Similarly, about one-half of the $24.8 trillion (= $12.6 + $2.4 + $9.0 + $0.7 + $0.1) equity market consists of non-U.S. stocks.

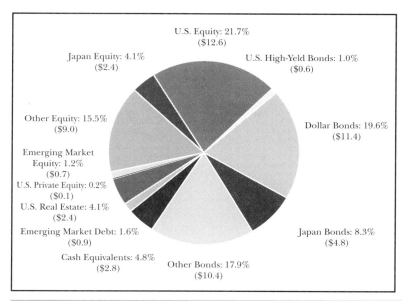

FIGURE 26.1 Total Investable Capital Market Portfolio, Year-End 1998, Preliminary (trillions of U.S. dollars)

Source: Provided by Brinson Partners, Inc. (Chicago, 1999).

A different perspective on the stock market capitalization at the end of April 1999 in the developed markets followed by Morgan Stanley Capital International is provided in columns (2) and (3) of Table 26.1. The largest market for common stocks is the United States, followed by Japan and the United Kingdom. In total, these three countries make up 72.6% of the total market capitalization of the developed stock markets. Notably behind in the fourth and fifth positions are Germany and France. These five countries represent 81.4% of the total. How Morgan Stanley calculates international stock market indices involving these countries is discussed next.

26.1.1 INTERNATIONAL EQUITY INDICES

In most countries, there are indices of overall stock values and of the values of stocks within various industry or economic sectors. Such indices can be used for assessing "market moves" within the country and, more importantly, for comparative performance measurement. Important indices include the Financial Times-Stock Exchange 100 Index (often referred to as FT-SE, or the "Footsie") for the London Stock Exchange; the Nikkei 225 Average for the Tokyo Stock Exchange; and the TSE 300 Composite Index for the Toronto Stock Exchange. As shown in Figure 26.2(a), these and other indices are published daily in *The Wall Street Journal.*[4]

On the international level, the indices produced by Morgan Stanley Capital International are also widely used for such purposes.[5] Each index is based on a value-weighted portfolio of stocks (using total shares outstanding) in a particular country. Nearly all of these stocks can be purchased by foreigners. Values for each of the national indices (plus various industry indices for each country) are given both in the local currency and in U.S. dollars on the basis of exchange rates at the time. The stocks selected for each index are designed to represent about 60% of the aggregate market value of the particular country's equity markets.[6] A listing of the countries with the largest and most mature stock markets is presented in Table 26.1.

TABLE 26.1 World Stock Market Capitalization, April 1999

Market Capitalization

Country (1)	Dollars[a] (billion U.S.) (2)	Percentage (3)
Austria	$ 25.3	.1%
Belgium	120.8	.7
Denmark	61.1	.4
Finland	135.5	.8
France	729.0	4.3
Germany	770.4	4.5
Ireland	37.9	.2
Italy	369.2	2.2
Netherlands	477.1	2.8
Norway	33.8	.2
Portugal	41.4	.2
Spain	233.1	1.4
Sweden	179.7	1.1
Switzerland	557.3	3.3
U.K.	1,801.4	10.6
Total Europe	5,573.0	32.7
Australia	235.7	1.4
Hong Kong	199.1	1.2
Japan	1,830.5	10.8
Malaysia	48.7	.3
New Zealand	16.7	.1
Singapore	70.0	.4
Total Pacific	2,400.7	14.1
Canada	338.3	2.0
U.S.	8707.1	51.2
Total North America	9,045.4	53.1
Total World	$17,019.1	100.0%

[a]Measured in billions of U.S. dollars. Individual percentage figures may not sum to the total due to rounding.

Source: Adapted from *Morgan Stanley Capital International Global Investment Monitor* (April 30, 1999): 3.

The individual country indices are combined into various regional indices. Furthermore, all of these indices are used to compute a "World" index based on 23 countries with developed capital markets (see Table 26.1), an "Emerging Markets" index based on 25 countries, and an "All-Country World" index based on the combined 48 countries. These indices are formed using weights based on market capitalization to produce value-weighted indices. Alternative versions of these indices are also calculated using gross domestic product (GDP) to form weights. Some countries with well-established stock markets but relatively small economies (such as the United Kingdom) have less weight in a GDP-weighted index than in a market capitalization-weighted index compared with countries with large economies but relatively small stock markets (such as Germany).

Morgan Stanley also calculates the "Europe, Australia, Far East" (EAFE) index, which is widely used by U.S. investors as a benchmark when evaluating the performance of international portfolio managers. The index excludes the United States and Canada and is currently based on the stock performance in the remaining 21 countries listed in Table 26.1. Several of the Morgan Stanley individual country indices are published daily in *The Wall Street Journal,* as shown in Figure 26.2(b), with the World and EAFE indices at the bottom.

26.1.2 EMERGING MARKETS

emerging markets

In recent years many countries have initiated organized stock exchanges or highly active over-the-counter stock markets. In general, these countries have in common a relatively low (compared with Western countries) level of per capita gross domestic product, improving political and economic stability, a currency convertible into Western countries' currencies (or at least some means for foreigners to repatriate income and capital gains), and most importantly, securities available for investment by foreigners. Such countries have what are referred to as **emerging markets.**

Investments in emerging market stocks have proven attractive to a number of institutional investors who, in many cases, invest directly in those securities, or when that is not possible, through country funds (such as the Indonesia Fund; see Chapter 23). Because many emerging market economies at various times have undergone rapid growth and because their stock markets are not highly developed and therefore are less efficient, there is considerable opportunity for relatively high returns from emerging market investments. However, there is also a relatively high level of risk involved, as witnessed by the meltdown of several Asian emerging stock markets in 1997 and 1998.

As mentioned earlier, Morgan Stanley Capital International currently defines 25 countries as emerging markets and publishes stock market indices for each of these countries as well as various regional stock market indices and an overall emerging markets index.[7] Also popular are various country, regional, and composite indices produced by the International Financial Corporation (IFC), including the IFC Global and Investable emerging markets indices.

26.2 Risk and Return from Foreign Investing

political risk
exchange risk

Investing in a foreign security involves all the risks associated with investing in a domestic security plus some additional risks. The investor expects to receive cash flows in the future from the foreign security. However, these cash flows will be in a foreign currency and thus will be of little use to the investor if they cannot be converted into the investor's domestic currency. The additional risks associated with foreign investing arise from uncertainties associated with converting these foreign cash flows into domestic currency. They are known as **political risk** and **exchange** (or currency) **risk.**[8]

Political risk refers to uncertainty about the *ability* of an investor to convert the profits from a foreign investment into domestic currency. For example, a foreign government might restrict, tax, or completely prohibit the exchange of one currency for another. Because such policies change from time to time, the ability of an investor to repatriate foreign cash flows may be subject to some uncertainty. If there is a possibility of complete expropriation, then the political risk may be very large.

Exchange risk refers to uncertainty about the *rate* at which a foreign currency can be converted into the investor's domestic currency in the future. When a foreign security is bought, the rate at which future foreign cash flows can be converted into domestic currency is uncertain, and it is this uncertainty that is known as exchange risk.

(a) Foreign Stock Market Indices

Stock Market Indexes

EXCHANGE	INDEX	3/4/99 CLOSE	NET CHG		PCT CHG		YTD NET CHG		YTD PCT CHG	
Argentina	Merval Index	383.83	+	9.05	+	2.41	−	46.23	−	10.75
Australia	All Ordinaries	2885.30	−	4.60	−	0.16	+	71.90	+	2.56
Belgium	Bel-20 Index	3282.98	−	11.43	−	0.35	−	231.53	−	6.59
Brazil	Sao Paulo Bovespa	9508.00	+	354.00	+	3.87	+	2724.00	+	40.15
Britain	London FT 100-share	6101.40	+	53.10	+	0.88	+	218.80	+	3.72
Britain	London FT 250-share	5314.80	+	27.90	+	0.53	+	460.10	+	9.48
Canada	Toronto 300 Comp.	6268.71	+	88.37	+	1.43	−	217.23	−	3.35
Chile	Santiago IPSA	114.01	+	3.54	+	3.20	+	14.01	+	14.01
China	Dow Jones China 88	117.55	−	0.30	−	0.25	−	3.65	−	3.01
China	Dow Jones Shanghai	147.61	−	0.03	−	0.02	−	1.73	−	1.16
China	Dow Jones Shenzhen	141.47	+	0.16	+	0.11	−	3.86	−	2.66
Europe	DJ Stoxx (Euro)	288.09	+	2.90	+	1.02	+	8.89	+	3.18
Europe	DJ Stoxx 50 (Euro)	3441.05	+	44.78	+	1.32	+	120.80	+	3.64
Euro Zone	DJ Euro Stoxx (Euro)	298.84	+	3.13	+	1.06	+	0.47	+	0.16
Euro Zone	DJ Euro Stoxx 50 (Euro)	3434.49	+	40.54	+	1.19	+	92.17	+	2.76
France	Paris CAC 40	4087.99	+	83.83	+	2.09	+	145.33	+	3.69
Germany	Frankfurt DAX	4678.72	−	18.95	−	0.40	−	323.67	−	6.47
Germany	Frankfurt Xetra DAX	4722.69	+	54.17	+	1.16	−	283.88	−	5.67
Hong Kong	Hang Seng	9912.76	−	9.64	−	0.10	−	135.82	−	1.35
India	Bombay Sensex	3601.96	−	38.46	−	1.06	+	546.55	+	17.89
Italy	Milan MIBtel	23923.00	+	533.00	+	2.28	+	228.00	+	0.96
Japan	Tokyo Nikkei 225	14183.45	+	13.09	+	0.09	+	341.28	+	2.47
Japan	Tokyo Nikkei 300	220.39	+	0.95	+	0.43	+	4.30	+	1.99
Japan	Tokyo Topix Index	1105.11	+	5.30	+	0.48	+	18.12	+	1.67
Malaysia	DJ Malaysia	96.46	+	0.48	+	0.50	−	12.68	−	11.62
Mexico	I.P.C. All-Share	4218.12	+	90.74	+	2.20	+	257.34	+	6.50
Netherlands	Amsterdam AEX	515.92	−	3.24	−	0.62	−	22.44	−	4.17
Singapore	Straits Times	1433.41	+	17.60	+	1.24	+	40.68	+	2.92
South Africa	Johannesburg Gold	934.30	+	18.40	+	2.01	+	62.80	+	7.21
South Korea	Composite	532.29	−	2.20	−	0.41	−	30.17	−	5.36
Spain	IBEX 35	9834.30	+	126.70	+	1.31	−	2.30	−	0.02
Sweden	Stockholm General	3332.63	+	4.22	+	0.13	+	98.17	+	3.04
Switzerland	Zurich Swiss Market	7106.80	+	120.70	+	1.73	−	53.90	−	0.75
Taiwan	Weighted Index	6393.74	−	9.40	−	0.15	−	24.69	−	0.38

(b) Morgan Stanley Indices

	MAR. 3	MAR. 2	% FROM 12/31/98	
U.S.	1200.8	1200:1	+	0.4
Britain	1790.8	1794.5	+	2.8
Canada	728.2	735.1	−	2.4
Japan	707.8	702.9	+	1.7
France	1264.7	1276.9	+	1.1
Germany	630.0	648.4	−	4.5
Hong Kong	5616.2	5605.3	−	5.5
Switzerland	880.0	877.9	−	1.3
Australia	583.5	584.9	+	2.0
World Index	**1123.5**	**1126.6**	−	**2.3**
EAFE MSCI-p	**1332.7**	**1340.8**	−	**5.1**

As calculated by Morgan Stanley Capital International Perspective, Geneva. Each index, calculated in local currencies, is based on the close of 1969 equaling 100.

FIGURE 26.2 International Equity Indices, March 4, 1999

Source: Reprinted by permission of *The Wall Street Journal,* Dow Jones & Company, Inc., March 5, 1999, p. C16. All rights reserved worldwide.

26.2.1 MANAGING EXCHANGE RISK

To an extent, exchange risk can be reduced by hedging in the forward (or futures) market for foreign currency. In the case of default-free fixed-income securities, it may be possible to completely eliminate such risk in this way. For example, assume that a one-year pure-discount bond paying 1,000 British pounds at maturity can be purchased for 900 British pounds. Furthermore, assume that a forward contract can be signed whereby the investor will receive $1,600 for delivering 1,000 British pounds a year from now because the *forward exchange rate* is $1.60 per pound. The rate of return *in British pounds* (a pound is denoted "£") on this security is 11.11% $\left[= (£1,000 - £900)/£900\right]$.

If the *spot* (that is, current) *exchange rate* were $1.65 per pound, then the cost of this bond to an American investor would be $1,485 (= 900 × $1.65). Thus, the rate of return *in U.S. dollars* on this British security would be 7.74% $\left[= ($1,600 - $1,485)/$1,485\right]$. Except for political risk, this is a certain return because exchange risk has been completely removed by hedging with a forward contract.

Unfortunately, it is not possible to completely hedge the exchange risk associated with risky investments. Forward contracts can be made to cover expected cash flows, but if the actual cash flows are larger or smaller than expected, then some of the foreign currency may have to be exchanged at the spot rate prevailing at the time the cash is received. Because future spot rates usually cannot be predicted with complete certainty, overall risk will be affected. As a practical matter, this "unhedgeable" risk is likely to be small in many cases involving fixed-income securities, but it can be large in the case of equities. Nevertheless, the cost of hedging foreign investments, regardless of whether they are fixed-income securities or equities, may exceed the benefit (see the Money Matters box later in the chapter).

It is important to differentiate between two very different approaches to managing exchange risk. The first approach is *passive currency management,* which involves a strategy of permanently controlling a portfolio's exposure to currency risk. For example, a foreign stock portfolio manager may choose to use forward contracts to consistently remove half of the portfolio's currency exposure. Although an attempt might be made initially to examine the effect such a strategy has on the portfolio's level of risk, afterward all decisions with respect to currency management are mechanical. The second approach is *active currency management,* which involves a strategy of frequently changing currency exposures to take advantage of perceived short-run mispricings among currencies. In this approach, the effect of such a strategy on the portfolio's level of risk is constantly taken into consideration.

Passive currency management requires the investor to set a policy concerning the desired level of exchange risk. This acceptable risk level is predicated on the investor's risk tolerance as well as the investor's assumptions about the long-run levels of volatilities and correlations of the currencies in the portfolio. Active currency management, on the other hand, involves moving away from the investor's normally desired levels of currency exposures. It assumes that currency markets are at times in disequilibrium. Furthermore, it assumes that the investor can add value by appropriately altering the portfolio's currency exposures as the disequilibrium corrects or shifts.

Unfortunately, both of these currency management approaches have become known as "hedging." Yet only passive currency management is truly hedging in the sense of attempting to eliminate or reduce unwanted risk. Active currency management, like any other active management strategy, might very well add risk to a portfolio, not reduce it.[9]

If an investor chooses to actively manage the currency exposure of a diversified foreign portfolio, then there are several ways of doing so. First, the investor could manage the currency exposures directly or hire a *currency specialist* to perform that function. Second, after deciding who is to manage these exposures, the investor must determine how integrated the currency management and security selection decisions should be. At one extreme, the currency management and security selection decisions are made independently. In that case, when a currency specialist is used, that manager is often referred to as a *currency overlay* manager (that is, the currency management is *overlaid* on top of the foreign security portfolio). Judgments on the amount and types of currency exposures to put in place are made without any consideration of which foreign securities are in the portfolio. This type of currency management is not likely to reduce the risk of a portfolio. At the other extreme, decisions about which securities to purchase and how to manage the resulting currency exposures are made at the same time by one manager, keeping in mind how the two decisions affect each other. This type of currency management is likely to reduce the risk of a portfolio. A middle course involves making such decisions sequentially; the investor selects the portfolio of foreign securities first and then a currency specialist chooses the make-up of the portfolio's currency exposures on the basis of the securities selected. Not surprisingly, one study found that the best approach was the joint-decision approach and the least desirable approach was the one in which the security selection and currency management decisions were made independently.[10]

26.2.2 FOREIGN AND DOMESTIC RETURNS

Changes in exchange rates can cause major differences between the returns obtained by domestic investors and the returns obtained by unhedged foreign investors. Consider a U.S. investor and a Swiss investor, both of whom purchase shares of a Swiss company whose stock does not pay dividends and is traded only in Switzerland. Let the price of the stock in Swiss francs be P_0 at the beginning of a period and P_1 at the end of the period. The **domestic return,** denoted r_D, is

domestic return

$$r_D = \frac{P_1 - P_0}{P_0} \tag{26.1}$$

For example, if $P_0 = 10$ Swiss francs and $P_1 = 12$ Swiss francs, then $r_D = 20\%$ $[= (12 - 10)/10]$.

For the Swiss investor, r_D is the stock's return. Not so for the U.S. investor. Assume that at the beginning of the period the price (in dollars) of one Swiss franc is $.50. Denoting this exchange rate (that is, the exchange rate at the beginning of the period) as X_0, the cost of a share to the U.S. investor will be $X_0 P_0$. In the example, this cost will be $5 (= $.50 \times 10$).

Now assume that the exchange rate rises to $.55 per Swiss franc at the end of the period. Denoting this by X_1, the ending value of the stock for the U.S. investor will be $X_1 P_1$. In the example, this value will be $6.60 (= $.55 \times 12$).

foreign return

The **foreign return** (that is, the return to a foreign investor), denoted r_F, is

$$r_F = \frac{X_1 P_1 - X_0 P_0}{X_0 P_0} \tag{26.2}$$

In the example, the foreign (that is, U.S.) investor would have earned a return of $r_F = 32\%$ $[= (\$6.60 - \$5.00)/\$5.00]$ on an investment in the Swiss firm's stock.

In effect, the U.S. investor made two investments: (1) an investment in a Swiss stock and (2) an investment in the Swiss franc. Accordingly, the overall return to the U.S. investor can be decomposed into a return on the investment in the Swiss stock and a

Currency Risk: To Hedge or Not to Hedge

 Investors in securities denominated in currencies other than those of their home country incur a risk not borne by their domestic investor counterparts: currency risk. For investors in foreign assets, currency (or exchange) risk is the variability in portfolio returns caused by fluctuations in the rate at which foreign currencies can be converted into their home currency. Whether investors in foreign securities should attempt to minimize currency risk in their portfolios has become a topic of considerable controversy in recent years.

As the text describes, the return on an investor's foreign portfolio can be divided into two components: a domestic (also called local) return and a currency (also called foreign exchange) return. Likewise, foreign portfolio risk can be decomposed into domestic risk, currency risk, and any possible interaction between the two. Most studies indicate that currency risk can increase total portfolio risk by 15% to 100% of the underlying domestic risk.

Investors can choose whether to bear currency risk. Through a variety of techniques, currency risk can be "hedged" and almost eliminated. The most popular means of hedging currency risk is to purchase units of the investor's home currency in the forward market equal to the expected value of the foreign investment. For example, consider a U.S. investor holding 1,000 shares of a Japanese company selling for 4,000 yen per share. He or she can purchase dollars for delivery six months from today at a rate of 125 yen per dollar. (The forward market is similar to the futures market; see Chapter 25.) By purchasing $32,000 for delivery six months from today to be paid for with 4 million yen, the investor insulates himself or herself from changes in the exchange rate between the yen and the dollar for the next six months.

Despite the availability of effective hedging tools, why do many investors in foreign securities choose not to hedge their currency risks and instead remain exposed to exchange rate fluctuations? Considered next are the primary arguments in support of and in opposition to currency risk hedging.

Proponents of hedging currency risk contend that a no-hedge policy violates one of the basic laws of modern portfolio theory: Only accept risks for which adequate compensation is expected to be earned. They view currencies as having zero expected returns. That is, in a world in which capital is free to flow across borders, there is no reason to expect the value of foreign currencies to move systematically in one direction relative to an investor's home currency. However, exchange rates do fluctuate, generating additional risk for an investor in foreign securities. Proponents view currency risk as uncompensated and believe that risk-averse investors should seek its minimization. Investors who do not hedge would seem to be passing up an opportunity to reduce portfolio risk while not diminishing portfolio returns. Proponents point out that the reduction in portfolio variability gained by hedging currency risk can be substantial.

Opponents of currency hedging generally concede that forgoing hedging means accepting additional uncompensated risks. (However, one school of thought contends that currency risk should be systematically rewarded by the market.) Nevertheless, they believe that market "frictions" cause the costs of currency hedging to outweigh the risk reduction benefits. That is, significant expenses may be incurred by an investor managing currency risk. Currency dealers must be compensated for facilitating hedging transactions. Custodian banks must be paid for record keeping. Investment managers charge fees for maintaining the hedge. Estimates of the total cost of hedging typically range from .25% to .50% per year of the value of the hedged assets, enough to convince opponents that currency risk hedging may not be cost-effective.

In addition, some hedging opponents question the wisdom of hedging for an investor who spends a high percentage of his or her income on goods produced abroad. Suppose the value of foreign currencies declines relative to the investor's home currency (thereby negatively affecting the investor's foreign portfolio returns, other things being equal). The declining relative value of the foreign currencies also reduces the effective cost of foreign-produced goods to the investor. In a sense the investor's own consumption basket serves as a hedge against currency risk in his or her portfolio.

Of additional importance to the discussion is the fact that the total risk (variance) of a portfolio containing foreign securities increases with the square of the amount of unhedged currency risk (assuming zero correlation between currency and domestic returns). On the other hand, the cost of hedging increases linearly. Thus, within a total portfolio of home country and foreign securities, there is some foreign allocation threshold (some observers say 15%) below which there should be no currency hedging and above which all incremental foreign positions should be completely hedged. Moreover, the longer the investor's time horizon is, the higher this threshold will be. This is because as the time horizon increases, currency risk declines due to mean reversion (that is, the tendency for currencies to move back toward "normal" relationships over time).

In the final analysis, an investor's optimal currency hedge depends on a number of factors, including the following:

1. Correlations between currencies
2. Correlations between domestic returns and currency returns
3. The cost of hedging
4. The portions of the investor's portfolio allocated to foreign securities
5. The variability of foreign asset returns
6. The variability of currency returns
7. The investor's consumption basket
8. The investor's level of risk aversion
9. The investor's time horizon
10. The premium earned (if any) for holding foreign currencies

These factors are difficult to quantify, making it hard to build a strong case for or against currency hedging. Moreover, as investors differ in both their financial circumstances and their beliefs about the characteristics of currencies and security markets, it is not surprising that everything from zero hedges to fully hedged positions occurs.

return on the investment in the Swiss franc. Consider a U.S. investor who had purchased a Swiss franc at the beginning of the period. If the U.S. investor subsequently sold the franc at the end of the period, the return on foreign currency, denoted r_C, would be

$$r_C = \frac{X_1 - X_0}{X_0} \tag{26.3}$$

In the example, $r_C = 10\%$ [= ($.55 - $.50)/$.50].

From Equations (26.1), (26.2), and (26.3), it can be shown that

$$1 + r_F = (1 + r_D)(1 + r_C) \tag{26.4}$$

which can be rewritten as

$$r_F = r_D + r_C + r_D r_C \tag{26.5}$$

In the example, Equation (26.5) reveals that $r_F = 32\%$ [= .20 + .10 + (.20 × .10)].

The last term in this equation ($r_D r_C$) will generally be smaller than the two preceding ones because it equals their product, and both are generally less than 1.0. Thus, Equation (26.5) can be restated as an approximation:

$$r_F \cong r_D + r_C \tag{26.6}$$

It can now be seen that the return on a foreign security (r_F) can be approximated by summing the domestic return on the security (r_D) and the return on foreign currency (r_C). In the example, the precise value for r_F was 32%. Use of the approximation indicates its value is equal to 30% (= .20 + .10). Thus, the approximation is in error by 6% $\left(= \frac{2}{32}\right)$, a relatively small amount.

26.2.3 EXPECTED RETURNS

Equation (26.6) leads directly to the proposition that the expected return on a foreign security will approximately equal the expected domestic return plus the expected return on foreign currency:

$$\bar{r}_F \cong \bar{r}_D + \bar{r}_C \tag{26.7}$$

It might be tempting for an investor to purchase a foreign security that has a high expected return in its host country on the belief that the security will have a high expected return to the foreign investor. However, Equation (26.7) reveals this type of logic to be flawed. Just because a foreign security has a high value for $\bar{r}_D$ does not mean that it has a high value for $\bar{r}_F$ because $\bar{r}_C$ can be negative. Consider an example of an investment in bonds. The expected domestic returns of fixed-income securities in countries with high expected inflation rates will typically be high. However, a foreign investor in a country with a lower expected inflation rate should expect a *negative* return on foreign currency because his or her currency can be expected to *appreciate* relative to that of the country with the higher expected inflation rate. Thus, in evaluating the expected return on the foreign security, there is good news (a high expected domestic return $\bar{r}_D$) and bad news (a negative expected return on foreign currency $\bar{r}_C$). On balance, the expected foreign return, $\bar{r}_F$, might not be as exceptional as first thought when just $\bar{r}_D$ was considered. Indeed, if markets were completely integrated, it would be reasonable to expect the values of $\bar{r}_D$ and $\bar{r}_C$ to roughly sum to an amount $\bar{r}_F$ that is equal to the expected return on an equivalent bond in the investor's own country. When government securities are involved, this relationship is known as **interest-rate parity.**

interest-rate parity

As an example, assume that an investor can buy either one-year Treasuries in the United States that have a yield of 5% or similar one-year German governments that are at 7%, where both securities have no coupons before they mature. Both securities are free from default risk, call risk, and political risk. Interest-rate parity states that the expected return from owning either security is the same. Interest-rate parity exists because, in the market's view, the German mark is expected to depreciate against the dollar so that at the end of the year, the 2% extra return a U.S. investor would earn from holding the German security will be exactly offset by a currency loss when it is exchanged for dollars. Applying Equation (26.5) to this situation results in the following equation:

$$.05 = .07 + \bar{r}_C + .07\bar{r}_C$$

which has the solution $\bar{r}_C = -1.87\%$ (or, using Equation (26.6) as an approximation, -2%). According to interest-rate parity, the German security has a 2% higher yield because the mark is expected to fall by roughly 2%. Indeed, the one-year dollar–mark forward rate should be roughly 2% lower than the spot rate, meaning that if the spot rate is $.60 per mark, then the one-year forward rate should be about $.5888 [= .60 × (1 − .0187)] per mark. In sum, an investor should not expect to make more by investing in fixed-income securities of a country that has higher interest rates than in the investor's home country.

Columns (2) and (3) of Table 26.2(a) indicate what the average excess returns [that is, returns over the London Interbank Offered Rate (LIBOR), an estimate of the risk-free rate] were for the stocks and bonds of six countries as well as the United States for a 200-month period. These averages were measured from the perspective of a U.S. investor and hence represent the historical average value of r_F. The table indicates that, although the stock and bond averages for the six countries are very similar to the U.S. averages, there are some notable differences among individual countries. For both stocks and bonds, the Canadian market had an average return that was much lower than the U.S. average, whereas the U.K. and Japanese averages were notably higher.[11]

26.2.4 FOREIGN AND DOMESTIC RISKS

Having seen in Equation (26.7) that the expected return on a foreign security consists of two components, it is appropriate that the risk of the foreign security be evaluated next. As before, consider a U.S. investor and a Swiss investor who have purchased shares

TABLE 26.2 Security Returns[a]

(a) EXCESS RETURNS AND STANDARD DEVIATIONS

Country (1)	Average Excess Return (%)		Standard Deviation (%)	
	Stocks (2)	Bonds (3)	Stocks (4)	Bonds (5)
Australia	4.5	−.8	21.9	5.5
Canada	.9	−1.5	18.3	7.8
France	4.8	−.1	22.2	4.5
Germany	4.7	.9	18.3	4.5
Japan	7.3	2.1	17.8	6.5
U.K.	8.6	1.2	24.7	9.9
U.S.	5.2	−.3	16.1	6.8
Average (excluding U.S.)	5.1	.3	20.5	6.4
Average	5.1	.2	19.9	6.5

(b) CORRELATIONS BETWEEN FOREIGN AND U.S. STOCKS AND BONDS[b]

Country (1)	U.S. Stocks with Foreign		U.S. Bonds with Foreign	
	Stocks (2)	Bonds (3)	Stocks (4)	Bonds (5)
Australia	.48	.24	−.05	.20
Canada	.74	.31	.18	.82
France	.50	.21	.20	.31
Germany	.43	.23	.17	.50
Japan	.41	.12	.11	.28
U.K.	.58	.23	.12	.28
Average	.52	.22	.12	.40

[a]Results are given from the U.S. investor's perspective and are in excess of LIBOR.

[b]Correlation of U.S. stocks with U.S. bonds was .32.

Source: Adapted from Fischer Black and Robert Litterman, "Global Portfolio Optimization," *Financial Analysts Journal*, 48, no. 5. (September/October 1992): 30–31.

of a Swiss company. The domestic variance, denoted σ_D^2, is the risk that the Swiss investor faces with respect to the Swiss stock. Correspondingly, the foreign variance, denoted σ_F^2, is the risk that the U.S. investor faces with respect to the Swiss stock. On the basis of Equation (26.5), it can be shown that the foreign variance consists of three components:

$$\sigma_F^2 = \sigma_D^2 + \sigma_C^2 + 2\rho_{DC}\sigma_D\sigma_C \qquad (26.8)$$

where σ_C^2 is the variance associated with the currency return to a U.S. investor from investing in Swiss francs and later exchanging them for U.S. dollars, and ρ_{DC} is the correlation coefficient between the return on the Swiss stock and the return on Swiss francs.[12] Table 26.2(b) provides estimates of the size of other correlations from the perspective of a U.S. investor (more on this later).

For example, assume the domestic variance is 225 (meaning the domestic standard deviation, σ_D, is $\sqrt{225}$ or 15%) and the currency variance is 25 (meaning the currency standard deviation, σ_C, is $\sqrt{25}$ or 5%). If $\rho_{DC} = 0$, then Equation (26.8) indicates that the foreign variance is 250 (= 225 + 25). Accordingly, the foreign standard deviation is 15.8% (= $\sqrt{250}$), which is only slightly greater than the domestic standard deviation of 15%.

Columns (4) and (5) of Table 26.2(a) provide the standard deviations of the excess returns for six foreign countries along with the United States from the perspective of a U.S. investor. Hence it provides estimates of the value of σ_F for the 200-month period. The six-country average standard deviation for both stocks and bonds is similar to the respective U.S. values, with the United Kingdom having notably larger values for both stocks and bonds.

Table 26.3 provides evidence on the relative magnitudes of the three types of risk. Standard deviations of monthly values over a 10-year period are shown for domestic risk (corresponding to σ_D), currency risk (corresponding to σ_C), and foreign risk (corresponding to σ_F), where the latter two types of risk have been measured from the perspective of a U.S. investor. The last column represents the ratio of foreign risk to domestic risk. Thus, a ratio greater than one can be taken as an indication that the risk to a U.S. investor is greater than the risk to a domestic investor. Indeed, with the exception of Hong Kong stocks, all the ratios are greater than 1, suggesting that fluctuations in currency exchange rates increased the risk a U.S. investor would have faced in buying foreign securities. Although the exact values of these ratios have undoubtedly changed since the study was conducted, in general the conclusion—that exchange risk typically increases the risk to U.S. investors from buying foreign securities—remains valid today.

The importance of currency risk can easily be exaggerated. Calculations such as those in Table 26.3 assume that investors purchase only domestic goods and services and convert all proceeds from foreign investments into their own currency before engaging in any spending for consumption purposes. But most people buy foreign goods and many buy foreign services as well (for example, as tourists). The cheaper another country's currency relative to one's own, the more attractive purchases of its goods and services will be. Other things being equal, it may make sense to invest more in countries whose products and scenery are admired, for the effective currency risk is likely to be smaller there than elsewhere.

26.3   International Listings

The common stocks of many firms are traded not only on the major stock exchange in their home country but also on an exchange in at least one foreign country. For this reason foreign investors no longer have to engage in foreign currency transactions when

TABLE 26.3 Risks for Domestic and U.S. Investors Based on Historical Values

	Domestic Risk (1)	Currency Risk (2)	Foreign Risk (3)	Foreign Domestic Risk (4)
(a) Stocks				
Australia	24.62%	9.15%	27.15%	1.10
Belgium	13.28	11.02	18.76	1.41
Canada	18.92	4.16	20.29	1.07
Denmark	15.41	10.28	17.65	1.15
France	22.00	10.24	25.81	1.17
Germany	13.87	11.87	18.39	1.33
Hong Kong	47.95	5.63	45.80	.96
Italy	24.21	8.58	26.15	1.08
Japan	16.39	10.42	19.55	1.19
Netherlands	16.37	10.97	18.91	1.16
Norway	28.61	8.89	29.92	1.05
Singapore	35.82	6.52	36.03	1.01
Spain	16.71	9.10	20.26	1.21
Sweden	15.05	8.89	18.06	1.20
Switzerland	16.80	14.67	21.40	1.27
U.K.	28.94	8.84	31.61	1.09
U.S.	16.00	.00	16.00	1.00
(b) Bonds				
Canada	6.16	4.16	7.93	1.29
France	4.39	10.24	11.80	2.69
Germany	6.91	11.87	14.35	2.08
Italy	6.53	10.42	14.36	2.20
Netherlands	7.16	10.97	13.61	1.90
Switzerland	4.33	14.67	15.33	3.54
U.K.	12.30	8.84	16.29	1.32
U.S.	8.96	.00	8.96	1.00

Source: Adapted from Bruno Solnik and Bernard Noetzlin, "Optimal International Asset Allocation," *Journal of Portfolio Management,* 9, no. 1 (Fall 1982): 13.

American Depositary Receipts (ADRs)

buying and selling the firm's stock. It is also possible for foreign investors to escape certain taxes and regulations to which they would be subject if the security were bought in the firm's home country. There are two methods of trading such internationally listed foreign securities in the United States that involve the use of ordinary shares and **American Depositary Receipts (ADRs).** In addition, investors can invest in foreign stock market indices through the use of World Equity Benchmark Shares (WEBS will be discussed shortly).

26.3.1 ORDINARIES

The first way foreign securities may be traded in the United States is for the shares of the firm to be traded directly in U.S. dollars, just as the shares of a typical U.S. firm are. Canadian firms generally are traded in this manner in the United States; at year-end

1998, none of the 69 Canadian firms with their stocks listed on the NYSE involved ADRs. Stocks traded in this form are referred to as *ordinary shares* or simply *ordinaries*.

26.3.2 AMERICAN DEPOSITARY RECEIPTS

The second way foreign securities may be traded in the United States is with ADRs.[13] American Depositary Receipts are financial assets that are issued by U.S. banks and represent indirect ownership of a certain number of shares of a specific foreign firm that are held on deposit in a bank in the firm's home country. The advantage of ADRs over direct ownership is that the investor need not worry about the delivery of the stock certificates or converting dividend payments from a foreign currency into U.S. dollars. The depository bank automatically does the converting for the investor and forwards all financial reports from the firm. The investor pays the bank a small fee for these services. Typically, non-Canadian firms use ADRs. For example, Mexican firms are traded in this manner in the United States; at year-end 1998, all 28 Mexican firms with their stocks listed on the NYSE used ADRs.

Table 26.4 displays the extent of foreign stock listings in the United States at year-end 1998. As the table shows, 880 foreign firms were listed on either the NYSE, AMEX, or Nasdaq.

One study that examined the diversification implications of investing in ADRs found that such securities were of notable benefit to U.S. investors.[14] Specifically, a sample of 45 ADRs was examined and compared with a sample of 45 U.S. securities. When an index based on all NYSE-listed stocks was used, the betas of the ADRs had an average value of .26, which was much lower than the average beta of 1.01 for the U.S. securities. Furthermore, the correlation of the ADRs' returns with those of the NYSE market portfolio averaged .33, whereas U.S. securities had a notably higher average correlation of .53.

Given these two observations, it is not surprising that portfolios formed from U.S. securities and ADRs had much lower standard deviations than portfolios consisting of just U.S. securities. For example, portfolios consisting of 10 U.S. securities had an average monthly standard deviation of 5.50%, whereas a 10-security portfolio split evenly between U.S. securities and ADRs had an average monthly standard deviation of 4.41%. Thus, it seems that investing in ADRs brings significant benefits in terms of risk reduction.[15]

The SEC currently requires foreign firms to prepare their financial statements using U.S. generally accepted accounting principles (GAAP) if they want their shares or ADRs

TABLE 26.4	Foreign Company Listings in the United States, Year-End 1998		
	Number of Issuers	*Canadian Issuers*	*Mexican Issuers*
NYSE	379	69	28
AMEX	60	37	2
Nasdaq	441	145	4
Total	880	251	34

Source: 1999 Nasdaq-Amex Fact Book & Company Directory (Washington, DC: The Nasdaq-Amex Market Group, 1999): pp. 9, 53; *New York Stock Exchange Fact Book 1998 Data* (New York: New York Stock Exchange, 1999): pp. 64–65.

to be listed on a U.S. exchange or on Nasdaq.[16] One consequence of this requirement is that many large and actively traded foreign firms have decided against listing their shares in the United States. This decision has caused U.S. exchanges to fear that certain foreign exchanges that do not have such reporting requirements (particularly London) will gain trading business at the expense of the U.S. exchanges. In response to the complaints of the exchanges, the SEC argues that this requirement is necessary to protect U.S. investors and that it would be patently unfair to U.S. firms if they had to meet such requirements but their foreign competitors did not have to do so. One thing is certain: This conflict between the exchanges and the SEC over this issue will not go away soon.[17]

26.3.3 WORLD EQUITY BENCHMARK SHARES

World Equity Benchmark Shares (WEBS)

World Equity Benchmark Shares (WEBS) are a unique type of international investment. Each WEBS share represents a portfolio of stocks in a given country that is designed to generate investment results that generally correspond to the performance of a given Morgan Stanley Capital International (MSCI) country index. Currently there are WEBS from 17 countries listed on the AMEX that can be traded just like any common stock listed there. For example, an investor not only can purchase WEBS for a given country, but can short sell them too, with all trades being settled in U.S. dollars. Otherwise, purchasing WEBS is similar to purchasing shares of a passively managed mutual fund (see Chapter 23). Net asset values of WEBS are published daily, dividend and capital gain distributions are made periodically, and their closing prices and trading volume can be found daily in the AMEX stock listings. Thus, WEBS offer investors a convenient way to diversify a portfolio internationally. The 17 countries that currently have WEBS listed on the AMEX are Australia, Austria, Belgium, Canada, France, Germany, Hong Kong, Italy, Japan, Malaysia, Mexico, Netherlands, Singapore, Spain, Sweden, Switzerland, and the United Kingdom.

26.4 Correlations between Markets

If all economies were completely integrated (and there were no specialization by countries in terms of industries, products, and so on), then stock markets in different countries would move together, and little advantage could be gained through international diversification. However, this is not the case. Table 26.2(b) shows the correlations of returns on stocks and bonds in six countries with the returns of stocks and bonds in the United States. There are three general observations:

1. With the exception of Canada, the correlations of foreign stocks with U.S. stocks are low, suggesting there are sizable potential diversification advantages to a U.S. stock investor of investing in the stocks of these five countries.[18]
2. The correlations of foreign bonds with U.S. bonds are low, with the exception of Canadian bonds.[19] Again, this observation suggests that there are sizable potential diversification advantages to a U.S. bond investor of investing in the bonds of these five countries.
3. The correlations of foreign bonds with U.S. stocks and the correlations of foreign stocks with U.S. bonds are all generally low. Once again, there are sizable potential advantages to diversification; but now the advantages are in diversifying across both asset classes and countries. That is, for a given level of risk, a U.S. stock investor would find it advantageous to buy foreign bonds, and a U.S. bond investor would find it advantageous to buy foreign stocks.

The bottom line is that international diversification is beneficial. Earlier, Figure 8.10 showed how diversification in general reduces the total risk of a portfolio. Similarly, Figure 26.3 shows that internationally well-diversified portfolios have lower levels of risk than those that are diversified just among domestic securities. Investors can either increase their expected return without increasing their risk or decrease their risk without decreasing their expected return by judiciously adding foreign securities to their portfolios.[20] Consequently, the efficient set of domestic securities, denoted *DD* in Figure 26.4, is dominated by the efficient set constructed from both domestic and foreign securities, denoted *FF.*

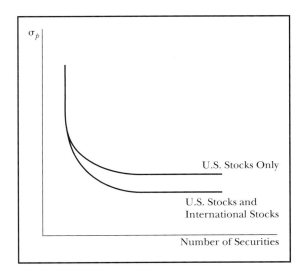

FIGURE 26.3 The Effects of International Diversification on Total Portfolio Risk

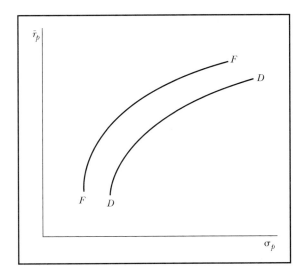

FIGURE 26.4 Efficient Set with (*FF*) and without (*DD*) International Diversification

Summary

1. Investing in a foreign security involves all the risks associated with investing in a domestic security, plus political and exchange (currency) risks associated with converting foreign cash flows into domestic currency.
2. The return on a foreign security can be decomposed into a domestic return and a return on the currency in which the security is denominated.
3. Passive currency management refers to the process of controlling a portfolio's exposure to exchange risk on a long-term policy basis. Active currency management refers to the process of altering a portfolio's exposure to foreign currencies based on a near-term forecast of relative valuations among currencies.
4. Because of interest-rate parity, the expected return from owning government securities of either one of two countries is the same, provided they are both free from political risk and default risk.
5. The standard deviation of return on a foreign security is a function of the security's domestic return standard deviation, the foreign currency return standard deviation, and the correlation between the two returns.
6. Exchange risk can be reduced by hedging in the forward or futures market for foreign currency.
7. Investments in ADRs seem to bring U.S. investors significant risk reduction benefits similar to the benefits obtained by investing directly in foreign securities.
8. Investors can take positions in WEBS for as many as 17 countries, thereby making it possible to passively invest in diversified foreign country stock portfolios.
9. Purchasing domestic and foreign securities typically results in an efficient frontier whose portfolios have more favorable risks and returns than those associated with the efficient frontier resulting from purchasing just domestic securities.

Questions and Problems

1. What types of political risks are relevant only for foreign investors? What types are relevant for both foreign and domestic investors? To what extent and in what manner would you expect the current prices of securities in a particular country to reflect these types of political risk?
2. Using a recent *Wall Street Journal,* find the exchange rate between German marks, British pounds, and U.S. dollars. Lyle Luttrell, a British citizen, is planning a trip to Germany and has budgeted expenses of 30 pounds per day. At current exchange rates, into how many dollars and marks does 30 pounds translate?
3. Why would an investor wish to hedge the currency risk in a portfolio of foreign securities? What considerations are relevant to making the decision whether to hedge?
4. Smead Jolly is a U.S. investor who has the opportunity to convert $1 into 130 Japanese yen and 1.90 German marks. Given this information, into how may yen should Smead be able to convert one mark?
5. How might a U.S. citizen or company use currency futures to hedge against exchange-rate risk?
6. Wickey McAvoy, a U.S. citizen, holds a portfolio of French common stocks. Last year the portfolio produced an 8% return, denominated in French francs. During that year the franc appreciated 20% against the U.S. dollar. What was Wickey's return measured in U.S. dollars?
7. Tris Speaker bought a Japanese stock one year ago when it sold for 280 yen per share and the exchange rate was $0.008 per yen. The stock now sells for 350 yen and the exchange rate is $0.010 per yen. The stock paid no dividends during the year. What was Tris's rate of return on this stock? What would be the rate of return on the stock to a Japanese investor?

8. Why is international diversification attractive to an investor who already has a well-diversified domestic portfolio?

9. Ownie Carroll owns a portfolio composed of U.S. stocks and bonds. Interested in further diversifying the portfolio, Ownie decides to add investments in Canadian common stocks. Ownie's broker, Slick Castleman, voices the opinion that the Canadian securities would not be particularly effective risk-reducing investments. Discuss the logic behind Slick's opinion.

10. Peek-a-Boo Veach, a U.S. citizen, estimates that a diversified portfolio of Norwegian common stocks has a standard deviation of 24%. Peek-a-Boo also estimates that the standard deviation of the U.S. and Norwegian currency return is 7%. Finally, Peek-a-Boo estimates the correlation between the dollar-krone currency return and the Norwegian stock market return to be 0.20. Given this information, what should Peek-a-Boo conclude is the standard deviation for a U.S. investor investing solely in the Norwegian stock market?

11. Why does a foreign security with a high expected *domestic* return relative to what an investor could earn in his or her home country not necessarily have a high expected *foreign* return for that investor?

12. Assume that the one-year U.S. riskfree rate is 6%. Moon Gibson, an investor knowledgable concerning the implications of interest-rate parity, expects the U.K. pound to appreciate by 3% next year relative to the U.S. dollar. What does that expectation imply about the current one-year U.K. riskfree rate?

13. Lin Storti, a U.S. citizen, is considering investing in both U.S. and Zanistan common stock index funds. Lin estimates the following market characteristics:

U.S. market expected return	20%
U.S. market standard deviation	18
Zanistan market expected return	30
Zanistan market standard deviation	30
U.S.–Zanistan expected currency return	0
U.S.–Zanistan currency return standard deviation	10
Zanistan domestic return and U.S.–Zanistan currency return correlation	0.15

Further, Lin estimates that the U.S. and Zanistan markets are uncorrelated as is the U.S. market return (or the Zanistan market return) and the U.S.–Zanistan currency exchange rate. If Lin plans to hold a portfolio with 60% invested in the U.S. index fund and 40% invested in the Zanistan index fund, what is the expected return and standard deviation of Lin's portfolio?

14. Discuss why mutual funds and WEBS are a particularly cost-effective means for small investors to own foreign securities.

15. Is a low correlation between the price movements of two countries' market indices a sufficient condition to ensure that a portfolio containing securities of both countries dominates a portfolio containing only domestic securities?

Endnotes

1. Some people also believe that investing in tangible assets such as collectibles (like Chinese ceramics, coins, gems, paintings, and stamps), precious metals (like gold and silver), and various privately-traded equity investments (such as investments in venture capital, leveraged buy-outs, and real estate) brings additional diversification benefits. Although not a tangible asset, commodity futures (discussed in Chapter 25) also are believed to have diversification benefits. See, for example, Burton G. Malkiel, *A Random Walk down Wall Street* (New York: W. W. Norton, 1990): pp. 304–309, William M. Taylor, "The Estimation of Quality-Adjusted Auction Returns with Varying Transaction Intervals," *Journal of Financial and Quantitative Analysis,* 27, no. 1 (March 1992): 131–142; James E. Pesando, "Art as an Investment: The Market for Modern Prints," *American Economic Review,* 83, no. 5 (December 1993): 1075–1089; William N. Goetzmann, "Accounting

for Taste: Art and the Financial Markets over Three Centuries," *American Economic Review,* 83, no. 5 (December 1993): 1370–1376; Josh Lerner, "Venture Capitalists and the Oversight of Private Firms," *Journal of Finance,* 50, no. 1 (March 1995): 301–318; Thomas J. Healey and Donald J. Hardy, "Growth in Alternative Investments," *Financial Analysts Journal,* 53, no. 4 (July/August 1997): 58–65; David E. Tierney and Jeffery V. Bailey, "Opportunistic Investing," *Journal of Portfolio Management,* 23, no. 3 (Spring 1997): 69–78; and Stephen L. Nesbitt and Hal W. Reynolds, "Benchmarks for Private Market Investments," *Journal of Portfolio Management,* 23, no. 4 (Summer 1997): 85–90.

2. For a discussion of the difficulties in measuring the size of the world market, see Roger G. Ibbotson, Laurence B. Siegel, and Kathryn S. Love, "World Wealth: Market Values and Returns," *Journal of Portfolio Management,* 12, no. 1 (Fall 1985): 4–23.

3. A detailed study of bonds outstanding at the end of 1989 found that 57% was government debt, 22% was local corporate debt, 9% was "crossborder" debt (that is, foreign bonds and Eurobonds), and 12% was "other domestic" debt. See Roger G. Ibbotson and Laurence B. Siegel, "The World Bond Market: Market Values, Yields, and Returns," *Journal of Fixed Income,* 1, no. 1 (June 1991): 90–99.

4. *The Wall Street Journal* also publishes daily a set of Dow Jones stock market indices for 33 countries. These country indices are combined into three regional indices (Americas; Europe/Africa; Asia/Pacific; there are other regional indices that exclude certain countries) and a World Stock Index that are also reported daily. For a discussion of European stock markets, see Gabriel Hawawini, *European Equity Markets: Price Behavior and Efficiency,* Monograph Series in Finance and Economics #1984-4/5 (New York University Salomon Center, Leonard N. Stern School of Business, 1984). Also see Victor A. Canto, "Everything You Always Wanted to Know about the European Monetary System, the ECU and ERM, But Didn't Know Who to Ask," *Financial Analysts Journal,* 47, no. 6 (November/December 1991): 22–25.

5. For a discussion of the Morgan Stanley indices, see Campbell R. Harvey, "The World Price of Covariance Risk," *Journal of Finance,* 46, no. 1 (March 1991): 111–157.

6. For more on these and other indices, see Chapter 5 in Bruno Solnik, *International Investments* (Reading, MA: Addison-Wesley, 1991); and John Markese, "An Investor's Guide to the International Marketplace," *AAII Journal,* 14, no. 7 (August 1992): 29–32.

7. For more on emerging markets, see Vihang Errunza, "Emerging Markets: A New Opportunity for Improving Global Portfolio Performance," *Financial Analysts Journal,* 39, no. 5 (September/October 1983): 51–58;

Vihang Errunza and Etienne Losq, "How Risky Are Emerging Markets? Myths and Perceptions versus Theory and Evidence," *Journal of Portfolio Management,* 14, no. 1 (Fall 1987): 62–67; Vihang Errunza and Prasad Padmanabhan, "Further Evidence on the Benefits of Portfolio Investments in Emerging Markets," *Financial Analysts Journal,* 44, no. 4 (July/August 1988): 76–78; and Christopher B. Barry, John W. Peavy, and Maurico Rodriquez, "Performance Characteristics of Emerging Capital Markets," *Financial Analysts Journal,* 54, no. 1 (January/February 1998): 72–80.

8. The effects these types of risk have on asset pricing has been considered by a number of people. For a discussion and list of references, see Chapters 1 and 5 in Solnik, *International Investments.*

9. The relationship of passive currency management to active currency management is similar to the relationship between strategic asset allocation and tactical asset allocation discussed in Chapter 17.

10. See Philippe Jorion, "Mean/Variance Analysis of Currency Overlays," *Financial Analysts Journal,* 50, no. 3 (May/June 1994): 48–56. The integration issue of managing a foreign portfolio's currency exposures and security holdings is essentially the same as the integration of the security selection and asset allocation decisions discussed in Chapter 17.

11. In a study of monthly stock returns using the Morgan Stanley indices, it was found that the return on Japanese stocks was inexplicably high. See Harvey, "The World Price of Covariance Risk."

12. The importance of accurately estimating the correlations between asset and currency returns in determining whether to hedge a portfolio is stressed in Victor S. Filatov and Peter Rappoport, "Is Complete Hedging Optimal for International Bond Portfolios?" *Financial Analysts Journal,* 48, no. 4 (July/August 1992): 37–47.

13. The London Stock Exchange began trading many of these ADRs in August 1987, with prices quoted in U.S. dollars.

14. Dennis T. Officer and J. Ronald Hoffmeister, "ADRs: A Substitute for the Real Thing?" *Journal of Portfolio Management,* 13, no. 2 (Winter 1987): 61–65. See also Leonard Rosenthal, "An Empirical Test of the Efficiency of the ADR Market," *Journal of Banking and Finance,* 7, no. 1 (March 1983): 17–29. For a summary article, see Amar Gande "American Depositary Receipts: Overview and Literature Survey," *Financial Markets, Institutions & Instruments,* 6, no. 5 (1997): 61–84.

15. A study of U.S. multinationals found that the percentage of a firm's sales that were overseas varied directly with a measure of how sensitive the firm's stock price was to an index of the dollar's value. That is, the greater the percentage, the larger the positive effect

of dollar depreciations on the firm's profits and hence on its stock returns. Accordingly, investing in U.S. firms that have a large percentage of their sales overseas may be beneficial. See Philippe Jorion, "The Exchange-Rate Exposure of U.S. Multinationals," *Journal of Business,* 63, no. 3 (July 1990): 331–345; and "The Pricing of Exchange Rate Risk in the Stock Market," *Journal of Financial and Quantitative Analysis,* 26, no. 3 (September 1991): 363–376.

16. An article published in 1993 stated that at that time there were 722 ADRs listed in the U.S. over-the-counter market. (Large bid–ask spreads are common for these thinly traded ADRs, thereby limiting the ability to invest profitably in them.) In comparison, at year-end 1993, there were 536 foreign companies (with 213 of them being ADRs) that had their shares listed on a U.S. exchange. See Franklin R. Edwards, "Listing of Foreign Securities on U.S. Exchanges," *Journal of Applied Corporate Finance,* 5, no. 4 (Winter 1993): 28–36.

17. Rule 144A (see Chapters 3 and 13), which permits the issuance of unregistered securities on a private placement basis, was intended in part to accommodate foreign issuers of stock that did not want to meet the SEC's financial reporting requirements. For more on the reporting requirements for foreign firms that want their securities traded in the United States, see Frederick D. S. Choi, "Financial Reporting Requirements for Non–U.S. Registrants: International Market Perspectives," *Financial Markets, Institutions & Instruments,* 6, no. 5 (December 1997): 23–44.

18. Another study found that stocks in Austria and Spain had slightly negative correlations with U.S. stocks, whereas stocks in Norway had a correlation of .01; see Roger G. Ibbotson, Richard C. Carr, and Anthony W. Robinson, "International Bond and Equity Portfolios," *Financial Analysts Journal,* 38, no. 4 (July/August 1982): 61–83. Yet another study of 11 countries revealed an average intercountry correlation coefficient of .234; see D. Chinhyung Cho, Cheol S. Eun, and Lemma W. Senbet, "International Arbitrage Pricing

Theory: An Empirical Investigation," *Journal of Finance,* 41, no. 2 (June 1986): 313–329. A third study of 10 equity markets found that the average correlation was .43, and the largest correlation of any of the countries with the United States was .52 (the U.K.); see Gary L. Gastineau, "The Currency Hedging Decision: A Search for Synthesis in Asset Allocation," *Financial Analysts Journal,* 51, no. 3 (May/June 1995): 8–17. In addition, the correlations between emerging markets and the United States have historically been near zero; see the references given in endnote 7. For a multiperiod approach that indicates the benefits from international diversification, particularly for highly risk-averse investors, see Robert R. Grauer and Nils H. Hakansson, "Gains from International Diversification: 1968–85 Returns on Portfolios of Stocks and Bonds," *Journal of Finance,* 42, no. 3 (July 1987): 721–739. Although the correlations between the U.S. and foreign stock markets is surely much less than 1, the actual values are highly dependent on the time period studied.

19. Similar results were found in another study. A negative correlation between the bonds in Italy and the United States was observed. See Ibbotson, Carr, and Robinson, "International Bond and Equity Portfolios."

20. Unfortunately, one study found that the benefits from international diversification are lessened just when these benefits are most needed by investors. Specifically, the low correlations between market returns appear to increase when markets become more volatile. See Patrick Odier and Bruno Solnik, "Lessons for International Asset Allocation," *Financial Analysts Journal,* 49, no. 2 (March/April 1993): 63–77. Another study found that the diversification benefits from international investing was not because different countries have different industrial structures. Hence, international diversification efforts should be aimed more at investing in different countries than in different industries. See Steven L. Heston and K. Geert Rouwenhorst, "Does Industrial Structure Explain the Benefits of International Diversification?" *Journal of Financial Economics,* 36, no. 1 (August 1994): 3–27.

Glossary

Abnormal Return The return earned on a financial asset in excess of that required on securities of similar risk. It is also frequently referred to as alpha.

Account Executive (alternatively, **Registered Representative**) A representative of a brokerage firm whose primary responsibility is servicing the accounts of individual investors.

Accounting Earnings (alternatively, **Reported Earnings**) A firm's revenues less its expenses. Equivalently, dividends paid to shareholders plus the change in the firm's book value of the equity.

Accrued Interest Interest earned, but not yet paid.

Active Management A form of investment management that involves buying and selling financial assets with the objective of earning positive abnormal returns.

Active Position The difference between the percentage of an investor's portfolio invested in a particular financial asset and the percentage of a benchmark portfolio invested in that same asset.

Adjusted Beta An estimate of a security's future beta, derived initially from historical data but modified by the assumption that the security's "true" beta has a tendency over time to move toward the market average of 1.0.

Aggressive Stocks Stocks that have betas greater than one.

Allocationally Efficient Market A market for securities in which those firms with the most promising investment opportunities have access to the needed funds.

Alpha The difference between a security's or portfolio's expected return and its equilibrium expected return (which is its fair return, given its riskiness).

American Depositary Receipts (ADRs) Financial assets issued by U.S. banks that represent indirect ownership of a certain number of shares of a specific foreign firm. These shares are held on deposit in a bank in the firm's home country.

American Option An option that can be exercised any time up until and including its expiration date.

Anomaly An empirical regularity that is not predicted by any known asset pricing model.

Approved List A list of securities that an investment organization deems worthy of accumulation in a given portfolio. For an organization that uses an approved list, typically any security on the list may be purchased by the organization's portfolio managers without additional authorization.

Arbitrage The simultaneous purchase and sale of the same, or essentially similar, security in two different markets at advantageously different prices.

Arbitrage Portfolio A portfolio that requires no investment, has no sensitivity to any factor, and has a positive expected return, and thus provides inflows in some circumstances and requires no outflows under any circumstances.

Arbitrage Pricing Theory An equilibrium model of asset pricing that states that the expected return on a security is a linear function of the security's sensitivity to various common factors.

Arbitrageur A person who engages in arbitrage.

Asked (or **Ask**) **Price** (alternatively, **Offered**) The price at which a market-maker is willing to sell a specified quantity of a particular security.

Asset Allocation The process of determining the optimal division of an investor's portfolio among available asset classes.

Asset Class A broadly defined generic group of financial assets, such as stocks or bonds.

Asset Pricing Model An equilibrium model that describes why assets with different specific characteristics have different expected returns.

Asymmetric Information A situation in which one party has more information than another party.

At the Money An option whose exercise price is roughly equal to the market price of its underlying asset.

693

Attribute See **Factor Loading.**

Automated Bond System (ABS) A computer system established by the New York Stock Exchange to facilitate the trading of inactive bonds that are typically investment grade.

Average Tax Rate The total amount of taxes paid expressed as a percentage of the total income subject to tax.

Bank Discount Basis A method of calculating the interest rate on a pure-discount, fixed-income security that uses the principal of the security as the security's cost.

Bankers Acceptance A type of money market instrument. It is a promissory note issued by a business debtor, with a stated maturity date, arising out of a business transaction. A bank, by endorsing the note, assumes the obligation. If this obligation becomes actively traded, it is referred to as a bankers acceptance.

Basis The difference between the spot price of an asset and the futures price of the same asset.

Basis Point $\frac{1}{100}$ of 1%.

Basis Risk The risk to a futures investor of the basis widening or narrowing.

Benchmark Portfolio A portfolio against which the investment performance of an investor can be compared for the purpose of determining investment skill. A benchmark portfolio represents a relevant and feasible alternative to the investor's actual portfolio and, in particular, is similar in terms of risk exposure.

Best-Efforts Basis A security underwriting in which the members of the investment banking group serve as agents instead of dealers, agreeing only to obtain for the issuer the best price that the market will pay for the security.

Beta (alternatively, **Beta Coefficient** or **Market Beta**) A relative measure of the sensitivity of an asset's return to changes in the return on the market portfolio. Mathematically, the beta coefficient of a security is the security's covariance with the market portfolio divided by the variance of the market portfolio.

Beta Coefficient See **Beta.**

Bid–Ask Spread The difference between the price that a market-maker is willing to pay for a security and the price at which the market-maker is willing to sell the same security.

Bidder In the context of a corporate takeover, the firm making a tender offer to the target firm.

Bid Price The price at which a market-maker is willing to purchase a specified quantity of a particular security.

Block A large order (usually 10,000 shares or more) to buy or sell a security.

Block House A brokerage firm with the financial capacity and the trading expertise to deal in block trades.

Bond Ratings An indicator of the creditworthiness of specific bond issues. These ratings are often interpreted as an indication of the relative likelihood of default on the part of the respective bond issuers.

Bond Swapping A form of active bond management that entails the replacement of bonds in a portfolio with other bonds to enhance the yield of the portfolio.

Book Value of the Equity The sum of the cumulative retained earnings and other balance sheet entries classified under stockholders' equity, such as common stock and capital contributed in excess of par value.

Book Value per Share A corporation's book value of the equity divided by the number of its common shares outstanding.

Bottom-Up Forecasting A sequential approach to security analysis that entails first making forecasts for individual companies, then for industries, and finally for the economy. Each level of forecasts is conditioned on the previous level of forecasts.

Broker An agent who facilitates the buying and selling of securities for investors.

Call Market A security market in which trading is allowed only at specified times. At those times, persons interested in trading a particular security are brought together and a market clearing price is established.

Call Money Rate The interest rate paid by brokerage firms to banks on loans used to finance margin purchases by the brokerage firm's customers.

Call Option A contract that gives the buyer the right but not the obligation to buy a specific number of shares of a company from the option writer at a specific purchase price during a specific time period.

Call Premium The difference between the call price of a bond and the par value of the bond.

Call Price The price that an issuer must pay bondholders when an issue is retired prior to its stated maturity date.

Call Provision A provision in some bond indentures that permits an issuer to retire some or all of the bonds in a particular bond issue prior to the bonds' stated maturity date.

Capital Asset Pricing Model (CAPM) An equilibrium model of asset pricing that states that the expected return on a security is a positive linear function of the security's sensitivity to changes in the market portfolio's return.

Capital Gain (or **Loss**) For financial assets, the difference between the current market value of the asset and the original cost of the asset.

Capital Market Line The set of portfolios obtainable by combining the market portfolio with riskfree borrowing or lending. Assuming homogeneous expectations and perfect markets, the Capital Market Line represents the efficient set.

Capital Markets Financial markets in which financial assets with a term-to-maturity of typically more than one year are traded.

Capitalization of Income Method of Valuation An approach to valuing financial assets. It is based on the concept that the "fair" or intrinsic value of a financial asset is equal to the discounted value of future cash flows generated by that asset.

Capitalization-Weighted Market Index See **Value-Weighted Market Index.**

Cash Account An account maintained by an investor with a brokerage firm in which deposits (cash and the proceeds from security sales) must fully cover withdrawals (cash and the costs of security purchases).

Cash Matching A form of immunization that involves the purchase of bonds that generate a stream of cash inflows identical in amount and timing to a set of expected cash outflows during a given period of time.

CATS See **Computer-Assisted Trading System.**

Certainty Equivalent The return on a riskfree investment that makes the investor indifferent between it and a particularly risky investment.

Certificate of Deposit A form of time deposit issued by banks and other financial institutions.

Certificate of Incorporation See **Charter.**

Characteristic Line A simple linear regression model expressing the relationship between the excess return on a security and the excess return on the market portfolio.

Charter (alternatively, **Certificate of Incorporation**) A document issued by a state to a corporation. It specifies the rights and obligations of the corporation's stockholders.

Chartist A technical analyst who relies primarily on stock price and volume charts when evaluating securities.

Circuitbreakers Established by the New York Stock Exchange, a set of limits on market price movements as measured by the Dow Jones Industrial Average. Depending on the magnitude of the price change, breaking through those limits on the downside results in closing the exchange.

Close See **Closing Price.**

Closed-End Investment Company A managed investment company, with an unlimited life, that does not stand ready to purchase its own shares from its owners and seldom issues new shares beyond its initial offering.

Closing Price (alternatively, **Close**) The price at which the last trade of the day took place in a particular security.

Closing Purchase The purchase of an option contract by an investor that is designed to offset, and thereby cancel, the previous sale of the same option contract by the investor.

Closing Sale The sale of an option contract by an investor that is designed to offset, and thereby cancel, the previous purchase of the same option contract by the investor.

Coefficient of Determination (alternatively, **R-Squared**) In the context of a simple linear regression, the proportion of the variation in the dependent variable that is related to the variation in (that is, "explained by") the independent variable.

Coefficient of Nondetermination In the context of a simple linear regression, the proportion of the variation in the dependent variable that is not related to variation in (that is, "not explained by") the independent variable. Equivalently, one minus the coefficient of determination.

Collateralized Mortgage Obligation A type of mortgage-backed security designed to allocate a mortgage pool's principal and interest payments among investors in accordance with their preferences for prepayment risk.

Commercial Paper A type of money market instrument. It represents unsecured promissory notes of large, financially sound corporations.

Commission The fee an investor pays to a brokerage firm for services rendered in the trading of securities.

Commission Broker A member of an organized security exchange who takes orders that the public has placed with brokerage firms and sees that these orders are executed on the exchange.

Commodity Futures Trading Commission (CFTC) A federal agency established by the Commodity Futures Trading Commission Act of 1974 that approves (or disapproves) the creation of new futures contracts and regulates the trading of existing futures contracts.

Common Stock Legal representation of an equity (or ownership) position in a corporation.

Competitive Bidding With respect to selecting an underwriter, the process of an issuer soliciting bids on the underwriting and choosing the underwriter offering the best overall terms.

Composite Stock Price Tables Price information provided on all stocks traded on the national exchanges, the regional stock exchanges, the Nasdaq system, and the Instinet system.

Compounding The payment of interest on interest.

Computer-Assisted Order Routing and Execution System (CORES) A computer system for trading all but the 150 most active stocks on the Tokyo Stock Exchange.

Computer-Assisted Trading System (CATS) A computer system for trading stocks on the Toronto Stock Exchange that involves a computer file containing a publicly accessible limit order book.

Consolidated Quotations System A system that lists current bid–asked prices of specialists on the national and regional stock exchanges and of certain over-the-counter dealers.

Consolidated Tape A system that reports trades that occur on the national stock exchanges, the regional stock exchanges, the Nasdaq system, and the Instinet system.

Constant-Growth Model A type of dividend discount model in which dividends are assumed to exhibit a constant growth rate.

Consumer Price Index A cost-of-living index that is representative of the goods and services purchased by U.S. consumers.

Contingent Deferred Sales Charge A fee charged by a mutual fund to its shareholders if they sell their shares within a few years after initially purchasing them.

Contingent Immunization A form of bond management that entails both passive and active elements. Under contingent immunization, as long as favorable results are obtained, the bond portfolio is actively managed. However, if unfavorable results occur, then the portfolio is immediately immunized.

Continuous Market A security market in which trades may occur at any time during business hours.

Convexity The tendency for bond prices to change asymmetrically relative to yield changes. Typically, for a given yield change, a bond will rise in price more if the yield change is negative than it will fall in price if the yield change is positive.

CORES See **Computer-Assisted Order Routing and Execution System.**

Corporate Governance The relationship between corporate management and the firm's shareholders.

Correlation Coefficient A statistical measure similar to covariance, in that it measures the degree of mutual variation between two random variables. The correlation coefficient rescales covariance to facilitate comparison among pairs of random variables. The correlation coefficient is bounded by the values −1 and +1.

Cost of Carry The differential between the futures and spot prices of a particular asset. It equals the interest forgone less the benefits plus the costs of ownership.

Cost-of-Living Index A collection of goods and services, and their associated prices, designed to reflect changes over time in the cost of making normal consumption expenditures.

Counterparty Risk The risk posed by the possibility that the person or organization with which an investor has entered into a financial contract may fail to honor the contract.

Coupon Payments The periodic payment of interest on a bond.

Coupon Rate The annual dollar amount of coupon payments made by a bond expressed as a percentage of the bond's par value.

Coupon Stripping The process of separating and selling the individual cash flows of Treasury notes or bonds.

Covariance A statistical measure of the relationship between two random variables. It measures the extent of mutual variation between two random variables.

Covered Call Writing The process of writing a call option on an asset owned by the option writer.

Cross-Deductibility An arrangement among federal and state tax authorities that permits state taxes to be deductible expenses for federal tax purposes, and federal taxes to be deductible expenses for state tax purposes.

Cumulative Dividends A common feature of preferred stock that requires that the issuing corporation pay all previously unpaid preferred stock dividends before any common stock dividends may be paid.

Cumulative Voting System In the context of a corporation, a method of voting in which a stockholder is permitted to give any one candidate for the board of directors a maximum number of votes equal to the number of shares owned by that shareholder times the number of directors being elected.

Currency Risk See **Exchange Risk.**

Current Yield The annual dollar amount of coupon payments made by a bond expressed as a percentage of the bond's current market price.

Customer's Agreement See **Hypothecation Agreement.**

Date of Record The date, established quarterly by a corporation's board of directors, on which the stockholders of record are determined for the purpose of paying a cash or stock dividend.

Day-of-the-Week Effect (alternatively, **Weekend Effect**) An empirical regularity whereby stock returns appear to be lower on Mondays than on other days of the week.

Day Order A trading order the broker will attempt to fill only during the day on which it is entered.

Dealer (alternatively, **Market-Maker**) A person who facilitates the trading of financial assets by maintaining an inventory in particular securities. The dealer buys for and sells from this inventory, profiting from the difference in the buying and selling prices.

Dealer's Spread The bid–ask spread quoted by a security dealer.

Debenture A bond that is not secured by specific property.

Debit Balance The dollar amount owed by an investor to a broker.

Debt Refunding The issuance of new debt for the purpose of paying off currently maturing debt.

Dedicated Portfolio A portfolio of bonds that provides its owner with cash inflows that are matched against a specific stream of cash outflows.

Default Premium The difference between the promised and expected yield-to-maturity on a bond arising from the possibility that the bond issuer might default on the bond.

Defensive Stocks Stocks that have betas less than one.

Delist The process of removing a security's eligibility for trading on an organized security exchange.

Delta See **Hedge Ratio.**

Demand-to-Buy Schedule A description of the quantities of a security that investors are prepared to purchase at alternative prices.

Depository Trust Company A central computerized depository for securities registered in the names of member firms. Members' security certificates are immobilized, and computerized records of ownership are maintained. This permits electronic transfer of the securities from one member to another as trades are conducted between the members' clients.

Discount Broker An organization that offers a limited range of brokerage services and charges fees substantially below those of brokerage firms that provide a full range of services.

Discount Factor The present value of one dollar to be received from a security in a specified number of years.

Discount Rate The interest rate used in calculating the present value of future cash flows. The discount rate reflects not only the time value of money, but also the riskiness of the future cash flows.

Discounting The process of calculating the present value of a given stream of future cash flows.

Discretionary Order A trading order that permits the broker to set the specifications for the order.

Disintermediation A pattern of funds flow whereby investors withdraw funds from financial intermediaries, such as banks and savings and loans, because market interest rates exceed the maximum interest rates that these organizations are permitted to pay. The investors reinvest their withdrawn funds in financial assets that pay interest rates not subject to ceilings.

Distribution Fee (or **12b-1 Fee**) An annual fee charged by a mutual fund to its shareholders to pay for advertising, promoting, and selling the fund to new investors, as well as certain shareholder services.

Diversification The process of adding securities to a portfolio to reduce the portfolio's unique risk and, thereby, the portfolio's total risk.

Dividend Decision The process of determining the amount of dividends that a corporation will pay its shareholders.

Dividend Discount Model The term used for the capitalization of income method of valuation as applied to common stocks. All variants of dividend discount models assume that the intrinsic value of a share of common stock is equal to the discounted value of the dividends forecast to be paid on the stock.

Dividend Yield The current annualized dividend paid on a share of common stock, expressed as a percentage of the current market price of the corporation's common stock.

Dividends Cash payments made to stockholders by the corporation.

Dollar-Weighted Return A method of measuring the performance of a portfolio during a particular period of time. It is the discount rate that makes the present value of cash flows into and out of the portfolio, as well as the portfolio's ending value, equal to the portfolio's beginning value.

Domestic Return The return on an investment in a foreign financial asset, excluding the impact of exchange rate changes.

Double Auction Bidding for a security among both buyers and sellers that may occur when the specialist's bid–ask spread is large enough to permit sales at one or more prices within the spread.

Duration A measure of the average maturity of the stream of payments generated by a financial asset. Mathematically, duration is the weighted average of the lengths of time until the asset's remaining payments are made. The weights in this calculation are the proportion of the asset's total present value represented by the present value of the respective cash flows.

Earnings per Share A corporation's accounting earnings divided by the number of its common shares outstanding.

Earnings-Price Ratio The reciprocal of the price-earnings ratio.

Earnings Yield The earnings-price ratio of a stock, expressed as a percentage.

Econometric Model A statistical model designed to explain and forecast certain economic phenomena.

Economic Earnings The change in the economic value of the firm plus dividends paid to shareholders.

Economic Value of the Firm The aggregate market value of all securities issued by the firm.

Effective Duration A measure of a bond's duration that accounts for the ability of either the bond's issuer or holder to cause the actual stream of cash payments to differ from that which would be received if the bond were paid off as promised over its entire life.

Efficient Diversification The process of creating diversification in a portfolio by selecting securities in a manner that explicitly considers the standard deviations and correlations of the securities.

Efficient Market A market for securities in which every security's price equals its investment value at all times, implying that a specified set of information is fully and immediately reflected in market prices.

Efficient Portfolio A portfolio within the feasible set that offers investors both maximum expected return for varying levels of risk and minimum risk for varying levels of expected return.

Efficient Set (Frontier) The set of efficient portfolios.

Efficient Set Theorem The proposition that investors will choose their portfolios only from the set of efficient portfolios.

Electronic Communications Networks (ECNs) Fourth market computerized systems designed to automatically execute investors' buy and sell orders.

Emerging Markets Financial markets in countries that have a relatively low level of per capita gross domestic product, improving political and economic stability, a currency that is convertible into Western countries' currencies, and securities available for investment by foreigners.

Empirical Regularities Differences in returns on securities that occur with regularity from period to period.

Endogenous Variable In the context of an econometric model, an economic variable that represents the economic phenomena explained by the model.

Equal-Weighted Market Index A market index in which all the component securities contribute equally to the value of the index, regardless of the various attributes of those securities.

Equity Premium The difference between the expected rate of return on common stocks and the riskfree return.

Equity Swap A contract between two counterparties where one pays the other a fixed stream of cash flows and in return receives a varying stream whose cash flows are regularly reset based on the performance of a given stock market index.

Equivalent Yield The annualized yield-to-maturity on a fixed-income security sold on a discount basis.

Eurobond A bond that is offered outside of the country of the borrower and usually outside of the country in whose currency the security is denominated.

Eurodollar Certificate of Deposit A certificate of deposit denominated in U.S. dollars and issued by banks domiciled outside of the United States.

Eurodollar Deposit A U.S. dollar-denominated time deposit held at a bank domiciled outside of the United States.

European Option An option that can be exercised only on its expiration date.

Ex Ante Before the fact; future.

Ex Distribution Date The date on which ownership of stock is determined for purposes of paying stock dividends or issuing new shares because of stock splits. Owners purchasing shares before the ex distribution date receive the new shares in question. Owners purchasing shares on or after the ex distribution date are not entitled to the new shares.

Ex Dividend Date The date on which ownership of stock is determined for purposes of paying cash dividends. Owners purchasing shares before the ex dividend date receive the dividend in question. Owners purchasing shares on or after the ex dividend date are not entitled to the dividend.

Ex Post After the fact; historical.

Ex Post Alpha A portfolio's alpha calculated on an *ex post* basis. Mathematically, during an evaluation interval, it is the difference between the average return on the portfolio and the average return on a benchmark portfolio.

Ex Post Selection Bias In the context of constructing a security valuation model, the use of securities that have performed well and the avoidance of securities that have performed poorly, making the model seem more effective than it truly is.

Excess Return The difference between the return on a security and the return on the riskfree asset.

Exchange Distribution or **Acquisition** A trade involving a large block of stock on an organized security exchange whereby a brokerage firm attempts to execute the order by finding enough offsetting orders from its customers.

Exchange Risk (alternatively, **Currency Risk**) The uncertainty in the return on a foreign financial asset because of unpredictability regarding the rate at which the foreign currency can be exchanged into the investor's own currency.

Exercise Price (alternatively, **Strike Price**) In the case of a call option, the price at which an option buyer may purchase the underlying asset from the option writer. In the case of a put option, the price at which an option buyer may sell the underlying asset to the option writer.

Exogenous Variable In the context of an econometric model, an economic variable taken as given and used in the model to explain the model's endogenous variables.

Expectations Hypothesis A relationship between the futures price of an asset and the expected spot price of the asset on the delivery date of the contract. It states that the futures price will equal the expected spot price.

Expected Holding Period Return (alternatively, **Expected Return**) The return on a security (or portfolio) that an investor anticipates receiving over a holding period.

Expected Return See **Expected Holding Period Return.**

Expected Return Vector A column of numbers that correspond to the expected returns for a set of securities.

Expected Value See **Mean.**

Expected Yield-to-Maturity The yield-to-maturity on a bond calculated as a weighted average of all possible yields that the bond might produce under different scenarios of default or late payments, where the weights are the probabilities of each scenario's occurring.

Expiration Date The date on which the right to buy or sell a security under an option contract ceases.

Externally Efficient Market A market for securities in which information is quickly and widely disseminated, thereby allowing each security's price to adjust rapidly in an unbiased manner to new information so that it reflects investment value.

Face Value See **Principal.**

Factor (alternatively, **Index**) An aspect of the investment environment that influences the returns of financial assets. To the extent that a factor influences a significant number of financial assets, it is termed common or pervasive.

Factor Loading (alternatively, **Attribute** or **Sensitivity**) A measure of the responsiveness of a security's returns to a particular common factor.

Factor Model (alternatively, **Index Model**) A return-generating process that attributes the return on a security to the security's sensitivity to the movements of various common factors.

Factor Risk That part of a security's total risk that is related to moves in various common factors and, hence, cannot be diversified away.

Factor Risk Premium The expected return over and above the riskfree rate on a portfolio that has unit sensitivity to a particular factor and zero sensitivity to all other factors.

Fallen Angel A speculative-grade bond that was of investment grade when originally issued.

Feasible Set (alternatively, **Opportunity Set**) The set of all portfolios that can be formed from the group of securities being considered by an investor.

Federally Sponsored Agency A privately owned organization with government backing that issues securities and uses the proceeds to support the granting of various types of special-purpose loans.

Fill-or-Kill (FOK) Order A trading order that is canceled if the broker is unable to completely execute it immediately.

Financial Analyst (alternatively, **Security Analyst** or **Investment Analyst**) An individual who analyzes financial assets to determine the investment characteristics of those assets and to identify mispricings among those assets.

Financial Asset See **Security.**

Financial Institution See **Financial Intermediary.**

Financial Intermediary (alternatively, **Financial Institution**) An organization that issues financial claims against itself and uses the proceeds of the issuance primarily to purchase financial assets issued by individuals, partnerships, corporations, government entities, and other financial intermediaries.

Financial Investment An investment in financial assets.

Financial Leverage The use of debt to fund a portion of an investment.

Financial Market (alternatively, **Security Market**) A mechanism designed to facilitate the exchange of financial assets by bringing buyers and sellers of securities together.

Firm Commitment An arrangement between underwriters and a security issuer whereby the underwriters agree to purchase at the offering price all of the issue not bought by the public.

Fixed Income Pricing System (FIPS) A bond market, run by the Nasdaq Stock Market, that is devoted to trading high-yield bonds.

Floating Rate (alternatively, **Variable Rate**) A rate of interest on a financial asset that may vary during the life of the asset, depending on changes in a specified indicator of current market interest rates.

Floor Broker (alternatively, **Two-Dealer Broker**) A member of an organized security exchange who assists commission brokers when there are too many orders flowing into the market for the commission brokers to handle alone.

Floor Order Routing and Execution System (FORES) A computer system for trading the 150 most active stocks on the Tokyo Stock Exchange.

Floor Trader (alternatively, **Registered Competitive Market-Maker** or **Registered Trader**) A member of an organized security exchange who trades solely for his or her own account and is prohibited by exchange rules from handling public orders.

Foreign Return The return on an investment in a foreign financial asset, including the impact of exchange rate changes.

FORES See **Floor Order Routing and Execution System.**

Forward Contract A contract made at a given date wherein money will be loaned at a future date and repaid at an agreed-on point further in the future. More generally, a contract made at a given date that involves delivery of an asset at an agreed-on future date, with payment occurring at delivery.

Forward Rate The interest rate that links the current spot interest rate over one holding period to the current spot interest rate over a longer holding period. Equivalently, the interest rate agreed on at a point in time when the associated loan will be made at a future date.

Fourth Market A secondary security market in which investors (typically, financial institutions) trade securities directly with one another, bypassing the brokers and dealers on organized security exchanges and the over-the-counter market.

Fundamental Analysis A form of security analysis that seeks to determine the intrinsic value of securities based on underlying economic factors. These intrinsic values are compared to current market prices to estimate current levels of mispricing.

Futures (Futures Contract) An agreement between two investors under which the seller promises to deliver a specific asset on a specific future date to the buyer for a predetermined price to be paid on the delivery date. Both buyer and seller must maintain deposits with their broker to assure each other of complying with the terms of the agreement.

Futures Commission Merchant (FCM) A firm that carries out orders submitted by customers involving futures.

Futures Option (alternatively, **Options on Futures**) An option contract for which the deliverable asset is a specific futures contract.

General Obligation Bond A municipal bond that is backed by the full faith and credit of the issuing agency.

Generally Accepted Accounting Principles (GAAP) Accounting rules established by recognized U.S. authorities, such as the Financial Accounting Standards Board (FASB).

Geometric Mean Return The compounded per period average rate of return on a financial asset during a specified time interval.

Good-till-Canceled (GTC) Order See **Open Order.**

Growth Stock A stock that has experienced or is expected to experience rapidly increasing earnings per share and is often characterized as having low earnings-to-price and book-value-to-market-value ratios.

Hedge Ratio (alternatively, **Delta**) The expected change in the value of an option per dollar change in the market price of the underlying asset.

Hedger An investor in futures or options contracts whose primary objective is to offset an otherwise risky position.

High-Yield Bonds See **Speculative-Grade Bonds.**

Historical Beta An estimate of a security's beta, derived solely from historical returns. Equivalently, the slope of the market model or the *ex post* characteristic line.

Holding Period The length of time over which an investor is assumed to invest a given sum of money.

Holding Period Return (alternatively, **Rate of Return**) The percentage change in the value of an investment in a financial asset (or portfolio of financial assets) during a specific time period.

Holdout Sample See **Out-of-Sample Data.**

Holiday Effect The observation that average stock returns have been abnormally high on the trading day immediately before a federal holiday.

Homogeneous Expectations A situation in which all investors possess the same perceptions with regard to the expected returns, standard deviations, and covariances of securities.

Horizon Analysis A form of active bond management where a single holding period is selected for analysis and possible yield structures at the end of the period are considered. Bonds with the most attractive expected returns under the alternative yield structures are selected for the portfolio.

Hypothecation Agreement (alternatively, **Customer's Agreement**) A legal arrangement between a brokerage firm and an investor that permits the brokerage firm to pledge the investor's securities as collateral for bank loans, provided the securities were purchased through the investor's margin account.

Idiosyncratic Risk See **Nonfactor Risk.**

Immunization A bond portfolio management technique that permits an investor to meet a promised stream of cash outflows with a high degree of certainty.

Implied Return See **Internal Rate of Return.**

Implied (or **Implicit**) **Volatility** The risk of an asset derived from an options valuation model, assuming that an option on the asset is fairly priced by the market.

In the Money In the case of a call option, an option whose exercise price is less than the current market price of its underlying asset. In the case of a put option, an option whose exercise price is greater than the current market price of its underlying asset.

Indenture A legal document formally describing the terms of the legal relationship between a bond issuer and bondholders.

Index See **Factor.**

Index Arbitrage An investment strategy that involves buying a stock index futures contract and selling the individual stocks in the index, or selling a stock index futures contract and buying the individual stocks in the index. The strategy is designed to take advantage of a mispricing between the stock index futures contract and the underlying stocks.

Indexation A method of linking payments associated with a bond to the price level in order to provide a certain real return on the bond.

Index Fund A passively managed investment in a diversified portfolio of financial assets designed to mimic the investment performance of a specific market index.

Index Model See **Factor Model.**

Indifference Curve All combinations of portfolios, considered in terms of expected returns and risk, that provide an investor with an equal amount of satisfaction.

Individual Retirement Account (IRA) A tax-advantaged means for people to set aside income and avoid taxes on the subsequent earnings until those earnings and the original funds are withdrawn.

Industrial Development Bond (IDB) A form of revenue bond used to finance the purchase or construction of industrial facilities that are leased by the issuing municipality to firms on a favorable basis.

Inefficient Portfolio A portfolio that does not satisfy the criteria of an efficient portfolio and, hence, does not lie on the efficient set.

Inflation The rate of change in a price index during a certain period of time. Equivalently, the percentage change in the purchasing power of a unit of currency during a certain period of time.

Inflation-Indexed Security A security whose real return is certain if held to maturity.

Information Content of Dividends Hypothesis The proposition that dividend announcements contain inside information about a corporation's future prospects.

Initial Margin Requirement The minimum percentage of a margin purchase (or short sale) price that must come from the investor's own funds.

Initial Public Offering (IPO) (alternatively, **Unseasoned Offering**) The first offering of the shares of a company to the public.

Initial Wealth The value of an investor's portfolio at the beginning of a holding period.

Inside Quotes [alternatively, **National Best Bid or Offer (NBBO)**] The highest bid price and the lowest asked price for a given stock offered by a group of dealers in a particular stock.

Insider Narrowly defined, an officer or director of a corporation or a stockholder who owns a "significant" proportion of a corporation's stock. More broadly defined, anyone who has access to information that is both "materially" related to the value of a corporation's securities and unavailable to the general public.

Instinet Acronym for Institutional Network. A computerized communications system that provides price quotations and order execution for fourth market participants.

Interest Rate Parity An explanation for why spot and futures exchange rates differ. It asserts that such differences result from different interest rates in the two countries.

Interest Rate Risk The uncertainty in the return on a fixed-income security caused by unanticipated fluctuations in the value of the asset because of changes in interest rates.

Interest Rate Swap A contract between two counterparties where one pays the other a fixed stream of cash flows and in return receives a varying stream whose cash flows are regularly reset based on the level of a given interest rate.

Intermarket Spread Swap A type of bond swap where an investor moves out of one market segment and into another because the investor believes that one segment is significantly underpriced relative to the other.

Intermarket Trading System (ITS) An electronic communications network that links the national and regional organized security exchanges and certain over-the-counter dealers. The network provides market-maker price quotes and allows participating brokers and dealers to route orders to market-makers offering the best prices.

Internal Rate of Return (alternatively, **Implied Return**) The discount rate that equates the sum of the present value of future cash flows expected to be received from a particular investment to the cost of that investment.

Internalization A form of preferencing whereby broker-dealers who are members of the New York Stock Exchange take their customers orders and fill them internally instead of sending them to an exchange floor for execution.

Internally Efficient Market A market for securities in which brokers and dealers compete fairly so that the cost of transacting is low and the speed of transacting is high.

Intrinsic Value of an Option The value of an option if it were exercised immediately. Equivalently, the mar-ket price of the asset on which a call option is written less the exercise price of the option (or the exercise price less the market price of the asset, in the case of a put option), or zero, whichever is larger.

Investment The sacrifice of certain present value for (possibly uncertain) future value.

Investment Analyst See **Financial Analyst.**

Investment Banker (alternatively, **Underwriter**) An organization that acts as an intermediary between issuers and the ultimate purchasers of securities in the primary security market.

Investment Committee With a traditional investment organization, a group of senior management responsible for establishing the organization's broad investment strategy.

Investment Company A type of financial intermediary that obtains money from investors and uses that money to purchase financial assets. In return, the investors receive shares in the investment company, and thus indirectly own a proportion of the financial assets that the company itself owns.

Investment Environment The financial structure in which investors operate, consisting of the kinds of marketable securities available for purchase or sale and how and where these securities are bought and sold.

Investment-Grade Bonds Bonds that possess bond ratings that permit them to be purchased by the vast majority of institutional investors, particularly regulated financial institutions. Usually, investment grade bonds have a BBB (Standard & Poor's) or Baa (Moody's) or higher bond rating.

Investment Manager See **Portfolio Manager.**

Investment Policy A component of the investment process that involves determining an investor's objectives, particularly his or her attitude toward the trade-off between expected return and risk.

Investment Process The set of procedures by which an investor decides what marketable securities to invest in, how extensive those investments should be, and when the investments should be made.

Investment Style The method an investor uses to take positions in certain types of securities or the types of securities an investor holds.

Investment Value The present value of a security's future prospects as estimated by well-informed market participants.

January Effect An empirical regularity whereby stock returns have historically been higher in January, on average, than in other months of the year.

Junk Bonds See **Speculative-Grade Bonds.**

Keogh Plan A tax-advantaged means by which people who are self-employed (or without access to an employer-sponsored retirement plan) can set aside income on a before-tax basis and invest tax-free until the original funds and subsequent earnings are later withdrawn.

Letter Stock (alternatively, **Restricted Stock**) Stock that is unregistered and sold directly to the purchaser, rather than through a public offering. Such stock must be held at least one year and cannot be sold even at that time unless ample information on the company is available and the amount sold is a relatively small percentage of the total shares outstanding.

Leveraged Buyout A situation in which a private investment group, using substantial amounts of debt financing, buys all the shares of a publicly held firm, thereby gaining control of the firm.

Limit Order A trading order that specifies a limit price at which the broker is to execute the order. The trade will be executed only if the broker can meet or better the limit price.

Limit Order Book (alternatively, **Specialist's Book**) The records kept by the specialist identifying the unfilled limit, stop, and stop limit orders that brokers want to execute in a particular security.

Limit Price The price specified when a limit order is placed with a broker, defining the maximum purchase price or minimum selling price at which the order can be executed.

Limited Liability An aspect of the corporate form of organization that prevents common stockholders from losing more than their investment if the corporation should default on its obligations.

Liquidity (alternatively, **Marketability**) The ability of investors to convert securities to cash at a price similar to the price of the previous trade in the security, assuming that no significant new information has arrived since the previous trade. Equivalently, the ability to sell an asset quickly without making a substantial price concession.

Liquidity Preference (Premium) Theory An explanation of the term structure of interest rates. It holds that the term structure is a result of the preference of investors for short-term securities. Investors can be induced to hold longer term securities only if they expect to receive a higher return.

Liquidity Premium The expected incremental return of longer term securities over shorter term securities that compensates investors for the greater interest rate risk entailed in holding longer term securities.

Listed Security A security that is traded on an organized security exchange.

Load Charge A sales charge levied by a mutual fund when an investor buys its shares. Sometimes it is levied when the investor sells the fund's shares.

Load Fund A mutual fund that has a load charge.

Local (alternatively, **Scalper**) A member of an organized futures exchange who trades for his or her own account and has a very short holding period.

Long Hedger A hedger who offsets risk by buying futures contracts.

Low-Load Fund A mutual fund that has a relatively small load charge, usually 3.5% or less.

M-Squared (M^2) An *ex post* risk-adjusted measure of portfolio performance that compares a portfolio's average return to what it would have earned if the portfolio had been invested with the same degree of total risk as the market portfolio.

Maintenance Margin Requirement The minimum collateral that a brokerage firm requires investors to keep in their margin accounts.

Majority Voting System (alternatively, **Straight Voting System**) In the context of a corporation, a system of "one share, one vote" for each seat to be filled on the board of directors. Equivalently, a method of voting in which a stockholder is permitted to give any one candidate for the board of directors a maximum number of votes equal to the number of shares owned by that shareholder.

Managed Investment Company An investment company with a portfolio that may be altered at the discretion of the company's portfolio manager.

Management Buyout A situation in which the existing management of a publicly owned firm, perhaps joined by an outside investment group, buys all the shares of the existing stockholders, thereby gaining complete control of the firm.

Margin Account An account maintained by an investor with a brokerage firm in which securities may be purchased by borrowing a portion of the purchase price from the brokerage firm, or may be sold short by borrowing the securities from the brokerage firm.

Margin Call A demand on an investor by a brokerage firm to increase the collateral or decrease the debit balance in the investor's margin account. The margin call is initiated when the investor's collateral falls below the minimum amount determined by the maintenance margin requirement.

Margin Purchase The purchase of securities financed by borrowing a portion of the purchase price from a brokerage firm.

Marginal Tax Rate The amount of taxes, expressed as a percentage, paid on each additional dollar of taxable income received.

Marginal Utility The extra utility that a person derives from engaging in an extra unit of economic activity.

Markdown The difference in prices between what an investor's broker receives and what the investor receives for a security sold in the over-the-counter market.

Marked (or **Marking**) **to Market** The daily process of adjusting the equity in an investor's account to reflect the daily changes in the market value of the account's assets and liabilities.

Market Beta See **Beta.**

Market Capitalization The aggregate market value of a security, equal to the market price per unit of the security multiplied by the total number of outstanding units of the security.

Market Discount Bond A bond initially issued at par that sells at a price below par in the secondary market.

Market Discount Function The set of discount factors on all default-free bonds across the spectrum of terms-to-maturity.

Market Index A collection of securities whose prices are averaged to reflect the overall investment performance of a particular set of financial assets.

Market-Maker See **Dealer.**

Market Model A simple linear model that expresses the relationship between the return on a security and the return on a market index.

Market Order A trading order that instructs the broker to buy or sell a security immediately at the best obtainable price.

Market Portfolio A portfolio consisting of an investment in all securities. The proportion invested in each security equals the percentage of the total market capitalization represented by the security.

Market Risk (alternatively, **Systematic Risk**) The portion of a security's total risk that is related to moves in the market portfolio and, hence, cannot be diversified away.

Market Segmentation Theory An explanation of the term structure of interest rates. It holds that various investors and borrowers are restricted by law, preference, or custom to certain maturity ranges. Spot rates in each market segment are determined by supply and demand conditions there.

Market Timing A form of active management that entails shifting an investor's funds between a surrogate market portfolio and the riskfree asset, depending on the investor's perception of their relative near-term prospects.

Marketability See **Liquidity.**

Marking to Market See **Marked to Market.**

Markup The difference in prices between what an investor pays and what the investor's broker pays for a security purchased in the over-the-counter market.

Maturity Date The date on which a bond issuer promises to repay investors the principal of the bond.

May Day The date (May 1, 1975) that the New York Stock Exchange ended its fixed-commission rate requirement and permitted member firms to negotiate commission rates with customers.

Mean (alternatively, **Expected Value**) A measure of central tendency of the probability distribution of a random variable that equals the weighted average of all possible outcomes using their probabilities as weights.

Median The outcome of a random variable where there is an equal probability of observing a value greater or less than it.

Member Corporation See **Member Firm.**

Member Firm (alternatively, **Member Corporation** or **Member Organization**) A brokerage firm with one or more memberships in an organized security exchange.

Member Organization See **Member Firm.**

Merger A form of corporate takeover in which two firms combine their operations and become one firm. Mergers are usually negotiated by the managements of the two merging corporations.

Mispriced Security A security that is trading at a price substantially different from its investment value.

Mode The one outcome of a random variable that has the highest probability of occurring.

Modified Duration The duration of a bond divided by the quantity 1 plus the bond's yield. For one percentage point change in yields, it measures the change in the opposite direction of the bond's price.

Money Manager See **Portfolio Manager.**

Money Markets Financial markets in which financial assets with a term-to-maturity of typically one year or less are traded.

Mortgage Bond A bond that is secured by the pledge of specific property. In the event of default, bondholders are entitled to obtain the property in question and sell it to satisfy their claims on the issuer.

Multiple-Growth Model A type of dividend discount model in which dividends are assumed to grow at different rates for specifically defined time periods.

Municipal Bond A bond issued by a state or local unit of government.

Mutual Fund See **Open-End Investment Company.**

Naked Call Writing The process of writing a call option on a stock that the option writer does not own.

Naked Put Writing The process of writing a put option on a stock when the writer does not have sufficient cash (or securities) in his or her brokerage account to purchase the stock.

Nasdaq International An early morning system for trading NYSE, AMEX, and Nasdaq securities through the use of a dealer network.

National Association of Securities Dealers (NASD) A self-regulatory agency that establishes rules and regulations and monitors the activities of brokers and dealers in the over-the-counter market.

National Association of Securities Dealers Automated Quotations (Nasdaq) An automated nationwide communications network operated by the NASD that connects dealers and brokers in the over-the-counter market. Nasdaq provides current bid-asked price quotes to market participants.

National Best Bid or Offer (NBBO) See **Inside Quotes.**

National Market System (Nasdaq/NMS) A segment of Nasdaq comprised of issues with relatively large trading volumes. More detailed trading information is provided on stocks included in Nasdaq/NMS than on other over-the-counter stocks.

NBBO See **National Best Bid or Offer.**

Neglected Firm Effect An empirical observation that firms followed by relatively few security analysts have had abnormally high returns.

Net Asset Value The market value of an investment company's assets, less any liabilities, divided by the number of shares outstanding.

Net Present Value The present value of future cash flows expected to be received from a particular investment less the cost of that investment.

No-Growth Model See **Zero-Growth Model.**

No-Load Fund A mutual fund that does not have a load charge.

Nominal Return The percentage change in the value of a financial asset, where the beginning and ending values of the asset are not adjusted for inflation over the time of the investment.

Nonfactor Risk (alternatively, **Idiosyncratic Risk**) The portion of a security's total risk that is not related to moves in various common factors and, hence, can be diversified away.

Nonmarket Risk See **Unique Risk.**

Nonsatiation A condition whereby investors are assumed to always prefer higher levels of terminal wealth to lower levels of terminal wealth.

Normal Backwardation A relationship between the futures price of an asset today and the expected spot price of the asset on the delivery date of the contract. Normal backwardation states that the futures price will be less than the expected spot price.

Normal Contango A relationship between the futures price of an asset today and the expected spot price of the asset on the delivery date of the contract. Normal contango states that the futures price will be greater than the expected spot price.

Normal Distribution A symmetrical bell-shaped probability distribution, completely described by its mean and standard deviation.

Normative Economics A form of economic analysis that is prescriptive in nature, dealing with what "ought to be."

Odd Lot An amount of stock that is less than the standard unit of trading, generally from 1 to 99 shares.

Offered (or **Offer**) **Price** See **Asked Price.**

On-the-Run Issues The most recently issued Treasury securities of a given maturity.

Open-End Investment Company (alternatively, **Mutual Fund**) A managed investment company with an unlimited life that stands ready at all times to purchase its shares from its owners and usually will continuously offer new shares to the public.

Open Interest The number of a particular futures or options contract that are outstanding at a particular point in time.

Open Order (alternatively, **Good-till-Canceled (GTC) Order**) A trading order that remains in effect until it is either filled or canceled by the investor.

Operating Expense Ratio The percentage of an investment company's average assets that are used to pay for management fees, administrative expenses, and other operating expenses in a given year.

Opportunity Set See **Feasible Set.**

Optimal Portfolio The feasible portfolio that offers an investor the maximum level of satisfaction. This portfolio represents the tangency between the efficient set and an indifference curve of the investor.

Option A contract between two investors in which one investor grants the other the right to buy (or sell) a specific asset at a specific price within a specific time period.

Options on Futures See **Futures Option.**

Order Specification The investor's instructions to a broker regarding the particular characteristics of a trading order, including the name of the security's issuing firm, whether to buy or sell, order size, maximum time the order is to be outstanding, and the type of order to be used.

Organized Exchange A central physical location where trading of securities is done under a set of rules and regulations.

Original Issue Discount (OID) Security A bond that was originally issued at a price below its par value.

Out-of-Sample Data (alternatively, **Holdout Sample**) In the context of constructing a security valuation model, information that is obtained from periods different from those used to estimate and formulate the valuation model. Out-of-sample data can be used to test the model's validity.

Out of the Money In the case of a call option, an option whose exercise price is greater than the market price of its underlying asset. In the case of a put option, an option whose exercise price is less than the market price of its underlying asset.

Overmargined (alternatively, **Unrestricted**) A situation in which the collateral in a margin account has risen above the minimum amount determined by the initial margin requirement.

Overpriced Security (alternatively, **Overvalued Security**) A security whose expected return is less than its equilibrium expected return. Equivalently, a security with a negative alpha.

Oversubscription Privilege The opportunity given shareholders who have exercised their rights in a rights offering to buy shares that were not purchased in the offering.

Overvalued Security See **Overpriced Security.**

Par Value The nominal value of shares of common stock as legally carried on the books of a corporation.

Par Value of Bond See **Principal.**

Participation Certificate A bond that represents an ownership interest in a pool of fixed-income securities. The holders of the certificates receive the interest and principal payments on the pooled securities in proportion to their ownership of the pool.

Passive Investment System (alternatively, **Passive Management**) The process of buying and holding a well-diversified portfolio.

Passive Management See **Passive Investment System.**

Payout Ratio The percentage of a firm's earnings paid to shareholders in the form of cash dividends.

Pegging The process by which investment bankers attempt to stabilize the price of an underwritten security in the secondary market for a period of time after the initial offering date.

Perfect Markets Security markets in which no impediments to investing exist. These impediments include finite divisibility of securities, taxes, transaction costs, and costly information.

Performance Margin The initial margin that must be posted by a futures buyer or seller.

Pink Sheets Written published quotations on over-the-counter stocks that are not listed on Nasdaq.

Plus Tick See **Up Tick.**

Poison Pill A strategy used by corporations to ward off hostile takeovers. The targeted company gives its shareholders certain rights that can be exercised only in the event of a hostile takeover, and that, once exercised, will be extremely onerous to the acquirer.

Political Risk The uncertainty in the return on a foreign financial asset because of the possibility that the foreign government might take actions that are detrimental to the investor's financial interests, such as restricting the ability of the investor to convert profits into his or her own currency.

Portfolio Construction (alternatively, **Security Selection**) A component of the investment process that involves identifying which assets to invest in and determining the proportion of funds to invest in each of the assets.

Portfolio Manager (alternatively, **Investment Manager** or **Money Manager**) An individual who uses the information provided by financial analysts to manage a portfolio of financial assets on behalf of others.

Portfolio Performance Evaluation A component of the investment process involving periodic analysis of how a portfolio performed in terms of both returns earned and risk incurred.

Portfolio Revision A component of the investment process involving periodically repeating the process of setting investment policy, conducting security analysis, and constructing a portfolio.

Portfolio Turnover Rate A measure of how much buying and selling occurs in a portfolio during a given period of time.

Positive Economics A form of economic analysis that is descriptive in nature, dealing with "what is."

Preemptive Rights When a corporation plans an issuance of new common shares, the right of existing shareholders to purchase the new shares in proportion to the number of shares that they currently own.

Preferred Habitat Theory An explanation of the term structure of interest rates. Similar to the market segmentation theory, it holds that various investors and borrowers have segments of the market in which they prefer to operate. However, these investors are assumed to be willing to leave their desired maturity segments if there are significant differences in yields between the various segments.

Preferred Stock A hybrid form of security that has characteristics of both common stocks and bonds.

Premium The price of an option contract.

Price-Earnings Ratio A corporation's current stock price divided by its earnings per share.

Price Impact The effect on the price of a security resulting from a trade in that security. Price impact is the result of several factors including size of the trade, demand for immediate liquidity, and presumed information of the individual or organization placing the order.

Price Relative The price of a security at the end of one period divided by its price at the end of the previous period. If a dividend is paid during the period, it is added to the end-of-period price.

Price-Weighted Market Index A market index in which the contribution of a security to the value of the index is a function of the security's current market price.

Primary Market The market in which securities are sold at the time of their initial issuance.

Principal (alternatively, **Face Value** or **Par Value of Bond**) The nominal value of a bond that is repaid to bondholders at the maturity date.

Private Placement The direct sale of a newly issued security to a small number of large institutional investors.

Probabilistic Forecasting A form of security analysis that begins with a series of economic scenarios, along with their respective probabilities of occurrence. Under each of these scenarios, accompanying projections are made as to the prospects for various industries, companies, and stock prices.

Probability Distribution A model describing the relative frequency of possible values that a random variable can assume.

Promised Yield-to-Maturity The yield-to-maturity on a bond calculated assuming that all promised cash flows are received on a full and timely basis.

Prospectus The official selling circular that must be given to purchasers of new securities whose offering is registered with the Securities and Exchange Commission. The prospectus provides various information about the issuer's business, its financial condition, and the nature of the security being offered.

Proxy The signing by a shareholder of a power of attorney, thereby authorizing a designated party to cast all of the shareholder's votes on any matter brought up at the corporation's annual meeting, or any special meeting.

Proxy Fight An attempt by dissident shareholders to solicit proxies to vote against corporate incumbents.

Purchasing Group See **Syndicate.**

Purchasing-Power Risk The risk experienced by investors in financial assets because of uncertainty about the impact of inflation on the real returns produced by those financial assets.

Pure Discount Bond (alternatively, **Zero Coupon Bond** or **Pure Discount Security**) A bond that promises to make only one payment to its owner.

Pure Discount Security See **Pure Discount Bond.**

Pure Factor Play See **Pure Factor Portfolio.**

Pure Factor Portfolio (alternatively, **Pure Factor Play**) A portfolio that possesses a unit sensitivity to one factor and no sensitivity to any other factor and has negligible zero nonfactor risk.

Pure Yield Pickup Swap A type of bond swap where an investor exchanges one bond for another to obtain a higher yield for the long term, with little attention paid to the near-term outlook for the bond's respective market segment or the market as a whole.

Putable Bond A bond that offers the owner the option to present the bond to the issuer in exchange for cash equal to the bond's face value at a time chosen by the owner.

Put-Call Parity The relationship between the market price of a put and a call that have the same exercise price, expiration date, and underlying stock.

Put Option A contract that gives the buyer the right but not the obligation to sell a specific number of shares of a company to the writer at a specific price within a specific time period.

R-Squared See **Coefficient of Determination.**

Random Diversification The process of creating diversification in a portfolio by randomly selecting securities without regard to the standard deviations and correlations of the securities.

Random Error Term The difference between the actual value of a random variable and the predicted value based on some model.

Random Variable A variable that takes on alternative values as described by a particular probability distribution.

Random Walk (or **Random Walk Model**) In general, a situation in which changes in the value of a random variable are independent and identically distributed. When applied to common stocks, it refers to a situation in which security price changes are independent and identically distributed, meaning that the size of a security's price change from one period to the next can be viewed as being determined by the spin of a roulette wheel.

Rate Anticipation Swap A type of bond swap where an investor exchanges bonds that are expected to perform relatively poorly for those that are expected to perform relatively well, given an anticipated movement in interest rates.

Rate of Return See **Holding Period Return.**

Real Estate Investment Trust (REIT) An investment fund, similar to an investment company, whose investment objective is to hold primarily real estate–related assets, either through mortgages, construction and development loans, or equity interests.

Real Investment An investment involving some kind of tangible asset, such as land, equipment, or buildings.

Real Return The percentage change in the value of an investment in a financial asset, where the ending value and interim cash flows of the asset are adjusted for inflation during the time of the investment.

Realized Capital Gain (or Loss) A capital gain (or loss) on an asset that is recognized, for tax purposes, through the sale or exchange of the asset.

Red Herring A preliminary prospectus that provides much of the information in the final prospectus but is not an offer to sell the security, nor does it display an actual offering price.

Redemption Fee A fee levied by an investment company when an investor sells his or her shares back to the investment company within a few days of purchase.

Regional Brokerage Firm An organization offering brokerage services that specializes in trading the securities of companies located in a particular region of the country.

Regional Exchange An organized exchange that specializes in trading the securities of companies located in a particular region of the country.

Registered Competitive Market-Maker See **Floor Trader.**

Registered Representative See **Account Executive.**

Registered Trader See **Floor Trader.**

Registrar A designated agent of a corporation responsible for canceling and issuing shares of stock in the corporation as these shares are issued or traded.

Registration Statement A document filed with the Securities and Exchange Commission prior to initiating a public security offering.

Reinvestment-Rate Risk The uncertainty in the return on a fixed-income asset caused by unanticipated changes in the interest rate at which cash flows from the asset can be reinvested.

Repo Rate The rate of interest involved in a repurchase agreement.

Repurchase Agreement A type of money market instrument that involves the sale of a financial asset from one investor to another. The investor selling the asset simultaneously agrees to repurchase it from the purchaser on a stated future date at a predetermined price, which is higher than the original transaction price.

Repurchase Offer An offer by the management of a corporation to buy back some of its own stock.

Residual Standard Deviation See **Standard Deviation of the Random Error Term.**

Restricted Account A margin account in which the collateral has fallen below the minimum amount determined by initial margin requirement but remains above the minimum amount determined by maintenance margin requirement.

Restricted Stock See **Letter Stock.**

Retention Ratio The percentage of a firm's earnings that are not paid to shareholders but instead are retained by the firm. Equivalently, one minus the payout ratio.

Return-Generating Process A statistical model that describes how the returns on a security are produced.

Return on Equity The earnings of a firm divided by the firm's book value of the equity.

Revenue Bond A municipal bond that is backed solely by the revenues from a designated project, authority, or agency, or by the proceeds from a specific tax.

Reverse Stock Split A form of stock split whereby the number of shares is reduced and the par value per share is increased.

Reversing Trade The purchase or sale of a futures (or options) contract designed to offset, and thereby cancel, the previous sale or purchase of the same contract.

Reward-to-Variability Ratio See **Sharpe Ratio.**

Reward-to-Volatility Ratio (Treynor Ratio) An *ex post* risk-adjusted measure of portfolio performance where risk is defined as the market risk of the portfolio. Mathematically, during an evaluation period, it is the excess return of a portfolio divided by the beta of the portfolio.

Rights Options issued to existing shareholders that permit them to buy a specified number of new shares at a designated subscription price. For each shareholder this number is proportional to the number of existing shares currently owned by the shareholder.

Rights Offering The sale of new stock conducted by first offering the stock to existing shareholders in proportion to the number of shares owned by each shareholder.

Risk The uncertainty associated with the end-of-period value of an investment.

Risk-Averse Investor An investor who prefers an investment with less risk over one with more risk, assuming that both investments offer the same expected return.

Risk-Neutral Investor An investor who has no preference between investments with varying levels of risk, assuming that the investments offer the same expected return.

Risk Premium The expected increase in terminal wealth (or expected return) associated with a risky investment over the increase that would occur if a riskless investment were made in order to compensate the investor for the risk incurred.

Risk-Seeking Investor An investor who prefers an investment with more risk over one with less risk, assuming that both investments offer the same expected return.

Risk Structure The set of yields-to-maturity across bonds that possess different degrees of default risk but are similar with respect to other attributes.

Risk Tolerance The trade-off between risk and expected return demanded by a particular investor.

Riskfree Asset An asset whose return during a given holding period is certain and known at the beginning of the holding period.

Riskfree Borrowing The act of borrowing funds that are to be repaid with a certain rate of interest.

Riskfree Lending (Investing) The act of investing in an asset whose cash flows are certain over the investor's holding period.

Round Lot An amount of stock that is equal to a standard unit of trading, generally 100 shares or a multiple of 100 shares.

SAEF See **SEAQ Automated Execution Facility.**

Scalper See **Local.**

SEAQ Automated Execution Facility (SAEF) A small-order execution system, similar to the Small Order Execution System of Nasdaq, that is used on the London Stock Exchange.

Seat The designation of membership in an organized exchange. By holding a seat, the member has the privilege of executing trades using the facilities provided by the exchange.

Secondary Distribution A means of selling a block of stock previously issued where the shares are sold away from an organized exchange after the close of trading in a manner similar to the sale of new issues of common stock.

Secondary (Security) Market The market in which securities are traded that have been issued at some previous point in time.

Sector Selection The stage in the investment process where the investment manager determines the appropriate combination of the sectors within each asset class.

Securities and Exchange Commission (SEC) A federal agency established by the Securities Exchange Act of 1934 that regulates the issuance of securities in the primary market and the trading of securities in the secondary market.

Securities Investor Protection Corporation (SIPC) A quasi-governmental agency that insures the accounts of clients of brokerage firms against loss caused by any of the firms' failure.

Securitization The process in which a sponsor buys a group of assets (for example, mortgages); places those assets in a pool; and sells ownership positions in the pool. These ownership positions are represented by certificates issued in proportion to the investors' individual contributions to the pool.

Security (alternatively, **Financial Asset**) A claim to receive prospective future benefits under certain conditions.

Security Analysis A component of the investment process that involves determining the prospective future benefits of a security, the conditions under which such benefits will be received, and the likelihood that such conditions will occur.

Security Analyst See **Financial Analyst.**

Security Market See **Financial Market.**

Security Market Line Derived from the Capital Asset Pricing Model, a linear relationship between the expected returns on securities and the risk of those securities, with risk expressed as the security's beta (or equivalently, the security's covariance with the market portfolio).

Security Selection See **Portfolio Construction.**

Selectivity An aspect of security analysis that entails forecasting the price movements of individual securities.

Self-Regulation A method of governmental regulation where the rules and standards of conduct in security markets are set by firms that operate in these markets, subject to the oversight of various federal agencies such as the SEC and CFTC.

Selling Group A group of investment banking organizations that, as part of a security underwriting, are responsible for selling the security.

Semistrong-Form Market Efficiency A level of market efficiency in which all relevant publicly available information is fully and immediately reflected in security prices.

Sensitivity See **Factor Loading.**

Separation Theorem A feature of the Capital Asset Pricing Model in which the optimal combination of risky assets for an investor can be determined without any knowledge about the investor's preferences toward risk and return.

Serial Bond A bond issue with different portions of the issue maturing at different dates.

Settle (or **Settlement**) **Price** The representative price for a futures contract determined during the closing period of the futures exchange.

Settlement Date The date after a security has been traded on which the buyer must deliver cash to the seller and the seller must deliver the security to the buyer.

Sharpe Ratio (alternatively, **Reward-to-Variability Ratio**) An *ex post* risk-adjusted measure of portfolio performance where risk is defined as the standard deviation of the portfolio's returns. Mathematically, during an evaluation period, it is the excess return of a portfolio divided by the standard deviation of the portfolio's returns.

Shelf Registration Under Securities and Exchange Commission Rule 415, issuers may register securities in advance of their issuance and sell these securities up to a year later.

Short Hedger A hedger who offsets risk by selling futures contracts.

Short Interest The number of shares of a given company that have been sold short and, as of a given date, have loans that remain outstanding.

Short Sale The sale of a security that is not owned by an investor but rather is borrowed from a broker. The investor eventually repays the broker in kind by purchasing the same security in a subsequent transaction.

Sinking Fund Periodic payments made by a bond issuer to reduce, in an orderly manner, the amount of outstanding principal on a bond issue during the life of the bond.

Size Effect (alternatively, **Small Firm Effect**) An empirical regularity whereby stock returns appear to differ consistently across the spectrum of market capitalization. During extended periods of time, smaller capitalization stocks have outperformed larger capitalization stocks on a risk-adjusted basis.

Small Cap Issues Less actively traded stocks that are listed on Nasdaq.

Small Firm Effect See **Size Effect.**

Small Order Execution System (SOES) A computer system associated with Nasdaq that provides for automatic order execution by routing the order to the market-maker with the best quote.

Special Offering or Bid A trade involving a large block of stock on an organized security exchange whereby a number of brokerage firms attempt to execute the order by soliciting offsetting orders from their customers.

Specialist A member of an organized exchange who has two primary functions. First, the specialist maintains an orderly market in assigned securities by acting as a dealer, buying and selling from his or her inventory of securities to offset temporary imbalances in the number of buy and sell orders. Second, the specialist facilitates the execution of limit, stop, and stop limit orders by acting as a broker. This is done by maintaining a limit order book and executing these orders as they are triggered.

Specialist Block Purchase or Sale The accommodation of a relatively small block trade by a specialist who buys or sells from his or her inventory at a price negotiated with the seller or buyer.

Specialist's Book See **Limit Order Book.**

Speculative-Grade Bonds (alternatively, **Junk Bonds** or **High-Yield Bonds**) Bonds that are not investment-grade bonds. Usually, speculative bonds have a BB (Standard & Poor's) or Ba (Moody's) or lower rating.

Speculator An investor in futures contracts whose primary objective is to make a profit from buying and selling these contracts.

Split-Funding A situation in which an institutional investor divides its funds among two or more professional money managers.

Spot Market The market for an asset that involves the immediate exchange of the asset for cash.

Spot Price The purchase price of an asset in the spot market.

Spot Rate The annual yield-to-maturity on a pure-discount security.

Standard Deviation A measure of the dispersion of possible outcomes around the expected value of a random variable.

Standard Deviation of the Random Error Term (alternatively, **Residual Standard Deviation**) In the context of simple linear regression, a measure of the dispersion of possible outcomes of the random error term.

Standard Error of Alpha The standard deviation of a security's estimated alpha, as derived from the *ex post* characteristic line.

Standard Error of Beta The standard deviation of a security's estimated beta, as derived from the *ex post* characteristic line.

Standardized Unexpected Earnings The difference between a firm's actual earnings for a given period and an estimate of the firm's expected earnings, with this quantity divided by the standard deviation of the firm's previous earnings forecast errors.

Standby Agreement An arrangement between a security issuer and an underwriter as part of a rights offering. The underwriter agrees to purchase at a fixed price all securities not purchased by current stockholders.

Stochastic Process Risk In the context of immunization, the risk that the yield curve will shift in a way that prevents an immunized bond portfolio from producing its expected cash inflows.

Stock Dividend An accounting transaction that distributes stock to existing shareholders in proportion to the number of shares currently owned by the shareholders. A stock dividend entails a transfer from retained earnings to the capital stock account of a dollar amount that is equal to the market value of the distributed stock.

Stock Split Similar to a stock dividend, an accounting transaction that increases the amount of stock held by existing shareholders in proportion to the number of shares currently owned by the shareholders. A stock split entails a reduction in the par value of the corporation's stock and the simultaneous exchange of a multiple number of new shares for each existing share.

Stop Limit Order A trading order that specifies both a stop price and a limit price. If the security's price reaches or passes the stop price, then a limit order is created at the limit price.

Stop Loss Order See **Stop Order.**

Stop Order (alternatively, **Stop Loss Order**) A trading order that specifies a stop price. If the security's price reaches or passes the stop price, then a market order is created.

Stop Price The price specified by an investor when a stop order or a stop limit order is placed that defines the price at which the market order or limit order for the security is to become effective.

Straddle An options strategy that involves buying (or writing) both a call and a put on the same asset, with the options having the same exercise price and expiration date.

Straight Voting System See **Majority Voting System.**

Street Name An arrangement between an investor and a brokerage firm where the investor maintains an account in which the investor's securities are registered in the name of the brokerage firm.

Strike Price See **Exercise Price.**

Strong-Form Market Efficiency A level of market efficiency in which all relevant information, both public and private, is fully and immediately reflected in security prices.

Subordinated Debenture A debenture whose claims, in the event of bankruptcy, are junior to other bonds issued by the firm, including certain other debentures.

Subscription Price The price at which holders of rights are permitted to purchase shares of stock in a rights offering.

Substitution Swap A type of bond swap where an investor exchanges one bond with a lower yield for another with a higher yield, yet both bonds have essentially the same financial characteristics.

Super Designated Order Turnaround (SuperDot) A set of special procedures established by the New York Stock Exchange to handle routine small trading orders. Using these procedures, participating member firms can route orders directly to the specialist for immediate execution.

Supply-to-Sell Schedule A description of the quantities of a security that investors are prepared to sell at alternative prices.

Swap Bank Typically a commercial or investment bank that sets up equity, interest rate, and other kinds of swaps between interested counterparties.

Syndicate (alternatively, **Purchasing Group**) A group of investment banking organizations that, as part of a security underwriting, are responsible for purchasing the security from the issuer and reselling it to the public.

Systematic Risk See **Market Risk.**

Takeover An action by an individual or a firm to acquire controlling interest in a corporation.

Target Firm A firm that is the subject of a takeover attempt.

Taxable Municipal Bond A municipal bond whose income is fully taxable by the federal government.

Tax-Exempt Bond A security whose income is not taxable by the federal government.

Technical Analysis A form of security analysis that attempts to forecast the movement in the prices of securities based primarily on historical price and volume trends in those securities.

Tender Offer A form of corporate takeover in which a firm or individual offers to buy some or all of the shares of a target firm at a stated price. This offer is publicly advertised, and material describing the bid is mailed to the target's stockholders.

Term Bond A bond issue where all of the bonds mature on the same date.

Term Structure The set of yields-to-maturity across bonds that possess different terms-to-maturity but are similar with respect to other attributes.

Term-to-Maturity The time remaining until a bond's maturity date.

Terminal Wealth The value of an investor's portfolio at the end of a holding period. Equivalently, the investor's initial wealth multiplied by one plus the rate of return earned on the investor's portfolio during the holding period.

Third Market A secondary security market where exchange-listed securities are traded over the counter.

Tick The standard unit in which prices are quoted, which in 1999 is $\$\frac{1}{16}$ for most stocks.

Time Value (Time Premium) The excess of the market price of an option over its intrinsic value.

Time-Weighted Return A method of measuring the performance of a portfolio during a particular period of time. Effectively, it is the return on one dollar invested in the portfolio at the beginning of the measurement period.

Timing An aspect of security analysis that entails forecasting the price movements of asset classes relative to one another.

Top-Down Forecasting A sequential approach to security analysis that entails first making forecasts for the economy, then for industries, and finally for individual companies. Each level of forecasts is conditional on the previous level of forecasts made.

Total Risk The standard deviation of the return on a security or portfolio.

Trading Halt A temporary suspension in the trading of a security on an organized exchange.

Trading Post The physical location on the floor of an organized exchange where a specialist in a particular stock is located and where all orders involving the stock must be taken for execution.

Transfer Agent A designated agent of a corporation, usually a bank, that administers the transfer of shares of a corporation's stock between old and new owners.

Treasury Bill A type of money market instrument. A pure-discount security issued by the U.S. Treasury with a maximum term-to-maturity of one year.

Treasury Bond A security issued by the U.S. Treasury with a term-to-maturity of more than seven years. Interest is paid semiannually, and principal is returned at maturity.

Treasury Note A security issued by the U.S. Treasury with a term-to-maturity between one and seven years. Interest is paid semiannually, and principal is returned at maturity.

Treasury Stock Common stock that has been issued by a corporation and then later repurchased by the corporation in the open market or through a tender offer. This stock does not include voting rights or rights to receive dividends and is equivalent economically to unissued stock.

Triple Witching Hour The date when options on individual stocks and market indices, futures on market indices, and options on market index futures expire simultaneously.

Trustee An organization, usually a bank, that serves as the representative of bondholders. The trustee acts to protect the interests of bondholders and facilitates communication between them and the issuer.

Turn-of-the-Month Effect An empirical regularity whereby stock returns seem to be abnormally high during a four-day period beginning on the last trading day of the month.

Two-Dollar Broker See **Floor Broker.**

Unbiased Expectations Theory An explanation of the term structure of interest rates. It holds that a forward rate represents the average opinion of the expected future spot rate for the time period in question.

Undermargined A situation in which the collateral in a margin account has fallen below the minimum amount determined by maintenance margin requirement.

Underpriced Security (alternatively, **Undervalued Security**) A security whose expected return is greater than its equilibrium expected return. Equivalently, a security with a positive expected alpha.

Undervalued Security See **Underpriced Security.**

Underwrite The process by which investment bankers bring new securities to the primary security market.

Underwriter See **Investment Banker.**

Unique Risk (alternatively, **Nonmarket Risk** or **Unsystematic Risk**) The portion of a security's total risk that is not related to moves in the market portfolio and, hence, can be diversified away.

Unit Investment Trust An unmanaged investment company with a finite life that raises an initial sum of capital from investors and uses the proceeds to purchase a fixed portfolio of securities (typically bonds).

Unrealized Capital Gain (or **Loss**) A capital gain (or loss) on an asset that has not yet been recognized for tax purposes through the sale or exchange of the asset.

Unrestricted See **Overmargined.**

Unseasoned Offering See **Initial Public Offering (IPO).**

Unsystematic Risk See **Unique Risk.**

Upstairs Dealer Market An adjunct to organized exchanges where block houses that are member firms handle large block trades. The block houses act as both agents and principals lining up trading partners to take the other side of the block orders.

Up Tick (alternatively, **Plus Tick**) A trade in a security made at a price higher than the price of the previous trade in that same security.

Uptick Rule Refers to Rule 10a-1, which the SEC made under the Securities Exchange Act of 1934, stating that a short sale can only be made on either a plus tick or a zero-plus tick.

Utility The relative enjoyment or satisfaction that a person derives from economic activity such as work, consumption, or investment.

Value Stock Typically, a stock is characterized as having high earnings-to-price and book-value-to-market-value ratios.

Value-Weighted Market Index (alternatively, **Capitalization-Weighted Market Index**) A market index in which the contribution of a security to the value of the index is a function of the security's market capitalization.

Variable Rate See **Floating Rate.**

Variance The squared value of the standard deviation.

Variance–Covariance Matrix A table that symmetrically arrays the covariances between a number of random variables. Variances of the random variables lie on the diagonal of the matrix, whereas covariances between the random variables lie symmetrically above and below the diagonal.

Variation Margin The amount of cash that an investor must provide to meet a margin call on a futures contract.

Volatility The standard deviation of the rate of return on the underlying asset to an option contract.

Wash Sale The sale and subsequent purchase of a "substantially identical" security solely for the purpose of generating a tax-deductible capital loss.

Weak-Form Market Efficiency A level of market efficiency in which all previous security price and volume data are fully and immediately reflected in current security prices.

Weekend Effect See **Day-of-the-Week Effect.**

World Equity Benchmark Shares (WEBS) A type of international investment where each share represents ownership of a portfolio of stocks in a given country. The portfolio is designed to generate investment results that generally correspond to the performance of a given Morgan Stanley Capital International (MSCI) country index. These shares are listed on the American Stock Exchange, and can be traded just like any common stock.

Wrap Account A type of account at a brokerage firm that involves having a broker provide the investor with advice. All fees for financial planning, investment management, and securities trading are "wrapped" into one annual fee.

Yield See **Yield-to-Maturity.** Can also be used to refer to a stock's dividend yield or its earnings yield or a bond's current yield.

Yield Curve A visual representation of the term structure of interest rates.

Yield Spread The difference in the promised yields-to-maturity of two bonds.

Yield Structure The set of yields-to-maturity across bonds differing in terms of a number of attributes including term-to-maturity, coupon rate, call provisions, tax status, marketability, and likelihood of default.

Yield-to-Call The yield-to-maturity of a callable bond calculated assuming that the bond is called at the earliest possible time.

Yield-to-Maturity (alternatively, **Yield**) For a particular fixed-income security, the single interest rate (with interest compounded at some specified interval) that, if paid by a bank on the amount invested in the security, would enable the investor to obtain all the payments made by that security. Equivalently, the discount rate that equates the present value of fu-ture promised cash flows from the security to the current market price of the security.

Zero Coupon Bond See **Pure-Discount Bond.**

Zero-Growth Model (alternatively, **No-Growth Model**) A type of dividend discount model in which dividends are assumed to maintain a constant value in perpetuity.

Zero-Plus Tick A trade in a security made at a price equal to that of the previous trade in that security but higher than that of the last trade made in the security at a different price.

References

CHAPTER 1

1. Historical returns on U.S. security markets can be obtained from

   Roger G. Ibbotson and Rex A. Sinquefield, *Stocks, Bonds, Bills, and Inflation: The Past and the Future* (Charlottesville, VA: Financial Analysts Research Foundation, 1983). Note that the Financial Analysts Research Foundation has been renamed the Research Foundation of the ICFA. It can be contacted by calling (804) 980-3647.

   Stocks, Bonds, Bills, and Inflation 1999 Yearbook (Chicago: Ibbotson Associates, 1999). This annual yearbook of monthly and annual data can be purchased for $100 by calling (800) 758-3557 or by contacting the publisher at <www.ibbotson.com>.

   Global Financial Data provides a free treasure trove of data at their Web site, <www.globalfindata.com>.

2. Additional historical data on U.S. common stock returns can be found in

   Jack W. Wilson and Charles P. Jones, "A Comparison of Annual Common Stock Returns: 1871–1925 and 1926–85," *Journal of Business,* 60, no. 2 (April 1987): 239–258.

   Jeremy J. Siegel, *Stocks for the Long Run* (New York: McGraw-Hill, 1998).

   Charles P. Jones and Jack W. Wilson, "Probabilities Associated with Common Stock Returns," *Journal of Portfolio Management,* 22, no. 1 (Fall 1995): 21–32.

3. The historical relative returns of U.S. stocks versus bonds are studied in

   Jeremy J. Siegel, "The Equity Premium: Stock and Bond Returns Since 1802," *Financial Analysts Journal,* 48, no. 1 (January/February 1992): 28–38.

   Peter L. Bernstein, "What Rate of Return Can You Reasonably Expect . . . or What Can the Long Run Tell Us about the Short Run?" *Financial Analysts Journal,* 53, no. 2 (March/April 1997): 20–28.

4. Comparable Japanese data for a more limited time period are presented in

   Yasushi Hamao, "A Standard Data Base for the Analysis of Japanese Security Markets," *Journal of Business,* 64, no. 1 (January 1991): 87–102.

5. Historical data on bond market returns are presented in

   Roger G. Ibbotson and Laurence B. Siegel, "The World Bond Market: Market Values, Yields, and Returns," *Journal of Fixed Income,* 1, no. 1 (June 1991): 90–99.

   Jack W. Wilson and Charles P. Jones, "Long-Term Returns and Risk for Bonds," *Journal of Portfolio Management,* 23, no. 3 (Spring 1997): 9–14.

6. The volatility of common stocks is examined in

   G. William Schwert, "Why Does Stock Market Volatility Change over Time?" *Journal of Finance,* 44, no. 5 (December 1989): 1115–1153.

   Peter Fortune, "An Assessment of Financial Market Volatility: Bills, Bonds, and Stocks," *New England Economic Review* (November/December 1989): 13–28.

7. For a discussion and analysis of U.S. common stock indices, see

   G. William Schwert, "Indexes of U.S. Stock Prices from 1802 to 1987," *Journal of Business,* 63, no. 3 (July 1990): 399–426.

8. For a discussion of using historical capital markets return data in making portfolio decisions, see

   Maria Crawford Scott, "Planning Assumptions: Will the Real Long-Term Return Please Stand Up?" *AAII Journal,* 19, no. 10 (November 1997): 10–12.

9. Investment policy is discussed in

   Charles D. Ellis, *Investment Policy* (Homewood, IL: Dow Jones-Irwin, 1985).

   Keith D. Ambachtsheer, *Pension Funds and the Bottom Line: Managing the Corporate Pension Fund as a Financial Business* (Homewood, IL: Dow Jones-Irwin, 1986).

Keith D. Ambachtsheer, "Pension Fund Asset Allocation: In Defense of the 60/40 Equity/Debt Asset Mix," *Financial Analysts Journal,* 43, no 5 (September/October 1987): 14–24.

Wayne H. Wagner, "The Many Dimensions of Risk," *Journal of Portfolio Management,* 15, no. 2 (Winter 1988): 35–39.

Editorial Board, "Investment Policy Statement," *Financial Analysts Journal,* 46, no. 5 (September/October 1990): 14–15.

Walter R. Good and Douglas A. Love, "Reactions to the Pension Investment Policy Statement," *Financial Analysts Journal,* 47, no. 2 (March/April 1991): 7–10.

Jeffery V. Bailey, "Investment Policy: The Missing Link," in Frank J. Fabozzi (ed.), *Pension Fund Investment Management* (New Hope, PA: Frank J. Fabozzi Associates, 1997): 17–30.

CHAPTER 2

1. For a discussion of the mechanics of purchasing and selling securities, along with margin purchasing and short selling, see

   George Sofianos, "Margin Requirements on Equity Instruments," *Federal Reserve Bank of New York Quarterly Review,* 13, no. 2 (Summer 1988): 47–60.

   DeWitt M. Foster, *The Stockbroker's Manual* (Miami: Pass, 1990). Copies can be obtained by calling (305) 270-2550.

   James J. Angel, "An Investor's Guide to Placing Stock Orders," *AAII Journal,* 15, no. 4 (April 1993): 7–10.

   J. Randall Woolridge and Amy Dickinson, "Short Selling and Common Stock Prices," *Financial Analysts Journal,* 50, no. 1 (January/February 1994): 20–28.

   Gordon J. Alexander, "On Back-Testing 'Zero-Investment' Strategies," *Journal of Business,* 73, no. 2 (April 2000): 255–278.

2. An interesting discussion of margin requirements and their impact on market volatility is contained in

   David A. Hsieh and Merton H. Miller, "Margin Requirements and Market Volatility," *Journal of Finance,* 45, no. 1 (March 1990): 3–29.

3. A study that examines levels and changes in short interest is

   Averil Brent, Dale Morse, and E. Kay Stice, "Short Interest: Explanations and Tests," *Journal of Financial and Quantitative Analysis,* 25, no. 2 (June 1990): 273–289.

4. For a discussion of short selling and the up-tick rule, see

   Gordon J. Alexander and Mark A. Peterson, "Short Selling on the New York Stock Exchange and the Effects of the Uptick Rule," *Journal of Financial Intermediation,* 8, no. 1 (January 1999): 1–27.

CHAPTER 3

1. A good reference source for U.S. stock markets is

   Robert A. Schwartz, *Equity Markets* (New York: Harper & Row, 1988).

2. Other valuable sources are the following fact books, which are updated annually, and Web sites

   New York Stock Exchange, *Fact Book: 1998 Data,* 1999; <www.nyse.com>

   The Nasdaq-Amex Market Group, *1999 Nasdaq-Amex Fact Book & Company Directory,* 1999; <www.nasd.com> or <www.nasdaq.com> or <www.nasdr.com>

   London Stock Exchange, *Stock Exchange Official Yearbook;* <www.londonstockex.co.uk>

   Toronto Stock Exchange Press, *1999 Official Trading Statistics;* <www.tse.com>

   Tokyo Stock Exchange, *Tokyo Stock Exchange 1999 Fact Book;* <www.tse.or.jp/eindex.html>

   Readers should also consider the Securities and Exchange Commission's Web site: <www.sec.gov>

3. For a description of foreign stock markets, see

   Giuseppe Tullio and Giorgio P. Szego, eds., "Equity Markets: An International Comparison: Part A," *Journal of Banking and Finance,* 13, nos. 4/5 (September 1989): 479–782.

   Giuseppe Tullio and Giorgio P. Szego, eds., "Equity Markets: An International Comparison: Part B," *Journal of Banking and Finance,* 14, nos. 2/3 (August 1990): 231–672.

   Roger D. Huang and Hans R. Stoll, *Major World Equity Markets: Current Structure and Prospects for Change,* Monograph Series in Finance and Economics 1991–1993 (New York: New York University Salomon Center, 1991).

   Roger D. Huang and Hans R. Stoll, "The Design of Trading Systems: Lessons from Abroad," *Financial Analysts Journal,* 48, no. 5 (September/October 1992): 49–54.

   Bruce N. Lehman and David M. Modest, "Trading and Liquidity on the Tokyo Stock Exchange: A Bird's Eye View," *Journal of Finance,* 49, no. 3 (July 1994): 951–984.

   Alexandros Benos and Michel Crouhy, "Changes in the Structure and Dynamics of European Securities Markets," *Financial Analysts Journal,* 52, no. 3 (May/June 1996): 37–50.

4. Other useful sources of information on market microstructure are

   James L. Hamilton, "Off-Board Trading of NYSE-Listed Stocks: The Effects of Deregulation and the National Market System," *Journal of Finance,* 42, no. 5 (December 1987): 1331–1345.

Ian Domowitz, "The Mechanics of Automated Execution Systems," *Journal of Financial Intermediation,* 1, no. 2 (June 1990): 167–194.

Lawrence E. Harris, *Liquidity, Trading Rules, and Electronic Trading Systems,* Monograph Series in Finance and Economics 1990–1994 (New York: New York University Salomon Center, 1990).

Peter A. Abken, "Globalization of Stock, Futures, and Options Markets," *Federal Reserve Bank of Atlanta Economic Review,* 76, no. 4 (July/August 1991): 1–22.

Joel Hasbrouck, George Sofianos, and Deborah Sosebee, "New York Stock Exchange Systems and Procedures," NYSE Working Paper 93–01, 1993.

Maureen O'Hara, *Market Microstructure Theory* (Cambridge, MA: Blackwell, 1995).

Hans Stoll, "Reconsidering the Affirmative Obligation of Market Makers," *Financial Analysts Journal,* 54, no. 5 (September/October 1998): 72–82.

5. For a discussion of the effects of listing and delisting on a firm's stock, see

Gary C. Sanger and John J. McConnell, "Stock Exchange Listings, Firm Value, and Security Market Efficiency: The Impact of NASDAQ," *Journal of Financial and Quantitative Analysis,* 21, no. 1 (March 1986): 1–25.

John J. McConnell and Gary C. Sanger, "The Puzzle in Post-Listing Common Stock Returns," *Journal of Finance,* 42, no. 1 (March 1987): 119–140.

Gary C. Sanger and James D. Peterson, "An Empirical Analysis of Common Stock Delistings," *Journal of Financial and Quantitative Analysis,* 25, no. 2 (June 1990): 261–272.

6. Empirical studies that examine the costs of trading include

Harold Demsetz, "The Cost of Transacting," *Quarterly Journal of Economics,* 82, no. 1 (February 1968): 33–53.

Walter Bagehot, "The Only Game in Town," *Financial Analysts Journal,* 27, no. 2 (March/April 1971): 12–14, 22.

Larry J. Cuneo and Wayne H. Wagner, "Reducing the Cost of Stock Trading," *Financial Analysts Journal,* 31, no. 6 (November/December 1975): 35–44.

Gilbert Beebower and William Priest, "The Tricks of the Trade," *Journal of Portfolio Management,* 6, no. 2 (Winter 1980): 36–42.

Jack L. Treynor, "What Does It Take to Win the Trading Game?" *Financial Analysts Journal,* 37, no. 1 (January/February 1981): 55–60.

Thomas F. Loeb, "Trading Cost: The Critical Link between Investment Information and Results," *Financial Analysts Journal,* 39, no. 3 (May/June 1983): 39–44.

Wayne H. Mikkelson and M. Megan Partch, "Stock Price Effects and Costs of Secondary Distributions," *Journal of Financial Economics,* 14, no. 2 (June 1985): 165–194.

Robert W. Holthausen, Richard W. Leftwich, and David Mayers, "The Effect of Large Block Transactions on Security Prices," *Journal of Financial Economics,* 19, no. 2 (December 1987): 237–267.

Stephen A. Berkowitz, Dennis E. Logue, and Eugene E. Noser, Jr., "The Total Cost of Transactions on the NYSE," *Journal of Finance,* 43, no. 1 (March 1988): 97–112.

André F. Perold, "The Implementation Shortfall: Paper versus Reality," *Journal of Portfolio Management,* 14, no. 3 (Spring 1988): 4–9.

Lawrence R. Glosten and Lawrence E. Harris, "Estimating the Components of the Bid/Ask Spread," *Journal of Financial Economics,* 21, no. 1 (May 1988): 123–142.

Joel Hasbrouck, "Trades, Quotes, Inventories, and Information," *Journal of Financial Economics,* 22, no. 2 (December 1988): 229–252.

Hans R. Stoll, "Inferring the Components of the Bid–Ask Spread: Theory and Empirical Tests," *Journal of Finance,* 44, no. 1 (March 1989): 115–134.

Robert W. Holthausen, Richard W. Leftwich, and David Mayers, "Large-Block Transactions, the Speed of Response, and Temporary and Permanent Stock-Price Effects," *Journal of Financial Economics,* 26, no. 1 (July 1990): 71–95.

Mark Edwards and Wayne Wagner, "Best Execution," *Financial Analysts Journal,* 49, no. 1 (January/February 1993): 65–71.

F. Douglas Foster and S. Viswanathan, "Variations in Trading Volume, Return Volatility, and Trading Costs: Evidence on Recent Price Formation Models," *Journal of Finance,* 48, no. 1 (March 1993): 187–211.

Hans R. Stoll, "Equity Trading Costs In-the-Large," *Journal of Portfolio Management,* 19, no. 4 (Summer 1993): 41–50.

Joel Hasbrouck and George Sofianos, "The Trades of Market Makers: An Empirical Analysis of NYSE Specialists," *Journal of Finance,* 48, no. 5 (December 1993): 1565–1593.

Ananth Madhavan and Seymour Smidt, "An Analysis of Changes in Specialist Inventories and Quotations" *Journal of Finance,* 48, no. 5 (December 1993): 1595–1628.

Mitchell A. Petersen and David Fialkowski, "Posted versus Effective Spreads: Good Prices or Bad Quotes?" *Journal of Financial Economics,* 35, no. 3 (June 1994): 269–292.

Jack L. Treynor, "The Invisible Costs of Trading," *Journal of Portfolio Management,* 22, no. 1 (Fall 1995): 71–78.

Donald B. Keim and Ananth Madhavan, "The Cost of Institutional Equity Trades," *Financial Analysts Journal,* 54, no. 4 (July/August 1998): 50–69.

Mark Edwards and Wayne H. Wagner, "Capturing the Research Advantage," *Journal of Portfolio Management,* 25, no. 3 (Spring 1999): 18–24.

7. For a comparison of trading costs on Nasdaq and the NYSE, see

Roger D. Huang and Hans R. Stoll, "Competitive Trading of NYSE Listed Stocks: Measurement and Interpretation of Trading Costs," *Financial Markets, Institutions & Instruments,* 5, no. 2 (1996).

Roger D. Huang and Hans R. Stoll, "Dealer versus Auction Markets: A Paired Comparison of Execution Costs on NASDAQ and NYSE," *Journal of Financial Economics,* 41, no. 3 (July 1996): 313–357.

Michele LaPlante and Chris J. Muscarella, "Do Institutions Receive Comparable Execution in the NYSE and Nasdaq Markets? A Transaction Study of Block Trades," *Journal of Financial Economics,* 45, no. 1 (July 1997): 97–134.

8. For a historical essay on the development of American capital markets, which includes a significant discussion of regulation, see

George David Smith and Richard Sylla, "The Transformation of Financial Capitalism: An Essay on the History of American Capital Markets," *Financial Markets, Institutions & Instruments,* 2, no. 2 (1993).

9. For more on the adverse selection problem that dealers face in setting spreads, see

Lawrence R. Glosten and Paul R. Milgrom, "Bid, Ask, and Transaction Prices in a Specialist Market with Heterogeneously Informed Traders," *Journal of Financial Economics,* 14, no. 1 (March 1985): 71–100.

Albert S. Kyle, "Continuous Auctions and Insider Trading," *Econometrica,* 53, no. 6 (November 1985): 1315–1335.

Murugappa Krishnan, "An Equivalence between the Kyle (1985) and the Glosten–Milgrom (1985) Models," *Economic Letters,* 40 (1992): 333–338.

Steven V. Mann, "How Do Security Dealers Protect Themselves from Traders with Private Information: A Pedagogical Note," *Financial Practice and Education,* 5, no. 1 (Spring/Summer 1995): 38–44.

Michael J. Brennan and Avanidhar Subrahmanyam, "Investment Analysis and Price Formation in Securities Markets," *Journal of Financial Economics,* 38, no. 3 (July 1995): 361–381.

CHAPTER 4

1. Discussion and examination of the demand curves for stocks are contained in

Andrei Shleifer, "Do Demand Curves Slope Down?" *Journal of Finance,* 41, no. 3 (July 1986): 579–590.

Lawrence Harris and Eitan Gurel, "Price and Volume Effects Associated with Changes in the S&P 500: New Evidence for the Existence of Price Pressures," *Journal of Finance,* 41, no. 4 (September 1986): 815–829.

Stephen W. Pruitt and K. C. John Wei, "Institutional Ownership and Changes in the S&P 500," *Journal of Finance,* 44, no. 2 (June 1989): 509–513.

2. For articles presenting arguments that securities are "overpriced" due to short-sale restrictions, see

Edward M. Miller, "Risk, Uncertainty, and Divergence of Opinion," *Journal of Finance,* 32, no. 4 (September 1977): 1151–1168.

Douglas W. Diamond and Robert E. Verrecchia, "Constraints on Short-Selling and Asset Price Adjustment to Private Information," *Journal of Financial Economics,* 18, no. 2 (June 1987): 277–311.

3. Allocational, external, and internal market efficiency are discussed in

Richard R. West, "Two Kinds of Market Efficiency," *Financial Analysts Journal,* 31, no. 6 (November/December 1975): 30–34.

4. Many observers believe that the following articles are the seminal pieces on efficient markets

Paul Samuelson, "Proof That Properly Anticipated Prices Fluctuate Randomly," *Industrial Management Review,* 6 (1965): 41–49.

Harry V. Roberts, "Stock Market 'Patterns' and Financial Analysis: Methodological Suggestions," *Journal of Finance,* 14, no. 1 (March 1959): 1–10.

Eugene F. Fama, "Efficient Capital Markets: A Review of Theory and Empirical Work," *Journal of Finance,* 25, no. 5 (May 1970): 383–417.

———, "Efficient Capital Markets: II," *Journal of Finance,* 46, no. 5 (December 1991): 1575–1617.

5. For an extensive discussion of efficient markets and related evidence, see

George Foster, *Financial Statement Analysis* (Englewood Cliffs, NJ: Prentice Hall, 1986), Chapters 9 and 11.

Stephen F. LeRoy, "Capital Market Efficiency: An Update," *Federal Reserve Bank of San Francisco Economic Review,* no. 2 (Spring 1990): 29–40. A more detailed version of this paper can be found in Stephen F. LeRoy, "Efficient Capital Markets and Martingales," *Journal of Economic Literature,* 27, no. 4 (December 1989): 1583–1621.

Peter Fortune, "Stock Market Efficiency: An Autopsy?" *New England Economic Review* (March/April 1991): 17–40.

Stephen A. Ross, Randolph W. Westerfield, and Jeffrey F. Jaffe, *Corporate Finance* (Boston: Irwin/McGraw Hill, 1996), Chapter 13.

Richard A. Brealey and Stewart C. Myers, *Principles of Corporate Finance* (New York: Irwin McGraw-Hill, 2000), Chapter 13.

6. Interesting overviews of efficient market concepts are presented in

Robert Ferguson, "An Efficient Stock Market? Ridiculous!" *Journal of Portfolio Management,* 9, no. 4 (Summer 1983): 31–38.

Bob L. Boldt and Harold L. Arbit, "Efficient Markets and the Professional Investor," *Financial Analysts Journal,* 40, no. 4 (July/August 1984): 22–34.

Fischer Black, "Noise," *Journal of Finance,* 41, no. 3 (July 1986): 529–543.

Keith C. Brown, W. V. Harlow, and Seha M. Tinic, "How Rational Investors Deal with Uncertainty (Or, Reports of the Death of Efficient Markets Theory Are Greatly Exaggerated)," *Journal of Applied Corporate Finance,* 2, no. 3 (Fall 1989): 45–58.

Ray Ball, "The Theory of Stock Market Efficiency: Accomplishments and Limitations," *Journal of Applied Corporate Finance,* 8, no. 1 (Spring 1995): 4–17.

Peter Bernstein, "Where, Oh Where Are the .400 Hitters of Yesteryear?" *Financial Analysts Journal,* 54, no. 6 (November/December 1998): 50–61.

CHAPTER 5

1. A good reference source for reading about the federal tax code is

John L. Kramer and Thomas R. Pope, eds., *Prentice Hall's Federal Taxation: Comprehensive, 2000* (Upper Saddle River, NJ: Prentice Hall, 1999).

J. K. Lasser Institute, *J. K. Lasser's Your Income Tax 2000* (New York: JKL Publishing, 2000).

2. For a valuable book that provides a framework for analyzing how tax rules affect decision making, see

Myron S. Scholes and Mark A. Wolfson, *Taxes and Business Strategy* (Upper Saddle River, NJ: Prentice Hall, 1992).

3. The relationship between taxation and portfolio management and performance evaluation is discussed in

Robert H. Jeffrey and Robert D. Arnott, "Is Your Alpha Big Enough to Cover Its Taxes?" *Journal of Portfolio Management,* 19, no. 3 (Spring 1993): 15–25.

Laurence B. Siegel and David Montgomery, "Stocks, Bonds, and Bills after Taxes and Inflation," *Journal of Portfolio Management,* 21, no. 2 (Winter 1995): 17–25.

Roberto Apelfeld, Gordon B. Fowler, Jr., and James P. Gordon Jr., "Tax-Aware Equity Investing," *Journal*

of Portfolio Management, 22, no. 2 (Winter 1996): 18–28.

William Ghee and Willaim Reichenstein, "The After-Tax Returns from Different Savings Vehicles," *Financial Analysts Journal,* 52, no. 4 (July/August 1996): 62–72.

David M. Stein, "Measuring and Evaluating Portfolio Performance after Taxes," *Journal of Portfolio Management,* 24, no. 2 (Winter 1998): 117–124.

4. A web site that contains tax information is

<www.irs.ustreas.gov>

CHAPTER 6

1. The seminal work linking interest rates and inflationary expectations is

Irving Fisher, *The Theory of Interest* (New York: Macmillan, 1930).

2. For a review article and test of this linkage, see, respectively,

Herbert Taylor, "Interest Rates: How Much Does Expected Inflation Matter?" *Federal Reserve Bank of Philadelphia Business Review* (July–August 1982): 3–12.

Jacob Boudoukh and Matthew Richardson, "Stock Returns and Inflation: A Long-Horizon Perspective," *American Economic Review,* 83, no. 5 (December 1993): 1346–1355.

3. The relationship between real interest rates and inflation is discussed in

George G. Pennachi, "Identifying the Dynamics of Real Interest Rates and Inflation: Evidence Using Survey Data," *Review of Financial Studies,* 4, no. 1 (1991): 53–86.

4. The following papers present an analysis of the effect of inflation on the accounting treatment of corporate earnings:

Franco Modigliani and Richard A. Cohn, "Inflation and the Stock Market," *Financial Analysts Journal,* 35, no. 2 (March/April 1979): 24–44.

Kenneth R. French, Richard S. Ruback, and G. William Schwert, "Effects of Nominal Contracting on Stock Returns," *Journal of Political Economy,* 91, no. 1 (February 1983): 70–96.

William H. Beaver, Paul A. Griffin, and Wayne R. Landsman, "How Well Does Replacement Cost Income Explain Stock Return [sic]?" *Financial Analysts Journal,* 39, no. 2 (March/April 1983): 26–30, 39.

William C. Nordby, "Applications of Inflation-Adjusted Accounting Data," *Financial Analysts Journal,* 39, no. 2 (March/April 1983): 33–39.

Charles G. Callard and David C. Kleinman, "Inflation-Adjusted Accounting: Does It Matter?" *Financial Analysts Journal,* 41, no. 3 (May/June 1985): 51–59.

5. For a discussion of the relationship between inflation rates and the returns on stocks, bonds, and real estate, see

Eugene F. Fama and G. William Schwert, "Asset Returns and Inflation," *Journal of Financial Economics,* 5, no. 2 (November 1977): 115–146.

6. Other papers dealing with the relationship between inflation and stock returns can be found at the end of the following survey articles

David P. Ely and Kenneth J. Robinson, "The Stock Market and Inflation: A Synthesis of the Theory and Evidence," *Federal Reserve Bank of Dallas Economic Review* (March 1989): 17–29.

Andrew B. Abel, "The Equity Premium Puzzle," *Federal Reserve Bank of Philadelphia Business Review* (September–October 1991): 3–14.

7. The equity premium has also been reviewed and analyzed in

Jeremy J. Siegel, "The Equity Premium: Stock and Bond Returns Since 1802," *Financial Analysts Journal,* 48, no. 1 (January/February 1992): 28–38, 46.

Narayana Kocherlakota, "The Equity Premium: It's Still a Puzzle," *Journal of Economic Literature,* 34, no. 1 (March 1996): 42–71.

8. The tendency of certain types of common stocks to offer better inflation hedges is discussed in

Douglas K. Pearce and V. Vance Roley, "Firm Characteristics, Unanticipated Inflation, and Stock Returns," *Journal of Finance,* 43, no. 4 (September 1988): 965–981.

Christopher K. Ma and M. E. Ellis, "Selecting Industries as Inflation Hedges," *Journal of Portfolio Management,* 15, no. 4 (Summer 1989): 45–48.

Yaman Asikoglu and Metin R. Ercan, "Inflation Flow-Through and Stock Prices," *Journal of Portfolio Management,* 18, no. 3 (Spring 1992): 63–68.

9. International evidence on the relationship between stock returns and inflation is provided by

Bruno Solnik, "The Relation between Stock Prices and Inflationary Expectations: The International Evidence," *Journal of Finance,* 38, no. 1 (March 1983): 35–48.

N. Bulent Gultekin, "Stock Market Returns and Inflation: Evidence from Other Countries," *Journal of Finance,* 38, no. 1 (March 1983): 49–65.

10. The CPI and other indices of inflation can be found at the Bureau of Labor Statistics Web site:

<www.bls.gov/datahome.htm>

CHAPTER 7

1. The seminal work developing the mean–variance model is credited to Harry Markowitz, co-winner of the 1990 Nobel Prize in economics, who developed his ideas in

Harry M. Markowitz, "Portfolio Selection," *Journal of Finance,* 7, no. 1 (March 1952): 77–91.

Harry M. Markowitz, *Portfolio Selection: Efficient Diversification of Investments* (New York: Wiley, 1959). (A reprint of this book that also contains some new material is available from Basil Blackwell, in Cambridge, MA, copyright 1991.)

2. Although utility theory can be traced back to the work of Daniel Bernoulli in the early part of the eighteenth century, the modern notion of utility theory was developed in

John von Neumann and Oskar Morgenstern, *Theory of Games and Economic Behavior* (New York: Wiley, 1944).

Kenneth J. Arrow, *Essays in the Theory of Risk-Bearing* (Chicago: Markham, 1971).

3. Significant other work in utility theory is reviewed in

Paul J. H. Schoemaker, "The Expected Utility Model: Its Variants, Purposes, Evidence and Limitations," *Journal of Economic Literature,* 20, no. 2 (June 1982): 529–563.

4. For an introduction to uncertainty and utility theory, see

Mark P. Kritzman, ". . . About Uncertainty," *Financial Analysts Journal,* 47, no. 2 (March/April 1991): 17–21.

Mark Kritzman, ". . . About Utility," *Financial Analysts Journal,* 48, no. 3 (May/June 1992): 17–20.

5. For a description of various alternative measures of risk, see

Mark Kritzman, ". . . About Higher Moments," *Financial Analysts Journal,* 50, no. 5 (September/October 1994): 10–17.

Leslie A. Balzer, "Measuring Investment Risk: A Review," *Journal of Investing,* 4, no. 3 (Fall 1995): 5–16.

Frank A. Sortino and Hal J. Forsey, "On the Use and Misuse of Downside Risk," *Journal of Portfolio Management,* 22, no. 2 (Winter 1996): 35–43.

Robert A. Olsen, "Investment Risk: The Experts' Perspective," *Financial Analysts Journal,* 53, no. 2 (March/April 1997): 62–66.

6. Behavioral finance is discussed in the entire second part of the October 1986 issue of the *Journal of Business* and the entire November/December issue of the *Financial Analysts Journal.* Also see

Richard H. Thaler, *Quasi Rational Economies* (New York: Russel Sage, 1991).

Daniel Kahneman and Mark W. Riepe, "Aspects of Investor Psychology," *Journal of Portfolio Management,* 24, no. 4 (Summer 1998): 52–65.

Robert A. Olsen, "Behavioral Finance and Its Implications for Stock-Price Volatility," *Financial Analysts Journal,* 54, no. 2 (March/April 1998): 10–18.

CHAPTER 8

1. As mentioned in the Chapter 7 references, the seminal work developing the mean–variance model is credited to Harry Markowitz. Also see

   Harry M. Markowitz, "The Early History of Portfolio Theory: 1600–1960," *Financial Analysts Journal,* 55, no. 4 (July/August 1999): 5–16.

2. The technique used for determining the location of the efficient set, along with the composition of the "corner portfolios" that lie on it, was developed in

   Harry M. Markowitz, "The Optimization of a Quadratic Function Subject to Linear Constraints," *Naval Research Logistics Quarterly,* 3, nos. 1–2 (March–June 1956): 111–133.

3. The market model, initially mentioned by Markowitz in a footnote on page 100 of his book, was developed in

   William F. Sharpe, "A Simplified Model for Portfolio Analysis," *Management Science,* 9, no. 2 (January 1963): 277–293.

4. An extensive discussion of the market model can be found in Chapters 3 and 4 of

   Eugene F. Fama, *Foundations of Finance* (New York: Basic Books, 1976).

5. For discussions of how diversification reduces market risk, see

   John L. Evans and Stephen H. Archer, "Diversification and the Reduction of Dispersion: An Empirical Analysis," *Journal of Finance,* 23, no. 5 (December 1968): 761–767.

   W. H. Wagner and S. C. Lau, "The Effect of Diversification on Risk," *Financial Analysts Journal,* 27, no. 6 (November/December 1971): 48–53.

   Meir Statman, "How Many Stocks Make a Diversified Portfolio?" *Journal of Financial and Quantitative Analysis,* 22, no. 3 (September 1987): 353–363.

   Gerald D. Newbould and Percy S. Poon, "The Minimum Number of Stocks Needed for Diversification," *Financial Practice and Education,* 3, no. 2 (Fall 1993): 85–87.

   Dirk P. M. De Wit, "Naïve Diversification," *Financial Analysts Journal,* 54, no. 4 (July/August 1998): 95–100.

6. A discussion of some statistical problems encountered in partitioning total risk is contained in

   Bert Stine and Dwayne Key, "Reconciling Degrees of Freedom When Partitioning Risk: A Teaching Note," *Journal of Financial Education,* 19 (Fall 1990): 19–22.

7. The use of optimization techniques to create and manage portfolios is discussed in

   J. D. Jobson and Bob Korkie, "Putting Markowitz Theory to Work," *Journal of Portfolio Management,* 7, no. 4 (Summer 1981): 70–74.

   Gordon J. Alexander and Jack Clark Francis, *Portfolio Analysis* (Upper Saddle River, NJ: Prentice Hall, 1986), Chapter 6.

   Peter A. Frost and James E. Savarino, "Portfolio Size and Estimation Risk," *Journal of Portfolio Management,* 12, no. 4 (Summer 1986): 60–64.

   ———, "For Better Performance: Constrain Portfolio Weights," *Journal of Portfolio Management,* 15, no. 1 (Fall 1988): 29–34.

   Richard O. Michaud, "The Markowitz Optimization Enigma: Is 'Optimized' Optimal?" *Financial Analysts Journal,* 45, no. 1 (January/February 1989): 31–42.

   Philippe Jorion, "Portfolio Optimization in Practice," *Financial Analysts Journal,* 48, no. 1 (January/February 1992): 68–74.

   Vijay K. Chopra and William T. Ziemba, "The Effects of Errors in Means, Variances, and Covariances on Optimal Portfolio Choice," *Journal of Portfolio Management,* 19, no. 2 (Winter 1993): 6–11.

   Kenneth L. Fisher and Meir Statman, "The Mean–Variance-Optimization Puzzle: Security Portfolios and Food Portfolios," *Financial Analysts Journal,* 53, no. 4 (July/August 1997): 41–50.

   David Eichorn, Francis Gupta, and Eric Stubbs, "Using Constraints to Improve the Robustness of Asset Allocation," *Journal of Portfolio Management,* 24, no. 3 (Spring 1998): 41–48.

   George Chow, Eric Jacquier, Mark Kritzman, and Kenneth Lowry, "Optimal Portfolios in Good Times and Bad," *Financial Analysts Journal,* 55, no. 3 (May/June 1999): 65–73.

CHAPTER 9

1. Credit for extending Markowitz's model to include riskfree lending and borrowing belongs to

   James Tobin, "Liquidity Preference as Behavior Towards Risk," *Review of Economic Studies,* 26, no. 1 (February 1958): 65–86.

   James Tobin, "The Theory of Portfolio Selection," in F. H. Hahn and F. P. R. Brechling, (eds.), *The Theory of Interest Rates* (London: Macmillan, 1965).

2. For a discussion of various mean–variance models that involve different sets of assumptions regarding riskfree lending and borrowing, margin purchasing, and short selling, see

Eugene F. Fama, *Foundations of Finance* (New York: Basic Books, 1976), Chapters 7 and 8.

Gordon J. Alexander and Jack Clark Francis, *Portfolio Analysis* (Upper Saddle River, NJ: Prentice Hall, 1986), Chapter 4.

3. For a discussion of how to determine the composition of portfolios on the efficient set under a variety of different assumptions, see

Edwin J. Elton, Martin J. Gruber, and Manfred D. Padberg, "Simple Criteria for Optimal Portfolio Selection," *Journal of Finance,* 31, no. 5 (December 1976): 1341–1357.

Gordon J. Alexander, "Short Selling and Efficient Sets," *Journal of Finance,* 48, no. 4 (September 1993): 1497–1506.

Edwin J. Elton and Martin J. Gruber, *Modern Portfolio Theory and Investment Analysis* (New York: Wiley, 1995), Chapters 6 and 9.

CHAPTER 10

1. Credit for the initial development of the CAPM is usually given to

William F. Sharpe, "Capital Asset Prices: A Theory of Market Equilibrium under Conditions of Risk," *Journal of Finance,* 19, no. 3 (September 1964): 425–442.

John Lintner, "The Valuation of Risk Assets and the Selection of Risky Investments in Stock Portfolios and Capital Budgets," *Review of Economics and Statistics,* 47, no. 1 (February 1965): 13–37; and "Security Prices, Risk, and Maximal Gains from Diversification," *Journal of Finance,* 20, no. 4 (December 1965): 587–615.

Jan Mossin, "Equilibrium in a Capital Asset Market," *Econometrica,* 34, no. 4 (October 1966): 768–783.

2. The Sharpe and Lintner papers were compared in

Eugene F. Fama, "Risk, Return, and Equilibrium: Some Clarifying Comments," *Journal of Finance,* 23, no. 1 (March 1968): 29–40.

3. For a comparison of the market model and CAPM betas, see

Harry M. Markowitz, "The 'Two Beta' Trap," *Journal of Portfolio Management,* 11, no. 1 (Fall 1984): 12–20.

4. It has been argued that the CAPM is virtually impossible to test because (a) the only testable hypothesis of the CAPM is that the "true" market portfolio lies on the efficient set (when this happens securities' expected returns and betas have a positive linear relationship) and (b) the "true" market portfolio cannot be meaningfully measured. See

Richard Roll, "A Critique of the Asset Pricing Theory's Tests: Part I. On Past and Potential Testability of the Theory," *Journal of Financial Economics,* 4, no. 2 (March 1977): 129–176.

5. Despite Roll's critique, several tests of the CAPM have been conducted. Some of them are summarized in

Gordon J. Alexander and Jack Clark Francis, *Portfolio Analysis* (Upper Saddle River, NJ: Prentice Hall, 1986), Chapter 10.

Edwin J. Elton and Martin J. Gruber, *Modern Portfolio Theory and Investment Analysis* (New York: John Wiley, 1995), Chapter 15.

6. Recently some people have concluded that the CAPM is no longer relevant based on the following test results that show that the relationship between beta and average stock returns is flat

Eugene F. Fama and Kenneth R. French, "The Cross-Section of Expected Stock Returns," *Journal of Finance,* 47, no. 2 (June 1992): 427–465.

———, "Common Risk Factors in the Returns on Stocks and Bonds," *Journal of Financial Economics,* 33, no. 1 (February 1993): 3–56.

James L. Davis, "The Cross-Section of Realized Stock Returns: The Pre-COMPUSTAT Evidence," *Journal of Finance,* 49, no. 5 (December 1994): 1579–1593.

Eugene F. Fama and Kenneth R. French, "The CAPM Is Wanted, Dead or Alive," *Journal of Finance,* 51, no. 5 (December 1996): 1947–1958.

7. CAPM test results have been challenged by others, such as the following:

Louis K. C. Chan and Josef Lakonishok, "Are the Reports of Beta's Death Premature?" *Journal of Portfolio Management,* 19, no. 4 (Summer 1993): 51–62.

Fischer Black, "Beta and Return," *Journal of Portfolio Management,* 20, no. 1 (Fall 1993): 8–18.

S. P. Kothari, Jay Shanken, and Richard D. Sloan, "Another Look at the Cross-Section of Expected Stock Returns," *Journal of Finance,* 50, no. 1 (March 1995): 185–224.

Ravi Jagannathan and Ellen R. McGrattan, "The CAPM Debate," Federal Reserve Bank of Minneapolis, *Quarterly Review,* 19, no. 4 (Fall 1995): 2–17.

Kevin Grundy and Burton Makiel, "Report of Beta's Death Have Been Greatly Exaggerated," *Journal of Portfolio Management,* 22, no. 3 (Spring 1996): 36–44.

Ravi Jagannathan and Zhenyu Wang, "The Conditional CAPM and the Cross-Section of Expected Returns," *Journal of Finance,* 51, no. 1 (March 1996): 3–53.

8. For an assertion that the use of modern investment theory does not depend on successful testing of the CAPM, see

Harry M. Markowitz, "Nonnegative or Not Nonnegative: A Question about CAPMs," *Journal of Finance,* 38, no. 2 (May 1983): 283–295.

9. An interesting Web site that presents a wealth of information on the Dow Jones Averages can be found at

<www.averages.dowjones.com>

CHAPTER 11

1. General discussions of factor models can be found in

William F. Sharpe, "Factors in New York Stock Exchange Security Returns, 1931–1979," *Journal of Portfolio Management,* 8, no. 4 (Summer 1982): 5–19; and "Factor Models, CAPMs, and the ABT [sic]," *Journal of Portfolio Management,* 11, no. 1 (Fall 1984): 21–25.

Mark Kritzman, ". . . About Factor Models," *Financial Analysts Journal,* 49, no. 1 (January/February 1993): 12–15.

Gregory Connor, "The Three Types of Factor Models: A Comparison of Their Explanatory Power," *Financial Analysts Journal,* 51, no. 3 (May/June 1995): 42–46.

Richard C. Grinold and Ronald N. Kahn, *Active Portfolio Management* (Chicago: Probus, 1995), Chapter 3.

2. Empirical papers that attempt to identify relevant factors and to estimate the magnitudes of the associated values include

Benjamin F. King, "Market and Industry Factors in Stock Price Behavior," *Journal of Business,* 39, no. 1 (January 1966): 139–170.

George J. Feeney and Donald D. Hester, "Stock Market Indices: A Principal Components Analysis," in Donald D. Hester and James Tobin, eds., *Risk Aversion and Portfolio Choice* (New York: Wiley, 1967).

Edwin J. Elton and Martin J. Gruber, "Estimating the Dependence Structure of Share Prices—Implications for Portfolio Selection," *Journal of Finance,* 28, no. 5 (December 1973): 1203–1232.

James J. Farrell, Jr., "Analyzing Covariation of Returns to Determine Homogeneous Stock Groupings," *Journal of Business,* 47, no. 2 (April 1974): 186–207.

Barr Rosenberg and Vinay Marathe, "The Prediction of Investment Risk: Systematic and Residual Risk," in *Proceedings of the Seminar on the Analysis of Security Prices* (Center for Research in Security Prices, University of Chicago, Graduate School of Business, November 1975).

Robert D. Arnott, "Cluster Analysis and Stock Price Movement," *Financial Analysts Journal,* 36, no. 6 (November/December 1980): 56–62.

Tony Estep, Nick Hanson, and Cal Johnson, "Sources of Value and Risk in Common Stocks," *Journal of Portfolio Management,* 9, no. 4 (Summer 1983): 5–13.

Nai-Fu Chen, Richard Roll, and Stephen A. Ross, "Economic Forces and the Stock Market," *Journal of Business,* 59, no. 3 (July 1986): 383–403.

Robert D. Arnott, Charles M. Kelso, Jr., Stephen Kiscadden, and Rosemary Macedo, "Forecasting Factor Returns: An Intriguing Possibility," *Journal of Portfolio Management,* 16, no. 1 (Fall 1989): 28–35.

Eugene F. Fama and Kenneth R. French, "The Cross-Section of Expected Stock Returns," *Journal of Finance,* 47, no. 2 (June 1992): 427–465.

―――, "Common Risk Factors in the Returns on Stocks and Bonds," *Journal of Financial Economics,* 33, no. 1 (February 1993): 3–56.

James L. Davis, "The Cross-Section of Realized Stock Returns: The Pre-COMPUSTAT Evidence," *Journal of Finance,* 49, no. 5 (December 1994): 1579–1593.

Eugene F. Fama and Kenneth R. French, "Size and Book-to-Market Factors in Earnings and Returns," *Journal of Finance,* 50, no. 1 (March 1995): 131–155.

S. P. Kothari, Jay Shanken, and Richard G. Sloan, "Another Look at the Cross-Section of Expected Stock Returns," *Journal of Finance,* 50, no. 1 (March 1995): 185–224.

Eugene F. Fama and Kenneth R. French, "Multifactor Explanations of Asset Pricing Anomalies," *Journal of Finance,* 51, no. 1 (March 1996): 55–84.

William C. Barbee, Jr., Sandip Mukherji, and Gary A. Raines, "Do Sales-Price and Debt-Equity Explain Stock Returns Better Than Book-Market and Firm Size?" *Financial Analysts Journal,* 52, no. 2 (March/April 1996): 56–60.

Kent Daniel and Sheridan Titman, "Evidence on the Characteristics of Cross Sectional Variation in Stock Returns," *Journal of Finance,* 52, no. 1 (March 1997): 1–33.

3. Several recent papers have argued that a factor model that distinguished value stocks from growth stocks is more appropriate than the Fama-French model

Josef Lakonishok, Andrei Shleifer, and Robert W. Vishny, "Contrarian Investment, Extrapolation, and Risk," *Journal of Finance,* 49, no. 5 (December 1994): 1541–1578.

Louis K. C. Chan, Narasimhan Jegadeesh, and Josef Lakonishok, "Evaluating the Performance of Value versus Glamour Stocks: The Impact of Selection Bias," *Journal of Financial Economics,* 38, no. 3 (July 1995): 269–296.

Rafael La Porta, Josef Lakonishok, Andrei Shleifer, and Robert Vishny, "Good News for Value Stocks: Further Evidence on Market Efficiency," *Journal of Finance,* 52, no. 2 (June 1997): 859–874.

4. Fixed-income factor models are discussed in

Ronald N. Kahn and Deepak Gulrajani, "Risk and Return in the Canadian Bond Market," *Journal of Portfolio Management,* 19, no. 3 (Spring 1993): 86–92.

5. For more on BARRA's factor models, see

<www.barra.com/MktIndices/default.asp>

CHAPTER 12

1. Credit for the initial development of APT belongs to

Stephen A. Ross, "The Arbitrage Theory of Capital Asset Pricing," *Journal of Economic Theory,* 13, no. 3 (December 1976): 341–360; and "Risk, Return, and Arbitrage," in Irwin Friend and James L. Bicksler (eds.), *Risk and Return in Finance,* vol. 1 (Cambridge, MA: Ballinger, 1977), Section 9.

2. Ross's initial presentation of APT was clarified in

Gur Huberman, "A Simple Approach to Arbitrage Pricing Theory," *Journal of Economic Theory,* 28, no. 1 (October 1982): 183–191.

Jonathan E. Ingersoll, Jr., "Some Results in the Theory of Arbitrage Pricing," *Journal of Finance,* 39, no. 4 (September 1984): 1021–1039.

3. The fundamental asset pricing equation of Ross's APT is approximately correct for all but a small number of assets. When additional assumptions are made, all assets will be priced with, at most, negligible error. Some of the papers (also see the papers cited in references 7 and 9) that address this issue are

Nai-fu Chen and Jonathan E. Ingersoll, Jr., "Exact Pricing in Linear Factor Models with Finitely Many Assets: A Note," *Journal of Finance,* 38, no. 3 (June 1983): 985–988.

Gary Chamberlain and Michael Rothschild, "Arbitrage, Factor Structure, and Mean–Variance Analysis on Large Asset Markets," *Econometrica,* 51, no. 5 (September 1983): 1281–1304.

Gary Chamberlain, "Funds, Factors, and Diversification in Arbitrage Pricing Models," *Econometrica,* 51, no. 5 (September 1983): 1305–1323.

Philip H. Dybvig, "An Explicit Bound on Individual Assets' Deviations from APT Pricing in a Finite Economy," *Journal of Financial Economics,* 12, no. 4 (December 1983): 483–496.

Mark Grinblatt and Sheridan Titman, "Factor Pricing in a Finite Economy," *Journal of Financial Economics,* 12, no. 4 (December 1983): 497–507.

Gregory Connor, "A Unified Beta Pricing Theory," *Journal of Economic Theory,* 34, no. 1 (October 1984): 13–31.

Robert A. Jarrow, "Preferences, Continuity, and the Arbitrage Pricing Theory," *Review of Financial Studies,* 2, no. 1 (Summer 1988): 159–172.

4. Nontechnical descriptions of APT can be found in

Richard W. Roll and Stephen A. Ross, "Regulation, the Capital Asset Pricing Model, and the Arbitrage Pricing Theory," *Public Utilities Fortnightly,* 111, no. 11 (May 26, 1983): 22–28.

Richard Roll and Stephen A. Ross, "The Arbitrage Pricing Theory Approach to Strategic Portfolio Planning," *Financial Analysts Journal,* 40, no. 3 (May/June 1984): 14–26.

Dorothy H. Bower, Richard S. Bower, and Dennis E. Logue, "A Primer on Arbitrage Pricing Theory," *Midland Corporate Finance Journal,* 2, no. 3 (Fall 1984): 31–40.

Richard C. Grinold and Ronald N. Kahn, *Active Portfolio Management* (Chicago: Probus, 1995), Chapter 7.

5. Some of the attempts to identify the number of factors that are priced are

Richard Roll and Stephen A. Ross, "An Empirical Investigation of the Arbitrage Pricing Theory," *Journal of Finance,* 35, no. 5 (December 1980): 1073–1103.

Stephen J. Brown and Mark I. Weinstein, "A New Approach to Testing Asset Pricing Models: The Bilinear Paradigm," *Journal of Finance,* 38, no. 3 (June 1983): 711–743.

Phoebus J. Dhrymes, Irwin Friend, and N. Bulent Gultekin, "A Critical Reexamination of the Empirical Evidence on the Arbitrage Pricing Theory," *Journal of Finance,* 39, no. 2 (June 1984): 323–346.

Richard Roll and Stephen A. Ross, "A Critical Reexamination of the Empirical Evidence on the Arbitrage Pricing Theory: A Reply," *Journal of Finance,* 39, no. 2 (June 1984): 347–350.

Phoebus J. Dhrymes, Irwin Friend, Mustafa N. Gultekin, and N. Bulent Gultekin, "New Tests of the APT and Their Implications," *Journal of Finance,* 40, no. 3 (July 1985): 659–674.

Charles Trzcinka, "On the Number of Factors in the Arbitrage Pricing Model," *Journal of Finance,* 41, no. 2 (June 1986): 347–368.

Gur Huberman, Shmuel Kandel, and Robert F. Stanbaugh, "Mimicking Portfolios and Exact Arbitrage

Pricing," *Journal of Finance,* 42, no. 1 (March 1987): 1–9.

Dolores A. Conway and Marc R. Reinganum, "Stable Factors in Security Returns: Identification Using Cross Validation," *Journal of Business and Economic Statistics,* 6, no. 1 (January 1988): 1–15.

Edwin Burmeister and Marjorie B. MacElroy, "Joint Estimation of Factor Sensitivities and Risk Premia for the Arbitrage Pricing Theory," *Journal of Finance,* 43, no. 3 (July 1988): 721–735.

Bruce N. Lehmann and David M. Modest, "The Empirical Foundations of the Arbitrage Pricing Theory," *Journal of Financial Economics,* 21, no. 2 (September 1988): 213–254.

Gregory Connor and Robert A. Korajczyk, "Risk and Return in an Equilibrium APT: Application of a New Test Methodology," *Journal of Financial Economics,* 21, no. 2 (September 1988): 255–289.

Stephen J. Brown, "The Number of Factors in Security Returns," *Journal of Finance,* 44, no. 5 (December 1989): 1247–1262.

Ravi Shukla and Charles Trzcinka, "Sequential Tests of the Arbitrage Pricing Theory: A Comparison of Principal Components and Maximum Likelihood Factors," *Journal of Finance,* 45, no. 5 (December 1990): 1541–1564.

Eugene F. Fama and Kenneth R. French, "Common Risk Factors in the Returns on Stocks and Bonds," *Journal of Financial Economics,* 33, no. 1 (February 1993): 3–56.

Jianping Mei, "A Semiautoregression Approach to the Arbitrage Pricing Theory," *Journal of Finance,* 48, no. 2 (June 1993): 599–620.

Gregory Connor and Robert A. Korajczyk, "A Test for the Number of Factors in an Approximate Factor Model," *Journal of Finance,* 48, no. 4 (September 1993): 1263–1291.

Jianping Mei, "Explaining the Cross-Section of Returns via a Multi-Factor APT Model," *Journal of Financial and Quantitative Analysis,* 28, no. 3 (September 1993): 331–345.

John Geweke and Guofu Zhou, "Measuring the Pricing Error of the Arbitrage Pricing Theory," *Review of Financial Studies,* 9, no. 2 (Summer 1996): 557–587.

6. A few of the previous papers also identified factors. Other papers that identified factors are

Tony Estep, Nick Hansen, and Cal Johnson, "Sources of Value and Risk in Common Stocks," *Journal of Portfolio Management,* 9, no. 4 (Summer 1983): 5–13.

Nai-fu Chen, Richard Roll, and Stephen A. Ross, "Economic Forces and the Stock Market," *Journal of Business,* 59, no. 3 (July 1986): 383–403.

Marjorie B. McElroy and Edwin Burmeister, "Arbitrage Pricing Theory as a Restricted Nonlinear Multivariate Regression Model," *Journal of Business and Economic Statistics,* 6, no. 1 (January 1988): 29–42.

Michael A. Berry, Edwin Burmeister, and Marjorie B. McElroy, "Sorting Out Risks Using Known APT Factors," *Financial Analysts Journal,* 44, no. 2 (March/April 1988): 29–42.

7. It has been argued that the APT cannot be meaningfully tested and is of questionable practical use. These arguments and their rebuttals have been provided by

Jay Shanken, "The Arbitrage Pricing Theory: Is It Testable?" *Journal of Finance,* 37, no. 5 (December 1982): 1129–1140.

Phoebus J. Dhrymes, "The Empirical Relevance of Arbitrage Pricing Models," *Journal of Portfolio Management,* 10, no. 4 (Summer 1984): 35–44.

Stephen A. Ross, "Reply to Dhrymes: APT Is Empirically Relevant," *Journal of Portfolio Management,* 11, no. 1 (Fall 1984): 54–56.

Phoebus J. Dhrymes, "On the Empirical Relevance of APT: Comment," *Journal of Portfolio Management,* 11, no. 4 (Summer 1985): 70–71.

Stephen A. Ross, "On the Empirical Relevance of APT: Reply," *Journal of Portfolio Management,* 11, no. 4 (Summer 1985): 72–73.

Philip H. Dybvig and Stephon A. Ross, "Yes, the APT Is Testable," *Journal of Finance,* 40, no. 4 (September 1985): 1129–1140.

Christian Gilles and Stephen F. LeRoy, "On the Arbitrage Pricing Theory," *Economic Theory,* 1, no. 3 (1991): 213–229.

Jay Shanken, "The Current State of Arbitrage Pricing Theory," *Journal of Finance,* 47, no. 4 (September 1992): 1569–1574.

8. Fama and French argue that stock prices are set according to a three-factor APT in

Eugene F. Fama and Kenneth R. French, "Multi-Factor Explanations of Asset Pricing Anomalies," *Journal of Finance,* 51, no. 1 (March 1996): 55–83.

9. For a discussion of the relationships between the APT and the CAPM, see

Robert Jarrow and Andrew Rudd, "A Comparison of the APT and CAPM: A Note," *Journal of Banking and Finance,* 7, no. 2 (June 1983): 295–303.

William F. Sharpe, "Factor Models, CAPMs, and the ABT [sic]," *Journal of Portfolio Management,* 11, no. 1 (Fall 1984): 21–25.

Jay Shanken, "Multi-Beta CAPM or Equilibrium-APT?: A Reply," *Journal of Finance,* 40, no. 4 (September 1985): 1189–1196.

K. C. John Wei, "An Asset-Pricing Theory Unifying the CAPM and APT," *Journal of Finance,* 43, no. 4 (September 1988): 881–892.

10. For a discussion of the APT in an international context, see

Bruno Solnik, "International Arbitrage Pricing Theory," *Journal of Finance,* 38, no. 2 (May 1982): 449–457.

11. Web sites of investment consultants using APT include

Advanced Portfolio Technologies <www.apt.co.uk/home.htm>

BIRR Portfolio Analysis, Inc. <www.birr.com>

CHAPTER 13

1. Corporate governance issues are discussed in

Bevis Longstreth, "Corporate Governance: There's Danger in New Orthodoxies," *Journal of Portfolio Management,* 21, no. 3 (Spring 1995): 47–52.

Adrei Shliefer and Robert W. Vishny, "A Survey of Corporate Governance," *Journal of Finance,* 52, no. 2 (June 1997): 737–783.

John Byrd, Robert Parrino, and Gunnar Pritsch, "Stockholder-Manager Conflicts and Firm Value," *Financial Analysts Journal,* 54, no. 3 (May/June 1998): 14–30.

Mark Latham, "Corporate Monitoring: New Shareholder Power Tool," *Financial Analysts Journal,* 54, no. 5 (September/October 1998): 9–15.

Paul W. MacAvoy and Ira M. Millstein, "The Active Board of Directors and Its Effect on the Performance of the Large Publicly Traded Corporation," *Journal of Applied Corporate Finance,* 11, no. 4 (Winter 1999): 8–20.

Rafael La Porta, Florencio Lopez-De Silanes, and Andrei Shleifer, "Corporate Ownership around the World," *Journal of Finance,* 54, no. 2 (April 1999): 471–517.

2. For a discussion of the motivations for takeovers and the associated consequences, see

Michael C. Jensen and Richard S. Ruback, "The Market for Corporate Control: The Scientific Evidence," *Journal of Financial Economics,* 11, nos. 1–4 (April 1983): 5–50.

Richard Roll, "The Hubris Hypothesis of Corporate Takeovers," *Journal of Business,* 59, no. 1, pt. 2 (April 1986): 197–216.

Michael C. Jensen, "Corporate Control and the Politics of Finance," *Journal of Applied Corporate Finance,* 4, no. 2 (Summer 1991): 13–33.

Andrei Shleifer and Robert W. Vishny, "The Takeover Wave of the 1980s," *Journal of Applied Corporate Finance,* 4, no. 3 (Fall 1991): 49–56.

Jack Treynor, "The Value of Control," *Financial Analysts Journal,* 49, no. 5 (July/August 1993): 6–9.

J. Fred Weston, Kwang S. Chung, and Susan E. Hoag, *Mergers, Restructuring, and Corporate Control* (Upper Saddle River, NJ: Prentice Hall, 1998).

3. For a study of how risk arbitrageurs (investors who buy and sell stocks of firms involved in takeovers and divestitures) are able to earn substantial returns, see

David F. Larcker and Thomas Lys, "An Empirical Analysis of the Incentives to Engage in Costly Information Acquisition: The Case of Risk Arbitrage," *Journal of Financial Economics,* 18, no. 1 (March 1987): 111–126.

4. Some interesting studies of stock repurchases are

Larry Y. Dann, "Common Stock Repurchases: An Analysis of Returns to Bondholders and Stockholders," *Journal of Financial Economics,* 9, no. 2 (June 1981): 113–138.

Theo Vermaelen, "Common Stock Repurchases and Market Signaling: An Empirical Study," *Journal of Financial Economics,* 9, no. 2 (June 1981): 139–183.

Aharon R. Ofer and Anjan V. Thakor, "A Theory of Stock Price Reponses to Alternative Corporate Cash Disbursement Methods: Stock Repurchases and Dividends," *Journal of Finance,* 42, no. 2 (June 1987): 365–394.

George M. Constantinides and Bruce D. Grundy, "Optimal Investment with Stock Repurchase and Financing as Signals," *Review of Financial Studies,* 2, no. 4 (1989): 445–465.

Josef Lakonishok and Theo Vermaelen, "Anomalous Price Behavior around Repurchase Tender Offers," *Journal of Finance,* 45, no. 2 (June 1990): 455–477.

Robert Comment and Gregg A. Jarrell, "The Relative Signalling Power of Dutch-Auction and Fixed-Price Self-Tender Offers and Open-Market Share Repurchases," *Journal of Finance,* 46, no. 4 (September 1991): 1243–1271.

Laurie Simon Bagwell, "Dutch Auction Repurchases: An Analysis of Shareholder Heterogeneity," *Journal of Finance,* 47, no. 1 (March 1992): 71–105.

David Ikenberry, Josef Lakonishok, and Theo Vermaelen, "Market Underreaction to Open Market Share Repurchases," *Journal of Financial Economics,* 39, no. 2/3 (October/November 1995): 181–208.

5. Stock splits and stock dividends are examined in

Eugene F. Fama, Lawrence Fisher, Michael C. Jensen, and Richard Roll, "The Adjustment of Stock Prices to New Information," *International Economic Review,* 10, no. 1 (February 1969): 1–21.

Sasson Bar-Yosef and Lawrence D. Brown, "A Reexamination of Stock Splits Using Moving Betas,"

Journal of Finance, 32, no. 4 (September 1977): 1069–1080.

Guy Charest, "Split Information, Stock Returns, and Market Efficiency—I," *Journal of Financial Economics,* 6, no. 2/3 (June/September 1978): 265–296.

Thomas E. Copeland, "Liquidity Changes Following Stock Splits," *Journal of Finance,* 34, no. 1 (March 1979): 115–141.

J. Randall Woolridge, "Ex-Date Stock Price Adjustment to Stock Dividends: A Note," *Journal of Finance,* 38, no. 1 (March 1983): 247–255.

J. Randall Woolridge and Donald R. Chambers, "Reverse Splits and Shareholder Wealth," *Financial Management,* 12, no. 3 (Autumn 1983): 5–15.

Mark S. Grinblatt, Ronald W. Masulis, and Sheridan Titman, "The Valuation Effects of Stock Splits and Stock Dividends," *Journal of Financial Economics,* 13, no. 4 (December 1984): 461–490.

Josef Lakonishok and Baruch Lev, "Stock Splits and Stock Dividends: Why, Who, and When," *Journal of Finance,* 42, no. 4 (September 1987): 913–932.

Christopher G. Lamoureux and Percy Poon, "The Market Reaction to Stock Splits," *Journal of Finance,* 42, no. 5 (December 1987): 1347–1370.

Michael J. Brennan and Thomas E. Copeland, "Stock Splits, Stock Prices, and Transactions Costs," *Journal of Financial Economics,* 22, no. 1 (October 1988): 83–101.

Maureen McNichols and Ajay Dravid, "Stock Dividends, Stock Splits, and Signaling," *Journal of Finance,* 45, no. 3 (July 1990): 857–879.

Robert S. Conroy, Robert S. Harris, and Bruce A. Benet, "The Effects of Stock Splits on Bid–Ask Spreads," *Journal of Finance,* 45, no. 4 (September 1990): 1285–1295.

David A. Dubofsky, "Volatility Increases Subsequent to NYSE and AMEX Stock Splits," *Journal of Finance,* 46, no. 1 (March 1991): 421–431.

Michael J. Brennan and Patricia J. Hughes, "Stock Prices and the Supply of Information," *Journal of Finance,* 46, no. 5 (December 1991): 1665–1691.

Michael T. Maloney and J. Harold Mulherin, "The Effects of Splitting on the Ex: A Microstructure Reconciliation," *Financial Management,* 21, no. 4 (Winter 1992): 44–59.

H. Kent Baker, Aaron L. Phillips, and Gary E. Powell, "The Stock Distribution Puzzle: A Synthesis of the Literature on Stock Splits and Stock Dividends," *Financial Practice and Education,* 5, no. 1 (Spring/Summer 1995): 24–37.

Eugene Pilotte and Timothy Manuel, "The Market's Response to Recurring Events: The Case of Stock Splits," *Journal of Financial Economics,* 41, no. 1 (May 1996): 111–127.

Chris J. Muscarella and Michael R. Vetsuypens, "Stock Splits: Signaling or Liquidity? The Case of ADR 'Solo Splits'," *Journal of Financial Economics,* 42, no. 1 (September 1996): 3–26.

David L. Ikenberry, Graeme Rankine, and Earl K. Stice, "What Do Stock Splits Really Signal?" *Journal of Financial and Quantitative Analysis,* 31, no. 3 (September 1996): 357–375.

James J. Angel, "Tick Size, Share Prices, and Stock Splits," *Journal of Finance,* 52, no. 2 (June 1997): 655–681.

James J. Angel, "Picking Your Tick: Toward a New Theory of Stock Splits," *Journal of Applied Corporate Finance,* 10, no. 3 (Fall 1997): 59–68.

6. References for the relationship between size and return are included in the endnotes. The characteristics of value and growth stocks are described in

Ken Gregory, "Fund Investment Strategies: Growth versus Value Investing," *AAII Journal,* 11, no. 9 (October 1989): 22–25.

David E. Tierney and Kenneth J. Winston, "Using Generic Benchmarks to Present Manager Styles," *Journal of Portfolio Management,* 17, no. 4 (Summer 1991): 33–36.

John Bajkowski, "A Question of Style: Growth and Value Investing," *AAII Journal,* 14, no. 5 (June 1992): 33–37.

John Bajkowski, "Creating Stock Screens That Make Practical Sense," *AAII Journal,* 15, no. 6 (July 1993): 34–37.

Louis K. C. Chan, Narasimhan Jegadeesh, and Josef Lakonishok, "Evaluating the Performance of Value versus Glamour Stocks: The Impact of Selection Bias," *Journal of Financial Economics,* 38, no. 3 (July 1995): 269–296.

Rafael La Porta, Josef Lakonishok, Andrei Shleifer, and Robert Vishny, "Good News for Value Stocks: Further Evidence on Market Efficiency," *Journal of Finance,* 52, no. 2 (June 1997): 859–874.

Kent Daniel and Sheridan Titman, "Characteristics or Covariances?" *Journal of Portfolio Management,* 24, no. 4 (Summer 1998): 24–33.

7. For more on investment banking, see the citations in the endnotes and

Stephen A. Ross, Randolph W. Westerfield, and Jeffrey F. Jaffee, *Corporate Finance* (Chicago: Irwin, 1996), Chapters 19–20.

Richard A. Brealey and Stewart C. Myers, *Principles of Corporate Finance* (New York: Irwin McGraw-Hill, 2000), Chapter 15.

8. Many of the studies conducted concerning various empirical regularities are cited in the endnotes. Also see

Donald B. Keim, "The CAPM and Equity Return Regularities," *Financial Analysts Journal*, 42, no. 3 (May/June 1986): 19–34.

Michael Smirlock and Laura Starks, "Day-of-the-Week and Intraday Effects in Stock Returns," *Journal of Financial Economics*, 17, no. 1 (September 1986): 197–210.

Richard H. Thaler, "Anomalies: The January Effect," *Journal of Economic Perspectives*, 1, no. 1 (Summer 1987): 197–201; and "Anomalies: Seasonal Movements in Security Prices II—Weekend, Holiday, Turn of the Month, and Intraday Effects," *Journal of Economic Perspectives*, 1, no. 2 (Fall 1987): 169–177.

Douglas K. Pearce, "Challenges to the Concept of Market Efficiency," *Federal Reserve Bank of Kansas City Economic Review*, 72, no. 8 (September/October 1987): 16–33.

Elroy Dimson, ed., *Stock Market Anomalies* (Cambridge, England: Cambridge University Press, 1988).

Robert A. Haugen and Josef Lakonishok, *The Incredible January Effect* (Homewood, IL: Dow Jones-Irwin, 1988).

Burton G. Malkiel, *A Random Walk down Wall Street* (New York: W. W. Norton, 1990), Chapter 8.

Eugene F. Fama, "Efficient Capital Markets: II," *Journal of Finance*, 46, no. 5 (December 1991): 1575–1617.

Narasimhan Jegadeesh, "Does Market Risk Really Explain the Size Effect?" *Journal of Financial and Quantitative Analysis*, 27, no. 3 (September 1992): 337–351.

Mark D. Griffiths and Robert W. White, "Tax-Induced Trading and the Turn-of-the-Year Anomaly: An Intraday Study," *Journal of Finance*, 48, no. 2 (June 1993): 575–598.

Rick A. Cooper and Joel M. Shulman, "The Year-End Effect in Junk Bond Prices," *Financial Analysts Journal*, 50, no. 5 (September/October 1994): 61–65.

Josef Lakonishok, Andrei Shliefer, and Robert W. Vishny, "Contrarian Investment, Extrapolation, and Risk," *Journal of Finance*, 49, no. 5 (December 1994): 1541–1578.

David K. Musto, "Portfolio Disclosures and Year-End Price Shifts," *Journal of Finance*, 52, no. 4 (September 1997): 1563–1588.

Richard W. Sias and Laura T. Starks, "Institutions and Individuals at the Turn-of-the-Year," *Journal of Finance*, 52, no. 4 (September 1997): 1543–1562.

9. For a tongue-in-cheek article on anomalies that shows that market returns are influenced by superstition because returns on Friday the 13th are, on average, abnormally low, see

Robert W. Kolb and Ricardo J. Rodriguez, "Friday the Thirteenth: 'Part VII'—A Note," *Journal of Finance*, 42, no. 5 (December 1987): 1385–1387.

10. The behavior of beta coefficients has been extensively studied. See, for example,

Marshall Blume, "On the Assessment of Risk," *Journal of Finance*, 26, no. 1 (March 1971): 1–10.

Robert A. Levy, "On the Short-Term Stationarity of Beta Coefficients," *Financial Analysts Journal*, 27, no. 6 (November/December 1971): 55–62.

William F. Sharpe and Guy M. Cooper, "Risk-Return Classes of New York Stock Exchange Common Stocks, 1931–1967," *Financial Analysts Journal*, 28, no. 2 (March/April 1972): 46–54.

Robert S. Hamada, "The Effect of the Firm's Capital Structure on the Systematic Risk of Common Stocks," *Journal of Finance*, 27, no. 2 (May 1972): 435–452.

Marshall Blume, "Betas and Their Regression Tendencies," *Journal of Finance*, 30, no. 3 (June 1975): 785–795.

Barr Rosenberg and Vinay Marathe, "The Prediction of Investment Risk: Systematic and Residual Risk," *Proceedings of the Seminar on the Analysis of Security Prices*, Center for Research in Security Prices, University of Chicago, Graduate School of Business, November 1975.

Barr Rosenberg and James Guy, "Prediction of Beta from Investment Fundamentals," *Financial Analysts Journal*, 32, no. 3 (May/June 1976): 60–72; and no. 4 (July/August 1976): 62–70.

Meir Statman, "Betas Compared: Merrill Lynch versus Value Line," *Journal of Portfolio Management*, 7, no. 2 (Winter 1981): 41–44.

Diana R. Harrington, "Whose Beta Is Best?" *Financial Analysts Journal*, 39, no. 5 (July/August 1983): 67–73.

Barr Rosenberg, "Prediction of Common Stock Investment Risk," *Journal of Portfolio Management*, 11, no. 1 (Fall 1984): 44–53.

———, "Prediction of Common Stock Betas," *Journal of Portfolio Management*, 11, no. 2 (Winter 1985): 5–14.

Gordon J. Alexander and Jack Clark Francis, *Portfolio Analysis* (Upper Saddle River, NJ: Prentice Hall, 1986), pp. 185–192.

George Foster, *Financial Statement Analysis* (Upper Saddle River, NJ: Prentice Hall, 1986), Chapter 10.

Frank K. Reilly and David J. Wright, "A Comparison of Published Betas," *Journal of Portfolio Management*, 14, no. 3 (Spring 1988): 64–69.

Thomas E. Copeland and J. Fred Weston, *Financial Theory and Corporate Policy* (Reading, MA: Addison-Wesley, 1988), Chapter 13.

Louis K. C. Chan and Josef Lakonishok, "Robust Measurement of Beta Risk," *Journal of Financial and Quantitative Analysis,* 27, no. 2 (June 1992): 265–282.

Stephon A. Ross, Randolph W. Westerfield, and Jeffrey Jaffe, *Corporate Finance* (Chicago: Irwin, 1996): 322, 469.

Richard A. Brealey and Stewart C. Myers, *Principles of Corporate Finance* (New York: Irwin McGraw-Hill, 2000): 224–227, 554–555.

CHAPTER 14

1. The role of financial analysts is discussed in

    Peter L. Bernstein, "The Expected Return of the Security Analyst," *Financial Analysts Journal,* 54, no. 2 (March/April 1998): 4–8.

2. Studies concerning the value of the CFA designation include

    Christopher M. Brockman and Robert Brooks, "The CFA Charter: Adding Value to the Market," *Financial Analysts Journal,* 54, no. 6 (November/December 1998): 50–61.

    Kenneth R. Miller, and Christopher B. Tobe, "Value of the CFA Designation to Public Pension Funds," *Financial Analysts Journal,* 55, no. 2 (March/April 1999): 21–26.

3. For a discussion of contrarian investment strategies, see, in addition to the references in Table 14.1 and Endnotes 12 and 15, the following:

    David Dremen, *Contrarian Investment Strategies* (New York: Random House, 1979).

    Paul Zarowin, "Short-Run Market Overreaction: Size and Seasonality Effects," *Journal of Portfolio Management,* 15, no. 3 (Spring 1989): 26–29.

    Paul Zarowin, "Does the Stock Market Overreact to Corporate Earnings Information?" *Journal of Finance,* 44, no. 5 (December 1989): 1385–1399.

    Jennifer Conrad, Mustafa N. Gultekin, and Gautam Kaul, "Profitability of Short-Term Contrarian Portfolio Strategies," unpublished paper, University of Michigan, 1991.

    Victor L. Bernard, Jacob K. Thomas, and Jeffery S. Abarbanell, "How Sophisticated Is the Market in Interpreting Earnings News?" *Journal of Applied Corporate Finance,* 6, no. 2 (Summer 1993): 54–63.

    Josef Lakonishok, Andrei Shleifer, and Robert W. Vishny, "Contrarian Investment, Extrapolation, and Risk," *Journal of Finance,* 49, no. 5 (December 1994): 1541–1578.

    Ray Ball, S. P. Kothari, and Charles E. Wasley, "Can We Implement Research on Stock Trading Rules?" *Journal of Portfolio Management,* 21, no. 2 (Winter 1995): 54–63.

    Ray Ball, S. P. Kothari, and Jay Shanken, "Problems in Measuring Portfolio Performance: An Application to Contrarian Investment Strategies," *Journal of Financial Economics,* 38, no. 1 (May 1995): 79–107.

    Tim Loughran and Jay Ritter, "Long-Term Market Overreaction: The Effect of Low-Priced Stocks," *Journal of Finance,* 51, no. 5 (December 1996): 1959–1970.

    S. P. Kothari and Jerold Warner, "Measuring Long-Horizon Security Price Performance," *Journal of Financial Economics,* 43, no. 3 (March 1997): 301–339.

4. Closely related to the issue of contrarian investment strategies is the issue of how stock price levels in one period are related to stock price levels in a subsequent period. This issue, like the usefulness of contrarian strategies, is open to debate. Two of the earliest papers and two recent ones that contradict them are

    Eugene F. Fama and Kenneth R. French, "Permanent and Temporary Components of Stock Prices," *Journal of Political Economy,* 96, no. 2 (April 1988): 246–273.

    James M. Poterba and Lawrence H. Summers, "Mean Reversion in Stock Prices: Evidence and Implications," *Journal of Financial Economics,* 22, no. 1 (October 1988): 27–59.

    Myung Jig Kim, Charles R. Nelson, and Richard Startz, "Mean Reversion in Stock Prices? A Reappraisal of the Empirical Evidence," *Review of Economic Studies,* 58, no. 3 (May 1991): 515–528.

    Grant McQueen, "Long-Horizon Mean-Reverting Stock Prices Revisited," *Journal of Financial and Quantitative Analysis,* 27, no. 1 (March 1992): 1–18.

5. Momentum strategies are discussed in

    Narasimhan Jegadeesh and Sheridan Titman, "Returns to Buying Winners and Selling Losers: Implications for Stock Market Efficiency," *Journal of Finance,* 48, no. 1 (March 1993): 65–91.

6. Moving average and trading range breakout strategies are discussed in

    William Brock, Josef Lakonishok, and Blake LeBaron, "Simple Technical Trading Rules and the Stochastic Properties of Stock Returns," *Journal of Finance,* 47, no. 5 (December 1992): 1731–1764.

7. Basic concepts used by fundamental analysts are presented in

    John Bajkowski, "Financial Statement Analysis: A Look at the Balance Sheet," *AAII Journal,* 21, no. 1 (January 1999): 7–10.

John Bajkowski, "Financial Statement Analysis: A Look at the Income Statement," *AAII Journal,* 21, no. 3 (April 1999): 23–26.

John Bajkowski, "Financial Statement Analysis: A Look at the Cash Flow Statement," *AAII Journal,* 21, no. 5 (June 1999): 26–29.

John Bajkowski and Wayne A. Thorp, "Frequently Asked Questions about Financial Statements," *AAII Journal,* 21, no. 9 (October 1999): 23–26.

8. The reaction of stock prices to the publication of analysts' recommendations is discussed in the sources given in Table 14.8 and in

Peter Lloyd-Davies and Michael Canes, "Stock Prices and the Publication of Second-Hand Information," *Journal of Business,* 51, no. 1 (January 1978): 43–56.

John C. Groth, Wilbur G. Lewellen, Gary G. Schlarbaum, and Ronald C. Lease, "An Analysis of Brokerage House Securities Recommendations," *Financial Analysts Journal,* 35, no. 1 (January/February 1979): 32–40.

Clark Holloway, "A Note on Testing an Aggressive Investment Strategy Using Value Line Ranks," *Journal of Finance,* 36, no. 3 (June 1981): 711–719.

Thomas E. Copeland and David Mayers, "The Value Line Enigma (1965–1978): A Case Study of Performance Evaluation Issues," *Journal of Financial Economics,* 10, no. 3 (November 1982): 289–321.

James H. Bjerring, Josef Lakonishok, and Theo Vermaelen, "Stock Prices and Financial Analysts' Recommendations," *Journal of Finance,* 38, no. 1 (March 1983): 187–204.

Gur Huberman and Shmuel Kandel, "Value Line Rank and Firm Size," *Journal of Business,* 60, no. 4 (October 1987): 577–589.

———, "Market Efficiency and Value Line's Record," *Journal of Business,* 63, no. 2 (April 1990): 187–216.

Pu Liu, Stanley D. Smith, and Azmat A. Syed, "Stock Price Reactions to *The Wall Street Journal*'s Securities Recommendations," *Journal of Financial and Quantitative Analysis,* 25, no. 3 (September 1990): 399–410.

Philip Heitner, "Isn't It Time to Measure Analysts' Track Records?" *Financial Analysts Journal,* 47, no. 3 (May/June 1991): 5–6.

Donna R. Philbrick and William E. Ricks, "Using Value Line and IBES Analyst Forecasts in Accounting Research," *Journal of Accounting Research,* 29, no. 2 (Autumn 1991): 397–417.

John Affleck-Graves and Richard R. Mendenhall, "The Relation between the Value Line Enigma and Post-Earnings-Announcement Drift," *Journal of Financial Economics,* 31, no. 1 (February 1992): 75–96.

John Markese, "The Role of Earnings Forecasts in Stock Price Behavior," *AAII Journal,* 14, no. 4 (April 1992): 30–32.

Rajiv Sant and Mir A. Zaman, "Market Reaction to *Business Week* 'Inside Wall Street' Column: A Self-Fulfilling Prophecy," *Journal of Banking and Finance,* 20, no. 4 (May 1996): 617–643.

Jennifer Francis and Leonard Soffer, "The Relative Informativeness of Analysts' Stock Recommendations and Earnings Forecast Revisions," *Journal of Accounting Research,* 35, no. 2 (Autumn 1997): 193–211.

9. The "Heard on the Street" column from *The Wall Street Journal* also sometimes discusses takeover rumors. For an analysis of the effects these rumors have on stock prices, see

John Pound and Richard Zeckhauser, "Clearly Heard on the Street: The Effect of Takeover Rumors on Stock Prices," *Journal of Business,* 63, no. 3 (July 1990): 291–308.

10. For a discussion of the neglected-firm effect, see

Avner Arbel and Paul Strebel, "Pay Attention to Neglected Firms!" *Journal of Portfolio Management,* 9, no. 2 (Winter 1983): 37–42.

Avner Arbel, Steven Carvel, and Paul Strebel, "Giraffes, Institutions, and Neglected Firms," *Financial Analysts Journal,* 39, no. 3 (May/June 1983): 57–63.

Craig G. Beard and Richard W. Sias, "Is There a Neglected-Firm Effect?" *Financial Analysts Journal,* 53, no. 5 (September/October 1997): 19–23.

11. Insider trading has been examined in a number of studies. Some of the major ones are

Jeffrey F. Jaffe, "Special Information and Insider Trading," *Journal of Business,* 47, no. 3 (July 1974): 410–428.

Joseph E. Finnerty, "Insiders and Market Efficiency," *Journal of Finance,* 31, no. 4 (September 1976): 1141–1148.

Herbert S. Kerr, "The Battle of Insider Trading and Market Efficiency," *Journal of Portfolio Management,* 6, no. 4 (Summer 1980): 47–58.

Wayne Y. Lee and Michael Solt, "Insider Trading: A Poor Guide to Market Timing," *Journal of Portfolio Management,* 12, no. 4 (Summer 1986): 65–71.

H. Nejat Seyhun, "Insiders' Profits, Costs of Trading, and Market Efficiency," *Journal of Financial Economics,* 16, no. 2 (June 1986): 189–212.

———, "The Information Content of Aggregate Insider Trading," *Journal of Business,* 61, no. 1 (January 1988): 1–24.

Michael S. Rozeff and Mir A. Zaman, "Market Efficiency and Insider Trading: New Evidence," *Journal of Business,* 61, no. 1 (January 1988): 25–44.

Ji-Chai Lin and John S. Howe, "Insider Trading in the OTC Market," *Journal of Finance,* 45, no. 4 (September 1990): 1273–1284.

Lisa K. Meulbroek, "An Empirical Analysis of Illegal Insider Trading," *Journal of Finance,* 47, no. 5 (December 1992): 1661–1699.

Mustafa Chowdhury, John S. Howe, and Ji-Chai Lin, "The Relation between Aggregate Insider Transactions and Stock Market Returns," *Journal of Financial and Quantitative Analysis,* 28, no. 3 (September 1993): 431–437.

Carr Bettis, Don Vickrey, and Donn W. Vickrey, "Mimickers of Corporate Insiders Who Make Large-Volume Trades," *Financial Analysts Journal,* 55, no. 5 (September/October 1997): 52–66.

12. Leading books on technical analysis, financial statement analysis, and fundamental analysis are, respectively,

George Foster, *Financial Statement Analysis* (Upper Saddle River, NJ: Prentice Hall, 1986).

Sidney Cottle, Roger Murray, and Frank Block, *Graham and Dodd's Security Analysis* (New York: McGraw-Hill, 1988).

Robert D. Edwards and John Magee, *Technical Analysis of Stock Trends* (New York: AMACOM, 1997).

13. Information sources for investing are described in

Maria Crawford Scott and John Bajkowski, "Sources of Information for the Simplified Approach to Valuation," *AAII Journal,* 16, no. 3 (April 1994): 29–32.

John Markese, "Picking Common Stocks: What Seems to Work, At Least Sometimes," *AAII Journal,* 16, no. 5 (June 1994): 24–27.

14. The new FASB reporting rules for earnings per share are discussed in

Ross Jennnings, Marc J. LeClere, and Robert B. Thompson II, "Evidence on the Usefulnesss of Alternative Earnings per Share Measures," *Financial Analysts Journal,* 53, no. 6 (November/December 1997): 24–32.

Ralph P. Goldsticker and Pankaj Agrrawal, "The Effects of Blending Primary and Diluted EPS Data," *Financial Analysts Journal,* 55, no. 2 (March/April 1999): 51–60.

15. Some interesting Web sites that contain a wealth of data, including analysts' reports, analysts' recommendations, criteria for evaluating stocks, stock screening programs, hot picks, and earnings forecasts, are

<www.bigcharts.com>

<www.stockscreener.com>

<www.dayinvestor.com>

<www.moneycentral.msn.com/investor/home.asp>

<www.businessweek.com/investor/frame/markets.htm>

<www.ndir/stocks.selection.html>

<www.zachs.com>

<www.firstcall.com/us/buysidenav.htm>

CHAPTER 15

1. The foundation for dividend discount models was laid out in

John Burr Williams, *The Theory of Investment Value* (Amsterdam: North-Holland, 1964). The original edition was published in 1938.

2. The constant-growth and multiple-growth models were subsequently developed by

M. J. Gordon, "Dividends, Earnings, and Stock Prices," *Review of Economics and Statistics,* 41, no. 2 (May 1959): 99–105.

Nicholas Molodovsky, Catherine May, and Sherman Chottiner, "Common Stock Valuation: Principles, Tables and Application," *Financial Analysts Journal,* 21, no. 2 (March/April 1965): 104–123.

3. For interesting extensions of the multiple-growth DDM, see

Patricia M. Fairfield, "P/E, P/B and the Present Value of Future Dividends," *Financial Analysts Journal,* 50, no. 4 (July/August 1994): 23–31.

Joseph R. Gordon and Myron J. Gordon, "The Finite Horizon Expected Return Model," *Financial Analysts Journal,* 53, no. 3 (May/June 1997): 52–61.

William J. Hurley and Lewis D. Johnson, "Stochastic Two-Phase Dividend Discount Models," *Journal of Portfolio Management,* 23, no. 4 (Summer 1997): 91–98.

Yulin Yao, "A Trinomial Dividend Valuation Model," *Journal of Portfolio Management,* 23, no. 4 (Summer 1997): 99–103.

4. For more on DDMs, see the entire November/December 1985 issue of the *Financial Analysts Journal* and *Damodaran on Valuation: Security Analysis for Investment and Corporate Finance* by Aswath Damodaran (New York: Wiley, 1994), particularly Chapter 6. Some of the problems in using dividend discount models are discussed in

Richard O. Michaud and Paul L. Davis, "Valuation Model Bias and the Scale Structure of Dividend Discount Returns," *Journal of Finance,* 38, no. 2 (May 1982): 563–573.

Adam K. Gehr, Jr., "A Bias in Dividend Discount Models," *Financial Analysts Journal,* 48, no. 1 (January/February 1992): 75–80.

5. For a discussion of how to estimate the discount rate *k* used with DDMs, see the entire issue of *Financial*

Markets, Institutions & Instruments, 3, no. 3 (1994) and

Eugene F. Fama and Kenneth R. French, "Industry Costs of Equity," *Journal of Financial Economics,* 43, no. 2 (February 1997): 153–193.

Bradford Cornell, John I. Hirshleifer, and Elizabeth P. James, "Estimating the Cost of Equity Capital," *Contemporary Finance Digest,* 1, no. 1 (Autumn 1997): 5–26.

6. For more on how to measure and use P/E ratios, see

John Markese, "Will the Real P/E Please Stand Up?" *AAII Journal,* 11, no. 9 (October 1989): 32–34.

Robert J. Angell and Alonzo Redman, "How to Judge a P/E? Examine the Expected Growth Rate," *AAII Journal,* 12, no. 3 (March 1990): 16–17.

John Baijkowski, "Price-Earnings Ratios and Fundamental Stock Valuation," *AAII Journal,* 13, no. 6 (July 1991): 33–36.

7. The issue of market volatility has been studied using dividend discount models. These studies compare the actual levels of various stock market indices with their intrinsic values, calculated by determining the present value of rational forecasts of subsequent dividends paid on the stocks in the indices. The main observation is that the actual levels fluctuate far more over time than the intrinsic values. A conclusion some people draw from these studies is that there is excess volatility in stock prices and hence markets are not efficient. This hotly debated topic was introduced in

Stephen F. LeRoy and Richard D. Porter, "The Present-Value Relation: Tests Based on Implied Variance Bounds," *Econometrica,* 49, no. 3 (May 1981): 555–574.

Robert J. Shiller, "Do Stock Prices Move Too Much to Be Justified by Subsequent Changes in Dividends?" *American Economic Review,* 71, no. 3 (June 1981): 421–436.

8. For more on market volatility, see

Robert J. Shiller, "Theories of Aggregate Stock Price Movements," *Journal of Portfolio Management,* 10, no. 2 (Winter 1984): 23–37.

———, *Market Volatility* (Cambridge, MA: MIT Press, 1989).

Stephen F. LeRoy, "Efficient Capital Markets and Martingales," *Journal of Economic Literature,* 27, no. 4 (December 1989): 1583–1621.

———, "Capital Market Efficiency: An Update," *Federal Reserve Bank of San Francisco Economic Review* (Spring 1990): 29–40.

Lucy F. Ackert and Brian F. Smith, "Stock Price Volatility, Ordinary Dividends, and Other Cash Flows to Shareholders," *Journal of Finance,* 48, no. 4 (September 1993): 1147–1160.

Bong-Soo Lee, "The Response of Stock Prices to Permanent and Temporary Shocks to Dividends," *Journal of Financial and Quantitative Analysis,* 30, no. 1 (March 1995): 1–22.

CHAPTER 16

1. The seminal paper on dividend policy that established both the "dividend irrelevancy theorem" and the notion that earnings are the basis for the market value of the firm was written by two Nobel laureates in economics:

Merton H. Miller and Franco Modigliani, "Dividend Policy, Growth, and the Valuation of Shares," *Journal of Business,* 34, no. 4 (October 1961): 411–433.

2. The Lintner model of dividend behavior and some studies that empirically tested it are

John Lintner, "Distribution of Incomes of Corporations among Dividends, Retained Earnings, and Taxes," *American Economic Review,* 46, no. 2 (May 1956): 97–113.

John A. Brittain, *Corporate Dividend Policy* (Washington, DC: The Brookings Institution, 1966).

Eugene F. Fama and Harvey Babiak, "Dividend Policy: An Empirical Analysis," *Journal of the American Statistical Association,* 63, no. 324 (December 1968): 1132–1161.

Eugene F. Fama, "The Empirical Relationship between the Dividend and Investment Decisions of Firms," *American Economic Review,* 64, no. 3 (June 1974): 304–318.

Terry A. Marsh and Robert C. Merton, "Dividend Behavior for the Aggregate Stock Market," *Journal of Business,* 60, no. 1 (January 1987): 1–40.

Bong-Soo Lee, "Time-Series Implications of Aggregate Dividend Behavior," *Review of Financial Studies,* 9, no. 2 (Summer 1996): 589–618.

3. The determinants of recent dividend behavior are similar to those in the Lintner model from the 1950s, according to

H. Kent Baker, Gail E. Farrelly, and Richard B. Edelman, "A Survey of Management Views on Dividend Policy," *Financial Management,* 14, no. 3 (Autumn 1985): 78–84.

4. A summary of the literature on signaling can be found in

Thomas E. Copeland and J. Fred Weston, *Financial Theory and Corporate Policy* (Reading, MA: Addison-Wesley, 1988), pp. 501–507, 584–588.

5. The information content of dividends hypothesis, closely linked to the signaling literature, has been the subject of much research. Some of the more important papers are

R. Richardson Pettit, "Dividend Announcements, Security Performance, and Capital Market Efficiency," *Journal of Finance,* 27, no. 5 (December 1972): 993–1007.

Ross Watts, "The Information Content of Dividends," *Journal of Business,* 46, no. 2 (April 1973): 191–211.

Joseph Aharony and Itzak Swary, "Quarterly Dividend and Earnings Announcements and Stockholders' Returns: An Empirical Analysis," *Journal of Finance,* 35, no. 1 (March 1980): 1–12.

Clarence C. Y. Kwan, "Efficient Market Tests of the Informational Content of Dividend Announcements: Critique and Extension," *Journal of Financial and Quantitative Analysis,* 16, no. 2 (June 1981): 193–206.

Paul Asquith and David W. Mullins, Jr., "The Impact of Initiating Dividend Payments on Shareholders' Wealth," *Journal of Business,* 56, no. 1 (January 1983): 77–96.

James A. Brickley, "Shareholder Wealth, Information Signaling and the Specially Designated Dividend: An Empirical Study," *Journal of Financial Economics,* 12, no. 2 (August 1983): 187–209.

J. Randall Woolridge, "Dividend Changes and Stock Prices," *Journal of Finance,* 38, no. 5 (December 1983): 1607–1615.

Terry E. Dielman and Henry R. Oppenheimer, "An Examination of Investor Behavior during Periods of Large Dividend Changes," *Journal of Financial and Quantitative Analysis,* 19, no. 2 (June 1984): 197–216.

Paul M. Healy and Krishna G. Palepu, "Earnings Information Conveyed by Dividend Initiations and Omissions," *Journal of Financial Economics,* 21, no. 2 (September 1988): 149–175.

P. C. Venkatesh, "The Impact of Dividend Initiation on the Information Content of Earnings Announcements and Returns Volatility," *Journal of Business,* 62, no. 2 (April 1989): 175–197.

Larry H. P. Lang and Robert H. Litzenberger, "Dividend Announcements: Cash Flow Signalling versus Free Cash Flow Hypothesis," *Journal of Financial Economics,* 24, no. 1 (September 1989): 181–191.

Harry DeAngelo, Linda DeAngelo, and Douglas J. Skinner, "Dividends and Losses," *Journal of Finance,* 47, no. 5 (December 1992): 1837–1863.

Keith M. Howe, Jia He, and G. Wenchi Kao, "One-Time Cash Flow Announcements and Free Cash-Flow Theory: Share Repurchases and Special Dividends," *Journal of Finance,* 47, no. 5 (December 1992): 1963–1975.

Roni Michaely, Richard H. Thaler, and Kent L. Womack, "Price Reactions to Dividend Initiations and Omissions: Overreaction or Drift?" *Journal of Finance,* 50, no. 2 (June 1995): 573–608.

6. The relationship between economic and accounting earnings is discussed in

Fischer Black, "The Magic in Earnings: Economic Earnings versus Accounting Earnings," *Financial Analysts Journal,* 36, no. 6 (November/December 1980): 19–24.

7. For a study on the timing of dividend announcements as well as a listing of other studies concerning dividend announcements, see

Avner Kalay and Uri Loewenstein, "The Informational Content of the Timing of Dividend Announcements," *Journal of Financial Economics,* 16, no. 3 (July 1986): 373–388.

Aharon R. Ofer and Daniel R. Siegel, "Corporate Financial Policy, Information, and Market Expectations: An Empirical Investigation of Dividends," *Journal of Finance,* 42, no. 4 (September 1987): 889–911.

8. For a review of the literature dealing with dividends, see

James S. Ang, *Do Dividends Matter? A Review of Corporate Dividend Theories and Evidence,* Monograph Series in Finance and Economics #1987-2 (New York: New York-University Salomon Center, Leonard N. Stern School of Business, 1987).

9. Time-series models of annual and quarterly earnings per share are discussed in

George Foster, "Quarterly Accounting Data: Time-Series Properties and Predictive-Ability Results," *Accounting Review,* 52, no. 1 (January 1977): 1–21.

George Foster, *Financial Statement Analysis* (Upper Saddle River, NJ: Prentice Hall, 1986), Chapter 7.

Ross L. Watts and Jerold L. Zimmerman, *Positive Accounting Theory* (Upper Saddle River, NJ: Prentice Hall, 1986), Chapter 6.

10. The relationship between earnings announcements and stock prices has been documented in many studies. See the following as well as their citations:

Ray Ball and Philip Brown, "An Empirical Evaluation of Accounting Income Numbers," *Journal of Accounting Research,* 6, no. 2 (Autumn 1968): 159–178.

William H. Beaver, "The Information Content of Annual Earnings Announcements," *Empirical Research in Accounting: Selected Studies,* Supplement to *Journal of Accounting Research,* 6 (1968): 67–92.

Leonard Zacks, "EPS Forecasts—Accuracy Is Not Enough," *Financial Analysts Journal,* 35, no. 2 (March/April 1979): 53–55.

Dale Morse, "Price and Trading Volume Reaction Surrounding Earnings Announcements: A Closer Examination," *Journal of Accounting Research,* 19, no. 2 (Autumn 1981): 374–383.

James M. Patell and Mark A. Wolfson, "The *Ex Ante* and *Ex Post* Effects of Quarterly Earnings Announcements Reflected in Stock and Option Prices," *Journal of Accounting Research,* 19, no. 2 (Autumn 1981): 434–458.

Richard J. Rendleman, Jr., Charles P. Jones, and Henry A. Latane, "Empirical Anomalies Based on Unexpected Earnings and the Importance of Risk Adjustments," *Journal of Financial Economics,* 10, no. 3 (November 1982): 269–287.

James M. Patell and Mark A. Wolfson, "The Intraday Speed of Adjustment of Stock Prices to Earnings and Dividend Announcements," *Journal of Financial Economics,* 13, no. 2 (June 1984): 223–252.

George Foster, Chris Olsen, and Terry Shevlin, "Earnings Releases, Anomalies, and the Behavior of Security Returns," *Accounting Review,* 59, no. 4 (October 1984): 574–603.

Catherine S. Woodruff and A. J. Senchack, Jr., "Intradaily Price-Volume Adjustments of NYSE Stocks to Unexpected Earnings," *Journal of Finance,* 43, no. 2 (June 1988): 467–491.

The entire issue of the *Journal of Accounting and Economics,* 15, no. 2/3 (June/September 1992).

Anthony Bercel, "Consensus Expectations and International Equity Returns," *Financial Analysts Journal,* 50, no. 4 (July/August 1994): 76–80.

Beverly R. Walther, "Investor Sophistication and Market Earnings Expectations," *Journal of Accounting Research,* 35, no. 2 (Autumn 1997): 157–179.

11. Some of the studies that have examined possible explanations for the "post-earnings-announcement drift" in stock prices are

Richard J. Rendleman, Jr., Charles P. Jones, and Henry A. Latane, "Further Insight into the Standardized Unexpected Earnings Anomaly: Size and Serial Correlation Effects," *Financial Review,* 22, no. 1 (February 1987): 131–144.

Victor L. Bernard and Jacob K. Thomas, "Post-Earnings-Announcement Drift: Delayed Price Response or Risk Premium?" *Journal of Accounting Research,* 27 (Supplement 1989): 1–36.

Robert N. Freeman and Senyo Tse, "The Multiperiod Information Content of Accounting Earnings: Confirmations and Contradictions of Previous Earnings Reports," *Journal of Accounting Research,* 27 (Supplement 1989): 49–79.

Victor L. Bernard and Jacob K. Thomas, "Evidence That Stock Prices Do Not Fully Reflect the Implications of Current Earnings for Future Earnings," *Journal of Accounting and Economics,* 13, no. 4 (December 1990): 305–340.

Richard R. Mendenhall, "Evidence on the Possible Underweighting of Earnings-Related Information," *Journal of Accounting Research,* 29, no. 1 (Spring 1991): 170–179.

Ray Ball, "The Earnings-Price Anomaly," *Journal of Accounting and Economics,* 15, no. 2/3 (June/September 1992): 319–345.

Jeffery S. Abarbanell and Victor L. Bernard, "Tests of Analysts' Overreaction/Underreaction to Earnings Information as an Explanation for Anomalous Stock Price Behavior," *Journal of Finance,* 47, no. 3 (July 1992): 1181–1207.

Ray Ball and Eli Bartov, "How Naïve Is the Stock Market's Use of Earnings Information?" *Journal of Accounting and Economics,* 21, no. 3 (June 1996): 319–337.

12. There have been numerous studies concerning the earnings forecasts made by security analysts. Some of the studies are

Lawrence D. Brown and Michael S. Rozeff, "The Superiority of Analyst Forecasts as Measures of Expectations: Evidence from Earnings," *Journal of Finance,* 33, no. 1 (March 1978): 1–16.

Lawrence D. Brown and Michael S. Rozeff, "Analysts Can Forecast Accurately!" *Journal of Portfolio Management,* 6, no. 3 (Spring 1980): 31–34.

John G. Cragg and Burton G. Malkiel, *Expectations and the Structure of Share Prices* (Chicago: University of Chicago Press, 1982), particularly pages 85–86 and 165.

Dan Givoly and Josef Lakonishok, "Properties of Analysts' Forecasts of Earnings: A Review and Analysis of the Research," *Journal of Accounting Literature,* 3 (Spring 1984): 117–152.

Dan Givoly and Josef Lakonishok, "The Quality of Analysts' Forecasts of Earnings," *Financial Analysts Journal,* 40, no. 5 (September/October 1984): 40–47.

Philip Brown, George Foster, and Eric Noreen, *Security Analyst Multi-Year Earnings Forecasts and the Capital Markets* (Sarasota, FL: American Accounting Association, 1985).

John M. Hassell and Robert H. Jennings, "Relative Forecast Accuracy and the Timing of Earnings Forecast Announcements," *Accounting Review,* 61, no. 1 (January 1986): 58–75.

Gary A. Benesh and Pamela P. Peterson, "On the Relation between Earnings Changes, Analysts' Forecasts and Stock Price Fluctuations," *Financial Analysts Journal*, 42, no. 6 (November/December 1986): 29–39, 55.

Lawrence D. Brown, Robert L. Hagerman, Paul A. Griffin, and Mark Zmijewski, "Security Analyst Superiority Relative to Univariate Time-Series Models in Forecasting Quarterly Earnings," *Journal of Accounting and Economics*, 9, no. 1 (April 1987): 61–87.

Robert Conroy and Robert Harris, "Consensus Forecasts of Corporate Earnings: Analysts' Forecasts and Time-Series Methods," *Management Science*, 33, no. 6 (June 1987): 725–738.

Lawrence D. Brown, Robert L. Hagerman, Paul A. Griffin, and Mark Zmijewski, "An Evaluation of Alternative Proxies for the Market's Assessment of Unexpected Earnings," *Journal of Accounting and Economics*, 9, no. 2 (July 1987): 159–193.

Patricia C. O'Brien, "Analysts' Forecasts as Earnings Expectations," *Journal of Accounting and Economics*, 10, no. 1 (January 1988): 53–83.

Werner F. De Bondt and Richard H. Thaler, "Do Security Analysts Overreact?" *American Economic Review*, 80, no. 2 (May 1990): 52–57.

Lawrence D. Brown and Kwon-Jung Kim, "Timely Aggregate Analyst Forecasts as Better Proxies for Market Earnings Expectations," *Journal of Accounting Research*, 29, no. 2 (Autumn 1991): 382–385.

Ashiq Ali, April Klein, and James Rosenfeld, "Analysts' Use of Information about Permanent and Transitory Earnings Components in Forecasting Annual EPS," *Accounting Review*, 67, no. 1 (January 1992): 183–198.

Scott E. Stickel, "Reputation and Performance among Security Analysts," *Journal of Finance*, 47, no. 5 (December 1992): 1811–1836.

David N. Dreman, "Analyst Forecasting Errors," *Financial Analysts Journal*, 52, no. 3 (May/June 1995): 77–80.

David N. Dreman and Michael A. Berry, "Analyst Forecasting Errors and Their Implications for Security Analysis," *Financial Analysts Journal*, 51, no. 3 (May/June 1995): 30–41.

Lawrence D. Brown, "Analyst Forecasting Errors and Their Implications for Security Analysis: An Alternative Perspective," *Financial Analysts Journal*, 52, no. 16 (January/February 1996): 40–47.

Robert A. Olsen, "Implications of Herding Behavior for Earnings Estimation, Risk Assessment, and Stock Returns," *Financial Analysts Journal*, 52, no. 4 (July/August 1996): 37–41.

Maribeth Collier and Teri Lombardi Yohn, "Management Forecasts and Information Asymmetry: An Examination of Bid–Ask Spreads," *Journal of Accounting Research*, 35, no. 2 (Autumn 1997): 181–191.

Lawrence D. Brown, "Analyst Forecasting Errors: Additional Evidence," *Financial Analysts Journal*, 53, no. 6 (November/December 1997): 81–88.

Maribeth Collier and Teri Lombardi Yohn, "Management Forecasts: What Do We Know?" *Financial Analysts Journal*, 54, no. 1 (January/February 1998): 58–62.

Huong Ngo Higgins, "Analyst Forecasting Performance in Seven Countries," *Financial Analysts Journal*, 54, no. 3 (May/June 1998): 58–62.

Michael J. Ho and Robert S. Harris, "Market Reactions to Messages from Brokerage Rating Systems," *Financial Analysts Journal*, 54, no. 1 (January/February 1998): 49–57.

Vijay Kumra Chopra, "Why So Much Error in Analysts' Earnings Forecasts?" *Financial Analysts Journal*, 54, no. 6 (November/December 1998): 50–61.

Kirt C. Butler and Hakan Saraoglu, "Improving Analysts' Negative Earnings Forecasts," *Financial Analysts Journal*, 55, no. 3 (May/June 1999): 34–48.

13. Web sites that provide earnings forecasts include
    <www.bigcharts.com>
    <www.zachs.com>
    <www.dayinvestor.com/engine/index.html>
    <www.firstcall.com/us/buysidenav.htm>

CHAPTER 17

1. Investment management is discussed in
    William F. Sharpe, "Decentralized Investment Management," *Journal of Finance*, 36, no. 2 (May 1981): 217–234.

    Jeffery V. Bailey and Robert D. Arnott, "Cluster Analysis and Manager Selection," *Financial Analysts Journal*, 42, no. 6 (November/December 1986): 20–28.

    Richard A. Brealey, "Portfolio Theory versus Portfolio Practice," *Journal of Portfolio Management*, 16, no. 4 (Summer 1990): 6–10.

    William F. Sharpe, "The Arithmetic of Active Management," *Financial Analysts Journal*, 47, no. 1 (January/February 1991): 7–9.

    Robert H. Jeffery, "Do Clients Need So Many Portfolio Managers?" *Journal of Portfolio Management*, 18, no. 1 (Fall 1991): 13–19.

    C. B. Garcia and F. J. Gould, "Some Observations on Active Manager Performance and Passive Indexing," *Financial Analysts Journal*, 47, no. 6 (November/December 1991): 11–13.

Richard C. Grinold and Ronald N. Kahn, *Active Portfolio Management* (Chicago: Probus, 1995).

2. Investment management for an individual investor is discussed in

Burton G. Malkiel, *A Random Walk down Wall Street* (New York: W. W. Norton, 1996), particularly Chapter 12.

3. Assessment of investor risk tolerance is discussed in

Gail Farrelly and Dean LeBaron, "Assessing Risk Tolerance Levels: A Prerequisite for Personalizing and Managing Portfolios," *Financial Analysts Journal,* 45, no. 1 (January/February 1989): 14–16.

W. V. Harlow and Keith C. Brown, "Understanding and Assessing Financial Risk Tolerance: A Biological Perspective," *Financial Analysts Journal,* 46, no. 6 (November/December 1990): 50–62.

William B. Riley, Jr., and K. Victor Chow, "Asset Allocation and Individual Risk Aversion," *Financial Analysts Journal,* 48, no. 6 (November/December 1992): 32–37.

Karen Hube, "Time for Investing's Four-Letter Word," *Wall Street Journal,* January 23, 1998, pp. C1, C17.

4. An extensive discussion of risk tolerance is included in

William F. Sharpe, *Asset Allocation Tools* (Redwood City, CA: Scientific Press, 1987), Chapter 2.

———, "Integrated Asset Allocation," *Financial Analysts Journal,* 43, no. 5 (September/October 1987): 25–32.

5. Active versus passive management is discussed in

Eric H. Sorensen, Keith L. Miller, and Vele Samak, "Allocating between Active and Passive Management," *Financial Analysts Journal,* 54, no. 5 (September/October 1998): 18–31.

Glen A. Larsen, Jr., and Bruce G. Resnick, "Empirical Insights on Indexing," *Journal of Portfolio Management,* 25, no. 1 (Fall 1998): 51–60.

Albert Ferguson, "The Index Fund Advantage: Low-Cost Passive Investing," *AAII Journal,* 21, no. 4 (May 1999): 6–10.

6. Market timing, asset allocation, and investment styles are discussed in

Keith P. Ambachtsheer, "Portfolio Theory and the Security Analyst," *Financial Analysts Journal,* 28, no. 6 (November/December 1972): 53–57.

Jack L. Treynor and Fischer Black, "How to Use Security Analysis to Improve Portfolio Selection," *Journal of Business,* 46, no. 1 (January 1973): 66–86.

William F. Sharpe, "Likely Gains from Market Timing," *Financial Analysts Journal,* 31, no. 2 (March/April 1975): 60–69.

———, "Major Investment Styles," *Journal of Portfolio Management,* 4, no. 2 (Winter 1978): 68–74.

Keith P. Ambachtsheer and James L. Farrell Jr., "Can Active Management Add Value?" *Financial Analysts Journal,* 35, no. 6 (November/December 1979): 39–47.

Robert D. Arnott and James N. von Germeten, "Systematic Asset Allocation," *Financial Analysts Journal,* 39, no. 6 (November/December 1983): 31–38.

Jess H. Chua and Richard S. Woodard, *Gains from Market Timing,* Monograph Series in Finance and Economics #1986-2 (New York: New York University Salomon Center, Leonard N. Stern School of Business).

Richard A. Brealey, "How to Combine Active Management with Index Funds," *Journal of Portfolio Management,* 12, no. 2 (Winter 1986): 4–10.

William F. Sharpe, "Integrated Asset Allocation," *Financial Analysts Journal,* 43, no. 5 (September/October 1987): 25–32.

André F. Perold and William F. Sharpe, "Dynamic Strategies for Asset Allocation," *Financial Analysts Journal,* 44, no. 1 (January/February 1988): 16–27.

William F. Sharpe, "Asset Allocation," in John L. Maginn and Donald L. Tuttle (eds.), *Managing Investment Portfolio: A Dynamic Process* (Boston, MA: Warren, Gorham & Lamont, 1990), Chapter 7.

David E. Tierney and Kenneth Winston, "Defining and Using Dynamic Completeness Funds to Enhance Total Fund Efficiency," *Financial Analysts Journal,* 46, no. 4 (July/August 1990): 49–54.

Craig B. Wainscott, "The Stock–Bond Correlation and Its Implications for Asset Allocation," *Financial Analysts Journal,* 46, no. 4 (July/August 1990): 55–60, 79.

John Markese, "All Eggs in One Basket, or a Basket for Each Egg?" *AAII Journal,* 12, no. 7 (August 1990): 31–33.

David E. Tierney and Kenneth Winston, "Using Generic Benchmarks to Present Manager Styles," *Journal of Portfolio Management,* 17, no. 4 (Summer 1991): 33–36.

P. R. Chandy and William Reichenstein, "Timing Strategies and the Risk of Missing Bull Markets," *AAII Journal,* 13, no. 7 (August 1991): 17–19.

William F. Sharpe, "Asset Allocation: Management Style and Performance Measurement," *Journal of Portfolio Management,* 18, no. 2 (Winter 1992): 7–19.

P. R. Chandy and William Reichenstein, "Stock Market Timing: A Modest Proposal," *AAII Journal,* 14, no. 4 (April 1992): 7–10.

Mark Hulbert, "Market Timing Strategies: Taxes Are a Drag," *AAII Journal,* 14, no. 7 (August 1992): 18–20.

Maria Crawford Scott, "Asset Allocation among the Three Major Categories," *AAII Journal,* 15, no. 4 (April 1993): 13–16.

Mark Hulbert, "Bond Market Timing: Even More Tough Than Timing the Stock Market," *AAII Journal,* 16, no. 3 (April 1994): 11–13.

Joseph B. Ludwig, "The Market Timing Approach: A Guide to the Various Strategies," *AAII Journal,* 16, no. 4 (May 1994): 11–14.

Richard Bernstein, *Style Investing* (New York: Wiley, 1995).

T. Daniel Coggin, Frank J. Fabozzi, and Robert Arnott (eds.), *The Handbook of Equity Style Management* (New Hope, PA: Frank J. Fabozzi Associates, 1997).

7. Investing in an international context is discussed in Chapter 26 (see the references listed there) and in

Robert D. Arnott and Roy D. Henriksson, "A Disciplined Approach to Global Asset Allocation," *Financial Analysts Journal,* 45, no. 2 (March/April 1989): 17–28.

Carlo Capaul, Ian Rowley, and William F. Sharpe, "International Value and Growth Stock Returns," *Financial Analysts Journal,* 49, no. 1 (January/February 1993): 27–36.

Jess Lederman and Robert A. Klein, eds., *Global Asset Allocation: Techniques for Optimizing Portfolio Management* (New York: Wiley, 1994).

Lucie Chaumeton, Gregory Connor, and Ross Curds, "A Global Stock and Bond Model," *Financial Analysts Journal,* 52 no. 6 (November/December 1996): 65–74.

8. For a discussion of portfolio revision procedures, see

Gordon J. Alexander and Jack Clark Francis, *Portfolio Analysis* (Upper Saddle River, NJ: Prentice Hall, 1986), pp. 221–228.

William F. Sharpe, *Asset Allocation Tools* (Redwood City, CA: Scientific Press, 1987), pp. 65–68.

9. Swaps are discussed in many of the textbooks on options and futures listed in the references for Chapters 24 and 25. Also see the following and their references:

Robert H. Litzenberger, "Swaps: Plain and Fanciful," *Journal of Finance,* 47, no. 3 (July 1992): 831–850.

John F. Marshall and Vipul K. Bansal, *Financial Engineering* (Boston: Blackwell, 1995).

Charles W. Smithson, Clifford W. Smith, Jr., and D. Sykes Wilford, *Managing Financial Risk: A Guide to Derivative Products, Financial Engineering, and Value Maximization* (Burr Ridge, IL: Irwin, 1995).

Frank J. Fabozzi, Franco Modigliani, and Michael G. Ferri, *Foundations of Financial Markets and Institutions* (Upper Saddle River, NJ: Prentice Hall, 1998).

Robert W. Kolb, *Futures, Options, and Swaps* (Malden, MA: Blackwell, 2000).

Also see the Web site for the International Swaps and Derivatives Association, an industry association for the participants in swaps and other privately negotiated derivatives transactions, at <www.isda.org>.

10. The International Swaps and Derivatives Association (see footnote 13) has the following Web site that contains information regarding swaps:

<www.isda.org>

CHAPTER 18

1. The use of portfolio benchmarks for performance evaluation is discussed in

Richard Roll, "Performance Evaluation and Benchmark Errors (I)," *Journal of Portfolio Management,* 6, no. 4 (Summer 1980): 5–12.

Richard Roll, "Performance Evaluation and Benchmark Errors (II)," *Journal of Portfolio Management,* 7, no. 2 (Winter 1981): 17–22.

Gary P. Brinson, Jeffrey J. Diermeier, and Gary G. Schlarbaum, "A Composite Portfolio Benchmark for Pension Plans," *Financial Analysts Journal,* 42, no. 2 (March/April 1986): 15–24.

Mark P. Kritzman, "How to Build a Normal Portfolio in Three Easy Steps," *Journal of Portfolio Management,* 13, no. 4 (Summer 1987): 21–23.

Jeffery V. Bailey, Thomas M. Richards, and David E. Tierney, "Benchmark Portfolios and the Manager/Plan Sponsor Relationship," *Journal of Corporate Finance,* 4, no. 4 (Winter 1988): 25–32.

Arjun Divecha and Richard C. Grinold, "Normal Portfolios: Issues for Sponsors, Managers, and Consultants," *Financial Analysts Journal,* 45, no. 2 (March/April 1989): 7–13.

Edward P. Rennie and Thomas J. Cowhey, "The Successful Use of Benchmark Portfolios: A Case Study," *Financial Analysts Journal,* 46, no. 5 (September/October 1990): 18–26.

Jeffery V. Bailey, "Are Manager Universes Acceptable Performance Benchmarks?" *Journal of Portfolio Management,* 18, no. 3 (Spring 1992): 9–13.

Jeffery V. Bailey, "Evaluating Benchmark Quality," *Financial Analysts Journal,* 48, no. 3 (May/June 1992): 33–39.

Martin L. Leibowitz, Lawrence N. Bader, Stanley Kogelman, and Ajay R. Dravid, "Benchmark Departures and Total Fund Risk: A Second Dimension of Diversification," *Financial Analysts Journal,* 51, no. 5 (September/October 1995): 40–48.

2. The four measures of risk-adjusted performance were initially developed in

Jack L. Treynor, "How to Rate Management of Investment Funds," *Harvard Business Review,* 43, no. 1 (January/February 1965): 63–75.

William F. Sharpe, "Mutual Fund Performance," *Journal of Business,* 39, no. 1 (January 1966): 119–138; and "The Sharpe Ratio," *Journal of Portfolio Management,* 21, no. 1 (Fall 1994): 49–58.

Michael C. Jensen, "The Performance of Mutual Funds in the Period 1945–1964," *Journal of Finance,* 23, no. 2 (May 1968): 389–416; and "Risk, the Pricing of Capital Assets, and the Evaluation of Investment Portfolios," *Journal of Business,* 42, no. 2 (April 1969): 167–185.

Franco Modigliani and Leah Modigliani, "Risk-Adjusted Performance," *Journal of Portfolio Management,* 23, no. 2 (Winter 1997): 45–54.

3. More sophisticated measures of portfolio performance that also measure market timing ability were initially developed by

Jack L. Treynor and Kay K. Mazuy, "Can Mutual Funds Outguess the Market?" *Harvard Business Review,* 44, no. 4 (July/August 1966): 131–136.

Robert C. Merton, "On Market Timing and Investment Performance I. An Equilibrium Theory of Value for Market Forecasts," *Journal of Business,* 54, no. 3 (July 1981): 363–406.

Roy D. Henriksson and Robert C. Merton, "On Market Timing and Investment Performance II. Statistical Procedures for Evaluating Forecasting Skill," *Journal of Business,* 54, no. 4 (October 1981): 513–533.

4. There have been many criticisms leveled at the various measures of portfolio performance that are presented in this chapter. One of the most formidable critiques was

Richard Roll, "Ambiguity When Performance Is Measured by the Security Market Line," *Journal of Finance,* 33, no. 4 (September 1978): 1051–1069.

5. APT-based measures of portfolio performance have been developed by

Gregory Connor and Robert Korajczyk, "Performance Measurement with the Arbitrage Pricing Theory: A New Framework for Analysis," *Journal of Financial Economics,* 15, no. 3 (March 1986): 373–394.

Bruce N. Lehmann and David M. Modest, "Mutual Fund Performance Evaluation: A Comparison of Benchmarks and Benchmark Comparisons," *Journal of Finance,* 42, no. 2 (June 1987): 233–265.

Nai-Fu Chen, Thomas E. Copeland, and David Mayers, "A Comparison of Single and Multifactor Portfolio Performance Methodologies," *Journal of Financial and Quantitative Analysis,* 22, no. 4 (December 1987): 401–417.

Edwin J. Elton, Martin J. Gruber, and Christopher R. Blake, "Fundamental Economic Variables, Expected Returns, and Bond Fund Performance," *Journal of Finance,* 50, no. 4 (September 1995): 1229–1256.

6. Developments in measuring portfolio performance are discussed in the references to Chapter 23 and in

Stanley J. Kon, "The Market-Timing Performance of Mutual Fund Managers," *Journal of Business,* 56, no. 3 (July 1983): 323–347.

Anat R. Admati and Stephen A. Ross, "Measuring Investment Performance in a Rational Expectations Equilibrium Model," *Journal of Business,* 58, no. 1 (January 1985): 1–26.

Philip H. Dybvig and Stephen A. Ross, "Differential Information and Performance Measurement Using a Security Market Line," *Journal of Finance,* 40, no. 2 (June 1985): 383–399.

——, "The Analytics of Performance Measurement Using a Security Market Line," *Journal of Finance,* 40, no. 2 (June 1985): 401–416.

Mark Kritzman, "How to Detect Skill in Management Performance," *Journal of Portfolio Management,* 12, no. 2 (Winter 1986): 16–20.

Ravi Jagannathan and Robert A. Korajczyk, "Assessing the Market Timing Performance of Managed Portfolios," *Journal of Business,* 59, no. 2, pt. 1 (April 1986): 217–235.

Anat R. Admati, Sudipto Bhattacharya, Paul Pfleiderer, and Stephen A. Ross, "On Timing and Selectivity," *Journal of Finance,* 41, no. 3 (July 1986): 715–730.

Gary P. Brinson, L. Randolph Hood, and Gilbert L. Beebower, "Determinants of Portfolio Performance," *Financial Analysts Journal,* 42, no. 4 (July/August 1986): 39–44.

William Breen, Ravi Jagannathan, and Aharon R. Ofer, "Correcting for Heteroscedasticity in Tests for Market Timing Ability," *Journal of Business,* 59, no. 4, pt. 1 (October 1986): 585–598.

Robert E. Cumby and David M. Modest, "Testing for Market Timing Ability: A Framework for Forecast Evaluation," *Journal of Financial Economics,* 19, no. 1 (September 1987): 169–189.

Larry J. Lockwood and K. Rao Kadiyala, "Measuring Investment Performance with a Stochastic Parameter Regression Model," *Journal of Banking and Finance,* 12, no. 3 (September 1988): 457–467.

Alex Kane and Gary Marks, "Performance Evaluation of Market Timers: Theory and Evidence," *Journal of Financial and Quantitative Analysis,* 23, no. 4 (December 1988): 425–435.

Mark Grinblatt and Sheridan Titman, "Portfolio Performance Evaluation: Old Issues and New Insights," *Review of Financial Studies,* 2, no. 3 (1989): 393–421.

Cheng-few Lee and Shafiqur Rahman, "Market Timing, Selectivity, and Mutual Fund Performance: An Empirical Investigation," *Journal of Business,* 63, no. 2 (April 1990): 261–278.

Michel Gendron and Christian Genest, "Performance Measurement under Asymmetric Information and Investment Constraints," *Journal of Finance,* 45, no. 5 (December 1990): 1655–1661.

Cheng-few Lee and Shafiqur Rahman, "New Evidence on Timing and Security Selection Skill of Mutual Fund Managers," *Journal of Portfolio Management,* 17, no. 2 (Winter 1991): 80–83.

Gary P. Brinson, Brian D. Singer, and Gilbert L. Beebower, "Determinants of Portfolio Performance II: An Update," *Financial Analysts Journal,* 47, no. 3 (May/June 1991): 40–48.

Chris R. Hensel, D. Don Ezra, and John H. Ilkiw, "The Importance of the Asset Allocation Decision," *Financial Analysts Journal,* 47, no. 4 (July/August 1991): 65–72.

Eric J. Weigel, "The Performance of Tactical Asset Allocation," *Financial Analysts Journal,* 47, no. 5 (September/October 1991): 63–70.

G. L. Beebower and A. P. Varikooty, "Measuring Market Timing Strategies," *Financial Analysts Journal,* 47, no. 6 (November/December 1991): 78–84, 92.

L. R. Glosten and R. Jagannathan, "A Contingent Claim Approach to Performance Evaluation," *Journal of Empirical Finance,* 1, no. 2 (January 1994): 133–160.

Wayne E. Ferson and Rudi Schadt, "Measuring Fund Strategy and Performance in Changing Economic Conditions," *Journal of Finance,* 51, no. 2 (June 1996): 425–461.

Zhiwu Chen and Peter Knez, "Portfolio Performance Measurement: Theory and Applications," *Review of Financial Studies,* 9, no. 2 (Summer 1996): 511–555.

Jeffery V. Bailey, "Evaluating Investment Skill with a VAM Graph," *Journal of Investing,* 5, no. 2 (Summer 1996): 64–71.

Stan Beckers, "Manager Skill and Investment Performance: How Strong Is the Link?" *Journal of Portfolio Management,* 23, no. 4 (Summer 1997): 9–23.

7. A description of various market indices can be found at the following Web sites:

<www.averages.dowjones.com>

<www.msci.com/index2.html>

<www.nasd.com>

<www.nyse.com/search/search.htm>

<www.russell.com/toc/toc.htm>

<www.standardpoor.com>

<www.wilshire.com/indexes/indexes.htm>

8. Monthly return series beginning in 1975 for various U.S. stock market indices can be downloaded over the Web at

<www.barra.com/MktIndices/default.asp>

CHAPTER 19

1. A concise summary description of the various types of money market instruments is contained in

Timothy Q. Cook and Timothy D. Rowe, *Instruments of the Money Market* (Federal Reserve Bank of Richmond, 1993).

Gunter Dufey and Ian Giddy, *The International Money Market* (Upper Saddle River, NJ: Prentice Hall, 1994).

2. The following contain thorough descriptions of the various types of fixed-income securities discussed in this chapter

Suresh Sundaresan, *Fixed Income Markets and Their Derivatives* (Cincinnati, OH: South-Western, 1997), Chapters 1–2, 8–10.

Frank J. Fabozzi, Franco Modigliani, and Michael G. Ferri, *Foundations of Financial Markets and Institutions* (Upper Saddle River, NJ: Prentice Hall, 1998), Chapters 16, 17, 20–25.

3. For a discussion of coupon stripping, see

Miles Livingston and Deborah Wright Gregory, *The Stripping of U.S. Treasury Securities,* Monograph Series in Finance and Economics #1989-1 (New York: New York University Salomon Center, Leonard N. Stern School of Business).

Deborah W. Gregory and Miles Livingston, "Development of the Market for U.S. Treasury STRIPS," *Financial Analysts Journal,* 48, no. 2 (March/April 1992): 68–74.

Phillip R. Daves, Michael C. Ehrhardt, and John M. Wachowicz, Jr., "A Guide to Investing in U.S. Treasury STRIPS," *AAII Journal,* 15, no. 1 (January 1993): 6–10.

Phillip R. Daves and Michael C. Ehrhardt, "Liquidity, Reconstitution, and the Value of U.S. Treasury STRIPS," *Journal of Finance,* 47, no. 1 (March 1993): 315–329.

4. For a discussion of the market for securities issued by the U.S. Treasury, see

Peter Wann, *Inside the U.S. Treasury Market* (New York: Quorum Books, 1989).

Saikat Nandi, "Treasury Auctions: What Do the Recent Models Tell Us?" *Federal Reserve Bank of*

Atlanta Economic Review, 82, no. 4 (Fourth Quarter 1997): 4–15.

5. A Web site for the U.S. Treasury that contains links to sites for information on Treasury securities, including U.S. savings bonds, is

   <www.publicdebt.treas.gov>

6. For a discussion of the U.S. Treasury's inflation-indexed securities, see

   Richard Roll, "U.S. Treasury Inflation-Indexed Bonds: The Design of a New Security," *Journal of Fixed Income,* 6, no. 3 (December 1996): 28.

   Jeffrey M. Wrase, "Inflation-Indexed Bonds: How Do They Work?" *Federal Reserve Bank of Philadelphia Business Review* (July–August 1997): 3–16.

   Robert J. Angell and Alonzo L. Redman, "Inflation-Indexed Treasuries: How Good Are They?" *AAII Journal,* 20, no. 3 (April 1998): 22–24.

   R. McFall Lamm, Jr., "Asset Allocation Implications of Inflation Protection Securities," *Journal of Portfolio Management,* 24, no. 4 (Summer 1998): 66–77.

   Richard W. Kopcke and Ralph C. Kimball, "Inflation-Indexed Bonds: The Dog That Didn't Bark," *New England Economic Review* (January/February 1999): 3–24.

7. For a discussion of mortgage-backed securities, see

   Earl Baldwin and Saundra Stotts, *Mortgage-Backed Securities: A Reference Guide for Lenders & Issuers* (Chicago: Probus, 1990).

   Sean Becketti and Charles S. Morris, *The Prepayment Experience of FNMA Mortgage-Backed Securities,* Monograph Series in Finance and Economics #1990-3 (New York: New York University Salomon Center, Leonard N. Stern School of Business).

   Eduardo S. Schwartz and Walter N. Torous, "Prepayment, Default, and the Valuation of Mortgage Pass-Through Securities," *Journal of Business,* 65, no. 2 (April 1992): 221–239.

   Andrew Carron, "Understanding CMOs, REMICs, and Other Mortgage Derivatives," *Journal of Fixed Income,* 2, no. 1 (June 1992): 25–43.

   Albert J. Golly, Jr., "An Individual Investor's Guide to the Complex World of CMOs," *AAII Journal,* 14, no. 6 (July 1992): 7–10.

   Frank J. Fabozzi and Franco Modigliani, *Mortgage & Mortgage-Backed Securities Markets* (Boston: Harvard Business School Press, 1992).

   Michael D. Joehnk and Matthew J. Hassett, "Getting a Grip on the Risks of CMO Prepayments," *AAII Journal,* 15, no. 5 (June 1993): 8–12.

   Frank J. Fabozzi, Charles Ramsey, and Frank R. Ramirez, *Collateralized Mortgage Obligations: Structure and Analysis* (Summit, NJ: Frank J. Fabozzi Associates, 1993).

8. For a discussion of municipal bonds, see

   Peter Fortune, "The Municipal Bond Market, Part I: Politics, Taxes, and Yields," Federal Reserve Bank of Boston, *New England Economic Review* (September/October 1991): 13–36.

   Peter Fortune, "The Municipal Bond Market, Part II: Problems and Policies," Federal Reserve Bank of Boston, *New England Economic Review* (May/June 1992): 47–64.

9. For a discussion of the foreign bond and Eurobond markets, see

   Bruno Solnik, *International Investments* (Reading, MA: Addison-Wesley, 1991), Chapters 6–7.

   J. Orlin Grabbe, *International Financial Markets* (New York: Elsevier Science, 1996), Chapter 12.

10. For a discussion of the Eurocredit market, see

    Arie L. Melnik and Steven E. Plaut, *The Short-Term Eurocredit Market,* Monograph Series in Finance and Economics #1991-1 (New York: New York University Salomon Center, Leonard N. Stern School of Business, 1991).

11. For a discussion of how government bond markets function in the United Kingdom, Japan, and Germany, see

    Thomas J. Urich, *U.K., German and Japanese Government Bond Markets,* Monograph Series in Finance and Economics #1991-2 (New York: New York University Salomon Center, Leonard N. Stern School of Business, 1991).

12. The accuracy of reported prices for corporate bonds is analyzed in

    Kenneth P. Nunn, Jr., Joanne Hill, and Thomas Schneeweis, "Corporate Bond Price Data Sources and Risk/Return Measurement," *Journal of Financial and Quantitative Analysis,* 21, no. 2 (June 1986): 197–208.

    Oded Sarig and Arthur Warga, "Bond Price Data and Bond Market Liquidity," *Journal of Financial and Quantitative Analysis,* 24, no. 3 (September 1989): 367–378.

    Arthur D. Warga, "Corporate Bond Price Discrepancies in the Dealer and Exchange Markets," *Journal of Fixed Income,* 1, no. 3 (December 1991): 7–16.

13. The market for preferred stock is discussed in

    Arthur L. Houston, Jr., and Carol Olson Houston, "Financing with Preferred Stock," *Financial Management,* 19, no. 3 (Autumn 1990): 42–54.

14. An extensive discussion of the private placement market for corporate debt is contained in

Mark Carey, Stephen Prowse, John Rea, and Gregory Udell, "The Economics of Private Placements: A New Look," *Financial Markets, Institutions & Instruments,* 2, no. 3 (1993).

Cynthia J. Campbell, "Private Security Placements and Resales to the Public under Rule 144," *Corporate Finance Review* (July/August 1997): 11–16.

George A. Martin, "Private Debt: Past, Present, and Future: Part I," *Journal of Alternative Investments,* 1, no. 1 (Summer 1998): 29–40.

15. Distressed securities are discussed in

Allen Michel, Israel Shaked, and Christopher McHugh, "After Bankruptcy: Can Ugly Ducklings Turn into Swans?" *Financial Analysts Journal,* 54, no. 3 (May/June 1998): 31–40.

16. Here are some Web sites that contain a wealth of information about fixed-income securities:

<www.bog.frb.fed.us/>

<www.fms.treas.gov/bulletin/index.html>

<www.intex.com/homepage/coverage.htm>

<www.investinginbonds.com>

<www.msrb.org>

<www.muniauction.com>

<www.munidirect.com>

<www.psa.com>

<www.stls.frb.org/fred/>

CHAPTER 20

1. Many of the fundamental concepts having to do with bonds are discussed in

Homer Sidney and Martin L. Leibowitz, *Inside the Yield Book: New Tools for Bond Market Strategy* (Upper Saddle River, NJ: Prentice Hall, 1972).

Marcia Stigum, *The Money Market,* 3rd ed. (Homewood, IL: Business One Irwin, 1990).

Frank J. Fabozzi, ed., *The Handbook of Fixed-Income Securities,* 5th ed. (Homewood, IL: Irwin Professional, 1997).

2. A discussion of the zero-coupon Treasury bond market is presented in

Deborah W. Gregory and Miles Livingston, "Development of the Market for U.S. Treasury STRIPS," *Financial Analysts Journal,* 48, no. 2 (March/April 1992): 68–74.

3. A brief overview of the term structure of interest rates is contained in

Mark Kritzman, ". . . About the Term Structure of Interest Rates," *Financial Analysts Journal,* 49, no. 4 (July/August 1993): 14–18.

4. For a thorough review of term structure theories and the associated empirical evidence, see

John H. Wood and Norma L. Wood, *Financial Markets* (San Diego, CA: Harcourt Brace Jovanovich, 1985), Chapter 19.

Peter A. Abken, "Innovations in Modeling the Term Structure of Interest Rates," Federal Reserve Bank of Atlanta, *Economic Review,* 75, no. 4 (July/August 1990): 2–27.

Steven Russell, "Understanding the Term Structure of Interest Rates: The Expectations Theory," Federal Reserve Bank of St. Louis, *Review,* 74, no. 4 (July/August 1992): 36–50.

Frederic S. Mishkin and Stanley G. Eakins, *Financial Markets and Institutions* (Reading, MA: Addison-Wesley, 1998), Chapter 6.

Frank J. Fabozzi, Franco Modigliani, and Michael G. Ferri, *Foundations of Financial Markets and Institutions* (Upper Saddle River, NJ: Prentice Hall, 1998), Chapter 12.

James C. Van Horne, *Financial Market Rates and Flows* (Upper Saddle River, NJ: Prentice Hall, 1998), Chapter 6.

5. For an intriguing tax-based explanation of why the yield curve has usually been upward sloping, see

Richard Roll, "After-Tax Investment Results from Long-Term versus Short-Term Discount Coupon Bonds," *Financial Analysts Journal,* 40, no. 1 (January/February 1984): 43–54.

Ricardo J. Rodriguez, "Investment Horizon, Taxes and Maturity Choice for Discount Coupon Bonds," *Financial Analysts Journal,* 44, no. 5 (September/October 1988): 67–69.

6. The yield curve is displayed daily at

<www.bloomberg.com/markets/C13.html>

<www.bloomberg.com/markets/index.html>

CHAPTER 21

1. For a detailed discussion of bond valuation and the attributes of bonds that are important in their pricing, see

Karlyn Mitchell, "The Call, Sinking Fund, and Term-to-Maturity Features of Corporate Bonds: An Empirical Investigation," *Journal of Financial and Quantitative Analysis,* 26, no. 2 (June 1991): 201–222.

Frank J. Fabozzi, *Valuation of Fixed Income Securities* (Summit, NJ: Frank J. Fabozzi Associates, 1994).

———, ed., *Advances in Fixed Income Valuation Modeling and Risk Management* (New Hope, PA: Frank J. Fabozzi Associates, 1997).

Suresh Sundaresan, *Fixed Income Markets and Their Derivatives* (Cincinnati, OH: Southwestern, 1997).

James C. Van Horne, *Financial Market Rates and Flows* (Upper Saddle River, NJ: Prentice Hall, 1998).

2. Putable bonds are discussed in

Leland E. Crabbe and Panos Nikoulis, "The Putable Bond Market: Structure, Historical Experience, and Strategies," *Journal of Fixed Income,* 7, no. 3 (December 1997): 47–60.

3. Some of the many studies that have investigated the relationship between historical measures of a firm's performance and its bond ratings are

Thomas F. Pogue and Robert M. Soldofsky, "What's in a Bond Rating?" *Journal of Financial and Quantitative Analysis,* 4, no. 2 (June 1969): 201–228.

R. R. West, "An Alternate Approach to Predicting Corporate Bond Ratings," *Journal of Accounting Research,* 8, no. 1 (Spring 1970): 118–125.

George E. Pinches and Kent A. Mingo, "A Multivariate Analysis of Industrial Bond Ratings," *Journal of Finance,* 30, no. 1 (March 1975): 201–206.

Robert S. Kaplan and Gabriel Urwitz, "Statistical Models of Bond Ratings: A Methodological Inquiry," *Journal of Business,* 52, no. 2 (April 1979): 231–261.

Ahmed Belkaoui, *Industrial Bonds and the Rating Process* (Westport, CT: Quorum Books, 1983).

4. Bond ratings have been studied in

Steven Katz, "The Price Adjustment Process of Bonds to Rating Reclassifications: A Test of Bond Market Efficiency," *Journal of Finance,* 29, no. 2 (May 1974): 551–559.

Paul Grier and Steven Katz, "The Differential Effects of Bond Rating Changes among Industrial and Public Utility Bonds by Maturity," *Journal of Business,* 49, no. 2 (April 1976): 226–239.

Mark I. Weinstein, "The Effect of a Rating Change Announcement on Bond Price," *Journal of Financial Economics,* 5, no. 3 (December 1977): 329–350.

Douglas J. Lucas and John G. Lonski, "Changes in Corporate Credit Quality 1970–1990," *Journal of Fixed Income,* 1, no. 4 (March 1992): 7–14.

Edward I. Altman and Duen Li Kao, "Rating Drift in High-Yield Bonds," *Journal of Fixed Income,* 1, no. 4 (March 1992): 15–20.

Edward I. Altman, "The Implications of Bond Ratings Drift," *Financial Analysts Journal,* 48, no. 3 (May/June 1992): 64–75.

John R. M. Hand, Robert W. Holthausen, and Richard W. Leftwich, "The Effect of Bond Rating Agency Announcements on Bond and Stock Prices," *Journal of Finance,* 47, no. 2 (June 1992): 733–752.

Lea V. Carty and Jerome S. Fons, "Measuring Changes in Corporate Credit Quality," *Journal of Fixed Income,* 4, no. 1 (June 1994): 27–41.

Richard Cantor and Frank Packer, "The Credit Rating Industry," *Journal of Fixed Income,* 5, no. 3 (December 1995): 10–34.

Gailen Hite and Arthur Warga, "The Effect of Bond-Rating Changes on Bond Price Performance," *Financial Analysts Journal,* 53, no. 3 (May/June 1997): 35–51.

Allen Michel, Israel Shaked, and Christopher McHugh, "After Bankruptcy: Can Ugly Ducklings Turn into Swans?" *Financial Analysts Journal,* 54, no. 3 (May/June 1998): 31–40.

Jeff Jewel and Miles Livingston, "A Comparison of Bond Ratings from Moody's, S&P and Fitch," *Financial Markets, Institutions & Instruments,* 8, no. 4 (1999).

5. Municipal bond ratings are discussed in

John E. Petersen, *The Rating Game* (New York: The Twentieth Century Fund, 1974).

Robert W. Ingram, Leroy D. Brooks, and Ronald M. Copeland, "The Information Content of Municipal Bond Rating Changes: A Note," *Journal of Finance,* 38, no. 3 (June 1983): 997–1003.

George Foster, *Financial Statement Analysis* (Upper Saddle River, NJ: Prentice Hall, 1986), Chapter 14.

6. Default premiums and risks are discussed in

W. Braddock Hickman, *Corporate Bond Quality and Investor Experience* (Princeton, NJ: Princeton University Press, 1958).

Harold G. Fraine and Robert H. Mills, "The Effect of Defaults and Credit Deterioration on Yields of Corporate Bonds," *Journal of Finance,* 16, no. 3 (September 1961): 423–434.

Thomas R. Atkinson and Elizabeth T. Simpson, *Trends in Corporate Bond Quality* (New York: Columbia University Press, 1967).

Gordon Pye, "Gauging the Default Premium," *Financial Analysts Journal,* 30, no. 1 (January/February 1974): 49–52.

Ricardo J. Rodriguez, "Default Risk, Yield Spreads, and Time to Maturity," *Journal of Financial and Quantitative Analysis,* 23, no. 1 (March 1988): 111–117.

Edward I. Altman, "Measuring Corporate Bond Mortality and Performance," *Journal of Finance,* 44, no. 4 (September 1989): 909–922.

Paul Asquith, David W. Mullins, Jr., and Eric D. Wolff, "Original Issue High Yield Bonds: Aging Analysis of Defaults, Exchanges, and Calls," *Journal of Finance,* 44, no. 4 (September 1989): 923–952.

Marshall E. Blume and Donald B. Keim, "Realized Returns and Defaults on Low-Grade Bonds: The Cohort of 1977 and 1978," *Financial Analysts Journal,* 47, no. 2 (March/April 1991): 63–72.

Marshall E. Blume, Donald B. Keim, and Sandeep A. Patel, "Returns and Volatility of Low-Grade Bonds, 1977–1989," *Journal of Finance,* 46, no. 1 (March 1991): 49–74.

Bradford Cornell and Kevin Greene, "The Investment Performance of Low-Grade Bond Funds," *Journal of Finance,* 46, no. 1 (March 1991): 29–48.

Jerome S. Fons and Andrew E. Kimball, "Corporate Bond Defaults and Default Rates 1970–1990," *Journal of Fixed Income,* 1, no. 1 (June 1991): 36–47.

Marshall E. Blume and Donald B. Keim, "The Risk and Return of Low-Grade Bonds: An Update," *Financial Analysts Journal,* 47, no. 5 (September/October 1991): 85–89.

Edward I. Altman, "Defaults and Returns on High-Yield Bonds through the First Half of 1991," *Financial Analysts Journal,* 47, no. 6 (November/December 1991): 67–77.

Bradford Cornell, "Liquidity and the Pricing of Low-Grade Bonds," *Financial Analysts Journal,* 48, no. 1 (January/February 1992): 63–67, 74.

Edward I. Altman, "Revisiting the High-Yield Bond Market," *Financial Management,* 21, no. 2 (Summer 1992): 79–92.

Martin S. Fridson, "Fraine's Neglected Findings: Was Hickman Wrong?" *Financial Analysts Journal,* 50, no. 5 (September/October 1994): 43–53.

7. The classic study on yield spreads is

Lawrence Fisher, "Determinants of Risk Premiums on Corporate Bonds," *Journal of Political Economy,* 67, no. 3 (June 1959): 217–237.

8. Yield spreads are also discussed in

George Foster, *Financial Statement Analysis* (Upper Saddle River, NJ: Prentice Hall, 1986), pp. 510–511.

Martin S. Fridson and Jeffrey A. Bersh, "Spread versus Treasuries as a Market-Timing Tool for High-Yield Investors," *Journal of Fixed Income,* 4, no. 1 (June 1994): 63–69.

Martin S. Fridson and Jon G. Jonsson, "Spread versus Treasuries and the Riskiness of High-Yield Bonds," *Journal of Fixed Income,* 5, no. 3 (December 1995): 79–88.

9. Predicting and analyzing bankruptcy has been a subject of much research; see the following papers and their citations:

William H. Beaver, "Financial Ratios as Predictors of Failure," *Empirical Research in Accounting: Selected Studies, 1966,* supplement to *Journal of Accounting Research,* 4, (1966): 71–111.

———, "Market Prices, Financial Ratios and the Prediction of Failure," *Journal of Accounting Research,* 6, no. 2 (Autumn 1968): 179–192.

Edward I. Altman, "Financial Ratios, Discriminant Analysis and the Prediction of Corporate Bankruptcy," *Journal of Finance,* 23, no. 4 (September 1968): 589–609.

Edward B. Deakin, "A Discriminant Analysis of Predictors of Business Failure," *Journal of Accounting Research,* 10, no. 1 (Spring 1972): 167–179.

R. Charles Moyer, "Forecasting Financial Failure: A Re-examination," *Financial Management,* 6, no. 1 (Spring 1977): 11–17.

Edward I. Altman, Robert G. Haldeman, and P. Narayanan, "Zeta Analysis: A New Model to Identify Bankruptcy Risk of Corporations," *Journal of Banking and Finance,* 1, no. 1 (June 1977): 29–54.

James A. Ohlson, "Financial Ratios and the Probabilistic Prediction of Bankruptcy," *Journal of Accounting Research,* 18, no. 1 (Spring 1980): 109–131.

Joseph Aharony, Charles P. Jones, and Itzhak Swary, "An Analysis of Risk and Return Characteristics of Corporate Bankruptcy Using Capital Market Data," *Journal of Finance,* 35, no. 4 (September 1980): 1001–1016.

Ismael G. Dambolena and Sarkis J. Khoury, "Ratio Stability and Corporate Failure," *Journal of Finance,* 35, no. 4 (September 1980): 1017–1026.

Edward I. Altman, "The Success of Business Failure Prediction Models: An International Survey," *Journal of Banking and Finance,* 8, no. 2 (June 1984): 171–198.

Cornelius J. Casey and Norman J. Bartczak, "Cash Flow—It's Not the Bottom Line," *Harvard Business Review,* 62, no. 4 (July–August 1984): 61–66.

Cornelius Casey and Norman Bartczak, "Using Operating Cash Flow Data to Predict Financial Distress: Some Extensions," *Journal of Accounting Research,* 23, no. 1 (Spring 1985): 384–401.

James A. Gentry, Paul Newbold, and David T. Whitford, "Classifying Bankrupt Firms with Funds Flow Components," *Journal of Accounting Research,* 23, no. 1 (Spring 1985): 146–160.

———, "Predicting Bankruptcy: If Cash Flow's Not the Bottom Line, What Is?" *Financial Analysts Journal,* 41, no. 5 (September/October 1985): 47–56.

Maggie Queen and Richard Roll, "Firm Mortality: Using Market Indicators to Predict Survival," *Financial Analysts Journal,* 43, no. 3 (May/June 1987): 9–26.

Ismael G. Dambolena and Joel M. Shulman, "A Primary Rule for Detecting Bankruptcy: Watch the

Cash," *Financial Analysts Journal,* 44, no. 5 (September/October 1988): 74–78.

James M. Gahlon and Robert L. Vigeland, "Early Warning Signs of Bankruptcy Using Cash Flow Analysis," *Journal of Commercial Bank Lending,* 71, no. 4 (December 1988): 4–15.

Abdul Aziz and Gerald H. Lawson, "Cash Flow Reporting and Financial Distress Models: Testing of Hypotheses," *Financial Management,* 18, no. 1 (Spring 1989): 55–63.

Douglas J. Lucas, "Default Correlation and Credit Analysis," *Journal of Fixed Income,* 4, no. 4 (March 1995): 76–87.

Jean Helwege and Paul Kleiman, "Understanding Aggregate Default Rates of High-Yield Bonds," *Journal of Fixed Income,* 7, no. 1 (June 1997): 55–61.

Martin S. Fridson, M. Christopher Garman, and Sheng Wu, "Real Interest Rates and the Default Rate on High-Yield Bonds," *Journal of Fixed Income,* 7, no. 2 (September 1997): 29–34.

10. Some interesting Web sites to explore some of the topics discussed in this chapter are

<www.finpipe.com>

<www.investinginbonds.com>

CHAPTER 22

1. There have been many tests of efficiency in the bond market. Endnotes 1 through 11 contain citations of several of them. Some of the others are cited in

Frank J. Fabozzi and T. Dessa Fabozzi, *Bond Markets, Analysis and Strategies* (Upper Saddle River, NJ: Prentice Hall, 1989): 300–303. Chapter 4 of this book also contains an extensive discussion of the concepts of convexity and duration.

2. Books that discuss convexity, duration, and many related investment strategies are

Gerald O. Bierwag, *Duration Analysis* (Cambridge, MA: Ballinger, 1987).

Frank J. Fabozzi, *Bond Markets, Analysis and Strategies* (Upper Saddle River, NJ: Prentice Hall, 1996).

Kenneth D. Garbade, *Fixed Income Analytics* (Cambridge, MA: MIT Press, 1996).

Suresh Sundaresan, *Fixed Income Markets and Their Derivatives* (Cincinnati OH: South-Western, 1997).

3. A method for measuring convexity is given by

Robert Brooks and Miles Livingston, "A Closed-Form Equation for Bond Convexity," *Financial Analysts Journal,* 45, no. 6 (November/December 1989): 78–79.

4. The concept of duration and its use to measure interest-rate risk was initially developed by

Frederick R. Macaulay, *Some Theoretical Problems Suggested by the Movement of Interest Rates, Bond Yields, and Stock Prices in the United States Since 1856* (New York: National Bureau of Economic Research, 1938).

J. R. Hicks, *Value and Capital,* 2d ed. (Oxford, England: Clarendon Press, 1946; the first edition was published in 1939).

Michael H. Hopewell and George G. Kaufman, "Bond Price Volatility and Term to Maturity: A Generalized Respecification," *American Economic Review,* 63, no. 4 (September 1973): 4749–4753.

5. For interesting articles describing the development of the concept of duration (as well as immunization), see

Roman L. Weil, "Macaulay's Duration: An Appreciation," *Journal of Business,* 46, no. 4 (October 1973): 589–592.

Frank K. Reilly and Rupinder S. Sidhu, "The Many Uses of Bond Duration," *Financial Analysts Journal,* 36, no. 4 (July/August 1980): 58–72.

G. O. Bierwag, George G. Kaufman, and Alden Toevs, "Duration: Its Development and Use in Bond Portfolio Management," *Financial Analysts Journal,* 39, no. 4 (July/August 1983): 15–35.

6. For alternative methods of calculating duration, see

Jess H. Chua, "A Generalized Formula for Calculating Bond Duration," *Financial Analysts Journal,* 44, no. 5 (September/October 1988): 65–67.

Sanjay K. Nawalkha and Nelson J. Lacey, "Closed-Form Solutions of Higher-Order Duration Measures," *Financial Analysts Journal,* 44, no. 6 (November/December 1988): 82–84.

7. For the initial development and subsequent supportive tests of immunization, see

F. M. Redington, "Review of the Principles of Life-Office Valuations," *Journal of the Institute of Actuaries,* 78, no. 3 (1952): 286–315.

Lawrence Fisher and Roman L. Weil, "Coping with the Risk of Interest-Rate Fluctuations: Returns to Bondholders from Naive and Optimal Strategies," *Journal of Business,* 44, no. 4 (October 1971): 408–431.

G. O. Bierwag and George G. Kaufman, "Coping with the Risk of Interest-Rate Fluctuations: A Note," *Journal of Business,* 50, no. 3 (July 1977): 364–370.

Charles H. Gushee, "How to Immunize a Bond Investment," *Financial Analysts Journal,* 37, no. 2 (March/April 1981): 44–51.

G. O. Bierwag, George G. Kaufman, Robert Schweitzer, and Alden Toevs, "The Art of Risk Management in Bond Portfolios," *Journal of Portfolio Management,* 7, no. 2 (Spring 1981): 27–36.

Gerald O. Bierwag, *Duration Analysis* (Cambridge, MA: Ballinger, 1987), Chapter 12.

Donald R. Chambers, Willard T. Carleton, and Richard W. McEnally, "Immunizing Default-Free Bond Portfolios with a Duration Vector," *Journal of Financial and Quantitative Analysis,* 23, no. 1 (March 1988): 89–104.

Iraj Fooladi and Gordon S. Roberts, "Bond Portfolio Immunization," *Journal of Economics and Business,* 44, no. 1 (February 1992): 3–17.

8. For some interesting articles involving duration, convexity, and immunization, see

Mark L. Dunetz and James M. Mahoney, "Using Duration and Convexity in the Analysis of Callable Bonds," *Financial Analysts Journal,* 44, no. 3 (May/June 1988): 53–72.

Bruce J. Grantier, "Convexity and Bond Portfolio Performance: The Benter the Better," *Financial Analysts Journal,* 44, no. 6 (November/December 1988): 79–81.

Jacques A. Schnabel, "Is Benter Better: A Cautionary Note on Maximizing Convexity," *Financial Analysts Journal,* 46, no. 1 (January/February 1990): 78–79.

Robert Brooks and Miles Livingston, "Relative Impact of Duration and Convexity on Bond Price Changes," *Financial Practice and Education,* 2, no. 1 (Spring/Summer 1992): 93–99.

Mark Kritzman, ". . . About Duration and Convexity," *Financial Analysts Journal,* 48, no. 6 (November/December 1992): 17–20.

Gerald O. Bierwag, Iraj Fooladi, and Gordon S. Roberts, "Designing an Immunized Portfolio: Is M-Squared the Key?" *Journal of Banking and Finance,* 17, no. 6 (December 1993): 1147–1170.

Edward J. Kane and Stephen A. Kane, "Teaching Duration of Annuities and Portfolio Net Worth from a Financial Engineering Perspective," *Financial Practice and Education,* 5, no. 2 (Fall/Winter 1995): 144–148.

Don M. Chance and James V. Jordan, "Duration, Convexity, and Time as Components of Bond Returns," *Journal of Fixed Income,* 6, no. 2 (September 1996): 88–96.

Nicola Carcano and Silverio Foresi, "Hedging against Interest Rate Risk: Reconsidering Volatility-Adjusted Immunization," *Journal of Banking and Finance,* 21, no. 2 (February 1997): 127–141.

Antony C. Cherin and Robert C. Hanson, "Consistent Treatment of Interest Payments in Immunization Examples," *Financial Practice and Education,* 7, no. 1 (Spring/Summer 1997): 122–126.

Joel R. Barber and Mark L. Copper, "Is Bond Convexity a Free Lunch?" *Journal of Portfolio Management,* 24, no. 1 (Fall 1997): 113–119.

Lee Thomas and Ram Willner, "Measuring the Duration of an Internationally Diversified Bond Portfolio," *Journal of Portfolio Management,* 24, no. 1 (Fall 1997): 93–100.

9. Some of the research that is critical of the use of duration, convexity, and immunization is mentioned in endnote 23. Other critical research includes

Jonathan E. Ingersoll, Jr., Jeffrey Skelton, and Roman L. Weil, "Duration Forty Years Later," *Journal of Financial and Quantitative Analysis,* 13, no. 4 (November 1977): 627–650.

Ronald N. Kahn and Roland Lochoff, "Convexity and Exceptional Return," *Journal of Portfolio Management,* 16, no. 2 (Winter 1990): 43–47.

Antti Ilmanen, "How Well Does Duration Measure Interest Rate Risk?" *Journal of Fixed Income,* 1, no. 4 (March 1992): 43–51.

10. For a discussion of how to use nondefault-free bonds in an immunized portfolio, see

Gordon J. Alexander and Bruce G. Resnick, "Using Linear and Goal Programming to Immunize Bond Portfolios," *Journal of Banking and Finance,* 9, no. 1 (March 1985): 35–54.

G. O. Bierwag and George G. Kaufman, "Durations of Nondefault-Free Securities," *Financial Analysts Journal,* 44, no. 4 (July/August 1988): 39–46, 62.

Gerald O. Bierwag, Charles J. Corrado, and George G. Kaufman, "Computing Durations for Bond Portfolios," *Journal of Portfolio Management,* 17, no. 1 (Fall 1990): 51–55.

———, "Durations for Portfolios of Bonds Priced on Different Term Structures," *Journal of Banking and Finance,* 16, no. 4 (August 1992): 705–714.

Antti Ilmanen, Donald McGuire, and Arthur Warga, "The Value of Duration as a Risk Measure for Corporate Debt," *Journal of Fixed Income,* 4, no. 1 (June 1994): 70–76.

Martin Leibowitz, Stanley Kogelman, and Lawrence N. Bader, "Spread Immunization: Portfolio Improvements through Dollar-Duration Matching," *Journal of Investing,* 4, no. 3 (Fall 1995): 49–56.

Iraj J. Fooladi, Gordon S. Roberts, and Frank Skinner, "Duration for Bonds with Default Risk," *Journal of Banking and Finance,* 21, no. 1 (January 1997): 1–16.

11. For a discussion of the effect of call risk on duration (and immunization), see

Kurt Winkelmann, "Uses and Abuses of Duration and Convexity," *Financial Analysts Journal,* 45, no. 5 (September/October 1989): 72–75.

12. For a discussion of how to use duration to measure the risk of foreign bonds, see

Steven I. Dym, "Measuring the Risk of Foreign Bonds," *Journal of Portfolio Management,* 17, no. 2 (Winter 1991): 56–61.

Steven Dym, "Global and Local Components of Foreign Bond Risk," *Financial Analysts Journal,* 48, no. 2 (March/April 1992): 83–91.

Lee Thomas and Ram Willner, "Measuring the Duration of an Internationally Diversified Bond Portfolio," *Journal of Portfolio Management,* 24, no. 1 (Fall 1997): 93–100.

13. Dedicated bond portfolios and contingent immunization are discussed in

Martin L. Leibowitz and Alfred Weinberger, "Contingent Immunization—Part I: Risk Control Procedures," *Financial Analysts Journal,* 38, no. 6 (November/December 1982): 17–31.

———, "Contingent Immunization—Part II: Problem Areas," *Financial Analysts Journal,* 39, no. 1 (January/February 1983): 39–50.

Martin L. Leibowitz, "The Dedicated Bond Portfolio in Pension Funds—Part I: Motivations and Basics," *Financial Analysts Journal,* 42, no. 1 (January/February 1986): 69–75.

———, "The Dedicated Bond Portfolio in Pension Funds—Part II: Immunization, Horizon Matching, and Contingent Procedures," *Financial Analysts Journal,* 42, no. 2 (March/April 1986): 47–57.

14. For a discussion of horizon analysis and bond swaps, see

Sidney Homer and Martin L. Leibowitz, *Inside the Yield Book* (Upper Saddle River, NJ: Prentice Hall, 1972), Chapters 6 and 7.

Martin L. Leibowitz, "Horizon Analysis for Managed Bond Portfolios," *Journal of Portfolio Management,* 1, no. 3 (Spring 1975): 23–34.

———, "An Analytic Approach to the Bond Market," in Sumner N. Levine (ed.), *Financial Analyst's Handbook* (Homewood, IL: Dow Jones-Irwin, 1975), pp. 226–277.

Marcia Stigum and Frank J. Fabozzi, *The Dow Jones-Irwin Guide to Bond and Money Market Investments* (Homewood, IL: Dow Jones-Irwin, 1987), Chapter 16.

15. For a discussion of various yield curve strategies, see

Jerome S. Osteryoung, Gordon S. Roberts, and Daniel E. McCarty, "Ride the Yield Curve When Investing Idle Funds in Treasury Bills?" *Financial Executive,* 47, no. 4 (April 1979): 10–15.

Edward A. Dyl and Michael D. Joehnk, "Riding the Yield Curve: Does It Work?" *Journal of Portfolio Management,* 7, no. 3 (Spring 1981): 13–17.

Marcia Stigum and Frank J. Fabozzi, *The Dow Jones-Irwin Guide to Bond and Money Market Investments* (Homewood, IL: Dow Jones-Irwin, 1987), 270–272.

Frank J. Jones, "Yield Curve Strategies," *Journal of Fixed Income,* 1, no. 2 (September 1991): 43–51.

Robin Grieves and Alan J. Marcus, "Riding the Yield Curve: Reprise," *Journal of Portfolio Management,* 18, no. 4 (Summer 1992): 67–76.

Robin Grieves, Steven V. Mann, Alan J. Marcus, and Pradipkumar Ramanlal, "Riding the Bill Curve," *Journal of Portfolio Management,* 25, no. 3 (Spring 1999): 74–82.

16. More on bond investment strategies is contained in

Ehud I. Ronn, "A New Linear Programming Approach to Bond Portfolio Management," *Journal of Financial and Quantitative Analysis,* 22, no. 4 (December 1987): 439–466.

Michael C. Ehrhardt, "A New Linear Programming Approach to Bond Portfolio Management: A Comment," *Journal of Financial and Quantitative Analysis,* 24, no. 4 (December 1989): 533–537.

Randall S. Hiller and Christian Schaack, "A Classification of Structured Bond Portfolio Modeling Techniques," *Journal of Portfolio Management,* 17, no. 1 (Fall 1990): 37–48.

Frank J. Fabozzi, *Bond Markets, Analysis and Strategies* (Upper Saddle River, NJ: Prentice Hall, 1996), in particular Chapters 20–22.

Antti Ilmanen, "Market Rate Expectations and Forward Rates," *Journal of Fixed Income,* 6, no. 2 (September 1996): 8–22.

Antti Ilmanen, "Does Duration Extension Enhance Long-Term Expected Returns?" *Journal of Fixed Income,* 6, no. 2 (September 1996): 23–36.

17. Bond portfolio performance evaluation is discussed in

Wayne H. Wagner and Dennis A. Tito, "Definitive New Measures of Bond Performance and Risk," *Pension World,* 13, no. 5 (May 1977): 10–12.

Wayne H. Wagner and Dennis A. Tito, "Is Your Bond Manager Skillful?" *Pension World,* 13, no. 6 (June 1977): 9–13.

Peter O. Dietz, H. Russell Fogler, and Donald J. Hardy, "The Challenge of Analyzing Bond Portfolio Returns," *Journal of Portfolio Management,* 6, no. 3 (Spring 1980): 53–58.

Mark Kritzman, "Can Bond Managers Perform Consistently?" *Journal of Portfolio Management,* 9, no. 4 (Summer 1983): 54–56.

Robert N. Anthony, "How to Measure Fixed-Income Performance Correctly," *Journal of Portfolio Management,* 11, no. 2 (Winter 1985): 61–65.

Peter O. Dietz and Jeannette R. Kirschman, "Evaluation Portfolio Performance," in John L. Maginn and Donald L. Tuttle (eds.), *Managing Investment Portfolio: A Dynamic Process* (Boston, MA: Warren, Gorham & Lamont, 1990), Chapter 14.

Ronald N. Kahn, "Bond Performance Analysis: A Multi-Factor Approach," *Journal of Portfolio Management,* 18, no. 1 (Fall 1991): 40–47.

Christopher R. Blake, Edwin J. Elton, and Martin J. Gruber, "The Performance of Bond Mutual Funds," *Journal of Business,* 66, no. 3 (July 1993): 371–403.

Edwin J. Elton, Martin J. Gruber, and Christopher R. Blake, "Fundamental Economic Variables, Expected Returns, and Bond Fund Performance," *Journal of Finance,* 50, no. 4 (September 1995): 1229–1256.

18. For interesting discussions of what mix of bonds and stocks is appropriate for investors, see

Martin L. Leibowitz and William S. Krasker, "The Persistence of Risk: Stocks versus Bonds over the Long Term," *Financial Analysts Journal,* 44, no. 6 (November/December 1988): 40–47.

Paul A. Samuelson, "The Judgment of Economic Science on Rational Portfolio Management: Indexing, Timing and Long-Horizon Effects," *Journal of Portfolio Management,* 16, no. 1 (Fall 1989): 4–12.

Martin L. Leibowitz and Terence C. Langetieg, "Shortfall Risk and the Asset Allocation Decision: A Simulation Analysis of Stock and Bond Profiles," *Journal of Portfolio Management,* 16, no. 1 (Fall 1989): 61–68.

Keith P. Ambachtscheer, "The Persistence of Investment Risk," *Journal of Portfolio Management,* 16, no. 1 (Fall 1989): 69–71.

Kirt C. Butler and Dale L. Domian, "Risk, Diversification, and the Investment Horizon," *Journal of Portfolio Management,* 17, no. 3 (Spring 1991): 41–47.

Peter L. Bernstein, "Are Stocks the Best Place to Be in the Long Run?" *Journal of Investing,* 5, no. 2 (Summer 1996): 6–9.

Ravi Jagannathan and Narayana R. Kotcherlakota, "Why Should Older People Invest Less in Stocks Than Younger People?" *Federal Reserve Bank of Minneapolis Quarterly Review,* 20, no. 3 (Summer 1996): 11–23.

19. Empirical regularities in the bond market have been investigated by

Eric C. Chang and J. Michael Pinegar, "Return Seasonality and Tax-Loss Selling in the Market for Long-Term Government and Corporate Bonds," *Journal of*

Financial Economics, 17, no. 2 (December 1986): 391–415.

Eric C. Chang and Roger D. Huang, "Time-Varying Return and Risk in the Corporate Bond Market," *Journal of Financial and Quantitative Analysis,* 25, no. 3 (September 1990): 323–340.

Susan D. Jordan and Bradford D. Jordan, "Seasonality in Daily Bond Returns," *Journal of Financial and Quantitative Analysis,* 26, no. 2 (June 1991): 269–285.

Kam C. Chan and H. K. Wu, "Another Look on Bond Market Seasonality: A Note," *Journal of Banking and Finance,* 19, no. 6 (September 1995): 1047–1054.

20. Key rate durations are discussed in

Robert R. Reitano, "Non-Parallel Yield Curve Shifts and Durational Leverage," *Journal of Portfolio Management,* 16, no. 4 (Summer 1990): 62–67.

Thomas S. Y. Ho, "Key Rate Durations: Measures of Interest Rate Risks," *Journal of Fixed Income,* 2, no. 2 (September 1992): 29–44.

Bennett W. Golub and Leo M. Tilman, "Measuring Yield Curve Risk Using Principal Components Analysis, Value at Risk, and Key Rate Durations," *Journal of Portfolio Management,* 23, no. 4 (Summer 1997): 72–84.

21. Some interesting Web sites that discuss duration, convexity, and bond strategies are

<www.contingencyanalysis.com/measureduration.htm>

<www.finpipe.com/bondstr.htm>

<www.investinginbonds.com>

CHAPTER 23

1. Good reference sources for information on investment companies are

Investment Companies Yearbook (to order, write: CDA Investment Technologies, Inc., 1355 Piccard Drive, Rockville, MD 20850).

Mutual Fund Fact Book (to order, write: Investment Company Institute, 1401 H Street, N.W., Suite 1200, Washington, DC 20005-2148). Also see the Investment Company Institute's Web site at <www.ici.org>.

The Individual Investor's Guide to No-Load Mutual Funds (to order, write: American Association of Individual Investors, 625 North Michigan Avenue, Research Department, Chicago, IL 60611-3110).

Morningstar Mutual Funds (to order this biweekly publication, write: Morningstar, Inc., 225 West Wacker Drive, Chicago, IL 60606).

William J. Baumol, Stephen M. Goldfeld, Lilli A. Gordon, and Michael F. Koehn, *The Economics of Mutual Fund Markets: Competition versus Regulation* (Boston: Kluwer Academic Publishers, 1990).

John C. Bogle, *Bogle on Mutual Funds* (Burr Ridge, IL: Irwin, 1994).

Peter Fortune, "Mutual Funds, Part I: Reshaping the American Financial System," *New England Economic Review,* Federal Reserve Bank of Boston (July/August 1997): 45–72.

2. Although annual management fees of investment companies are usually a given percentage of the market value of the assets under management, performance-based fees are allowed. In addition to the January/February 1987 issue of the *Financial Analysts Journal,* which is devoted to this topic, see

Laura T. Starks, "Performance Incentive Fees: An Agency Theoretic Approach," *Journal of Financial and Quantitative Analysis,* 22, no. 1 (March 1987): 17–32.

Mark Grinblatt and Sheridan Titman, "How Clients Can Win the Gaming Game," *Journal of Portfolio Management,* 13, no. 4 (Summer 1987): 14–23.

Joseph H. Golec, "Do Mutual Fund Managers Who Use Incentive Compensation Outperform Those Who Don't?" *Financial Analysts Journal,* 44, no. 6 (November/December 1988): 75–78.

Mark Grinblatt and Sheridan Titman, "Adverse Risk Incentives and the Design of Performance-Based Contracts," *Management Science,* 35, no. 7 (July 1989): 807–822.

Jeffery V. Bailey, "Some Thoughts on Performance-Based Fees," *Financial Analysts Journal,* 46, no. 4 (July/August 1990): 31–40.

Philip Halpern and Isabelle I. Fowler, "Investment Management Fees and Determinants of Pricing Structure in the Industry," *Journal of Portfolio Management,* 17, no. 2 (Winter 1991): 74–79.

Keith C. Brown, W. V. Harlow, and Laura T. Starks, "Of Tournaments and Temptations: An Analysis of Managerial Incentives in the Mutual Fund Industry," *Journal of Finance,* 51, no. 1 (March 1996): 85–110.

Tarun Chordia, "The Structure of Mutual Fund Charges," *Journal of Financial Economics,* 41, no. 1 (May 1996): 3–39.

Robert Ferguson and Dean Leistikow, "Investment Management Fees: Long-Run Incentives," *Journal of Financial Engineering,* 6, no. 1 (March 1997): 1–30.

Peter Tufano and Matthew Sevick, "Board Structure and Fee-Setting in the U.S. Mutual Fund Industry," *Journal of Financial Economics,* 46, no. 3 (December 1997): 321–355.

3. The imposition of 12b-1 distribution fees by mutual funds has been contentious. See

Stephen P. Ferris and Don M. Chance, "The Effect of 12b-1 Plans on Mutual Fund Expense Ratios: A Note," *Journal of Finance,* 42, no. 4 (September 1987): 1077–1082.

Charles Trzcinka and Robert Zweig, *An Economic Analysis of the Cost and Benefits of S.E.C. Rule 12b-1,* Monograph Series in Finance and Economics #1990-1 (New York: New York University Salomon Center, Leonard N. Stern School of Business, 1990).

4. For a discussion of the distribution fees associated with the various classes of mutual fund shares, see

Miles Livingston and Edward S. O'Neal, "The Cost of Mutual Fund Distribution Fees," *Journal of Financial Research,* 21, no. 2 (Summer 1998): 205–218.

5. Closed-end investment companies known as "country funds" have been examined by

Catherine Bonser-Neal, Greggory Brauer, Robert Neal, and Simon Wheatley, "International Investment Restrictions and Closed-End Country Fund Prices," *Journal of Finance,* 45, no. 2 (June 1990): 523–547.

Gordon Johnson, Thomas Schneeweis, and William Dinning, "Closed-End Country Funds: Exchange Rate and Investment Risk," *Financial Analysts Journal,* 49, no. 6 (November/December 1993): 74–82.

6. For evidence on the performance of international funds, see

Andre L. Farber, "Performance of Internationally Diversified Mutual Funds," in Edwin J. Elton and Martin J. Gruber (eds.), *International Capital Markets* (Amsterdam: North-Holland, 1975), pp. 298–309.

R. S. Woodward, "The Performance of U.K. Investment Trusts as Internationally Diversified Portfolios over the Period 1968 to 1977," *Journal of Banking and Finance,* 7, no. 3 (September 1983): 417–426.

Jess H. Chua and Richard S. Woodward, *Gains from Market Timing,* Monograph Series in Finance and Economics #1986-2 (New York: New York University Salomon Center, Leonard N. Stern School of Business, 1982).

Robert E. Cumby and Jack D. Glen, "Evaluating the Performance of International Mutual Funds," *Journal of Finance,* 45, no. 2 (June 1990): 497–521.

Cheol S. Eun, Richard Kolodny, and Bruce G. Resnick, "U.S.-Based International Mutual Funds: A Performance Evaluation," *Journal of Portfolio Management,* 17, no. 3 (Spring 1991): 88–94.

7. Studies of mutual fund performance are discussed and cited in

Gordon J. Alexander and Jack Clark Francis, *Portfolio Analysis* (Upper Saddle River, NJ: Prentice Hall, 1986), Chapter 13.

Bruce N. Lehmann and David M. Modest, "Mutual Fund Performance Evaluation: A Comparison of Benchmarks and Benchmark Comparisons," *Journal of Finance,* 42, no. 2 (June 1987): 233–265.

Richard A. Ippolito, "Efficiency with Costly Information: A Study of Mutual Fund Performance," *Quarterly Journal of Economics,* 104, no. 1 (February 1989): 1–23.

Mark Grinblatt and Sheridan Titman, "Mutual Fund Performance: An Analysis of Quarterly Portfolio Holdings," *Journal of Business,* 62, no. 3 (July 1989): 393–416.

Cheng-few Lee and Shafiqur Rahman, "Market Timing, Selectivity, and Mutual Fund Performance: An Empirical Investigation," *Journal of Business,* 63, no. 2 (April 1990): 261–278.

Cheng F. Lee and Shafiqur Rahman, "New Evidence on Timing and Security Selection Skill of Mutual Fund Managers," *Journal of Portfolio Management,* 17, no. 2 (Winter 1991): 80–83.

John C. Bogle, "Selecting Equity Mutual Funds," *Journal of Portfolio Management,* 18, no. 2 (Winter 1992): 94–100.

Ravi Shukla and Charles Trzcinka, "Performance Measurement of Managed Portfolios," *Financial Markets, Institutions & Instruments,* 1, no. 4 (1992).

Mark Grinblatt and Sheridan Titman, "The Persistence of Mutual Fund Performance," *Journal of Finance,* 47, no. 5 (December 1992): 1977–1984.

———, "Performance Measurement without Benchmarks: An Examination of Mutual Fund Returns," *Journal of Business,* 66, no. 1 (January 1993): 47–68.

Edwin J. Elton, Martin J. Gruber, Sanjiv Das, and Matthew Hlavka, "Efficiency with Costly Information: A Reinterpretation of Evidence from Managed Portfolios," *Review of Financial Studies,* 6, no. 1 (1993): 1–22.

Richard A. Ippolito, "On Studies of Mutual Fund Performance," *Financial Analysts Journal,* 49, no. 1 (January/February 1993): 42–50.

Darryll Hendricks, Jayendu Patel, and Richard Zeckhauser, "Hot Hands in Mutual Funds: Short-Run Persistence of Relative Performance, 1974–1988," *Journal of Finance,* 48, no. 1 (March 1993): 93–130.

Mark Grinblatt, Sheridan Titman, and Russ Wermers, "Momentum Strategies, Portfolio Performance, and Herding: A Study of Mutual Fund Behavior," *American Economic Review,* 85, no. 5 (December 1995): 1088–1105.

Christopher R. Blake, Edwin J. Elton, and Martin J. Gruber, "The Performance of Bond Mutual Funds," *Journal of Business,* 66, no. 3 (July 1993): 371–403.

John Bogle, *Bogle on Mutual Funds* (Burr Ridge, IL: Irwin, 1994), Chapter 4.

Mark Grinblatt and Sheridan Titman, "A Study of Monthly Mutual Fund Returns and Performance Evaluation Techniques," *Journal of Financial and Quantitative Analysis,* 29, no. 3 (September 1993): 419–444.

William N. Goetzmann and Roger G. Ibbotson, "Do Winners Repeat?" *Journal of Portfolio Management,* 20, no. 2 (Winter 1994): 9–18.

Edwin J. Elton and Martin J. Gruber, *Modern Portfolio Theory and Investment Analysis* (New York: Wiley, 1995), Chapter 24.

Burton G. Malkiel, "Returns from Investing in Equity Mutual Funds," *Journal of Finance,* 50, no. 2 (June 1995): 549–572.

Stephen J. Brown and William N. Goetzmann, "Performance Persistence," *Journal of Finance,* 50, no. 2 (June 1995): 679–698.

Edwin J. Elton, Martin J. Gruber, and Christopher R. Blake, "Fundamental Economic Variables, Expected Returns, and Bond Fund Performance," *Journal of Finance,* 50, no. 4 (September 1995): 1229–1256.

Ronald N. Kahn and Andrew Rudd, "Does Historical Performance Predict Future Performance?" *Financial Analysts Journal,* 51, no. 6 (November/December 1995): 43–52.

Edwin J. Elton, Martin J. Gruber, and Christopher R. Blake, "The Persistence of Risk-Adjusted Mutual Fund Performance," *Journal of Business,* 69, no. 2 (April 1996): 133–157.

Wayne E. Ferson and Rudi W. Schadt, "Measuring Fund Strategy and Performance in Changing Economic Conditions," *Journal of Finance,* 51, no. 2 (June 1996): 425–461.

Mark M. Carhart, "On Persistence in Mutual Fund Performance," *Journal of Finance,* 51, no. 1 (March 1997): 57–82.

8. *Survivorship bias* refers to the problems incurred in mutual fund studies because unskilled portfolio managers are usually fired whereas the skilled ones are not. These problems are examined in

Stephen J. Brown, William Goetzmann, Roger G. Ibbotson, and Stephen A. Ross, "Survivorship Bias in Performance Studies," *Review of Financial Studies,* 5, no. 4 (1992): 553–580.

Edwin J. Elton, Martin J. Gruber, and Christopher R. Blake, "Survivorship Bias and Mutual Fund Performance," *Review of Financial Studies,* 9, no. 4 (Winter 1996): 1097–1120.

9. For a discussion of Morningstar's risk-adjusted ratings and style analysis of mutual funds, see

William F. Sharpe, "Morningstar's Performance Measures," unpublished paper, Graduate School of Business, Stanford University, 1997. This paper can be found on the Web at <www.stanford.edu/~wfsharpe/art/stars/stars0.htm>.

Marshall Blume, "An Anantomy of Morningstar Ratings," *Financial Analysts Journal,* 54, no. 2 (March/April 1998): 19–27.

William F. Sharpe, "Morningstar's Risk-Adjusted Ratings," *Financial Analysts Journal,* 54, no. 4 (July/August 1998): 21–33.

John C. Bogle, "The Implications of Style Analysis for Mutual Fund Performance Evaluation," *Journal of Portfolio Management,* 24, no. 4 (Summer 1998): 34–42.

10. For a discussion and extensive set of references regarding closed-end funds, see, along with the citations given in the chapter, the following papers:

Rex Thompson, "The Information Content of Discounts and Premiums on Closed-End Fund Shares," *Journal of Financial Economics,* 6, no. 2/3 (June/September 1978): 151–186.

Greggory A. Brauer, " 'Closed-End Fund Shares' Abnormal Returns and the Information Content of Discounts and Premiums," *Journal of Finance,* 43, no. 1 (March 1988): 113–127.

Kathleen Weiss, "The Post-Offering Price Performance of Closed-End Funds," *Financial Management,* 18, no. 3 (Autumn 1989): 57–67.

Charles M. C. Lee, Andrei Shleifer, and Richard H. Thaler, "Anomalies: Closed-End Mutual Funds," *Journal of Economic Perspectives,* 4, no. 4 (Fall 1990): 153–164.

John W. Peavey, III, "Returns on Initial Public Offerings of Closed-End Funds," *Review of Financial Studies,* 3, no. 4 (1990): 695–708.

Charles M. C. Lee, Andrei Shleifer, and Richard H. Thaler, "Investor Sentiment and the Closed-End Fund Puzzle," *Journal of Finance,* 46, no. 1 (March 1991): 75–109.

Albert J. Fredman and George Cole Scott, "An Investor's Guide to Closed-End Fund Discounts," *AAII Journal,* 13, no. 5 (May 1991): 12–16.

James Brickley, Steven Manaster, and James Schallheim, "The Tax-Timing Option and Discounts on Closed-End Investment Companies," *Journal of Business,* 64, no. 3 (July 1991): 287–312.

J. Bradford DeLong and Andrei Shleifer, "Closed-End Fund Discounts," *Journal of Portfolio Management,* 18, no. 2 (Winter 1992): 46–53.

Nai-fu Chen, Raymond Kan, and Merton H. Miller, "Are the Discounts on Closed-End Funds a Sentiment Index?" and "A Rejoinder," *Journal of Finance,* 48, no. 2 (June 1993): 795–800 and 809–810.

Navin Chopra, Charles M. C. Lee, Andrei Shleifer, and Richard H. Thaler, "Yes, Discounts on Closed-End Funds Are a Sentiment Index," and "Summing Up," *Journal of Finance,* 48, no. 2 (June 1993): 801–808 and 811–812.

Jeffrey Pontiff, "Closed-End Fund Premia and Returns: Implications for Financial Market Equilibrium," *Journal of Financial Economics,* 37, no. 3 (March 1995): 341–370.

Michael Barclay, Clifford Holderness, and Jeffrey Pontiff, "Concentrated Ownership and Discounts on Closed-End Funds," *Journal of Applied Corporate Finance,* 8, no. 1 (Spring 1995): 32–42.

Jeffrey Pontiff, "Excess Volatility and Closed-End Funds," *American Economic Review,* 87, no. 1 (March 1997): 155–169.

11. Open-ending of closed-end investment companies is discussed in

Greggory A. Brauer, " 'Open-Ending' Closed-End Funds," *Journal of Financial Economics,* 13, no. 4 (December 1984): 491–507.

James A. Brickley and James S. Schallheim, "Lifting the Lid on Closed-End Investment Companies: A Case of Abnormal Returns," *Journal of Financial and Quantitative Analysis,* 20, no. 1 (March 1985): 107–117.

Jeffrey Pontiff, "Costly Arbitrage: Evidence from Closed-End Funds," *Quarterly Journal of Economics,* 111, no. 4 (November 1996): 1135–1151.

12. There is a wealth of information on investment companies that is available on the Web. In addition to sites that are kept by mutual fund management companies, information can be found at these independent sites:

<www.lipperweb.com>

<www.micropal.com>

<www.mfcafe.com>

<www.moodys.com/mfund/index.html>

<www.morningstar.net>

<www.quote.lycos.com/quotecom/>

13. A Web site devoted to investing in index funds is <www.indexfundsonline.com>

14. The Investment Company Institute, the trade asociation for investment companies in the United States, has an extensive Web site at

<www.ici.org>

CHAPTER 24

1. Investment strategies involving options are discussed in many papers. Here are three of the most notable ones:

Robert C. Merton, Myron S. Scholes, and Mathew L. Gladstein, "The Returns and Risk of Alternative Call-Option Portfolio Investment Strategies," *Journal of Business,* 51, no. 1 (April 1978): 183–242.

———, "The Returns and Risk of Alternative Put-Option Portfolio Investment Strategies," *Journal of Business,* 55, no. 1 (January 1982): 1–55.

Aimee Gerberg Ronn and Ehud I. Ronn, "The Box Spread Arbitrage Conditions: Theory, Tests, and Investment Strategies," *Review of Financial Studies,* 2, no. 1 (1989): 91–107.

2. A description and comparison of the specialist and market-maker systems for trading options are presented by

Robert Neal, "A Comparison of Transaction Costs between Competitive Market-Maker and Specialist Structures," *Journal of Business,* 65, no. 2 (July 1992): 317–334.

3. The binomial option pricing model was initially developed in

William F. Sharpe, *Investments* (Upper Saddle River, NJ: Prentice Hall, 1978), Chapter 14.

4. A short while later the following two papers expanded on Sharpe's model:

John C. Cox, Stephen A. Ross, and Mark Rubinstein, "Option Pricing: A Simplified Approach," *Journal of Financial Economics,* 7, no. 3 (September 1979): 229–263.

Richard J. Rendleman, Jr., and Brit J. Bartter, "Two-State Option Pricing," *Journal of Finance,* 34, no. 5 (December 1979): 1093–1110.

5. For more on the theory of binomial models, see

Daniel B. Nelson and Krishna Ramaswamy, "Simple Binomial Processes as Diffusion Approximations in Financial Models," *Review of Financial Studies,* 3, no. 3 (1990): 393–430.

6. Two seminal papers on option pricing are

Robert C. Merton, "Theory of Rational Option Pricing," *Bell Journal of Economics and Management Science,* 4, no. 1 (Spring 1973): 141–183.

Fischer Black and Myron Scholes, "The Pricing of Options and Corporate Liabilities," *Journal of Political Economy,* 81, no. 3 (May/June 1973): 637–654.

7. The Black–Scholes option pricing model assumes that the riskfree rate is constant for the life of the option. Four interesting papers that relax this assumption are

Ramon Rabinovitch, "Pricing Stock and Bond Options When the Default-Free Rate Is Stochastic," *Journal of Financial and Quantitative Analysis,* 24, no. 4 (December 1989): 447–457.

Stuart M. Turnbull and Frank Milne, "A Simple Approach to Interest-Rate Option Pricing," *Review of Financial Studies,* 4, no. 1 (1991): 87–121.

Jason Z. Wei, "Valuing American Equity Options with a Stochastic Interest Rate: A Note," *Journal of Financial Engineering,* 2, no. 2 (June 1993): 195–206.

T. S. Ho, Richard C. Stapleton, and Marti G. Subrahmanyam, "The Valuation of American Options with Stochastic Interest Rates: A Generalization of the Geske–Johnson Technique," *Journal of Finance,* 52, no. 2 (June 1997): 827–840.

8. The Black–Scholes model also assumes that the volatility of the underlying asset is constant for the life of the option. For papers that relax this assumption, see

Andrew A. Christie, "The Stochastic Behavior of Common Stock Variances: Value, Leverage, and Interest Rate Effects," *Journal of Financial Economics,* 10, no. 4 (December 1982): 407–432.

John Hull and Alan White, "The Pricing of Options on Assets with Stochastic Volatilities," *Journal of Finance,* 42, no. 2 (June 1987): 281–300.

Herb Johnson and David Shanno, "Option Pricing When the Variance Is Changing," *Journal of Financial and Quantitative Analysis,* 22, no. 2 (June 1987): 143–151.

Louis O. Scott, "Option Pricing When the Variance Changes Randomly: Theory, Estimation, and an Application," *Journal of Financial and Quantitative Analysis,* 22, no. 4 (December 1987): 419–438.

James B. Wiggins, "Option Values under Stochastic Volatility: Theory and Empirical Estimates," *Journal of Financial Economics,* 19, no. 2 (December 1987): 351–372.

Marc Chesney and Louis Scott, "Pricing European Currency Options: A Comparison of the Modified Black–Scholes Model and a Random Variance Model," *Journal of Financial and Quantitative Analysis,* 24, no. 3 (September 1989): 267–284.

Thomas J. Finucane, "Black–Scholes Approximations of Call Option Prices with Stochastic Volatilities: A Note," *Journal of Financial and Quantitative Analysis,* 24, no. 4 (December 1989): 527–532.

Steven L. Heston, "A Closed-Form Solution for Options in Stochastic Volatility with Applications to Bond and Currency Options," *Review of Financial Studies,* 6, no. 2 (1993): 327–343.

Stephen Figlewski, "Forecasting Volatility," *Financial Markets, Institutions & Instruments,* 6, no. 1 (1997): 1–88.

9. For a discussion of how the possibility of default by the writer affects the prices of options, see

Herb Johnson and Rene Stulz, "The Pricing of Options with Default Risk," *Journal of Finance,* 42, no. 2 (June 1987): 267–280.

10. For a discussion of transaction costs and their impact on the Black–Scholes model, see

John E. Gilster, Jr., and William Lee, "The Effects of Transactions Costs and Different Borrowing and Lending Rates on the Option Pricing Model: A Note," *Journal of Finance,* 39, no. 4 (September 1984): 1215–1222.

Hayne E. Leland, "Option Pricing and Replication with Transactions Costs," *Journal of Finance,* 40, no. 5 (December 1985): 1283–1301.

Phelim P. Boyle and Ton Yorst, "Option Replication in Discrete Time with Transactions Costs," *Journal of Finance,* 47, no. 1 (March 1992): 271–293.

11. For an interesting paper on static analysis of calls, see

Don M. Chance, "Translating the Greek: The Real Meaning of Call Option Derivatives," *Financial Analysts Journal,* 50, no. 4 (July/August 1994): 43–49.

12. FLEX options are discussed in

James J. Angel, Gary L. Gastineau, and Clifford J. Weber, "Reducing the Market Impact of Large Stock Trades," *Journal of Portfolio Management,* 24, no. 1 (Fall 1997): 69–76.

13. Many textbooks are devoted exclusively to options or have options as a primary subject. Most cover everything discussed in this chapter but in more detail and with a more complete list of citations. Here are a few:

Robert A. Jarrow and Andrew Rudd, *Option Pricing* (Homewood, IL: Irwin, 1983).

John C. Cox and Mark Rubinstein, *Options Markets* (Upper Saddle River, NJ: Prentice Hall, 1985).

Richard M. Bookstaber, *Option Pricing and Investment Strategies* (Chicago: Probus Publishing, 1987).

Peter Ritchken, *Options: Theory, Strategy, and Applications* (Glenview, IL: Scott, Foresman, 1987).

Alan L. Tucker, *Financial Futures, Options, and Swaps* (St. Paul, MN: West, 1991).

David A. Dubofsky, *Options and Financial Futures* (New York: McGraw-Hill, 1992).

Hans R. Stoll and Robert E. Whaley, *Futures and Options* (Cincinnati, OH: South-Western, 1993).

Fred D. Arditti, *Dervatives* (Boston: Harvard Business School Press, 1996).

John C. Hull, *Introduction to Futures and Options Markets* (Upper Saddle River, NJ: Prentice Hall, 1998).

Don M. Chance, *An Introduction to Derivatives* (Fort Worth, TX: The Dryden Press, 1998).

Robert W. Kolb, *Futures, Options & Swaps* (Malden, MA: Blackwell, 2000).

Robert Jarrow and Stuart Turnbull, *Derivative Securities* (Cincinnati, OH: South-Western, 2000).

14. The various exchanges where options are traded all have Web sites containing useful information about their products (the NYSE withdrew from the option trading business in 1997):

Chicago Board Options Exchange: <www.cboe.com>

Philadelphia Stock Exchange: <www.phlx.com>

American Stock Exchange: <www.nasdaq-amex.com>

Pacific Exchange: <www.pacificex.com>

15. "Open outcry" has long been the official trading standard of the NYSE, setting it apart from Nasdaq. See

Louis Engel and Henry R. Hecht, *How to Buy Stocks* (Boston: Little, Brown, 1994), Chapter 12.

CHAPTER 25

1. Many books either are devoted exclusively to futures or have futures as one of their primary subjects. Most cover everything discussed in this chapter in more detail and with a more complete list of citations. Here are a few:

Stephen Figlewski, *Hedging with Financial Futures for Institutional Investors* (Cambridge, MA: Ballinger, 1986).

Edward W. Schwarz, Joanne M. Hill, and Thomas Schneeweis, *Financial Futures* (Homewood, IL: Irwin, 1986).

Commodity Trading Manual (Chicago: Chicago Board of Trade, 1989).

Darrell Duffie, *Futures Markets* (Upper Saddle River, NJ: Prentice Hall, 1989).

Daniel R. Siegel and Diane F. Siegel, *Futures Markets* (Hinsdale, IL: Dryden, 1990).

Alan L. Tucker, *Financial Futures, Options, & Swaps* (St. Paul, MN: West, 1991).

David A. Dubofsky, *Options and Financial Futures* (New York: McGraw-Hill, 1992).

Hans R. Stoll and Robert E. Whaley, *Futures and Options* (Cincinnati, OH: South-Western, 1993).

Robert T. Daigler, *Financial Futures and Markets: Concepts and Strategies* (New York: HarperCollins, 1994).

Fred D. Arditti, *Derivatives* (Boston: Harvard Business School Press, 1996).

Don M. Chance, *An Introduction to Derivatives* (Fort Worth, TX: Dryden, 1998).

Robert W. Kolb, *Futures, Options & Swaps* (Malden, MA: Blackwell, 2000).

Robert Jarrow and Stuart Turnbull, *Derivative Securities* (Cincinnati, OH: South-Western, 2000).

John C. Hull, *Options, Futures, and Other Derivative Securities* (Upper Saddle River, NJ: Prentice Hall, 2000).

2. For a discussion of the market structure of futures exchanges, see

Sanford J. Grossman and Merton H. Miller, "Liquidity and Market Structure," *Journal of Finance,* 43, no. 3 (July 1988): 617–633.

Michael J. Fishman and Francis A. Longstaff, "Dual Trading in Futures Markets," *Journal of Finance,* 47, no. 2 (June 1992): 643–671.

3. For a more complete discussion of margin and marking to market, see

Robert W. Kolb, Gerald D. Gay, and William C. Hunter, "Liquidity Requirements for Financial Futures Investments," *Financial Analysts Journal,* 41, no. 3 (May/June 1985): 60–68.

Don M. Chance, *The Effect of Margins on the Volatility of Stock and Derivative Markets: A Review of the Evidence,* Monograph Series in Finance and Economics #1990-2 (New York: New York University Salomon Center, Leonard N. Stern School of Business, 1990).

Ann Kremer, "Clarifying Marking to Market," *Journal of Financial Education,* 20 (November 1991): 17–25.

4. The concepts of spreads and basis are discussed in

Martin L. Leibowitz, *The Analysis of Value and Volatility in Financial Futures,* Monograph Series in Finance and Economics #1981-3 (New York: New York University Salomon Center, Leonard N. Stern School of Business, 1981).

5. Foreign currency markets are discussed in

J. Orlin Grabbe, *International Financial Markets* (Upper Saddle River, NJ: Prentice Hall, 1996), Part 2.

6. Interest-rate futures were shown to be useful in immunizing bond portfolios by

Robert W. Kolb and Gerald D. Gay, "Immunizing Bond Portfolios with Interest Rate Futures," *Financial Management,* 11, no. 2 (Summer 1982): 81–89.

Jess B. Yawitz and William J. Marshall, "The Use of Futures in Immunized Portfolios," *Journal of Portfolio Management,* 11, no. 2 (Spring 1985): 51–58.

7. Using futures to hedge bond portfolios is discussed in

Richard Bookstaber and David P. Jacob, "The Composite Hedge: Controlling the Credit Risk of High-Yield Bonds," *Financial Analysts Journal,* 42, no. 2 (March/April 1986): 25–35.

Robin Grieves, "Hedging Corporate Bond Portfolios," *Journal of Portfolio Management,* 12, no. 4 (Summer 1986): 23–25.

8. Stock index futures and their relationship to the market crash in October 1987 have been heavily researched. Some of the papers are

Paula A. Tosini, "Stock Index Futures and Stock Market Activity in October 1987," *Financial Analysts Journal,* 44, no. 1 (January/February 1988): 28–37.

F. J. Gould, "Stock Index Futures: The Arbitrage Cycle and Portfolio Insurance," *Financial Analysts Journal,* 44, no. 1 (January/February 1988): 48–62.

Lawrence Harris, "The October 1987 S&P 500 Stock-Futures Basis," *Journal of Finance,* 44, no. 1 (March 1989): 77–99.

Marshall E. Blume, A. Craig MacKinlay, and Bruce Terker, "Order Imbalances and Stock Price Movements on October 19 and 20, 1987," *Journal of Finance,* 44, no. 4 (September 1989): 827–848.

Lawrence Harris, "S&P 500 Cash Stock Price Volatilities," *Journal of Finance,* 44, no. 5 (December 1989): 1155–1175.

Hans R. Stoll and Robert E. Whaley, "The Dynamics of Stock Index and Stock Index Futures Returns," *Journal of Financial and Quantitative Analysis,* 25, no. 4 (December 1990): 441–468.

Kolak Chan, K. C. Chan, and G. Andrew Karolyi, "Intraday Volatility in the Stock Index and Stock Index Futures Markets," *Review of Financial Studies,* 4, no. 4 (1991): 657–684.

Avanidhar Subrahmanyam, "A Theory of Trading in Stock Index Futures," *Review of Financial Studies,* 4, no. 1 (1991): 17–51.

Kolak Chan, "A Further Analysis of the Lead-Lag Relationship between the Cash Market and Stock Index Futures Market," *Review of Financial Studies,* 5, no. 1 (1992): 123–152.

9. Papers on index arbitrage and program trading include

A. Craig MacKinlay and Krishna Ramaswamy, "Index-Futures Arbitrage and the Behavior of Stock Index Futures Prices," *Review of Financial Studies,* 1, no. 2 (Summer 1988): 137–158.

Michael J. Brennan and Eduardo S. Schwartz, "Arbitrage in Stock Index Futures," *Journal of Business,* 63, no. 1, part 2 (January 1990): S7–S31.

Hans R. Stoll and Robert E. Whaley, "Program Trading and Individual Stock Returns: Ingredients of the Triple-Witching Brew," *Journal of Business,* 63, no. 1, part 2 (January 1990): S165–S192.

Gary L. Gastineau, "A Short History of Program Trading," *Financial Analysts Journal,* 47, no. 5 (September/October 1991): 4–7.

10. Forward and futures prices were shown to be equal when interest rates are constant over time in

John C. Cox, Jonathan E. Ingersoll, and Stephen A. Ross, "The Relation between Forward Prices and Futures Prices," *Journal of Financial Economics,* 9, no. 4 (December 1981): 320–346.

11. The performance of commodity funds, which are investment companies that speculate in futures, has not been attractive, according to

Edwin J. Elton, Martin J. Gruber, and Joel C. Rentzler, "Professionally Managed, Publicly Traded

Commodity Funds," *Journal of Business,* 60, no. 2 (April 1987): 175–199.

12. Construction and performance of the Goldman Sachs Commodity Index is described in

Scott L. Lummer and Lauence B. Siegel, "GSCI Collateralized Futures: A Hedging and Diversification Tool for Institutional Portfolios," *Journal of Investing,* 2, no. 2 (Summer 1993): 75–82.

13. The relationships among futures, options, and futures options are discussed in

Clifford W. Smith, Jr., Charles W. Smithson, and D. Sykes Wilford, "Managing Financial Risk," *Journal of Applied Corporate Finance,* 1, no. 4 (Winter 1989): 27–48.

Charles W. Smithson, Clifford W. Smith, Jr., and D. Sykes Wilford, *Managing Financial Risk: A Guide to Derivative Products, Financial Engineering, and Value Maximization* (Homewood, IL: Irwin, 1995).

14. The seminal paper on the pricing of futures options is

Fischer Black, "The Pricing of Commodity Contracts," *Journal of Financial Economics,* 3, nos. 1, 2 (January/March 1976): 167–179.

15. For a thought-provoking book that covers futures markets, among other subjects, see

Merton H. Miller, *Financial Innovations and Market Volatility* (Cambridge, MA: Blackwell, 1991).

16. The various exchanges where futures are traded all have Web sites containing useful information about their products.

Chicago Board of Trade: <www.cbot.com>

Chicago Mercantile Exchange: <www.cme.com>

Coffee, Sugar & Cocoa Exchange: <www.csce.com>

Kansas City Board of Trade: <www.kcbt.com>

MidAmerica Commodity Exchange: <www.midam.com>

Minneapolis Grain Exchange: <www.mgex.com>

New York Board of Trade: <www.nybot.com>

New York Cotton Exchange/New York Futures Exchange: <www.nyce.com>

New York Mercantile Exchange/Commodity Exchange: <www.nymex.com>

17. The Commodity Futures Trading Commission, the federal regulator of trading in futures contracts that was established in 1974, has a Web site at

<www.cftc.gov>

CHAPTER 26

1. Books devoted to understanding international financial markets and investing include

Bruno Solnik, *International Investments* (Reading, MA: Addison-Wesley, 1991).

Roger G. Ibbotson and Gary P. Brinson, *Global Investing* (New York: McGraw-Hill, 1993).

Piet Sercu and Raman Uppal, *International Financial Markets and the Firm* (Cincinnati, OH: South-Western, 1995).

J. Orlin Grabbe, *International Financial Markets* (Upper Saddle River, NJ: Prentice Hall, 1996).

2. Foreign stock market indices are studied in

Campbell R. Harvey, "The World Price of Covariance Risk," *Journal of Finance,* 46, no. 1 (March 1991): 111–157.

Richard Roll, "Industrial Structure and the Comparative Behavior of International Stock Market Indices," *Journal of Finance,* 47, no. 1 (March 1992): 3–41.

Seth J. Masters, "The Problem with Emerging Markets Indices," *Journal of Portfolio Management,* 24, no. 2 (Winter 1998): 93–100.

3. Investing internationally in bonds has been studied by

Kenneth Cholerton, Pierre Pieraerts, and Bruno Solnik, "Why Invest in Foreign Currency Bonds?" *Journal of Portfolio Management,* 12, no. 4 (Summer 1986): 4–8.

Haim Levy and Zvi Lerman, "The Benefits of International Diversification of Bonds," *Financial Analysts Journal,* 44, no. 5 (September/October 1988): 56–64.

Paul Burik and Richard M. Ennis, "Foreign Bonds in Diversified Portfolios: A Limited Advantage," *Financial Analysts Journal,* 46, no. 2 (March/April 1990): 31–40.

Roger G. Ibbotson and Laurence B. Siegel, "The World Bond Market: Market Values, Yields, and Returns," *Journal of Fixed Income,* 1, no. 1 (June 1991): 90–99.

Victor S. Filatov, Kevin M. Murphy, Peter M. Rappoport, and Russell Church, "Foreign Bonds in Diversified Portfolios: A Significant Advantage," *Financial Analysts Journal,* 47, no. 4 (July/August 1991): 26–32.

Mark Fox, "Different Ways to Slice the Optimization Cake," *Financial Analysts Journal,* 47, no. 4 (July/August 1991): 32–36.

Richard M. Ennis and Paul Burik, "A Response from Burik and Ennis," *Financial Analysts Journal,* 47, no. 4 (July/August 1991): 37.

Fischer Black and Robert Litterman, "Asset Allocation: Combining Investors Views with Market Equilibrium," *Journal of Fixed Income,* 1, no. 2 (September 1991): 7–19.

Shmuel Hauser and Azriel Levy, "Effect of Exchange Rate and Interest Rate Risk on International Fixed-

Income Portfolios," *Journal of Economics and Business,* 43, no. 4 (November 1991): 375–388.

Mark R. Eaker and Dwight M. Grant, "Currency Risk Management in International Fixed-Income Portfolios," *Journal of Fixed Income,* 1, no. 3 (December 1991): 31–37.

Steven Dym, "Global and Local Components of Foreign Bond Risk," *Financial Analysts Journal,* 48, no. 2 (March/April 1992): 83–91.

John Markese, "Foreign Bond Funds: What Are You Buying Into?" *AAII Journal,* 14, no. 10 (November 1992): 28–31.

Kent G. Becker, Joseph E. Finnerty, and Kenneth J. Kopecky, "Economic News and Intraday Volatility in International Bond Markets," *Financial Analysts Journal,* 49, no. 3 (May/June 1993): 65, 81–86.

Richard M. Levich and Lee R. Thomas, "The Merits of Active Currency Risk Management: Evidence from International Bond Portfolios," *Financial Analysts Journal,* 49, no. 5 (September/October 1993): 63–70.

Claude B. Erb, Campbell R. Harvey, and Tadas E. Viskanta, "National Risk in Global Fixed-Income Allocation," *Journal of Fixed Income,* 4, no. 2 (September 1994): 17–26.

Antti Ilmanen, "Time-Varying Expected Returns in International Bond Markets," *Journal of Finance,* 50, no. 2 (June 1995): 481–506.

Claude B. Erb, Campbell R. Harvey, and Tadas E. Viskanta, "The Influence of Political, Economic, and Financial Risk on Expected Fixed-Income Returns," *Journal of Fixed Income,* 6, no. 2 (June 1996): 7–30.

Richard Cantor and Frank Packer, "Determinants and Impacts of Sovereign Ratings," *Journal of Fixed Income,* 6, no. 3 (December 1996): 76–91.

4. Investing internationally in stocks has also been studied by

Jeff Madura and Wallace Reiff, "A Hedge Strategy for International Portfolios," *Journal of Portfolio Management,* 12, no. 1 (Fall 1985): 70–74.

Lee R. Thomas, III, "Currency Risks in International Equity Portfolios," *Financial Analysts Journal,* 44, no. 2 (March/April 1988): 68–71.

Fischer Black, "Universal Hedging: Optimizing Currency Risk and Reward in International Equity Portfolios," *Financial Analysts Journal,* 45, no. 4 (July/August 1989): 16–22.

Warren Bailey and Rene M. Stulz, "Benefits of International Diversification: The Case of Pacific Basin Stock Markets," *Journal of Portfolio Management,* 16, no. 4 (Summer 1990): 57–61.

Mark R. Eaker and Dwight Grant, "Currency Hedging Strategies for Internationally Diversified Equity Portfolios," *Journal of Portfolio Management,* 17, no. 1 (Fall 1990): 30–32.

John E. Hunter and T. Daniel Coggin, "An Analysis of the Diversification Benefit from International Equity Investment," *Journal of Portfolio Management,* 17, no. 1 (Fall 1990): 33–36.

Martin L. Leibowitz and Stanley Kogelman, "Return Enhancement from 'Foreign' Assets: A New Approach to the Risk Return Trade-Off," *Journal of Portfolio Management,* 17, no. 4 (Summer 1991): 5–13.

Mark Eaker, Dwight Grant, and Nelson Woodard, "International Diversification and Hedging: A Japanese and U.S. Perspective," *Journal of Economics and Business,* 43, no. 4 (November 1991): 363–374.

Wayne E. Ferson and Campbell R. Harvey, "The Risk and Predictability of International Equity Returns," *Review of Financial Studies,* 6, no. 3 (1993): 527–566.

Steven L. Heston and K. Geert Rouwenhorst, "Does Industrial Structure Explain the Benefits of International Diversification?" *Journal of Financial Economics,* 36, no. 1 (August 1994): 3–27.

Wayne E. Ferson and Campbell R. Harvey, "Sources of Risk and Expected Returns in Global Equity Markets," *Journal of Banking and Finance,* 18, no. 4 (September 1994): 775–803.

Claude B. Erb, Campbell R. Harvey, and Tadas E. Viskanta, "Expected Returns and Volatility in 135 Countries," *Journal of Portfolio Management,* 22, no. 3 (Spring 1996): 46–59.

———, "Inflation and World Equity Selection," *Financial Analysts Journal,* 51, no. 6 (November/December 1995): 28–42.

Rex A. Sinquefield, "Where Are the Gains from International Diversification?" *Financial Analysts Journal,* 52, no. 1 (January/February 1996): 8–14.

Claude B. Erb, Campbell R. Harvey, and Tadas E. Viskanta, "Political Risk, Economic Risk, and Financial Risk," *Financial Analysts Journal,* 52, no. 6 (November/December, 1996): 29–46.

Bruno Solnik, Cyril Boucrelle, and Yann Le Fur, "International Market Correlation and Volatility," *Financial Analysts Journal,* 52, no. 5 (September/October 1996): 17–34.

5. Many of the previously cited papers include a discussion of hedging foreign exchange risk. Also see

Andre F. Perold and Evan C. Schulman, "The Free Lunch in Currency Hedging: Implications for Investment Policy and Performance Standards," *Financial Analysts Journal,* 44, no. 3 (May/June 1988): 45–50.

Fischer Black, "Universal Hedging: Optimizing Currency Risk and Reward in International Equity Portfolios," *Financial Analysts Journal,* 45, no. 4 (July/August 1989): 16–22.

————, "Equilibrium Exchange Rate Hedging," *Journal of Finance,* 45, no. 3 (July 1990): 899–907.

Stephen L. Nesbitt, "Currency Hedging Rules for Plan Sponsors," *Financial Analysts Journal,* 47, no. 2 (March/April 1991): 73–81.

Ira G. Kawaller, "Managing the Currency Risk of Non-Dollar Portfolios," *Financial Analysts Journal,* 47, no. 3 (May/June 1991): 62–64.

Evi Kaplanis and Stephen M. Schaefer, "Exchange Risk and International Diversification in Bond and Equity Portfolios," *Journal of Economics and Business,* 43, no. 4 (November 1991): 287–307.

Michael Adler and Bhaskar Prasad, "On Universal Currency Hedges," *Journal of Financial and Quantitative Analysis,* 27, no. 1 (March 1992): 19–38.

Mark Kritzman, "...About Currencies," *Financial Analysts Journal,* 48, no. 2 (March/April 1992): 27–30.

Kenneth Froot, "Currency Hedging over Long Horizons," NBER Working Paper No. 4355, May 1993.

Mark Kritzman, "The Minimum-Risk Currency Hedge Ratio and Foreign Asset Exposure," *Financial Analysts Journal,* 49, no. 5 (September/October 1993): 77–79.

Ira G. Kawaller, "Foreign Exchange Hedge Management Tools: A Way to Enhance Performance," *Financial Analysts Journal,* 49, no. 5 (September/October 1993): 79–80.

Jack Glen and Philippe Jorion, "Currency Hedging for International Portfolios," *Journal of Finance,* 48, no. 5 (December 1993): 1865–1886.

John Markese, "How Currency Exchange Rates Can Affect Your International Returns," *AAII Journal,* 16, no. 2 (February 1994): 29–31.

Bernard Dumas and Bruno Solnik, "The World Price of Foreign Exchange Risk," *Journal of Finance,* 50, no. 2 (June 1995): 445–479.

Gary L. Gastineau, "The Currency Hedging Decision: A Search for Synthesis in Asset Allocation," *Financial Analysts Journal,* 51, no. 3 (May-June 1995): 8–17.

Kenneth J. Winston and Jeffery V. Bailey, "Investment Policy Implications of Currency Hedging," *Journal of Portfolio Management,* 22, no. 4 (Summer 1996): 50–57.

Bruno Solnik, "Global Asset Management," *Journal of Portfolio Management,* 24, no. 4 (Summer 1998): 43–51.

6. International asset allocation has been studied by

Philippe Jorion, "Asset Allocation with Hedged and Unhedged Foreign Stocks and Bonds," *Journal of Portfolio Management,* 15, no. 4 (Summer 1989): 49–54.

Fischer Black and Robert Litterman, "Global Portfolio Optimization," *Financial Analysts Journal,* 48, no. 5 (September/October 1992): 28–43.

Patrick Odier and Bruno Solnik, "Lessons for International Asset Allocation," *Financial Analysts Journal,* 49, no. 2 (March/April 1993): 63–77.

Bruno Solnik, "The Performance of International Asset Allocation Strategies Using Conditional Information," *Journal of Empirical Finance,* 1, no. 1 (June 1993): 33–55.

Philippe Jorion, "Mean/Variance Analysis of Currency Overlays," *Financial Analysts Journal,* 50, no. 3 (May/June 1994): 48–56.

Mark W. Griffin, "Why Do Pension and Insurance Portfolios Hold So Few International Assets?" *Journal of Portfolio Management,* 23, no. 4 (Summer 1997): 45–50.

Roger G. Clarke and R. Matthew Tullis, "How Much International Exposure Is Advantageous in a Domestic Portfolio?" *Journal of Portfolio Management,* 25, no. 2 (Winter 1999): 33–44.

7. For an interesting paper that examines the market crash of October 1987 from a worldwide perspective, and related papers, see

Richard Roll, "The International Crash of October 1987," *Financial Analysts Journal,* 44, no. 5 (September/October 1988): 19–35.

Mervyn A. King and Sushil Wadhwani, "Transmission of Volatility between Stock Markets," *Review of Financial Studies,* 3, no. 1 (1990): 5–33.

Yasushi Hamao, Ronald W. Masulis, and Victor Ng, "Correlations in Price Changes and Volatility across International Stock Markets," *Review of Financial Studies,* 3, no. 2 (1990): 281–307.

C. Sherman Cheung and Clarence C. Y. Kwan, "A Note on the Transmission of Public Information across International Stock Markets," *Journal of Banking and Finance,* 16, no. 4 (August 1992): 831–837.

Jeremy J. Siegel, "Equity Risk Premia, Corporate Profit Forecasts, and Investor Sentiment around the Stock Market Crash of October 1987," *Journal of Business,* 65, no. 4 (October 1992): 557–570.

8. In addition to the references provided in endnote 7, emerging markets are also discussed in

W. Scott Bauman, "Investment Research Analysis in an Emerging Market: Singapore and Malaysia," *Financial Analysts Journal,* 45, no. 12 (November/December 1989): 60–67.

Jarrod W. Wilcox, "Global Investing in Emerging Markets," *Financial Analysts Journal,* 48, no. 1 (January/February 1992): 15–19.

Warren Bailey and Joseph Lim, "Evaluating the Diversification Benefits of the New Country Funds," *Journal of Portfolio Management,* 18, no. 3 (Spring 1992): 74–80.

Arjun B. Divecha, Jamie Drach, and Dan Stefek, "Emerging Markets: A Quantitative Perspective," *Journal of Portfolio Management,* 18, no. 1 (Fall 1992): 41–50.

Mark Mobius, *The Investor's Guide to Emerging Markets* (Burr Ridge, IL: Irwin, 1995).

Christopher B. Barry and Larry J. Lockwood, "New Directions in Research on Emerging Capital Markets," *Financial Markets, Institutions & Instruments,* 4, no. 5 (1995): 15–36.

Campbell R. Harvey, "Predictable Risk and Returns in Emerging Markets," *Review of Financial Studies,* 8, no. 3 (Fall 1995): 773–816.

Jonathan M. Kelly, Luis F. Marins and John H. Carlson, "The Relationship between Bonds and Stocks in Emerging Countries," *Journal of Portfolio Management,* 24, no. 3 (Spring 1998): 110–122.

Sandeep A. Patel and Asani Sarkar, "Crises in Developed and Emerging Markets," *Financial Analysts Journal,* 54, no. 6 (November/December 1998): 50–61.

Geert Bekaert and Michael S. Urias, "Is There a Free Lunch in Emerging Markets Equities?" *Journal of Portfolio Management,* 25, no. 3 (Spring 1999): 83–95.

Seth J. Masters, "After the Fall," *Journal of Portfolio Management,* 26, no. 1 (Fall 1999): 18–26.

9. Discussions of international and global factor models can be found in some of the previously cited papers and in

Richard Grinold, Andrew Rudd, and Dan Stefek, "Global Factors: Fact or Fiction?" *Journal of Portfolio Management,* 15, no. 1 (Fall 1989): 79–88.

Martin Drummen and Heinz Zimmermann, "The Structure of European Stock Returns," *Financial Analysts Journal,* 48, no. 7 (July/August 1992): 15–26.

Claude B. Erb, Campbell R. Harvey, and Tadas E. Viskanta, "Country Risk and Global Equity Selection," *Journal of Portfolio Management,* 21, no. 2 (Winter 1995): 74–83.

Stan Beckers, Gregory Connor and Russ Curds, "National versus Global Influences on Equity Returns," *Financial Analysts Journal,* 52, no. 2 (March/April 1996): 31–39.

Bala Arshanapalli, T. Daniel Coggin, and John Doukas, "Multifactor Asset Pricing Analysis of International Value Investment Strategies," *Journal of Portfolio Management,* 24, no. 4 (Summer 1998): 10–23.

10. Information on WEBS can be found at <www.websontheweb.com>. Also see

Ajay Khoran, Edward Nelling, and Jeffrey J. Trester, "The Emergence of Country Index Funds," *Journal of Portfolio Management,* 24, no. 4 (Summer 1998): 78–84.

Selected Solutions to End-of-Chapter Questions and Problems

CHAPTER 1

2. 18.2%
3. a. 30.0%
   b. –13.3%
   c. 4.0%
5. Small stock average return: 21.24%
   Small stock standard deviation: 19.94%
   Common stock average return: 15.35%
   Common stock standard deviation: 13.63%

CHAPTER 2

2. Total assets: $15,000
   Total liabilities: $6,750
3. a. $8,000
   b. $12,000
   c. $7,000
4. No; minimal collateral is $4,285.71
5. $30,000
7. 17.1%
8. a. 56.0%
   b. –65.2%
   c. 36.7%, –30.0%
9. Total assets: $18,750
   Total liabilities: $12,500
10. a. $2,900
    b. $6,100
11. No; minimal collateral is $33,750
13. –20.0%
14. a. –27.6%
    b. 43.6%

CHAPTER 5

4. Preferred stock after-tax return: 6.2%
   Corporate bond after-tax return: 6.5%
6. $15,012.50

9. a. 6.7%
   b. 8.3%
   c. 9.0%
10. Choose the taxable bond
    Municipal bond tax-equivalent yield: 7.1%
11. Tax bill if gain is short-term: $28,625.50
    Tax bill if gain is long-term: $26,494.50
14. a. 6.1%
    b. 23.5%
    c. 29.6%

CHAPTER 6

1. 8.8%
2. a. 20.0%
   b. 13.4%
   c. –7.4%
4. Arithmetic average inflation rate:
   1899–1915: 2.3%
   1916–1919: 16.4%
   1920–1934: –2.2%
   1935–1951:4.2%
   1952–1965: 1.3%
   1966–1981: 7.1%
   1982–1998: 3.3%
5. a. $0.78
   b. $0.62
   c. $0.50
6. $20,286.85
7. 8.1%
9. Nominal value triples in 12.7 years
   Real value triples in 29.5 years

CHAPTER 7

6. 18.3%
7. 34.6%

759

9. 11.6%
11. a. 34.1%
    b. 25.0%
    c. 9.2%
12. a. 8.8%
    b. 4.7%
13. Expected return: 8.5%
    Standard deviation: 10.1%
14. Covariance: –52.1
    Correlation: –.98
15. –10.3

CHAPTER 8

7. Minimum standard deviation when $\rho = -1$: 9.2%
   Maximum standard deviation when $\rho = +1$: 23.3%
8. 12.3%
12. 1.03%
14. 19.7%
15. Portfolio 1 standard deviation: 25.0%
    Portfolio 2 standard deviation: 22.1%

CHAPTER 9

2. a. 17.0%
   b. 14.0%
   c. 12.5%
3. Risky portfolio weight: 1.46
4. a. 26.0%
   b. 18.0%
   c. 14.0%
5. 11.0%
11. b. Expected return: 9.0%
       Standard deviation: 10.2%
    c. Expected return: 8.0%
       Standard deviation: 7.7%

CHAPTER 10

5. $\bar{r}_p = 5.0\% + 39\sigma_p$
6. 15.8%
10. $\beta_A = 1.30$
    $\beta_B = 0.80$
    $\beta_C = 1.00$
12. c. Security A expected return: 9.4%
       Security B expected return: 10.8%

CHAPTER 11

5. a. 1,069.3
   b. 43.8
   c. 33.4%
6. 22.4%
7. Standard deviation of security A: 28.9%
   Standard deviation of security B: 26.3%
8. 22.5, 2.25, 0.225
9. 220, 20

11. Sensitivity to factor 1: 0.28
    Sensitivity to factor 2: 4.60
    Sensitivity to factor 3: 0.24
17. Expected return: 15.5%
13. Security A standard deviation: 64.8%
    Security B standard deviation: 30.2%
    Covariance (A, B): 1,936.5

CHAPTER 12

4. $X_2 = .15$
   $X_3 = -.35$
6. Weight of security B: $-.10$
   Weight of security C: $-.10$
9. 26.0%
11. $rf = 5.0\%$
13. 13.6%

CHAPTER 13

2. a. 750,001
   b. 250,001
6. a. 1,380,000, $34.78
   b. 1,600,000, $30.00
   c. 400,000, $120.00
7. 0.67
8. 0.84
9. a. 1.18
   b. –0.05
   c. 1.45
   d. 0.91

CHAPTER 14

6. ROA = 13.7%
   ROE = 41.1%
7. a. 15.0
   b. $6.00
   c. 5.0
   d. 1.7%
   e. 25.0%

CHAPTER 15

1. $25.82
2. $1,978.10
3. 7.0%
4. a. $6.52
   b. 8.0%
5. $80.00
6. $52.00
7. 12.0%
8. $106.83
9. a. $35.00
   b. $46.34
   c. 6.0%, 3.13
10. $73.03
12. $44.00

13. 10.60

17. 16.41%

CHAPTER 16

2. a. Purchase $400,000 of new equity
    b. Sell $400,000 of existing equity
    c. No action
6. D_1 = $13.0 million
    D_2 = $15.7 million
    D_3 = $15.3 million
    D_4 = $13.6 million
    D_5 = $14.4 million
7. 0.59
13. $4.87
15. SUE_6 = −0.03
    SUE_7 = +1.14
    SUE_8 = +0.77
    SUE_9 = −0.91

CHAPTER 17

6. 64.8
9. 8.7%
13. Quarter 1: $1,750,000 (S to D)
    Quarter 2: $1,200,000 (D to S)
    Quarter 3: $350,000 (S to D)
    Quarter 4: $300,000 (D to S)

CHAPTER 18

1. 12.7%
2. 18.8%
3. 10.5%
4. 9.4%
6. 40.7%, 43.0%
8. a. 1.967
    b. 1.130
    c. 1.478
97. a. 15.0
    b. 18.7
    c. 18.7
    d. 120.0
11. a. 3.5%
    b. 4.5%
12. 0.8%
13. *Ex post* alpha: +.05%
    Reward-to-volatility: .55
    Sharpe ratio: .06
14. *Ex post* alpha: +3.42
    Reward-to-volatility: 7.88
    Sharpe ratio: 0.33

CHAPTER 19

1. a. 13.0%
    b. 13.4%
6. 12.8%

12. Corporate bond after-tax return: 6.3%

15. a. 14.9%
    b. 10.4%

CHAPTER 20

1. a. 7.0%
    b. 9.0%
2. $939.26, 1,066.23
3. 10.0%
4. One-year spot rate: 7.5%
    Two-year spot rate: 4.0%
    Three-year spot rate: 2.8%
5. Three-year discount factor: .810
    Four-year discount factor: .731
    Five-year discount factor: .650
6. Forward rate from year 1 to year 2: 6.0%
    Forward rate from year 2 to year 3: 8.5%
    Forward rate from year 3 to year 4: 8.5%
7. One-year spot rate: 10.0%
    Two-year spot rate: 9.8%
    Three-year spot rate: 9.5%
    Four-year spot rate: 9.2%
8. a. One-year discount factor: .909
    Two-year discount factor: .819
    Three-year discount factor: .749
    b. Forward rate from today to year 1: 10.0%
    Forward rate from year 1 to year 2: 11.0%
    Forward rate from year 2 to year 3: 9.4%
    c. $1,470.20
9. a. 6.1%
    b. 6.2%
10. 9.0%, 9.9%
13. Yield on one-year pure discount bond: 10.0%
    Yield on two-year pure discount bond: 12.0%
14. 0.54%
15. 6.2%

CHAPTER 21

1. $5,583.95
2. Bond's intrinsic value: $937.82
3. a. $9,366.03
    b. 12.0%
4. Change in five-year bond's price: −7.6%
    Change in ten-year bond's price: −12.3%
6. 107 basis points
7. a. 9.0%
    b. 12.8%
8. 12.9%
9. Actual yield with 15% reinvestment rate: 9.7%
    Actual yield with 0% reinvestment rate: 8.0%
12. 7.6%

CHAPTER 22

1. $10,000.00, $8,770.68, $12,316.36

2. Price of bond *A*: $10,912.50
   Price of bond *B*: $10,388.70
3. −7.2%, 8.0%
4. Proportion of five-year bond's price increase due to change in present value of principal: 79.1%
   Proportion of twenty-year bond's price increase due to change in present value of principal: 42.4%
5. 10% coupon bond's price increase: 14.1%
   8% coupon bond's price increase: 14.7%
6. 2.8 years
7. 2.6 years
8. 3.4 years
10. −.98%
14. Overall rate of return: 50.9%

CHAPTER 23

1. $17.60
4. a. $12.45
   b. $11.45
5. 8.0%
7. −1.9%
8. Year 1: 6.6%
   Year 2: 14.8%
   Year 3: −2.1%

CHAPTER 24

5. $4.87
6. $3.27
7. $5.08
10. .40
11. 216 contracts
12. $12.40
14. $2.19

CHAPTER 25

3. a. $1,050.00
   b. $3,050.00
   c. $50.00; Zack will receive a margin call
6. $4,280,00
7. $5,164,286.00
13. a. 204

CHAPTER 26

4. 68.42 yen/DM
6. 29.6%
7. 56.3%, 25.0%
10. 26.3%
12. 2.9%
13. 24.0%, 17.0%

Index